My goal in writing this book is creating the foundation for you to learn about the important issues and concepts in labor relations in an engaging and enjoyable fashion. Studying labor relations can be both intellectually stimulating and fun! Labor relations has been influenced by everything from violent strikes to religious writings, from libertarians to Marxists, from radical union leaders to great industrialists. You will encounter not one, but two characters named Big Bill, the brazen yet grandmotherly Mother Jones, and the still-missing Jimmy Hoffa—not to mention the colorful language of labor relations that includes yellow dog contracts, the blue flu, hot cargo, whipsawing, and a narcotic effect. You can enrich your studies by listening to union folk songs and watching *Norma Rae, On the Waterfront, Matewan, Billy Elliot,* and other films. Studying labor relations should draw on scholarship in industrial relations, management, economics, history, psychology, sociology, political science, law, working class and women's studies, and philosophy and I hope you find this diversity both stimulating and interesting.

At the same time, labor relations can be controversial and many people have strongly formed opinions of labor unions, even if they've had little or no firsthand experience with them. I encourage you to approach this book and your labor relations course with an open mind. As you will see, whether labor unions are good or bad largely depends on how one thinks the employment relationship works, especially the extent to which one believes that labor markets are competitive. You do not need to change your beliefs about the employment relationship (and by extension, labor unions), but you do need to understand other perspectives and respect those with other views—just as they must respect your viewpoint. Try to learn from your classmates with different perspectives, and engage them in reasoned and respectful discussions with an open mind. I've worked hard to include a diversity of materials in this textbook to help you understand labor relations from multiple perspectives, and to foster lively classroom exercises and discussions. Be an active yet respectful learner in your classroom!

Lastly, U.S. labor relations is often equated to negotiating thick contracts full of detailed work rules. This is undeniably an important part of labor relations, and it will receive the necessary attention in this book, but do not sell labor relations short by limiting your expectations to this narrow view. I wrote this book so that you can learn not only *how* the traditional labor relations processes work (like negotiating contracts), but also *why* the processes exist. Ultimately, labor relations is not about negotiating work rules, it is about trying to balance the economic and human needs of a democratic society and foster broadly shared prosperity. As you learn about the existing processes, continually ask yourself how they contribute (or not) to balancing these needs, and whether there are better ways of achieving these objectives—with traditional unions, with new types of unions, or without any unions at all—in the world of work of the 21st century. Even if you are a current or future manager or union leader with practical concerns, this deep understanding of the pros and cons of the labor relations processes—not just a simple grasp of how things currently work—is necessary because the labor relations system is in flux. Designing new policies, practices, and strategies that are effective hinges on a deep understanding of the employment relationship and the past, present, and future of labor relations.

Enjoy your stimulating journey through the fascinating world of labor relations!

John W. Budd

Labor Relations
Striking a Balance

Second Edition

John W. Budd
University of Minnesota

McGraw-Hill
Irwin

Boston   Burr Ridge, IL   Dubuque, IA   New York   San Francisco   St. Louis
Bangkok   Bogotá   Caracas   Kuala Lumpur   Lisbon   London   Madrid   Mexico City
Milan   Montreal   New Delhi   Santiago   Seoul   Singapore   Sydney   Taipei   Toronto

McGraw-Hill
Irwin

LABOR RELATIONS: STRIKING A BALANCE

Published by McGraw-Hill/Irwin, a business unit of The McGraw-Hill Companies, Inc., 1221 Avenue of the Americas, New York, NY, 10020. Copyright © 2008 by The McGraw-Hill Companies, Inc. All rights reserved. No part of this publication may be reproduced or distributed in any form or by any means, or stored in a database or retrieval system, without the prior written consent of The McGraw-Hill Companies, Inc., including, but not limited to, in any network or other electronic storage or transmission, or broadcast for distance learning. Some ancillaries, including electronic and print components, may not be available to customers outside the United States.

This book is printed on acid-free paper.

2 3 4 5 6 7 8 9 0 CCW/CCW 0 9 8

ISBN   978-0-07-340489-9
MHID   0-07-340489-6

Editorial director: *John E. Biernat*
Executive editor: *John Weimeister*
Editorial assistant: *Heather Darr*
Executive marketing manager: *Rhonda Seelinger*
Project manager: *Kristin Bradley*
Manager, New book production: *Heather D. Burbridge*
Lead designer: *Matthew Baldwin*
Senior photo research coordinator: *Jeremy Cheshareck*
Media project manager: *Joyce J. Chappetto*
Cover design: *Studio Montage*
Cover image: *© Digital Vision*
Typeface: *10/12 Times New Roman*
Compositor: *Laserwords Private Limited Chennai India*
Printer: *Courier Westford*

Library of Congress Cataloging-in-Publication Data

Budd, John W.
    Labor relations: striking a balance / John W. Budd.—2nd ed.
      p. cm.
    Includes index.
    ISBN-13: 978-0-07-340489-9 (alk. paper)
    ISBN-10: 0-07-340489-6 (alk. paper)
    1. Industrial relations—United States. I. Title.
HD8066.B83 2008
331.880973—dc22

                                        2006034509

www.mhhe.com

To the University of Minnesota—its faculty, staff, and students make studying and teaching labor relations rewarding

And to my family—for the rewards of their love and support

About the Author

John W. Budd is a professor in the Industrial Relations Center at the University of Minnesota's Carlson School of Management where he holds an Industrial Relations Landgrant Professorship. He is a *Phi Beta Kappa* graduate of Colgate University and received M.A. and Ph.D. degrees from Princeton University. Professor Budd has taught labor relations to undergraduates, professional Master's students, and Ph.D. candidates and has received multiple departmental teaching awards as well as an Excellence in Education award from the Industrial Relations Research Association (IRRA). He has served on the IRRA's Education Committee and has published journal articles on teaching labor relations. Professor Budd's main research interests are in industrial relations, especially labor relations. He is the author of the award-winning *Employment with a Human Face: Balancing Efficiency, Equity, and Voice* (Cornell University Press), a co-editor of *The Ethics of Human Resources and Industrial Relations* (Labor and Employment Relations Association), and has published numerous articles in *Industrial and Labor Relations Review, Industrial Relations,* the *Journal of Labor Economics,* the *British Journal of Industrial Relations*, the *Journal of Industrial Relations, Labor Studies Journal,* and other journals and edited volumes. He received the IRRA Outstanding Young Scholar Award in 1998 and serves on the editorial boards of *Industrial and Labor Relations Review* and *Working USA.* Professor Budd is also Director of Graduate Studies for the University of Minnesota's graduate program in Human Resources and Industrial Relations, one of the oldest and largest such graduate programs in the United States. He is a distant cousin of Frederick Winslow Taylor.

Preface

The traditional approach to studying U.S. labor relations focuses on an uncritical exploration of how the existing labor processes work: how unions are organized, how contracts are negotiated, and how grievances are resolved. And since U.S. unions have typically used these processes to win detailed work rules, there is a tendency to equate labor relations with work rules, and to therefore structure labor relations courses and textbooks around the examination of these work rules. In other words, traditional labor relations textbooks are dominated by rich descriptions of the *how, what,* and *where* of the major labor relations processes. But what's missing is the *why*. Labor relations is not about work rules. Labor relations processes and work rules are simply a means to more fundamental ends or objectives. What are these objectives? Under what conditions are collectively bargained work rules a desirable or undesirable method for achieving these objectives? In the world of work of the 21st century, are there better ways of pursuing these objectives? These are the central and engaging questions of labor relations—questions ignored by textbooks that narrowly focus on how the existing labor relations processes and detailed work rules operate in practice.

The importance of moving beyond a process-based focus in studying labor relations is underscored by the fact that today's labor relations processes are under attack from all directions. Business professionals, labor leaders, and diverse academics frequently criticize the operation of contemporary U.S. labor relations, albeit usually for different reasons. Analyzing whether the labor relations system needs updating and evaluating alternative options for reform require an intellectual framework that is rooted in the objectives of the employment relationship. A description of how the current processes work without any discussion of what the processes are trying to achieve fails to provide the basis for determining whether the processes are working, and fails to supply metrics for judging alternative strategies, policies, and processes.

This textbook presents labor relations as a system for striking a balance between the employment relationship goals of efficiency, equity, and voice, and between the rights of labor and management. It is important to examine these goals to discover what motivates contemporary U.S. labor relations processes, and to evaluate whether these processes remain effective in the 21st century. What are the differing assumptions (such as whether labor markets are competitive) that underlie alternative mechanisms for achieving efficiency, equity, and voice? Why is a balance important? How do both the external environment and individual decision making determine labor relations outcomes, and therefore the extent to which these goals are balanced? These questions provide the framework for analyzing the existing processes—especially organizing, bargaining, dispute resolution, and contract administration—as well as the major pressures on these processes—workplace flexibility, employee involvement, and globalization. An important theme is that the current processes are one option for balancing workplace objectives and rights, but that this system is under fire from many directions. The book therefore concludes with chapters to promote reflection on the strengths and weaknesses of the current system and the possibilities for reform. This material includes a comparative examination of labor relations systems from other countries and a consideration of varied U.S. reform proposals that include changes in union and corporate behavior as well as public policies.

This textbook therefore replaces the tired paradigm of "labor relations equals detailed work rules" with the dynamic paradigm of "labor relations equals balancing workplace goals and rights." This is *not* to say that the existing processes are unimportant. Labor law, union organizing, bargaining, dispute resolution, and contract administration are central topics that are thoroughly covered in the heart of this book using diverse historical and contemporary examples. Current and future labor relations practitioners will certainly learn the ins and outs of the traditional labor relations processes. But this is no longer sufficient for effective practice because labor relations practices are in flux. As such, the labor relations processes are not presented in this textbook as self-evidently good; they are placed in the broader context of the nature of the employment relationship to foster a deep understanding of labor relations. The logic and relevance of the existing labor relations processes are more readily understood when explicitly linked to the beliefs about the employment relationship that underlie these processes. This deep understanding further provides the foundation for critically evaluating future directions for labor relations and labor policy—what labor relations strategies, policies, and practices can most effectively strike a balance among the workplace goals and rights of workers and employers in the environment of the 21st century?

ORGANIZATION

Labor Relations: Striking a Balance has four parts and is written for upper-level undergraduates and professional-level graduate students. Part I provides the intellectual framework for studying labor relations: the objectives of the employment relationship (Chapter 1); the neoclassical economics, human resource management, industrial relations, and critical (or radical or Marxist) industrial relations models of the employment relationship (Chapter 2); and the determinants of labor relations outcomes, especially the external environment as well as individual decision making including ethics (Chapter 3). Part II focuses on the New Deal industrial relations system—today's U.S. labor relations system: its historical development (Chapter 4), labor law (Chapter 5), the strategies, structures, and conflicting rights of labor and management (Chapter 6), how new unions are organized (Chapter 7), how contracts are negotiated (Chapter 8), how bargaining disputes are resolved (Chapter 9), and how grievances over the application of the contracts are resolved (Chapter 10). Part II is intended to provide a thorough understanding of these processes to help develop effective management professionals and labor advocates, as well as for thinking more critically about future directions for U.S. labor relations.

Part III focuses on three issues that are putting particular strain on the New Deal industrial relations system in the 21st century: workplace flexibility and employee involvement (Chapter 11) as well as globalization (Chapter 12). Part IV reflects on the current state of U.S. labor relations and future options for reform. One avenue for thinking about alternatives for U.S. labor relations is to examine how labor relations in other countries seeks to balance efficiency, equity, and voice (Chapter 13). Lastly, the final chapter integrates the material from the other chapters to explicitly discuss reform alternatives—changes in union strategies, corporate behavior, and labor law for the world of work of the 21st century. Throughout the chapters, engaging historical and contemporary examples are combined with concrete issues for both practice and policy to develop a deep understanding of the past, present, and future of U.S. labor relations for managers, unionists, workers, and anyone concerned with the employment relationship.

The first edition of *Labor Relations: Striking a Balance* was very well received by instructors and students alike. In fact, it was recognized with a Texty excellence award from the Textbook and Academic Authors Association for the best textbook in accounting, business, economics, and management in 2005. As such, this second edition refines and updates rather than overhauls the successful approach of the first edition. The biggest changes are to Chapter 2 which has been rewritten to use stereotypes and media portrayals of unions to motivate a streamlined exploration of whether unions are good or bad. Chapter 1's discussion of the continued relevance of labor relations in the 21st century has also been expanded. All of the chapters have been updated to reflect the latest research, statistics, and contemporary developments, including recent NLRB rulings and the formation of the Change to Win federation in 2005.

KEY FEATURES

- Extensive supporting pedagogical materials (discussed below).

- A rich intellectual framework for understanding both the current labor relations system and possible alternatives. This framework focuses on three conceptual elements: the objectives of the employment relationship (efficiency, equity, and voice), differing views of labor markets and conflict, and labor relations outcomes as the product of the environment and individual decision-making, including ethics.

- Comprehensive, even-handed coverage of the New Deal industrial relations system—including history, law, and all of the major labor relations processes—as well as current pressures (workplace flexibility, employee involvement, and globalization) and multiple alternative directions for union strategies, corporate behavior, and labor law. Engaging historical and contemporary examples are used to illustrate many issues. These examples are drawn from a wide variety of industries, occupations, and demographic groups.

- Discussion of whether labor rights are human rights. Moreover, the clash between property rights and labor rights is highlighted as a central conflict in labor relations. This theme is used to increase the understanding of the legal doctrines that underlie the labor relations processes by seeking to balance these competing rights.

- A serious treatment of ethics integrated throughout the text. Unlike any other labor relations textbook, major ethical theories and principles are discussed (Chapter 3). Many chapters ask students to apply these principles to important labor relations issues.

- Contemporary management and union strategic issues integrated throughout the text, including integrative bargaining, workplace flexibility, work teams, reengineering, leadership, change management, the organizing model of union representation, and social movement unionism.

- Separate chapters on globalization and comparative labor relations systems. The comparative chapter discusses labor relations in representative industrialized countries (Canada, Great Britain, Ireland, France, Germany, Sweden, Australia, and Japan) as well as in Mexico, eastern Europe, and Asian developing countries and the debate over convergence of policies and practices. The globalization chapter is unique among labor relations textbooks and explores the pros and cons of globalization, debates over free or fair trade, the use of corporate codes of conduct and the International Labor Organization to promote labor rights, transnational union collaboration, issues for international managers, and ethical concerns.

- Issues specific to public sector labor relations integrated throughout the text rather than relegated to a special topics chapter.

- Explicit discussions of four schools of thought on the employment relationship—pluralist industrial relations, critical industrial relations, human resource management, and neoclassical economics—and the importance of these different perspectives in understanding conflicting views of labor unions and labor policies.

- Inclusion of diverse scholarship on labor relations incorporated throughout the text to promote a broad understanding of the subject, and to create an engaging, interesting book for the reader that draws on many disciplines and perspectives.

- Appendix A includes selected portions of the U.S. Constitution and the full text of the National Labor Relations Act, the International Labor Organization's Declaration of Philadelphia, and the United Nations' Universal Declaration of Human Rights.

- The Zinnia and Service Workers Local H-56: An accompanying online bargaining simulation for students to experience the collective bargaining process by renegotiating a hotel's union contract. The simulation is structured around Web sites for the hotel and the union and all of the necessary materials are online at *www.thezinnia.com.*

LEARNING AIDS

Labor Relations: Striking a Balance combines a rich intellectual framework and the latest issues and debates in labor relations with extensive pedagogical aids. My teaching philosophy embraces contemporary developments in learning theory by using active learning strategies that are responsive to a diversity of learning styles. In my own teaching of labor relations, this approach has resulted in a very stimulating classroom environment as well as multiple teaching awards. Helping instructors create similar learning environments to facilitate enriched student learning is an important objective of this textbook. Significant learning aids in this textbook include:

- Numerous boxes and case studies to promote classroom discussion appear throughout each chapter. Boxes are also used extensively to summarize and reinforce important elements of each chapter.
- Varied active learning exercises to foster an active learning approach and increase student participation are included in the text and supplementary materials.
- Each chapter begins with an advance organizer, list of learning objectives, and outline to prepare students for the chapter's material. Each chapter concludes with a list of key terms (boldfaced in the chapter), reflection questions, and a list of suggested readings.
- Each chapter includes multiple Internet exploration exercises (not just Web links) to further promote reflection and construction of knowledge.
- Visual learning aids such as diagrams, pictures, cartoons, timelines, and charts are used to help students with diverse learning styles connect with the material.
- Eight labor law discussion cases in Chapters 5, 7, 8, 9, and 11 help students apply important legal concepts. Ten grievance discussion cases in Chapter 10 help students wrestle with the central elements of contract administration.
- The accompanying Web-based bargaining simulation at *www.thezinnia.com* also promotes active learning. Rather than reading a spoon-fed narrative, students must explore the Web sites of a fictitious employer and union to learn about the bargaining environment.
- The textbook Web site includes links and suggested *BusinessWeek* articles for each chapter to further integrate the textbook with real-world examples and business concerns. Self-quizzes allow students to test their knowledge by answering five true-false and five multiple-choice questions per chapter. The textbook Web site is at *www.mhhe.com/budd 2e.*

TEACHING AIDS

Labor Relations: Striking a Balance includes and is supplemented with a variety of teaching aids to help instructors create a dynamic learning environment, including:

- An instructor's manual includes chapter outlines, learning objectives, lecture ideas, teaching tips, active learning exercises, ideas for using technology in the classroom, and suggestions for videos and other supplementary materials. A glossary of key terms and answers to the end-of-chapter questions are also included.
- Detailed teaching notes for all of the text's labor law and grievance cases that appear in Chapters 5, 7, 8, 9, 10, and 11 are contained in the instructor's manual.

- Tips and hints for using the accompanying online collective bargaining simulation, The Zinnia and Service Workers Local H-56 available at *www.thezinnia.com*, are outlined in the instructor's manual.

- An instructor's resource CD includes PowerPoint slides of the diagrams, pictures, cartoons, and timelines from the book that help students with diverse learning styles connect with the material.

- A test bank is included in the instructor's manual and in electronic format on the instructor's CD. The test bank contains approximately 100 questions per chapter in a variety of types, such as true-false, multiple choice, essay, and matching.

- An instructor's manual includes a unique "Pedagogical Introduction to Teaching Labor Relations" that discusses the use of active learning techniques and other best practices to help instructors engage students with diverse learning styles.

Acknowledgments

I am indebted to numerous individuals for their direct and indirect assistance in the creation of both editions of *Labor Relations: Striking a Balance*. I must first thank my family—Gwen, Gregory, Cecily, Elizabeth, and Bert—for their continued support, patience, good humor, stress relief, and occasional proofreading. For the first edition, my colleague John Fossum was instrumental in helping me get started while John Weimeister and the McGraw-Hill/Irwin team encouraged me to be innovative while providing the editorial support to improve and refine my ideas. The editorial coordinators—Trina Hauger on the first edition and Heather Darr on the second—have been especially helpful, supportive, and responsive. I continue to be indebted to the University of Minnesota human resources and industrial relations students over the years that have tolerated my classroom experimentation and provided feedback for improvements. I am similarly grateful to many professors at Minnesota and elsewhere, numerous human resources professionals, and union leaders for sharing their experiences, expertise, and encouragement. The staff of the Industrial Relations Center's Georgianna Herman Reference Room deserve special thanks for their helpfulness in identifying references and sources. I am also grateful to Mary Walker for her assistance—which was always requested without warning—and good cheer.

The first edition was greatly improved by the careful feedback I received from the reviewers, each of whom deserves individual recognition: Alex Colvin (Penn State), Victor Devinatz (Illinois State), Richard Hannah (Middle Tennessee), Michael LeRoy (Illinois), Barb Rau (Wisconsin–Oshkosh), William Ross (Wisconsin–LaCrosse), Howard Stanger (Canisius), and Jim Wanek (Boise State). The second edition was similarly improved by the helpful comments of: Robert A. Figler (The University of Akron), James Randall Nutter (Geneva College, Phillip Ettman (westfield State College), Matthew M. Bodah (University of Rhode Island), James E. Wanek (Boise state University).

Minneapolis, Minnesota
July 2006

Brief Contents

Contents

Labor Relations
Striking a Balance

Part **One**

Foundations

It's tempting to study labor relations by focusing on key processes such as how contracts are negotiated. But we cannot effectively understand and analyze these processes unless we know the context in which these processes are situated. The first three chapters therefore provide a foundation for studying labor relations by discussing the objectives of the employment relationship, outlining key models of the employment relationship, and exploring the determinants of labor relations outcomes.

Chapter **One**

Contemporary Labor Relations: Objectives, Practices, and Challenges

Advance Organizer

You probably have preconceived notions about labor relations and labor unions—perhaps from your parents, from the news media, or from personal experiences. Now it is time to think more carefully about labor relations in an open-minded way. The starting point for studying labor relations is the objectives of the employment relationship. The U.S. labor relations system represents an attempt to achieve and balance these objectives, but this system faces important pressures and continues to be criticized from many directions.

Learning Objectives

By the end of the chapter, you should be able to:

1. **Understand** why studying labor relations is important, and how it can be fascinating.
2. **Define** the objectives of the employment relationship (efficiency, equity, and voice) and of labor relations (striking a balance).
3. **Describe** the basic features of the contemporary U.S. labor relations system—exclusive representation, collective bargaining, detailed contracts, and private sector union density decline.
4. **Discuss** the current pressures on the U.S. labor relations system—on the corporate side, workplace flexibility and employment involvement (stemming at least partly from globalization); on the labor side, low union density, a representation gap, and difficulties organizing new workers.
5. **Determine** that there are many different options for structuring labor relations systems as illustrated by examples from around the world.

Contents

I consider it important, indeed urgently necessary, for intellectual workers to get together, both to protect their own economic status and also, generally speaking, to secure their influence in the political field. . . . In the meantime the intellectual worker, due to his lack of organization, is less well protected against arbitrariness and exploitation than a member of any other calling.[1]

[1] Albert Einstein, *Out of My Later Years* (New York: Philosophical Library, 1950), p. 179.

And thus, Albert Einstein became a charter member of a labor union at Princeton University in 1938. Before becoming President of the United States, Ronald Reagan was President of the Screen Actors Guild (twice!), the labor union of actors, actresses, and stuntplayers. Millions of less famous people—perhaps even your parents, or grandparents, or you—have been represented by labor unions around the world. Even housewives in the United States, Europe, and South America have formed unions. But why?

While many labor unions today appear to be large, bureaucratic organizations, the essence of a **labor union** is a formal or informal group of workers who join together to influence the nature of their employment. Perhaps they are seeking improved wages and benefits, or protections against arbitrary treatment and discharge, or a greater voice in workplace decision making. This is fundamentally what labor relations is about: collective workplace protection, influence, and voice.

One way to study labor relations is to focus on the major processes of labor relations. In particular, there is the union organizing process (how unions are formed). There is the collective bargaining process (how contracts are negotiated after unions are formed). And there is the contract administration process (how grievances over the application of the contract are resolved after contracts are negotiated). These are very important processes in U.S. labor relations, and they are the focus of the middle part of this book.

But these processes are embedded in the larger context of important underlying themes. The foundation of studying any work-related subject is the objectives of the employment relationship. When you work, what do want to get out of it? Money? Health insurance? A feeling of accomplishment? A sense of self-worth? Other things? When you work, how would you like to be treated? Like a machine? Or with dignity and respect? Would you be satisfied to always have someone else telling you how your job should be done, or would you like to have input into the nature of your job? What does your employer want?

Now think about society at large. From this perspective, what should be the goals of work? This book is based on three objectives of the employment relationship: **efficiency, equity,** and **voice.**[2] Efficiency is productive use of scarce resources for economic prosperity, equity is the provision of fair labor standards for both material outcomes and personal treatment (for example, a decent wage and respectful, nondiscriminatory treatment), and voice is the ability of employees to have meaningful input into workplace decisions. Sometimes these three objectives work together, such as when equitable treatment and employee voice increase commitment, reduce turnover, and therefore improve productivity and quality (efficiency). Unfortunately, these goals often conflict with each other—equitable treatment might reduce flexibility and therefore efficiency, or employee voice might make decision making more cumbersome and therefore less efficient. The sharpest conflicts are typically between efficiency on the one hand, and equity and voice on the other. But equity and voice can also clash, such as when unions centralize their power to better achieve equity but in the process become less responsive to individual needs and voice. Labor relations, therefore, must strike a balance between these three conflicting goals.[3] More specifically, labor relations studies how employee representation through independent labor unions contributes towards achieving a balance between efficiency, equity, and voice. This is the first major theme of this book.

Furthermore, it is the official policy of the United States to "encourag[e] the practice and procedure of collective bargaining" and to protect workers' rights to join together for

---

[2] John W. Budd, *Employment with a Human Face: Balancing Efficiency, Equity, and Voice* (Ithaca, NY: Cornell University Press, 2004).

[3] Jack Barbash, *The Elements of Industrial Relations* (Madison, WI: University of Wisconsin Press, 1984). Budd, *Employment with a Human Face.* John R. Commons, *Industrial Goodwill* (New York: McGraw-Hill, 1919). Sidney Webb and Beatrice Webb, *Industrial Democracy* (London: Longmans, Green, and Co., 1897).

"negotiating the terms and conditions of their employment" and for "other mutual aid or protection."[4] U.S. policy, at least as written in the law, is not to tolerate collective bargaining, but to *encourage* it. And according to the United Nations's Universal Declaration of Human Rights, "Everyone has the right to form and to join trade unions for the protection of his interests" (§23). But why? Why should society encourage or discourage the formation of labor unions? This is the second major theme of this book.

Lastly, what do labor unions do? U.S. unions are stereotypically associated with inflated wages and restrictive work rules.[5] However, unions secure better wages to provide decent living standards for their members; they negotiate extensive work rules to protect their members against unfair treatment by management. Moreover, unions provide voice and representation to individual workers. The labor movement can also be an advocate for working people in the social and political arenas. Based on these and other activities, why do some workers support unions while others oppose them? Why do employers typically oppose unions? And if labor unions are a good thing, how should they be structured and promoted in the world of work of the 21st century? This is the third theme of this book.

PLAN OF THE BOOK

This book is structured around four parts. Part I provides a framework for thinking about the major themes for studying labor relations. The objectives of the employment relationship are presented in this chapter. In Chapter 2, four different views of labor unions in the employment relationship are presented from the perspectives of neoclassical economics, human resource management, industrial relations, and critical (or radical or Marxist) industrial relations. The industrial relations viewpoint shapes the existing U.S. policies on collective bargaining, so a thorough understanding of this school of thought is essential, and this understanding is best achieved through contrasts with the other three schools. Lastly, understanding labor relations requires understanding the determinants of labor relations outcomes—why do workers unionize (or not)? Why do firms invest in nonunion locations (or not)? Chapter 3 therefore explores the major factors that determine labor relations outcomes, including ethics. These chapters provide the foundation for the remainder of the book.

Part II focuses on the New Deal industrial relations system—today's U.S. labor relations system. The important topics are this system's historical development (Chapter 4), labor law (Chapter 5), the strategies, structures, and conflicting rights of labor and management (Chapter 6), how unions are formed (Chapter 7), how contracts are negotiated (Chapter 8), how bargaining disputes are resolved (Chapter 9), and how grievances over the application of the contracts are resolved (Chapter 10). The thorniest problems of labor relations are those in which efficiency, equity, and voice conflict with each other. As described in Chapter 6, these conflicts are often clashes between property rights and labor rights. Striking a balance between labor rights and property rights is a major task of labor relations, and the processes described in Part II are the existing U.S. institutional framework for trying to balance property rights and labor rights. On a practical level, a thorough understanding of these processes is necessary to be an effective management professional or labor advocate.

Part III focuses on three issues that are putting particular strain on the New Deal industrial relations system in the 21st century: employee involvement, workplace flexibility, and globalization. These three pressures are discussed in Chapters 11 and 12. These are important issues

---

[4] National Labor Relations Act (1935), section 1.

[5] William J. Puette, *Through Jaundiced Eyes: How the Media View Organized Labor* (Ithaca, NY: ILR Press, 1992).

for business, policy makers, and labor unions and also reflect struggles with efficiency, equity, and voice and trying to strike a balance between labor rights and property rights. Consequently, these issues are critical for both policy and practice.

The goals of Parts I–III are to develop a deep understanding of the current state of U.S. labor relations—its goals, major processes, and current pressures. But many individuals from nearly every viewpoint—pro-business or pro-union, liberal or conservative, Republican or Democrat, academic or practitioner—have called for reform of the existing U.S. labor relations system. Thus, Part IV reflects on this current state of affairs and future options for reform. Other countries wrestle with the same goal of balancing efficiency, equity, and voice, and Chapter 13 presents some major comparative examples of different labor relations systems. In a global economy, it is important to understand how things work in other countries to be a better manager or labor leader, but there are also lessons for reflection and reform. Chapter 14 returns to the starting question: What should labor relations do? What should labor relations seek to accomplish? And in light of the material in Parts I–III, what reforms are needed—in union strategies, corporate strategies, and labor law? This concluding chapter therefore integrates the past lessons with directions for the future.

The major components of the book are captured in the conceptual model in Box 1.1. At either end of the diagram, employers and employees have their goals (Chapter 1). As conditioned by both the external environment (laws, economic trends, social norms, and the like) and individual decision making (motivation, attitudes, ethics, and other influences), labor and management strategies and structures are determined, and outcomes result. Important outcomes include worker reactions to workplace injustice—including whether or not to unionize, contract terms, strikes, grievances, firm performance, and employment trends. The elements of this model are explored in greater detail in Chapter 3. The goals, strategies, processes, and outcomes of the New Deal industrial relations system are a product of a particular institutional environment which is the focus of Part II. Part III analyzes two big changes in the environment and Part IV questions how the environment can be structured to produce desired outcomes in the future.

But it all starts with the objectives of the employment relationship.

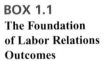

BOX 1.1
The Foundation of Labor Relations Outcomes

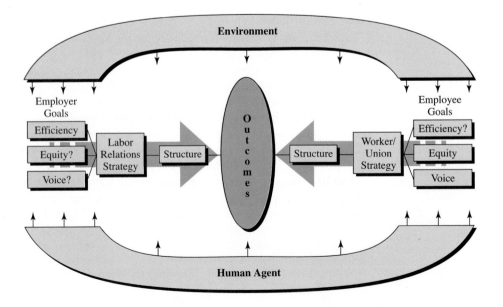

THE OBJECTIVES OF THE EMPLOYMENT RELATIONSHIP

The study of labor relations is based on the employment relationship's objectives. What do employees, employers, and society want to gain from employment? This book is structured around three employment relationship objectives: efficiency, equity, and voice. In brief, efficiency is the effective, profit-maximizing use of labor, equity encompasses fair labor standards in terms of both material outcomes and personal treatment, and voice is the ability to have meaningful input into decisions.[6] Efficiency is a standard of economic or business performance; equity is a standard of treatment; voice is a standard of employee participation. The following discussion presents each of these three dimensions in more detail. The reasons for equity and voice might appear philosophical, but the important thing to note is the diversity of arguments for each of these standards; they do not rely on one, narrow justification. Moreover, the reasons might seem to have little to do with business, but employment is not merely an economic transaction; it is also related to psychological fulfillment, human dignity, and the values of a democratic society.[7] Remember this broad perspective not only for the following discussion of efficiency, equity, and voice, but also for your entire study of labor relations.

Efficiency

Efficiency is the effective use of scarce resources and, because of the clear implications for competitiveness, economic development, and economic prosperity, efficiency is an important objective of the employment relationship. The standard economic definition of efficiency is Pareto optimality—no one can be made better off without making someone else worse off.[8] Otherwise, if someone can be made better off without harming someone else, the current situation is wasteful (inefficient) and resources are not being utilized as effectively as they can be. For the purposes of the employment relationship, focus on this last part—is labor being utilized effectively? Are products and services being produced at the desired quality at a competitive, profitable cost? Is economic prosperity as high as it can be?

A basic result in economics is that every perfectly competitive equilibrium is Pareto optimal (efficient). Therefore, neoclassical economics emphasizes the importance of competitive markets, including competitive labor markets.[9] In the legal arena, the efficiency of self-interested individuals exchanging in free markets is fostered by the common law elements of well-defined property-rights, the freedom to enter into contracts, and protections against property damage.[10] These economic and legal theories are mutually reinforcing. Consumers, workers, corporations, suppliers, investors, and other economic agents will maximize their individual welfare. If they can enter into contracts as equals in competitive

---

[6] Budd, *Employment with a Human Face.*

[7] Randy Hodson, *Dignity at Work* (Cambridge: Cambridge University Press, 2001). Russell Muirhead, *Just Work* (Cambridge, MA: Harvard University Press, 2004).

[8] Daniel M. Hausman and Michael S. McPherson, *Economic Analysis and Moral Philosophy* (Cambridge: Cambridge University Press, 1996).

[9] Roger Backhouse, *A History of Modern Economic Analysis* (New York: Blackwell, 1985). George J. Borjas, *Labor Economics,* 2nd ed. (Boston: McGraw-Hill/Irwin, 2000). George R. Boyer and Robert S. Smith, "The Development of the Neoclassical Tradition in Labor Economics," *Industrial and Labor Relations Review* 54 (January 2001), pp. 199–223.

[10] Richard A. Epstein, "In Defense of the Contract at Will," *University of Chicago Law Review* 51 (Fall 1984), pp. 947–82. Richard A. Posner, *Economic Analysis of Law,* 3rd edition (Boston: Little, Brown, 1986). Stewart J. Schwab, "The Law and Economics Approach to Workplace Regulation," in Bruce E. Kaufman (ed.), *Government Regulation of the Employment Relationship* (Madison, WI: Industrial Relations Research Association, 1997), Chapter 3.

markets, individual welfare maximization produces socially optimal, efficient outcomes. Unless these assumptions are violated, laissez faire economic and legal policies allow freely adjusting prices—for inputs and outputs—to signal scarcity and relative worth and therefore guide as an invisible hand the participants to efficiency.

Something that prevents the invisible hand from producing efficient outcomes is called a market failure. Market failures are controversial because many believe that trying to correct a market failure, such as through government regulation or subsidies, can make things worse, not better.[11] For example, a common neoclassical economics argument is that increasing the minimum wage does more harm than good because it results in greater unemployment. There are also problems with the administration and enforcement of public policies.[12] While keeping these issues in mind, consider some possible market failures.

Some market failures stem from features of real-world labor markets that are assumed away in the perfectly competitive neoclassical labor market. Perfect competition depends on employers and employees being economic and legal equals in the labor market, but various real-world market imperfections can favor the employer. Employees likely have incomplete information about dismissal policies, accident risks, or pensions.[13] Individual workers without the resources to purchase expertise will not be the legal equal of corporations with their cadre of lawyers. Internal labor markets, unvested pension benefits, and employer-specific health insurance can increase a firm's leverage by making workers less mobile.[14] Lack of savings or other resources can further reduce employees' mobility. These factors can turn perfect competition into excessive or destructive competition that drives wages and working conditions down.[15] At its worst, superior employer bargaining power can result in low wages, long hours, dangerous conditions, and arbitrary or abusive supervisory practices, but it can also be detrimental to efficiency by undermining trust, cooperation, and motivation. Or consider what was once called "industrial parasitism"—a company profits from paying low wages with no health insurance while society pays for nutritious food for workers' families and for visits to hospital emergency rooms for health care.[16]

Other market failures stem from the human side of labor. Neoclassical economics disregards the human side of labor—workers with feelings and aspirations—so that it may be possible to increase efficiency by incorporating psychological and social concerns. Contemporary human resource management emphasizes fair treatment—distributive and

---

[11] John T. Addison and Barry T. Hirsch, "The Economic Effects of Employment Regulation: What Are the Limits?" in Bruce E. Kaufman (ed.), *Government Regulation of the Employment Relationship* (Madison, WI: Industrial Relations Research Association, 1997), Chapter 4.

[12] David Weil, "Implementing Employment Regulation: Insights on the Determinants of Regulatory Performance," in Bruce E. Kaufman (ed.), *Government Regulation of the Employment Relationship* (Madison, WI: Industrial Relations Research Association, 1997), Chapter 12. Stephen M. Befort, "Labor and Employment Law at the Millennium: A Historical Review and Critical Assessment," *Boston College Law Review* 43 (March 2002), pp. 351–460.

[13] Paul C. Weiler, *Governing the Workplace: The Future of Labor and Employment Law* (Cambridge: Harvard University Press, 1990). Addison and Hirsch, "The Economic Effects of Employment Regulation."

[14] Weiler, *Governing the Workplace.* Thomas C. Buchmueller and Robert G. Valletta, "The Effects of Employer-Provided Health Insurance on Worker Mobility," *Industrial and Labor Relations Review* 49 (April 1996), pp. 439–55. Teresa Ghilarducci, "Pensions and the Uses of Ignorance by Unions and Firms," *Journal of Labor Research* 11 (Spring 1990), pp. 203–16.

[15] Bruce E. Kaufman, "Labor Markets and Employment Regulation: The View of the 'Old' Institutionalists," in Bruce E. Kaufman (ed.), *Government Regulation of the Employment Relationship* (Madison, WI: Industrial Relations Research Association, 1997), Chapter 1.

[16] Webb and Webb, *Industrial Democracy,* pp. 766–67.

BOX 1.2
Efficiency in the Employment Relationship

Dimensions	Rationale
Market-Based Transactions and Contracts	Allocative Efficiency, Economic Prosperity
Minimum Labor Standards (Wages, Hours, Safety, Family Leave, Advance Notice, Child Labor)	Externalities (Social Cost, Purchasing Power), Asymmetric Information
Income Maintenance (Unemployment Insurance, Workers' Compensation, Pension Standards)	Asymmetric Information, Costly Dispute Resolution, Liquidity Constraints
Industrial Peace	Externalities (Social Cost)
Increased Labor Bargaining Power	Externalities (Social Cost, Purchasing Power), Mobility Costs
Workplace Public Goods	Externalities (Free Riders)
Equality of Opportunity	Externalities (Social Cost)
Employee Representation / Participation	Coordination Failure, Asymmetric Information
Just Cause Dismissal	Coordination Failure, Costly Dispute Resolution

procedural justice—as an important mechanism for reducing turnover and improving employee loyalty, motivation, and performance.[17] As discussed in the next chapter, labor unions might enhance efficiency by increasing workers' sense of equity and voice.[18]

In sum, because of the importance of using scarce resources effectively to promote economic prosperity, efficiency is a primary objective of the employment relationship. In theory, perfect competition yields efficient outcomes, but in real-world labor markets, there may be market failures and efficiency might be improved through government regulations, labor unions, or other mechanisms. Market proponents argue that many of these enhancements do more harm than good, but wide-ranging possibilities are summarized in Box 1.2 to stimulate broad reflection about the possible elements of an efficient employment relationship. In short, the need for efficient workplaces is widely accepted; disagreements arise over how to achieve this goal.

Equity

Equity in the employment relationship is a set of fair labor standards that respect human dignity and liberty and include both material outcomes and personal treatment (see Box 1.3).[19] In industrial relations, the particular concern with equity is rooted in the sometimes abusive and exploitive employment practices of the early 20th century, such as long hours at low

---

[17] Tove Helland Hammer, "Nonunion Representational Forms: An Organizational Behavior Perspective," in Bruce E. Kaufman and Daphne Gottlieb Taras (eds.), *Nonunion Employee Representation: History, Contemporary Practice, and Policy* (Armonk, NY: M.E. Sharpe, 2000), Chapter 8. Robert Folger and Russell Cropanzano, *Organizational Justice and Human Resource Management* (Thousand Oaks, CA: Sage, 1998).

[18] Richard B. Freeman and James L. Medoff, *What Do Unions Do?* (New York: Basic Books, 1984). Bruce E. Kaufman and David I. Levine, "An Economic Analysis of Employee Representation," in Bruce E. Kaufman and Daphne Gottlieb Taras (eds.), *Nonunion Employee Representation: History, Contemporary Practice, and Policy* (Armonk, NY: M.E. Sharpe, 2000), Chapter 7.

[19] Budd, *Employment with a Human Face.*

BOX 1.3
Equity in the Employment Relationship

Dimensions	Rationale
Minimum Labor Standards (Wages, Hours, Safety, Family Leave, Advance Notice, Child Labor)	Human Dignity (Moral and Religious)
Balanced Distribution of Income	Political Equality / Liberty
Equality of Opportunity	Human Dignity (Moral and Religious) Political Equality / Liberty Due Process Rights
Just Cause Dismissal	Human Dignity (Moral and Religious) Political Equality / Liberty Due Process Rights

wages in dangerous working conditions.[20] As such, the push for equitable employment outcomes focused to a large degree on minimum standards—minimum wages, maximum hours, minimum safety standards, just cause protections against arbitrary discharge and favoritism, and restrictions on child labor. In human resource management, the emphasis on equity focuses on general fairness. In particular, equity theory defines fairness in terms of relative inputs and outputs, that is, between effort and reward.[21] A person sees an outcome as fair when the ratio of the individual's outputs to inputs equals the analogous ratio for someone else. In the labor movement, this is associated with the famous slogan "a fair day's pay for a fair day's work"; in human resource management this is associated with distributive justice.[22] Political equality, social stability, and workplace fairness also imply that a balanced distribution of income is a desirable, equitable outcome of the employment relationship.[23]

Human resource management often advocates equitable treatment of employees to enhance both employee and organizational welfare. In short, equity is important if workplace justice improves organizational efficiency and effectiveness. Workplace equity, however, can also be based on political theories of liberty and democracy, moral views of human dignity, humanistic psychology theories of human nature, and religious beliefs about the sanctity of human life. These reasons might seem abstract, but it's important to appreciate the wide-ranging sources of support for equity as an objective of the employment relationship.

First, the lack of at least minimum standards and nondiscriminatory treatment is counter to the basic ideals of political democracy with free and equal citizens.[24] Citizens are not able to function as political equals when they lack a basic level of material well-being. Moreover,

---

[20] Kaufman, "Labor Markets and Employment Regulation."

[21] J. Stacy Adams, "Inequity in Social Exchange," in Leonard Berkowitz (ed.), *Advances in Experimental Social Psychology,* Volume 2 (New York: Academic Press, 1965), pp. 267–99.

[22] Folger and Cropanzano, *Organizational Justice and Human Resource Management.* Jerald Greenberg, "A Taxonomy of Organizational Justice Theories," *Academy of Management Review* 12 (January 1987), pp. 9–22.

[23] Paul Osterman, Thomas Kochan, Michael J. Piore, and Richard M. Locke, *Working in America: A Blueprint for the New Labor Market* (Cambridge: MIT Press, 2001). Michael J. Sandel, *Democracy's Discontent: America in Search of a Public Philosophy* (Cambridge, MA: Harvard University Press, 1996).

[24] John Rawls, *Political Liberalism* (New York: Columbia University Press, 1993). John Rawls, *Justice as Fairness: A Restatement* (Cambridge, MA: Harvard University Press, 2001). Sandel, *Democracy's Discontent.* Joshua Cohen and Joel Rogers, *On Democracy* (New York: Penguin, 1983). Frank I. Michelman, "The Supreme Court 1968 Term—Foreword: On Protecting the Poor Through the Fourteenth Amendment," *Harvard Law Review* 83 (November 1969), pp. 7–59. Robin West, "Rights, Capabilities, and the Good Society," *Fordham Law Review* 69 (April 2001), pp. 1901–32. Rebecca E. Zietlow, "A Substantive Approach to Equal Justice Under Law," *New Mexico Law Review* 28 (Summer 1998), pp. 411–50.

as enshrined in the U.S. Constitution, a democratic society must guarantee equal protection and due process to its citizens which obligates society to provide minimum standards.

Second, the lack of equity violates basic principles of human dignity. In the philosophy of Immanuel Kant, the basic value of human life implies that actions must "treat humanity whether, in your own person or in that of another, always as an end and never as a means only."[25] Paying unfair wages or managing people in a discriminatory fashion violates this basic principle. Humanistic psychology in the tradition of Abraham Maslow also supports workplace equity because providing the basic standards needed for self-development and actualization—which are the elements of workplace equity listed in Box 1.3—should be a critical goal of society.[26]

Third, the standard of equity in the employment relationship also derives from religious views on the sanctity of human life and respect for human dignity. Labor is very important in both the Old and New Testaments of the Bible and Moses has been labeled "history's greatest labor leader" for freeing the Israelite workers from Egyptian exploitation.[27] In Judaism, "a social justice imperative appears repeatedly in Talmudic decisions concerning worker rights" which results in important standards regarding the payment of wages, hours of work, and sick and disability pay.[28] In Islam, one Hadith of the Holy Prophet can be interpreted as requiring a living wage for workers and many teachings emphasize justice and fairness. Equitable distribution of wealth and lack of discrimination or favoritism are also important.[29]

The Catholic Church's papal encyclicals have been the most explicit. In the first encyclical on social thought, *Rerum Novarum* ("On the Condition of Workers," 1891), Pope Leo XIII wrote "justice demands that the dignity of human personality be respected in [workers]. . . . It is shameful and inhuman, however, to use men as things for gain and to put no more value on them than what they are worth in muscle and energy" (§31). Why? Because "no one may with impunity outrage the dignity of man, which God Himself treats with great reverence, nor impede his course to that level of perfection which accords with eternal life in heaven" (§57). Consequently, *Rerum Novarum* advocates a platform of workplace equity: a living wage, health standards, a limit on work hours, and restrictions on child labor.

These principles are reaffirmed in Pope John Paul II's *Centesimus Annus* ("The Hundredth Year," 1991):

> God has imprinted his own image and likeness on man (cf. Gen. 1:26), conferring upon him an incomparable dignity, as [*Rerum Novarum*] frequently insists. In effect, beyond the rights which man acquires by his own work, there exists rights which do not correspond to any work he performs, but which flow from his essential dignity as a person (§11).

While also affirming the importance of private property, the efficiency of the "modern business economy," and the "legitimate role of profit," *Centesimus Annus* asserts that "the market be appropriately controlled by the forces of society and by the State, so as to guarantee that the basic needs of the whole of society are satisfied" (§32 and 35). Thus, fulfilling moral and spiritual development in human beings created by God is another rationale for why fair employment standards and treatment are necessary in the employment relationship.

---

[25] Norman E. Bowie, *Business Ethics: A Kantian Perspective* (Malden, MA: Blackwell, 1999), p. 43.

[26] Abraham H. Maslow, *Toward a Psychology of Being* (Princeton, NJ: Van Nostrand, 1968). John Lawrence Hill, "Law and the Concept of the Core Self: Toward a Reconciliation of Naturalism and Humanism," *Marquette Law Review* 80 (Winter 1997), pp. 289–390.

[27] Joseph Husslein, *Bible and Labor* (New York: Macmillan, 1924).

[28] Michael S. Perry, *Labor Rights in the Jewish Tradition* (New York: Jewish Labor Committee, 1993), p. 1. Israel Weisfeld, *Labor Legislation in the Bible and Talmud* (New York: Yeshiva University Press, 1974).

[29] Khalil-ur-Rehman, *The Concept of Labour in Islam* (Karachi: Arif Publications, 1995). Suzanne Haneef, *What Everyone Should Know About Islam and Muslims* (Chicago: Library of Islam, 1996).

BOX 1.4
Voice in the
Employment
Relationship

Dimensions	Rationale
Industrial Democracy	Political Equality / Liberty / Democracy
Employee Decision Making and Autonomy	Human Dignity (Moral and Religious) Psychological / Social Needs Property Rights (Stakeholder Theory)
Free Speech	Liberty / Human Dignity (Moral)
Political Employee Voice	Political Equality / Liberty

Voice

Voice is the ability to have *meaningful* input into decisions (see Box 1.4).[30] Workers should be able to express unpopular views in the workplace. To back this up, workers should be protected from arbitrary treatment and have access to fair dispute resolution procedures when disagreements arise. And either directly or through representatives, workers should be able to participate in workplace decision making. Synonyms for "voice" might include empowerment, participation, and democracy. Employee voice includes both individual and collective voice, and collective voice includes both nonunion employee representation and independent employee representation. Labor unions are the primary example of independent employee representation because they are independent of managerial authority. With nonunion employee representation, management establishes and ultimately controls the nature of the collective voice mechanism. This is a vital distinction to remember throughout this book.

In human resource management, voice is closely related to procedural justice—the extent to which organizational procedures are fair.[31] In particular, procedural justice largely depends on allowing input as part of a process: for example, being able to discuss your performance and its evaluation with your supervisor or being able to present evidence and participate in your own grievance hearing when facing discipline.[32] Forms of employee voice are also an important part of many recent corporate efforts to improve competitiveness and quality via employee involvement programs and the creation of high performance work systems.[33] Workplace voice can provide a formal mechanism for employees to contribute productivity-improving ideas. Direct participation can fulfill individual needs for personal growth and development which in turn enhances performance through increased job satisfaction and motivation.[34] Employee representation, union or nonunion, can also possibly

[30] Budd, *Employment with a Human Face.*

[31] Folger and Cropanzano, *Organizational Justice and Human Resource Management.* John Thibaut and Laurens Walker, *Procedural Justice: A Psychological Analysis* (Hillsdale, NJ: Lawrence Erlbaum Associates, 1975).

[32] Robert Folger and Mary A. Konovsky, "Effects of Procedural and Distributive Justice on Reactions to Pay Raise Decisions," *Academy of Management Journal* 32 (March 1989), pp. 115–30. Thibaut and Walker, *Procedural Justice.*

[33] Peter Cappelli and David Neumark, "Do 'High-Performance' Work Practices Improve Establishment-Level Outcomes?" *Industrial and Labor Relations Review* 54 (July 2001), pp. 737–75. Brian E. Becker and Mark A. Huselid, "High Performance Work Systems and Firm Performance: A Synthesis of Research and Managerial Implications," in Gerald R. Ferris (ed.), *Research in Personnel and Human Resources Management,* Volume 15 (Stamford, CT: JAI Press, 1998), pp. 53–101. Eileen Appelbaum and Rosemary Batt, *The New American Workplace: Transforming Work Systems in the United States* (Ithaca, NY: ILR Press, 1994). Barry Bluestone and Irving Bluestone, *Negotiating the Future: A Labor Perspective on American Business* (New York: Basic Books, 1992).

[34] Hammer, "Nonunion Representational Forms." Lewis D. Solomon, "Perspectives on Human Nature and Their Implications for Business Organizations," *Fordham Urban Law Journal* 23 (Winter 1996), pp. 221–56.

improve efficiency by providing better two-way communication between employees and management. Employee representation plans can also increase cooperation and reduce turnover by facilitating trust and a sense of fairness.[35]

In industrial relations, employee voice is largely rooted in political theories of liberty and democracy—hence the term **industrial democracy**—and is not dependent on increasing productivity or efficiency.[36] Industrial democracy is premised on the belief that workers in a democratic society are entitled to the same democratic principles of participation in the workplace:

> It is a fundamental doctrine of political democracy that one should have some voice in regard to matters that vitally affect him. . . . [A worker's] life is a factory life; and it is the incidents of factory life over which he needs some control. If there is an argument for giving him a vote, even more is there an argument for giving him a voice in the conditions of shop and factory.[37]

If the U.S. Constitution guarantees free speech, why shouldn't this extend to the workplace? The idea of "might makes right" is rejected in the U.S. political arena; why should it be acceptable in the employment relationship? Because when employees are denied free speech and are subjected to the coercive power of employers, the democratic principle of liberty is violated, even in the workplace.[38] The 19th century socialist labor leader Eugene V. Debs was more blunt: "so long as one man depends upon the will of another or more often the whim and caprice of another for employment, he is a slave."[39]

It is also argued that participation in civil and political life is critical to political democracy, but that much of one's life is spent at work which is often undemocratic.[40] Consequently, an additional political argument for industrial democracy is to create citizens who are trained in participatory democracy. In other words, the workplace should be a school or training ground for democracy, both practically and psychologically.[41] To reinforce this point, note that the workplace is the "single most significant site of regular and ongoing interaction among adult citizens of different racial and ethnic identities."[42] As such, the ability to have workplace conversations that are not stifled by authoritarian managers—in other words, workplace voice—is critical for breaking down racial barriers and strengthening a diverse and inclusive democracy. Workplace voice institutions such as labor unions

---

[35] Kaufman and Levine, "An Economic Analysis of Employee Representation."

[36] Webb and Webb, *Industrial Democracy.* W. Jett Lauck, *Political and Industrial Democracy, 1776–1926* (New York: Funk and Wagnalls, 1926). Milton Derber, *The American Idea of Industrial Democracy, 1865–1965* (Urbana, IL: University of Illinois Press, 1970). Nelson Lichtenstein and Howell John Harris (eds.), *Industrial Democracy in America: The Ambiguous Promise* (Washington, DC: Woodrow Wilson Center Press, 1993).

[37] J.A. Estey, *The Labor Problem* (New York: McGraw-Hill, 1928), p. 208. Roy J. Adams, "Universal Joint Regulation: A Moral Imperative," *Proceedings of the Forty-Third Annual Meeting* (Madison, WI: Industrial Relations Research Association, 1991), pp. 319–27. Brian Towers, *The Representation Gap: Change and Reform in the British and American Workplace* (Oxford: Oxford University Press, 1997).

[38] Burton Hall, "Collective Bargaining and Workers' Liberty," in Gertrude Ezorsky (ed.), *Moral Rights in the Workplace* (Albany: State University of New York Press, 1987), pp. 161–170. Kurt Nutting, "Work and Freedom in Capitalism," in Gertrude Ezorsky (ed.), *Moral Rights in the Workplace* (Albany: State University of New York Press, 1987), pp. 97–104. Compare Epstein, "In Defense of the Contract at Will."

[39] Quoted in Hall, "Collective Bargaining and Workers' Liberty," p. 162.

[40] Carole Pateman, *Participation and Democratic Theory* (London: Cambridge University Press, 1970). Karl E. Klare, "Workplace Democracy and Market Reconstruction: An Agenda for Legal Reform," *Catholic University Law Review* 38 (Fall 1988), pp. 1–68. Cynthia Estlund, *Working Together: How Workplace Bonds Strengthen a Diverse Democracy* (Oxford: Oxford University Press, 2003). Paul Brest, "Further Beyond the Republican Revival: Toward Radical Republicanism," *Yale Law Journal* 97 (July 1988), pp. 1623–31.

[41] Pateman, *Participation and Democratic Theory.*

[42] Estlund, *Working Together*, p. 5.

are essential features of modern, balanced democracies that champion equity and voice in the political arena.[43] In sum, "democratic values are important in the workplace. . . . Real participation in industrial society is critical to a democratic society."[44]

Workplace voice through participative management (in which employees can set goals and make decisions) has also been advocated on moral and religious grounds. In particular, it has been argued that autonomy, meaningful work, and interpersonal contact are basic human needs. Therefore, there is an ethical imperative to provide workers with participative management on the job.[45] Abraham Maslow's famous theory of needs has similarly been used to advocate employee participation in decision making to promote personal growth.[46] Catholic social doctrine mandates employee participation in decision making as necessary for moral and spiritual development and because human beings are part of God's ongoing creation.[47] The stakeholder theory of the corporation also asserts that all stakeholders—employees, customers, suppliers, and others—not just shareholders or owners have sufficient "stakes" in the company to deserve the right to participate in decision making.[48] As such, employees are entitled to workplace voice as stakeholders. Note that participative management and stakeholder theory advocate employee voice but are not arguments specifically for labor unions. In fact, participative management goes beyond traditional union behavior in encouraging direct democracy rather than representation. Like equity, then, voice can be pursued in various ways and is supported as a critical dimension of the employment relationship by many different perspectives—moral, religious, psychological, political, and in some cases, economic.

Isn't Efficiency Enough?

In public conversations about work, efficiency is often the only consideration because business leaders, investment bankers, economists, conservative politicians, and others focus on promoting economic prosperity through free-market initiatives. Profits, not wages, are seen as the critical barometer of corporate health and shareholder interests trump the interests of other stakeholders. The mainstream media's coverage of work-related issues has similarly elevated the importance of consumers over workers in the American "social imagination."[49] Debates over labor unions, minimum wage laws, and paid family or sick leave are reduced to debates over their effects on labor costs and competitiveness. The old saying of "what's good for General Motors is good for the country" is perhaps more widely believed than ever, especially if it was updated to "what's good for Wal-Mart is good for the world." Moreover, conservative social theorists suggest that business is not designed to be a "training ground for democracy" and does not have an obligation to provide personal and moral development.[50] Managers are responsible to investors while workers freely choose to subordinate their interests to managerial

---

[43] Nelson Lichtenstein, *State of the Union: A Century of American Labor* (Princeton, NJ: Princeton University Press, 2002).

[44] William B. Gould, *Agenda for Reform: The Future of Employment Relationships and the Law* (Cambridge, MA: MIT Press, 1993), p. 32.

[45] Norman E. Bowie, *Business Ethics: A Kantian Perspective* (Malden, MA: Blackwell, 1999). Marshall Sashkin, "Participative Management Is an Ethical Imperative," *Organizational Dynamics* 12 (Spring 1984), pp. 5–22.

[46] Solomon, "Perspectives on Human Nature and Their Implications for Business Organizations."

[47] Michael J. Naughton, "Participation in the Organization: An Ethical Analysis from the Papal Social Tradition," *Journal of Business Ethics* 14 (November 1995), pp. 923–35.

[48] Thomas Donaldson and Lee E. Preston, "The Stakeholder Theory of the Corporation: Concepts, Evidence, and Implications," *Academy of Management Review* 20 (January 1995), pp. 65–91.

[49] Rick Fantasia and Kim Voss, *Hard Work: Remaking the American Labor Movement* (Berkeley: University of California Press, 2004). Christopher R. Martin, *Framed! Labor and the Corporate Media* (Ithaca, NY: Cornell University Press, 2004).

[50] Stephen M. Bainbridge, "Corporate Decision Making and the Moral Rights of Employees: Participatory Management and Natural Law," *Villanova Law Review* 43 (1998), pp. 741–828.

directives in return for compensation in the form of wages and benefits. These commentators suggest that workers who wish to exercise "democracy" in publicly traded corporations buy stock in the company and voice their concerns at shareholder meetings. So when studying labor relations or other work-related topics, isn't it enough to just consider efficiency issues?

Suppose an employer believed it was efficient to hire only African-American janitors and white managers—or vice versa. Is this acceptable? If not, it means that there must be social and human boundaries on efficiency.[51] These boundaries are equity and voice. In practice, the boundaries can often be quite weak. For example, the U.S. employment relationship is governed by the employment-at-will doctrine.[52] A classic statement of this doctrine is the ruling that "all may dismiss their employees at will, be they many or few, for good cause, for no cause or even for cause morally wrong, without being thereby guilty of legal wrong."[53] Although employees typically do not realize it, employers therefore have wide latitude for firing workers for many reasons—or no reason at all (see Box 1.5). In fact, the United States is unique among industrialized countries in the strength of at-will employment and the corresponding lack of just cause discharge protections—that is, protections against being arbitrarily fired for reasons not related to job performance or business need.[54] There are a few exceptions to the employment-at-will doctrine in the United States, but these are limited to several legislative restrictions (especially antidiscrimination laws), contractual restrictions (most widely associated with union contracts), and a patchwork of state-by-state judicial exceptions (such as firing someone for refusing to break the law).

The fact that workers are human beings forces us to pay attention to equity and voice in addition to efficiency. In earlier agrarian and crafts-based societies, the quality of life for you and your family was critically linked to your property such as your farm land or workshop, but in today's industrial or postindustrial society, modern workers and their families are often completely dependent on *jobs*, not property. Moreover, working adults spend much of their lives at work and "the workplace is the single most important site of cooperative interactivity and sociability among adult citizens outside the family."[55] The quality of employment and the nature of the workplace are therefore very important for society. Work is not simply an economic transaction; work is a fully human activity such that employees are entitled to fair treatment and opportunities to have input into decisions that affect their daily lives. We must pay attention to the extent to which workers' interests are subordinated to shareholders' and consumers' interests and we must recognize the pervasiveness of inequality—economic inequality exacerbates social inequalities in schooling, health, housing, and political participation.[56] In other words, equity and voice along with efficiency are the central objectives of the employment relationship.

Moreover, in addition to decent wages and fair treatment, workers want a voice in the workplace. A 1994 survey revealed that 63 percent of American workers want more influence over "company decisions that affect your job or work life."[57] Individuals indicated they

---

[51] I am grateful to Alex Colvin for suggesting this example.

[52] Jay M. Feinman, "The Development of the Employment at Will Rule," *American Journal of Legal History* 20 (1976), pp. 118–135.

[53] *Payne v. Western and Atlantic R.R. Co.*, 81 Tenn. 507, 519–520 (1884), *overruled on other grounds.* Hutton v. Watters, 179 S.W. 134, 138 (Tenn. 1915).

[54] Hoyt N. Wheeler and Jacques Rojot (eds.), *Workplace Justice: Employment Obligations in International Perspective* (Columbia: University of South Carolina Press, 1992). Clyde W. Summers, "Individual Protection Against Unjust Dismissal: Time for a Statute," *Virginia Law Review* 62 (April 1976), pp. 481–532. Befort, "Labor and Employment Law at the Millennium."

[55] Estlund, *Working Together*, p. 7.

[56] Kathryn M. Neckerman (ed.), *Social Inequality* (New York: Russell Sage Foundation, 2004). Muirhead, *Just Work.*

[57] Richard B. Freeman and Joel Rogers, *What Workers Want* (Ithaca, NY: ILR Press, 1999).

Instructions: For each of the following scenarios, indicate whether you believe a court of law would find the discharge to be lawful or unlawful, *not* what you would like the result to be. In each case, the employee is *not* represented by a union and was *not* discharged because of his or her race, sex, national origin, religion, age, or disability. Except for question 7, there is no formal written or oral agreement between the employee and employer stating the terms of employment.

	Lawful	Unlawful	Correct
1. Company discharges Employee in order to hire another person to do the same job at a lower wage. Employee's job performance has been satisfactory. The discharge is:	_____	_____	18 %
2. Company discharges Employee because of unsatisfactory job performance. The discharge is:	_____	_____	92 %
3. Employee is discharged because Company mistakenly believes Employee has stolen money. Employee is able to prove in court that Company is mistaken. Employee's job performance has been satisfactory. The discharge is:	_____	_____	10 %
4. Company discharges Employee because there is no longer enough work. The discharge is:	_____	_____	79 %
5. Employee is accused of dishonesty. Supervisor knows that Employee is not dishonest, but discharges him anyway, because she dislikes Employee personally. Employee's job performance has been satisfactory. The discharge is:	_____	_____	8 %
6. Employee discovers that Company has been violating the law by charging customers for services which were not actually provided. Employee is discharged because she refuses to participate in Company's illegal billing practices. The discharge is:	_____	_____	88 %
7. Company's Employee Handbook states that "Company will resort to dismissal for just and sufficient cause only." Based on this statement, Employee leaves his current job to work for Company. Employee performs his job satisfactorily for several years. Company discharges Employee in order to hire another person to do the same job at a lower wage. The discharge is:	_____	_____	16 %

Note: the percentage correct refers to the fraction of respondents in Pauline Kim's 1996 survey of 336 unemployed workers in Missouri who answered the question correctly. The correct answer to question 7 depends on the state you are in.

Source: Pauline T. Kim, "Bargaining with Imperfect Information: A Study of Worker Perceptions of Legal Protection in an At-Will World," *Cornell Law Review* 83 (November 1997), pp. 105–60.

Answers: The discharge is lawful in questions 1–5 (unless you live in Montana). The discharge in question 6 is unlawful. In Missouri and 20 other states, the discharge in question 7 is lawful.

would enjoy their jobs more and their business would be more competitive if they had a greater voice in the workplace. The survey also reveals an important dichotomy between managers and employees: managers prefer to deal with workers one-on-one, but half of workers prefer to deal with management as a group. A majority of workers also indicated that they would like representation that is independent of management. The Internet and e-mail are also helping workers exercise their voice in both union and nonunion workplaces (see Box 1.6).

Workplace CyberVoice

Box 1.6

In what must be one of the first instances of employee voice being facilitated by communications technology, hundreds of telegraph operators conducted an online meeting in the mid-1800s. The employees were from 33 offices along 700 miles of telegraph line stretching from Boston to the Canadian border with Maine. They conducted the meeting, and even passed resolutions, "electronically" using Morse code. Modern information technologies such as the Internet, World Wide Web, and e-mail have an even greater potential to enhance workplace voice in both nonunion and unionized settings on a much broader scale.

A large, nonunion technology company, for example, established a company-wide electronic bulletin board for employees to discuss issues. Case study evidence shows that this enabled management to better share information with the employees. But more important for issues of employee voice, this electronic communication provided a forum for employees to express their concerns to management and to discuss issues with other employees.

In fact, employees were able to join together and succeeded in getting policies changed. In response to a proposed change in the company's profit-sharing plan, hundreds of messages were posted on the electronic bulletin board and after a number of electronic conversations among employees and management, the plan was revised. Moreover, a number of employees subsequently formed a group which met with management in person and ultimately resulted in the creation of an Employee-Executive Forum for discussion of employee issues (in person). While this forum was not successful on a long-term basis, the case study illustrates the potential of information technology to enhance workplace voice.

In a more traditional union setting, dock workers represented by the Maritime Union of Australia went on strike in 1998. News of this strike appeared on the LabourStart Web site (www.labourstart.org) and discussion of the strike then spread by e-mail as well. U.S. and Canadian stevedores pledged solidarity and threatened to boycott Australian shipping. This international solidarity, clearly facilitated by electronic communication, is credited with the union's eventual victory in this strike.

When 17 protesting South Korean union leaders were arrested in December 1999, a news item appeared on the LabourStart Web site and an e-mail plea was sent to labor organizations around the world. These postings included the e-mail address of the President of Korea and the resulting international messages in support of the arrested individuals is believed to have caused their release within 48 hours.

The use of e-mail communication between remote workers has also been prominent in recent contract negotiations at several major airlines. In one case, three Northwest Airlines flight attendants independently launched a mass e-mail campaign, a Web site with dissenting information, and another Web site with a threaded discussion forum criticizing the tentative contract agreed to by their union. The costs are minimal—e-mail is essentially free and one of the Web sites was started after the individual discovered that their Internet service provider included a free Web site with their subscription. But this grassroots effort caused the rank and file to reject the contract. This would have been extremely unlikely without the availability of e-mail and an online bulletin board.

The Internet and information technologies can clearly add another dimension to employee voice and industrial democracy—among unions and informal groups of individuals, and within both nonunion and unionized settings. And no Morse code is required.

Sources: Tom Standage, *The Victorian Internet: The Remarkable Story of the Telegraph and the Nineteenth Century's Online Pioneers* (New York: Walker, 1998), p. 133; Libby Bishop and David I. Levine, "Computer-Mediated Communication as Employee Voice: A Case Study," *Industrial and Labor Relations Review* 52 (January 1999), pp. 213–33; Eric Lee, "How the Internet Is Changing Unions," *WorkingUSA* 4 (Fall 2000), pp. 56–72; Tony Kennedy, "Renegades Went Online to Block NWA Contract," *Star Tribune* (Minneapolis, September 1, 1999), p. 1D.

The centrality of voice in contemporary labor relations is further underscored by the frequency of this theme in union literature and campaigns. Recent materials produced by the American Federation of Labor–Congress of Industrial Organizations (AFL–CIO), the umbrella federation of most U.S. labor unions, emphasize themes such as "A Voice for America's Working Families" and "Together we can make our voice heard." Another example is shown in Box 1.7. The AFL–CIO's counterpart in Great Britain, the Trades Union Congress (TUC), similarly emphasizes voice. Thus, a number of social commentators, labor leaders, and even workers themselves want a workplace that provides fairly distributed outcomes

BOX 1.7
AFL–CIO Palm Card
Emphasizing Voice
(circa 2002)

(front)

Today's
You have a voice. Make it heard.
Unions

(back)

Television ads now running in your community are spreading the good news about today's unions. Take advantage of heightened public interest by talking to people about unions. Tell them:

- *Unions are working people working together to solve problems.*

- *Unions give workers a voice on the job about safety, security, pay, benefits—and about the best ways to get the work done.*

- *Unions stand for fair treatment of all working people—on the job, in our communities and in the economy.*

(equity) and participation in decision making (voice), in addition to the production of goods and services profitably and effectively (efficiency). Whether union or not, each business organization must consider ways to respond to these sometimes conflicting desires.

CONTEMPORARY U.S. LABOR RELATIONS

The three objectives of efficiency, equity, and voice provide a rich framework for understanding labor relations. Why might society want to encourage some type of unionism and why might workers support unionization? Because labor unions can help strike a balance between efficiency, equity, and voice. The U.S. labor relations system is premised on the belief that the invisible hand of markets and the visible hand of human resource managers cannot create efficiency, equity, and voice by themselves. In particular, U.S. labor law assumes that corporations have significantly greater bargaining power than individual, nonunion workers that can result in substandard wages and benefits, discriminatory treatment, autocratic supervision, long hours, and dangerous working conditions. These outcomes do not fulfill the desired objectives: low pay and worker unrest can cause inefficiencies through lack of consumer purchasing

"The demand for organization and collective action has been misunderstood, it is claimed, because of the belief among a large number of citizens that its purpose was simply to secure better wages and better physical conditions. It has been urged, however, by a large number of witnesses before the commission that this is a complete misconception of the purposes for which workers desire to form organizations. It has been pointed out with great force and logic that the struggle of labor for organization is not merely an attempt to secure increased measure of the material comforts of life, but is a part of the age-long struggle for liberty; that this struggle is sharpened by the pinch of hunger and the exhaustion of body and mind by long hours and improper working conditions; but that even if men were well fed they would still struggle to be free. It is not denied that the exceptional individual can secure an economic sufficiency either by the sale of his unusual ability or talent or by sycophantic subservience to some person in authority, but it is insisted that no individual can achieve freedom by his own efforts. Similarly, while it is admitted that in some cases exceptional employers treat their employees with the greatest justice and liberality, it is held to be a social axiom that no group of workers can become free except by combined action, nor can the mass hope to achieve any material advance in their condition except by collective effort."

Source: U.S. Commission on Industrial Relations, *Final Report and Testimony Submitted to Congress by the Commission on Industrial Relations* (Washington, DC: U.S. Government Printing Office, 1916), p. 62. The Commission on Industrial Relations was a nine-person investigative panel created by Congress in 1912 that included both labor and employer representatives. The commission held 154 days of hearings and produced an 11-volume report.

power and disruptions of the economy because of strikes and other disputes; long hours at low pay under dangerous and discriminatory conditions violate equity; and employer dictation of employment conditions as well as autocratic supervision fail to provide employee voice and are counter to the standards of democracy (see Box 1.8).

As will be developed in later chapters, U.S. labor law therefore protects union activity to promote efficiency, equity, and voice:

- **Efficiency:** increasing the purchasing power of workers and reducing disruptive strike activity
- **Equity:** achieving fair standards and protections against exploitation
- **Voice:** providing democracy in the workplace.

If a majority of workers in a specific workplace want union representation, then their employer has a legal obligation to bargain with the union over wages, hours, and other terms and conditions of employment. Workers cannot be fired or otherwise discriminated against because of their support for a union. Employers cannot threaten employees or undertake other actions for the sole purpose of preventing unionization. The rationale for these legal protections is to allow workers to unionize to equalize bargaining power between employees and employers to strike a balance between efficiency, equity, and voice.

When the system is working effectively, efficiency, equity, and voice are achieved through **collective bargaining.** In collective bargaining, representatives of the employer and the employees negotiate the terms and conditions of employment that will apply to the employees. The major subjects of bargaining are listed in Box 1.9. Note that these subjects include much more than basic compensation (often called economic items) and include a number of issues related to personnel policies and work rules (often called language issues). For all of these items, the crucial feature of collective bargaining is that management's traditional authority to unilaterally establish terms and conditions of employment is

- **Compensation**—wages, fringe benefits, vacations and holidays, shift premiums, profit sharing
- **Personnel Policies and Procedures**—layoff, promotion, and transfer policies, overtime and vacation rules
- **Employee Rights and Responsibilities**—seniority rights, job standards, workplace rules
- **Employer Rights and Responsibilities**—management rights, just cause discipline and discharge, subcontracting, safety standards
- **Union Rights and Responsibilities**—recognition as bargaining agent, bulletin board, union security, dues checkoff, shop stewards, no strike clauses
- **Dispute Resolution and Ongoing Decision Making**—grievance procedures, committees, consultation, renegotiation procedures

replaced by bilateral negotiations. Employers cannot single-handedly dictate compensation, policies, and work rules; rather, workers have a collective voice when employment conditions are being determined.

In the United States, when the collective bargaining process results in terms that are approved by both upper management and the union members, the provisions are written down and bound into a legally enforceable collective bargaining agreement, also called a union contract. Traditionally, these contracts have been very detailed and legalistic, and over the last few decades they have grown very thick. While an extreme example, the first contract between the United Automobile Workers (UAW) and General Motors in 1937 was only a page long whereas recent UAW–General Motors contracts are hundreds of pages long and divided into several volumes.

Beginning in the 1980s, business pressures for competitiveness and quality have pressured the collective bargaining process in at least three major ways. First, the business need for flexibility (efficiency) clashes with lengthy, 100-page contracts that spell out detailed work rules (equity). As a result, there has been experimentation with shorter, less detailed (less restrictive) contracts, such as the UAW–Saturn agreement (see Box 1.10). Flexible compensation systems to promote and reward high performance employees can also clash with equity if these systems are perceived as overly subjective, competitive, or unfair. Second, the business need for cooperation and employee involvement clashes with the traditionally adversarial bargaining process in which labor and management use aggressive tactics to extract as many gains or concessions from the other side as their power will allow. As a result, some advocate mutual gains, integrative, or "win-win" bargaining which embraces a culture of joint problem solving rather than competition and conflict. Third, the need for both flexibility and involvement is not well-served by a process in which contracts are renegotiated every three years or so with little productive communication (voice) in between these formal negotiating periods. More bargaining relationships, therefore, are establishing mechanisms to foster ongoing communication, such as joint labor–management committees. These examples demonstrate the framework of environmental influences on strategies and outcomes as shown in Box 1.1. Moreover, because of these challenges, it is imperative that students of labor relations study not only the existing processes, but also consider reform possibilities.

The current legal framework in the U.S. private sector dates back to the Wagner Act (or National Labor Relations Act—NLRA) in 1935—hence the label "New Deal industrial relations system" because of its genesis during President Franklin Roosevelt's New Deal during the Great Depression. That this framework is over 70 years old further reinforces the pressures for reform. The decades around the Depression, and especially immediately after

BOX 1.10
The Thickness of U.S. Union Contracts
These boxes show the relative height of each contract as viewed from the side.

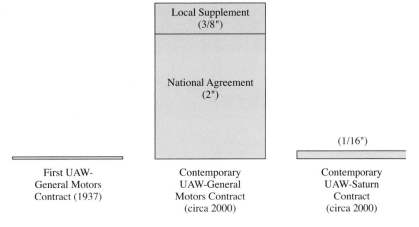

First UAW-General Motors Contract (1937)

Local Supplement (3/8")

National Agreement (2")

Contemporary UAW-General Motors Contract (circa 2000)

(1/16")

Contemporary UAW-Saturn Contract (circa 2000)

World War II, were characterized by mass manufacturing, very sharp distinctions between manual (blue collar) and managerial (white collar) workers, and American domination of world markets. Many argue that labor law is outdated because none of these business features remain true. Rather, the business climate of the 21st century is characterized by flexible methods of production, the rise of knowledge workers and the blurring of traditional distinctions between brawn and brains, and intense global competition. This changed environment cannot be ignored in any study of labor relations (see Box 1.11).

U.S. labor law is also criticized by union supporters, not as much for being outdated, but rather for being too weak. This is directly related to the other significant trend that every student should be aware of, and that also points towards the need for reform: the current state of the U.S. labor movement. In 2005, there were an estimated 15.7 million union members, and another 1.5 million workers covered by union contracts, but who are not union members. But Box 1.12 reveals several important features of labor union membership in the postwar period. First, while the overall number of union members grew into the 1970s, it has declined since then. Moreover, much of the growth after the 1950s was in the public sector. In the private sector, there were roughly the same number of union members in 1965 and 1980 whereas in the public sector, there were twice as many union members in 1980. In the 1990s, total union membership was relatively stable, but this is because a continued decline in private sector membership was offset by an increase in public sector membership.

The more significant measure of the state of organized labor is **union density**—the percentage of workers that are union members. Overall, union density in 2005 was 12.5 percent.[58] But private sector union density in the United States has declined since 1955 from about 35 percent to only 7.8 percent of the workforce. In the public sector, in sharp contrast, union density jumped in the early 1960s, when the first laws protecting public sector unionizing efforts were enacted, increased steadily for 15 years, and after a slight decline, has leveled off at around 37 percent.

It is well-accepted that private sector U.S. union density has been declining for at least 50 years. The reasons for this long decline, however, are controversial.[59] One possible explanation is that employment in traditionally unionized industries such as manufacturing has declined while employment in nonunion industries such as the service industry has increased. Related structural, or compositional, changes include regional and demographic

[58] U.S. Bureau of Labor Statistics News Release, *www.bls.gov/news.release/union2.toc.htm* (accessed May 10, 2006).

[59] Towers, *The Representation Gap*.

Continuing Pressures on the New Deal Industrial Relations System

Box 1.11

MANAGEMENT'S PERSPECTIVE

- Adversarial negotiations create distrust and acrimony rather than trust and cooperation.
- Need to supplement high-level, periodic negotiations with ongoing low-level communication and problem-solving mechanisms.
- Lengthy, detailed contracts inhibit flexibility and involvement.
- Labor law is outdated: these are things of the past:
  - Us v. them (management v. labor)
  - Bureaucratic production
  - American domination of world markets

LABOR'S PERSPECTIVE

- Labor law is weak: penalties are minimal, delays are frequent, employers can use captive audience speeches and permanent strike replacements, secondary boycotts are prohibited.
- Private sector union density is less than 10 percent.
- Workers need protection more than ever in the global economy.

BOX 1.12
U.S. Union Membership, 1950–2005

Source: U.S. Department of Labor.

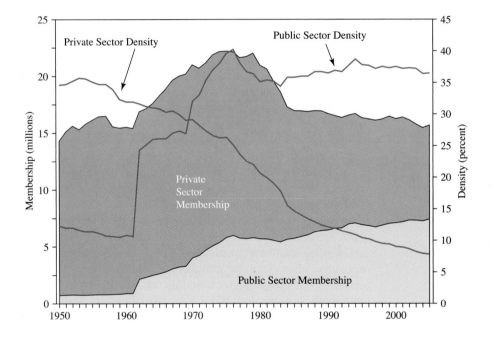

shifts, such as faster employment growth in southern states, increased number of women in the labor force, and increases in education and skill levels.[60] These structural factors may explain part of the decline, but they also beg important questions about why certain industries, occupations, regions, or workers are more or less receptive to unionization.

[60] Gary N. Chaison and Joseph B. Rose, "The Macrodeterminants of Union Growth and Decline," in George Strauss, Daniel G. Gallagher, and Jack Fiorito (eds.), *The State of the Unions* (Madison, WI: Industrial Relations Research Association, 1991), Chapter 1.

A second possibility is that demand for union services has declined.[61] This explanation has three components. One, demand can decline because unions are not doing a good job responding to the needs of a changing workforce. Related to this dimension is that U.S. unions have traditionally devoted few resources towards organizing new workers, though some unions are trying to change this practice.[62] Two, if employers have improved their responsiveness to employees' needs, then this can reduce demand for union protection and advocacy. Three, it is possible that increased protective legislation has provided a substitute for unions.[63] Examples include the Civil Rights Act and Equal Pay Act (and related laws pertaining to age and disability discrimination) forbidding discriminatory employment practices, the Occupational Safety and Health Act providing workplace safety standards, and the Family and Medical Leave Act which establishes unpaid leave for parental, family, and medical reasons. In short, workers no longer need unions to win these basic protections and benefits.

The third, and most controversial, possible reason for the decline in U.S. union density is employer resistance or opposition. Relative to their peers in other industrialized countries, American managers appear to be exceptionally hostile toward unions and have significantly stronger traditions of using union avoidance tactics.[64] Rather than invest in unionized plants or workplaces, U.S. companies often invest in their nonunion operations.[65] Moreover, it is argued that many companies actively fight union organizing drives by firing union supporters, interrogating workers about their support for a union, making threats and promises, hiring anti-union consultants, manipulating the legal system to frustrate and delay organizing campaigns, and in unionized companies, forcing strikes and then hiring replacement workers to bust unions.[66]

One factor that seems to support the significance of employer opposition is the existence of a **representation gap:** employees say that they want more representation in the workplace than they have.[67] Approximately one-third of nonunion workers would like a union in their workplace which implies a desired union density rate of roughly 40 percent

---

[61] Henry S. Farber and Alan B. Krueger, "Union Membership in the United States: The Decline Continues," in Bruce E. Kaufman and Morris M. Kleiner (eds.), *Employee Representation: Alternatives and Future Directions* (Madison, WI: Industrial Relations Research Association, 1993), Chapter 3.

[62] Paula B. Voos, "Union Organizing: Costs and Benefits," *Industrial and Labor Relations Review* 36 (July 1983), pp. 576–91. Richard W. Hurd, "Contesting the Dinosaur Image: The Labor Movement's Search for a Future," *Labor Studies Journal* 22 (Winter 1998), pp. 5–30.

[63] James T. Bennett and Jason E. Taylor, "Labor Unions: Victims of Their Political Success?" *Journal of Labor Research* 22 (Spring 2001), pp. 261–73.

[64] Sanford M. Jacoby, "American Exceptionalism Revisited: The Importance of Management," in Sanford M. Jacoby (ed.), *Masters to Managers: Historical and Comparative Perspectives on American Employers* (New York: Columbia University Press, 1991), Chapter 8. Daphne Gottlieb Taras, "Collective Bargaining Regulation in Canada and the United States: Divergent Cultures, Divergent Outcomes," in Bruce E. Kaufman (ed.), *Government Regulation of the Employment Relationship* (Madison, WI: Industrial Relations Research Association, 1997), Chapter 8. Fantasia and Voos, *Hard Work*.

[65] Thomas A. Kochan, Harry C. Katz, and Robert B. McKersie, *The Transformation of American Industrial Relations* (New York: Basic Books, 1986).

[66] Weiler, *Governing the Workplace*. Freeman and Medoff, *What Do Unions Do?* John J. Lawler, *Unionization and Deunionization: Strategy, Tactics, and Outcomes* (Columbia: University of South Carolina Press, 1990). Fantasia and Voos, *Hard Work*.

[67] Freeman and Rogers, *What Workers Want*. Richard B. Freeman and Joel Rogers, "Who Speaks for Us? Employee Representation in a Nonunion Labor Market," in Bruce E. Kaufman and Morris M. Kleiner (eds.), *Employee Representation: Alternatives and Future Directions* (Madison, WI: Industrial Relations Research Association, 1993), Chapter 1. Seymour Martin Lipset and Noah M. Meltz, with Rafael Gomez and Ivan Katchanovski, *The Paradox of American Unionism: Why Americans Like Unions More Than Canadians Do but Join Much Less* (Ithaca, NY: Cornell University Press, 2004).

in the private sector.[68] The difference between the desired union density rate of 40 percent and the actual private sector rate of 10 percent is the private sector representation gap. Interestingly, this desired figure is roughly the same as the public sector density rate of 37 percent. This is thought-provoking because the scope for fighting unionization by public sector employers is less than in the private sector—the local board of education cannot shut down a school and move it to Mexico (or more importantly, threaten to) in response to a union organizing drive. Perhaps private sector union density would also be close to 40 percent if managerial opposition was more limited, as is the case in the public sector? This evidence regarding the importance of private sector employer opposition to unionization attempts is only suggestive, but the representation gap is a significant feature of U.S. labor relations.

Union membership trends might also be caught in a vicious spiral. In Great Britain it appears that much of the union membership decline in that country can be explained not by union members becoming nonunion, but by a sharp increase in the number of workers who are never unionized.[69] This implies that unionized workers are satisfied with their unions, but that there are fewer opportunities for nonunion workers to experience unionization. Like some consumer products, however, union membership might only be fully appreciated after you have a chance to experience it firsthand.[70] In the United States, Canada, and Great Britain, younger workers are significantly less likely than older workers to be union members.[71] So if new entrants to the labor force are increasingly less likely to experience unionization they are less likely to develop an appreciation for unions and, in turn, union membership will continue to decline. With this decline, even fewer workers will experience unionization, and the vicious cycle of low union experience and low union demand builds on itself.

The decline in private sector union density is one of the central features of contemporary U.S. labor relations and serves as an important backdrop to the study of labor relations. This decline is likely the result of all of the above-mentioned factors, though there are still major disagreements as to their relative importance. These different factors should be remembered when considering the need for labor relations reform. The explanations based on structural changes and declining demand for unionization due to improved corporate policies and employment laws imply that little reform is warranted. On the other hand, if union density has declined because of unresponsive union behavior, labor relations reform must look at transforming unions. But if employer opposition is key, then labor law should be reformed to close the representation gap.

A GLOBAL SNAPSHOT OF LABOR RELATIONS

The question of whether U.S. labor relations needs to be reformed, and if so, how, are very important questions that will be revisited in several places in this book. An important theme, therefore, is that there is more than one way to try to balance efficiency, equity, and voice.

[68] Freeman and Rogers, *What Workers Want.* Freeman and Rogers, "Who Speaks for Us?"

[69] Alex Bryson and Rafael Gomez, "Why Have Workers Stopped Joining Unions? The Rise in Never-Membership in Britain," *British Journal of Industrial Relations* 43 (March 2005), pp. 67–92.

[70] Rafael Gomez and Morley Gunderson, "The Experience Good Model of Trade Union Membership," in Phanindra V. Wunnava (ed.), *The Changing Role of Unions: New Forms of Representation* (Armonk, NY: M. E. Sharpe, 2004), pp. 92–112.

[71] Alex Bryson, Rafael Gomez, Morley Gunderson, and Noah Meltz, "Youth-Adult Differences in the Demand for Unionization: Are American, British, and Canadian Workers All That Different?" *Journal of Labor Research* 26 (Winter 2005), pp. 155–68.

The current U.S. system represents one attempt, with strengths and weaknesses, but other systems or methods are possible. To emphasize that there are many options, it is useful to briefly look at the basic dimensions of labor relations systems from several other countries. These countries will be explored in greater detail in Chapter 13, by which time you will have a greater understanding of how the U.S. system works. For the present time, try to appreciate the differences across these countries in very broad strokes. Also remember that they all have the same goal: striking a balance between efficiency, equity, and voice.

The basic dimensions to consider are summarized in Box 1.13. As already discussed, union density in the United States is less than 15 percent and has generally been falling. Bargaining for union contracts usually takes place at the workplace or company level and results in detailed, legalistic, legally enforceable contracts. Unions have a business unionism philosophy—full acceptance of capitalism with the goal of getting labor's fair share of the profits by strong, pragmatic collective bargaining. If a union represents a majority of employees in a workplace, they are legally designated as the **exclusive representative** of those employees. In other words, no other union can represent those employees. This last concept distinguishes North American labor relations from many other countries in which there may be multiple unions in a single workplace. Also, public policy intervenes in the processes, but not the outcomes. For example, labor law regulates how the parties must act during bargaining, but does not concern itself with the outcome of the bargaining process. The major struggle in

BOX 1.13   Labor Relations around the World: A Snapshot

	Union Density	Bargaining Level	Key Features	Current Questions
United States	15 percent Falling	Mostly Workplace or Company	Exclusive Representation Business Unionism Detailed Contracts	How to Protect Workers with Low Union Density and Promote Efficiency with Bureaucratic Unionism
Canada	35 percent Stable	Mostly Workplace or Company	Exclusive Representation Moving Towards Social Unionism	Are the Small Legal or Social Differences with the U.S. Significant?
Mexico	25 percent	Government Control	Detailed Contracts Strong Constitutional Protections, but Weak, Tightly Controlled Unions	How to Manage Tension Between State Control, Emerging Independent Labor Unions, and Competitiveness
Great Britain	30 percent Falling	Mostly Workplace or Company	Voluntarism Wildcat Strikes Labour Party	Does Voluntarism Yield Unpredictable Labor Relations and Harm Competitiveness?
Germany	30 percent (90% Coverage) Stable	Industry	Codetermination Extension of Agreements to Entire Industry Many Mandated Benefits	Generous Benefits and Extensive Consultation, but Is It Flexible Enough?
Australia	30 percent Falling	Occupational Awards Workplace Negotiations	Arbitration Awards Craft or Occupation Unions Wildcat Strikes	Are Decentralization and Deregulation the Answers to International Competition?
Japan	25 percent Falling	Company	Enterprise Unions Cooperative Relationships Spring Labor Offensive	Flexibility and Cooperation, or Management Domination?

U.S. labor relations is how to protect and represent workers when union density is so low while also achieving competitiveness with a traditionally bureaucratic system of employee representation (recall the thick General Motors contract in Box 1.10).

Canadian labor law is modeled after U.S. labor law, so the nature of bargaining is similar and the resulting contracts have been similar. There are some cultural and seemingly small legal differences, however, which have caused outcomes to diverge from those in the United States.[72] Union density has remained more stable, though Canada also has a larger public sector which accounts for at least some of this difference with the United States, and unions are moving towards a social unionism philosophy in which labor has more of a social activist role—a workplace focus on collective bargaining is supplemented with political protests, social demonstrations, and alliances with other activist groups.

The remaining North American country, Mexico, is broadly representative of labor relations in developing countries. In particular, the primary theme is appearance versus reality. On paper, Mexican law provides much stronger protections for employees and unions than in either the United States or Canada, but the extent of enforcement can be questioned.[73] Moreover, labor negotiations and unions have traditionally been controlled by the government as part of a larger economic development strategy. As in many other developing countries, this results in sharp clashes between independent labor unions and a government interested in fostering competitiveness and foreign investment.

In contrast to the strong protections in Mexican labor law, and even the regulation of the key labor relations processes in the United States and Canada, labor relations in Great Britain have historically been characterized by voluntarism. Though there is some regulation of union behavior and affairs, labor relations are characterized as voluntary because, unlike in the United States, there is little scope for using the law to compel labor–management bargaining or enforcing contracts.[74] Instead, unions and companies voluntarily agree to bargain (or not), and abide by their agreements (or not), based on their relative power. If management thinks a union has sufficient power to make it costly for the employer to refuse to bargain or abide by the contract, then management will bargain or follow the contract. Otherwise, it will not. This can make labor relations less predictable and more turbulent, as indicated by historically higher levels of wildcat strikes over grievances.[75]

If Great Britain's labor relations are fragmented and turbulent, Germany's are institutionalized and centralized. Collective bargaining generally takes place at an industry and regional level between the dominant industry union and the employers' federation. The resulting agreement is often extended to the entire industry.[76] The agreements only contain economic items, especially wages, additional bonuses or benefits, and working time. Unlike the United States, there is no concept of exclusive representation—there can be members of several unions representing the same type of workers in the same workplace. This system of collective bargaining is complemented by a mandatory system of codetermination which includes

---

[72] Taras, "Collective Bargaining Regulation in Canada and the United States." Lipset and Meltz, *The Paradox of American Unionism.*

[73] Stephen F. Befort and Virginia E. Cornett, "Beyond the Rhetoric of the NAFTA Treaty Debate: A Comparative Analysis of Labor and Employment Law in Mexico and the United States," *Comparative Labor Law Journal* 17 (Winter 1996), pp. 269–313.

[74] Mick Marchington, John Goodman, and John Berridge, "Employment Relations in Britain," in Greg J. Bamber, Russell D. Lansbury, and Nick Wailes (eds.), *International and Comparative Employment Relations: Globalisation and the Developed Market Economies* (London: Sage, 2004), pp. 36–66.

[75] Royal Commission on Trade Unions and Employers' Associations, 1965–8. Chairman: Lord Donovan, *Report,* Cmnd. 3623 (London: HMSO, 1968). Towers, *The Representation Gap.*

[76] Berndt K. Keller, "Employment Relations in Germany," in Greg J. Bamber, Russell D. Lansbury, and Nick Wailes (eds.), *International and Comparative Employment Relations: Globalisation and the Developed Market Economies* (London: Sage, 2004), pp. 211–53.

workplace-level works councils as well as employee representation on corporate boards of directors. Works councils are bodies of elected worker representatives that are legally empowered to information and consultation over numerous workplace issues such as overtime, safety, transfers, discipline, the pace of work, and the introduction of new technology. While union members are often active in works councils, collective bargaining is legally distinct from works councils and the presence of a works council is not dependent on the presence of a union. Along with a high level of mandated benefits and social safety nets providing equity, this system of codetermination provides a strong system of employee voice, but the pressure is on efficiency and competitiveness. While there are differences, works councils are also found in other European countries.[77]

As an example of yet another system of labor relations, a major feature of Australian labor relations is a centralized system of arbitration awards.[78] In general, a federal or state arbitration commission issues an award that specifies the minimum standards for pay and working conditions, often for an occupation. Unions and employers are free to negotiate more generous terms. Because of the importance of the national and regional awards, this is a centralized system, but also has a high degree of workplace disputes over grievances. To improve flexibility and responsiveness to firm-specific conditions, there have been efforts at decentralizing the system by encouraging more reliance on enterprise bargaining and less on the arbitration awards through recent policy changes.

Lastly, a key feature of Japan's system of labor relations is enterprise unionism.[79] An enterprise union represents all of the workers, often blue and white collar, at a single enterprise or company. Unlike U.S. industrial unions which often represent all production workers at multiple firms, an enterprise union is limited to one company. Because enterprise unions only represent workers at a single company, there is generally a cooperative attitude because the company's performance affects wages and working conditions for the entire membership of the union. The resulting flexibility and participation is often cited as a model of labor relations on the corporate side because it promotes efficiency, but the important question on the union side is the extent to which enterprise unions are sufficiently independent to represent workers' interests of equity and voice. In other words, the harshest critics view enterprise unions as management-dominated, sham unions.

The labor relations systems of each of these countries will be explored in greater detail later in this book. These brief snapshots, however, emphasize that there are a variety of possibilities for trying to balance efficiency, equity, and voice, and that many countries face the same pressures of globalization, flexibility, and decentralization. Moreover, these comparative examples broadly illustrate many of the continuing debates over U.S. labor relations. Some advocate the deregulation of labor relations, but is a system of voluntarism too turbulent? Some advocate greater institutionalization of codetermination and employee rights to information and consultation as in German works councils, but is this too bureaucratic or cumbersome? Others advocate moving more towards enterprise unions as in Japan, but is this simply a weakening of unions—a reduction in equity and voice—for management's benefit—increased efficiency? There are no easy answers to

[77] Joel Rogers and Wolfgang Streeck (eds.), *Works Councils: Consultation, Representation, and Cooperation in Industrial Relations* (Chicago: University of Chicago Press, 1995).

[78] Russell D. Lansbury and Nick Wailes, "Employment Relations in Australia," in Greg J. Bamber, Russell D. Lansbury, and Nick Wailes (eds.), *International and Comparative Employment Relations: Globalisation and the Developed Market Economies* (London: Sage, 2004), pp. 119–45.

[79] Yasuo Kuwahara, "Employment Relations in Japan," in Greg J. Bamber, Russell D. Lansbury, and Nick Wailes (eds.), *International and Comparative Employment Relations: Globalisation and the Developed Market Economies* (London: Sage, 2004), pp. 277–305.

these important and fascinating questions, but one objective of this book is to develop your understanding of labor relations, intellectually and procedurally, so that you can develop your own informed views on these issues.

THE CONTINUED RELEVANCE OF LABOR RELATIONS

Many are tempted to dismiss unions as a relic from a bygone era and to dismiss studying labor relations as unimportant for business careers in the 21st century. But not so fast. Yes, unions represent less than 15 percent of the U.S. workforce, but this still affects a large number of workers and many of the country's leading companies. Contrary to popular stereotypes, unions are not relevant only to blue-collar occupations; doctors, nurses, lawyers, teachers, writers, professional athletes, college professors, and even graduate students are represented by unions. Labor relations therefore continues to be a very relevant and dynamic area of study and practice.

All managers and business professionals—not just human resource managers—can benefit from learning about labor relations. This is obviously true for those who are or will be working in companies where unions are present, but the study of labor relations has important benefits for other business professionals as well. Consider the four scenarios in Box 1.14. In a nonunion workplace, which of the actions can you legally take? Each of these actions is illegal under U.S. labor law, essentially because they are undermining union-like activities—even in a nonunion workplace. This is because a union does not have to be a large, formal, bureaucratic organization; a union is simply a group of workers acting together to influence their working conditions. Wage and benefit packages from union contracts can also influence nonunion compensation through a threat effect—the threat that dissatisfied workers will unionize causes nonunion firms to at least partially match union wage and benefit terms.[80] Studying labor relations also reveals the consequences of poorly managing a workforce. Thus, an understanding of labor relations is important for all current and future managers.

Studying labor relations can also help current and future business leaders appreciate the broader historical, social, and political influences on business and to better deal with the realities of managing a business in a complex world. Stylized economic models conveniently assume a neat world of perfect competition and rational agents; most business courses consider only the objectives of business and consumers. In contrast, studying labor relations considers the goals of workers and society and does not shy away from the conflicts that can arise between competing groups, especially in a real world characterized by imperfect competition. Labor relations can therefore help everyone understand and resolve conflict—in the workplace, in business relationships, and in everyday personal interactions. Studying labor relations also reveals how work and business are embedded in a very complex environment—at various points in this book, we will consider market forces, individual emotions, managerial strategies, forms of work organization, constitutional and legal issues, history, questions of human rights, negotiation and conflict resolution strategies, debates over globalization, ethical challenges, and much more. These topics contain important lessons for all business leaders because the principles apply to many business and social issues, not just those pertaining to labor relations. For others that are interested in work and workers, labor relations is an engaging subject for thinking about the world of work—what we want to gain from work, how work should be structured, the rights of labor, and other questions that greatly affect the type of society we live in.

---

[80] Lawrence M. Kahn, "The Effect of Unions on the Earnings of Nonunion Workers," *Industrial and Labor Relations Review* 31 (January 1978), pp. 205–16.

Scenario One You implement a new pay-for-performance program and five employees together decide to refuse to work until the program is withdrawn. Can you fire the employees?

Scenario Two You are interviewing applicants for a Web designer position in your organization. One applicant has a Graphic Communications International Union day planner and pen. Can you refuse to hire this qualified individual because you don't want any union troublemakers in your organization?

Scenario Three You overhear two employees discussing a union during a break in the employee cafeteria. Can you stop their conversation?

Scenario Four You want to change your company's health care insurance provider, but only if the employees feel that it is a positive change. Can you handpick an employee committee to represent the other employees in discussions about new health insurance options?

This also implies that the study of labor relations is not confined to a business analysis of problems nor to a description of how existing processes work, though these are important and will be thoroughly covered in this book. U.S. labor relations is a system in flux. Business, unions, and employees are confronted with diversity and experimentation in both business and human resources practices. As a result, a deeper understanding of the underlying issues—the goals of the employment relationship, how labor markets operate, major environmental pressures—is required in order to devise new business practices, union strategies, and public policies in a turbulent world with weak processes and institutions. This book examines the current U.S. labor relations processes, but also seeks to provide a rich foundation for not only understanding the logic of these processes, but also for critically evaluating them and for considering whether reforms are needed. This approach also raises critical questions about how workers should be treated and valued in society. Box 1.15 shows that individuals who defraud shareholders can be sentenced to 25 years in jail, but someone who willfully violates federal workplace safety standards that results in a worker's death faces maximum jail time of only six months—even lower than the prison sentence for harassing a wild burro. A deeper analysis of the employment relationship provides the basis for questioning whether this is appropriate, or if reforms are needed.

The continued relevance of labor relations is also illustrated by the close connection between labor relations and contemporary events. The 9/11 terrorist attacks in 2001 spurred thousands of police, firefighters, and other unionized rescue workers to heroic duty and left thousands of unionized hotel and airline workers without jobs as the tourism and travel industries collapsed.[81] After 9/11, airport screeners became federal employees and were denied the right to be represented by a union for the purpose of collective bargaining. More recently, new federal personnel systems for the Departments of Defense and Homeland Security allow collective bargaining rights to be curtailed and eliminated in the name of

---

[81] C. Jeffrey Waddoups and Vincent H. Eade, "Hotels and Casinos: Collective Bargaining During a Decade of Expansion," in Paul F. Clark, John T. Delaney, and Ann C. Frost (eds.), *Collective Bargaining in the Private Sector* (Champaign, IL: Industrial Relations Research Association, 2002), pp. 137–77. Nancy Brown Johnson, "Airlines: Can Collective Bargaining Weather the Storm?" in Paul F. Clark, John T. Delaney, and Ann C. Frost (eds.), *Collective Bargaining in the Private Sector* (Champaign, IL: Industrial Relations Research Association, 2002), pp. 15–53.

BOX 1.15
The Relative Value of Workers? Selected Federal Criminal Penalties

Protected Group	Violation	Maximum Fine	Maximum Imprisonment
Shareholders	Defrauding shareholders of publicly traded companies	$250,000	25 years
Wildlife	Maliciously causing the death or harassment of any wild free-roaming horse or burro	$2,000	One year
Employees	Willful violation of OSHA safety standards causing death to any employee	$10,000	Six months
Shareholders	Discriminating against an employee for reporting actions that might defraud shareholders (whistleblowing)	$250,000	10 years
Employees	Discriminating against an employee because of their race, sex, religion, age, or union membership.	None	None

Sources: Sarbanes-Oxley Act (U.S. Code, Title 18, Chapter 73, Sections 807 and 1514a); Wild Free-Roaming Horses and Burros Act (Title 16, Chapter 30, Section 113); National Labor Relations Act (Title 29, Chapter 7, Subchapter II); Age Discrimination in Employment Act (Title 29, Chapter 14); Occupational Safety and Health Act (Title 29, Chapter 15, Section 666); Title 42, Chapter 21, Subchapter VI.

national security.[82] Educational reform of public schools is another contemporary issue that is closely intertwined with labor relations.[83] These are all highly charged, complex issues; regardless of what one thinks of the particulars, they clearly demonstrate the continued relevance of labor relations.

Lastly, labor relations continues to have great relevance for society. An analysis of the recent production of Firestone tires indicates that defective tires, which resulted in numerous deaths, were significantly more likely to have been produced during two critical periods of labor–management conflict—when management demanded concessions and when permanent strike replacements were used.[84] Twenty-five people died in a fire because the fire exits were locked at a chicken processing plant in North Carolina.[85] The year? 1911? No, 1991. Office workers in a San Francisco telemarketing "factory" had to raise their hands to get permission to use the restroom, and supervisors prohibited workers from having drinks at their desk so there would be less need to use the bathroom. The year? 1925? No, 1995. In fact, some chicken processing plants have rules against using the bathroom "on company time" more than once a week.[86]

[82] Ruben F. Garcia, "Labor's Fragile Freedom of Association Post-9/11," *University of Pennsylvania Journal of Labor and Employment Law* 8 (Winter 2006), pp. 283–351.

[83] Tom Loveless (ed.), *Conflicting Missions? Teachers Unions and Educational Reform* (Washington, DC: Brookings Institution Press, 2000).

[84] Alan B. Krueger and Alexandre Mas, "Strikes, Scabs and Tread Separations: Labor Strife and the Production of Defective Bridgestone/Firestone Tires," *Journal of Political Economy* 112 (April 2004), pp. 253–89.

[85] Ralph Estes, *Tyranny of the Bottom Line: Why Corporations Make Good People Do Bad Things* (San Francisco: Berrett-Koehler, 1996).

[86] Marc Linder and Ingrid Nygaard, *Void Where Prohibited: Rest Breaks and the Right to Urinate on Company Time* (Ithaca, NY: ILR Press, 1998), p. 2.

While it is unfair to characterize all employers in such terms, it is equally inaccurate to wish away contemporary abuses. Modern sweatshops continue to exist, in the United States and around the globe.[87] Appalling behavior that recalls the foreman's empire of 100 years ago continues today in the form of quid pro quo sexual harassment—demands for sexual conduct in return for job-related benefits or as a threat to avoid negative consequences such as "sleep with me or you will be fired."[88] The U.S. Equal Employment Opportunity Commission receives over 15,000 sexual harassment charges each year and one study found that 25 percent of charges include allegations of quid pro quo harassment.[89] Experimental evidence also indicates that racial discrimination persists—fictitious résumés with African-American names such as Lakisha and Jamal are less likely to lead to a job interview than similar résumés with names that sound White such as Emily and Greg.[90] Workers also continue to be fired for numerous reasons that at best are unrelated to job performance and at worst are illegal and reprehensible: trying to form a union, their race or age, refusing to falsify medical records, and even because of who they were dating or living with.[91] As working hours and contingent employment (such as part-time or temporary work) again increase, even the nature of professional work has been labeled a "white collar sweatshop" as cell phones, laptops, home fax machines, and other technologies combine with the pressures to always be accessible lead to overwork, stress, and burnout.[92] The power of collective action as one method for redressing perceived injustices is underscored by the rise of the Association of BellTel Retirees and other retiree organizations—often comprised of retired white collar managers and executives—to challenge unilateral corporate reduction of cost-of-living increases and health-care benefits for retirees.[93]

One of the most significant economic trends over the last two decades has been the increase in wage and income inequality.[94] Between 1979 and 2000, family income for the poorest 20 percent of households increased by 6.4 percent whereas for the richest 20 percent,

[87] Edna Bonacich and Richard P. Appelbaum, *Behind the Label: Inequality in the Los Angeles Apparel Industry* (Berkeley: University of California Press, 2000). Karl Schoenberger, *Levi's Children: Coming to Terms with Human Rights in the Global Marketplace* (New York: Atlantic Monthly Press, 2000). Pamela Varley, Carolyn Mathiasen, and Meg Voorhes (eds.), *The Sweatshop Quandary: Corporate Responsibility on the Global Frontier* (Washington, DC: Investor Responsibility Research Center, 1998).

[88] Ann Juliano and Stewart J. Schwab, "The Sweep of Sexual Harassment Cases," *Cornell Law Review* 86 (March 2001), pp. 548–602. Joan S. Weiner, "Understanding Unwelcomeness in Sexual Harassment Law: Its History and a Proposal for Reform," *Notre Dame Law Review* 72 (1997), pp. 621–53. Linda LeMoncheck and James P. Sterba (eds.), *Sexual Harassment: Issues and Answers* (New York: Oxford University Press, 2001).

[89] *www.eeoc.gov/stats/harass.html* (accessed January 10, 2002). Juliano and Schwab, "The Sweep of Sexual Harassment Cases."

[90] Marianne Bertrand and Sendhil Mullainathan, "Are Emily and Greg More Employable than Lakisha and Jamal? A Field Experiment on Labor Market Discrimination," *American Economic Review* 94 (September 2004), pp. 991–1013.

[91] Weiler, *Governing the Workplace*. Terry Morehead Dworkin, "It's My Life—Leave Me Alone: Off The-Job Employee Associational Privacy Rights," *American Business Law Journal* 35 (Fall 1997), pp. 47–104.

[92] Jill Andresky Fraser, *White-Collar Sweatshop: The Deterioration of Work and Its Rewards in Corporate America* (New York: W.W. Norton, 2001). Juliet B. Schor, *The Overworked American: The Unexpected Decline of Leisure* (New York: Basic Books, 1991).

[93] "Revenge of the Retirees," *BusinessWeek* (November 18, 2002).

[94] Lawrence Mishel, Jared Bernstein, and John Allegretto, *The State of Working America, 2004–2005* (Ithaca, NY: ILR Press, 2005). Peter Gottschalk, "Inequality, Income Growth, and Mobility: The Basic Facts," *Journal of Economic Perspectives* 11 (Spring 1997), pp. 21–40. Peter Gottschalk and Timothy Smeeding, "Cross-National Comparisons of Earnings and Income Inequality," *Journal of Economic Literature* 35 (June 1997), pp. 633–87. Gary Burtless, "International Trade and the Rise in Earnings Inequality," *Journal of Economic Literature* 33 (June 1995), pp. 800–16.

family income increased by 70 percent.[95] Additionally, more than 10 percent of U.S. residents are estimated to be living in poverty, including between 20 and 25 percent of African Americans and Hispanics, and over one-third of African-American children under the age of six.[96] The apparent link between increasing inequality and weakening labor market institutions and laws, such as declining unionization and inflation eroded minimum wage standards, underscores the continued relevance of labor relations.[97]

Finally, the corporate scandals of 2001–2002—the collapse of Enron, bankruptcy of WorldCom, arrest of the CEO of Adelphia, and charges against the CEO of Tyco International (for stealing $170 million from his company and for $430 million in improper stock sales)—underscore the power and potential for abuse of unchecked individual self-interest.[98] According to *BusinessWeek,* an "astounding" number of companies had to restate their reported earnings between 1997 and 2001 as companies succumbed to the pressure to produce earnings growth by resorting to misleading accounting techniques. "Corrupted by the chase for an ever-greater piece of the action, accountants, lawyers, analysts, and managers have shirked their duty on a scale not seen since the 1920s." *BusinessWeek* is obviously not accusing everyone of being corrupt but recognizes that there is a need for regulation, or a system of checks and balances, to prevent abuse.[99] The same logic applies to the labor market and the employment relationship. Labor relations is the analysis of such problems. Labor relations is about striking a balance between efficiency, equity, and voice.

Key Terms

labor union, *4*	industrial democracy, *13*	representation gap, *23*
efficiency, *4*	collective	exclusive
equity, *4*	bargaining, *19*	representation, *25*
voice, *4*	union density, *21*	

Reflection Questions

1. In a concise paragraph, paraphrase what you have learned about labor relations to explain to a potential employer why studying labor relations will make you a stronger job candidate.

2. Interview workers, union officials, and/or managers who have been involved in a union organizing drive (or look in a newspaper). What issues were emphasized in the organizing drive? Are the issues examples of efficiency, equity, or voice?

3. Alexander Hamilton wrote, "In the general course of human nature, a power over a man's subsistence amounts to a power over his will" (Federalist No. 79, 1788). With respect to the 21st century employment relationship, do you agree? What are the implications for labor policy?

[95] Mishel, Bernstein, and Allegretto, *The State of Working America,* p. 62.

[96] Mishel, Bernstein, and Allegretto, *The State of Working America,* pp. 316–19.

[97] John DiNardo, Nicole Fortin, and Thomas Lemieux, "Labor Market Institutions and the Distribution of Wages, 1973–1992: A Semi-Parametric Approach." *Econometrica* 64 (September 1996), pp. 1001–44. David Card, "The Effect of Unions on Wage Inequality in the U.S. Labor Market," *Industrial and Labor Relations Review* 54 (January 2001), pp. 296–315. John W. Budd and Brian P. McCall, "The Grocery Stores Wage Distribution: A Semi-Parametric Analysis of the Role of Retailing and Labor Market Institutions," *Industrial and Labor Relations Review* 54 (March 2001), pp. 484–501. Harry C. Katz and Owen Darbishire, *Converging Divergences: Worldwide Changes in Employment Systems* (Ithaca, NY: ILR Press, 2000).

[98] More generally, see Estes, *Tyranny of the Bottom Line.*

[99] "Special Report: The Enron Scandal," *BusinessWeek* (January 28, 2002). Quote is from p. 32. "Restoring Trust in Corporate America," *BusinessWeek* (June 24, 2002). "The Rise and Fall of Dennis Kozlowski," *BusinessWeek* (December 23, 2002).

4. As an employee, what kind of voice would you like on a job? Would this make you more productive? Should whether or not you are more productive be the only criterion for whether or not you should have this voice in the workplace?

5. Winston Churchill said, "Democracy is the worst form of Government except all those other forms that have been tried from time to time" (House of Commons speech, November 11, 1947). Is this statement also applicable to the workplace?

Internet Exploration

1. Find a union contract on the Internet (or obtain an actual contract from a library, friend, or contact). What provisions increase efficiency? Decrease efficiency? Provide equity? Provide voice?

2. Search the Internet for Papal encyclicals or statements about labor in other religious denominations. Are these good principles for the employment relationship? If so, how should society ensure that they are fulfilled? Note: the major encyclical on labor is "On the Condition of Workers" (*Rerum Novarum,* 1891) by Pope Leo XIII which was followed by "Reconstruction of the Social Order" (*Quadragesimo Anno,* 1931) by Pope Pius XI, "A Call to Action" (*Octogesima Adveniens,* 1971) by Pope Paul VI, and "On Human Work" (*Laborem Exercens,* 1981) and "The Hundredth Year" (*Centesimus Annus,* 1991) by Pope John Paul II.

Additional Reading

Bamber, Greg J., Russell D. Lansbury, and Nick Wailes (eds.), *International and Comparative Employment Relations: Globalisation and the Developed Market Economies* (London: Sage, 2004).

Budd, John W., *Employment with a Human Face: Balancing Efficiency, Equity, and Voice* (Ithaca, NY: Cornell University Press, 2004).

Fantasia, Rick, and Kim Voss, *Hard Work: Remaking the American Labor Movement* (Berkeley: University of California Press, 2004).

Freeman, Richard B., and Joel Rogers, *What Workers Want* (Ithaca, NY: ILR Press, 1999).

Lichtenstein, Nelson, *State of the Union: A Century of American Labor* (Princeton, NJ: Princeton University Press, 2002).

Osterman, Paul, Thomas Kochan, Richard Locke, and Michael J. Piore, *Working in America: A Blueprint for the New Labor Market* (Cambridge: MIT Press, 2001).

Turner, Lowell, Harry C. Katz, and Richard W. Hurd (eds.), *Rekindling the Movement: Labor's Quest for Relevance in the Twenty-First Century* (Ithaca, NY: ILR Press, 2001).

Chapter **Two**

Labor Unions: Good or Bad?

Advance Organizer

Stereotypes of unions are pervasive (what are yours?). Understanding labor relations requires replacing these stereotypes with informed views. Employee representation through labor unions and collective bargaining is one way to pursue a balance among efficiency, equity, and voice. But how labor union representation compares to other possible ways of structuring the employment relationship—in short, whether unions are good or bad—depends on how one thinks labor markets and the employment relationship work, not on stereotypes.

Learning Objectives

By the end of the chapter, you should be able to:

1. **Explain** the four distinct schools of thought on the employment relationship—neoclassical economics, human resource management, industrial relations, and critical or Marxist industrial relations.

2. **Understand** how different views of labor unions are fundamentally rooted in the basic assumptions of these four schools of thought.

3. **Discuss** various roles of labor unions in the employment relationship and in society.

4. **Identify** alternative methods for making workplace rules.

5. **Compare** employee representation through labor unions to other methods of workplace governance.

Contents

It's not hard to find passionately held views of labor unions. Search for labor union blogs in Google, for example, and you will easily find exchanges such as:

> *Posted by J.*: Forty years of proud union membership, excellent wages, terrific benefits, wonderful retirement, all brought to me by my union

> *Posted by R.*: J, I'm glad you have enjoyed those benefits and high wages all these years—no one's denying that a union is generally very good for its members—the problem is that they are generally very bad for everyone else. Here's how . . .

- Unions shift the extra cost of those wages and benefits to the consumer. . . .
- They drive whole industries out of business and overseas, ultimately lessening the number of jobs in this country. . . .
- They promote laziness and a sense of entitlement, which is a very dangerous thing. . . . [1]

---

[1] *http://www.nathannewman.org/laborblog/archive/003635.shtml* (accessed May 12, 2006).

The common sentiment among Americans that unions are outdated is also often repeated in blog postings; for example:

> *Posted by C.*: Hopefully no one is behind the unions anymore; unless they are pushing them the rest of the way over the cliff. They served a very good purpose 50–100 years ago when they helped push labor issues and worker treatment to the forefront. Now, their bloated wage/benefit packages and refusal to compromise threatens hundreds of thousands of jobs at UAW plants, and in the airline industry.[2]

The mainstream media in the United States—that is, the major TV networks and newspapers that are themselves corporations concerned with making profits—reinforce important stereotypes of labor unions.[3] In general terms, the media report on issues from a consumer rather than worker perspective while also emphasizing the accomplishments of business leaders and entrepreneurs. As representatives of producers rather than consumers and as proponents of collective rather than individual actions, unions are therefore implicitly devalued. When unions are explicitly discussed in the news, strikes and corruption are repeated topics. Even though strikes are rare in practice, they are the most frequent news story in the media, and such stories often convey images about worker greed, inflation, consumer inconvenience, and violence.

Other elements of popular culture reinforce similar stereotypes.[4] TV sitcoms and dramas rarely include labor unions; when such issues arise, it is often a reference to union corruption or strikes. The characters on the TV shows *Married with Children, Spin City, WKRP in Cincinnati, ER, Trapper John, MD, Fraggle Rock,* and *Mona the Vampire* have all had to deal with garbage strikes; on *All in the Family*, Archie Bunker was on strike for four episodes and was portrayed at the conclusion of the strike as not being any better off than before the strike. In an episode of *Seinfeld*, when George wonders about becoming a movie projectionist, Jerry says "But you gotta know how to work the projector. . . . And it's probably a union thing." George then scoffs, "Those unions" and gives up being a projectionist because he figures that he won't be able to break the union's alleged stranglehold on the occupation. Stereotypes about restrictive union work rules or the protection of lazy workers are also reinforced through jokes on sitcoms or in comic strips. One *Dilbert* comic portrays a union steward as wanting to add PDAs and laptops to the list of things that employees should not be able to move because "that's union work." The *Wizard of Id* comic shown in Box 2.1 combines the popular stereotypes of strikes and lazy union workers.

It's important for students of labor relations to recognize their own stereotypes and to replace them with an informed understanding of the central issues in labor relations, and to appreciate multiple perspectives on labor relations and labor unions. As such, this chapter presents four different schools of thought on labor unions. This provides the foundation for accurately assessing what unions do and whether they are good or bad. In short, these schools of thought are essential for understanding labor relations.

---

[2] *http://blog.washingtonpost.com/thefix/2005/12/aflcio_asks_whos_on_our_side.html* (accessed May 12, 2006).

[3] William J. Puette, *Through Jaundiced Eyes: How the Media View Organized Labor* (Ithaca, NY: ILR Press, 1992). Christopher R. Martin, *Framed! Labor and the Corporate Media* (Ithaca, NY: Cornell University Press, 2004).

[4] Puette, *Through Jaundiced Eyes*. Pepi Leistyna, *Class Dismissed: How TV Frames the Working Class* [DVD] (Northampton, MA: Media Education Foundation, 2005).

BOX 2.1 Union Stereotypes in the *Wizard of Id*

Source: *Wizard of Id* by Brant Parker (June 22, 2000) © 2000 Creators Syndicate, Inc.

THE LABOR PROBLEM

Since there is more agreement that unions were once useful, this section considers the historical example of the labor conditions of the early 20th century which were labeled the "labor problem." Turning then to the question of how to solve this labor problem provides the opportunity to consider four different schools of thought on the employment relationship. Understanding these four intellectual perspectives is the basis for a reasoned rather than stereotypical or naïve consideration of labor unions and labor–management relations. It is perhaps easier to tackle these perspectives in a historical context because we have fewer preconceived ideas, but at the end of the discussion, the strong relevance for contemporary labor relations should also be clear.

Today's critical issues in human resources and industrial relations are perhaps familiar to you. Growing labor market disparities. Problems of low-wage workers trying to move out of poverty and support families. Corporate pressures for cost controls, quality, and flexibility to compete in a global, information-rich economy. The need to educate individuals as lifelong learners because of ever-changing technologies. Problems of work–life balance, especially for working mothers.[5] But what about at the start of the previous century? The critical human resources and industrial relations issue in the early 1900s was the labor problem: undesirable outcomes that stem from an inequitable and contentious, or perhaps even oppressive and exploitative, employment relationship.[6] Many important dimensions

---

[5] Paul Osterman, Thomas Kochan, Richard Locke, and Michael J. Piore, *Working in America: A Blueprint for the New Labor Market* (Cambridge: MIT Press, 2001). Jeffrey Pfeffer, *Competitive Advantage Through People: Unleashing the Power of the Work Force* (Boston: Harvard Business School Press, 1994). Edward E. Potter and Judith A. Youngman, *Keeping America Competitive: Employment Policy for the Twenty-First Century* (Lakewood, CO: Glenbridge Publishing, 1995). Jody Heymann, *The Widening Gap: Why America's Working Families Are in Jeopardy and What Can Be Done About It* (New York: Basic Books, 2000).

[6] Bruce E. Kaufman, *The Origins and Evolution of the Field of Industrial Relations in the United States* (Ithaca, NY: ILR Press, 1993). Bruce E. Kaufman, "Labor Markets and Employment Regulation: The View of the 'Old' Institutionalists," in Bruce E. Kaufman (ed.), *Government Regulation of the Employment Relationship* (Madison, WI: Industrial Relations Research Association, 1997), Chapter 1. J. A. Estey, *The Labor Problem* (New York: McGraw-Hill, 1928). E. E. Cummins, *The Labor Problem in the United States* (New York, D. Van Nostrand, 1932). William E. Barns, *The Labor Problem: Plain Questions and Practical Answers* (New York: Harper and Brothers, 1886). Carroll R. Daugherty, *Labor Problems in American Industry* (Boston: Houghton Mifflin, 1933). Warren B. Catlin, *The Labor Problem in the United States and Great Britain* (New York: Harper and Brothers, 1926).

of the labor problem are captured, in the observers' and participants' own words, in the testimony from around 1900 reported in Box 2.2.

The first three entries in Box 2.2 highlight the long hours that were often the norm. The president of the employers' National Association of Manufacturers was satisfied with a standard workweek of between 54 and 57 hours. More generally, a 1909 government survey revealed that only 15 percent of wage earners had a standard workweek of less than 54 hours, and in the South, over 20 percent had standard workweeks of more than 60 hours.[7] Another government survey found that among iron and steel industry workers in 1910, over 40 percent worked more than 72 hours per week and about 20 percent worked more than 84 hours per week.[8]

These long hours were often for low pay. The fourth entry in Box 2.2 claims that wages paid to children in Georgia were as low as 15 or 20 cents per day. Around 1910, most male workers earned less than $15 per week which meant that at least half of working class families had annual incomes below the $800 that was estimated "as a reasonable minimum for healthful, efficient, and decent living"[9] Impoverished conditions were widespread in spite of the fact that less than half of families depended solely on a male breadwinner—25 percent received income from renting rooms to boarders and 15 percent from children working.[10] The fifth and sixth entries in Box 2.2 describe the poor living conditions in Philadelphia and Boston.

The long hours at low pay were often in dangerous and unhealthy conditions. In March 1911, a fire at the Triangle Shirtwaist Company in New York City killed 146 workers because of inadequate and locked fire exits.[11] A 1915 federal study in New York City found that among the two-thirds of garment workers with the lowest pay, over 5 percent had tuberculosis.[12] The emphasis on breaking work into specialized tasks caused what was labeled "new strain"—foreshadowing today's repetitive strain and carpal tunnel injuries.[13] One source estimates that industrial accidents resulted in 25,000 deaths, 25,000 permanent disability cases, and 2,000,000 temporary disability cases per year which implies that during World War I, U.S. casualties were greater in the workplace than on the battlefield.[14]

The long hours at low pay in dangerous and unhealthy conditions were also marked by great insecurity. Many lived with a constant fear of unemployment. Companies might hire workers on a short-term basis, perhaps for only one day at a time with the foreman selecting the day's employees each morning from among those massed outside the factory gate.[15] A 1909 government investigation of nearly 30,000 male workers found that only 37 percent did not have any time lost from work over the course of a full year; half of the workers lost four or more months.[16] As mentioned in the previous paragraph, there were

[7] W. Jett Lauck and Edgar Sydenstricker, *Conditions of Labor in American Industries: A Summarization of the Results of Recent Investigations* (New York: Funk and Wagnalls, 1917), p. 185.

[8] Lauck and Sydenstricker, *Conditions of Labor in American Industries*, p. 186. Interchurch World Movement of North America, *Report on the Steel Strike of 1919* (New York: Harcourt, Brace and Howe, 1920).

[9] Lauck and Sydenstricker, *Conditions of Labor in American Industries*, pp. 29, 376. Seth D. Harris, "Conceptions of Fairness and the Fair Labor Standards Act," *Hofstra Labor and Employment Law Journal* 18 (Fall 2000), pp. 19–166. Cummins, *The Labor Problem in the United States*.

[10] Lauck and Sydenstricker, *Conditions of Labor in American Industries*, p. 254.

[11] Leon Stein, *The Triangle Fire* (Philadelphia: Lippincott, 1962).

[12] Lauck and Sydenstricker, *Conditions of Labor in American Industries*, p. 347. Cummins, *The Labor Problem in the United States*, pp. 90–94.

[13] Lauck and Sydenstricker, *Conditions of Labor in American Industries*, p. 327.

[14] Ezekiel H. Downey, *Workmen's Compensation* (New York: Macmillan, 1924), p. 1.

[15] Lauck and Sydenstricker, *Conditions of Labor in American Industries*, pp. 157–60. Sanford M. Jacoby, *Employing Bureaucracy: Managers, Unions, and the Transformation of Work in American Industry, 1900–1945* (New York: Columbia University Press, 1985).

[16] Lauck and Sydenstricker, *Conditions of Labor in American Industries*, p. 77.

TESTIMONY OF NATIONAL ASSOCIATION OF MANUFACTURERS PRESIDENT

Ten hours [of work] has been fixed as the legal day in [Pennsylvania], and it has been very satisfactory. Many of our trades are now working 57 hours a week. More of our factory force is employed only 54 hours a week, yet in the same branches where we employ them 54 some other manufacturers keep them 60. . . .

TESTIMONY OF SOUTHERN INDUSTRIAL CONVENTION VICE PRESIDENT

Well, it is possible to work them a good deal more than 70 hours in the general work [in the South]. Now, you take sawmills all through the South, Georgia included, and they work their help from sun to sun. It frequently amounts to 14 or 15 hours in the summer, and they never think of working less than 11 hours; that is the least they expect to work, but very often it is 14.

TESTIMONY OF NORTH CAROLINA COMMISSIONER OF LABOR

A great many of the [North Carolina cotton] mills work what they call a 66-hour week; but as they stop at 12 o'clock on Saturday, they work more than 11 hours a day. I am sorry to say that we have no law on that subject. I am sorry to say that some of the mills work over 12 hours, and just as long as they can.

TESTIMONY OF INTERNATIONAL TYPOGRAPHICAL UNION PRESIDENT

The capitalist who owns the factory in Massachusetts has been transferring his industry nearer to the cotton fields; and we find that, in the State of Georgia, where industrial conditions are not as good as in the State of Massachusetts, the man who has been subject in the State of Massachusetts to all these [labor, inspection, and compulsory education] laws has been living under them, has been putting rails around his machinery, has been boxing in his belting, has been refusing to employ in his factory a child under the age of 14 years, and has been putting on every floor of his factory separate closets for male and female labor, has been giving Saturday half holidays for his employees, and abolishing the company store and complying with the law of the State of Massachusetts—when he goes to the State of Georgia and transfers his business there he does not put any railing around his machinery; he does not box in his belting; he employs children

9, 10, or 12 years of age at wages as low as 15 or 20 cents per day, and works them from the time the light shines in the morning until it is dark at night; and in his factory he has no closets, no sanitary conditions, such as are required in the State of Massachusetts; he simply does as he pleases and acts in a most tyrannical and unchristian-like manner.

TESTIMONY OF CHIEF DEPUTY COLLECTOR OF INTERNAL REVENUE, PHILADELPHIA

We visited the so-called slums of Philadelphia and found hundreds of shops where clothing was being manufactured under the most vile conditions. The rooms in which they were being made were very small and greatly crowded—no thought of sanitation or air. Frequently we found that the clothing in course of manufacture was being used to soften the floors, that would otherwise be hard to sleep upon; and in many, many instances we found vermin creeping over the garments as we found them in the sweat shops. There were very, very few of what would be called shops at the present time. They were altogether in homes of private families, houses that ought to be used for living purposes, rooms that ought to be used for living purposes. . . .

[In one shop a man] was working upon this coat. The [man] sat upon a table, working hard, with a view of accomplishing his task before night. Alongside of him was his little baby, about 2 years old, perhaps, without a stitch of clothing on, and you could not lay a 10-cent piece upon a part of its body that was clean. It was slobbering and playing around the father while he was manufacturing or making this coat. Sitting with him were 2 or 3 boys, who were looking after some little detail parts of the coat, and on the floor were at least half a dozen or dozen small spring chickens, that were running in and out. . . .

TESTIMONY OF HEAD OF SOUTH END HOUSE, BOSTON

Of this population of 40,000 [comprising Boston's south end], fully one-half live in tenement houses— that is, where the families have from 1 to 4 rooms. One-fifth of the population lives in higher grade tenements and apartment houses, and nearly all the remainder live in lodging houses. In this entire district, . . . there are less than 100 families who have residences of their own—that is, who have entire houses to themselves. . . .

In this district there is a great lack of sanitary facilities on account of the increase of inhabitants per house; that is, these old houses which formerly were used as residences of well-to-do citizens and formerly accommodated one family, now accommodate a number of families, and accommodate two or three or four times as many people as they were intended for; so that the bathing facilities and water closet facilities and all that are very inadequate to the present number of inhabitants. Where there are houses that have been specially built as tenement houses there appears the evil of the ventilating shaft and the dark inside rooms. . . . Of course this state of things means dampness, darkness, and bad air. The crowding of the houses puts immorality and uncleanliness at a premium.

TESTIMONY OF OHIO STATE BOARD OF ARBITRATION SECRETARY

Wages did not at any time enter into [the causes of the streetcar strike in Cleveland]. There was no question of wages, no dispute whatever on that subject between the company and the men. The men claimed that for a long time the company had established unjust rules; that they were arbitrary in their dealings with the men. They would refuse men a hearing; men were suspended for very trifling causes and frequently discharged. . . . They were not allowed sufficient times for meals . . . in fact, they were not even allowed time for the necessaries of nature.

TESTIMONY OF BOOT AND SHOE WORKERS' UNION SECRETARY-TREASURER

There are about 100 subdivisions of labor in the manufacture of a shoe, varying more or less according to the factory and methods and the kind of shoe made. . . .

Question: The workman only knows how to perform the labor of one particular department?

Answer: That is all, and he becomes a mere machine. . . . Now, take the proposition of a man operating a machine to nail on 40 to 60 pairs cases of heels in a day. That is 2,400 pairs, 4,800 shoes, in a day. One not accustomed to it would wonder how a man could pick up and lay down 4,800 shoes in a day, to say nothing of putting them on a jack into a machine and having them nailed on. That is the driving method of the manufacture of shoes under the minute subdivisions.

Sources: United States Industrial Commission, *Report of the Industrial Commission on the Relations and Conditions of Capital and Labor Employed in Manufactures and General Business* [Volume 7 of the Commission's Reports] (Washington, DC: Government Printing Office, 1901), pp. 132, 280, 363, 472, 496, 789. United States Industrial Commission, *Report of the Industrial Commission on the Relations and Conditions of Capital and Labor Employed in Manufactures and General Business* [Volume 14 of the Commission's Reports] (Washington, DC: Government Printing Office, 1901), pp. 198, 252–254. The Industrial Commission was a 19 person investigative panel created by Congress in 1898 that included senators, congressmen, and industry representatives. The commission produced 19 volumes of reports and testimony on various circumstances relating to labor, business, immigration, and agriculture.

significant dangers of industrial accidents and disease. And in the foreman's empire system of complete management control, there was the fear of arbitrary dismissal (see the seventh entry in Box 2.2).[17] Workers could be, and were, fired for any reason—poor performance, absenteeism, ethnicity, union sympathies, age, failing to provide the foreman with extra services (such as raking his leaves . . . or worse), or simply as a demonstration to others of the foreman's absolute power.

These important dimensions of the labor problem—long hours, low wages, unsafe conditions, and insecurity—were reinforced and worsened by the managerial mind-set of "workers as machines." Labor was frequently viewed as just another input in the production

[17] Nelson Lichtenstein, "'The Man in the Middle': A Social History of Automobile Industry Foremen," in Nelson Lichtenstein and Stephen Meyer (eds.), *On the Line: Essays in the History of Auto Work* (Urbana: University of Illinois Press, 1989), Chapter 7. Jacoby, *Employing Bureaucracy.* Lizabeth Cohen, *Making a New Deal: Industrial Workers in Chicago, 1919–1939* (Cambridge: Cambridge University Press, 1990). Susan A. Glenn, *Daughters of the Shtetl: Life and Labor in the Immigrant Generation* (Ithaca, NY: Cornell University Press, 1990). Nancy F. Gabin, *Feminism in the Labor Movement: Women and the United Auto Workers, 1935–1975* (Ithaca, NY: Cornell University Press, 1990). Meghan Cope, "'Working Steady': Gender, Ethnicity, and Change in Households, Communities, and Labor Markets in Lawrence, Massachusetts, 1930–1940," in Andrew Herod (ed.), *Organizing the Landscape: Geographical Perspectives on Labor Unionism* (Minneapolis: University of Minnesota Press, 1998), Chapter 9.

process no different from machines or raw materials. With mass manufacturing methods emphasizing repetitive, narrowly defined tasks by individual workers to achieve high output, workers had no contact with the final product and minimal control over the content of their jobs. This is reminiscent of Adam Smith's famous example of the 18 steps used to make a single pin, and even in 1776, he recognized that this division of labor had both efficiency advantages and negative social consequences (since it renders human beings "stupid and ignorant").[18] The final entry in Box 2.2 describes how the production of a shoe was divided into 100 specialized operations, and the worker who, for example, nailed heels to 4,800 shoes in a single day was "a mere machine." In modern human resource management terms, employees had no ownership in their work. And if workers are simply machines, they are not entitled to equity or voice; the sole concern of the owner of a machine is efficiency!

These primary conditions of the labor problem were widespread and not limited to manufacturing industries in urban areas. Thousands of Mexican Americans and Mexican immigrants migrated through the Southwest and Midwest following agricultural planting and harvesting seasons earning perhaps $1 a day and living in appalling conditions.[19] In the public sector, police officers regularly worked more than 70 hours per week out of vermin-infested stations.[20] Across the private and public sectors then, the poor conditions of the labor problem were a problem for two broad reasons. First is the societal or human perspective. Put simply, people should have better lives than this. This is partly an economic issue—workers should be able to afford decent housing, clothing, food, and the like; in other words, equity is important. But as emphasized by employee voice, the labor problem is more than a material concern. In particular, one should question whether treating workers as commodities, even as a valuable one, in an autocratic relationship, even if benevolent, fulfills the standards of a democratic society.

There is also the business perspective on why the labor problem is a problem. Are the workers motivated? loyal? productive? Absenteeism and turnover were very costly. At Ford, the absenteeism rate in 1913 was 10 percent, and the annual turnover rate was 370 percent which caused Henry Ford to offer the then large sum of five dollars a day in 1914 as an attempt to tackle these problems.[21] Also, with significant numbers living below the poverty line, a second business problem was that they lacked consumer purchasing power. In the words of one union president in 1899, "as the workingman is himself the consumer, he can not purchase unless he has that with which to purchase."[22] The unskilled workers at Ford, for example, couldn't afford to buy the cars they produced until the five-dollar-a-day plan was implemented. Last, strikes and other forms of industrial conflict that resulted from the labor problem in both the private and public sectors were costly to business, and society more generally.

[18] Adam Smith, *An Inquiry into the Nature and Causes of the Wealth of Nations* (1776) (Edwin Cannan (ed), New York: The Modern Library, 1937), p. 734 (Book V, Chapter I, Article 2d).

[19] Zaragosa Vargas, *Labor Rights Are Civil Rights: Mexican American Workers in Twentieth-Century America* (Princeton, NJ: Princeton University Press, 2005).

[20] Joseph E. Slater, *Public Workers: Government Employee Unions, the Law, and the State, 1900–1962* (Ithaca, NY: Cornell University Press, 2004).

[21] Stephen Meyer, *The Five Dollar Day: Labor Management and Social Control in the Ford Motor Company, 1908–1921* (Albany: State University of New York Press, 1981), p. 80.

[22] United States Industrial Commission, *Report of the Industrial Commission on the Relations and Conditions of Capital and Labor Employed in Manufactures and General Business* [Volume 7] (Washington, DC: Government Printing Office, 1901), p. 397.

FOUR SCHOOLS OF THOUGHT ON THE EMPLOYMENT RELATIONSHIP

The labor problem embodies the ultimate human resources and industrial relations problem: balancing efficiency, equity, and voice. To understand how to solve a problem, you need to analyze the problem's underlying causes. But beliefs on the cause of the labor problem differ between four schools of thought: the neoclassical economics school, the human resource management school, the industrial relations school, and the critical industrial relations school. Understanding and appreciating the basic assumptions of these four schools are essential for understanding not only labor relations, but also the entire field of human resources and industrial relations—past, present, and future.

The Neoclassical Economics School

First, consider the **neoclassical economics school** of thought. This school focuses on the economic activity of self-interested agents, such as firms and workers, in competitive markets.[23] Under some assumptions (such as perfect information), competition among firms, workers, consumers, investors, and suppliers in competitive markets yields optimal prices, output, wages, and consumption. In economics jargon, a Pareto optimal equilibrium is reached and no one can be made better off without making someone else worse off.

In standard economic thought, efficiency, equity, and voice are achieved. Competition yields prices equal to the value of what's being purchased so outcomes are efficient. These outcomes are fair because the amount employees are paid equals the value they contribute to the production process. And voice is expressed through freely participating or abstaining from transactions—if you don't like your working conditions, vote with your feet and quit, and find an employer who treats workers better.[24] In other words, to adherents of the neoclassical economics school, the conditions of the labor problem are not exploitation. Employees are free to choose among jobs and an employer who is not responsive to workers will be unable to hire anyone.

If there is a labor problem, what should be done? Ensure competition. In the neoclassical economics school, the best protection an employee has against his or her current employer is not the government, a lawyer, or a union, but rather other employers.[25] If there is insufficient labor market competition because of excess unemployment, the appropriate policy response is a macroeconomic policy to stimulate the economy and thus reduce unemployment. Or if competition is prevented because of a barrier such as a government regulation, then the policy response is to remove this barrier. As long as there is competition, employment outcomes are not seen as a "problem" (with its negative connotations) in this school of thought. Outcomes are value-free so there may be the labor *situation* (which simply describes the outcomes), but not the labor *problem* (which implies that the outcomes are undesirable).

What is the role of labor unions in the neoclassical economics school of thought? Unions are labor market monopolies that try to restrict the supply of labor. By threatening to strike, unions use their monopoly power to raise wages above the competitive level; this situation

[23] Roger Backhouse, *A History of Modern Economic Analysis* (New York: Blackwell, 1985). George J. Borjas, *Labor Economics,* 3rd ed. (Boston: McGraw-Hill/Irwin, 2005). George R. Boyer and Robert S. Smith, "The Development of the Neoclassical Tradition in Labor Economics," *Industrial and Labor Relations Review* 54 (January 2001), pp. 199–223. Leo Troy, *Beyond Unions and Collective Bargaining* (Armonk, NY: M. E. Sharpe, 1999).

[24] Leo Troy, *Beyond Unions and Collective Bargaining*.

[25] Milton Friedman and Rose Friedman, *Free to Choose: A Personal Statement* (New York: Harcourt Brace Jovanovich, 1980), p. 246. Paul C. Weiler, *Governing the Workplace: The Future of Labor and Employment Law* (Cambridge: Harvard University Press, 1990).

BOX 2.3
"King Debs,"
Cartoon from
Harper's Weekly
(July 14, 1894)

KING DEBS.

distorts employment and output levels throughout the economic system.[26] Moreover, the economics view of work is that it is a lousy activity only endured to earn money. As such, companies rely on the threat of unemployment to motivate otherwise disinterested workers. Unions are seen as interfering with the discipline of the market by protecting lazy workers. In sum, to those who believe in perfect competition, unions are bad because their monopoly power interferes with the efficient operation of the economy. This is the neoclassical economics view, and it is graphically captured by the cartoon from 1894 in Box 2.3. The cartoon portrays union leader Eugene Debs as a powerful king that is able to use a strike to control the railroads, and therefore shut down shipments of food, passengers, mail, coal, and freight, and by extension to close factories. In other words, labor unions are powerful monopolies that are harmful to the economy and the public.

It is important to note that this vision of unions as harmful monopolies relies on a set of fairly strong assumptions pertaining to perfectly competitive markets. First, the standard economic model assumes that goods and services are private—you consume only what you purchase. But some aspects of the workplace are public goods. Safety provisions, heating, lighting, ventilation, just cause discipline and discharge provisions, or grievance procedures, benefit everyone regardless of whether someone "pays" for it. With individual decision making there is a free-rider problem and too little of these beneficial public goods will be provided (analogous to standard societal examples such as national defense). Second, in the standard economic model, mobility and transactions costs are assumed to be zero. Moreover, in competitive markets, compensation and employment conditions are determined by the intersection of supply and demand as shaped by what economists call the marginal worker (the individual who is on the margin of joining or leaving the company with small changes in compensation and employment conditions). For the firm to retain the optimal number of workers, employment conditions must satisfy the marginal worker.

[26] Friedman and Friedman, *Free to Choose*. Morgan O. Reynolds, *Power and Privilege: Labor Unions in America* (New York: Universe Books, 1984). Dan C. Heldman, James T. Bennett, and Manuel H. Johnson, *Deregulating Labor Relations* (Dallas: Fisher Institute, 1981).

If mobility and transactions costs are zero, then anyone who doesn't like these terms and conditions of employment and can get a better deal elsewhere is assumed to be able to easily quit and change jobs. But for workers with seniority, children, a mortgage, and/or doctors through a specific health insurance plan, quitting can be risky and costly. As such, a nonunion workplace might include a group of less mobile workers who are effectively locked into their jobs but who are also not satisfied by the compensation package that is tailored to younger, more mobile, marginal workers. Third, the standard economic model assumes that workers are purely rational. If we relax this assumption, then trust, communication, respect, and fairness become important.

Weakening these assumptions results in a very different economic perspective on labor unions.[27] First, having a collective voice mechanism such as a union in the workplace internalizes both the costs and benefits of workplace public goods and solves the free-rider problem. Workers likely respond positively to these workplace public goods which can increase productivity and efficiency. Second, with a union, employment conditions are determined by bargaining, not the market and the marginal worker. As political organizations, unions are concerned with satisfying a majority of the workers. This is often referred to as the median voter model: if union leaders can satisfy the median worker, they will have satisfied at least 50 percent and will be reelected. Thus, terms and conditions of employment that are determined by collective bargaining will reflect the preferences of a majority of the workers, who are likely to be older and less likely to leave the firm than the marginal workers. This can increase economic efficiency. Third, a regular consultation process between management and a union provides a visible avenue for sustained communication and a forum for employees to voice concerns or resolve grievances. This consultation can promote employee commitment by promoting a sense of dignity, respect, and procedural justice which in turn can enhance economic efficiency.

More generally, note that standard economic models rely on exit for expressing displeasure. If you don't like your job, quit; if you feel a store is too expensive, shop elsewhere. But there is an alternative to exit: communication or voice.[28] Instead of quitting an undesirable job, you can communicate your displeasure to your boss, discuss the situation, and try to work out improvements. If the strong neoclassical economics assumptions necessary for perfect competition are fulfilled, then exit is costless. But voice can be better than exit if exit is costly. As a result, by replacing exit with collective voice, unions can increase economic efficiency if real-world workplaces do not satisfy the simplifying assumptions of the standard neoclassical economics model of perfect competition. If there are workplace public goods, if quitting a job is costly for workers or employers, or if trust and fairness are important to workers, then collective voice in the workplace can be socially beneficial.

Unions therefore have **two economic faces,** a monopoly face and a collective voice/institutional response face.[29] The monopoly face is the dominant neoclassical

[27] Richard B. Freeman and James L. Medoff, "The Two Faces of Unionism," *The Public Interest* (Fall 1979), pp. 69–93. Richard B. Freeman and James L. Medoff, *What Do Unions Do?* (New York: Basic Books, 1984). Bruce E. Kaufman and David I. Levine, "An Economic Analysis of Employee Representation," in Bruce E. Kaufman and Daphne Gottlieb Taras (eds.), *Nonunion Employee Representation: History, Contemporary Practice, and Policy* (Armonk, NY: M. E. Sharpe, 2000), Chapter 7. Alan Manning, *Monopsony in Motion: Imperfect Competition in Labor Markets* (Princeton, NJ: Princeton University Press, 2003). Tove Helland Hammer, "Nonunion Representational Forms: An Organizational Behavior Perspective," in Bruce E. Kaufman and Daphne Gottlieb Taras (eds.), *Nonunion Employee Representation: History, Contemporary Practice, and Policy* (Armonk, NY: M. E. Sharpe, 2000), Chapter 8.

[28] Albert O. Hirschman, *Exit, Voice, and Loyalty: Responses to Decline in Firms, Organizations, and States* (Cambridge: Harvard University Press, 1970).

[29] Freeman and Medoff, "The Two Faces of Unionism." Freeman and Medoff, *What Do Unions Do?* James T. Bennett and Bruce E. Kaufman, "What Do Unions Do?: A Twenty-Year Perspective," *Journal of Labor Research* 25 (Summer 2004), pp. 339–49.

economics view of unions in which unions use their monopoly power in the labor market to raise wages for their members above the competitive level which often proves to be harmful for everyone else. The collective voice face is a second side of unions in which they add collective voice to the workplace and potentially improve outcomes for workers *and* employers. In this face, unions don't raise compensation; rather they represent the collective voice of the workers to alter the mix of the compensation package (for example, more health insurance benefits in lieu of a wage increase, holding total costs constant) to better satisfy a majority of the workforce.

So weakening the strong neoclassical economics assumptions to make them more realistic results in a more nuanced economic model in which unions might not simply be harmful monopolies that always reduce aggregate economic welfare. Nevertheless, the neoclassical view of monopoly labor unions is deeply engrained in economic thought and continues to be the dominant mainstream view. Moreover, labor unions are not singled out in this dominant mainstream view. The same reasoning applies to other government interventions in the labor market, such as minimum wage policies, and to monopolies in other sectors, such as corporate monopolies. The role of government is not to establish labor standards, only to promote competition. The role of law is to protect individual freedoms which are necessary for competition.[30] Remembering the fundamental assumptions that underlie *perfect* competition, and the resulting benefits, is important for understanding one view of the labor problem, and for appreciating important arguments against labor unions and other labor market policies as solutions to historical and contemporary labor problems.

The Human Resource Management School

The second school of thought to consider is the **human resource management school,** or what was formerly called the personnel management school.[31] While the neoclassical economics school focuses on markets, which are external to the firm, proponents of the human resource management school focus their attention inside the firm. In short, this school of thought believes that the labor problem stems from poor management. This is easy to remember: "PM" can stand for both personnel management and poor management.

Recall from above that in the early 1900s, foremen used the drive system—motivation by intimidation and fear—to manage workers.[32] This was a very autocratic and authoritarian management system in which workers were viewed as a commodity or a machine, and thus exploited. A common mind-set was to drive employees to get maximum production for the least cost, and when they broke down (from exertion, age, or injury), discard them and get fresh workers to replace them—as you would with a machine. Hence, there was little concern with how low the wage rates might be, how long the hours, how dangerous the conditions, or how arbitrary the hiring and firing procedures. Moreover, scientific management and the movement to large-scale mass manufacturing and assembly lines tended to reduce workers' tasks to their simplest components and this emphasis on specialization led to monotony, boredom, and deskilling.[33]

---

[30] Richard A. Epstein, *Simple Rules for a Complex World* (Cambridge: Harvard University Press, 1995). Richard A. Posner, *Economic Analysis of Law*, 3rd ed. (Boston: Little, Brown, 1986).

[31] Kaufman, *The Origins and Evolution of the Field of Industrial Relations in the United States.*

[32] Jacoby, *Employing Bureaucracy*. Daniel Nelson, *Managers and Workers: Origins of the Twentieth-Century Factory System in the United States, 1880–1920* (Madison: University of Wisconsin Press, 1995).

[33] Meyer, *The Five Dollar Day*. Harry Braverman, *Labor and Monopoly Capital: The Degradation of Work in the Twentieth Century* (New York: Monthly Review Press, 1974).

This school of thought, therefore, presents a very different underlying cause of the labor problem than in the neoclassical economics school: poor management. The resulting solution to the labor problem is then quite simple: better management. More generally, these solutions to the labor problem are reflected in today's human resource management philosophy: align the interests of workers and the firm via better management. To create motivated and efficient workers, firms should design and implement better supervisory methods, selection procedures, training methods, compensation systems, and evaluation and promotion mechanisms. And if workers want justice, security, respect, and opportunities for advancement, then design human resource management policies that are responsive to these needs to create motivated and efficient employees. With these new policies, workers will be motivated and productive, proponents claim, and efficiency is achieved. Since management policies are responsive to the needs of employees, equity is also achieved. Voice is typically informal, such as in open-door dispute resolution procedures in which workers individually discuss complaints with their managers.

The human resource management philosophy is depicted in the cartoon from a 1928 issue of *Forbes* shown in Box 2.4. The pilgrim, representing business, brings home the Thanksgiving bounty to stockholders, workers, and the government. It is significant that business is clearly depicted as the provider, with a passive role for both labor and government, but also that the gun is labeled "new methods." The new, in the 1920s, methods of the personnel management school, along with other improved business practices in accounting and other areas, can produce healthy returns for all.[34]

What is the role of unions in the human resource management school of thought? As with the dominant view in the neoclassical economics school, unions are not viewed as a positive institution, but for different reasons. In the human resource management school, unions are perceived as adversarial and inimical to cooperation.[35] A popular saying in

BOX 2.4
"Bringing Home the Turkey," Cartoon from *Forbes* (December 1, 1928)

[34] Jacoby, *Employing Bureaucracy.*

[35] Kaufman, *The Origins and Evolution of the Field of Industrial Relations in the United States.* Thomas A. Mahoney and Mary R. Watson, "Evolving Modes of Work Force Governance: An Evaluation," in Bruce E. Kaufman and Morris M. Kleiner (eds.), *Employee Representation: Alternatives and Future Directions* (Madison, WI: Industrial Relations Research Association, 1993), Chapter 4.

human resource management circles is "companies get the union they deserve." If companies are following the human resource management school's ideas of effective management, then workers will be satisfied and will not support a union. But if a company is practicing "bad management" (recall the drive system, for example), workers will seek unionization to combat these poor practices. In other words, unions are a fever—a sign of unhealthy human resources practices—and a healthy company shouldn't have one. This reveals a significant irony and tension within human resource management—human resources professionals have greater influence in companies when there is a threat of unionization, but an important objective is often to keep unions out.[36] In fact, critics of human resource management see it as nothing more than a sophisticated (albeit gentle) antiunion device.[37]

The human resource management school of thought also believes that unions are unnecessary "third parties" which prevent employers and employees from getting "closer together." This remains a very popular theme today. It is interesting to note, however, that in the 1920s many in this school of thought felt that workers should have some type of voice and representation. Having representation, it was believed, would help companies treat employees with respect, create a cooperative, constructive relationship, and foster loyalty which are all important goals in the human resource management school.[38] Thus, in these nonunion representation plans, management would meet and confer with worker representatives. But there would not be bargaining and the representation plans did not have any authority outside management. These were not independent unions, which again in this school of thought are adversarial and inimical to cooperation, but were another management strategy for creating a motivated, productive workforce (and also for preventing independent unions, see Chapter 11). In sum, the labor problem would not be solved with labor unions, but with effective management practices.

The Industrial Relations School

The third school of thought is the **industrial relations school,** formerly the institutional labor economics school.[39] In this school, the labor problem is believed to stem from an inequality of bargaining power between corporations and individual workers. Recall that at the turn of the century in 1900, the "modern" economic system was still emerging. The emergence of large corporations which separated the owners of the production process from a new wage-earning class who did the manual work was relatively new.[40] Institutional labor economists accepted this modern corporation as being an efficient organization of mass production, but rejected the neoclassical economics belief in perfect competition. Rather, institutional labor economists believed that there were many market imperfections: persistent unemployment;

[36] Sanford M. Jacoby, *The Embedded Corporation: Corporate Governance and Employment Relations in Japan and the United States* (Princeton, NJ: Princeton University Press, 2005).

[37] Karen Legge, *Human Resource Management: Rhetorics and Realities* (Basingstoke: Macmillan Press, 1995).

[38] Bruce E. Kaufman, "The Case for the Company Union," *Labor History* 41 (August 2000), pp. 321–50. Bruce E. Kaufman, "Accomplishments and Shortcomings of Nonunion Employee Representation in the Pre-Wagner Act Years: A Reassessment," in Bruce E. Kaufman and Daphne Gottlieb Taras (eds.), *Nonunion Employee Representation: History, Contemporary Practice, and Policy* (Armonk, NY: M. E. Sharpe, 2000), Chapter 2.

[39] Bruce E. Kaufman, *The Global Evolution of Industrial Relations: Events, Ideas, and the IIRA* (Geneva: International Labour Office, 2004). Kaufman, *The Origins and Evolution of the Field of Industrial Relations in the United States.* Kaufman, "Labor Markets and Employment Regulation." Yuval P. Yonay, *The Struggle Over the Soul of Economics: Institutionalist and Neoclassical Economists in America Between the Wars* (Princeton, NJ: Princeton University Press, 1998). Boyer and Smith, "The Development of the Neoclassical Tradition in Labor Economics." Stephen M. Hills, *Employment Relations and the Social Sciences* (Columbia: University of South Carolina Press, 1995).

[40] Nelson Lichtenstein et al., *Who Built America? Working People and the Nation's Economy, Politics, Culture, and Society,* Volume 2 (New York: Worth Publishing, 2000).

company towns dominated by a single employer; lack of worker savings and other safety nets; and large, monopolistic employers with undue influence in markets, politics, and the legal system. In other words, "often the invisible guiding hand of competition is all thumbs."[41]

As a result of these imperfections, individual wage earners have vastly inferior bargaining power relative to employers. With greater bargaining power, employers can pay low wages for working long hours under dangerous working conditions. This greater bargaining power also allows managers to be autocratic and authoritarian. In short, in the industrial relations school, unequal bargaining power is the primary cause of the labor problem.[42] The labor market is characterized not by competition, but by bargaining, and society is worse off if either side has too much power. These problems are compounded by business cycles which create additional insecurities.

The struggle for a balance between labor and management is richly illustrated in Box 2.5. The laborer, clad only in shorts and a headband, is struggling with the capitalist, complete with ruffled collar and puffy pantaloons, for power, as represented by the pendulum. When there is a balance of power in the middle of the spectrum labeled "equity," there is an abundant harvest for both to share. However, when capital has too much power, the result is despotism and the cornucopia is flowing with the weapons of dictators such as shackles. At the same time, at the other end of the spectrum when labor is too powerful, anarchy results, and the cornucopia is filled with the weapons of anarchists, such as daggers and bombs. This is a great characterization of the industrial relations school of thought—and for much of this book, and the study and practice of labor relations. This pendulum imagery will also be important in later chapters as labor law struggles to find a balance between the rights of employers and labor.

Compared to the other schools of thought, in the industrial relations school the causes of the labor problem are very different, and so the solutions are also different. **Most important for labor relations, if the labor problem stems from inequality of bargaining**

BOX 2.5
Striking a Balance between Labor and Capital, *Survey* **(February 7, 1914)**

[41] Garth Mangum and Peter Philips (eds.), *Three Worlds of Labor Economics* (Armonk, NY: M. E. Sharpe, 1988), pp. 4–5.
[42] Kaufman, *The Origins and Evolution of the Field of Industrial Relations in the United States*. Kaufman, "Labor Markets and Employment Regulation." John W. Budd, Rafael Gomez, and Noah M. Meltz, "Why a Balance Is Best: The Pluralist Industrial Relations Paradigm of Balancing Competing Interests," in Bruce E. Kaufman (ed.), *Theoretical Perspectives on Work and the Employment Relationship* (Champaign, IL: Industrial Relations Research Association, 2004), pp. 195–227.

power, then the solution is to increase workers' bargaining power by forming labor unions and pursuing collective bargaining.[43]

The Critical Industrial Relations School

The fourth school of thought to consider is the **critical industrial relations school**, traditionally labeled "Marxist industrial relations" and also referred to as a political economy or a radical perspective. The underlying thesis of this school of thought is that the class or ideology that has the greatest power in society can design and control institutions to serve their own interests.[44] For example, in the 1880s railroad titan James J. Hill set up trust funds to create and manage a Catholic seminary to train local priests so that these priests could in turn Americanize Irish immigrants and preach to them about the importance of diligence and respect for authority—values that Hill wanted in his largely Irish-Catholic workforce.[45] More recently, the profit-based corporate media often portray labor issues through the eyes of consumers, not workers, and corporations are often believed to wield great influence when shaping global trading arrangements. Corporations can therefore shape the broader social context of labor relations to serve their own interests and, in the view of the critical school, maintain their dominance over labor.[46]

In Marxist industrial relations, employment practices are viewed similarly—employers are seen as structuring the organization of work organization, human resource management practices, and labor law to serve the class interests of capital at the expense of labor.[47] The division of labor is a strategy to make labor easily replaceable and therefore weak, fair treatment through progressive human resources policies is pursued primarily to prevent unionization, and legal protection of unions is enacted with legal restraints to keep them in check. Thus, the cause of the labor problem is believed to be control of both society's institutions and the means of production by the capitalist class. In this school of thought, the solution to the labor problem is therefore worker control, ultimately by replacing capitalism with socialism.

As such, labor unions can be important in critical industrial relations. Strong, militant unions can aid workers' struggles with capitalism by mobilizing and raising the consciousness of the working class, and fighting for improved compensation, better working conditions, and greater control over workplace decision making. The anarcho-syndicalist perspective within the critical school also sees radical unions as the key revolutionary vehicle for overthrowing capitalism and creating a society managed by workers. In contrast, proponents of socialism envision a political rather than revolutionary movement away from capitalism, and under socialism, unions would no longer be needed as representatives of

[43] Kaufman, *The Origins and Evolution of the Field of Industrial Relations in the United States.* Kaufman, "Labor Markets and Employment Regulation."

[44] Anthony Giles and Gregor Murray, "Industrial Relations Theory and Critical Political Economy," in Jack Barbash and Noah M. Meltz (eds.), *Theorizing in Industrial Relations: Approaches and Applications* (Sydney: Australian Centre for Industrial Relations Research and Teaching, 1997), pp. 77–120. John Godard, "Beyond Empiricism: Towards a Reconstruction of IR Theory and Research," in David Lewin and Donna Sockell (eds.), *Advances in Industrial and Labor Relations,* Volume 6 (Greenwich, CT: JAI Press, 1994), pp. 1–35. Richard Hyman, *Industrial Relations: A Marxist Introduction* (London: Macmillan, 1975).

[45] Mary Lethert Wingerd, *Claiming the City: Politics, Faith, and the Power of Place in St. Paul* (Ithaca, NY: Cornell University Press, 2001).

[46] Martin, *Framed!* Joseph E. Stiglitz, *Globalization and Its Discontents* (New York: W. W. Norton, 2002).

[47] Braverman, *Labor and Monopoly Capital.* Karl E. Klare, "Judicial Deradicalization of the Wagner Act and the Origins of Modern Legal Consciousness, 1937–1941," *Minnesota Law Review* 62 (March 1978), pp. 265–339. Legge, *Human Resource Management.* David Montgomery, *Workers' Control in America: Studies in the History of Work, Technology, and Labor Struggles* (Cambridge, England: Cambridge University Press, 1979).

the working class (though they might still exist to aid the state in educating and mobilizing workers). In spite of these differing views, many adherents to the various perspectives within critical industrial relations are critical of the pragmatic, collective bargaining focus of U.S. unions (and many unions around the world) which does not do enough to challenge capital's power in the workplace and which reinforces capitalism rather than educating and leading the working class toward worker control or socialism.

The critical industrial relations school of thought does not have widespread acceptance in the United States, but there is greater support in Great Britain and elsewhere. However, even if one does not accept this Marxist or critical viewpoint, it adds another perspective which is important for a complete understanding of labor relations. Moreover, this school of thought forces a critical examination of institutions that might otherwise be naïvely considered neutral. In particular, "free markets" are not actually free in the sense of having no regulation. "Free" markets are regulated by common-law rules, which support competition, but are not necessarily value- or outcome-neutral.[48] For example, a determination of whether employee picketing of a business is allowed or not—or whether only 1 or 100 pickets are allowed—is not a neutral legal finding: restricting picketing benefits employers and allowing picketing benefits labor. A critical perspective also provides an important lens for considering work-related public policies. For example, by some accounts, government-funded job training programs for disadvantaged workers have largely been reduced to training positive attitudes such as a strong work ethic and submission to authority. While these attitudes might be important for labor market success, the critical perspective argues that in the absence of good-paying jobs, such "training" programs simply reinforce the power of employers by teaching workers to accept lousy working conditions and to not question the authority of employers.[49]

The Fundamental Assumptions of Human Resources and Industrial Relations

The labor problem of the early 20th century—low wages for long hours of dangerous work under autocratic supervision and periods of insecurity—can therefore be traced to four possible underlying causes: market failures, poor management, unequal bargaining between employers and individual employees, or domination of labor by the capitalist class. In turn, these lead to four different views of labor unions (see Box 2.6). Underlying these views are four fundamental assumptions of how markets work and the nature of employment:

1. Is labor a commodity?
2. Are employers and employees equals in self-regulating, competitive labor markets?
3. What is the nature of conflict between employers and employees?
4. Is employee voice important?[50]

Each of the four schools of thought answers these questions in different ways. First, what is the nature of labor? Neoclassical economics views the purpose of the economic system as consumption. Work is an unpleasant activity that one endures only to earn money which can then be used to buy things (including leisure). Labor is just another commodity or machine in the production process. Work is endured to earn income, but does not provide intrinsic rewards. The alternative view of labor is embraced by the other

[48] Karl E. Klare, "Workplace Democracy and Market Reconstruction: An Agenda for Legal Reform," *Catholic University Law Review* 38 (Fall 1988), pp. 1–68.

[49] Gordon Lafer, *The Job Training Charade* (Ithaca, NY: Cornell University Press, 2002).

[50] John W. Budd, *Employment with a Human Face: Balancing Efficiency, Equity, and Voice* (Ithaca, NY: Cornell University Press, 2004).

BOX 2.6
Four Schools of Thought on Labor Unions

In Each School of Thought . . .	Labor Unions Are . . .
Neoclassical Economics	*Bad:* Monopolies that benefit a few at the expense of everyone else.
Human Resource Management (formerly, Personnel Management)	*Unnecessary:* Effective management policies are best. Also, unions add unproductive conflict.
Industrial Relations (formerly, Institutional Labor Economics)	*Important:* Necessary to counter corporate bargaining power and to balance efficiency, equity, and voice in democratic, capitalist societies.
Critical Industrial Relations (formerly, Marxist Industrial Relations)	*Important but inadequate:* One key vehicle for aiding labor's struggle against capitalists and for protecting workers, but because of capitalism's inherent imbalances greater sociopolitical changes are needed for true reform.

three schools (human resource management, industrial relations, and critical industrial relations): labor is comprised of human beings with aspirations and feelings. Work fulfills important psychological and social needs and provides more than extrinsic, monetary rewards. Industrial relations, for example, views the purpose of the economic system as facilitating self-development and self-realization, not just consumption. Work has intrinsic value and labor should not be viewed as a commodity or machine. In management and organization theory, these differing views of labor are embedded in Theory X and Theory Y.[51] Theory X, the traditional control model, assumes that people dislike work and have little ambition. In contrast, Theory Y assumes that, under the right conditions, individuals can derive satisfaction from work and will ambitiously pursue various goals if they are committed to them. This is sometimes referred to as the "control versus commitment" dilemma.

Second, are employers and employees equals in the labor market and the legal arena? The assertion that employers and employees are equal is equivalent to believing that the traditional neoclassical economics assumptions, such as perfect information and no transactions costs, are fulfilled. The other schools of thought, however, believe that employers and employees are not equals in the labor market and in the legal arena. Imperfect information, mobility costs, and tilted benefit structures can give firms monopsony (single-buyer) power. Lack of worker savings and persistent unemployment can cause individual workers to have inferior bargaining power relative to employers. These factors can turn perfect competition into excessive or destructive competition which drives wages and working conditions down.[52] In the legal arena, individual workers with imperfect information or without the resources to purchase legal expertise will be at a disadvantage. Admittedly, inequality of bargaining power is difficult to observe, but as one scholar notes, "it is almost unheard of . . . that an *employee* abuses his power to quit at will by using it to coerce his employer to violate its legal obligations or forfeit its statutory rights."[53]

Third, what is the nature of conflict between employers and employees? Three different answers distinguish the human resource management, industrial relations, and critical industrial relations schools of thought—and are therefore very important. The human resource

[51] Douglas McGregor, *The Human Side of Enterprise* (New York: McGraw-Hill, 1960).
[52] Kaufman, "Labor Markets and Employment Regulation."
[53] Weiler, *Governing the Workplace*, p. 58 (emphasis added).

management school has a **unitarist view** of employment relationship conflict.[54] Conflict is not seen as an inherent or a permanent feature of the employment relationship; conflict is seen as a manifestation of poor human resource management policies. Fundamentally, employees and employers have a unity of interests and therefore, effective management policies can align these interests for the benefit of all.

In contrast, the industrial relations school sees the workplace as characterized by multiple interests—that is, a plurality of interests—so this school embraces a **pluralist view** of conflict in the employment relationship. Some of these interests are shared—both employers and employees want their organizations to be successful—but for other issues, it is believed that there is an inherent conflict of interest between employers and employees. In its most simple form, employers' drive for higher profits conflicts with labor's push for higher wages. To be clear, the pluralist belief in an inherent conflict of interest does not mean that all workplace issues involve conflict, but rather is a rejection of the unitarist view that all workplace issues can be structured as a shared interest. In other words, the pluralist view is that employment relationship conflict is mixed motive—some issues are conflictual and some involve mutual interests.[55] Employees want their employers to be profitable, but their desires for higher wages, better benefits, increased security, favorable working conditions, and input into decision making (equity and voice) clash with employers' pressures for lower labor costs, flexibility, and high output (efficiency).

Believers in pluralist workplace conflict therefore see government laws and labor unions as balancing this conflict—striking a balance between efficiency, equity, and voice. Because some conflict is inherent, it is unwise to rely on managerial goodwill to protect workers and to rely on management-initiated programs to provide employee voice. When times get bad enough, even enlightened management can be tempted to put their interests above those of the workers (recall the 2001–2002 corporate scandals at Enron and elsewhere, or the 25 deaths because of locked exit doors at the North Carolina chicken processing plant). And unlike the neoclassical economics school, the industrial relations school does not believe it is sufficient to rely on economic markets to place a check on this conflict of interest. Labor unions, independent of managerial authority, provide checks and balances in the workplace and are therefore essential for protection *and* participation—equity *and* voice.[56]

The view of employment relationship conflict also distinguishes the critical industrial relations school. In this school, there is an inherent conflict between employers and employees, but it is significantly broader than the limited economic conflict in the pluralist view. Conflict is not limited to higher wages or better benefits; it is a social conflict of unequal power relations, or **class conflict.**[57] As such, the critical industrial relations school believes that the pluralist limitation of the concept of "power" to bargaining power, rather than greater social relations, is superficial.[58] Unequal social relations are believed to pervade all capitalist institutions and it is therefore inadequate to think about *balancing* the conflict

[54] Alan Fox, *Beyond Contract: Work, Power and Trust Relations* (London: Farber and Farber, 1974). David Lewin, "IR and HR Perspectives on Workplace Conflict: What Can Each Learn from the Other?" *Human Resource Management Review* 11 (Winter 2001), pp. 453–85.

[55] Thomas A. Kochan, "On the Paradigm Guiding Industrial Relations Theory and Research: Comment on John Godard and John T. Delaney, 'Reflections on the "High Performance" Paradigm's Implications for Industrial Relations as a Field,'" *Industrial and Labor Relations Review* 53 (July 2000), pp. 704–11. Richard E. Walton and Robert B. McKersie, *A Behavioral Theory of Labor Negotiations* (New York: McGraw-Hill, 1965).

[56] Weiler, *Governing the Workplace.*

[57] Giles and Murray, "Industrial Relations Theory and Critical Political Economy." Godard, "Beyond Empiricism."

[58] Hyman, *Industrial Relations.*

There are a number of reasons why human resource managers might want to develop a strategy for providing employee voice. Before reading further, create a list of reasons. Here are some possibilities:

- Learning about employee ideas for improved productivity, quality, and cost savings.
- Increasing employee satisfaction and loyalty (therefore improving productivity and reducing turnover).
- Decentralizing decision making to improve responsiveness and flexibility to changing business needs.
- Providing a substitute for a union (Is this ethical?).
- Increasing employees' problem-solving, communication, and decision-making skills.
- Making work more democratic.

Choose a specific nonunion, business situation (such as a hotel, automobile assembly line, retail food manufacturing marketing group, or insurance company sales force) and determine what type of employee voice mechanism should be implemented. Why? Outline the structure of the employee voice mechanism (examples: voluntary or mandatory, individual or group, decision-making authority or just talk) and a strategy for making it successful.

Now consider the same business situation in the presence of a union. How might the voice mechanism you developed be improved with a union? How might the voice mechanism be less effective with a union? Are your answers to these two questions from the perspective of the company or the employees?

Additional Reading: William C. Byham and Jeff Cox, *Zapp!: The Lightning of Empowerment: How to Improve Productivity, Quality, and Employee Satisfaction* (New York: Ballantine, 1998). Richard S. Wellins, William C. Byham, and Jeanne M. Wilson, *Empowered Teams: Creating Self-Directed Work Groups that Improve Quality, Productivity, and Participation* (San Francisco: Jossey-Bass, 1991). Ronald E. Purser and Steven Cabana, *The Self-Managing Organization: How Leading Companies Are Transforming the Work of Teams for Real Impact* (New York: Free Press, 1998). Edward Cohen-Rosenthal and Cynthia E. Burton, *Mutual Gains: A Guide to Union-Management Cooperation* (Ithaca, NY: ILR Press, 1993).

between labor and management because management always has the upper hand—their domination is built into the entire political, legal, economic, and social structure.

Fourth, is employee voice important? Employee voice is an important component of many contemporary human resources strategies (see Box 2.7). With a unitarist view of conflict, workplace voice can successfully be provided through policies that encourage individual voice or through a nonunion employee representation plan.[59] As the name suggests, an employee representation plan is like a labor union to the extent that employee representatives communicate employee interests to management, but it is not independent. Management, not the employees, typically controls how the plans are structured, when they meet, and what topics are covered.[60] Company management can unilaterally create and disband nonunion employee representation committees.

In contrast, if employment relationship conflict is in fact of a pluralist nature (the industrial relations belief in the existence of some inherent conflicts of interest), then it follows that industrial democracy can only be achieved by traditional labor unions that are independent of management.[61] Such labor unions have power independent of management: they have the right to strike and control how they will select officers and other internal organizational issues. Only independent unions can fight for the protection necessary for industrial democracy such as free speech and due process protections. Taking this one step further, if

---

[59] Kaufman, "The Case for the Company Union." John Leitch, *Man to Man: The Story of Industrial Democracy* (New York: Forbes, 1919).

[60] Bruce E. Kaufman and Daphne Gottlieb Taras (eds.), *Nonunion Employee Representation: History, Contemporary Practice, and Policy* (Armonk, NY: M. E. Sharpe, 2000).

[61] Patricia A. Greenfield and Robert J. Pleasure, "Representatives of Their Own Choosing: Finding Workers' Voice in the Legitimacy and Power of Their Unions," in Bruce E. Kaufman and Morris M. Kleiner (eds.), *Employee Representation: Alternatives and Future Directions* (Madison, WI: Industrial Relations Research Association, 1993), Chapter 5. W. Jett Lauck, *Political and Industrial Democracy, 1776–1926* (New York: Funk and Wagnalls, 1926).

labor–management conflict is embedded throughout society and is not limited to the employment relationship (as believed by the critical industrial relations school), then labor unions ultimately are inadequate for challenging the power of employers. The sometimes-intense debates about nonunion employee representation plans, independent yet conservative labor unions (that is, unions that focus on collective bargaining in a specific workplace rather than on a more general class struggle), and more militant unions continues to be a very important issue in U.S. labor relations and will be addressed in later chapters.[62] Differing assumptions about employment relationship conflict underlie these debates. Understanding these assumptions are therefore critical for understanding labor relations.

THE CONTINUED RELEVANCE OF THE LABOR PROBLEM

Thinking about differing views of labor unions and the four models of the employment relationship that underlie them is usefully pursued in the historical context of the labor problem. Our views of today's employment relationship are powerfully shaped by our limited personal experiences so it can be easier to acknowledge the poor working conditions of earlier eras and think more open-mindedly about various causes and solutions. But this is not intended as a purely historical exercise; while the working conditions for many workers have improved over the last 100 years, the fundamental issues surrounding the four schools of thought on the employment relationship are timeless and apply to today's employment relationship as much as 100 years ago.

To understand labor unions and labor relations, it is imperative to understand the beliefs of the different schools of thought on the labor problem. These four intellectual frameworks provide the keys to a reasoned rather stereotypical understanding of labor unions and to appreciating the basis for differing views on whether unions are good or bad (recall Box 2.6). More generally, these four schools of thought continue to be the key frameworks for analyzing all aspects of the employment relationship in the 21st century and for thinking about how to improve employment issues. In fact, how to balance the employment relationship goals of efficiency, equity, and voice is a critical question for all eras. The focus of this book is how employee representation and collective bargaining help and hinder the achievement of these goals, but there are other options for structuring the employment relationship that do not involve labor union representation. Some might argue that human resource management, government laws, or unregulated, competitive markets are better mechanisms for trying to strike a balance between efficiency, equity, and voice. To better understand labor unions, it is important to explicitly compare collective bargaining to these alternative methods for determining wages and other terms and conditions of employment.

Workplace Governance

All workplaces need rules. In addition to standard rules of behavior and performance, these rules also include compensation and benefits, and policies and procedures. Some of these rules might be written, for example, in an employee handbook, in a union contract, or posted on a bulletin board. Others might be unwritten. Or some might simply be "The workers must do whatever the boss says." But at a more fundamental level, who gets to make these rules? In other words, what are the rules for making the rules?[63] Are they dic-

---

[62] Kaufman and Taras, *Nonunion Employee Representation*. Kaufman and Kleiner, *Employee Representation*. Kaufman, "The Case for the Company Union." Sheldon Friedman, Richard W. Hurd, and Rudolph A. Oswald (eds.), *Restoring the Promise of American Labor Law* (Ithaca, NY: ILR Press, 1994).

[63] John T. Dunlop, *Industrial Relations Systems* (New York: Holt, 1958). Hugh Armstrong Clegg, *The Changing System of Industrial Relations in Great Britain* (Oxford, England: Basil Blackwell, 1979).

tated by the marketplace? Are they established unilaterally by management? Are they mandated by government laws? Or do they result from negotiations between employers and labor unions? Whoever gets to make the rules, gets to rule (or govern), the workplace. Thus, a comparison of the alternative rules for making rules is the question of **workplace governance**.[64] This determines the nature of the balance that is struck between efficiency, equity, and voice. And though it is called workplace governance because of the focus on how workplace rules are determined, note that the ramifications are much broader and determine the quality of life for retirees, spouses, dependents, and communities.

Analyzing the question of workplace governance is particularly instructive for understanding labor relations because it provides the context for evaluating whether unions are good or bad. The statement that unions are good is really the belief that unions achieve a better balance between efficiency, equity, and voice than alternative mechanisms. The assertion that unions are bad is actually the belief that alternative mechanisms strike a better balance. Moreover, analyzing workplace governance reveals that these evaluations are critically related to the underlying assumptions about the nature of markets and employment outlined earlier in this chapter. Supporters of free markets, human resource management, or labor unions have different fundamental beliefs about the value of work, how labor markets work, and the nature of conflict between employers and employees. Understanding these differing beliefs is essential for understanding the evolution of the U.S. labor relations systems, the operation of the processes in practice, and the possible need for reform.

There are six major possibilities for creating workplace rules, that is, for governing the workplace: competitive labor markets, human resource management, human resource management with employee participation (voice), worker control, bargaining with independent employee representatives (labor unions), and statutory government regulation.[65] These six alternatives are summarized in Box 2.8.

Laissez faire reliance on competitive labor markets includes two central critical features: standard neoclassical economic theories plus common-law legal rules that protect individual liberties to enter into contracts. Workplace rules—again, broadly defined to include implicit and explicit rules governing compensation, benefits, working conditions, and performance standards—result from self-interested individuals interacting in free markets. Workplace rules will favor management (lower wages, less generous benefits, shorter vacations, and the like) when labor demand is low and/or labor supply is high; rules will favor employees (higher wages, good benefits, training opportunities, and the like) when labor demand is high and/or labor supply is low. But the rules always result from the invisible hand of market forces. This can be thought of as a system of individual representation—workers looking out for their own interests in competitive markets—in contrast to the union model of collective representation.[66]

In the human resource management model of workplace governance, managers establish employment conditions. They are perhaps constrained to a range of alternatives established by the marketplace, but within this range managers choose specific terms and conditions of employment. For example, salary surveys always indicate that wages are not equal, even for a single occupation in a single location, and managers decide whether to set salaries below, at, or above the market average. The prime mover of workplace rules is therefore not markets, but management. This option of workplace governance contains a

---

[64] Weiler, *Governing the Workplace*. Kaufman, *The Origins and Evolution of the Field of Industrial Relations in the United States*. Thomas A. Kochan, "Labor Policy for the Twenty-First Century," *University of Pennsylvania Journal of Labor and Employment Law* 1 (Spring 1998), pp. 117–31. Estey, *The Labor Problem*. John R. Commons, *Industrial Goodwill* (New York: McGraw-Hill, 1919).

[65] Budd, *Employment with a Human Face*.

[66] Troy, *Beyond Unions and Collective Bargaining*.

BOX 2.8   Options for Workplace Governance

Governance Mechanism	Workplace Determined By:	Key Feature	Question Marks
1. Competitive labor markets	Competition among firms for employees; competition among individuals for jobs.	Competitive markets promote efficiency and provide protections against abuses.	What if markets are not competitive? Should humans be solely at the mercy of markets?
2. Human resource management	Human resource managers.	Human resources policies can align the interests of employers and employees and promote efficiency and equity.	What prevents managerial abuses of its authority and power?
3. Human resource management with voice	Human resource managers in consultation with employees, or by employees within parameters established by managers who have veto power.	Human resources policies and employee participation in decision making can align the interests of employers and employees and promote efficiency, equity, and voice.	What prevents managerial abuses of its authority and power? Is management-controlled voice meaningful?
4. Worker control	Workers or their representatives.	Workers' interests served by having them in control.	What prevents exploitation of investors? How is efficiency achieved?
5. Government regulation	Legislatures or government agencies.	Laws can establish uniform standards for all that are not dependent on the vagaries of markets, managers, or worker power.	How to establish and enforce regulations for many diverse workplaces? Do regulations stifle efficiency?
6. Independent employee representation	Jointly by employers and employees (especially, collective bargaining).	Collective bargaining can equalize power between employees and employers while involving both sides in decision making.	Are unions adversarial and harmful to efficiency? What if unions are weak or absent?

variety of human resource management strategies or philosophies. One possibility is the set of practices advocated by many human resource management scholars and practitioners which treat employees as assets: using valid and reliable selection measures to hire and promote employees, providing training and development opportunities, supporting respectful methods of supervision, promoting distributive and procedural justice, compensating employees in a manner that rewards performance and provides more than a living wage, and providing benefits that foster personal growth, security, and work–life balance.[67] However, traditional autocratic management policies are also possible in this governance option.[68] The distinguishing feature is that the policies, practices, and conditions are unilaterally determined by management.

Employee voice is not a very important component of both the autocratic and the "employees as assets" versions of human resource management. In contrast, strategic human resource management often advocates practices such as direct employee participation in

[67] Raymond A. Noe, John R. Hollenbeck, Barry Gerhart, and Patrick M. Wright, *Human Resource Management: Gaining a Competitive Advantage,* 5th ed. (Boston: Irwin/McGraw-Hill, 2005).

[68] George Strauss, "HRM in the USA: Correcting Some British Impressions," *International Journal of Human Resource Management* 12 (September 2000), pp. 873–97.

decision making through self-directed work teams or quality circles, indirect participation through some form of committee or employee representation, and dispute resolution procedures that include important due process elements.[69] This is the third option for workplace governance: human resource management with employer-initiated employee participation. Note carefully that these employee voice mechanisms are established and directed by management. Employee voice is not independent of managerial authority; this is a crucial distinction between these mechanisms and labor unions.

In the human resource management models with and without voice, management is ultimately in control. The opposite possibility is worker control, such as in producer cooperatives or models of worker control and ownership under socialism. This is more than employee participation, it is employee control over organizational objectives and rule making.[70] This is also more than many employee stock ownership plans in which employees have a financial stake, but not control rights.[71] Rather, workers instead of managers unilaterally establish the terms and conditions of employment. Perhaps the leading U.S. example of worker self-governance was the craft union model of the early 20th-century unions, before the dominance of mass manufacturing. These unions often unilaterally established work rules and enforced them through refusing to work on any other terms and by fining or expelling members who undermined these standards.[72]

Another possibility for governing the workplace is to replace the unilateral authority of the human resource management or worker control models with a system of shared, bilateral authority in which employee voice is independent of managerial authority.[73] The major example of this shared control mechanism is collective bargaining. Workplace rules are not determined by competitive markets or unilaterally by either managers or workers, but are determined via negotiations between two parties with broadly equal bargaining power.

Last, workplace rules can be set by statutory government regulation.[74] Major U.S. examples of governing the workplace via government regulation include the Fair Labor Standards Act (to establish a minimum wage and maximum work hours), Title VII of the Civil Rights Act (to provide equal opportunity), and the Occupational Safety and Health Act (to establish minimum safety standards). Ideally, this system provides protection to everyone and standards can be determined by rational debate rather than bargaining or market power. On the other hand, regulations are determined by a central authority, not the workplace participants so it can be very difficult to shape agreements to fit particular needs and situations, and enforcement can be inconsistent, lax, and/or expensive.[75]

So what determines which system of workplace governance is best? To answer this question we need to put these governance alternatives together with the intellectual models outlined earlier in the chapter—individual opinions on the preferred system of workplace

---

[69] Gary C. McMahan, Meghna Virick, and Patrick M. Wright, "Alternative Theoretical Perspectives for Strategic Human Resource Management Revisited: Progress, Problems, and Prospects," in Patrick Wright et al. (eds.), *Research in Personnel and Human Resources Management, Supplement 4: Strategic Human Resources Management in the Twenty-First Century* (Stamford, CT: JAI Press, 1999), pp. 99–122. Hammer, "Nonunion Representational Forms."

[70] Avner Ben-Ner and Derek C. Jones, "Employee Participation, Ownership, and Productivity: A Theoretical Framework," *Industrial Relations* 34 (October 1995), pp. 532–54.

[71] John Godard, *Industrial Relations, the Economy, and Society,* 3rd ed. (Concord, Ontario: Captus Press, 2005).

[72] Montgomery, *Workers' Control in America.*

[73] Weiler, *Governing the Workplace.*

[74] Bruce E. Kaufman (ed.), *Government Regulation of the Employment Relationship* (Madison, WI: Industrial Relations Research Association, 1997).

[75] Weiler, *Governing the Workplace.*

governance are rooted in how one thinks the employment relationship works. If, as assumed in the neoclassical economics school of thought, labor is simply an economic factor of production (in other words, just another commodity) and employers and employees are economic and legal equals, then the appropriate workplace governance mechanism is reliance on competitive markets. Similarly, the assumptions of the human resource management school of thought lead to a human resource management model of workplace governance and the assumptions of the critical industrial relations school lead to worker control or socialism as the preferred workplace governance model.

Or if one believes that the employment relationship is characterized by unequal bargaining power as in the industrial relations school, then there are two important governance mechanisms for balancing the goals of employers and employees: statutory government regulation and labor unions. Government regulation can try to establish labor standards, but does not involve employee voice whereas labor unions can try to counter corporate bargaining power and also provide voice that is independent of managerial authority. Box 2.9 summarizes the linkages between the key assumptions of human resources and industrial relations, the four schools of thought on the employment relationship, and the various alternatives for governing the workplace. Understanding these linkages is the key to understanding all aspects of employment, evaluating solutions to historical and contemporary labor problems, and considering whether unions are good or bad.

Solving Labor Problems

U.S. political and legal thought during the 1800s and early 1900s was dominated by laissez faire views consistent with the neoclassical economics school, especially the supremacy of the freedom to enter into any type of economic relationship—including employment—without government or union interference. Very few laws were passed that set even minimal labor standards, and many of those that were enacted did not last long because they were ruled unconstitutional. For example, beginning in 1912 some states passed minimum wage laws, for women and children only, but this came to an end in 1923 when the U.S. Supreme Court declared the District of Columbia's law unconstitutional because the law violated the rights of parties to freely enter into economic relationships (generally referred to as the "freedom to contract" where contract is widely defined as an economic relationship and is not limited to written contracts).[76]

The severity of the Great Depression in the 1930s, however, called into serious question the wisdom of the laissez faire legal and economic philosophy.[77] It was during this time period, as part of President Roosevelt's New Deal, that U.S. labor law was fashioned (and upheld by the courts). **As a consequence, U.S. laws pertaining to labor unions and collective bargaining reflect the central belief of the industrial relations school that unions are needed to counter corporate bargaining power and provide industrial democracy.**[78] National labor policy is based on the assumption that the pluralist conflict in the employment relationship is best resolved via collective bargaining to balance efficiency, equity, and voice. This is supplemented by government laws to establish additional standards and safety nets. For

[76] *Adkins v. Children's Hospital*, 261 U.S. 525 (1923). Harris, "Conceptions of Fairness and the Fair Labor Standards Act." Elizabeth Brandeis, "Labor Legislation," in John R. Commons (ed.) *History of Labor in the United States, 1896–1932,* Volume 3 (New York: Macmillan, 1935), pp. 399–741.

[77] Stanley Vittoz, *New Deal Labor Policy and the American Industrial Economy* (Chapel Hill: University of North Carolina Press, 1987).

[78] Melvyn Dubofsky, *The State and Labor in Modern America* (Chapel Hill: University of North Carolina Press, 1994). Yonay, *The Struggle Over the Soul of Economics.* Thomas A. Kochan, Harry C. Katz, and Robert B. McKersie, *The Transformation of American Industrial Relations* (New York: Basic Books, 1986). Budd, *Employment with a Human Face.*

BOX 2.9
The Intellectual
Foundations
of the Options
for Governing
the Workplace

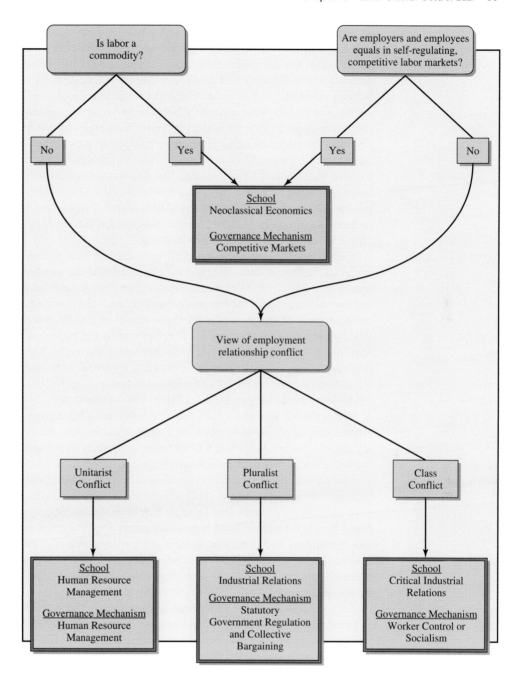

example, the Fair Labor Standards Act of 1938 established a national minimum wage, mandated overtime for hours above a standard workweek (now 40 hours), and restricted child labor. The Social Security Act of 1935 not only established old-age assistance and insurance, but also effectively created a system of state unemployment insurance programs.

Collective bargaining was a very important model of workplace governance in the postwar period, but in the latter part of the 20th century, the nonunion human resource management model came to dominate. This transformation resulted from the growth of nonunion companies and from heavily unionized companies becoming less unionized through the construction of new nonunion plants in the southern United States.[79] Consistent with a human resource management workplace governance model, in this time period after World War II, government laws to strengthen worker bargaining power through unions and social safety nets have been largely nonexistent. In contrast to the New Deal policies of the 1930s, postwar public policies concede employees' dependence on employers by avoiding mandating specific benefits and instead requiring nondiscrimination and disclosure requirements for employer-controlled terms and conditions of employment. As just one example, rather than requiring employers to provide health insurance or pensions, government regulations require those that do to file annual reports so that employees can monitor these plans. More recently, the free-market model of workplace governance is again becoming dominant (as it was before the New Deal). With little threat of unionization or new employment laws in the United States, finance has trumped human resources in many organizations.[80] Public policies that support free trade and deregulation further increase the emphasis on competitive markets.

Each of these shifts represent different views on how to solve that generation's labor problems consistent with changing beliefs about how the employment relationship works (recall Box 2.9). In spite of the rise of the nonunion human resource management model and the reemergence of the free market model, the U.S. system of labor relations is founded on the beliefs of the industrial relations school in the context of the early 20th-century labor problem. Understanding the development of the New Deal industrial relations system, therefore, grows out of an examination of the early 20th-century labor problem. Moreover, since contemporary labor relations continues to be dominated by laws rooted in the industrial relations school's principles, understanding the logic of current practices and strategies requires an appreciation of this school of thought.

But again, all four schools of thought continue to have great practical relevance—the laissez faire emphasis of neoclassical economics dominates national and international policy debates, today's corporate human resources policies are rooted in the principles of the human resource management school of thought, and critical scholars continue to make important contributions to our understanding of employment issues. And the principles of the industrial relations school continue to appear in practice in many places around the globe, such as in New Zealand's Employment Relations Act of 2000 which is based on the belief that "there is an inequality of bargaining power in many employment relationships" such that "employers and employees share many common interests, but they also have separate interests" which means that "productive employment relationships depend on . . . promoting areas of common interest and managing competing interests in a way that maintains and builds relationships."[81]

Last, while some of the details may have changed, the United States and every other developed and developing country in the 21st century continue to struggle with the modern equivalent of the labor problem. All three dimensions of efficiency, equity, and voice are very relevant to the employment relationship of today. Modern sweatshops, in the United States and elsewhere, continue to exist and exploit workers (compare Boxes 2.10 and 2.11). Wage and income inequality has increased at the end of the 20th century. The arbitrary power of supervisors persists as illustrated by the thousands of complaints of quid pro quo sexual harassment filed with the U.S. Equal Employment Opportunity Commission.

---

[79] Kochan, Katz, and McKersie, *The Transformation of American Industrial Relations.*

[80] Jacoby, *The Embedded Corporation.*

[81] "In Good Faith: Collective Bargaining Under the Employment Relations Act 2000" (Wellington: New Zealand Department of Labour, 2001), p. 8, available at
http://www.ers.dol.govt.nz/publications/pdfs/A5_good_faith_bargain.pdf (accessed May 22, 2006).

BOX 2.10
**Garment Factory
Workers Sitting at
Long Tables Probably
in New York City,
circa 1900**

(ILGWU Archives, Kheel
Center, Cornell University).

BOX 2.11
**Garment Factory
Workers Sitting
at Long Tables,
New York City, 1991**

(American Social History
Project).

Workers in many occupations want a stronger voice in the workplace, and there is increasing recognition that this is a fundamental human right. At the same time, private and public sector organizations continue to struggle with issues of competitiveness, productivity, and quality. Efficiency, equity, and voice continue to be critical themes for policy makers and practitioners, workers and employers. The seemingly historical discussion of the labor problem continues to have great relevance for us in the 21st century both intellectually and practically.

WHAT DO U.S. UNIONS DO?

So, are unions good or bad? The four schools of thought and the labor problem discussion reveal that the evaluation of labor unions fundamentally depends on the nature of work, how labor markets operate, the nature of employment relationship conflict, and the importance of employee voice (recall Boxes 2.6 and 2.9). In neoclassical economics, unions are harmful because they are monopolies that negatively affect economic efficiency. Unions may exist, but they are bad. The preferred method of workplace governance is reliance on competitive markets. In the human resource management school, unions are an indication that management is not successfully creating motivated and efficient workers via firm-created human resource management policies. Unions may exist, but they are unnecessary. The preferred workplace governance method is human resource management. In critical industrial relations thought, unions are either management tools of worker suppression or worker tools of power and revolution, though neither of these are mainstream U.S. beliefs. The desired mechanisms for governing the workplace are worker control or socialism.

But within the intellectual framework of the industrial relations school, unions are a critical part of the solution to the labor problem because collective, not individual, bargaining is needed to match corporate bargaining power and because independent employee voice is important in a democratic society. Unions provide their members with protection and participation, equity and voice. The preferred method of workplace governance is a combination of government standards and labor union representation. So one important method for answering the question of whether unions are good or bad is conceptual in nature. A second approach to addressing this question is to look at the empirical research record about what unions do in practice, and whether, on balance, these things are beneficial or harmful and to whom.

Evaluating the Two Economic Faces of Unionism

The two economic faces of the union model described earlier in this chapter is a very popular framework for empirically considering what unions do and for evaluating this track record.[82] With two economic faces, unions can have both positive and negative economic effects—negative effects from the monopoly face, positive effects from the collective voice face. What happens in practice? The research on the effects of unions on U.S. workers and workplaces is summarized in Box 2.12; it should be noted further that while much of the research focuses on the private sector, the two economics faces model is also applicable to the public sector.[83] Unionized workers in the United States are generally estimated to have wages approximately 15 percent higher or more than

---

[82] Freeman and Medoff, "The Two Faces of Unionism." Freeman and Medoff, *What Do Unions Do?* Bennett and Kaufman, "What Do Unions Do?"

[83] Morley Gunderson, "Two Faces of Union Voice in the Public Sector," *Journal of Labor Research* 26 (Summer 2005), pp. 393–413.

Source: See text.

BOX 2.12
What Do Unions Do?

Dimension	Estimated Effect of U.S. Unions
Efficiency	
Job satisfaction	Union workers are less satisfied on average, but probably because their working conditions are different.
Turnover	Reduced turnover.
Productivity	Mixed evidence—controversial effects.
Profits	Reduced profitability.
Equity	
Wage levels	Higher wages (15 percent higher, on average).
Wage distribution	Compressed (less unequal) wage structure.
Fringe benefits	Increased likelihood of benefits being offered.
Just cause discipline and discharge	Nearly universal in union contracts; rare elsewhere.
Public policies	Assistance with exercising rights (e.g., workers compensation).
Seniority	Increased importance of seniority provisions in personnel changes.
Voice	
Collective negotiations	Management is required to bargain with a certified union.
Grievance procedures	Nearly universal presence of formal grievance procedures in union contracts; few nonunion procedures with same level of due process and representation.

nonunion workers (a **union wage premium**).[84] Unions also reduce wage inequality and CEO pay.[85] With respect to other terms and conditions of employment, research finds that unions increase the likelihood of fringe benefits, seniority rights, and just cause discipline and discharge provisions.[86] For example, unionized workers are at least 15 percentage points more likely to have employer-provided health insurance and pensions than similar nonunion workers.[87] In an economics framework, the union wage premium is attributed to monopoly power while the other dimensions can represent both the monopoly face and the collective voice face. Consider fringe benefits, for example. In the monopoly face, unions increase the overall amount of fringe benefits while in the collective voice face, the composition of the benefits package is rearranged

[84] Alison L. Booth, *The Economics of the Trade Union* (Cambridge, England: Cambridge University Press, 1995). H. Gregg Lewis, *Union Relative Wage Effects: A Survey* (Chicago: University of Chicago Press, 1986). Barry T. Hirsch, "Reconsidering Union Wage Effects: Surveying New Evidence on an Old Topic," *Journal of Labor Research* 25 (Spring 2004), pp. 233–66. David G. Blanchflower and Alex Bryson, "What Effect Do Unions Have on Wages Now and Would Freeman and Medoff Be Surprised?" *Journal of Labor Research* 25 (Summer 2004), pp. 383–414.

[85] David Card, Thomas Lemieux, and W. Craig Riddell, "Unions and Wage Inequality," *Journal of Labor Research* 25 (Fall 2004), pp. 519–62. Rafael Gomez and Konstantinos Tzioumis, "What Do Unions Do to CEO Pay?" unpublished working paper, London School of Economics, 2004.

[86] Richard B. Freeman and Morris M. Kleiner, "The Impact of New Unionization on Wages and Working Conditions," *Journal of Labor Economics* 8 (January 1990), pp. S8–S25.

[87] John W. Budd, "Non-Wage Forms of Compensation," *Journal of Labor Research* 25 (Fall 2004), pp. 597–622.

to better satisfy the preferences of the workers. Research suggests that the overall effect of union on fringe benefits is split equally between these two faces.[88]

In terms of efficiency, there is a lot of research on the effects of unions on productivity.[89] In the monopoly face, firms are forced to pay higher wages so they will respond by hiring better workers, but this negatively affects productivity (if it was optimal to increase productivity via higher wages, firms would already have done this by themselves—a union is not needed to raise wages!). Moreover, strict work rules, which unions are able to win because of their monopoly power, reduce productivity. On the other hand, research evidence supports the presence of a **shock effect**—that is, the presence of a union shocks managers out of complacency and forces them to develop better managerial practices and policies that improve workplace efficiencies including more formal human resources policies such as training programs and objective rather than subjective selection tests.[90] Moreover, in the voice face unions can increase productivity in several ways. Grievance procedures, seniority provisions, and other public goods or provisions that reflect the preferences of the average worker, can increase morale, improve communication between managers and employees, and reduce turnover which can all increase productivity. One study finds that the heart attack mortality rate is lower in hospitals with unionized nurses relative to similar nonunion hospitals, perhaps because of improved work climate, communication, and trust.[91] Overall, however, the results are mixed. Some research finds that unions are associated with increased productivity, but this finding is not universal with other studies finding no or negative effects of unions on productivity and organizational effectiveness.[92] In contrast to this mixed track record on productivity, the presence of a union is usually found to be associated with lower profitability.[93] In other words, even when unions raise productivity, these gains do not offset the higher unionized labor costs. Research also finds that unions reduce employment growth, but are not more likely to drive firms out of business.[94]

Unions have also been found to have other important effects in the workplace. Union voice gives workers an alternative to quitting when they are dissatisfied with a job and research finds that unionized workers are in fact less likely to quit than similar nonunion workers.[95] For many years this created a puzzle because early research indicated that unionized workers were less satisfied with their jobs—but if they were less satisfied, then

[88] Freeman and Medoff, *What Do Unions Do?* Budd, "Non-Wage Forms of Compensation."

[89] Freeman and Medoff, *What Do Unions Do?* Barry T. Hirsch, "What Do Unions Do for Economic Performance?" *Journal of Labor Research* 25 (Summer 2004), pp. 415–55. Christos Doucouliagos and Patrice LaRoche, "What Do Unions Do to Productivity? A Meta-Analysis," *Industrial Relations* 42 (October 2003), pp. 650–91.

[90] Anil Verma, "What Do Unions Do to the Workplace? Union Effects on Management and HRM Policies," *Journal of Labor Research* 26 (Summer 2005), pp. 415–49.

[91] Michael Ash and Jean Ann Seago, "The Effect of Registered Nurses' Unions on Heart-Attack Mortality," *Industrial and Labor Relations Review* 57 (April 2004), pp. 422–42.

[92] Hirsch, "What Do Unions Do for Economic Performance?" Doucouliagos and LaRoche, "What Do Unions Do to Productivity?" Verma, "What Do Unions Do to the Workplace?"

[93] Hirsch, "What Do Unions Do for Economic Performance?" Richard S. Ruback and Martin B. Zimmerman, "Unionization and Profitability: Evidence from the Capital Market," *Journal of Political Economy* 92 (December 1984), pp. 1134–57.

[94] Hirsch, "What Do Unions Do for Economic Performance?" Richard B. Freeman and Morris M. Kleiner, "Do Unions Make Enterprises Insolvent?" *Industrial and Labor Relations Review* 52 (July 1999), pp. 510–27. John Dinardo and David S. Lee, "Economic Impacts of New Unionization on Private Sector Employers: 1984–2001," *Quarterly Journal of Economics* 119 (November 2004), pp. 1383–1441.

[95] Richard B. Freeman, "The Exit-Voice Tradeoff in the Labor Market: Unionism, Job Tenure, Quits, and Separations," *Quarterly Journal of Economics* 94 (June 1980), pp. 643–73. Tove Helland Hammer and Ariel Avgar, "The Impact of Unions on Job Satisfaction, Organizational Commitment, and Turnover," *Journal of Labor Research* 26 (Spring 2005), pp. 241–66.

why would they quit less often?[96] Later research, however, revealed that there does not appear to be significant union–nonunion differences in job satisfaction once one accounts for differences in working conditions and workplace climate.[97] Moreover, there shouldn't be a puzzle because quitting isn't necessarily the most frequent response to dissatisfaction—adaptation, for example, is often personally less costly.[98] The collective voice face can perhaps help unionized workers adapt as well as change their working conditions. Another thing that unions do is facilitate the receipt of benefits to which workers are already entitled. For example, unions can provide information to employees about benefit plans through union newsletters and can protect against retaliation for exercising their rights.[99] Consistent with this union facilitation effect, research finds that unions appear to improve employee awareness of their employer's family-friendly policies, help employees file valid unemployment insurance and workers' compensation claims, and increase employer compliance with nondiscrimination laws.[100]

The model of two economic faces of unionism undermines the single-mindedness of the neoclassical economics tradition in which unions are seen as socially harmful monopolies, which makes the question of whether unions are good or bad more complex. Even within the neoclassical economics paradigm in which unions are traditionally viewed very negatively, the collective voice face of unionism can improve efficiency and improve social welfare. At the same time, it is important not to push the two faces of unionism model too far. The evidence in support of unions improving productivity, for example, is mixed and it is difficult to make the case for unions on this basis. But one shouldn't have to. The economic effects of unions—on workers, productivity, and competitiveness—are certainly important, but they should not be the *sole* basis for evaluating labor unions and employee representation (recall efficiency *and* equity *and* voice). Unions were not established as productivity-enhancing mechanisms and should not be evaluated only in this vein.

Moreover, while this model is often referred to as the "two faces of unionism," it should more accurately be thought of as the "two neoclassical economics faces of unionism." In the industrial relations school of thought, for example, higher wages are not considered a negative monopoly effect but are an essential purpose of unions and reflect a better balance between corporate and employee bargaining power. In fact, to address the social ills of the labor problem and to boost consumer purchasing power, U.S. labor law was explicitly

[96] Richard B. Freeman, "Job Satisfaction as an Economic Variable," *American Economic Review* 68 (May 1978), pp. 135–41. George J. Borjas, "Job Satisfaction, Wages, and Unions," *Journal of Human Resources* 14 (Spring 1979), pp. 21–40.

[97] Jeffrey Pfeffer and Alison Davis-Blake, "Unions and Job Satisfaction: An Alternative View," *Work and Occupations* 17 (August 1990), pp. 259–83. Michael E. Gordon and Angelo S. DeNisi, "A Re-Examination of the Relationship Between Union Membership and Job Satisfaction," *Industrial and Labor Relations Review* 48 (January 1995), pp. 226–36. Keith A. Bender and Peter J. Sloane, "Job Satisfaction, Trade Unions, and Exit-Voice Revisited," *Industrial and Labor Relations Review* 51 (January 1998), pp. 222–40. Alex Bryson, Lorenzo Cappellari, and Claudio Lucifora, "Does Union Membership Really Reduce Job Satisfaction?" *British Journal of Industrial Relations* 42 (September 2004), pp. 439–59.

[98] Hammer and Avgar, "The Impact of Unions on Job Satisfaction, Organizational Commitment, and Turnover."

[99] Budd, "Non-Wage Forms of Compensation."

[100] John W. Budd and Karen Mumford, "Trade Unions and Family-Friendly Policies in Britain," *Industrial and Labor Relations Review* 57 (January 2004), pp. 204–22. John W. Budd and Brian P. McCall, "Unions and Unemployment Insurance Benefits Receipt: Evidence from the CPS," *Industrial Relations* 43 (April 2004), pp. 339–55. Barry T. Hirsch, David A. Macpherson, and J. Michael DuMond, "Workers' Compensation Recipiency in Union and Nonunion Workplaces," *Industrial and Labor Relations Review* 50 (January 1997), pp. 213–36. Mark Harcourt, Geoffrey Wood, and Sondra Harcourt, "Do Unions Affect Employer Compliance with the Law? New Zealand Evidence for Age Discrimination," *British Journal of Industrial Relations* 42 (September 2004), pp. 527–41.

intended to *help* unions *raise* wages! As such, the empirical evidence that unions raise wages, increase the probability of receiving health insurance and other employee benefits, facilitate the receipt of social insurance benefits, reduce income inequality, and negotiate for grievance procedures with just cause discipline and discharge provisions is interpreted in the pluralist industrial relations school of thought as evidence that unions help promote economic and social justice.

Labor unions can also provide a sense of community in the workplace and counter some negative psychological effects of the lack of ownership in one's work.[101] Similarly, collective voice mechanisms like unions can enhance a democratic society by promoting workplace interactions among workers from diverse backgrounds.[102] And as will be discussed in Chapter 4, the Knights of Labor in the 1800s emphasized moral and spiritual reform. In fact, the Catholic Church advocates for labor unions not only as a vehicle for improving working conditions but also for the spiritual improvements that can come when workers enjoy a better life. As articulated by Pope John Paul II in the Papal encyclical *Laborem Exercens* ("On Human Work," 1981),

> The experience of history teaches that [labor unions] are an indispensable element of social life, especially in modern industrialized societies. . . . It is always to be hoped that, thanks to the work of their unions, workers will not only *have* more, but above all *be* more: in other words, that they will realize their humanity more fully in every respect.[103]

Theories of the Labor Movement

In the United States, it is common to focus on the workplace when thinking about labor unions. To wit, the four views of labor unions revealed by the neoclassical economics, human resource management, industrial relations, and critical industrial relations schools of thought capture the central debates over the workplace roles of unions. However, unions are not purely workplace institutions, and any discussion of what unions do should look beyond the workplace. At this point it is also useful to distinguish labor unions from the labor movement. A **labor movement** is a form of a social movement in which workers and unions from multiple workplaces join together to pursue common interests, most frequently in the political and social arenas.

More specifically, the labor movement provides a voice for workers in the political arena.[104] Labor unions, or their associated political action committees, endorse candidates for political offices, mobilize get out the vote efforts, campaign on behalf of candidates, and lobby and make donations to lawmakers. During the administration of President George W. Bush, for example, the AFL–CIO has lobbied against privatization of Social Security, for an increase in the minimum wage, for enactment of a new ergonomics standard to reduce workplace injuries, for extended unemployment benefits for survivors of hurricanes Katrina and Rita, and for rights for immigrant workers. European labor movements continue to lobby for European policies to combat unemployment and poverty while labor

---

[101] Frank Tannenbaum, *A Philosophy of Labor* (New York: Alfred A. Knopf, 1951). Simeon Larson and Bruce Nissen (eds.), *Theories of the Labor Movement* (Detroit: Wayne State University Press, 1987).

[102] Cynthia Estlund, *Working Together: How Workplace Bonds Strengthen a Diverse Democracy* (Oxford: Oxford University Press, 2003).

[103] Pope John Paul II, *On Human Work: Encyclical Laborem Exercens* (1981), §20.

[104] Taylor E. Dark, *The Unions and the Democrats: An Enduring Alliance* (Ithaca, NY: ILR Press, 2001). John Delaney and Susan Schwochau, "Employee Representation Through the Political Process," in Bruce E. Kaufman and Morris M. Kleiner (eds.), *Employee Representation: Alternatives and Future Directions* (Madison, WI: Industrial Relations Research Association, 1993), Chapter 8. Jo-Ann Mort, *Not Your Father's Union Movement: Inside the AFL-CIO* (New York: Verso, 1998). J. David Greenstone, *Labor in American Politics* (New York: Knopf, 1969).

movements around the world are allied in campaigns to include labor rights in free trade agreements. In many countries, unions are also closely intertwined with political parties such as the Labour Party in Great Britain or the Workers' Party in Brazil.

As with the workplace role of labor unions, evaluating the political and social roles of labor movements depends on our frame of reference. From the perspective of neoclassical economics in which labor unions are labor market monopolies, a labor movement's political activities are also seen as the use of power to benefit unionized workers at the expense of others. At the other end of the spectrum, the critical industrial relations model sees labor movements that are active in the political and social arenas as critical for countering the dominant power of employers in these arenas. Taking this one step further, some labor movements see themselves as agents of radical reform and, outside North America, it's not uncommon to have unions aligned with socialist or communist political parties.

Last, recall that the industrial relations school of thought is rooted in the belief that the workplace encompasses a plurality of employer and employee interests. Extending this perspective to the political and social arenas, a democratic society is seen as a pluralist society in which there are numerous groups with common and conflicting interests—corporations, consumers, farmers, workers, homeowners, and the like. From this frame of reference then, the labor movement is a representative of workers in the political arena just as the Chamber of Commerce represents business and AARP represents senior citizens. Unions are therefore seen as balancing the economic power of employers in the workplace, and as balancing the political power of employers and their allies in the political arena. Labor unions can also be important organizations in civil society where individuals gather to socialize, discuss issues, pursue charitable goals, and form a sense of community.[105] From a pluralist perspective then, the labor movement makes important contributions in the political and civil arenas in contemporary democratic societies, and the relationship between a vibrant, independent labor movement and a healthy, balanced democratic society must be remembered when evaluating the labor unions.[106]

In sum, whether labor unions are good or bad is a difficult, complex question. There are undoubtedly specific examples in which most would agree that a specific labor union was either harmful (for example, with a corrupt, predatory leadership) or beneficial (for example, winning basic protections against an exploitative, sweatshop employer). On a broader scale, however, thinking about the labor problem and the question of workplace governance reveals the basis for evaluating labor unionism. There are four primary schools of thought on these questions—neoclassical economics, human resource management, industrial relations, and critical industrial relations—and each has its own beliefs about the nature of markets and the employment relationship. Consequently, each school of thought has its own views about labor unions and labor movements—good, bad, or indifferent. Understanding these differing views, and where they come from, is critical for understanding labor relations. And appreciating these views is critical for thinking not only about the past, but also the future.

In particular, it is difficult to understand U.S. labor law, and the U.S. system of labor relations, from the perspectives of the neoclassical economics, human resource management, and critical industrial relations schools of thought. **The intellectual foundations of the U.S. system of labor relations come from the industrial relations school of thought.** Labor laws protecting employees' rights to form unions were passed because of the belief

[105] Peter Levine, "The Legitimacy of Labor Unions," *Hofstra Labor and Employment Law Journal* 18 (Spring 2001), pp. 527–71.
[106] Nelson Lichtenstein, *State of the Union: A Century of American Labor* (Princeton, NJ: Princeton University Press, 2002).

that labor market competition is not among equals, that it is not wise to rely on managerial benevolence, and that employee voice is important in a democratic society. One does not need to agree with this pluralist industrial relations philosophy, but it is imperative to remember this intellectual foundation when studying and practicing U.S. labor relations.

Key Terms

neoclassical economics school, *42*

two economic faces of unionism, *44*

human resource management school, *45*

industrial relations school, *47*

critical industrial relations school, *49*

unitarist view of conflict, *52*

pluralist view of conflict, *52*

class conflict, *52*

workplace governance, *55*

union wage premium, *63*

shock effect, *64*

labor movement, *66*

Reflection Questions

1. Mother Jones, a very colorful figure in U.S. labor history who will be introduced in Chapter 4, said in 1913, "The world is suffering, today, from an industrial yellow fever, not less fatal, but I am certain, as preventable."[107] Yellow fever was caused by mosquitoes so Mother Jones continued, "Search for the mosquito! That ought to be a slogan with investigators on both sides of the labor question." What is the mosquito that causes the labor problem in each of the four schools of thought?

2. How are the major premises of the neoclassical economics and industrial relations schools consistent with Box 2.4? How would you change the label on the gun to make this into a neoclassical economics cartoon? an industrial relations cartoon?

3. Review Box 2.5. Sketch a similar diagram to capture the range of outcomes possible within the human resource management school. (*Hint*: use a pendulum but not necessarily a power struggle between labor and management.)

4. Think of jobs you or someone you know has had. What was undesirable about these jobs? Was the pay too low? hours too long? were you treated poorly? Which of the four schools of thought best explains the causes of these undesirable aspects? What would you try to do to redress these undesirable features?

5. Four simple (!) questions: (a) Is labor just another commodity?, (b) Are employers and employees equals in self-regulating, competitive labor markets?, (c) Is there an inherent conflict of interest between employees and employers? and (d) Is employee voice important?

Internet Exploration

1. Explore the online exhibit about the 1911 Triangle Shirtwaist Factory fire (*www.ilr.cornell.edu/trianglefire*). What were working conditions like? Search the Internet for information on sweatshops in the 21st century. How do these compare to sweatshops of the early 20th century? If modern sweatshops are a problem, what should be done?

2. The major union federations in the United States, Canada, and Great Britain are the AFL–CIO (*www.aflcio.org*), Canadian Labour Congress (*www.clc-ctc.ca*), and the Trades Union Congress (*www.tuc.org.uk*), respectively. Explore their Web sites, or those of individual unions, and look for examples of the different types of union roles outlined in Box 2.12. Can you find examples of all seven? Compare the sites of the three major federations to that of the Industrial Workers of the World (*www.iww.org* or *http://www.iww.org.uk/*).

---

[107] Elliot J. Gorn, *Mother Jones: The Most Dangerous Woman in America* (New York: Hill and Wang, 2001), p. 195.

Additional
Reading

Budrys, Grace, *When Doctors Join Unions* (Ithaca, NY: Cornell University Press, 1997).

Freeman, Richard B., and James L. Medoff, *What Do Unions Do?* (New York: Basic Books, 1984).

Kaufman, Bruce E., *The Origins and Evolution of the Field of Industrial Relations in the United States* (Ithaca, NY: ILR Press, 1993).

Larson, Simeon, and Bruce Nissen (eds.), *Theories of the Labor Movement* (Detroit: Wayne State University Press, 1987).

Rosenblum, Jonathan D., *Copper Crucible: How the Arizona Miners' Strike of 1983 Recast Labor-Management Relations in America* (Ithaca, NY: ILR Press, 1998).

Weiler, Paul C., *Governing the Workplace: The Future of Labor and Employment Law* (Cambridge: Harvard University Press, 1990).

Chapter Three

Labor Relations Outcomes: Individuals and the Environment

Advance Organizer

The previous chapters emphasize the objectives of the employment relationship and different perspectives on how to achieve these objectives. But how are actual outcomes determined? Labor relations outcomes are the result of labor and management strategies interacting in a multidimensional environment in which choices are also shaped by individual decision-making behaviors, including ethics.

Learning Objectives

By the end of the chapter, you should be able to:

1. **Understand** that employment outcomes are the product of the employment environment and features of behavioral decision making, including ethics.

2. **Analyze** the basic elements of the employment environment and behavioral decision making.

3. **Discuss** the importance of ethics in studying, practicing, and reforming labor relations.

4. **Identify** the central elements of major ethical theories and their relevance to labor relations.

Contents

Central to studying and practicing labor relations is understanding what determines labor relations outcomes. What factors cause employees to join together to form a union or go on strike? What determines whether unions win wage increases or are forced to grant wage concessions? What factors influence whether a company invests in nonunion rather than union locations? None of these events is a random occurrence. Rather, they take place in a system that shapes actions and outcomes. Just as scientists try to figure out how the physical world works, the primary focus of industrial relations research is trying to figure out how the labor relations system causes various outcomes.

Later chapters outline the institutional aspects of different labor relations systems and revisit key elements, such as the legal environment in Chapter 5 and the bargaining environment in Chapter 8; this chapter focuses more generally on what determines diverse labor relations outcomes within any institutional framework. In other words, the framework presented in this chapter applies to all labor relations systems. It is a building block for understanding labor relations generally, not just the existing U.S. system specifically, and therefore appears here as the final of the three foundational chapters in this book. Mastery of labor relations as a student and practitioner is incomplete without knowing how to model and therefore predict labor relations outcomes.

Modeling labor relations outcomes frequently starts with the environment—laws, economic trends, and technology, for example—especially in research in industrial relations and economics.[1] At the same time, the nature of human decision making and behavior—such as social interactions and person-specific needs, feelings, and mental processes—have long been central in psychology, sociology, and organizational behavior.[2] Putting these two approaches together means that we should think about labor relations outcomes as resulting from environmental pressures and behavioral characteristics. In Box 1.1 at the beginning of Chapter 1, then, outcomes are shown as being pressured from above by the environment and from below by the human agent. But there's more to the story—employers, employees, and unions have goals which are pursued by strategies. In Box 1.1, therefore, employers start on the left and work in toward the center by forming goals and strategies that are influenced by the environment and individual decision making. Employees and unions similarly work toward the center of Box 1.1 from the right, as influenced by environment and individual decision making. And then there is one last complication: labor and management interact at different levels—in the workplace, at a functional policy-making level, and at higher strategic levels.[3] Putting all these elements together yields a conceptual model of the determinants of labor relations outcomes as summarized in Box 3.1.[4]

The employment environment can be divided into seven categories:

- Legal
- Economic
- Technical
- Political
- Social
- Business
- Institutional

Note carefully that the external environment in this framework is important, but it does not completely determine outcomes. Managers, unions, and employees have choices within the

---

[1] John T. Dunlop, *Industrial Relations Systems* (New York: Holt, 1958).

[2] Bruce E. Kaufman, "Models of Man in Industrial Relations Research," *Industrial and Labor Relations Review* 43 (October 1989), pp. 72–88. Bruce E. Kaufman, "Expanding the Behavioral Foundations of Labor Economics," *Industrial and Labor Relations Review* 52 (April 1999), pp. 361–392. Tony J. Watson, *Sociology, Work and Industry*, 3rd ed. (London: Routledge, 1995).

[3] Thomas A. Kochan, Harry C. Katz, and Robert B. McKersie, *The Transformation of American Industrial Relations* (New York: Basic Books, 1986).

[4] John W. Budd, *Employment with a Human Face: Balancing Efficiency, Equity, and Voice* (Ithaca, NY: Cornell University Press, 2004).

BOX 3.1
The Determinants of Labor Relations Outcomes

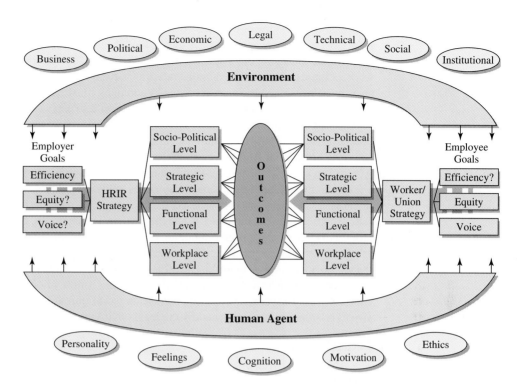

boundaries or parameters established by the external environment.[5] The factors that shape these choices can be summarized into five major elements of human decision making:

- Cognition
- Motivation
- Personality
- Feelings
- Ethics

Because of the importance of ethics for both understanding and evaluating labor relations behaviors and outcomes, this element is explored in more detail than the others in the middle of the chapter.[6] The chapter concludes with two examples to illustrate the usefulness of modeling labor relations outcomes as in Box 3.1.

THE LABOR RELATIONS ENVIRONMENT

Legal

The legal system in every country establishes the framework for labor–management interactions. The clearest component of the **legal environment** is the set of laws explicitly pertaining to labor relations. In the United States, the National Labor Relations Act (NLRA) establishes the processes for forming new unions and for bargaining union

---

[5] Kochan, Katz, and McKersie, *The Transformation of American Industrial Relations.*

[6] Budd, *Employment with a Human Face.* John W. Budd and James G. Scoville (eds.), *The Ethics of Human Resources and Industrial Relations* (Champaign, IL: Labor and Employment Relations Association, 2005).

contracts. This framework will be covered in detail in Part II of this book, but as an example, if U.S. workers want to form a union, the NLRA explicitly requires that a majority of the workers must support a specific union. The NLRA further provides the steps that the workers must go through to demonstrate this majority support. The U.S. legal framework also specifies what subjects a union and a company must bargain over, when it is legal to strike, and what each side can and cannot do during a strike.

The legal environment is not confined to labor law, however. Some U.S. employment standards are established by the Fair Labor Standards Act (minimum wages and overtime payments), the Civil Rights Act (nondiscrimination), the Occupational Health and Safety Act (workplace safety), and the Family and Medical Leave Act (unpaid leave), to name just a few major laws. Tax laws, bankruptcy codes, and deregulation acts can also affect labor relations.[7] Common law—law based on tradition and precedent rather than created by statutes enacted by lawmakers—is also important. For example, common law doctrine on property rights affects union organizing by forbidding union organizers from the employer's premises. Perhaps most significantly, the U.S. employment relationship is governed by the employment-at-will doctrine (recall Box 1.5).[8] In the absence of legislative (especially antidiscrimination laws) or contractual restrictions (most widely associated with union contracts), employees can generally be discharged or quit at any time for any reason. This at-will relationship is established by the legal environment.

Economic

The **economic environment** includes the labor market, the market for the employer's products or services, markets for other factors of production, and the state of the overall economy. Within the framework established by common and/or statutory laws, the economic environment critically determines workers' employment options. If the labor market is tight—that is, if unemployment is low and jobs are easy to find—a frustrated employee might quit and find a better job elsewhere. Or because a tight labor market makes it hard for employers to find new employees, a frustrated employee might use his or her leverage to win favorable gains from an employer. In a loose or weak labor market with high levels of unemployment, employees might be reluctant to form a union for fear of being fired and unable to find a new job. Similarly, employees might be less willing to strike when the labor market is weak and collective bargaining settlements are therefore expected to favor the employer.

For employers, the economic environment determines their labor and product market opportunities and constraints.[9] Increased competitive pressures, whether from globalization, domestic nonunion competition, or deregulation, are perhaps the single most important change in the labor relations environment in the postwar period. Labor demand—the strength of an employer's need for employees—is a derived demand; it is derived from employers' competitive positions in markets for their goods and services.[10] Labor demand

---

[7] Michael H. Belzer, *Sweatshops on Wheels: Winners and Losers in Trucking Deregulation* (New York: Oxford University Press, 2000). Howard R. Stanger, "Newspapers: Collective Bargaining Decline Amidst Technological Change," in Paul F. Clark, John T. Delaney, and Ann C. Frost (eds.), *Collective Bargaining in the Private Sector* (Champaign, IL: Industrial Relations Research Association, 2002), Chapter 5.

[8] Jay M. Feinman, "The Development of the Employment at Will Rule," *American Journal of Legal History* 20 (1976), pp. 118–35.

[9] John R. Commons, *Industrial Goodwill* (New York: McGraw-Hill, 1919). Dunlop, *Industrial Relations Systems.* Thomas A. Kochan and Harry C. Katz, *Collective Bargaining and Industrial Relations: From Theory to Policy and Practice,* 2nd ed. (Homewood, IL: Irwin, 1988).

[10] Alfred Marshall, *Principles of Economics,* 8th ed. (New York: Macmillan, 1920).

for airline pilots stems from their role in satisfying customers' demands for flights. As routes, types of aircraft, and passengers' needs change, the demand for pilots changes accordingly. Employers that do not deliver competitive products and services will face declining market share and therefore declining labor demand. Increased competitive pressures through globalization, increased nonunion competition, and deregulation have therefore placed significant pressures on labor relations in the United States, and around the globe. Globalization also makes it easier to replace high-wage domestic employees with low-wage labor in other countries through international trade or by opening up foreign subsidiaries.[11]

Several major pieces of the U.S. economic environment are summarized in Box 3.2. The recessions, indicated by the shaded regions, and the unemployment rate portray the cyclical nature of the U.S. economy as the economy strengthens and weakens over the business cycle. The sharp increase in unemployment in the early 1980s, for example, accompanied an intense period of **concession bargaining** in which many unions agreed to wage, benefit, and work rule concessions (or give-backs) to try to save jobs.[12] Increased globalization is represented by the import share trend (imports as a fraction of gross domestic product) which quadruples between 1960 and 2000. Globalization represents a major shift in the environment and is the focus of Chapter 12. Lastly, the series for average real wages for high school graduates and college graduates show that real wages for high school graduates have been stagnant since the 1970s and that the earnings gap between less-educated and more-educated workers has increased.

Technical

The third dimension of the environment is the **technical** context that includes the nature of production, work organization, and technology.[13] The technical context includes whether the workplace is fixed (as in a factory) or variable (as in transportation industries),

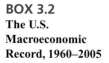

BOX 3.2
The U.S. Macroeconomic Record, 1960–2005

Sources: U.S. Department of Commerce. U.S. Department of Labor. National Bureau of Economic Research. Lawrence Mishel, Jared Bernstein, and Sylvia Allegretto, *The State of Working America, 2004–2005* (Ithaca, NY: ILR Press, 2005).

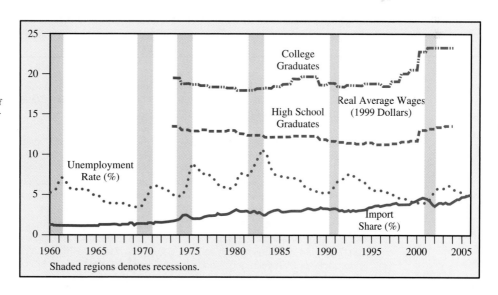

[11] Dani Rodrik, *Has Globalization Gone Too Far?* (Washington, DC: Institute for International Economics, 1997).

[12] Paula B. Voos (ed.), *Contemporary Collective Bargaining in the Private Sector* (Madison, WI: Industrial Relations Research Association, 1994).

[13] Dunlop, *Industrial Relations Systems.*

the degree of workforce and workplace stability, the size and hours of the workforce, and the workers' job content and responsibilities. The technical context defines the issues of importance for employees and employers. The concerns of truck drivers are likely different from nurses; the concerns of trucking company managers are likely different from hospital administrators. The technical context also establishes workplace-level social relations among co-workers which may critically influence how employees react to perceived injustices. The portion of the technical context that includes formal organizational structures, including work structures, is also very important for labor relations. Work structures—such as hierarchical, assembly-line production methods or team-based production with high dependence on co-workers—can serve as methods of employee control.[14] Moreover, some of the biggest challenges for employers, employees, policymakers, and unions is devising new behaviors, policies, and strategies—and therefore employment outcomes—as workplaces move from mass manufacturing to flexible specialization.[15]

Technology is also a very important element of the labor relations environment. The central debate over technology is whether technological change is skill-biased or deskilling, though the answer likely depends on the context including the composition of the specific innovation and how management chooses to deploy it.[16] **Skill-biased technological change** upgrades the skill requirements of technical jobs and results in greater demand for high skills—in other words, it is biased in favor of skilled workers. This phenomenon is often associated with information technology and is a leading explanation for the increased wage gap between low and high skilled workers.[17] An example from manufacturing is the increased need for skilled workers to use computer-based machinery. In contrast, **deskilling** technological change reduces the skills required for a specific job. In grocery stores, technological change that allows case-ready meat—meat that arrives from a processing plant already cut and packaged—reduces the skilled meatcutter job in the store to an unskilled stock clerk position. Scanning technology similarly reduces the skills required for checkout clerks. Deskilling is often associated with scientific management efforts to reduce

[14] Mike Parker and Jane Slaughter, "Advancing Unionism on the New Terrain," in Bruce Nissen (ed.), *Unions and Workplace Reorganization* (Detroit: Wayne State University Press, 1997), pp. 208–25. Watson, *Sociology, Work and Industry.*

[15] Eileen Appelbaum and Rosemary Batt, *The New American Workplace: Transforming Work Systems in the United States* (Ithaca: ILR Press, 1994). Barry Bluestone and Irving Bluestone, *Negotiating the Future: A Labor Perspective on American Business* (New York: Basic Books, 1992). Peter Cappelli, *The New Deal at Work: Managing the Market-Driven Workforce* (Boston: Harvard Business School Press, 1999). Charles C. Heckscher, *The New Unionism: Employee Involvement in the Changing Corporation* (New York: Basic Books, 1988). David I. Levine, *Reinventing the Workplace: How Business and Employees Can Both Win* (Washington, DC: Brookings, 1995).

[16] John W. Budd and Brian P. McCall, "The Grocery Stores Wage Distribution: A Semi-Parametric Analysis of the Role of Retailing and Labor Market Institutions," *Industrial and Labor Relations Review* 54 (March 2001), pp. 484–501. Clair Brown and Ben Campbell, "Technical Change, Wages, and Employment in Semiconductor Manufacturing," *Industrial and Labor Relations Review* 54 (March 2001), pp. 450–65. Larry W. Hunter, Annette Bernhardt, Katherine L. Hughes, and Eva Skuratowicz, "It's Not Just the ATMs: Technology, Firm Strategies, Jobs, and Earnings in Retail Banking," *Industrial and Labor Relations Review* 54 (March 2001), pp. 402–24.

[17] David H. Autor, Lawrence F. Katz, and Alan B. Krueger, "Computing Inequality: Have Computers Changed the Labor Market?" *Quarterly Journal of Economics* 113 (November 1998), pp. 1169–213. Eli Berman, John Bound, and Stephen Machin, "Implications of Skill-Biased Technological Change: International Evidence," *Quarterly Journal of Economics* 113 (November 1998), pp. 1245–79. Jonathan E. Haskel and Matthew J. Slaughter, "Does the Sector Bias of Skill-Biased Technological Change Explain Changing Skill Premia?" *European Economic Review* 46 (December 2002), pp. 1757–83.

complex jobs to simple, repetitive tasks and is argued to be a management tool for gaining control of the workplace.[18]

Political

The **political** context explicitly captures political influences beyond laws and the legal environment. For example, during World War II, many unions refrained from striking because of a fear that interference with the war effort would lead to anti-union government interference.[19] With respect to employer behavior, it is commonly believed that the firing of the public-sector air traffic controllers by President Ronald Reagan during the (illegal) PATCO strike in 1981 created a climate in which it was acceptable for private-sector employers to actively fight unions and resist their legal strikes (see Chapter 4).[20] The British government's role in defeating the 1984–85 National Union of Mineworkers strike is viewed similarly (see Chapter 13).[21] Box 3.3 further describes the various roles that a government can play in labor relations.

Business and labor can also lobby political leaders for favorable treatment. In Minneapolis, the hotel employees union successfully pressured the city to include provisions for employer neutrality in any organizing campaigns at a hotel that was being developed with public assistance.[22] In this case, the political environment affects the labor relations environment by making it easier for unions to organize new workplaces. Unions that represent workers at public utilities such as phone companies can lobby for rate increases (so the employer can afford higher wages) and mandated service improvements (which might require hiring additional employees). In fact, some employee groups rely on political lobbying rather than collective bargaining to improve wages and working conditions. As an example, the International Union of Gambling Employees does not pursue collective bargaining but tries to protect the interests of casino dealers by filing lawsuits to alleviate problems of secondhand smoke and by lobbying for better safety standards with respect to repetitive-motion injuries.[23] Because of their shunning of collective bargaining, such groups are often referred to as associations rather than unions. Associations can grow into "full-fledged" unions that engage in collective bargaining.[24] For example, the National Educational Association started as a lobbying association on behalf of teachers but now also bargains for them.

Social

The workplace or workgroup-level **social** context of employment is emphasized in sociology, social psychology, and organizational behavior. Workgroups, for example, can have at

[18] Harry Braverman, *Labor and Monopoly Capital: The Degradation of Work in the Twentieth Century* (New York: Monthly Review Press, 1974). David Montgomery, *Workers' Control in America: Studies in the History of Work, Technology, and Labor Struggles* (Cambridge: Cambridge University Press, 1979).

[19] James B. Atleson, *Labor and the Wartime State: Labor Relations and Law During World War II* (Urbana: University of Illinois Press, 1998). Nelson Lichtenstein, *Labor's War at Home: The CIO in World War II* (Cambridge: Cambridge University Press, 1982).

[20] Steve Babson, *The Unfinished Struggle: Turning Points in American Labor, 1877–Present* (Lanham, MD: Rowman and Littlefield, 1999). Nelson Lichtenstein, *State of the Union: A Century of American Labor* (Princeton, NJ: Princeton University Press, 2002). Paul C. Weiler, *Governing the Workplace: The Future of Labor and Employment Law* (Cambridge: Harvard University Press, 1990).

[21] Brian Towers, *The Representation Gap: Change and Reform in the British and American Workplace* (Oxford: Oxford University Press, 1997).

[22] John W. Budd and Paul K. Heinz, "Union Representation Elections and Labor Law Reform: Lessons from the Minneapolis Hilton," *Labor Studies Journal* 20 (Winter 1996), pp. 3–20.

[23] C. Jeffrey Waddoups and Vincent H. Eade, "Hotels and Casinos: Collective Bargaining During a Decade of Expansion," in Paul F. Clark, John T. Delaney, and Ann C. Frost (eds.), *Collective Bargaining in the Private Sector* (Champaign, IL: Industrial Relations Research Association, 2002), Chapter 4.

[24] Casey Ichniowski and Jeffrey S. Zax, "Today's Associations, Tomorrow's Unions," *Industrial and Labor Relations Review* 43 (January 1990), pp. 191–208.

The government (or in academic discussions, "the state") has several roles in labor relations. The role that receives the most attention, and which will be covered in detail in Chapter 5, is the *regulative* role. Labor law regulates individuals, unions, and companies in the context of union organizing, collective bargaining, and other collective activities while employment law regulates the individual employment relationship. The regulative role provides the legal context of the bargaining environment. But there are four other roles a government can assume: an employer role, a facilitative role, a structural role, and a constitutive role.

The government as *employer* is the subject of public sector labor relations. Note that in the United States, the federal and state governments make the rules for their own behavior because they are both the regulator of public sector labor laws and the employer of public sector employees. In this situation, the government has a vested interest in making laws that favor its role as employer, especially with respect to employees that provide essential services.

In the *facilitative* role, the government facilitates the nature of labor relations by establishing social norms or attitudes and by providing various services. The PATCO and NUM strikes in the 1980s are often credited with establishing anti-union climates in the United States and Great Britain (see Boxes 4.24 and 13.5). This contributes to the political and social dimensions of the labor relations environment. Moreover, by providing training, statistics, and mediation, the government can facilitate the practice of labor relations.

The *structural* role of government consists of economic policies that help shape or structure the economic environment for labor relations. This includes fiscal policy, monetary policy, international trade agreements, and social safety nets (such as unemployment insurance, Social Security, workers' compensation, and welfare).

In the *constitutive* role, the government establishes how economic and social relationships, including the employment relationship, are established or constituted. A government that establishes a capitalist, market-based economy emphasizes the importance of property rights; labor rights are often of secondary importance. For example, managers have a fiduciary obligation to serve the shareholders, but no corresponding obligation to employees.

In sum, the constitutive dimension establishes the broadest parameters for labor relations (such as a capitalistic society), and within this overall system, the regulative role creates the legal framework for labor relations, the structural role partially determines the economic climate, and the facilitative role contributes towards the attitudinal climate and the capabilities of the parties. In U.S. labor relations, the regulative role is generally the focal point, but these other roles of government are intertwined and should not be overlooked.

Source: John Godard, *Industrial Relations, the Economy, and Society,* 3rd ed. (Concord, Ontario: Captus Press, 2005).

least four major social functions: socialization of employees to workplace norms, solidarity in defense against managerial abuse, support of personal space, and affirmation of workplace identities.[25] Social norms—standards to which conformity is expected—in the workplace can shape worker behavior; restraints on working too fast such as by limiting piece-rate output among workers is a classic example.[26] Workplace-level employee solidarity and social identification are also important factors in shaping whether workers will try to correct perceived workplace injustices individually or collectively, and are thus very important for labor relations outcomes.[27] The social context also includes corporate or organizational culture.

Beyond the workplace or corporation, the social part of the labor relations environment can favor labor or management depending on the extent of social support for each group. In other words, employment outcomes can be influenced by public attitudes towards labor

[25] Randy Hodson, *Dignity at Work* (Cambridge: Cambridge University Press, 2001).

[26] Jack Barbash, *The Elements of Industrial Relations* (Madison: University of Wisconsin Press, 1984). Hodson, *Dignity at Work.*

[27] John E. Kelly, *Rethinking Industrial Relations: Mobilization, Collectivism and Long Waves* (London: Routledge, 1998). Hodson, *Dignity at Work.*

unions. The success of the Teamsters' strike against UPS in 1997 is widely credited to public support for the problem of part-time workers that was an important issue in the strike.[28] In a comparative context, the relative success of labor unions in Canada versus the United States can be partially explained by greater social acceptance of collective action, and therefore lack of acceptability of anti-union management behavior.[29]

The social context of the labor relations environment also includes broad social and demographic trends. The labor force participation rate—the fraction of a certain set of individuals that are working or want to work—among women increased sharply in the last few decades of the 20th century. Educational attainment, on average, is increasing, so the workforce is more skilled than in earlier eras, though there are also significant numbers of high school dropouts and others that are at-risk for lacking the necessary skills in the 21st century job market. The workforce is also becoming more diverse as more entrants to the labor force are from various ethnic backgrounds. All of these trends put pressure on the employment relationship and pose significant challenges for both employers and unions. Union organizing drives among female-dominated clerical workers and immigrant-dominated janitors, for example, will be described in Chapter 7.

Business

A dominant factor—perhaps even *the* dominant factor—in contemporary labor relations, and the world economy more generally, is the corporation (see Box 3.4). As a result, factors relating to business comprise another important dimension of the employment environment. One element of the **business** dimension of the labor relations environment is the nature of corporate governance—that is, how rules and decisions regarding resource allocation (such as investment) within corporations are made. The dominant U.S. model of corporate governance is the shareholder model.[30] The shareholders—the owners of a company through the ownership of stock—are viewed as the key group in the corporation because they bear the risk of making a profit or loss. Other groups within the company, such as employees, are viewed as always receiving the fixed payment for their services that was agreed upon in advance, such as wage and salary payments. As such, only shareholders are viewed as having the desire to see the corporation's resources put to the most productive uses, and economic performance will therefore be best when corporate decisions seek to maximize shareholder value. U.S. corporate governance arrangements—such as election of the board of directors by the shareholders—support this emphasis on shareholder value. In terms of the labor relations environment, a strong shareholder value model of corporate governance establishes a corporate preoccupation with short-term .financial results and also usually denies employees or unions meaningful participation in corporate governance and decisions over investments, mergers, and other major business activities. Alternative corporate governance arrangements, such as having employee representation on the board of directors as in Germany, yield different labor relations climates.[31]

[28] Matt Witt and Rand Wilson, "The Teamsters' UPS Strike of 1997: Building a New Labor Movement," *Labor Studies Journal* 24 (Spring 1999), pp. 58–72.

[29] Daphne Gottlieb Taras, "Collective Bargaining Regulation in Canada and the United States: Divergent Cultures, Divergent Outcomes," in Bruce E. Kaufman (ed.), *Government Regulation of the Employment Relationship* (Madison, WI: Industrial Relations Research Association, 1997), Chapter 8.

[30] Margaret M. Blair, *Ownership and Control: Rethinking Corporate Governance for the Twenty-First Century* (Washington, DC: Brookings, 1995). Mary O'Sullivan, *Contests for Corporate Control: Corporate Governance and Economic Performance in the United States and Germany* (Oxford: Oxford University Press, 2000).

[31] Sanford M. Jacoby, "Employee Representation and Corporate Governance: A Missing Link," *University of Pennsylvania Journal of Labor and Employment Law* 3 (Spring 2001), pp. 449–89. Sanford M. Jacoby, *The Embedded Corporation: Corporate Governance and Employment Relations in Japan and the United States* (Princeton, NJ: Princeton University Press, 2005).

A dominant—perhaps even *the* dominant factor—in contemporary labor relations, and the world economy more generally, is the corporation. A corporation is an organization that is allowed by law to function essentially as a person with specific rights (such as the ability to purchase property) and duties (such as abiding by the law). Investors purchase shares of the corporation and these shareholders therefore collectively own the corporation (these shares might also be called "stocks" and these shareholders might therefore be called "stockholders"). These shares might be publicly traded on a stock market (a publicly traded company) or not (a privately owned company). Note carefully that the shareholders own, but do not manage, the corporation. Investors purchase shares with the expectation that the executives and managers will work hard on their behalf, make a profit, and increase the values of the shares.

Corporations have come to dominate the economic landscape only in the last 200 years. In the 1600s, pepper and other spices from southeastern Asia were in great demand in Europe. But spice voyages were very risky—one storm, an encounter with pirates, an outbreak of scurvy, or some other hazardous event could wipe out the entire investment. To avoid the potential for a huge loss in a single voyage, merchants bid for "shares" of a voyage. Moreover, as spice voyages, mines, and utilities became bigger and more complex, their expense could no longer be financed by a sole merchant or by a small number of partners. As such, the now common practice of purchasing shares in a corporation was born. Early corporations, however, were viewed with suspicion. Prior to this time, even the largest businesses were partnerships in which the owners knew each other personally and were all actively involved in running the business. The separation of ownership and management inherent in a corporation was a significant break from what people were familiar with. Many feared that when shareholders did not personally know the managers, the managers would be able to take advantage of the shareholders. In fact, corruption was widespread and corporations were banned in England from 1720 until 1825.

By pooling resources, corporations can be very efficient economic organizations and with the rise of railroads in the 1800s, corporations became widespread. Individual investors, however, still faced a significant risk—*personal* liability for a company's debts regardless of the amount of the initial investment. In the late 1800s, England and the United States enacted limited liability laws so now individual investors can lose only the amount of their initial investment (not their house, cars, personal savings, and the like). At this same time, through various court rulings, the legal nature of a corporation developed into that of a person "with its own identity, separate from the flesh-and-blood people who were its owners and managers and empowered, like a real person, to conduct business in its own name, acquire assets, employ workers, pay taxes, and to go court to assert its rights and defend its actions."

As a result, corporations have taken on a life of their own. And it is largely a single-minded life. So that managers cannot take advantage of shareholders, corporations are legally bound to make money for the shareholders. Managers must act in the interests of shareholders—not in the interests of workers, consumers, or the environment except to the extent that these interests are aligned with increased profits. Supporters emphasize the incredible economic efficiencies which can result. But detractors caution against placing too much faith in corporate self-interest—a corporation is in business to make money, not to promote other things that real humans value such as democracy, empathy, relationships, justice, and dignity—especially when, unlike a real person that can be put in jail, it is hard to punish corporations for their transgressions.

So what's the bottom line? For a corporation, it is returning profits to shareholders. This undeniably creates great economic wealth, but also provides incentives for resisting unions, polluting the environment, and avoiding taxes. For a society, the bottom line should be more than just profits. Corporations are not real people—they are created through the legal system and given certain privileges (recall limited liability, for example) in return for serving the public interest. It is therefore legitimate for a labor relations system—as well as national and global economic systems—to ensure that corporations continue to serve the public interest.

Source: Joel Bakan, *The Corporation: The Pathological Pursuit of Profit and Power* (New York: Free Press, 2004). Quote is from p. 16. Howard Gospel and Andrew Pendleton (ed.), *Corporate Governance and Labour Management: An International Comparison* (Oxford: Oxford University Press, 2005). Thom Hartmann, *Unequal Protection: The Rise of Corporate Dominance and the Theft of Human Rights* (New York: Rodale, 2002). Majorie Kelly, *The Divine Right of Capital: Dethroning the Corporate Aristocracy* (San Francisco: Berrett-Koehler, 2001). Penny Le Couteur and Jay Burreson, *Napoleon's Buttons: How 17 Molecules Changed History* (New York: Jeremy P. Tarcher/Putnam, 2003).

A second element of the business dimension of the labor relations environment is business strategy.[32] Business strategies affect human resource management strategies and therefore can affect individual behavior through rewards, incentives, and controls. In the steel minimill industry (minimills start with scrap metal; they do not make steel from raw materials), for example, mills with business strategies that emphasize low-cost production use human resources practices like narrowly defined jobs, intense supervision, and limited training whereas mills with business strategies that emphasize responsiveness to customers' needs use human resources practices like broadly defined jobs, self-managed teams, and extensive training.[33] In fact, Wal-Mart is so large and pervasive that its business and employment practices influence not only other sectors of retail trade, but perhaps are also creating the template for 21st-century capitalism more generally.[34] Business strategies also determine labor relations strategies, such as how strenuously to try to avoid unionization. General Motors's drive to build low-cost automobiles led to its Southern strategy of trying to open new, nonunion plants in the 1970s, and Wal-Mart's business model puts constant downward pressure on labor costs which in turn creates strong incentives to fight any unionization attempts. Labor relations strategies are discussed in greater detail in Chapter 6.

Institutional

The **institutional** context includes the varied influences on the employment relationship that stem from the presence of nonmarket institutions and organizations. Primary elements of this dimension of the labor relations environment are the philosophy, structure, and strength of the labor movement. U.S. unions have traditionally had a business unionism philosophy with a pragmatic focus on workplace issues such as wages, benefits, and work rules.[35] In contrast, European unions often have more of a social unionism philosophy in which unions are part of a broader network of community, social, and political activist groups. Labor relations outcomes in a system of business unionism stem from collective bargaining and grievance resolution; outcomes in a social unionism system are the product of social and political activism. History is another element of the institutional context of the employment relationship. The central role of seniority in U.S. union contracts can be traced back to abusive examples of favoritism by supervisors in the early 20th century.[36] Bureaucratic forms of representation, a weak shop steward system, and widespread no-strike clauses can be traced back to the pressures for discipline and military production during World War II.[37] The current system of grievance arbitration was also developed in this same period, and in turn was heavily influenced by the experiences

[32] Kochan, Katz, and McKersie, *The Transformation of American Industrial Relations.* Peter Cappelli and Harbir Singh, "Integrating Strategic Human Resources and Strategic Management," in David Lewin, Olivia S. Mitchell, and Peter D. Sherer (eds.), *Research Frontiers in Industrial Relations and Human Resources* (Madison, WI: Industrial Relations Research Association, 1992), Chapter 5.

[33] Jeffrey B. Arthur, "The Link Between Business Strategy and Industrial Relations Systems in American Steel Minimills," *Industrial and Labor Relations Review* 45 (April 1992), pp. 488–506.

[34] Nelson Lichtenstein (ed.), *Wal-Mart: The Face of Twenty First Century Capitalism* (New York: The New Press, 2006).

[35] Robert Franklin Hoxie, *Trade Unionism in the United States* (New York: D. Appleton, 1917).

[36] David Brody, "Workplace Contractualism in Comparative Perspective," in Nelson Lichtenstein and Howell John Harris (eds.), *Industrial Democracy in America: The Ambiguous Promise* (Washington, DC: Woodrow Wilson Center Press, 1993), Chapter 8. Carl Gersuny and Gladis Kaufman, "Seniority and the Moral Economy of U.S. Automobile Workers, 1934–1946," *Journal of Social History* 18 (Spring 1985), pp. 463–75.

[37] Atleson, *Labor and the Wartime State.* Lichtenstein, *Labor's War at Home.*

of the Amalgamated Clothing Workers in the 1920s.[38] The nature of management resistance to unions, and therefore the shape and state of the U.S. labor movement, has important historical origins in the economics, politics, and ideologies of the early 1900s.[39]

The institutional context also includes community groups. Unions can join with civil rights groups, religious leaders, and other activists to promote living wage standards, nondiscriminatory treatment, immigrants' rights, affordable housing, local economic development, and other community goals.[40] In the international arena, the labor movement is allied with environmental groups in pursuit of their common goal of restraining free trade with labor and environmental standards. Two other very important aspects of the institutional context are discussed in later chapters: union strategies (Chapter 6) and bargaining structure (Chapter 8).

INDIVIDUAL DECISION MAKING

In addition to the environment, the second key element for studying labor relations behavior and outcomes is the nature of individual decision making.[41] Employees, managers, shareholders, and union leaders make choices.[42] The seven dimensions of the labor relations environment provide the broad parameters and constraints on the available choices, but within the set of feasible choices, what determines the actions of employees, managers, shareholders, and union leaders? This is the human agent—or individual decision-making—portion of Box 3.1. Mainstream economics assumes that individual decisions always reflect rational maximization of individual welfare in the face of the constraints of the external environment. Psychology incorporates mental states and processes into the decision-making process while sociology emphasizes the importance of informal and formal social structures. The varied influences on individual decision-making behavior can be captured by five categories: cognition, motivation, personality, feelings, and ethics. The first four will be briefly reviewed here; the question of ethics will then be explored in greater detail.

[38] Steve Fraser, "Dress Rehearsal for the New Deal: Shop-Floor Insurgents, Political Elites, and Industrial Democracy in the Amalgamated Clothing Workers," in Michael H. Frisch and Daniel J. Walkowitz (eds.), *Working-Class America: Essays on Labor, Community, and American Society* (Urbana: University of Illinois Press, 1983), pp. 212–55. Nelson Lichtenstein, "Great Expectations: The Promise of Industrial Jurisprudence and its Demise, 1930–1960," in Nelson Lichtenstein and Howell John Harris (eds.), *Industrial Democracy in America: The Ambiguous Promise* (Washington, DC: Woodrow Wilson Center Press, 1993), Chapter 6.

[39] Daniel R. Ernst, *Lawyers Against Labor: From Individual Rights to Corporate Liberalism* (Urbana: University of Illinois Press, 1995). Sanford M. Jacoby, "American Exceptionalism Revisited: The Importance of Management," in Sanford M. Jacoby (ed.), *Masters to Managers: Historical and Comparative Perspectives on American Employers* (New York: Columbia University Press, 1991), Chapter 8. Ruth O'Brien, *Workers' Paradox: The Republican Origins of New Deal Labor Policy, 1886–1935* (Chapel Hill: The University of North Carolina Press, 1998).

[40] Lichtenstein, *State of the Union*. Paul Johnston, "Organize for What? The Resurgence of Labor as a Citizenship Movement," in Lowell Turner, Harry C. Katz, and Richard W. Hurd (eds.), *Rekindling the Movement: Labor's Quest for Relevance in the Twenty-First Century* (Ithaca, NY: ILR Press, 2001), Chapter 2. John Russo and Brian R. Corbin, "Work, Organized Labor, and the Catholic Church: Boundaries and Opportunities for Community/Labor Coalitions," in Bruce Nissen (ed.), *Which Direction for Organized Labor: Essays on Organizing, Outreach, and Internal Transformation* (Detroit: Wayne State University Press, 1999), Chapter 5.

[41] Budd, *Employment with a Human Face*. Kaufman, "Models of Man in Industrial Relations Research." Kaufman, "Expanding the Behavioral Foundations of Labor Economics."

[42] Kochan, Katz, and McKersie, *The Transformation of American Industrial Relations*.

Cognition

Cognition is the processing of information and knowledge. The mainstream economics model of cognition is rational choice. Individuals are assumed to fully process all relevant information to maximize their personal welfare. Everyone is assumed to be fully capable of rational choice. An important alternative to pure rational choice is bounded rationality.[43] Boundedly rational individuals strive for optimal actions, but cognitive limitations—the inability to process all relevant information and alternatives in a reasonable amount of time—mean that individuals satisfy instead of optimize. In other words, individuals do things that are deemed "good enough," not optimal. "Rules of thumb" are an important decision-making aid in models of bounded rationality. In addition to cognitive processing limitations, pure rational choice might also be impeded by frustration, social influences, instinct, habit, and learning.[44] Cognitive ability is widely believed to be the single best predictor of job performance.[45]

Motivation

Motivation is a drive to do something. A range of motivators for human behavior are possible: survival, money, conformity with social norms, pleasure, or psychological fulfillment. Three theories of motivation are relevant for understanding labor relations outcomes: needs, justice, and concern for others. Maslow's famous hierarchy of needs posits that individuals first satisfy their most basic needs—food, water, and air—and then pursue safety needs, and then love, esteem, and finally self-actualization.[46] Fairness or justice is a second important motivator of individual decision making.[47] Equity theory emphasizes distributive justice—fairness in the distribution of rewards. Individual behavior is thought to be motivated by the creation of fair (equitable) outcomes relative to a comparison group.[48] A classic example is reducing how hard you work if you believe you are underpaid compared to the pay and effort level of your co-workers. Comparisons with a peer group—in other words, "orbits of coercive comparisons"—can therefore be important motivators of workplace behaviors, outcomes, and union bargaining goals.[49] In addition to distributive justice, procedural justice—fairness in the process of making workplace decisions—can also be

[43] James G. March and Herbert A. Simon, *Organizations* (New York: Wiley, 1958). Herbert A. Simon, *Models of Bounded Rationality* (Cambridge: MIT Press, 1982).

[44] Albert Bandura, *Social Foundations of Thought and Action: A Social Cognitive Theory* (Englewood Cliffs, NJ: Prentice-Hall, 1986). Jennifer J. Halpern, "Bonded Rationality: The Rationality of Everyday Decision Making in a Social Context," in Jennifer J. Halpern and Robert N. Stern (eds.), *Debating Rationality: Nonrational Aspects of Organizational Decision Making* (Ithaca, NY: Cornell University Press, 1998), Chapter 9. Geoffrey M. Hodgson, "The Approach of Institutional Economics," *Journal of Economic Literature* 36 (March 1998), pp. 166–92. Hoyt N. Wheeler, *Industrial Conflict: An Integrative Theory* (Columbia: University of South Carolina Press, 1985).

[45] Frank L. Schmidt and John E. Hunter, "The Validity and Utility of Selection Methods in Personnel Psychology: Practical and Theoretical Implications of 85 Years of Research Findings," *Psychological Bulletin* 124 (September 1998), pp. 262–74.

[46] Abraham H. Maslow, "A Theory of Human Motivation," *Psychological Review* 50 (July 1943), pp. 370–96.

[47] Stephen W. Gilliland and David Chan, "Justice in Organizations: Theory, Methods, and Applications," in Neil Anderson et al. (eds.), *Handbook of Industrial, Work and Organizational Psychology*, Volume 2 (London: Sage, 2001), Chapter 8. Daniel Kahneman, Jack L. Knetsch, and Richard Thaler, "Fairness as a Constraint on Profit Seeking: Entitlements in the Market," *American Economic Review* 76 (September 1986), pp. 728–41.

[48] J. Stacy Adams, "Inequity in Social Exchange," in Leonard Berkowitz (ed.), *Advances in Experimental Social Psychology*, Volume 2 (New York: Academic Press, 1965), pp. 267–99.

[49] Arthur M. Ross, *Trade Union Wage Policy* (Berkeley: University of California Press, 1948).

important.[50] Labor union emphases on seniority-based layoffs and promotions reflect a desire to guard against violations of procedural justice by replacing managerial favoritism with an objective criterion for decision making; civil rights legislation also seeks procedural justice by prohibiting arbitrary discrimination. Lastly, concern for other people can also motivate behavior. This concern may stem from pressure to conform to social norms, from social or biological needs to belong to groups, or from altruism.[51] The most fundamental descriptions of the extent to which we should care about others (directly or indirectly through concerns for processes) are ethical theories; these are addressed in more detail later in this chapter.

Personality

Personality is an enduring dispositional quality or stable mental state.[52] The most widely recognized set of personality dimensions in psychology is the Big Five: extraversion, agreeableness, neuroticism (emotional stability), conscientiousness, and openness to experience. The employment-related research on personality focuses to a much greater extent on outcomes like job performance than on issues specific to labor relations. Conscientiousness, in particular, is related to job performance.[53] Personality also appears partially linked to job satisfaction, health, safety, and stress on the job, and leadership.[54] In a labor relations application, extroverted individuals seem to prefer working in groups than individually which then underlies a more favorable disposition towards unions because unions involve group rather than individual action.[55] Other facets of labor relations in which personality might be important include union organizing (do certain personality types make better organizers?), contract negotiations (do personality clashes make negotiations more difficult?), and dispute resolution (do certain personality types make better mediators?).

Feelings

While a person's personality is fixed (or close to it), the category of feelings includes three distinct psychological concepts that vary over time and with experiences—attitudes, moods, and emotions. Attitudes are the most stable and are generally believed to develop through experience. In the context of employment, a central attitude is job satisfaction—your attitude toward your job. Job satisfaction is believed to be related to absenteeism, tar-

[50] John Thibaut and Laurens Walker, *Procedural Justice: A Psychological Analysis* (Hillsdale, NJ: Lawrence Erlbaum Associates, 1975).

[51] Avner Ben-Ner and Louis Putterman, "Values and Institutions in Economic Analysis," in Avner Ben-Ner and Louis Putterman (eds.), *Economics, Values, and Organization* (Cambridge: Cambridge University Press, 1998), pp. 3–69. Richard Dawkins, *The Selfish Gene* (New York: Oxford University Press, 1976). Hodson, *Dignity at Work.*

[52] Robert T. Hogan, "Personality and Personality Measurement," in Marvin D. Dunnette and Leaetta M. Hough (eds.), *Handbook of Industrial and Organizational Psychology,* Volume 2, 2nd ed. (Palo Alto: Consulting Psychologists Press, 1992), Chapter 13.

[53] Murray R. Barrick and Michael K. Mount, "The Big Five Personality Dimensions and Job Performance: A Meta-Analysis," *Personnel Psychology* 44 (Spring 1991), pp. 1–26.

[54] Peter M. Hart and Cary L. Cooper, "Occupational Stress: Toward a More Integrated Framework," in Neil Anderson et al. (eds.), *Handbook of Industrial, Work and Organizational Psychology,* Volume 2 (London: Sage, 2001), Chapter 5. Leaetta M. Hough and Deniz S. Ones, "The Structure, Measurement, Validity, and Use of Personality Variables in Industrial, Work, and Organizational Psychology," in Neil Anderson et al. (eds.), *Handbook of Industrial, Work and Organizational Psychology,* Volume 1 (London: Sage, 2001), Chapter 12. Timothy A. Judge, Daniel Heller, and Michael K. Mount, "Five-Factor Model of Personality and Job Satisfaction: A Meta-Analysis," *Journal of Applied Psychology* 87 (June 2002), pp. 530–41.

[55] Jeffrey D. Houghton, "Extraversion and Organizational Work Beliefs as Pre-Employment Predictors of Union Attitudes," *Journal of Behavioral and Applied Management* 1 (Winter/Spring 2000), pp. 115–26.

diness, employee turnover, workplace aggression, and support for unionizing.[56] In addition to job satisfaction, a worker's sense of identification with the values and objectives of his or her employer (organizational commitment) can also affect employment outcomes.[57] Support for unionization in an individual's workplace is also related to attitudes toward unions—such as favorable beliefs about unions in general, union loyalty, and a feeling that a union can help achieve the worker's goals (union instrumentality).[58] On the management side, attitudes toward employee participation in business decision making and toward unions are related to human resources and industrial relations strategies and practices.[59]

In contrast to attitudes which are targeted toward specific things, moods are feelings of a general nature and are not linked to specific triggers. Emotions are similar to moods, but are more intense, short-lived, and linked to specific causal factors.[60] Having a positive outlook is a mood; being angry at a co-worker is an emotion. Positive moods can be linked to increased work motivation, greater levels of helping co-workers, increased flexibility, improved leadership effectiveness, reduced absenteeism, and increased cooperation in bargaining.[61] Since emotions are more closely linked than moods with specific triggers, they can prompt behaviors directed toward the specific cause, and can momentarily overwhelm other goals and behavioral patterns.[62] For example, strikes might result from employees' intense frustration toward an employer that blocks the employees' peaceful attempts to satisfy their goals.[63]

[56] Theresa M. Glomb, Piers D. G. Steel, and Richard D. Arvey, "Office Sneers, Snipes, and Stab Wounds: Antecedents, Consequences, and Implications of Workplace Violence and Aggression," in Robert G. Lord, Richard J. Klimoski, and Ruth Kanfer (eds.), *Emotions in the Workplace: Understanding the Structure and Role of Emotions in Organizational Behavior* (San Francisco: Jossey-Bass, 2002), Chapter 7. Howard E. Miller and Joseph G. Rosse, "Emotional Reserve and Adaptation to Job Dissatisfaction," in Jeanne M. Brett and Fritz Drasgow (eds.), *The Psychology of Work: Theoretically Based Empirical Research* (Mahwah, NJ: Lawrence Erlbaum, 2002), Chapter 10. Hoyt. N. Wheeler and John A. McClendon, "The Individual Decision to Unionize," in George Strauss, Daniel G. Gallagher, and Jack Fiorito (eds.), *The State of the Unions* (Madison, WI: Industrial Relations Research Association, 1991), Chapter 2. Barry A. Friedman, Steven E. Abraham, and Randall K. Thomas, "Factors Related to Employees' Desire to Join and Leave Unions," *Industrial Relations* 45 (January 2006), pp. 102–10.

[57] John P. Meyer and Natalie J. Allen, *Commitment in the Workplace: Theory, Research, and Application* (Thousand Oaks, CA: Sage, 1997). Julian Barling, Clive Fullagar, and E. Kevin Kelloway, *Organizational Behavior and the Psychology of Unions* (New York: Oxford University Press, 1992).

[58] Daniel G. Gallagher and George Strauss, "Union Membership Attitudes and Participation," in George Strauss, Daniel G. Gallagher, and Jack Fiorito (eds.), *The State of the Unions* (Madison, WI: Industrial Relations Research Association, 1991), Chapter 4. Wheeler and McClendon, "The Individual Decision to Unionize." Heejoon Park, Patrick P. McHugh, and Matthew M. Bodah, "Revisiting General and Specific Union Beliefs: The Union-Voting Intentions of Professionals," *Industrial Relations* 45 (April 2006), pp. 270–89.

[59] John Godard, "Whither Strategic Choice: Do Managerial IR Ideologies Matter?" *Industrial Relations* 36 (April 1997), pp. 206–28.

[60] Joseph P. Forgas and Jennifer M. George, "Affective Influences on Judgments and Behavior in Organizations: An Information Processing Perspective," *Organizational Behavior and Human Decision Processes* 86 (September 2001), pp. 3–34. Howard M. Weiss, "Conceptual and Empirical Foundations for the Study of Affect at Work," in Robert G. Lord, Richard J. Klimoski, and Ruth Kanfer (eds.), *Emotions in the Workplace: Understanding the Structure and Role of Emotions in Organizational Behavior* (San Francisco: Jossey-Bass, 2002), Chapter 2.

[61] Forgas and George, "Affective Influences on Judgments and Behavior in Organizations." Alice M. Isen, "Positive Affect and Decision Making," in Michael Lewis and Jeannette M. Haviland-Jones (eds.), *Handbook of Emotions,* 2nd ed. (New York: Guilford Press, 2000), Chapter 27.

[62] George Lowenstein, "Out of Control: Visceral Influences on Behavior," *Organizational Behavior and Human Decision Processes* 65 (March 1996): pp. 272–92.

[63] Wheeler, *Industrial Conflict.*

INTRODUCTION TO BUSINESS ETHICS

The final dimension of the human agent or individual decision making in Box 3.1 is ethics. Comparing ethical theories is a valuable way of considering different perspectives on labor relations that illuminates why individuals, employers, unions, or elected officials make specific choices. Studying ethics in labor relations also provides a basis for judging whether reforms in behavior and laws are needed. In light of the business scandals at Enron and elsewhere early in the 21st century, ethics has received increased attention in business. But for ethics to be useful, a firm understanding of alternative theories is required. This section therefore provides an introduction to business ethics. The following section applies business ethics to labor relations.

Suppose a major employer in your community closes a local facility, lays off the workers, and opens a new plant in another country to take advantage of lower labor costs. How do you feel? Is this acceptable because it improves economic efficiency which will benefit consumers through lower prices? Or because business owners have a right to use their private property as they choose? Alternatively, is this plant closing troubling because it treats workers simply as factors of production? Or because it doesn't seem fair as some benefit at the expense of others? Or because it doesn't seem like the right thing to do? Or because it doesn't respect relationships and communities that have been established?

Each of these responses represents a different moral standard for whether the action is right or wrong. Business ethics studies moral standards as they apply to the business context and is therefore important for both understanding and evaluating labor relations behaviors, policies, and outcomes. While ethics studies right and wrong, you should not narrowly view ethics as simply providing restrictions on your behavior. Rather, think of business ethics as an important motivating force for behavior.[64] An ethical framework that emphasizes efficiency produces very different behaviors than one that emphasizes interpersonal relationships. As such, ethics is the final dimension of individual decision making that determines in labor relations outcomes in Box 3.1. Consideration of different ethical theories, therefore, provides the framework for a better understanding of labor relations strategies, policies, and outcomes. Six ethical theories are useful to consider: the ethics of . . .

- . . . Utility
- . . . Liberty
- . . . Duty
- . . . Fairness
- . . . Virtue
- . . . Care[65]

These six frameworks are summarized in Box 3.5 and are described in greater detail below. While many challenges in labor law represent conflicts between labor rights and property rights, many clashes in labor relations behavior reflect conflicting ethical frameworks. If labor and management seem to be at odds in a specific situation, ask whether each side is approaching the problem from a different ethical framework. Even if this does not resolve the conflict, it will facilitate a fuller understanding of the situation.

---

[64] Robert C. Solomon, *Ethics and Excellence: Cooperation and Integrity in Business* (New York: Oxford University Press, 1992). John W. Budd and James G. Scoville, "Moral Philosophy, Business Ethics, and the Employment Relationship," in John W. Budd and James G. Scoville (eds.), *The Ethics of Human Resources and Industrial Relations* (Champaign, IL: Labor and Employment Relations Association, 2005), pp. 1–21.

[65] Budd, *Employment with a Human Face.*

BOX 3.5   **Six Ethical Frameworks**

Ethics of . . .	Influential Thinkers	Focal Point	Tools	Immoral Acts
Utility	Jeremy Bentham John Stuart Mill	Greatest good for the greatest number	Cost-benefit analysis	Inefficient or welfare-reducing behavior
Liberty	John Locke	Freedom as the negative right to be left alone	Property rights	Forcing individuals to use themselves or their property against their will (Including taxation for redistribution)
Duty	Immanuel Kant	Respect for human dignity	Categorical imperative	Treating others in ways you would not want to be treated; Treating people only as means, not also as ends
Fairness	John Rawls	Justice through liberty, equal opportunity, and concern for the least well-off	Veil of ignorance; difference principle	Placing efficiency above liberty, equal opportunity, and concern for the least well-off
Virtue	Aristotle	Moral character to achieve happiness (flourishing)	Specific virtues (such as friendliness and truthfulness)	Actions contrary to virtues (vices) which prevent flourishing
Care	Carol Gilligan	Nurturing personal relationships	Caring for people	Failing to develop special relationships; relationships based on exploitation, disrespect, or injustice

In addition to developing a better understanding of labor relations, the use of business ethics can also help us evaluate labor relations practices, systems, and outcomes. It is easy to say that a labor relations system should strike a balance between efficiency, equity, and voice, but how can we evaluate a system to see if an appropriate balance has been achieved? Ethical theories describe what should be of fundamental importance in society and these standards provide a way of evaluating specific labor relations practices and outcomes. Of course, there are differing views of which ethical standards are best, but these theories provide for the basis for debating these standards.

Lastly, an understanding of business ethics can help managers and labor union officials in decision making. Business and labor leaders face numerous, complex issues with conflicting obligations, trade-offs between costs and benefits, clashes between principles and outcomes, and winners and losers. The study of business ethics can help you become "more comfortable facing moral complexity" and can provide "a renewed sense of purpose and vision" for business and labor leaders struggling with this complexity.[66] This is especially important in the context of human resources and industrial relations because of the direct impact on workers' lives, and is also particularly important in the workplace of the 21st century with the potential for electronic monitoring, genetic testing, and other emerging

[66] Solomon, *Ethics and Excellence*, pp. 4–5.

88 Part One *Foundations*

BOX 3.6 Business Metaphors Can Justify Harmful Behavior

Mythical Metaphor	Negative Consequences	Reality
"It's a Jungle Out There"	Business is viewed as uncivilized, lacking rules, and dominated by a killer instinct. Survival-of-the-fittest mentality justifies selfish behavior.	Business requires cooperation, shared interests, and agreed-upon rules of conduct. Humans need to be members of communities, not atomistic, isolated individuals.
War Metaphors: employees as troops, competitors as the enemy, strategies as plans of attack, cash as a war chest, competition as a battle.	Emphasis on beating competition (rather than producing an excellent product or service) by any means necessary. Hierarchical, authoritarian, military-like chain of command.	Business is about excellent products and services, not winning. Business requires cooperation, shared interests, and agreed-upon rules of conduct.
Machine Metaphors: employees as cogs, corporations as machines, knowledge as input, rest periods as downtime.	Emphasis on static efficiency rather than dynamic effectiveness. Employees as impersonal machines without needs, rights, and knowledge.	Companies are human communities. Effective management requires more than manipulation and adjustment.
Game Metaphors: playing players, coaches, and scorecards.	Emphasis on keeping score (money) and winning. Emphasis on thrills and challenges with no regard for the public ("spectators").	Business is an integral part of fields, society, not a sideshow for entertainment. Corporate "playing fields" are not isolated from society and business is not just about winning through profits.

Source: Adapted from Robert C. Solomon, *Ethics and Excellence: Cooperation and Integrity in Business* (New York: Oxford University Press, 1992).

issues.[67] Studying business ethics will not provide easy answers to these difficult issues, but it will help you more fully identify and evaluate the consequences of alternative courses of action.

Many of the major theories in business ethics imply a broader conception of business than simply making profits. These theories also discount the popular emphasis on competition over cooperation as the driving force in business. Rather, it is emphasized that business is "a fully human activity" that requires a sense of community, extensive cooperation, and a deeper purpose than simply making money.[68] Box 3.6 presents some common metaphors that capture very narrow views of business. The rhetorical power of these metaphors is illustrated by the negative practices that these metaphors support. In studying business ethics, and labor relations, try to break through these narrow metaphors.

Subjectivism and Relativism

Before considering each of the six ethical frameworks, it is important to consider potential objections to evaluating behavior using ethics. If we say that someone did something morally wrong or that a law should prevent certain actions, we are asserting that there are universal moral standards that everyone should follow. But consider the objections in

[67] Paul Schumann, "A Moral Principles Framework for Human Resource Management Ethics," *Human Resource Management Review* 11 (Spring/Summer 2001), pp. 93–111. Richard S. Rosenberg, "The Technological Assault on Ethics in the Modern Workplace," in John W. Budd and James G. Scoville (eds.), *The Ethics of Human Resources and Industrial Relations* (Champaign, IL: Labor and Employment Relations Association, 2005), pp. 141–71.

[68] Solomon, *Ethics and Excellence,* p. 16.

1. "Don't be judgmental. Moral judgments are oppressive. Morality is a private matter, and as no one is in a position to know what is right for others, so no one has the right to condemn their behavior. Moral opinions differ, as do lifestyles; we should recognize this and be tolerant. We should live and let live."

2. "'Right' and 'wrong' can only mean right and wrong in a particular culture. It is totally misguided to use the standards of one culture (invariably one's own) to pass a moral judgment on an action performed within the context of a different culture. As no one can be said to be right or wrong in a dispute like this, it's better simply to say 'You're right from your side and I'm right from mine.' Respect the diversity of cultures. No one is right, so live and let live."

Source: Chris Horner and Emrys Westacott, *Thinking Through Philosophy* (Cambridge University Press, 2000), pp. 120 and 126.

Box 3.7. The first objection ("Morality is a private matter") is called **ethical subjectivism.** Moral judgments are feelings, not facts, so each person is entitled to his or her own ethical standards. The second objection ("Respect the diversity of cultures") is called **ethical relativism.** No single ethical theory is universal either because of specific historical or cultural factors or because people's reasons for differing ethical beliefs are equally valid.

Most philosophers reject these claims of subjectivism and relativism, at least in their strongest forms which do not allow any universal judgments.[69] First, note that diversity of views does not necessarily make them equally valid. Taken to their logical conclusions, subjectivism and relativism prevent condemnation of Nazi Germany's unconscionable atrocities in the Holocaust. This is difficult to justify. Second, tolerance is itself an ethical belief—to assert that everyone should be tolerant of all views is a universal prescription! Similarly, the statement that "morality is a private matter" asserts that individual freedom is more important than the consequences of actions—this, too, is a concrete, universal ethical statement.[70] Thus, subjectivism and relativism both have internal contradictions. Third, while there are clear cross-cultural differences in norms of behavior, there is more fundamental agreement than initially meets the eye.[71] Thus, it is widely accepted that at least some universal moral standards exist. There is not agreement on what the standards should be, but it is reasonable to debate universal standards that should apply to others. Labor and management may have different ethical systems, but this does not mean that both are correct, or that it is pointless to establish a societal standard. The six ethical frameworks presented next therefore provide the basis not only for understanding labor relations behavior, but for evaluating such behavior and for designing public policies to fulfill ethical standards.

Utility

The **ethics of utility**—utilitarianism—focuses on maximizing net social welfare (utility). As such, the key to utilitarianism is creating the "greatest good for the greatest number." Utilitarianism is a consequentialist moral theory: actions are judged simply by their consequences. Actions are morally good if they maximize aggregate welfare in which the greatest

[69] Michael C. Brannigan, *Ethics Across Cultures* (Boston: McGraw-Hill, 2005). James Rachels, *The Elements of Moral Philosophy*, 4th ed. (Boston: McGraw-Hill, 2003).

[70] Chris Horner and Emrys Westacott, *Thinking Through Philosophy* (Cambridge University Press, 2000).

[71] Manuel G. Velasquez, *Business Ethics: Concepts and Cases,* 4th ed. (Upper Saddle River, NJ: Prentice Hall, 1998). Tom L. Beauchamp and Norman E. Bowie (eds.), *Ethical Theory and Business,* 5th ed. (Upper Saddle River, NJ: Prentice Hall, 1997).

benefits are produced with the least costs compared to alternative actions.[72] In fact, the utilitarian calculation of totaling costs and benefits is the same cost-benefit analysis used in the economic analysis of policy or business decisions. Cost-benefit analysis operationalizes utilitarianism.[73] This is graphically illustrated by the Ford Motor Company's calculation in the 1960s that moving the gas tank in its new small car, the Pinto, would cost $137 million in manufacturing expenses but would only save $49 million in preventing the expected 180 deaths, 180 serious burn injuries, and 2,100 burned cars.[74] As the costs outweighed the benefits, Ford did not modify the design of its now-notorious exploding Pinto. In the ethics of utility, this was morally acceptable. If the negative aspects of unions described in Chapter 2 outweigh the socially beneficial contributions, then in utilitarian terms, labor unions are socially harmful and should not be allowed.

Economic efficiency also provides a very strong link between utilitarianism, economics, and business. Standard economic theory indicates that "the greatest good for the greatest number" is achieved through competitive markets, profit-maximizing behavior, and efficiency. Consequently, "the enterprise of business harbors a fundamentally utilitarian conception of the good society."[75] Union avoidance strategies to maximize profits as well as human resource management strategies to provide equity because it improves the bottom line reflect a utilitarian belief system: "managerial opposition to unions is pragmatic, and motivated by competitive pressures . . . they evaluate unionism as a net cost in the cost/benefit ratio of the performance of the company, and that is why they oppose unionization."[76] These decisions are not independent of ethics, they are the ethics of utility.

The logic of the utilitarian-economics-business thinking is powerful: individuals pursuing their self-interests in competitive markets will maximize efficiency, and therefore welfare. Moreover, employee compensation packages will equal the value that employees contribute. More productive workers will earn a higher wage, less productive workers will earn less. Because of a popular belief that hard work should be rewarded accordingly, this theoretical prediction has evolved into a value statement that "factors of production *ought to be paid* the value of their marginal product" which has been called "marginal productivity justice."[77] This is a utilitarian ethical philosophy, but outside of economics, business, and conservative political thought, the *normative* value of this logic is not well-accepted. Especially troublesome to critics is that in this framework, the ends justify the means.[78] Rights and virtues are irrelevant, distributive justice and minimum living standards are not a concern, and communities and relationships are only important so far as they increase aggregate welfare. Only the consequences matter.

Liberty

The **ethics of liberty,** or libertarianism, emphasizes individual freedom. In this ethical system, restrictions on anyone's behavior are only justified if they are needed to prevent

---

[72] Velasquez, *Business Ethics*. Beauchamp and Bowie (eds.), *Ethical Theory and Business*. Daniel M. Hausman and Michael S. McPherson, *Economic Analysis and Moral Philosophy* (Cambridge: Cambridge University Press, 1996).

[73] Hausman and McPherson, *Economic Analysis and Moral Philosophy*.

[74] Velasquez, *Business Ethics*.

[75] Beauchamp and Bowie, *Ethical Theory and Business*, p. 22.

[76] Leo Troy, *Beyond Unions and Collective Bargaining* (Armonk, NY: M.E. Sharpe, 1999), p. 54.

[77] Peter D. McClelland, *The American Search for Justice* (Cambridge, MA: Basil Blackwell, 1990), pp. 19 and 59 (emphasis in original).

[78] Beauchamp and Bowie, *Ethical Theory and Business*. Norman E. Bowie, *Business Ethics: A Kantian Perspective* (Malden, MA: Blackwell, 1999). Hausman and McPherson, *Economic Analysis and Moral Philosophy*. Solomon, *Ethics and Excellence*. Velasquez, *Business Ethics*.

harm to others. Unless your actions harm others, you should be free to do as you please. Strong property rights are therefore central to the libertarian philosophy and the role of government is to protect the individual and his or her property. Taxes and other forms of redistribution from the wealthy to the poor that are not purely voluntary are seen as coercive takings of private property which violate the primary right of liberty. As long as the distribution of wealth in society is the result of fair acquisition and exchange (such as the lack of coercion and fraud), then it is just, even if it is extremely unequal.[79]

Like utilitarianism, the ethics of liberty strongly advocates free markets. While utilitarianism supports free markets because they are viewed as the best way to achieve efficiency and to maximize utility, libertarianism supports free markets because of the primacy of liberty. Individuals should have the right to interact with others in free markets. Chapter 5 will show that this primacy of property rights and the freedom to pursue unregulated economic relationships dominated U.S. labor law before the 1930s. Moreover, continuing struggles with labor rights versus property rights in U.S. labor law, such as in whether union organizers can be banned from private premises, partly reflect the libertarian view of the sanctity of property rights.

Libertarianism can be criticized for its narrow conception of liberty. In simple terms, are people who are starving truly free? Why should the freedom from harm to private property always trump other freedoms such as the freedom from hunger?[80] Fraud, slavery, theft, and other actions also question the justice of existing patterns of property rights and resources which then undermines the libertarian premise that free marketplace transactions are just. Recall further that the industrial relations school believes that labor and management have unequal bargaining power and asymmetric information (Chapter 2). If this is true, the extent to which unregulated marketplace transactions are free—and therefore just—is questionable.

Duty

Traditionally, the most important contrast to the ethics of utility is the **ethics of duty** because, rather than judging actions based on their consequences, judgments are based on the action itself. Most literally, people have a duty to act in certain ways, for example not to lie, even if it does not produce the best outcome. The most important advocate of the ethics of duty is the 18th century German philosopher Immanuel Kant. Kantian moral philosophy is based on the **categorical imperative:**

> Act only on that maxim by which you can at the same time will that it should become a universal law.[81]

Box 3.8 contains three formulations of the categorical imperative that Kant argued are equivalent. These principles are based on the view that human beings are rational and therefore capable of self-determination and self-governance.[82] Everyone is therefore entitled to dignity and respect. Using someone simply to increase your own wealth, for example, treats them only as a means and violates the intrinsic value and sanctity of human life (Formula of the End Itself). Since everyone has equal intrinsic value, universal application of standards of behavior is critical (Formula of the Universal Law). Note that this means that you must be willing to be treated as you treat others, similar to the Golden Rule. And

---

[79] Robert Nozick, *Anarchy, State, and Utopia* (New York: Basic Books, 1974).

[80] Jack Donnelly, *Universal Human Rights in Theory and Practice* (Ithaca, NY: Cornell University Press, 1989). Alan Gerwith, *The Community of Rights* (Chicago: University of Chicago Press, 1996).

[81] Immanuel Kant, *Groundwork of the Metaphysics of Morals* (1785), 17/402.

[82] Bowie, *Business Ethics.* Roger J. Sullivan, *Immanuel Kant's Moral Theory* (Cambridge: Cambridge University Press, 1989).

Three Equivalent Formulations of Kant's Categorical Imperative

Box 3.8

1. Act only on that maxim by which you can at the same time will that it should become a universal law (Formula of Universal Law).

2. Act in such a way that you always treat humanity, whether in your own person or in the person of any other, never simply as a means, but always at the same time as an end (Formula of the End Itself).

3. So act as if you were through your maxims a law-making member of a kingdom of ends (Formula of the Kingdom of Ends).

Source: Immanuel Kant, *Groundwork of the Metaphysics of Morals* (1785), 17/402, 66–67/429, 80/436.

everyone's intrinsic value must be respected in social interactions (Formula of the Kingdom of Ends). A full respect for human dignity and a moral kingdom of ends also requires concern for the welfare of others.

The moral principles embodied in the categorical imperative specify our duties—we have a duty to act such that our actions are universal and never treat individuals as only a means, even at the expense of aggregate welfare. In terms of labor relations, this implies that workers are entitled to equity and voice. To refuse to hire someone because of their race, gender, or union sympathies, for example, violates the first formulation of the categorical imperative if we are not willing to be discriminated against in the same manner. Discrimination also violates the Formula of the End Itself because discriminatory treatment for arbitrary reasons violates the equal sanctity of all human life.[83]

It can also be argued that Kantian moral philosophy also gives managers a moral obligation to stockholders to pursue profits to increase shareholder wealth: a manager that ignores profitability violates an implied promise between managers and shareholders and thus violates the categorical imperative. But this is not the same as *maximizing* shareholder wealth at the expense of all other concerns.[84] Therefore, an employment relationship guided by the Kantian ethics of duty should provide efficiency *and* equity *and* voice.

Kant's emphasis on universal, unwavering rules can be criticized for understating the importance of virtues, or what it means to be a good person in everyday life.[85] Universal rules are also challenged by situations such as protecting an innocent person by telling a lie. Proponents of property rights and liberty object to the Kantian implication of concern for others rather than a focus on individual liberties. Kantian moral philosophy also ignores the development of relationships.

Fairness

The most important example of the **ethics of fairness,** or justice, is John Rawls's theory of distributive justice which adds a concern with the distribution of outcomes to the Kantian standards of equality and freedom.[86] Rawlsian justice is based on individuals determining societal standards and outcomes from behind a "veil of ignorance" in which they do not yet know their own characteristics (such as race, gender, social status, and abilities). In very

---

[83] Norman E. Bowie and Ronald F. Duska, *Business Ethics,* 2nd ed. (Englewood Cliffs, NJ: Prentice Hall, 1990).

[84] Bowie, *Business Ethics.*

[85] Solomon, *Ethics and Excellence.*

[86] John Rawls, *A Theory of Justice* (Cambridge, MA: Harvard University Press, 1971).

The Principles of Rawlsian Justice   Box 3.9

1. Each person is to have an equal right to the most extensive total system of equal basic liberties compatible with a similar system of liberty for all (Liberty Principle).
2. Social and economic inequalities are to be arranged so that they are both:
   a. to the greatest benefit of the least advantaged (Difference Principle), and
   b. attached to offices and positions open to all under conditions of fair equality of opportunity (Principle of Equal Opportunity).

Source: John Rawls, *A Theory of Justice* (Cambridge, MA: Harvard University Press, 1971), pp. 83 and 250.

simple terms, think of this as dividing a cake without knowing which piece you'll receive. The principles that Rawls believes rational, self-interested, and equal individuals will agree to are shown in Box 3.9. The first principle, the liberty principle, is the highest priority and includes the right to vote, freedom of speech, freedom from oppression, private property rights, and freedom from arbitrary arrest and seizure. Principle 2a, the difference principle, allows inequalities in outcomes, but these inequalities must also benefit the least well-off members of society. Principle 2b emphasizes equality of opportunity—differential outcomes are allowed, but these should reflect legitimate differences in ability and effort, not arbitrary or discriminatory factors. In short, Rawlsian fairness combines political liberty with equal opportunity and distributive justice. Efficiency is important, but it does not trump political liberties, equal opportunity, and concern for the least well-off. The importance of this Rawlsian ethics of fairness for labor relations is to highlight the importance of social justice.

Virtue

The previous four ethical theories may strike you as cold and unfeeling—there is an emphasis on outcomes or duties or rights or difference principles, but where is human goodness or moral character? In contrast, the **ethics of virtue** focuses on the type of person each individual ought to be. This framework can be traced back to Aristotle over two thousand years ago in ancient Greece. In this tradition, virtues are the characteristics that make a person a good human being and are necessary to live a good life as part of, and in service to, a social community. Moral behavior flows from virtues—not by the application of rules, but from the virtuous moral character of individuals. A contemporary Aristotelian ethical framework is described in Box 3.10. Note the importance of using virtues to serve not only your own interests, but also greater social purposes as well.

As applied to business ethics, virtue ethics sees corporations as human communities with a vital sense of purpose that contribute to, and have responsibilities in, the larger social community.[87] Corporations are collections of mutually dependent individuals, not isolated competitors, and individual excellence and virtues contribute to the success of the individual and the community. As a member of the global community, corporate excellence is defined by service to the broader community, not by a singular focus on making money. Service in the form of quality goods and services will result in profits if done well, but a blind focus on profits should not be the sole driving force: profit is "a means of encouraging and rewarding hard work and investment, building a better business, and serving society better," not "an end in itself."[88] As applied to labor relations, actions that undermine

[87] Solomon, *Ethics and Excellence.*
[88] Solomon, *Ethics and Excellence,* p. 47.

Community People are not primarily individualists, but are members of organized social groups with extensive shared and communal interests. Human meaning and identification stems from being part of communities.

Excellence Individual qualities of moral character—virtues—necessary for living the good life. Requires serving social purposes, not just individual needs. Important contemporary virtues include:

Honesty	Fairness	Trust
Friendliness	Honor	Loyalty
Compassion	Charisma	Justice

Membership Roles for each individual (in personal life, business, and society) provide the context for using the virtues. These roles might conflict, but context-specific virtues should not override greater social purposes.

Integrity Unity of character and moral courage. Requires harnessing all of the virtues to create a whole person.

Judgment With virtues instead of universal rules, and with conflicting roles, individuals need good judgment to develop integrity and make good (ethical) decisions. Generally requires consideration of all options, interests, and consequences.

Holism Concern for the whole. Virtues should be the driving force for all behavior. All virtues should be harnessed to create integrity and good judgment. Integrity and good judgment should be directed toward the greater social purposes of the relevant communities.

Source: Robert C. Solomon, *Ethics and Excellence: Cooperation and Integrity in Business* (New York: Oxford University Press, 1992).

---

a holistic sense of community are unethical. Moreover, if the adjectives for an employer or a union are vices, such as greedy, selfish, dishonest, or corrupt, then the employer or the union is acting unethically.[89] In the ethics of virtue, labor relations should instead be characterized by cooperation, integrity, honesty, fairness, and tolerance.

Care

The **ethics of care** highlights the importance of special, interpersonal relationships such as with parents, children, neighbors, co-workers, or friends. Caring in this sense refers not to simply caring *about* something, but caring *for* someone—nurturing their well-being.[90] This ethical framework was initially developed in the 1980s using feminist theories, especially the claim that the feminine voice consists of "defining the self and proclaiming its worth on the ability to care for and protect others."[91] Thus, moral judgments are not based on rules or principles; rather, the ethics of care relies on the deeper context of each particular situation, especially the implications for relationships. This framework is similar to a specialized version of virtue ethics with a focus on those virtues that are important to personal relationships such as sympathy, compassion, fidelity, love, and friendship.[92] Moreover, within the ethics of care it is acceptable —and maybe even encouraged—to treat people you have relationships with differently. But in developing and nurturing these special relationships, one must guard against positive nurturing becoming discriminatory favoritism, especially in the workplace.[93]

---

[89] Schumann, "A Moral Principles Framework for Human Resource Management Ethics."

[90] Nel Noddings, *Caring: A Feminine Approach to Ethics and Moral Education* (Berkeley: University of California Press, 1984). Velasquez, *Business Ethics.*

[91] Carol Gilligan, *In a Different Voice: Psychological Theory and Women's Development* (Cambridge, MA: Harvard University Press, 1982), p. 79.

[92] Beauchamp and Bowie, *Ethical Theory and Business.*

[93] Velasquez, *Business Ethics.*

While the ethics of care is rooted in feminist theory, it is certainly not relevant only to women. As applied to labor relations, the ethics of care focuses our attention on the relationships between employers and employees and between companies and the local communities. Deceiving employees is unethical because this demonstrates a lack of care.[94] Because this ethical framework legitimizes special treatment, corporate decisions such as whether to invest in an existing unionized plant or open a new nonunion plant in another location should pay particular attention to the existing relationships with the current workers and the local community.

BUSINESS ETHICS IN LABOR RELATIONS

The use of business ethics in labor relations is important in providing a basis for evaluating behavior and outcomes.[95] Many participants and observers, both pro-business and pro-labor, in the U.S. labor relations system feel that it needs fixing. In other words, the labor relations system is not fulfilling some basic standards. But what are those standards? The six ethical frameworks provide the basic standards against which both the labor relations system and the participants' behavior should be evaluated. Similarly, when you find yourself confronted with difficult decisions—as a manager, employee, or union leader—these six ethical theories provide a framework for analyzing your options and the associated positive and negative consequences. Box 3.11 provides a template that incorporates the six ethical theories into a process for analyzing morally complex problems. This template can be applied to ethical questions in later chapters and to real-world situations you confront.

But business ethics is not only the evaluation of right and wrong; it is also the study of the underlying basis for decision making. As emphasized in the model of labor relations outcomes portrayed in Box 3.1, it is important to consider both the environment and individual decision making when trying to understand labor relations outcomes. The external environment establishes the parameters for decision makers, but specific actions within these parameters result from choices made by individual employees, managers, union leaders, and shareholders. One important influence on these choices is ethics. As a concrete example of managerial choice, consider the owner's response to a 1995 fire that destroyed the Massachusetts factory of leading fleece-maker Malden Mills. The owner chose to rebuild the Massachusetts factory rather than moving to a country with lower labor costs and also chose to continue to pay all of the dislocated workers their full wages and benefits instead of laying them off. The environment provided the owner with options, but the owner's ethical framework, in this case an emphasis on the special relationships with the workers and local community, determined the final course of action.[96] While this owner's decisions are not typical, other business decisions made with a sole focus on efficiency and profit maximization also represent an underlying ethical framework—the ethics of utility. In fact, the widespread frequency of corporate and professional association codes of ethics underscores the belief that ethical foundations shape behavior. One view of the ethical obligations of human resource

---

[94] Schumann, "A Moral Principles Framework for Human Resource Management Ethics."

[95] John T. Delaney, "Ethical Challenges in Labor Relations," in John W. Budd and James G. Scoville (eds.), *The Ethics of Human Resources and Industrial Relations* (Champaign, IL: Labor and Employment Relations Association, 2005), pp. 203–28.

[96] Velasquez, *Business Ethics.*

For a proposed action . . .

1. **Identify the benefits.** Be as specific as possible about people or groups of people whose material, financial, or personal well-being will be improved.

2. **Identify the harms.** Be as specific as possible about people or groups of people whose material, financial, or personal well-being will be worsened.

3. **Identify rights.** Be as specific as possible about people or groups of people whose rights will be exercised or strengthened.

4. **Identify rights violations.** Be as specific as possible about people or groups of people whose rights will be violated or weakened.

5. **Identify the impact to the person making the decision.**

6. **State the moral problem.** Use the format "Is it right that (insert decision maker and action) given that (insert harms and rights violations)?" [For example, is it right that company XYZ hires workers to replace strikers given that the strikers will potentially lose their jobs, the union may be broken, and the local residents may be divided by violence?]

7. **Consider the ethics of utility.** Total the overall costs and benefits. Is net welfare improved or worsened? Does the proposed action increase or decrease efficiency?

8. **Consider the ethics of duty.** Does the action respect human dignity? Does it treat people only as a means? Should the action be universal? Would you accept being treated in this way?

9. **Consider the ethics of liberty.** Does the action violate individual liberty? If some rights are exercised and some are harmed, can they be prioritized? Does liberty take precedence over outcomes?

10. **Consider the ethics of fairness.** Is distributive justice respected? Do the least well-off benefit from this action? Would you choose this course of action from behind a veil of ignorance knowing that you might either benefit or be harmed by the action after the veil is lifted?

11. **Consider the ethics of virtue.** Is this action consistent with individual excellence and virtues in service of a larger social purpose? Could you be proud of this action?

12. **Consider the ethics of care.** How does the action affect special relationships? Does it nurture relationships?

13. **Identify several alternatives.** Be simultaneously creative and realistic.

14. **Support your decision.** What are the three most important ethical principles that support your decision as morally right?

Adapted from LaRue Tone Hosmer, "Standard Format for the Case Analysis of Moral Problems," *Teaching Business Ethics* 4 (May 2000), pp. 169–80.

managers is the Society of Human Resource Management's (SHRM) code of ethics (see Box 3.12).

As such, ethics is not just philosophy—it provides an additional framework for a better understanding of labor relations (see Box 3.13). Arguments against labor unions on the grounds that they impair efficiency or intrude on property rights reflect utilitarian and libertarian ethical beliefs. Arguments for labor unions because they provide equity and voice that respect human dignity, fairness, and the importance of community reflect the ethics of duty, justice, virtue, and care. In fact, the campaign to form a union of Harvard University clerical and technical workers in the 1980s was largely inspired by the ethics of care's emphasis on developing interpersonal relationships (see Chapter 7). The continuing managerial drive for greater flexibility in deploying labor and the continued resistance by workers and unions reflects in part a clash between utilitarian concerns with efficiency and Kantian concerns with the quality of human life. The sometimes violent protests over increasing globalization stem from the utilitarian emphasis on free trade to increase efficiency clashing with the other ethical frameworks that emphasize human rights and fairness. To understand behavior and outcomes—and in making your own decisions—pay attention to both the environment and ethics. This is equally true for both labor and management.

Ethics in Action: The Society for Human Resource Management (SHRM) Code of Ethics   Box 3.12

THE SIX CORE PRINCIPLES OF THE SHRM CODE OF ETHICAL AND PROFESSIONAL STANDARDS IN HUMAN RESOURCE MANAGEMENT

- *Professional responsibility:* HR professionals are responsible for adding value to the organizations they serve and contributing to the ethical success of those organizations. They accept professional responsibility for their individual decisions and actions and are advocates for the profession, engaging in activities that enhance its credibility and value.

- *Professional development:* HR professionals must strive to meet the highest standards of competence and commit to strengthen their competencies on a continuous basis.

- *Ethical leadership:* HR professionals are expected to exhibit individual leadership as a role model for maintaining the highest standards of ethical conduct.

- *Fairness and justice:* HR professionals are ethically responsible for promoting and fostering fairness and justice for all employees and their organizations.

- *Conflicts of interest:* HR professionals must maintain a high level of trust with stakeholders. In the interest of professional integrity, they must protect the interests of stakeholders and should not engage in activities that create actual, apparent or potential conflicts of interest.

- *Use of information:* HR professionals consider and protect the rights of individuals, especially in the acquisition and dissemination of information while ensuring truthful communications and facilitating informed decision making.

Reflection Questions

1. In the first principle, should "value" only mean "profits"?

2. In the third principle, what should the "highest standards of ethical conduct" consist of?

3. Is a legal union avoidance campaign consistent with SHRM's code of ethical standards?

Source: *www.shrm.org/ethics* (accessed on May 29, 2006). The full code also includes description of each principle's intent and guidelines for implementation.

BOX 3.13
Examples of Ethical Foundations in Labor Relations

The Ethics of . . .	Labor Relations Examples
Utility	A management desire to be "union free" based on a cost/benefit analysis. Provision of equity and voice only because they increase productivity.
Liberty	Employer participation in the union organizing process because of their rights of private property and free speech.
Duty	Employees are entitled to voice because they are rational, human beings who should not be treated only as a means to some other end.
Fairness	Unions negotiating compressed wage structures which narrow the gap between unskilled and skilled workers in the name of fairness.
Virtue	"Might does not make right." Rather, establish productive workplaces or engage in collective bargaining based on excellence and integrity.
Care	Recent union initiatives to organize workers by developing special relationships with the workers, especially in female-dominated occupations.

LEVELS OF DECISION MAKING

Individuals and organizations make choices within the parameters of the environment and are influenced by ethics and other elements of the human agent. In labor relations, these choices are made within four tiers: the sociopolitical, strategic, functional, and workplace tiers.[97] The sociopolitical level encompasses the broad social and political arenas while the other three levels are focused on companies, labor unions, and their interaction. On the corporate side, the strategic level is where strategic decisions are made regarding business and human resources strategies (see Chapter 6). At the other end, the workplace level is where production occurs. If there is an employee involvement plan or a grievance procedure, these are part of the workplace level. The functional level is in between the corporate boardroom and the local workplace. Specific policies, rather than broad strategic directions, are established at this level. In large corporations, these levels are likely to be visibly distinct. In a smaller organization, these levels might overlap. In a small restaurant, the restaurant owner may be the primary management person making strategic, functional, and daily workplace level decisions. And while these decisions are interrelated, it is useful to think about them separately. This provides a more complete understanding of labor relations goals, strategies, and outcomes.

On the union side, the strategic level includes the headquarters' and executive officers' responsibilities of national unions.[98] Broad policies on collective bargaining goals, a political agenda, and strategies for organizing new members are determined at this level. Representation of individual employees through the grievance procedure, building relationships with union and nonunion workers, and participating in joint labor—management workplace committees, such as safety and health committees, occur at the workplace level. The functional level of union organizations is where collective bargaining occurs. As with the corporate side, this level is between the union boardroom and the local workplace.

Interactions occur between unions and management on all four levels. While most strategic activity might occur within each organization, some U.S. companies, and many in other countries such as Germany, have employee or union representatives on the corporate board of directors.[99] At Northwest Airlines, for example, the three largest unions each obtained a seat on the corporation's board of directors as part of a massive concessions package in 1993. As a result, the unions have had input into decisions over executive compensation and possible mergers with other airlines, gained access to information about the airline's strategic plans, and added a worker's perspective to the board. On the other hand, this representation didn't stop the protests of frustrated flight attendants from causing the company's annual meeting in 1999 to be canceled after 20 minutes and didn't prevent the airline from permanently replacing more than 4,000 mechanics during a strike in 2005. The interactions between labor and management at the functional and workplace level are readily seen in all unionized workplaces. The most visible example at the functional level is the collective bargaining process of negotiating union contracts (Chapter 8). At the workplace level, managers and unions interact through steps of grievance procedures (Chapter 10) and in joint committees (Chapter 11). Strikes (Chapter 9) and union organizing drives (Chapter 7) involve both the functional and workplace levels. A union corporate campaign that seeks to generate public pressure on a company through adverse social and political reactions is an example of a sociopolitical activity (Chapter 9).

[97] Kochan, Katz, and McKersie, *The Transformation of American Industrial Relations.* Thomas A. Kochan, Robert B. McKersie, and Peter Cappelli, "Strategic Choice and Industrial Relations Theory," *Industrial Relations* 23 (Winter 1984), pp. 16–39.

[98] Kochan, Katz, and McKersie, *The Transformation of American Industrial Relations.* Kochan, McKersie, and Cappelli, "Strategic Choice and Industrial Relations Theory."

[99] Larry W. Hunter, "Can Strategic Participation Be Institutionalized? Union Representation on American Corporate Boards," *Industrial and Labor Relations Review* 51 (July 1998), pp. 557–78.

EMPLOYEE REACTIONS TO WORKPLACE INJUSTICE

Putting all of the elements of Box 3.1 together—the environment, the human agent including ethics, and the levels of decision making—provides an important framework for understanding labor relations. As one important example, many of the central questions of labor relations can be phrased in terms of workplace injustice: Does workplace injustice cause workers to support unions? Do unions more effectively prevent and redress workplace injustices than alternative mechanisms such as laws, courts, markets, human resource management policies, or individual activities? Does workplace injustice increase strikes and other forms of labor conflict? Box 3.1 provides the framework for considering the options for workers' reactions to workplace injustice and the factors that shape these reactions. The possible outcomes in Box 3.1 are the possible responses to workplace injustice: exit, individual voice, collective voice, resistance, and silence.

One of the most well-known models for considering responses to dissatisfaction is the exit-voice model.[100] In the employment relationship, exit means quitting. In terms of Box 3.1, whether a worker quits is likely influenced by the economic environment and the prospects for finding a comparable new job. Feelings are also important: workers who are loyal to their employer are less likely to exit (quit).[101] Workers who stay with their employer have four alternatives for dealing with injustice. They can discuss the injustice with their managers on an individual basis (individual voice) or as a group (collective voice). Alternatively, dissatisfied workers can remain silent or try to rectify the situation through active, unilateral resistance.[102] Resistance includes what economists call shirking and what psychologists call work withdrawal: absenteeism, reduced work effort, work avoidance.[103] More aggressive forms of resistance include sabotage, theft, or workplace violence.[104] These choices are influenced by many of the dimensions of the environment and individual decision making presented in Box 3.1. The legal or institutional environment might protect or foster certain forms of voice while social norms or the technical context of the workplace (such as an assembly line) may constrain certain forms of resistance.[105] If undocumented immigrants have a more difficult time finding new jobs than native workers, then they will be more likely to fight for improved conditions in their existing jobs than to quit and look for better conditions

[100] Albert O. Hirschman, *Exit, Voice, and Loyalty: Responses to Decline in Firms, Organizations, and States* (Cambridge: Harvard University Press, 1970).

[101] Karen Boroff and David Lewin, "Loyalty, Voice, and Intent to Exit a Union Firm: A Conceptual and Empirical Analysis," *Industrial and Labor Relations Review* 51 (October 1997), pp. 50–63. Hirschman, *Exit, Voice, and Loyalty*. Andrew A. Luchak, "What Kind of Voice Do Loyal Employees Use?" *British Journal of Industrial Relations* 41 (March 2003), pp. 115–34.

[102] Brian Bemmels, "Exit, Voice, and Loyalty in Employment Relationships," in David Lewin, Daniel J.B. Mitchell, and Mahmood Zaidi (eds.), *The Human Resource Management Handbook, Part 2* (Greenwich, CT: JAI Press, 1997), pp. 245–59. Boroff and Lewin, "Loyalty, Voice, and Intent to Exit a Union Firm." Craig C. Pinder and Karen P. Harlos, "Employee Silence: Quiescence and Acquiescence as Responses to Perceived Injustice," in Gerald R. Ferris (ed.), *Research in Personnel and Human Resources Management*, Volume 20 (Amsterdam: JAI Press, 2001), pp. 331–69.

[103] Kathy A. Hanisch and Charles L. Hulin, "General Attitudes and Organizational Withdrawal: An Evaluation of a Causal Model," *Journal of Vocational Behavior* 39 (August 1991), pp. 110–28. Hodson, *Dignity at Work*.

[104] John W. Budd, Richard D. Arvey, and Peggy Lawless, "Correlates and Consequences of Workplace Violence," *Journal of Occupational Health Psychology* 1 (April 1996), pp. 197–210. Glomb, Steel, and Arvey, "Office Sneers, Snipes, and Stab Wounds." Jerald Greenberg, *The Quest for Justice on the Job: Essays and Experiments* (Thousand Oaks, CA: Sage, 1996). Hodson, *Dignity at Work*.

[105] Hodson, *Dignity at Work*.

elsewhere.[106] Attitudes such as low self-esteem or low perceived control over outcomes may underlie a silent response while emotions may trigger aggressive resistance.[107]

Labor unions are formal institutions of collective voice and thus represent a critical option for employee reactions to workplace injustices.[108] Voice is exercised through bargaining over the terms of employment (Chapter 8) and by filing grievances (Chapter 10). The intersection between collective voice and resistance is a strike (Chapter 9). The environmental and behavioral predictors of support for unionization will be discussed in Chapter 7, but to help set the stage for the remainder of this book, it is useful to emphasize that understanding why workers unionize amounts to understanding when, why, and how workers choose collective action over other responses to workplace injustice. In other words, under what conditions will workers mobilize as a group?[109] The answer to this question is undoubtedly complex, but Box 3.1 captures the major elements—feelings of frustration, motivation to redress injustices, individual and social attitudes and ethics towards collective rather than individual action, and the relative power of various alternatives as determined by the environment.[110]

EMPLOYER REACTIONS TO COMPETITIVE PRESSURES

From the perspective of employees, the nature of reactions to workplace injustice is a recurring theme throughout the study of labor relations. On the employer side, perhaps the most important theme is the nature of reactions to unions and competitive pressures. Thus, another important application of Box 3.1 is considering the factors that shape employers' reactions to unions. The economic environment is of obvious importance as it determines a firm's competitive position. In particular, increased competition—from domestic nonunion companies and from international companies—starting in the 1970s caused stronger anti-union responses by companies than in the 1950s which resulted in significant investments in nonunion rather than union facilities.[111] Business pressures for flexibility and competitiveness in the global economy of the 21st century further push unionized employers to reshape their union contracts and to improve their adversarial relationships with labor unions (Chapters 11 and 12). In fact, just the announcement that Wal-Mart was expanding into southern California prompted unionized grocery stores to demand large health insurance cuts which resulted in a six-month strike by nearly 60,000 grocery workers in 2003. Competitive pressures further push nonunion employers like Wal-Mart and many others to aggressively keep unions out. A favorable (to business) political and social climate in the 1980s is also believed to have allowed employers to use strike replacements on a wider scale than previously—an action allowable by the legal environment.[112] And not to be overlooked are managerial values.[113] Ethical beliefs shape employer reactions to unions,

[106] Immanuel Ness, *Immigrants, Unions, and the New U.S. Labor Market* (Philadelphia: Temple University Press, 2005).

[107] Bemmels, "Exit, Voice, and Loyalty in Employment Relationships." Pinder and Harlos, "Employee Silence." Wheeler, *Industrial Conflict.*

[108] Richard B. Freeman and James L. Medoff, *What Do Unions Do?* (New York: Basic Books, 1984). Kelly, *Rethinking Industrial Relations.*

[109] Kelly, *Rethinking Industrial Relations.*

[110] Hodson, *Dignity at Work.* Kelly, *Rethinking Industrial Relations.* Wheeler, *Industrial Conflict.*

[111] Kochan, Katz, and McKersie, *The Transformation of American Industrial Relations.*

[112] Jonathan D. Rosenblum, *Copper Crucible: How the Arizona Miners' Strike of 1983 Recast Labor–Management Relations in America,* 2nd ed. (Ithaca, NY: ILR Press, 1998).

[113] Kochan, Katz, and McKersie, *The Transformation of American Industrial Relations.*

especially the goal of remaining union-free in order to make business decisions free from interference and consistent with the ethics of utility and liberty. Remember the dimensions of Box 3.1 when studying the development of the U.S. labor relations system, its current operation, and the pressures for change.

This chapter concludes Part I of this book that provides an overall framework for thinking about the objectives of the employment relationship, different viewpoints on the role of labor unions in serving these objectives which are rooted in competing schools of thought on markets and conflict, and the determinants of specific labor relations outcomes. This chapter helps lay the foundation for understanding the present U.S. labor relations system—the New Deal industrial relations system discussed next in Part II—by highlighting the importance of the different dimensions of the environment and individual choices. As you will see, the establishment of the New Deal industrial relations system reflects explicit ethical decisions to structure the legal environment to promote specific labor relations outcomes. But then in Part III, three tremendous changes in the environment are explored: the pressures of employee involvement, workplace flexibility, and globalization. These changes have altered the environment so significantly as to call into question the continued viability and wisdom of the New Deal system. The New Deal system and these pressures for reform cannot be understood without appreciating the objectives of the employment relationship, different viewpoints on labor markets and employment relationship conflict, and the role of the environment and individual decision making in shaping labor relations outcomes.

Key Terms

legal environment, *73*
economic environment, *74*
concession bargaining, *75*
technical environment, *75*
skill-biased technological change, *76*
deskilling, *76*

political environment, *77*
social environment, *77*
business environment, *79*
institutional environment, *81*
ethical subjectivism, *89*
ethical relativism, *89*

ethics of utility, *89*
ethics of liberty, *90*
ethics of duty, *91*
categorical imperative, *91*
ethics of fairness, *92*
ethics of virtue, *93*
ethics of care, *94*

Reflection Questions

1. Suppose you are dissatisfied with your pay. What are you likely to do in response? What elements of the environment and individual decision making will influence your reaction? Does your answer change if you feel abused or harassed rather than dissatisfied with your pay?

2. Should soldiers be allowed to join unions? (*Hint:* consider both the environment and ethics.)

3. Suppose you face a moral dilemma in the workplace. What standards would you use when deciding what to do? How do these standards fit into the six ethical frameworks described here?

4. Consider a company whose employees are trying to form a union. Use the template in Box 3.11 to outline how the company's response to this organizing drive might be shaped by each of the six ethical frameworks. Does ethical behavior equal legal behavior?

Internet Exploration

1. Identify a local company or some other business organization that is of interest. Search the Internet to find information on the economic environment for that company. Try to find labor market information as well as company-level, industry-level, and economy-wide information regarding consumer demand and ability to pay. Are there trends in other dimensions of the labor relations environment that are relevant for this company?

2. Find examples of corporate codes of ethics. Alternatively, find codes of ethics for professional associations in your areas of interest (for example, accounting or marketing). Do they reflect a specific ethical theory? What would you add to the codes? As a human resources manager, should you make sure they are followed? If so, how would you do this?

Additional
Reading

Bowie, Norman E., *Business Ethics: A Kantian Perspective* (Malden, MA: Blackwell Publishers, 1999).

Budd, John W., *Employment with a Human Face: Balancing Efficiency, Equity, and Voice* (Ithaca, NY: Cornell University Press, 2004).

Dunlop, John T., *Industrial Relations Systems,* revised edition (Boston: Harvard Business School Press, 1993).

Hodson, Randy, *Dignity at Work* (Cambridge: Cambridge University Press, 2001).

Kelly, John E., *Rethinking Industrial Relations: Mobilization, Collectivism and Long Waves* (London: Routledge, 1998).

Kochan, Thomas A., Harry C. Katz, and Robert B. McKersie, *The Transformation of American Industrial Relations* (New York: Basic Books, 1986).

Solomon, Robert C., *Ethics and Excellence: Cooperation and Integrity in Business* (New York: Oxford University Press, 1992).

Towers, Brian, *The Representation Gap: Change and Reform in the British and American Workplace* (Oxford: Oxford University Press, 1997).

Part Two

The U.S. New Deal Industrial Relations System

The New Deal industrial relations system is the set of labor relations policies and practices that grew out of the New Deal economic policies during the Great Depression in the 1930s and that attempt to balance efficiency, equity, and voice. Even though it is over 70 years old, the New Deal industrial relations system still governs U.S. labor relations today. The next seven chapters therefore describe the development of this system and its current operation, especially with respect to how unions are organized, how contracts are negotiated, and how disputes are resolved.

Chapter **Four**

Historical Development

Advance Organizer

The contemporary U.S. labor relations system can be studied simply as it exists today without any reference to the past. But this is not very satisfying. Today's laws, philosophies, processes, organizations, and strategies have evolved out of experiences from 10, 50, and even 150 years ago. To better understand the current system—and its future challenges—this chapter presents important events, organizations, and strategies from the history of U.S. labor relations.

Learning Objectives

By the end of the chapter, you should be able to:

1. **Understand** why workers have tried to form unions throughout U.S. history and the influences on their successes and failures.
2. **Identify** the major events in U.S. labor history including what happened and why each event is significant.

3. **Compare** the major organizations in labor history and their contrasting strategies, including labor strategies for promoting collective action among workers and business strategies for discouraging or repressing such action.
4. **Understand** how studying the historical record deepens the understanding of the current labor relations system and alternatives for reform.

Contents

The current U.S. labor relations system is a product of history. Some of this history is relatively recent—such as President Reagan's firing of the striking air traffic controllers in 1981—while other aspects might seem like ancient history—such as the Great Uprising of 1877—but it is all very relevant to a richer understanding of labor relations. Workers' efforts to form unions are better appreciated against the backdrop of changes in the nature of work and the growth of corporate power. The continued emphasis on seniority rights in U.S. union contracts is more fully comprehended when placed in the context of the abuses of all-powerful supervisors in the early 1900s. Union hostility towards nonunion forms of employee representation is rooted in corporate manipulation of company unions in the 1930s. U.S. labor laws that emphasize representation elections stem from the historical record of strike activity and labor–management conflict.

Two related yet distinct types of historical elements are emphasized throughout this chapter: events and organizational strategies. Every student of labor relations should be aware of the major events in U.S. labor history. These events often visibly reveal the leading issues and conflicts of a certain era, and also altered the course of labor relations. It is thus difficult to understand labor relations without discussing these events. At the same time, the history of labor relations contains a rich tapestry of organizations and strategies. Some of these organizations and strategies continue to exist today, others have passed into the annals of history. A broad historical investigation provides the opportunity to therefore consider a wider range of organizational strategies than currently exist in 21st century labor relations. This wider analysis simultaneously sharpens our understanding of each organizational strategy through contrasts with others while also broadening the set of ideas for future options. As an example, today's U.S. unions are dominated by a business unionism philosophy, but an investigation of several historical labor organizations reveals significantly different philosophies. Examination of these philosophies and their accompanying strategies enriches the understanding of business unionism and also provides potential ideas for labor union strategies in the future.

Consideration of major events and organizational strategies in the history of U.S. labor relations also illustrates the twin roles of the environment and choice discussed in the previous chapter. As the chapter unfolds, pay attention to how the external environment—the economic climate, technology, immigration, and the like—affect events and organizations. At the same time, do not reduce workers, unions, managers, and corporations to mere puppets of the environment. History reveals choices that are actively made by individuals and organizations within the environment. This history is also more than just labor history— the study of workers and their unions. The historical development of U.S. labor relations also involves important components of social, business, economic, and legal history. The historical development of U.S. labor law is discussed in Chapter 5; our concern for the rest of this chapter is the rich fabric of events, organizations, and strategies that weave together with social, economic, business, and labor history to reveal the historical development of the U.S. labor relations system.

FROM LOCAL TO NATIONAL ORGANIZATIONS

In the 21st century, we take working for someone else as natural. Most workers today are *employees* selling their labor in return for a wage or a salary. Only about 10 percent are self-employed.[1] And half of employees today work for large organizations with 500 or more employees. These patterns are taken for granted today because they have been true for much of the 20th century, but it is essential to appreciate that these patterns are the result of tremendous, tumultuous economic and social changes that occurred in the 1800s—changes typically summarized as "industrialization." At the end of the 1700s, a large majority of free people were self-employed as farmers, shopkeepers, blacksmiths, shoemakers, and the like.[2] In major cities, a few skilled workers might have worked as employees for a master craftsman, but these businesses were small and local. The early "large" businesses were in the iron industry and employed perhaps 25 employees.[3] Slightly more than one hundred years later, U.S. Steel employed 170,000 employees, Ford's Highland Park factory outside Detroit had 15,000 employees, and the era of self-employment was over.[4] The roots of the modern labor relations system lie in this massive change in the nature of work, and of industrial society.

[1] Robert W. Fairlie and Bruce D. Meyer, "Trends in Self-Employment Among White and Black Men During the Twentieth Century," *Journal of Human Resources* 35 (Autumn 2000), pp. 643–69.

[2] Melvyn Dubofsky and Foster Rhea Dulles, *Labor in America: A History,* 6th ed. (Wheeling, IL: Harlan Davidson, 1999).

[3] Joseph G. Rayback, *A History of American Labor* (New York: Free Press, 1966).

[4] Nelson Lichtenstein et al., *Who Built America? Working People and the Nation's Economy, Politics, Culture, and Society,* Volume 2 (New York: Worth Publishing, 2000). William Serrin, *Homestead: The Glory and Tragedy of an American Steel Town* (New York: Vintage Books, 1992).

The rise of large-scale corporations is typically associated with efficiency gains from specialization—it's faster and cheaper to produce a car with many unskilled workers doing small, repetitive tasks along an assembly line than with a single, skilled craftsperson building the entire car.[5] But this comes later. Starting in the 1820s, large textile mills were constructed outside of Boston and Philadelphia, some of them employing 500 workers under one roof. This was not driven entirely by specialization—the work could be done at home using a hand loom. Advances in water- and later steam-powered machinery helped spur industrialization, but large-scale factories using power looms were also constructed to take advantage of direct labor supervision and control:

> If workers came to the mill to work twelve hours instead of coming there to pick up yarn to weave at home, output would be steady, thievery reduced, and the continuous labor of a hundred souls in one room guaranteed under the eyes of the overseer (note the name), his assistant, and their two runners. In one room, four people—two managers and two clerks—could control a hundred workers.[6]

This control was reinforced by harsh penalties: a quarter of a day's wages was the penalty for being 15 minutes late to work, two days' pay for missing one day without a reason, and two weeks' worth for quitting without permission.[7] Immigration provided a steady influx of cheap labor to staff the mills. These textile mills were the beginnings of U.S. big business that combined technological advances in power, large-scale wage labor, and bureaucratic, centralized management functions financed by large amounts of investment capital.[8]

While the textile industry illustrates the beginnings of industrialization, the railroad industry overwhelmingly determined the nature of business competition and organization.[9] Spurred by advances in steel and steam-powered engines, the development of the railroads drastically improved transportation in the 1850s. What was a three-week trip from New York to Chicago was reduced to three days, and local markets for many products expanded into national markets. With a greatly enlarged set of possible customers, mass production of shoes, clothes, watches, tools, and many other products became economically feasible. But the railroads also perfected the central dimensions of big business—bureaucratic, centralized control (and hence, impersonal work) and a concentration of wealth and power (and hence, monopoly power in markets and society)—that would later spread to many other industries.[10]

Quite naturally, the forms and functions of labor unions paralleled these changes in work and business organization. The earliest examples of union-like activity in the United States were short-term actions triggered by specific complaints, such as a strike by fishermen on a Maine island in 1636 protesting the withholding of a year's wages or a strike by twenty journeymen tailors in 1768 in New York City protesting a reduction in wages (see Box 4.1).[11] It was not until the 1790s that Philadelphia shoemakers formed the first

---

[5] Alfred D. Chandler, Jr., *The Visible Hand: The Managerial Revolution in American Business* (Cambridge: Harvard University Press, 1977).

[6] Charles Perrow, *Organizing America: Wealth, Power, and the Origins of Corporate Capitalism* (Princeton, NJ: Princeton University Press, 2002), p. 66.

[7] Cynthia J. Shelton, *The Mills of Manayunk: Industrialization and Social Conflict in the Philadelphia Region, 1787–1837* (Baltimore: Johns Hopkins University Press, 1986).

[8] Perrow, *Organizing America.*

[9] Chandler, *The Visible Hand.* Perrow, *Organizing America.*

[10] Perrow, *Organizing America.*

[11] Philip S. Foner, *First Facts of American Labor* (New York: Holmes and Meier, 1984). Rayback, *A History of American Labor.*

Early U.S. Labor Organizations: Some Firsts   Box 4.1

LOCAL ACTIVITIES

First Strike Over Economic Issues: Richmond Island, Maine, fishermen, over the employer's withholding of a year's wages (1636)

First Strike by Black Workers: Charleston, South Carolina, chimney sweeps, for higher wages (1763)

First Strike by a Permanent Union: Philadelphia shoemakers (1792)

First Trade Agreement: Philadelphia shoemakers and their employers (1799)

First Women Workers in a Strike: Weavers in Pawtucket, Rhode Island (1824)

First Organizations Using the Word "Union": The Nailers' Union and the Weavers' Union, both of New York City (1825)

First Permanent Union of Women Workers: The Lowell Female Labor Reform Association, at the Lowell, Massachusetts, textile mills (1845)

First Union of Black Workers: The Colored Caulkers' Trade Union Society of Baltimore (1866)

NATIONAL ACTIVITIES

First National Union: The National Cooperative Association of Journeymen Cordwainers (1836)

First National Trade Agreement: Iron puddlers and their employers (1866)

First National Union of Women Workers: The Daughters of St. Crispin, of shoemakers (1867)

Source: Philip S. Foner, *First Facts of American Labor* (New York: Holmes and Meier, 1984).

permanent union. The first organizations were local in nature and focused on a single skilled occupation—shoemakers, printers, carpenters, and tailors. These local craft unions established work standards and a minimum wage rate; union members agreed not to work for any employer paying less.[12] Their permanency, however, was tenuous. Some strikes were ruled to be illegal criminal conspiracies (see Chapter 5) and depressions in 1819 and 1837 severely crippled the early labor unions because union members were desperate for any work they could get.[13] This importance of the legal and economic environment for labor relations is a universal theme from the 18th to the 21st centuries.

As business organizations became larger and more national in scope, so too did labor unions. National rather than local unions began to develop in the 1850s—necessitated by the ability of manufactured goods to be shipped via the railroads, and likely facilitated by the ability of union leaders to travel via the railroads (see Box 4.2). The increasingly nonlocal scope of union activity is underscored by the shoemakers strike in 1860 that involved 20,000 workers in several New England states.[14] While the budding national unions were craft unions—of printers, plumbers, and railroad engineers, for example—some also included craft occupations in factory settings, especially iron molders and machinists.[15] The iron molders' experience in a stove foundry is perhaps illustrative of many transformations during the 19th century: with the advent of the railroads, iron stove manufacturers tried to capture national market share through mass manufacturing methods. Previously, each iron molder used skill and discretion to mold an entire stove, but with a mass manufacturing system, the parts of the stove were divided and each molder was relegated to repetitively making one part. The work became impersonal and subject to constant pressure to reduce labor costs. The National Molders Union was thus formed in 1859 in reaction to these changing conditions. One year later it had 44 locals ranging from St. Louis to New York to

[12] Rayback, *A History of American Labor.*
[13] Dubofsky and Dulles, *Labor in America.*
[14] Dubofsky and Dulles, *Labor in America.*
[15] Rayback, *A History of American Labor.*

BOX 4.2
A Timeline of Labor History up to 1875

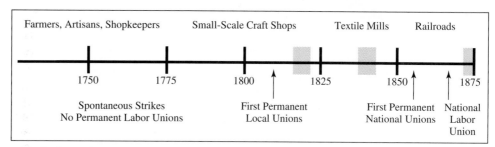

Note: Shading indicates economic recessions.

Toronto.[16] After the Civil War, this union became the Iron Molders' International Union which, for a time, was the strongest in the country and its features were a direct forerunner to today's unions—centralized and national control, a per capita tax on all union members, creation of a national strike fund to support striking workers, and an emphasis on strong collective bargaining.[17]

The next step in the development of U.S. labor organizations was the creation of a national labor federation representing unions from different occupations or industries. The first such federation was the **National Labor Union** which was founded in 1866.[18] The National Labor Union only lasted six years, but it established a precedent for the labor movement by uniting diverse unions into a single federation—foreshadowing today's AFL–CIO. Moreover, the National Labor Union sharply contrasts with other U.S. union approaches and therefore helps broaden our thinking about possible union strategies. In particular, the National Labor Union primarily emphasized political activity to bring about legal reform. In addition to campaigning for the eight-hour working day (rather than the 10-or-more-hour day common at the time) through maximum hour legislation, the National Labor Union favored currency and banking reform, women's suffrage, and ultimately, a national labor political party.

THE GREAT UPRISING OF 1877

The 1870s ushered in an era of intense and violent labor conflict that would continue into the 20th century. A massive depression caused severe unemployment and wage cuts. One study estimates that only 20 percent of the labor force worked regularly for an entire year and that wages in various industries had fallen by 30 to 60 percent.[19] Union membership plummeted. A six-month coal strike in eastern Pennsylvania in 1875 ended when workers agreed to a 20 percent wage *reduction*. This strike involved open battles between strikers and company-paid police, and the use of company spies.[20] As the strike dragged on, the miners were increasingly led by a young group of Irish miners who belonged to a secret

[16] Jonathan Grossman, *William Sylvis, Pioneer of American Labor* (New York: Columbia University Press, 1945).

[17] Dubofsky and Dulles, *Labor in America.*

[18] Dubofsky and Dulles, *Labor in America.* Grossman, *William Sylvis, Pioneer of American Labor.* Rayback, *A History of American Labor.*

[19] Rayback, *A History of American Labor.*

[20] Richard O. Boyer and Herbert M. Morais, *Labor's Untold Story* (Pittsburgh: United Electrical, Radio, and Machine Workers of America, 1955). Kevin Kenny, *Making Sense of the Molly Maguires* (New York: Oxford University Press, 1998).

The Pinkerton National Detective Agency   Box 4.3

Lurking in the shadows of many of the bitterest labor conflicts of the 19th century is the Pinkerton National Detective Agency. Founded in 1850 by Allan Pinkerton, the Pinkerton agency started off protecting railroads against criminal activity (including dishonest conductors) and then gathering intelligence as spies during the Civil War. After the war, Pinkerton detectives tracked some of the most notorious criminals of the era, including Jesse James and Butch Cassidy and the Sundance Kid. The company logo became an unblinking eye above the motto "we never sleep" which is the source of the expression "private eye."

In labor relations, the Pinkerton agency provided both guards and detectives. The Philadelphia and Reading Railroad hired the agency in 1873 to infiltrate the secret association of its Irish coal miners—the alleged Molly Maguires. An agent successfully became a secretary of the local union and sent numerous reports to the company on labor activity. Though never proved, some accused this spy of being an *agent provocateur*—that is, of initiating violence in order to get the Molly Maguires in trouble. Thereafter, Pinkerton detectives were used extensively as labor spies, and charges of being *agents provocateur* more than once accompanied their discovery. As evidence of the pervasiveness of Pinkerton spies, one Pinkerton operative even infiltrated the legal defense team for the radical union leader Big Bill Haywood who was accused of conspiring to murder the former governor of Idaho in retaliation for breaking a miners' strike in 1899. In the 1930s, Pinkertons were still being used as spies inside various labor unions—in fact, at least 50 members of the United Auto Workers were actually Pinkerton agents.

In addition to infiltrating unions, the Pinkerton agency provided armed guards to companies. Pinkerton guards were involved in at least 70 strikes between 1877 and 1892, often accompanied by violence. By one account, the Pinkerton agency had 2,000 active agents and 30,000 in reserve—a total greater than the standing army of the United States at the time. In fact, the intense gun battles between Pinkertons and strikers, such as when 300 Pinkertons descended upon Homestead, Pennsylvania, in 1892, made the Pinkertons look more like a mercenary army than the protectors of corporate private property. By the end of the 19th century, 24 states had outlawed the importation of armed guards from other states.

In the 20th century, strikebreaking became big business and numerous agencies specialized in providing both strikebreakers and armed guards. While not nearly as violent, union-avoidance consulting still remains a thriving business in the 21st century. The Knights of Labor have long faded from U.S. history, but the Pinkerton National Detective Agency pioneered these "Knights of Capital."

Sources: Jeremy Brecher, *Strike!* (Boston: South End Press, 1972). J. Anthony Lukas, *Big Trouble: A Murder in a Small Western Town Sets Off a Struggle for the Soul of America* (New York: Simon and Schuster, 1997). Frank Morn, *"The Eye That Never Sleeps:" A History of the Pinkerton National Detective Agency* (Bloomington: Indiana University Press, 1982). Stephen H. Norwood, *Strikebreaking and Intimidation: Mercenaries and Masculinity in Twentieth-Century America of the Labor Movement* (Chapel Hill: University of North Carolina Press, 2002). Robert Michael Smith, *From Blackjacks to Briefcases: A History of Commercialized Strikebreaking and Unionbusting in the United States* (Athens: Ohio University Press, 2003). Frederick Voss and James Barber, *We Never Sleep: The First Fifty Years of the Pinkertons* (Washington, DC: Smithsonian Institution Press, 1981).

---

fraternal society. This group was widely publicized as controlled by the Molly Maguires, a secret Irish terrorist organization, that allegedly led a campaign of murder and arson during the strike. The coal company hired an agent of the Pinkerton National Detective Agency—an organization that emerges repeatedly in employers' strikebreaking efforts in U.S. labor history—to infiltrate the Molly Maguires (see Box 4.3). The truth may never be known, but many historians believe that this agent was unable to gather evidence of criminal activity, and in fact may have instigated such activity as an *agent provocateur*. But in the aftermath of the strike, against the backdrop of a public frenzy fearful of the Molly Maguires and opposed to Irish immigration and organized labor, the agent's testimony—perhaps all fabricated—convicted 24 Molly Maguires for murder. Ten were hanged.

But this was just the beginning. In response to a 10 percent wage cut (on top of wage cuts in earlier years of the depression), workers on one railroad and then another, and another, went on strike in July 1877. The strike quickly spread until railroad activity in large sections of the country was affected. Large crowds stopped trains, spiked switches, and took over depots and roundhouses (see Box 4.4). Two hundred federal troops were first

BOX 4.4
Violence During the Great Uprising of 1877
Workers Forcibly Stopping a B&O Train in Martinsburg, West Virginia, July 17, 1877

Source: *Frank Leslie's Illustrated Newspaper* (August 4, 1877)

A Pittsburgh Train Yard After a Night of Destruction Prompted by the Killing of Workers by the State Militia, July 22, 1877

Source: *Frank Leslie's Illustrated Newspaper* (August 11, 1877)

sent to Martinsburg, West Virginia, and violence flared elsewhere. Nine people were killed in rioting in Baltimore; the state militia fired into a crowd in Pittsburgh killing 20 and prompting a night of conflict, fire, and destruction that resulted in $5,000,000 of railroad property damage.[21]

These events became the **Great Uprising of 1877** because it was much more than a railroad strike. More workers were involved than in any other labor conflict of the 1800s.[22] Many of these workers were not railroad workers—coal miners, iron workers, and others significantly aided the railroad workers in many locations. Black longshoring workers in Texas and sewer workers in Kentucky struck for higher pay.[23] Chicago and St. Louis experienced general strikes in which thousands of workers shut down many businesses in the two cities. State militia and federal troops were used to forcefully end demonstrations and restore order in many locations. Yet in spite of its widespread intensity, the uprising ended nearly as quickly as it began and railroad traffic resumed normal operations at the end of the month.

The Great Uprising of 1877 is probably more notable for what it represents than what it accomplished. The numerous strikes clearly reflected pent-up grievances of workers—in many industries and locations—struggling with the forces of industrialization and the conflict between labor and capital. The uprising also demonstrates the shared concerns of workers and is often used to define the beginning of the modern era in U.S. labor relations—

---

[21] Jeremy Brecher, *Strike!* (Boston: South End Press, 1972). Dubofsky and Dulles, *Labor in America.* Philip S. Foner, *The Great Uprising of 1877* (New York: Monad Press, 1977). Rayback, *A History of American Labor.*

[22] Rayback, *A History of American Labor.*

[23] Brecher, *Strike!* Foner, *The Great Uprising of 1877.*

one in which capital and labor are often sharply at odds. By some accounts, business fears of future labor insurrections led to more aggressive strategies to repress labor activity.[24] Alternatively, by showing that federal and state troops would protect business property, the events of 1877 may have made big business "emboldened to confront labor rather than bargain with it."[25] In either case, the Great Uprising of 1877 lays the foundation for future labor–management conflict, not cooperation. Lastly, the greater social aspects should not be overlooked. Some of the violent attacks on railroad property may have resulted not from work-related grievances, but from frustration with the dangerous invasion of railroads into local communities, often against the wishes of local residents and small retail shop-owners.[26] But whether rooted in work or community, individuals turned to collective action, protest, and sometimes violence when they felt otherwise powerless.

UPLIFT UNIONISM

One union that survived the depression of 1873–1878 was the Noble and Holy Order of the Knights of Labor. The **Knights of Labor** started as a union in the garment industry and emphasized secrecy to prevent employers from breaking it. Like many fraternal organizations of the time, the Knights of Labor initially had various rituals, passwords, and secret signs.[27] If a member wanted to know if someone else was a member, they would say "I am a worker" to which the correct response was "I too earn my bread with the sweat of my brow."[28] The top leader was called the Grand Master Workman. As the union expanded outside the garment industry, secrecy was dropped in 1881. For a brief time in the mid-1880s, the Knights of Labor was the most influential labor organization in the United States with over 100,000 members in 1885 and 700,000 in 1886.[29] Yet its decline was equally rapid and 15 years later the organization had effectively faded away.

The Knights of Labor is traditionally considered the major U.S. example of **uplift unionism,** a philosophy in which a union "aspires chiefly to elevate the moral, intellectual, and social life of the worker."[30] A primary concern of the Knights of Labor was the moral worth, not just the material wealth of a person.[31] Decent wages and working conditions were important because they served "the divine nature of man" (see Box 4.5). Shorter working hours were needed so that workers would have greater time for education and moral betterment. As such, the Knights of Labor was a very inclusive organization that emphasized education and cooperation over conflict.

Organizationally, the Knights of Labor consisted of numerous local assemblies—as many as 1,500 at one point.[32] There were two types of assemblies: trade and mixed. Trade assemblies were often very similar to typical local unions in which all of the members

---

[24] Dubofsky and Dulles, *Labor in America.*

[25] Perrow, *Organizing America,* p. 179.

[26] David O. Stowell, *Streets, Railroads, and the Great Strike of 1877* (Chicago: University of Chicago Press, 1999).

[27] Gregory S. Kealey and Bryan D. Palmer, *Dreaming of What Might Be: The Knights of Labor in Ontario, 1880–1900* (Cambridge: Cambridge University Press, 1982). Rayback, *A History of American Labor.*

[28] Kealey and Palmer, *Dreaming of What Might Be,* p. 286.

[29] Norman J. Ware, *The Labor Movement in the United States 1869–1895: A Study in Democracy* (New York: D. Appleton, 1929).

[30] Robert Franklin Hoxie, *Trade Unionism in the United States* (New York: D. Appleton, 1917), p. 47.

[31] Philip Taft, *Organized Labor in American History* (New York: Harper and Row, 1964).

[32] Ware, *The Labor Movement in the United States 1869–1895.*

belonged to a single occupation (or trade). Mixed assemblies, as the name suggests, contained a mixture of different occupations. Membership in the Knights of Labor was therefore open to nearly everyone. In fact, the Knights of Labor wanted to unite all "producers" that included the equivalent of today's white collar and professional workers as well as farmers, shopkeepers, and even employers.[33] The central conflict was not with employers, it was with those who controlled money and who were perceived as not working (producing)—bankers, stockbrokers, and lawyers.[34] And consistent with the emphasis on morality, gamblers and liquor dealers were also excluded. But otherwise, the Knights of Labor was broadly inclusive and emphasized the solidarity of all producers—including African Americans and women—as underscored by its motto "An injury to one is a concern to all."[35]

To accomplish its goals, the Knights of Labor emphasized cooperation.[36] The ultimate goal was replacing capitalism with a system of producer cooperatives in which producers (not bankers and absentee owners) owned and controlled businesses. The bringing together of capital and labor into small-scale cooperatives was believed to harmonize the interests of labor and capital (ending labor conflict) and avoid the problems of monopoly. As importantly, workers would regain a sense of control and autonomy—which industrialization and wage work were removing—and work would be restored to its noble purpose of serving personal and psychological needs and serving God. This latter goal rests on the then-common assumption that producing a tangible product (a barrel or a plow, for example) was superior to contributing a less tangible service (management expertise or investment capital, for example).[37] This view may seem simplistic today, but it is again important to remember that industrialization was a new phenomenon and that corporations and the nature of employment as we know it today were just emerging and were causing great upheavals throughout society. As such, the Knights of Labor's reform agenda sought to replace capitalism with a different system rather than simply cushion capitalism's perceived negative

[33] Melton Alonza McLaurin, *The Knights of Labor in the South* (Westport, CT: Greenwood Press, 1978).
[34] Hoyt N. Wheeler, *The Future of the American Labor Movement* (Cambridge: Cambridge University Press, 2002).
[35] Kealey and Palmer, *Dreaming of What Might Be*. Ware, *The Labor Movement in the United States 1869–1895*.
[36] McLaurin, *The Knights of Labor in the South*. Ware, *The Labor Movement in the United States 1869–1895*.
[37] Ware, *The Labor Movement in the United States 1869–1895*.

effects on workers.[38] At the same time, the proposed reform was not socialism—the cooperatives would be privately, not publicly, owned.[39] In fact, replacing the wage system with producer cooperatives was seen as a way to restore democracy, because capitalism's inequalities and the wage system's degradation of workers were viewed as undermining the values and skills needed for a healthy, participative democracy.[40]

A major component of the Knights of Labor's strategy was education. Education was the route to moral betterment and civil improvement, and also the way to articulate the need for economic reform.[41] In contrast, the use of strikes and boycotts was viewed very negatively, at least by the top leadership. Economic weapons might be able to obtain higher wages and shorter working hours, but remember that in the philosophy of the Knights of Labor, these economic improvements were not important in their own right. Broader reform to serve the divine nature of man could not be achieved through strikes and boycotts (believed the national leadership). And strikes and boycotts are not particularly consistent with the Knights of Labor's religious and moral theme. There was also a practical element to this emphasis on education over strikes and boycotts: the leaders remembered labor's defeats during the strikes of the 1870s (recall the Molly Maguires and the Great Uprising of 1877).[42] The leadership therefore favored arbitration over strikes—and arbitration was essentially viewed as educating employers about how workers should be treated.[43]

The reality of strike activity, however, did not always match these theoretical ideals. In fact, the emphasis on solidarity meant that one of the first actions of the Knights of Labor was to create a strike fund to provide financial support to striking workers—remember, "An injury to one is a concern to all."[44] And strikes indeed did occur.[45] In fact, the Knights of Labor's largest success was arguably the 1885 Southwest System rail strike in which they won a startling victory over this very large railroad system controlled by robber baron Jay Gould.[46] This strike is popularly viewed as the first instance where a U.S. union stood equal to a large, powerful corporation and as causing the Knights of Labor's dramatic growth in 1886.[47] Victory was short-lived, however. The leadership's lack of emphasis on collective bargaining resulted in letting Gould settle for very weak language—not even union recognition was achieved.[48] In fact, only a year later Gould successfully broke a violent strike with the help of Pinkerton spies, and the Knights of Labor faded from the Southwest System.

Contributing to this defeat—and the overall demise of the Knights of Labor—was the most famous event that the Knights of Labor is associated with: the **Haymarket Tragedy.** A very significant movement during the mid-1880s was the drive for the eight-hour working day. In 1884, May 1, 1886, was established by the forerunner of the American Federation of Labor as the effective date for the eight-hour day. This is the modern origin of May Day—International Workers' Day—celebrated in many countries around the world,

[38] Wheeler, *The Future of the American Labor Movement.*

[39] McLaurin, *The Knights of Labor in the South.*

[40] Clayton Sinyai, *Schools of Democracy: A Political History of the American Labor Movement* (Ithaca, NY: Cornell University Press, 2006). Josiah Bartlett Lambert, *"If the Workers Took a Notion": The Right to Strike and American Political Development* (Ithaca, NY: Cornell University Press, 2005).

[41] Wheeler, *The Future of the American Labor Movement.*

[42] Ware, *The Labor Movement in the United States 1869–1895.*

[43] Kealey and Palmer, *Dreaming of What Might Be.*

[44] Ware, *The Labor Movement in the United States 1869–1895.*

[45] Kealey and Palmer, *Dreaming of What Might Be.* McLaurin, *The Knights of Labor in the South.*

[46] Dubofsky and Dulles, *Labor in America.* Ware, *The Labor Movement in the United States 1869–1895.*

[47] John R. Commons, *History of Labour in the United States,* Volume II (New York: Macmillan, 1918).

[48] Ware, *The Labor Movement in the United States 1869–1895.*

but not officially in the United States. Numerous strikes occurred in 1886 in support of this May 1 deadline. In Chicago 40,000 went on strike on May 1, 1886, and 80,000 paraded while being watched by police and armed Pinkertons from nearby rooftops.[49] Two days later, a battle between strikers and their replacements at the McCormick Reaper Works resulted in the death of at least two strikers when police fired upon them. A protest was called for May 4, 1886, in Haymarket Square.

Perhaps three thousand attended the rally in Haymarket Square—including the mayor in order to deter trouble. After a few speeches, the crowd started to disperse. On his way out, the mayor told the police that the speeches were tame.[50] The police then arrived on the scene and ordered the remaining 200–300 participants to leave. As the final speaker was stepping down, a bomb flew over the small crowd and exploded in the middle of the police. The police responded by firing on the remaining crowd. Seven police ultimately died as a result of the riot, though only one death can be unquestionably linked to the bomb; bullet wounds were involved in the other deaths—many from their fellow police. At least four members of the crowd were killed by the police. The bomb thrower was never identified, but the Haymarket Tragedy caused near hysteria that anarchists and radicals were starting an uprising. Depictions in the media were sensationalized. In "the most celebrated trial of the late nineteenth century," eight anarchist leaders were found guilty of murder for the killing of the police.[51] The evidence was fabricated, the judge was exceptionally biased, and all of the jurors openly admitted to being prejudiced against the defendants. One juror was even a relative of one of the dead policemen. Four of the eight defendants were hanged.

The Knights of Labor was not directly involved in the Haymarket Tragedy. One of the defendants was a member, but the Haymarket demonstration was called by anarchists, not the Knights of Labor. The striking McCormick employees were not led by the Knights of Labor. In fact, consistent with the national leadership's emphasis on education rather than conflict, the Knights of Labor encouraged workers to write essays on the eight-hour day rather than strike in May 1886.[52] But the Knights of Labor was the most visible labor organization at that time and the public backlash against labor greatly weakened the Knights of Labor. The Knights of Labor was also undone by employers' antiunion activities, including the use of strikebreakers and labor spies. And the Knights of Labor suffered from conflicts with workers, trade assemblies, and independent trade unions that wanted more vigorous campaigns for short-term bread and butter issues: wages, hours of work, and working conditions.[53]

PURE AND SIMPLE CRAFT UNIONISM

In response to the perceived failure of the Knights of Labor's leadership to address everyday working issues, representatives from 25 national unions—such as the Iron Molders' Union, International Typographical Union, United Brotherhood of Carpenters, and the Cigar Makers' International Union—created a new labor federation in December 1886 called the **American Federation of Labor** (AFL).[54] The first president of the AFL was

[49] Paul Avrich, *The Haymarket Tragedy* (Princeton, NJ: Princeton University Press, 1984).

[50] Avrich, *The Haymarket Tragedy,* p. 204.

[51] Avrich, *The Haymarket Tragedy,* p. 260.

[52] Dubofsky and Dulles, *Labor in America.*

[53] Dubofsky and Dulles, *Labor in America.* Ware, *The Labor Movement in the United States 1869–1895.*

[54] Dubofsky and Dulles, *Labor in America.* Philip Taft, *The A.F. of L. in the Time of Gompers* (New York: Harper and Brothers, 1957).

BOX 4.6
A Timeline of Labor History between 1875 and 1925

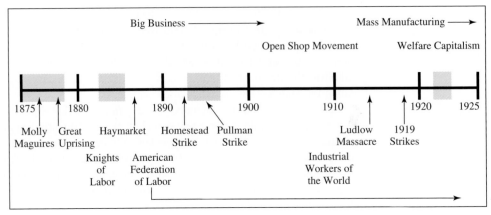

Note: Shading indicates economic depressions.

Samuel Gompers, an official from the Cigar Makers' International Union, who would eventually be president with only a one-year interruption until his death nearly 40 years later in 1924. The AFL and Gompers are both very central figures in the development of U.S. labor relations (see Box 4.6).

It is important to understand that the AFL was a union *federation,* not a labor union per se. The member unions, not the AFL, pursued the primary labor relations functions of bargaining with employers, leading strikes, and resolving grievances. The AFL was a support organization for the independent unions.[55] The AFL sometimes coordinated bargaining and strikes when multiple unions were involved, and provided financial assistance to striking unions. The AFL also resolved jurisdictional disputes when more than one union wanted to represent the same group of workers and, to a lesser extent, provided education and political lobbying. The AFL initiated organizing drives in occupations without a national union, but with the goal of ultimately creating a new national union for that occupation.[56] In contrast with the Knights of Labor, each union that joined the AFL was explicitly granted the autonomy to control its own affairs.[57] But it is nevertheless useful to discuss the AFL because its philosophies are representative of the member unions and would dominate U.S. labor relations until the Great Depression in the 1930s.

The AFL and its affiliated unions are the classic example of a **business unionism** philosophy (see Box 4.7).[58] In contrast to the uplift unionism of the Knights of Labor, the business unionism of the AFL and its unions emphasizes immediate improvements in basic employment conditions—wages, hours, and working conditions. Business unionism accepts capitalism and the need for employers to make a profit, but seeks to win labor's fair share of the profits through collective bargaining. The main weapon to make collective bargaining effective was the strike. This is a pragmatic, business-like approach to employee representation, or unionism "pure and simple"—not an idealistic approach based on morality and cooperatives (or at the other extreme, revolution). In the words of Gompers, "Economic betterment—today, tomorrow, in home and shop, was the foundation upon which trade unions have been built."[59] Business unionism continues to be the dominant philosophy of U.S. labor unions in the 21st century.

[55] Dubofsky and Dulles, *Labor in America.*

[56] Taft, *The A.F. of L. in the Time of Gompers.*

[57] Dubofsky and Dulles, *Labor in America.* Taft, *The A.F. of L. in the Time of Gompers.*

[58] Hoxie, *Trade Unionism in the United States.*

[59] Samuel Gompers, *Seventy Years of Life and Labor* (New York: E.P. Dutton, 1925), p. 286.

One of the earliest definitions of business unionism remains accurate today:

> It aims chiefly at more, here and now, for the organized workers of the craft or industry, in terms mainly of higher wages, shorter hours, and better working conditions, regardless for the most part of the welfare of the workers outside the particular organic group, and regardless in general of political and social considerations, except in so far as these bear directly upon its own economic ends. It . . . accepts as inevitable, if not as just, the existing capitalistic organization and the wage system, as well as existing property rights and the binding force of contract. It regards unionism mainly as a bargaining institution and seeks its ends chiefly through collective bargaining, supported by such methods as experience from time to time indicates to be effective in sustaining and increasing its bargaining power.

This describes the AFL craft unions in the first part of the 20th century, the CIO industrial unions three decades later, and today's private and public sector AFL–CIO unions. But why is this called business unionism?

> The truth is that the outlooks and ideals of this dominant type of unionism are those very largely of a business organization. Its successful leaders are essentially business men and its union are organized primarily to do business with employers—to bargain for the sale of the product it controls.

Source: Robert Franklin Hoxie, *Trade Unionism in the United States* (New York: D. Appleton, 1917), pp. 45–46 and 336.

Beyond a business unionism philosophy, there are several additional central features of the AFL unions. Most AFL unions wholeheartedly endorsed a system of **craft unionism.** In this approach, unions were divided along craft lines; that is, by occupation or trade. In this way, each union could focus on the unique concerns of workers in that occupation and overcome a weakness of the Knights of Labor. Moreover, the craft unionism of the AFL was focused on *skilled* crafts—such as printers, machinists, carpenters, cigar makers, and iron molders. Most of the AFL unions were openly hostile towards unskilled labor and only represented skilled workers. In fact, the Knights of Labor's inclusion of unskilled workers was an important point of frustration among the trade unions that led to the formation of the AFL.[60] The structure of the AFL unions was further guided by the principle of **exclusive jurisdiction** which meant that there would be one and only one union per craft. For example, there was one carpenters union that was entitled to represent carpenters—this union could not represent other occupations, and no other union could represent carpenters. An important function of the AFL was to resolve jurisdictional disputes, but as with other issues, the AFL lacked formal power to force rulings on the member unions.[61]

By the 1890s, industrialization and the factory system were firmly in place. There were 160,000 miles of railroad tracks, coal provided power for a vast range of machines so that most major industries were mechanized, and the United States was truly becoming an industrial nation.[62] Andrew Carnegie's steel plant in Homestead, Pennsylvania, employed over 3,000 workers; large meat-packing plants in Chicago employed twice as many.[63] By 1900, almost 1,500 factories had over 500 workers.[64] Workers were increasingly becoming

[60] Dubofsky and Dulles, *Labor in America.*

[61] Taft, *The A.F. of L. in the Time of Gompers.*

[62] Daniel Nelson, *Managers and Workers: Origins of the Twentieth Century Factory System in the United States, 1880–1920,* 2nd ed. (Madison: University of Wisconsin Press, 1994). Rayback, *A History of American Labor.*

[63] Rick Halpern, *Down on the Killing Floor: Black and White Workers in Chicago's Packinghouses, 1904–54* (Urbana: University of Illinois Press, 1997). Serrin, *Homestead.*

[64] Lichtenstein et al., *Who Built America?*

subservient to machines, but skilled craftsmen in many industries—iron rollers, glass blowers, and coal miners, to name just a few—still had special knowledge of the production processes and therefore had some discretion or control over their work and their helpers.[65] Or in the words of the militant union leader Big Bill Haywood, "The manager's brains are under the workman's cap."[66] AFL unions and their members generally accepted this factory system (some sooner than others), but sought to maintain skilled worker control over the production process in addition to decent wages and hours of work.

As such, an important activity of the AFL unions was establishing and maintaining job standards through work rules. These rules frequently pertained to apprenticeship standards, tasks reserved for union members, undesirable or unskilled job duties that union members did not have to do (to prevent the degradation of the craft), work allocation procedures, and other standards.[67] Before the 1900s, these work rules were often established unilaterally by the unions and enforced by refusing to work on any other terms and by fining or expelling members who undermined these standards.[68] Wage rates might be negotiated with employers, but skilled workers believed that their skilled status as craftsmen entitled them to establish work standards. Control over decision making was seen as necessary to promote human dignity and to reinforce the mental and civic skills needed for being active participants in a democratic society.[69] A critical struggle in the development of U.S. labor relations in the early 20th century therefore revolves around employers' efforts to weaken this level of worker control and establish supervisory supremacy over production decisions.[70]

One of the most violent examples of this struggle for control of the workplace was the **Homestead strike** in 1892 at the steel mill owned by Andrew Carnegie in Homestead, Pennsylvania. Of the 3,800 workers at the mill, the 800 most-skilled belonged to the Amalgamated Association of Iron and Steel Workers, an AFL-affiliated craft union. The Amalgamated at Homestead was the last union in Carnegie's operations and he was determined to wrest control of Homestead away from the skilled union members—and their 58 pages of work rules—when their contract expired in 1892 (see Box 4.8).[71] The mill was run by Henry Clay Frick who had already used Pinkertons to protect strikebreakers in his coal mines. With Carnegie vacationing at his castle in Scotland, Frick's final offer to the union amounted to a 12–15 percent wage cut. When the union refused, Frick shut down the mill on July 1, 1892, and announced that the mill would reopen on July 6 as a nonunion operation. Union members watched the railroad stations and the river that bordered the mill for any sign of the importation of strikebreakers.

At 1:00 AM on July 6, two barges were spied on the river and by sunrise hundreds of workers—skilled and unskilled—were on the mill property along the river armed with rifles, pistols, rocks, and fence posts. The barges contained 300 armed Pinkertons who were supposed to secretly secure the mill property so that strikebreakers could be brought in. When the Pinkertons tried to come ashore, a gun battle broke out. No one knows who fired first, but the battle raged for hours. The workers even fired upon the barges with an

---

[65] David Montgomery, *Workers' Control in America: Studies in the History of Work, Technology, and Labor Struggles* (Cambridge: Cambridge University Press, 1979). Nelson, *Managers and Workers.*

[66] Quoted in Montgomery, *Workers' Control in America,* p. 9.

[67] Selig Perlman, *A Theory of the Labor Movement* (New York: Macmillan, 1928).

[68] Montgomery, *Workers' Control in America.*

[69] Sinyai, *Schools of Democracy.*

[70] Montgomery, *Workers' Control in America.* Nelson, *Managers and Workers.* Christopher L. Tomlins, *The State and the Unions: Labor Relations, Law, and the Organized Labor Movement, 1880–1960* (Cambridge: Cambridge University Press, 1985).

[71] Brecher, *Strike!* Serrin, *Homestead.*

You are in charge of a steel mill in the 1890s. A craft union represents less than one-quarter of the mill's employees; the rest are not represented by a union. The contract with this union is expiring. What do you do to prepare for negotiations with the union?

Now suppose that this particular mill is the only operation in your company with a union. And your boss is vacationing out of the country and has left clear instructions that he doesn't want any union interference in his company. And your boss is one of the richest men in the world. Remember that in the 1890s there aren't any laws protecting workers' rights to belong to unions. How do you approach negotiations?

In 1892 at the Homestead Works owned by Andrew Carnegie, Henry Clay Frick prepared for negotiations with the Amalgamated Association of Iron and Steel Workers by ordering the construction of a fence all around the mill and running down to the river that bordered the mill. This fence was 11 feet high and made with 2-inch boards and topped with barbed wire. Every 25 feet there was a three-inch hole at shoulder height. The workers called this "Fort Frick." A second component of Frick's negotiation preparations was to contract with the Pinkerton National Detective Agency for 300 armed Pinkertons. These guards were to secretly enter the mill via the river and secure the mill for the strikebreakers that Frick was presumably also arranging to bring in from other states. Lastly, Frick's final offer to the union was for a 12–15 percent wage reduction. When this was refused, he closed the mill for the fourth of July holiday and reopened it on a nonunion basis. The existing employees had to reapply for jobs.

Sources: Jeremy Brecher, *Strike!* (Boston: South End Press, 1972). William Serrin, *Homestead: The Glory and Tragedy of an American Steel Town* (New York: Vintage Books, 1992).

old cannon. The Pinkertons surrendered in the afternoon, but still had to endure walking a gauntlet between two rows of workers and townspeople in which they were beaten and stoned, in spite of the efforts of the union leaders to prevent further harm. At least seven strikers and three Pinkertons died. On July 12, 4,000 soldiers of the Pennsylvania militia arrived in Homestead and secured the mill. Aided by new technology that reduced the skills needed for steelmaking, strikebreakers reopened the mill seven days later.[72]

By October, perhaps a thousand strikebreakers had been brought in—guarded by the state militia—and perhaps 100 of the strikers had returned to work. By the end of November, the strike was officially over; only 400 of the 2,200 strikers that had reapplied for jobs were rehired.[73] In 1892, profits in Carnegie's steel operations were $4 million, and by the end of decade they would be $40 million; Carnegie sold these operations in 1901 for $480 million.[74] In the year after the strike, wages for skilled workers were significantly reduced while the 12-hour workday continued. A union would not return to the Homestead mill until the 1930s—with the protection of a new labor law and the efforts of an industrial union to organize all of the workers, skilled and unskilled alike.

In a decade filled with many violent clashes between strikers, strikebreakers, Pinkertons, and other armed agents, and of strikes broken by state militia or federal troops—from a streetcar strike in New Orleans to a miners' strike in Coeur d'Alene, Idaho—the second great labor history event of the 1890s was the **Pullman strike** in 1894. The Pullman Palace Car Company produced Pullman railroad cars in Pullman, Illinois. During the depression that started in 1893, Pullman cut wages by an average of 28 percent and laid off about one-quarter of the workers.[75] Management pay and the stockholders' dividends were

[72] Brecher, *Strike!* Serrin, *Homestead.*

[73] Serrin, *Homestead.*

[74] David Montgomery, *The Fall of the House of Labor* (Cambridge: Cambridge University Press, 1987). Serrin, *Homestead.*

[75] Susan Eleanor Hirsch, *After the Strike: A Century of Labor Struggle at Pullman* (Urbana: University of Illinois Press, 2003).

not reduced, nor was the rent charged to workers for company-owned housing.[76] After rent was deducted from his paycheck, one worker was reportedly left with a paycheck for two cents. Pullman workers joined an independent union led by Eugene V. Debs: the American Railway Union which included both railroad employees and workers that made railroad cars (as at Pullman). Unlike the AFL craft unions with their principle of exclusive jurisdiction, the American Railway Union included multiple occupations—though as was common at the time, only white workers.

In May 1894, three grievance committee members at Pullman were discharged. When Pullman refused to arbitrate any disputed issues, workers struck and Pullman closed the plant. In solidarity, the railroad workers who belonged to the American Railway Union refused to handle Pullman cars on the railroads. The railroads fired anyone who adhered to this boycott, and the rest of each train crew often struck in support of these discharges. The Pullman dispute therefore quickly expanded into a national railroad strike (recall Box 2.3). The railroads started to put Pullman cars behind the mail cars so when workers detached the Pullman cars, the mail would be disrupted. In July 1894, federal troops were therefore called in and placed on the trains. This drastically changed the tenor of the strike and violence erupted. In various conflicts, 13 people ended up dead and more than 700 railroad cars were destroyed by looting in Chicago. Debs was arrested for conspiracy to disrupt the mail and served six months in jail. With federal troops protecting the trains and the leader of the American Railway Union in jail, the strike died out.[77]

WORKERS OF THE WORLD UNITE!

The first part of the new century—the early 1900s—was marked by sharp contrasts. The richest 1 percent of households controlled 45 percent of total U.S wealth around 1900—the highest ever.[78] Almost unimaginable wealth was accumulated by industrialists like Carnegie, Rockefeller, Morgan, and Vanderbilt while millions of workers and their families, including many new immigrants, struggled with day-to-day survival. Whether in rural, company-owned towns or urban tenements, families lived in fear of unemployment, accidents, poor health, and making ends meet.[79] While railroad tycoon Jay Gould earned $10,000,000 a year, the average unskilled worker earned $10 a week which meant his family could barely afford a run-down, two-room (not two bedroom) apartment without running water.[80] Many children therefore had to work to supplement family incomes (see Box 4.9). This period was an era of tremendous industrial growth, but also of relatively stagnant wages and dangerous working conditions.[81]

The early 20th century was the age of big business. The increased size and power of major corporations was graphically illustrated by the trusts—the companies that were able

[76] Brecher, *Strike!* Dubofsky and Dulles, *Labor in America.*

[77] Brecher, *Strike!* Dubofsky and Dulles, *Labor in America.* Hirsch, *After the Strike.*

[78] J. Bradford DeLong, "Robber Barons," in Anders Aslund and Tatyana Maleva (eds.), *Series of Lectures on Economics: Leading World Experts at the Carnegie Moscow Center* (Moscow: Carnegie Endowment for International Peace, 2002), Chapter 4.

[79] James R. Green, *The World of the Worker: Labor in Twentieth-Century America* (New York: Hill and Wang, 1980).

[80] Matthew Josephson, *The Robber Barons: The Great American Capitalists, 1861–1901* (New York: Harcourt, Brace, and Company, 1934), p. 378. Lichtenstein et al., *Who Built America?*, p. 176.

[81] Melvyn Dubofsky, *Industrialism and the American Worker, 1865–1920,* 2nd ed. (Arlington Heights, IL: Harlan Davidson, 1985). Rayback, *A History of American Labor.*

A vivid illustration of why union leaders and social reformers fought for institutional checks and balances—through unions, laws, or otherwise—in the early 20th century labor market is the problem of child labor. Many of the first textile mill workers in the 1830s were women and children. Compared to men, women and children were less productive on small New England farms and therefore mill owners could attract them into the factories at a cheaper wage. By 1900, child labor had greatly expanded to the point that it was hard to ignore as a societal issue. To wit, it was estimated that nearly two million children aged 10–14 (20 percent of this age group) were gainfully employed in 1900. In many cases, these were not safe, part-time after-school jobs, but rather were dangerous and dirty jobs in which children worked more hours than many adults today.

To spur change, several social reformers and philanthropists formed the National Child Labor Committee (NCLC) in 1904. For the NCLC, Lewis Hine took over 7,000 black and white photographs, often disguising himself as a fire inspector, insurance salesman, or photographer of machines rather than child workers. These photographs remain very powerful images of the abusive nature of child labor. Two of his photographs are reproduced here; the source note points to collections of larger numbers of photographs. These were some of the worst industries for child labor:

- *The coal industry.* Breaker boys worked 9 or 10 hours per day hunched over fast-moving conveyors of coal picking out rocks from the coal and breathing in thick coal dust. Others worked with their fathers half a mile underground loading coal into cars.

- *Textile mills.* Girls were spinners that spun cotton into yarn on large spinning frames for nine or more hours a day, perhaps six days a week. They received a break when boys were brought in several times a day to frantically replace all of the full bobbins of yarn with empty ones. These boys were called doffers and either played or swept the factory in between doffing.

- *Glass making.* Boys worked on teams with skilled glass blowers doing various unskilled aspects of glass making. The pace was very quick (to keep up with the glass blowers who were paid piece rates) and the furnaces were extremely hot. Because molten glass had to be kept at a constant temperature day and night, many glass-making factories worked around the clock. Boys would often work the day shift one week and the night shift the next.

- *Agriculture and food processing.* From almost their birth, children would accompany their parents into the fields and food processing plants, and would start helping when they were old enough—perhaps at age 3 or 4. A study of a cranberry bog harvest

Breaker Boys at the Ewen Breaker, South Pittston, Pennsylvania (1911)
Photograph by Lewis Hine who wrote "The dust was so intense at times as to obscure the view. This dust penetrated the utmost recesses of the boys' lungs. A kind of slave driver sometimes stands over the boys, prodding or kicking them into obedience."

Source: U.S. National Archives

Young Textile Mill Workers, London, Tennessee (1910)

Photograph by Lewis Hine who wrote "Two of the tiny workers, a raveler and a looper in London Hosiery Mills."

Source: U.S. National Archives

found that half of the child pickers were less than 10 years old. Lewis Hine also photographed children harvesting cotton and sugar beets, shucking oysters and shrimp, and preparing vegetables for canning.

- *Messenger services.* In cities, many boys worked day and night as messengers. Remember, the telephone was not yet completely established, so messengers were used to relay many communications as well as parcels. But the messenger boys also worked at night, running errands for hotels, restaurants, and whorehouses.

Source: Russell Freedman, *Kids at Work: Lewis Hine and the Crusade Against Child Labor* (New York: Clarion Books, 1994) [good source of photographs]. Hugh D. Hindman, *Child Labor: An American History* (Armonk, NY: M. E. Sharpe, 2002). John R. Kemp, *Lewis Hine: Photographs of Child Labor in the New South* (Jackson: University of Mississippi Press, 1986) [good source of photographs]. A large number of Lewis Hines photographs are also available online through the U.S. National Archives at *arcweb.archives. gov/arc/basic_search.jsp* (enter "523064" in the keyword search box).

to monopolize and dominate their industry. By 1905, the Standard Oil Company refined nearly 25 million barrels of oil (85 percent of the market), U.S. Steel had over 150,000 employees and 200 mills (60 percent of the steel industry), and International Harvester manufactured over 500,000 agricultural harvesting machines (85 percent of the market).[82] The size of individual factories also continued to grow because the economical use of new mechanized production methods often required a large-scale operation—for example, steel mills were not cost effective unless they produced at least 2,500 tons a day.[83] The rise of big

[82] Eliot Jones, *The Trust Problem in the United States* (New York: Macmillan, 1923). Serrin, *Homestead.*
[83] David Brody, *Workers in Industrial America: Essays on the Twentieth Century Struggle* (New York: Oxford University Press, 1980).

business created important contrasts, especially between large corporations and individual workers, and between professional managers and unskilled laborers. Scientific management, or "Taylorism" after Frederick Winslow Taylor, decomposed skilled jobs into basic repetitive tasks and, as a result, created professional, scientifically trained managers and unskilled occupations.[84] When Henry Ford added the assembly line to narrowly defined jobs in 1913, the mass manufacturing model was established for much of the rest of the century.

The labor movement was also rife with contrasts. In the Homestead Strike, skilled and unskilled workers stood together, but this was the exception rather than the rule. Most of the AFL-affiliated craft unions focused exclusively on skilled, white, crafts*men* to the exclusion of unskilled, minority, and female workers.[85] Even the American Railway Union, which embraced unskilled workers, discriminated against African-American workers. There was also tension between the dominant craft union approach and a perceived need by other workers and union leaders for industrial unionism—that is, organizing workers of all occupations within an industry into a single union. Though affiliated with the AFL, the United Mine Workers (UMW) is an early example of an industrial union because they tried to unionize all employees in the mining industry—led in part by the very colorful Mother Jones (see Box 4.10).[86] The UMW also stood out from other unions of the time in its acceptance of African-American workers.[87]

The labor movement's views on the AFL's business unionism and pure and simple unionism philosophies is another sharp contrast in this time period. During the Pullman strike, the Gompers-led AFL refused to support Eugene Debs's industrial union, the American Railway Union. While this refusal may partly reflect a pragmatic decision not to join a losing cause, it also reflects a fundamental difference between the conservative business unionism philosophy and more militant alternatives.[88] In fact, as Gompers and other AFL leaders watched judges and the armed forces violently repress strikes and labor demonstrations that were publicly labeled as radical—such as the Great Uprising of 1877 and the eight-hour-day strikes of 1886—the conservatism of business unionism in seeking narrow economic gains for workers rather than more radical reforms to capitalism was reinforced.[89] In contrast, other labor leaders reacted to this repression by pursuing more radical, militant approaches. From 1905 to 1925, the visible radical and militant approach was the **Industrial Workers of the World** (IWW), often referred to by its nickname the "Wobblies" (see Box 4.11). The perspective of the IWW was cleverly captured by one of its most well-known leaders, Big Bill Haywood: "I've never read Marx's *Capital*, but I have the marks of capital all over me."[90]

---

[84] Robert Kanigel, *The One Best Way: Frederick Winslow Taylor and the Enigma of Efficiency* (New York, Penguin, 1997). Montgomery, *Workers' Control in America*. Nelson, *Managers and Workers*. Frederick Winslow Taylor, *The Principles of Scientific Management* (New York: Harper and Brothers, 1911).

[85] Philip S. Foner, *Organized Labor and the Black Worker, 1619–1981* (New York: International Publishers, 1981). William H. Harris, *The Harder We Run: Black Workers Since the Civil War* (New York: Oxford University Press, 1982). Taft, *The A.F. of L. in the Time of Gompers*.

[86] Elliot J. Gorn, *Mother Jones: The Most Dangerous Woman in America* (New York: Hill and Wang, 2001).

[87] Foner, *Organized Labor and the Black Worker*. Harris, *The Harder We Run*.

[88] Nick Salvatore, *Eugene V. Debs: Citizen and Socialist* (Urbana: University of Illinois Press, 1982).

[89] Lambert, *If the Workers Took a Notion*.

[90] J. Anthony Lukas, *Big Trouble: A Murder in a Small Western Town Sets Off a Struggle for the Soul of America* (New York: Simon and Schuster, 1997), p. 233.

Mother Jones: The Most Dangerous Woman in America Box 4.10

One of the most colorful and determined individuals in the U.S. labor movement in the early 1900s was Mother Jones. Born as Mary Harris in 1837 in Cork, Ireland, she emigrated to Canada with her family as a teenager. She moved to the United States on her own at the age of 23 and a few years later was in Memphis and married to George Jones, an iron molder and union member. A yellow fever epidemic spread through Memphis in 1867 killing her husband and all four of her children. She was only 30 and yet she had experienced religious persecution in Ireland, the Irish potato famine, racial and ethnic hatred in the aftermath of the Civil War, and now yellow fever.

She moved to Chicago and became a seamstress, only to have her belongings destroyed in the great Chicago fire of 1871. She was likely in Chicago during the Great Uprising of 1877 and the Haymarket Tragedy in 1886 and probably attended meetings of the Knights of Labor in this time period. In the 1890s—when she was nearly 60 years old—Mary Jones developed into Mother Jones—a grandmotherly figure dressed in long, black Victorian dresses who traveled the country raising hell on behalf of workers and their families, especially in the coal wars of Pennsylvania, West Virginia, and Colorado. From her experiences, she developed a sense of radicalism in which worker power, militancy, and ultimately control was needed to counter the overwhelming economic and political power of big business in order to secure decent lives for the working class as well as true democracy. One of her most well-known slogans was "Pray for the dead and fight like hell for the living."

Mother Jones often served as a union organizer for the United Mine Workers. Before the 1930s, organizing usually meant leading a strike because companies would not recognize a union unless forced to. The issues in many of the strikes were similar—pay was determined by the ton, but workers did not trust the scales and the supervisors who weighed their coal; mine work was exceptionally dangerous; workers were shadowed by armed guards; company-owned stores and housing further exploited the miners and their families; and the local governments were controlled by the mine owners. Mother Jones would therefore travel around coal country rallying the rank and file workers with fiery speeches, leading public demonstrations to put pressure on the corporate enemies, and raising money to feed the families of strikers. Her fighting spirit is revealed by her December 1902 description of a West Virginia coal strike:

> The wind blows cold this morning, but these cruel coal barons do not feel the winter blast; their babes, nay even their poodle dogs are warm and have a comfortable breakfast, while these slaves of the caves, who in the past have moved the commerce of the world, are out on the highways without clothes or shelter. Nearly 3,000 families have been thrown out of the corporation shacks to face the cold blasts of winter weather.

While not an advocate of unprovoked violence, she didn't hesitate to urge workers to protect their families: "I am not going to say to you don't molest the [mine] operators. It is they who hire the dogs to shoot you. I am not asking you to do it, but if he is going to oppress you, deal with him." Unlike the AFL unions of the time, she also emphasized broad-based solidarity among diverse workers:

> The enemy seeks to conquer by dividing your ranks, by making distinctions between North and South, between American and foreign. You are all miners, fighting a common cause, a common master. The iron heel feels the same to all flesh. Hunger and suffering and the cause of your children bind more closely than a common tongue. . . . If it is my fortune to live to see the industrial chain broken from every workingman's child in America, and if then there is one black child in Africa in bondage, there I shall go.

Mother Jones (circa 1915)

Source: *International Socialist Review* (December 1915)

Her fiery independence was also demonstrated in her willingness to clash with national union leaders when she thought they were compromising with business owners too readily, and in her contempt for judges who tried to clamp down on her speeches. In fact, the experiences of Mother Jones reveals the extent to which workers' civil liberties were violated to repress union activity. In West Virginia she was arrested in 1902 for violating a judge's order that prevented all demonstrations, even those on union property. In Colorado in 1914, a National Guard general deported her from mining country to Denver and arrested her upon her return—twice. She was jailed for a total of three months and never had charges filed against her. In contrast, the mine owners' armed guards were rarely ever even detained for killing strikers and their families.

Mine owners and others hated and feared Mother Jones for the power she had to inspire, even in her 70s, rank and file workers of nearly all skills and ethnic origins to fight for a better life. She is perhaps the most vivid personification of the "outside agitator" frequently attacked by management, even today. It should be obvious that outside agitation does not cause the conditions that spark worker discontent, but nevertheless, Mother Jones "held great power over mine families . . . [her] speeches articulated the discontents of the coal towns; her body offered a model of physical courage; her spirit taught hope and perseverance." To those in power, she was therefore the most dangerous woman in America between 1900 and 1920.

Source: Elliot J. Gorn, *Mother Jones: The Most Dangerous Woman in America* (New York: Hill and Wang, 2001). Quotations are from pp. 98–99, 106, 175, and 183

The IWW is the major U.S. example of **revolutionary unionism,** a philosophy that emphasizes

> the complete harmony of interests of all wage workers as against the representatives of the employing class, and seeks to unite the former, skilled and unskilled together, into one homogeneous fighting organization. It repudiates, or tends to repudiate, the existing institutional order and especially individual ownership of production means, and the wage system.[91]

In terms of the intellectual schools of thought presented in Chapter 2, this philosophy is rooted in critical, Marxist, or radical industrial relations thought that believes in classbased employment relationship conflict. Revolutionary unionism therefore tries to create a working class solidarity rather than solidarity by occupation or industry, and ultimately seeks the overthrow of capitalism. Revolutionary unionism therefore embraces the labor movement as an agent for revolution.

Founded in 1905 out of frustration with the discrimination and conservatism of the AFL, the IWW was explicitly inclusive and radical. Recall that the American Railway Union lost the Pullman strike when, among other things, the AFL and craft-based railroad unions refused to help. Events like this one underlie the IWW's industrial union emphasis on working class solidarity and inclusiveness. Its goal was to form "One Big Union" that embraced all workers—skilled and unskilled, young and old, native-born and immigrant, white and nonwhite, male and female—across all industries. The radical component of the IWW's philosophy can also be traced to events like the Pullman strike and miners' strikes in Cripple Creek, Colorado, and Coeur d'Alene, Idaho, in which the strike leaders felt that elected officials, judges, police, and the army helped employers break strikes. As such, these leaders turned to more radical viewpoints which emphasized the need for worker control of economic and political institutions.[92] In fact, one of the founders of the IWW was Eugene Debs, leader of the American Railway Union during the Pullman strike; another was Big Bill Haywood, one of the leaders of the Western Federation of Miners during the western coal wars. Mother Jones was also present at the founding, although she was not

[91] Hoxie, *Trade Unionism in the United States,* p. 48.
[92] Melvyn Dubofsky, *We Shall Be All: A History of the Industrial Workers of the World,* abridged ed. (Urbana: University of Illinois Press, 2000). Salvatore, *Eugene V. Debs.*

It's not immediately obvious how one goes from "Industrial Workers of the World" (IWW) to the nickname "Wobblies." In fact, there are at least four potential origins for this nickname:

- An immigrant worker in the early 1900s allegedly referred to the IWW, in broken English, as the "I-Wobble-U-Wobble-U" (or by some accounts, "I-Wobble-Wobble"). This is the leading explanation.

—or—

- The nickname "Wobbly" might have come from "wobbly saw"—a popular saw in lumber camps where there were IWW members.

—or—

- IWW detractors allegedly started the "Wobbly" nickname because of the IWW's instability or as a way of accusing individual members of being drunks, and then the nickname was adapted by the IWW as a convenience.

—or—

- It may have been the case that "wobbly" was a code name for sabotage, a tactic of the IWW.

Source: *www.iww.org/culture/official/wobbly.shtml* (accessed April 23, 2003).

active afterwards.[93] Putting the inclusive and radical elements together, the "One Big Union" was to engage in the class struggle with the capitalists (see Box 4.12).

The intense conflicts of the Pullman strike, the miners strikes, and elsewhere also shaped the IWW's tactics. Big Bill Haywood and others grew convinced that employers so effectively controlled elected officials and judges that reform could not be achieved through voting.[94] Rather direct worker action was emphasized:

> As defined by Wobblies, direct action included any step taken by workers at the point of production that improved wages, reduced hours, and bettered conditions. It encompassed conventional strikes, intermittent strikes, silent strikes, passive resistance, sabotage and the ultimate direct action measure: the general strike.[95]

This direct action philosophy is called syndicalism. Unlike the Knights of Labor, the IWW did not overlook short-term improvements in working conditions—these short-term improvements were viewed as important victories for bettering workers, and for advancing the larger struggle against the capitalists. Signed contracts, however, were viewed negatively by the IWW as legitimizing the capitalist system and restricting the IWW's ability to choose when to engage in direct action (rather than having to wait until a contract expires). The IWW also developed a rich tapestry of songs, poems, stories, skits, and visual images to convey their message and reinforce working class solidarity.[96] In fact, today's most well-known union song, "Solidarity Forever," was originally a Wobbly song (see Box 4.13).

Consistent with the IWW's inclusiveness, its biggest victory was the Lawrence, Massachusetts, textile workers strike in 1912.[97] After a wage reduction, workers spontaneously walked out and within three days, 20,000 employees were on strike. Many of the strikers were Italian immigrants, but there were also significant numbers from Germany, Poland,

[93] Gorn, *Mother Jones.*

[94] Dubofsky, *We Shall Be All.* Patrick Renshaw, *The Wobblies: The Story of Syndicalism in the United States* (Garden City, NY: Doubleday, 1967).

[95] Dubofsky, *We Shall Be All,* p. 90.

[96] Joyce L. Kornbush (ed.), *Rebel Voices: An I.W.W. Anthology* (Ann Arbor: University of Michigan Press, 1964).

[97] Dubofsky, *We Shall Be All.* Dubofsky and Dulles, *Labor in America.* Anne Huber Tripp, *The I.W.W. and the Paterson Silk Strike of 1913* (Urbana: University of Illinois Press, 1987).

The Philosophy of the Industrial Workers of the World

Box 4.12

"The working class and the employing class have nothing in common. There can be no peace so long as hunger and want are found among the millions of working people and the few, who make up the employing class, have all the good things of life.

Between these two classes a struggle must go on until the workers of the world organize as a class, take possession of the earth and the machinery of production, and abolish the wage system.

. . . conditions can be changed and the interest of the working class upheld only by an organization formed in such a way that all its members in any one industry, or in all industries if necessary, cease work whenever a strike or lockout is on in any department thereof, thus making an injury to one an injury to all.

Instead of the conservative motto, 'A fair day's wage for a fair day's work,' we must inscribe on our banner the revolutionary watchword, 'Abolition of the wage system.'

It is the historic mission of the working class to do away with capitalism. The army of production must be organized, not only for the everyday struggle with capitalists, but also to carry on production when capitalism shall have been overthrown. By organizing industrially we are forming the structure of the new society within the shell of the old."

Source: Preamble to the IWW Constitution (1908).

Russia, and elsewhere—at least 25 nationalities in all.[98] Two IWW officials took over the task of managing the strike, establishing picket lines, and feeding striking workers and their families. It was an intense strike: dynamite was planted to discredit the IWW, martial law was declared after a clash killed one worker, the strike leaders were arrested, and police brutality made national news. The strikers maintained their unity, however, and after two months the textile companies agreed to the strikers' demands. The IWW also fought on behalf of miners, loggers, and migratory agricultural workers in the West—sometimes with success, sometimes without.[99]

Unsurprisingly, employers and AFL unions were hostile towards the IWW and its radical agenda. World War I further heightened fears and led to greater repression of the IWW.[100] In fact, as part of an anticommunist Red Scare, Big Bill Haywood and 100 other Wobblies were found guilty of essentially opposing the war and sent to prison in 1918. An IWW leader was lynched in Montana. And in Bisbee, Arizona, labor radicalism met corporate vigilantism: the sheriff and 2,000 anti-IWW townspeople rounded up 1,200 striking copper miners in the middle of the night at gunpoint, put them on railroad cattle cars, and forcibly deported them to the New Mexico desert where they were stranded without food or water in the July heat.[101] A railroad company provided transportation; the telegraph company agreed not to let any messages leave Bisbee. The IWW survived in a meaningful way for only a few more years.

While the IWW continues to exist today, its greatest activity occurred between 1905 and 1925. Even during this time period, there was probably no more than 60,000 Wobblies at

---

[98] Renshaw, *The Wobblies*.

[99] Dubofsky, *We Shall Be All*.

[100] Dubofsky, *We Shall Be All*. Renshaw, *The Wobblies*.

[101] Dubofsky, *We Shall Be All*. Renshaw, *The Wobblies*. Jonathan D. Rosenblum, *Copper Crucible: How the Arizona Miners' Strike of 1983 Recast Labor–Management Relations in America* (Ithaca, NY: ILR Press, 1998).

The folk song "Solidarity Forever" is probably the U.S. labor movement's unofficial anthem. It is widely embraced today by many mainstream unions and is often sung at rallies, demonstrations, and picket lines. However, it was written by the Wobbly songwriter Ralph Chaplin in 1915 to be "full of revolutionary fervor." If you want to sing along, the tune is that of the "Battle Hymn of the Republic." Go ahead, try it! Or search in Google for "solidarity forever mp3" and listen online.

Solidarity Forever
When the union's inspiration through the workers' blood shall run
There can be no power greater anywhere beneath the sun,
Yet what force on earth is weaker than the feeble strength of one?
But the Union makes us strong.

Chorus:
Solidarity forever!
Solidarity forever!
Solidarity forever!
For the Union makes us strong.

Is there aught we hold in common with the greedy parasite
Who would lash us into serfdom and would crush us with his might?
Is there anything left to us but to organize and fight?
For the Union makes us strong.

It is we who plowed the prairies; built the cities where they trade;
Dug the mines and built the workshops; endless miles of railroad laid;
Now we stand outcast and starving, 'midst the wonders we have made;
But the Union makes us strong.
All the world that's owned by idle drones is ours and ours alone.
We have laid the wide foundations, built it skyward stone by stone.
It is ours, not to slave in, but to master and to own
While the Union makes us strong.
They have taken untold billions that they never toiled to earn,
But without our brain and muscle not a single wheel can turn.
We can break their haughty power, gain our freedom when we learn
That the Union makes us strong.
In our hands is placed a power greater than their hoarded gold,
Greater than the might of armies magnified a thousand-fold.
We can bring to birth a new world in the ashes of the old
For the Union makes us strong.

Note: The quote is from Joyce L. Kornbush (ed.), *Rebel Voices: An I.W.W. Anthology* (Ann Arbor: University of Michigan Press, 1964), p. 26.

any one time and though its revolutionary aims were not embraced by others, the IWW's inclusiveness and emphasis on social justice provided sparks (and sometimes, tactics) for industrial unions that would mushroom in the 1930s.[102] In the short run, however, the IWW's radicalism likely contributed to increased employer hostility toward labor unions.

THE OPEN SHOP MOVEMENT AND WELFARE CAPITALISM

Until the Great Depression of the 1930s, employer resistance to unions in the 20th century largely consisted of the open shop movement and then the strategy of welfare capitalism. Craft unions wanted to control the standards of their craft—to maintain wages by restricting entry to skilled workers, and to maintain worker dignity by having workers rather than employers determining all aspects of work. A central goal of the AFL craft unions was therefore the closed shop—a workplace closed to all except union members (and the union controlled who could become a member). Naturally, employers strenuously opposed the closed shop

[102] Dubofsky and Dulles, *Labor in America*.

BOX 4.14
Open Shop Advertisement, Minneapolis (circa 1921)

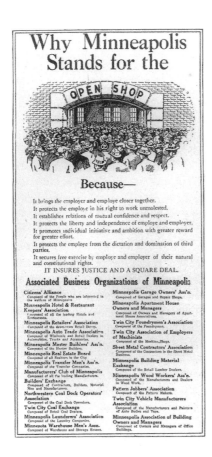

because they wanted to control hiring and the nature of work.[103] Beginning around 1903, employers launched a large-scale effort to achieve what they labeled the open shop. This label should not be taken literally—an open shop is not open to all workers, union and nonunion (or white and black). Rather, an open shop is a thoroughly nonunion operation. The **open shop movement** is therefore a concerted drive by employers and their employers' associations in the early 1900s to create and maintain union-free workplaces.

To the public, the open shop movement emphasized an ideology of individual freedom. Unions were portrayed as violating individual liberties by denying workers the ability to choose where to work and on what terms.[104] This was a very public campaign, as underscored by the advertisement from 1921 shown in Box 4.14. In the advertisement, note the emphasis on *individual* liberties: "the right to work unmolested" (in other words, without a union), the "independence" of employees, "individual initiative," and the "free exercise . . . of their natural and constitutional rights." This rhetoric of individualism went so far that the open shop movement was renamed the American Plan in the 1920s.[105] Employers further used the rhetoric of individual liberty to argue that unions should not be allowed to in-

[103] Montgomery, *Workers' Control in America.*

[104] Hirsch, *After the Strike.* William Millikan, *A Union Against Unions: The Minneapolis Citizens Alliance and Its Fight Against Organized Labor, 1903–1947* (St. Paul: Minnesota Historical Society, 2001).

[105] Irving Bernstein, *The Lean Years: A History of the American Worker, 1920–1933* (Boston: Houghton Mifflin, 1960). Dubofsky and Dulles, *Labor in America.* Taft, *Organized Labor in American History.*

terfere with management's control of its private property—its business.[106] As such, the advertisement in Box 4.14 further equates the open shop with the "liberty and independence" of the employer that protects the employer's "natural and constitutional rights."

Not heavily publicized, however, was that this drive for individual liberty was conducted by sophisticated local and national alliances of powerful employers and employers' associations.[107] In other words, the open shop movement consisted of well-orchestrated *collective* activity by business—in contrast, when labor engaged in collective activity, it was labeled "un-American." Even in the 1880s, "the capacity of New York's industrialists to organize [against labor] was extraordinary."[108] In Minneapolis, over 200 employers formed an organization in 1903 called the Citizens Alliance which openly promoted the open shop and fought unions until the 1940s. In the name of *individual* liberty, the Citizens Alliance created a trade school to educate skilled workers who were also schooled in the importance of individualism, blacklisted union supporters, operated a network of hundreds of labor spies, and recruited a private army when necessary. Dues payments to the Citizens Alliance were used to provide financial assistance to struck employers (just like a union strike fund) and if this was not enough, the business community threatened to boycott businesses that agreed to a union's terms (just like a union boycott).[109] These activities and the recruitment of strikebreakers were facilitated by national employers' associations such as the National Association of Manufacturers (just like a union might get support from the AFL). Employers were also often successful in using court-ordered injunctions to break strikes (see Chapter 5). And Minneapolis was not unique: there were hundreds of open shop organizations in major cities around the country in the first few decades of the 20th century.[110]

Some employers also exploited racial tensions to foster an open shop. Many AFL craft unions were very discriminatory and openly hostile towards anyone except white men. The Pullman Company trained African-American workers for skilled positions to keep the skilled labor force divided by racial tension and therefore nonunion. Pullman locations in which the labor movement was weaker saw fewer numbers of African-American workers hired for skilled positions because the threat of unionization was not as strong. Worker solidarity across occupations was also weakened through racial and gender segregation—on Pullman cars, for example, conductors were always white and porters were always black; men cleaned the exterior of the railroad cars, women the interior. As another example of discrimination, to keep wages low female clerical workers were fired when they got married.[111]

The open shop movement was sometimes characterized by open warfare. Professional strikebreaking companies were formed that provided a complete array of strikebreaking services: trained workers, armed guards, food and medical supplies, cots, and the like (see Box 4.15).[112] In other cases, police and the National Guard were used to repress strikes—

---

[106] Thomas Klug, "Employers' Strategies in the Detroit Labor Market, 1900–1929," in Nelson Lichtenstein and Stephen Meyer (eds.), *On the Line: Essays in the History of Auto Work* (Urbana: University of Illinois Press, 1989), Chapter 3. Millikan, *A Union Against Unions.*

[107] Millikan, *A Union Against Unions.*

[108] Sven Beckert, *The Monied Metropolis: New York City and the Consolidation of the American Bourgeoisie, 1850–1896* (Cambridge, England: Cambridge University Press, 2001), p. 292.

[109] Millikan, *A Union Against Unions.*

[110] Dubofsky and Dulles, *Labor in America.*

[111] Hirsch, *After the Strike.*

[112] Stephen H. Norwood, *Strikebreaking and Intimidation: Mercenaries and Masculinity in Twentieth-Century America of the Labor Movement* (Chapel Hill: University of North Carolina Press, 2002). Robert Michael Smith, *From Blackjacks to Briefcases: A History of Commercialized Strikebreaking and Unionbusting in the United States* (Athens: Ohio University Press, 2003).

Who Was the Most-Favored Strikebreaker? Box 4.15

Between 1890 and 1940, strikebreaking was a highly profitable business in U.S.—but not European—labor relations. Numerous strikebreaking agencies specialized in providing armed guards, labor spies, and replacement workers to struck firms—perhaps by the thousands on very short notice. One agency advertised that it could deliver 10,000 strikebreakers within 72 hours. These private armies often clashed violently with strikers and their supporters. Strikebreaking agencies managed the recruitment, training, compensation, feeding, housing, security, and work of the strikebreakers. In fact, these agencies often assumed complete control over the operation of struck firms.

Which of these four groups do you think was the preferred strikebreaker?

- African Americans?
- Criminals?
- The Unemployed?
- College Students?

Each of these were used in large numbers as strikebreakers. But college students were preferred! College students were instrumental in breaking these and other strikes in the early 20th century:

Minneapolis flour millers strike (1903): University of Minnesota students

New York subway strike (1905): Columbia students

Pacific Gas and Electric Company strike (1913): Stanford students

Boston police strike (1919): Harvard students

New England telephone operators strike (1919): MIT students

Pennsylvania Railroad strike (1920): Princeton students

San Francisco dockworkers strike (1934): University of California-Berkeley students

College students were especially attractive for several reasons. Unlike the other groups listed above, college students were generally from the upper class and therefore had no sympathy for the working class. African Americans and the unemployed often developed sympathy for those on strike—especially if they were lured into being strikebreakers by not being informed that the available jobs were because of a strike. College students were more skilled than the other groups and yet athletes and others still had the brawn to endure not only physical work, but also confrontations with strikers. Finally, unlike the other groups of strikebreakers, college students were viewed by the public as respectable and therefore helped with the struck firm's public relations (consider the public's reaction to having college students versus criminals operate local transit systems).

From the perspective of the college students, strikebreaking was simply another adventurous extracurricular activity—like wild fraternity parties—and a chance to assert their masculinity—like playing football. And college presidents often encouraged strikebreaking to the pleasure of wealthy trustees and donors. Some even created courses to help prepare students for strikebreaking, such as courses at MIT and Harvard in railroad engineering.

Source: Stephen H. Norwood, *Strikebreaking and Intimidation: Mercenaries and Masculinity in Twentieth-Century America of the Labor Movement* (Chapel Hill: University of North Carolina Press, 2002).

sometimes violently and illegally. During one strike, the National Guard used military tribunals to prosecute more than 100 civilian strikers while denying them defense attorneys; other violations of strikers' civil liberties were common.[113] The Ludlow Massacre is often used to illustrate the extent to which employers would go to maintain an open shop.[114] In 1913 workers struck the Rockefeller-owned coal mines in southern Colorado for union recognition and improvements in wages and working conditions. The strikers were forced out of their company-owned homes and moved into tent colonies, including one in Ludlow. Guerilla warfare essentially broke out between strikers and the company's private army.[115] The stockholders were told that this strike was over the closed shop and John D. Rockefeller, Jr., testified before a congressional hearing in April 1914 that he would

[113] Lambert, *If the Workers Took a Notion.*

[114] Dubofsky and Dulles, *Labor in America.*

[115] Gorn, *Mother Jones.*

stand by the principle of the open shop even if, as the question was posed to him, "it costs all your property and kills all your employees."[116] Two weeks later, a gun battle broke out between the strikers and the Colorado militia that was staffed essentially by company hirelings and guards. After the shooting killed perhaps 10 strikers, the militia overran the tent colony at Ludlow. The tents were soaked with kerosene and lit on fire. Two women and 11 children died hiding in a hole under a tent.[117] The Rockefeller-owned mine never did recognize the union. Four million workers were involved in strikes in 1919, including a general strike that paralyzed Seattle, huge coal mine, textile, and steel strikes, and a strike by Boston police.[118] In 1921, upwards of 10,000 frustrated coal miners fought a week-long armed battle at Blair Mountain, West Virginia, against deputies funded by nonunion mine owners determined to keep the United Mine Workers out of southern West Virginia. Federal troops caused the miners to give up the battle and the mines remained nonunion until the 1930s.[119]

The negative publicity of this type of violence and the destructiveness of bitter strikes caused some companies to switch from aggressively suppressing unions to avoiding unions through less confrontational, and perhaps more positive, methods. Dating back to the late 1800s, some companies implemented a strategy of welfare work.[120] Welfare work tried to create harmony between workers and their employers by creating a family-like company spirit and providing for the enhanced welfare of workers. Elements of welfare work included attractive company housing, recreational programs, libraries, landscaped factory grounds, profit-sharing, and pension plans. The structure of work, however, was determined by scientific management and the push to decompose and standardize job tasks; workers were literally driven by supervisors in the foreman's empire. In the aftermath of the Ludlow Massacre and the labor shortages and unrest of World War I, welfare work evolved into the creation of the personnel management function, and the 1920s is thereby characterized by welfare capitalism.

Welfare capitalism sought to win worker loyalty and increase efficiency by improving supervisory practices, implementing orderly hiring and firing procedures, providing wage incentives, offering protective insurance benefits, creating a positive culture, improving the physical work environment and safety, and providing employee voice.[121] Depending on one's perspective, welfare capitalism represents either a sophisticated managerial strategy to control the workplace and prevent unionization, or the beginnings of

[116] H. M. Gitelman, *Legacy of the Ludlow Massacre: A Chapter in American Industrial Relations* (Philadelphia: University of Pennsylvania Press, 1988), p. 15.

[117] Dubofsky and Dulles, *Labor in America.* Gitelman, *Legacy of the Ludlow Massacre.* Gorn, *Mother Jones.*

[118] Lichtenstein et al., *Who Built America?* Joseph E. Slater, *Public Workers: Government Employee Unions, the Law, and the State, 1900–1962* (Ithaca, NY: Cornell University Press, 2004).

[119] Robert Shogan, *The Battle of Blair Mountain: The Story of America's Largest Labor Uprising* (Boulder, CO: Westview Press, 2004).

[120] Sanford M. Jacoby, *Employing Bureaucracy: Managers, Unions, and the Transformation of Work in American Industry, 1900–1945* (New York: Columbia University Press, 1985). Nelson, *Managers and Workers.*

[121] Bernstein, *The Lean Years.* Lizabeth Cohen, *Making a New Deal: Industrial Workers in Chicago, 1919–1939* (Cambridge: Cambridge University Press, 1990). Jacoby, *Employing Bureaucracy.* Sanford M. Jacoby, *Modern Manors: Welfare Capitalism Since the New Deal* (Princeton: Princeton University Press, 1997). Gerald Zahavi, *Workers, Managers and Welfare Capitalism: The Shoeworkers and Tanners of Endicott Johnson, 1890–1950* (Urbana: University of Illinois Press, 1988).

today's strategic human resource management and high performance workplaces.[122] Nevertheless, union avoidance was at least one important aspect of welfare capitalism—"the labor movement was . . . being killed with kindness."[123] Note further that employers lobbied against legislating the same types of benefits provided by welfare capitalism—employers wanted their employees to be dependent on, and therefore loyal and tied to, the company, not the government, a local community, or a union (a pattern that continues today).[124]

The most controversial aspect of welfare capitalism—then and now—was the attempt to provide employee voice or industrial democracy through employee representation plans or company unions. One of the first examples was the Rockefeller Plan, crafted to offset the negative publicity of the Ludlow Massacre, in which a committee of equal numbers of managers and elected employee representatives would meet to resolve labor issues.[125] These types of employee representation plans are often called company unions because they are similar to a union in that workers and managers meet to discuss work issues, but they are established and often run by the company. By the mid-1920s it was estimated that there were over 400 company unions covering more than one million workers.[126]

The debate over company unions—which still rages today (see Chapter 11)—is whether they provide legitimate employee voice, or are management-dominated schemes that are manipulated to keep independent unions out. In other words, are company unions sham unions? Company unions could not strike and did not have the authority to force management to discuss specific issues. But they did provide an open channel of communication with management and a forum to present grievances; to prevent unionization, companies made concessions to the employee representatives at least some of the time. Unlike the AFL craft unions at the time, the Pullman Company's employee representation plans were integrated, and African-American workers served as representatives equal to whites.[127] Pullman also negotiated wage increases and other improvements with the employee representation plans several times in the 1920s.[128] However, these agreements coincided with periods of union activity when the threat of unionization was high. The company also discriminated against workers that did not support the employee representation plans. The struggle by the Brotherhood of Sleeping Car Porters, an independent union, to organize the Pullman porters was portrayed in no uncertain terms as a drive to break porters from the chains of the company-dominated representation plan (see Box 4.16). The Brotherhood of Sleeping Car Porters would eventually become the first African-American union to sign a contract with a major corporation, but not until the great union upsurge in the New Deal of the 1930s.

[122] Bruce E. Kaufman, "The Case for the Company Union," *Labor History* 41 (August 2000), pp. 321–50. David Fairris, *Shopfloor Matters: Labor-Management Relations in Twentieth-Century American Manufacturing* (London: Routledge, 1997).

[123] Dubofsky and Dulles, *Labor in America,* p. 235. Bernstein, *The Lean Years.*

[124] Cohen, *Making a New Deal.* Jennifer Klein, *For All These Rights: Business, Labor, and the Shaping of America's Public–Private Welfare State* (Princeton, NJ: Princeton University Press, 2003).

[125] Gitelman, *Legacy of the Ludlow Massacre.* Bruce E. Kaufman, "Accomplishments and Shortcomings of Nonunion Employee Representation in the Pre-Wagner Act Years: A Reassessment," in Bruce E. Kaufman and Daphne Gottlieb Taras (eds.), *Nonunion Employee Representation: History, Contemporary Practice, and Policy* (Armonk, NY: M. E. Sharpe, 2000), Chapter 2. Kaufman, "The Case for the Company Union." John D. Rockefeller, Jr., *The Personal Relation in Industry* (New York: Boni and Liveright, 1923).

[126] Bernstein, *The Lean Years.* Dubofsky and Dulles, *Labor in America.*

[127] Hirsch, *After the Strike.*

[128] Hirsch, *After the Strike.*

BOX 4.16
Aided by Truth and Education, the Brotherhood of Sleeping Car Porters Seeks to Break the Chains of Pullman's Employee Representation Plan

Source: *The Messenger* (September 1926)

A NEW DEAL FOR WORKERS: LEGAL PROTECTION AND INDUSTRIAL UNIONS

On October 24, 1929, the stock market unexpectedly crashed. Consumer purchasing slowed and unemployment increased. Weak farm prices put farmers out of business; panics wiped out savings accounts and banks closed. And then the economy plunged into the Great Depression. By 1933, the country's gross national product had declined by 29 percent, the steel industry was operating at 12 percent of capacity, the unemployment rate was nearly 25 percent with 15 million unemployed workers, and many others were only working part-time.[129] Many companies that had implemented welfare capitalism programs in the 1920s abandoned them and slashed wages and jobs.[130] Bread lines, evictions, and cardboard settlements of homeless families became common; thousands roamed the country looking for work. Today's unemployment insurance system had yet to be created, and the local poverty relief programs could not keep up with the incredible needs. While economic activity partially rebounded in the mid-1930s, mass unemployment was a problem throughout the decade and the Great Depression effectively lasted for the entire 1930s (see Box 4.17). The widespread poverty is hard to describe in words, and at the time, no one knew when it would end.

---

[129] Irving Bernstein, *A Caring Society: The New Deal, the Worker, and the Great Depression* (Boston: Houghton Mifflin, 1985). Lichtenstein et al., *Who Built America?* Cass R. Sunstein, *The Second Bill of Rights: FDR's Unfinished Revolution and Why We Need it More than Ever* (New York: Basic Books, 2004).

[130] Jacoby, *Modern Manors*. Chiaki Moriguchi, "Did American Welfare Capitalists Breach Their Implicit Contracts During the Great Depression? Preliminary Findings from Company-Level Data," *Industrial and Labor Relations Review* 59 (October 2005), pp. 51–81.

BOX 4.17
A Timeline of Labor History between 1925 and 1970

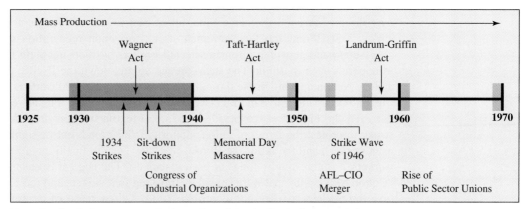

Note: Shading indicates economic depressions; light shading indicates recessions.

The severity of the Great Depression shook the intellectual foundations of the U.S. economy. The wisdom of relying on the invisible hand of free markets and the nation's elite—big business in particular, but not the government—to promote widespread economic prosperity and security was discarded. Franklin Delano Roosevelt was elected President in 1932 and pledged "a new deal for the American people."[131] The New Deal program of the Roosevelt presidency would ultimately create an active government role in guaranteeing the welfare and security of the population, including federally mandated minimum wages and overtime premiums, unemployment insurance and social security systems, and through the Wagner Act in 1935, explicit protections for workers trying to form unions. With respect to the schools of thought from Chapter 2, government policy follows pluralist industrial relations thought rather than neoclassical economics in this time period.

As will be described in Chapter 5, even before the Wagner Act in 1935, New Deal legislation starting with the National Industrial Recovery Act (NIRA) in 1933 encouraged and emboldened workers to form unions. The AFL unions enjoyed a modest resurgence and employers rushed to establish company unions to avoid independent unionization. In fact, membership in company unions nearly equaled membership in AFL unions with each group having between 2.5 and 3 million members.[132] But the NIRA was weak and there were tremendous strikes in 1934 as workers again clashed with employers who refused to recognize their independent unions.

A successful strike for recognition at an auto parts plant in Toledo resulted in an extended battle between strikers (joined by the unemployed) and the Ohio National Guard.[133] In Minneapolis, 3,000 truck drivers and helpers struck after the trucking companies refused to bargain with Teamsters Local 574.[134] By infiltrating the union, the business leaders'

[131] David M. Kennedy, *Freedom from Fear: The American People in Depression and War, 1929–1945* (New York: Oxford University Press, 1999), p. 98. Lichtenstein et al., *Who Built America?* p. 393. Sunstein, *The Second Bill of Rights.*

[132] Dubofsky and Dulles, *Labor in America.*

[133] Irving Bernstein, *Turbulent Years: A History of the American Worker, 1933–1941* (Boston: Houghton Mifflin, 1970). Brecher, *Strike!* Philip A. Korth and Margaret R. Beegle, *I Remember Like Today: The Auto-Lite Strike of 1934* (East Lansing: Michigan State University Press, 1988).

[134] Bernstein, *Turbulent Years.* Philip Korth, *Minneapolis Teamsters Strike of 1934* (East Lansing: Michigan State University Press, 1995). Millikan, *A Union Against Unions.*

Citizens Alliance lured strikers into an alley where they were brutally beaten by police. After additional violence, Local 574 agreed to an election to see if workers wanted to unionize, but the employers refused. Martial law was declared and the National Guard took over the city. Around the same time, all of San Francisco was paralyzed by a general strike.[135] San Francisco longshoremen struck for union recognition and an end to the shape-up system in which foremen selected workers by choosing them from a large crowd of hopefuls each morning. The strike spread up and down the Pacific coast. After police and the National Guard broke through the picket lines, 130,000 workers from many industries and occupations in San Francisco struck in support of the longshoremen. And this was not even the biggest strike of 1934—375,000 textile workers from Maine to Alabama struck to protest the firing of union supporters, the stretch-out (assigning more looms to each worker), and the failure of Roosevelt's New Deal to fulfill its promises of justice for workers.[136] Interestingly, songs of protest such as "The Big Fat Boss and the Worker" and "Cotton Mill Colic" that were spread by traveling folk singers and radio broadcasts helped give the workers a voice and contributed to a shared sense of oppression and struggle across otherwise isolated mill towns.[137]

In 1935, Congress passed the Wagner Act which encouraged unionization, enacted legal protections for workers, and outlawed company unions. The Wagner Act will be presented in detail in Chapter 5; the key point at this juncture is that the government became supportive of union organizing and bargaining. By 1941, union membership tripled to about 8.4 million, or 23 percent of workers.[138] This explosion in union membership is certainly connected to the new legal protections of the Wagner Act, but a second issue is also tremendously important: the rise of industrial unionism. Recall that the AFL emphasized craft unionism—organizing *skilled* workers into unions by craft or occupation. Craft unionism "reflected the industrial world of a half-century earlier: small shops, a simple technology, and the highly skilled workman."[139] In contrast, **industrial unionism** seeks to organize all of the workers in a workplace or industry regardless of their occupations or their skill levels.

The mismatch between craft unionism and the emerging modern workplace was vividly revealed in the 1919 steel strike. At the start of a coordinated drive to unionize steelworkers at the end of World War I, no less than 24 AFL unions claimed jurisdiction over various occupations. When the steel industry refused to negotiate, over 300,000 workers went on strike in 1919 for union recognition and the eight-hour day (instead of the existing 12). The steel companies used all of the tactics of the open shop movement—strikebreakers, negative publicity campaigns associating unionism with radicalism, blacklisting, and the use of martial law and state militia—so there were many reasons for the strike's complete failure. But attempting to organize the industry along craft lines with 24 different unions contributed to this failure: the individual unions insisted on following their own procedures,

[135] Bernstein, *Turbulent Years.* Brecher, *Strike!* Bruce Nelson, *Workers on the Waterfront: Seamen, Longshoremen, and Unionism in the 1930s* (Urbana: University of Illinois Press, 1988). David F. Selvin, *A Terrible Anger: The 1934 Waterfront and General Strikes in San Francisco* (Detroit: Wayne State University Press, 1996).

[136] Bernstein, *Turbulent Years.* Brecher, *Strike!* Janet Irons, *Testing the New Deal: The General Textile Strike of 1934 in the American South* (Urbana: University of Illinois Press, 2000). John A. Salmond, *The General Textile Strike of 1934: From Maine to Alabama* (Columbia: University of Missouri Press, 2002).

[137] Vincent J. Roscigno and William F. Danaher, *The Voice of Southern Labor: Radio, Music, and Textile Strikes, 1929–1934* (Minneapolis: University of Minnesota Press, 2004).

[138] Bernstein, *Turbulent Years.*

[139] Bernstein, *Turbulent Years,* p. 353.

some fought over jurisdictional issues, organizers were uncoordinated, and each union was unwilling to contribute the financial resources needed to counter the steel industry.[140] The steel industry would not be unionized until the late 1930s, and then, by an industrial union, not multiple craft unions.

Industrial unions emerged as a significant force in the mid-1930s, but the roots of industrial unionism are much older. The Knights of Labor and the Industrial Workers of the World were both industrial unions. In fact, in 1913 Mother Jones accurately saw into the future: "I know Industrial Unionism is coming, and you can't stop it."[141] Mother Jones had extensive experience with industrial unionism, because even though it was part of the AFL, the United Mine Workers was an industrial union for the coal industry—by a special AFL exception, it represented all workers in the mines and around them, including skilled workers typically represented by other AFL craft unions (such as carpenters).[142] Several other unions within the AFL, such as the Amalgamated Clothing Workers, were also essentially industrial unions.[143]

The rise of industrialized, mass manufacturing industries created huge numbers of unskilled and semiskilled factory workers in autos, rubber/tires, farm and construction machinery, airplanes, electrical products, and elsewhere. The jurisdictional disputes between competing unions that had plagued the AFL since the 1890s intensified with the rise of these mass manufacturing industries.[144] The issue boiled over at the AFL's convention in 1935.[145] On the one side were the old-line, conservative craft union leaders that looked down upon the unskilled mass production workers and who saw industrial unionism as a threat to their own power. One such leader was the other Big Bill in U.S. labor history: Big Bill Hutcheson, leader of the Carpenters union, who wanted jurisdiction over any worker who worked with wood. On the other side were the leaders of unions that were already organized along industrial lines, led by the president of the United Mine Workers, John L. Lewis. Lewis particularly wanted to aggressively organize the steel industry to strengthen his union's power in coal (since coal fed, and was often owned by, the steel industry), and felt that an industrial union approach was necessary (recall the 1919 strike). Personality conflicts between various leaders magnified the disagreements. At the 1935 convention, Lewis was (again) unable to muster sufficient AFL support for launching mass production, industrial union organizing drives. To underscore this conflict, Hutcheson called Lewis a bastard; the 225-pound Lewis responded by sending the equally large Hutcheson sprawling with a punch to the jaw.

Within a month, Lewis and the leaders of seven other unions formed the Committee for Industrial Organization (CIO) to pursue unionization of the mass manufacturing industries through industrial unionism. These unions were later suspended from the AFL. Mass production workers were ripe for unionization—the work was physically difficult, the hours

---

[140] David Brody, *Steelworkers in America: The Nonunion Era* (Cambridge: Harvard University Press, 1960). David Brody, *Labor in Crisis: The Steel Strike of 1919* (Philadelphia: J. B. Lippincott, 1965).

[141] Gorn, *Mother Jones,* p. 193.

[142] Taft, *The A.F. of L. in the Time of Gompers.*

[143] Steve Fraser, "Dress Rehearsal for the New Deal: Shop-Floor Insurgents, Political Elites, and Industrial Democracy in the Amalgamated Clothing Workers," in Michael H. Frisch and Daniel J. Walkowitz (eds.), *Working-Class America: Essays on Labor, Community, and American Society* (Urbana: University of Illinois Press, 1983), pp. 212–55.

[144] Taft, *The A.F. of L. in the Time of Gompers.* Philip Taft, *The A.F. of L. from the Death of Gompers to the Merger* (New York: Harper and Brothers, 1959).

[145] Bernstein, *Turbulent Years.* Dubofsky and Dulles, *Labor in America.* Taft, *The A.F. of L. from the Death of Gompers to the Merger.*

were long, and the supervision was arbitrary and abusive. Workers were looking for more equity, but also voice:

> When Armour's pork division grievance committee complained to the plant superintendent about a speed-up and the lack of a relief man, Superintendent Renfro responded, "You've been getting along for a good many years this way. What's the difference now?" Crawford Love, hog-kill steward, told him frankly, "The difference is this. I've been up there for eighteen years, and for eighteen years we've been breaking our hearts for the company, but now we've got a chance to say something about it."[146]

The CIO launched or supported organizing drives in the auto, steel, rubber, and radio industries, and would become a very visible force in U.S. society (see Box 4.18).[147] The intense conflicts and ultimate successes of these drives are revealed by the events between 1936 and 1941 in autos and steel.

In spite of the Wagner Act, the major auto and steel makers took a hard line against unionizing attempts. As in the 19th century, companies extensively used labor spies to infiltrate unions and thereby weaken or break them.[148] In fact, a government investigation found that one local union of General Motors workers was so thoroughly infiltrated that after the company fired all of the workers that they found out were members, only seven members were left. All were officers, and all were spies working for seven different agencies.[149] More generally, the Pinkertons alone infiltrated 93 separate unions.[150] While General Motors relied on espionage, Ford did not hesitate to supplement spying with brass knuckles. Ford's infamous Service Department of over several thousand ex-boxers, violent criminals, and thugs arbitrarily ruled the factories with intimidation and force. Union organizers in several cities were brutally beaten in broad daylight while police watched, and one was even tarred and feathered.[151]

BOX 4.18
The Visibility of the Rise of the CIO

Source: *Common Sense* (December 1937)

"WHAT! . . . YOU, TOO, DOC?"

---

[146] Cohen, *Making a New Deal,* p. 321.

[147] Walter Galenson, *The CIO Challenge to the AFL: A History of the American Labor Movement, 1925–1941* (Cambridge: Harvard University Press, 1960).

[148] Jerold S. Auerbach, *Labor and Liberty: The LaFollette Committee and the New Deal* (Indianapolis: Bobbs-Merrill, 1966).

[149] Norwood, *Strikebreaking and Intimidation.*

[150] Smith, *From Blackjacks to Briefcases.*

[151] Norwood, *Strikebreaking and Intimidation.*

Against this backdrop, the watershed **General Motors sit-down strike** began in December 1936 when workers in Flint, Michigan, took over two Chevrolet plants by sitting down and refusing to work or leave the plant.[152] At the time, Flint was the heart of General Motors, the world's premiere corporation, and the most important issue was getting General Motors to recognize the United Auto Workers (UAW) as the employees' bargaining agent. Mass production unionism in some respects depended upon success at General Motors, but this sit-down took even Lewis and the leaders of the fledgling UAW by surprise. Workers in Cleveland, Toledo, Detroit, and elsewhere followed suit, but the center of the strike was Flint. General Motors's injunction against this seizure of its plants was discredited when the UAW revealed that the judge owned General Motors stock. Strict discipline was maintained inside the plants by union leaders and company property was not damaged; food was brought to the strikers by outside union members and the women's auxiliary. In early January 1937, police tried to recapture one plant with tear gas, but in the Battle of the Running Bulls, they were repulsed by fire hoses and strikers who threw two-pound car door hinges at them from the roof. The battle ended when women broke through the police lines and joined the picket line in front of the plant, an action which led to the formation of the Women's Emergency Brigade (see Box 4.19).[153]

The governor then ordered the National Guard to Flint to preserve peace and a stalemate ensued. General Motors refused to negotiate until its plants were evacuated, but the UAW figured that if the plants were evacuated, General Motors would not have any incentive to bargain. In early February, the UAW further demonstrated its power by taking possession of Flint's large Chevrolet engine plant after a deception and mobilization effort worthy of a military battle and with the help of the Women's Emergency Brigade. Faced with a governor that refused to order the National Guard to forcibly evacuate the plants—likely with considerable bloodshed and loss of life—(but who also pressured Lewis and the

BOX 4.19
The Women's Emergency Brigade Outside a Chevrolet Plant in Flint, Michigan (1937)
The sticks they are carrying were used to break the windows to release the tear gas affecting the sit-down strikers.

Source: Flint Labor Museum and Learning Center.

[152] Bernstein, *Turbulent Years.* Brecher, *Strike!* Sidney Fine, *Sit-down: The General Motors Strike of 1936–1937* (Ann Arbor: University of Michigan Press, 1969). John Barnard, *American Vanguard: The United Autoworkers during the Reuther Years, 1935–1970* (Detroit: Wayne State University Press, 2004).
[153] Sol Dollinger and Genora Johnson Dollinger, *Not Automatic: Women and the Left in the Forging of the Auto Workers' Union* (New York: Monthly Review Press, 2000).

UAW to settle) and with pressure from President Roosevelt to settle, General Motors agreed to recognize the UAW on February 11, 1937, and the six-week strike ended. With the exception of Ford— whose Service Department's violence suppressed unionization until 1941—this victory at General Motors was followed by a strong wave of unionization throughout the auto industry.

The ramifications of the UAW's victory in the General Motors sit-down strike spread beyond the auto industry, too. In 1936 Lewis and the CIO created the Steel Workers Organizing Committee (SWOC) to unionize the steel industry.[154] The steel industry was full of employee representation plans / company unions so the companies and the SWOC vied for the workers' support.[155] In the aftermath of the UAW's sit-down strike and with the SWOC apparently winning more support than the company unions, the dominant steelmaker, U.S. Steel, announced in March 1937 that it had secretly negotiated an agreement with Lewis. As indicative of the contrast with the 1890s Homestead era, Henry Clay Frick's portrait was removed from the boardroom when the agreement was signed.

But perhaps Frick's spirit lived on in Little Steel, a handful of "smaller" steel manufacturers relative to the giants in the steel industry, though still quite large. Little Steel matched the terms of U.S. Steel's contract with the SWOC, but refused to recognize the union, and in May 1937 the workers struck. Outside of Republic Steel in Chicago, the police defied the courts by arresting peacefully picketing workers. A protest was thus called for Memorial Day. Marching to the steel mill, strikers and their families met a line of police that refused to let them proceed. Police fired into the crowd, killing 10 of the marchers. Seven of them were shot in the back. More than 50 were injured from gunfire or billy clubs. After this Memorial Day Massacre, as the event became known, the Little Steel strike was lost. Union recognition would finally be achieved in 1941. The SWOC would eventually become the United Steelworkers of America, and with the UAW, be among the most important industrial unions in the postwar period.

After the CIO organizing drives resulted in viable unions, it formally became the **Congress of Industrial Organizations** (CIO) in 1938—a union federation of industrial unions to rival the AFL federation of craft unions. There were now roughly 35 industrial unions affiliated with the CIO and their growth was spectacular. Conservative estimates reveal that by 1941 the CIO had 2.85 million members—an increase of two million members from 1936.[156] CIO industrial unions dominated the auto, steel, and rubber industries. The wave of CIO energy was not limited to the industrial centers of the Midwest. For example, CIO unions led organizing drives and strikes of Mexican-American workers throughout the Southwest and West—such as pecan shellers in Texas, sugar beet harvesters in Colorado, copper miners in Arizona, and cannery workers in California.[157] As such, the CIO achieved the broadest base of support that the U.S. labor movement has ever known:

> The CIO had successfully organized the unskilled workers into industrial unions and broken through the narrow lines of craft unionism fostered by the AFL. It had welcomed, as the [AFL] had never done, immigrants, blacks, and women, without regard to race, sex, or nationality.[158]

---

[154] Paul F. Clark, Peter Gottlieb, and Donald Kennedy (eds.), *Forging a Union of Steel: Philip Murray, SWOC, and the United Steelworkers* (Ithaca, NY: ILR Press, 1987).

[155] Bernstein, *Turbulent Years.*

[156] Galenson, *The CIO Challenge to the AFL,* p. 585.

[157] Zaragosa Vargas, *Labor Rights Are Civil Rights: Mexican American Workers in Twentieth Century America* (Princeton, NJ: Princeton University Press, 2005).

[158] Dubofsky and Dulles, *Labor in America,* p. 290.

On the other hand, by the end of the decade, the CIO unions were becoming centralized—partly out of necessity when dealing with massive corporations—and grassroots initiatives increasingly took a backseat to leadership control.[159] Accompanying this shift was a movement from community-based to workplace-based unionism. With the decreased emphasis on community and an increased portrayal of the workplace and unionism in masculine terms (recall Box 4.16), women were relegated to marginal roles.[160] Most CIO unions "wanted women to join unions, organize auxiliaries, and even shape union culture, but they did not make much room for them on center stage" and "by reinforcing the patriarchal family, the CIO did not encourage workers to challenge traditional gender relationships as much as ethnic and racial ones."[161] These issues have become significant concerns in the workplace of the 21st century.

It is also important not to overstate the differences between the two federations by the start of World War II. In its first years, the CIO unions relied heavily on aggressive workplace tactics—as most visibly demonstrated by the sit-down strikes—and were significantly aided by communists, socialists, and other radicals.[162] But unfavorable legal rulings—most visibly, a 1939 Supreme Court decision that sit-down strikes are illegal—set the CIO unions on the path toward embracing the AFL's business unionism philosophy that emphasizes stable, workplace collective bargaining to improve wages and working conditions.[163] Moreover, the AFL had a larger membership and made gains during the 1930s as well (see Box 4.20).[164] Much of the CIO's success was in durable goods manufacturing where large corporations dominated. The more decentralized AFL unions grew significantly in other sectors with smaller employers: trucking, construction, service industries, and retail trade. Industrial unionism, therefore, might be well-suited to mass manufacturing, but other models might better fit other situations.

WARTIME AND POSTWAR LABOR RELATIONS

World War II was particularly important for the development of U.S. labor relations.[165] War production ended the mass unemployment problem of the 1930s. This new labor market power allowed unions to strengthen their weak spots—such as at Ford and Little Steel in 1941. At the same time, government leaders wanted to keep union militancy under control so that strikes would not interfere with the production of airplanes, tanks, and other defense products. A National War Labor Board (NWLB) was created by President Roosevelt which had a tripartite structure—it consisted of representatives of business, labor,

---

[159] Cohen, *Making a New Deal.* Nelson Lichtenstein, *The Most Dangerous Man in Detroit: Walter Reuther and the Fate of American Labor* (New York: Basic Books, 1995).

[160] Elizabeth Faue, *Community of Suffering and Struggle: Women, Men, and the Labor Movement in Minneapolis, 1915–1945* (Chapel Hill: University of North Carolina Press, 1991).

[161] Cohen, *Making a New Deal,* p. 359.

[162] Robert H. Zieger and Gilbert J. Gall, *American Workers, American Unions: The Twentieth Century,* 3rd ed. (Baltimore: Johns Hopkins Press, 2002). James Gray Pope, "Worker Lawmaking, Sit-Down Strikes, and the Shaping of American Industrial Relations, 1935–1958," *Law and History Review* 24 (Spring 2006), pp. 45–113.

[163] Bernstein, *Turbulent Years. NLRB v. Fansteel Metallurgical Corp.,* 306 U.S. 240 (1939).

[164] Christopher L. Tomlins, "AFL Unions in the 1930s: Their Performance in Historical Perspective," *Journal of American History* 65 (March 1979), pp. 1021–42.

[165] James B. Atleson, *Labor and the Wartime State: Labor Relations and Law During World War II* (Urbana: University of Illinois Press, 1998). Dubofsky and Dulles, *Labor in America.* Nelson Lichtenstein, *Labor's War at Home: The CIO in World War II* (Cambridge: Cambridge University Press, 1982). Taft, *Organized Labor in American History.* Zieger and Gall, *American Workers, American Unions.*

A. Philip Randolph and the Brotherhood of Sleeping Car Porters   Box 4.20

Before the rise of automobiles and airplanes, long-distance passenger travel was via railroads. The most luxurious method of railroad travel was in a Pullman sleeping car. Passengers' every needs were handled by porters who were a combination of host and servant. And all 10,000 Pullman porters were African-American men. Being a Pullman porter was probably the best job a recently freed slave could obtain—it was a position of prestige and paid more than unskilled laborer jobs. At the same time, the job was full of indignities: the company exclusively hired African-American workers to fit racist stereotypes that blacks were servile and that whites would find it more luxurious to be served by blacks; porters were subjected to bigotry from passengers and other railroad employees (conductors, for example, were always white) in a segregated society.

Porters had to pay for their uniforms and even the rags used to shine the passengers' shoes. They could be ordered to make an extra trip without any advance notice and a porter filling in for a sick porter might not get paid for six hours of preparation work such as making beds. Until the 1920s, all porters were referred to as "George"—after the company founder's name, George Pullman. To redress these inequities and indignities, porters turned to unionization. In the early 1920s, Pullman created an employee representation plan to forestall unionizing activity. In frustration, some workers formed the Brotherhood of Sleeping Car Porters (BSCP) in 1925 and asked A. Philip Randolph to be its leader.

The BSCP fought battles on several fronts in the 1920s. Though the BSCP was a craft union, the AFL would not grant the BSCP status as a national union on par with other AFL unions until 1935. For its part, the company fired or reassigned union supporters and continued to use the representation plan to reduce support for the union (recall Box 4.16). It was the representation plan that supposedly "won" the termination of the "George" policy, although many porters credited union pressure. In the early 1930s, the BSCP's membership of roughly 4,000 fell to 650 during the Depression, but the BSCP continued its struggle to become the recognized union for Pullman porters.

Under the tireless leadership of Randolph, the BSCP rebounded during the upsurge of union activity and legislative support in Roosevelt's New Deal. The BSCP finally won an election to represent the porters in 1935—as such, it was not only the CIO industrial unions that thrived in this period. Two years later, the BSCP became the first African-American union to sign a contract with a major U.S. corporation. Randolph went on to become an important civil rights leader, and in many respects, the struggle of the BSCP laid the foundation for the postwar civil rights movement. The 1955 bus boycott in Montgomery, Alabama, after Rosa Parks was arrested, was organized by a Pullman porter. And A. Philip Randolph organized the 1963 March on Washington in which Martin Luther King delivered his famous "I have a dream" speech.

Sources: William H. Harris, *Keeping the Faith: A. Philip Randolph, Milton P. Webster, and the Brotherhood of Sleeping Car Porters, 1925–37* (Urbana: University of Illinois Press, 1991). Jack Santino, *Miles of Smiles, Years of Struggle: Stories of Black Pullman Porters* (Urbana: University of Illinois Press, 1989). Larry Tye, *Rising from the Rails: Pullman Porters and the Making of the Black Middle Class* (New York: Henry Holt, 2004).

and government. The NWLB's function was to resolve labor disputes to keep war production moving along. The end result was that organized labor essentially traded its right to strike in return for enhanced security in the workplace. This further institutionalized labor unions—union membership rose by 6 million workers to a union density of 36 percent—but also enhanced the power of union leaders at the expense of the rank and file, and ultimately created a bureaucratic form of unionism. In particular, rank and file militancy was channeled into bureaucratic grievance procedures (see Chapter 10). The NWLB also created fringe benefits such as holiday pay, shift differentials, and health insurance benefits in order to work around wage controls. All of these features—bureaucratic, centralized unions, formal grievance procedures, and fringe benefits—remain central in U.S. labor relations today, and can be traced to the wartime need for stable production. Lastly, wartime production demands drew women into factory work in unprecedented numbers—think,

"Rosie the Riveter"—but unions did little to prevent their equally quick postwar purge; unionism as a male institution was reinforced.[166]

The end of World War II brought on the **Great Strike Wave of 1945–46.** For the 12 months beginning August 1945, 4,600 strikes occurred involving 4.9 million workers and resulted in nearly 120 million worker-days lost.[167] There were large strikes in autos, steel, coal, rail, oil refining, longshoring, meat packing, and electrical products. This level of strike activity surpasses any other year in U.S. history. Compared to earlier periods of significant strike activity, however, the great strike wave of 1945–46 was relatively peaceful. But what explains such a strike wave? Important causes include decreased employee earnings with the inevitable postwar slowdown in production, rising prices with the lifting of price controls, and a renewed drive by management to reassert its workplace control and cost discipline (which had waned during the war because costs could be passed through to government contracts).[168] This strike wave led to major changes in the Wagner Act through the passage of the Taft-Hartley Act in 1947 (see Chapter 5).

The strike with the most lasting significance during this wave was the UAW strike at General Motors.[169] Walter Reuther, the ambitious leader of the UAW (see Box 4.21), wanted to link workers' and consumers' interests and therefore demanded a 30 percent wage increase without an increase in auto prices. Reuther demanded that General Motors open its financial books when it claimed that it could not afford such an increase and 200,000 General Motors went on strike in November 1945. General Motors reacted very negatively to this perceived incursion into the management of its business and was adamant about retaining its right to manage—in the boardroom and on the shop floor. After 113 days, Reuther declared victory, but it is corporate America that won: General Motors did not open its books and retained its right to manage. This established the postwar model of union representation: unions could negotiate for higher wages, better benefits, and favorable seniority provisions, but would not be involved in production decisions. From this point forward, union contracts progressively increased in length and detail; shop floor activism was controlled by the workplace rule of law.[170] The workplace rule of law was increasingly enforced by college-educated foremen under pressure to speed up the pace of work; grievance resolution became more formal and injury rates increased.[171]

The largely bureaucratic nature of U.S. unions was further cemented in the late 1940s and 1950s when opposition groups within the major CIO unions were driven out under the guise of rooting out communists during the beginnings of the Cold War.[172] Allegedly communist-controlled unions were expelled from the CIO.[173] This led to raiding attempts as

[166] Ruth Milkman, "Rosie the Riveter Revisited: Management's Postwar Purge of Women Automobile Workers," in Nelson Lichtenstein and Stephen Meyer (eds.), *On the Line: Essays in the History of Auto Work* (Urbana: University of Illinois Press, 1989), Chapter 6.

[167] Taft, *Organized Labor in American History,* p. 567.

[168] Zieger and Gall, *American Workers, American Unions.*

[169] Lichtenstein, *Labor's War at Home.* Lichtenstein, *The Most Dangerous Man in Detroit.* Barnard, *American Vanguard.*

[170] Victor G. Devinatz, "An Alternative Strategy: Lessons from the UAW Local 6 and the FE, 1946–52," in Cyrus Bina, Laurie Clements, and Chuck Davis (eds.), *Beyond Survival: Wage Labor in the Late Twentieth Century* (Armonk, NY: M.E. Sharpe, 1996), Chapter 7. Kim Moody, *An Injury to All: The Decline of American Unionism* (London: Verso, 1988). Fairris, *Shopfloor Matters.*

[171] David Fairris, "Institutional Change in Shopfloor Governance and the Trajectory of Postwar Injury Rates in U.S. Manufacturing, 1946–1970," *Industrial and Labor Relations Review* 51 (January 1998), pp. 187–203.

[172] Moody, *An Injury to All.* Zieger and Gall, *American Workers, American Unions.*

[173] Taft, *Organized Labor in American History.*

The Most Dangerous Man in Detroit

In the early 1900s, Mother Jones was the most dangerous woman in America (Box 4.10), but in the immediate postwar period Walter Reuther was the most dangerous man in Detroit. Born in 1907 to German immigrant parents, Reuther moved to Detroit in 1927 lured by the possibility of working as a skilled die maker in the world's biggest and most celebrated auto factory: Ford's River Rouge plant (a die is a large piece of hardened metal used to stamp flat pieces of metal into the shapes—such as a hood—necessary to make cars and other products; making a die is skilled and careful work). He worked at Ford for more than five years and quickly rose to a leader position. Reuther was simultaneously becoming more enthusiastic about the socialist ideas taught to him by his parents earlier in life.

Intrigued by the Soviet five-year plan to industrialize, he left Ford in 1932 to work with his brother in a Soviet auto plant initially established by Ford. Before getting to the Soviet Union, the brothers traveled around Europe networking with socialist activists in several countries, and witnessing firsthand the rise of the antisocialist Nazi regime in Germany. By 1936, Reuther was back in Detroit and actively involved in the organizing efforts of the newly emerging United Auto Workers (UAW) union—usually working quite closely with communist and socialist activists who were the most active organizers in 1930s Detroit. He quickly became a member of the UAW Executive Board and in 1937 was beaten by Ford's Service Department goons when passing out union literature to Ford workers. This highly publicized event became known as the Battle of the Overpass, and elevated Reuther's visibility.

The UAW of the 1930s and 1940s was rife with intense political factions; suffice it to say that Reuther distanced himself from the communists and socialists and consolidated his power. But a broad and ambitious vision of labor's role in the economy and society remained important to him:

> The kind of labor movement we want is not committed to a nickel-in-the-pay-envelope philosophy. We are building a labor movement, not to patch up the world so men can starve less often and less frequently, but a labor movement that will remake the world so that the working people will get the benefit of their labor.

During World War II he famously proposed a plan in which the corporations, organized labor, and the government would work together to produce 500 planes a day. At the end of the war, he demanded that General Motors raise wages 30 percent without increasing car prices in a bid to link workers with consumers into a broad force. The strike lasted 113 days and Reuther failed to establish the desired link.

In 1946 he was elected president of the UAW—a position he would hold for the rest of his life. Under his leadership—which was principled yet tightly controlling—the UAW won great gains in living standards for autoworkers through collective bargaining. These gains, however, never matched Reuther's social vision and in fact went in the opposite direction: the companies agreed to generous wages and benefits in return for retaining the right to manage the business. Detailed, formal contracts became the norm. With the UAW representing nearly the entire auto industry, Reuther was the most powerful man in Detroit in the 1950s. Nationally, he was perhaps the most visible union leader of his generation.

In the 1960s, Reuther turned his social vision towards the civil rights movement. In fact, he played a key role in the 1963 March on Washington, was one of the lead marchers, and gave a speech just before Martin Luther King's "I have a dream" speech. To the end he was trying to broaden the mainstream labor movement's "nickel-in-the-pay-envelope" philosophy—Reuther died in a plane crash in 1970 en route to a UAW worker education center he was helping build in northern Michigan.

It is ironic that Reuther was the most dangerous man in Detroit—a reflection of the power of his union at the bargaining table—while his vision for broader social and economic equality and justice

UAW President Walter Reuther (left) and Martin Luther King (waving) leading the June 1963 civil rights march in Detroit. Later that summer, Reuther, King, A. Philip Randolph (president of the Brotherhood of Sleeping Car Porters), and other civil rights leaders would lead the famous march on Washington, DC highlighted by King's "I have a dream" speech. The Civil Rights Act was passed the next year.

Source: Walter P. Reuther Library, Wayne State University.

could never be achieved solely at the bargaining table. It was during the turbulent times of the early 1900s when Mother Jones was associated with the specter of class warfare that a labor leader could be the most dangerous woman in America. By the 1950s, unions had been contained to the workplace, and in spite of his tremendous efforts, Walter Reuther could only be the most powerful man in Detroit.

Sources: Nelson Lichtenstein, *The Most Dangerous Man in Detroit: Walter Reuther and the Fate of American Labor* (New York: Basic Books, 1995). John Barnard, *American Vanguard: The United Autoworkers during the Reuther Years, 1935–1970* (Detroit: Wayne State University Press, 2004). The quote is from Melvyn Dubofsky and Foster Rhea Dulles, *Labor in America: A History*. 6th ed. (Wheeling, IL: Harlan Davidson, 1999), p. 349.

CIO unions tried to win bargaining rights in units represented by the expelled unions, such as the UAW's multi-year raiding campaign against the locals of the expelled Farm Equipment Workers.[174] This raiding activity was in addition to the ongoing raids between AFL and CIO unions. These raids consumed precious resources for very little gain and in 1955, the AFL and CIO reconciled. A single, united federation was born: the American Federation of Labor–Congress of Industrial Organizations (AFL–CIO).[175]

Public attention to the labor movement in the 1950s largely focused on allegations of union corruption—as captured by the classic 1954 movie *On the Waterfront* in which Marlon Brando portrays a boxer wrestling with his guilt over providing muscle for a corrupt union boss on the New Jersey docks. Fears of union corruption and the presence of mafia-infiltrated local unions led to the passage of a major federal law (the Landrum-Griffin Act) in 1959 and will therefore be discussed further in the next chapter. The 1960s witnessed the start of another upsurge in union membership, this time among teachers, police, and other employees of various local, state, and federal governments.[176] As in the private sector, public sector workers' attempts to unionize to fight low wages, onerous working conditions, and other indignities date back to the early 1800s. Government employers fought back with yellow dog contracts and restrictive legislation. In 1959, Wisconsin passed the first law protecting public sector collective bargaining and since that time, the federal government and a number of other states have followed; as a result, public sector union density exploded. The development of firefighter unions illustrates the trajectory of public sector unionism (see Box 4.22). In contrast to this rise in public sector unionism, postwar U.S. union density in the private sector peaked at around 35 percent in the mid-1950s, (recall Box 1.12). For private sector unions, the remaining decades of the 20th century would be years of turbulence and decline.

One source of turbulence in the labor movement was the civil rights movement in the 1960s. The question of race and ethnicity in the U.S. labor movement is a thorny one.[177] There is no question that African-American and Mexican-American workers faced pervasive discrimination and were often relegated to the most menial, dangerous, and low-paying jobs. Throughout the historical development of U.S. labor relations, there are

[174] Devinatz, "An Alternative Strategy."

[175] Taft, *The A.F. of L. from the Death of Gompers to the Merger*. Taft, *Organized Labor in American History*.

[176] Slater, *Public Workers*.

[177] Foner, *Organized Labor and the Black Worker*. Halpern, *Down on the Killing Floor*. Harris, *The Harder We Run*. Michael K. Honey, *Southern Labor and Black Civil Rights: Organizing Memphis Workers* (Urbana: University of Illinois Press, 1997). Timothy J. Minchin, *The Color of Work: The Struggle for Civil Rights in the Southern Paper Industry, 1945–1980* (Chapel Hill: University of North Carolina Press, 2001). Alan Draper, *Conflict of Interests: Organized Labor and the Civil Rights Movement in the South 1954–1968* (Ithaca, NY: ILR Press, 1994). Robert Rodgers Korstad, *Civil Rights Unionism: Tobacco Workers and the Struggle for Democracy in the Mid-Twentieth-Century South* (Chapel Hill: University of North Carolina Press, 2003). Vargas, *Labor Rights Are Civil Rights*.

Public Sector Labor Relations: The Development of Firefighters Unions

Box 4.22

The development of public unions parallels the private sector and reflects many of the same important themes such as worker frustration and union success tied to the business cycle and public opinion. As an example, consider professional firefighters. Professional firefighters date back to the 1850s when steam-powered pumps ended the need for numerous volunteers to pump water at a fire by hand. The first worker organizations among firefighters were mutual aid or benevolent societies in the late 1800s in which workers would contribute money to a central fund to pay accident and death benefits to firefighters or their families.

The first firefighter union was established in Chicago in 1901, and it later affiliated with the AFL. During World War I, labor shortages increased workers' leverage and it's estimated that by 1918 one-quarter of the country's full-time firefighters were unionized. The unions started as local in nature and then joined together in 1918 to form the International Association of Fire Fighters. Early issues that seem to have sparked workers to unionize included pay, working hours, and political favoritism. There were a variety of firefighter strikes during this time period, but the most notorious public sector strike was by Boston police in 1919. The governor, Calvin Coolidge who would become president of the United States, sent in the National Guard to end significant looting. As a result, public sector unionism was viewed very negatively and many jurisdictions outlawed public sector strikes, if not public sector unions entirely.

In Illinois, the firefighters unions in some cities disbanded while others continued but without legal protection. Firefighters, and other public sector employees, increasingly turned to state and local political lobbying to win gains such as wage increases or safety improvements. For example, Illinois firefighters successfully lobbied for a state minimum wage law in 1937 and a state-mandated reduction in weekly work hours in 1941.

The private sector unionization wave during the New Deal of the 1930s spurred organizing among firefighters, but it's important to remember that this was done without legal protection. Public sector unions therefore continued to be dependent on political power. Some states started passing laws to protect public sector unionization in the 1960s, but not Illinois. Nationally, public sector union membership grew significantly in this time period. In Illinois even without protective legislation, in the social turbulence of the late 1960s, firefighter frustration over wages and working conditions resulted in a number of strikes.

Without a regularized or legally sanctioned mechanism for settling disputes, conflicts continued. In one extreme case, firefighters in Normal, Illinois, went on strike in 1978. The striking firefighters were sentenced to 42 days in jail for violating a restraining order, and the fire station was declared to be a work release center so the firefighters spent half of their time in jail and half of their time on "work release" protecting the city against fires. After a 56-day strike, which included the use of private-sector strikebreakers serving as firefighters, a contract was signed. After other strikes, including a 23-day strike in Chicago in 1980, Illinois passed a public sector collective bargaining law in 1985. As in the private sector, the development of public sector unionization followed a path of turbulence to stability.

Source: Michael G. Matejka, *Fiery Struggle: Illinois Fire Fighters Build a Union, 1901–1985* (Chicago: Illinois Labor History Society, 2002).

---

examples where unions contributed to this problem—either passively or actively—and other examples where unions fought to break down discriminatory practices. The AFL craft unions are most well-known for their history of excluding African-American workers, but even the progressive CIO leaders like Walter Reuther had difficulties ending discriminatory practices that were embedded in rank and file workers and their local unions. For example, the southern workplace was largely segregated until the 1960s—at paper mills, for example, there were separate entrances, pay clocks, pay windows, bathrooms, water fountains, and cafeterias for blacks and whites.[178] From 1946 to 1953, the CIO aggressively

[178] Minchin, *The Color of Work.*

BOX 4.23
A Timeline of Labor
History since 1970

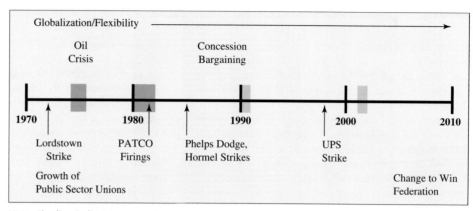

Note: Shading indicates economic recessions.

tried to organize workers in the South, but this "Operation Dixie" failed partly because many southern white workers refused to join together with African-American workers.[179] Where unions did exist in the South, black workers were commonly segregated into Jim Crow locals with seniority ladders separate from white workers. As such, labor relations reflected larger societal patterns of discrimination.

During the civil rights movement in the 1960s, the Brotherhood of Sleeping Car Porters and the UAW contributed significant amounts of money and leadership, while the AFL–CIO generally remained on the sidelines or provided assistance quietly. In fact, these two unions played instrumental roles in the 1963 March on Washington, famously remembered for Martin Luther King's "I have a dream" speech. The Civil Rights Act of 1964 outlawed discriminatory practices by both employers and unions, but issues of social and economic justice continue to be closely intertwined. In Memphis in 1968, black sanitation workers were outraged when two African-American workers were killed by lightning because they could not enter the whites-only lounge.[180] It was during the ensuing strike that Martin Luther King was assassinated.

Another source of turbulence for the U.S. labor movement is the economy. The stability of the mass manufacturing system was undermined by the oil crisis of the 1970s and by increased globalization (see Chapters 11 and 12). Intense competitive pressures resulted in a period of concession bargaining in the early 1980s (See Box 4.23). Under the threat of significant job loss, many unions agreed to wage freezes or cuts, benefits reductions, and a loosening of work rules. The most visible examples were in the auto and steel industries.[181] More generally, the 1980s is believed to represent the return of a much more adversarial labor–management climate. In 1981 President Reagan fired the air traffic controllers during the illegal PATCO strike and hired replacement workers (see Box 4.24). To many observers, the PATCO strike emboldened private sector employers to take a hard-line approach with their unions, though the true linkage may never be known.[182] With or without the PATCO strike as a model, there were a number of bitter strikes in the 1980s and 1990s involving management's use of permanent strike replacements: the Phelps-Dodge copper strike in Arizona (1983), the Hormel meatpacking

[179] Barbara S. Giffith, *Operation Dixie and the Defeat of the CIO* (Philadelphia: Temple University Press, 1988).

[180] Harris, *The Harder We Run.*

[181] John P. Hoerr, *And the Wolf Finally Came: The Decline of the American Steel Industry* (Pittsburgh: University of Pittsburgh, 1988). Harry C. Katz, *Shifting Gears: Changing Labor Relations in the U.S. Automobile Industry* (Cambridge: MIT Press, 1985).

[182] Michael H. LeRoy, "The PATCO Strike: Myths and Realities," in Paula B. Voos (ed.), *Proceedings of the Forty-Ninth Annual Meeting* (Madison, WI: Industrial Relations Research Association, 1997), pp. 15–22.

Arguably the most significant U.S. labor relations event in the latter part of the 20th century is the failed strike by air traffic controllers belonging to the Professional Air Traffic Controllers Organization (PATCO) in 1981. Against a backdrop of long-term private sector union membership decline and robust unionism in the public sector, it is perhaps appropriate that this event occurred in the public sector: air traffic controllers are U.S. federal government employees that work for the Federal Aviation Administration (FAA), a government agency. As will be discussed in Chapter 5, it is illegal for unions of federal government employees to strike.

Being an air traffic controller is stressful; a mistake can cause a plane crash. Controllers first formed a union in 1968—a common time period for the formation of public sector unions. During the 1970s, PATCO fought with the FAA over wages and working conditions, and several times engaged in coordinated sick-outs since striking was illegal. In June 1981, PATCO negotiators tentatively accepted a new contract that (if approved by Congress) would give substantial pay raises, increased severance pay, and an enhanced voice in operating and safety policy making. The membership rejected this agreement. President Reagan warned that strikers would be discharged because federal sector strikes are illegal, but on August 3, 1981, PATCO went on strike. Military controllers, retirees, supervisors, and air traffic controllers who did not strike were used by the FAA and after 10 days, the system was working at about 70 percent of normal capacity. Four hours after the start of the strike, President Reagan gave the strikers 48 hours to return to work or be fired. Over 11,000 did not return and were fired. PATCO was decertified.

There are two competing views on why the PATCO membership struck. One view is that PATCO figured that a disruption of air traffic would force Congress to grant them the legal right to strike and to negotiate wages (which is also illegal in the federal sector), but that the union leadership blundered by overestimating its power. As such, the workers foolishly turned down a generous contract. The alternative view is that the workers were striking out of frustration with autocratic, even paramilitary, FAA supervisors and managers. As such, the Reagan administration is also to blame for taking an exceptionally hard line during negotiations and the strike. In either case, the firing of the striking air traffic controllers was a very public and devastating defeat for organized labor. By many accounts (but not all), the failed PATCO strike established an antiunion climate in which it was acceptable for private sector employers to aggressively weaken or break unions during the 1980s and 1990s.

As a footnote, the new controllers voted to unionize in 1987 and are now represented by the National Air Traffic Controllers Association.

Questions

1. Was it ethically acceptable for the air traffic controllers to strike? (*Hint:* use the ethical analysis template from Box 3.11.)

2. Was it ethically acceptable for President Reagan to fire the striking air traffic controllers? (*Hint:* use the ethical analysis template from Box 3.11.)

Note: These questions do not ask whether the actions were legal or illegal—that issue is clear. The question is whether the actions were ethical.

Sources: Herbert R. Northrup, "The Rise and Demise of PATCO," *Industrial and Labor Relations Review* 37 (January 1984), pp. 167–84. Richard W. Hurd and Jill K. Kriesky, "Communications: 'The Rise and Demise of PATCO' Reconstructed," *Industrial and Labor Relations Review* 40 (October 1986), pp. 115–22.

strike in Minnesota (1985), the International Paper strike in Maine (1987), the Greyhound bus strike (1990), the Ravenswood aluminum strike in West Virginia (1990), the Bridgestone-Firestone tire strike in Illinois (1995), and the Detroit newspaper strike (1995), to name just a few.[183] Harkening back to the earlier era of the Pinkertons, the

[183] Julius Getman, *The Betrayal of Local 14* (Ithaca, NY: ILR Press, 1998). Dave Hage and Paul Klauda, *No Retreat, No Surrender: Labor's War at Hormel* (New York: William Morrow, 1989). Tom Juravich and Kate Bronfenbrenner, *Ravenswood: The Steelworkers' Victory and the Revival of American Labor* (Ithaca, NY: Cornell University Press, 1999). Barbara Kingsolver, *Holding the Line: Women in the Great Arizona Mine Strike of 1983* (Ithaca, NY: ILR Press, 1989). Peter Rachleff, *Hard-Pressed in the Heartland: The Hormel Strike and the Future of the Labor Movement* (Boston: South End Press, 1993). Rosenblum, *Copper Crucible*. Bruce M. Meyer, *The Once and Future Union: The Rise and Fall of the United Rubber Workers, 1935–1995* (Akron, OH: University of Akron Press, 2002).

provision of antiunion consultants, armed guards, and surveillance forces continues to be big business.[184] At the same time, labor relations practices have become more divergent—as some relationships have become more adversarial, others are trying to create stronger union–management partnerships (see Chapter 11).[185]

The labor movement at the beginning of the 21st century is struggling, yet has pockets of vibrancy. As will be discussed in later chapters, the sharp increase in immigrant workers in industries such as meatpacking and in occupations such as janitors provides great challenges and opportunities for U.S. unions.[186] Globalization continues to undermine labor's bargaining power and private sector union density has sunk to less than 10 percent, though it continues to hover between 35 and 40 percent in the public sector (recall Box 1.12). Public sector unionism, therefore, is one of the labor movement's strongest areas and cannot be ignored in contemporary labor relations.[187] Many of the strikes noted in the previous paragraph ended in defeat for the strikers, though in 1997 the Teamsters mobilized rank and file militancy, built public support for the plight of part-time workers, and won a very visible strike at the United Parcel Service. Against this backdrop of labor–management conflict in a competitive global economy, President Clinton appointed a distinguished committee of academics and practitioners to investigate future directions for labor relations in 1993.[188] This "Commission on the Future of Worker-Management Relations" (popularly referred to as the "Dunlop Commission" after its leader, Professor John Dunlop) issued recommendations for reducing conflict and improving productivity, but with continued political gridlock between Democrats and Republicans, these recommendations were received with "thundering silence."[189]

The economic and political environment continues to pressure the labor movement to change. Union mergers have washed away many of the historical distinctions between craft and industrial unions.[190] Today, diverse occupations and industries are frequently represented in a single, general union. The United Steelworkers represents not only steelworkers, but also employees across the entire manufacturing spectrum plus nurses, public school food service workers, and public sector clerical, technical, and professional employees. **General unionism** has largely replaced craft unionism and industrial unionism.

Frustration with the direction of the labor movement even resulted in a rare contested election for the leadership of the AFL–CIO. In 1995, John Sweeney, president of the Service Employees International Union (SEIU), and a slate of insurgents defeated the

---

[184] Norwood, *Strikebreaking and Intimidation.* Smith, *From Blackjacks to Briefcases.*

[185] Harry C. Katz and Owen Darbishire, *Converging Divergences: Worldwide Changes in Employment Systems* (Ithaca NY: ILR Press, 2000).

[186] Ruth Milkman (ed.), *Organizing Immigrants: The Challenge for Unions in Contemporary California* (Ithaca, NY: ILR Press, 2000). Immanuel Ness, *Immigrants, Unions, and the New U.S. Labor Market* (Philadelphia: Temple University Press, 2005).

[187] Slater, *Public Workers.*

[188] Commission on the Future of Worker–Management Relations, *Fact Finding Report* (Washington, DC: U.S. Departments of Labor and Commerce, 1994). Commission on the Future of Worker-Management Relations, *Report and Recommendations* (Washington, DC: U.S. Departments of Labor and Commerce, 1994).

[189] Samuel Estreicher, "Freedom of Contract and Labor Law Reform: Opening Up the Possibilities for Value-Added Unionism," *New York University Law Review* 71 (June 1996), pp. 827–49 at 827. Symposium, *Journal of Labor Research* 17 (Winter 1996).

[190] Gary Chaison, *Union Mergers in Hard Times: The View From Five Countries* (Ithaca, NY: ILR Press, 1996). Gary Chaison, *When Unions Merge* (Lexington, MA: Lexington Books, 1986).

longtime officials selected by outgoing AFL–CIO president, Lane Kirkland. Sweeney has tried to shake up the AFL–CIO and its affiliate unions by devoting significant resources to union organizing and political mobilization—including a program called Union Summer in which college students spend a summer working on organizing campaigns. Even more dramatic than the contested election in 1995 were the events 10 years later. The Sweeney administration failed to reverse the continued decline in union density so several unions called for more changes in the AFL–CIO, especially (another) renewed emphasis on new organizing and less emphasis on political activity. This launched a surprisingly open and frank year-long discussion in union halls and in cyberspace regarding the future of the AFL–CIO. These debates came to a head when the SEIU (Sweeney's old union now under the leadership of Andy Stern), the Teamsters, UNITE HERE (a large union of textile and hotel workers), and the United Food and Commercial Workers (UFCW) announced that they were boycotting the 2005 AFL–CIO convention. These four unions then broke away from the AFL–CIO and with the United Brotherhood of Carpenters, the Laborers' International Union, and the United Farm Workers, formed a new labor federation, the **Change to Win** federation. Change to Win seeks to aggressively increase the resources devoted to organizing new members and will likely deemphasize electoral politics in order to pay for additional organizing activity. The seven unions of Change to Win represent around 6 million workers while the member unions of the AFL–CIO represent about 9 million workers. It remains to be seen whether this new federation is successful, and the extent to which the two federations cooperate or compete. Whether the structural changes resulting from union mergers and from the breakup of the AFL–CIO can overcome the effects of globalization and other environmental factors is a major question for the future of U.S. labor relations.

In conclusion, the largest unions and watershed strikes in various eras often involve traditional blue collar occupations—railroad workers in the 1870s, skilled craft steel workers in the 1890s, coal miners in the early 1900s, semiskilled auto assemblers in the 1930s—but the history of U.S. labor is not strictly a blue collar affair. During the 20th century, waitresses, actors, university clerical workers and professors, teachers, hotel and casino workers, journalists, athletes, agricultural workers, nurses, and airline pilots unionized.[191] Even doctors, university teaching assistants, and nude models have tried to form unions. The details may differ, but the fundamental reasons are universal: to seek greater equity and increased voice in the workplace through collective action with co-workers. Studying labor history reveals the various forces that may cause workers to seek unionization and the wide-ranging organizational and policy strategies in response. And thus, the historical record provides a rich foundation for understanding the development of the U.S. labor relations system and options for its future.

[191] Paul F. Clark, John T. Delaney, and Ann C. Frost (eds.), *Collective Bargaining in the Private Sector* (Champaign, IL: Industrial Relations Research Association, 2002). Dorothy Sue Cobble, *Dishing It Out: Waitresses and Their Unions in the Twentieth Century* (Urbana: University of Illinois Press, 1991). Susan Ferriss and Ricardo Sandoval, *The Fight in the Fields: Cesar Chavez and the Farmworkers Movement* (New York: Harcourt Brace, 1997). Leon Fink and Brian Greenberg, *Upheaval in the Quiet Zone: A History of Hospital Workers' Union, Local 1199* (Urbana: University of Illinois Press, 1989). Toni Gilpin, et al., *On Strike for Respect: The Clerical and Technical Workers' Strike at Yale University, 1984–85* (Urbana: University of Illinois Press, 1995). John P. Hoerr, *We Can't Eat Prestige: The Women Who Organized Harvard* (Philadelphia: Temple University Press, 1997). George E. Hopkins, *Flying the Line: The First Half Century of the Air Line Pilots Association* (Washington, DC: The Air Line Pilots Association, 1982). Marjorie Murphy, *Blackboard Unions: The AFT and the NEA, 1900–1980* (Ithaca, NY: Cornell University Press, 1990).

Key Terms

National Labor Union, *109*
Great Uprising of 1877, *111*
Knights of Labor, *112*
uplift unionism, *112*
Haymarket Tragedy, *114*
American Federation of
Labor, *115*
business unionism, *116*
craft unionism, *117*

exclusive jurisdiction, *117*
Homestead strike, *118*
Pullman strike, *119*
Industrial Workers of the
World, *123*
revolutionary
unionism, *125*
open shop movement, *129*
welfare capitalism, *132*

industrial unionism, *136*
General Motors sit-down
strike, *139*
Congress of Industrial
Organizations, *140*
Great Strike Wave of
1945–46, *143*
general unionism, *149*
Change to Win, *150*

Reflection Questions

1. The AFL, IWW, and CIO were all created out of frustration with the existing dominant form of unionism at the time. Explain. Also, what does this imply about the future of U.S. unionism?

2. Violence—by companies and their agents, by unions and their workers, by governments and their soldiers—is a recurring theme in U.S. labor history. To Mother Jones, this violence "means that the workers would rather die fighting to protect their women and children than to die in death-trap mines producing more wealth for the Rockefellers to use in crushing their children."[192] Do you agree? Develop other explanations or interpretations. Try to construct alternatives in which unions or workers are responsible, companies are responsible, and the government or the system is responsible.

3. It's been written that "The attempt of persons to understand the forces remaking their world and, by organization, to control them, constitutes, indeed, the major motif of the social history of the late nineteenth century."[193] Describe how this statement applies to workers and their unions in different periods of labor history. How were employers more successful than employees in controlling these forces through creating and shaping their organizations?

4. Recall Box 4.13. How are the lyrics of "Solidarity Forever" consistent with the IWW's beliefs? How is it ironic that today's mainstream unions have adopted this song as their own? What parts of the lyrics would today's mainstream unions agree with?

5. Look at the reasons listed by the employers for being nonunion in the open shop handout in Box 4.14. How would an AFL leader have responded to these reasons? Is the open shop movement consistent with today's human resource management approach?

6. Describe how the Knights of Labor, American Federation of Labor, and the Industrial Workers of the World differed in their views of efficiency, equity, and voice. How about employers? What were their views on efficiency, equity, and voice during the open shop movement? Did these views change during the period of welfare capitalism?

Internet Exploration

1. Explore some online labor history exhibits (for example, see *www.reuther.wayne.edu/exhibits/stories.html*, *www.library.arizona.edu/exhibits/bisbee/*, or *www.chicagohistory.org/dramas/*). To what extent did these events result from managerial choices? labor choices? the environment? How did they influence subsequent actions and events?

2. Search the Web for events in labor history that occurred in your city, state, or region. How are these events consistent with and/or different from the major themes of the time periods of labor history outlined in this chapter?

[192] Gorn, *Mother Jones*, p. 216
[193] Sigmund Diamond, *The Nation Transformed: The Creation of an Industrial Society* (New York: George Braziller, 1963), p.18.

3. Listen to some oral histories of workers (for example, see *www.bridgeporthistory.org* or *depts.washington.edu/civilr/interviews.htm*). How do the experiences of individual workers fit into the larger sweep of labor history?

4. While not a significant presence in today's U.S. labor movement, the IWW still exists. Explore its web site at *www.iww.org*. Are the beliefs, goals, and tactics different from the 1905–1920 period?

Additional
Reading

Bruno, Robert, *Steelworker Alley: How Class Works in Youngstown* (Ithaca, NY: Cornell University Press, 1999).

Dubofsky, Melvyn, and Foster Rhea Dulles, *Labor in America: A History,* 6th ed. (Wheeling, IL: Harlan Davidson, 1999).

Cohen, Lizabeth, *Making a New Deal: Industrial Workers in Chicago, 1919–1939* (Cambridge: Cambridge University Press, 1990).

Gompers, Samuel, *Seventy Years of Life and Labor* (New York: E.P. Dutton, 1925).

Gorn, Elliot J., *Mother Jones: The Most Dangerous Woman in America* (New York: Hill and Wang, 2001).

Hirsch, Susan Eleanor, *After the Strike: A Century of Labor Struggle at Pullman* (Urbana: University of Illinois Press, 2003).

Jacoby, Sanford M., *Employing Bureaucracy: Managers, Unions, and the Transformation of Work in American Industry, 1900–1945* (New York: Columbia University Press, 1985).

Lichtenstein, Nelson, et al., *Who Built America? Working People and the Nation's Economy, Politics, Culture, and Society,* Volume 2 (New York: Worth Publishing, 2000).

Markowitz, Gerald and David Rosner, *"Slaves of the Depression": Workers' Letters About Life on the Job* (Ithaca, NY: Cornell University Press, 1987).

Minchin, Timothy J., *The Color of Work: The Struggle for Civil Rights in the Southern Paper Industry, 1945–1980* (Chapel Hill: University of North Carolina Press, 2001).

Norwood, Stephen H., *Strikebreaking and Intimidation: Mercenaries and Masculinity in Twentieth-Century America of the Labor Movement* (Chapel Hill: University of North Carolina Press, 2002).

Serrin, William, *Homestead: The Glory and Tragedy of an American Steel Town* (New York: Vintage Books, 1992).

Sinyai, Clayton, *Schools of Democracy: A Political History of the American Labor Movement* (Ithaca, NY: Cornell University Press, 2006).

Slater, Joseph E., *Public Workers: Government Employee Unions, the Law, and the State, 1900–1962* (Ithaca, NY: Cornell University Press, 2004).

Chapter Five

Labor Law

Advance Organizer

It is impossible to understand contemporary U.S. labor relations without a careful examination of labor law. U.S. labor law grants rights to workers, unions, and companies, gives them responsibilities, and makes certain behaviors illegal. The major labor relations processes are therefore critically shaped by the specific provisions of labor law. A foundation for understanding these processes is studying labor law.

Learning Objectives

By the end of the chapter, you should be able to:

1. **Understand** how a legal system can be used to either promote or repress unionization.
2. **List** the major provisions of U.S. labor law and their underlying logic and rationale, especially with respect to the Wagner Act, Taft-Hartley Act, and Landrum-Griffin Act.
3. **Understand** the role of the National Labor Relations Board and similar state agencies in U.S. labor relations.
4. **Compare** the similarities and differences between U.S. private and public sector law.

5. **Discuss** the criticisms of U.S. labor law and possible directions for reform.

Contents

U.S. labor relations has been closely intertwined with the U.S. legal system for over two centuries. Since the New Deal in the 1930s, U.S. labor laws have explicitly protected workers' union activity primarily by making it illegal for companies to prevent unionization through intimidation or manipulation. Prior to that time, there were few laws that specifically targeted union activity, but business laws and judicial rulings on conspiracy and other issues were applied to workers' actions. In fact, it's very difficult to imagine a labor relations system in which at least some aspects of the law are not important. Suppose we throw out all existing labor laws with the intent of letting labor and management do what they choose. Would you let workers take over the employer's factory during a strike? Would you let supervisors threaten physical harm to employees that support a union? Would you allow violent or destructive picketing to the same extent as peaceful picketing? Most people would probably answer no to these questions which then injects legal rulings into labor relations. Labor relations is always critically shaped by the legal system—whether there are explicit labor laws or not.

Consequently, to understand labor relations it is imperative to consider the legal aspects. The major processes in today's U.S. labor relations system—organizing new unions, bargaining contracts, and resolving disputes and grievances—are not entirely legal in nature, but labor law has defined very important aspects of these processes. Throughout this chapter, therefore, do not divorce these legal elements—whether they be court decisions or provisions in labor laws—from the underlying objectives. In addition to learning how labor law works, dig deeper and make the connections between the how and the why. Understanding the objectives of labor law and their intellectual foundations makes the operation of specific legal provisions more readily comprehensible. In particular, the New Deal industrial relations system seeks to balance efficiency, equity, and voice in the U.S. employment relationship and is rooted in the industrial relations school of thought (recall Chapter 2). This perspective determined what form today's labor laws took, what provisions were written into them, and what language was used. All of these legal details will make much more sense if you keep this objective of balancing efficiency, equity, and voice in mind.

Another important strategy for understanding U.S. labor law is recognizing the theme of striking a balance between property rights and labor rights. To balance efficiency, equity, and voice, many legal rules and court decisions try to balance property rights and labor rights. You might not agree with the specific balance in a certain case, but in many areas of labor law it is very instructive to consider the conflicting rights and how they are weighed against each other. Before the New Deal in the 1930s, legal doctrine generally favored property rights and individual liberty—consistent with the neoclassical economics school of thought. As such, if there were conflicting rights, private property and individual liberty often won out over the interests or rights of labor. But today's laws seek a balance—consistent with the industrial relations school of thought.

This evolution in the legal doctrine pertaining to unions and union activity represents a shift from common law to statutory law, and within statutory law a shift from business law to labor law. Common law is a body of law based on customs, traditions of acceptable behavior, and judicial precedent—often stemming back to English legal principles from several centuries ago (see Box 5.1).[1] Important areas of common law include conspiracy, breach of contract, property rights, and the employment-at-will doctrine. In contrast, statutory law consists of laws enacted by legislatures, not judges. Three categories of statutory law are particularly relevant for labor relations: business law (laws applying to businesses, such as antitrust laws), labor law (laws written explicitly for unions and union activity), and employment law (laws pertaining to the individual rather than the collective employment relationship). Between 1800 and 1932, workers who tried to act collectively to influence their wages and working conditions were subjected to common law principles, and starting in 1890, also to business laws. The year 1932 marks the birth of U.S. labor law, so since that time, unions and union activity have first and foremost been governed by statutory laws written explicitly for labor relations activities (see Box 5.2). It is to these developments that we now turn.

---

[1] Norman F. Cantor, *Imagining the Law: Common Law and the Foundations of the American Legal System* (New York: HarperCollins, 1997). Mary Ann Glendon, Michael Wallace Gordon, and Paolo G. Carozza, *Comparative Legal Traditions in a Nutshell,* 2nd ed. (St. Paul: West Group, 1999).

Common Law Laws based on custom and judicial precedent, dating back several centuries into English jurisprudence. Examples include conspiracy, property rights, and employment-at-will. With statutory law, one of the two major categories of law.

Conspiracy: Common law doctrine making it a crime for two or more individuals to plot to deprive someone else of their rights or property.

Contract: A legally binding and enforceable agreement between two parties governed by common law.

Yellow Dog Contract: An agreement sometimes required by employers before the 1930s in which employees would agree not to join or support a union.

Injunction: A court order requiring an individual or an organization to stop a proposed or current action on the belief that the action would cause irreparable harm or damage. A common example in the 1800s was a court order preventing picketing.

Due Process: Core standards of legal treatment, such as the right to a fair trial and to hear and present evidence.

Statutory Law Laws (statutes) passed by legislatures. With common law, one of the two major categories of law. Business, labor, and employment law are three examples. The implementation of statutory law is shaped by judicial interpretation of the written statutes; over time, the accumulation of judicial precedents creates a body of case law for a particular statute.

Business Law: Laws written to govern business activities. A major example of business law is antitrust law to prevent monopolies, especially the Sherman Antitrust Act (1890).

Labor Law: Laws written to govern the collective employment relationship (unions and union activity). Major examples include the Wagner Act (1935) and Taft-Hartley Act (1947).

Employment Law: Laws written to govern the individual employment relationship. Major examples include minimum wage, antidiscrimination, occupational safety, and family leave legislation. Some legislation was passed in the 1930s, but the large expansion in employment law started in the 1960s.

THE COMMON LAW OF LABOR RELATIONS: CONSPIRACIES AND INJUNCTIONS

In the beginning, there was no labor law. But there were (and are) common-law doctrines pertaining to conspiracy, property rights, and breach of contract. Throughout the 19th century and in the first three decades of the 20th century, workers who collectively tried to influence their wages and working conditions by trying to form unions, striking, and leading boycotts were subjected to these common-law doctrines. Recall from Chapter 4 that Philadelphia shoemakers formed the first permanent union in the United States in the 1790s. The Philadelphia shoemakers also have the dubious honor of marking the start of the **conspiracy doctrine** in labor relations as they were the first union convicted of being an illegal conspiracy in 1806. By joining together and refusing to work unless their terms were met, the shoemakers were viewed as conspiring to harm the community because shoe prices and unemployment would increase and profits would fall. *Individual* attempts to influence wages and working conditions are consistent with individual freedom, but in traditional economics thought that emphasizes free market competition, the *collective* aspect of union activity was viewed as particularly pernicious and harmful—and thus was viewed as an illegal conspiracy.[2] Note that conspiracy is a criminal offense so prosecution required a

---

[2] Charles O. Gregory and Harold A. Katz, *Labor and the Law,* 3rd ed. (New York: Norton, 1979). Benjamin J. Taylor and Fred Witney, *Labor Relations Law,* 5th ed. (Englewood Cliffs, NJ: Prentice Hall, 1987).

1806	Philadelphia shoemakers found guilty of conspiracy
1842	*Commonwealth v. Hunt*: unions are not illegal conspiracies per se, but their actions might be
1880s	Labor injunctions start to be used
1890	Sherman Antitrust Act bans trusts or monopolies
1895	*In re Debs*: Supreme Court affirms that labor injunctions are constitutional
1908	*Dunbury Hatters*: Supreme Court applied the Sherman Antitrust Act to labor unions
1914	Clayton Act updates the Sherman Antitrust Act
1917	*Hitchman Coal and Coke*: Supreme Court affirms that yellow dog contracts are legal
1932	Norris-LaGuardia Act restricts federal injunctions and ends enforceability of yellow dog contracts
1934	Amendments to the Railway Labor Act restrict company-dominated unions and create union recognition procedures
1935	*Schecter Poultry*: Supreme Court rules that the National Industrial Recovery Act is unconstitutional
1935	Wagner Act encourages and protects union activity
1937	*Jones and Laughlin*: Supreme Court upholds the constitutionality of the Wagner Act
1938	Fair Labor Standards Act establishes minimum wages and overtime premium
1947	Taft-Hartley Act tries to rebalance the Wagner Act
1959	Landrum-Griffin Act creates standards for internal union democracy
1960s	Rise of public sector labor law
1964	Civil Rights Act prohibits employment discrimination
1970	Occupational Safety and Health Act establishes standards for safe workplaces
1978	Civil Service Reform Act formalizes earlier policies on federal sector labor relations
1990	Americans with Disabilities Act prohibits discrimination against individuals with disabilities
1993	Family and Medical Leave Act provides 12 weeks of family and medical leave
2006	Pension Protection Act changes funding rules and disclosure requirements for traditional pension plans while also encouraging personal retirement savings

jury trial. In the early 1800s, jurors had to own property so the juries included employers and merchants, not workers.[3]

In 1842, the Massachusetts Supreme Court ruled in *Commonwealth v. Hunt* that while some union actions might be conspiratorial and therefore illegal, labor unions are not per se unlawful conspiracies. This case is viewed as a landmark in granting unions some element of legal legitimacy, and ultimately marks the beginning of the end for the application

[3] Taylor and Witney, *Labor Relations Law.*

of the conspiracy doctrine to labor relations.[4] Starting in the 1880s, the application of common law to labor relations was dominated by the use of **injunctions**—court-ordered restraints on action to prevent harm or damage to someone else.[5] One study estimates that at least 4,300 injunctions were issued between 1880 and 1930 with increased activity in each decade of that time period.[6] Injunctions were most frequently issued to stop or severely limit picketing during strikes, though there are also cases of prohibiting employees from striking or even from unionizing.

Central to the increased use of injunctions, and to their controversy, is that temporary restraining orders and injunctions are issued by judges without a full hearing. In theory, the purpose of these orders is to preserve the status quo until a full hearing with witnesses, evidence, and the like can be held. In practice, full hearings rarely occurred because the strike would be over before then. In fact, rather than maintaining the status quo, injunctions contributed towards breaking strikes in several ways: by turning public opinion away from strikers because of a perception that they were lawbreakers, by draining the union's financial and human resources through legal proceedings, and most importantly, by demoralizing strikers through fear and confusion.[7] As such, injunctions had powerful effects, and sweeping injunctions could be quickly issued without a full hearing based on questionable evidence and in response to a standard, generic request that was nearly identical to employers' submissions in hundreds of other injunction cases. In short, the potential for abuse was very high, and the injunction was a powerful antiunion legal weapon in the late 1800s and early 1900s.

The use of injunctions in labor disputes was rooted in the property rights area of common law. If a strike caused physical destruction of the employer's factory, machines, railroad cars, and the like, the link between property and an injunction to prevent irreparable harm is clear. But "property" in the U.S. common law tradition is significantly broader than tangible physical assets—intangibles such as the right to do business, to hire and fire employees, and interact with customers are also part of a corporation's property rights.[8] As such, any strike or boycott that threatened to interfere with the employer's business could potentially be challenged by an injunction. Note that if the law is applied equally, then judges should grant injunctions equally when a company's right to conduct business is threatened by the actions of either a union or another business. But in practice labor seems to have been treated more harshly—judges frequently refused to grant injunctions to restrain potentially harmful business actions yet often restrained union actions even though the same legal principles applied to both situations.[9]

In the 1900s, the use of labor injunctions was also applied to **yellow dog contracts**.[10] A yellow dog contract is a promise by a worker not to join or support a union; refusal to agree to such conditions meant either termination or not being hired. The courts viewed these contracts as legally enforceable, binding contracts because, in their view, employees entered into them voluntarily and were not economically coerced into agreement because

[4] Gregory and Katz, *Labor and the Law.* Taylor and Witney, *Labor Relations Law.*
[5] Felix Frankfurter and Nathan Greene, *The Labor Injunction* (New York: Macmillan, 1930). Gregory and Katz, *Labor and the Law.* Taylor and Witney, *Labor Relations Law.*
[6] William E. Forbath, *Law and the Shaping of the American Labor Movement* (Cambridge: Harvard University Press, 1991).
[7] Frankfurter and Greene, *The Labor Injunction.* Taylor and Witney, *Labor Relations Law.* Edwin E. Witte, *The Government in Labor Disputes* (New York: McGraw-Hill, 1932).
[8] Taylor and Witney, *Labor Relations Law.*
[9] William E. Forbath, "The New Deal Constitution in Exile," *Duke Law Journal* 51 (October 2001), pp. 165–222.
[10] Gregory and Katz, *Labor and the Law.* Joel Seidman, *The Yellow-Dog Contract* (Baltimore: Johns Hopkins University Press, 1932). Taylor and Witney, *Labor Relations Law.* Witte, *The Government in Labor Disputes.*

BOX 5.3

Court-ordered injunctions to protect employers' property rights and liberty to make yellow dog contracts were common in the first three decades of the 20th century.

Source: *The Striker* from *Minneapolis Labor Review,* October 23, 1936. www.minneapolisunions.org

THE STRIKER

of a lack of other jobs. As such, a union's attempt to unionize the employees could result in an injunction because an outside third party should not be allowed to try to break up valid contracts. If a union ignores such an injunction, there can be significant penalties for contempt of court, so yellow dog contracts were an effective antiunion device. Some states passed laws outlawing yellow dog contracts, but they were ruled unconstitutional because they violated the liberty to freely make contracts.[11] Putting all of these elements together, organized labor felt that employers and judges were abusing property rights and the Constitution to break strikes and unions (see Box 5.3).

THE BUSINESS LAW OF LABOR RELATIONS: UNIONS AS CORPORATIONS

Recall from Chapter 4 that corporations increased in size during the 19th century, and towards the end of the 1800s, some were huge monopolies or trusts that dominated entire industries. As a result, Congress passed the Sherman Antitrust Act in 1890 to outlaw monopolies and prevent the accompanying negative economic and social effects. Note that this is statutory law, not common law, and is premised on the neoclassical economics promotion of competition. This law remains in effect today and served as the basis for breaking up AT&T in the 1980s, for the U.S. Football League's suit against the NFL in the 1980s, and for lawsuits over breaking up Microsoft between 1997 and 2001. Violators can be punished by having to pay triple damages. Sections 1 and 2 are shown in Box 5.4—read the passages with the following question in mind: Does the Sherman Antitrust Act apply to labor unions?

The Sherman Antitrust Act does not explicitly include or exclude labor unions.[12] *If* a union is viewed as a "combination . . . in restraint of trade or commerce" or represents an attempt "to monopolize any part of the trade or commerce," then this Act applies to unions

---

[11] For example, *Adair v. U.S.,* 208 U.S. 161 (1908). *Coppage v. State of Kansas,* 236 U.S. 1 (1915).
[12] Taylor and Witney, *Labor Relations Law.*

The Sherman Antitrust Act (1890)

Box 5.4

Section 1. Every contract, combination in the form of trust or otherwise, or conspiracy, in restraint of trade or commerce among the several States, or with foreign nations, is declared to be illegal.

Section 2. Every person who shall monopolize, or attempt to monopolize, or combine or conspire with any other person or persons, to monopolize any part of the trade or commerce among the several States, or with foreign nations, shall be deemed guilty of a felony. . . .

as well as corporations. The question of whether the Sherman Antitrust Act applies to labor unions went all the way to the Supreme Court in the **Danbury Hatters case** (1908).[13] After a failed strike, the United Hatters of North America initiated a nationwide boycott of hats made by a Danbury, Connecticut, nonunion company in 1902.[14] In the *Danbury Hatters* case, the Supreme Court ruled that the union boycott violated the Sherman Antitrust Act and a later ruling held individual union members responsible for over $200,000 in damages.[15] In a different case, Samuel Gompers and the American Federation of Labor were found guilty of violating the Act by placing a stove company on its "We Don't Patronize" list in its magazine.[16] Free speech was forced to take a back seat to antitrust law.[17] Given that the neoclassical economics school of thought views labor unions as labor market monopolies, it is unsurprising that the Supreme Court ruled that the Sherman Antitrust Act applied to labor unions.

During this time period Congress was debating a follow-up act to clarify some of the weaknesses of the Sherman Antitrust Act. Organized labor lobbied very hard for this legislation to exempt unions from antitrust law.[18] This new law was the Clayton Act (1914) which Gompers hailed as a great victory for labor because it included the statement "the labor of a human being is not a commodity or article of commerce." But contrary to labor's proclamations, the Clayton Act simply gave unions the legal right to exist, it did not unambiguously exempt them from antitrust laws.[19] In fact, other aspects of the Clayton Act actually increased labor's burdens under antitrust laws because it became easier for employers to seek injunctions. As an illustration of how the courts could narrowly interpret the law to labor's disadvantage, the Clayton Act stated that

> no such restraining order or injunction shall prohibit any person or persons, whether singly or in concert, from terminating any relation of employment, or from ceasing to perform any work or labor, or from recommending, advising, or persuading others by peaceful means to do so (section 20).

This statement allows peaceful strikes and picketing. But the Supreme Court so narrowly construed this language that *any* picketing that involved even two people was *assumed* not to be peaceful, and could therefore be prevented with an injunction:

> We think that the strikers and their sympathizers engaged in the economic struggle should be limited to one representative for each point of ingress and egress in the plant or place of business and that all others be enjoined from congregating or loitering at the plant or in the

[13] *Loewe v. Lawlor,* 208 U.S. 274 (1908).
[14] Daniel R. Ernst, *Lawyers Against Labor: From Individual Rights to Corporate Liberalism* (Urbana: University of Illinois Press, 1995).
[15] *Lawlor v. Loewe,* 235 U.S. 522 (1915).
[16] *Gompers v. Bucks Stove and Range Company,* 221 U.S. 418 (1911).
[17] Taylor and Witney, *Labor Relations Law.*
[18] Ernst, *Lawyers Against Labor.*
[19] Taylor and Witney, *Labor Relations Law.*

neighboring streets by which access is had to the plant, that such representatives should have the right of observation, communication and persuasion, but with special admonition that their communication, arguments and appeals shall not be abusive, libelous or threatening, and that they shall not approach individuals together but singly, and shall not in their single efforts at communication or persuasion obstruct an unwilling listener by importunate following or dogging his steps. . . . The purpose should be to prevent the inevitable intimidation of the presence of groups of pickets, but to allow missionaries.[20]

In fact, even the word "picket" is too sinister; the court instead allowed single "missionaries."

Between 1890 and 1932, therefore, business law was applied to union activities in ways unfavorable to organized labor (as were common-law injunctions and the coercive force of the police, militia, and army). Perhaps the most important development in this era, however, is the emergence of the legal view that unions are legitimate but need to be controlled by legal regulation to make sure they are serving the public interest.[21] The 19th century philosophy of Gompers and the AFL was that unions were voluntary associations of workers, not incorporated organizations. As such, freedoms to unionize, strike, and boycott were rooted in individual liberty and the government should not interfere.[22] But the *Danbury Hatters* case reveals a risk—individual members were liable for damages—and the unwillingness of the courts to sanction all voluntary actions, such as nationwide boycotts. At this same time, the industrial relations school of thought developed its pluralist rather than individualist vision—corporations and unions are both formal institutions that should serve the public interest and counterbalance each other (recall Chapter 2). In this business law era, adherents to this school successfully laid the foundation for transforming the legal treatment of unions (and corporations) from voluntary associations beyond the state's control to legally sanctioned organizations with corresponding rights and obligations in a pluralist society—including serving the public interest and living up to their collective bargaining agreements. Republicans, too, wanted labor controlled so both they and the industrial relations school promoted responsible unionism.[23] This institutionalized rather than voluntaristic vision of labor unions—legally sanctioned, tightly regulated, and party to enforceable union contracts—would become even more firmly cemented in the labor laws of the 1930s and 1940s, and still dominates U.S. labor relations today.

KEEPING COURTS OUT OF LABOR RELATIONS: THE NORRIS-LAGUARDIA ACT

Because of the potential for abuse, especially with all of the power concentrated in a single judge's hands with no checks and balances, the labor injunction was widely despised not only by union leaders and members, but also by sympathetic lawmakers and reformers. In fact, the AFL supported at least one anti-injunction proposal in Congress in every year between 1895 and 1914.[24] Several events in the early 1920s brought anti-injunction legislation to the fore once again. Narrow Supreme Court rulings such as the case quoted above allowing only a sole missionary on the picket line deflated labor's faith in the Clayton Act.

---

[20] *American Steel Foundries v. Tri-City Central Trades Council*, 257 U.S. 184, 206-7 (1921).

[21] Ernst, *Lawyers Against Labor*. Ruth O'Brien, *Workers' Paradox: The Republican Origins of New Deal Labor Policy, 1886–1935* (Chapel Hill: The University of North Carolina Press, 1998).

[22] Clayton Sinyai, *Schools of Democracy: A Political History of the American Labor Movement* (Ithaca, NY: Cornell University Press, 2006).

[23] O'Brien, *Workers' Paradox*. Christopher L. Tomlins, *The State and the Unions: Labor Relations, Law, and the Organized Labor Movement, 1880–1960* (Cambridge: Cambridge University Press, 1985).

[24] Witte, *The Government in Labor Disputes*.

The Norris-LaGuardia Act (1932)   Box 5.5

Section 2. Whereas under prevailing economic conditions, developed with the aid of governmental authority for owners of property to organize in the corporate and other forms of organization, the individual unorganized worker is commonly helpless to exercise actual liberty of contract and to protect his freedom of labor, and thereby to obtain acceptable terms and condition of employment, wherefore, though he should be free to decline to associate with his fellows, it is necessary that he have full freedom of association, self-organization, and designation of representatives of his own choosing, to negotiate the terms and conditions of employment, and that he shall be free from the interference, restraint, and coercion of the employers of labor, or their agents, in the designation of such representatives or in self-organization or in other concerted activities for the purpose of collective bargaining or other mutual aid or protection; therefore, the following definitions of and limitations upon the jurisdiction and authority of the courts of the United States are enacted.

And in 1922, Judge James Wilkerson issued "one of the most notorious injunctions in American legal history" during a strike by railroad shop workers.[25] Not only did this expansive injunction make striking illegal regardless of how peaceful, it restricted free speech by banning any type of "persuasion" to convince workers to strike and even made it illegal to "annoy any employees of said railroad companies."[26]

Between 1924 and 1931, anti-injunction legislation failed to get enough votes in Congress. But with the onset of the Great Depression in the early 1930s, the political composition of Congress changed and in 1932, the **Norris-LaGuardia Act** was enacted.[27] The policy declaration for this Act is presented in Box 5.5. Note carefully the intellectual foundations: organized corporations (essentially individual shareholders that have unionized by pooling their resources and hiring experts to look out for their best interests) are significantly more powerful than unorganized individual workers, and this imbalance in bargaining power forces workers to accept substandard wages and working conditions (recall the conditions of the labor problem from Chapter 2). As such, in the industrial relations school of thought, workers should be able to unionize to equalize corporate power and thus obtain decent wages and working conditions. But how to promote this unionization? The last 20 words in Box 5.5 reveal the answer: the Norris-LaGuardia Act seeks to protect unionization efforts by limiting the "jurisdiction and authority of the courts of the United States." In other words, this Act seeks to remove the courts from labor relations.

More concretely, the Norris-LaGuardia Act forbids federal courts from issuing injunctions that interfere with strikes, payment of strike benefits, publicizing a dispute (as long as it is not fraudulent), peaceful picketing, and workers joining unions.[28] The conditions under which injunctions can be issued were also severely limited. As such, the popular name for this Act is the federal anti-injunction act. The Act further makes yellow dog contracts unenforceable and ends the criminal conspiracy doctrine of labor unions. Finally, by broadly defining permissible labor disputes, the Act effectively exempts labor unions from the Sherman Antitrust Act. The Norris-LaGuardia Act, therefore, marks the end of the

[25] Melvin Dubofsky, *The State and Labor in Modern America* (Chapel Hill: University of North Carolina Press, 1994), p. 95. Colin J. Davis, *Power at Odds: The 1922 National Railroad Shopmen's Strike* (Urbana: University of Illinois Press, 1997).
[26] Frankfurter and Greene, *The Labor Injunction,* p. 254.
[27] Dubofsky, *The State and Labor in Modern America.* Forbath, *Law and the Shaping of the American Labor Movement.*
[28] Gregory and Katz, *Labor and the Law.* Taylor and Witney, *Labor Relations Law.*

common law and business law eras in labor relations, and the start of the labor law era which still governs labor relations today. At the same time, it is important to emphasize that the Norris-LaGuardia Act simply tries to remove the courts from labor relations. The Act does not provide labor unions or workers with any new rights or enforcement mechanisms. These are the next steps toward today's labor law.

PRELUDES TO A NATIONAL POLICY: THE NATIONAL INDUSTRIAL RECOVERY ACT AND RAILWAY LABOR ACT

Franklin Delano Roosevelt was elected President of the United States several months after the passage of the Norris-LaGuardia Act in 1932. The Great Depression had been wreaking economic havoc for three years, and yet 1933 was to be even worse.[29] Widespread unemployment, poverty, homelessness, and hunger shook the country's faith in the wisdom of relying on laissez faire government policies to support the invisible hand of free markets to promote economic prosperity and security. Roosevelt promised "a new deal for the American people" which meant creating an *active* government role in promoting and guaranteeing the welfare of the population.[30] The industrial relations school of thought, not neoclassical economics or human resource management, underlies this New Deal philosophy (recall Chapter 2): because of imperfect markets, a conflict of interest in the employment relationship between workers and owners, and the importance of employees as human beings, government regulation and labor unions are important for balancing power between employees and employers which promotes economic stability and prosperity as well as fairness and democracy—efficiency, equity, and voice.[31]

But at the beginning of the Roosevelt presidency, the existing piece of labor legislation was passive, not active: the Norris-LaGuardia Act simply tried to remove the courts from labor relations by clamping down on the rampant use of labor injunctions by judges hostile to unions. The Norris-LaGuardia Act did not actively protect or promote union activity—it did little to combat the employers' open shop tactics described in Chapter 4: infiltrating unions with spies, using armed guards and professional strikebreaking agencies to break strikes, firing union activists, creating racial tension to divide workers, and using nonunion employee representation plans (company unions) to prevent the creation of independent labor unions. On the other hand, the most pressing issue in 1933 was not union resistance, it was massive unemployment. As such, one of the early New Deal initiatives was the National Industrial Recovery Act (NIRA) in 1933. The NIRA contained a public works program to create jobs and an ambitious framework for establishing industry codes of fair competition. Each industry was to create a code of marketing, production, pricing, and employment standards to prevent destructive competition and to stabilize the industry and promote economic recovery.[32] Over 500 industry codes were created, and

[29] David M. Kennedy, *Freedom from Fear: The American People in Depression and War, 1929–1945* (New York: Oxford University Press, 1999). Nelson Lichtenstein et al., *Who Built America? Working People and the Nation's Economy, Politics, Culture, and Society,* Volume 2 (New York: Worth Publishing, 2000).
[30] Cass R. Sunstein, *The Second Bill of Rights: FDR's Unfinished Revolution and Why We Need It More than Ever* (New York: Basic Books, 2004).
[31] John W. Budd, *Employment with a Human Face: Balancing Efficiency, Equity, and Voice* (Ithaca, NY: Cornell University Press, 2004). Thomas A. Kochan, Harry C. Katz, and Robert B. McKersie, *The Transformation of American Industrial Relations* (New York: Basic Books, 1986).
[32] Ellis W. Hawley, *New Deal and the Problem of Monopoly: A Study in Economic Ambivalence* (Princeton: Princeton University Press, 1966). Colin Gordon, *New Deals: Business, Labor, and Politics in America, 1920–1935* (New York: Cambridge University Press, 1994).

with respect to labor conditions, their greatest (or only?) success was eliminating child labor.[33]

Echoing the declaration of the Norris-LaGuardia Act, and over the opposition of business, section 7(a) of the NIRA also specified that each industry code of fair competition must contain the following:

> Employees shall have the right to organize and bargain collectively through representatives of their own choosing, and shall be free from the interference, restraint, and coercion of the employers of labor, or their agents, in the designation of such representatives or in self-organization or in other concerted activities for the purpose of collective bargaining or other mutual aid or protection.

This language emboldened workers to focus their pent-up frustration on unionizing, but the lack of specific enforcement provisions could not prevent continued employer opposition.[34] A National Labor Board was added to help settle labor disputes, but without specific enforcement powers it was ineffective.[35] The National Labor Board was comprised of representatives of labor, employers, and the government; the chair was Senator Robert Wagner of New York (see Box 5.6).

The ineffectiveness of the NIRA and the National Labor Board in achieving industrial peace was starkly demonstrated by the intense strikes of 1934 described in Chapter 4: the Toledo Auto-Lite strike, the Minneapolis Teamsters strike, and the San Francisco general strike. Employers also established sham company unions in an attempt to minimally comply with the NIRA without recognizing independent labor unions.[36] And the broader failure of the NIRA to restructure power relations between workers and employers, improve wages and working conditions, and reduce unemployment is graphically illustrated by the 170,000 Southern textile workers who went on strike in 1934.[37] In contrast to the New Deal's promise of justice for the working class and reduced unemployment, layoffs increased as the remaining textile mill hands were worked to exhaustion by the stretch-out (assigning more looms to each worker). And in spite of section 7(a), thousands of union supporters were blatantly fired. Since the NIRA's textile industry code was written and administered by the owners of the mills, workers struck out of extreme frustration and a sense of powerlessness. Various institutions failed the workers and the strike was a major defeat, but it highlighted the need for new legislation.

The NIRA's fate was sealed when it was ruled unconstitutional by the Supreme Court in May 1935 because of its overbroad regulation of economic activity.[38] But Senator Wagner

---

[33] Irving Bernstein, *A Caring Society: The New Deal, the Worker, and the Great Depression* (Boston: Houghton Mifflin, 1985).

[34] Irving Bernstein, *Turbulent Years: A History of the American Worker, 1933–1941* (Boston: Houghton Mifflin, 1970). Dubofsky, *The State and Labor in Modern America.* Janet Irons, *Testing the New Deal: The General Textile Strike of 1934 in the American South* (Urbana: University of Illinois Press, 2000). Stanley Vittoz, *New Deal Labor Policy and the American Industrial Economy* (Chapel Hill: University of North Carolina Press, 1987).

[35] Dubofsky, *The State and Labor in Modern America.* James A. Gross, *The Making of the National Labor Relations Board: A Study in Economics, Politics, and the Law* (Albany: State University of New York Press, 1974). Taylor and Witney, *Labor Relations Law.*

[36] Bruce E. Kaufman, "Accomplishments and Shortcomings of Nonunion Employee Representation in the Pre- Wagner Act Years: A Reassessment," in Bruce E. Kaufman and Daphne Gottlieb Taras (eds.), *Nonunion Employee Representation: History, Contemporary Practice, and Policy* (Armonk, NY: M. E. Sharpe, 2000), Chapter 2. Daniel Nelson, "The AFL and the Challenge of Company Unionism, 1915–1937," in Bruce E. Kaufman and Daphne Gottlieb Taras (eds.), *Nonunion Employee Representation: History, Contemporary Practice, and Policy* (Armonk, NY: M. E. Sharpe, 2000), Chapter 3. O'Brien, *Workers' Paradox.*

[37] Irons, *Testing the New Deal.*

[38] *Schecter Poultry Corp. v. United States,* 295 U.S. 495 (1935). Bernstein, *Turbulent Years.*

Senator Robert F. Wagner: Father of U.S. Labor Law

Box 5.6

The development of U.S. labor law is a complex story with many events and actors, but if there is a single father of U.S. labor law, it would arguably be Senator Robert F. Wagner. Wagner was born in Germany in 1877, the youngest of seven children, and emigrated to New York City with his family when he was nine years old. As the youngest, Wagner was able to attend public school while everyone else worked to make ends meet. He passed the entrance exams to the City College of New York and was able to attend tuition-free, and captain the football team, while being supported by his oldest brother. His brother then helped him finance law school and he graduated in 1900 with honors.

Wagner became involved in New York politics and was elected to the New York State Assembly in 1904, and to the New York State Senate in 1908. In the aftermath of the horrendous 1911 Triangle Shirt Waist factory fire in which over 100 seamstresses died when the fire exits (such as they were) were locked, Wagner was chairman of the New York State Factory Investigating Commission. As part of this commission, Wagner spent four years comprehensively touring factories all across the state and saw firsthand the deplorable conditions that many individuals worked and lived in—and was reminded of his own childhood poverty. In response, Wagner sponsored numerous state laws to improve fire safety, establish safety standards for machinery, limit child labor, and control tenement home work. This would continue to be the foundation for his thinking throughout his political career: the need for government to place checks and balances on economic markets to protect the unlucky and promote prosperity for all.

Wagner was a state judge in Manhattan between 1919 and 1926 and was reluctant to issue labor injunctions. In fact, he became the first judge to issue an injunction compelling an employer rather than a union to abide by the terms of the collective bargaining agreement it had agreed to. He was elected to the U.S. Senate in 1926 where he immediately continued to champion workers' issues: his first speech in the Senate was on the problem of unemployment. Both before and after his colleague from the New York State Senate, Franklin Delano Roosevelt, was elected president in 1932, Wagner advocated using public spending to create jobs to increase workers' purchasing power which would both improve their living standards and further boost the economy by giving them money to spend. As one of the most respected and influential senators of the time, Wagner was instrumental in shaping the National Industrial Recovery Act (NIRA) which contained a large public works component.

When strikes erupted after the NIRA's section 7(a) guaranteed workers the right to organize, Wagner was appointed to head the National Labor Board. It was this appointment that would shift Wagner's attention from public works projects to collective bargaining. As Wagner witnessed labor relations firsthand, he became convinced that the way to achieve economic prosperity and decent working and living standards was through equality of bargaining power between labor and management. Without this equality, companies were able to keep wages low which, Wagner believed, not only maintained substandard living conditions and threatened democracy by leaving workers voiceless and powerless, but also kept the economy depressed because of insufficient purchasing power. And Wagner witnessed how company-dominated unions were powerless to raise wages, and therefore not a worthy substitute for independent labor unions.

Wagner therefore continued to press for stronger labor relations legislation—in addition to strong public works programs, unemployment insurance, and a social security program—that would achieve industrial peace and economic prosperity that "rests upon freedom, not restraint; upon equality, not subservience; upon cooperation, not dominance." In 1935, Wagner successfully mustered sufficient support for the National Labor Relations Act, commonly and appropriately referred to as the Wagner Act which continues today as the basis of U.S. labor law. Wagner continued to champion the government's role in improving economic and social issues, including public housing and fair employment practices, until he was forced to retire from the Senate in 1949 due to health problems. His last speech on the Senate floor was, unsurprisingly, in objection to the Taft-Hartley Act that substantially modified his Wagner Act in 1947. He died in his old Manhattan neighborhood in 1953, but his legacy of progressive labor policies remains.

Source: J. Joseph Huthmacher, *Senator Robert F. Wagner and the Rise of Urban Liberalism* (New York: Atheneum, 1968). Quote is from p. 193.

had already been working for over a year to craft a stronger labor relations law that would have the teeth necessary to counter corporate resistance and thus improve U.S. capitalism by creating increased worker purchasing power, industrial peace, fairness, and industrial democracy through unionization.[39] Moreover, there were already the experiences of a major industry to draw on—the railroad industry. Recall from Chapter 4 that some of the most destructive strikes in labor history centered on the railroad industry, including the Great Uprising of 1877 and the Pullman Strike of 1894. As railroads were also the backbone of the entire economy, congressional efforts to achieve industrial peace specifically in this industry date back to the Arbitration Act of 1888.[40] A series of attempts to improve the regulation of railroad labor relations culminated in the passage of the **Railway Labor Act** in 1926.[41] Airlines were added to the Act in 1936 and both industries are still regulated by this Act today.[42]

The primary purpose of the Railway Labor Act is to avoid strikes and other forms of labor–management conflict which disrupt interstate commerce and weaken the economy. Thus, the Act protects the rights of *employees* to form labor unions, provides for government mediation of bargaining disputes, and establishes adjustment boards to resolve grievances. Consistent with American values, note the importance of individualism—unions specifically are not granted rights; rather, individual employees are granted the right to select a union to represent them if they so choose. Moreover, these rights are procedural (such as the right to choose a bargaining representative or to engage in collective bargaining) rather than substantive (such as a specific wage rate) which is also consistent with the individual liberty to make your own choices. As such, U.S. labor policy has important Republican origins.[43]

But how to make the individual choice about unionization effective? A major failure of the initial Railway Labor Act was failing to provide a mechanism for determining when an employer would have to recognize a union as the employees' representative.[44] In fact, while nonunion employee representation plans sometimes served workers' needs in other industries, the railroad industry extensively manipulated company unions to keep independent labor unions out—before and after the passage of the Railway Labor Act in 1926.[45] Consequently, the Act was substantially strengthened in 1934 by restricting company-dominated unions and by establishing the National Mediation Board to conduct secret ballot elections to determine whether a union would represent the employees. If a union wins support from a majority of the workers, the union is certified as the exclusive representative of all the workers in that craft or class and the company must bargain with that union. Senator Wagner's efforts at a national labor policy developed along very similar lines.

As a third prelude to a national labor relations law, there was also the philosophy of some union leaders like Sidney Hillman, leader of the Amalgamated Clothing Workers (ACW)

[39] Irving Bernstein, *The New Deal Collective Bargaining Policy* (Berkeley: University of California Press, 1950). Bernstein, *Turbulent Years*. O'Brien, *Workers' Paradox*. Vittoz, *New Deal Labor Policy and the American Industrial Economy*.
[40] Gerald G. Eggert, *Railroad Labor Disputes: The Beginnings of Federal Strike Policy* (Ann Arbor, University of Michigan Press, 1967).
[41] Charles M. Rehmus, "Evolution of Legislation Affecting Collective Bargaining in the Railroad and Airline Industries," in Charles M. Rehmus (ed.), *The Railway Labor Act at Fifty: Collective Bargaining in the Railroad and Airline Industries* (Washington, DC: National Mediation Board, 1976), Chapter I.
[42] Douglas L. Leslie (ed.), *The Railway Labor Act* (Washington, DC: Bureau of National Affairs, 1995).
[43] O'Brien, *Workers' Paradox*.
[44] Dana E. Eischen, "Representation Disputes and their Resolution in the Railroad and Airline Industries," in Charles M. Rehmus (ed.), *The Railway Labor Act at Fifty: Collective Bargaining in the Railroad and Airline Industries* (Washington, DC: National Mediation Board, 1976), Chapter II.
[45] Nelson, "The AFL and the Challenge of Company Unionism."

union. The garment industry was traditionally characterized by runaway, destructive competition—anyone could sew clothes as a subcontractor, so desperate workers undercut each other. Purchasing power was low, working and living conditions were lousy, and larger manufacturers were undercut. In the 1910s and 1920s, the ACW successfully brought stability and order to the garment industry through strong collective bargaining and an orderly grievance procedure. The militancy of small work groups was replaced by the discipline of "responsible" union leaders and union contracts. This was an early example of a union working cooperatively with employers and the government to create economic stability, increased purchasing power, and fair economic outcomes while also providing some form of employee voice. This experience proved to be a "dress rehearsal for the New Deal."[46]

SOLVING LABOR PROBLEMS: THE WAGNER ACT

When the NIRA was ruled unconstitutional in 1935, President Roosevelt finally endorsed Senator Wagner's efforts at creating stronger labor legislation, and relatively quickly, one of the most radical pieces of U.S. legislation was passed.[47] **The Wagner Act,** or the National Labor Relations Act (NLRA), was signed into law by President Roosevelt on July 5, 1935. This Act builds upon the previous legislative attempts to promote and protect workers' abilities to unionize in the private sector—if they so choose (see Box 5.7). **As amended in 1947 and 1959, the Wagner Act remains the centerpiece of today's U.S. labor law in the private sector.** In other words, corporate and union leaders in the 21st century must thoroughly understand the objectives and provisions of the Wagner Act. The Wagner Act declares:

> The inequality of bargaining power between employees who do not possess full freedom of association or actual liberty of contract and employers who are organized in the corporate or other forms of ownership association substantially burdens and affects the flow of commerce, and tends to aggravate recurrent business depressions, by depressing wage rates and the purchasing power of wage earners in industry and by preventing the stabilization of competitive wage rates and working conditions within and between industries. . . . It is declared to be the policy of the United States to eliminate the causes of certain substantial obstructions to the free flow of commerce and to mitigate and eliminate these obstructions when they have occurred by encouraging the practice and procedure of collective bargaining and by protecting the exercise by workers of full freedom of association, self-organization, and designation of representatives of their own choosing, for the purpose of negotiating the terms and conditions of their employment or other mutual aid or protection.

The Wagner Act is rooted in the industrial relations school's principle beliefs (see Box 5.8). From other intellectual perspectives, the Wagner Act is difficult to understand and is viewed as a harmful protection of monopoly labor (neoclassical economics), unnecessary support of adversarial third parties (human resource management), or an imperfect attempt to empower labor that inadequately challenges capital's power (critical industrial

---

[46] Steve Fraser, "Dress Rehearsal for the New Deal: Shop-Floor Insurgents, Political Elites, and Industrial Democracy in the Amalgamated Clothing Workers," in Michael H. Frisch and Daniel J. Walkowitz (eds.), *Working-Class America: Essays on Labor, Community, and American Society* (Urbana: University of Illinois Press, 1983), pp. 212–55.

[47] Bernstein, *The New Deal Collective Bargaining Policy.* Dubofsky, *The State and Labor in Modern America.*

Senator Wagner Presents His Labor Relations Bill to Congress (March 1935)

Box 5.7

"Mr. Chairman and members of the committee, the National Labor Relations bill does not present a single novel principle for the consideration of Congress. It is designed to further the equal balance of opportunity among all groups that we have always attempted to preserve despite the technological forces driving us toward excessive concentration of wealth and power.

. . .

I am not pleading for any special group. It is well recognized today that the failure to spread adequate purchasing power among the vast masses of the consuming public disrupts the continuity of business operations and causes everyone to suffer.

. . .

The government policy of fixing minimum wages and maximum hours is not a definitive solution. It is merely the foundation upon which can be built the mutual endeavors of a revived industry and a rehabilitated labor. This process of economic self-rule must fail unless every group is equally well represented. In order that the strong may not take advantage of the weak, every group must be equally strong. Not only is this common sense; but it is also in line with the philosophy of checks and balances that colors our political thinking. It is in accord with modern democratic concepts which reject the merger of all group interests into a totalitarian state.

. . .

Our alternatives are clear. If we allow section 7(a) [of the NIRA] to languish, we shall be confronted by intermittent periods of peace at the price of economic liberty, dangerous industrial warfare, and dire depressions. On the other hand, if we clarify that law and bolster it by adequate enforcement agencies, we shall do much to round out the program for a balanced economic system founded upon fair dealing and common business sense."

Source: National Labor Relations Board, *Legislative History of the National Labor Relations Act 1935* (Washington, DC: U.S. Government Printing Office, 1949), pp. 1408–13.

relations).[48] But in the industrial relations school, unequal bargaining power is at the heart of the labor problem and therefore equalizing bargaining power through unionization will solve these ills (recall Chapter 2). As such, one does not need to agree with the industrial relations school, but understanding its perspective is critical for understanding U.S. labor law and its goal of protecting union activity to strike a balance between efficiency, equity, and voice:

- **Efficiency:** increasing the purchasing power of workers, reducing disruptive strike activity, and largely maintaining employer's property rights[49]
- **Equity:** achieving fair employment conditions and protections against exploitation[50]
- **Voice:** providing democracy in the workplace.[51]

[48] Dan C. Heldman, James T. Bennett, and Manuel H. Johnson, *Deregulating Labor Relations* (Dallas: Fisher Institute, 1981). Karl E. Klare, "Judicial Deradicalization of the Wagner Act and the Origins of Modern Legal Consciousness, 1937–1941," *Minnesota Law Review* 62 (March 1978), pp. 265–339. David Montgomery, *Workers' Control in America: Studies in the History of Work, Technology, and Labor Struggles* (Cambridge: Cambridge University Press, 1979). Morgan O. Reynolds, *Power and Privilege: Labor Unions in America* (New York: Universe Books, 1984). Katherine V. W. Stone, "The Post-War Paradigm in American Labor Law," *Yale Law Journal* 90 (June 1981), pp. 1509–80. Tomlins, *The State and the Unions.* Leo Troy, *Beyond Unions and Collective Bargaining* (Armonk, NY: M. E. Sharpe, 1999).

[49] Bruce E. Kaufman, "Why the Wagner Act? Reestablishing Contact with Its Original Purpose," in David Lewin, Bruce E. Kaufman, and Donna Sockell (eds.), *Advances in Industrial and Labor Relations,* Volume 7 (Greenwich, CT: JAI Press, 1996), pp. 15–68. Kochan, Katz, and McKersie, *The Transformation of American Industrial Relations.*

[50] Bernstein, *The New Deal Collective Bargaining Policy.* William E. Forbath, "Caste, Class, and Equal Citizenship," *Michigan Law Review* 98 (October 1999), pp. 1–91.

[51] Craig Becker, "Democracy in the Workplace: Union Representation Elections and Federal Labor Law," *Minnesota Law Review* 77 (February 1993), pp. 495–603.

The Intellectual Foundations of the Wagner Act

Box 5.8

The Wagner Act (1935) is based on the fundamental assumptions of the industrial relations school of thought:

- Labor is more than a commodity,
- Labor and management are not economic or legal equals (in other words, there is an imbalance of bargaining power),
- There is at least some conflict of interest between workers and employers that cannot be resolved by unitarist management policies, but this is pluralist employment relationship conflict, not class-based or societal conflict, and
- Employee voice is important.

Source: John W. Budd, *Employment with a Human Face: Balancing Efficiency, Equity, and Voice* (Ithaca, NY: Cornell University Press, 2004).

In the later words of Senator Wagner, "The spirit and purpose of the law is to create a free and dignified workingman who had the economic strength to bargain collectively with a free and dignified employer in accordance with the methods of democracy."[52]

The full text of the Wagner Act can be found in an appendix at the end of this book and the central provisions are summarized in Box 5.9. The core of the Wagner Act, section 7, echoes the NIRA's section 7(a):

> Employees shall have the right to self-organization, to form, join, or assist labor organizations, to bargain collectively through representatives of their own choosing, and to engage in other concerted activities for the purpose of collective bargaining or other mutual aid or protection.

Note that this protects more than formal union activities like bargaining a contract—spontaneous acts by small groups of nonunion employees can also be protected by section 7 (see Box 5.10). The remainder of the Wagner Act essentially tries to make section 7 a reality rather than hollow words. As such, the Act builds off of earlier legislative failures and shortcomings in four important ways:

- Granting a certified, majority-status union the right to be the exclusive representative of the relevant employees,
- Specifying a certification procedure for establishing whether a majority of workers wants union representation,
- Defining illegal employer actions that undermine section 7, and
- Creating an independent agency, the National Labor Relations Board (NLRB), to enforce the Act.

Let's consider each of these in turn.

First, the Wagner Act explicitly establishes **exclusive representation** when a union has the support of a majority of a group of employees. In other words, with majority support a union is the *only* representative of that group of workers—there cannot be another union or a company union representing some of the employees in the group. Exclusive representation is unique to North America and stems from Senator Wagner's experience under the NIRA which did not mandate exclusive representation.[53] Without exclusivity, companies

---

[52] Leon H. Keyserling, "Why the Wagner Act?" in Louis G. Silverberg (ed.), *The Wagner Act: After Ten Years* (Washington, DC: Bureau of National Affairs, 1945), pp. 5–33 at 31.
[53] Gross, *The Making of the National Labor Relations Board.* O'Brien, *Workers' Paradox.*

Box 5.9

The Central Provisions of the Wagner Act (1935)

Sections 3–6	Creates the National Labor Relations Board (NLRB) to resolve representation questions and adjudicate unfair labor practices
Section 7	Guarantees employees the right to form unions, bargain collectively, and engage in other concerted activities for mutual aid and protection
Section 8	Defines five employer unfair labor practices:

(1) To interfere with, restrain, or coerce employees in the exercise of the rights guaranteed in section 7

(2) To dominate or interfere with the formation or administration of any labor organization or contribute financial or other support to it

(3) By discrimination in regard to hire or tenure of employment or any term or condition of employment to encourage or discourage membership in any labor organization

(4) To discharge or otherwise discriminate against an employee because he has filed charges or given testimony under this Act

(5) To refuse to bargain collectively with the representatives of his employees

Section 9	Establishes exclusive representation for unions that have majority support and grants them rights of collective bargaining over wages, hours of employment, and other conditions of employment. Empowers the NLRB to define appropriate bargaining units and to determine majority support via a secret ballot election or other suitable means.

Note: The full text is in an appendix.

established company unions even when a majority of employees wanted an independent union, and then manipulated the company unions to weaken the independent unions. Exclusive representation was established by the Wagner Act to prevent this problem. Note that any cutoff could have been specified for determining when a union becomes the exclusive representative—when 40 percent, 60 percent, 80 percent, etc., of the workers are in favor. But using a simple majority as the decision rule is the most consistent with democracy and is therefore what the Wagner Act specifies.

Establishing the principle of exclusive representation with majority support next begs the question of how to determine majority support, and therefore union recognition, in practice. Recall from labor history that before 1935 the primary method for forcing employers to recognize unions was by striking. In fact, the major strikes in 1934 were over recognition, so this issue was fresh in Senator Wagner's mind. These strikes were very disruptive to the economy as well as workers' lives and the Wagner Act sought to help both by replacing these strikes with an orderly procedure. What's the natural method in a democratic society for determining what a majority of individuals prefer? A secret ballot vote. So the Wagner Act allows for secret ballot elections to determine whether a majority of workers support a specific union. Technically, the Wagner Act allowed secret ballot elections or "any other suitable method," but elections are now the dominant method and this will be the focus of Chapter 7 on union organizing. If a union is certified as the exclusive representative of a group of workers after a secret ballot election, then the employer must bargain with that union over wages, hours, and other terms and conditions of employment (Chapter 8). In the absence of a certified exclusive representative with majority support, the obligation to bargain with

"Employees shall have the right to self-organization, to form, join, or assist labor organizations, to bargain collectively through representatives of their own choosing, and to engage in other concerted activities for the purpose of collective bargaining or other mutual aid or protection" (The Wagner Act, section 7).

Indicate whether each scenario is protected activity under section 7.

	Protected, or Not?
1. Trying to form a union to negotiate wages and working conditions.	_____
2. Going on strike and peacefully picketing for improved benefits.	_____
3. Destroying company property while striking for improved benefits.	_____
4. Discussing wages with your co-workers.	_____
5. Individually meeting with your supervisor to ask for improved lighting for you and two co-workers.	_____
6. Circulating a flyer among co-workers to build support for a plan for employees to buy the company.	_____
7. In a nonunion workplace, joining with several co-workers and refusing to work until the company provides a paid lunch break.	_____
8. In a nonunion workplace, joining with several co-workers and refusing to work overtime until the company increases the overtime pay, but continuing to do all other duties.	_____
9. Requesting that a co-worker be present when you think you will be disciplined.	_____
10. Sending an e-mail message to co-workers pointing out the disadvantages of your employer's new vacation plan.	_____
11. Distributing obscene or malicious cartoons to protest a supervisor's actions.	_____
12. Refusing to work under conditions that you reasonably believe pose a high risk of death or serious injury.	_____

Answers are at the end of the chapter.

a union that represents a minority of the workers has interestingly and perhaps inappropriately faded away (see Box 5.11).[54]

In order to make the organizing and bargaining processes effective, the third major element of the Wagner Act is to specify illegal employer actions which are called **unfair labor practices** (see Box 5.12). The first unfair labor practice [section 8(a)(1)] prohibits employers from interfering, restraining, or coercing employees who are exercising their section 7 rights. Section 8(a)(1) is the "universal enforcer" because it covers all employer violations of employee rights.[55] As a result, this is the only unfair labor practice that is technically necessary to enforce the Wagner Act, but four other unfair labor practices were included to reinforce the illegality of four of the most problematic issues at the time.[56] Employers are explicitly reminded that they cannot fire or otherwise discriminate against employees who are trying to form a union [section 8(a)(3)]. It is also reinforced that it is illegal for companies to dominate a labor organization [8(a)(2)]—this bans company unions which Senator Wagner experienced as being sham unions that management manipulated to prevent workers from forming legitimate, independent unions.[57] Company unions

[54] Charles J. Morris, *The Blue Eagle at Work: Reclaiming Democratic Rights in the American Workplace* (Ithaca, NY: Cornell University Press, 2005).
[55] Morris, *The Blue Eagle at Work*, p. 101.
[56] Morris, *The Blue Eagle at Work*.
[57] Samuel Estreicher, "Nonunion Employee Representation: A Legal/Policy Perspective," in Bruce E. Kaufman and Daphne Gottlieb Taras (eds.), *Nonunion Employee Representation: History, Contemporary Practice, and Policy* (Armonk, NY: M. E. Sharpe, 2000), Chapter 9.

Since the 1940s, U.S. labor relations has emphasized exclusive representation with majority support. But consider a situation in which some workers, but less than 50 percent, want a union to collectively bargain for them. Around the time of the Wagner Act in the mid-1930s, it was not uncommon for companies to bargain with a union in this situation and the resulting contract would apply only to union members. In fact, the famous 1937 General Motors sit-down strike discussed in Chapter 4 resulted in a members-only agreement because the UAW did not have majority support. In this situation, the union is called a minority union or a nonmajority union because it represents only a minority of the workers, not a majority. It's clear from section 7 of the Wagner Act that workers have the right to engage in this type of concerted activity, but does a company have an obligation to bargain with a nonmajority union when there is no majority union present?

It has recently been argued that yes, a company must bargain with a nonmajority union—failure to do so interferes with an employee's section 7 rights and is therefore a section 8(a)(1) unfair labor practice. Section 8(a)(5) was added late in the drafting of the Wagner Act and was intended to make it explicit that a company must treat a union with majority support as the exclusive representative because there was significant employer resistance to exclusive representation (employers wanted to be able to continue to use company unions even when a majority of workers supported an independent union). But section 8(a)(5) was not intended to limit employers' bargaining obligation to cases of majority support.

Perhaps ironically, in the late 1930s and early 1940s, unions were so successful in winning majority support that the use of nonmajority unionism faded away. And with it, the legal doctrine that employers must bargain with nonmajority unions also faded from memory. As a result, without majority support a union today is considered a nonentity in the workplace and U.S. labor relations has become in essence an all or nothing affair—a union is seen as either entitled to represent all of the employees, or none. But nonmajority unionism can provide representation groups of workers who would otherwise be denied the opportunity, and can also provide the means for unions to demonstrate their effectiveness and generate majority support. Whether unions will revive their use of nonmajority unionism, and whether the legal system will support a return to the legislative intent of the Wagner Act and obligate employers to bargain with nonmajority unions (again, only in the absence of a union with majority support), remains to be seen.

Source: Charles J. Morris, *The Blue Eagle at Work: Reclaiming Democratic Rights in the American Workplace* (Ithaca, NY: Cornell University Press, 2005).

were also perceived as weak and thus undermined Senator Wagner's objective of increasing employee bargaining power to prevent destructive competition, increase workers' purchasing power, and therefore stimulate the economy.[58] This unfair labor practice received renewed attention in the 1990s as it potentially hinders corporate employee involvement initiatives; this issue will be addressed in detail in Chapter 11. Last, in the 1930s, some employers would agree to bargain with a union that had majority support, but would not recognize the union as the exclusive representative of all of the employees (in other words, the employer would only agree to apply the resulting contractual terms to union members). To promote stable collective bargaining arrangements, section 8(a)(5) explicitly reminds employers that when a union has majority support, the employer must recognize the union as the exclusive representative of *all* employees and bargain with it accordingly.[59] In short, it is an unfair labor practice for an employer to refuse to bargain with a certified, majority union as the exclusive representative; this will be discussed in Chapter 8.

But how to conduct the secret ballot elections and enforce the unfair labor practices? The final component of the Wagner Act is the creation of the **National Labor Relations**

[58] Bruce E. Kaufman, "The Case for the Company Union," *Labor History* 41 (August 2000), pp. 321–50.
[59] Morris, *The Blue Eagle at Work*.

Examples of Employer Unfair Labor Practices

Box 5.12

Section 8(a)(1)—interference, restraint, or coercion that undermines section 7

- Circulating an antiunion petition
- Surveillance of union activities beyond what's necessary for security of company property
- Threatening employees with job loss or demotion or physical harm if they support a union
- Promising benefits such as wage increases if employees reject a union
- Interrogating employees about their union sympathies
- Preventing employees from talking about a union or wearing union buttons when it doesn't interfere with their work duties or customers
- Note: All of the examples provided below for sections 8(a)(2)–8(a)(5) also violate section 8(a)(1)

Section 8(a)(2)—domination of a labor organization (company union ban)

- Initiating the formation of a union
- Providing financial support to a union
- Creating a nonunion employee representation plan
- Creating a labor–management committee that discusses wages and working conditions with some give-and-take with management, but in which managers retain decision-making power and control the committee's agenda, structure, and continued existence

Section 8(a)(3)—discrimination to encourage or discourage union membership

- Firing a union supporter or someone trying to form a union

- Transferring a union supporter to a less desirable job or promoting a union opponent to a better job
- Firing a worker for contacting a union organizer
- Refusing to hire someone because of past union sympathies or membership
- Closing part of a business for antiunion reasons

Section 8(a)(4)—discrimination for filing charges or testifying under the NLRA

- Firing a worker who files an unfair labor practice charge

Section 8(a)(5)—refusal to bargain with a certified union

- Refusing to meet with a certified union
- Failing to bargain in good faith, that is, without a sincere attempt to reach agreement
- Never making counterproposals
- Changing wages, benefits, or other terms of employment without negotiating first
- Dealing directly with individual employees to circumvent the union
- Refusing to provide relevant information
- Refusing to bargain with a certified union as the exclusive representative of *all* bargaining unit employees (in other words, insisting on bargaining over terms that will only apply to union members)

Board (NLRB).[60] The NLRB is an independent federal agency devoted to conducting representation elections and adjudicating unfair labor practices. The NLRB now has two parts—i) a General Counsel's office that conducts representation elections and investigates and prosecutes unfair labor practices, and ii) a five-member board of presidential appointees (also called the National Labor Relations Board, or the Board for short) that hears and decides cases. If a group of workers or a union wants an employer to recognize

[60] Gross, The Making of the National Labor Relations Board. National Labor Relations Board, *NLRB: The First 50 Years* (Washington, DC: 1985).

and bargain with a union, they generally approach a regional office of the NLRB's General Counsel's office to manage the process and determine—usually through a secret ballot vote—whether the union has majority support. This process will be discussed in detail in Chapter 7.

If someone believes an unfair labor practice has occurred, they can file charges with an NLRB regional office. If the regional office finds merit in the charge, a hearing will be held before an administrative law judge in which evidence can be presented and witnesses examined and cross-examined. The administrative law judge issues a formal decision that can be appealed by the General Counsel to the five-member Board. Violators can be ordered to cease and desist from their illegal activities and, when relevant, to offer reinstatement with back pay to illegally discharged workers. The NLRB can seek enforcement of its rulings in federal court. While the NLRB is criticized by some as weak—for example, punitive damages or fines are not allowed—this is a significantly stronger enforcement mechanism than appeared in previous labor laws. The NLRB currently receives approximately 30,000 unfair labor practice allegations and requests for over 5,000 representation elections each year.[61]

The Wagner Act was immediately very controversial.[62] Strong laissez faire proponents attacked the Act as greatly extending the federal government's reach into private affairs and therefore as interfering with economic efficiency as well as individual and corporate liberty. In contrast, New Deal reformers felt that the overall structure of private property and economic exchange was maintained: the Wagner Act "did not dictate the terms and conditions of employment, but rather endorsed a process by which the parties could shape their own substantive contract terms."[63] As such, the Act protects worker choice regarding unionization and provides an affirmative obligation for employers to bargain with a majority union, but does not require agreement or specific outcomes. Senator Wagner further argued that his Act increased rather than decreased individual freedom by granting workers the same opportunities to join together as enjoyed by employers (see Box 5.13). Some business leaders even hoped that unions could help stabilize their industries by preventing marginal employers from undercutting wage rates and labor standards and by increasing workers' purchasing power.[64]

Nevertheless, many employers openly flaunted the new law.[65] Recall from Chapter 4 that the historic General Motors sit-down strike and Memorial Day Massacre occurred in 1937—*after* the passage of the Wagner Act. In fact, nearly two-thirds of the tremendous number of strikes in 1937 were exactly the type the Act sought to prevent: union recognition strikes.[66] On the legal front, the new NLRB spent its first two years defending its existence.[67] Federal judges issued injunctions against the NLRB, and most strikingly, two months after the passage of the Wagner Act, conservative lawyers attached to the American Liberty League declared that the Wagner Act was unconstitutional.[68] The American

---

[61] National Labor Relations Board, *Seventieth Annual Report of the Relations Board* (Washington, DC: Government Printing Office, 2005)

[62] Bernstein, *Turbulent Years*. Dubofsky, *The State and Labor in Modern America*. Gross, *The Making of the National Labor Relations Board*.

[63] Kochan, Katz, and McKerise, *The Transformation of American Industrial Relations*, P. 24.

[64] Gordon, *New Deals*.

[65] Jerold S. Auerbach, *Labor and Liberty: The LaFollette Committee and the New Deal* (Indianapolis: Bobbs-Merrill, 1966). Dubofsky, *The State and Labor in Modern America*.

[66] James B. Atleson, *Labor and the Wartime State: Labor Relations and Law During World War II* (Urbana: University of Illinois Press, 1998).

[67] Gross, *The Making of the National Labor Relations Board*. Taylor and Witney, *Labor Relations Law*.

[68] Bernstein, *Turbulent Years*. Gross, *The Making of the National Labor Relations Board*. National Lawyers Committee of the American Liberty League, *Report on the Constitutionality of the National Labor Relations Act* (September 5, 1935).

The Wagner Act Hearings: Senator Wagner Questions an Employers' Association Representative (1934)

Box 5.13

MR. TORREY (of the Employers' Association of North Jersey). On behalf of the managements of 200 manufacturing businesses located in the vicinity of Newark, N.J., we are opposing the measure before this committee, because we believe it to be inequitable, economically unsound, pregnant with class antagonism, and therefore contrary to sound public policy.

. . .

SENATOR WAGNER. You think that most men that join labor organizations, join because somebody clubs them into joining a labor organization, and if it wasn't for that, you think men would much prefer, as employees, to deal individually, although they may be one in 10,000, with the employer? That is your idea, isn't it?

MR. TORREY. That is my personal conviction.

. . .

SENATOR WAGNER. Well, why do you find it necessary to organize your manufacturers into one organization? Why didn't you act individually? Why don't you act individually?

MR. TORREY. I did not organize them, sir.

SENATOR WAGNER. Well, they are organized.

MR. TORREY. Why they decided to organize, I cannot tell you, except that they felt it advisable to have a common ground on which they could meet for discussion, interchange of opinion, information with regard to any common problems, affecting all of the individuals involved.

SENATOR WAGNER. Don't you think workers have an equal interest?

. . .

MR. TORREY. . . . All [of this bill's] provisions tend to array employees as a class against employers as a class. This is an essential characteristic of the bill. It is directly counter to the spirit of cooperation, toleration, and national unity.

SENATOR WAGNER. May I ask you there, the organization of employers into an association—does that have the effect of arraying class against class, or is it only the organization of the workers causes this array of class against class?

MR. TORREY. It depends.

SENATOR WAGNER. In other words, you think that one side ought to be permitted to organize but not the other; isn't that it?

. . .

MR. TORREY. . . . It is our opinion that an effect, practical effect—psychological effect, if you will, of the enactment of this bill, would be to extend to a very large extent the labor monopoly under the present American Federation of Labor Unions.

SENATOR WAGNER. Well, I hear that statement made, and I do not know where you got such a notion, when all that we are attempting to do is make the worker a free man, so that he may be permitted to bargain collectively, even though he may encounter an employer, such as you have referred to, who does not believe in labor organizations and won't deal with any labor organizations, or any organization of workers, call it what you will. There isn't anything in here at all that does any more than give the worker freedom.

Source: National Labor Relations Board, *Legislative History of the National Labor Relations Act 1935* (Washington, DC: U.S. Government Printing Office, 1949), pp. 512–16.

Liberty League was bankrolled by major corporations and in that period of misinformation and resistance, this pronouncement fueled the legal attacks on the NLRB as well as continued opposition to unions and the new law. Not until the Supreme Court's 1937 ruling in ***NLRB v. Jones and Laughlin Steel Corp.*** which declared the Act constitutional could the NLRB wholeheartedly attend to the business of enforcing the nation's new labor policy (see Box 5.14).[69]

[69] *NLRB v. Jones and Laughlin Steel Corporation*, 301 U.S. 1 (1937).

The Wagner Act radically increased Congressional regulation of what had been private affairs, and hence was very controversial. A conservative group of lawyers declared the Act unconstitutional and in spite of their lack of jurisdiction, this declaration summed up the opinion of many. In fact, some believe that some lawmakers voted for the Act under the assumption that it would be struck down by the Supreme Court as unconstitutional. There were two major elements to why many believed Congress was exceeding its powers granted by the U.S. Constitution.

First, remember that Congress can only regulate specific things such as war, immigration, banking, and interstate and foreign commerce. Where's the power to regulate labor relations? Congress based its power to govern labor unions and collective bargaining on its constitutional authority to regulate interstate commerce, but this justification was not widely accepted in 1935. Railroads were clearly part of interstate commerce, but the Wagner Act applied to manufacturing, coal mining, retail stores, and other businesses that operated in fixed locations. Many argued that a strike at a single manufacturing facility disrupted *production*, but not interstate *commerce*. Earlier Supreme Court decisions rejected a connection between labor relations and interstate commerce, except for railroads.

Second, the Constitution's fifth amendment guarantees that no one will "be deprived of life, liberty, or property, without due process of law." It was widely argued that regulating labor relations deprived companies and individuals of their liberty and property rights without due process—employers cannot establish company unions or fire workers because of union status, for example, and unionized employees have to work at the terms negotiated by the union, not themselves. In fact, numerous Supreme Court rulings in the first three decades of the 20th century struck down various employment laws on this basis of violating the liberty to contract.

With so much opposition to the Wagner Act and the NLRB, it wasn't hard to find a test case for the courts to decide these legal questions. In 1936, the NLRB ruled that steel manufacturer Jones and Laughlin was guilty of violating the Act by firing employees for trying to form a union. Jones and Laughlin fought the case by arguing that they did not affect interstate commerce and thus were not covered by the Act. A federal appeals court agreed. However, the Supreme Court agreed to hear the case. By a slim 5–4 vote, the Supreme Court upheld the constitutionality of the Wagner Act in its 1937 decision in *NLRB v. Jones and Laughlin Steel Corp.* by ruling that strikes in manufacturing affected interstate commerce and that employers were not denied due

process of law. In the shadow of Roosevelt's court-packing plan and the sit-down strikes—two very serious crises—the Court indicated that in an advanced, integrated economy, strikes in one establishment affect businesses in other states. With respect to due process, the Court followed an earlier Railway Labor Act ruling and stated that the Act did not interfere with employers' normal ability to hire and fire employees; rather, the target of the Act is protecting free employee choice of bargaining representatives.

This is a landmark decision which not only upheld the constitutionality of the Wagner Act, thus giving legitimacy to the U.S. system of labor relations, but also provided the legal foundation for additional government laws pertaining to employment such as minimum wage and civil rights legislation.

Sources: Richard C. Cortner, *The Jones & Laughlin Case* (New York, Knopf, 1970). James A. Gross, *The Making of the National Labor Relations Board: A Study in Economics, Politics, and the Law* (Albany: State University of New York Press, 1974). Benjamin J. Taylor and Fred Witney, *Labor Relations Law*, 5th ed. (Englewood Cliffs, NJ: Prentice Hall, 1987).

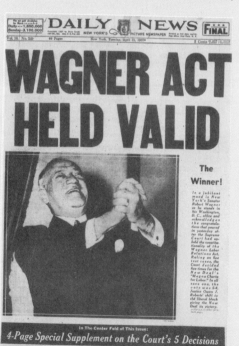

Senator Wagner Celebrating the Supreme Court's Upholding of the Constitutionality of the Wagner Act (April 1937)

Source: Front Cover of the *New York Daily News* (April 13, 1937)

REBALANCING THE SYSTEM: THE TAFT-HARTLEY ACT

While the Wagner Act / National Labor Relations Act (NLRA) grew out of the experience of earlier laws, it was a major increase in government intervention in economic and social affairs and continued to be controversial even after its constitutionality was affirmed: "Scarcely had the ink dried on the President's signature establishing the NLRA as part of our national policy when bills to repeal or amend the Act began pouring into the congressional mills."[70] In the decade after the Wagner Act, union membership nearly quadrupled from four million to more than 15 million and many felt that unions were too strong, lacked a sense of public responsibility, were controlled by communists or corrupt union bosses, and should be bound by the same responsibilities and restrictions that employers faced under the Wagner Act.[71] Remember, the Wagner Act only specified employer unfair labor practices—unions were not restricted in any way. The pressures for reforming (or discarding) the Wagner Act boiled over with the Great Strike Wave of 1945–46 that followed the end of World War II. Recall from Chapter 4 that for the 12 months beginning in August 1945, 4,600 strikes occurred involving 4.9 million workers and resulted in nearly 120 million worker-days lost.[72] There were large strikes in autos, steel, coal, rail, oil refining, longshoring, meat packing, and electrical products. This level of strike activity surpasses any other year in U.S. history, and magnified the perceived need to bring unions under control.

A popular framework for thinking about labor law is to consider a pendulum which can range from high bargaining power for labor on one side to high bargaining power for companies on the other side (recall Box 2.5). If the pendulum is too far to one side, either labor or management will have too much power which will be bad for society as a whole. For much of the 19th and early 20th centuries, the absence of specific laws pertaining to collective bargaining left labor relations subject to common-law and business-law rulings shaped by classical economic beliefs on the importance of free markets. The pendulum favored employers—injunctions were issued, strikes were broken, union leaders jailed, and union supporters blacklisted. The Wagner Act in 1935 sought to move the pendulum to the middle of the power spectrum by restraining employers' abilities to repress unionization. However, by 1946 many believed that the Wagner Act had overcorrected the earlier problems: the pendulum swung all the way through the middle and too far towards labor. Proposals for reform sought to correct the perceived excesses of the Wagner Act to move the pendulum to the middle of the spectrum.[73]

Unlike today when labor issues are rarely on the national agenda, labor relations issues in the 1930s and 1940s were a big deal. In fact, 17 bills to reform labor law were introduced on the opening day of Congress in 1947—the first Congress controlled by Republicans since 1930 (see Box 5.15).[74] The proposal that was ultimately enacted later in 1947 was the **Taft-Hartley Act,** also known as the Labor Management Relations Act. The Taft-Hartley Act significantly amends the Wagner Act. These Acts are still the basis of U.S. labor law and together are often referred to as the National Labor Relations Act (NLRA). While the opening of the Wagner Act emphasizes inequalities between labor and management and therefore the need to promote collective bargaining, the Taft-Hartley Act, in contrast, declares:

> Industrial strife . . . can be avoided or substantially minimized if employers, employees, and labor organizations each recognize under law one another's legitimate rights in their relations

---

[70] Harry A. Millis and Emily Clark Brown, *From the Wagner Act to Taft-Hartley: A Study of National Labor Policy and Labor Relations* (Chicago: University of Chicago Press, 1950), p. 332.

[71] Millis and Brown, *From the Wagner Act to Taft-Hartley.*

[72] Philip Taft, *Organized Labor in American History* (New York: Harper and Row, 1964), p. 567.

[73] Fred A. Hartley, *Our New National Labor Policy: The Taft-Hartley Act and the Next Steps* (New York: Funk and Wagnalls, 1948).

[74] Millis and Brown, *From the Wagner Act to Taft-Hartley.*

"During the last few years, the effects of industrial strife have at times brought our country to the brink of general economic paralysis. Employees have suffered, employers have suffered—and above all, the public has suffered.

. . .

During the 6 years preceding the enactment of the National Industrial Recovery Act of 1933, the United States had an average of 753 strikes a year, involving an average of 297,000 workers; during the next 6 years 2,541 strikes per year involving an average of 1,181,000 workers; and during the next 5 years—that is, through 1944—3,514 strikes a year involving an average of 1,508,000 workers.

In 1945 approximately 38,000,000 man-days of labor were lost as a result of strikes. And that total was trebled in 1946, when there were 116,000,000 man-days lost and the number of strikes hit a new high of 4,985. The resulting loss in national wealth is staggering.

. . .

For the last 14 years, as a result of labor laws ill-conceived and disastrously executed, the American workingman has been deprived of his dignity as an individual. He has been cajoled, coerced, intimidated, and on many occasions beaten up, in the name of the splendid aims set forth in section 1 of the National Labor Relations Act. His whole economic life has been subject to the complete domination and control of unregulated [labor union] monopolists. . . . He has been forced into labor organizations against his will. . . . He has been prohibited from expressing his own mind on public issues. He has been denied any voice in arranging the terms of his own employment. He has frequently against his will been called out on strikes. . . . In many cases his economic life has been ruled by Communists and other subversive influences.

. . .

The employer's plight has likewise not been happy. He has witnessed the productive efficiency in his plants sink to alarmingly low levels. He has been required to employ or reinstate individuals who have destroyed his property and assaulted other employees. . . . He has seen the loyalty of his supervisors undermined by the compulsory unionism imposed upon them by the National Labor Relations Board.

. . .

The bill attacks the problem in a comprehensive—not in a piecemeal—fashion. It is neither drastic, oppressive, nor punitive. . . . It does not take away any rights guaranteed by the existing National Labor Relations Act. It does, however, go to the root of the evils and provides a fair, workable, and long-overdue solution to the problem."

Source: National Labor Relations Board, *Legislative History of the Labor Management Relations Act, 1947* (Washington, DC: U.S. Government Printing Office, 1948), pp. 294–96.

with each other, and above all recognize under law that neither party has any right in its relations with any other to engage in acts or practices which jeopardize the public health, safety, or interest. It is the purpose and policy of this Act . . . to prescribe the legitimate rights of both employees and employers . . . , to provide orderly and peaceful procedures for preventing the interference by either with the legitimate rights of the other, to protect the rights of individual employees in their relations with labor organizations . . . , and to protect the rights of the public in connection with labor disputes affecting commerce.

To accomplish these objectives, the Taft-Hartley Act amends and adds to the Wagner Act in diverse and far-reaching ways; the full text is in the appendix, and the major provisions are summarized in Box 5.16. These changes can be usefully divided into four categories:

- Restrictions on union actions
- Enhanced rights of individuals
- Explicit rights of employers
- Revised dispute resolution procedure.[75]

[75] Taylor and Witney, *Labor Relations Law.*

The Central Changes of the Taft-Hartley Act (1947)

Box 5.16

Section 2	Excludes supervisors and independent contractors
Sections 3–6	Expands and restructures the National Labor Relations Board (NLRB)
Section 7	Guarantees employees the right to refrain from forming unions, bargaining collectively, and engaging in other concerted activities
Section 8(a)	Modifies the third employer unfair labor practice to outlaw the closed shop
Section 8(b)	Defines six union unfair labor practices:

(1) To restrain or coerce employees in the exercise of the rights guaranteed in section 7

(2) To cause an employer to discriminate against employees except for failure to pay required union dues

(3) To refuse to bargain collectively with the employer

(4) To engage in secondary boycotts and certain forms of strikes and picketing

(5) To require excessive or discriminatory membership fees

(6) To force an employer to pay for services not performed (featherbedding)

[(7) is added in 1959: To picket an employer to demand recognition except in limited circumstances]

Section 8(c)	Grants employers the right to express views and opinions except for threats and promises (employer free speech)
Section 8(d)	Defines the bargaining obligation as meeting in good faith with respect to wages, hours, and other terms and conditions of employment, but as not requiring agreement
Section 9	Specifies secret ballot elections for determining questions of majority support for both certification and decertification cases
Section 14(b)	Allows states to pass right-to-work laws
Sections 201–204	Creates the Federal Mediation and Conciliation Service to provide voluntary mediation
Sections 206–210	Empowers the U.S. President to petition a court to suspend a strike that is deemed a national emergency strike

Note: The full text is in an appendix

Union actions are restricted in the Taft-Hartley Act primarily through the addition of six union unfair labor practices (a seventh is added in 1959 that restricts picketing for union recognition). The Wagner Act's employer unfair labor practices remain and appear in section 8(a); section 8(b) is created for the union unfair labor practices. The first three parallel the employer unfair labor practices: to restrain or coerce employees in the exercise of the rights guaranteed in section 7 [8(b)(1)], to cause or attempt to cause an employer to discriminate against employees except for failing to pay any required union dues [8(b)(2)], and to refuse to bargain collectively with the employer [8(b)(3)].

Of the remaining three, only 8(b)(4) is significant.[76] This unfair labor practice prohibits unions from engaging in secondary boycotts and other forms of strikes and picketing that then tend to involve "innocent" employers. The term *secondary boycott* comes from the fact that a secondary rather than primary employer is being targeted—that is, a company that does not directly employ the workers who are involved in the dispute. For example, consider a union of brewery workers that is on strike against the maker of a certain beer that is sold in a local grocery store. A secondary boycott would occur if the union pickets

[76] Taylor and Witney, *Labor Relations Law.*

the grocery store to tell consumers not to shop at the store. This is illegal because the grocery store is a secondary employer; the workers on strike do not work for the grocery store, they work for the primary employer—the beer maker. In contrast, it would be legal for the union and its members to "picket the product" outside the grocery store and tell consumers not to buy the specific brand of beer because of a labor dispute—this action specifically targets the primary employer and is therefore acceptable. But telling consumers to completely boycott the store is going too far.

Union actions are also restricted by a change that outlaws **closed shop** agreements. A closed shop agreement is a provision negotiated into a collective bargaining agreement that requires the employer to only hire union members. In other words, the workplace is closed to all except union members. Employers viewed this as especially pernicious because the employer is deprived of hiring whomever they choose; rather, they must hire union members. In contrast, a **union shop** allows anyone to be hired, but to remain employed, workers must join the union within a certain amount of time (30–90 days is common). An **agency shop** is similar, but rather than joining the union, workers need to pay dues. Both are allowed by the Taft-Hartley Act, though later Supreme Court rulings render union shops enforceable only as agency shops in which workers can only be forced to pay the fraction of union dues that is germane to bargaining and administering union contracts (see Chapter 10); union shop clauses cannot be used to compel workers to formally join unions.[77] Moreover, section 14(b) of the Act allows states to pass right-to-work laws—laws that prohibit union and/or agency shop agreements.[78] There are 22 such states—called right-to-work states—so union actions are further restricted in these states with respect to these types of membership provisions (see Box 5.17).

The second major category of Taft-Hartley Act provisions is enhancing the rights of individuals. These provisions again reflect the view that unions were too strong and the perceived need to bolster individual rights. Section 7 is expanded to explicitly provide individuals with the right to refrain from concerted activity and section 9 is revised to add

BOX 5.17
Right-to-Work States (unshaded) with Date of Enactment

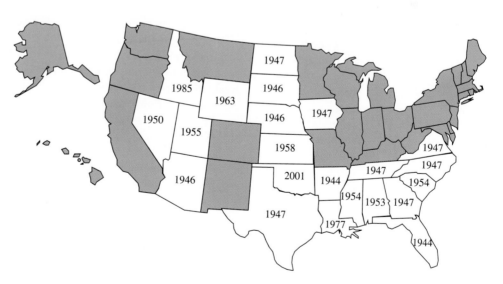

77 *NLRB v. General Motors*, 373 U.S. 734 (1963). *Communication Workers of America v. Beck*, 487 U.S. 735 (1988).
78 Raymond Hogler, "The Historical Misconception of Right to Work Laws in the United States: Senator Robert Wagner, Legal Policy, and the Decline of American Unions," *Hofstra Labor and Employment Law Journal* 23 (Fall 2005), pp. 101–52.

a decertification procedure—the certification process in reverse in which individuals can oust their bargaining agent if they no longer desire union representation. Employers are also explicitly granted rights by the Taft-Hartley Act, especially by the employer's free speech provision [section 8(c)]. This provision explicitly permits employers to express views on unionization as long as these expressions do not contain threats or promises. This is an important aspect of union organizing campaigns and will therefore be discussed in Chapter 7. Additionally, to serve employers' demands for unquestioned loyalty among supervisors, supervisors were excluded from protection of the Act. Supervisors can try to unionize, but it's not an unfair labor practice to fire them in response. Another right granted to employers is the ability to file unfair labor practice charges against unions.[79]

Lastly, the Taft-Hartley Act addressed various dispute resolution mechanisms. The NLRB was sharply attacked by business since its creation, and the Act restructured the NLRB to separate the investigation/prosecution and judicial aspects of the agency (unlike all other federal agencies) and also prevented it from undertaking economic analyses—changes which significantly weakened the agency and forced it to become singularly legal rather than pragmatic.[80] The Board was also expanded to five members. To facilitate the resolution of bargaining disputes, the Act created the Federal Conciliation and Mediation Service (FMCS) to provide voluntary mediation to labor and management negotiators. Also, the U.S. President was authorized by the Act to petition the courts to stop strikes that "imperil the national health or safety." This national emergency strike provision is unsurprising when one remembers that this Act was passed in the aftermath of the tremendous strike wave in 1945–46, though its provisions are used only infrequently. President Bush used this power to stop a dispute that shut some Pacific Coast docks in 2002; before that, President Carter's request to stop a 1978 coal strike was denied by the courts.

In sum, if unions were too powerful, then these various amendments to the Wagner Act that were implemented by the Taft-Hartley Act in 1947 can be viewed as restoring a needed balance between individuals, unions, and employers. On the other hand, organized labor saw the Taft-Hartley Act as an opportunistic effort by business and conservative politicians to roll back labor's protections and therefore labeled it the "Slave Labor Act."[81] This label might be more accurate for the original proposal in the House of Representatives than the final law that was passed, but it clearly underscores labor's strong opposition.[82] In this view, restrictions on secondary boycotts undermined union solidarity and prevented the strong from aiding the weak; the employer's free speech provision legitimized employer interference in what should be a worker-only issue (whether to join a union); not protecting supervisor unions relegated the labor movement to only representing blue collar workers; and the Act generally made unions even more dependent on government control.[83] Though no longer in effect, union leaders also felt victimized by the Taft-Hartley requirement that union leaders sign an affidavit swearing that they are not communists. Many unions had already purged communists from their organizations, but the Taft-Hartley Act now publicly

[79] Taylor and Witney, *Labor Relations Law.*
[80] James A. Gross, *The Reshaping of the National Labor Relations Board: National Labor Policy in Transition 1937–1947* (Albany: State University of New York Press, 1981). James A. Gross, *Broken Promise: The Subversion of U.S. Labor Relations Policy, 1947–1994* (Philadelphia: Temple University Press, 1995). Tomlins, *The State and the Unions.*
[81] Joseph G. Rayback, *A History of American Labor* (New York: Free Press, 1966). Tomlins, *The State and the Unions.*
[82] Dubofsky, *The State and Labor in Modern America.* Taft, *Organized Labor in American History.*
[83] Nelson Lichtenstein, *State of the Union: A Century of American Labor* (Princeton, NJ: Princeton University Press, 2002). Tomlins, *The State and the Unions.*

equated unionism with communism (no one else had to sign affidavits, just union leaders).[84] Advocates of the industrial relations school of thought opposed the Taft-Hartley Act amendments as injecting too much government regulation into labor relations (such as with very broad and vague union unfair labor practices).[85] President Truman vetoed the Taft-Hartley Act, but his veto was easily overridden by an alliance of Republicans and conservative Southern Democrats. As such, the Taft-Hartley Act remains at the heart of U.S. labor law—and by some accounts, organized labor's weakness—in the 21st century.

FIGHTING UNION CORRUPTION: THE LANDRUM-GRIFFIN ACT

In 1956 a New York journalist appeared on national television with dark glasses and bandaged hands and generated widespread public outrage for corruption in the labor movement. After publishing a newspaper column on organized crime in the New York garment and trucking industries, Victor Riesel had been blinded in an acid attack linked to New York gangster Johnny Dio.[86] A congressional investigating committee was formed in response, and through the McClelland committee hearings in 1957–1959, the American public would learn about the links between Teamsters leader Jimmy Hoffa, Johnny Dio, and other organized crime figures and their use of sweetheart contracts (in return for kickbacks, union officials would ignore an employer's violations of the contract such as substandard wages, though they would still collect union dues), personal loans from union health and welfare funds, and violence to keep resistant employers and employees in line.[87] In fact, the committee would eventually publish 58 volumes of hearings and reports—34 on the Teamsters, and the remainder on four other unions.[88] The McClelland committee concluded that rank and file union members lacked a voice and often the right to vote in internal union affairs, national union leaders abused their power over locals and union finances, and violence was used to keep members in line. As this represented just 5 out of 200 or so national unions, it's important not to overstate the extent of union corruption, but nevertheless there were (and continue to be) unfortunate examples of mafia-infiltrated unions and of corrupt union leaders.[89]

Congress responded by debating various bills to address concerns with union democracy, financial transparency, and some revisions to the National Labor Relations Act (NLRA) (see Box 5.18). As a result, the **Landrum-Griffin Act** was passed in 1959.[90] As emphasized by its opening declaration, this Act focuses on internal union affairs:

> In order to accomplish the objective of a free flow of commerce it is essential that labor organizations, employers, and their officials adhere to the highest standards of responsibility and ethical conduct in administering the affairs of their organizations, particularly as they affect labor–management relations. The Congress further finds, from recent investigations in the labor and management fields, that there have been a number of instances of breach

[84] Lichtenstein, *State of the Union*. Sinyai, *Schools of Democracy*.
[85] Dubofsky, *The State and Labor in Modern America*. Millis and Brown, *From the Wagner Act to Taft-Hartley.*
[86] Thaddeus Russell, *Out of the Jungle: Jimmy Hoffa and the Remaking of the American Working Class* (New York: Knopf, 2001).
[87] R. Alton Lee, *Eisenhower and Landrum-Griffin: A Study in Labor–Management Politics* (Lexington: University Press of Kentucky, 1990). Russell, *Out of the Jungle*. Taft, *Organized Labor in American History.*
[88] Janice R. Bellace and Alan D. Berkowitz, *The Landrum-Griffin Act: Twenty Years of Federal Protection of Union Members' Rights* (Philadelphia: Industrial Research Unit, University of Pennsylvania, 1979).
[89] James B. Jacobs, *Mobsters, Unions, and Feds: The Mafia and the American Labor Movement* (New York: New York University Press, 2006).
[90] Bellace and Berkowitz, *The Landrum-Griffin Act*. Lee, *Eisenhower and Landrum-Griffin*. Taylor and Witney, *Labor Relations Law.*

Representative Landrum Introduces a Labor–Management Reform Bill (1959)

Box 5.18

"Mr. Chairman, together with the gentleman from Michigan [Representative Griffin], I have today introduced a nonpartisan bill, dealing with the tremendously vital issue of labor-management reform legislation. We did so only after the most thorough consideration, and in light of what we feel to be absolutely necessary in this field, if free and democratic processes in the industrial relations of our great Nation are to survive.

. . .

I would call to the Members' attention that the interim report of the McClelland committee found that there has been a significant lack of democratic processes in certain unions, that one-man dictatorships have thrived—in some instances for 20 to 30 years—and that through intimidation and fear, the rank and file union member has been deprived of a voice in his own union affairs.

. . .

One of the basic underlying principles of both the Wagner Act of 1935 and the Taft-Hartley Act of 1947 has been the rights of employees—under the first to be free from employer domination, under the second to be free from union domination. That further legislation, however, dealing with union democracy is needed in 1959 cannot be challenged. As one union official put it in his testimony:

We believe that the control of the union by its membership is the best way to insure its democracy and keep the officers in line—I believe that the best demonstration of democracy in action, is where the people directly handle their own union business.

This [our] bill seeks to accomplish, by insuring effective membership control.

The [previous] bill also purports to contain reporting provisions, under which the goldfish-bowl approach would enable union members to see for themselves wrongdoing and take effective and corrective action. . . . Under the bill we propose, all unions of whatever size would be required to report pertinent financial data, informing the membership of possible conflicts of interest, and other shady deals . . .

. . .

In conclusion, Mr. Chairman, let me say that the bill the gentleman from Michigan and I have introduced is not an antiunion bill, it is not a union busting bill, it is not an anticollective bargaining bill. It would not impinge in any way upon the lawful and legitimate purposes and activities of American labor unions. It is a bill which would restore the control of union affairs to union members."

Source: National Labor Relations Board, *Legislative History of the Labor-Management Reporting and Disclosure Act of 1959*, Volume II (Washington, DC: U.S. Government Printing Office, 1959), pp. 1517–19.

of trust, corruption, disregard of the rights of individual employees, and other failures to observe high standards of responsibility and ethical conduct which require further and supplementary legislation that will afford necessary protection of the rights and interests of employees and the public generally as they relate to the activities of labor organizations, employers, labor relations consultants, and their officers and representatives.

To achieve union democracy, the Landrum-Griffin Act creates a Bill of Rights for union members which guarantees all union members equal rights of participation in internal union affairs including voting and expressing views (see Box 5.19). Democratic standards for the election of union officers are also established.

Increased democracy should reduce union corruption, but the Landrum-Griffin Act explicitly tries to prevent union corruption and labor racketeering in three additional ways. One, unions and their officers are required to disclose financial records by filing reports with the U.S. Department of Labor. In fact, the formal name of the Landrum-Griffin Act is the Labor–Management Reporting and Disclosure Act. This is intended to increase the transparency of union governance to prevent abuse—foreshadowing the attempts to increase

Title I: Bill of Rights of Members of Labor Organizations

- Equal rights for all union members to nominate candidates for office, vote in union elections, attend meetings, and participate in deliberations
- Freedom of speech and assembly for union members
- Dues amounts must be approved by a majority vote
- Safeguards against improper discipline or expulsion of union members
- All union members are entitled to receive a copy of the collective bargaining agreement

Title II: Reporting by Labor Organizations and Employers

- Unions must adopt a constitution and bylaws and file it with the Department of Labor
- Unions must report the following information to the Department of Labor:
- Name and title of officers as well as their salaries and any loans made to them
- Initiation fees and dues
- Procedures for auditing financial records, approving contracts, and the like
- Financial assets, liabilities, receipts, and expenditures
- Union members are entitled to look at union records to verify this information
- Officers and employees of unions must report financial interests, transactions, or loans between them and any business whose employees are represented by the union
- Employers must report payments or loans to union officials
- Employers must report any contracts with labor relations consultants

Title III: Trusteeships

- Unions must report and justify trusteeships to the Department of Labor
- Standards for trusteeships are outlined

Title IV: Union Elections

- All national unions must elect officers through democratic procedures at least every five years
- All local unions must elect officers through a secret ballot vote at least every three years
- Neither union funds nor employer donations can be used to finance a campaign for union office
- Mailing lists of union members must be made equally available to all candidates for office

Title V: Safeguards for Labor Organizations

- Union officers have a fiduciary duty to the union and its members
- Significant loans to officers and employees of the union are prohibited
- Convicted criminals of certain offenses (e.g., bribery, extortion, embezzlement, murder) are prohibited from holding positions of authority in labor unions within five years of ending their prison sentence

Title VI: Miscellaneous Provisions

- Picketing to extort an employer is illegal

Title VII: NLRA Amendments

- Permanently replaced strikers are only allowed to vote in NLRB elections that occur within 12 months of the start of the strike
- Some loopholes with respect to section 8(b)(4)'s ban on secondary boycotts are closed
- A seventh union unfair labor practice [(8(b)(7)] is added restricting picketing for union recognition
- Hot cargo agreements are banned
- Prehire agreements in the construction industry are allowed

Note: The full text is available on the internet at *http://www4.law.cornell.edu/uscode/29/ch11.html*.

the transparency of corporate governance 40 years later in the wake of the Enron scandal. Two, the Act restricts the use of union trusteeships. National unions have the power to take over the operation of a local union and replace the elected officers with an appointed trustee and the Act tries to ensure that this power is used for legitimate purposes (cleaning up a corrupt local) rather than illegitimate ones (removing local leaders that are political opponents of the national leadership and/or installing a corrupt leader who is beholden to the national leadership). Three, the Landrum-Griffin Act also establishes the fiduciary responsibility of union leaders.

While the overwhelming purpose of the Landrum-Griffin Act is to increase internal union democracy and prevent union corruption, it also amended the National Labor Relations Act in a few minor ways. The rights of permanently replaced strikers to participate in NLRB elections were confined to the first 12 months of a strike, the section 8(b)(4) restrictions on secondary boycotts were revised, a seventh union unfair labor practice [section 8(b)(7)] was added that restricted picketing for union recognition, and hot cargo agreements were outlawed [section 8(e)]. In labor relations, hot cargo are goods that are made by nonunion workers or by a company that is on strike and a hot cargo agreement is a clause negotiated into union contracts giving union members the right to refuse to handle hot cargo. The Landrum-Griffin Act also created special exceptions in various areas for the construction industry because of the short-term nature of employment in that industry.

EXTENSIONS TO GOVERNMENT EMPLOYEES: PUBLIC SECTOR LABOR LAW

The next major developments in U.S. labor law occur in the public sector—government employees at a federal, state, and local level—not in the private sector. In fact, by 1959 the legislative framework for private sector labor law is nearly completely established, but it is on the verge of erupting in the public sector. The National Labor Relations Act (NLRA) applies to private sector employers and workers nationwide. In contrast, public sector labor law has 51 separate jurisdictions—the U.S. federal government for federal employees and the 50 states for state and local government workers in each state. It is therefore important to remember that there can be significant differences in public sector labor law across different jurisdictions.

Public sector unionization dates back to the 19th century—there was a strike in 1836 in the federal shipyards, a national teachers union was established in 1857, postal workers formed unions as early as 1863, and firefighters and police began organizing around the turn of the century.[91] However, in the wake of a 1919 strike by police in Boston that resulted in looting and violence, public sentiment became, in the words of Calvin Coolidge who was governor of Massachusetts at the time, "there is no right to strike against the public safety by anybody, anywhere, any time."[92] As such, early laws and legal rulings treated attempts to bargain with governments as interfering with the responsibility of *elected* government officials to establish public policies and protect the public interest. The worsening of public sector employment conditions in the 1950s as well as a new legal respect for the freedom of association began to change the strong aversion to public sector unions.[93] The

[91] Joseph E. Slater, *Public Workers: Government Employee Unions, the Law, and the State, 1900–1962* (Ithaca, NY: Cornell University Press, 2004). Richard C. Kearney, *Labor Relations in the Public Sector,* 2nd ed. (New York: Marcel Dekker, 1992).
[92] Francis Russell, *A City in Terror: 1919, The Boston Police Strike* (New York: Viking, 1975), p. 191. Sterling D. Spero, *Government as Employer* (New York: Remsen Press, 1948).
[93] Kearney, *Labor Relations in the Public Sector.* B.V.H. Schneider, "Public-Sector Labor Legislation—An Evolutionary Analysis," in Benjamin Aaron, Joyce M. Najita, and James L. Stern (eds.), *Public-Sector Bargaining,* 2nd ed. (Washington, DC: Bureau of National Affairs, 1988), Chapter 6.

first public sector law that gave government employees the right to engage in collective bargaining was passed by Wisconsin in 1959; the federal government and a number of other states followed in the 1960s. Since that time, union membership in the public sector has increased from less than 1 million in 1960 to over 7 million in 2000—that is, from a union density of 10 percent to nearly 40 percent (recall Box 1.12).

In the federal sector, President Kennedy established limited bargaining rights, exclusive representation, and unfair labor practices with Executive Order 10988 in 1962.[94] Subsequent presidents revised this initial structure and the resulting bargaining system was codified into law by Congress in 1978 through the **Civil Service Reform Act.**[95] This Act protects most federal sector workers, though supervisors, the military, security agencies (like the FBI), the Post Office, and several other agencies are excluded. Postal employees are covered under the NLRA (but cannot strike) while it is illegal for military personnel to unionize. The major elements of the labor relations system for federal workers set forth in the Civil Service Reform Act parallel the NLRA framework—it's based on the principle of exclusive representation with majority support, certification elections, employer and union unfair labor practices, and an agency (the Federal Labor Relations Authority) that administers elections and unfair labor practice charges (see Box 5.20). At the same time, there are some important differences in the details between the two systems. In particular, strikes are prohibited, wages and benefits are excluded from bargaining, and unions with minority but not majority support have consultation rights so that the federal agency must consult with the union before making changes in working conditions (see Chapter 14). As long as one remembers that it is an oversimplification, labor law for federal employees can be summarized as "the NLRA without the right to strike."

Labor relations for state and municipal workers is governed by the laws and courts of each state. First note that the courts have decided that preventing public sector workers from unionizing violates freedom of assembly and speech (this differs from the private sector because in the public sector the employer is a government), but there is not a constitutional right of bargaining.[96] Thus, questions of public sector labor law focus on bargaining. With this in mind, it is useful to consider four categories of state public sector bargaining laws: comprehensive laws, narrow laws, no laws, and prohibitive laws. Comprehensive laws broadly grant nearly all government occupations—teachers, firefighters, police, state employees, and the like—the right to collectively bargain while narrow laws apply to one or several occupations only. For example, Hawaii, Iowa, and New York have comprehensive laws while Wyoming's narrow law only covers firefighters and Indiana's only teachers. States with no laws are silent on whether public sector bargaining is legal or not, while prohibitive laws ban it. All told, 25 states have comprehensive laws, 16 have narrow laws or executive orders, eight have no laws, and one state prohibits bargaining (see Box 5.21).[97] In states with no laws, bargaining still occurs—this underscores the important distinction between unprotected and illegal union activity.[98]

Unsurprisingly, the bargaining laws (where present) vary tremendously from state to state in the operational details. Most prohibit strikes for all employees—the sentiment of "there is no right to strike against the public safety by anybody, anywhere, any time" is still

[94] Schneider, "Public-Sector Labor Legislation."

[95] Kearney, *Labor Relations in the Public Sector.* Taylor and Witney, *Labor Relations Law.*

[96] Kearney, *Labor Relations in the Public Sector.* Taylor and Witney, *Labor Relations Law.*

[97] John Lund and Cheryl L. Maranto, "Public Sector Labor Law: An Update," in Dale Belman, Morley Gunderson, and Douglas Hyatt (eds.), *Public Sector Employment in a Time of Transition* (Madison, WI: Industrial Relations Research Association, 1996), Chapter 1. Schneider, "Public-Sector Labor Legislation—An Evolutionary Analysis."

[98] Schneider, "Public-Sector Labor Legislation—An Evolutionary Analysis."

BOX 5.20   The Civil Service Reform Act and the NLRA: Similar . . . but Different

Major Features of the Civil Service Reform Act	Comparison with the NLRA	
	Similar	Different
Grants employees the right to form unions and engage in collective bargaining	✓	
Applies to many federal government employees		X
Exclusive representation with majority support is a key principle	✓	
Unfair labor practices are specified	✓	
An agency conducts elections to determine majority support and adjudicates unfair labor practice charges	✓	
A union with the support of 10 percent but less than 50 percent of the bargaining unit has consultation rights		X
Negotiable issues exclude wages and benefits; bargaining is generally limited to policies and procedures		X
Explicitly grants management rights (the right to determine mission and budgets, to hire, assign, direct employees, and other managerial functions) to managers		X
Strikes are prohibited		X

Note: The full text of the Civil Service Reform Act is available on the Internet at *http://www4.law.cornell.edu/uscode/5/pIIIspFch71.html*

widespread—but differ on the type of dispute resolution procedure used as a substitute (see Chapter 9). Some states allow strikes for nonessential workers—teachers, bus drivers, state workers, college professors—while banning strikes for essential workers—firefighters, police, prison guards. Some states harshly penalize strikers—New York's Taylor law imposes a "two for one" penalty for each day someone is on strike: their lost pay for the day plus a fine equal to their day's pay.[99] Beyond the dispute resolution procedures, there are operational differences in the scope of bargaining, the legality of the agency shop, and the wording of unfair labor practices. But the laws are generally based on exclusive representation with majority rule, certification elections, unfair labor practices, and administration via a specialized agency.[100] As long as one remembers that it is an oversimplification, labor law for state and municipal employees—where it exists—can be summarized as "the NLRA usually without the right to strike."

It is estimated that approximately one-third of public sector workers (excluding the military) are not covered by a bargaining law.[101] Moreover, 20 to 25 percent of private sector workers lack the protections of the NLRA because they are supervisors or independent contractors, or because they work for businesses that are too small to be covered or in industries such as agriculture that are excluded.

---

[99] Janet McEneaney and Robert P. Hebdon, "Public Sector Labor Law and Experience in New York State," in Joyce M. Najita, and James L. Stern (eds.), *Collective Bargaining in the Public Sector: The Experience of Eight States* (Armonk, NY: M. E. Sharpe, 2001), Chapter 7.
[100] Kearney, *Labor Relations in the Public Sector.*
[101] General Accounting Office, *Collective Bargaining Rights: Information on the Number of Workers with and without Bargaining Rights*, GAO-02-835 (Washington, DC: United States General Accounting Office, 2002).

BOX 5.21   **Four Types of State Public Sector Bargaining Laws**

Comprehensive	Narrow	No Law	Prohibitive
(bargaining rights for nearly all occupations)	(no bargaining rights for some occupations)	(bargaining neither protected nor banned)	(bargaining is prohibited)
(25 states)	(16 states)	(8 states)	(1 state)
Alaska*	Alabama	Arizona	North Carolina
California*	Georgia	Arkansas	
Connecticut	Idaho	Colorado*	
Delaware	Indiana	Louisiana*	
Florida	Kentucky	Mississippi	
Hawaii*	Maryland	South Carolina	
Illinois*	Michigan	Virginia	
Iowa	Missouri	West Virginia	
Kansas	Nevada		
Maine	North Dakota		
Massachusetts	Ohio*		
Minnesota*	Oklahoma		
Montana*	Tennessee		
Nebraska	Texas		
New Hampshire	Utah		
New Jersey*	Wyoming		
New Mexico			
New York			
Oregon*			
Pennsylvania*			
Rhode Island			
South Dakota			
Vermont*			
Washington			
Wisconsin			

Note: * denotes right to strike for teachers and/or state workers (by law or court ruling).

Sources: John Lund and Cheryl L. Maranto, "Public Sector Labor Law: An Update," in Dale Belman, Morley Gunderson, and Douglas Hyatt (eds.), *Public Sector Employment in a Time of Transition* (Madison, WI: Industrial Relations Research Association, 1996), Chapter 1. B.V.H. Schneider, "Public-Sector Labor Legislation—An Evolutionary Analysis," in Benjamin Aaron, Joyce M. Najita, and James L. Stern (eds.), *Public-Sector Bargaining*, 2nd ed. (Washington, DC: Bureau of National Affairs, 1988), Chapter 6.

LABOR LAW IN PRACTICE: NLRB DECISIONS AND REFORM

The statutes that comprise both private and public sector U.S. labor law are quite static. In the private sector, in particular, the bulk of today's laws on labor–management relations were written in 1935 and 1947. The Landrum-Griffin Act made some minor modifications, but the major focus of that Act was internal union affairs rather than interactions between labor and management. In 1974 the NLRA was amended to include private sector hospitals and to provide stringent notice requirements before hospital unions could strike.[102] These are the only changes since 1947 worth mentioning here. However, beyond the static statutes, there is a second important component of labor law that is much more dynamic and voluminous: the accumulated body of case law developed through National Labor Relations Board (NLRB) and court decisions and precedents. The same is true, albeit on a smaller scale, for public sector labor law.

The NLRA contains numerous general standards—interference, restraint, domination, discrimination, good faith—but in practice what do these standards mean? It is the responsibility of the NLRB to apply the facts of specific cases to these general principles of the law to determine if violations have occurred (you can try this with the end of chapter exercises in Boxes 5.24–5.26). When the NLRB hears a case, it issues a written decision that may serve as a precedent for future cases (see Box 5.22). Between 1935 and 2005, the NLRB issued 345 volumes of decisions. It's difficult to keep up with all of these rulings, but labor relations professionals need to be generally aware of this body of case law. Moreover, some NLRB and court precedents are so important that they have become part of everyday labor relations jargon: *Beck* rights (from the 1988 Supreme Court decision *Communication Workers of America v. Beck* described in Chapter 10), the *Mackay* doctrine (Chapter 9), *Weingarten* rights (Chapter 10), the *Borg-Warner* doctrine (chapter 8), the *Excelsior* list (Chapter 7), and the *Wright Line* test, to name some of the most important.

The ***Wright Line* test** illustrates the importance of precedents for guiding legal decision making, and is doubly important because it pertains to the heart of U.S. labor law: the dividing line between legitimate employee discipline and discharge on the one hand, and unlawful retaliation for union activity on the other (an 8(a)(3) unfair labor practice). Under the *Wright Line* test, established by the 1980 NLRB decision of this name, the NLRB General Counsel (the prosecution) must first show that (1) the disciplined or discharged employee was engaged in protected activity, (2) the employer was aware of the activity, and (3) the activity was a substantial or motivating reason for the employer's action.[103] If the General Counsel establishes these facts, the burden of proof then shifts to the employer to prove that it would have taken the same action even if the employee had not engaged in protected activity. Human resource managers, therefore, must be able to document that employee discipline and termination is applied consistently and for valid job-related reasons, and that the reasons for discipline are not a pretext for discriminating against concerted activity. This is an important example of how labor law matters for the everyday practice of labor relations, even in nonunion situations.

A major theme in many areas that the NLRB has to adjudicate is balancing property rights with labor rights. The *Wright Line* test tries to balance employers' rights and needs to discipline and discharge poor performers with employees' rights to engage in protected activity under the NLRA. Preventing employees from wearing pro-union buttons and other insignia interferes with protected activity and therefore violates section 8(a)(1)—unless the employer can demonstrate a legitimate business need. Employers can use surveillance equipment to monitor employees to maintain security, but overly aggressive surveillance that might be used to retaliate against union supporters is viewed by the NLRB as going beyond the need to protect property rights and violates labor rights. Sticky issues in labor law pertaining to union organizing, bargaining, and strikes will be presented in subsequent chapters —these issues also often involve difficulties balancing property rights with labor rights.

[102] Taylor and Witney, *Labor Relations Law.*
[103] 251 NLRB 1083 (1980) [approved by the Supreme Court in *NLRB v. Transportation Management Corp.,* 462 U.S. 403 (1983)].

Looking at real NLRB decisions can help understand not only the application of the NLRA but also how the U.S. labor law system operates. The following decision illustrates the common elements of NLRB decisions. By convention, this case can be cited as *News Journal Company,* 331 NLRB No. 117 (2000) or as *News Journal Company,* 331 NLRB 1331 (2000). From these citations we see that this decision is part of the 331st volume of NLRB decisions and is the 117th decision in this volume and begins on page 1331. Citations for other legal decisions are similar; for example, *NLRB v. Katz,* 369 U.S. 736 (1962) refers to a 1962 U.S. Supreme Court decision in volume 369 that starts on page 736 of that volume.

Unfair labor practices cases are first heard by an administrative law judge who issues a written opinion that includes a statement of the issues, a review of the factual background information, a legal analysis, conclusions of law, and if necessary, remedies (see the following example). In the *News Journal Company* case, a union (the Newspaper Guild) accused the employer (The News Journal Company) of violating section 8(a)(1) and

8(a)(5) by granting wage increases to certain employees without bargaining over them, but the law judge did not agree, so he dismissed the case. This decision was appealed to the NLRB in Washington by the NLRB's General Counsel. Three members of the NLRB considered the case and affirmed the judge's dismissal of the case. Note carefully that in the published decisions, the NLRB's decision appears before the administrative law judge's decision, even though chronologically the law judge's decision occurs first.

In *News Journal Company,* the NLRB affirmed the law judge's decision without any discussion. In other cases, the NLRB might overturn or expand upon the law judge's decision. Also, this case is presented here because it is concise—most cases are more complicated and have longer descriptions of the facts and more complex legal analyses. Note, however, that even in this case the law judge relied on previous NLRB and court precedents when making his determination.

Note: Numerous NLRB decisions can be accessed at www.nlrb.gov.

Gannett Co., Inc., d/b/a The News Journal Company and The Newspaper Guild of Greater Philadelphia, Local No. 10 a/w The Newspaper Guild, AFL–CIO–CLC. Case 4–CA–26797

August 25, 2000

DECISION AND ORDER

BY MEMBERS FOX, LIEBMAN, AND BRAME

On February 18, 2000, Administrative Law Judge Bruce D. Rosenstein issued the attached decision. The General Counsel filed exceptions and a supporting brief which the Charging Party joined. The Respondent filed an answering brief.

The National Labor Relations Board has delegated its authority in this proceeding to a three-member panel.

The Board has considered the record in light of the exceptions and briefs, and has decided to affirm the judge's rulings, findings,[1] and conclusions, and to adopt the recommended Order.

ORDER

The complaint is dismissed.

Margaret M. McGovern, Esq., and *Anne C. Ritterspach, Esq.,* for the General Counsel.

Joyce T. Bailey, Esq., of Arlington, Virginia, for the Respondent Employer.

Laurence M. Goodman, Esq., of Philadelphia, Pennsylvania, for the Charging Party.

DECISION

STATEMENT OF THE CASE

Bruce D. Rosenstein, Administrative Law Judge. This case was tried before me on October 27, 1999, in Philadelphia, Pennsylvania, pursuant to a complaint and notice of hearing (the complaint) issued by the Regional Director for Region 4 of the National Labor

---

[1] The General Counsel and the Charging Party have excepted to some of the judge's credibility findings. The Board's established policy is not to overrule an administrative law judge's credibility resolutions unless the clear preponderance of all the relevant evidence convinces us that they are incorrect. *Standard Dry Wall Products,* 91 NLRB 544 (1950), enfd. 188 F.2d 362 (3d Cir. 1951). We have carefully examined the record and find no basis for reversing the findings.

In affirming the judge's decision, Member Fox and Member Liebman note that significantly more employees with satisfactory ratings at the end of their probationary period received raises from 1993 through September 1997 than received them from October 1997 through 1999. In some cases, a numerical showing is sufficient to establish a discontinuation of past practice and, hence, a violation. *Electrical South, Inc.,* 327 NLRB 270 (1998). Here, however, the Respondent adduced evidence, which was credited by the judge, that the decision to award postprobationary merit wage increases was highly subjective and depended on numerous criteria, including budget, skill, and area of specialty, and the General Counsel failed to show that executive editors who approved those raises prior to October 1997 applied different criteria than current Executive Editor Jane Amari in determining whether to give merit increases.

Relations Board (the Board) on August 27, 1998. The complaint, based on an original and amended charge filed by The Newspaper Guild of Greater Philadelphia, Local 10 a/w The Newspaper Guild, AFL–CIO–CLC (the Charging Party or the Union), alleges that Gannett Co., Inc., d/b/a The News Journal Company (the Respondent or Employer), has engaged in certain violations of Section 8(a)(1) and (5) of the National Relations Act (the Act).[1] The Respondent filed a timely answer to the complaint denying that it had committed any violations of the Act.

ISSUES

The complaint alleges that about July 1997,[2] Respondent discontinued its practice of considering and, when appropriate, granting wage increases to the editorial unit employees on successful completion of their 90-day probationary periods.

On the entire record, including my observation of the demeanor of the witnesses, and after considering the briefs filed by the General Counsel, the Charging Party, and the Respondent, I make the following.

FINDINGS OF FACT
I. JURISDICTION

The Respondent is a corporation engaged in the publishing and distribution of publications, with a place of business in New Castle, Delaware, where it derived gross revenues in excess of $200,000 during the past year and held membership in or subscribed to various interstate news services, including the Associated Press. The Respondent admits, and I find, that it is an employer engaged in commerce within the meaning of Section 2(2), (6), and (7) of the Act and that the Union is a labor organization within the meaning of Section 2(5) of the Act.

II. ALLEGED UNFAIR LABOR PRACTICES
A. Background

On December 14, 1989, the Union was certified as the exclusive collective-bargaining representative of the editorial unit. Since that time, the parties have been operating without a collective-bargaining agreement. However,

[1] The Regional Director consolidated Case 4–CA–26670 with the subject case. After the opening of the hearing, the parties entered into an informal Board settlement with the posting of a notice, which I approved on the record subject to compliance with its terms and conditions (Jt. Exh. 3). Likewise, I approved the General Counsel's motion to sever that case from the subject case. Therefore, this decision will only address the issues in Case 4–CA–26797.

[2] All dates are in 1997 unless otherwise indicated.

since at least 1995, they have been engaged in negotiations to reach an agreement. Since October 1997, Jane Amari has been Respondent's executive editor and is responsible for all personnel related decisions of the approximately 150 employees on the editorial staff. This includes all hiring decisions, reviewing performance appraisals written by first-line supervisors, and determining whether employees should receive pay increases after completing their 90-day probationary periods. In order to assist Amari in finalizing performance appraisals and salary decisions, a manager's wage and salary administration guide is followed (R. Exh. 2). It details the procedure for conducting performance appraisals and, at section 4.4, merit increases, states in pertinent part that "Employees should not expect automatic increases and should not expect 12 month increases unless their accomplishments justify it."

B. Discussion and Analysis

The General Counsel asserts in paragraph 6 of the complaint that Respondent maintained a practice that employees who performed at a satisfactory level or higher routinely received wage increases after completion of their 90-day probationary periods. In or about July 1997, the practice was discontinued and a number of employees did not receive a wage increase after the completion of their 90-day probationary periods. The General Counsel opines that the Respondent engaged in this conduct without notice to the Union and without affording the Union an opportunity to bargain with respect to this conduct.

Respondent contends that no firm practice ever existed that editorial employees automatically receive wage increases after completion of their 90-day probationary periods. Rather, it is discretionary, subject to an independent review of the executive editor as to whether individual employees are eligible to receive wage increases.

The evidence discloses that first-line supervisors prepare a performance evaluation after employees complete their first 90 days of employment and award a score from 1 through 5 on the rating system with 3 to 3.5 being average. On occasions, the first-line supervisor will recommend that a wage increase is appropriate. The executive editor then reviews all of the employee performance appraisals and makes an independent decision as to whether a wage increase is warranted. The parties' submitted an exhibit that depicts the history of wage increases for employees in the editorial department who completed their 90-day probationary periods from May 1994 to May 1999 (Jt. Exh. 1). That document conclusively shows that three employees, who completed their 90-day probationary periods from May 1994 to the end of June 1997, did not receive a wage increase. Likewise, the document establishes that between July 1997 and May 1999, 17 employees received wage increases while 28 employees did not receive wage increases despite being rated satisfactory or higher after completing their 90-day probationary periods.

Both Executive Editor Amari and former Executive Editor Bennie Ivory (September 1995 to June 1997) credibly testified that the decision to grant wage increases to employees after completion of their 90-day probationary periods is not automatic. Rather, it is within the exclusive discretion of the executive editor, and is based on a number of factors including budget considerations, the evaluation of the employee's performance, the amount of money the employee is currently earning, and whether granting a wage increase might be a factor in retaining an individual on the staff. For example, Amari testified that although employee Hurlock was rated outstanding after completing his 90-day probationary period, he was not given a wage increase because he was a part-time sports clerk. Subsequently, Hurlock was hired as a full-time employee.

The Board previously held in *Oneita Knitting Mills,* 205 NLRB 500 fn. 1 (1973), that "An employer with a past history of a merit increase program neither may discontinue that program . . . nor may he any longer . . . exercise his discretion with respect to such increases, once an exclusive bargaining representative is selected. *NLRB v. Katz,* [369] U.S. 736 (1962). What is required is a maintenance of preexisting practices, i.e., the general outline of the program; however, the implementation of that program (to the extent that discretion has existed in determining the amounts or timing of the increases), becomes a matter as to which the bargaining agent is entitled to be consulted." The Board further addressed the issue of a respondent discontinuing the practice of granting merit increases to employees after they successfully completed a 90-day probationary period in *Dynatron/Bondo Corp.,* 323 NLRB 1263 (1997). In that case, while finding a violation of the Act when the employer totally discontinued giving merit increases to employees, the Board principally relied on a number of factors including that merit was the sole fixed criterion for granting the raise, the timing of granting the raise was consistent, the amount of the raise fell within a narrow range, the majority of employees received the raises, and the increase had been granted over a significant period of time.

In stark contrast, the merit increases in the subject case have not been totally discontinued. Additionally, other factors beside merit are utilized in determining whether a merit increase is awarded and the dollar amount of the increase ranges from 100 percent to zero rather than remaining in a narrow range.

Based on the foregoing, I am not convinced that an established practice was in effect that employees automatically received wage increases if they were rated satisfactory or higher after completion of their 90-day probationary periods. Indeed, the evidence establishes that both before and after July 1997, a number of employees did not receive wage increases after completion of their 90-day probationary periods. Likewise, the record discloses that during the same period, a number of employees did receive wage increases after completion of their 90-day probationary periods. Thus, as required under *Oneita Knitting Mills,* the Respondent here maintained its existing practice of using a number of factors including the discretion of the executive editor in determining whether a merit increase was given to employees after completion of the 90-day probationary period. Accordingly, it follows that if there was no change in past practice in July 1997, Respondent was not required to notify or bargain with the Union. Under these circumstances, I find that since there was no change in the practice of granting wage increases to employees after completion of their 90-day probationary periods, Respondent did not violate Section 8(a)(1) and (5) of the Act. See *Selkirk Metalbestos,* 321 NLRB 44 (1996); *Haddon Craftsmen,* 297 NLRB 462 (1989).

CONCLUSIONS OF LAW

1. Respondent is an employer engaged in commerce within the meaning of Section 2(6) and (7) of the Act.
2. The Union is a labor organization within the meaning of Section 2(5) of the Act.
3. Respondent did not engage in violations of Section 8(a)(1) and (5) of the Act by discontinuing its practice of granting wage increases to employees after successful completion of their 90-day probationary periods.

On these findings of fact and conclusions of law and on the entire record, I issue the following recommended[3]

ORDER

The complaint is dismissed.

[3] If no exceptions are filed as provided by Sec. 102.46 of the Board's Rules and Regulations, the findings, conclusions, and recommended Order shall, as provided in Sec. 102.48 of the Rules, be adopted by the Board and all objections to them shall be deemed waived for all purposes.

NLRB case law—the dynamic, interpretive aspect of labor law—enables the law to accommodate new situations that were not present in 1935 and 1947 and to therefore balance property rights and labor rights in a changing environment. For example, are a company's restrictions on the use of its e-mail system by employees a legitimate use of property rights, or does it violate labor rights by interfering with concerted activity such as discussing working conditions? Such questions must be answered by the NLRB through its decisions. The NLRB framework for adjudicating U.S. labor law, however, is not without its critics. The five-person board that decides cases are political appointees and few deny that there are important political influences on major NLRB rulings (see Box 5.23). One critic goes so far as to assert that "national labor policy is in shambles in part because its meaning seems to depend on which political party won the last election."[104] Other labor supporters argue that the NLRB lacks sufficient remedial powers—in particular, the lack of punitive damages means that employers find it cost effective to commit unfair labor practices. If this is true, the penalties for labor law violators need to be strengthened. Unions are also very critical of the ways in which employers can manipulate NLRB hearings and judicial appeals to create legal delays that frustrate union organizing and bargaining.

Beyond the operation of the NLRB, there are a number of ongoing labor law controversies. As more and more employees are asked to exercise independent judgment or delegate minor tasks to co-workers, who exactly is and is not a supervisor under the NLRA has become a contentious legal issue, especially as employers have tried to increasingly exclude nurses and others from coverage under the Act.[105] The increased importance of undocumented immigrant workers for the U.S. economy highlights another controversial area: undocumented workers are protected under the NLRA, but the 2002 *Hoffman Plastic* Supreme Court decision denies backpay awards to undocumented workers when their NLRA rights are violated.[106] The NLRA protects the right to strike, but the Supreme Court allows employers to use permanent strike replacements.[107] One can even argue that judges have completely rewritten the NLRA through these types of legal rulings that significantly weaken the original law.[108] As such, there continue to be calls to reform some of the substantive aspects of the NLRA.[109] Union proponents favor expanding the coverage of the

[104] Gross, *Broken Promise*, p.275.

[105] Marley S. Weiss, "*Kentucky River* at the Intersection of Professional and Supervisory Status: Fertile Delta or Bermuda Triangle," in Laura J. Cooper and Catherine L. Fisk (eds.), *Labor Law Stories* (New York: Foundation Press, 2005), pp. 353–98.

[106] *Hoffman Plastic Compounds, Inc. v. NLRB*, 535 U.S. 137 (2002). Catherine L. Fisk and Michael J. Wishnie, "The Story of *Hoffman Plastic Compounds, Inc. v. NLRB:* Labor Rights Without Remedies for Undocumented Immigrants," in Laura J. Cooper and Catherine L. Fisk (eds.), *Labor Law Stories* (New York: Foundation Press, 2005), pp. 399–438. Steven E. Abraham, Adrienne E. Eaton, and Paula B. Voos, "Supreme Court Supervisory Status Decisions: The Impact on the Organizing of Nurses," in Richard N. Block et al. (eds.), *Justice on the Job: Perspectives on the Erosion of Collective Bargaining in the United States* (Kalamazoo, MI: Upjohn, 2006), pp. 163–89.

[107] Julius G. Getman and Thomas C. Kohler, "The Story of *NLRB v. Mackay Radio and Telegraph Co.*: The High Cost of Solidarity," in Laura J. Cooper and Catherine L. Fisk (eds.), *Labor Law Stories* (New York: Foundation Press, 2005), pp. 13–53.

[108] Ellen Dannin, *Taking Back the Workers' Law: How to Fight the Assault on Labor Rights* (Ithaca, NY: Cornell University Press, 2006).

[109] Stephen F. Befort, "Labor and Employment Law at the Millennium: A Historical Review and Critical Assessment." *Boston College Law Review* 43 (March 2002), pp. 351–460. Charles B. Craver, *Can Unions Survive? The Rejuvenation of the American Labor Movement* (New York: New York University Press, 1993). Sheldon Friedman, Richard W. Hurd, Rudolph A. Oswald, and Ronald L. Seeber (eds.), *Restoring the Promise of American Labor Law* (Ithaca, NY: ILR Press, 1994). William B. Gould, *Agenda for Reform: The Future of Employment Relationships and the Law* (Cambridge: MIT Press, 1993).

The five board members of the NLRB that decide NLRB cases are presidential appointees and with the election of President George W. Bush, the NLRB has three Republicans and two Democrats. Most NLRB decisions are unanimous which indicates that a pro-labor or pro-management leaning isn't important for interpreting the NLRA in many instances. But some of the most controversial and consequential decisions are split along party lines. As such, changing from a Democratic to a Republican presidency or vice versa can have significant effects on the legal climate of U.S. labor relations.

The following Clinton-era precedents were overruled and reversed in the Bush era:

- Granting *Weingarten* rights for nonunion employees. As will be discussed in Chapter 12, it is well accepted that unionized employees may request that a union representative be present when disciplinary action is anticipated. The Clinton-era board extended this same right to nonunion workers; the Bush-era board reversed by denying nonunion workers *Weingarten* rights.

- Making graduate assistants employees under the NLRA. For many years, the NLRB considered graduate teaching and research assistants to be students, not employees, and therefore not protected by the NLRA. The Clinton-era board brought graduate assistants under the NLRA by ruling that they were also employees; the Bush-era board reversed so that graduate assistants are again not covered by the NLRA.

- Including temporary employees in a bargaining unit with permanent employees. Prior to the Clinton-era board, an employer could prevent the creation of a single bargaining unit that includes both permanent and temporary employees on the basis that their employers were different (the regular employer versus the temporary agency). The Clinton-era board developed conditions under which permanent and temporary employees could be combined into a single bargaining unit even if one of the employers objects; the Bush-era board reversed so that permanent and temporary employees cannot be combined without the employers' consent.

Source: *http://www.lawmemo.com/emp/articles/nlrbreversals.htm* (accessed July 3, 2006).

NLRA to include supervisors, streamlining the certification election process to determine majority support, and banning the use of permanent strike replacements. These issues will be addressed in subsequent chapters, and while Congress has debated various reform proposals, none have passed. A recent example is the Employee Free Choice Act which was introduced in Congress in 2003 and 2005, but as of mid-2006, had not been debated or voted on. This bill would provide for certifying unions based on signed authorization cards rather than an election, authorize the use of first contract arbitration, and mandate stiffer penalties for violators.

Others criticize the NLRA framework for reducing labor unions to economic agents such that workers are only legally protected when they pursue their narrow economic interests such as higher wages rather than seeing the freedom of association and the right to strike as fundamental civil liberties that support democracy.[110] Taking this one step further, critical scholars advocate more sweeping changes to U.S. labor law that would shift labor law away from seeing unions as limited workplace advocates of workers (as in the industrial relations school) toward broader visions of unions as key institutions of the working class across workplaces and throughout the political and economic aspects of society (as in the critical industrial relations school).[111] Such changes might entail weakening the

[110] Josiah Bartlett Lambert, *"If the Workers Took a Notion": The Right to Strike and American Political Development* (Ithaca, NY: Cornell University Press, 2005).

[111] George Feldman, "Unions, Solidarity, and Class: The Limits of Liberal Labor Law," *Berkeley Journal of Employment and Labor Law* 15 (1994), pp. 187–272. Karl E. Klare, "Workplace Democracy and Market Reconstruction: An Agenda for Legal Reform," *Catholic University Law Review* 38 (Fall 1988), pp. 1–68. Katherine Van Wezel Stone, "Labor and the Corporate Structure: Changing Conceptions and Emerging Possibilities," *University of Chicago Law Review* 55 (Winter 1988), pp. 73–173.

dominance of employers' property rights, increasing union participation in corporate governance, and removing barriers to broad-based working class solidarity like the prohibition on secondary boycotts. In a very different vein, advocates of using joint (nonunion) labor–management committees for improving workplace issues lobby for a loosening of the section 8(a)(2) ban on company-dominated unions; this too has been considered by Congress, but has not been enacted (see Chapter 11).[112] Still others favor repealing the NLRA. Adherents of the neoclassical economics school see the NLRA as interfering with the achievement of economic prosperity through free markets and individual action; this view implies that the NLRA should be discarded.[113]

In contrast, an alternative view is that the assumptions of the NRLA—especially a sharp divide between managers and workers in stable, mass manufacturing industries—no longer match the world of work in the 21st century based on knowledge workers in a global system of flexible production.[114] The industrial relations school of thought then implies that new institutions should be created to place checks and balances on free markets, promote efficiency, equity, and voice, and balance property rights with labor rights.[115] These various perspectives of labor law reform are very important for thinking about future directions for U.S. labor relations, and they will be revisited in Chapter 14. But first, the next few chapters discuss the major processes of the current U.S. labor relations system—union organizing, bargaining, and grievance resolution. Understanding the development of the NLRA out of the industrial relations school of thought is a critical foundation for understanding these processes.

POSTSCRIPT: THE RISE OF EMPLOYMENT LAW

In U.S. legal and business circles, it is common to distinguish between labor law, which focuses on workers' *collective* actions, and **employment law,** which pertains to *individual* employment rights. Recall from Chapter 1 and Box 1.5 that in the absence of explicit laws, the U.S. employment relationship is governed by the employment-at-will doctrine which means that employees can be hired under any conditions and fired at any time for *any* reason. Under the employment-at-will doctrine, outstanding job performers can be fired because their supervisor dislikes them, because of their gender or race, or for any other arbitrary reason—and in return, employees are free to quit at any time.

The earliest attempts to temper the at-will doctrine occurred in the area of safety and health as various states enacted laws specifying minimum safety standards around 1900, though these laws were generally ineffective.[116] Many states also passed workers' compensation laws between 1910 and 1920, and they are now universal. Because of these workers' compensation policies, employees do not have to sue their employers in court to collect damages if they are

---

[112] Michael H. LeRoy, "Employee Participation in the New Millennium: Redefining a Labor Organization Under Section 8(a)(2) of the NLRA," *Southern California Law Review* 72 (September 1999), pp. 1651–723. Edward E. Potter and Judith A. Youngman, *Keeping America Competitive: Employment Policy for the Twenty-First Century* (Lakewood, CO: Glenbridge Publishing, 1995).

[113] Richard A. Epstein, "A Common Law for Labor Relations: A Critique of the New Deal Labor Legislation," *Yale Law Journal* 92 (July 1983), pp. 1357–1408. Heldman, Bennett, and Johnson, *Deregulating Labor Relations.* Morgan O. Reynolds, *Making America Poorer: The Cost of Labor Law* (Washington, DC: Cato Institute, 1987). Morgan Reynolds, "A New Paradigm: Deregulating Labor Relations," *Journal of Labor Research* 17 (Winter 1996), pp. 121–28.

[114] Charles C. Heckscher, *The New Unionism: Employee Involvement in the Changing Corporation* (New York: Basic Books, 1988).

[115] Budd, *Employment with a Human Face.*

[116] John F. Burton, Jr. and James R. Chelius, "Workplace Safety and Health Regulations: Rationale and Results," in Bruce E. Kaufman (ed.), *Government Regulation of the Employment Relationship* (Madison, WI: Industrial Relations Research Association, 1997), Chapter 7.

injured on the job; rather, employees are now guaranteed a set schedule of benefits.[117] This tempers the at-will doctrine by requiring workers' compensation insurance and by prohibiting employees from being fired in retaliation for filing a valid workers' compensation claim. That workers' compensation laws were passed so much earlier than other employment laws is perhaps explained by the fact that *employers* benefit substantially because they are shielded from litigation expenses and the possibility of very large damage awards.

During the Great Depression, adherents to the industrial relations school of thought believed that both unionization and government regulation of the employment relationship were necessary for balancing efficiency, equity, and voice. Unions can help equalize bargaining power between employers and unionized employees while government laws can ensure minimum standards for all employees.[118] Consequently, the New Deal period not only included the passage of the Wagner Act promoting unionization, but also advanced employment law through the passage of the Social Security Act (1935) and the Fair Labor Standards Act (FLSA, 1938). The Social Security Act establishes what has grown into OASDHI: old age, survivors, disability, and health insurance which provides monetary assistance and health care coverage from the federal government to retirees, the disabled, and their dependents. This legislation also establishes a system of state unemployment insurance benefits programs administered under the Federal Unemployment Tax Act. The FLSA creates a federal, national minimum wage, a mandatory overtime premium for covered workers for hours worked in excess of a weekly standard (now 40 hours), and restrictions on child labor.

As noted earlier, private sector labor law was largely enacted before 1960. By that time, employment law largely consisted of various forms of social insurance (workers' compensation, unemployment insurance, social security) and protective employment standards (minimum wages, maximum hours, and child labor restrictions). Between the 1960s and the present, private sector labor law has received little attention by lawmakers while employment law has exploded.[119] Consistent with the civil rights movement of the 1960s, many of the new employment laws target discriminatory employment practices. The Equal Pay Act of 1963 prohibits discriminating between men and women in determining compensation for equal jobs. Title VII of the Civil Rights Act of 1964 establishes the principle of equal employment opportunity by prohibiting employment discrimination by both employers and unions on the basis of race, color, religion, sex, or national origin. The Age Discrimination in Employment Act (1967) extends Title VII's prohibitions to age discrimination for employees over the age of 40 and the Americans with Disabilities Act (1990) adds disabled individuals to the list of protected classes. The Civil Rights Act of 1991 strengthens these nondiscriminatory laws by adding the possibility of compensatory and punitive damages, not just backpay.

Other employment laws passed since the 1960s provide for mandated employment conditions beyond the wage, hours, and child labor provisions specified by the FLSA. The Occupational Safety and Health Act (1970) obligates employers to provide a safe workplace and empowers the Occupational Safety and Health Administration (OSHA) to determine specific safety standards that employers must comply with. The Employee Retirement Income Security Act (ERISA, 1974) establishes basic requirements for employer-sponsored pension plans and other benefits to protect employees against abuse and loss of benefits; some of these requirements and protections were strengthened in 2006 in the Pension Protection Act. The Worker Adjustment and Retraining Act (WARN, 1989) requires

---

[117] Dawn D. Bennett-Alexander and Laura P. Hartman, *Employment Law for Business,* 4th. ed. (Boston: McGraw-Hill/Irwin, 2004).

[118] Bruce E. Kaufman, "Labor Markets and Employment Regulation: The View of the 'Old' Institutionalists," in Bruce E. Kaufman (ed.), *Government Regulation of the Employment Relationship* (Madison, WI: Industrial Relations Research Association, 1997), Chapter 1.

[119] Bennett-Alexander and Hartman, *Employment Law for Business.*

employers to provide advance notice of mass layoffs and the Family and Medical Leave Act (FMLA, 1993) guarantees employees 12 weeks of unpaid leave for caring for themselves, their parents, or their children. Lastly, state courts have developed a patchwork of limited exceptions to the employment-at-will doctrine such as when a dismissal violates a public policy or when an employee handbook constitutes a valid employment contract.

The rise of employment law is a critical feature of the modern U.S. employment relationship and is significant for labor relations. On a practical level, these laws directly affect labor relations by providing standards that both employers and unions must fulfill, such as nondiscrimination or family leave. Moreover, research frequently finds that unions facilitate the fulfillment of the promises of employment law such as the receipt of unemployment insurance benefits.[120] On a broader level, the sufficiency of employment law protections against the potential abuses of the employment-at-will doctrine provides an important basis for evaluating the need for labor unions in the 21st century employment relationship. In other words, does employment law provide nonunion workers with sufficient levels of equity and voice? By some accounts, employment law has made unions obsolete by providing basic protections and the rise of employment law may therefore underlie the long-term decline in union density.[121] On the other hand, other observers might feel that the exceptions to the employment-at-will doctrine are still quite limited. Age discrimination, for example, is permissible towards workers under the age of 40, and many other areas are untouched by employment law—workers have been fired for living with someone without being married, smoking, drinking, motorcycling, and other legal activities outside of work.[122] Workers can even be fired for saying "blacks have rights too" to a co-worker.[123] In contrast to the standard of just cause discipline and discharge prevalent in union contracts (Chapter 10), the current nonunion exceptions to the employment-at-will doctrine do not amount to broad protections against unfair dismissal for nonunion workers. Whether this narrowness of employment law is evaluated as sufficient for the 21st-century employment relationship (as in the neoclassical economics and human resource management schools of thought) or not (as in the industrial relations and critical industrial relations schools of thought) has important ramifications for the future role of labor unions.

Key Terms

conspiracy doctrine, *155*	unfair labor practices, *170*	agency shop, *179*
injunction, *157*	National Labor Relations Board, *171*	Landrum-Griffin Act, *181*
yellow dog contract, *157*		Civil Service Reform Act, *185*
Danbury Hatters case, *159*	*NLRB v. Jones and Laughlin Steel Corp., 174*	*Wright Line* test, *188*
Norris-LaGuardia Act, *161*	Taft-Hartley Act, *176*	employment law, *194*
Railway Labor Act, *165*	closed shop, *179*	
The Wagner Act, *166*	union shop, *179*	
exclusive representation, *168*		

[120] John W. Budd and Brian P. McCall, "The Effect of Unions on the Receipt of Unemployment Insurance Benefits," *Industrial and Labor Relations Review* 50 (April 1997), pp. 478–92. David Weil, "Implementing Employment Regulation: Insights on the Determinants of Regulatory Performance," in Bruce E. Kaufman (ed.), *Government Regulation of the Employment Relationship* (Madison, WI: Industrial Relations Research Association, 1997), Chapter 12.

[121] James T. Bennett and Jason E. Taylor, "Labor Unions: Victims of Their Political Success?" *Journal of Labor Research* 22 (Spring 2001), pp. 261–73.

[122] Terry Morehead Dworkin, "Its My Life—Leave Me Alone: Off-the-Job Employee Associational Privacy Rights." *American Business Law Journal* 35 (Fall 1997), pp. 47–104.

[123] *Bigelow v. Bullard*, 901 P.2d 630 (Nev. 1995).

Reflection Questions

1. A Kenyan proverb states, "When elephants fight, it is the grass that suffers." How is U.S. labor law premised on this belief? Describe specific provisions in U.S. labor law that are intended to address this concern.

2. Outline the arguments in support of the Taft-Hartley Act. Outline the opposing arguments (in other words, that Taft-Hartley was heartily daft).

3. In U.S. politics, the Democratic party has generally been more supportive of labor unions while the Republican party has been more hostile. Explain how it makes sense that the Wagner Act was sponsored by a Democrat, the Taft-Hartley Act by two Republicans, and the Landrum-Griffin Act by one of each.

4. One of the main tasks of the NLRB is applying the facts of a certain case to the general principles of the NLRA to determine if an unfair labor practice has been committed. To gain a greater understanding of this process, answer the questions in the Labor Law Discussion Cases in Boxes 5.24–5.26.

5. In both the private and public sectors, a sharp increase in union membership coincides with the passage of protective legislation. A longstanding debate is whether increased demand for unionization causes new legislation or vice versa.[124] Explain how causality can work in both directions. In which direction is labor law more important? Which direction do you think is more realistic?

6. Draw pictures to represent the NLRA's employer and union unfair labor practices.

7. Reconsider the examples of protected and unprotected concerted activity in Box 5.10. For each one explain how the ruling tries to balance property rights and labor rights.

Internet Exploration

1. Find a state bargaining law online. Is this a comprehensive law? How is it similar to the NLRA framework? How is it different?

2. Explore the websites of the National Labor Relations Board (*www.nlrb.gov*) and the National Mediation Board (*www.nmb.gov*). How are these agencies similar? Different?

3. Whether or not graduate assistants are protected by labor law in terms of trying to organize unions and bargain collectively depends on whether the university is public or private, and for the public sector, what state it's located in. Explore the Coalition of Graduate Employee Unions Web site (*www.cgeu.org*) to learn about the employment issues of concern for graduate students and the differing levels of legal coverage. Is it good or bad that there are such great legal differences across sectors?

4. Search the Web for statements on the need to reform the NLRA. Try to find pro-business and pro-union perspectives. What are the important issues? Why?

Additional Reading

Dubofsky, Melvin, *The State and Labor in Modern America* (Chapel Hill: University of North Carolina Press, 1994).

Ernst, Daniel R., *Lawyers Against Labor: From Individual Rights to Corporate Liberalism* (Urbana: University of Illinois Press, 1995).

Gross, James A., *Broken Promise: The Subversion of U.S. Labor Relations Policy, 1947–1994* (Philadelphia: Temple University Press, 1995).

Hardin, Patrick, and John E. Higgins, Jr. (eds.), *The Developing Labor Law: The Board, the Courts, and the National Labor Relations Act* (Washington, DC: BNA Books, 2001).

O'Brien, Ruth, *Workers' Paradox: The Republican Origins of New Deal Labor Policy, 1886–1935* (Chapel Hill: The University of North Carolina Press, 1998).

Ray, Douglas E., Calvin William Sharpe, and Robert N. Strassfield, *Understanding Labor Law* (New York: Mathew Bender, 1999).

[124] Gregory M. Saltzman, "Bargaining Laws as a Cause and Consequence of the Growth of Teacher Unions," *Industrial and Labor Relations Review* 38 (April 1985), pp. 335–51.

Background

Bird Engineering manufactures go-carts and minibikes in Nebraska and annually purchases and sells goods and services valued in excess of $50,000 from/to sources outside of Nebraska. The plant includes a lunchroom and a break room which include vending machines, but no cafeteria. The vending machines contain "chips, cookies, peanuts, sometimes rolls, soup, hot chocolate, and coffee." None of the employees are represented by a labor union.

Production is very cyclical with peak production in November so night shifts and temporary employees are generally added to various production departments beginning in August. Because of "thefts of employee and company property, the unauthorized use of company property, suspicion of drinking during lunch breaks, and employees returning tardy from lunch breaks," management implemented a "closed campus" rule for night-shift employees. Under this new policy, night-shift employees were prohibited from leaving the plant during the night-shift lunch break. This is legal by Nebraska state law.

The welding department added a night shift a week after the closed campus rule was instituted and consequently the welding department was not aware of this rule. After management found out that the welding department was violating the closed campus rule, five night-shift employees of the welding department were called to the supervisor's office and informed of the closed campus rule and told by their supervisor that they would be terminated if they left the plant building during their lunch break. The five employees protested that the policy was illegal and asked to be granted permission to leave for lunch since they did not bring any lunch with them to work that day. Their request was denied.

The five employees decided to protest the closed campus rule by following their past practice and leaving the premises for lunch. Termination slips were issued to them when they returned from their lunch outing 30 minutes later.

That same evening, at about 10:30 P.M. (the normal lunch break time for the night shift), a sixth employee, Christina Hodgeman, was preparing to go to her van and eat her lunch when her supervisor informed her that if she left the building she would be fired. Hodgeman normally ate her lunch in her van in the parking lot and had been told when she was hired a month ago that employees were permitted to go to the parking lot but should clock out. She had been absent the previous three days because of the flu and asked permission to go to her van to get her lunch and medication. This request was denied. Feeling that she needed her medication, Hodgeman responded "Well, if there's no other alternative, then write me out a termination slip." The supervisor obliged.

National Labor Relations Act Excerpt

RIGHTS OF EMPLOYEES. SECTION 7.

Employees shall have the right to self-organization, to form, join, or assist labor organizations, to bargain collectively through representatives of their own choosing, or to engage in other concerted activities for the purpose of collective bargaining or other mutual aid or protection, and shall also have the right to refrain from any or all of such activities except to the extent that such right may be affected by an agreement requiring membership in a labor organization as a condition of employment as authorized in section 8(a)(3).

UNFAIR LABOR PRACTICES. SECTION 8.

(a) It shall be an unfair labor practice for an employer
   (1). to interfere with, restrain, or coerce employees in the exercise of the rights guaranteed in section 7;

Questions

1. Are the six employees covered by the NLRA? Does it matter that they are not represented by a labor union?

2. Consider the five employees who left together. Assuming that the employees are covered by the NLRA, did Bird Engineering violate section 8(a)(1) by firing the five employees? In other words, were they discharged for activities that are protected by section 7? (*Hint:* if the employees were on strike, it was protected activity. If their action was insubordination, it is not protected.)

3. Consider the sixth employee who went to her van to get her medicine. Assuming that the employees are covered by the NLRA, did Bird Engineering violate section 8(a)(1) by firing her?

4. If Bird Engineering violated the NLRA, what is the appropriate remedy?

Background

La Gloria Gas and Oil Company operates a Texas refinery that employs 14 truck drivers that are not represented by a union. The drivers deliver oil products to various industrial clients, sometimes several hours away. Linda Taylor, a former state trooper, works part-time for La Gloria monitoring the drivers' driving patterns by secretly following them. Every two weeks to six months she submits written reports to the company listing various infractions she observes: following too closely, speeding, failing to stop at railroad tracks, missing a mud flap, and the like. No driver had been disciplined or discharged for the violations reported by Taylor.

One of the drivers, Jose Garcia, questioned his supervisor, Chris Mueller, about why the drivers didn't receive any benefits and was told in response, "You work for La Gloria, so you got what you want, but there's no benefits." Around the same time, Garcia received some union literature. He then contacted a union organizer and talked with some other drivers about unionizing. He met with the organizer at the union hall a couple of times. With two other drivers, he also met with the organizer at a local restaurant. All of these events occurred in a span of about six weeks.

The day after the meeting at the restaurant, supervisor Mueller approached another worker who was at that meeting and asked, "What's the rumors that I am hearing?" The worker explained that the drivers had met with a union organizer because they were upset at the lack of benefits. He did not name the other workers at the meeting. The next day, a similar exchange occurred with another worker who was at the restaurant. Both workers indicated that Mueller was agitated and upset and remarked that the refinery would probably get rid of the trucks if the drivers unionized which would also put him out of a job. Mueller was even more upset when Garcia's name came up.

Two days later, Taylor monitored Garcia's driving and called in a report to Mueller the next day. Taylor indicated that Garcia intermittently exceeded the speed limit, ran a red light, and left his turn signal on for a long time. Mueller then fired Garcia for these traffic violations and for two prior incidents of insubordination. Garcia denies that he ran a red light and tailgated. Garcia denies being disciplined for the prior incidents of insubordination. The written memos in his personnel file are questionable—they contain little factual documentation and could have been made after the fact.

Discussion

Section 8(a)(3) of the NLRA makes it an unfair labor practice for an employer "to encourage or discourage membership in any labor organization" "by discrimination in regard to hire or tenure of employment or any term or condition of employment." The scenario in this case is a classic 8(a)(3) unfair labor practice question. The employer claims to have valid, job-related reasons for disciplining or firing an employee while the employee feels that these reasons are an excuse to justify firing a union supporter. The question for the NLRB is whether the employer's claims are legitimate, or are instead simply a pretext for firing the employee because of his union activity. It is very important for management and union practitioners to understand how the NLRB analyzes and decides these cases.

When an alleged 8(a)(3) violation hinges on the employer's motivation (such as valid job performance issues versus retribution for union activity), the NLRB applies the framework established by *Wright Line,* 251 NLRB 1083 (1980) [approved by the Supreme Court in *NLRB v. Transportation Management Corp.,* 462 U.S. 403 (1983)]. In this framework, the General Counsel (the prosecution) must first show that (1) the employee was engaged in protected activity, (2) the employer was aware of the activity, and (3) the activity was a substantial or motivating reason for the employer's action. If the General Counsel establishes these facts, the burden of proof then shifts to the employer to prove that it would have taken the same action even if the employees had not engaged in protected activity.

Questions

1. How would you argue the first three requirements on behalf of the discharged employee: (1) Garcia was engaged in protected activity, (2) the employer was aware of the activity, and (3) the activity was a substantial or motivating reason for Garcia's discharge?

2. Assuming that the first three requirements are established, how would you argue on behalf of the employer that Garcia would have been discharged even if he had not engaged in his protected activity?

3. If you were a member of the NLRB, how would you rule? What is the remedy?

Box 5.26

Labor Law Discussion: Is Body Language Protected Activity?

Background

The Health Care and Retirement Corporation (HCR) owns and operates over 100 nursing homes in 27 states. Corporate headquarters is in Toledo, Ohio. One of the nursing homes is located in rural Ohio and is called Heartland. Heartland is a 100-bed facility with about 65 people employed in the nursing department (10 staff nurses [8 licensed practical nurses, 2 registered nurses] and 55 nurses aides). None of the employees at Heartland are represented by a union.

The nurse aides have the most contact with the residents of Heartland—bathing, dressing, feeding, emptying bed pans, etc. The nurses are responsible for making sure that the needs of the residents are fulfilled—checking on the health status of the residents, administering medicine, communicating with physicians. Nurses also perform the duties of nurse aides when an insufficient number of nurse aides show up for work.

While night-shift nurses have little to do with assigning aides' duties, the day-shift nurses are responsible for telling each aide what residents he/she is responsible for. The nature of the aides' work makes them fairly interchangeable. Also, assignments are often done by following old patterns and/or letting the aides decide coverage among themselves. Nurses are responsible for trying to find replacement aides when an aide does not show up for work, but have no authority to order an aide to come in. Nurses have no authority to authorize overtime. Disciplining and performance appraisals of the aides are conducted by the Director of Nursing, not a staff nurse (although nurses can make comments about an aide's performance on an "employee counseling form"). At night and on weekends, the staff nurses are the most senior personnel at the facility. The Director of Nursing (or an assistant) is on call and is normally contacted when nonroutine matters arise.

Barbara Young was hired in July to be the new administrator at Heartland. She was quite inexperienced, however, and was overworked. In December, Ms. Young switched the Heartland's pharmacy from a local pharmacy (whose owner had very close ties with the community) to a chain pharmacy located 40 miles away. This drastically increased the paperwork duties of the nurses (although it is perhaps the case that this increased paperwork was because Heartland and the local pharmacy were not completing the forms required by state regulations). The community was offended by this action and Heartland experienced a drop in new admissions (some of this discontent in the community was fueled by the nurses).

The Director of Nursing position was vacant between December and February of the next year. The facility was understaffed, especially among nurse aides, and little was being done to hire new personnel. In January, three staff nurses asked to meet with Young. They wished to discuss several actions by Young that the nurses thought were detrimental to the residents and affected the work of the nurses and aides. Young replied that, due to her busy schedule, they should set up an appointment for later in the week.

Instead, the three nurses traveled to corporate headquarters in Toledo the next day where they met with a vice president and with Bob Custer, HCR's director of human resources. In this meeting, the three nurses expressed four primary problems:

> i) there were an insufficient number of aides employed at Heartland (and substandard wages and recruiting perpetuated this ongoing problem),
> ii) little discipline was taken with regard to aides' absenteeism which placed more burden on the aides who showed up for work,
> iii) the pharmacy switch, and
> iv) communications problems between Young and Heartland's nurses.

The nurses were told that an investigation would be launched to investigate their complaints and that they would not be harassed for speaking out.

A week later, Custer met with the Heartland's department heads (Young was not present). The department heads liked Young, knew the nurses had complained about Young, and assumed that Custer would fire her. The department heads supported Young in their meeting with Custer and also talked about the unprofessional behavior of the three nurses. Custer subsequently asked each person at the meeting for the names of the people he/she thought responsible for the tension at Heartland. Two of the three nurses appeared on every response; the third was on many.

Custer also met with Young. During their discussion, Young remarked to Custer about the three nurses' lack of cooperation with management. Young also mentioned that some employees had, among other things, started a rumor about an affair between Custer and Young. A few days later, Custer met with the facility's aides. The complaints about Heartland were greatest among those aides who worked the same shift as the three nurses. Custer took this as further evidence that the three nurses were the root of the problem.

During February, the three nurses received a variety of disciplinary notices. Their disciplinary notices for missing an "in-service" (internal training session) are typical: only six nurses attended, but the three were the only absent nurses to receive warnings. Additionally, Heartland's policy is to give two weeks' notice before any mandatory in-service—in this instance, only a few days' notice was given. As a second example, a state audit found many minor mistakes by all of the nurses in their unit, but only the three were disciplined.

In March, HR Director Custer met with the Heartland's nurses to announce:

i) the pay for aides would be increased to hire more aides,
ii) Young would not be fired, and
iii) the pharmacy situation would not be changed back.

Custer perceived the "demeanor and tone" of the meeting to be "resistance to change, emphatic refusal to get on board and make Heartland a good facility." Custer believed the three nurses were responsible for this attitude among the nurses and concluded that they should be fired. The "demeanor" of the meeting, Custer admitted, was conveyed to him by the three nurses crossing their arms and rolling their eyes as Custer talked. Custer therefore concluded that the three nurses were unwilling to change their mode of operation and attitude to improve the facility. Thus, Custer decided that they should be fired. When they refused to resign, they were fired.

Questions

1. Are the nurses covered by the NLRA? Remember that the NLRA excludes supervisors from protection under the Act using the following definition:

2(11) The term "supervisor" means any individual having authority, in the interest of the employer, to hire, transfer, suspend, lay off, recall, promote, discharge, assign, reward, or discipline other employees, or responsibly to direct them, or to adjust their grievances, or effectively to recommend such action, if in connection with the foregoing the exercise of such authority is not of a merely routine or clerical nature, but requires the use of independent judgment.

2. Create a list of possible reasons that the three nurses were fired. Determine whether each reason is protected by section 7.

3. If you were a member of the NLRB, would you rule that HCR violated section 8(a)(1) of the NLRB by discharging the three nurses (assuming that they are covered by the NLRA)? Why or why not?

Answers to Box 5.10

1. Protected — This is the classic form of concerted activity that the Wagner Act seeks to protect—employees joining together to increase their bargaining power to improve their employment conditions.

2. Protected — Striking or threatening to strike is the primary way for employees to succeed in improving their employment conditions as envisioned by the Wagner Act.

3. Unprotected — While strikes are central to the Wagner Act framework, the section 7 rights are not unlimited and they do not protect outrageous or illegal behavior such as destroying company property, vandalism, or violence.

4. Protected — The Wagner Act empowers employees to work together to improve their employment conditions.

5. Protected — Even though the meeting is attended by an individual, not a group, that individual is acting on behalf of others and therefore is concerted activity.

6. Unprotected — This one is tricky. Circulating a flyer is concerted activity, but building support for employee ownership is an issue for the workers as owners, not employees. The Act promotes the improvement of working conditions; ownership issues are beyond the scope and therefore beyond the protection of the Act.

7. Protected — This is a strike and is therefore protected. Being represented by a union is not necessary. Nonunion employees are entitled to engage in collective actions to improve their working conditions.

8. Unprotected — By selectively picking and choosing what policies to obey, workers are engaging in a partial strike which is insubordination, not a protected strike. This is essentially an attempt to "have your cake and eat it too" rather than making a sincere protest.

9. Protected — This is another form of mutual aid and protection. This specific scenario will be discussed in Chapter 10.

10. Protected — This is the same as #4 but using information technologies.

11. Unprotected — Actions that are malicious, defamatory, or insubordinate lose protection. Spontaneous outbursts of profanity can be protected if they result from the "heat of the moment" and frustration over working conditions.

12. Protected — Consistent with the spirit of the Wagner Act, employees have the right to protect themselves from harm. But if the situation is not truly dangerous, then a refusal to work is insubordination which is not protected by the Act.

Additional Reading: Calvin William Sharpe, " 'By Any Means Necessary'—Unprotected Conduct and Decisional Discretion Under the National Labor Relations Act," *Berkeley Journal of Employment and Labor Law* 20 (1999), pp. 203–53.

Chapter **Six**

Labor and Management: Strategies, Structures, and Rights

Advance Organizer

The previous two chapters have described the historical development and legal framework of the U.S. labor relations system. This chapter examines the structure and strategies used by labor unions and employers to achieve efficiency and/or equity and/or voice. Some strategies can involve mutual gains while others conflict. Balancing these conflicts is the central issue in labor relations and labor law.

Learning Objectives

By the end of the chapter, you should be able to:

1. **Compare** the traditional U.S. union strategies (especially, business unionism, job control unionism, and the servicing model) and their alternatives (especially, social unionism, employee empowerment unionism, and the organizing model).

2. **Understand** the structure of unions and the labor movement in the United States.

3. **Discuss** the range of possible management strategies toward labor unions and how they relate to human resource strategies and business strategies.

4. **Determine** the relative importance of property rights and labor rights in U.S. labor relations and why these competing human rights should be balanced.

Contents

The heart of labor relations is conflict between the goals of employees and employers. This can be an intimidating image, but it shouldn't be. It doesn't mean that labor and management are consumed in an all-out war and continually attack each other. In fact, on a daily basis the striking feature of most workplaces is the amount of cooperation, not conflict or competition.[1] But what sets labor relations apart from human resource management and labor economics is the study of conflict in the employment relationship. As described in Chapter 2, labor relations scholars and practitioners who adhere to the pluralist industrial relations school of thought believe that there is an inherent conflict of interest in the employment relationship. While employees and employers have shared interests, conflict is also natural and to be

---

[1] John Godard, *Industrial Relations, the Economy, and Society,* 3rd ed. (Concord, Ontario: Captus Press, 2005). Robert C. Solomon, *Ethics and Excellence: Cooperation and Integrity in Business* (New York: Oxford University Press, 1992). Cynthia Estlund, *Working Together: How Workplace Bonds Strengthen a Diverse Democracy* (Oxford: Oxford University Press, 2003).

expected, not pathological and to be suppressed. Labor relations therefore seeks to design systems and policies to manage this conflict to create productive workplaces that balance efficiency with equity and voice. In other words, the task is to effectively manage conflict and harness the shared interests for mutual gain.

The objectives of the employment relationship are efficiency, equity, and voice. This chapter describes the strategies and structures for achieving the efficiency, equity, and voice goals of employees, unions, and employers. For labor, efficiency is usually a way to achieve the primary objectives of equity and voice—profitable companies can better afford equitable wage and benefit packages and provide job security. But employers have the opposite perspective: equity and voice are important primarily to the extent that they foster the main objective of efficiency—employees who are treated fairly and provided with a voice might be more loyal and productive.

Because of these differing perspectives on efficiency, equity, and voice, conflicts are likely. Labor's desired form of employee voice might reduce efficiency by making decision making more cumbersome and by increasing employee bargaining power. Equitable, seniority-based layoff or promotion policies might reduce managerial flexibility and efficiency. These are labor–management conflicts of interest. Companies have an interest in lower wages and employees are interested in higher wages. Employees desire security and managers desire flexibility. These conflicts will generally be resolved privately by individuals, unions, and companies, for example through bargaining. But at a more fundamental level, there is also an underlying conflict between property rights and labor rights. Companies have a right to use their private property to pursue profits while employees have rights to unionize and seek basic living standards. These conflicts are resolved by policymakers and judges. **The U.S. labor relations system seeks to balance property rights and labor rights in order to promote a balanced resolution of conflicts of interest.**

This is a critical theme to remember throughout this book. When trying to understand and evaluate labor law, ask how property rights are conflicting with labor rights. For example, should the law allow union organizers to talk to employees in the workplace which is the employer's private property? Should management be allowed to hire replacement workers for striking employees which serves the employer's property rights to conduct business while potentially harming the employees' rights to engage in collective bargaining? When trying to understand and evaluate union contracts, ask how property rights are conflicting with labor rights. Do seniority-based promotion policies strike a good balance between property rights and labor rights? When thinking about whether the U.S. labor relations system needs to be reformed, ask whether property rights and labor rights could be better balanced in a different system. On a global level, the sometimes violent protests in Seattle and other locations that have accompanied international summits on free trade and globalization reflect frustration with perceived imbalances in the promotion of property rights over labor (and environmental) rights in free trade agreements.[2] Labor rights versus property rights is an important issue for the 21st century.

LABOR GOALS AND STRATEGIES

What does labor want? This is a famous question in labor relations. In what is perhaps more labor relations legend than fact, Samuel Gompers, the longtime president of the American Federation of Labor (AFL), is reported to have simply said, "More." His true answer is contained in Box 6.1. The goals presented in Box 6.1 are hard to argue with and

[2] Marjorie Cohn, "The World Trade Organization: Elevating Property Interests Above Human Rights," *Georgia Journal of International and Comparative Law* 29 (Summer 2001), pp. 427–40.

"We want more school houses and less jails; more books and less arsenals; more learning and less vice; more constant work and less crime; more leisure and less greed; more justice and less revenge; in fact, more of the opportunities to cultivate our better natures, to make manhood more noble, womanhood more beautiful and childhood more happy and bright. These in brief are the primary demands made by the Trade Unions in the name of labor."

Samuel Gompers
President of the American Federation of Labor, 1886–1894, 1896–1924
Address of August 1893

Source: Stuart B. Kaufman and Peter J. Albert (eds.), *The Samuel Gompers Papers, Volume 3, Unrest and Depression, 1891–94* (Urbana: University of Illinois Press, 1989), p. 396.

might be summarized by fairness and respect based on dignity and social justice—or equity and voice. This section investigates the common strategies that are used to support the broad objectives of equity and voice.

In considering union strategies, it is important to clearly distinguish between the scope and soul of employee representation (see Box 6.2). The *scope* of representation describes the breadth of the representation activities—in particular, whether union activity is concentrated in the workplace or in the broader political and social arenas. A focus on collective bargaining is a workplace scope of representation; a focus on social activism and political lobbying is a broader scope.

In contrast, the *soul* of representation captures how the representation is pursued or delivered, especially regarding the extent of rank and file participation. U.S. labor unions are often categorized as employing either a servicing model or organizing model of representation.[3] In the **servicing model,** a union is like an insurance company. Workers pay dues and in return they are protected against bad times: arbitrary supervisors, the vagaries of markets, accidents, and the like. In this conceptualization, workers do not participate in a union, they consume union services, especially collectively bargained contracts and representation in the grievance procedure. Workers are serviced by union officials: problems are solved *for* the workers, not *by* the workers. This is a passive form of employee representation and the soul of the representation process consists of union officials. In contrast, the **organizing model** views unions as an institution of worker participation. This includes a strategy of organizing new unions not by professional, full-time union staff members, but by internal organizers: existing workers who talk about forming a union with their coworkers and thereby create more internal organizers. But the organizing model is a philosophy that extends beyond the process of forming new unions, it is a conceptualization of labor unions as institutions of empowerment and mobilization. In this model, problems are not solved for workers, they are involved in their resolution; workers do not consume equity and voice, they participate in their attainment and continually serve as internal organizers to create vibrant unions. This is an active form of representation, and the soul of the representation process consists of the rank and file union members. In short, the servicing model sees the relationship between a worker and his or her union as a narrow economic exchange; the organizing model sees this as more of a social exchange.[4]

[3] Andy Banks and Jack Metzgar, "Participating in Management: Union Organizing on a New Terrain," *Labor Research Review* 14 (Fall 1989), pp. 1–55. Bill Fletcher, Jr. and Richard W. Hurd, "Beyond the Organizing Model: The Transformation Process in Local Unions," in Kate Bronfenbrenner, et al. (eds.), *Organizing to Win: New Research on Union Strategies* (Ithaca, NY: ILR Press, 1998), pp. 37–53.

[4] Ed Snape and Tom Redman, "Exchange or Covenant? The Nature of the Member-Union Relationship," *Industrial Relations* 43 (October 2004), pp. 855–73.

BOX 6.2
The Soul and Scope of Employee Representation

		Scope of Representation	
		Workplace (Business Unionism)	Social Arena (Social Unionism)
Soul of Representation	Union Officials (Passive Servicing Model)	Job Control Unionism, Traditional Craft Unionism	European Social Partnerships
	Union Members (Active Organizing Model)	Employee Empowerment Unionism	Social Movement Unionism

In terms of the scope of representation, U.S. unions have traditionally had a **business unionism** philosophy (recall Box 4.7).[5] This is a workplace scope and the key to achieving equity and voice is through strong collective bargaining in the workplace which allows unions to win wage gains, fringe benefits, grievance procedures, and protective work rules. This philosophy fully embraces capitalism and the need for employers to make a profit. Labor's goal is to win their fair share of the profits through collective bargaining. John L. Lewis, long-time president of the United Mine Workers and leader of the industrial union movement in the 1930s, clearly described the U.S. business unionism outlook:

> Trade unionism is a phenomenon of capitalism quite similar to the corporation. One is essentially a pooling of labor for the purpose of common action in production and sales. The other is a pooling of capital for exactly the same purpose. The economic aims of both are identical—gain.[6]

In other words, this is a business-like approach to employee representation, or unionism "pure and simple."[7]

An abusive variant of business unionism can be called hold-up unionism or jungle unionism.[8] If unrestrained competition, especially in periods of high unemployment, leads to individual needs for survival, a jungle unionism strategy is to take whatever you need or can by whatever means necessary—like the law of the jungle. Among the "best" (or perhaps "worst" is more appropriate) examples are the tactics of Jimmy Hoffa's Teamsters in 1930s and 1940s in which strikes and boycotts were readily supplemented with bombings, brawls, flying squadrons, and other means of violence and coercion to organize drivers and warehouse workers in the highly competitive Detroit transportation, retail, and wholesale industries.[9] It is important, however, not to generalize the pattern of a handful of corrupt unions to the many that are not.

Within the business unionism philosophy, the pursuit of equity and voice by U.S. unions since World War II has been dominated by **job control unionism.** This philosophy involves a workplace scope of representation and a passive soul of representation (consistent with the servicing model of representation) (see Box 6.2). Job control unionism consists of very detailed and legalistic union contracts, enforced by a formal grievance procedure, that tie employee rights to very narrowly defined jobs while removing labor from decision

---

[5] Robert Franklin Hoxie, *Trade Unionism in the United States* (New York: D. Appleton, 1917).

[6] Sidney Lens, *The Crisis of American Labor* (New York, 1959), p. 81.

[7] David Brody, "Labor's Crisis in Historical Perspective," in George Strauss, Daniel G. Gallagher, and Jack Fiorito (eds.), *The State of the Unions* (Madison, WI: Industrial Relations Research Association, 1991), Chapter 8.

[8] Hoxie, *Trade Unionism in the United States.* Thaddeus Russell, *Out of the Jungle: Jimmy Hoffa and the Remaking of the American Working Class* (New York: Knopf, 2001).

[9] Russell, *Out of the Jungle.*

making.[10] Through much of the 20th century, the dominant method of work organization was scientific management in which jobs were divided into very specialized tasks. A typical example is assembly-line production in which each worker repeats just a few operations on each item as it passes by on the assembly line, although narrow job classifications can be found in many occupations and industries—grocery store checkout clerks, financial services data entry clerks, and hotel room cleaners, for example. In addition to creating detailed job classifications, employers have traditionally been adamant about maintaining their managerial prerogatives—discipline, production, scheduling, marketing, pricing, investment, and other managerial functions.[11] Faced with this environment, unions have pursued equity and voice by winning predictable wage increases, generous fringe benefits, seniority-based layoff and promotion systems, limitations on discipline and discharge for just cause only, and grievance procedures. The result is job control unionism: a sharp break between collective bargaining over wages and rights linked to jobs on the one hand, and managerial authority over business functions on the other (see Box 6.3).

Faced with increased foreign and nonunion competition and greater pressures for flexibility and quality, the rigidities of job control unionism have been under attack since the 1980s (see Chapter 11). Labor and management have experimented with different ways of moving away from job control unionism and some can be loosely grouped together as **employee empowerment unionism** (see Box 6.3).[12] While retaining a workplace scope of representation, this model seeks to achieve a more active soul of representation. Rather than establishing standardized outcomes, such as a certain job classification receives a certain wage or the person with the least seniority is laid off first as are typical in job control unionism, employee empowerment unionism establishes the framework of procedures in which workers are then empowered to determine their own outcomes. Consider union strategies in professional sports. These unions focus less on negotiating specific outcomes and instead have established the parameters within which individual players negotiate their own salaries.[13] These parameters include minimum standards and provisions for resolving disputes. A similar model is used for actors and might also be appropriate for college professors, doctors, and other occupations.

Professional athletes and actors are perhaps unique examples because the individual employees are negotiating their own salaries, but as companies move toward teamwork and various mechanisms for employee involvement and decision making, examples of employee empowerment unionism are increasing. Skill-based pay is one example: labor and management negotiate the parameters of the system, and workers are empowered to be responsible for upgrading their skills and reaping rewards for doing so. Union involvement in establishing standards for a team to select new members or a team leader is another example in which the union's role is not negotiating outcomes, but negotiating processes for empowering individual employees. Lastly, the clerical workers at Harvard University bargained for a problem-solving system that replaces a traditional grievance procedure with a framework that empowers employees to resolve their own workplace problems.[14]

---

[10] Harry C. Katz, *Shifting Gears: Changing Labor Relations in the U.S. Automobile Industry* (Cambridge: MIT Press, 1985). Thomas A. Kochan, Harry C. Katz, and Robert B. McKersie, *The Transformation of American Industrial Relations* (New York: Basic Books, 1986).

[11] Howell John Harris, *The Right to Manage: Industrial Relations Policies of American Business in the 1940s* (Madison: University of Wisconsin Press, 1982).

[12] John W. Budd, *Employment with a Human Face: Balancing Efficiency, Equity, and Voice* (Ithaca, NY: Cornell University Press, 2004).

[13] Roger I. Abrams, *The Money Pitch: Baseball Free Agency and Salary Arbitration* (Philadelphia: Temple University Press, 2000). Kenneth M. Jennings, *Swings and Misses: Moribund Labor Relations in Professional Baseball* (Westport, CT: Praeger, 1997).

[14] John Hoerr, *We Can't Eat Prestige: The Women Who Organized Harvard* (Philadelphia: Temple University Press, 1997).

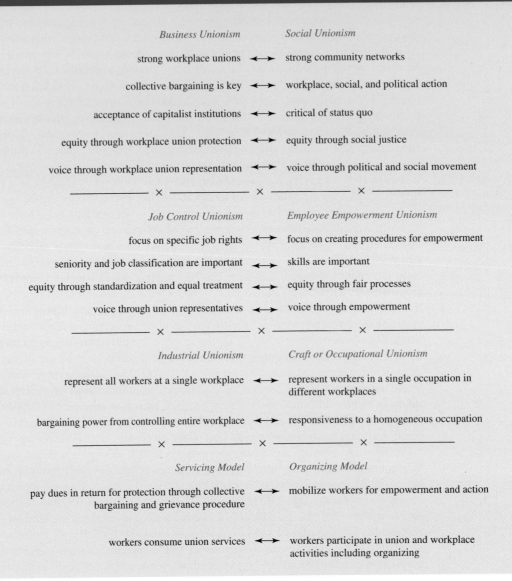

Business Unionism · Social Unionism

strong workplace unions	←→	strong community networks
collective bargaining is key	←→	workplace, social, and political action
acceptance of capitalist institutions	←→	critical of status quo
equity through workplace union protection	←→	equity through social justice
voice through workplace union representation	←→	voice through political and social movement

Job Control Unionism · Employee Empowerment Unionism

focus on specific job rights	←→	focus on creating procedures for empowerment
seniority and job classification are important	←→	skills are important
equity through standardization and equal treatment	←→	equity through fair processes
voice through union representatives	←→	voice through empowerment

Industrial Unionism · Craft or Occupational Unionism

| represent all workers at a single workplace | ←→ | represent workers in a single occupation in different workplaces |
| bargaining power from controlling entire workplace | ←→ | responsiveness to a homogeneous occupation |

Servicing Model · Organizing Model

| pay dues in return for protection through collective bargaining and grievance procedure | ←→ | mobilize workers for empowerment and action |
| workers consume union services | ←→ | workers participate in union and workplace activities including organizing |

Returning to the broader category of business unionism (of which job control and employee empowerment are two variants), this workplace scope of representation contrasts with the **social unionism** philosophy that is frequently observed in Europe. Adherents to a social unionism philosophy see labor unions as more than workplace mechanisms for winning economic gains; rather, unions are viewed as integral participants in a country's civic and political activities (see Box 6.3). In other words the scope of representation is the broader social and political arena. Labor's influence comes less from strong bargaining power in the workplace and more from social and political power. The pursuit of equity and voice is not limited to negotiating favorable contract language governing the rules of the workplace, but extends to broader concerns of social justice throughout society.

Like business unionism, however, the soul of social unionism can be union leaders with passive rank and file participation—consistent with a servicing model of representation—or active union member participation—consistent with an organizing model of representation (see Box 6.2). European social partnership arrangements in which the top union and business leaders negotiate agreements with the government on broad social and economic issues are examples of social unionism with passive rank and file participation (see Chapter 13). Active union lobbying for minimum wage increases, civil rights legislation, or other broad reforms without grassroots participation is another example. In contrast, social *movement* unionism embraces labor unions as part of a broader social movement of community, social, and political activist groups that relies on active grassroots participation and mobilization.[15] Advocates of a greater social unionism orientation for the U.S. labor movement are generally reacting against the passive servicing model and therefore focus on social movement unionism with widespread rank and file participation. Social movement unionism in the United States is often advocated as a basis for revitalizing the labor movement by providing the means to increase organizing, especially among traditionally overlooked groups such as immigrant workers, and to resist management demands for concessions.[16]

Equity and voice can therefore be pursued through business unionism or social unionism, and within business unionism, through a strategy of job control unionism or employee empowerment unionism. Another important comparison to consider is industrial unionism versus craft unionism (see Box 6.3). **Craft unionism,** or occupational unionism, involves a single union representing only workers in a single occupation or craft, such as separate unions for electricians, carpenters, and painters. This is prevalent today in the construction industry and it might also be well-suited to the workforce of the future if workers are increasingly mobile and identify more with an occupation than with a specific company.[17] In contrast, **industrial unionism** focuses on an industry rather than a craft. Industrial unions seek to represent workers of all occupations within an industry. For example, an industrial union at an appliance factory represents janitors, assembly-line workers, and skilled workers such as electricians; an industrial union at a hotel represents employees who work at the front desk, in the bar, restaurant, and kitchen, on the loading dock, in the back office, at the bellstand, in the laundry room, and in the rooms as cleaners.

In sum, contemporary U.S. unions have employed several strategies for achieving equity and voice. The dominant postwar model is on the left-hand side of Box 6.3: the pursuit of job control unionism through industrial unions with a business unionism philosophy and a servicing model of delivery. In this mode, equity is achieved through generous wage and benefit packages, seniority-based layoff and promotion procedures, restrictions on discipline and discharge for just cause only, and due process protections in the grievance procedure. Voice is achieved through representation at the bargaining table and in the grievance procedure. Collective bargaining is institutionalized and the union contract becomes the

---

[15] Lowell Turner and Richard W. Hurd, "Building Social Movement Unionism: The Transformation of the American Labor Movement," in Lowell Turner, Harry C. Katz, and Richard W. Hurd (eds.), *Rekindling the Movement: Labor's Quest for Relevance in the Twenty-First Century* (Ithaca, NY: ILR Press, 2001), Chapter 1. Paul Johnston, "Organize for What? The Resurgence of Labor as a Citizen Movement," in Turner, Katz, and Hurd, *Rekindling the Movement: Labor's Quest for Relevance in the Twenty-First Century,* Chapter 2.

[16] Ray M. Tillman and Michael S. Cummings (eds.), *The Transformation of U.S. Unions: Voices, Visions, and Strategies from the Grassroots* (Boulder, CO: Lynne Rienner Publishers, 1999). Rick Fantasia and Kim Voss, *Hard Work: Remaking the American Labor Movement* (Berkeley: University of California Press, 2004).

[17] Dorothy Sue Cobble, "Lost Ways of Unionism: Historical Perspectives on Reinventing the Labor Movement," in Turner, Katz, and Hurd, *Rekindling the Movement: Labor's Quest for Relevance in the Twenty-First Century,* Chapter 4. Katherine V. W. Stone, *From Widgets to Digits: Employment Regulations for the Changing Workplace.* (Cambridge, England: Cambridge University Press, 2004).

"workplace rule of law."[18] But the alternatives on the right-hand side of Box 6.3 can also balance efficiency, equity, and voice. As will be discussed in Chapter 14, determining which strategies are best for the 21st century is an important debate in labor relations.

THE STRUCTURE OF THE U.S. LABOR MOVEMENT

The primary focus of this chapter is the strategies of labor and management used to achieve efficiency, equity, and voice, but it is instructive to also consider the structure of the U.S. labor movement. Recall from Chapter 1 that an important trend is a long-term decline in U.S. union membership. Union density—the fraction of workers who belong to or are covered by a union—has been falling in the private sector since the 1950s and is now less than 10 percent. In the public sector, union density has hovered between 35 and 40 percent since 1980.

According to the U.S. Department of Labor, in 2005 there were 15,685,000 union members in the private and public sectors combined. An additional 1.5 million workers were covered by union contracts but were not union members, which brings the total number of U.S. workers covered by unions to 17,223,000, or 13.7 percent of all employed workers. As shown in Box 6.4, union density is significantly higher in full-time than in part-time jobs and is slightly higher among men than women. Moreover, relative to whites, union density is higher among African-American workers but lower among workers of Hispanic origin. These figures also imply that 43 percent of union members are women, at least 35 percent are members of minority groups, and 47 percent are in the public sector.

BOX 6.4
U.S. Union Membership and Coverage Statistics, 2005

	Union Members		Workers Covered by a Union Contract	
	Number	**Percent**	**Number**	**Percent**
Total	15,685,000	12.5	17,223,000	13.7
Full-time workers	14,207,000	13.7	15,551,000	15.0
Part-time workers	1,441,000	6.5	1,630,000	7.4
White				
Men	7,275,000	13.4	7,858,000	14.4
Women	5,245,000	10.8	5,897,000	12.2
Black				
Men	1,062,000	16.1	1,166,000	17.7
Women	1,115,000	14.2	1,225,000	15.6
Hispanic origin				
Men	1,093,000	10.6	1,185,000	11.5
Women	700,000	10.2	796,000	11.6

Source: U.S. Department of Labor. Figures are for workers 16 years and older.

[18] David Brody, *Workers in Industrial America* (New York: Oxford University Press, 1980), p. 217. Victor G. Devinatz, "An Alternative Strategy: Lessons from the UAW Local 6 and the FE, 1946–52," in Cyrus Bina, Laurie Clements, and Chuck Davis (eds.), *Beyond Survival: Wage Labor in the Late Twentieth Century* (Armonk, NY: M. E. Sharpe, 1996), Chapter 7.

Box 6.5 illustrates the range of union coverage across different occupations, industries, and states. Union density is quite low for sales and managerial positions, but is between 15 and 20 percent for blue-collar manual occupations, and over 40 percent for teachers. A similar pattern is evident across industries with service-related industries having low union coverage and manufacturing, construction, transportation, and utilities being above average. Lastly, there are significant regional differences in union membership. Southern and southwestern states generally have the lowest union densities while northern, industrial states have the highest. These differences in union densities can have important effects on bargaining power and labor relations outcomes.

Most union members have the greatest contact with their local union. A local union may represent many workers from a single workplace—an *industrial local*—or workers in a single occupation from several workplaces—a *craft local*—or multiple occupations in multiple workplaces in multiple industries—an *amalgamated local.* Craft and amalgamated locals are likely to have an elected business agent to administer the contracts that have been negotiated with the various employers. Most work sites also have one or more elected or appointed shop stewards. These individuals are the primary point of contact for most unionized employees, and the stewards' most important responsibility is processing grievances that have been filed within their work groups. Local unions are governed by a president and executive committee who are democratically elected. There may also be a negotiation committee and/or a grievance committee. Some local unions may be active in local politics and in trying to organize new members.

The local leadership positions, including the shop stewards, can be either full-time or part-time depending on the size and complexity of the local union. In some cases, this local union may be an independent organization and not part of a national union. Employees at Kodak and TRW have traditionally had their own independent local unions. But nearly all local unions are part of a **national union.**

There are approximately 100 national unions in the United States. The largest are the National Education Association (NEA) with over 2.5 million members and the Teamsters, United Food and Commercial Workers (UFCW), Service Employees International Union (SEIU), and American Federation of State, County, and Municipal Employees (AFSCME) each with over 1 million members. The NEA has over 14,000 locals and the UFCW has 950 locals. Some national unions are called "internationals" because they also have locals in Canada; for example, the UFCW's full name is the United Food and Commercial Workers International Union.

While local unions are the focal point of most rank and file members' contact with the union, the greatest power and authority generally lies with the national unions. National unions charter the local unions and often have final approval authority over local actions. While keeping in mind that the labor movement has diverse structures so that generalizations do not apply universally, most national unions are responsible for organizing new members, providing research and training, lobbying legislators, providing strike benefits, and supervising the collective bargaining process. When bargaining with larger companies, the national union may directly handle collective bargaining. With smaller companies, a local union's negotiating committee may take the lead, but often with the support and advice of a national union staff member.

The national unions are structured to support these activities. National unions generally have a number of departments, divisions, and regions. Departments consist of specialized staff in important functional areas. Common departments include organizing, collective bargaining, research, education or training, and government affairs. Divisions or conferences focus on important industries or occupations within a national union and provide the opportunity for coordination and networking within these areas. For example, the International Brotherhood of Boilermakers has divisions for construction, railroad, ship building,

BOX 6.5
Union Contract
Coverage by
Industry, Occupation,
and State, 2005

	Percent
Occupation	
Farming, Fishing, and Forestry	4.3
Management, Business, and Financial	5.9
Sales and Office Occupations	8.2
Service Occupations	12.6
Installation, Maintenance, and Repair	18.1
Construction and Extraction	18.5
Production, Transportation, and Material Moving	19.1
Professional and Educational	20.7
Industry	
Private Wage and Salary Workers	8.5
Financial Activities	2.8
Agriculture	3.0
Professional and Business Services	3.1
Leisure and Hospitality	3.5
Other Services	3.5
Wholesale and Retail Trade	5.9
Education and Health Services	9.4
Mining	9.5
Manufacturing	13.7
Construction	13.8
Information	14.4
Transportation and Utilities	25.1
Government workers	40.5
State	33.1
Federal	35.0
Local	45.8

States			
Lowest Five		**Highest Five**	
South Carolina	3.3	New York	27.5
North Carolina	3.9	Hawaii	26.7
Arkansas	6.0	Alaska	24.1
Georgia	6.0	New Jersey	21.7
Utah	6.1	Michigan	21.4

Source: U.S. Department of Labor.

and appliances. It is also common for national unions to have regional or district offices to help better serve the local unions. The basic nature of a typical national union is summarized in Box 6.6.

As with the local unions, national unions are governed through traditional, democratic methods. National union officers are elected on a periodic basis either directly by the

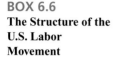

BOX 6.6
**The Structure of the
U.S. Labor
Movement**

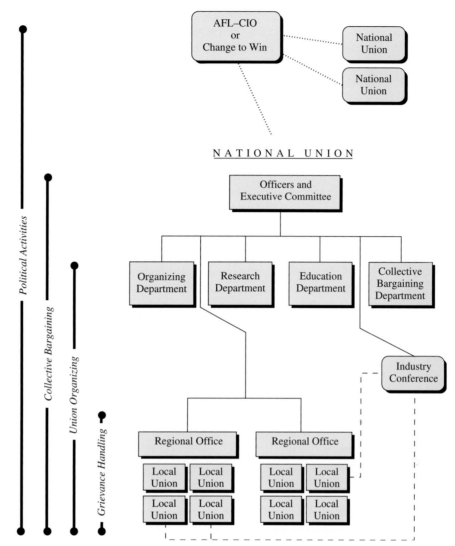

membership or indirectly through elected delegates. Each national union has a constitution which spells out the union's bylaws and procedures. Overall policy directions and changes to the constitution are done through periodic conventions attended by delegates elected by the union's membership. While unions have increased the use of formal human resources, financial, and strategic planning processes, improving the management and strategic planning skills of union leaders is needed.[19]

Since providing voice is one of the primary roles of labor unions, it is imperative that unions are democratic. Democracy in unions is also championed because of the belief that democratic unions more effectively represent their members.[20] **Union democracy** can be

[19] Thomas A. Hannigan, *Managing Tomorrow's High-Performance Unions* (Westport, CT: Quorum Books, 1998). David Weil, *Turning the Tide: Strategic Planning for Labor Unions* (Lexington, MA: Lexington Books, 1994). Paul F. Clark and Lois S. Gray, "Changing Administrative Practices in American Unions: A Research Note," *Industrial Relations* 44 (October 2005), pp. 654–58.

[20] George Strauss, "Union Democracy," in George Strauss, Daniel G. Gallagher, and Jack Fiorito (eds.), *The State of the Unions* (Madison, WI: Industrial Relations Research Association, 1991), Chapter 6. Robert Bruno, *Reforming the Chicago Teamsters: The Story of Local 705* (DeKalb: Northern Illinois Press, 2003).

analyzed along three dimensions: procedural, behavioral, and substantive.[21] Procedurally, U.S. law (the Landrum-Griffin Act of 1959) mandates basic democratic procedures within unions including free speech and election provisions. Behaviorally, unions appear to be more democratically vibrant at the local than the national level. While participation rates of rank and file members at local union meetings are low, attendance rises when voting on contracts and strikes. Many national leaders are regularly reelected while there is greater turnover of leaders at the local level. Even if officer turnover is low, however, the presence of an opposition can keep the leadership responsive to the membership.[22] This is the substantive dimension and between 70 and 80 percent of union members report being at least somewhat satisfied with their ability to influence local union leaders, bargaining agendas, and the selection of national leaders.[23] While there is room for improvement, the generally positive record on the substantive dimension is adequate if one accepts the servicing model of unionism (recall Box 6.3). Advocates for the organizing model, however, point to the dismal record along the behavioral dimension of democracy as a major obstacle to creating a vibrant labor movement, especially because of entrenched union bureaucracies and socially conservative union leaders.[24] Managerial pressures for employee involvement in workplace decision making can also undermine union democracy by eroding employee commitment to their union and lowering participation in union affairs.[25] In extreme cases, union leaders can be corrupt and unions can be infiltrated by the mafia (as portrayed in the HBO series *The Sopranos*).[26] National unions can use trusteeships to clean up local abuses, and in the worst instances, corrupt officials can be prosecuted under the federal Racketeer Influenced and Corrupt Organizations Act (RICO), as was the case for the national leadership of the Teamsters in 1989.

Historically, it was easy to distinguish between national craft unions representing workers in a single craft, such as the United Brotherhood of Carpenters or the International Brotherhood of Electrical Workers, and national industrial unions representing all workers in a single industry, such as the United Steelworkers of America (USW) or the United Auto Workers (UAW). But unions have diversified and merged over the years so there is now less of a distinction.[27] In fact, today many U.S. unions represent workers from very diverse occupations and industries. For example, after merging with another major union in 2005 (and more than 10 other unions before that), the USW officially became the United Steel, Paper and Forestry, Rubber, Manufacturing, Energy, Allied Industrial and Service Workers International Union. The USW represents not only workers in numerous metal and manufacturing industries, but also nurses, pharmacists, home health aides, librarians, zookeepers,

[21] Hannigan, *Managing Tomorrow's High-Performance Unions.* Strauss, "Union Democracy."

[22] Russell, *Out of the Jungle.*

[23] Richard B. Freeman and Joel Rogers, *What Workers Want* (Ithaca, NY: ILR Press, 1999). Daniel G. Gallagher and George Strauss, "Union Membership Attitudes and Participation," in George Strauss, Daniel G. Gallagher, and Jack Fiorito (eds.), *The State of the Unions* (Madison, WI: Industrial Relations Research Association, 1991), Chapter 4. Robert Bruno, "Consenting to be Governed: Union Transformation and Teamster Democracy," in David Lewin and Bruce Kaufman (eds.), *Advances in Industrial and Labor Relations,* Volume 11 (Amsterdam: Elsevier Science, 2002), pp. 95–122.

[24] Tillman and Cummings, *The Transformation of U.S. Unions.* Nelson Lichtenstein, *State of the Union: A Century of American Labor* (Princeton, NJ: Princeton University Press, 2002). Fantasia and Voss, *Hard Work.*

[25] Ann C. Frost, "Union Involvement in Workplace Decision Making: Implications for Union Democracy," *Journal of Labor Research* 21 (Spring 2000), pp. 265–86.

[26] James B. Jacobs, *Mobsters, Unions, and Feds: The Mafia and the American Labor Movement* (New York: New York University Press, 2006). Bruno, *Reforming the Chicago Teamsters.*

[27] Gary Chaison, *Union Mergers in Hard Times: The View From Five Countries* (Ithaca, NY: ILR Press, 1996). Gary Chaison, *When Unions Merge* (Lexington, MA: Lexington Books, 1986).

bus drivers, police officers, university clerical workers, and many others. Many U.S. unions today would therefore be better described as a **general union** rather than as a true industrial or craft union.

One persistent question for the U.S. labor movement is whether the increased strength that the national unions gain by increasing their membership and financial base through mergers and diverse organizing activity outweighs the potential problems with being responsive to the increasingly disparate needs and situations of individual workers. One critic has gone so far as to characterize opportunistic mergers and organizing activity as "nickel-and-dime business unionism" which lacks a coherent strategy for representing diverse workers.[28] A related question relates to union competition for members, or **rival unionism.** Merger activity reduces interunion competition, as when one of the Teamsters' fiercest rivals, the Brewery Workers, joined the Teamsters. But diverse organizing activity among general unions increases competition among unions, as when the Steelworkers compete with both service employee and nurses unions to organize nursing home employees. The question for the labor movement is whether this competition is a waste of precious resources or whether it causes better representation. The former is a popular view, but as a counterexample, it appears that many truck drivers and warehouse workers significantly benefited from competition between the Teamsters and rival unions in the 1930s–1950s as the threat of losing members to rivals caused union leaders to bargain more aggressively and win greater gains.[29] Perhaps the benefits of competition that cause corporations to innovate and strive for better goods and services also apply to labor unions.

Last, at the top of the structure of each country's labor movement is one or more national labor federations. A labor federation is an association of labor unions that provides support and leadership to the labor movement. Between 1955 and 2005, there was one major national labor federation in the United States, the American Federation of Labor–Congress of Industrial Organizations (**AFL–CIO**). The AFL–CIO is comprised of 53 national unions that represent nearly 9 million workers. A fraction of the union dues collected by each member union is forwarded to the AFL–CIO to fund its operations.

Box 6.7 shows the organizational structure of the AFL–CIO. As with the national unions, there are specialized departments, called programmatic departments, as well as divisions for specific industries or occupations, called trade and industrial departments. Specialized departments include civil and human rights, international affairs, organizing, and several pertaining to the AFL–CIO's political function: legislative, political, and public policy. Trade and industrial departments include building and construction trades, food and allied services, maritime trades, and professional employees. The AFL–CIO also has affiliated state federations and local labor councils which provide opportunities for the labor movement to cooperate at the state and local levels. Box 6.7 also emphasizes the AFL–CIO's relationship with a number of other groups. The AFL–CIO plays an important leadership role in the direction and coordination of the U.S. labor movement, but it is important to remember that most of the organizing, negotiating, and grievance handling is done by local and national unions, not the AFL–CIO. The AFL–CIO is a support organization, analogous to the National Association of Manufacturers or the Chamber of Commerce on the employer side. As such, its main functions are political lobbying, research, education, and overall coordination and direction.

The AFL–CIO and individual unions also have international links and alliances with labor movements from around the globe. The AFL–CIO is a member of the International Trade Union Confederation (ITUC)—a federation of national union federations. Similarly, individual unions participate in international organizations for their industries. For example, the UAW belongs to the International Metalworkers Federation. These

---

[28] Kim Moody, *An Injury to All: The Decline of American Unionism* (London: Verso, 1988), p. 205.

[29] Russell, *Out of the Jungle.*

BOX 6.7   AFL–CIO Organization Chart

Source: http://www.aflcio.org/aboutus/thisisthealfcio/organizationchart.cfm (accessed July 3, 2006).

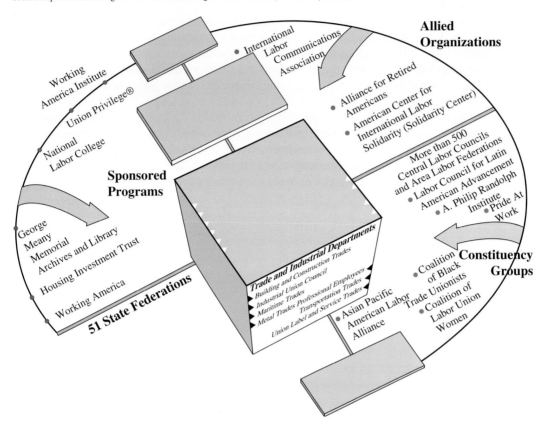

organizations provide the same type of communication, coordination, research, and education functions as the AFL–CIO, but at a global level.

To further appreciate the power structure of the U.S. labor movement, it is instructive to compare it to the levels of government in the United States. Local unions are like state governments—they have their own elected officials and can pursue their own policies and conduct their own activities, but subject to the ultimate approval of a superior authority. For state governments, the superior authority is the U.S. federal government and for local unions it is their parent national union. Thus, national unions are like the federal government—they have the ultimate authority. The AFL–CIO is like the United Nations—it provides overall leadership and important services, but membership is voluntary. Neither the AFL–CIO nor the United Nations has the authority to compel its members to comply with its decisions.

In a very dramatic turn of events, the AFL–CIO is no longer the sole U.S. labor federation at the national level. Frustration with the continued decline of the U.S. labor movement led to unusually open and pointed calls for a change in the direction and leadership of the AFL–CIO in 2004. In particular, several union presidents pressed for significantly shifting the AFL–CIO's spending from political activities (such as lobbying and get-out-the-vote drives) to organizing activities (especially campaigns to unionize nonunion workplaces). From this, several unions left the AFL–CIO in 2005 and formed a new labor federation, the **Change to Win** federation. This federation includes only seven unions, but they are among the largest and represent a total of 6 million workers. This breakup of the AFL–CIO rippled throughout the structure of the labor movement, especially at the local and state level where AFL–CIO–affiliated central labor councils and state federations were forced to expel local unions affiliated with Change to Win. The resulting loss of membership, leaders, and financial support—the Oregon state AFL–CIO, for example, lost more than half its membership—caused the national AFL–CIO leadership to rethink this approach and the federations are experimenting with solidarity charters that allow local unions from both federations to work together on a local and state level. It is too early to assess the long-term influence of the Change to Win federation and the sustainability of the solidarity charters.

MANAGEMENT GOALS AND STRATEGIES

To think about managerial strategies in labor relations, consider two possible management attitudes toward labor unions: acceptance or avoidance. Theoretically, there is a third possibility: union encouragement, but there is little doubt that except in rare situations, U.S. management prefers to be nonunion.[30] To the extent that management works toward remaining nonunion, or becoming nonunion if already unionized, this is **union avoidance.** To the extent that management accepts, perhaps begrudgingly, the presence of a union or a drive to establish a union, this is union acceptance. How these attitudes translate into labor relations strategies depends on the organization's approach to human resources more generally, which is, in turn, rooted in its business strategy.

It is common to divide business strategies into two general types: cost leadership strategies (emphasizing low cost) and differentiation strategies (emphasizing product quality and features).[31] A cost leadership business strategy is likely pursued through a human resources strategy that seeks to minimize labor costs (see Box 6.8). Efficiency stems from low costs and high output so labor is driven and treated as a commodity or machine. Equity and voice are not important to management; efficiency through high output and low cost is key. A stereotypical example is a traditional mass-production assembly line where supervisors push employees to work harder and threaten them with discipline or discharge if they fail to produce. Such approaches are consistent with the well-known Theory X of management in which workers are assumed to dislike work and must therefore be commanded and controlled through threat of punishment.[32] The result is a human resources approach that is largely autocratic.

In contrast, a differentiation business strategy is likely pursued through a human resources strategy that develops, rewards, and perhaps even empowers employees to create a loyal and productive workforce (see Box 6.8). Equity and voice are important components of this strategy because fair treatment and protective benefits (equity) and individual voice mechanisms such as open-door policies can foster loyalty, satisfaction, and therefore productivity. In contrast to the traditional Theory X, this human resources strategy is consistent with Theory Y in which management motivates employees by establishing conditions of commitment and responsibility.[33] More extensive approaches might even employ a strategic business partner HR strategy in which employees are seen as a source of competitive advantage; employees are thus empowered in high-performance workplaces.[34] In management theory, this approach is

[30] Sanford M. Jacoby, *Modern Manors: Welfare Capitalism since the New Deal* (Princeton, NJ: Princeton University Press, 1997). Freeman and Rogers, *What Workers Want*. Kochan, Katz, and McKersie, *The Transformation of American Industrial Relations*.

[31] Michael E. Porter, *Competitive Strategy* (New York: Free Press, 1980).

[32] Douglas McGregor, *The Human Side of Enterprise* (New York: McGraw-Hill, 1960).

[33] McGregor, *The Human Side of Enterprise*.

[34] Eileen Appelbaum and Rosemary Batt, *The New American Workplace: Transforming Work Systems in the United States* (Ithaca, NY: ILR Press, 1994).

BOX 6.8
Human Resources Patterns and Labor Relations Strategies

	Human Resources and Industrial Relations Patterns	
	Autocratic	**Paternalistic/Strategic**
Business Strategy	Cost Leadership	Differentiation
Human Resources Strategy	Minimize Labor Costs	Develop, Reward, and Empower Employees
Supervision	Drive	Inspire
Management's View of		
Efficiency	Low Cost and High Output	Loyal, Productive, and Empowered Workforce
Equity	Not Important	Fair Treatment; Protective Benefits
Voice	Not Important	Open-Door Policies; Formal Employee Involvement Programs
Employees as	Commodities or Machines	Assets
Labor Relations Strategy		
If Union Acceptance	Adversarial	Participatory
If Union Avoidance	Suppression	Substitution

similar to Theory Z which features participative decision making.[35] The overall approach is paternalistic, or in the high-performance model, strategic.

The autocratic and paternalistic/strategic patterns help reveal the importance of managerial attitudes toward unions (see the last two rows of Box 6.8). First consider the autocratic approach. A union acceptance strategy in this type of organization would likely consist of very adversarial negotiations in which labor and management negotiators challenge and threaten each other during negotiations. Strikes and grievance activity would also be expected to be higher than average as management fights to keep labor costs down and unions react to this aggressiveness. But management does not seek to oust the union. In contrast, a union avoidance strategy in an autocratic organization is **union suppression** (see Box 6.9).[36] Some might call this union busting. Union suppression tactics include harassment, demotion, or firing of union supporters. Recall from Chapter 5 that this behavior is illegal in the United States, but studies suggest that it is nevertheless common.[37] Another set of union suppression tactics involves either proactively or reactively shifting work from locations that are unionized (or are threatening to unionize): plant closings, outsourcing, bankruptcies, and double-breasting (the opening of nonunion operations

[35] William G. Ouchi, *Theory Z: How American Business Can Meet the Japanese Challenge* (Reading, MA: Addison-Wesley, 1981).

[36] Thomas A. Kochan and Harry C. Katz, *Collective Bargaining and Industrial Relations: From Theory to Policy and Practice*, 2nd ed. (Homewood, IL: Irwin, 1988).

[37] Freeman and Rogers, *What Workers Want*. Paul C. Weiler, *Governing the Workplace: The Future of Labor and Employment Law* (Cambridge: Harvard University Press, 1990). Kate Bronfenbrenner and Tom Juravich, "It Takes More than House Calls: Organizing to Win with a Comprehensive Union Building Strategy," in Kate Bronfenbrenner, et al. (eds.), *Organizing to Win: New Research on Union Strategies* (Ithaca, NY: ILR Press, 1998), pp. 19–36. John J. Lawler, *Unionization and Deunionization: Strategy, Tactics, and Outcomes* (Columbia: University of South Carolina Press, 1990).

BOX 6.9
Union Avoidance
Tactics

Union Suppression	Union Substitution
Firing or Harassing Union Supporters	Above-Market Pay and Benefits
Screening Out Pro-Union Applicants	Opportunities for Training and Development
Plant Closings / Bankruptcy	Respectful Supervision
Double-Breasting / Relocation	Complaint or Grievance Procedures
Subcontracting / Outsourcing	Employment Security
Nonunion Investment	Attitude Surveys
Facilitating Decertification	Information Sharing
Surface Bargaining Use of Permanent Strike Replacements	Committees and Participatory Mechanisms Such as Quality Circles

in the same market, a popular strategy in construction). Recent examples include the outsourcing of jobs to low-wage countries in the private sector and the privatization of services in the public sector. Decisions to not make new investments in unionized facilities in favor of targeting new investment toward nonunion locations are also part of a union suppression strategy.[38] Last, an aggressive union suppression strategy in a unionized workplace might include tactics to decertify (kick out) the union, engage in surface bargaining (going through the motions without intending to reach agreement), and use permanent strike replacements to take the jobs of union supporters. These tactics will be covered in greater detail in later chapters, and as will be discussed, many are of questionable legality.

In an autocratic organization, a union avoidance strategy is union suppression; in a paternalistic/strategic organization, a union avoidance strategy is **union substitution**.[39] In short, management adopts policies and practices to keep unions out by making them unnecessary (see Box 6.9). Central features of this strategy include paying above-market wages and benefits (often comparable to unionized compensation packages), providing employment security, giving employees opportunities for training and development, and instituting informal grievance procedures, or at least complaint mechanisms. Authoritarian supervisors are replaced with more respectful, coaching methods of supervision, and attitude surveys are used to monitor employee satisfaction. Employees are made to feel like they are part of the organization, and have voice, through information sharing and participatory mechanisms such as quality circles. Through these equity and voice mechanisms, employers hope to create not only loyal and productive workers, but also workers who feel that they do not need a union. This is essentially the goal of welfare capitalism and modern human resource management.[40] In fact, one of the very first health insurance plans ever developed stemmed from an attempt by DuPont to expand its employee insurance benefits and thwart an organizing drive.[41] Union substitution tactics are generally legal when pursued as a consistent human resource management strategy but, for example, if compensation is manipulated in response to a specific union-organizing drive then this might be illegal interference under section 8(a)(1) of the National Labor Relations Act. Moreover, voice mechanisms that are viewed as company-dominated unions violate section 8(a)(2); this important controversy will be discussed in Chapter 11.

[38] Kochan, Katz, and McKersie, *The Transformation of American Industrial Relations*.

[39] Kochan and Katz, *Collective Bargaining and Industrial Relations*.

[40] Jacoby, *Modern Manors*. Karen Legge, *Human Resource Management: Rhetorics and Realities* (Basingstoke: Macmillan Press, 1995). Jennifer Klein, *For All These Rights: Business, Labor, and the Shaping of America's Public-Private Welfare State* (Princeton, NJ: Princeton University Press, 2003).

[41] Klein, *For All These Rights*.

Last, a union acceptance attitude in a paternalistic/strategic organization results in a participatory labor relations strategy in which the union is enlisted as a partner to help the business create high-performance work systems. In this system, the nature of employee involvement programs, work teams, and other practices are jointly determined by representatives of management and the workers rather than unilaterally imposed by management. This has the potential for being more effective than in a nonunion situation because a union has the potential to better articulate true employee concerns and individuals will speak more freely when employees are not afraid of management reprisal.[42] A popular example is the automaker Saturn in which unionized employee teams are responsible for production and have decision-making authority.[43]

As emphasized in the model of the environment and ethics (Box 3.1), managerial labor relations strategies are a product of corporate goals, the environment, and values. Research has shown that while the relationship between business strategy and labor relations strategy is complex, weaker product market conditions and fewer unionized plants in the company are both associated with a higher chance that companies will pursue union avoidance rather than acceptance strategies.[44] Or consider the U.S. steel minimill industry (minimills start with scrap metal, they do not make steel from raw materials). In this industry, firms with a cost leadership strategy are significantly more likely to have human resources and industrial relations practices similar to the autocratic culture in Box 6.8. Minimills with a differentiation business strategy are more likely to be similar to the paternalistic/strategic pattern in Box 6.8.[45] Quality is also an important objective in many organizations. Box 6.10 describes W. Edwards Deming's famous strategy for achieving quality and asks you to consider what might determine whether labor unions help or hinder such initiatives.

The history of human resources and industrial relations in the U.S. automobile industry is also a good example of these different labor relations strategies. Henry Ford implemented a form of paternalistic welfare capitalism with his five-dollar-a-day plan in 1914.[46] This is consistent with a union avoidance strategy in the paternalistic pattern of Box 6.8. After a recession in the early 1920s, however, Ford adopted a more antagonistic strategy and aggressively fought any attempts at unionization by its workers for the next 20 years. Ford became famous for its so-called Service Department—essentially an internal police force composed of criminals and informers—which used spying, intimidation, and violence to suppress union activity.[47]

In the postwar period, the United Auto Workers (UAW) became entrenched at Ford and resistance to unions became prohibitively expensive. Ford then adopted a union acceptance

---

[42] Barry Bluestone and Irving Bluestone, *Negotiating the Future: A Labor Perspective on American Business* (New York: Basic Books, 1992). Adrienne E. Eaton and Paula B. Voos, "Productivity-Enhancing Innovations in Work Organization, Compensation, and Employee Participation in the Union versus the Nonunion Sectors," in David Lewin and Donna Sockell (eds.), *Advances in Industrial and Labor Relations*, Volume 6 (Greenwich, CT: JAI Press, 1994), pp. 63–109.

[43] Saul A. Rubinstein and Thomas A. Kochan, *Learning from Saturn: Possibilities for Corporate Governance and Employee Relations* (Ithaca, NY: ILR Press, 2001).

[44] William N. Cooke and David G. Meyer, "Structural and Market Predictors of Corporate Labor Relations Strategies," *Industrial and Labor Relations Review* 43 (January 1990), pp. 280–93. Andrew Pendleton, "The Evolution of Industrial Relations in UK Nationalized Industries," *British Journal of Industrial Relations* 35 (June 1997), pp. 145–72.

[45] Jeffrey B. Arthur, "The Link Between Business Strategy and Industrial Relations Systems in American Steel Minimills," *Industrial and Labor Relations Review* 45 (April 1992), pp. 488–506.

[46] Stephen Meyer, *The Five Dollar Day: Labor Management and Social Control in the Ford Motor Company, 1908–1921* (Albany: State University of New York Press, 1981).

[47] Meyer, *The Five Dollar Day.* Nelson Lichtenstein, *The Most Dangerous Man in Detroit: Walter Reuther and the Fate of American Labor* (New York: Basic Books, 1995). Stephen H. Norwood, *Strikebreaking and Intimidation: Mercenaries and Masculinity in Twentieth-Century America of the Labor Movement* (Chapel Hill: University of North Carolina Press, 2002).

One of the contemporary challenges for business, managers, and employees is achieving exceptional levels of quality in the production and delivery of goods and services. To serve this goal, quality guru W. Edwards Deming articulated 14 points for management:

1. Create constancy of purpose toward improvement of product and service, with the aim to become competitive and to stay in business, and to provide jobs.

2. Adopt the new philosophy. We are in a new economic age. Western management must awaken to the challenge, must learn their responsibilities, and take on leadership for change.

3. Cease dependence on inspection to achieve quality. Eliminate the need for inspection on a mass basis by building quality into the product in the first place.

4. End the practice of awarding business on the basis of price tag. Instead, minimize total cost. Move toward a single supplier for any one item, on a long-term relationship of loyalty and trust.

5. Improve constantly and forever the system of production and service, to improve quality and productivity, and thus constantly decrease costs.

6. Institute training on the job.

7. Institute leadership. The aim of supervision should be to help people and machines and gadgets to do a better job. Supervision of management is in need of overhaul as well as supervision of production workers.

8. Drive out fear, so that everyone may work effectively for the company.

9. Break down barriers between departments. People in research, design, sales, and production must work as a team, to foresee problems of production and in use that may be encountered with the product or service.

10. Eliminate slogans, exhortations, and targets for the work force asking for zero defects and new levels of productivity. Such exhortations only create adversarial relationships, as the bulk of the causes of low quality and low productivity belong to the system and thus lie beyond the power of the workforce.

11. a. Eliminate work standards (quotas) on the factory floor. Substitute leadership.

    b. Eliminate management by objective. Eliminate management by numbers, numerical goals. Substitute leadership.

12. a. Remove barriers that rob the hourly worker of his right to pride of workmanship. The responsibility of supervisors must be changed from sheer numbers to quality.

    b. Remove barriers that rob people in management and in engineering of their right to pride of workmanship. This means, *inter alia*, abolishment of the annual merit rating and of management by objective.

13. Institute a vigorous program of education and self-improvement.

14. Put everybody in the company to work to accomplish the transformation. The transformation is everybody's job.

Questions

1. Do you agree with these principles?
2. How can unions help pursue these 14 principles?
3. How might unions hinder these 14 principles?
4. What factors determine whether a union helps or hinders achievement of these 14 principles?

Source: W. Edward Deming, *Out of the Crisis* (Cambridge, MA: Center for Advanced Engineering Study, MIT, 1986), pp. 23–24.

strategy that accepted, but sought to contain, the presence of the UAW (recall the discussion of job control unionism from earlier in this chapter). Since the 1980s, however, competitive price and quality issues have caused Ford to adopt more of a participative strategy in which union members are empowered with greater input into production decisions.[48] Similarly, in the 1970s General Motors tried a union avoidance strategy (its "Southern strategy") of opening new, nonunion plants in the southern United States. The UAW was successful in pressuring General Motors to end this policy because of its corporate-wide leverage.[49] Today, General Motors has more of a union acceptance strategy, although it is generally believed to lag behind Ford in terms of employee involvement.

[48] Bluestone and Bluestone, *Negotiating the Future*.
[49] Kochan, Katz, and McKersie, *The Transformation of American Industrial Relations*.

The auto and other manufacturing industries, however, are no longer the pacesetters for the rest of American business. Rather, some argue that Wal-Mart is creating the template for 21st-century capitalism in the United States and around the world.[50] In particular, Wal-Mart is obsessive about continually and aggressively reducing costs in order to "squeeze more out of every penny."[51] Wal-Mart's business model is therefore highly centralized to take advantage of standardized policies, scale economies, and data mining.[52] Wal-Mart's human resources strategies fit with this business strategy—policies are centralized and standardized, store managers' labor costs are carefully policed by Wal-Mart's headquarters, worker behavior is tightly proscribed, and wages and benefits are low.[53] With respect to unions, Wal-Mart is aggressively antiunion. If a manager suspects any union activity, a rapid response team is dispatched from headquarters to squelch this threat; antiunion videos are shown, supervisors meet with employees one-on-one, employees are closely watched, and union supporters are reportedly fired.[54] When butchers in one store voted for a union, Wal-Mart ceased employing butchers by switching to only selling prepackaged meats in all of its stores. When employees at a store in Quebec voted to unionize, Wal-Mart closed the store. These are classic examples of a union suppression strategy, and are consistent with a 21st-century business model that emphasizes low costs.

CONFLICTING GOALS MEANS BALANCING RIGHTS

There are various labor and management strategies to achieve specific goals that serve the broad employment relationship objectives of efficiency, equity, and voice. While remembering that labor and management can have many common goals, many of the critical difficulties in labor relations arise from conflicting goals or interests. Equity and voice can often conflict with efficiency. A major theme of labor relations is therefore striking a balance between these conflicting goals and interests.

Much of this book pertains to how the U.S. labor relations system attempts to achieve this balance, and alternatives for reform if the system isn't working. But how do we judge if the system is not working? The distinct labor and management views are straightforward: labor evaluates a system based on the degree to which equity and voice are achieved while management focuses on efficiency. But as a society, how should a system be judged? Are certain goals more important than others? At a fundamental level, this becomes a question of rights: if the goals of labor and management conflict, what rights does each party have? Are certain rights more important than others? If unionization reduces efficiency but increases equity and voice, should management have rights to prevent unions or should workers have rights to form unions? If strikes benefit workers but harm companies, what rights should employees have to strike? Or what rights should management have to prevent

[50] Nelson Lichtenstein (ed.), *Wal-Mart: The Face of Twenty-First Century Capitalism* (New York: The New Press, 2006).

[51] Ellen Israel Rosen, "How to Squeeze More out of a Penny," in Nelson Lichtenstein (ed.), *Wal-Mart: The Face of Twenty-First Century Capitalism* (New York: The New Press, 2006), pp. 243–59.

[52] James Hoopes, "Growth Through Knowledge: Wal-Mart, High Technology, and the Ever Less Visible Hand of the Manager," in Nelson Lichtenstein (ed.), *Wal-Mart: The Face of Twenty-First Century Capitalism* (New York: The New Press, 2006), pp. 83–104. Charles Fishman, *The Wal-Mart Effect: How the World's Most Powerful Company Really Works—and How It's Transforming the American Economy* (New York: Penguin Press, 2006).

[53] Rosen, "How to Squeeze More out of a Penny." Barbara Ehrenreich, *Nickel and Dimed: On (Not) Getting By in America* (New York: Henry Holt, 2001).

[54] Steven Greenhouse, "At a Small Shop in Colorado, Wal-Mart Beats a Union Once More," *New York Times*, February 26, 2005.

or counteract strikes? Note that these questions of rights apply to "big picture" questions about the nature of a labor relations system as determined by a legal framework; there are also important conflicts of interests (for example, over the level of wages) which the participants directly resolve themselves. For the remainder of this chapter, focus on the bigger picture conflicts of rights. Later chapters will illustrate that how a society resolves these conflicts of rights will critically shape how conflicts of interests are resolved.

The rights of business are primarily property rights. Property rights have long been viewed in U.S. political and social thought as one of the most important rights because they are critical for liberty.[55] The U.S. Bill of Rights makes deprivation of "life, liberty, or property, without due process of law" a cornerstone of individual freedoms. This is because property rights traditionally provided autonomy and thus established the boundaries or limits on legitimate government.[56] In other words, property rights are "the guardian of every other right."[57] As such, in U.S. labor relations property rights have dominated or trumped all others. But is this desirable?

This classical or natural rights view of property rights is no longer the dominant reason for property rights. Recall from the last chapter's discussion of labor injunctions that in the late 1800s U.S. courts "dephysicalized" property by expanding property rights to include value as well as physical things.[58] Intangible property rights now include the right to conduct business, the value of goodwill, and trade secrets. Thus, in legal, political, and economic thinking, the modern view of property rights is as a bundle of economic rights.[59] It is well-accepted that these bundles are both government-created and a source of protection *against* government coercion. The function of property rights today is not only liberty, but also economic efficiency.

Moreover, in an industrial society dominated by wage earners, rather than in an agrarian society populated by small farmers, property rights are "no longer the source of autonomy for most people."[60] In fact, it can be argued that in a wage-earning society, property rights are a source of coercion, not protection against it. Strong property rights of corporations over both physical and intangible property, such as a broad right to conduct business, give organizations the right to deny others the ability to work, and therefore survive. This is a complete reversal of the classical notion of property rights as the source of freedom.[61]

Lastly, property rights from ancient to modern times have rarely been absolute. Even the conservative U.S. Supreme Court in the late 19th and early 20th centuries that placed great emphasis on property rights upheld some legislation infringing on corporate property rights when it felt the public interest was truly served, such as an Oregon law that limited the hours of women in factories and laundries.[62]

[55] James W. Ely, *The Guardian of Every Other Right: A Constitutional History of Property Rights* (New York: Oxford University Press, 1998).

[56] Jennifer Nedelsky, *Private Property and the Limits of American Constitutionalism.* (Chicago: University of Chicago Press, 1990).

[57] Ely, *The Guardian of Every Other Right.*

[58] Kenneth J. Vandevelde, "The New Property of the Nineteenth Century: The Development of the Modern Concept of Property," *Buffalo Law Review* 29 (Spring 1980), pp. 325–67. William E. Forbath, *Law and the Shaping of the American Labor Movement* (Cambridge: Harvard University Press, 1991).

[59] Gregory S. Alexander, *Commodity and Proprietary: Competing Visions of Property in American Legal Thought, 1776–1970* (Chicago: University of Chicago Press, 1997). Thomas W. Merrill, and Henry E. Smith, "What Happened to Property in Law and Economics?" *Yale Law Journal* 111 (November 2001), pp. 357–98.

[60] Nedelsky, *Private Property and the Limits of American Constitutionalism,* p. 234.

[61] John R. Commons, *Legal Foundations of Capitalism* (New York: Macmillan, 1924). Alexander, *Commodity and Proprietary.*

[62] *Muller v. Oregon,* 208 U.S. 412 (1908). Michael J. Phillips, "The Progressiveness of the Lochner Court," *Denver University Law Review* 75 (1998), pp. 453–505.

In sum, in contrast to the historic emphasis on private property as a fundamental freedom against coercive governments, the dominant modern economic and legal view is that property rights are bundles of rights that are essential for economic efficiency and development. As such, property rights are important. But when they conflict with labor rights, should property rights always be assumed to be more important? To address this question we need to consider the importance of labor rights.

ARE LABOR RIGHTS HUMAN RIGHTS?

There is a growing international consensus that the rights of workers to important dimensions of equity and voice are **human rights.** This is an important issue to consider as part of the question of the relative rights of labor and corporations. A timeline of the development of human rights thought is presented in Box 6.11.

Visions of human rights can be traced back to various early religious and moral philosophy traditions, including all of the major religions, which "share a universal interest in addressing the integrity, worth, and dignity of all persons, and, consequently, the duty toward other people."[63] The roots of human rights are therefore both religious and moral, Western and non-Western. The prime foundation of human rights is the belief that there are basic rights that everyone is entitled to simply by being human.[64] These rights are "essential to the adequate functioning of a human being" and do not depend on "varying social circumstances and degrees of merit."[65] Thus, there is common affirmation that intrinsic human value and inherent dignity endow humans with a set of basic rights. Or in the words of the U.S. Declaration of Independence, all people "are endowed by their Creator with certain unalienable rights." But what are these rights?

At the time of the Declaration of Independence in 1776, the focus was on first generation human rights: civil and political rights. These included private property rights, freedom of speech, religion, and assembly, and the right to due process. Agitation for these rights continued through the 19th century. First there was the fight against slavery, resulting in the 13th amendment to the U.S. Constitution in 1865 ending slavery in the United States. This fight then raised questions about the oppression of women, which resulted in the 19th amendment in 1920 granting U.S. women the right to vote.[66] The worldwide attention to slavery also provided the opportunity for reformers to expand awareness of other forms of economic exploitation, such as sweatshop conditions in the mills and mines of mid-19th-century Europe (see Box 6.12):

> What good were civil rights such as freedom of speech or political rights for voting, asked those who suffered, to people like themselves who had no food, no home, no clothing, no medical care, or no prospect of an education? What were the benefits of freedom from slavery or serfdom if the alternative was destitution?[67]

---

[63] Paul Gordon Lauren, *The Evolution of International Human Rights: Visions Seen* (Philadelphia: University of Pennsylvania Press, 1998), p. 5. Michael J. Perry, *The Idea of Human Rights: Four Inquiries* (New York: Oxford University Press, 1998). Jerome J. Shestack, "The Jurisprudence of Human Rights," in Theodor Meron (ed.), *Human Rights in International Law: Legal and Policy Issues* (Oxford: Oxford University Press, 1984), Chapter 3.

[64] Jack Donnelly, *Universal Human Rights in Theory and Practice*, 2nd ed. (Ithaca, NY: Cornell University Press, 2003).

[65] Michael Freeden, *Rights* (Minneapolis: University of Minnesota Press, 1991), p. 7. Shestack, "The Jurisprudence of Human Rights," p. 74.

[66] Lauren, *The Evolution of International Human Rights*. James MacGregor Burns and Stewart Burns, *A People's Charter: The Pursuit of Rights in America* (New York: Alfred A. Knopf, 1991).

[67] Lauren, *The Evolution of International Human Rights,* p. 54.

BOX 6.11
Human Rights Timeline

Adapted from Paul Gordon Lauren, *The Evolution of International Human Rights: Visions Seen* (Philadelphia: University of Pennsylvania Press, 1998). James MacGregor Burns and Stewart Burns, *A People's Charter: The Pursuit of Rights in America* (New York: Alfred A. Knopf, 1991). Alan S. Rosenbaum (ed.), *The Philosophy of Human Rights: International Perspectives* (Westport, CT: Greenwood Press, 1980).

First Generation: Civil and Political Rights

1500 B.C.	Birth of Hinduism—*sanctity of human life and noninjury to others*
1300 B.C	Birth of Judaism—*sacredness of human life and equality of all*
500 B.C.	Birth of Confucianism and Buddhism—*harmony, compassion, and duty*
400 B.C.	Greek Philosophy (Plato, Aristotle)—*principles of a just society*
100 B.C.	Roman Philosophy (Cicero)—*universal, egalitarian natural law*
30 A.D.	Birth of Christianity—*sacredness of human life and compassion*
600	Birth of Islam—*sanctity of human life, equality, and charity*
1215	Magna Carta—*liberties of citizens, limits on rulers*
1270	St. Thomas Aquinas—*Catholic analysis of moral life and natural law*
1690	John Locke—*natural rights to preserve life, liberty, and property*
1776	Declaration of Independence (U.S.)— *inalienable rights to life, liberty, and the pursuit of happiness*
1780	Immanuel Kant—*universal moral law of treating people as ends in themselves, not as means; also advocates a federation of nations to punish aggressor nations*
1789	Declaration of the Rights of Man and Citizen (France)—*universal natural rights to liberty, property, security, and resistance to oppression*
1791	Bill of Rights (U.S.)—*freedom of speech, religion, assembly, from unreasonable search and seizure, and right to due process*

Second Generation: Economic and Social Rights

1800s	Industrial Revolution—*rise of wage work and factories*
1833	Abolition Act (Great Britain)—*ends slavery in the British Empire*
1841	Treaty of London (Russia, France, Prussia, Austria, and Great Britain)—*abolishes slavery*
1848	Seneca Falls Declaration—*launches the women's rights movement*
1864	Geneva Convention—*forms the Red Cross and protects the rights of wounded and captured soldiers*
1865	13th Amendment to the Constitution (U.S.)—*frees slaves*
1891	*Rerum Novarum* (Pope Leo XIII)—*rights and justice for wage earners*
1914–1918	World War I—*eight million killed, 20 million wounded; all were equal in death, why not in life?*
1919	Founding of the International Labor Organization (ILO)—*promotion of workers' rights and peace through social justice*
1920	19th Amendment to the Constitution (U.S.)—*gives women the right to vote*
1929–1939	Great Depression—*in 1933, U.S. unemployment rate is 25 percent*
1939–1945	World War II—*25 million military and 30 million civilian casualties (not including the Holocaust victims)*
1941–1945	Holocaust—*killing of six million Jewish people in Nazi Germany*
1941	President Franklin Roosevelt issues call for four freedoms worldwide—*freedom of speech, of religion, from want, and from fear*
1944	President Franklin Roosevelt calls for an economic bill of rights—*rights to a useful job, earnings to obtain adequate food, clothing, shelter, and recreation, medical care, education and protection against insecurity from old age, sickness, accidents and unemployment*
1944	Declaration of Philadelphia—*reaffirmation of ILO's principles and workers' rights to material well-being and dignity*
1945	Founding of the United Nations by 51 Countries—*to promote peace, justice, social progress, and human rights*
1948	United Nations Declaration of Universal Rights—*statement of civil, political, social, and economic rights for all because of inherent human dignity*

Third Generation: Environmental, Cultural, and Developmental Rights

1950–1960	De-colonization of Asia and Africa
1964	Civil Rights Act (U.S.)—*forbids racial, gender, and religious discrimination*
1976	The United Nations International Covenants on Civil and Political Rights and on Economic, Social and Cultural Rights Enter into Force—*parties to the treaties must comply with international human rights standards*
1998	ILO Declaration of Fundamental Principles and Rights at Work—*all countries have an obligation to promote freedom of association and collective bargaining, equality and nondiscrimination, and the abolition of forced and child labor*
1999	United Nations Challenges Business to Embrace the Global Compact—*respect for human rights, labor, and the environment in worldwide corporate behavior*
2003	United Nations issues "Norms on the Responsibilities of Transnational Corporations and Other Business Enterprises with Regard to Human Rights"—*business has an obligation to respect human rights, including collective bargaining rights*

Before the rise of widespread media and easy international communication, novels were an important factor in spreading information about abuse and suffering, and therefore were instrumental in increasing support for international human rights. Some important examples include:

Dead Souls (1842) by Nikolai Gogol	Serfs
Uncle Tom's Cabin (1852) by Harriet Beecher Stowe	Slaves
Hard Times (1854) by Charles Dickens	19th-century workers
A Doll's House (1879) by Henrik Ibsen	Women
Germinal (1885) by Emile Zola	19th-century workers
The Jungle (1906) by Upton Sinclair	Early 20th-century workers
The Grapes of Wrath (1939) by John Steinbeck	Migrant workers

From this movement grew a second generation of human rights—positive economic and social rights in which governments have a responsibility for ensuring adequate standards of living including employment opportunities, income, housing, medical care, safety, and education. Workers' rights received further attention at the end of World War I, partly because of labor's sacrifices during the war and partly as a strategy to further continued peace which led to the creation of the **International Labor Organization** (ILO) in 1919.[68]

The ILO is now a specialized agency of the United Nations and is the chief international authority on, and promoter of, labor standards pertaining to union organizing and collective bargaining, forced labor, discrimination, and other conditions of work. To this end, a primary activity of the ILO is adopting conventions which specify minimum labor standards. Member countries are obligated to submit the conventions to their national legislatures for ratification and to fulfill their provisions. As of 2005, the ILO had passed 185 conventions. Technical assistance to help implement these standards is also provided. The ILO has a unique tripartite structure of government, employer, and worker representatives, and most countries are now members.

The Great Depression in the 1930s further increased calls for economic and social rights.[69] In the aftermath of World War II, and Hitler's assertion of national sovereignty over Nazi Germany's right to commit incredible atrocities in the Holocaust, the United Nations was formed in 1945 "to save succeeding generations from the scourge of war" and to "reaffirm faith in fundamental human rights, in the dignity and worth of the human person, in the equal rights of men and women of nations large and small" (United Nations Charter). The Universal Declaration of Human Rights was adopted and proclaimed by the United Nations' General Assembly in 1948 and integrates second generation economic and social rights with first generation civil and political rights and is reproduced in the appendix to this book.

With respect to employment rights, consider the ILO's fundamental objective as proclaimed in the 1944 Declaration of Philadelphia (also reproduced in Appendix A):

> All human beings, irrespective of race, creed or sex, have the right to pursue both their material well-being and their spiritual development in conditions of freedom and dignity, of economic security and equal opportunity.

[68] Lauren, *The Evolution of International Human Rights.*

[69] Cass R. Sunstein, *The Second Bill of Rights: FDR's Unfinished Revolution and Why We Need It More than Ever* (New York: Basic Books, 2004).

Excerpts from the Eight Fundamental Conventions of the International Labor Organization (ILO)

Box 6.13

According to the ILO, "Eight ILO Conventions have been identified by the ILO's Governing Body as being fundamental to the rights of human beings at work, irrespective of levels of development of individual member States. These rights are a precondition for all the others in that they provide for the necessary implements to strive freely for the improvement of individual and collective conditions of work."

Freedom of Association

Freedom of Association and Protection of the Right to Organize Convention, 1948 (No. 87)

Workers and employers, without distinction whatsoever, shall have the right to establish and, subject only to the rules of the organization concerned, to join organizations of their own choosing without previous authorization.

Right to Organize and Collective Bargaining Convention, 1949 (No. 98)

Workers shall enjoy adequate protection against acts of anti-union discrimination in respect of their employment.

Abolition of Forced Labor

Forced Labor Convention, 1930 (No. 29)

Abolition of Forced Labor Convention, 1957 (No. 105)

Equality

Discrimination (Employment and Occupation) Convention, 1958 (No. 111)

Equal Remuneration Convention, 1951 (No. 100)

Elimination of Child Labor

Minimum Age Convention, 1973 (No. 138)

Worst Forms of Child Labor Convention, 1999 (No. 182)

Note: The United States ratified C. 105 in 1991 and C. 182 in 1999. As of 2005, the United States was therefore one of only six (out of 178) countries that had ratified two or fewer of these fundamental conventions. The other five countries are Myanmar, Samoa, the Solomon Islands, Timor-Leste, and Vanuatu.

These objectives are reinforced by several articles of the Universal Declaration of Human Rights and the eight fundamental ILO conventions. In particular, in the Universal Declaration human rights include just and favorable conditions of work including pay sufficient for an existence worthy of human dignity, equal pay for equal work, reasonable working hours, periodic paid holidays, unemployment and disability insurance, and the right to form labor unions. The eight fundamental ILO conventions specify that freedom of association and collective bargaining, the abolition of forced labor, equal opportunity and pay, and the elimination of child labor are "fundamental to the rights of human beings at work" (see Box 6.13).

The United States has not ratified many ILO conventions.[70] Nevertheless, the basic dimensions of workplace equity and voice are recognized worldwide as human rights. The history of human rights illustrates why these are human rights: they stem from the basic feature of being human and are necessary to fulfill the inherent dignity of human beings. Underlying this inherent dignity are the common beliefs of the major religions that humans are created in the image of God and the common beliefs of the intrinsic value and equality of human beings

[70] Richard McIntyre and Matthew M. Bodah, "The United States and ILO Conventions 87 and No. 98: The Freedom of Association and Right to Bargain Collectively," in Richard N. Block et al. (eds.), *Justice on the Job: Perspectives on the Erosion of Collective Bargaining in the United States* (Kalamazoo, MI: Upjohn, 2006), pp. 231–47. Edward E. Potter, "A Pragmatic Assessment from the Employers' Perspective," in James A. Gross (ed.), *Workers' Rights as Human Rights* (Ithaca, NY: Cornell University Press, 2003), pp. 118–35.

in many secular and political philosophies. Note that this emphasizes the human aspect of employees; it rejects the traditional neoclassical economics view of labor as a commodity.[71]

Human dignity and freedom are violated if people are not able to maintain a minimal standard of living and are subjected to onerous working hours in dangerous or unhealthy conditions.[72] Due process protections against arbitrary and discriminatory discipline and discharge are essential for human dignity as is freedom of speech.[73] Denying workers the freedom of association, "denies individuals what they need to live a fully human life"—human dignity—and undermines democracy—freedom.[74] Thus, strong arguments can be made that equity and voice are human rights.

So how do labor rights stack up against property rights? Property rights continue to have significant symbolic, mythic, and rhetorical power.[75] Labor relations needs to break through this myth of the sanctity of property rights. In labor relations, property rights serve economic efficiency. This makes them important, but not sacred. The sanctity of property rights is further reinforced by a persistent belief that laissez faire orderings are natural, apolitical, or free of regulation. But they are instead state-created and enforced.[76] For example, whether nonviolent picketing of an employer's business is ruled as violating the owner's property rights is not an apolitical or neutral legal determination—either way, the decision will affect labor and management's relative power and therefore alter the distribution of wages and profits.

The rhetorical power of property rights also makes labor rights seem secondary. The history of human rights, however, illustrates that contemporary human rights include both first generation civil and political rights and second generation economic and social rights. Workplace equity and voice are intimately intertwined with the inherent dignity of human beings. As such, labor rights can be considered human rights and should not be accorded secondary status relative to efficiency-enhancing property rights. Rather, labor relations must balance the competing claims of labor rights and property rights. In other words, both property rights and labor rights are accepted human rights. As such, they should not be ranked or ordered; they should be balanced.[77]

This chapter started by discussing common labor and management strategies for achieving the goals of efficiency, equity, and voice. The tough issues in labor relations are when the goals and strategies of labor and management conflict. The philosophy of the U.S. labor relations system is that labor and management should freely interact and resolve

---

[71] Hoyt N. Wheeler, "Viewpoint: Collective Bargaining Is a Fundamental Human Right," *Industrial Relations* 39 (July 2000), pp. 535–39.

[72] James A. Gross, "The Broken Promises of the National Labor Relations Act and the Occupational Safety and Health Act: Conflicting Values and Conceptions of Rights and Justice," *Chicago-Kent Law Review* 73 (1998), pp. 351–87. J. M. Spectar, "Pay Me Fairly, Kathie Lee! The WTO, the Right to a Living Wage, and a Proposed Protocol," *New York Law Journal of International and Comparative Law* 20 (2000), pp. 61–92.

[73] Hoyt N. Wheeler, "Employee Rights as Human Rights," *Bulletin of Comparative Labour Relations* 28 (1994), pp. 9–18.

[74] James A. Gross, "A Human Rights Perspective on U.S. Labor Relations Law: A Violation of the Freedom of Association," *Employee Rights and Employment Policy Journal* 3 (1999), pp. 65–103 at 71. Roy J. Adams, "Choice or Voice? Rethinking American Labor Policy in Light of the International Human Rights Consensus," *Employee Rights and Employment Policy Journal* 5 (2001), pp. 521–48. Human Rights Watch, *Unfair Advantage: Workers' Freedom of Association in the United States under International Human Rights Standards* (Washington, DC, 2000).

[75] Nedelsky, *Private Property and the Limits of American Constitutionalism.* Alexander, *Commodity and Proprietary.*

[76] Nedelsky, *Private Property and the Limits of American Constitutionalism.* Karl E. Klare, "Workplace Democracy and Market Reconstruction: An Agenda for Legal Reform," *Catholic University Law Review* 38 (Fall 1988), pp. 1–68.

[77] Budd, *Employment with a Human Face.*

their own conflicts within a framework that appropriately respects the rights of each party involved. Consequently, discussions of conflicting goals turn into discussions of conflicting rights. Labor history reveals the economic and social costs of unbalanced rights (Chapter 4). The evolution of labor law described in the previous chapter is therefore a move from the dominance of property rights (recall labor injunctions and yellow dog contracts) to an explicit statutory framework in which the National Labor Relations Act grants labor rights to employees while respecting the property rights of employers.

Many of the tensions or conflicts in labor relations can be understood as conflicts between property rights and labor rights. The standard U.S. union organizing process discussed in the next chapter is a vivid illustration of the conflict between property rights and labor rights in U.S. labor relations. In short, it is a human right to form unions, but do property and free speech rights give employers the right to participate in the union organizing process? Or to fire union supporters? Can property rights be used by employers to restrict union organizers and therefore potentially interfere with labor rights to organize unions? Can labor rights be used by employees to force employers to bargain over work design issues, plant closings, or other questions intimately related to property rights (Chapter 8)? Should employers be able to hire replacement workers during a strike because of their property rights to conduct business; or should replacement workers be illegal because they interfere with labor rights to engage in collective bargaining (Chapter 9)? Does videotaping picketing workers support property rights by protecting the employer's property, or does it violate labor rights by intimidating workers who are exercising their voice?

There aren't easy answers to these questions. But rooting these questions in the conflicting goals and rights of workers and employers provides the framework for trying to tackle these questions. The specific processes in contemporary U.S. labor relations that are intended to handle the conflicting workplace goals and rights are the subject of the next few chapters. Afterward, to consider whether the U.S. labor relations system needs to be reformed, ask whether property rights and labor rights—and therefore the goals of labor and management and the resulting outcomes—could be better balanced with different processes, strategies, and/or structures.

Key Terms

servicing model, *205*	craft unionism, *209*	Change to win, *216*
organizing model, *205*	industrial unionism, *209*	union avoidance, *217*
business unionism, *206*	national union, *211*	union suppression, *218*
job control unionism, *206*	union democracy, *213*	union substitution, *219*
employee empowerment	general union, *215*	human rights, *224*
unionism, *207*	rival unionism, *215*	International Labor
social unionism, *208*	AFL–CIO, *215*	Organization, *226*

Reflection Questions

1. Of the union strategies in Box 6.3, which ones do you think are best for the 21st-century world of work? Are some of the strategies always better or does it depend on the environment?

2. Describe the pros and cons of union mergers for (i) two unions that represent workers in the same industry, and (ii) two unions that represent workers in different industries. Should U.S. law encourage, discourage, or remain neutral on union mergers?

3. There is longstanding debate over "American exceptionalism"—the extent to which the low levels of support for unionization and a socialist movement make the United States unique among industrialized, democratic countries. There might also be a management side: American management has been exceptionally antiunion compared to managers in

other countries.[78] Why do you think this is?

4. It is almost universally accepted that labor unions, but not companies, must be democratic. Why is there this dichotomy? What does this dichotomy imply about the organizational structures and sources of power for labor unions and for corporations?

5. What should people be entitled to as human beings? Why? How should these things be provided?

Internet Exploration

1. Find some descriptions of national union structures on various union websites (on many sites there is a link for "About Union Name"). How similar are the structures? Can you find differences in structures that are related to differences in the environment? Here are some example Web sites: the American Postal Workers Union (*www.apwu.org*), International Brotherhood of Boilermakers (*www.boilermakers.org*—look under "who we are"), International Longshore and Warehouse Union (ILWU) (*www.ilwu.org*), and the United Auto Workers (UAW) (*www.uaw.org*). Additional union links can be found at *www.aflcio.org/aboutus/unions/* and *www.changetowin.org/members.html.*

2. Find the AFL–CIO state federation or central labor council closest to you (see *www.aflcio.org/aboutus/unioncities/*.) What types of activities and issues is it emphasizing? How does this support the local labor movement?

3. Find and explore the Web sites for the AFL–CIO and Change to Win. In what ways are the messages and strategies of the two federations similar? Different? Are workers better off when the labor movement has a single, unified federation or multiple, competing national federations?

4. Go to the Global Compact Web site (*www.unglobalcompact.org*) and explore various statements and materials about the compact. What do you think of this Global Compact? Are the objectives laudable? If so, are there better alternative methods for achieving them? Do companies violate human rights by investing in countries with poor human rights records?

Additional Reading

Barling, Julian, Clive Fullagar, and E. Kevin Kelloway, *The Union and its Members: A Psychological Approach* (New York: Oxford University Press, 1992).

Fantasia, Rick, and Kim Voss, *Hard Work: Remaking the American Labor Movement* (Berkeley: University of California Press, 2004).

Gross, James A. (ed.), *Workers' Rights as Human Rights* (Ithaca, NY: Cornell University Press, 2003).

Hannigan, Thomas A., *Managing Tomorrow's High-Performance Unions* (Westport, CT: Quorum Books, 1998).

Human Rights Watch, *Unfair Advantage: Workers' Freedom of Association in the United States Under International Human Rights Standards* (Washington, DC, 2000).

Kochan, Thomas A., Harry C. Katz, and Robert B. McKersie, *The Transformation of American Industrial Relations* (New York: Basic Books, 1986).

Lauren, Paul Gordon, *The Evolution of International Human Rights: Visions Seen* (Philadelphia: University of Pennsylvania Press, 1998).

Lowell Turner, Harry C. Katz, and Richard W. Hurd (eds.), *Rekindling the Movement: Labor's Quest for Relevance in the Twenty-First Century* (Ithaca, NY: ILR Press, 2001).

---

[78] Sanford M. Jacoby, "American Exceptionalism Revisited: The Importance of Management," in Sanford M. Jacoby (ed.), *Masters to Managers: Historical and Comparative Perspectives on American Employers* (New York: Columbia University Press, 1991), Chapter 8.

Chapter Seven

Union Organizing

Advance Organizer

In the U.S. labor relations system, if a group of employees wants their employer to bargain with them collectively rather than individually, they typically will need to form a union and formally demonstrate that a majority of the employees support the union. This chapter discusses the behavioral, strategic, and legal aspects of this union organizing process.

Learning Objectives

By the end of the chapter, you should be able to:

1. **Discuss** the basic procedural steps and legal standards for how new unions are formed in the United States. This is called the organizing process.

2. **Explain** the determinants of whether individuals vote for or against a union in a representation election

3. **Understand** the tactics used by employers to weaken individual support for unions and why these tactics are controversial.

4. **Understand** the traditional tactics used by unions to strengthen individual support for unions and the pressures for developing new strategies.

5. **Compare** the pros and cons of the existing certification election process and options for reform.

Contents

The previous chapter described the organizational structure of U.S. unions—which are typically large, bureaucratic organizations with many members and locations (like many corporations). In contrast, to start this chapter, return to the fundamental conception of a labor union described in Chapter 1: a group of workers who join together to influence the nature of their employment. Suppose this group wants their employer to bargain with them as a group rather than as individuals—perhaps to get improved wages and benefits, or to have some input into workplace policies, or to secure standards for objective treatment. The employer is unlikely to agree to formally bargain with this informal group. To force the employer to bargain with them, the employees must *organize* themselves into a union.

You can probably think of numerous ways in which a union can be formed. A few employees could initiate a strike and then round up support (as in the 1930s sit-down strikes), union supporters could get workers to sign a petition and present the results to management along with a threat to strike if management ignores their request, or the employees could have a secret ballot election in which the union and employer must abide by the decision of the majority. Since the passage of the National Labor Relations Act (NLRA) in 1935, U.S. public policy has favored the last option. Most U.S. unions are organized (formed) through secret ballot elections administered by the National Labor Relations

Board (NLRB). The first major U.S. labor relations process—the organizing process—is therefore largely shaped by the NLRA and the procedural and legal aspects of NLRB elections. These elections are known as **representation elections,** because they are to answer questions of who the employees want to represent them. The most significant type of representation election is a certification election—an election to determine if the union will be certified as the bargaining agent of the employees. The U.S. union organizing process, and therefore this chapter, is largely about certification elections—how employees can get an election held, legal and illegal election conduct by both labor and management, union and employer strategies to affect how employees vote, determinants of individual voting, and criticisms of the election process.

THE ORGANIZING TIMELINE

Most union organizing drives—that is, campaigns to organize nonunion workers into unions to gain recognition of the unions by their employers—follow a common sequence of steps (see Box 7.1). The first step is initiation. In theory, there are three possible initiators of an organizing drive: one or more employees, a union, or an employer. The last possibility might seem odd, but as an example, in the 1960s and 1970s some agricultural companies signed contracts with the Teamsters rather than risk having their employees choose the more militant United Farm Workers. Note that this interferes with employee free choice and therefore employer-initiated organizing drives are illegal [section 8(a)(1) unfair labor practices under the NLRA]. As such, our concern is with employee- or union-initiated campaigns.

An employee-initiated organizing drive is perhaps the classic scenario. Low pay, excessive overtime, harsh supervision, lack of respect and voice, or numerous other things cause dissatisfied employees to talk with each other about forming a union to increase their collective strength. These employees might then try to form a union on their own or, more frequently, contact a union organizer that works for an existing union in their area, industry, or occupation. In either case, this is an employee-initiated campaign.

Alternatively, unions may initiate organizing campaigns by advertising, distributing information, and trying to contact employees to show the benefits of unionization. There are two types of union-initiated campaigns: strategic and opportunistic. Strategic campaigns are those in which organizing a particular workplace will enhance a union's ability to effectively represent existing employees. For example, the United Auto Workers (UAW) frequently try to organize the nonunion U.S. manufacturing plants of the Japanese auto companies such as Honda in order to maintain its bargaining power in that industry. On the other hand, opportunistic campaigns involve an attempt to increase a union's membership by organizing dissatisfied workers that are "ripe" for unionization, but that do not have a strategic fit with the existing membership, such as when the United Steelworkers of America try to organize nursing home workers.

In any case, once an organizing drive has been initiated, the next step in the union organizing timeline is building support (see Box 7.1). This generally involves meeting with interested employees outside the workplace and distributing information. If an organizing drive is going to continue, sooner or later employees will have to concretely express support for having a union represent them. The most important method in U.S. labor relations for showing this support is to sign an **authorization card.** An authorization card is a preprinted form containing something like "I authorize [union name] to represent me for the purposes of collective bargaining" which employees fill out and sign (see Box 7.2). Collecting signed authorization cards is a critical part of the union organizing process because they demonstrate the interest in unionization to three important players: union organizers, the

BOX 7.1
The Union
Organizing Process

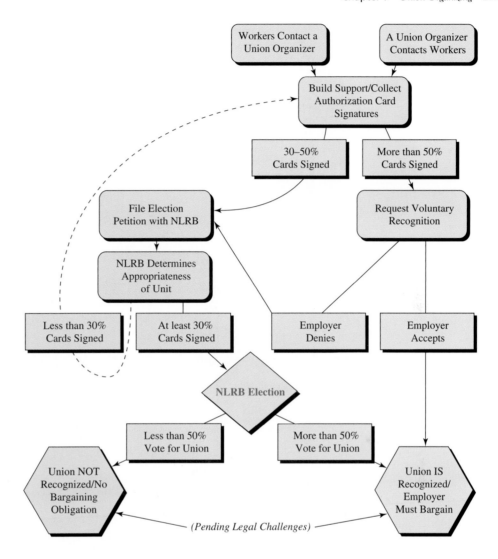

employer, and if necessary, the NLRB. Some union organizers will not continue to devote their time and resources to a campaign if they cannot collect a certain number of signatures in a certain time period.[1]

More importantly, authorization cards can be used to show the employer that a majority of employees want union representation. If a union gathers signed cards from more than 50 percent of the employees, it can ask the employer to recognize the union as the bargaining agent of the employees. If the employer is agreeable, a neutral party can examine the cards and determine if truly more than 50 percent of the employees signed cards. If so, the employer can recognize the union and is then obligated to bargain with the union. This is called voluntary recognition, and when this occurs, the union organizing process is over (see Box 7.1). Recognition based on the authorization cards is also called a **card-check election** or a majority signup procedure. Both employers and unions violate the NLRA by agreeing to recognize a union when the union lacks majority support.[2]

[1] Ken Gagala, *Union Organizing and Staying Organized* (Reston, VA: Reston Publishing Company, 1983).
[2] *International Ladies' Garment Workers (Bernhard-Altmann Texas Corp.) v. NLRB,* 366 U.S. 731 (1961).

BOX 7.2

A Union Flyer with Authorization Card for University of California (UC) Professional Employees

www.upte.org

UC staff professionals are central to the University's research, medical and educational missions, but often our work is not given the recognition it deserves. We need an effective organization to give us a voice in determining our future at the University. The ability to negotiate a union contract will guarantee that our voices will be heard.

We need to have a say in how our compensation system works. Increasing workloads, uncertain job security, and rising health care costs can no longer remain unchallenged. Thousands of other UC employees have already won the right to collectively negotiate with the University over the issues important to them. Now it's our turn to get the recognition we deserve.

UPTE

UNIVERSITY PROFESSIONAL & TECHNICAL EMPLOYEES, CWA 9119

Take a step for *real* change by filling out the card below. It will be given to the California Public Employment Relations Board with a petition for a secret ballot election to give UC staff professionals an opportunity to vote for UPTE-CWA representation.

Professionals eligible to sign a card: Administrative Analysts, Student Affairs Officers, Programmer Analysts, Administrative Specialists, Accountants, Program Reps, Analysts, Computer Network Technicians, Statisticians, Library Asst. V., Senior & Principal Writers & Editors, Learning Skills Counselors and other job titles.

Questions? Please call (510) 704-UPTE.

UPTE is the union for UC professional and technical employees at the campuses, medical centers and national labs. UPTE is a democratic, member-run union. Since 1990 UPTE-CWA has won union elections benefiting more than 11,000 UC technical, research and health care professionals. With UPTE-CWA as their representative these employees have made many gains on the job including better wages, more layoff protections and enhanced career development.

Now it's our turn to have a voice at the bargaining table. Imagine the power of thousands of UC staff professionals joining together to work for solutions that benefit all employees.

PLEASE MAIL THIS CARD TO UPTE, PO Box 4443, BERKELEY, CA 94704. DO NOT FAX.

Campus _____

Authorization Card

Yes! I want UPTE-CWA Local 9119 to be my union for the purpose of negotiating wages, hours and working conditions with the University of California.

Please print legibly

Name _____ Home Phone ( ) _____
       LAST   FIRST   MIDDLE INITIAL

Home Address _____

City/State/Zip _____

Job Title/Classification _____ Department _____

Work Mailing Address _____ Work Phone ( ) _____

Actual Work Location_____ Email _____
       BUILDING and ROOM

Date _____ Signature _____

Unions are increasingly pushing for card-check elections, but they are the exception rather than the norm because employers typically refuse to recognize unions voluntarily. So what happens after an employer declines a request for voluntary recognition? First consider the pre-NLRA era before 1935. In this era, employees had only one option: step up the pressure on the company to force it to change its stance. As a result, employees would launch a **recognition strike**—a strike to try to compel the employer to recognize their union. Recall from Chapter 4 that the Ludlow Massacre, the 1934 general strikes in San Francisco and Minneapolis, the General Motors sit-down strike, and the Memorial Day Massacre all resulted from recognition strikes. And recall further how costly these strikes were—in terms of loss of human life, human suffering, lost profits, and disruption of economic activity. A major goal of the NLRA is to replace these costly recognition strikes with an orderly alternative. What is the natural, orderly mechanism in a democratic society for determining the wishes of the majority? An election.

The passage of the NLRA in 1935, therefore, created a certification procedure in which employees can petition the NLRB to have an election to determine if a union has the support of a majority of the employees. The NLRA does not ban recognition strikes per se (though the Landrum-Griffin Act restricts recognition picketing to 30 days) but rather tries to make them obsolete by providing employees with a safer alternative that does not involve lost wages and the risk of being replaced by a new employee during a strike. Most recognition questions today are settled through NLRB representation elections rather than through strikes.

Contemporary examples reinforce the NLRA's logic. For example, graduate student teaching assistants at Yale University have been trying to form a union since the early 1990s.[3] A major complicating factor, however, has been whether in the eyes of the law these individuals are employees or students. Except for a period between 2000 and 2004, the NLRB has ruled that graduate assistants at private universities are students, not employees, and are therefore not covered under the NLRA and not entitled to use the certification election process. Rather, the law of the jungle prevails and the only way for the graduate assistants to force Yale to recognize their union is through economic pressure tactics. In fact, at the end of the Fall semester in 1995, the Graduate Employees and Students Organization (GESO) led a grade strike—the graduate assistants refused to hand in grades for the classes they were teaching—to try to force the university to recognize the GESO as their union. The strike failed and the conflict between the graduate assistants and the university continues to fester. Yale graduate assistants struck again for a week in 2005 to try to win recognition for their union. This time, they were joined by Columbia University teaching assistants also striking for recognition. Whether in the form of sit-down strikes, grade strikes, or traditional strikes, U.S. labor law tries to prevent this type of disruptive activity by using secret ballot elections to decide questions of representation.

NLRB REPRESENTATION ELECTIONS

There are several types of NLRB representation elections that correspond to different questions of representation, but all have the same goal—to determine the wishes of the majority of the employees. The most frequent type is the **certification election** which is used in a nonunion location to ascertain if a majority of employees want to become unionized—that is, to designate a specific union as their bargaining agent. If so, the NLRB uses the election results to *certify* this union as the bargaining agent (hence the name, certification election). Most certification elections have just one union on the ballot (so the choice

[3] See *www.yaleunions.org*.

BOX 7.3
Some Notable NLRB Representation Elections

First	December 1935: Fort Wayne (Indiana) knitting mill employees
Longest	112 Days: Maritime seaman on 20 ships (1965)
Most Remote	Island of Tinian (Northern Marianas): Micronesian Telecommunications Co. employees (1984)
Most Complex	Bituminous coal industry: 2,200 staffers providing ballots to 311,000 eligible workers at 2,000 mines in 31 states in 22 hours (1945)
Largest	Steel industry: 686,000 workers (1945)
Largest in a Single Plant	Ford's River Rouge Plant (Dearborn, Michigan): 78,000 eligible workers (1941)
Smallest	Two employees: Various instances, including one election for two grave diggers

Source: National Labor Relations Board, NLRB: The First 50 Years (Washington, DC: 1985).

is between a specific union and no union) but some have multiple unions vying for representation rights. In these cases, run-off elections between the top vote getters might be needed to determine the wishes of the majority.

The opposite of a certification election is a **decertification election.** This type of election is used to determine if a majority of unionized employees no longer wish to be represented by their union. If so, this union is decertified and loses the right to represent and bargain for these employees. A small number of decertification elections decertify the existing union and certify a new union—this is a raid election in which employees can choose between their existing union, a challenging (raiding) union, and no union. Most decertification elections result in a workplace going from union to nonunion. The NLRB conducts between 3,500 and 4,000 representation elections each year; approximately 85 percent are certification elections (see Box 7.3).[4] Unions win roughly half of certification elections and lose about two-thirds of decertification elections. This chapter largely focuses on certification elections. Most of the issues discussed are similar for decertification elections.

A group of employees or a union can petition the NLRB to conduct a certification election *if* they can support this petition by demonstrating that there is sufficient interest among the employees for such an election. Sufficient interest is defined by the NLRB as 30 percent. This is perhaps the most important use of signed authorization cards—the typical way to demonstrate sufficient interest is to provide signed authorization cards from at least 30 percent of the employees. Many unions will wait until they have cards from more than 50 percent, but 30 percent is the legal minimum. Authorization cards are presumed valid for one year. Thirty percent is also the threshold for demonstrating that there is sufficient interest for holding a decertification election, though this would be demonstrated through signatures on an employee petition or other means, not by authorization cards.

In addition to verifying sufficient interest, there are several other details that the NLRB must deal with before scheduling a representation election. First, unless there are unusual circumstances, the NLRB will not allow more than one election in a 12-month period. Second,

---

[4] National Labor Relations Board, *Seventieth Annual Report of the National Labor Relations Board* (Washington, DC: Government Printing Office, 2005).

elections will not be authorized within 12 months of any union certification.[5] Third, a de-certification election cannot be held when there is a valid collective bargaining agreement in place (up to a limit of three years). This is called the "contract bar doctrine."

Finally, the NLRB must handle the most contentious aspect of the petition—defining the occupations and geographical locations included in a certification election. A union will be certified as the exclusive bargaining representative for the employees when a majority of them support the union, but what set of employees does this refer to? For example, in a grocery store, does this mean just full-time cashiers, all cashiers, all hourly employees, all employees including managers, or some other group? For a grocery chain with multiple stores in a single city, is the unit limited to a single store or does it include multiple locations? When a petition for a certification election is filed with the NLRB, a definition of the relevant jobs and locations is proposed by the party filing the petition. But if the employer objects to this definition, then the NLRB must make a determination. Section 9(b) of the NLRA states that the NLRB "shall decide in each case whether, in order to assure to employees the fullest freedom in exercising the rights guaranteed by this Act, the unit appropriate for the purposes of collective bargaining shall be the employer unit, craft unit, plant unit, or subdivision thereof." As such, the group of occupations and locations relevant to the certification election is referred to as the **appropriate bargaining unit**—employees in these occupations can vote in the election and will be represented by the union if the union wins the election.

But how to determine the appropriate unit? Because supervisors and managers are excluded from the NLRA, these employees are excluded from NLRB–defined bargaining units. Security guards cannot be in the same unit with other employees. Otherwise, the NLRB's determination of the appropriate bargaining unit is generally based on grouping together the jobs that share a community of interest. In manufacturing, it's common to include all production and maintenance employees in a single facility—this is called an industrial unit because it follows the industrial unionism model. Drivers, clerical employees, and workers at other locations of the same employer may or may not be included based on specific circumstances, such as whether there are common human resources policies or significant similarities and interactions between employee groups.[6] In contrast, under the Railway Labor Act, bargaining units are narrow in terms of occupation, but broad in terms of geography and include all of an employer's locations.[7] But under the NLRA there is great diversity: some units span many occupations and diverse locations while, under other circumstances, the NLRB might rule that a single occupation in one location is appropriate (a craft rather than industrial unit). In some cases, a bargaining unit consists of only two employees. The NLRB's determination of the appropriate bargaining unit can be contentious because each side—the union and the employer—wants the unit defined to maximize their chances of winning the election (see Box 7.4). In fact, unions fare significantly better in smaller rather than larger elections, and in elections with more homogeneous rather than heterogeneous skill groups.[8]

Once the appropriate bargaining unit is determined, note carefully that the petition for a certification election might not be supported any longer by signed authorization cards from at least 30 percent of the relevant employees. For example, in the Harvard University case

[5] Douglas E. Ray, Calvin William Sharpe, and Robert N. Strassfield, *Understanding Labor Law* (New York: Mathew Bender, 1999).

[6] Ray, Sharpe, and Strassfield, *Understanding Labor Law.*

[7] Douglas L. Leslie (ed.), *The Railway Labor Act* (Washington, DC: Bureau of National Affairs, 1995).

[8] Rebecca S. Demsetz, "Voting Behavior in Union Representation Elections: The Influence of Skill Homogeneity and Skill Group Size," *Industrial and Labor Relations Review* 47 (October 1993), pp. 99–113. Henry S. Farber, "Union Success in Representation Elections: Why Does Unit Size Matter?" *Industrial and Labor Relations Review* 54 (January 2001), pp. 329–48.

Harvard University's medical area consists of its medical, dental, and public health schools and is located about three miles from the main Harvard campus. The medical area employs approximately 1,200 clerical and technical workers. These employees are similar to the 2,400 clerical and technical workers throughout the rest of the university in typing manuscripts, handling correspondence, and performing technical duties, though in the medical area the work is more medically oriented and perhaps includes more health hazards. There are relatively more technical workers than clerical workers in the medical area as compared to the rest of Harvard. Of the Harvard clerical and technical employees in the medical area that transfer jobs, approximately 80 percent stay within the medical area. Human resources policies are established centrally for all of Harvard. The medical area is the only campus unit to have its own human resources office. This office is responsible for hiring new employees, but must comply with the centrally established job classification and wage system.

In the early 1970s, a handful of women employed in Harvard University's medical area started a group to bring attention to discriminatory treatment against female workers. Out of frustration with Harvard's unresponsiveness, this movement grew into a campaign to unionize, and in 1975 a petition was filed with the NLRB to conduct an election for clerical and technical employees in the medical area.

Questions

1. As the human resources director for Harvard University, do you object to the definition of the bargaining unit? In other words, would you rather have an election for all clerical and technical workers at Harvard, not just those in the medical area? What are the risks and benefits?

2. As the NLRB, how do you decide on the appropriate bargaining unit if Harvard objects?

Source: *Harvard College,* 229 NLRB No. 97 (1977). *Harvard College,* 269 NLRB No. 151 (1984).

---

discussed in Box 7.4, when the NLRB expanded the bargaining unit in 1984 to include all Harvard University clerical and technical workers, not just those in the medical area, the size of the bargaining unit tripled from 1,200 to 3,600 employees. The union had been collecting cards only in the medical area, so with this expansion, it no longer had 30 percent. In this situation, the union must return to the start of the timeline—building support and collecting signed authorization cards (recall Box 7.1). In the Harvard University case, the union spent nearly four additional years collecting enough cards to demonstrate sufficient interest for a certification election based on the new unit; not all unions are successful in this endeavor.[9]

Once all of the details are ironed out—sufficient interest, timeliness, and unit definition—the NLRB will schedule an election. Elections are supervised and monitored by NLRB officials and usually take place at the employees' work site—in factories, warehouses, offices, restaurants, movie studios, sports stadiums, train yards, and aboard ships. In special circumstances, mail ballots are allowed. Each eligible worker can vote using a secret ballot. Voter turnout is often quite high—around 80 percent on average.[10] Elections are typically held within six to eight weeks after a petition is filed, though challenges to the unit definition can drastically lengthen the election timetable. It is in this time period that the most intense campaigning by both unions and employers takes place, all with the intent of shaping how each individual worker votes in the election.

---

[9] John P. Hoerr, *We Can't Eat Prestige: The Women Who Organized Harvard* (Philadelphia: Temple University Press, 1997).

[10] National Labor Relations Board, *Seventieth Annual Report of the National Labor Relations Board.*

INDIVIDUAL VOTING DECISIONS

In the most common scenario, an individual worker voting in a representation election receives a ballot preprinted with "Do you wish to be represented for the purpose of collective bargaining by [union name]" and is instructed to mark the appropriate box—Yes or No. An important question in labor relations is what influences whether individual workers vote "yes" to form a union, or "no" to remain nonunion. For starters, research on U.S. workers typically reveals that demographic factors such as age and gender are *not* important predictors of how people vote in representation elections.[11] Rather, the voting decision is believed to be much more practical and focused on the perceived costs and benefits of unionization as well as on individual attitudes towards unions. As such, two starting points for the voting decision are typically identified: job dissatisfaction and a desire to maximize one's own utility or well-being.[12] In the job dissatisfaction models, only dissatisfied workers will consider unionizing. In very broad terms, these can be thought of as psychological models as they are rooted in dissonance between desired and actual employment conditions. In contrast, the utility-maximization models are economic models: rational workers will consider unionization if it increases their well-being; job dissatisfaction is not required.[13] Most studies emphasize dissatisfaction rather than utility maximization.[14]

Job dissatisfaction or utility maximization are only the starting points, however. In order for these features to translate into a "yes" vote for unionization, three additional items are important: (1) a worker needs to feel that the union will be effective in improving things in their specific workplace, (2) a worker usually must not have negative views about unions in general, and (3) the social environment of the workplace is favorable to unionization (see Box 7.5). The first item is called **union instrumentality**: the degree to which an individual thinks a union will be instrumental (successful) in improving their workplace.[15] Unsurprisingly, workers who do not think a union will make a positive difference in their workplace will not be very likely to vote for a union, even if they are dissatisfied with their wages, working conditions, or other aspects of their jobs. Workers' fears that a union will bring conflict to the

[11] Julian Barling, Clive Fullagar, and E. Kevin Kelloway, *The Union and its Members: A Psychological Approach* (New York: Oxford University Press, 1992). Jack Fiorito and Angela Young, "Union Voting Intentions: Human Resource Policies, Organizational Characteristics, and Attitudes," in Kate Bronfenbrenner et al. (eds.), *Organizing to Win: New Research on Union Strategies* (Ithaca, NY: ILR Press, 1998), pp. 232–46. Hoyt. N. Wheeler and John A. McClendon, "The Individual Decision to Unionize," in George Strauss, Daniel G. Gallagher, and Jack Fiorito (eds.), *The State of the Unions* (Madison, WI: Industrial Relations Research Association, 1991), Chapter 2. Stuart A. Youngblood, Angelo S. DeNisi, Julie L. Molleston, and William H. Mobley, "The Impact of Work Environment, Instrumentality Beliefs, Perceived Labor Union Image, and Subjective Norms on Union Voting Intentions," *Academy of Management Journal* 27 (September 1984), pp. 576–90.

[12] Wheeler and McClendon, "The Individual Decision to Unionize."

[13] Henry S. Farber and Daniel H. Saks, "Why Workers Want Unions: The Role of Relative Wages and Job Characteristics," *Journal of Political Economy* 88 (April 1980), pp. 349–69.

[14] Barling, Fullagar, and Kelloway, *The Union and its Members.* Jeanne M. Brett, "Why Employees Want Unions," *Organizational Dynamics* 8 (Spring 1980), pp. 47–59. Richard B. Freeman and Joel Rogers, *What Workers Want* (Ithaca, NY: ILR Press, 1999). Julius B. Getman, Stephen B. Goldberg, and Jeanne B. Herman, *Union Representation Elections: Law and Reality* (New York: Russell Sage, 1976). Thomas A. Kochan, "How American Workers View Labor Unions," *Monthly Labor Review* 102 (April 1979), pp. 23–31. Steven L. Premack and John E. Hunter, "Individual Unionization Decisions," *Psychological Bulletin* 103 (1988), pp. 223–34.

[15] Barling, Fullagar, and Kelloway, *The Union and its Members.* Brett, "Why Employees Want Unions." Satish P. Deshpande and Jack Fiorito, "Specific and General Beliefs in Union Voting Models," *Academy of Management Journal* 32 (December 1989), pp. 883–97. Kochan, "How American Workers View Labor Unions." Youngblood et al., "The Impact of Work Environment, Instrumentality Beliefs, Perceived Labor Union Image, and Subjective Norms on Union Voting Intentions."

BOX 7.5
The Individual Voting Decision in NLRB Representation Elections

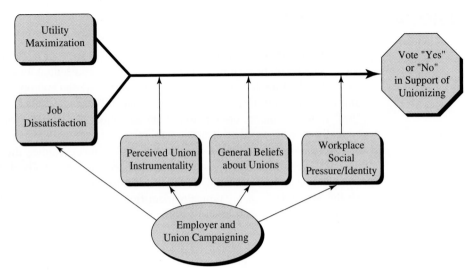

workplace can be viewed as an important (negative) dimension of union instrumentality.[16] In fact, union instrumentality is believed by some to be the most consistent predictor of union support.[17] Workers' beliefs that their unions lack instrumentality also increase the likelihood that they vote against union representation in decertification elections.[18]

A second item often identified as important for determining whether dissatisfied workers will vote for a union is attitudes toward unions in general.[19] While union instrumentality is a belief about a specific union in your specific workplace, this second dimension pertains to broader images of unions. On the negative side, these general attitudes might include unions as autocratic, discriminatory, corrupt, outdated, bureaucratic, and too strong. In contrast, general positive attitudes can include beliefs that unions improve working conditions, help ensure that workers are treated fairly, and lobby for needed protective labor legislation. Positive attitudes might stem from previous experience in unionized workplaces or from having a parent or a spouse who is a union member.

The third item that affects whether job dissatisfaction translates into a pro-union vote pertains to social aspects of the workplace. At one level, this involves what has been labeled social pressure. Social pressure measures the extent to which an individual thinks his

[16] Larry Cohen and Richard W. Hurd, "Fear, Conflict, and Union Organizing," in Kate Bronfenbrenner et al. (eds.), *Organizing to Win: New Research on Union Strategies* (Ithaca, NY: ILR Press, 1998), pp. 181–96.

[17] Jack Fiorito, Daniel G. Gallagher, and Charles R. Greer, "Determinants of Unionism: A Review of the Literature," in Kenneth M. Rowland and Gerald R. Ferris (eds.), *Research in Personnel and Human Resource Management, Volume 4* (Greenwich, CT: JAI Press, 1986), pp. 269–306.

[18] Barling, Fullagar, and Kelloway, *The Union and its Members.* Barry A. Friedman, Steven E. Abraham, and Randall K. Thomas, "Factors Related to Employees' Desire to Join and Leave Unions," *Industrial Relations* 45 (January 2006), pp. 102–10.

[19] Julian Barling, E. Kevin Kelloway, and Eric H. Bremermann, "Preemployment Predictors of Union Attitudes: The Role of Family Socialization and Work Beliefs," *Journal of Applied Psychology* 76 (October 1991), pp. 725–31. Brett, "Why Employees Want Unions." Deshpande and Fiorito, "Specific and General Beliefs in Union Voting Models." Getman, Goldberg, and Herman, *Union Representation Elections.* Kochan, "How American Workers View Labor Unions." Wheeler and McClendon, "The Individual Decision to Unionize." Heejoon Park, Patrick P. McHugh, and Matthew M. Bodah, "Revisiting General and Specific Union Beliefs: The Union-Voting Intentions of Professionals," *Industrial Relations* 45 (April 2006), pp. 270–89. Seymour Martin Lipset and Noah M. Meltz, with Rafael Gomez and Ivan Katchanovski, *The Paradox of American Unionism: Why Americans Like Unions More than Canadians Do But Join Much Less* (Ithaca, NY: Cornell University Press, 2004).

or her co-workers support the union, especially good co-workers.[20] More generally, social aspects of the workplace capture the basic fact that unionization is ultimately a social or collective rather than individual activity.[21] Workplace-level employee solidarity and social identification are important factors in determining whether workers will try to correct perceived workplace injustices individually or collectively.[22] In other words, if workplace solidarity is low and workers have more of an individual rather than collective social identity, job dissatisfaction is not likely to translate into pro-union support. Interestingly, it therefore can be the case that low-wage immigrant workers are more likely to unionize than low-wage native workers because of the greater collective social identity of immigrant workers that results when they self-select or are forced into living together and working in concentrated occupational niches such as New York City's West African grocery delivery workers or Pakistani "black-car" drivers.[23]

Lastly, it is important to note that the description of individual decisions to unionize captured by Box 7.5 is distinctly North American. In the United States and Canada, the decision to join a union is very closely linked to collective representation in the workplace. In Europe collective bargaining often occurs at the industry level and does not depend on whether a majority of workers in a workplace support a specific union (see Chapter 13). As such, an alternative explanation for why workers join unions focuses on political and ideological beliefs, but this is more appropriate in Europe.[24] Furthermore, since collective bargaining is so tightly linked with workplace-level union support in the United States, each NLRB representation election is a very important contest for both unions and companies. Consequently, campaigning by both sides to affect whether individuals vote for or against union representation is a very significant component of the U.S. union organizing process.

NLRB ELECTION STANDARDS

In the days and weeks leading up to NLRB representation elections, employers and unions typically conduct intense campaigns to bolster support for their side. Unions try to create a social climate in the workplace that supports collective rather than individual action while highlighting reasons why employees should be dissatisfied with their jobs, how the union will be effective in improving their jobs (union instrumentality), and that unions in general are a positive societal force. On the other hand, employers try to make employees feel satisfied with their jobs, question the effectiveness and need for unions in improving the workplace, negatively portray unions as dues-hungry or corrupt, and emphasize the value of individual rather than collective action. In short, employer and union campaigns try to affect the key determinants of how individuals vote in representation elections (see Box 7.5). Various campaign tactics will be discussed in the next two sections, but first ask yourself whether there should be any limits or restrictions on employer and union campaigning. It's critical not to lose sight of the fact that NLRB representation elections are not about employers or unions. Rather, the NLRA authorizes these elections to determine whether or not the *workers* want union representation.

---

[20] Jeanette A. Davy and Frank Shipper, "Voter Behavior in Union Certification Elections: A Longitudinal Study," *Academy of Management Journal* 36 (February 1993), pp. 187–99.

[21] John E. Kelly, *Rethinking Industrial Relations: Mobilization, Collectivism and Long Waves* (London: Routledge, 1998). Hoyt N. Wheeler, *Industrial Conflict: An Integrative Theory* (Columbia: University of South Carolina Press, 1985).

[22] Brett, "Why Employees Want Unions." Randy Hodson, *Dignity at Work* (Cambridge: Cambridge University Press, 2001). Kelly, *Rethinking Industrial Relations*.

[23] Immanuel Ness, *Immigrants, Unions, and the New U.S. Labor Market* (Philadelphia: Temple University Press, 2005).

[24] Wheeler and McClendon, "The Individual Decision to Unionize."

The key legal standard for NLRB representation elections is therefore employee free choice. Campaigning by employers and unions is permitted by the NLRA's employer's free speech provision [section 8(c)]:

> The expressing of any views, argument, or opinion, or the dissemination thereof, whether in written, printed, graphic, or visual form, shall not constitute or be evidence of an unfair labor practice under any of the provisions of this Act, if such expression contains no threat of reprisal or force or promise of benefit.

But this right is not unlimited—threats and promises are not allowed. Why? Because threats and promises can interfere with employee free choice. Union supporters might not vote for a union if they are afraid that they will lose their job if the union wins; employees who do not favor unionization might not vote against a union if union organizers have threatened them with physical violence. More generally, to promote the underlying standard of employee free choice, the NLRB has used the NLRA to establish boundaries for employer and union campaigning—campaign tactics that hamper, restrict, or interfere with *employee* free choice in deciding whether to have union representation are prohibited.[25] This is similar to the familiar standards for political elections for government offices—well-informed voters are important for democracy, but buying votes through bribes or violence undermines democracy and is not allowed.

In particular, the NLRB evaluates election conduct using its **laboratory conditions doctrine,** also known as the *General Shoe* doctrine (after the name of the NLRB decision that created this doctrine):

> In election proceedings, it is the [NLRB's] function to provide a laboratory in which an experiment may be conducted, under conditions as nearly ideal as possible, to determine the uninhibited desires of the employees. It is our duty to establish those conditions; it is also our duty to determine whether they have been fulfilled. When, in the rare extreme case, the standard drops too low, because of our fault or that of others, the requisite laboratory conditions are not present and the experiment must be conducted over again.[26]

When the NLRB feels that election campaigning or conduct causes employees to vote differently from their true preferences, the election results will be thrown out and a new election conducted (see Box 7.6). The clearest violations of laboratory conditions are the NLRA's employer and union unfair labor practices: interfering with or coercing employees [sections 8(a)(1) and 8(b)(1)], establishing a company-dominated, sham union [8(a)(2)], and discriminating against employees on the basis of union support [8(a)(3)]. The classic example is firing union activists. This can affect the outcome of an election in several ways. Pro-union votes are kept from the election. Key individuals in spreading information about the union and creating a workplace climate supportive of collective action are removed. And other employees may be afraid to support the union for fear of being fired next. Firing (or otherwise discriminating against) union activists because of their union support therefore interferes with employee free choice and is illegal. Threatening to close a plant if a union wins an election or promising wage increases if the union loses amount to buying votes and interfere with free choice. These actions are therefore prohibited. Improving wages, benefits, and working conditions before an election in order to defeat a union is also illegal interference.

But the laboratory conditions standard goes beyond unfair labor practices.[27] In other words, election conduct does not need to rise to the severity of a clear unfair labor practice in order to

---

[25] National Labor Relations Board, *Outline of Law and Procedure in Representation Cases* (Washington, DC: U.S. Government Printing Office, 2005). Ray, Sharpe, and Strassfield, *Understanding Labor Law.* Benjamin J. Taylor and Fred Witney, *Labor Relations Law,* 7th ed. (Englewood Cliffs, NJ: Prentice Hall, 1996).

[26] *General Shoe Corp.,* 77 NLRB 124, 127 (1948).

[27] Taylor and Witney, *Labor Relations Law.*

Labor Law Discussion: Does a Meeting with a Supervisor Interfere with Employee Free Choice?

Box 7.6

BACKGROUND

The International Association of Bridge, Structural, and Ornamental Iron Workers was conducting an organizing drive at a plant of the NVF Company. The election unit was determined to be all production and maintenance employees including truck drivers, shipping and receiving clerks, and all other plant clerical employees, employed by NVF Company at its Hartwell, Georgia, facility, but excluding all office clerical employees, professional employees, guards, and supervisors as defined in the NLRA. An election to determine union certification was scheduled for August 16.

During the months of July and August leading up to the election, Matt Rust, general manager of the Hartwell plant, called employees into his office in groups of five or six. The purpose of the meetings was to discuss the upcoming NLRB election. Rust's remarks were not coercive, but he did express NVF's reasons for wanting the employees to vote against union representation. He solicited the employees to vote against the union. Approximately 95 percent of the employees eligible to vote participated in this type of meeting with Rust.

The employees were familiar with the general manager's office from prior experiences. For example, employees previously visited that office to obtain loans or discuss grievances. There was no other suitable location to hold such meetings.

The results of the election held on August 16 were as follows:

International Association of Bridge, Structural and Ornamental Iron Workers . . . . 64 votes

No Union . . . . 95 votes

Shortly after the election of August 16, the union filed timely objections with the NLRB.

POTENTIALLY RELEVANT PRECEDENT

In *General Shoe Corp.* (1948), the company president brought into his office 25 groups of 20–25 employees on the day before a certification election. Each group was read the same intemperate antiunion address. The employer had also instructed foremen to propagandize employees in their homes. The NLRB invalidated the results of the election because one could not assume that the results "represented the employees' own true wishes." This decision was not, however, based on the finding of an unfair labor practice.

Questions

1. Should the election be ruled invalid? On what basis? If so, what is the appropriate remedy?
2. Do the size of the groups (five or six) and the percentage of voters involved (95%) matter?

violate laboratory standards and therefore trigger a new election. For example, employer or union campaign tactics that serve to inflame racial prejudices are not necessarily unfair labor practices, but they can create a distorted environment in which employee free choice is affected. Lies and other distortions or misrepresentations of facts are also not unfair labor practices but can undermine free choice. Even though the NLRB has largely abandoned the view that lies and misrepresentations by themselves distort laboratory conditions—its logic is that workers can see through such propaganda—in extreme cases where the "pervasiveness of misrepresentation or the artfulness of deception during an election campaign renders employees so unable to separate truth from untruth that their free and fair choice is affected," a new election will be held.[28] Lastly, the actions of a third party—that is, individuals not under the direction of the employer or the union, such as individual employees, the mayor or chief of police, or business and labor union leaders from other companies and unions—cannot be unfair labor practices, but nevertheless can negatively impact laboratory conditions (see Box 7.7).

---

[28] *Dayton Hudson Dept. Store v. NLRB,* 987 F.2d 359, 365 (6th Cir. 1993), on remand 314 NLRB No. 129 (1994), affd. 79 F.3d 546 (1996).

Labor Law Discussion: Does Community Activity Interfere with Laboratory Conditions?

Box 7.7

BACKGROUND

The International Hod Carriers' Building and Common Laborers' Union of America was conducting an organizing drive of production employees at the Monarch Rubber Company. An election to determine the preference of a majority of the workers for collective representation was scheduled for Friday, July 19.

On Thursday, July 18, the local newspaper, the *Times Record*, ran the following full-page advertisement:

The Times Record   Thursday July 18   A10
Proudly serving Roane County since 1932

Dear Monarch Rubber Employee,

On the eve of the union election, one should fully consider the advantages and disadvantages of having a Union.

The advantages and benefits to be obtained *without* a Union are clear: full employment, improved working conditions, increased earnings, and a larger future plant, to name but a few.

The disadvantages of voting *for* a Union are: intermittent unemployment, AND, by union domination—

a complete LOSS OF YOUR JOB!

WE URGE ALL MONARCH RUBBER EMPLOYEES TO VOTE TO KEEP THEIR JOBS!

VOTE <u>AGAINST</u> THE UNION.

Sponsored by: A Group of Business People

The results of the election held on Friday, July 19, were as follows:

International Hod Carriers' Building and Common Laborers' Union of America . . . . 54 votes

No Union . . . . 58 votes

There were 121 eligible voters. Seven ballots were challenged by the union. On July 24, the union filed timely objections with the National Labor Relations Board.

Upon investigation, it was found that on July 10, Samuel Quail, publisher of the *Times Record*, met with Kristin Day, vice president of Monarch Rubber. Quail showed Day the text of the newspaper ad. Day pointed out various items in the ad that did not pertain to the situation at Monarch Rubber. Furthermore, Quail informed Day of his intention to approach the Chamber of Commerce about sponsoring the ad. Day did not respond to this remark.

On July 15, Quail met with the treasurer of the Roane County Chamber of Commerce. In spite of Quail's exhortation, the organization would not sponsor, nor pay for, the newspaper advertisement. Consequently, Quail inserted the advertisement in Thursday's (July 18) edition of the *Times Record* free of charge and without a sponsor.

Upon seeing the advertisement in the paper, Day contacted Quail and disavowed any and all responsibility for the ad.

Questions

1. Should the election be ruled invalid? If so, what is the appropriate remedy?
2. Does Monarch Rubber have any responsibility for the ad? Does it matter?

EMPLOYER CAMPAIGNING

Employer campaign tactics try to influence the four key determinants of individual voting decisions—job dissatisfaction, union instrumentality, general union attitudes, and collective social identity (recall Box 7.5). At a minimum, these tactics usually include providing pro-company and antiunion information and opinions to the employees. This is generally legal. Some companies are more aggressive and supplement this information with the manipulation of wages, benefits, working conditions, and job assignments as well as with threats, promises, rumors, layoffs, and firings. Antiunion committees might be formed, supervisors might be reassigned, and parties might be thrown. Many of these more aggressive activities can distort laboratory conditions and are therefore essentially prohibited. These efforts might be led by full-time antiunion consultants.

Information and opinions are shared with employees in a variety of methods. Supervisors might meet with employees individually or in small groups. Letters or e-mail messages might be sent to workers (see Box 7.8). The letters in Box 7.8 are representative of common employer messages: the first letter tries to weaken workers' perceptions of union instrumentality and the second portrays unions more generally in negative terms. Strikes and paying dues are also frequent themes. Another important employer tactic for sharing information and opinions is the **captive audience meeting**—a group meeting held in the workplace during working hours in which employees are forced to listen to management's antiunion and pro-company presentations (captive audience speeches). Such meetings are legal as long as they are not within 24 hours of the election.[29] Captive audience meetings are hotly debated—employers justify them on the basis of property and free speech rights; unions criticize them as providing employers with an unfair advantage in communicating with, and perhaps pressuring, the employees.

BOX 7.8
Management Campaign Letters to Employees

Source: Adapted from actual letters from a company's website modified to preserve anonymity.

Dear Employee of ABC:

With the election expected to be soon, many employees continue to ask:

EXACTLY WHAT CAN THE UNION GUARANTEE ME IF THEY GET ELECTED?

Not Much. Here are the facts.

FACT: If the union wins the election, it wins only the right to bargain with ABC as your exclusive negotiating agent.

FACT: While the union and ABC both would be required by law to bargain "in good faith," the law would not require ABC to agree with the union on any union proposal or promise made to you during the campaign (your supervisor has proof).

FACT: If the union made demands to which ABC could not or would not agree, the union would ultimately have two choices:

1. DROP THEIR DEMAND, OR

2. STRIKE

FACT: Bargaining for a first contract is often a lengthy and complex process with uncertain results . . . and while bargaining goes on, your wages and benefits are **FROZEN** until changed, if at all, by a contract.

FACT: If and when a contract is finally agreed to, you may wind up with more, the same, or less than you now have.

I hope this is helpful. We've heard that the union organizers are promising employees "big" pay raises, "free" day care, etc. Sadly, as other employees have found out, there is often a **big** difference between what unions promise and what they actually deliver. It's just one more reason to vote "**NO**" union.

Sincerely,

W. Leiserson
Senior Vice President, Human Resources

---

[29] *Peerless Plywood Co.,* 107 NLRB 427 (1954).

BOX 7.8
(Continued)

Dear Employee:

"Member Decline Threatens U.S. Unions"

That's the headline of a recent news story about the current state of union membership. As you can see, union officials are worried; and they should be. Despite their recent efforts, union membership as a percentage of the total U.S. workforce continues to drop—from a high of 35% in 1955 to just 13.5% last year.

And just how do these union officials intend to solve this problem? At their recent convention in Las Vegas, they decided:

1. to spend more of their members' money on political campaigns, and

2. to raise the dues payments that union members now pay!

In fact, the same union that is chasing you here at ABC has already announced their plan **to increase members' dues each year for the next three years!** (See your supervisor for proof).

Ask yourself:

• **Do I want to pay money to help unions bail themselves out?**

• **Would I want my money spent on political campaigns?**

• **If unions have so much to offer employees, why aren't there more "takers"?**

If you have questions, please feel free to see your supervisor or any other member of management.

Sincerely,

W. Leiserson
Senior Vice President, Human Resources

All of these forms of communication are legal unless the employer is too aggressive and makes threats or promises. Sometimes, however, there is a fine line between predictions or opinions on the one hand, and threats on the other.[30] Suppose an employer tells employees that if a union increases labor costs too much then the plant will have to close. Is this an opinion, a prediction, or a threat? Or suppose an employer tells employees that similar facilities have closed after being organized by this same union. Is this a factual statement or an implied threat? It depends. Predictions based on objective facts that some events will likely occur because of forces beyond the employer's control (like competitive forces) are legal; statements that convey the impression that these events are inevitable or at the discretion of the employer are threats. A legal conversation between a supervisor and an employee also becomes illegal if it turns into an interrogation of the employee's views on unionization. A visit to an employee's home by a management official is grounds for invalidating an election—because the employer controls an employee's job, visiting him or her at home is viewed as intimidating and coercive.[31]

Related to the issue of communication, another employer campaign tactic is to use no solicitation rules. The employer can use its private property rights to prohibit outside

---

[30] National Labor Relations Board, *Outline of Law and Procedure in Representation Cases.* Taylor and Witney, *Labor Relations Law.*

[31] *Plant City Welding and Tank Co.,* 119 NLRB 131 (1957).

organizations from entering the workplace and interacting with workers. As long as these rules are equally enforced for all types of outside organizations, then union organizers can be denied access to employees in the workplace, except in extreme circumstances when unions have no other access to employees (such as in remote mining camps).[32] Union organizers can even be banned from parking lots in shopping malls.[33] Note carefully that this applies to outside union organizers, not the employer's employees.[34] Employees can discuss unionization in the workplace, but such conversations can be restricted to nonwork hours, and if it interferes with production or customers, to nonwork locations such as an employee cafeteria.[35] As such, some unions, especially in the construction industry, have tried a tactic called salting in which paid union organizers try to get hired as regular employees (and therefore "salt" or enrich the workplace) for the purpose of organizing the workers.[36] In a controversial ruling, the Supreme Court has ruled that salts are employees under the NLRA and therefore protected against discrimination in hiring and firing.[37]

Restrictions on both employees and nonemployee union organizers must be equally enforced. Consider an organization that allows its employees to sell Girl Scout cookies in working areas but restricts employee discussions of unions to nonwork areas, or allows Boy Scouts into the workplace to sell Christmas wreaths but prohibits union organizers from the premises. Isolated charitable acts will be overlooked.[38] But if employees are allowed to repeatedly sell Girl Scout cookies to other workers during work time, then such activities are likely not disruptive. To then restrict discussions of unionization by claiming that it is disruptive to work is disingenuous and amounts to discriminating against union activity.[39] For the same reason, discriminatory enforcement of no solicitation rules is illegal interference with employee rights to organize unions.[40]

The use of outside union-avoidance consultants and lawyers is also a prominent component of employers' campaigns.[41] Consultants can help managers take advantage of tactics such as captive audience meetings and train supervisors in union-avoidance methods. Unions, however, view union-avoidance consultants as another element of a deck stacked in favor of employers who can hold captive-audience meetings, ban union organizers from the workplace, and hire expensive consultants to lead sophisticated communications and public relations campaigns. Moreover, at least some union-avoidance consultants aggressively seek to break unions by resorting to almost any means necessary—a less publicly visible descendant of the aggressive strikebreaking agencies like the Pinkertons in the 19th century (Chapter 4). This is labor relations at its worse: lies, threats, promises, manipulation, harassment, espionage, abuse, and firings (see Box 7.9).[42] In one extreme case, a 17-year employee with no record of violence challenged his plant manager to let the

---

[32] *NLRB v. Babcock & Wilcox Co.,* 351 U.S. 105 (1956).

[33] *Lechmere, Inc. v. NLRB,* 112 U.S. 841 (1992). Cynthia L. Estlund, "Labor, Property, and Sovereignty after *Lechmere," Stanford Law Review* 46 (January 1994), pp. 305–59.

[34] Ray, Sharpe, and Strassfield, *Understanding Labor Law.*

[35] *Republic Aviation v. NLRB,* 324 U.S. 793 (1945).

[36] Cory R. Fine, "Union Salting: Reactions and Rulings since *Town and Country," Journal of Labor Research* 23 (Summer 2002), pp. 475–85. James L. Fox, " 'Salting' the Construction Industry," *William Mitchell Law Review* 24 (1998), pp. 681–712.

[37] *NLRB v. Town and Country Electric,* 516 U.S. 85 (1995).

[38] *Hammary Mfg. Corp.,* 265 NLRB 57 (1982).

[39] *New York Telephone Company,* 304 NLRB No. 33 (1991).

[40] *NLRB v. Stowe Spinning Co.,* 336 U.S. 226 (1949). *Price Chopper,* 325 NLRB 186 (1997).

[41] John J. Lawler, *Unionization and Deunionization: Strategy, Tactics, and Outcomes* (Columbia: University of South Carolina Press, 1990).

[42] Martin Jay Levitt and Terry Conrow, *Confessions of a Union Buster* (New York: Crown Publishers, 1993).

Marty Levitt spent more than 20 years as a union-avoidance consultant aggressively directing campaigns to prevent unions from winning representation elections. And then he had a change of heart and publicly revealed his past activities offering a glimpse into some portion of the big business of labor relations consulting. Here are some of his revelations:

"There are many forms of union busting. Some labor consultants and attorneys take on unions that already represent a work force, squeezing negotiators at the bargaining table, forcing workers out on strike, harassing union officers. My career took another path. I refined the specialty . . . called "counterorganizing drives," battling nonunion employees as they struggled to win union representation. The enemy was the collective spirit. I got hold of that spirit while it was still a seedling; I poisoned it, choked it, bludgeoned it if I had to, anything to be sure that it would never blossom into a united work force, the dreaded foe of any corporate tyrant.

"For my campaigns I identified two key targets: the rank-and-file workers and their immediate supervisors. The supervisors served as my front line. I took them hostage on the first day and sent them to antiunion boot camp. I knew that people who didn't feel threatened wouldn't fight. So through hours of seminars, rallies, and one-on-one encounters, I taught the supervisors to despise and fear the union. I persuaded them that a union-organizing drive was a personal attack on them, a referendum on their leadership skills, and an attempt to humiliate them. I was friendly, even jovial at times, but always unforgiving as I compelled each supervisor to feel he was somehow to blame for the union push and consequently obliged to defeat it.

. . .

"Although I took on the supervisors face to face, my war on union activists was covert. To stop a union proponent—a "pusher," in the antiunion lexicon—the buster will go anywhere, not just to the lunch room, but into the bedroom if necessary. The buster is not only a terrorist; he is also a spy. My team and I routinely pried into workers' police records, personnel files, credit histories, medical records, and family lives in search of a weakness that we could use to discredit union activists.

"Once in a while, a worker is impeccable. So some consultants resort to lies. To fell the sturdiest union supporters in the 1970s, I frequently launched rumors that the targeted worker was gay or was cheating on his wife. . . . If even the nasty stories failed to muzzle an effective union proponent, the busters might get the worker fired.

. . .

"Not only were working people crushed by the cruelty of the union busters, but the companies themselves were raped, as consultants and attorneys conspired to wring as much as they could out of their clients. The executives paid whatever they were asked, the consultants having convinced them that a union-organizing effort amounted to the worst crisis of their business lives. In the end I understood that a union-busting campaign left a company financially devastated and hopelessly divided and almost invariably created an even more intolerable work environment than before. . . ."

Questions

1. Show how the type of union busting described here is unethical in all six ethical theories presented in Chapter 3.
2. Given that this type of union busting is unethical in all six perspectives, why do some managers hire such consultants? Why do some people become union-busting consultants? Is it simply because some people are unethical, or are there more complex reasons?

Reprinted with permission of International Creative Management, Inc. Copyright © 1993 by Martin Jay Levitt and Terry Conrow.

employees talk with a union organizer. The following day the employer notified the local sheriff that this employee was threatening workers so the sheriff's deputies surrounded him at gunpoint on his way to work and forcibly took him to the local hospital. Based on what the employer told the sheriff, the employee was involuntarily committed to a mental hospital. He was held for two weeks against his will and forcibly injected with anti-psychotic drugs until a lawyer could obtain his release. This happened in 1999 in South Carolina.[43]

[43] *http://abcnews.go.com/onair/2020/2020_000128_unions_feature.html* (accessed August 14, 2003).

With the help of attorneys and consultants, another employer tactic is delay.[44] By challenging the proposed bargaining unit definition in the election petition, the employer can slow down the election timeline and delay the election date for a couple of months, or more. The 1975 unit determination case for Harvard University clerical and technical workers (recall Box 7.4) was stretched out by the university's lawyers to include more than 20 days of hearings, and in a similar case at Yale University, the university's lawyers submitted a witness list of over 300 individuals.[45] Why is delay a significant tactic in the employer's favor? The employer gains more time to campaign against the union, employee turnover may result in the loss of union supporters, perceptions of union instrumentality might be weakened as the union appears helpless to counter the employer's legal maneuverings, and critical union momentum is lost.

Employer campaigning during NLRB representation elections is a controversial topic in U.S. labor relations. Some argue that union representation is a question solely for workers so that employers should not be granted rights as formal participants in the process—free speech should be allowed, but not the right to object to the definition of the unit, to use special campaign tactics like captive audience speeches, and to challenge the results (see Box 7.10).[46] The usual counterarguments are that the employers' property rights grant them the right to participate in the process, that unions are too powerful without a fair counterweight of employer campaigning, and that employers need to speak for the antiunion employees and deliver their message.

More pragmatically, there is also significant debate over the practical questions of the prevalence and significance of employer campaigning. Some campaign tactics are hard to observe or measure (such as informal supervisor conversations with employees) and most are undertaken quietly (especially the illegal ones). Using NLRB data on illegal discharge unfair labor practices, one study estimates that one of every 20 pro-union voters in NLRB elections are discriminatorily discharged.[47] Another study critiques this estimate as overstating the number of firings in representation elections, but nonetheless agrees that such firings are a significant problem.[48] In either case, employees perceive the chances of retribution for organizing activity to be high: in one survey, 41 percent of nonunion respondents agreed that "it is likely I will lose my job if I tried to form a union," and 79 percent of all respondents said it is "very" or "somewhat" likely that "nonunion workers will get fired if they try to organize a union."[49] More generally, research seems to reveal a pattern of broad-based employer campaigning during NLRB representation elections.[50] This research

[44] Lawler, *Unionization and Deunionization*. Levitt and Conrow, *Confessions of a Union Buster.* Paul Weiler, "Promises to Keep: Securing Workers' Rights to Self-Organization Under the NLRA," *Harvard Law Review* 96 (June 1983), pp. 1769–827.

[45] Toni Gilpin, Gary Isaac, Dan Letwin, and Jack McKivigan, *On Strike for Respect: The Clerical and Technical Workers' Strike at Yale University, 1984–85* (Urbana: University of Illinois Press, 1995). Hoerr, *We Can't Eat Prestige.*

[46] Paul C. Weiler, "A Principled Reshaping of Labor Law for the Twenty-First Century," *University of Pennsylvania Journal of Labor and Employment Law* 3 (Winter 2001), pp. 177–206. Weiler, "Promises to Keep."

[47] Weiler, "Promises to Keep."

[48] Robert J. LaLonde and Bernard D. Meltzer, "Hard Times for Unions: Another Look at the Significance of Employer Illegalities," *University of Chicago Law Review* 58 (Summer 1991), pp. 953–1014.

[49] Richard B. Freeman, and Joel Rogers, "Who Speaks for Us? Employee Representation in a Nonunion Labor Market," in Bruce E. Kaufman and Morris M. Kleiner (eds.), *Employee Representation: Alternatives and Future Directions* (Madison, WI: Industrial Relations Research Association, 1993), Chapter 1 at p. 31.

[50] Kate Bronfenbrenner, "The Role of Union Strategies in NLRB Certification Elections," *Industrial and Labor Relations Review* 50 (January 1997), pp. 195–212. Kate Bronfenbrenner and Tom Juravich, "It Takes More than House Calls: Organizing to Win with a Comprehensive Union Building Strategy," in Kate Bronfenbrenner et al. (eds.), *Organizing to Win: New Research on Union Strategies* (Ithaca, NY: ILR Press, 1998), pp. 19–36. Richard B. Freeman and Morris M. Kleiner, "Employer Behavior in the Face of Union Organizing Drives," *Industrial and Labor Relations Review* 43 (April 1990), pp. 351–65. Lawler, *Unionization and Deunionization.*

The Case Against Employer Campaigning   Box 7.10

"The major counter-argument [to proposals to limit employer campaigning] made by employers—especially the majority who do not engage in this most egregious breaking of labor law tradition—is that they are denied what should be their equal right to campaign for the allegiance of employee voters. This is said to be the equivalent of a political election that allows the Democratic party, but not the Republicans, to campaign effectively for voter support in political elections.

"The fallacy in that analogy and argument is that it mistakenly assumes that an affirmative vote for the union . . . means that the union is now *governing* employers (or even employees). All that a successful employee verdict does is give the union the mandate to *represent* employees in negotiations with the employer under labor law. Under employment law, we would never dream of suggesting that the employer should have an affirmative right and opportunity to campaign against the employee's decision about whether to hire a law firm (and if so, which one) when challenging employer policies regarding occupational safety or sexual harassment, for example.

. . .

"The more apt political analog of the role of the employer in a representation election is the role of a foreign government in an American election. Canada, for example, has a significant interest in which party is elected to govern the United States; selection of one party rather than the other may make life considerably easier or more difficult for the Canadian government in negotiations over defense, trade, natural resources, energy, foreign investment, and so on. Yet no one would argue that Canadian government agencies should therefore have a right to participate in an American election campaign in order to try to persuade United States citizens to vote for a party that would be favorable to Canadian interests. After all, it is the job of the United States government to advance the interests of its own citizens when those interests conflict with the interests of Canadians; Canadians have their own government to defend their interests irrespective of the electoral verdict in the United States.

. . .

"The law should not restrain the employer's freedom to say what it will about collective bargaining—censorship in the representation campaign has the same offensive flavor that it has in politics or in the arts—but there is no principle of fairness that requires that the representation process be structured to facilitate employer opposition to unionization."

Source: Paul C. Weiler, "A Principled Reshaping of Labor Law for the Twenty-First Century," *University of Pennsylvania Journal of Labor and Employment Law* 3 (Winter 2001), pp. 177–206 at 190 (emphases in original). Paul Weiler, "Promises to Keep: Securing Workers' Rights to Self-Organization Under the NLRA," *Harvard Law Review* 96 (June 1983), pp. 1769–827 at 1814–15.

often relies on the reports of union organizers so it might overstate (if organizers or their inside sources intentionally or unintentionally inflate the amount of employer resistance) or understate (if organizers do not observe all of the campaigning) the true level of employer campaigning. With this in mind, Box 7.11 presents some typical statistics. Note that a large fraction of employers reportedly use outside consultants, one-on-one meetings between workers and supervisors, and multiple captive audience meetings.

But do these tactics matter? This is the most debated question of all. Relative to their peers in other industrialized countries, American managers appear to be exceptionally hostile toward unions and have significantly stronger traditions of using union avoidance tactics.[51] Various studies find that employer antiunion campaign tactics reduce the likelihood that employees vote for unions in NLRB representation elections and that unions are less

[51] Sanford M. Jacoby, "American Exceptionalism Revisited: The Importance of Management," in Sanford M. Jacoby (ed.), *Masters to Managers: Historical and Comparative Perspectives on American Employers* (New York: Columbia University Press, 1991), Chapter 8. Daphne Gottlieb Taras, "Collective Bargaining Regulation in Canada and the United States: Divergent Cultures, Divergent Outcomes," in Bruce E. Kaufman (ed.), *Government Regulation of the Employment Relationship* (Madison, WI: Industrial Relations Research Association, 1997), Chapter 8.

BOX 7.11
**The Frequency of
Employer Campaign
Tactics**

Used Outside Consultant	87%
One-on-One Meetings with Supervisors	76%
Five or More Captive Audience Meetings	64%
Used Antiunion Committee	50%
Changed Benefits	29%
Discharged Workers Not Reinstated	26%
Gave Wage Increase	24%
Five or More Company Letters Mailed to Workers	24%

Source: Kate Bronfenbrenner and Tom Juravich, "It Takes More than House Calls: Organizing to Win with a Comprehensive Union Building Strategy," in Kate Bronfenbrenner et al. (eds.), *Organizing to Win: New Research on Union Strategies* (Ithaca, NY: ILR Press, 1998), pp. 19–36.

likely to win these elections.[52] In contrast, a famous study in the 1970s found that most workers already had their minds made up before employer campaigning began and therefore that employer tactics do not matter.[53] On the other hand, a reanalysis of this study's data revealed that since many elections are decided by thin margins, captive audience meetings as well as illegal threats and actions towards union supporters can affect enough votes to shift the outcome of the election.[54] And so the debate continues.

In sum, by many accounts employers devote a lot of time and money to campaigning against unions in NLRB representation elections. Some campaign tactics are legal—though still criticized by labor supporters; other tactics are illegal and union busting can be "a very dirty business."[55] Given the resources spent on campaigning, managers must perceive them as effective in reducing the likelihood that a union organizing drive will be successful. Moreover, the evidence points towards the presence of significant incentives to avoid unions at all costs. One-third of nonunion managers believe that their career will be harmed if their employees unionize.[56] And they are probably right: in one study, managers in establishments without any union organizing activity had a 21 percent chance of being promoted and a 2 percent chance of being fired; in similar establishments that experienced an organizing drive, not a single manager was promoted and 15 percent were fired.[57]

UNION CAMPAIGNING

Like employers, unions can campaign to influence the four key determinants of individual voting decisions in NLRB representation elections (recall Box 7.5). An example of a union campaign flyer is shown in Box 7.12—note the emphasis on the implicit messages regarding job dissatisfaction (all other employees have a *full* subsidy for dependent health care) and union instrumentality (if we unionize, we can also win a full subsidy). But beyond some of these basic similarities between employer and union campaigning, there are

[52]Bronfenbrenner, "The Role of Union Strategies in NLRB Certification Elections." Bronfenbrenner and Juravich, "It Takes More than House Calls." Freeman and Kleiner, "Employer Behavior in the Face of Union Organizing Drives." Lawler, *Unionization and Deunionization.*

[53] Getman, Goldberg, and Herman, *Union Representation Elections.*

[54] William T. Dickens, "The Effect of Company Campaigns on Certification Elections: *Law and Reality* Once Again," *Industrial and Labor Relations Review* 36 (July 1983), pp. 560–75.

[55]Levitt and Conrow, *Confessions of a Union Buster,* p. xi.

[56] Freeman and Rogers, *What Workers Want.*

[57] Freeman and Kleiner, "Employer Behavior in the Face of Union Organizing Drives."

BOX 7.12
A Union Campaign Flyer

www.yaleunions.org/geso

Got fully subsidized dependent health care?

Spring
Membership
Meeting:
Wed. April 26
5:30 pm
SSS-114

In 1998, due in great part to GESO organizing, Yale agreed to subsidize half of the cost of dependent health care. Like the rest of the employees on campus working over 20 hours per week, graduate students should be provided with a *full* subsidy, along with affordable child care and reasonable parental leave.

>>Contact an organizer. Show your support for these benefits so graduate students with families can worry about completing their degrees, not what will happen if their spouses or children become sick or injured.

The Graduate Employees & Students Organization

Organizing toward a written and binding contract.

For more information:
www.geso.org   or   203/624-5161

significant differences. Labor law tries to balance the rights of employers and unions during the organizing process, but because of employers' power over their property and employees, the tactics available to each side differ. From a behavioral and strategic rather than legal perspective, U.S. unions have not traditionally devoted extensive resources towards campaign tactics (though some unions are trying to change this practice).[58] Yet in many ways, unions need to make more important decisions than employers. In fact, the organizing process is perhaps the primary area of labor relations in which unions are the proactive rather than reactive party. Unions, not employers, need to figure out what type of representation philosophy fits best with various types of workers—factory workers, office employees, professionals, women, recent immigrants, and the like—and what type of campaign tactics support these philosophies.

From a legal standpoint, the laboratory conditions doctrine applies to union as well as employer actions. If union threats or harassment distort employee free choice, the election results can be invalidated and a new election held. NLRB rulings, however, have traditionally been less likely to conclude that union promises undermine laboratory conditions.[59] Rather, the NLRB typically holds the perspective that

---

[58] Paula B. Voos, "Union Organizing: Costs and Benefits," *Industrial and Labor Relations Review* 36 (July 1983), pp. 576–91. Richard W. Hurd, "Contesting the Dinosaur Image: The Labor Movement's Search for a Future," *Labor Studies Journal* 22 (Winter 1998), pp. 5–30.

[59] Taylor and Witney, *Labor Relations Law.*

Employees are generally able to understand that a union cannot obtain benefits automatically by winning an election but must seek to achieve them through collective bargaining. Union promises . . . are easily recognized by employees to be dependent on contingencies beyond the union's control and do not carry with them the same degree of finality as if uttered by an employer who has it within his power to implement promises of benefits.[60]

In fact, unions have little to offer employees except promises that they will try to win gains for the employees.[61] One of the vexing problems for unions, however, is how to get this message to the employees.

Recall from the previous section that employers can force employees to attend captive audience meetings and listen to captive audience speeches. At the same time, property rights can be used to enforce no-solicitation rules banning union organizers from the workplace and the surrounding private property such as parking lots. So how can union organizers contact employees? In lieu of workplace access, once a representation election is scheduled, a longstanding NLRB rule requires employers to provide the union with a list of names and addresses of the employees eligible to vote in the election. This is called an **Excelsior list** (named after the 1966 *Excelsior Underwear* decision) and must be provided within seven days.[62] Unions can then mail information to employees or visit them at home.[63] Unlike employers, unions are allowed home visits:

There is a substantial difference between the employment of the technique of individual interviews by employers on the one hand and by unions on the other. Unlike employers, unions often do not have the opportunity to address employees in assembled or informal groups, and never have the position of control over tenure of employment and working conditions which imparts the coercive effect to systematic individual interviews conducted by employers. Thus, not only do unions have more need to seek out individual employees to present their views, but, more important, lack the relationship with the employees to interfere with their choice of representatives thereby.[64]

Some employees might view home visits as invasions of privacy, but with no workplace access, unions are left with little choice. Some unions are also using websites to provide campaign information, but have to figure out how to direct employees to their sites.

Union campaigning has traditionally focused on the distribution of flyers and letters through mailings and handbilling (the classic picture of a union organizer standing outside the factory gate handing out flyers).[65] In both cases, individual workers are the passive recipients of information; there is no personal contact and they are not actively involved in building their union. Unions are increasingly supplementing these traditional tactics with new methods for developing personal relationships with workers—such as house calls and small group meetings—and for getting workers actively involved in the campaign—such as rallies and using workers as volunteer organizers (see Box 7.13). In fact, research has shown that these tactics are often more important than employer campaigning in influencing the outcome of NLRB representation elections, especially when used as a comprehensive union-building strategy.[66] Until these new campaign tactics become more widespread,

[60] *Smith Co.,* 192 NLRB 1098, 1101 (1971).

[61] Ray, Sharpe, and Strassfield, *Understanding Labor Law.*

[62] *Excelsior Underwear,* 156 NLRB 1236 (1966).

[63] Leonard Bierman, "Toward a New Model for Union Organizing: The Home Visits Doctrine and Beyond," *Boston College Law Review* 27 (December 1985), pp. 1–35.

[64] *Plant City Welding and Tank Co.,* 119 NLRB 131, 133–34 (1957).

[65] Richard B. Peterson, Thomas W. Lee, and Barbara Finnegan, "Strategies and Tactics in Union Organizing Campaigns," *Industrial Relations* 31 (Spring 1992), pp. 370–81.

[66] Bronfenbrenner, "The Role of Union Strategies in NLRB Certification Elections." Bronfenbrenner and Juravich, "It Takes More than House Calls."

The Frequency of Union Campaign Tactics   Box 7.13

The traditional union campaign tactics are mailings and handbilling. Tactics to create more personal contact with individual employees and to get them actively involved are starting to be used:

Made House Calls	58%
Used Solidarity Days (Supporters Wear Buttons, etc.)	56%
Held Union Rallies	41%
Made House Calls to at Least Half of the Unit	39%
Held 10 or More Small Group Meetings	39%
Used Coalitions with Community Groups	30%
Surveyed at Least 70% One-on-One	21%
Used 10 or More Rank-and-File Volunteers	17%

Source: Kate Bronfenbrenner and Tom Juravich, "It Takes More than House Calls: Organizing to Win with a Comprehensive Union Building Strategy," in Kate Bronfenbrenner et al. (eds.), *Organizing to Win: New Research on Union Strategies* (Ithaca, NY: ILR Press, 1998), pp. 19–36.

however, the conventional wisdom will likely continue to be true: more often than not, employer campaigning is more comprehensive, sophisticated, and aggressive (and expensive) compared to union campaigning.

Union organizing tactics are closely related to the type of message unions want to deliver. Passive campaign tactics like mailings and handbilling are consistent with the servicing model of union representation. Recall from the previous chapter that in this model, workers consume union services, especially collectively bargained contracts and representation in the grievance procedure. Problems are solved *for* the workers, not *by* the workers. And who is the source of these problems? Management. The employer is therefore portrayed in campaign literature as the enemy. The union is a source of protection, and unionism becomes "us versus them" adversarialism (see Box 7.14).

In contrast, the organizing model views unions as vehicles for worker participation and empowerment.[67] Problems are not solved *for* workers, workers are directly involved in solving their own problems. Workers do not consume equity and voice, they participate in their attainment. Traditional passive union campaign tactics cannot be used to organize a new union based on active rank-and-file participation. A different type of unionism requires a different type of campaigning. To be successful, these campaigns use the types of tactics listed in Box 7.13—extensive one-on-one personal contact, active rank and file volunteers, and rallies to build collective identity. Much of the focus of labor advocates today is on developing these active campaign tactics to increase organizing success and build stronger labor unions.[68]

These tactics that emphasize grassroots involvement rather than reliance on outside, full-time, paid union organizers reflect Saul Alinsky's "Iron Rule of Organizing:" "Never

[67] Andy Banks and Jack Metzgar, "Participating in Management: Union Organizing on a New Terrain," *Labor Research Review* 14 (Fall 1989), pp. 1–55. Bill Fletcher, Jr., and Richard W. Hurd, "Beyond the Organizing Model: The Transformation Process in Local Unions," in Kate Bronfenbrenner et al. (eds.), *Organizing to Win: New Research on Union Strategies* (Ithaca, NY: ILR Press, 1998), pp. 37–53.

[68] Kate Bronfenbrenner et al. (eds.), *Organizing to Win: New Research on Union Strategies*. Bruce Nissen (ed.), *Which Direction for Organized Labor? Essays on Organizing, Outreach, and Internal Transformations* (Detroit: Wayne State University Press, 1999). Ray M. Tillman and Michael S. Cummings (eds.), *The Transformation of U.S. Unions: Voices, Visions, and Strategies from the Grassroots* (Boulder, CO: Lynne Rienner Publishers, 1999). Lowell Turner, Harry C. Katz, and Richard W. Hurd (eds.), *Rekindling the Movement: Labor's Quest for Relevance in the Twenty-First Century* (Ithaca, NY: ILR Press, 2001).

BOX 7.14
A Union Campaign Flyer

www.teamstersjc3.org

Sometimes Things Are Not What They Seem!

Beware of Management's Tricks.

Management often tries to convince you that they are on your side. They say your interests are the same and that we are all just one big, happy family.

Management uses mandatory meetings on company time to trick you into believing that it's in your best interest to believe that a union is not needed here.

They tell you that management will take care of you. The truth is that they are in business to make money. If making money means paying you less and providing fewer benefits that is what they will do.

The company makes money because of your hard work. You need a union to protect your rights.

The only guarantee of keeping good wages and increasing your benefits is a union contract—not management's promises. Don't get the wool pulled over your eyes.

Let's Get It In Writing — A Union Contract!
Vote Teamsters — For a Better Future

*Local name, phone and any contact info

This handbill is not intended nor does it ask any employee to cease work or cease deliveries.

do for others what they can do for themselves."[69] In such a campaign, existing workers take the lead in talking with their co-workers about the possibility of unionizing. To put this in perspective, consider how differently you might react if you were approached by a full-time union organizer that you had never met or by a co-worker that you've known and respected for several years. Note also that existing employees have greater access to their co-workers than do outside union organizers because of the no-solicitation rules discussed earlier in this chapter. Beyond the benefits that flow from volunteer rank and file organizers being able to better connect with their co-workers, the extensive use of such volunteers can build a much stronger local union organization. Following the iron rule of organizing creates new leaders by increasing personal responsibility, confidence, communication skills, and self-respect, creates a sense of vibrancy and life through participation, and roots the local union more strongly into the local community.[70]

Many advocates believe that such tactics are necessary when employers seem to have the upper hand. As such, these new tactics can be aggressive and militant. A combination of very public rank and file activism and alliances with community groups has been effective in overcoming the language barriers and fears of immigrant workers by tapping into their strong social networks and by creating campaigns that are more responsive to the particular concerns of these workers.[71] Perhaps the most heralded successes in this regard are the Justice for Janitors campaigns to organize commercial-sector janitors in several major cities (see Box 7.15).

[69] Saul D. Alinsky, *Rules for Radicals: A Practical Primer for Realistic Radicals* (New York: Random House, 1971). Gagala, *Union Organizing and Staying Organized*.

[70] Bruce Nissen and Seth Rosen, "Community-Based Organizing: Transforming Union Organizing Programs from the Bottom Up," in Bruce Nissen (ed.), *Which Direction for Organized Labor? Essays on Organizing, Outreach, and Internal Transformations* (Detroit: Wayne State University Press, 1999), Chapter 3.

[71] Ruth Milkman (ed.), *Organizing Immigrants: The Challenge for Unions in Contemporary California* (Ithaca, NY: ILR Press, 2000). Ness, *Immigrants, Unions, and the New U.S. Labor Market*.

Organizing Immigrant Workers: The Justice for Janitors Campaigns

Organizing immigrant workers is a major challenge for the U.S. labor movement in the 21st century. In many major cities, a majority of the jobs that have traditionally been keys to union strength—manual jobs with little educational requirements—are held by recent immigrants. In fact, first and second generation immigrants were an important part of the development of the labor movement in the early 20th century, especially the rise of the CIO industrial unions. Particular issues for organizing immigrant workers include language barriers, high turnover, employer power, employers' attempts to manipulate ethnic conflict, and, among undocumented immigrants, the fear of deportation (note however that the NLRA does not exclude undocumented workers from its protections). It is not accurate, however, to assume that immigrant workers are not receptive to unionism; in fact, many have had positive experiences with unions or other efforts at challenging institutionalized authority in their home countries.

One of the most celebrated success stories of organizing immigrant workers is the Justice for Janitors campaigns created by the Service Employees International Union (SEIU) in the 1980s to organize janitors at large commercial properties in major cities such as Los Angeles and Washington, D.C. Organizing commercial janitors involves a number of special challenges, even beyond the fact that many are immigrant workers. In particular, building owners contract with cleaning services to provide janitorial services rather than directly hiring their own janitors. Consequently, it is very easy for building owners to switch contractors if one becomes unionized, and it is difficult to put pressure on the primary employer because it is not the building owner (even though the building owner essentially controls employment by choosing the contractor). Picketing a building, for example, is therefore an illegal secondary boycott. Furthermore, since cleaning services contractors have janitors at numerous properties around a city, organizing cannot focus on a single building—the appropriate bargaining unit as defined by the NLRB is all of the janitors working for a single contractor at all of its properties.

For all of these reasons, traditional union campaign tactics are not successful in organizing commercial janitors. In the mid-1980s, the SEIU launched a more militant strategy. Since the building owners hold the true

power but are shielded from NLRB elections because janitorial services are contracted out, the SEIU focuses on bringing public pressure to the owners and forcing them to support unionization without an election. To a large degree, this strategy depends critically on extensive rank and file involvement in organizing. To generate sufficient publicity and galvanize community support, the Justice for Janitors campaigns rely on extensive, if not daily, public demonstrations which would not be possible without high levels of worker involvement. To end these "in your face" tactics, building owners pressure the contractors to recognize the SEIU and negotiate union contracts. In Los Angeles, the number of unionized janitors went from less than 2,000 to over 20,000 as a result of a Justice for Janitors campaign.

The Justice for Janitors campaigns have been successful in winning contracts without NLRB elections by mobilizing the janitors to help themselves. By creating high levels of participation, these campaigns are able to harness the strong social networks within the immigrant communities and to develop strong alliances with other community groups such as churches and immigrant rights groups. Lastly, extensive rank and file participation forces unions to be more responsive to the particular interests and concerns of various groups of workers. These techniques are therefore being championed by the labor movement as not just good for organizing immigrant workers, but for organizing all workers.

Sources: Catherine L. Fisk, Daniel J. B. Mitchell, and Christopher L. Erickson, "Union Representation of Immigrant Janitors in Southern California," in Ruth Milkman (ed.), *Organizing Immigrants: The Challenge for Unions in Contemporary California* (Ithaca, NY: ILR Press, 2000), Chapter 8. Rachel Sherman and Kim Voss, " 'Organize or Die': Labor's New Tactics and Immigrant Workers," in Milkman (ed.), *Organizing Immigrants: The Challenge for Unions in Contemporary California*, Chapter 3. Roger Waldinger et al., "Helots No More: A Case Study of the Justice for Janitors Campaign in Los Angeles," in Kate Bronfenbrenner et al. (eds.), *Organizing to Win: New Research on Union Strategies* (Ithaca, NY: ILR Press, 1998), Chapter 6. Miriam J. Wells, "Immigration and Unionization in the San Francisco Hotel Industry," in Milkman (ed.), *Organizing Immigrants: The Challenge for Unions in Contemporary California*, Chapter 4. Jane Williams, "Restructuring Labor's Identity: The Justice for Janitors Campaign in Washington, D.C.," in Ray M. Tillman and Michael S. Cummings (eds.), *The Transformation of U.S. Unions: Voices, Visions, and Strategies from the Grassroots* (Boulder, CO: Lynne Rienner Publishers, 1999), Chapter 11.

But these tactics that emphasize rank and file involvement do not have to be aggressively militant. Clerical and technical workers at Harvard University were successfully organized by a grassroots campaign that focused on developing personal relationships.[72] This campaign explicitly rejected the traditional passive campaign tactics and the traditional "us versus them" adversarial mind-set (see Box 7.16). A prominent campaign theme was "It's not anti-Harvard to be pro-union." The workers were seeking empowerment, not protection. This philosophy is perhaps a good approach for organizing female workers, and it's no coincidence that the clerical and technical workers at Harvard and the lead organizers were overwhelmingly female.[73] In fact, this organizing style is rooted in the ethics of care (Chapter 3) which is rooted in feminist thought. This emphasis on empowerment, involvement, and by extension, independent judgment, can also be a good model for professional employees who are looking for additional workplace voice but do not view their employer as the enemy. Professional workers typically do not want outside third parties to "service" them and to create an adversarial, inflexible workplace.[74] In organizing campaigns, professionals therefore "respond best to a democratic structure that allows them to take control of their own organization and use it to gain influence and respect and to enhance their professionalism."[75] Again, unions are the proactive party in the organizing process and need to determine the best type of representation for different workplaces, and then develop comprehensive organizing campaigns to support them.

THE CERTIFICATION ELECTION PROCESS: HELP OR HINDRANCE?

The union certification process established by the NLRA in 1935 was initially a great victory for workers wanting union representation. The firing of union supporters was made illegal, and rather than having to strike for recognition, workers could petition the NLRB for a democratic determination of whether a majority of workers favored unionizing. In the first few years after 1935, the NLRB used a variety of methods to determine majority status: authorization cards, petitions, union membership applications, employee affidavits of membership, strike participation, and employee testimony.[76] The Taft-Hartley Act amendments in 1947, however, explicitly stated that if "a question of representation exists, [the NLRB] shall direct an election by secret ballot" [section 9(c)]. Later, the Supreme Court ruled that an employer can request a secret ballot election, even if majority status as indicated by signed authorization cards is not in doubt.[77] Early NLRB decisions also excluded employers from participating in the certification process, but the Supreme Court and section 8(c) of the Taft-Hartley Act explicitly authorize (noncoercive) employer participation in the process.[78]

The certification process has therefore changed from a quick procedure with minimal employer involvement to a formal and often lengthy election procedure with extensive employer participation, including not only campaigning but also legal challenges to proposed bargaining

[72] Hoerr, *We Can't Eat Prestige.*

[73] Marion Crain, "Gender and Union Organizing," *Industrial and Labor Relations Review* 47 (January 1994), pp. 227–48. Kris Rondeau and Gladys McKenzie, "Women's Ways of Organizing," *Labor Research Review* (1991), pp. 45–59.

[74] Cohen and Hurd, "Fear, Conflict, and Union Organizing." Victor G. Devinatz, "The Fears of Resource Standardization and the Creation of an Adversarial Workplace Climate: The Struggle to Organize a Faculty Union at Illinois State University," in David Lewin and Bruce Kaufman (eds.), *Advances in Industrial and Labor Relations, Volume 11* (Amsterdam: Elsevier, 2002), pp. 145–79.

[75] Cohen and Hurd, "Fear, Conflict, and Union Organizing," p. 195.

[76] Craig Becker, "Democracy in the Workplace: Union Representation Elections and Federal Labor Law," *Minnesota Law Review* 77 (February 1993), pp. 495–603.

[77] *Linden Lumber Division, Summer & Co. v. NLRB,* 419 U.S. 301 (1974).

[78] *NLRB v. Virginia Electric and Power Company,* 314 U.S. 469 (1941).

During the women's movement in the early 1970s, a handful of women employed in Harvard University's medical area started a group to bring attention to discriminatory treatment against female workers. Out of this grew a full-fledged push to unionize clerical and technical workers. A petition for an NLRB representation election for the medical area was first filed in 1975 and after the NLRB finally upheld this unit definition in 1977, workers voted against union representation 436 to 346. Another unsuccessful election was held in 1981. In this case, Harvard posted armed guards outside the polling place and the union lost 390 to 328. When a third petition was filed in 1983, the NLRB expanded the unit to include all clerical and technical employees throughout Harvard.

By the time the NLRB issued its unit determination ruling in 1984, the United Auto Workers (UAW) was leading the organizing drive. The UAW has a strong history of organizing industrial workers using traditional campaign tactics, especially passive handbilling that emphasizes the need for strong union protection against harsh working conditions and employers concerned more with profits than people. But the clerical and technical workers were predominantly women and were fighting against the paternalism of Harvard. They had no interest in replacing this with the paternalism of the UAW. And the Harvard employees were not anti-Harvard—they wanted more respect in a nonadversarial workplace. The local grassroots organizers (former Harvard employees) therefore emphasized trying to build one-on-one relationships rather than just getting signatures on authorization cards.

In 1985, the grassroots organizers split from the UAW and formed an independent organization: the Harvard Union of Clerical and Technical Workers (HUCTW). In 1986 the HUCTW gave up on letters, flyers, and other paper forms of communication—largely because they couldn't afford it, but also because they wanted to create an active campaign. "No longer could a prounion worker become an activist merely by handing out pieces of paper. Now she or he had to talk to people." The slogan "It's not anti-Harvard to be pro-union" became a central theme of the campaign. The union also emphasized broad issues such as voice and self-representation rather than specific issues like better wages:

We believe in self-representation. We are building our union for this reason, and *not* out of anger or negativity. Responsible, self-respecting adults should represent themselves in important matters affecting their lives. We have until now allowed Harvard to decide everything to do with our work lives. Now we are ready to participate as equals in making those decisions.

And the central campaign tactic became one-on-one organizing: "the objective of one-on-one organizing was to establish a personal relationship with each worker and to introduce him or her to other workers through union activities, so that in the end a very large number of workers were 'connected' to one another in a complex web of relationships." Feminist thought emphasizing the importance of relationships rather than outright power was thus incorporated into the labor movement.

To get an election, the HUCTW eventually turned to getting signed authorization cards and filed an election petition in 1988 supported by cards from 60 percent of the workers. Harvard actively campaigned against the union for the two months leading up to the election including the use of captive audience meetings. While remaining largely autonomous, the HUCTW was now affiliated with the American Federation of State, County, and Municipal Workers (AFSCME) and Harvard tried to paint a picture of a large, strike-prone, dues-hungry union that would bring conflict and rigidity into the workplace. But with the strong one-on-one relationships that had been developed, many workers were inoculated against this standard antiunion rhetoric.

In May 1988, the HUCTW won the NLRB representation election by a vote of 1,530 to 1,486 with 89 percent of the workers voting. Harvard filed objections accusing the union of illegal campaigning by having HUCTW balloons near the polling place and other activities. In October an Administrative Law Judge ruled in favor of the HUCTW. Harvard mulled appealing to the NLRB in Washington, but instead decided to recognize the union. After Harvard dropped its opposition to the union, a number of workers came forward and voluntarily joined the union and membership in the union jumped to 75 percent.

In June 1989, a contract was signed that contained wage and benefits improvements, maternity and child care benefits, a unique dispute resolution system in which workers are empowered to resolve their own problems, and no traditional work rules. Several years later, the person who led Harvard's campaign *against* the HUCTW offered the following assessment:

[The HUCTW] knew us better than we did. We didn't know our employees in this huge decentralized place. They organized employees that we didn't know existed. . . . If they had stayed with the UAW, they would have put out a flyer, and we would have put out a flyer, and we would have beaten them. [The HUCTW] understood intuitively what the people were hungering for and nurtured it. The approach was conflict-averse, a much more typical way for women. They want to be in relationships rather than putting up their dukes.

Source: John P. Hoerr, *We Can't Eat Prestige: The Women Who Organized Harvard* (Philadelphia: Temple University Press, 1997). Quotes are from pp. 155, 183, 197, and 211.

units and election results. Recall that during this evolution, private sector union density has fallen from 35 percent in the 1950s to less than 10 percent today. Some argue that employer resistance, including campaigning during representation elections, is primarily responsible for this extended decline in U.S. union density.[79] Three criticisms of the NLRA certification process are therefore expressed most frequently: unequal access to employees, the lack of penalties for violators of the NLRA, and the length of the election process.

Employers can conduct captive audience meetings and enforce no solicitation rules against union organizers while unions only get a list of employee addresses after the election date is set. To some, this unequal access to employees provides employers with an unfair advantage. Possibilities for reform include banning employer captive audience meetings, giving unions the right to hold captive audience meetings, or requiring a certain number of campaign debates.[80] In fact, for a few years in the 1950s, the NLRB granted unions a right of reply—if an employer used a captive audience speech, it also had to provide the union with an equal opportunity to address the employees.[81] Another possibility is to make *Excelsior* lists available at any time or after a union collects 30 percent signed authorization cards.[82] Others advocate greater union access to employees at work more generally.[83] In particular, rather than placing the burden on the union to show that no other channels of communication exist, the burden could be on the employer to show that greater access for union organizers interferes with the business (the current standard for attempts to restrict employees from discussing unionization).

[79] Gary N. Chaison and Joseph B. Rose, "The Macrodeterminants of Union Growth and Decline," in George Strauss, Daniel G. Gallagher and Jack Fiorito (eds.), *The State of the Unions* (Madison, WI: Industrial Relations Research Association, 1991), Chapter 1. Phil Comstock and Maier B. Fox, "Employer Tactics and Labor Law Reform," in Sheldon Friedman, Richard W. Hurd, Rudolph A. Oswald, and Ronald L. Seeber (eds.), *Restoring the Promise of American Labor Law* (Ithaca, NY: ILR Press, 1994), Chapter 6. Richard B. Freeman, "Why Are Unions Faring So Poorly in NLRB Representation Elections?" in Thomas A. Kochan (ed.), *Challenges and Choices Facing American Labor* (Cambridge: MIT Press, 1985), pp. 45–64. Michael Goldfield, *The Decline of Organized Labor in the United States* (Chicago: University of Chicago Press, 1987). James A. Gross, *Broken Promise: The Subversion of U.S. Labor Relations Policy, 1947–1994* (Philadelphia: Temple University Press, 1995). Weiler, "Promises to Keep."

[80] Bierman, "Toward a New Model for Union Organizing." Charles B. Craver, *Can Unions Survive? The Rejuvenation of the American Labor Movement* (New York: New York University Press, 1993). Samuel Estreicher, "Labor Law Reform in a World of Competitive Product Markets," *Chicago-Kent Law Review* 69 (1993), pp. 3–46.

[81] *Bonwit Teller, Inc.,* 96 NLRB 608 (1951).

[82] Craver, *Can Unions Survive?* Estreicher, "Labor Law Reform in a World of Competitive Product Markets." Randall J. White, "Union Representation Election Reform: Equal Access and the *Excelsior* Rule," *Indiana Law Journal* 67 (Winter 1991), pp. 129–67.

[83] Estlund, "Labor, Property, and Sovereignty after *Lechmere.*" Karl E. Klare, "Workplace Democracy and Market Reconstruction: An Agenda for Legal Reform," *Catholic University Law Review* 38 (Fall 1988), pp. 1–68. Sarah Korn, "Property Rights and Job Security: Workplace Solicitation by Nonemployee Union Organizers," *Yale Law Journal* 94 (December 1984), pp. 374–93.

A second criticism of the NLRA certification process is the lack of penalties for violators. When a company violates section 8(a)(3) by illegally discharging a union supporter, the worst penalty the company faces is minor: offering reinstatement with full backpay to the employee. And the company can reduce the backpay award by the amount the employee has earned elsewhere since their discharge. Many see this as an inadequate deterrent to violating the NLRA and propose reforming the NLRA to allow compensatory and punitive damage awards (as is the case under antidiscrimination laws such as the Civil Rights Act) rather than only allowing backpay awards.[84] With respect to elections, if the NLRB finds that laboratory conditions have been corrupted by employer, union, or third party actions, the typical remedy is to throw out the election results and conduct a new election. In some instances, this happens several times. In rare cases in which the NLRB believes that the union had majority support but extreme employer misconduct has eroded this support and has also been so pernicious as to make an election pointless, the NLRB can issue a ***Gissel bargaining order*** instead of trying to restore laboratory conditions and conducting a new election.[85] A *Gissel* bargaining order requires the employer to recognize and bargain with the union even though the usual election results are lacking. As such, there are three ways in which a union can win recognition: voluntary recognition, an NLRB representation election, and a bargaining order. But bargaining orders are only rarely issued and only for the most extreme cases in which multiple, severe unfair labor practices have been committed.

A third criticism of the NLRB certification process is the length of the process. Typically elections are not held until two months after the filing of the election petition, and employers' legal maneuverings can further lengthen this time period. Many believe that the worst violations occur during this time period when the campaigning on both sides is the most intense.[86] Consequently, an important reform proposal is for instant or expedited elections in which the NLRB would be required to hold an election soon after the petition is filed. In the Canadian province of Nova Scotia, for example, elections must be held within five days.[87] Others argue that this would simply compress the hostility into a shorter period of time and therefore advocate using card-check elections.[88] Under such a system, the NLRB could certify a union based on signed authorization cards without holding an election. This is common in Canada, and research shows that employer unfair labor practices are less significant in Canada and that management opposition under card-check regimes is significantly less effective in thwarting unionization efforts than in traditional election regimes.[89] The major concern with using card-check elections is whether signing a card always equates to supporting the union (maybe someone signs a card because of peer pressure), but the Canadian system includes

[84] Craver, *Can Unions Survive?* William B. Gould, *Agenda for Reform: The Future of Employment Relationships and the Law* (Cambridge: MIT Press, 1993).

[85] *NLRB v. Gissel Packing Company,* 395 U.S. 575 (1969). Taylor and Witney, *Labor Relations Law.*

[86] Commission on the Future of Worker-Management Relations, *Report and Recommendations* (Washington, DC: U.S. Departments of Labor and Commerce, 1994). Gould, *Agenda for Reform.* Weiler, "Promises to Keep."

[87] Sheila Murphy, "A Comparison of the Selection of Bargaining Representatives in the United States and Canada: *Linden Lumber, Gissel,* and the Right to Challenge Majority Status," *Comparative Labor Law Journal* 10 (Fall 1988), pp. 65–97. Weiler, "Promises to Keep."

[88] Stephen F. Befort, "Labor and Employment Law at the Millennium: A Historical Review and Critical Assessment." *Boston College Law Review* 43 (March 2002), pp. 351–460. Gould, *Agenda for Reform.*

[89] Murphy, "A Comparison of the Selection of Bargaining Representatives in the United States and Canada." Terry Thomason, "The Effect of Accelerated Certification Procedures on Union Organizing Success in Ontario," *Industrial and Labor Relations Review* 47 (January 1994), pp. 207–26. Chris Riddell, "Union Certification Success under Voting versus Card-Check Procedures: Evidence from British Columbia, 1978–1998," *Industrial and Labor Relations Review* 57 (July 2004), pp. 493–517.

various safeguards for this possibility (such as requiring a dues payment with a signed card or requiring a supramajority such as 60 percent to gain certification using cards).

NLRB elections are supposed to be the democratic method for settling representation questions. But it's questionable whether NLRB elections fulfill the standards for democratic elections.[90] Democratic elections should be free of intimidation, but many workers are fired for trying to form unions. Freedom of speech is essential for democratic elections, but employers can limit free speech in the workplace. Democratic elections also require reasonably balanced financial resources and access to voters, but employers typically have much greater resources and access to employees.

For labor supporters, therefore, the NLRB certification process has some major weaknesses. If these weaknesses are in fact responsible for the decline in U.S. union density, then reform is warranted. But there are other possible explanations for this decline. Structural, or compositional, changes are partly responsible: declining employment in traditionally unionized industries such as manufacturing combined with faster employment growth in Southern states, increased number of women in the labor force, and increases in education and skill levels.[91] This structural explanation, however, begs important questions about why certain industries, occupations, regions, or workers are more or less receptive to unionization. Another possible explanation is that the demand for unions by nonunion employees has declined—perhaps because of increased employment laws, improved human resource management practices, or unresponsive unions that have failed to stay in touch with the contemporary workforce.[92] There is no single, universally accepted answer to why union density has declined, but the true answer is critically important for determining whether reforms to the NLRB certification process are needed.

Without waiting for this academic debate to be settled, or for labor law to be reformed, more and more unions are explicitly trying to organize new workers outside of the NLRB certification process. In fact, the AFL–CIO claims that in recent years, more workers have been organized outside NLRB elections than through such elections.[93] The Justice for Janitors campaigns use public demonstrations to pressure commercial property owners and cleaning service contractors into recognizing unions without going through the NLRB election process (recall Box 7.15). Unions are also trying to organize outside the NLRB by negotiating neutrality and card-check agreements with employers in which employers agree to remain neutral in organizing drives and to recognize the union based on a card-check election.[94] For example, the Communication Workers of America (CWA) negotiated a card-check procedure with Cingular Wireless in 2001 in which Cingular agreed to recognize

[90] David L. Cingranelli, "International Election Standards and NLRB Representation Elections," in Richard N. Block et al. (eds.), *Justice on the Job: Perspectives on the Erosion of Collective Bargaining in the United States* (Kalamazoo, MI: Upjohn, 2006), pp. 41–56.

[91] Chaison and Rose, "The Macrodeterminants of Union Growth and Decline."

[92] James T. Bennett and Jason E. Taylor, "Labor Unions: Victims of Their Political Success?" *Journal of Labor Research* 22 (Spring 2001), pp. 261–73. Henry S. Farber and Alan B. Krueger, "Union Membership in the United States: The Decline Continues," in Bruce E. Kaufman and Morris M. Kleiner (eds.), *Employee Representation: Alternatives and Future Directions* (Madison, WI: Industrial Relations Research Association, 1993), Chapter 3. Leo Troy, *Beyond Unions and Collective Bargaining* (Armonk, NY: M. E. Sharpe, 1999).

[93] James Brudney, "Neutrality Agreements and Card Check Recognition: Prospects for Changing Paradigms," *Iowa Law Review* 90 (March 2005), pp. 819–86.

[94] Paul F. Clark, John T. Delaney, and Ann C. Frost (eds.), *Collective Bargaining in the Private Sector* (Champaign, IL: Industrial Relations Research Association, 2002). Adrienne E. Eaton and Jill Kriesky, "Union Organizing Under Neutrality and Card Check Agreements," *Industrial and Labor Relations Review* 55 (October 2001), pp. 42–59. Adrienne E. Eaton and Jill Kriesky, "Dancing with the Smoke Monster: Employer Motivations for Negotiating Neutrality and Card Check Agreements," in Richard N. Block et al. (eds.), *Justice on the Job: Perspectives on the Erosion of Collective Bargaining in the United States* (Kalamazoo, MI: Upjohn, 2006), pp. 139–60.

the CWA in any workplace in which a majority of the workers signed authorization cards. The neutral American Arbitration Association simply has to compare the signed cards with a list of unit employees provided by Cingular. Since that time, more than 15,000 Cingular employers have unionized with the CWA using this process, including network technicians, retail sales associates, and call center workers.

The Hotel Employees and Restaurant Employees union (now UNITE-HERE) has also occasionally been successful in pressuring local governments to include these types of provisions in lease agreements when new hotels are constructed with public funds. In one case, the union staffed a table in the employee cafeteria to talk with interested workers and after 32 days had sufficient cards to be recognized through a card-check election.[95] Compare this to the months (sometimes years) of hostility and warfare in standard NLRB elections. Lastly, workers outside the scope of the NLRA (or other pieces of legislation) of course must also organize outside the NLRB. A notable example is agricultural workers. In California, for example, before the passage of a state law in the mid-1970s established a recognition election process, Cesar Chavez and the United Farm Workers were forced to rely on national boycotts of grapes and lettuce as well as public demonstrations (such as a 340-mile protest march from Delano to Sacramento) to win recognition for field workers.[96] Interestingly, New Jersey enacted a law in 2005 in which public sector workers and private sector workers at companies too small to be covered by the NLRA can obtain recognition through a card-check procedure. Organizing outside the NLRB election process has become a very important issue in labor relations.

In a different vein, one can argue that the NLRA obligates employers to bargain with unions on a members-only basis when a union represents less than a majority of employees.[97] Therefore, another strategy for unions is to concentrate on building organizations within workplaces and signing up union members rather than on winning elections. The benefits that accrue to a small number of union members through members-only bargaining and representation can then build support among skeptical workers and perhaps ultimately create majority support and full-fledged exclusive representative status. This has the potential to drastically reshape the union organizing process, but conventional wisdom that emphasizes an all-or-nothing approach to winning majority support through NLRB elections is very deeply ingrained in U.S. labor relations. Only time will tell whether members-only organizing and bargaining takes hold both legally and practically.

This chapter focuses on the private sector union organizing process in the United States as governed by the NLRA and NLRB. This practice of using secret ballot elections to determine majority support and to bestow exclusive representation rights to a union is not representative of how unions are formed outside North America (see Chapter 13), but the process in the U.S. railway and airline industries under the Railway Labor Act and National Mediation Board is quite similar. Moreover, the organizing process in the U.S. public sector also closely follows the NLRA philosophy and machinery (at least for occupations covered by a public sector law) (see Box 7.17). And in all of these jurisdictions—the U.S. private and covered public sectors—the certification of a majority union as the exclusive representative of the employees only obligates the

[95] John W. Budd and Paul K. Heinz, "Union Representation Elections and Labor Law Reform: Lessons from the Minneapolis Hilton," *Labor Studies Journal* 20 (Winter 1996), pp. 3–20.

[96] Susan Ferriss and Ricardo Sandoval, *The Fight in the Fields: Cesar Chavez and the Farmworkers Movement* (New York: Harcourt Brace, 1997).

[97] Charles J. Morris, *The Blue Eagle at Work: Reclaiming Democratic Rights in the American Workplace* (Ithaca, NY: Cornell University Press, 2005).

Recall from Chapter 5 that federal government employees are covered by the Civil Service Reform Act while state and local government employees fall within the jurisdiction of each state. Not all state and local workers are covered by a collective bargaining law: 25 states have comprehensive laws, 16 have narrow laws or executive orders applying to limited occupations, eight have no laws, and one state prohibits bargaining. Consequently, the organizing process for public sector employees varies from jurisdiction to jurisdiction.

In states without laws, or for occupations outside the coverage of narrow laws, workers can still try to form unions, but there is no established legal machinery for granting recognition to these unions. This is analogous to the pre-1935 situation in the private sector. These workers therefore must resort to economic and political pressure tactics to try to win recognition. Workers can try to pressure local school boards and other government officials through demonstrations and lobbying, but the most powerful weapon is the recognition strike. In fact, Martin Luther King was assassinated while visiting Memphis to support sanitation workers who were striking for recognition. Firefighters (recall Box 4.22), teachers, college professors, and many other occupations in numerous states have won recognition for their unions through recognition strikes, or the threat of one. Graduate student teaching assistants are also exempted from many state bargaining laws, but students at the University of Massachusetts–Amherst and the University of Illinois used strikes, sit-ins, and class boycotts to pressure these universities into agreeing to elections which were won by unions.

For federal, state, and local government employees covered by bargaining laws, the union certification process typically closely parallels the NLRA system described in this chapter. In the federal sector, individuals who wish to be represented by a union must file a petition with the Federal Labor Relations Authority (FLRA). The FLRA clarifies any unit definition questions and if the petition is supported by 30 percent signed authorization cards, an election will be called (subject to the usual bars such as a contract already being in place). State laws are similar with state agencies handling the representation process. Like the NLRB, many jurisdictions use a "community of interest" standard to define appropriate bargaining units. Public sector bargaining units are often small—in one study, half of all (nonfederal) public sector elections were for bargaining units of less than 15 employees. Some states also allow for card-check elections if only one union is present and if management does not object. Some states also extensively use mail ballots.

Perhaps the most striking difference between private and public sector representation elections is the win rate. In the private sector, unions typically win about half of the elections; in the public sector the win rate is 85 percent. And the margin of victory is also significantly higher in the public sector: in elections won by unions, over 80 percent of employees, on average, vote for the union. It is widely believed that public sector employers do not aggressively campaign against unions during organizing drives. Perhaps this explains the stark differences in win rates between private and public sector elections?

Sources: Kate Bronfenbrenner and Tom Juravich, *Union Organizing in the Public Sector: An Analysis of State and Local Elections* (Ithaca, NY: ILR Press, 1995). Richard C. Kearney, *Labor Relations in the Public Sector*, 2nd ed. (New York: Marcel Dekker, 1992).

employer to bargain with the union. A contract is not guaranteed. In fact, 25 to 30 percent of newly unionized bargaining units fail to overcome managerial resistance and secure a first contract.[98] This second major process of U.S. labor relations is the topic of the next chapter: bargaining.

[98] Bronfenbrenner and Juravich, "It Takes More than House Calls." William N. Cooke, *Union Organizing and Public Policy: Failure to Secure First Contracts* (Kalamazoo, MI: W. E. Upjohn Institute for Employment Research, 1985).

Key Terms	NLRB representation election, *232*	decertification election, *236*	captive audience meeting, *245*
	authorization card, *232*	appropriate bargaining unit, *237*	*Excelsior* list, *253*
	card-check election, *233*	union instrumentality, *239*	*Gissel* bargaining order, *260*
	recognition strike, *235*	laboratory conditions doctrine, *242*	
	certification election, *235*		

Reflection Questions

1. Outline the pros and cons of the NLRA's union recognition process focused on secret ballot elections. Describe some alternative means for deciding questions of representation. What do you think would be best for the workplace and workforce of the 21st century? Refer back to Box 7.10—should employers be excluded from the representation process?

2. In a concise paragraph, paraphrase what you have learned about union strategies in organizing drives to describe these strategies to a new union organizer.

3. Bob Ulrich, CEO of nonunion retailer Target, justifies his company's antiunion philosophy by saying that Target "simply doesn't believe that third-party representation would add anything for our customers, our employees, or our shareholders. We just do not believe it's productive and adds value."[99] Critique this stance.

4. Box 7.18 contains four scenarios of union organizing drives that end with a different decision point for management. For each scenario, develop an HR strategy for responding to the organizing drive by (1) Outlining the various alternatives for responding to the union organizing drive, and (2) Developing and supporting a specific recommended course of action to present to upper management.

Internet Exploration

1. Search the Internet for Web sites for union avoidance management consultants (try searching for "union avoidance" or "union free"). Are these consultants good or bad for labor relations? What types of tactics are described on their Web sites? How do these tactics compare to those described by longtime consultant Martin Jay Levitt in his 1993 book *Confessions of a Union Buster?*

2. Search for union sites that are focused on organizing new workers, such as *www.walmartworkersneo.com* (*Hint:* search for "authorization card"). What types of issues are emphasized in the different campaigns? What tactics are used? What are the pros and cons of using Web sites for organizing?

3. Web sites like *www.cyberlodge.org* and *www.youareworthmore.org* feature online forums or bulletin boards for unorganized workers. Is this more consistent with a servicing or an organizing model of union representation? Is it ethical for a company to monitor these sites to see what its workers are saying?

4. Download the "Boys and Girls" episode (first aired February 2, 2006, in season two) of the NBC comedy series *The Office.* Why do the warehouse workers want to unionize? How is it about more than just wages and benefits? Evaluate the reaction of Michael's corporate boss (Jan) when she hears the news from Michael. Is it exaggerated or realistic? Evaluate her speech to the employees. Is it legal? A good approach?

Additional Reading

Bronfenbrenner, Kate, et al. (eds.), *Organizing to Win: New Research on Union Strategies* (Ithaca, NY: ILR Press, 1998).

Gall, Gregor (ed.), *Union Organizing: Campaigning for Trade Union Recognition* (London: Routledge, 2003).

[99] Chris Serres, "Teflon Target," *Star Tribune,* May 22, 2005, pp. D1, D4.

Hoerr, John P., *We Can't Eat Prestige: The Women Who Organized Harvard* (Philadelphia: Temple University Press, 1997).

Levitt, Martin Jay, and Terry Conrow, *Confessions of a Union Buster* (New York: Crown Publishers, 1993).

National Labor Relations Board, *Outline of Law and Procedure in Representation Cases* (Washington, DC: U.S. Government Printing Office, 2005). Also available online at *www.nlrb.gov/nlrb/legal/manuals/outline.asp.*

Ness, Immanuel, *Immigrants, Unions, and the New U.S. Labor Market* (Philadelphia: Temple University Press, 2005).

Ray, Douglas E., Calvin William Sharpe, and Robert N. Strassfield, *Understanding Labor Law* (New York: Mathew Bender, 1999).

For each of the four scenarios below, you are the HR manager and you need to:

1. Outline your various alternatives in responding to the union organizing drive.
2. Develop and support a specific recommended course of action to present to upper management.

Acme Auto Parts

Acme Auto Parts is a small nonunion manufacturer of auto parts located in a small town in the South. The work is repetitive and routine. There are no particular skill or educational requirements for the production employees. Acme sells nearly all of its parts to the Big Three automakers (Ford, General Motors, and Daimler-Chrysler) according to the specifications that they provide. The highly unionized Big Three have largely outsourced the manufacturing of parts. Many of their traditional parts suppliers have closed their unionized operations in Michigan and opened nonunion plants in the South and in Mexico. The Big Three, however, continue to face competitive cost pressures from the Japanese car companies and therefore are continually trying to wring cost concessions from their suppliers.

The parts workers at various companies that are still represented by the United Auto Workers (UAW) are faced with demands for concessions during every contract negotiation. The UAW is therefore trying to organize the nonunion parts factories. You have seen UAW organizers in town trying to contact Acme workers for the past few weeks. This morning you overheard two workers talking about the UAW.

The Zinnia

The Zinnia is a 300-room hotel in the central business district of a major Midwestern metropolitan area. This is a full-service hotel—a hotel providing a wide variety of services including food and beverage facilities and meeting rooms—that caters to individual business travelers, convention attendees, and local businesspeople who need meeting space. The Zinnia emphasizes outstanding service and amenities and is owned by a prominent local real estate magnate, Ms. Lucy Baldercash, who closely monitors the management and financial performance of her diversified properties.

Many of this city's major hotels are unionized and the Zinnia's wage rates are equal to the local union wage scale. You feel that while the Zinnia's employee benefit package is modest compared to what the union has been able to extract from your unionized competi-

tors, it is competitive with other low-skilled occupations in the area—and is particularly generous for the undocumented immigrants that you have quietly hired to fill the dishwashing and room cleaning positions. You also feel that your unionized competitors are saddled with myriad work rules that restrict flexibility.

The local union organizes aggressively and isn't afraid to have public marches and demonstrations in support of its goal of social justice. But you thought your workers were content and you were astonished to learn this morning that Zinnia workers have been quietly signing authorization cards. You received notice from the NLRB that a petition was filed by the local hotel union requesting an election covering back-of-the-house workers (kitchen, laundry, and room cleaning employees—not front-of-the-house employees like bellhops, bartenders, and waitresses) and that this petition was supported by signed authorization cards from 40 percent of the workers.

School District 273

School district 273 is a medium-sized public school district in a Northeastern state with a comprehensive bargaining law that includes teachers. The bargaining law allows strikes (except for police, firefighters, and prison guards) and also allows unions to be recognized through a card-check election if the employer does not object. Otherwise, a representation election will be conducted when a petition is supported by 30 percent signed authorization cards. No employees in district 273 are represented by a union though teachers in many of the neighboring districts are.

District 273 receives 75 percent of its funding from the state based on a statewide per-student funding formula; the remainder comes from local property taxes and fees. To balance the state budget, school funding was reduced by 10 percent. School budgets are also being squeezed by rising health care costs. Lastly, teachers are frustrated by the state's emphasis on standardized test scores and they feel they are losing control over educational standards and curriculum. A grassroots unionization effort started among some teachers at the district's high school near the beginning of the school year. It is now the middle of the school year and the leaders of this grassroots effort—which they are now calling the District 273 Teacher's Association—claim to have signed authorization cards from 70 percent of the teachers, including large numbers at all of the district's schools. They have asked the school board to voluntarily recognize their union and schedule bargaining sessions to hear their concerns and negotiate a contract that preserves teachers' input into the educational process.

Woodville HealthCare

Woodville HealthCare is a for-profit health care provider formed through the merger of several networks of physicians. It operates 50 managed-care clinics and employs 400 doctors in the West. The merger has resulted in a major restructuring of operations. Several clinics have been closed and a number of new operating guidelines have been implemented. Doctors are now required to see more patients, specialty medical procedures and nongeneric prescriptions must be approved by the medical authorization department, and expensive procedures can negatively affect a doctor's salary.

Some doctors contacted a national doctors union which is affiliated with one of the largest U.S. unions, and an organizing drive was launched. After a petition was filed with the NLRB, Woodville filed objections and argued that the doctors were supervisors and therefore excluded from the NLRA. The NLRB eventually ruled that 100 of the doctors had supervisory responsibilities, but that 300 were nonmanagerial doctors. Woodville then spent $200,000 (plus staff time) on an antiunion campaign leading up to last week's election for the 300 nonmanagerial doctors. The election results were 142 voting in favor of the union, 128 against.

This is a slim seven-vote margin and you have until tomorrow to decide whether to appeal the results of the election by filing objections with the NLRB. Several days before the election, the union's Web site reported salary figures for Woodville's top executives that were grossly inflated. You have also investigated several allegations of inappropriate union campaigning on the day of the election but have only uncovered weak evidence. Your attorney predicts that there is a 20 percent chance an appeal would be successful.

Chapter **Eight**

Bargaining

Advance Organizer

Once a union is organized by a group of employees and recognized by the employer through the process outlined in the previous chapter, the next goal of the employees is for the union to negotiate a contract with the employer. This chapter discusses the behavioral, strategic, and legal aspects of collectively bargaining contracts in U.S. labor relations.

Learning Objectives

By the end of the chapter, you should be able to:

1. **Understand** how union contracts are negotiated.
2. **Outline** the four subprocesses of bargaining (distributive bargaining, integrative bargaining, attitudinal structuring, and intraorganizational bargaining), their purposes, and their tactics.

3. **Explain** the legal parameters of the U.S. bargaining process.
4. **Discuss** the determinants and importance of bargaining power.
5. **Define** the different types of bargaining structures.
6. **Sketch** the typical bargaining timeline.

Contents

One of the main goals of the U.S. labor relations system is to allow employees to *negotiate* their terms and conditions of employment with their employer as a group, instead of individually taking or leaving whatever their employer offers unilaterally. Bargaining is therefore a central process of the U.S. labor relations system. In fact, bargaining is so important that (1) the term collective bargaining is often used to capture the entire sweep of labor relations, (2) the unit for a National Labor Relations Board (NLRB) representation election is defined by the National Labor Relations Act (NLRA) as the one most appropriate for collective bargaining (Chapter 7), and (3) a certified union is referred to as the bargaining agent of the employees.

The process of collective bargaining in U.S. labor relations almost always has the goal of producing a legally binding, written contract that specifies wages, benefits, layoff policies, grievance procedures, and many other terms and conditions of employment: "the union at work is the union negotiating a contract."[1] These contracts are called union contracts or collective bargaining agreements. When a union becomes newly certified as the bargaining agent for a previously nonunion set of employees, the next major objective of the employees is for the union to negotiate a union contract with the employer. Contracts typically last one to five years (three years is quite common) and must be renegotiated upon expiration. So bargaining is also important for established unions. This chapter is

---

[1] Arthur M. Ross, *Trade Union Wage Policy* (Berkeley: University of California Press, 1948), p. 11.

about bargaining union contracts—types of bargaining, bargaining tactics, the NLRA's legal parameters for union and employer negotiators, the influences on relative bargaining power, and strategic negotiating in a competitive environment.

BARGAINING SUBPROCESSES AND STRATEGIES

In a classic work, Richard Walton and Robert McKersie decomposed the overall labor negotiations process into four types of bargaining: distributive bargaining, integrative bargaining, attitudinal structuring, and intraorganizational bargaining (see Box 8.1).[2] In Walton and McKersie's terminology, these are the four subprocesses of negotiations: the four types of bargaining that take place in collective bargaining to negotiate a union contract. The first two subprocesses—distributive and integrative bargaining—are the major alternatives for negotiating terms and conditions of employment: adversarial bargaining over conflicts of interest or collaborative problem solving for issues of mutual gain. Attitudinal structuring pertains to broader concerns of managing the labor–management relationship, such as creating trust. Lastly, intraorganizational bargaining captures the debates and conflict resolution strategies used to reach a consensus *within* the union and *within* the employer's management ranks. Collective bargaining in both the private and public sectors is a mixture of all four subprocesses because mainstream industrial relations views employment relationship conflict as a **mixed motive** (a mixture of conflicts of interests and shared opportunities for mutual gain) (so both distributive and integrative bargaining are important), the employer–employee–union relationship is a long-term, ongoing affair (so attitudinal structuring is significant), and both employers and unions have constituencies with diverse interests (so intraorganizational bargaining is present).

Distributive Bargaining

Think of some bargaining situations in everyday life. What scenarios come to mind? Buying a car? Haggling with your roommate over who's going to wash the dishes? Trying to get your boss to give you a day off next week? One way to approach these bargaining situations

BOX 8.1   The Four Subprocesses of Labor Negotiations

Subprocess	Focus	Where the Subprocess Occurs
Distributive Bargaining	Resolving Conflicts of Interest; Often Adversarial	At the Bargaining Table between Labor and Management Negotiators
Integrative Bargaining	Solving Joint Problems (That Do Not Involve Conflicts of Interest) by Creating Solutions for Mutual Gains; Often Collaborative	At the Bargaining Table and in Brainstorming Sessions between Labor and Management Negotiators and Their Committees
Attitudinal Structuring	Changing Attitudes and the Overall Labor–Management Relationship; Often Trust-Building	At the Bargaining Table between Labor and Management Negotiators, but Spilling Over to Others
Intraorganizational Bargaining	Achieving Consensus within Each Group; Often Complex	Away from the Bargaining Table within Each Organization

Source: Richard E. Walton and Robert B. McKersie, *A Behavioral Theory of Labor Negotiations* (New York: McGraw-Hill, 1965).

[2] Richard E. Walton and Robert B. McKersie, *A Behavioral Theory of Labor Negotiations* (New York: McGraw-Hill, 1965).

is by assuming that there is a strict conflict of interest: you want a lower price for the car and the salesperson wants a higher price, you want your roommate to wash the dishes and your roommate wants you to, you want a day off next week and your boss wants you to work. In labor relations, the simplest example is bargaining over wages—employees want to receive higher wages, employers want to keep labor costs down. These types of bargaining scenarios are typically viewed as dividing up a fixed pie—the more dishes your roommate washes, the fewer you are stuck with, or paying out an extra $10,000 in wages reduces profits by $10,000. **Distributive bargaining** is the familiar type of negotiation used to resolve these conflicts of interests—in other words, to *distribute* the shares of the fixed pie.[3] In distributive bargaining, the more that one side receives, the less the other side receives, so this type of bargaining is also referred to as zero-sum bargaining.

Distributive bargaining is the classic vision of collective bargaining: union and management negotiators pounding the table demanding more (the union) or less (the employer) and both trying to drive the hardest bargain possible. Wages, benefits, working conditions, and work rules are all viewed as having a conflict of interest—improvements benefit the workers and harm the company's bottom line (and vice versa). But if both sides are trying so hard to win, why bargain at all? Negotiations are used to resolve conflict when the parties are interdependent.[4] Employers need workers to produce goods and services, workers need employers to earn a living. But not at all costs. Parties will pursue and enter into a negotiated agreement when the terms of this agreement are better than their alternatives. For workers, their alternatives include going on strike and looking for work elsewhere; for employers, the alternatives are taking a strike, trying to hire new employees, outsourcing, and moving. The Best Alternative to a Negotiated Agreement (BATNA) therefore determines what terms are minimally acceptable to either side.[5]

The expectation that a negotiated settlement will be better than a party's BATNA provides an incentive to bargain. The costs of a strike and hiring new employees give employers an incentive to bargain; the costs of unemployment and the uncertainties of trying to find a new job give employees an incentive to bargain. In distributive bargaining, each side's BATNA can be thought of as their threat point or their resistance point—they will resist accepting terms less favorable than their BATNA and will threaten to quit the negotiations and walk away if they cannot obtain terms at least equal to their BATNA. It is common to graphically represent this situation as shown in Box 8.2.[6] In the top half of Box 8.2, the union's resistance point is a 2 percent wage increase while the employer's resistance point is a 5 percent wage increase. There is thus a positive settlement or bargaining range and each side should be satisfied with any wage increase between 2 and 5 percent. In the bottom half of Box 8.2, however, a settlement is not expected: the maximum the employer is willing to offer is 2 percent and the minimum the union is willing to accept is 5 percent. If each side's BATNA is realistic, then these parties are better off with their alternatives than with negotiating a settlement.

The top half of Box 8.2 captures the traditional distributive bargaining scenario. Remember that the resistance points are the minimally acceptable terms. The parties also have a desired or target settlement. In distributive bargaining, each party's target is often

[3] Walton and McKersie, *A Behavioral Theory of Labor Negotiations.*

[4] Roy J. Lewicki, David M. Saunders, and Bruce Barry, *Negotiation,* 5th ed. (Boston: McGraw-Hill/Irwin, 2006).

[5] Roger Fisher, William Ury, and Bruce Patton, *Getting to YES: Negotiating Agreement Without Giving In,* 2nd ed. (New York: Penguin Books, 1991).

[6] Howard Raiffa, *The Art and Science of Negotiation* (Cambridge: Harvard University Press, 1982). Walton and McKersie, *A Behavioral Theory of Labor Negotiations.*

BOX 8.2
Distributive
Bargaining and the
Settlement Range

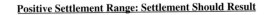

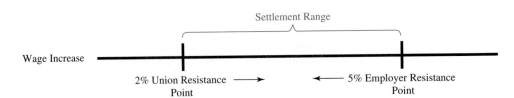

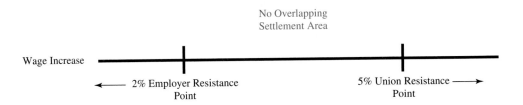

the other side's resistance point.[7] In other words, each side wants to win as much as possible without driving the other side to walk away. Consequently, the major distributive bargaining strategies and tactics are rooted in power: trying to strengthen the image of your own resistance point while seeking out and weakening the other side's impression of their own resistance point.[8] Such tactics include carefully controlling and selectively presenting the information shared with the other side (typically only the chief negotiator gets to speak at the bargaining table), reacting emotionally to statements made by the other side (or not reacting at all), "educating" the other side about the implications of their proposals, and staking out strong positions. Pressure tactics might also include increasing the other side's costs of not making an agreement such as through union rallies that disrupt production and bring negative publicity to the employer. The careful sequencing of offers, counteroffers, and concessions lies at the heart of the distributive bargaining process, and these tactics are designed to quicken the pace and generosity of the other side's concessions while reducing the need to make your own concessions. Hardball tactics such as lies, bluffs, threats, and intimidation are also sometimes used to achieve these ends, but may do more harm than good. A visible example of how concealing information can backfire is presented in Box 8.3. Whether these hardball tactics are ethical is also subject to debate (see Box 8.4).

With or without these hardball tactics, each side's maneuvers are designed to win the most for their side, and distributive bargaining is therefore typically adversarial. Adversarial conflicts of interests over wages, benefits, working conditions, and work rules are a central component of collective bargaining in U.S. labor relations. But remember that labor and management have critical areas of common interest. Both want productive work systems and organizations that are financially healthy so that employers can continue to provide quality jobs and returns on shareholders' investments. Finding the best solutions to these problems that involve mutual gain rather than conflicts of interest is pursued through a different type of bargaining: integrative bargaining.

---

[7] Walton and McKersie, *A Behavioral Theory of Labor Negotiations*.

[8] Lewicki, Saunders, and Barry, *Negotiation*. Walton and McKersie, *A Behavioral Theory of Labor Negotiations*.

Faced with bankruptcy, American Airlines sought $1.62 billion in concessions in February–April 2003 from the three unions that represent significant numbers of its employees. Within days after the rank and file voted to grudgingly approve the concession deals, the airline's filings to the Securities and Exchange Commission disclosed its plans to give bonuses to seven top executives and to provide special pension protections to 48 top executives. That these executive perks had been concealed from employees during the concessions talks caused a tremendous amount of anger and the unions threatened to not sign the concession agreements or to hold new ratification votes. In response, the American Airlines CEO resigned, and the airline barely avoided bankruptcy by renegotiating the concession agreements to be more favorable to the employees. Hiding these executive perks during negotiations proved to be a very costly bargaining tactic for American Airlines.

Source: Eric Torbenson, "American Flight Attendants Accept Concession Deal," *Dallas Morning News* (April 25, 2003).

Integrative Bargaining

Integrative bargaining seeks to unify (integrate) the common interests of the parties to a negotiation so that all can become better off.[9] Rather than trying to split a fixed pie as in distributive bargaining, integrative bargaining seeks to expand the size of the pie. Solving a production bottleneck by reconfiguring work flow, or reallocating a benefits package that holds costs steady but increases employee satisfaction, or implementing a training program that improves productivity and wage rates are three examples in which both employees and employers benefit. Such integrative outcomes, however, are unlikely to result from the adversarial tactics and limited sharing of information in distributive bargaining. Rather, integrative bargaining is joint problem solving that relies heavily on trust and full communication (see Box 8.5). Integrative bargaining is also referred to as win-win bargaining (because both sides win by expanding the pie) or mutual gains bargaining (because of the focus on creating mutual gains rather than resolving zero-sum conflicts).

An important strategy in integrative bargaining is focusing on interests rather than positions.[10] Negotiators in distributive bargaining are focused on positions: "I'll pay you $20,000 for this new car and not a nickel more," or "We demand a 5 percent wage increase." Such positions reinforce an adversarial bargaining climate as each side gets locked into defending its position. But this overlooks and obscures the more fundamental interests of each party that underlie its positions. Your interest is not getting a car for $20,000, it is obtaining safe, reliable, and affordable transportation; the union's interest is not getting a 5 percent raise, it is ensuring that the workers are rewarded for their contributions to the company and can live comfortably. There might be several ways of satisfying these basic interests—perhaps you could lease a car instead of buying one, or perhaps the union and company can provide rewards and security through a profit-sharing plan and a no-layoff guarantee. But these options will not be discovered when two adversarial negotiators are focused on defending their positions. Integrative bargaining requires revealing your true interests, and is therefore sometimes called interest-based bargaining.

[9] Walton and McKersie, *A Behavioral Theory of Labor Negotiations.*
[10] Fisher, Ury, and Patton, *Getting to YES.*

Ethics in Action: Is Bluffing Ethical?   Box 8.4

A classic *Harvard Business Review* article argued that business is like a poker game. Since bluffing is a well-known part of both poker and business that everyone does to win, bluffing is ethically acceptable. This theme has been taken up in discussions over labor negotiations often with the same conclusions: bluffing is part of the game and is therefore harmless because (a) everyone does it, and (b) you need to protect yourself against the bluffing of others.

But not everyone agrees. Critics emphasize the true nature of bluffing. Don't confuse bluffing with asking for a generous settlement. Opening a negotiation by asking for a 10 percent wage increase and then making compromises is not bluffing. This is readjusting your expectations after seeing the other side's resistance. Bluffing involves intentional deception. An employer claims that it has replacement workers already lined up to continue production if the regular employees strike, but it doesn't. A union claims that the employees will strike if the employer insists on any health insurance co-pays, though it knows they won't. These types of deceptions are what bluffing is about.

Questions

1. With this precise definition of bluffing, do you think bluffing is widespread in labor negotiations?
2. Is bluffing ethical? Does it matter if it is widespread in labor negotiations or not?

Sources: Albert Z. Carr, "Is Business Bluffing Ethical?" *Harvard Business Review* 46 (January–February 1968), pp. 143–53. Chris Provis, "Ethics, Deception and Labor Negotiation," *Journal of Business Ethics* 28 (November 2000), pp. 145–58.

BOX 8.5
Distributive and Integrative Bargaining

Distributive Bargaining		Integrative Bargaining
Conflict of Interest	*Conflict*	Common Interest
Distributing a Fixed Pie	*Imagery*	Integrating Interests to Increase the Size of the Pie
Positions	*Focus*	Interests
Of Minor Importance, Hindered	*Trust*	Critical, Facilitated
Tightly Controlled	*Information*	Free Flowing
Chief Spokesperson/Lead Negotiator Only	*Participation*	All Members of Negotiating Teams
Manipulating Perceptions of Positions, Increasing Costs of Delay	*Tactics*	Brainstorming, Using Objective Criteria
Table for Pounding	*Important Prop*	Flip Chart for Brainstorming
Winning Gains for Your Side through Bargaining Power	*Benefits*	Creating Joint Gain and Stronger Relationships
Too Aggressive? Harmful to the Relationship? How to Innovate?	*Risks*	Selling Out? Giving Up Too Much?
Stress	*Difficulties for Negotiators*	Giving Up Control, Selling Results to Constituents, Time Consuming
How to Prevent Adversarial Tactics from Damaging the Relationship?	*Question Marks*	How to Distribute the Increased Gains?
Adversarial Bargaining, Hard Bargaining, Traditional Bargaining	*Other Labels*	Win–Win Bargaining, Mutual Gains Bargaining, Interest-Based Bargaining
Positional Bargaining	*In Sum*	Joint Problem Solving

BOX 8.6
The Integrative Bargaining Circle Chart

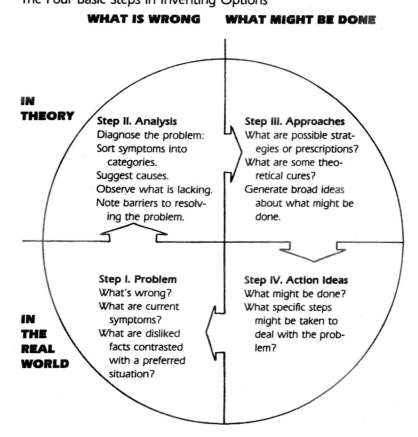

CIRCLE CHART
The Four Basic Steps in Inventing Options

WHAT IS WRONG   **WHAT MIGHT BE DONE**

IN THEORY

Step II. Analysis
Diagnose the problem:
Sort symptoms into categories.
Suggest causes.
Observe what is lacking.
Note barriers to resolving the problem.

Step III. Approaches
What are possible strategies or prescriptions?
What are some theoretical cures?
Generate broad ideas about what might be done.

IN THE REAL WORLD

Step I. Problem
What's wrong?
What are current symptoms?
What are disliked facts contrasted with a preferred situation?

Step IV. Action Ideas
What might be done?
What specific steps might be taken to deal with the problem?

Once the true interests are laid bare, the task of integrative bargaining becomes exploring possible ways of fulfilling these interests. In other words, integrative bargaining uses basic problem-solving strategies such as brainstorming. A circle chart for creating multiple ideas for satisfying the parties' interests is a useful tool for negotiators (see Box 8.6).[11] Note carefully that in contrast to the tight control of information in distributive bargaining, the brainstorming approach of integrative bargaining requires high levels of trust and extensive sharing of information.[12] And all members of each side's bargaining committee—not just the lead negotiators—are expected to participate and contribute ideas.[13] Lastly, after numerous options for solving a particular problem have been identified, the negotiators must select one. The literature on integrative bargaining emphasizes using objective criteria that are established in advance to select the best solution.[14] For example, in considering how to allocate overtime hours, the parties might agree in advance that each alternative will be evaluated against the standard of equal overtime earnings for all hourly employees.

[11] Fisher, Ury, and Patton, *Getting to YES.*

[12] Walton and McKersie, *A Behavioral Theory of Labor Negotiations.*

[13] Maurice B. Better, *Contract Bargaining Handbook for Local Union Leaders* (Washington, DC: Bureau of National Affairs, 1993).

[14] Fisher, Ury, and Patton, *Getting to YES.* Lewicki Saunders, and Barry, *Negotiation.*

One of the leading issues for established labor–management relationships is what type of bargaining to use. Many academics and consultants advocate replacing distributive with integrative bargaining in labor negotiations in order to create more cooperative partnerships to create healthy workplaces and organizations in a competitive environment.[15] But achieving this change in practice is exceptionally difficult.[16] This difficulty stems partially from the overly simplistic illusion of distributive *or* integrative bargaining. If the employment relationship is characterized by mixed motive conflict, then a mixture of distributive and integrative bargaining is appropriate for collective bargaining. In particular, what happens if integrative bargaining is successful? Increasing the size of the pie is not an end in itself—such gains are valuable because they can benefit specific stakeholders through higher profits, wages, or other means. Dividing the fruits of integrative bargaining is a task for distributive bargaining, so successful integrative bargaining ultimately creates a distributive bargaining situation later on.

While it is therefore overly simplistic to say that collective bargaining should use integrative bargaining instead of distributive bargaining, it is reasonable to question whether labor negotiations use integrative bargaining enough. It is common for people generally to *assume* that a negotiating situation involves a conflict of interest—this is a mythical fixed-pie bias.[17] As a result, labor negotiators default to distributive bargaining tactics—and miss opportunities for mutual gains through integrative bargaining. Instead, labor negotiators should start with integrative bargaining and then turn to distributive bargaining if it turns out that mutual gains are not possible.[18] Such a change is difficult. Negotiators need to overcome not only the mythical fixed-pie bias, but also their old habits and strategies that they believe are tried and true. Joint labor–management training in preparation for integrative bargaining is therefore often emphasized. And if collective bargaining is going to be a mix of distributive and integrative tactics, it is important that distributive bargaining over some issues does not poison the relationship and prevent the successful pursuit of integrative bargaining on other issues. Lastly, thinking of labor negotiations as a play with actors who perform their roles on a stage to satisfy the expectations of their audience highlights that labor and management negotiators find it difficult to engage in integrative bargaining because their constituents want their representatives to be forceful champions of their interests (see Box 8.7).[19] Corporate executives and union members want to see a distributive bargaining show. To some, therefore, integrative bargaining means selling out.

Attitudinal Structuring

The difficulties of trying to increase the amount of integrative bargaining pursued as part of the collective bargaining process underscores the importance of Walton and McKersie's third subprocess: **attitudinal structuring**.[20] Integrative bargaining produces joint gains, distributive bargaining divides these gains, and attitudinal structuring establishes the broad

[15] Edward Cohen-Rosenthal and Cynthia E. Burton, *Mutual Gains: A Guide to Union–Management Cooperation,* 2nd ed. (Ithaca, NY: ILR Press, 1993). David S. Weiss, *Beyond the Walls of Conflict: Mutual Gains Negotiating for Unions and Management* (Chicago: Irwin, 1996).

[16] Raymond A. Friedman, *Front Stage, Backstage: The Dramatic Structure of Labor Negotiations* (Cambridge, MA: MIT Press, 1994).

[17] Margaret A. Neale and Max H. Bazerman, *Cognition and Rationality in Negotiation* (New York: Free Press, 1991).

[18] Weiss, *Beyond the Walls of Conflict.*

[19] Friedman, *Front Stage, Backstage.*

[20] Walton and McKersie, *A Behavioral Theory of Labor Negotiations.*

The dramatic structure of labor negotiations closely parallels a theatrical play. The negotiators are actors and have roles, especially the lead negotiators with the leading parts. The audience for the actors' performances are other negotiators and the negotiators' constituents (upper management for management negotiators, union members for the union negotiators). These performances take place on a visible stage at the bargaining table. The audience has certain expectations of how the performance should proceed—that is, the constituents demand that their interests are being strongly represented. As such, the lead negotiators need to put on a show. Table-pounding and other aggressive tactics are used to demonstrate the strength of the negotiators not to each other, but to their audiences/constituents: "Getting members to be happy about the results is largely a matter of good theater—of enhancing confidence in the bargainer and using tensions to good effect." This theater takes place on the front stage of negotiations at the bargaining table for the other members of the bargaining committee to see.

But there is also a backstage—experienced lead negotiators often meet with each other in private outside of the limelight. No other members of the bargaining teams are present. In these meetings, the negotiators can step out of their public roles, share information, and explore wide-ranging options. In contrast with the distributive bargaining of the front stage, backstage interactions can have an integrative bargaining flavor. "While conflict is expressed in public, understanding is built up in private." This front-stage, backstage dichotomy is driven by the social structure of labor negotiations—negotiators have to demonstrate their leadership by satisfying the expectations of their constituents by being a strong advocate and also producing an agreement.

Implications for Novice Labor Relations Practitioners

Don't get emotionally involved! Table pounding, yelling, even personal attacks are likely a "show" or a performance for the audience. Don't take it personally, and don't get caught up in it. Know your role and the nature of the entire performance, and wait for your opportunity out of the spotlight backstage. This dramatic structure applies equally well to the grievance procedure. Be prepared for public performances during meetings and hearings to resolve grievances. Don't take it personally. In the words of one union rep: "I have had arbitration cases where I will bring in 25 guys and put the show on, and they don't remember I lost the case. They remember I worked over management."

Implications for Bargaining

The dramatic structure of labor negotiations means that negotiations are more complex than they appear on the surface. Negotiators have to decipher whether the other negotiator is putting on a show or trying to communicate a legitimate point. Negotiations will almost always go down the wire and settle at the last minute. To settle earlier risks leaving the audience dissatisfied and suspicious that the negotiators have not fought for their interests as strenuously as possible.

And perhaps most significantly, seeing labor negotiations as theater reveals the difficulty of switching from traditional adversarial bargaining to more integrative approaches. Traditional bargaining fulfills the social roles that negotiators must play: "The traditional process is stable because the public rituals that are so common to it—displays of opposition, representation, and control—help negotiators achieve their personal and strategic goals and to manage the many political pressures that they face." This is not to say that the traditional system is perfect—front-stage conflict can get out of hand, signals might be misread, and many participants are left out. But it does highlight the difficulties with changing to integrative bargaining. How can negotiators fulfill their social roles on a front stage of integrative bargaining when the audience still demands a distributive bargaining performance?

Source: Raymond A. Friedman, *Front Stage, Backstage: The Dramatic Structure of Labor Negotiations* (Cambridge, MA: MIT Press, 1994). Quotations are from pp. 87, 111, and 115.

quality of the relationship between labor and management. Distributive and integrative bargaining produce a written contract, attitudinal structuring creates a social contract.[21] Distributive and integrative bargaining are negotiation subprocesses for managing transactions;

[21] Robert B. McKersie and Richard E. Walton, "From the Behavioral Theory to the Future of Negotiations," in Thomas A. Kochan and David B. Lipsky (eds.), *Negotiations and Change: From the Workplace to Society* (Ithaca, NY: ILR Press, 2003), Chapter 17. Richard E. Walton, Joel E. Cutcher-Gershenfeld, and Robert B. McKersie, *Strategic Negotiations: A Theory of Change in Labor–Management Relations* (Boston: Harvard Business School Press, 1994).

attitudinal structuring is a negotiation subprocess for managing relationships.[22] In particular, the close personal interaction between labor and management negotiators that occurs during the bargaining process provides the opportunity for the parties to build trust and respect and therefore move towards a more cooperative and less conflict-laden relationship. This important issue of changing the nature of labor–management relationships is addressed in more detail in Chapter 11.

Intraorganizational Bargaining

If an unmarried person is buying a single used car from another unmarried person, the negotiators only need to concern themselves with the distributive and integrative bargaining subprocesses. If they anticipate repeated interactions, then attitudinal structuring will also be important in establishing the nature of their relationship. If one of them is married, that negotiator will also encounter *intra*organizational bargaining as the negotiator and his or her spouse try to reach consensus on the terms for buying or selling the car. **Intraorganizational bargaining** is the subprocess of the bargaining process that takes place within an organization—within the union and within the ranks of management.[23] The need for intraorganizational bargaining results from the presence of diverse interests within the constituency of a negotiator.

A diversity of interests is typically most visible on the union side. Employees with varying demographic characteristics may have different priorities: older employees might be particularly interested in retirement benefits, younger workers in vacation, female and minority employees in equal opportunities policies, and workers with children in health insurance benefits. Some occupations might be in competition for wage increases, especially in bargaining units that contain both skilled and unskilled jobs. This is quite common in manufacturing in which bargaining units include production as well as skilled maintenance workers. Airplane mechanics at most airlines are represented by the International Association of Machinists (IAM) along with baggage handlers and other ground workers. The Aircraft Mechanics Fraternal Association is trying to raid these IAM locals by convincing mechanics that they would be better off in a union that only represents skilled mechanics. These raids underscore the diversity of interests within many bargaining units. Lastly, in addition to differences in priorities for contract negotiations, employees might disagree about appropriate bargaining tactics with some supporting a more adversarial and distributive approach and others a more conciliatory or integrative approach.

Union leaders and rank and file workers also have differing priorities. Local union leaders might be more concerned with institutional issues such as union security, the number of union stewards, and access to employees at work; rank and file workers might be more concerned with bread and butter employment issues—compensation, benefits, and working conditions. That most U.S. unionized workers belong to diverse national or international unions (Chapter 6) further complicates the nature of intraorganizational bargaining. National union leaders need to strike a balance between the good of a specific bargaining unit and the greater good of all of the union's members. Intense conflicts, however, can arise when a local union wants to give concessions such as wage cuts or work rule changes to save their jobs and a national union objects to prevent a downward spiral throughout an industry—or vice versa (see Box 8.8).

---

[22] Leonard Greenhalgh and Roy J. Lewicki, "New Directions in Teaching Negotiations: From Walton and McKersie to the New Millennium," in Thomas A. Kochan and David B. Lipsky (eds.), *Negotiations and Change: From the Workplace to Society* (Ithaca, NY: ILR Press, 2003), Chapter 2.

[23] Walton and McKersie, *A Behavioral Theory of Labor Negotiations*.

On a Friday in April 1983, the large meatpacking company Wilson Foods filed for bankruptcy. Before the bankruptcy code was changed in 1984, employers used bankruptcy to void their collective bargaining agreements and when Wilson's employees returned to work on Monday, their hourly wages had been slashed from $10.69 to $6.50. Wilson was losing money because of nonunion competition, the recession of the early 1980s, and a decade of neglect as its parent corporation took out its profits without reinvesting. Other major meatpacking companies demanded concessions from their workers and by the end of 1983, much of the industry was paying between $6.00 and $8.25. Many of these workers were represented by the United Food and Commercial Workers (UFCW).

The national UFCW leadership acceded to the demands for concessions with the hopes of stabilizing employment and then gradually bargaining wages back up over time. But UFCW Local P-9, representing 1,500 workers at Hormel's flagship plant in Austin, Minnesota—maker of Spam and other products—wasn't inclined to go along with this plan. Hormel's plants were modern and the company was profitable. P-9 members felt that they were working harder than before and saw no reason to grant wage and benefit concessions to a profitable company. In 1984 six other UFCW locals at Hormel agreed to a concessions package that reduced wages to $9.00 for a year and then upped them to $10.00. Against the wishes of the national UFCW, Local P-9 refused to negotiate, so Hormel implemented the "me too" provision in its contract that allowed it to follow the industry wage pattern and cut wages at the Austin plant from $10.69 to $8.25 in October 1984. Local P-9 insisted that the "me too" clause only applied to wage *increases* but an arbitrator disagreed.

Local P-9's contract with Hormel expired in August 1985, and after a summer of unproductive bargaining sessions, they went on strike. A dissident faction within P-9 was formed and called itself P-10. The national UFCW unenthusiastically sanctioned the strike so that strikers could receive strike benefits. By some accounts, this strike stemmed partly from a failure of intraorganizational bargaining—the P-9 negotiating committee was unable or unwilling to prioritize and trim its exceedingly long list of demands, even though Hormel had greater bargaining leverage.

In December, federal mediators drafted a proposed contract that would essentially match the other Hormel plants. Hormel agreed to accept this proposal if P-9 members would. The national UFCW thought it was the best that could be achieved and recommended that Local P-9 members approve it. The leaders of Local P-9 thought everyone was selling them out. Neither the national UFCW leaders nor the Local P-9 leaders trusted the other to reveal the true results of a vote, so they both did their own. But the same result emerged: the proposal was rejected. The intraorganizational conflict over continuing the strike is revealed by the fact that 40 percent voted for the mediator's proposal.

By mid-February 1986, the Hormel plant in Austin was operating at almost full capacity with P-9 members who had crossed the picket lines and with newly hired replacement workers. With no contract in place and with replacement workers outnumbering P-9 members, the UFCW faced a serious threat of being decertified. The national UFCW leadership therefore began to publicly criticize the Local P-9 leadership. In March it withdrew authorization for the strike, and two months later placed Local P-9 in trusteeship and removed the local leaders. Local P-9 in return sued the UFCW—its parent union!—for $13 million for allegedly undermining its strike. This suit was dismissed and the UFCW ended the strike. By the time a contract was negotiated with Hormel in August 1986, the UFCW had brought Local P-9 back into cooperation with the other Hormel plants and they all negotiated the same terms.

The Hormel strike was one of the most bitter of the last part of the 20th century, and reveals several layers of intraorganizational conflict. The failure of Local P-9 to manage intraorganizational bargaining by narrowing their demands likely contributed to the strike. Within Local P-9, a majority clearly supported the strike, but there was a dissident group that fought for a settlement and significant numbers crossed the picket lines. Local P-9 also differed in their views from the six other Hormel locals and especially with the national UFCW leadership. The Local P-9 leaders strongly believed that they were just in resisting concessions from a profitable corporation, and they received zealous support from many labor activists from around the country. The national UFCW leadership in contrast felt that it was more prudent to preserve unionized employment at Hormel (and elsewhere in the meatpacking industry) and to wait for a more favorable environment to fight for improvements. It is hard to adequately describe the level of distrust and conflict between the Local P-9 leaders and the national UFCW leadership. Intraorganizational conflict typically does not create such a bitter and costly strike, but it is a central feature of the U.S. collective bargaining process.

Sources: Dave Hage and Paul Klauda, *No Retreat, No Surrender: Labor's War at Hormel* (New York: William Morrow, 1989). Peter Rachleff, *Hard-Pressed in the Heartland: The Hormel Strike and the Future of the Labor Movement* (Boston: South End Press, 1993).

Intraorganizational bargaining is more visible on the union side of the collective bargaining process because unions are political institutions—bargaining agendas are determined with rank and file input, leaders are elected, and contracts are approved by ratification votes (see Box 8.9).[24] But intraorganizational bargaining also occurs within the ranks of management.[25] In the bargaining process, top management is particularly concerned with the bottom line financial impact, human resources professionals worry about the principles that are affected or established, supervisors are interested in how works get done, and the negotiators want an agreement. As in the union case, these sometimes-conflicting priorities need to be dealt with before negotiations begin and as bargaining takes place.

Intraorganizational bargaining occurs in varying ways, and might include both distributive and integrative bargaining tactics. Elected union bargaining committees often use surveys of rank and file desires to establish bargaining agendas before negotiations begin. Management negotiating teams typically research problem areas in the current contract and get feedback or direction from various levels of managers. While negotiations are underway, the teams periodically provide bargaining updates to their constituents that are used to manage their expectations and help prepare them to accept a specific outcome. The bargaining teams frequently caucus during negotiations, and some of these committee-only meetings might involve heated discussions of bargaining priorities and strategies. Emotional outbursts, table-pounding, and other distributive bargaining tactics might be used to persuade your own team members of the benefits of a certain position. Once the negotiators reach a tentative agreement, the bargaining teams need to sell this agreement to their constituents, and this is another significant instance of intraorganizational bargaining in the collective bargaining process.

IN GOOD FAITH OVER TERMS AND CONDITIONS OF EMPLOYMENT

As revealed by Walton and McKersie's four subprocesses, labor and management negotiators have a number of tasks to accomplish and a variety of tactics to choose from to achieve them. But their choices are not unlimited. As with the union organizing process (Chapter 7), U.S. labor law regulates the bargaining *process* but not outcomes. In particular, labor law provides important boundaries for negotiators by placing limits on how negotiators can behave and by specifying what types of issues must be negotiated. The National Labor Relations Act (NLRA) specifies that it is an unfair labor practice both for employers and unions "to refuse to bargain collectively" [sections 8(a)(5) and 8(b)(3)] where

> To bargain collectively is the performance of the mutual obligation of the employer and the representative of the employees to meet at reasonable times and confer **in good faith with respect to wages, hours, and other terms and conditions of employment,** or the negotiation of an agreement, or any questions arising thereunder, and the execution of a written contract incorporating any agreement reached if requested by either party, but such obligation does not compel either party to agree to a proposal or require the making of a concession [section 8(d), emphasis added].

In other words, how must negotiators bargain? In good faith. Over what issues? Wages, hours, and other terms and conditions of employment.

Consider this second element first—issues for bargaining. The U.S. Supreme Court has empowered the National Labor Relations Board (NLRB) to classify bargaining issues into three categories of bargaining items: mandatory, permissive, and illegal. This is called the

---

[24] Ross, *Trade Union Wage Policy.*

[25] Friedman, *Front Stage, Backstage.* Walton and McKersie, *A Behavioral Theory of Labor Negotiations.*

One of the most famous academic debates in U.S. industrial relations was launched by an exchange between Professors John T. Dunlop and Arthur M. Ross that occurred in the 1940s: Are labor unions economic or political organizations? The economic approach models unions as trying to maximize some type of utility function, just as corporations are assumed to maximize profits and individuals are assumed to maximize their utility. Dunlop argued that unions act to maximize their wage bill—the aggregate income earned by its membership. In contrast, the political approach models unions as comprised of individuals with diverse preferences and leaders with goals of their own that do not translate into a single well-defined union objective. Ross argued that the major challenge of union leaders and negotiators is to reconcile these diverse and often conflicting preferences into concrete bargaining objectives and that this reconciliation is a political process based on the relative political power of various groups within the union.

In the economic approach, bargaining outcomes are a function of the external environment that determines union bargaining power—the unemployment rate, corporate profitability, whether technology can be easily substituted for expensive labor, and the like. In contrast, in the political approach, "orbits of coercive comparisons" (as Ross labeled them) are an important determinant of bargaining outcomes:

Comparisons are important to the worker. They establish the dividing line between a square deal and a raw deal. . . . Comparisons are crucially important within the union world . . . they measure whether one union has done as well as others. They show whether the negotiating committee has done a sufficiently skillful job of bargaining. They demonstrate to the union member whether he is getting his money's worth for his dues. A favorable contract ("the best contract in the industry") becomes an argument for reelection of officers, a basis for solidification and extension of membership, and an occasion for advancement within the union hierarchy.

So are unions economic or political institutions? Does bargaining reflect the external environment or internal union political struggles? Both Dunlop and Ross agreed that the answer is "both." Dunlop thought the economic aspects are more important and Ross believed that the political aspects are unwisely overlooked, but neither argued for an exclusively economic or political approach to understanding labor union behavior. With respect to the bargaining process, the political aspects—that is, intraorganizational bargaining—must not be ignored.

Sources: John T. Dunlop, *Wage Determination Under Trade Unions* (New York: Macmillan, 1944). Arthur M. Ross, *Trade Union Wage Policy* (Berkeley: University of California Press, 1948). Quote is from p. 51. Bruce E. Kaufman, "Models of Union Wage Determination: What Have We Learned Since Dunlop and Ross?" *Industrial Relations* 41 (January 2002), pp. 110–58.

Borg-Warner doctrine after the name of the Court's decision.[26] **Mandatory bargaining items** are wages, hours, and terms and conditions of employment. Employers and unions have an obligation to bargain over mandatory bargaining items. At the other end of the spectrum, illegal bargaining items are those that would violate the law—such as closed shop provisions, policies that involve racial discrimination, or the payment of wages below the legal minimum. Employers and unions are prohibited from bargaining over these items. The middle category—**permissive bargaining items**—includes everything not in the other two. Employers and unions can bargain over permissive items if they choose, but since they are outside the boundaries of the NLRA, the NLRB cannot order bargaining on these issues, and employees are not protected if they go on strike over these issues. When there are disputes between negotiators about whether something is a mandatory bargaining item—for example, prices in the company cafeteria—the NLRB issues a ruling indicating whether the specific issue is included in their interpretation of "wages, hours, and other terms and conditions of employment." Some prominent examples of mandatory and permissive bargaining items are listed in Box 8.10. One additional issue is called "effects bargaining." The decision to close a plant, for example, is not a mandatory bargaining item,

---

[26] *NLRB v. Wooster Division of Borg-Warner Corporation,* 356 U.S. 342 (1958).

BOX 8.10
Examples of Mandatory and Voluntary Bargaining Items

Mandatory	Permissive
Wage reductions/increases	Union representation on the board of directors
Bonus plans	Drug and alcohol screening for applicants
Health insurance payments	Benefits for retirees
Pension contributions	Interest arbitration
Work schedules and vacations	Bargaining unit expansion
Seniority provisions	Contract ratification procedures
Just cause discipline provisions	Plant closings
Grievance arbitration	
Food prices in the company cafeteria	
Lie detector and drug tests	
Subcontracting	
Effects of plant closings	

but the effects of that decision on the workers, such as layoff order or severance pay, are mandatory items.[27] As such, companies do not need to bargain over the decision to shutdown facilities, but they must bargain with unions over layoff procedures, severance packages, and other effects of these closings.

In the public sector, it is also common to use a mandatory/permissive distinction for bargaining items.[28] However, in some jurisdictions there are also greater restrictions on the allowable bargaining subjects. For federal government employees, the parties are prohibited from negotiating wages and benefits. These items are established through civil service rules; mandatory bargaining items include policies and procedures rather than wages and benefits. At the state and local level, some states allow for a broad scope of bargaining and a few provide for a narrow scope of bargaining.[29] At the narrow end, New Jersey only allows bargaining over mandatory items (there are no permissive items) and does not allow effects bargaining. At the broad end, Illinois and Pennsylvania are similar to the NLRA in requiring bargaining over wages, hours, and other terms and conditions of employment.

Employers and unions have an obligation to bargain in good faith over mandatory bargaining items. The dividing line between good faith and illegal bad faith bargaining, however, is not always clear, as illustrated by four major examples of bad faith bargaining: making unilateral changes, direct dealing, refusing to provide information, and surface bargaining (see Box 8.11). A **unilateral change** is when the employer changes wages, benefits, or other terms and conditions of employment without first bargaining with the union. This includes both during contract negotiations and when a contract is in force. An employer can only make unilateral changes in mandatory bargaining items after it has fulfilled its bargaining obligation by bargaining to an impasse. Unfortunately, "impasse" is another aspect of labor law that is fairly ambiguous and often requires NLRB interpretation of the specific facts of a case to make a ruling:

[27] *Fibreboard Paper Products Corporation v. NLRB,* 379 U.S. 203 (1964).

[28] B. V. H. Schneider, "Public-Sector Labor Legislation—An Evolutionary Analysis," in Benjamin Aaron, Joyce M. Najita, and James L. Stern (eds.), *Public-Sector Bargaining,* 2nd ed. (Washington, DC: Bureau of National Affairs, 1988), Chapter 6.

[29] Joyce M. Najita and James L. Stern (eds.), *Collective Bargaining in the Public Sector: The Experience of Eight States* (Armonk, NY: M. E. Sharpe, 2001).

Background

Winn-Dixie Stores, Inc., operates a multistate chain of retail food stores. Its volume of business is such that it is engaged in interstate commerce. The United Food and Commercial Workers is the authorized bargaining agent for all employees (with the standard exceptions) engaged in the receiving, shipping, and processing of all food products at the Winn-Dixie warehouse in Jacksonville, Florida.

The previous collective bargaining agreement expired in February and the two parties were continuing to negotiate a new agreement. On April 8, the company submitted a wage proposal to the union which would increase wages for employees in the bargaining unit by 56 to 81 cents per hour. The offer was rejected by the union. In letters dated April 17 and April 25, the union requested dates for the purpose of collective bargaining.

The company responded to the union in a letter dated May 3. The letter contained two proposals. First, the company suggested arranging a meeting to be held in early June. Second, the company proposed that the wage proposal dated April 8 "be put into effect immediately without prejudice to further bargaining on the subject." The union responded on May 6 by rejecting the wage proposal and emphasized its desire to bargain not only for "wage increases, but increases in pensions, vacations, hospitalization, and other fringe benefits as well as terms and conditions of employment."

The parties met for the purpose of collective bargaining on June 24. Each side discussed the current agreement section by section. Each side, for the most part, simply restated its previously announced bargaining positions. Additionally, the company again expressed its wish to implement the wage proposal of April 8. The company stated that such an increase was necessary to keep its wages competitive in the local labor market since Winn-Dixie warehouse employees had not received a wage increase in over 18 months. The company also stated that it did *not* intend to have the implementation of this wage increase foreclose further bargaining on the subject of wages. Again, the union would not agree to this wage proposal. The union preferred to first reach agreement on premium pay, holidays, vacations, the pension plan, and arbitration.

Similar negotiating sessions occurred on July 1 and July 2. At the second of these two meetings the company informed the union that as of July 7, it was implementing the proposed wage increase. The company further proposed that the union and the company post joint notice of this increase stating that it was an interim increase and further bargaining was still taking place. The union replied that it would not agree and that if the company implemented the increase, the union would file an unfair labor practice charge.

The company implemented the wage increase plan on July 7.

The Union's Position

The unilateral change for wages of employees represented by the union violates Sections 8(a)(5) and 8(a)(1) of the National Labor Relations Act.

The Company's Position

A unilateral change in wages or working conditions by an employer during negotiations, in the absence of an impasse, does not per se establish a failure of the duty to bargain. In fact, the union was given ample notice of the proposed changes and there was adequate time for the union to make counterproposals.

Questions

1. You are an administrative law judge who has to decide this case. With which party do you agree? Why?
2. Does it matter that there was no impasse?

Whether a bargaining impasse exists is a matter of judgment. The bargaining history, the good faith of the parties in negotiations, the length of the negotiations, the importance of the issue or issues as to which there is disagreement, the contemporaneous understanding of the parties as to the state of negotiations are all relevant factors.[30]

Once an impasse has been reached, however, the employer can legally implement the terms of its final offer to the union.[31]

[30] *Taft Broadcasting,* 163 NLRB 475, 478 (1967).
[31] *NLRB v. Katz,* 369 U.S. 736 (1962).

Direct dealing occurs when an employer illegally tries to circumvent and undermine a union by interacting directly with the employees with respect to bargaining issues. For example, an employer cannot survey employees to gauge their support for specific bargaining proposals or striking—these are issues for employees to convey through their union at the bargaining table and an employer survey erodes the union's bargaining power.[32] This does not mean that employers cannot communicate with its employees. Noncoercive communication from the employer to the employees that simply informs the employees about the status of negotiations is acceptable, but if it undermines the union (for example by questioning the union's effectiveness), then it is illegal direct dealing and violates the employer's obligation to bargain in good faith with the union.[33]

A third example of bad faith bargaining is refusing to provide information in certain situations. Upon request, an employer has an obligation to provide information to the union that is necessary for representing the workers effectively. Examples of legitimate requests that the employer must comply with include wage information for employees, job evaluation data, standards for merit raises, the results of a local wage survey, and health and safety statistics.[34] Perhaps the most contentious information requests pertain to union requests for corporate financial data. Such information is not deemed necessary for collective bargaining, so unions are not entitled to receive it. But, if an employer states that they cannot afford one of the union's bargaining proposals, the information becomes relevant and the employer is obligated to provide it.[35] There is a fine line in these types of cases: if an employer says that it *cannot* pay, then it must back this up by providing financial data; if an employer says that it *will not* pay because of a competitive disadvantage, there is no obligation to provide any financial information.[36] Unions must also comply with employer requests for information if it is relevant, although this situation arises less frequently than union requests.[37]

The fourth and most important example of bad faith bargaining is **surface bargaining.** Surface bargaining occurs when an employer or a union appears to be going through the motions of bargaining but is not sincerely trying to reach an agreement. Rather, good faith bargaining requires that the parties must make "a serious attempt to resolve differences and reach a common ground."[38] Surface bargaining is a multifaceted concept, and in each case the NLRB looks at the specific facts and the totality of conduct, including delaying tactics, unreasonable bargaining demands, failure to designate an agent with sufficient bargaining authority, withdrawal of already agreed-upon provisions, and arbitrary scheduling of meetings.[39] A difficulty with surface bargaining is distinguishing it from "hard bargaining." Proposals for wage cuts or other concessions that are justified by competitive concerns is hard bargaining and not illegal surface bargaining. A company can use its bargaining power to achieve a favorable settlement (hard bargaining), but not to undermine the sincere pursuit of an agreement (surface bargaining).

A well-known example of bad faith bargaining is called Boulwarism, after a Vice President of General Electric in the 1960s, Lemuel Boulware. Boulware would determine

---

[32] *Harris-Teeter Super Markets,* 310 NLRB 216 (1993).

[33] *United Technologies Corp.,* 274 NLRB 1069 (1985) enfd. 789 F.2d 121 (2d Cir. 1986).

[34] Linda G. Kahn, *Primer of Labor Relations,* 25th ed. (Washington, DC: Bureau of National Affairs, 1994).

[35] *NLRB v. Truitt Mfg. Co.,* 351 U.S. 149 (1956). Kenneth G. Dau-Schmidt, "The Story of *NLRB v. Truitt Manufacturing Co.* and *NLRB v. Insurance Agents' International Union*: The Duty to Bargain in Good Faith," in Laura J. Cooper and Catherine L. Fisk (eds.), *Labor Law Stories* (New York: Foundation Press, 2005), pp. 107–48.

[36] *Lakeland Bus Lines,* 335 NLRB No. 29 (2001).

[37] Bruce S. Feldacker, *Labor Guide to Labor Law,* 4th ed. (Upper Saddle River, NJ: Prentice Hall, 2000).

[38] *NLRB v. Insurance Agent's International Union,* 361 U.S. 477, 487 (1960).

[39] *Atlanta Hilton and Tower,* 271 NLRB 1600 (1984).

General Electric's desired contract based on its financial condition and an employee survey (a form of direct dealing) and then make one "take it or leave it" offer to the unions. Refusing to make any counterproposals is not consistent with a sincere desire to reach an agreement and is one element of surface bargaining. In fact, note carefully that when Boulware made a single "take it or leave it offer," no bargaining actually took place. Boulwarism is therefore an example of bad faith bargaining.

BARGAINING POWER AND THE BARGAINING ENVIRONMENT

Many labor relations outcomes reflect differences in relative **bargaining power** between labor and management. In fact, one of the critical reasons that U.S. labor law protects workers' efforts at forming unions and engaging in collective bargaining is to balance bargaining power between a company and a group of employees. But what is bargaining power? A popular conceptualization is "the ability to secure another's agreement on one's own terms" which in turn depends on the relative costs of agreeing and disagreeing.[40] If management calculates that it is more costly to disagree to a union's proposed contract terms, and therefore endure a strike, than it is to agree to the terms, then management will accept the terms. Unions face the same calculation. Thus, the side that can impose greater disagreement costs on the other will be in a more powerful position. Strikes are the most important way for unions to impose disagreement costs on employers, so relative bargaining power is closely related to a union's strike leverage. A union with strong strike leverage can impose significant costs on management through a strike, and labor in this situation has strong bargaining power relative to the employer. The contract terms that result from this negotiation are expected to favor the employees. The reverse is true if a union has weak strike leverage.

Analyzing relative bargaining power—or strike leverage—consists of identifying the important elements of the **bargaining environment.** The bargaining environment is the diverse set of external influences on labor and management as they sit at a bargaining table negotiating a contract. The broad dimensions of the bargaining environment were introduced in Chapter 3 as part of the foundation for thinking about labor relations outcomes more generally:

- Legal
- Economic
- Technical
- Political
- Social
- Business
- Institutional

Because of the importance of the bargaining environment in understanding labor relations, these dimensions are revisited here with an explicit focus on how these dimensions affect bargaining power. You can refer back to Chapter 3 for additional details on each of the dimensions.

To illustrate the various elements of the bargaining environment, this section will primarily use the grocery industry. The concepts derived from these examples are easily extended to other industries or occupations. Think about two or three grocery stores that you

---

[40] Neil W. Chamberlain and James W. Kuhn, *Collective Bargaining,* 2nd ed. (New York: McGraw-Hill, 1965), p. 170. Terry L. Leap and David W. Grigsby, "A Conceptualization of Collective Bargaining Power," *Industrial and Labor Relations Review* 39 (January 1986), pp. 202–13.

are familiar with. Are they big or small? Old or new? Warehouse style, traditional, or up-scale? What is the demographic composition of the employees? What training do you think they receive? What types of technology do you think the employees use? All of these questions are part of the bargaining environment in this industry. The importance of these environmental pressures is illustrated by the steady decline in the union wage premium in grocery stores and the across-the-board decrease in real wage levels for both lower and higher paid workers which stem from competitive pressures, changing technologies, and other factors.[41] More generally, the grocery store industry illustrates the seven categories of the bargaining environment (see Box 8.12).

Legal

The legal dimension of the bargaining environment includes labor law as well as other laws. The previous section describes the influence of the NLRA on establishing the parameters for bargaining by mandating good faith bargaining and by defining mandatory bargaining items. Grocery unions, therefore, cannot block the introduction of new technology such as scanners because this is not a mandatory bargaining item. As an example outside of labor law, grocery store wages are anchored by the level of the minimum wage which is altered through the Fair Labor Standards Act.[42]

Economic

Within the framework established by common and/or statutory laws, the economic environment critically determines strike leverage and relative bargaining power.[43] The economic environment includes the labor market, the market for the employer's products or

BOX 8.12
The Bargaining Environment: Examples from the Grocery Industry

Dimension	Examples
1. Legal	Unions cannot block the introduction of new technologies like scanners. Grocery stores can hire replacement workers during strikes. Grocery store wages are anchored by the level of the minimum wage.
2. Economic	Grocery store employees can be easily replaced in a loose labor market. Increased grocery store competition with restaurants and discount. retailers reduces the grocery industry's ability to pass costs to consumers.
3. Technical	Technological change reduces demand for skilled meat cutters. Increased store hours increase demand for workers.
4. Political	Unions can lobby against zoning permits for discount retailers that bring increased product market competition.
5. Social	Community might support a strike if it sympathizes with the plight of part-time grocery workers.
6. Business	Grocery workers likely to have higher bargaining power when the store's business strategy emphasizes customer service rather than low costs.
7. Institutional	Many unionized grocery stores are nearly completely unionized which gives the union the power to shut down the store during a strike.

[41] John W. Budd and Brian P. McCall, "The Grocery Stores Wage Distribution: A Semi-Parametric Analysis of the Role of Retailing and Labor Market Institutions," *Industrial and Labor Relations Review* 54 (March 2001), pp. 484–501.

[42] Budd and McCall, "The Grocery Stores Wage Distribution."

[43] John R. Commons, *Industrial Goodwill* (New York: McGraw-Hill, 1919). John T. Dunlop, *Industrial Relations Systems* (New York: Holt, 1958). Thomas A. Kochan and Harry C. Katz, *Collective Bargaining and Industrial Relations: From Theory to Policy and Practice,* 2nd ed. (Homewood, IL: Irwin, 1988).

services, markets for other factors of production, and the state of the overall economy. First, consider labor demand—the strength of an employer's need for employees. The importance of the economic environment partly results from the fact that labor is a derived demand.[44] In grocery stores, for example, labor demand for clerks, butchers, and other employees stems from their role in satisfying customers' demands for food. As customer preferences change to weekend shopping or more prepared foods, the demand for labor changes accordingly.

Labor's bargaining power is greater when labor demand is less elastic, that is, when labor demand is less responsive to wage changes. Marshall's conditions state that labor demand is less elastic when (1) labor is essential or difficult to replace, (2) demand for the resulting product or service is inelastic (less responsive to price changes), (3) labor accounts for a small fraction of the entire production cost, and (4) supply of the other factors of production is inelastic.[45] These conditions capture many aspects of the economic dimension of the bargaining environment.

The importance of the labor market is captured in the first dimension of Marshall's conditions. When the labor market is tight (low unemployment), it is more difficult to hire new employees, so labor's bargaining power will be higher. On the other hand, if grocery clerks, for example, do not need special skills, they are easily replaced by new hires and will have lower bargaining power. Strike leverage that comes from perishable products is also a form of labor being difficult to replace because perishable products imply the need for immediate replacement of employees. On the other hand, weakened strike leverage because of a large inventory of non-perishable goods is a form of labor being easy to replace. For example, think of a warehouse-format grocery store that is already stocked with huge quantities of boxed and canned goods. In this case, it might not take much labor to operate during a strike. Lastly, if it is easy to substitute machines for labor, for example, by replacing grocery checkout clerks with self-service checkout stations, then labor is more easily replaced and its bargaining power is lower.

Industry ability to pay, market concentration, and the nature of product market competition are captured by Marshall's second condition. With greater demand for takeout food, grocery stores face increased competition from restaurants. This competition makes product demand for grocery stores more dependent on price and quality which in turn reduces labor's bargaining power in grocery stores. For example, a wage increase for grocery employees cannot be passed along to consumers because they have significant alternatives. In many industries, though not in grocery stores, increased globalization reduces labor's bargaining power by making product demand more elastic through increased imports and by making the supply of other factors more elastic through increased capital mobility. Increased competitive pressure, whether from globalization, domestic nonunion competitors, or deregulation is perhaps the single most important change in the bargaining environment in the postwar period.

With respect to Marshall's third condition, grocery store employees are a large fraction of total costs; thus, even a small wage increase can translate into a large increase in total costs, so labor's power is lower. There is a tension between this condition and the first one, however: a union will generally have greater bargaining power if it represents all employees because it can be harder to replace the entire workforce during a strike. Marshall's fourth condition reveals that labor demand is also related to the availability of other factors of production. If the cost of self-service checkout stands declines, then labor's bargaining power also declines. The macroeconomic environment can also affect bargaining power through Marshall's conditions. When the economy is booming, consumers have more disposable income which might make the demand for groceries less responsive to price changes (less elastic) increasing labor's bargaining power.

---

[44] Alfred Marshall, *Principles of Economics,* 8th ed. (New York: Macmillan, 1920).

[45] Marshall, *Principles of Economics.* George J. Borjas, *Labor Economics,* 3rd ed. (Boston: McGraw-Hill/Irwin, 2005).

In addition to labor *demand* factors, the economic environment also affects labor *supply,* and therefore bargaining power. While labor demand captures an employer's demand for labor, labor supply captures the willingness of individuals to offer their services as workers. When the economy is booming, it is likely to be easier for workers and/or their spouses to find another job during a strike. This source of additional income can change the worker's labor supply decision and strengthen labor's bargaining position. The extent of union strike benefits, the amount of workers' savings, and whether striking workers are eligible for unemployment insurance can also factor into labor's bargaining power.

Technical

The third dimension of the environment is the technical context which includes the nature of production, work organization, and technology.[46] In the grocery industry, the increase in store size, hours of operation, and diversity of products and services are changes in the technical context. The development of the first self-service market in 1916 reduced the number of clerks as shoppers took over the labor of handling the merchandise.[47] The introduction of self-service meat counters in the late 1930s reduced demand for butchers and was only made possible by technological advances that produced efficient refrigerated meat cases and plastic wrap.[48] Beginning in the 1970s, additional technological innovations allowed a switch to boxed beef, prepackaged chicken and pork, and most recently, to case-ready meats in which much, if not all, of the processing and packaging is done at a meatpacking plant. This significantly reduces the demand for skilled meat cutters in retail grocery stores.[49] New scanning technology has transformed cashier tasks by increasing checkout speed and has transformed ordering tasks by using scanned checkout data in automatic reordering of products.[50]

A small part of the technological change in the grocery industry might be skill-biased, meaning that it upgrades the skill requirements of technical jobs and results in greater demand for high skills (in other words, is biased in favor of skilled workers). An example is the increased need for computer programmers to integrate scanning technology with inventory systems for ordering and marketing purposes. However, most of the grocery store uses of scanning technology, refrigeration, and even plastic wrap appear to be deskilling technological changes that reduce the skills required for jobs such as meat cutters and checkout clerks. In terms of Marshall's first condition, skill-biased technological change makes skilled workers harder to replace and therefore increases their bargaining power whereas deskilling technology has the opposite effect.

Political and Social

Labor's bargaining power is enhanced by a political and social climate supportive of labor unions, and is weakened by a political and social climate that is hostile towards organized labor. In fact, for collective bargaining in the public sector, the political environment is perhaps as important as the economic environment (see Box 8.13). In the grocery industry, union leaders can lobby local political leaders to deny zoning approval for Wal-Mart and other big-box retailers to try to limit nonunion competition. On a social level, grocery workers

[46] Dunlop, *Industrial Relations Systems.*

[47] James M. Mayo, *The American Grocery Store: The Business Evolution of an Architectural Space* (Westport, CT: Greenwood Press, 1993).

[48] Mayo, *The American Grocery Store.* John P. Walsh, *Supermarkets Transformed: Understanding Organizational and Technological Innovations* (New Brunswick, NJ: Rutgers University Press, 1993).

[49] Walsh, *Supermarkets Transformed.*

[50] Jean Kinsey, Ben Senauer, Robert P. King, and Paul F. Phumpiu, *Changes in Retail Food Delivery: Signals for Producers, Processors and Distributors* (St. Paul: University of Minnesota Retail Food Industry Center, 1996).

Public Sector Labor Relations: The Bargaining Environment

Box 8.13

The seven dimensions of the bargaining environment apply equally well to the private and public sectors. The *legal* environment provides the framework for public sector labor–management interactions (Chapter 5). In the *economic* environment, Marshall's conditions describe the nature of public sector labor demand. How public services are delivered, including the role of technological change, is captured by the *technical* context. Labor-saving technology, such as single-operator garbage trucks that hydraulically lift garbage cans, puts the same pressures on public sector collective bargaining as in the private sector.[1] The factors associated with the composition and structural forms of unionism in the *institutional* context operate in similar fashion in the public sector: unions must be responsive to changing demographic trends, internal union political pressures are important, and bargaining structures are relatively decentralized.

There are two key differences between the public and private sectors, however. First, while some services can be privatized or outsourced, essential services must still be provided. Public sector management does not have the option of moving to a different location in search of lower labor costs. This places an important constraint on the *business strategies* available to public sector managers. Second, public services are not bought and sold in economic markets; instead, the levels of services are ultimately determined by voters, taxpayers, and elected officials in the political arena. This heightens the importance of both the *political* and *social* dimensions of the bargaining environment.

In fact, these differences lead some to argue that public sector collective bargaining should be prohibited because public sector unions are too powerful.[2] In the private sector, if one brand of car is too expensive, consumers can purchase competing brands. Consumers are not dependent on a single manufacturer and the threat of lost business restrains labor's demands. In the public sector, when there is only one service provider—one police department, for example—residents are dependent on this sole source of services. It is argued that this dependence makes labor—the police officers, for example—too powerful economically and politically and therefore distorts both the provision of public services and the democratic process.

An examination of Marshall's conditions suggests that labor's bargaining is often higher in the public sector than in the private sector. It is difficult, though not impossible, to replace police officers, firefighters, and even college professors with computers or machines (condition #1). Because communities cannot do without essential public services—police, firefighters, prison guards, air traffic controllers—demand for public services is often inelastic or unresponsive to price changes (condition #2). Compared to the private sector, there are fewer alternatives for consumers (residents and taxpayers). On the other hand, many public services are labor intensive which lowers labor's bargaining power (condition #3), and there is little reason to expect that the elasticity of other production factors differs between the private and public sectors (condition #4).

Compared to the private sector, the political and social dimensions of the bargaining environment are particularly important in the public sector. During collective bargaining in the public sector, the extent to which elected officials are dependent—or not—on local union endorsements and union member votes for reelection affects a union's bargaining power. Unions can also strengthen their bargaining power by convincing the public that there is a need for mutually beneficial services such as additional police officers or smaller class sizes.[3] But at the same time, it is the political and social arenas, rather than economic markets, that place restraints on labor's power. The public's limited tolerance for paying for government services are reflected through taxpayer revolts, public ballot initiatives to limit or reduce taxes, and the prominence of tax reductions as a major campaign issue in local, state, and federal elections.[4]

In sum, while labor's bargaining power is expected to be higher in the public sector than in the private sector, the evidence does not support the contention that public sector unions have unlimited bargaining power.[5] Government budgets and taxpayer willingness-to-pay are limited. Some occupations face private sector competition. And many laws forbid public employees from striking.

[1] David Lewin, "Technological Change in the Public Sector: The Case of Sanitation Service," in Daniel B. Cornfield (ed.), *Workers, Managers, and Technological Change* (New York: Plenum, 1987), pp. 281–309.

[2] Harry Wellington and Ralph K. Winter, Jr., *The Unions and the Cities* (Washington, DC: Brookings Institution, 1971).

[3] Victor G. Devinatz, "The Real Difference Between the Old Unionism and the New Unionism: A New Strategy for U.S. Public Sector Unions," *Journal of Collective Negotiations in the Public Sector* 28 (1999), pp. 29–39. Joseph E. Slater, *Public Workers: Government Employee Unions, the Law, and the State, 1900–1962* (Ithaca, NY: Cornell University Press, 2004).

[4] David Lewin, Peter Feuille, Thomas A. Kochan, and John Thomas Delaney (eds.), *Public Sector Labor Relations: Analysis and Readings,* 3rd ed. (Lexington, MA: D.C. Heath, 1988).

[5] Lewin et al., *Public Sector Labor Relations.*

will have higher bargaining power if they have the support of the community—for example, if the community sympathizes with problems of part-time workers—and they pressure the employer to treat its employees fairly. Supermarkets also reflect broader social trends. Increases in female labor force participation and ethnic diversity cause grocery stores to stay open longer and to expand to accommodate more ready-to-eat foods, a greater variety of food items, and an array of convenience items such as video rentals, banks, and pharmacies.[51] Pressures for convenience also create increased competition for grocery stores from both "home-meal replacement" outlets (such as Boston Market) and supercenters (such as Wal-Mart) in which consumers can purchase both groceries and other consumer products at a single location. These social changes affect labor's bargaining power.

Business

The grocery industry is dominated by supermarkets that are part of regional or national chains such as Kroger (2,500 stores in 2006), Albertson's (1,700 stores), Safeway (1,500 stores), and Ahold USA (800 stores) which control one-third of U.S. grocery sales.[52] Financial pressures have been intense and the industry experienced a number of leveraged buyouts in recent years. Moreover, profit margins are slim and labor costs account for a large share of operating costs. Lastly, increases in income differences between high and low income families yield two broad groups of shoppers, price-conscious and convenience-oriented.[53] There are therefore two broad business strategies in the grocery industry: price-leadership and service. Labor's bargaining power is likely to be higher in the latter relative to the former.

The Wal-Mart supercenter business model is also placing intense pressure on the grocery industry. Because of its large volume of sales, Wal-Mart can undercut prices and still be profitable. That Wal-Mart is nonunion provides another cost advantage. The expansion of Wal-Mart's grocery operations has therefore drastically altered the bargaining environment between the UFCW and the unionized grocery chains. In fact, nearly 60,000 grocery workers struck for six months in 2003 when southern California grocery chains demanded drastic health insurance concessions in *anticipation* of future Wal-Mart expansion in the region.

Institutional

The institutional dimension captures the organizational characteristics of unionism in a specific bargaining situation. The union density rate in grocery stores is about 25 percent. The primary union in the industry is the United Food and Commercial Workers (UFCW) which represents nearly 900,000 grocery industry employees and is the result of a 1979 merger between the Retail Clerks and Amalgamated Meat Cutters unions. In some stores only the meat cutters are unionized, but the UFCW generally represents an entire store. However, not all of the premerger clerks and meat cutters contracts have been combined, so some stores and UFCW local unions continue to have divisions between these two groups that can weaken their bargaining power.[54] The most important part of the institutional dimension is the bargaining structure.

BARGAINING STRUCTURE

Recall from Chapter 7 that an appropriate bargaining unit is defined during the representation process. This unit is the minimal unit for collective bargaining. Once certified, however, multiple units can be combined into a single, larger bargaining unit for the purposes of negotiating

[51] Kinsey et al., *Changes in Retail Food Delivery.*
[52] *Progressive Grocer Annual Report* (New York, 2006).
[53] Kinsey et al., *Changes in Retail Food Delivery.*
[54] Jan Kainer, "Gender, Corporate Restructuring and Concession Bargaining in Ontario's Food Retail Sector," *Relations Industrielles* 53 (Winter 1998), pp. 183–206.

a contract if the parties agree. The resulting organizational structure for the collective bargaining process is called the **bargaining structure** and ranges between decentralized and centralized structures. A very decentralized bargaining structure involves a limited group of employees in a single workplace: for example, meat cutters in a single grocery store or school bus drivers in a single school district. At the other end of the range, a very centralized bargaining structure involves numerous occupations, locations, and companies. In the late 1960s, 26 unions representing 60,000 workers at 73 U.S. and Canadian locations in the copper industry—including mining, manufacturing, and refining operations—tried unsuccessfully to pursue very broad industrywide bargaining in which the unions would bargain as a single coalition with an employer's association representing the copper industry.[55] A more typical example of industrywide bargaining occurred between the basic steel manufacturers and the United Steelworkers union between the 1950s and 1980s.[56]

The conventional wisdom is that in many (but not all) situations, employers prefer decentralized bargaining structures in order to have local unions compete against one another for jobs (this is called "whipsawing") and to tailor contracts to local situations. Unions are generally believed to prefer more centralized structures because they can consolidate their power and prevent whipsawing by negotiating uniform contracts (this is called "taking wages out of competition"). Compared to many other countries (Chapter 13), the bargaining structure in the United States is typically decentralized. Before competitive pressures intensified in the 1970s, less than 15 percent of union contracts in manufacturing covered more than one employer and the most common bargaining structure consisted of multiple sites within a single company, but less than completely firmwide.[57] Since that time, the bargaining structure in the United States (and in many other countries) has become more decentralized.[58] Industrywide arrangements such as in basic steel have broken apart into company-by-company negotiations, and in previously firmcentered negotiations, plant-level variation has become more important. The leading explanations for this trend appear to be that employers have been able to use their greater bargaining leverage to force more decentralization and also that both firms and workers like the flexibility and opportunities for employee involvement in decision making allowed by decentralized bargaining structures (see Chapter 11).

Another aspect of the bargaining structure is **pattern bargaining.** For example, the United Auto Workers (UAW) explicitly selects either Ford, General Motors, or Chrysler as the target company for its auto industry contract negotiations every three years. The union then bargains exclusively with that target company until an agreement is reached. That target settlement is then used by the union as the pattern for subsequent negotiations in the auto industry and other manufacturing industries.[59] Note that this sequential bargaining process is an informal way of achieving a more centralized bargaining structure—unions are negotiating with one company at a time, but the contracts that follow the pattern all end up being quite similar (though not identical). Before the 1980s, pattern bargaining was a

---

[55] Jonathan D. Rosenblum, *Copper Crucible: How the Arizona Miners' Strike of 1983 Recast Labor–Management Relations in America* (Ithaca, NY: ILR Press, 1995).

[56] John P. Hoerr, *And the Wolf Finally Came: The Decline of the American Steel Industry* (Pittsburgh: University of Pittsburgh, 1988). Garth L. Mangum and R. Scott McNabb, *The Rise, Fall, and Replacement of Industrywide Bargaining in the Basic Steel Industry* (Armonk, NY: M. E. Sharpe, 1997).

[57] Wallace E. Hendricks and Lawrence M. Kahn, "The Determinants of Bargaining Structure in U.S. Manufacturing Industries," *Industrial and Labor Relations Review* 35 (January 1982), pp. 181–95.

[58] Harry C. Katz, "The Decentralization of Collective Bargaining: A Literature Review and Comparative Analysis," *Industrial and Labor Relations Review* 47 (October 1993), pp. 3–22.

[59] John W. Budd, "The Determinants and Extent of UAW Pattern Bargaining," *Industrial and Labor Relations Review* 45 (April 1992), pp. 523–39. Christopher L. Erickson, "A Re-Interpretation of Pattern Bargaining," *Industrial and Labor Relations Review* 49 (July 1996), pp. 615–34.

prominent feature of collective bargaining in many industries.[60] Consistent with the broad trend towards decentralization, pattern bargaining appears to have weakened since 1980, but has not disappeared.[61] In 1991 striking workers at Caterpillar rode a John Deere tractor on the picket line to emphasize the demand on their picket signs: "Wanted: John Deere Contract."[62] Both companies make heavy construction equipment. Pattern bargaining can help unions take wages out of competition, but there are also intraorganizational bargaining reasons: within the UAW, for example, internal union political pressures stemming from rank and file comparisons of different contracts cause negotiators to pattern contracts after each other, even across different industries.[63] Graphical representations of four major examples of the bargaining structure are presented in Box 8.14.

The tension inherent within different choices of the bargaining structure is power versus responsiveness. Decentralized bargaining can be more responsive to local needs—the issues

BOX 8.14
Bargaining Structures

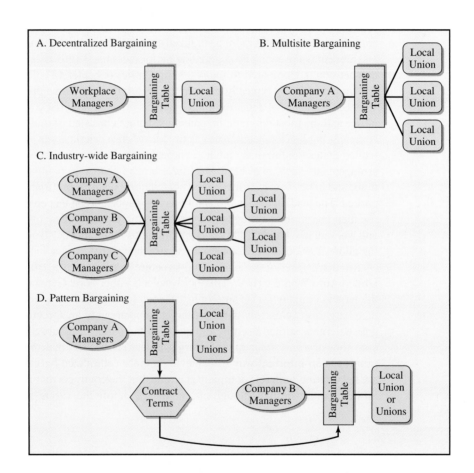

[60] Trevor Bain, "Flat Glass: Industrial Peace Revisited," *Industrial Relations* 8 (May 1969), pp. 259–68. George Seltzer, "Pattern Bargaining and the United Steelworkers," *Journal of Political Economy* 59 (August 1951), pp. 319–31.

[61] Budd, "The Determinants and Extent of UAW Pattern Bargaining." John W. Budd, "Institutional and Market Determinants of Wage Spillovers: Evidence from UAW Pattern Bargaining," *Industrial Relations* 36 (January 1997), pp. 97–116.

[62] Kevin Kelly, "CAT May Be Trying to Bulldoze the Immovable," *BusinessWeek* (December 2, 1991), p. 116.

[63] John W. Budd, "The Internal Union Political Imperative for UAW Pattern Bargaining," *Journal of Labor Research* 16 (Winter 1995), pp. 43–55.

are often more homogeneous and the negotiators are close to their constituents. But decentralized bargaining can be weak for labor. If a union is negotiating only for meat cutters in a single grocery store, the union likely has little strike leverage because management can weather the strike simply by replacing the small number of meat cutters and by continuing to earn profits at other grocery stores owned by the same company. Compare this weak strike leverage to the more common grocery store bargaining structures in which the UFCW negotiates a single contract for all grocery stores in a metropolitan area or for all stores in a single chain. In the former case, it is more difficult to hire replacement workers because of the number of positions that need to be filled while, in the latter scenario, a company in which all locations are shut down by a strike loses all sources of revenue. However, as negotiations become more centralized, the issues become more heterogeneous and the negotiators become farther removed from their constituents—on both the labor and management sides. The current trend is towards greater decentralization, in the United States and elsewhere, to be more responsive and flexible to local needs (for both workers and companies), but this is not without its costs and critics because of lost bargaining power for labor.

BARGAINING IN PRACTICE: CONTINUITY AND CHANGE

The previous sections outline the subprocesses of collective bargaining and their strategies, the legal parameters of the bargaining process, the determinants of bargaining power, and alternative bargaining structures. But how does bargaining play out in practice? A timeline of the negotiation process is shown in Box 8.15. A critical foundation for successful bargaining—collective and otherwise—is preparation. Since collective bargaining involves numerous, complex issues and the outcomes are very important to a wide range of stakeholders, preparation usually begins at least several months before bargaining begins. Preparation for particularly large, complex, or pattern-setting contracts might begin 18 months before the start of negotiations.[64] The management structure typically determines the responsibility for bargaining on the employer's side whereas union bargaining committees are usually elected by the rank and file. A national union staff representative might assist or lead the negotiations for the union.

Before face-to-face negotiations begin, each side should determine five things at a minimum: their interests (what they are really concerned about), options, legitimacy ("external standards or precedents that might convince [the parties] that a proposed agreement is fair"), the other side's interests, and their best alternative to a negotiated agreement (BATNA).[65] Because of the complexity of labor negotiations, these five items involve a lot of work. Determining the employer's interests requires reviewing the experiences under the current contract (were there a number of grievances from one part of the contract, for example), collecting external benchmarking data, and determining the strategic direction of the corporation. On the union side, interest identification often begins with input from the rank and file (such as through a survey) and also includes input from the national union. From these data collection efforts, both bargaining teams develop options, priorities, and strategies. Extensive checklists for both employer and union negotiators are available to help guide preparation activities.[66]

Sixty days before the existing contract expires, or 90 days in the health care industry, the parties provide official notification to each other and to the Federal Mediation and Conciliation Service that they intend to negotiate a new contract. The bargaining teams then establish

[64] Charles S. Loughran, *Negotiating a Labor Contract: A Management Handbook*, 3rd ed. (Washington, DC: Bureau of National Affairs, 2003).

[65] Roger Fisher and Danny Ertel, *Getting Ready to Negotiate: The Getting to YES Workbook* (New York: Penguin Books, 1995), p. 11.

[66] Better, *Contract Bargaining Handbook for Local Union Leaders.* Loughran, *Negotiating a Labor Contract.*

BOX 8.15
The Bargaining Timeline

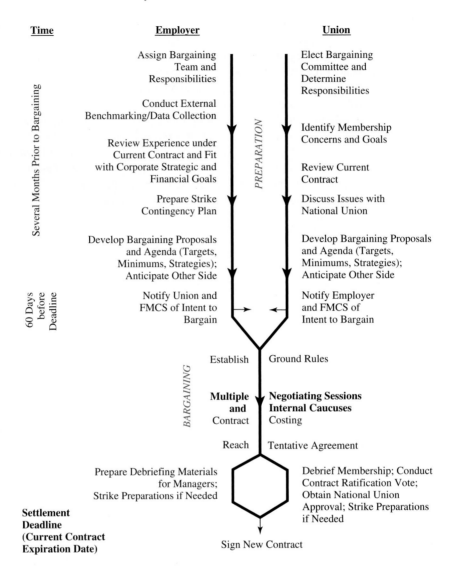

a schedule of bargaining sessions and establish ground rules. If the parties intend to use an integrative bargaining approach, a joint training session might also be completed at this time. It is traditional that the side that wants to make changes in the contract initially makes the opening proposals. When the company is healthy, unions present initial demands for improvements in wages, benefits, and work rules; when the company is struggling, employers open with demands for concessions in wages, benefits, and work rules. Negotiations then continue on the front stage and the back stage (recall Box 8.7) using distributive and/or integrative bargaining strategies and tactics. An important tool for evaluating proposals is contract costing—estimating the monetary costs of a specific contract provision (see Box 8.16).[67] Another common tool for negotiators is a bargaining book.[68] Each side uses three-ring binders to create a complete record of the negotiation including their agenda, proposals, supporting documents, proposals and materials received from the other side, and the minutes of each bargaining session.

[67] Michael H. Granoff, *How to Cost Your Labor Contract* (Washington, DC: Bureau of National Affairs, 1973).
[68] Better, *Contract Bargaining Handbook for Local Union Leaders.* Loughran, *Negotiating a Labor Contract.*

Contract Costing Example

Box 8.16

Contract Change All workers with at least five years of seniority will receive an extra week of paid vacation annually.

Costing this Change

200 workers × 5 days × 8 hours × $10.00 per hour ×
    (1)   (2)   (3)   (4)

 1.5 per hour = $120,000 per year
   (5)

1. Number of workers affected. There are currently 200 employees with at least five years of seniority, so assume 200.
2. Each worker gets five extra days of vacation per year with this contract change.
3. Standard working day is eight hours.
4. Need to replace each vacationing worker with another employee. Assume that the average hourly wage for all employees in the bargaining unit is $10 per hour.
5. Overtime premium. When existing employees work extra to take the places of vacationing employees, they are working overtime and receive time and a half.

Note that this is just an estimate and some complicating factors are ignored:

1. Turnover reduces the number of affected workers. But workers with four years of seniority this year will be eligible next year, workers with three will be eligible in two years, etc.
2. Some workers might not take all of their extra vacation days.
3. Some workers might not need to be replaced for an entire eight hours.
4. Since extra vacation is for workers with more seniority, they might need to be replaced with workers with higher seniority in which case the hourly wage for the replacements would be higher than the overall average of $10 per hour.
5. If there are extra workers or business is slow, the extra hours might not be overtime.

Also, if extra vacation increases morale and reduces turnover, the costs of this change can be offset by lower turnover costs (which includes the costs of recruitment, training, and lost productivity).

If successful, negotiations conclude with a tentative agreement. Union negotiators in particular must obtain formal approval before the settlement becomes official. Typically the approval process focuses on a contract ratification vote by the rank and file, though some union constitutions provide for approval by an elected executive committee. Some unions might also require the approval of the national union headquarters. Before a ratification vote, unions will usually have a membership meeting in which the terms of the agreement are presented to the rank and file and intraorganizational bargaining occurs as the leaders try to convince the members that the agreement is a good one. Union members then have the final say when they vote whether or not to accept the agreement.

On the employer side, management negotiators typically have the authority to agree to a final settlement and intraorganizational bargaining takes place prior to the final agreement. However, if the union is told in advance, it is legal for management negotiators to agree to a tentative settlement subject to upper management approval.[69] In this case, management negotiators may have to sell the agreement to their bosses just as the union negotiators must sell it to the rank and file. In collective bargaining, "it takes three agreements to achieve one agreement—that is, an agreement within each party as well as one across the table."[70] If the contract is not ratified or approved, the negotiators can continue negotiating or a strike may occur (Chapter 9). Once a contract settlement is approved, it is signed by the employer and the union and it is binding on both parties for the length specified in the contract (often three years).

[69] *Mid-Wilshire Health Care Center,* 337 NLRB No. 7 (2001).

[70] John T. Dunlop, *Dispute Resolution: Negotiation and Consensus Building* (Dover, MA: Auburn House Publishing, 1984), p. 10.

The process of collective bargaining in the public sector is usually similar to that in the private sector, but with a few additional complexities. Some states have sunshine laws that require public sector negotiations to take place in the public (that is, out in the sunshine).[71] More significantly, the management structures of public sector agencies are not as hierarchical as in the private sector and often a collection of elected officials and professional managers share or compete for decision-making authority.[72] And special interest groups, voters, and taxpayers might also try to have a strong voice in public decisions. Collective bargaining in the public sector is therefore sometimes characterized by **multilateral bargaining**—negotiations between more than two parties. Consider negotiations in a school district for a contract covering teachers. Important groups in these negotiations can include the teachers' union, the school superintendent, an elected school board, a parents organization like the PTA, taxpayers groups, and a state board of education. Even if only the first two are sitting at the bargaining table proper, the other groups can be vocal in trying to influence negotiations.

Multilateral bargaining also raises the possibility of an end run. Unions can appeal directly to these other groups for support who in turn can pressure the management officials at the bargaining table. For example, suppose the police union helped campaign for the city mayor during the last election. During negotiations for a new contract for police officers, the union can ask the mayor for support in the hope that the mayor will pressure the city's negotiating team to settle on terms favorable to the police officers. As such, the union makes an end run around the city's negotiators. As another form of an end run, unions can also improve the results of their bargaining by lobbying. By selling the public on the need for services such as additional firefighters or smaller class sizes, unions can increase the size of public sector budgets and thereby increase both compensation and employment.[73] Or in the opposite direction, some police unions have been able to roll back unfavorable local policies such as mandatory name tags by lobbying the legislature to enact laws outlawing such policies.[74]

In both the private and public sectors collective bargaining has traditionally been adversarial yet professional. But with the more challenging competitive environment that started in the late 1970s, collective bargaining has become increasingly divergent. On the one hand, a number of employers have tried to tackle labor cost issues through a forcing strategy: aggressive distributive bargaining tactics to force weakened labor unions to grant significant wage, benefit, and work rule concessions.[75] In fact, concession bargaining has been a prominent feature of the labor relations landscape in many industries since the 1980s. The most aggressive forcing strategies have often involved strikes and the use of replacement workers to take the place of striking workers (Chapter 9).[76] Unsurprisingly,

[71] Richard C. Kearney, *Labor Relations in the Public Sector*, 2nd ed. (New York: Marcel Dekker, 1992).

[72] Milton Derber, "Management Organization for Collective Bargaining in the Public Sector," in Benjamin Aaron, Joyce M. Najita, and James L. Stern (eds.), *Public-Sector Bargaining*, 2nd ed. (Washington, DC: Bureau of National Affairs, 1988), Chapter 3. Hervey A. Juris and Peter Feuille, *Police Unionism: Power and Impact in Public-Sector Bargaining* (Lexington, MA: Lexington Books, 1973). Thomas A. Kochan, "A Theory of Multilateral Bargaining in City Governments," *Industrial and Labor Relations Review* 27 (July 1974), pp. 525–42.

[73] Victor G. Devinatz, "The Real Difference Between the Old Unionism and the New Unionism: A New Strategy for U.S. Public Sector Unions," *Journal of Collective Negotiations in the Public Sector* 28 (1999), pp. 29–39. Jeffrey Zax and Casey Ichniowski, "The Effects of Public Sector Unionism on Pay, Employment, Department Budgets, and Municipal Expenditures," in Richard B. Freeman and Casey Ichniowski (eds.), *When Public Sector Workers Unionize* (Chicago: University of Chicago Press, 1988), Chapter 12.

[74] Juris and Feuille, *Police Unionism*.

[75] Walton, Cutcher-Gershenfeld, and McKersie, *Strategic Negotiations*.

[76] Julius Getman, *The Betrayal of Local 14* (Ithaca, NY: ILR Press, 1998). Dave Hage and Paul Klauda, *No Retreat, No Surrender: Labor's War at Hormel* (New York: William Morrow, 1989). Rosenblum, *Copper Crucible*. Walton, Cutcher-Gershenfeld, and McKersie, *Strategic Negotiations*.

many of these situations also witnessed an escalation in conflict that risked violence, continued distrust, and unanticipated costs to the employer.[77]

In contrast, other bargaining pairs have tried to develop a more cooperative relationship through attitudinal structuring. Attempts to change the bargaining relationship between an employer and union from adversarial to integrative highlight important issues of change management and leadership for both corporate and labor leaders. Negotiators often express frustration with both the personal costs—stressful, marathon negotiating sessions that include threats, bluffs, and perhaps personal attacks—and the organizational costs—limited participation except by chief negotiators and eleventh-hour settlements narrowly averting work stoppages—of adversarial bargaining sessions. Moreover, traditional bargaining sessions often reflect and contribute to an overall adversarial climate that pervades the entire labor–management relationship. Such a stereotypical, traditional relationship might include a culture of conflict, defensiveness, and entrenchment. There is little trust between the parties, and communication is limited to formal negotiating sessions every three years in which all of the problems of the last three years are aired. As such, attempts to move away from an adversarial bargaining relationship are often intimately related to broader desires to change the entire labor relations climate.

But such changes often run into sharp resistance. Resistance to many types of organizational changes often stem from inertia, self-interest, peer pressure, misunderstanding, and other reasons; these same elements underlie resistance to changing a bargaining relationship from adversarial to more integrative (see Box 8.17). Strong traditions of adversarial bargaining (inertia) combined with suspicions about the other side's motive for change (self-interest) and leadership fears of appearing weak or of "selling out" (misunderstanding and peer pressure) are particularly important when labor and management negotiators try to change the tenor of the bargaining relationship. Joint training programs to overcome resistance are therefore important.[78] Such programs can help address misperceptions of integrative bargaining, can involve negotiators from both sides to reduce the impression that a change is serving one side's hidden agenda, and can develop the participants' skills so that they are comfortable with the process. Training programs can also dispel the simplistic illusion of a choice between distributive *or* integrative bargaining. If the employment relationship is characterized by mixed motive conflict, then a combination of distributive and integrative bargaining in collective bargaining is best. Survey evidence shows that more than half of management and union negotiators have used integrative bargaining principles, but negotiators differ on how they rate traditional and integrative approaches— management negotiators rate the integrative approach higher than the traditional approach whereas union negotiators express the opposite ratings.[79]

This chapter mostly focuses on what might be called "institutional bargaining"— bargaining between unions and corporations or public sector organizations. This institutional bargaining is focused on the formal, periodic negotiation of a collective bargaining agreement. However, there is a very important second level of negotiations— daily contests between workers and managers over working conditions, performance expectations, and the like. This has been called fractional bargaining, but a more intuitive label is perhaps "employee bargaining."[80] Employee bargaining might take place

[77] Walton, Cutcher-Gershenfeld, and McKersie, *Strategic Negotiations.*

[78] Joel Cutcher-Gershenfeld, "Bargaining Over How to Bargain in Labor–Management Negotiations," *Negotiation Journal* 10 (October 1994), pp. 323–35.

[79] Joel Cutcher-Gershenfeld and Thomas Kochan, "Taking Stock: Collective Bargaining at the Turn of the Century," *Industrial and Labor Relations Review* 58 (October 2004), pp. 3–26.

[80] James W. Kuhn, *Bargaining and Grievance Settlements* (New York: Columbia University Press, 1962).

BOX 8.17

Resistance to Changing Bargaining Relationships from Adversarial to Integrative

Source: Column 1 is adapted from Thomas S. Bateman and Scott A. Snell, *Management: Competing in the New Era,* 5th ed. (Boston: McGraw-Hill/Irwin, 2002).

Resistance to Change Factors	Application to Labor Negotiations
General Reasons for Resistance to Change	
Inertia Difficult to try something new.	Strong tradition of adversarial negotiations in labor relations.
Timing Not a good time to try something new.	Difficult to change style or form in the middle of negotiations.
Surprise Sudden and unexpected occurrences can cause a negative reaction.	Management or labor might unilaterally develop a new approach and propose it to the other side without warning.
Peer Pressure Group norms might sharpen resistance to change.	Strong antiunion or antimanagement group sentiment can reinforce suspicions about the other side's motives for change.
Change-Specific Reasons for Resistance to Change	
Self-Interest A specific change might be harmful to a certain person or group.	The more powerful side might see a different bargaining style as weakening their position.
Misunderstanding Incomplete or false information about a proposed change might cause resistance.	Some view integrative bargaining methods as giving up power and selling out.
Different Assessments Different people might value elements of a change differently.	Management emphasis on efficiency; labor emphasis on equity and voice.

through the grievance procedure (Chapter 10), but it might also occur informally between individual workers and supervisors, and it is also an important element of quality circles, work teams, and other initiatives to involve workers in workplace decision making (Chapter 11). Many of the concepts presented in this chapter are equally instructive for employee bargaining: distributive versus integrative bargaining strategies, the importance of BATNA and the environment, and the need for careful preparation as the foundation for negotiating success.

Bargaining between unions and employers is one of the important processes of U.S. labor relations. Collective bargaining can serve efficiency, equity, and voice: efficiency is served by having the employers' interests represented at the bargaining table, equity can be achieved by harnessing the employees' collective strength to balance the employers' power and produce fair outcomes, and voice is fulfilled by having the terms and conditions of employment negotiated rather than unilaterally imposed by someone else. This is almost always operationalized in U.S. collective bargaining through written union contracts. The content and the resolution of disputes that arise under the terms of these contracts are the subjects of Chapter 10. But first, the next chapter discusses what happens if bargaining fails.

Key Terms	mixed motive conflict, *270* distributive bargaining, *271* integrative bargaining,*273* attitudinal structuring, *276* intraorganizational bargaining, *278* mandatory bargaining	item, *281* permissive bargaining item, *281* unilateral change, *282* direct dealing, *284* surface bargaining, *284* bargaining power, *285*	bargaining environment, *285* bargaining structure, *291* pattern bargaining, *291* multilateral bargaining, *296*

Reflection Questions

1. In a concise paragraph, paraphrase what you have learned about bargaining strategies to inform a friend about the options for negotiating his/her starting salary and other items for a new job.

2. Distributive bargaining is sometimes referred to as win–lose bargaining. Where does this label come from? How can it be misleading? Also, some people casually characterize any negotiated settlement as a win–win. Why is this accurate in layperson's terms but inaccurate in terms of how academics use the term "win–win"?

3. Choose one of the *HR Strategy* scenarios from Chapter 7 (Box 7.18) and assume that the union wins recognition. As an HR manager, how would you prepare for negotiations? What type of information would be important for you? What type of bargaining priorities and strategies would you develop? How would your answers change if you represented the union rather than management?

4. Use the three fictitious newspaper articles in Box 8.18 to analyze the bargaining environment for contract negotiations between copper producer Phelps Dodge and Morenci Miners Local 616. Create a traditional outline or a Mind Map (a radial outline) for one of the years. Use the seven major dimensions of the bargaining environment as your major categories. Note that the newspaper articles are based on fact, but have been embellished for educational use.

Internet Exploration

1. Search the Internet for descriptions of integrative bargaining in practice (for example, search for "teachers and interest-based bargaining," or some other occupation). What types of benefits are described? Are the areas of resistance consistent with Box 8.17?

2. Go to the NLRB website (*www.nlrb.gov*), find the section that contains NLRB decisions, and go to the search page. Search for "surface bargaining." What types of negotiator behaviors were ruled to be surface bargaining? What behaviors were acceptable as fulfilling the good faith bargaining standard?

3. Some unions use the Internet to publicize their bargaining goals and to keep their members informed about the status of negotiations. An extensive example is *www.geworkersunited.org.* You can find other sites by using the search term "bargaining update." What types of issues are emphasized on these sites? What issues seem common across different unions? What issues are specific to certain occupations? Do the sites suggest a more adversarial or cooperative bargaining relationship?

Additional Reading

Better, Maurice B., *Contract Bargaining Handbook for Local Union Leaders* (Washington, DC: Bureau of National Affairs, 1993).

Clark, Paul F., John T. Delaney, and Ann C. Frost (eds.), *Collective Bargaining in the Private Sector* (Champaign, IL: Industrial Relations Research Association, 2002).

Fisher, Roger, William Ury, and Bruce Patton, *Getting to YES: Negotiating Agreement Without Giving In,* 2nd ed. (New York: Penguin Books, 1991).

Friedman, Raymond A., *Front Stage, Backstage: The Dramatic Structure of Labor Negotiations* (Cambridge, MA: MIT Press, 1994).

Lewicki, Roy J., David M. Saunders, and Bruce Barry, *Negotiation,* 5th ed. (Boston: McGraw-Hill/Irwin, 2006).

Loughran, Charles S., *Negotiating a Labor Contract: A Management Handbook*, 3rd ed. (Washington, DC: Bureau of National Affairs, 2003).

Walton, Richard E., Joel E. Cutcher-Gershenfeld, and Robert B. McKersie, *Strategic Negotiations: A Theory of Change in Labor–Management Relations* (Boston: Harvard Business School Press, 1994).

Walton, Richard E. and Robert B. McKersie, *A Behavioral Theory of Labor Negotiations* (New York: McGraw-Hill, 1965).

BOX 8.18

Three Fictitious Newspaper Articles to Accompany Reflection Question No. 3

From the *Copper Era* (Clifton, Arizona):

PD, Miners Set to Bargain ... Again
Copper Prices Up; Local Union Confident

MORENCI, AZ; November 14, 1954. The rhetoric is heating up again in Clifton and Morenci as Mine-Mill local 616 prepares to negotiate a new collective bargaining agreement with Phelps Dodge. The Morenci Miners Local 616 represents 2,000 open-pit mine laborers and mill and smelter production workers. The major issues this year appear to be medical coverage and the length of the agreement. Collective bargaining agreements between Morenci Miners Local 616 and Phelps Dodge have been one-year agreements since the first contract was signed after a 107-day strike in 1946. This year, the International Union of Mine, Mill, and Smelter Workers has been pushing for three year contracts for its 100,000 members nationally. The local union enters negotiations confidently. "The miners know how important the union is" says longtime Local 616 president David Velasquez.

The copper industry continues to benefit from several economic trends and forces. Automobiles and housing construction are two primary consumers of copper and the postwar boom in both industries continues to push copper prices higher. Pending legislation to create a federally funded interstate highway network would probably continue strong automobile demand, experts contend. Adding to demand in recent years was the Korean conflict. Phelps Dodge, the third largest domestic copper producer, has consequently realized an average return on its investment of close to 20 percent while the other copper producers' returns have been between 8 and 16 percent.

Nationally, aggregate union ranks continue to swell with more and more members each year, but the Mine-Mill negotiations are set against a backdrop of union rivalry and competition.

While the 1952 deaths of AFL leader William Green and CIO leader Phillip Murray have reduced the fiery nature of the public feud between the two federations, and a no-raid agreement is rumored to be close to finalizing, there is still a long history of bitter divisions between the craft and industrial unions at Phelps Dodge. Morenci Miners Local 616 is one of 13 unions at the Morenci mine and the primarily Mexican-American miners local continues to be ostracized from the predominately white craft unions.

Adding to the inter-union conflict is the Mine-Mill's national leadership's Communist party sympathies. Mine-Mill and several other unions were expelled from the CIO in 1950 and the Steelworkers and Auto Workers unions have been trying to raid Mine-Mill locals ever since. A section of the Taft-Hartley Act has been used to deny Mine-Mill the protections of the National Labor Relations Board and the recently passed Communist Control Act opens up the national Mine-Mill leadership to criminal prosecution.

A planned union rally in Clifton was cut short by the arrival of the first television set in Clifton. Ironically, the first program broadcast was the trial of three leaders of the Farm Equipment Workers Union for alleged Communist activities. These trials are part of the ongoing investigations spearheaded by Senator Joseph McCarthy (R–WI). The mood could only have been more somber if the McClellan Committee hearings investigating union corruption had also been broadcast, but the Ed Sullivan Show followed the McCarthy hearing. Phelps Dodge continues to ban television sets in the company town of Morenci.

BOX 8.18
Continued

From the *Arizona Tribune* (Phoenix, Arizona):

USW-led Coalition to Bargain in Copper
Industrywide Strike Feared with New Bargaining Structure

SALT LAKE CITY, UT; March 16, 1967. Twenty-six unions have been meeting this week to hammer out plans for negotiating as a coalition against the copper industry when the major union contracts expire this summer. The coalition has been named the "Non-Ferrous Industry Conference" (NIC) and is being led by the United Steelworkers of America (USW), with significant assistance from the AFL–CIO's Industrial Union Department (IUD). Tomorrow the coalition members will vote on the NIC's bargaining goals, a 38-page booklet some have dubbed "Heaven in '67."

The coalition's main goal, however, is no secret: industrywide uniformity in collective bargaining agreements covering the Big Four copper companies' mining, manufacturing, and refining operations in the United States and Canada covering over 60,000 workers at 73 locations. A USW spokesperson said the two primary objectives are companywide master agreements and simultaneous expiration dates across the industry. This outcome would be a drastic departure from traditional copper bargaining. For example, in previous negotiations at Phelps Dodge, the second largest domestic copper producer with 15,000 employees nationally, management has agreed to similar contracts for its four Arizona mining properties, including milling and smelting operations, but separate negotiations have always been the rule for its refinery and fabrication operations located throughout the United States.

The 26 unions participating in the NIC are quite diverse and observers of the labor movement are watching with keen interest to see if the alliance holds. The diversity stems from copper's history of decentralized bargaining and representation. The USW primarily represents unskilled mine employees and mill and smelter production employees. The Operating Engineers represent power shovel operators, the Teamsters and various railroad craft unions represent workers who haul mined ore to mills, and numerous craft unions represent mill and smelter maintenance workers. The Auto Workers and other industrial unions represent myriad workers in copper refining and fabrication.

To explain the existing union solidarity in the NIC, experts point to 12 years of a united AFL–CIO and perhaps more importantly, to the recently finalized USW merger plans with the Mine, Mill, and Smelter Workers, or Mine-Mill. Mine-Mill has been plagued by Communist influences for two decades. The USW has been trying to raid Mine-Mill locals around the country for 15 years, but very rarely with success. Last year, a Supreme Court ruling reversed convictions against Mine-Mill leaders for allegedly lying on anticommunist oaths and in January, 40,000 Mine-Mill workers agreed to join the million member USW. A majority of workers in copper now belong to the USW and it comes as no surprise that the USW is leading the NIC. According to conference participants, Joseph Molony, a USW vice president, is likely to be named chief negotiator for the NIC. Some of the other 25 unions, however, are nervous that USW attention will be diverted once steel negotiations begin. Steel contracts expire next summer.

The Johnson administration has publicly declined comment; insiders say that Defense Secretary Clark Clifford and Treasury Secretary Henry Fowler will be kept apprised of developments at the bargaining table when talks begin next month. Armed conflict in Vietnam continues to increase and labor experts are certain that any strike would be on an industrywide basis. "The IUD appears determined to bring stability to copper bargaining via industrywide bargaining–a stance likely to require an industrywide strike," says Jim Scoville, assistant professor of economics at Harvard University. Such a strike, sources say, could have negative implications for the war effort and for the country's balance of payments. The Taft-Hartley Act gives the president powers to force an 80-day cooling-off period for national emergency strikes, but no one knows whether Johnson would invoke these powers if there was an industrywide strike.

Coincidentally, governors from five western states have been meeting in Phoenix this week to discuss matters of mutual concern. The governors unanimously endorsed a statement calling for productive negotiations between the unions and the copper industry. The Arizona governor is particularly apprehensive due to copper's importance to the state economy. Roughly 60 percent of U.S. copper comes from Arizona and 10 percent of earnings in Arizona comes from copper employment.

Copper prices have been rising for most of the decade, but industry analysts caution that new deposits of copper have recently been discovered in Africa and South America. Currently, imports amount to 5 percent of U.S. consumption. The Big Four copper companies targeted by the NIC account for nearly 90 percent of all U.S. copper mining, smelting, and refining. The Big Four are all engaged primarily in the nonferrous metals industry with little diversification. Phelps Dodge, in particular, is known for being self-financing and rarely borrows capital on the open market. An IUD spokesperson estimates that military-related U.S. copper consumption will amount to 600 million pounds in 1967, or enough to build more than 15 million cars. Sources at the Pentagon say that the government is considering a 10 percent "set aside" of all U.S. copper production for defense purposes. Several professors call this proposal "previously unheard of."

BOX 8.18
Continued

From the *New York Journal* (New York, New York):
Phelps Dodge, Copper Unions Open Talks
1982 Losses, Kennecott Settlement Seen as Complicating Factors

NEW YORK, NY; May 4, 1983. Negotiations over new collective bargaining agreements between copper producer Phelps Dodge and 13 unions began today in Phoenix. Phelps Dodge lost $74 million in 1982 as the worst recession since the 1930s shut down automobile factories and new construction—copper's biggest customers. Industry analysts disagree about whether copper prices will rebound any time soon. While negotiators refused comment, Phelps Dodge is reportedly seeking $2 per hour wage cuts, an end to cost-of-living adjustments (COLA), and benefits reductions. Industry leader and SOHIO subsidiary Kennecott, however, surprised the industry last month by agreeing to a new contract containing only minor benefits concessions. The Kennecott settlement, which preserves wage rates and the COLA clause, "dropped a bombshell on the industry" says George Hildebrand, a labor relations expert at Cornell University.

The 13 unions have joined forces as the "Unity Council" and are jointly negotiating contracts covering 2000 workers at Phelps Dodge's remote Arizona properties in Morenci, Ajo, Douglas, and Bisbee. Union contracts for Phelps Dodge's Tyrone, New Mexico mine, mill, and smelter complex expire next year. The Unity Council dates back to 1967 when the unions' attempt to impose industrywide contracts failed. Since that time, the copper unions have followed a practice known as pattern bargaining in which the first settlement in each bargaining round sets the pattern for subsequent negotiations. Consequently, settlements every three years at Phelps Dodge have followed the pattern set at Kennecott or Anaconda, but only after a strike each time. In the last bargaining round, Phelps Dodge withstood a 90-day strike before conceding to the unions' demands. Pattern bargaining and COLAs yielded an annual wage increase of roughly 15 percent in the 1970s according to Phelps Dodge.

In spite of these successes in the 1970s, observers argue that these are tough times for organized labor. President Reagan is widely believed to be unsympathetic, if not openly hostile, toward labor unions as illustrated by his appointments to the National Labor Relations Board and the firing of the air traffic controllers in 1981. Unions represent a smaller fraction of the workforce than at any other time since World War II and "employers are trying to bust unions like never before" says an AFL–CIO spokesperson. Organized labor has also criticized the Reagan administration's inflation-fighting tight monetary policy and the increased taxation of unemployment insurance benefits.

Labor is also fearful of a Supreme Court decision in *Belknap* v. *Hale*, which is expected some time this summer. A Kentucky court of appeals ruled that an employer who told new employees who were replacing striking workers that they were "permanent" could not discharge the replacements to make room for returning strikers without committing a breach of contract. Labor worries that the Supreme Court will affirm this ruling. Management has had the right to replace striking workers during a labor dispute since the 1938 *Mackay* ruling.

The copper industry has its own worries. Copper imports now account for over 20 percent of domestic consumption—and much of the imported copper is from state-owned mines in places like Chile and Zambia. Even after last month's modest copper price increase to 70¢ per pound, Phelps Dodge loses 10¢ on every pound of copper it produces. In addition to Phelps Dodge's $74 million loss for 1982, Anaconda lost $332 million, Kennecott $189 million, and ASARCO $38 million. According to industry insiders, however, Phelps Dodge is very close to introducing a new solvent extraction-electrowinning process which drastically reduces production costs, eliminates the need for smelting, and makes it cost-effective to extract copper from low-grade ore previously considered waste. Phelps Dodge's Douglas smelter employs 300 people and is the nation's largest polluter of sulfur dioxide.

The Unity Council is being led by the Steelworkers union (USW) a majority of Arizona miners. The Unity Council is following the broader industry goals established by the Nonferrous Industry Committee led by USW vice-president Frank McKee. McKee, 62, has publicly denounced the concession bargaining that has occurred in other industries, notably autos. His name is commonly mentioned as a possible successor to USW president Lloyd McBride who is seriously ill. George Seltzer, professor of industrial relations at the University of Minnesota, describes McKee as "a hard-line, bread and butter unionist."

The growing metropolis of Phoenix with its growing base of emerging companies is an odd setting for a classic Western standoff. But from Wall Street to Main Street Morenci, Arizona, where miners were laid off for six months last year and only two-thirds have returned to work, many eyes are focused on the negotiating table at a Phoenix hotel. Unlike many in the United States, the aging Morenci Miners, as they are known locally, have a strong understanding of history, but so, too, does Phelps Dodge.

Chapter **Nine**

Impasse, Strikes, and Dispute Resolution

Advance Organizer

The primary goal of the bargaining process described in the previous chapter is for labor and management negotiators to reach an agreement on the terms and conditions of employment, usually in the form of a written union contract. Sometimes, however, negotiations are unsuccessful and impasses are reached. This chapter outlines what happens when impasses occur and the alternative methods for their resolution.

Learning Objectives

By the end of the chapter, you should be able to:

1. **Explore** options for resolving bargaining disputes and impasses.
2. **Understand** different types of strikes and lockouts, their roles in labor relations, and their legal restrictions in the private and public sectors.
3. **Discuss** the controversies surrounding the use of strike replacements.
4. **Identify** other types of pressure tactics beyond strikes and lockouts and why they are being used more frequently than in the past.
5. **Compare** the major third-party dispute resolution mechanisms (mediation, arbitration, and fact-finding) and their strengths and weaknesses.

Contents

The previous chapter discussed the bargaining process, especially as it pertains to negotiating a union contract that specifies wages, benefits, and other terms and conditions of employment. This process is almost always successful. Of the thousands of intent to bargain notices filed annually with the Federal Mediation and Conciliation Service, less than three percent result in strikes.[1] Nevertheless, bargaining disputes or impasses and methods for their resolution are central topics in labor relations for several reasons. One, the possibility of an impasse, especially a strike, underlies all labor negotiations as the threat of a strike or other dispute is the source of bargaining power, and therefore greatly influences bargaining outcomes. Two, even though infrequent, major strikes can have devastating consequences for workers, employers, and the public and are therefore important to understand. Companies can lose customers and profits and see their stock prices decline; public sector agencies can lose the support of taxpayers and voters; workers can lose income and face severe emotional and financial strain, including

[1] Federal Mediation and Conciliation Service, *Annual Report* (Washington, DC: U.S. Government Printing Office, various years).

struggling to pay for food and rent; communities might be divided and suffer from economic losses; and the public can be deprived of important goods, services, and sources of transportation.

Three, some dispute resolution methods can be used before an impasse is reached (especially mediation), and others are designed to prevent an impasse from occurring (especially arbitration), and therefore their significance is greater than a low dispute rate might otherwise indicate. And lastly, the method used to resolve bargaining disputes is a defining feature of different labor relations systems or laws; students of labor relations should therefore understand the alternative methods and their advantages and disadvantages.

Before proceeding, it is important to clarify that there are two broad categories of disputes in labor relations: interest disputes and rights disputes. As the name suggests, **interest disputes** pertain to conflicts of interest—higher wages (the employees' interest) versus lower labor costs (the employer's interest), seniority-based layoffs versus merit-based layoffs, broad union input into managerial issues versus strict management rights to conduct business without interference. These conflicts of interest are the focus of contract negotiations. Compromises on these conflicts result in specific contractual terms—a wage and benefits package and language governing layoffs and management rights, for example. In contrast, rights disputes are disagreements over whether someone's rights have been violated. In labor relations, these rights are specified in the union contract. Rights disputes are therefore grievances—conflicts over the application and interpretation of the contract. The resolution of rights disputes is the focus of Chapter 10. The current chapter focuses on interest disputes—conflicts that occur during the negotiation of *new* contract terms, not over the interpretation of *existing* terms.

The National Labor Relations Act (NLRA) specifically states that negotiators do not have to reach an agreement: the good faith bargaining obligation "does not compel either party to agree to a proposal or require the making of a concession" [section 8(d)]. Public sector bargaining laws in many states use the same language. An interest dispute occurs when labor and management negotiators fail to agree with each other on a mutually acceptable set of terms and conditions of employment and therefore reach a bargaining impasse. Recall from the previous chapter that bargaining in good faith to an impasse fulfills each side's legal bargaining obligation. This is very significant because the employer is then free to implement the employment terms of its final offer (such as new wage rates or benefits packages) even over the objection of the union. But reaching an impasse is also significant because it is at this stage that the union, employer, or both typically increase their use of various pressure tactics—also known as economic weapons—to force the other side to make additional concessions at the bargaining table by increasing the other side's costs of disagreeing. The most well-known economic weapon for employees is the strike. In the public sector where striking is often illegal, a bargaining impasse often triggers a mandatory dispute resolution mechanism, especially mediation, arbitration, or fact-finding. This chapter is about these economic weapons and dispute resolution mechanisms.

STRIKES AND LOCKOUTS

A strike occurs when employees refuse to work until an employer changes its position on one or more issues. The *Oxford English Dictionary* traces this usage of the word *strike* to British sailors in 1768 who struck (lowered) their ships' sails to bringing shipping to a halt until their demands for a higher wage were met.[2] But by whatever name, strikes have occurred for thousands of years, including during construction of the pyramids in ancient Egypt. Even children around the turn of the century in 1900 struck for better pay and hours in various U.S. industries (see Box 9.1). A strike is fundamentally an expression of protest

[2] Marcus Rediker, *Between the Devil and the Deep Blue Sea: Merchant Seaman, Pirates, and the Anglo-American Maritime World, 1700–1750* (Cambridge: Cambridge University Press, 1987).

Strikes to protest and force improvements in substandard wages, hours, and working conditions have occurred throughout history. It is therefore no surprise that in situations with significant numbers of child workers, children have attempted to improve their jobs by striking. Some notable strikes by children in the United States include:

- *Patterson Cotton Mill Strike* (New Jersey, 1828). Children struck for three weeks to change their lunch hour back to noon and to reduce daily working hours from $13\frac{1}{2}$ to 9 hours. The strikers won the former but not the latter.

- *Lowell Textile Mill Strike* (Massachusetts, 1836). Two thousand women and girls, including some as young as 10 or 11 years old, struck when a rent increase at the company-owned boardinghouses amounted to a 12 percent reduction in pay. After a month the strike was broken by evicting the workers from the boardinghouses.

- *Newsies Strike* (New York City, 1899). At the turn of the century, newspapers in major cities were often sold by newspaper boys (newsies) between the ages of 8 and 15 hawking papers on street corners after school. The newsies bought the papers wholesale from the newspaper companies and kept whatever they took in from customers; unsold papers could not be returned. In 1899 two of the leading New York City publishers, William Randolph Hearst and Joseph Pulitzer, increased the wholesale price to the newsies while keeping the retail price unchanged. When the publishers refused to rescind this increase, newsies boycotted their papers. After two weeks of beating up newsies (and men) who broke the boycott and attacking delivery carts, and in spite of their leaders being bought off by the publishers, the strike ended with a victory—the papers did not rescind the price increase but they agreed to a policy of refunding newsies for their unsold papers each day.

- *Garment Workers Strike* (New York City and Philadelphia, 1909–1910). In late November 1909, 20,000 girls and young, unmarried women struck almost 500 sewing factories in New York City for better wages, reduced hours, no fees for supplies, improvements in safety, and union recognition. Hundreds of strikers were beaten on the picket lines and then arrested. The sewing companies tried moving production to Philadelphia, and five days before Christmas, garment workers in Philadelphia also struck. By late January and early February, most of the workers had won wage improvements, a shorter work week (52 hours), no supply fees, and an arbitration board to resolve grievances. The strike failed to win improvements in safety standards. A year later, a fire at one of the factories where workers demanded safety improvements—the Triangle Shirtwaist Company—killed 146 workers when oil-soaked rags caught on fire and the fire exits were locked.

Source: Susan Campbell Bartoletti, *Kids On Strike!* (Boston: Houghton Mifflin, 1999).

Children on strike attempting to reduce their work week from 60 to 55 hours in Philadelphia textile mills (cira 1900). After $2\frac{1}{2}$ months, the strikers ran out of money and returned to work without the reduced work week.
Source: Bettmann/CORBIS

and dissatisfaction, but it is also frequently intended to pressure the employer—by withholding their labor, strikers seek to increase the employer's cost of disagreement by depriving the employer of profits (private sector) or the ability to satisfy the demands of taxpayers and voters (public sector). If such actions are costly enough, the employer will accept the employees' demands and settle the strike.

There are a variety of reasons why employees might strike, so there are a number of different types of strikes. If employees are striking to force an employer to recognize and bargain with their union, it is called a recognition strike. A strike to protest an employer's unfair labor practice is an **unfair labor practice strike.** Striking to support other workers who are on strike (for example, by not crossing their picket line) is a sympathy strike. If a union strikes to force an employer to assign certain work to its members, this is a jurisdiction strike. Work stoppages over grievances during the life of union contracts are usually prohibited by the inclusion of no-strike clauses in the contracts and such strikes are therefore called wildcat strikes. Grievance arbitration is typically used instead of wildcat strikes (Chapter 10). Lastly, employees might strike to win better wages, benefits, and work rules—this is called an **economic strike.** These strikes stem from a bargaining impasse over mandatory bargaining items when negotiating a union contract. Economic strikes are the most frequent type of strikes in U.S. labor relations and are probably what most people think of when they think about strikes. Closely related to an economic strike is a **lockout**—an employer-initiated rather than worker-initiated work stoppage during a bargaining impasse. In an economic strike, the workers refuse to work until their terms are met; in a lockout, the employer tells the workers not to return until they agree to the employer's terms.

It is important to differentiate between types of strikes because U.S. legal doctrine in the private sector is different for each one (see Box 9.2). Jurisdiction strikes are prohibited by the NLRA. In contrast, unfair labor practice strikes and economic strikes are protected by

BOX 9.2   Types of Strikes

Category	Definition	Private Sector Strikers Protected by the NLRA?
Economic Strikes	Strikes over wages, benefits, and work rules (mandatory bargaining items) during contract negotiations. This is the classic form of strike in contemporary U.S. labor relations.	*Yes.* Workers cannot be disciplined or discharged. But workers can be replaced with both permanent and temporary strike replacements.
Unfair Labor Practice Strikes	Strikes in protest against an employer's unfair labor practice(s).	*Yes.* Workers cannot be disciplined or discharged or permanently replaced. But the NLRB must find that an unfair labor practice was committed.
Recognition Strikes	Strikes to force an employer to recognize and bargain with a union. Occurred frequently in labor history, but the NLRA encourages the use of representation elections instead.	*Yes, but can only picket for 30 days.* Workers are protected, but can be permanently replaced. Picketing for recognition is essentially limited to 30 days. After 30 days, can strike but not picket.
Sympathy Strikes	Strikes in support of other workers on strike.	*Maybe.* A no-strike clause in a contract might be a waiver of protection if the clause clearly includes sympathy strikes. In this case, workers are not protected and can be disciplined or discharged. Otherwise, sympathy strikes are protected, but strikers can be replaced.
Wildcat Strikes	Strikes over grievances while a contract is still in force (not during contract negotiations).	*Occasionally.* A no-strike clause in a contract usually waives protection, so workers can be disciplined or discharged. Otherwise, grievance strikes are protected, but strikers can be replaced.
Jurisdiction Strikes	Strikes over the assignment of work to bargaining unit employees.	*No.* Jurisdiction strikes are prohibited by the NLRA.
Noneconomic Strikes	Strikes over permissive bargaining items during contract negotiations.	*No.* The NLRA only protects workers' efforts to improve their wages, hours, and other terms and conditions of employment.

Note: The same taxonomy (columns 1 and 2) applies to public sector strikes, but strikes by government employees are more tightly regulated than in the private sector and are more likely to be unprotected or even illegal (column 3).

section 7 of the NLRA. As such, workers cannot be disciplined or discharged for participating in these types of strikes—to do so would be a section 8(a)(1) unfair labor practice. But as will be detailed in the next section, economic strikers can be permanently replaced. Remember that to be an economic strike, the dispute must be over mandatory bargaining items; permissive items are outside the boundaries of the NLRA, so strikes over these issues are not protected and workers can be fired for participating in such a strike. Strikes over grievances are considered protected activity under the NLRA, but no-strike clauses in union contracts frequently forfeit this protection. As such, employees who participate in wildcat strikes can often be disciplined. These various limitations on the right to strike, including the legality of permanent strike replacements, reveal that U.S. public policy sees striking as an economic activity to pursue things like higher wages rather than a civil liberty rooted in freedom of association.[3]

A key aspect of a strike is a picket line—strikers, their leaders, and their supporters march outside the struck employer's location(s) to publicize their dispute, convince the public not to patronize the business and workers not to cross the picket line, create solidarity among the strikers, and otherwise build support for their cause. In economic and unfair labor practice strikes, picketing is legal but is not without legal limitations. Picket line misconduct such as violence or vandalism is not protected by the NLRA and can therefore result in discipline and loss of recall rights at the end of the strike, as well as potential criminal prosecution. Moreover, mass picketing that blocks entrances to an employer's property is also illegal. Recall from Chapter 5 that injunctions were used in the early 20th century to severely restrain picketing. While not as extreme, injunctions by state courts are still used to restrain illegal picketing and it is not unusual for an injunction to limit picketing to a certain number of picketers at each entrance to an employer's property.

Picketing raises several other important issues. One, what about employees who want to work instead of strike and therefore cross their own union's picket line? This can be a very emotionally charged issue, but legally employees are allowed to do this. Moreover, unions have the right to discipline union members who cross the picket line, but union members also have the right to resign from the union and thus avoid discipline.[4] Discipline can consist of being expelled from the union and being assessed reasonable fines. Two, picketing gives rise to sympathy strikes—the refusal to cross another union's picket line. Sympathy strikes are protected by the NLRA, but sympathy strikers can be replaced. Moreover, a no-strike clause in a union contract might waive this protection.[5] Three, picketing to pressure an employer to recognize a union is explicitly limited by the NLRA to 30 days [section 8(b)(7)(C)]. Recognition strikes are legal, but after 30 days such strikes typically cannot also include picketing (though there are some exceptions).[6] U.S. labor law seeks to discourage recognition strikes by making the certification election process available to employees (Chapter 7), but recognition strikes are nevertheless allowed. Lastly, as will be discussed later in this chapter, the legality of picketing also becomes complex when more than one employer is involved.

The taxonomy of strikes presented in Box 9.2 also applies to public sector strikes, but all of the types of strikes are more likely to be illegal when conducted by government employees. Prohibiting public sector strikes is rooted in several traditional beliefs: that striking against the government is an unacceptable threat to the supreme authority of the

[3] Josiah Bartlett Lambert, *"If the Workers Took a Notion": The Right to Strike and American Political Development* (Ithaca, NY: Cornell University Press, 2005).

[4] Bruce S. Feldacker, *Labor Guide to Labor Law*, 4th ed. (Upper Saddle River, NJ: Prentice Hall, 2000).

[5] Benjamin J. Taylor and Fred Witney, *Labor Relations Law*, 7th ed. (Englewood Cliffs, NJ: Prentice Hall, 1996).

[6] *Local 707 Motor Freight Drivers (Claremont Polychemical Corp.)*, 196 NLRB 613 (1972).

government, that public sector employee bargaining power is too high because there are no market-based checks on their demands, and that government services are too critical to be interrupted. The commonly cited watershed event in creating widespread opposition to public sector strikes is the Boston police strike in 1919 that resulted in looting and violence when police officers walked off the job when their union leaders were suspended by the police commissioner.[7] In the midst of this lawlessness, the governor of Massachusetts (who would later become U.S. President), Calvin Coolidge, expressed what would become the common sentiment toward public sector strikes: "there is no right to strike against the public safety by anybody, anywhere, any time."[8] As such, strikes by federal government workers are prohibited and only 25 percent of states grant a right to strike (recall Box 5.21).[9] And even these laws are significantly more restrictive than the NLRA. For example, in Hawaii, only teachers, college faculty, and blue collar state and local workers can strike, only economic strikes are allowed, and only after mediation, fact-finding, and a 60-day cooling off period. Other types of strikes are illegal and all other employees are considered essential and must use arbitration instead of striking.[10] On the other hand, a number of states not only prohibit all strikes but also specify penalties for violators.[11] New York's Taylor law, for example, imposes a "two for one" strike penalty—for each day someone is on strike, they lose their pay for the day plus a fine equal to their day's pay.[12] In both the private and public sectors, however, illegal strikes do occur. For example, New York City transit workers struck for 60 hours in December 2005 and shut down the subway and bus system; strikers forfeited six days of pay under the Taylor Law's two for one penalty and a judge also fined the union $2.5 million for conducting an illegal strike.

There is also a concern in private sector labor law with strikes that seriously harm the public interest. Because of the critical importance of railroads for the early 20th century economy, the Railway Labor Act empowers the President of the United States to create a Presidential Emergency Board if a strike would "threaten substantially to interrupt interstate commerce to a degree such as to deprive any section of the country of essential transportation service" (section 10).[13] A Presidential Emergency Board has 30 days to investigate the dispute and issue a report which typically contains nonbinding recommendations for a settlement. After the report is issued, a strike can occur after a 30-day cooling off period. For the private sector more generally, the Taft-Hartley Act amendments to the NLRA in

[7] Sterling D. Spero, *Government as Employer* (New York: Remsen Press, 1948). Joseph E. Slater, *Public Workers: Government Employee Unions, the Law, and the State, 1900–1962* (Ithaca, NY: Cornell University Press, 2004).

[8] Francis Russell, *A City in Terror: 1919, The Boston Police Strike.* (New York: Viking, 1975), p. 191. Sterling D. Spero, *Government as Employer* (New York: Remsen Press, 1948).

[9] John Lund and Cheryl L. Maranto, "Public Sector Labor Law: An Update," in Dale Belman, Morley Gunderson, and Douglas Hyatt (eds.), *Public Sector Employment in a Time of Transition* (Madison, WI: Industrial Relations Research Association, 1996), Chapter 1.

[10] Joyce M. Najita, William J. Anzenberger, and Helene S. Tanimoto, "Essential Employee Strikes and Compulsory Arbitration Procedures: The Hawaii Public Sector Collective Bargaining Experience," in Joyce M. Najita and James L. Stern (eds.), *Collective Bargaining in the Public Sector: The Experience of Eight States* (Armonk, NY: M. E. Sharpe, 2001), Chapter 9.

[11] Lund and Maranto, "Public Sector Labor Law."

[12] Janet McEneaney and Robert P. Hebdon, "Public Sector Labor Law and Experience in New York State," in Joyce M. Najita and James L. Stern (eds.), *Collective Bargaining in the Public Sector: The Experience of Eight States* (Armonk, NY: M. E. Sharpe, 2001), Chapter 7.

[13] Donald E. Cullen, "Emergency Boards Under the Railway Labor Act," in Charles M. Rehmus (ed.), *The Railway Labor Act at Fifty: Collective Bargaining in the Railroad and Airline Industries* (Washington, DC: National Mediation Board, 1976), Chapter VI. Douglas L. Leslie (ed.), *The Railway Labor Act* (Washington, DC: Bureau of National Affairs, 1995). Charles M. Rehmus, "Emergency Strikes Revisited," *Industrial and Labor Relations Review* 43 (January 1990), pp. 175–90.

1947 created provisions for settling national emergency strikes following the Great Strike Wave of 1945–46.[14] When the President believes that a strike or threatened strike "will imperil the national health or safety" s/he can appoint a Board of Inquiry to investigate and report on the disputed issues (section 206). Upon receipt of this report, the President can seek a court-ordered injunction halting the strike or threatened strike for up to a maximum of 80 days. Additional changes to the NLRA in 1974 provided for Boards of Inquiry in the health care industry if a strike would "substantially interrupt the delivery of health care in the locality concerned" (section 213).

The NLRA's national emergency strike procedures have been used 36 times since 1947, mostly before 1970.[15] President Bush invoked these procedures to stop a West Coast dock workers lockout in 2002; before that, President Carter's request to stop a 15-week old 1978 coal strike was denied by the courts. With respect to the Railway Labor Act's provisions, 238 Presidential Emergency Boards were formed between 1934 and 2005. There have been 20 since 1990, three in the airline industry and 17 in the railroad industry, and over half of these were for commuter rail lines. These NLRA and Railway Labor Act emergency procedures are not always successful in resolving bargaining disputes, however. In some cases, strikes occur after the procedures have been exhausted while in others Congress legislates a settlement, either in the form of mandating specific conditions or requiring the submission of the dispute to binding arbitration. When all else fails, Presidents have also seized various industrial and transportation operations to maintain production, shipping, or fuel supplies—a tactic used 71 times between 1864 and 1952.[16] In fact, the entire railroad industry has been seized five times.

These emergency strikes and seizures are, of course, the exception rather than the rule. The most frequent form of strike is the economic strike—a work stoppage stemming from a bargaining impasse over mandatory bargaining items during negotiations for a union contract. Most work stoppages are economic strikes or lockouts, and often the public (as well as researchers) do not distinguish between the two. Research on the effects of strikes and lockouts affirms the rarity of strikes that should be considered emergencies. Work stoppages clearly have negative effects: productivity declines, profits are lost, stock prices fall, and workers lose income and suffer from stress, but these effects are generally confined to the specific employer and workers involved in the strike.[17]

The largest U.S. work stoppages for each year between 2000 and 2005 are listed in Box 9.3. Note the variety of industries, issues, and dispute lengths—one was only two days in length, another lasted six months. Box 9.3 underscores the fact that major work stoppages still occur, yet U.S. strike activity in the early 21st century is at an all-time low. The number of major strikes/lockouts (those involving at least 1,000 workers) exceeded 400 per year in the early 1950s, ranged between 250 and 425 in the early 1970s, and then plummeted from 187 in 1980 to 54 in 1985 to 22 in 2005 (see Box 9.4). Public sector strikes account for perhaps 15

[14] Donald E. Cullen, *National Emergency Strikes* (Ithaca, NY: New York State School of Industrial and Labor Relations, 1968). Harry A. Millis and Emily Clark Brown, *From the Wagner Act to Taft-Hartley: A Study of National Labor Policy and Labor Relations* (Chicago: University of Chicago Press, 1950). Rehmus, "Emergency Strikes Revisited."

[15] Cullen, *National Emergency Strikes.* Rehmus, "Emergency Strikes Revisited."

[16] John L. Blackman, Jr., *Presidential Seizure in Labor Disputes* (Cambridge: Harvard University Press, 1967).

[17] Brian E. Becker and Craig A. Olson, "The Impact of Strikes on Shareholder Equity," *Industrial and Labor Relations Review* 39 (April), pp. 425–38. Bruce E. Kaufman, "Research on Strike Models and Outcomes in the 1980s: Accomplishments and Shortcomings," in David Lewin, Olivia S. Mitchell, and Peter D. Sherer (eds.), *Research Frontiers in Industrial Relations and Human Resources* (Madison, WI: Industrial Relations Research Association, 1992), pp. 77–129. Charles R. Stoner and Raj Arora, "An Investigation of the Relationship Between Selected Variables and the Psychological Health of Strike Participants," *Journal of Occupational Psychology* 60 (March 1987), pp. 61–71.

2005

More than 30,000 New York City Metropolitan Transit Authority workers represented by the Transit Workers Union shut down subway and bus lines for 60 hours in December and faced monetary fines for this illegal strike. Major issue: pensions.

2004

Though only lasting four days, 102,000 workers represented by the Communications Workers of America struck telecommunications giant SBC Communications. Major issue: health care.

2003

A strike by the United Food and Commercial Workers (UFCW) against Vons prompted Albertsons and Ralph's to lock out their workers and as a result 67,300 workers in the southern California grocery industry were idled from October 2003 to February 2004. Major issue: health care.

2002

The Pacific Maritime Association locked out 10,500 workers represented by the International Longshore and Warehouse Union for 12 days. Ended through the intervention of President Bush under the NLRA's national emergency strike procedures. Major issue: technology implementation.

2001

The largest strike of the year was in the public sector: nearly 25,000 state government employees represented by the American Federation of State, County, and Municipal Employees and the Minnesota Association of Professional Employees struck the State of Minnesota for 14 days. Major issue: health insurance.

2000

Roughly 135,000 radio and television commercial actors belonging to the American Federation of Television and Radio Artists and the Screen Actors Guild went on strike against the Association of National Advertisers and the American Association of Advertising Agencies for six months. Major issue: compensation.

Source: Bureau of Labor Statistics Major Work Stoppages Program (*www.bls.gov/cba/home.htm*).

BOX 9.4
U.S. Major Strikes (1,000 workers or more), 1950–2005

Source: Bureau of Labor Statistics, U.S. Department of Labor.

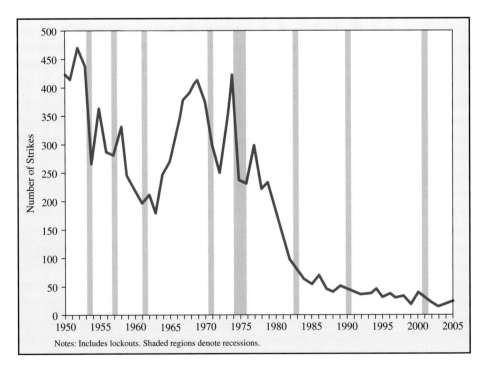

Notes: Includes lockouts. Shaded regions denote recessions.

percent of these major strikes (and of those, 40 percent are illegal public sector strikes).[18] Relative to the total economy, the number of working days lost because of strikes is minis-cule—in 2005, the days lost due to strikes involving at least 1,000 workers amounted to 1/100th of one percent of total working days. Even in the 1950s, this figure was only 1/5th of 1 percent of total working days.[19] There are a number of complicated data issues that make it difficult to know exactly what fraction of all negotiations result in strikes, but the best estimates are that the strike rate in large bargaining units (more than 1,000 workers) has declined from 15 percent in the 1970s to perhaps 5 percent in the 2000s.[20] Strike rates for all negotiations are even lower—perhaps even less than 1 percent in recent years.[21] Strike ac-tivity in Europe is also at a low level compared to previous years.[22]

This sharp decline in U.S. strike activity since 1980 begs the question of why strikes occur. A simple view starts with the important interaction between bargaining power and strikes. Recall from the previous chapter that the threat of a strike is a major determinant of bargaining power. If the economy is strong and employees are not worried about losing their jobs and replacement employees are difficult to find, the threat of a strike might be more viable than in a weak economy with significant anxiety about job loss and with large numbers of available replacements. A company that has a significant inventory of finished products (such as automobiles) is probably less threatened by a strike than a company with little inventory. A union that represents most of a company's employees, or most of an in-dustry's employees, can likely inflict greater economic losses and therefore has greater strike leverage and bargaining power than a union that only represents a small fraction of workers. The legality or illegality of being able to use replacement workers to continue production during a strike is another important determinant of the strength of a strike threat and therefore bargaining power. In fact, important bargaining tactics for both labor and management focus on strengthening or weakening the strike threat—such as building union solidarity to maximize the extent to which a strike affects an employer's bottom line, or on the part of management, arranging for replacement workers or moving production to other locations to minimize a strike's disruptions.

One might be tempted to therefore speculate that strike activity has declined since 1980 because labor's bargaining power has declined. But this confuses the *threat* of strikes with the *occurrence* of strikes. Bargaining power depends on the strength of the strike threat. If labor's bargaining power is high because employers face greater strike losses, employers should be more likely to give in to labor's demands before strikes occur. As such, the threat of a strike is higher and wages will be higher, but the actual occurrence of strikes is not higher than when labor's bargaining power is lower.[23] In short, bargaining power and the threat of a strike should affect the extent to which bargaining outcomes favor labor or man-agement (Chapter 8), but not the occurrence of strikes.

[18] Robert Hebdon, "Public Sector Dispute Resolution in Transition," in Dale Belman, Morley Gunderson, and Douglas Hyatt (eds.), *Public Sector Employment in a Time of Transition* (Madison, WI: Industrial Rela-tions Research Association, 1996), Chapter 3.

[19] "Major Work Stoppages in 2005," Bureau of Labor Statistics, U.S. Department of Labor (March 2, 2006).

[20] Sheena McConnell, "Cyclical Fluctuations in Strike Activity," *Industrial and Labor Relations Review* 44 (October 1990), pp. 130–43. Michael H. Cimini and John K. Steinmeyer, "What Can You Tell Me About Collective Bargaining Expirations and Work Stoppages?" *Compensation and Working Conditions Online*, May 28, 2003. Accessed June 23, 2003, at *http://www.bls.gov/opub/cwc/cb20030522ar01p1.htm*.

[21] Federal Mediation and Conciliation Service, *Annual Report.*

[22] European Industrial Relations Observatory, "Developments in Industrial Action—2000–2004," *EIRO Online* (Dublin: European Foundation for the Improvement of Living and Working Conditions, 2005). Accessed July 7, 2006, at *http://www.eiro.eurofound.eu.int/2005/06/update/tn0506101u.html*.

[23] Kaufman, "Research on Strike Models and Outcomes in the 1980s."

More generally, since strikes are costly for all involved, they seem irrational on a strict cost-benefit basis—in standard economic thought, rational negotiators should be able to figure out the poststrike settlement and agree to it without a strike and everyone would be better off.[24] And yet, strikes are not completely irrational because in practice strike activity is not random but instead is correlated with a number of factors (for example, the unemployment rate, bargaining unit size, contract duration, and in the public sector, strike penalties).[25] The economics approach to explaining why strikes occur typically focuses on problems of information (so, for example, rational negotiators cannot figure out the poststrike settlement ahead of time). Other approaches broaden the narrow dollars and cents focus of *economic* rationality and examine other explanations for strikes such as the pursuit of workplace voice.[26] These various approaches to explaining why strikes occur are discussed in Box 9.5.

So what explains the decline in strike activity? Before the 1980s, research often found that strikes were pro-cyclical: strike activity tracked the business cycle (more strikes during booms, fewer during recessions).[27] But as shown in Box 9.4, strike activity declined consistently through the 1980s and 1990s irrespective of the business cycle. Alternatively, many of the theories of strikes described in Box 9.5 hinge on the lack of full information possessed by negotiators and their constituents. Another explanation, therefore, is that information issues have improved, for example, through a decline in inflation uncertainty.[28] Lastly, there is a possible sociopolitical explanation: it is frequently argued that the steep decline in U.S. strike activity results from an increased acceptability of using strike replacements that started in the 1980s.[29] And thus, workers stopped striking so as not to lose their jobs.

STRIKE REPLACEMENTS

Less than three months after the NLRA was signed into law in 1935, a number of telegraph operators for the Mackay Radio and Telegraph Company went on strike in San Francisco. The company brought in operators from its branches in New York, Chicago, and Los Angeles to keep its business going during the strike. The strike didn't go well for the strikers and after four days they offered to return to work. However, five of the operators that were brought in from the other cities apparently decided that they liked San Francisco so much that they wanted to stay. As such, there were now five fewer openings and five of the striking operators were not allowed to return to their positions. These five strikers had been particularly active in the union and the strike—they were not, for example, the five employees with the lowest seniority or the lowest job performance ratings. An unfair labor practice

[24] Alison L. Booth, *The Economics of the Trade Union* (Cambridge: Cambridge University Press, 1995). John R. Hicks, *The Theory of Wages* (London: Macmillan, 1932). Barry T. Hirsch and John T. Addison, *The Economic Analysis of Unions* (Boston: Allen and Unwin, 1986).

[25] Kaufman, "Research on Strike Models and Outcomes in the 1980s." McConnell, "Cyclical Fluctuations in Strike Activity." Craig A. Olson, "Strikes, Strike Penalties, and Arbitration in Six States," *Industrial and Labor Relations Review* 39 (July 1986), pp. 539–51.

[26] John Godard, "Strikes as Collective Voice: A Behavioral Analysis of Strike Activity," *Industrial and Labor Relations Review* 46 (October 1992), pp. 161–75.

[27] Kaufman, "Research on Strike Models and Outcomes in the 1980s." McConnell, "Cyclical Fluctuations in Strike Activity." Albert Rees, "Industrial Conflict and Business Fluctuations," *Journal of Political Economy* 60 (October 1952), pp. 371–82.

[28] Cynthia L. Gramm, Wallace E. Hendricks, and Lawrence M. Kahn, "Inflation Uncertainty and Strike Activity," *Industrial Relations* 27 (Winter 1988), pp. 114–29.

[29] Jonathan D. Rosenblum, *Copper Crucible: How the Arizona Miners' Strike of 1983 Recast Labor–Management Relations in America,* 2nd ed. (Ithaca, NY: ILR Press, 1998). Robert H. Zieger and Gilbert J. Gall, *American Workers, American Unions: The Twentieth Century,* 3rd ed. (Baltimore: Johns Hopkins Press, 2002).

Why Do Strikes Occur? Box 9.5
A Multidisciplinary Research Question

In the textbook economics model, individuals are rational and possess perfect information. In this framework, it's very hard to explain why strikes occur. If labor and management negotiators have perfect information, they both know the terms of the contract settlement that will occur after a strike. The rational thing to do, therefore, is to agree to those terms without a strike and save everyone the expense of a strike.[1] But strikes obviously do occur. Why? Most explanations for strikes focus on the two assumptions embedded in the textbook economics model: perfect information and pure economic rationality.

Less than Perfect Information

Since rationality is at the heart of economics, most economic models of strikes focus instead on problems with the perfect information assumption. One of the first theories posited that strikes were mistakes that stemmed from imperfect information.[2] If union and management negotiators differ in their forecasts of inflation, for example, then even rational negotiators will not be able to agree in advance on the poststrike settlement and a strike might occur.[3] Along similar lines, uncertainty about the other side's power and future economic trends can cause miscalculation or a divergence between labor and management negotiators and thus strikes.[4] This is another information-related model because uncertainty stems from a lack of perfect information. Lastly, private or asymmetric information explanations have been developed.[5] Suppose a firm has better information about its profitability than the union. The union wants high-profit firms to pay high wages and will allow low-profit firms to pay lower wages. With private information about profitability, all firms will claim to be low-profit. Consequently, the union can use a strike to screen true profitability by giving the firm two choices: a high wage with no strike or a lower wage after a strike. High-profit firms will take the former, low-profit firms will choose the latter.

Two other economic models of strikes are also ultimately rooted in information issues. In the joint costs model, if the combined costs of a strike to labor and management are high, negotiators will work hard to avoid a strike.[6] On the other hand, if the joint costs of a strike are less than the expense of negotiating, strikes will occur. But how can the costs of a strike ever be less than negotiating? Because of information issues that make it costly (in terms of time and frustration) to negotiate contracts that deal with every possible future contingency that might arise. The last economic model is rooted in information issues between union leaders and the rank and file.[7] In this model, rational union and management negotiators agree on the optimal settlement that avoids a strike, but rank and file workers have unrealistically high expectations. In the absence of convincing information, it sometimes takes a strike to lessen the workers' expectation of a high settlement.

Beyond Pure Economic Rationality

Outside of economics there is often less attachment to assuming that individuals are always fully rational in a narrow, dollars and cents, self-interested manner. Models of strike activity in other disciplines therefore embrace a broader conception of rational behavior and incorporate sociological and psychological influences such as social identities and emotions.

Mobilization theory posits that workers will mobilize for collective action (as in a strike) if there are leaders present when workers (1) suffer from perceived injustice, (2) blame management rather than themselves for their problems, and (3) feel a sense of collective rather than individual identity in the workplace.[8] In this thinking, strikes are not simply calculated attempts to increase wages, but are also expressions of discontent through the exercise of collective voice.[9] As such, strikes will depend not only upon the costs and benefits of striking, but also on the social relations and climate of the workplace. Organizational stability or institutional turmoil within the workplace, unions, and the labor movement can also affect strike activity.[10]

Conservative business and political groups occasionally blame strikes on troublemaking agitators—often branded as Communists—who manufacture strikes by manipulating workers. While mobilization theory reveals the importance of leaders in collective action such as strikes, and while the personalities of labor and management negotiators can be important, it is inaccurate to blame strikes solely on manipulative leaders.[11] Legitimate worker dissatisfaction or injustice is needed to cause strikes.

A second category of models that broaden the pure economic rationality assumption are behavioral models rooted in psychology. Work in this vein focuses on

Continued

Continued

perception, motivation, and frustration.[12] If workers perceive situations differently from managers, are motivated to seek different goals than managers, and are frustrated in pursuit of these goals, strikes can result. Because of the powerful emotion of frustration, aggression can overwhelm pure economic calculations and result in strikes.[13]

Lastly, a final explanation for strikes is that they are used occasionally as practice to make sure employers continue to appreciate the strike threat and therefore concede to union demands in negotiations without an actual strike:

> Weapons grow rusty if unused, and a Union which never strikes may lose the ability to organize a formidable strike, so that its threats become less effective. The most able Trade Union leadership will embark on strikes occasionally, not so much to secure greater gains upon that occasion . . . . but in order to keep their weapon burnished for future use, and to keep employers thoroughly conscious of the Union's power.[14]

In sum, strikes involve complex interactions of human behavior and the surrounding environment, often in stressful and challenging situations. There are a variety of possible explanations for why strikes occur and few researchers probably believe that a single theory underlies all strikes. Rather, strikes likely stem from a combination of economic, social, organizational, political, and psychological factors. Explaining strikes continues to be a challenging, multidisciplinary research problem.[15]

[1] Barry T. Hirsch and John T. Addison, *The Economic Analysis of Unions* (Boston: Allen and Unwin, 1986).

[2] John R. Hicks, *The Theory of Wages* (London: Macmillan, 1932).

[3] Bruce E. Kaufman, "Bargaining Theory, Inflation, and Cyclical Strike Activity in Manufacturing," *Industrial and Labor Relations Review* 34 (April 1981), pp. 333–55.

[4] Jean-Michel Cousineau and Robert Lacroix, "Imperfect Information and Strikes: An Analysis of Canadian Experience, 1967–82," *Industrial and Labor Relations Review* 39 (April 1986), pp. 377–87. Cynthia L. Gramm, Wallace E. Hendricks, and Lawrence M. Kahn, "Inflation Uncertainty and Strike Activity," *Industrial Relations* 27 (Winter 1988), pp. 114–29. W. Stanley Siebert and John T. Addison, "Are Strikes Accidental?" *Economic Journal* 91 (June 1981), pp. 389–404.

[5] David Card, "Strikes and Wages: A Test of an Asymmetric Information Model," *Quarterly Journal of Economics* 105 (1990), pp. 625–59. Beth Hayes, "Unions and Strikes with Asymmetric Information," *Journal of Labor Economics* 2 (January 1984), pp. 57–83. Sheena McConnell, "Strikes, Wages, and Private Information," *American Economic Review* 79 (September 1989), pp. 801–15.

[6] John Kennan, "Pareto Optimality and the Economics of Strike Duration," *Journal of Labor Research* 1 (Spring 1980), pp. 77–94. Melvin W. Reder and George R. Neumann, "Conflict and Contract: The Case of Strikes," *Journal of Political Economy* 88 (October 1980), pp. 867–86.

[7] Orley Ashenfelter and George E. Johnson, "Bargaining Theory, Trade Unions, and Industrial Strike Activity," *American Economic Review* 59 (March 1969), pp. 35–49.

[8] John E. Kelly, *Rethinking Industrial Relations: Mobilization, Collectivism and Long Waves* (London: Routledge, 1998).

[9] John Godard, "Strikes as Collective Voice: A Behavioral Analysis of Strike Activity," *Industrial and Labor Relations Review* 46 (October 1992), pp. 161–75. Josiah Bartlett Lambert, *"If the Workers Took a Notion": The Right to Strike and American Political Development* (Ithaca, NY: Cornell University Press, 2005).

[10] Mario F. Bognanno, John W. Budd, and Young-Myon Lee, "Institutional Turmoil and Strike Activity in Korea," *Journal of Industrial Relations* 36 (September 1994), pp. 353–69. Arthur M. Ross and Paul T. Hartman, *Changing Patterns of Industrial Conflict* (New York: John Wiley and Sons, 1960).

[11] Ralph Darlington, " 'Wildcats' and 'Agitators': The Relationship Between Spontaneity and Leadership within Workplace Strike Activity," Paper Presented at the Canadian Industrial Relations Association Annual Meeting (June 2004).

[12] Stephen D. Bluen, "The Psychology of Strikes," in Cary L. Cooper and Ivan T. Robertson (eds.), *International Review of Industrial and Organizational Psychology, 1994*, Volume 9 (Chichester: John Wiley and Sons, 1994), Chapter 4. Ross Stagner and Hjalmar Rosen, *Psychology of Union–Management Relations* (Belmont, CA: Wadsworth, 1965).

[13] Hoyt N. Wheeler, *Industrial Conflict: An Integrative Theory* (Columbia: University of South Carolina Press, 1985).

[14] Hicks, *The Theory of Wages,* p. 146.

[15] Bruce E. Kaufman, "Research on Strike Models and Outcomes in the 1980s: Accomplishments and Shortcomings," in David Lewin, Olivia S. Mitchell, and Peter D. Sherer (eds.), *Research Frontiers in Industrial Relations and Human Resources* (Madison, WI: Industrial Relations Research Association, 1992), pp. 77–129.

charge was filed with the National Labor Relations Board (NLRB) alleging that the company violated the NLRA by discriminating against these five strikers for their active participation in the union and the strike.

In one of its earliest decisions pertaining to the NLRA, the Supreme Court in 1938 ruled against the Mackay Radio and Telegraph Company and found it guilty of discriminating against the five union activists. However, the Court emphasized that the key illegal act was singling out union activists. In an almost incidental remark, the Court indicated that absent such discrimination, it is legal to use employees to do the work of individuals on strike during an economic strike:

Nor was it an unfair labor practice to replace the striking employees with others in an effort to carry on the business. Although Section 13 [of the NLRA] provides, "Nothing in this Act shall be construed so as to interfere with or impede or diminish in any way the right to strike," it does not follow that an employer, guilty of no act denounced by the statute, has lost the right to protect and continue his business by supplying places left vacant by strikers. And he is not bound to discharge those hired to fill the places of strikers, upon the election of the latter to resume their employment, in order to create places for them.[30]

Employees used or hired to do the work of individuals on strike are called strike replacements. But note carefully that the Supreme Court did more than just allow employers to hire strike replacements—in the last sentence of this passage the Court also wrote that employers did not have to fire the replacements at the end of the strike in order to provide jobs to strikers who want to return to work. In other words, employers can hire **permanent strike replacements**—replacement workers that continue in their positions after the strike ends—as well as temporary strike replacements—replacement workers that are discharged at the end of the strike. This is known as the *Mackay* doctrine after the famous 1938 decision quoted above: **NLRB v. Mackay Radio and Telegraph Co.** Most other industrialized countries, however, do not allow permanent strike replacements (see Box 9.6).

Strikers that have been permanently replaced are not necessarily entitled to immediate reinstatement back to their old jobs once they end their strike. However, these employees cannot be fired in the literal sense—to do so would violate the NLRA's ban on discharging workers for engaging in protected activity [sections 8(a)(1) and 8(a)(3)]. Rather, at the conclusion of a strike, returning strikers are placed on a priority recall list and as jobs become available, employers must first offer jobs to the former strikers before hiring any brand new employees.[31] As a practical matter, the status of temporary or permanent replacements is determined by what the employer tells the replacement workers when they are hired.[32] If disputes arise later, the employer has the burden of proving that the replacements were told that they were permanent; otherwise they will be considered temporary and must be terminated when strikers make an unconditional offer to return to work.

Numerous other complications can arise (see Box 9.7). Perhaps the most significant is whether the strike is an economic strike or an unfair labor practice strike. The *Mackay* doctrine clearly establishes the legality of using permanent strike replacements in the former, but what about the latter? In other words, are replaced strikers entitled to *immediate* reinstatement at the conclusion of an unfair labor practice strike? On the one hand, providing immediate reinstatement might encourage reckless strikes that would be inconsistent with the NRLA's objective of industrial peace. On the other hand, not providing immediate reinstatement would allow the employer to gain from its illegal activity. It is now well-accepted legal doctrine that employers cannot use permanent replacements during an unfair labor practice strike—strikers in this case are entitled to immediate reinstatement—so that employers are not rewarded for their illegal

[30] *NLRB v. Mackay Radio and Telegraph Co.,* 304 U.S. 333, 345–46 (1938). Julius G. Getman and Thomas C. Kohler, "The Story of *NLRB v. Mackay Radio and Telegraph Co.*: The High Cost of Solidarity," in Laura J. Cooper and Catherine L. Fisk (eds.), *Labor Law Stories* (New York: Foundation Press, 2005), pp. 13–53. Lambert, *"If the Workers Took a Notion."* Samuel Estreicher, "Collective Bargaining Or 'Collective Begging'?: Reflections On Antistrikebreaker Legislation," *Michigan Law Review* 93 (December 1994), pp. 577–608. Michael H. LeRoy, "The *Mackay Radio* Doctrine of Permanent Striker Replacements and the Minnesota Picket Line Peace Act: Questions of Preemption," *Minnesota Law Review* 77 (April 1993), pp. 843–69. Jeffrey A. Spector, "Replacement and Reinstatement of Strikers in the United States, Great Britain, and Canada," *Comparative Labor Law Journal* 13 (Winter 1992), pp. 184–232.

[31] *NLRB v. Fleetwood Trailer Co.,* 389 U.S. 375 (1967).

[32] Douglas E. Ray, Calvin William Sharpe, and Robert N. Strassfield, *Understanding Labor Law* (New York: Mathew Bender, 1999).

Opponents of proposals to ban permanent strike replacements argue that such a ban would raise labor costs and harm international competitiveness. This argument means we need to look at other countries to see if a U.S. ban would put it out of line with its trading partners. In contrast, labor supporters that want to ban permanent strike replacements argue that the United States is already unique among industrialized, democratic countries in allowing permanent strike replacements. Sometimes it is even stated that only the United States and South Africa permit employers to use permanent strike replacements.

Is the *Mackay* doctrine another example of American exceptionalism in labor relations? Almost. In Canada, private sector labor law is generally controlled by the provinces and most provinces effectively ban permanent replacements. In British Columbia and Quebec, employers are prohibited from using both temporary and permanent replacements, and even are restricted in their ability to use existing employees from non-struck work locations. Manitoba and Prince Edward Island ban the use of permanent strike replacements. Lastly, Ontario, Alberta, and Saskatchewan do not explicitly ban permanent replacements, but effectively do by granting immediate reinstatement rights to striking employees.

European countries such as France, Germany, and Italy, ban the use of permanent strike replacements. In fact, as will be discussed in Chapter 13, many countries outside of North America have just cause protections which means that employees can only be dismissed for good reasons. Striking is typically not a valid reason for being dismissed, though there are exceptions. In Great Britain, for example, employees are protected against unfair dismissal. But not being reinstated after striking is only viewed as an illegal, unfair dismissal if only some are not reinstated. In effect, the use of permanent strike replacements in Great Britain is allowed as long as *all* of the strikers are replaced.

But what about likening the United States to South Africa? South Africa has traditionally been especially repressive of labor unions and strikers. In fact, until 1973 it was illegal for black workers to strike at all, and after 1973 nearly all strikes by black workers were declared to be illegal for one reason or another—and not only can illegal strikers be permanently replaced, they can be forcibly resettled to another part of the country. As such, it is perhaps inflammatory to compare the United States to South Africa in terms of allowing permanent strike replacements. On the other hand, after reforms in the 1990s, South Africa now restricts the use of permanent strike replacements.

In conclusion, the United States is not strictly alone in allowing the use of permanent strike replacements, but this does appear to be the exception rather than the rule. With respect to international competitiveness, most trading partners of the United States already ban the use of permanent strike replacements.

Source: John W. Budd, "The Effect of Strike Replacement Legislation on Employment," *Labour Economics* 7 (March 2000), pp. 245–47. Matthew W. Finkin, "Labor Policy and the Enervation of the Economic Strike," *University of Illinois Law Review 1990* (1990), pp. 547–74. Lennox S. Hinds, "The Gross Violations of Human Rights of the Apartheid Regime Under International Law," *Rutgers Race and Law Review* 1 (1999), pp. 231–317. Jeffrey A. Spector, "Replacement and Reinstatement of Strikers in the United States, Great Britain, and Canada," *Comparative Labor Law Journal* 13 (Winter 1992), pp. 184–232. An example of the South Africa comparison can be found in U.S. Congress, *Hearings on H.R. 5, The Striker Replacement Bill,* Hearings Before the Subcommittee on Labor–Management Relations of the Committee on Education and Labor, House of Representatives, March 6 and 13, 1991 (Washington, DC: U.S. Government Printing Office, 1991), p. 297.

actions.[33] As a result, striking workers will commonly claim that they are engaged in an unfair labor practice strike, but it is up to the NLRB to make that determination. This determination can be complicated; in short, if an unfair labor practice has "anything to do with" causing a strike or if it appears that the employer's unlawful conduct played a part in the employees' decision to strike, then the strike is an unfair labor practice strike.[34] Also, an employer's unfair labor practice during an economic strike can convert it to an unfair labor practice strike.

[33] *Mastro Plastics Corp. v. NLRB,* 350 U.S. 270 (1956).

[34] *NLRB v. Cast Optics Corp.,* 458 F.2d 398 (3d Cir. 1972), cert. denied 409 U.S. 850 (1972). *Larand Leisurelies,* 213 NLRB 197 (1974), enfd. 523 F.2d 814 (6th Cir. 1975).

Labor Law Discussion: Replacing Strikers by Inverse Seniority: Saving Costs or Coercing Employees?

Box 9.7

Background

Child Care Services, Inc. (CCSI), operates 12 child care centers. A local of the American Federation of State, County, and Municipal Employees (AFSCME) has represented employees at CCSI for over 15 years with the most recent collective bargaining agreement covering 80 nonprofessional employees (four teachers were covered by a separate contract). In anticipation of the June 30 expiration date, CCSI (represented by attorney Donald Barrister and executive director Susan Gruber) and AFSCME (represented by AFSCME staff rep Elaine Mendez and five bargaining unit members), bargained between April and June. However, the parties were unable to reach agreement.

In a final attempt to craft a settlement, the two parties met on June 27. At this bargaining session, the union presented a proposal consisting of a $1,500 per year wage increase, employer-paid health insurance, shift assignments, and a few other items. CCSI countered with a final offer of no wage increase and sharing of health care costs. Barrister also said that if there was a strike, the child care centers would be operated by permanent replacements and strikers would be replaced by inverse seniority. In other words, employees with the most seniority would be replaced first.

Later that evening, the union held a membership meeting and the negotiating committee briefed the membership on the day's events. Many employees were upset at CCSI's plans to replace employees by reverse seniority, especially since the negotiating committee would be the first to be replaced: the employees on the committee were 1st, 2nd, 5th, 9th, and 19th on the seniority list. By a large margin, those present voted to reject the company's final offer and to go on strike.

On July 1, 54 employees went on strike while 26 did not. Over the next few months, 34 replacements were hired. During the strike there was no mention of unfair labor practice allegations or the reverse seniority replacement plan. The picket signs read "On Strike for Fair Wages and Health Insurance." On July 25, Mendez met with Barrister and told him that the strike was over and made an unconditional offer to return to work. In January, CCSI began offering reinstatement to the strikers by seniority.

Questions

1. Recall that the *Mackay* doctrine grants employers the right to hire replacement workers during an economic strike. CCSI indicated that it would replace striking employees by inverse seniority. Does this plan violate the section 8(a)(1) of the NLRA or is it allowable under the *Mackay* doctrine?

2. Assuming that the replacement plan violated the NLRA and was therefore an unfair labor practice, was the strike then an unfair labor practice strike?

3. Were the strikers entitled to be reinstated as of July 25? Does it matter whether or not the strike was an unfair labor practice strike?

4. During the Administrative Law Judge hearings for this case, Gruber testified that the reason for replacing employees by reverse seniority was that it would save $40,000 because more senior employees are more expensive. However, it was unclear whether this explanation was offered to the union at the June 27 bargaining session or whether it was an afterthought used in defense during the hearings. Therefore, the NLRB remanded the case back to the Administrative Law Judge for further factual investigation. Why is it important whether the cost-savings rationale was offered to the union on June 27?

Whether a work stoppage is a strike or a lockout is also critically important for determining the legal use of replacement workers. Recall that a lockout is similar to an economic strike in that it is a work stoppage that results from a bargaining dispute, but that a lockout is initiated by the employer rather than the employees. It is useful to distinguish between defensive and offensive lockouts.[35] A defensive lockout occurs when the employer locks out the employees to prevent losses from an expected strike. If an employer handles perishable goods and expects a

---

[35] Ray, Sharpe, and Strassfield, *Understanding Labor Law.* Taylor and Witney, *Labor Relations Law.*

strike but the union will not reveal the timing of its strike plans, then the employer can lock out the employees to prevent losses stemming from the spoilage of its perishable products. This is a defensive action to protect the employer from significant economic losses. In contrast, an offensive lockout occurs when an employer takes the initiative to put pressure on the union to settle for more favorable terms. A common reason for this initiative is to control the timing of the work stoppage. Baseball players struck in 1994 just before the playoffs, so they had been paid for much of the season while the owners would lose significant amounts of revenue during this time of peak fan interest. After seeing this, the NBA and NHL owners locked out professional basketball and hockey players in 1994 and 1995 *before* their seasons began.[36]

Both defensive and offensive lockouts are legal (assuming an absence of illegal actions like surface bargaining) as long as they are to protect or support employers' bargaining positions. Lockouts are not legal if they are overly aggressive and appear to be an attempt to destroy the union. As such, employers can use *temporary* replacements during lockouts—this has been interpreted as legitimate support of a bargaining position.[37] But to maintain a balance between employees and employers, hiring *permanent* replacements is not allowed.[38] This would be too destructive of employee rights: an employer could lock employees out against their wishes, hire permanent replacements, and decertify the union. These outcomes are also possible with a strike, but note the critical difference—in a strike, the employees are choosing to go on a strike, in a lockout the employees are forced out.

The legal rulings that establish the doctrine surrounding the use of replacement workers in both strikes and lockouts largely date back to the 1960s and before. In fact, the *Mackay* decision was handed down in 1938, and was not controversial at that time.[39] The issue was a quiet one until the 1980s, but since that time it has been engulfed in perhaps the most intense debate in U.S. labor relations. The spark that set this debate afire was the 1981 firing of the striking air traffic controllers by President Reagan during the illegal PATCO strike (recall Box 4.24). Among labor supporters, it is frequently argued that this event set the tenor for labor relations in the 1980s and made it acceptable to replace workers during strikes—though the true linkage may never be known.[40] Two years later, copper producer Phelps Dodge showed that permanent strike replacements could be used to effectively break a strike and decertify a union in a legal, private sector strike.[41]

While permanently replaced strikers have the right to priority recall when jobs become available, the NLRA specifies that they are only eligible to vote in a decertification election within 12 months of the start of the strike. A decertification election at Phelps Dodge occurred 15 months after the strike began, and unsurprisingly the unions were decertified because all of the voters were either strike replacements or employees that crossed the picket lines. Permanent strike replacements were subsequently used in bitter strikes at Hormel (1985), International Paper (1987) (see Box 9.8), Greyhound (1990), Bridgestone-Firestone (1995), the Detroit News (1995), Northwest Airlines (2005), and elsewhere.[42]

[36] Michael H. LeRoy, "Lockouts Involving Replacement Workers: An Empirical Public Policy Analysis and Proposal to Balance Economic Weapons Under the NLRA," *Washington University Law Quarterly* 74 (Winter 1996), pp. 981–1057.

[37] *NLRB v. Brown,* 380 U.S. 278 (1965). *Harter Equipment,* 280 NLRB 597 (1986).

[38] *Harter Equipment,* 293 NLRB 647 (1989).

[39] Estreicher, "Collective Bargaining Or 'Collective Begging'?"

[40] Michael H. LeRoy, "The PATCO Strike: Myths and Realities," in Paula B. Voos (ed.), *Proceedings of the Forty-Ninth Annual Meeting* (Madison, WI: Industrial Relations Research Association, 1997), pp. 15–22.

[41] Barbara Kingsolver, *Holding the Line: Women in the Great Arizona Mine Strike of 1983* (Ithaca, NY: ILR Press, 1989). Rosenblum, *Copper Crucible.*

[42] Julius Getman, *The Betrayal of Local 14* (Ithaca, NY: ILR Press, 1998). Dave Hage and Paul Klauda, *No Retreat, No Surrender: Labor's War at Hormel* (New York: William Morrow, 1989). Peter Rachleff, *Hard-Pressed in the Heartland: The Hormel Strike and the Future of the Labor Movement* (Boston: South End Press, 1993).

In 1987–88, workers represented by the United Paperworkers International Union at the Jay, Maine, Lock Haven, Pennsylvania, and DePere, Wisconsin, plants of the International Paper Company struck for 17 months when the company demanded significant concessions. At the time, International Paper was earning record profits and refused to share its financial records with the union to justify the need for concessions. When the strikers were permanently replaced after a few weeks, the strike became very bitter and divided the union, families, and communities. Consider some perspectives of the participants in their own words:

A mill manager on the company's decision to use permanent strike replacements.
"We had enjoyed a stable workforce, with whom the Company had a constructive relationship. We did not provoke the strike, nor did we have any interest or intent in replacing that workforce when the dispute began. However, the union left us with no choice. By striking, the union put the Company in the position of either accepting conditions which would have clearly made the mill uncompetitive within the industry . . . or shutting down the mill, eliminating jobs not only there but in other parts of the Company and in the community dependent on our producing and fulfilling our orders. The only alternative allowing us to continue to fulfill our commitments to our other employees, customers, communities, and shareholders, was to hire permanent replacement workers."

The president of the United Paperworkers International Union on the company's demands.
"They were asking for stuff that we've had for 25 years in our contract [including the Christmas Day holiday]. And it was at a time when the profits with the company were setting records. And at the same time now, they gave the executives an average of a 38 percent increase in salary. It boggles your mind."

A mill worker/former union steward/one-time temporary supervisor on striking.
"If we had accepted this contract or not voted to strike and worked without one, they could have squeezed 1,200 workers [at another plant] until they relented to the contract which was offered them. [Note: three months earlier, Mobile, Alabama, workers continued working without a contract and International Paper locked them out and hired temporary replacements.]

Then . . . they could have squeezed us, and they could have done that to every plant . . . so we in essence would have been cutting our own throat anyway. This company was out to squeeze the worker and they were going to do it systematically throughout the United States. I have no doubt in my mind. I sat on both sides and could see it coming."

A replacement worker on taking the job of a striker.
"No. It wasn't really a hard decision. You had no choice, especially when you're in the construction business working like I was, $5.70 an hour. It doesn't take much to convince you—when somebody tells you you can make $16.00 an hour, and you've been trying to get into a paper mill. So if you have any family at all, then you'd be a fool not to go for it."

A local supporter of the union on the replacement workers.
"In my book there is no redeeming a scab under any circumstances whatsoever. That means never, ever. . . . Scabs epitomize self-interest and would likely run their mothers over if it meant an extra buck or two. Scabs are scumbags."

A striker on the impact of the strike and of using replacement workers on the community.
"It has put brother against brother, friend against friend, neighbor against neighbor. It will take many generations before the hurt and anger will heal."

Questions
1. Is it ethical for a company to use permanent strike replacements? How about temporary strike replacements?
2. Is it ethical for individuals to cross picket lines and become temporary or permanent strike replacements?
3. Is it ethical for unions and their supporters to attack strike replacements as "scabs" and try to prevent them from crossing picket lines?

Sources: Julius Getman, *The Betrayal of Local 14* (Ithaca, NY: ILR Press, 1998), pp. 32, 40, 71, 196, and 213. U.S. Congress, *Hearings on H.R. 5, The Striker Replacement Bill,* Hearings Before the Subcommittee on Labor–Management Relations of the Committee on Education and Labor, House of Representatives, March 6 and 13, 1991 (Washington, DC: U.S. Government Printing Office, 1991), p. 244.

These high-profile examples underlie the belief in the labor movement that the use of strike replacements exploded in the 1980s. Research indicates that replacements were used in 10–20 percent of strikes during the 1980s, but without comparable statistics for the earlier period, the extent to which this represents an increase remains an open question.[43]

Based on the results of these high-profile strikes, banning the use of permanent strike replacements is one of the labor movement's top legislative priorities. Labor argues that workers are essentially fired for striking, so other workers are afraid to strike. This destruction of the right to strike is argued to disrupt the balance of the U.S. labor relations system and give employers vastly greater power. And for employers that are determined to rid themselves of their unions, the use of permanent replacements allows them to accomplish this objective by forcing a strike through hard bargaining, hiring permanent strike replacements, and engineering a decertification election.[44] For labor, the use of permanent strike replacements is not about keeping a business operating during a strike—this could be accomplished with temporary replacements; it is about busting unions through intensified confrontation. That some companies use professional "security" companies (some would say "strikebreaking" companies)—the modern descendants of the Pinkerton Agency—that provide armed guards in combat fatigues or riot gear to intimidate strikers and protect replacement workers reinforces the suspicions of labor.[45] As another example, the U.S. Nursing Corporation specializes in providing nurses to hospitals during nurse strikes by recruiting nurses from around the country, arranging transportation to the strike locations, and providing housing for replacement nurses.

On the other hand, business argues that the current system is balanced and that banning permanent strike replacements would favor unions. Without the threat of being permanently replaced, it is argued that unions will strike more frequently for increased demands that will reduce competitiveness and jobs. To business, the use of permanent strike replacements is not about busting unions, it is about maintaining competitiveness. Between 1985 and 1995, the U.S. Congress considered, but did not pass, at least four proposals to limit the use of permanent strike replacements. And the debate goes on (see Box 9.9). In the public sector, only Minnesota bans the use of permanent strike replacements. And so the United States continues to be relatively unique among industrialized, democratic countries in allowing permanent strike replacements.

OTHER PRESSURE TACTICS

Labor's primary economic weapon is the strike, but this is not the only tactic for applying pressure on an employer. Boycotts, work slowdowns, and corporate campaigns are also designed to increase labor's bargaining power by imposing costs on employers, and to therefore win more favorable settlements for employees. Though the legality of such tactics is mixed, they have become more important and more frequent since the 1980s. The reason for this trend is straightforward: as the use of strike replacements (perceived or real) has

[43] Peter C. Cramton and Joseph S. Tracy, "The Use of Replacement Workers in Union Contract Negotiations: The U.S. Experience, 1980–1989," *Journal of Labor Economics* 16 (October 1998), pp. 667–701. Craig A. Olson, "The Use of Strike Replacements in Labor Disputes: Evidence from the 1880s to the 1980s" (unpublished paper, University of Wisconsin–Madison, 1991). John F. Schnell and Cynthia L. Gramm, "The Empirical Relations Between Employers' Striker Replacement Strategies and Strike Duration," *Industrial and Labor Relations Review* 47 (January 1994), pp. 189–206.

[44] Rick Fantasia and Kim Voss, *Hard Work: Remaking the American Labor Movement* (Berkeley: University of California Press, 2004).

[45] Stephen H. Norwood, *Strikebreaking and Intimidation: Mercenaries and Masculinity in Twentieth-Century America of the Labor Movement* (Chapel Hill: University of North Carolina Press, 2002). Robert Michael Smith, *From Blackjacks to Briefcases: A History of Commercialized Strikebreaking and Unionbusting in the United States* (Athens: Ohio University Press, 2003).

Labor and Business Square Off over Proposed Legislation to Ban Permanent Strike Replacements

Box 9.9

STATEMENT OF RICHARD L. TRUMKA, PRESIDENT, UNITED MINE WORKERS OF AMERICA

"For the men and women who labor in our Nation's factories, mines, and offices, the distinction between being fired and permanently replaced is, for all practical purposes, nonexistent. Either way, you lose your job—a high price to pay for exercising a right supposedly guaranteed under the law.

. . .

By raising the stakes of what should be a limited conflict over limited objectives, the employment of permanent strike replacements transforms an economic strike—a strike over the terms and conditions which will govern the strikers' employment when they resume work—into a life or death struggle which can only be settled by the economic destruction of one of the parties.

There are those who would argue that protecting workers from being permanently replaced will lead labor unions to make unreasonable demands and will only encourage unions to destroy an employer to achieve this goal. This argument is unreasonable on its face.

A union that starts off with the intent of destroying an employer is engaging in economic suicide. In fact, it is inconceivable that any responsible labor organization would ever set out on a course to permanently weaken—let alone destroy—a company with whom it has a bargaining relationship. . . . While some of the business community has claimed that striker replacement promotes compromise at the bargaining table, the opposite is in fact true. As we saw at Eastern Airlines, the use of permanent replacement workers causes strikes to be longer, more confrontational and tragic for the community.

. . .

The Mackay doctrine is, in fact, more glitter than substance. It is destructive to workers, communities and business; it is harmful to the public and to our economy and, despite its attraction to a certain type of management mentality, increasingly less likely to succeed in the long run. In fact, the legally sanctioned use of permanent replacement workers recreates the very conditions the [NLRA] sought to eliminate in 1935. Instead of enabling our economy to compete more effectively in the global marketplace of the 1990s, it will make our Nation increasingly less likely to do so."

STATEMENT OF STEVEN G. LAMB, MILL MANAGER, INTERNATIONAL PAPER

"Current law ensures that there are risks to both sides of failing to resolve a dispute and disrupting production. This bill [to ban permanent strike replacements] would eliminate the risks for one side and increase them for the other. What could possibly justify this dramatic shift in labor law?

Proponents of the legislation assert that the ability to hire permanent replacement workers during a strike negates the right of workers to strike, and results in their being "fired" for exercising that right. This assertion—while superficially appealing—ignores several basic facts.

First, being replaced is not tantamount to being fired, since the replaced worker, under existing law, has the preferential right to reinstatement as positions become available.

Second, current law is designed to protect the employee's right to strike and those protections are numerous; it is not designed to guarantee the employee a right to a job under any circumstances, nor to protect him against the laws of economics. . . . Similarly, the employer is not protected from the laws of economics. If he seeks to operate under terms and conditions unacceptable to employees, he will be unable to attract a workforce capable of producing a marketable product or service. The degree of risk for both employee and employer will vary with time, location, and circumstance, with the marketplace providing the ultimate balance.

If the law is changed to protect one party against the consequences of its actions, that balance will be tilted in a manner disruptive to the economy.

. . .

If this bill [to ban permanent strike replacements] is enacted, the consequences are likely to be broadly felt, as more American businesses are rendered unproductive by increased work stoppages and uncompetitive by inflationary labor demands. The result will be shrinking profitability, investment, and ultimately, jobs. Those pushing for passage of this bill are seeking to gain an advantage in the wrong arena—the arena of the past, confrontation, rather than the arena of the future, competitiveness. The arena of confrontation will close factory doors—for good; the arena of competitiveness will not."

Source: U.S. Congress, *Hearings on H.R. 5, The Striker Replacement Bill,* Hearings Before the Subcommittee on Labor-Management Relations of the Committee on Education and Labor, House of Representatives, March 6 and 13, 1991 (Washington, DC: U.S. Government Printing Office, 1991), pp. 240–45 and 287–89.

increased, labor unions have increasingly turned to tactics in which employees do not risk losing their jobs by being permanently replaced in a strike. Additionally, boycotts and corporate campaigns can also be used to increase the pressure on a struck employer, especially when a strike is being neutralized by the use of replacement workers. In short, unions believe that employers have escalated economic warfare through the use of strike replacements, and unions have responded by searching for alternatives to strikes and also by further escalating conflicts through the use of other pressure tactics. In the public sector, these other pressure tactics are more frequent when strikes are prohibited.[46]

One pressure tactic that has a long history in labor relations is the boycott. A boycott is a campaign to encourage a company's customers to stop doing business with it. In a bargaining dispute in the U.S. private sector, a boycott is generally legal if it narrowly targets the company directly involved in this bargaining dispute—in legal terms, the primary employer. But section 8(b)(4) of the NLRA prohibits **secondary boycotts**—boycotts that target secondary rather than primary employers. In general, a secondary employer is an organization that does not directly employ the workers who are involved in the dispute. Consider the employees of a hotel who are demanding wage and benefit improvements from the hotel's management. The hotel is the primary employer and the hotel's employees can legally launch a consumer boycott campaign by asking travelers to stay at a different hotel. But encouraging consumers to not patronize (in other words, to boycott) a local flower shop because it supplies flowers to the hotel is illegal because the flower shop is a secondary or neutral employer.

While this example might seem straightforward, note that the legal doctrine on boycotts can be quite complex.[47] What if the union just publicizes the fact that the flower shop does business with the hotel without explicitly asking consumers to boycott it? Or could the union boycott the flower shop if it is owned by the same corporate parent as the hotel? Or if the hotel's flower arrangements were done by hotel employees until the bargaining dispute at which time the work was contracted out to the flower shop? The answers to these three scenarios are probably, probably not, and probably, but more importantly, in all of these cases the NLRB tries to balance the rights of employees and employers.

Boycotts frequently involve picketing in order to publicize the boycott, and the legality of such conduct can be especially complex in the construction industry when employees of numerous companies are working at the same construction site. Suppose electricians are on strike against an electrical contractor, and they picket an entire construction site where they work alongside other construction trades that work for other contractors. This is called common situs picketing because it involves multiple employers at a common location or site. Common situs picketing that targets the entire worksite is illegal because it includes secondary or neutral employers.[48] It is now common for construction sites to include separate gates for different contractors so picketers are limited to the gate of their employer. But there can still be significant complications if the primary gate is too far removed from the public's eye, if there are mixed-use gates, or if there is a roving employer (such as a construction equipment repair company that is called to different job sites throughout the workday).[49] How the message is conveyed—for example, by the use of giant inflatable rats—can also be controversial (see Box 9.10). In all of these cases, the law seeks to balance the employees' right to publicize their dispute with the secondary or neutral employers' right to conduct business.

---

[46] Robert Hebdon and Robert Stern, "Do Public-Sector Strike Bans Really Prevent Conflict?" *Industrial Relations* 42 (July 2003), pp. 493–512.

[47] Ray, Sharpe, and Strassfield, *Understanding Labor Law.* Taylor and Witney, *Labor Relations Law.*

[48] *NLRB v. Denver Building Trades Council,* 341 U.S. 675 (1951).

[49] Feldacker, *Labor Guide to Labor Law.*

Without the NLRB's Muscle, Tony Soprano Loses to a Giant Inflatable Rat   Box 9.10

During season four of the hit TV drama *The Soprano's*, mob figures Carmine Lupertazzi and Tony Soprano are battling for cuts of a housing scam. After Tony has Carmine's new restaurant ransacked in the "Eloise" episode, Carmine tells Johnny Sack, "I haven't wanted to do this, but it's gotta be . . . call the union." Cut to Tony's construction site for the Esplanade project and, consistent with popular media stereotypes, a corrupt union business agent drives up with a giant inflatable rat in the back of his pickup—complete with pink beady eyes, two big teeth, and claws poised to strike—and announces that because of the use of nonunion laborers, the job site is shut down until further notice.

This is an example of art imitates life—giant inflatable rats ranging from 10 to 30 feet tall have become a common sight at labor disputes in New York and other major cities. During a musician's strike at Radio City Music Hall in New York City in 2005, striking workers were accompanied by a giant inflatable rat; management responded by putting a ferocious-looking inflatable cougar on top of the Radio City marquee. The use of inflatable rats has been especially common at construction sites to protest the use of nonunion labor as in *The Soprano's*. In this episode, if the laborers' union had set up a picket line to cause electricians and other workers of other contractors to quit working at the job site, this would have clearly been an illegal boycott under the NLRA's prohibition on secondary boycotts. But sometimes there aren't any pickets, just a giant inflatable rat as in *The Soprano's* episode.

Unions argue that this is free speech, but companies argue that this is illegal secondary picketing. In the absence of formal pickets, the NLRB has ruled that secondary "signal picketing" is illegal. Signal picketing is an action that effectively sends the same signal or message as picketing. So a debate has emerged: are giant inflatable rats signal pickets, and therefore illegal? To date, the NLRB has ruled that because employees know that the rat is a sign of labor protest, especially against "rat contractors" and their low wages and dangerous working conditions,

it is a signal picket. And at construction job sites where this signal picketing is secondary in nature—that is, it is aimed at pressuring a secondary employer—the use of giant inflatable rats is illegal. Rather than trying to outlast his mob rival with his job site shut down, Tony Soprano could have used the muscle of the NLRB.

Sources: Alison Grant, "Free Speech or Vermin: Employers Setting Legal Traps for Unions' Rat Inflatables, *Plain Dealer* (Cleveland), October 4, 2005. *Laborers' Eastern Region Organizing Fund*, 346 NLRB No. 105 (2006).

A second pressure tactic is the work slowdown. Slowdowns try to pressure employers by imposing costs through lowered productivity, but without employees leaving their jobs and going on strike (and therefore facing the risk of being permanently replaced). Slowdowns can take various forms. Perhaps the most creative is a **work-to-rule campaign** in which employees do their work by exactly following the employer's rules. For example, if there is a safety rule that all machines must be inspected before being used, a worker can spend 15 minutes at the start of each shift thoroughly checking every nut and bolt on the machine. And perhaps the machine will need to be inspected again after being turned off for lunch. Postal workers can check numerous zip codes, grocery clerks can do frequent price checks, and utility workers can scrupulously check for gas leaks. More generally, workers can frequently ask supervisors questions to make sure they understand their tasks. When overtime is voluntary, workers can refuse to work overtime. The legal status of such actions is unsettled. On the one hand, if workers are simply following management's rules, it's hard to argue that it is not acceptable.[50] On the other hand, if a work-to-rule campaign is interpreted as a withholding of work that has been traditionally provided (literally, slowing down work), then perhaps it is insubordination and is not protected by the NLRA.[51] The NLRB has yet to issue definitive rulings.

Another method for engaging in work slowdowns is the use of partial, quickie, or intermittent strikes.[52] A refusal to work overtime is a partial strike, a very short duration strike (such as one day, or even one hour) is a quickie strike, and a series of repeated quickie strikes amounts to an intermittent strike. The basic goal of these job actions is to disrupt the employer's operations, but by making these strikes a surprise and for very short periods of time, it is difficult for an employer to hire strike replacements. Such strikes, however, are often ruled to be insubordination, not legitimate protected activity, so employees can be disciplined and discharged for engaging in these types of strikes. In the public sector where strikes are often illegal, workers sometimes resort to quickie strikes by conducting coordinated days of mass absenteeism—for example, a number of police officers can catch the "blue flu" and all call in sick on the same day (see Box 9.11).[53] Work slowdowns are often part of a broader campaign of inside-the-workplace tactics—sometimes called an inside game strategy—that includes visible demonstrations of worker solidarity such as wearing armbands and holding rallies in the parking lot before work.[54]

The most recently developed economic pressure tactic—the **corporate campaign**—seeks to bolster these inside tactics with external pressure, typically directed at corporate headquarters by outsiders such as other members of the business and financial community, consumers, politicians, and government regulators. The union's strategy is to create negative publicity that causes these outsiders to pressure or withdraw support for the targeted company. It is common to trace the beginnings of corporate campaigns to the union campaign directed against the textile company J. P. Stevens in the late 1970s.[55] After years of being thwarted by union-busting techniques (such as firing union supporters), the textile workers union shifted its focus from the workplace to the corporate boardroom. Remember that it is common for a company's board of directors to include outside directors who are also executives from other companies. The J. P. Stevens board included the chairman of the cosmetics company Avon. When J. P. Stevens's aggressive antiunion conduct towards its female workers was publicized to women who used Avon products, Avon's chairman resigned from the J. P. Stevens board. The chairman of J. P. Stevens resigned from the board of a major bank when unions threatened to withdraw its pension funds from this bank. This type of high-level pressure is credited with causing J. P. Stevens to finally settle with the textile workers union.

Since that time, there has been great interest within the labor movement in using corporate campaigns to increase labor's power. In addition to pressuring corporate directors and

---

[50] *Central Illinois Public Service Company,* 326 NLRB No. 80 (1998).

[51] *Caterpillar, Inc.,* 322 NLRB No. 115 (1996).

[52] Michael H. LeRoy, "Creating Order Out of CHAOS and Other Partial and Intermittent Strikes," *Northwestern University Law Review* 95 (Fall 2000), pp. 221–70.

[53] Richard C. Kearney, *Labor Relations in the Public Sector,* 2nd ed. (New York: Marcel Dekker, 1992), p. 270.

[54] Dan LaBotz, *A Troublemaker's Handbook: How to Fight Back Where You Work—And Win!* (Detroit: Labor Notes, 1991).

[55] Hage and Klauda, *No Retreat, No Surrender.* Tom Juravich and Kate Bronfenbrenner, *Ravenswood: The Steelworkers' Victory and the Revival of American Labor* (Ithaca, NY: Cornell University Press, 1999). LaBotz, *A Troublemaker's Handbook.*

Blue Flu	Mass absenteeism among police officers, named after blue uniforms	Heal-In	Doctors refusing to release patients
Red Flu or Red Rash	Same as the blue flu, but for firefighters	Human Error Day	Intentional day of mistakes by clerical workers
Chalk Dust Fever	Same as the blue flu, but for teachers		
Budgetitus	Mass absenteeism among public sector workers in protest over budget issues		

Source: Richard C. Kearney, *Labor Relations in the Public Sector*. 2nd ed. (New York: Marcel Dekker, 1992), p. 270.

financial linkages with major banks, some corporate campaigns have expanded to also include the use of regulatory agencies, politicians, and activist organizations or causes. Such efforts can bring the labor movement into unexpected alliances. A corporate campaign against copper producer Phelps Dodge in the 1980s found support among college students who were involved in campus-based antiapartheid protests of corporate investment in South Africa. Labor activists are currently working with college students on the "Campaign to Stop Killer Coke" stemming from the killing of union supporters at Coca-Cola bottling plants in South America.[56] Corporate campaigns also find labor unions working closely with environmental groups—while there can be conflicts if workers see environmentalists as reducing jobs through environmental protections, they have also teamed up to push for sustainable jobs and a sustainable natural environment.[57] During labor disputes, these two groups also have a common interest in bringing a company's environmental violations to the attention of federal and state regulators. For example, the publicity and pressure generated in the above-mentioned Phelps Dodge corporate campaign caused the Environmental Protection Agency to fine the company $18 million for water pollution. Note that corporate campaigns might include boycotts, but corporate campaigns are comprehensive strategies that go beyond just the use of consumer boycotts.

Both the success and legality of corporate campaigns are debatable.[58] The campaigns against J. P. Stevens and Ravenswood Aluminum (see Box 9.12) are visible success stories; campaigns against Phelps Dodge, Hormel, and International Paper are visible failures.[59] Labor supporters see corporate campaigns as important tools for pressuring corporations who seem to hold all the power in a global economy, and in the process of conducting such campaigns, for building stronger, more vibrant labor organizations with greater rank and file participation and stronger linkages with other community groups.[60] Critics—who are also proponents of free markets—see corporate campaigns as manipulating the media and regulatory agencies to benefit unionized workers at the expense of consumers and nonunion

[56] www.killercoke.org.

[57] Laura Paskus, "In Search of Solidarity," *High Country News* 36 (May 24, 2004).

[58] Paul Jarley and Cheryl L. Maranto, "Union Corporate Campaigns: An Assessment," *Industrial and Labor Relations Review* 43 (July 1990), pp. 505–24. Charles R. Perry, "Corporate Campaigns in Context," *Journal of Labor Research* 17 (Summer 1996), pp. 329–43.

[59] Hage and Klauda, *No Retreat, No Surrender.* Getman, *The Betrayal of Local 14.* Juravich and Bronfenbrenner, *Ravenswood.* Rosenblum, *Copper Crucible.*

[60] Kate Bronfenbrenner and Tom Juravich, "The Evolution of Strategic and Coordinated Bargaining Campaigns in the 1990s: The Steelworkers' Experience," in Lowell Turner, Harry C. Katz, and Richard W. Hurd (eds.), *Rekindling the Movement: Labor's Quest for Relevance in the Twenty-First Century* (Ithaca, NY: ILR Press, 2001), Chapter 9. LaBotz, *A Troublemaker's Handbook.*

The Corporate Campaign against Ravenswood Aluminum

Box 9.12

At the end of October 1990, the Ravenswood Aluminum Company in Ravenswood, West Virginia, declared an impasse in its contract negotiations with Local 5668 of the United Steelworkers of America and locked out the 1,700 production and maintenance workers. Before the contract had even expired, several buses of replacement workers were idling in the company parking lot and the replacement workers entered the plant almost immediately after the start of the lockout. The company also brought in guards with military-style clothing, riot shields, and video cameras. Replacement workers did the production jobs; salaried employees worked 12-hour shifts, seven days a week, doing their regular jobs plus the maintenance and janitorial tasks of locked-out workers.

By January, the company was operating with between 750 and 1,100 replacement workers. Less than 1 percent of the union members had crossed the picket lines, but the union felt powerless to get the company to negotiate. Several union offers of significant concessions were summarily rejected without discussion by the company. The union filed unfair labor practice charges accusing the company of engaging in bad faith bargaining and in unilaterally implementing its final offer without reaching an impasse. But unfair labor practice cases take a while to be investigated and litigated by the NLRB; the Steelworkers wanted faster results. Consequently, the national Steelworkers leadership decided to launch a corporate campaign against Ravenswood Aluminum.

One track of the corporate campaign was to target consumers. Union members followed trucks from the Ravenswood plant to their destinations to determine what companies were using the finished aluminum products. These companies were then contacted by the union and Anheuser-Busch, Miller Brewing, and Stroh's ultimately agreed to not use aluminum from Ravenswood in its cans rather than risk the negative publicity of being tied to Ravenswood.

The second track of the Steelworkers' corporate campaign was targeting the owners and creditors of Ravenswood Aluminum. Working with researchers from the AFL–CIO and other labor activists, a Steelworkers team was able to trace the company's complex ownership structure. The offices of major investors in New York and Connecticut were then picketed. A significant piece of the ownership puzzle was Marc Rich, a commodities trader who had earlier fled the United States to Switzerland to avoid being convicted of fraud, tax evasion, and trading with the enemy (by violating the U.S. embargo of Iranian oil). In fact, Rich was America's most-wanted white-collar criminal. The Steelworkers then worked with European labor unions to further uncover the secret activities of Marc Rich. Demonstrations were held outside of Rich's Swiss offices and the unionists met with a major source of his financing in the Netherlands, NMB Postbank. This negative publicity started to scuttle Rich's deals with corporations and governments that were unaware of his shady dealings.

Lastly, when Ravenswood denied government safety inspectors access to the aluminum plant, the Steelworkers lobbied national politicians to investigate. This led to a wall-to-wall OSHA inspection and a December 1991 citation for over 200 health and safety violations and a $600,000 fine. Environmental investigations—more negative publicity for the company—were then launched and the company was sued for violating the Clean Water Act.

After more than a year of this intense corporate campaign, and with an unfair labor practice ruling looming, the CEO of Ravenswood Aluminum was ousted and negotiations began again in April 1992. Because of the corporate campaign, "This time the whole world was watching . . . the U.S. Congress, the international and national news media, and financial investors worldwide. This was no longer a simple negotiation between a local union and a West Virginia employer." At the end of June 1992, the workers ratified a new contract containing wage, pension, and safety improvements and returned to work victorious.

Source: Tom Juravich and Kate Bronfenbrenner, *Ravenswood: The Steelworkers' Victory and the Revival of American Labor* (Ithaca, NY: Cornell University Press, 1999). Quote is from p. 185.

workers, and as ineffective in stemming organized labor's decline.[61] Since corporate campaigns are outside of the workplace, the legality of these campaigns will be determined outside of labor law. In particular, companies have tried to challenge corporate campaigns by charging unions with blackmail, extortion, and other illegal interference in business relations, primarily under the same law used to prosecute the mafia (the Racketeer Influenced and Corrupt Organization Act, or RICO).[62] Free speech rights, however, have largely prevailed.[63]

THIRD-PARTY DISPUTE RESOLUTION

One way to settle a bargaining impasse is to let the parties resort to economic weapons—strikes, lockouts, corporate campaigns, boycotts, strike replacements, and the like. Escalating the costs of disagreement will bring the parties to a settlement, or the relationship will disintegrate as in the case of strikes that lead to decertification. In either case, the dispute is resolved. But economic weapons can be very costly dispute resolution mechanisms and the public interest might be better served by more proactive methods of resolving impasses. Third-party dispute resolution mechanisms use a neutral third party to settle bargaining impasses with the goal of avoiding costly strikes. In the private sector, a strong sense of property rights and the freedom to enter into economic contracts of one's own choosing means that the use of third-party dispute resolution mechanisms is usually voluntary—they are rarely forced on labor and management. In the public sector, however, the primacy of serving the public interest means that third-party dispute resolution mechanisms are often compulsory—labor and management must use them before or instead of striking.

The three primary third-party dispute resolution mechanisms are mediation, arbitration, and fact-finding. In mediation, the neutral third party is a mediator who tries to facilitate an agreement, but lacks the power to force an agreement. In arbitration, the neutral third party is an arbitrator who forces an agreement on both parties by issuing a ruling that specifies the settlement terms. In fact-finding, the neutral third party is a fact finder who investigates the dispute and makes nonbinding recommendations for a settlement. Hybrid mechanisms can also be created, such as med-arb in which the mediator becomes the arbitrator if mediation fails. These dispute resolution mechanisms differ in the amount of control the third party has over the dispute resolution process and the outcome (see Box 9.13).[64] A mediator has a high level of control over the negotiating process, but not the outcome; an arbitrator has the opposite—a high level of control over the outcome, but is not involved in the negotiating process. A fact finder lacks control over both the process and the outcome.

While mediators and arbitrators both serve critical functions as third-party neutrals in labor relations, the career paths and skills are typically different. Mediators can either be

[61] Thomas J. DiLorenzo, "The Corporate Campaign Against Food Lion: A Study of Media Manipulation," *Journal of Labor Research* 17 (Summer 1996), pp. 359–75. Herbert R. Northrup, "Expanding Union Power by Comprehensive Corporate Campaigns and Manipulation of the Regulatory Process," in Bruce E. Kaufman (ed.), *Government Regulation of the Employment Relationship* (Madison, WI: Industrial Relations Research Association, 1997), Chapter 17.

[62] Nathan Newman, "The Conflict of the Courts: RICO, Labor, and Legal Preemption in Union Comprehensive Campaigns," *Drake Law Review* 51 (2003), pp. 307–60.

[63] *Edward J. DeBartolo Corp. v. Florida Gulf Coast Building and Construction Trades Council*, 485 U.S. 568 (1988).

[64] Victor G. Devinatz and John W. Budd, "Third Party Dispute Resolution—Interest Disputes," in David Lewin, Daniel J. B. Mitchell, and Mahmood A. Zaidi (eds.), *The Human Resource Management Handbook Part II* (Greenwich, CT: JAI Press, 1997), pp. 95–135. Roy J. Lewicki, Stephen E. Weiss, and David Lewin, "Models of Conflict, Negotiation and Third Party Intervention: A Review and Synthesis," *Journal of Organizational Behavior* 13 (May 1992), pp. 209–52.

BOX 9.13
Options for Third-Party Dispute Resolution.

Source: Victor G. Devinatz and John W. Budd, "Third Party Dispute Resolution—Interest Disputes," in David Lewin, Daniel J. B. Mitchell, and Mahmood A. Zaidi (eds.), *The Human Resource Management Handbook Part II* (Greenwich, CT: JAI Press, 1997), pp. 95–135 at 96.

		Degree of Third-Party Control over the Negotiating Process	
		Low	High
Degree of Third-Party Control over the Outcome	Low	Fact-finding	Mediation
	High	Arbitration	Med-Arb

independent practitioners or full-time employees of mediation agencies at the federal level (the Federal Mediation and Conciliation Service and the National Mediation Board) or the state level (such as the Pennsylvania Bureau of Mediation Services). In contrast, arbitrators are usually either full-time, self-employed arbitrators or are lawyers or university professors (typically in law or industrial relations) who arbitrate on a part-time basis.[65] Both mediators and arbitrators rarely begin their careers in these positions; rather, individuals almost always develop expertise in labor relations in other ways before becoming mediators or arbitrators later in their careers. Significant experience negotiating contracts as either a management or labor negotiator seems particularly important for a career in mediation while arbitrators tend to start their labor relations careers as lawyers or professors. Methods for obtaining work also differ: for each particular dispute, mediators are often assigned by the relevant mediation agency; arbitrators are usually picked by the labor and management negotiators. As will become apparent in the following sections, mediators need to be well-trained in conflict resolution and communication strategies while arbitrators tend to need analytical skills. Neither will be successful, however, if they are not impartial and do not have a deep understanding of labor relations.

MEDIATION

Mediation is a dispute resolution process in which a neutral third party—the mediator—helps negotiators avoid or resolve an impasse by reaching an agreement. Note that unlike striking or going to arbitration, the use of mediation does not need to wait until an impasse occurs. By definition, mediators lack the authority to force a resolution by imposing a settlement on the negotiators; rather, mediation is essentially "assisted negotiation."[66] In practice, mediation involves a series of meetings with the mediator—some joint meetings with the union and management negotiating teams together, and some individual meetings with only the union or management negotiators. Through these meetings, the mediation process typically evolves through several stages.[67] The first stage is "setting the stage" in which the mediator collects information and establishes ground rules. One of the most important keys to success for mediators needs to be achieved during this stage: establishing a rapport such that the parties trust the mediator.[68] In the second stage, "problem solving," the mediator works on clarifying the

[65] Mario F. Bognanno and Charles J. Coleman (eds.), *Labor Arbitration in America: The Profession and Practice* (New York: Praeger, 1992).

[66] Lawrence Susskind and Jeffrey Cruikshank, *Breaking the Impasse: Consensual Approaches to Resolving Public Disputes* (New York: Basic Books, 1987).

[67] Christopher W. Moore, *The Mediation Process: Practical Strategies for Resolving Conflict,* 2nd ed. (San Francisco: Jossey-Bass, 1996). Dean G. Pruitt et al., "The Process of Mediation: Caucusing, Control, and Problem Solving," in M. Afzalur Rahim (ed.), *Managing Conflict: An Interdisciplinary Approach* (New York: Praeger, 1989), pp. 201–8.

[68] Stephen B. Goldberg, "The Secrets of Successful Mediators," *Negotiation Journal* 21 (July 2005), pp. 365–76.

disputed issues and on developing alternative solutions. The focus of the mediator in the third stage, "achieving a workable agreement," is encouraging the negotiators to reach a settlement.

A wide range of tactics can be used by mediators in these stages to help solve a bargaining impasse (see Box 9.14).[69] Depending on the types of tactics emphasized, individual mediators can be classified as orchestrators or dealmakers.[70] Orchestrators focus on trying to facilitate productive negotiations. This is the traditional view of mediation that targets improved dialogue between negotiators. In contrast, dealmakers see negotiations as over when they enter and are therefore not very concerned with facilitating renewed negotiations. Dealmakers focus their attention on the bargaining issues and trying to pressure the negotiators to make concessions. Orchestrators think that if they can improve the climate and structure of negotiations, then the parties will be able to resolve their differences on the issues. Dealmakers are more direct in their attempts to shape the final outcome— not the process—by getting the negotiators to change their positions and strike a deal. Dealmakers are more likely to produce agreements, but are also more likely to be perceived as antagonistic or biased which can reduce negotiators' acceptance of mediators.[71]

Depending on the sector, mediation can be voluntary or mandatory. Under the NLRA, mediation is voluntary. Employers and unions are required to notify the Federal Mediation and Conciliation Service (FMCS) that they will be renegotiating a contract. This advance notice provides the FMCS with the opportunity to offer the assistance of a mediator, but either party can refuse this offer. The Railway Labor Act, however, makes mediation mandatory for negotiators in the railway and airline industries. Railroads and airlines are prohibited from changing the existing terms and conditions of employment and unions are forbidden from striking until the National Mediation Board releases the parties from mediation. In difficult disputes, the parties may be kept in mediation longer than they would like, but the objective of the mediator, and of the Railway Labor Act, is to resolve disputes without strikes and other forms of conflict. The National Mediation Board is also obligated to offer arbitration to the parties as a method for resolving their dispute, but either party can reject this offer. If the parties are released from mediation and one party rejects arbitration, a strike can legally occur after a 30-day cooling-off period.

A diverse pattern of voluntary and mandatory mediation is also present in public sector labor law across different states. A majority of state laws include provisions for some type of mediation and some states have mediation agencies similar to the FMCS.[72] Public sector mediation is typically the first step in a multistep dispute resolution process. In states that allow public sector workers to strike, mediation is commonly required before strikes can legally occur (similar to the Railway Labor Act). Mediation is also frequently used before arbitration or fact-finding. In only a handful of states is mediation the final dispute resolution step.[73] In California, for example, if mediation fails to resolve a bargaining impasse for state employees, the terms and conditions of employment revert to those specified by the state's civil service laws.[74]

---

[69] Devinatz and Budd, "Third Party Dispute Resolution—Interest Disputes." Ahmid Karim and Richard Pegnetter, "Mediator Strategies and Qualities and Mediation Effectiveness," *Industrial Relations* 22 (Winter 1983), pp. 105–14.

[70] Deborah M. Kolb, *The Mediators* (Cambridge: MIT Press, 1983).

[71] Paul F. Gerhart and John E. Drotning, "Dispute Settlement and the Intensity of Mediation," *Industrial Relations* 19 (Fall 1980), pp. 352–59. Thomas A. Kochan and Todd Jick, "The Public Sector Mediation Process: A Theory and Empirical Examination," *Journal of Conflict Resolution* 22 (June 1978), pp. 209–38. Kolb, *The Mediators*. Gary L. Welton and Dean G. Pruitt, "The Mediation Process: The Effects of Mediator Bias and Disputant Power," *Personality and Social Psychology Bulletin* 13 (March 1987), pp. 123–33.

[72] Kearney, *Labor Relations in the Public Sector.*

[73] Hebdon, "Public Sector Dispute Resolution in Transition."

[74] Carol A. Vendrillo, "Collective Bargaining in California's Public Sector," in Joyce M. Najita and James L. Stern (eds.), *Collective Bargaining in the Public Sector: The Experience of Eight States* (Armonk, NY: M. E. Sharpe, 2001), Chapter 6.

To facilitate agreement and solve a bargaining impasse, mediators can try to . . .

. . . increase the level of objectivity among the negotiators by decreasing hostility, promoting cooperation, and focusing the negotiators away from personal conflicts and towards the bargaining issues.

. . . improve each negotiator's understanding of the other side's positions by accurately communicating information between the two sides.

. . . remove structural roadblocks in the negotiation process by changing the format of negotiations. Mediator tactics in this vein include revising agendas, chairing negotiating sessions, and forming subcommittees for specific issues.

. . . help shape new compromise proposals and make suggestions for mutual concessions.

. . . increase the perceived costs of disagreeing by highlighting the uncertainty of strikes or arbitration decisions.

. . . allow negotiators to save face. In particular, negotiators can make concessions under the guise of mediator pressure so as not to appear weak to their constituents and the other negotiators.

Sources: Victor G. Devinatz and John W. Budd, "Third Party Dispute Resolution—Interest Disputes," in David Lewin, Daniel J. B. Mitchell, and Mahmood A. Zaidi (eds.), *The Human Resource Management Handbook Part II* (Greenwich, CT: JAI Press, 1997), pp. 95–135. Ahmid Karim and Richard Pegnetter, "Mediator Strategies and Qualities and Mediation Effectiveness," *Industrial Relations* 22 (Winter 1983), pp. 105–14.

INTEREST ARBITRATION

Arbitration resolves disputes by the issuing of a settlement by a neutral third-party arbitrator (or panel of arbitrators) that is binding on the employer, union, and employees. A hearing is held, evidence is presented by each side, and an arbitrator issues a decision. This section focuses on **interest arbitration**—arbitration to resolve interest disputes that results in new contractual terms governing wages and terms and conditions of employment; grievance arbitration to settle rights disputes is also very important in U.S. labor relations and will be described in the next chapter. Unlike mediation and fact-finding, interest arbitration *imposes* a settlement on the parties to the dispute. As such, once invoked arbitration has a 100 percent settlement rate. But a common objective in labor relations is to have parties peacefully settle their own differences.[75] The typical standard for arbitration, therefore, is the extent to which the threat of arbitration encourages negotiated rather than arbitrated settlements.

The two primary forms of interest arbitration are conventional arbitration and final offer arbitration. In conventional arbitration, the arbitrator is not constrained in deciding the settlement terms. The employer likely argues for a certain wage increase, the union tries to justify a higher wage increase, and the arbitrator can choose any wage increase s/he believes is warranted. The uncertainty of what the arbitrator will choose and the loss of control by the negotiators over the settlement terms are thought to provide negotiators with an incentive to reach their own negotiated agreement without resorting to arbitration.[76] It has traditionally been believed that such a system suffers from the **chilling effect**.[77] In particular, if arbitrators simply split-the-difference between the positions of labor and management, then each side might hold back from making compromises during negotiations. Suppose you are the management negotiator and the union is demanding a 10 percent wage increase and you have offered 2 percent.

[75] George W. Taylor, *Government Regulation of Industrial Relations* (Englewood Cliffs, NJ: Prentice Hall, 1948).

[76] Frederic C. Champlin and Mario F. Bognanno, "A Model of Arbitration and the Incentive to Bargain," in David B. Lipsky and David Lewin (eds.), *Advances in Industrial and Labor Relations* (Greenwich, CT: JAI Press, 1986), pp. 153–90. Henry S. Farber and Harry C. Katz, "Interest Arbitration, Outcomes, and the Incentive to Bargain," *Industrial and Labor Relations Review* 33 (October 1979), pp. 55–63.

[77] Peter Feuille, "Final Offer Arbitration and the Chilling Effect," *Industrial Relations* 14 (October 1975), pp. 302–10.

If you make a concession to 4 percent and the union doesn't budge and you end up in arbitration, the wage increase will be 7 percent if the arbitrator splits-the-difference. If you had stayed at 2 percent, the arbitrator's award would have been less (6 percent). If negotiators follow this logic and refrain from making concessions during negotiations, then the bargaining process is "chilled" by the specter of conventional arbitration. Since many believe that arbitration should encourage negotiated settlements, the chilling effect is a significant concern in labor relations.

To try to lessen this potential chilling effect under conventional arbitration, final offer arbitration was created such that the arbitrator must choose between the union's final offer and the employer's final offer.[78] Final offer arbitration has two variations: (1) total package final offer arbitration in which the arbitrator must select one party's final offer on all the disputed contract terms (for example, wages, health insurance, holidays, etc.), and (2) issue-by-issue final offer arbitration in which the arbitrator can choose either party's final offer on an issue-by-issue basis. The underlying logic of final-offer arbitration is that since the arbitrator cannot choose a compromise value, it is riskier for a negotiator to present an extreme offer because this will increase the chances that the arbitrator chooses the other side's final offer.

However, if both sides present extreme offers, then final-offer arbitration is not necessarily any more risky than conventional arbitration, so both types of arbitration might induce a chilling effect. Additionally, if arbitrators weigh the reasonableness of each party's offer, then negotiators have an incentive to present moderate rather than extreme demands to the arbitrator in both types of arbitration (see Box 9.15).[79] As a result, the traditional thought on extreme offers undermining the value of conventional arbitration is overly simplistic. In fact, although dispute rates are higher under arbitration than strike regimes, the empirical research does not unequivocally support the superiority of either final-offer or conventional arbitration in encouraging negotiated settlements, nor does it find a pattern of extreme offers in either type of arbitration.[80]

In addition to the chilling effect, arbitration might have a **narcotic effect** — that is, negotiators might become addicted or overdependent on arbitration. For example, during difficult economic times if union negotiators settle for minimal gains for the employees, they risk being accused of being ineffective or of selling out. As such, the negotiators can instead take a tough bargaining stance and force arbitration. When the arbitrator awards minimal gains (as the economic environment warrants), the union negotiators can blame the arbitrator and deflect concerns about their own bargaining ability.[81] Similar incentives might be present among management negotiators. The narcotic effect posits that when negotiators see how they can "pass the buck" to the arbitrator, they will develop an overdependence on arbitration to settle their negotiations. In practice, the evidence in support of a narcotic effect is mixed.[82]

---

[78] Carl M. Stevens, "Is Compulsory Arbitration Compatible with Bargaining?" *Industrial Relations* 5 (February 1966), pp. 38–52.

[79] Henry S. Farber, "Splitting-the-Difference in Interest Arbitration," *Industrial and Labor Relations Review* 35 (October 1981), pp. 70–77.

[80] Orley Ashenfelter and David E. Bloom, "Models of Arbitrator Behavior: Theory and Evidence," *American Economic Review* 74 (March 1984), pp. 111–24. Frederic C. Champlin and Mario F. Bognanno, "'Chilling' Under Arbitration and Mixed Strike-Arbitration Regimes," *Journal of Labor Research* 6 (Fall 1985), pp. 375–87. Devinatz and Budd, "Third Party Dispute Resolution—Interest Disputes." Hebdon, "Public Sector Dispute Resolution in Transition." Craig A. Olson, "Final Offer versus Conventional Arbitration Revisited: Preliminary Results from the Lab" (unpublished paper, University of Wisconsin–Madison, 1994).

[81] Brian P. McCall, "Interest Arbitration and the Incentive to Bargain: A Principal-Agent Approach," *Journal of Conflict Resolution* 34 (March 1990), pp. 151–67.

[82] Richard J. Butler and Ronald G. Ehrenberg, "Estimating the Narcotic Effect of Public Sector Impasse Procedures," *Industrial and Labor Relations Review* 35 (October 1981), pp. 3–20. James R. Chelius and Marian M. Extejt, "The Narcotic Effect of Impasse-Resolution Procedures," *Industrial and Labor Relations Review* 38 (July 1985), pp. 629–38. Janet Currie, "Who Uses Interest Arbitration? The Case of British Columbia's Teachers, 1947–1981," *Industrial and Labor Relations Review* (April 1989), pp. 363–79. Thomas A. Kochan and Jean Baderschneider, "Dependence on Impasses Procedures: Police and Firefighters in New York State," *Industrial and Labor Relations Review* 31 (July 1978), pp. 431–39.

How Do Arbitrators Make Decisions?   Box 9.15

An arbitrator in an interest dispute is presented with arguments from both the union and employer as to what wage increases and other terms and conditions of employment the arbitrator should award in the arbitration decision. But how do arbitrators decide the terms of the award? The traditional wisdom in labor relations is that arbitrators split the difference between the final offers of labor and management. If the union requests two new paid holidays and the employer demands no new holidays, an arbitrator that splits the difference will award one additional paid holiday. An important debate is whether the traditional wisdom is accurate in practice—do arbitrators really just split the difference?

First note that while mediators typically work full-time for a mediation agency like the Federal Mediation and Conciliation Service, arbitrators are often independent and are frequently selected by the labor and management negotiators. An arbitrator that develops a reputation as biased in favor of either labor or management will not get selected and will quickly be out of work. Consequently, there is a powerful incentive for arbitrators to split the difference: splitting the difference is a simple way to appear fair or impartial and therefore to continue one's career as an arbitrator. Moreover, while splitting the difference is easiest under conventional arbitration, pseudo–splitting-the-difference behavior is also possible under final-offer arbitration. In issue-by-issue final-offer arbitration, for example, arbitrators can choose the union's offer on half of the issues and the employer's offer on the other half. In total package final-offer arbitration, the arbitrator can choose the union's final offer in one round and the employer's final offer in the next round (this is sometimes called a "flip-flop effect").

Now think about what's observed in practice. In states with final-offer arbitration, it's common to find average union win rates (a union win is when the union's final offer is selected) close to 50 percent. So arbitrators split the difference. Or do they? Arbitrators have more information about a dispute than the final offers of the parties. Arbitrators know the strength or weakness of the economic environment, the terms of other settlements with the same employer, and the terms of settlements in comparable bargaining units elsewhere. As such, it's likely that arbitrators have an independent view of a fair settlement. If arbitrators weigh the reasonableness of the final offers when making a decision, then union and management negotiators will position their offers around their estimate of the arbitrator's fair award belief. This behavior will yield union and management win rates close to 50 percent, and will yield awards that appear to split the difference. But in this scenario, it is not the final offers that determine the award via splitting the difference, it is the exact opposite—the expected award determines the final offers submitted by each side.

Consequently, one cannot determine whether arbitrators split the difference simply by observing win rates close to 50 percent or by observing arbitrator awards that are close to the middle of the final offers. Such observations might reflect splitting the difference, or they might reflect the negotiators' views of the arbitrator's fair award belief. More sophisticated analyses of arbitrator behavior suggest that arbitrators do not simply split the difference. In an experiment in which arbitrators were presented with hypothetical scenarios, the awards depended both upon the parties' final offers and on the facts of each scenario. Moreover, the facts were of much greater importance than the final offers.

In sum, labor relations needs to update its conventional wisdom regarding arbitrator behavior. Arbitrator awards are influenced by the final offers of the negotiators, but arbitrator decision making is more complex than a naïve model of splitting the difference. Arbitrators are also influenced by their own perceptions of a fair award based on the facts of the situation. This is consistent with provisions in some state laws that specify that arbitrators should base their awards on multiple criteria. For example, Oregon law (section 243.746) states that arbitrators must base their findings on (a) the interest and welfare of the public, (b) the financial ability of the public sector employer to meet the costs of the proposed contract, (c) the ability of the employer to attract and retain qualified personnel at the wage and benefit levels provided, (d) overall compensation presently received by the employees, (e) a comparison of the overall compensation of other employees performing similar services in comparable communities, (f) the cost of living, (g) the stipulations of the parties, and (h) other factors that are traditionally taken into consideration in the determination of wages, hours, and other terms and conditions of employment.

Sources: Orley Ashenfelter and David E. Bloom, "Models of Arbitrator Behavior: Theory and Evidence," *American Economic Review* 74 (March 1984), pp. 111–24. Max Bazerman and Henry S. Farber, "Arbitrator Decision Making: When Are Final Offers Important?," *Industrial and Labor Relations Review* 39 (October 1985), pp. 76–89. Henry S. Farber, "Splitting-the-Difference in Interest Arbitration," *Industrial and Labor Relations Review* 35 (October 1981), pp. 70–77. Richard A. Lester, *Labor Arbitration in State and Local Government* (Princeton, NJ: Princeton University Industrial Relations Section, 1984).

As with mediation, interest arbitration is voluntary in the private sector and often mandatory in the public sector. The most visible use of private sector interest arbitration is the final offer arbitration system used in major league baseball to determine player salaries. However, note that this arrangement is limited to a single issue (salary) and is not used to resolve bargaining disputes between the players' union and team owners. Another notable example of a voluntary interest arbitration arrangement in the private sector is the Experimental Negotiating Agreement (ENA) between the United Steelworkers of America and the major steel companies in the 1970s.[83] By agreeing to the ENA, the union and the steel companies gave up the right to conduct strikes or lockouts during national contract negotiations; rather, unresolved national-level bargaining issues would be settled by a three-member arbitration panel. The goal of this arrangement was to reduce customer stockpiling of steel prior to contract expiration (in anticipation of a strike), which resulted in layoffs even when a strike was avoided. During the life of the ENA, the negotiators never needed to invoke the arbitration mechanism and it was abandoned after the 1980 negotiations due to the companies' belief that it escalated labor costs. By some accounts, the most notable feature of the ENA was that no other bargaining pairs outside of steel adopted this model—rather, private sector negotiators strongly prefer to remain in control of determining their settlements, and private sector interest arbitration is largely a "nonevent."[84]

Most interest arbitration occurs in the public sector. In fact, more than 20 states have some form of *compulsory* arbitration statute for at least some public sector employees, especially essential occupations such as police officers and firefighters.[85] The specific details across states, however, vary.[86] In Hawaii, for example, police and fire disputes are resolved by mandatory conventional arbitration. In New Jersey, the statute allows the two parties to select the type of arbitration. If the two parties cannot agree, the statute mandates that final-offer arbitration be used with economic issues treated as a package and noneconomic issues chosen issue-by-issue. Michigan police and firefighter bargaining units are covered by a compulsory arbitration method in which economic issues are settled via issue-by-issue final-offer arbitration and noneconomic issues are settled via conventional arbitration. As yet a different example, Iowa uses a tri-offer arbitration system—the arbitrator in a dispute can choose from three offers on an issue-by-issue basis: the union's final offer, the employer's final offer, and a fact finder's recommendation. In the federal sector, bargaining disputes over terms and conditions of employment for postal employees that persist for 180 days are settled through interest arbitration using a panel of arbitrators. Empirical research generally supports the primary goal of these various forms of compulsory interest arbitration dispute resolution systems: preventing strikes.[87]

---

[83] John P. Hoerr, *And the Wolf Finally Came: The Decline of the American Steel Industry* (Pittsburgh: University of Pittsburgh, 1988).

[84] Peter Feuille, "Dispute Resolution Frontiers in the Unionized Workplace," in Sandra E. Gleason (ed.), *Workplace Dispute Resolution: Directions for the Twenty-First Century* (East Lansing: Michigan State University Press, 1997), Chapter 2.

[85] Hebdon, "Public Sector Dispute Resolution in Transition." Lund and Maranto, "Public Sector Labor Law." Craig A. Olson, "Dispute Resolution in the Public Sector," in Benjamin Aaron, Joyce M. Najita, and James L. Stern (eds.), *Public-Sector Bargaining*, 2nd ed. (Washington, DC: Bureau of National Affairs, 1988), Chapter 5.

[86] Richard A. Lester, *Labor Arbitration in State and Local Government* (Princeton, NJ: Princeton University Industrial Relations Section, 1984). Joyce M. Najita and James L. Stern (eds.), *Collective Bargaining in the Public Sector: The Experience of Eight States* (Armonk, NY: M. E. Sharpe, 2001).

[87] Janet Currie and Sheena McConnell, "Collective Bargaining in the Public Sector: The Effect of Legal Structure on Dispute Costs and Wages," *American Economic Review* 81 (December 1991), pp. 693–718. Casey Ichniowski, "Arbitration and Police Bargaining: Prescriptions for the Blue Flu," *Industrial Relations* 21 (Spring 1982), pp. 149–66. Olson, "Dispute Resolution in the Public Sector."

Some states (Wisconsin, for example) use a hybrid mediation–arbitration procedure, often referred to as "med-arb."[88] While many states that use arbitration also use mediation as a first-step, note carefully that med-arb is a special case in which the same neutral individual serves as both the mediator and the arbitrator. In other words, once the mediation process is exhausted, the mediator changes hats and becomes the arbitrator. The main advantage of med-arb over other third-party dispute resolution mechanisms is that the mediator–arbitrator develops detailed knowledge of the situation during the mediation phase which can then result in a better arbitration award if arbitration becomes necessary.[89] The threat of arbitration might also give the mediator-arbitrator more leverage during the mediation phase—in other words, med-arb can be thought of as "mediation with a club."[90] On the other hand, others worry that negotiators will not be completely forthcoming during the mediation phase for fear that the revealed information could be used against them during the arbitration phase.[91] There is also a concern that few individuals are effective at both mediation and arbitration because the important skills needed for each are different.[92] As with other methods of dispute resolution, med-arb has advantages and disadvantages, but med-arb underscores that there are numerous possibilities for designing systems of third-party dispute resolution.

FACT-FINDING

Fact-finding is a third party dispute resolution method in which a neutral third party—a fact finder—investigates a bargaining impasse and issues nonbinding recommendations for a settlement. Fact-finding is essentially nonbinding arbitration—there are typically hearings in which each side makes its case which are followed by a report containing specific terms of a settlement, but unlike in arbitration, these terms are not binding on the parties. But even without a binding award, it is hoped that the fact-finding report will resolve the bargaining dispute in at least three ways.[93] One, by establishing a set of unbiased settlement terms, the fact-finding report can help the negotiators reevaluate their positions and find an acceptable compromise settlement. Two, as with the narcotic effect for arbitration, a fact-finding report can provide an opportunity for union or management negotiators to save face by making concessions under the guise of following the report rather than appearing weak. Three, by making the fact-finding report public, the glare of the public spotlight can push the parties to a settlement—typically along the lines of the fact finder's recommendations because they are publicly viewed as neutral and fair.

But what happens if these avenues fail to produce a settlement? The public pressure that underlies the rationale of fact-finding frequently does not exist. As a last resort, a legislative body might need to intervene and legislate an end to the dispute. The fact-finding report is useful as a basis for the substance of this action, but one can question the efficiency of having to enact legislation to end each bargaining dispute. Moreover, absent legislative

[88] Devinatz and Budd, "Third Party Dispute Resolution—Interest Disputes." Lester, *Labor Arbitration in State and Local Government.*

[89] David A. Dilts and William J. Walsh, *Collective Bargaining and Impasse Resolution in the Public Sector* (New York: Quorum Books, 1988).

[90] Kearney, *Labor Relations in the Public Sector*, p. 347.

[91] W. Meagher, "New Frontiers in Dispute Resolution: Skills and Techniques," in Howard J. Anderson (ed.), *New Techniques in Labor Dispute Resolution* (Washington, DC: Bureau of National Affairs, 1976), pp. 166–77.

[92] Dilts and Walsh, *Collective Bargaining and Impasse Resolution in the Public Sector.*

[93] Devinatz and Budd, "Third Party Dispute Resolution—Interest Disputes." Hebdon, "Public Sector Dispute Resolution in Transition." Arnold M. Zack, "Improving Mediation and Fact-Finding in the Public Sector," *Labor Law Journal* 21 (May 1970), pp. 259–73.

Florida's public sector bargaining law is an example of a system that uses fact-finding as the final dispute resolution step. Here is an excerpt from the Florida statute:

447.403 Resolution of impasses.—

. . .

3. The fact finder shall hold hearings in order to define the area or areas of dispute, to determine facts relating to the dispute, and to render a decision on any and all unresolved contract issues. . . . Within 15 calendar days after the close of the final hearing, the fact finder shall transmit his or her recommended decision to the [Florida Public Employees Relations Commission] and to the representatives of both parties. . . .

4. If the public employer or the employee organization does not accept, in whole or in part, the recommended decision of the fact finder:

a. The chief executive officer of the governmental entity involved shall, within 10 days after rejection of a recommendation of the fact finder, submit to the legislative body of the governmental entity involved a copy of the findings of fact and recommended decision of the fact finder, together with the chief executive officer's recommendations for settling the disputed impasse issues. . . .

b. The employee organization shall submit its recommendations for settling the disputed impasse issues to such legislative body and to the chief executive officer;

c. The legislative body or a duly authorized committee thereof shall forthwith conduct a public hearing at which the parties shall be required to explain their positions with respect to the rejected recommendations of the fact finder;

d. Thereafter, the legislative body shall take such action as it deems to be in the public interest, including the interest of the public employees involved, to resolve all disputed impasse issues; and

e. Following the resolution of the disputed impasse issues by the legislative body, the parties shall reduce to writing an agreement which includes those issues agreed to by the parties and those disputed impasse issues resolved by the legislative body's action taken pursuant to paragraph (d). The agreement shall be signed by the chief executive officer and the bargaining agent and shall be submitted to the public employer and to the public employees who are members of the bargaining unit for ratification. If such agreement is not ratified by all parties . . . the legislative body's action taken pursuant to the provisions of paragraph (d) shall take effect as of the date of such legislative body's action for the remainder of the first fiscal year which was the subject of negotiations. . . .

Note: Florida law refers to fact finders as "special masters." The excerpt here has been changed by replacing "special master" with the more commonly used "fact finder" to avoid confusion.

action, important questions arise as to what happens next. If management can make unilateral changes after an unresolved impasse, what incentive does the employer have to bargain? Or if the status quo must be maintained and it is a concessionary environment, what incentive does the union have to bargain?

Nevertheless, fact-finding is firmly entrenched as an important component of U.S. labor relations. The emergency strike procedures in both the Railway Labor Act and the NLRA described earlier in this chapter are essentially fact-finding procedures. In the railroad industry in particular, Congress has occasionally legislated settlements based on the report of the Presidential Emergency Board when this report fails to generate sufficient pressure for the parties to settle voluntarily.[94] In the public sector, fact-finding is specified as the final dispute resolution step in many state bargaining laws.[95] The statutory language governing Florida's use of fact-finding is presented as an example in Box 9.16—note the explicit reliance on legislative action to end unresolved disputes, though this is not present in all state policies.

The widespread incorporation of fact-finding in state laws is perhaps a political compromise between unions' demands for binding arbitration and public sector employers' demands

[94] Rehmus, "Emergency Strikes Revisited."

[95] Kearney, *Labor Relations in the Public Sector.* Lund and Maranto, "Public Sector Labor Law."

for only mediation as the final step for resolving interest disputes.[96] But it is reasonable to question whether this compromise effectively serves the labor relations process. Unlike arbitration, fact-finding does not guarantee a resolution, and unlike mediation, it does little to help the negotiating process in order to facilitate productive bargaining and a settlement. In fact, fact-finding appears to actually increase labor conflict relative to public sector jurisdictions that settle disputes with strikes or arbitration.[97] In terms of Box 9.13, fact-finding has the worst of both worlds—low control over both the outcome and the negotiating process. As such, fact-finding is often evaluated negatively.[98]

WHAT'S BEST?

Bargaining impasses—threatened or real—are a central topic in labor relations. From a practical standpoint, preparing for any type of bargaining impasse, but especially a strike through the creation of a strike contingency plan, is complex and contains significant challenges for labor relations professionals on both the management and union sides (see Box 9.17). From a policy perspective, there are a number of ways of resolving bargaining impasses—allowing the parties to use their economic weapons, providing mediation, requiring binding arbitration, publicizing a fact finder's recommendations, and various hybrid combinations of these alternatives. This naturally begs the question of what is the best method for resolving interest disputes. But there is no simple answer to this question. No method is best along all dimensions; rather, each of the alternatives involve trade-offs. Like other aspects of labor relations, dispute resolution systems need to strike a balance between these trade-offs.

Strikes and lockouts can be particularly costly to employers, employees, and the public (in other words, detrimental to efficiency). But private sector unions and employers are almost always adamantly opposed to giving up the right to strike or to lock out employees. Employers insist on retaining control over the terms of the settlement (rather than handing control over to an arbitrator) while unions insist that striking is a fundamental right that underlies the ability of employees to achieve equity and voice. Whether the use of strike replacements destroys this right is an important question for the future of U.S. labor relations and again is a question of balancing the rights and interests of employers and employees.

With respect to third-party dispute resolution, the process and outcome dimensions of Box 9.13 capture the trade-offs between different methods.[99] Fact-finding lacks significant control over both the negotiating process and the outcome. If public sentiment is absent (as it commonly is), then fact-finding puts little pressure on the parties to resolve their dispute. Mediation lacks this same pressure, but at least helps the parties improve the negotiating process. Therefore, if the primary goal of the dispute resolution system is putting pressure on negotiators to settle and guaranteeing a settlement, then arbitration is best. However, if the goal of the dispute resolution system is assisting negotiators in resolving their own disputes—and thereby fostering healthy collective bargaining relationships—then mediation is best. In practice, therefore, many labor relations systems combine various dispute resolution methods—especially (usually voluntary) mediation with economic weapons in the private sector and (sometimes mandatory) mediation with fact-finding in the public sector. And as the labor relations environment changes, the search for the "best" dispute resolution procedure continues.

[96] Feuille, "Dispute Resolution Frontiers in the Unionized Workplace."
[97] Hebdon and Stern, "Do Public-Sector Strike Bans Really Prevent Conflict?"
[98] Devinatz and Budd, "Third Party Dispute Resolution—Interest Disputes." Feuille, "Dispute Resolution Frontiers in the Unionized Workplace."
[99] Devinatz and Budd, "Third Party Dispute Resolution—Interest Disputes."

Undertaking a strike is a daunting task for both labor and management, and therefore requires careful planning. Here are some major elements of developing a strike contingency plan:

Employer
- Appoint a strike coordinator
- Notify customers and suppliers of possible strike
- Prepare a security plan to protect the premises
- Develop either a shutdown plan or a plan for operating during the strike
- If planning to operate during the strike, assess how many employees will cross the picket line, how to use supervisors and managers, and the availability of strike replacements
- If using replacements, determine training needs, HR policies, and housing, food, recreational, and security needs
- Determine eligibility of strikers for health insurance, etc.
- Create a communications plan for communicating with the strikers
- Create a public relations plan
- Debrief participants on legal issues

Union
- Choose a strike committee to lead the strike
- Establish a strike headquarters
- Create a picket subcommittee to prepare picket signs and assign picket duty
- Communicate with the national union regarding strike benefits and other forms of support
- Establish support committees to reach out to other groups (other unions, food shelves, local banks and stores for lines of credit for strikers)
- Develop activities to maintain solidarity and morale among the strikers
- Determine a strategy for handling strike replacements and union members who cross the picket line
- Evaluate corporate campaign options
- Create a communications plan for communicating with the union members
- Create a public relations plan
- Debrief participants on legal issues

Questions

Recall the *HR Strategy* scenarios from Chapter 7 (Box 7.18) and assume that the union won recognition in each scenario.

1. As an HR manager developing a strike contingency plan, what particular concerns should you have in each scenario?

2. As a local union leader developing a strike contingency plan, what particular concerns should you have in each scenario?

3. For public sector negotiations in which strikes are illegal and bargaining impasses are instead resolved through arbitration, mediation, or fact-finding, which elements of the strike contingency plans presented in this box are unnecessary? Which elements should still be completed?

Sources: Maurice B. Better, *Contract Bargaining Handbook for Local Union Leaders* (Washington, DC: Bureau of National Affairs, 1993). Charles S. Loughran, *Negotiating a Labor Contract: A Management Handbook*, 3rd ed. (Washington, DC: Bureau of National Affairs, 2003).

Key Terms

interest dispute, *306*
unfair labor practice strike, *307*
economic strike, *308*
lockout, *308*
permanent strike

replacement, *317*
NLRB v. Mackay Radio and Telegraph Co., *317*
secondary boycott, *324*
work-to-rule campaign, *325*
corporate campaign, *326*

mediation, *330*
interest arbitration, *332*
chilling effect, *332*
narcotic effect, *333*
fact-finding, *336*

Reflection Questions

1. Not all forms of strikes are protected by the NLRA. What types are protected? Unprotected? Does this make sense, or should all types of strikes be treated equally?

2. In a concise paragraph, paraphrase what you have learned about strike replacements to explain to your parents or spouse why this is such a controversial issue in labor relations. Should the NLRA be revised to prohibit the use of temporary and/or permanent strike replacements?

3. List the pros and cons of interest arbitration. Why do you think the usage of interest arbitration in the private sector is so low?

4. A state legislature is writing a public sector bargaining law and asks you to design the law's impasse procedures (strike, arbitration, mediation, fact-finding, some combination, etc.). Outline a detailed plan. Do you allow workers to strike? Do you require any types of third party dispute resolution procedures? How would you sell this plan to the various interested parties?

Internet Exploration

1. Use labor news Web sites such as *www.labourstart.org* or *www.labornet.org* to find out about current strikes in the United States and in other countries. What are the main issues? How similar are the main issues across different strikes? Across countries?

2. Explore the Web site of Corporate Campaign, Inc. (*www.corporatecampaign.org*). What types of pressure tactics are emphasized? How do they increase the cost of disagreeing for a company or a public sector agency? How is a corporate campaign "better" than a strike (where "better" means winning gains for workers)? How is it worse? Do your answers change if the definition of "better" is promoting industrial peace?

3. Browse the Federal Mediation and Conciliation Service Web site (*www.fmcs.gov*). What types of activities does this agency pursue in order to promote dispute resolution? Does your state have comparable agency for public sector collective bargaining (see *www.alra.org/agindex.htm*)? If so, how does it compare to the FMCS? If not, should your state have a comparable public sector agency? Why or why not?

4. Insurance and legal disputes over a claim for damages or compensation can now be settled online through various Web sites.[100] Explore *www.cybersettle.com* to see how their process works. What are the advantages? What are the disadvantages? (*Hint:* think about the literature on arbitration to predict what counterproductive behaviors this settlement process might encourage.) Could such a system be used to settle labor disputes?

Additional Reading

Bartoletti, Susan Campbell, *Kids On Strike!* (Boston: Houghton Mifflin, 1999).

Devinatz, Victor G., and John W. Budd, "Third Party Dispute Resolution—Interest Disputes," in David Lewin, Daniel J. B. Mitchell, and Mahmood A. Zaidi (eds.), *The Human Resource Management Handbook Part II* (Greenwich, CT: JAI Press, 1997), pp. 95–135.

Filippelli, Ronald L. (ed.), *Labor Conflict in the United States: An Encyclopedia* (New York: Garland Publishing, 1990).

Juravich, Tom, and Kate Bronfenbrenner, *Ravenswood: The Steelworkers' Victory and the Revival of American Labor* (Ithaca, NY: Cornell University Press, 1999).

Kaufman, Bruce E., "Research on Strike Models and Outcomes in the 1980s: Accomplishments and Shortcomings," in David Lewin, Olivia S. Mitchell, and Peter D. Sherer (eds.), *Research Frontiers in Industrial Relations and Human Resources* (Madison, WI: Industrial Relations Research Association, 1992), pp. 77–129.

Lambert, Josiah Bartlett, *"If the Workers Took a Notion": The Right to Strike and American Political Development* (Ithaca, NY: Cornell University Press, 2005).

Moore, Christopher W., *The Mediation Process: Practical Strategies for Resolving Conflict,* 2nd ed. (San Francisco: Jossey-Bass, 1996).

Rosenblum, Jonathan D., *Copper Crucible: How the Arizona Miners' Strike of 1983 Recast Labor–Management Relations in America,* 2nd ed. (Ithaca, NY: ILR Press, 1998).

[100] William Krause, "Do You Want to Step Outside? An Overview of Online Alternative Dispute Resolution, "*John Marshall Journal of Computer and Information Law* 19 (Spring 2001), pp. 457–91.

Chapter **Ten**

Contract Clauses and Their Administration

Advance Organizer

The primary objective of most U.S. unions is to negotiate contracts with employers that specify wages, hours, and other terms and conditions of employment. The labor relations processes described in the previous chapters—union organizing, bargaining, and dispute resolution—largely lead the parties to such a contract. This chapter describes the types of clauses that are frequently found in union contracts and also how disputes (grievances) over the application of these clauses are resolved.

Learning Objectives

By the end of the chapter, you should be able to:

1. **Understand** the nature of U.S. union contracts.
2. **Explain** important contractual provisions that attach rights and obligations to employees, jobs, unions, and employers.
3. **Outline** how grievances are resolved, that is, how contracts are administered.

4. **Discuss** the importance of grievance arbitration in U.S. labor relations.
5. **Analyze** the pressures for changing the nature of U.S. union contracts and how they are administered.

Contents

The centerpiece of U.S. labor relations has long been union contracts that specify the rights and responsibilities of employees (including wages and other terms and conditions of employment), jobs, unions, and employers. Contracts come in a wide variety of sizes, shapes, formats, and colors: some are slim, others have grown into thick, multivolume documents (recall Box 1.10), some are pocket-sized bound booklets, others are three-ring binders. But in whatever form, the U.S. labor relations system—more so than in most other countries, and for better or worse—largely revolves around these contracts. Employees form unions (Chapter 7) to pursue collective bargaining (Chapter 8) in order to obtain contracts. Mediation helps parties reach agreement on contracts, and interest arbitration imposes contracts on the parties (Chapter 9).

Contracts are central to U.S. labor relations because of the belief that both industrial justice and efficiency are best achieved through written workplace rules. These rules are embodied in union contracts, also called collective bargaining agreements. Recall that under the employment-at-will doctrine, employers are generally free to establish whatever terms and conditions of employment they desire and to discharge workers at any time (and employees are free to quit at any time). Unions have long sought to protect workers by restricting this absolute authority: "Whether carved on stone by an ancient monarch or written in a Magna Charta [sic] by a King John, or embodied in collective agreement between a union and employer; the intent is the same, to subject the ruler to definite laws to which subjects or citizens may hold him when he attempts to exercise arbitrary power."[1] In unionized U.S. workplaces, these "definite laws" that restrict the employer's unilateral authority in order to promote employee equity and voice are spelled out in detailed, legally enforceable union contracts.

In spite of the detailed nature of many contract clauses, they can never anticipate or remove every ambiguity for all scenarios that will arise during the life of the contract. For example, to prevent an employer from repeatedly sending employees home for lack of work, suppose a contract indicates that all employees who report to work will be paid for at least four hours. What happens if employees are sent home because of a bomb scare? Are they entitled to four hours of pay? Alternatively, a contract might specify that promotions are based on seniority and ability. How are the two factors weighted when comparing two specific individuals? Nearly all contracts limit employee terminations to cases in which there is just cause. Is one unexcused absence just cause? How about sending a personal e-mail message from an office computer? In short, conflicts over the interpretation, application, and enforcement of the contract inevitably occur.

Interpreting, applying, and resolving conflicts regarding collective bargaining agreements is called **contract administration** and is a critical process in U.S. labor relations. Contract administration involves rights disputes. Recall from the previous chapter that there are two broad categories of disputes in labor relations: interest disputes and rights disputes. Interest disputes are conflicts of interest—such as over wage rates, benefits packages, or personnel policies—that are the focus of contract negotiations (Chapters 8 and 9). Once a union contract is in place, **rights disputes** are disagreements over whether someone's rights as specified in the contract have been violated. In other words, rights disputes are grievances—conflicts over the administration (that is, the application and interpretation) of the contract. Understanding the major types of clauses commonly found in U.S. union contracts and the resolution of grievances regarding the administration of these clauses is the central goal of this chapter.

U.S. labor relations traditionally embraces the belief that equity and voice are best balanced with efficiency through rules-based contracts enforced by a private system of industrial justice (grievance arbitration). This is the subject of this chapter. However, before proceeding it should be noted that this bureaucratic model is not without its critics. On the management side, rules-based contracts and the system of grievance arbitration that relies heavily on past practices and precedents are viewed as inhibiting the flexibility and innovation that are continually emphasized as necessary to compete in the 21st-century marketplace. These concerns will be addressed in detail in the next chapter. On the labor side, the bureaucratic system of representation is criticized for achieving stability at the expense of rank and file involvement and activism (recall the debate between the servicing and organizing models of union representation from Chapter 6).[2] Mobilizing worker power through grassroots activism (recall the inside-the-workplace pressure tactics from Chapter 9) is an

---

[1] William M. Leiserson, "Constitutional Government in American Industries," *American Economic Review* 12 (May 1922), pp. 58–79 at 75.

[2] Karl E. Klare, "Workplace Democracy and Market Reconstruction: An Agenda for Legal Reform," *Catholic University Law Review* 38 (Fall 1988), pp. 1–68. Kim Moody, *An Injury to All: The Decline of American Unionism* (London: Verso, 1988). Katherine V. W. Stone, "The Post-War Paradigm in American Labor Law," *Yale Law Journal* 90 (June 1981), pp. 1509–80.

alternative path for protecting workers' rights not typically chosen by U.S. unions.[3] Alternative forms of unionism will be discussed in Chapters 13 and 14. This chapter focuses on the path traditionally favored in U.S. labor relations: striking a balance between efficiency, equity, and voice through specific rules laid out in union contracts that are enforced through formal quasilegal grievance procedures (a servicing model of representation).

U.S. UNION CONTRACTS

As workers fought for workplace justice in the early decades of the 1900s, they frequently tried to force their employers to follow impartial rules: wages that were based on jobs rather than unfair manipulation of piece rates; promotions and layoffs based on seniority rather than managerial favoritism and discrimination.[4] This was a way of "introducing civil rights into industry, that is, of requiring that management be conducted by rule rather than by arbitrary decision."[5] An alternative quest for workplace justice focused on shop floor militancy and union control of work standards backed up by spontaneous strikes and slowdowns. Many union, as well as corporate, leaders preferred the rules-based approach—it supported management's desire for stability and discipline and also fulfilled union leaders' needs for countering managerial authority without having to resort to wildcat strikes that could undermine their own leadership positions.[6] Therefore, by 1930 the Amalgamated Clothing Workers union had negotiated numerous contracts in the garment industry that replaced the militancy of small work groups with the discipline of "responsible" union leaders.[7] Both workers and managers had to follow the negotiated work rules, performance standards, and disciplinary procedures that were enforced through a grievance procedure culminating with the rulings of impartial arbitrators. In 1940, General Motors agreed to a contract with the United Auto Workers that provided for an impartial umpire to settle grievances over seniority rights, discipline, and other contractual standards that remained unresolved through a four-step grievance procedure.[8]

Governmental pressures for industrial peace to promote war production during World War II further spread the use of grievance procedures and umpires/arbitrators while driving out wildcat strikes over grievances.[9] The strikes that followed the end of World War II, especially the UAW's strike against General Motors (Chapter 4), established that unions would negotiate for higher wages, better benefits, and favorable seniority provisions and

[3] Victor G. Devinatz, "An Alternative Strategy: Lessons from the UAW Local 6 and the FE, 1946–52," in Cyrus Bina, Laurie Clements, and Chuck Davis (eds.), *Beyond Survival: Wage Labor in the Late Twentieth Century* (Armonk, NY: M. E. Sharpe, 1996), Chapter 7.

[4] David Brody, "Workplace Contractualism in Comparative Perspective," in Nelson Lichtenstein and Howell John Harris (eds.), *Industrial Democracy in America: The Ambiguous Promise* (Washington, DC: Woodrow Wilson Center Press, 1993), Chapter 8.

[5] Sumner H. Slichter, *Unions Policies and Industrial Management* (Washington, DC: Brookings Institution, 1941), p. 1.

[6] Charles C. Heckscher, *The New Unionism: Employee Involvement in the Changing Corporation* (New York: Basic Books, 1988). Nelson Lichtenstein, "Great Expectations: The Promise of Industrial Jurisprudence and its Demise, 1930–1960," in Nelson Lichtenstein and Howell John Harris (eds.), *Industrial Democracy in America: The Ambiguous Promise* (Washington, DC: Woodrow Wilson Center Press, 1993), Chapter 6.

[7] Steve Fraser, "Dress Rehearsal for the New Deal: Shop-Floor Insurgents, Political Elites, and Industrial Democracy in the Amalgamated Clothing Workers," in Michael H. Frisch and Daniel J. Walkowitz (eds.), *Working-Class America: Essays on Labor, Community, and American Society* (Urbana: University of Illinois Press, 1983), pp. 212–55.

[8] Lichtenstein, "Great Expectations."

[9] James B. Atleson, *Labor and the Wartime State: Labor Relations and Law During World War II* (Urbana: University of Illinois Press, 1998). Nelson Lichtenstein, *Labor's War at Home: The CIO in World War II* (Cambridge: Cambridge University Press, 1982).

work rules, but would not be involved in business decisions. Section 301 of the Taft-Hartley amendments to the National Labor Relations Act (NLRA) in 1947 made these collective bargaining agreements enforceable in federal court.[10] Lastly, the Supreme Court confirmed that this enforceability applied to agreements to submit unresolved grievances to binding arbitration.[11] The postwar model of industrial self-government—complete with the law of the workplace (the contract and previous arbitration rulings), defense attorneys (union stewards), and court of appeals (the grievance procedure)—was thus cemented.[12] Note carefully that U.S. labor relations is therefore rooted in contract clauses and their administration through grievance procedures—an administration that is legalistic and orderly (not based on strike power) and that is private (relying on arbitrators not court judges).

Today's union contracts, therefore, are legally enforceable documents that specify the laws of the workplace, often in great detail. UAW contracts with the major automakers are hundreds of pages long, contracts with the U.S. Postal Service exceed 300 pages, the collective bargaining agreement between the National Football League and the players union is over 250 pages long, and the University of Minnesota clerical employees' contract approaches 150 pages. Not all contracts are this long, but even many of the shorter ones are between 25 and 50 pages long. Most contracts have a duration of three years.[13] Some include a reopener in which the parties can reopen the contract during its life to negotiate wage or benefit adjustments, but most are renegotiated upon expiration. The following five sections discuss the types of clauses that are frequently found in U.S. contracts—clauses that give rights to employees, jobs, unions, and managers, and that govern the resolution of conflicts that arise (see Box 10.1).

EMPLOYEE RIGHTS AND OBLIGATIONS

There are frequently four areas of employee rights granted in union contracts: just cause discipline and discharge, seniority rights, compensation, and grievance procedures. In return for these various rights, employees are obligated to follow the employer's work rules and supervisor's directions, and to abide by the provisions of the contract (such as not striking over grievances). Over 90 percent of private sector union contracts specify that employees can only be disciplined and discharged for "cause" or "just cause." Public sector contracts frequently contain this same language. As such, employees have the right to insist that there be valid, job-related reasons for being disciplined or fired. This is of obvious importance for both employees and employers, and is also a significant departure from the employment-at-will doctrine, and will therefore be discussed in more detail towards the end of this chapter.

A second category of employee rights pertains to **seniority.** A traditional union objective is to replace arbitrary or discriminatory treatment of workers with an objective standard to prevent favoritism, manipulation, and abuse. But how many truly objective standards exist in the employment relationship? Merit and ability, in particular, are often largely subjective. Seniority—length of employment with the employer—is objective (just count the number of days since being hired), and also resonates with basic ideas of fairness.[14] Seniority is therefore widely used

---

[10] Bruce S. Feldacker, *Labor Guide to Labor Law,* 4th ed. (Upper Saddle River, NJ: Prentice Hall, 2000).

[11] *Textile Workers Union of America v. Lincoln Mills,* 353 U.S. 448 (1957).

[12] Brody, "Workplace Contractualism in Comparative Perspective." David E. Feller, "A General Theory of the Collective Bargaining Agreement," *California Law Review* 61 (May 1973), pp. 663–856. Lichtenstein, "Great Expectations." Stone, "The Post-War Paradigm in American Labor Law."

[13] Unless otherwise noted, in this chapter the statistics on the frequency of union clauses in private sector agreements are from *Basic Patterns in Union Contracts,* 14th ed. (Washington, DC: Bureau of National Affairs, 1995).

[14] Barry Bluestone and Irving Bluestone, *Negotiating the Future: A Labor Perspective on American Business* (New York: Basic Books, 1992). Sumner H. Slichter, James J. Healy, and E. Robert Livernash, *The Impact of Collective Bargaining on Management* (Washington, DC: Brookings, 1960).

BOX 10.1 **The Major Components of Traditional U.S. Union Contracts**

Employee Rights . . .

- Just cause discipline and discharge
- Seniority rights in layoffs, promotions, etc.
- Compensation (benefits, call-in pay, etc.)
- Fair hearing through the grievance procedure

Job Rights . . .

- Job holders entitled to a certain wage rate
- Specific tasks must be done within the bargaining unit and by certain jobs

Union Rights . . .

- Exclusive bargaining agent
- Union bulletin board in the workplace
- Union leader access to the workplace
- Shop stewards
- Union security and dues checkoff clauses

Management Rights . . .

- Hire and fire (with just cause)
- Determine job content and workforce size
- Establish production standards and rules of conduct
- Decide what to produce and how and where to make it

. . . and Obligations

- Obey work rules
- Follow supervisor's orders
- Abide by the contract
- Accept arbitrators' awards

. . . and Obligations

- Fulfill job standards

. . . and Obligations

- Abide by the contract, including not striking over grievances
- Accept arbitrators' awards

. . . and Obligations

- Abide by the contract, including not making unilateral changes
- Just cause discipline and discharge
- Safety standards
- Accept arbitrators' awards

Grievance Procedure

- Employees, the union, and management meet to resolve disputes over the application and enforcement of the contract
- Typically a multistep procedure in which unresolved grievances are appealed to higher levels in the organization
- The final step is frequently binding rights arbitration

Other

- Contracts are legally enforceable (in the United States)
- Contracts are usually several years in duration

in union contracts as a criterion for allocating employment opportunities. Seniority is at least partly a factor (sometimes, the only factor) in nearly 90 percent of private sector contracts and can also be found in a variety of public sector contracts. Layoffs are therefore frequently done by inverse seniority—workers with lower seniority are laid off before those with more ("last hired, first fired"). Bumping rights further grant more senior employees the right to bump less senior workers out of their positions during layoffs. Seniority is also a factor in promotions (two-thirds of private sector contracts) and transfers (more than half of private sector contracts) with more senior employees having priority (at least partly) over less senior ones. More senior employees usually receive more vacation days, and in some cases get the first opportunities at overtime (though most contracts specify that overtime should be allocated equally).

In allocating employment opportunities, seniority is typically either a sole, determining, or secondary factor (see Box 10.2). Consider the case of several workers all of whom request to be promoted into a single job that opens up. When seniority is the sole factor, the worker with the longest length of service receives the promotion. If seniority is the determining factor, then among the workers who are minimally qualified for the job, the worker with greatest seniority receives the promotion. When seniority is a secondary factor, the

Seniority as the Sole Factor

"The Company will give forty-eight (48) hours notice of layoffs caused by reduction in production schedules. Probationary employees shall be laid off first. Should the reduction of force be such that the layoff of regular employees becomes necessary, the regular employees with the least seniority shall be laid off first." [From a contract at an auto parts company]

Seniority as the Determining Factor

"When it is necessary, because of a lack of work, to reduce the number of persons within a classification, the employees within that classification with the least amount of seniority shall be cut back, provided those employees remaining in that classification possess the skills required to do the work. Cutback employees shall exercise seniority held in another classification(s) than the one from which they are cut back, in the reverse order of their job ladder progression, provided they are able to perform the work without further training other than the normal "break in" period." . . . Cutback

employees who do not possess sufficient seniority to remain in the plant will be laid off." [From a contract at a chemical plant]

Seniority as a Secondary Factor

"When, in the judgment of Board of Education, decline in enrollment, reduction of program, or any other reason requires reduction in staff, the administration shall attempt to accomplish same by attrition. In the event necessary reduction in staff cannot be adequately accomplished by attrition, the administration shall base its decision as to resulting contract renewals on the relative skill, ability, competence, and qualifications of available staff to do the available work. If a choice must be made between two or more staff members of equal skill, ability, competence, and qualifications to do the available work, contract renewals will be given to the staff member with the greater full-time continuous length of service in the school district." [From a contract covering public school teachers]

worker with greatest seniority among those with relatively equal ability receives the promotion. Seniority is more likely to be the sole factor for layoffs than for promotions or transfers. As such, promotions and transfers are fertile areas for grievances—individuals vying for promotions have differing perspectives on the very ambiguous nature of "minimal qualifications" and "equal ability," and unions and employers have different views of the relative weight to be accorded to seniority and ability.[15]

A third category of employee rights frequently granted by union contracts is compensation. Unionized workers are significantly more likely than nonunion employees to receive benefits such as health insurance, pensions, life insurance, and the like.[16] Numerous collective bargaining agreements contain provisions pertaining to overtime compensation, premium pay for weekends, rest periods, severance pay, supplemental unemployment benefits, and holidays. A majority of private sector contracts also give employees the right to reporting pay and call-in pay. Reporting pay guarantees that employees will be paid for a certain number of hours (typically four) if they report for work as scheduled but the employer doesn't have sufficient work. Call-in pay is similar and pertains to situations in which employees are called in to work by the employer.

Lastly, nearly every U.S. union contract contains a grievance procedure in which employees are entitled to file a challenge to managerial actions that they feel violate their rights under the contract. The final step of the grievance procedure is almost always binding arbitration. While only a small fraction of grievances reach the final arbitration step, the possibility of arbitration by a third party neutral can promote fair consideration of

[15] *Grievance Guide,* 11th ed. (Washington, DC: Bureau of National Affairs, 2003). Alan Miles Ruben (ed.), *Elkouri and Elkouri: How Arbitration Works*, 6th ed. (Washington, DC: Bureau of National Affairs, 2003).

[16] John W. Budd, "Non-Wage Forms of Compensation," *Journal of Labor Research* 25 (Fall 2004), pp. 597–622. Richard B. Freeman and James L. Medoff, *What Do Unions Do?* (New York: Basic Books, 1984).

employee grievances at lower levels.[17] Through the grievance procedure then, union contracts grant employees the right to a fair hearing when there is a workplace problem. In return, employees are obligated to seek an orderly resolution to their grievance through the specified channels and not to use strikes or other economic weapons to pressure management for a settlement. At the same time, it's important to remember that this bureaucratic approach to justice restricts grievances to specific contractual violations; this restriction, in turn, significantly limits worker influence over day-to-day work issues.[18] Because of the importance of the grievance procedure to the operation of workplace labor relations in the United States, this topic is revisited in greater detail later in the chapter.

JOB RIGHTS AND OBLIGATIONS

Union contracts can also convey rights and obligations to jobs. Unions representing blue collar workers frequently negotiate wage rates that are tied to specific jobs, not individuals.[19] In other words, the holder of a specific job is entitled to a certain wage rate by virtue of holding that job irrespective of their individual characteristics. At a food processing plant, there might be a single pay rate for bulk unloaders, one for machine operators, another for janitors, and one for machine repairers—and you can read them all in the contract. This is not universally true—salaries for community college professors might be a function of each faculty member's educational credentials and years of teaching experience while professional athletes typically negotiate their own salaries individually within the parameters determined by the union contract, but tying wages to jobs rather than individuals is a significant component of the traditional U.S. union contract for blue collar workers.

Another aspect of job rights pertains to work assignments such that certain jobs are entitled to perform certain tasks.[20] Unions seek such job rights because of a concern that the employer might whittle away the union-represented jobs by having supervisors expand their duties. Some contracts therefore explicitly prohibit supervisors from doing bargaining unit work (with some exceptions such as training new employees or emergencies). Subcontracting and outsourcing restrictions try to prevent the loss of union jobs by limiting the farming out of work to other employers. Another fear that underlies union pursuit of job rights is that management might try to replace higher-skilled jobs with lower-skilled, and therefore lower-paying, jobs. Some contracts therefore include general language requiring that a job's usual tasks be assigned to those jobs, such as "The Company agrees that, to the extent practicable, such work assignments will be made consistent with the principal job duties and skills of an employee's classification" (chemical plant contract). As this concern is particularly sharp among skilled workers—since they face the greatest risk for having their jobs diluted and even deleted— contractual language for job rights is frequently most explicit in guaranteeing certain tasks for skilled job classifications (see Box 10.3). In return for these various categories of job rights, the holders of these jobs must fulfill the performance standards for these jobs.

[17] Trevor Bain, "Third Party Dispute Resolution—Rights Disputes," in David Lewin, Daniel J. B. Mitchell, and Mahmood A. Zaidi (eds.), *The Human Resource Management Handbook Part II* (Greenwich, CT: JAI Press, 1997), pp. 219–44. Peter Feuille, "Dispute Resolution Frontiers in the Unionized Workplace," in Sandra E. Gleason (ed.), *Workplace Dispute Resolution: Directions for the Twenty-First Century* (East Lansing: Michigan State University Press, 1997), Chapter 2.

[18] David Fairris, *Shopfloor Matters: Labor–Management Relations in Twentieth-Century American Manufacturing* (London: Routledge, 1997).

[19] Harry C. Katz, *Shifting Gears: Changing Labor Relations in the U.S. Automobile Industry* (Cambridge: MIT Press, 1985). Slichter, Healy, and Livernash, *The Impact of Collective Bargaining on Management*.

[20] Slichter, Healy, and Livernash, *The Impact of Collective Bargaining on Management*.

Auto Industry Examples

"Operators will remove their drill heads when there is a change in operation or going from one part to another as part of their normal setup. . . . The appropriate [skilled] Tradesman will be responsible for the removal of drill heads that are being removed for the sole purpose of being repaired. When repairs are completed, it will be the duties of the Tradesman to replace drill heads and make necessary alignment."

"When a Skilled Tradesman is assigned a job, he will be able to remove switches, guards, hydraulic lines, air lines, etc, in order to perform his work. He will not repair any portion of the job that is not in his classification. If any wires have to be disconnected, this will be done by electricians. In the event a piece of equipment is either dismantled for moving or a new machine is set up, the appropriate [skilled] Tradesman will be utilized."

Grocery Store Examples

"Meat helpers' work is limited to marking, weighing, labeling, wrapping, cleaning cases, stocking and displaying of smoked meats, stocking and displaying of luncheon meats, and cleaning any and all tools. Meat helpers may wait upon customers and use the knife or slicers when necessary to finish a product already supplied by the [skilled] meat cutters as in the sale to an individual customer. . . . There must be a minimum of one (1) journeyman meat cutter on duty any time a meat helper is on duty."

"Food Handler's work includes marking, stocking, displaying and weighing of all pre-processed, fresh, frozen and smoked, meat, poultry and fish, including receiving of meat products, fresh and frozen, the storage of all the above mentioned products, and the cleaning of cases. These employees shall not be allowed to work in the processing areas of the meat department including wrapping or service case."

UNION RIGHTS AND OBLIGATIONS

A third category of clauses frequently found in collective bargaining agreements provides unions with rights and obligations. It is probably universal for one of the first sections of the contract to include a recognition clause in which the employer recognizes the union as the exclusive bargaining agent for the bargaining unit and affirms the union's right as the representative of the employees. A broadly written recognition clause can help unions maintain their strength by including new occupations within the bargaining unit, such as when new editorial positions are created when a traditional newspaper launches an online paper.[21] Unions are also concerned with maintaining recognition rights if a business is sold or if a public sector operation is privatized. Under favorable conditions, various legal rulings indicate that a successor employer will have to recognize and bargain with the union, but in order to try to cement this continued recognition, some unions negotiate a successorship clause into their contract.[22] Such a clause requires a successor employer to recognize and bargain with the existing union; a strong successorship clause further obligates the successor employer to abide by the union contract.

To facilitate communication between a union and the employees, it is common for unions to negotiate rights for union leaders to use a bulletin board on company premises and to enter the workplace to meet with employees (without interfering with their

[21] Howard R. Stanger, "Newspapers: Collective Bargaining Decline Amidst Technological Change," in Paul F. Clark, John T. Delaney, and Ann C. Frost (eds.), *Collective Bargaining in the Private Sector* (Champaign, IL: Industrial Relations Research Association, 2002), Chapter 5.

[22] Thomas Benjamin Huggett, "Successor Clauses: What They Are and Why Every Union Should Have One," *Catholic University Law Review* 46 (Spring 1997), pp. 835–905.

work). To help the union be an effective representative of the workers, unions also negotiate for workplace systems of shop stewards. Stewards are employees who are elected by the rank and file or appointed by the union leadership to be the first line of advocates for the workers in ensuring that the contract is not violated. For most workers, stewards are the personification of the union—when there is a problem, employees typically contact their steward.[23] Contracts frequently include clauses in which employers recognize the right of stewards to investigate grievances, and some contracts further specify the number of stewards, grant them special seniority rights ("superseniority"), and indicate that the company will pay the steward for their time conducting legitimate union business.

The most controversial clauses within the category of union rights pertain to issues of dues and mandatory membership. Recall from Chapter 5 that there are three types of **union security clauses:** (1) a closed shop, requiring the employer to hire only union members, (2) a union shop, requiring employees to become union members after hired in order to keep their jobs, and (3) an agency shop, requiring employees to pay union dues after hired in order to keep their jobs. The NLRA outlaws the closed shop. Right-to-work laws outlaw union and agency shops. But in the 28 states that are not right-to-work states, unions are allowed to negotiate union or agency shop provisions into their contracts with employers. Between 1947 and 1951, union shop clauses had to be ratified by the bargaining unit through a special union-shop election supervised by the National Labor Relations Board (NLRB). This requirement was repealed because union shop clauses were approved in 97 percent of the elections, but it underscores the special attention that union security clauses receive.[24] In fact, employees can still petition the NLRB to hold a special deauthorization poll (not to be confused with a decertification election; see Chapter 7) in which the employees can vote to revoke a union shop clause. In 2005, there were 59 such polls and union shop clauses were revoked in 16.[25]

The Supreme Court has further determined that union shop clauses are only enforceable as agency shops—workers can be forced to pay dues, but not join the union.[26] In other words, when a union shop or agency shop clause is included in the collective bargaining agreement, a worker can be fired for failing to pay dues, but not for refusing to join the union. Furthermore, workers only need to pay the amount of dues that go towards collective bargaining and contract administration. This right to pay less than full union dues is called *Beck* rights—named after the 1988 Supreme Court case that established this right (see Box 10.4).[27] In principle, this sounds straightforward, but in practice it is complex. Some union expenses are clearly germane to bargaining and administering contracts—salaries for union staff that negotiate contracts or arbitrator fees, for example—and some are not—such as union publications, social activities, and political lobbying. But what about organizing new members? This does not directly support bargaining and contract administration for existing union members, but it supports these activities indirectly by increasing union power. Whether organizing expenses can be charged to employees that exercise their *Beck* rights has been intensely debated. The NLRB has ruled that organizing

---

[23] David Prosten, *The Union Steward's Complete Guide* (Annapolis, MD: Union Communication Services, 1997). Robert M. Schwartz, *The Legal Rights of Union Stewards,* 4th ed. (Cambridge, MA: Work Rights Press, 2006).

[24] Benjamin J. Taylor and Fred Witney, *Labor Relations Law,* 7th ed. (Englewood Cliffs, NJ: Prentice Hall, 1996).

[25] National Labor Relations Board, *Seventieth Annual Report of the National Labor Relations Board* (Washington, DC: Government Printing Office, 2005), p. 17.

[26] *NLRB v. General Motors,* 373 U.S. 734 (1963).

[27] *Communication Workers of America v. Beck,* 487 U.S. 735 (1988).

Except in right-to-work states, it is common for unions to negotiate union shop clauses into their collective bargaining agreements. However, the Supreme Court has interpreted the NLRA to only require the payment of dues: union membership is "whittled down to its financial core" [*NLRB v. General Motors Corp.*, 373 U.S. 734, 742 (1963)]. Workers can thus satisfy a union shop requirement by paying dues; they do not need to formally join the union. This might seem like a distinction without a difference, but consider two points:

1. Nonmembers cannot vote in union elections or to ratify contracts, and
2. Nonmembers do not have to pay full union dues.

With respect to this last point, the courts have determined that nonmembers only need to pay dues that go towards collective bargaining and contract administration (*Beck* rights). As such, nonmembers might only pay 75 percent of the amount of full union dues (the actual amount varies from union to union).

Questions

1. Union shop clauses are legal, but a court will only enforce them as equivalent to agency shop clauses. Is it ethical for a union steward to show the contract's union shop clause to a new employee to get them to join the union? Before quickly jumping to answer, remember that contracts are ratified by majority votes.
2. Should a union steward have a legal obligation to inform employees of their *Beck* rights?
3. Should employers have a legal obligation to inform employees of their rights under the NLRA, such as being able to discuss wages and working conditions with their co-workers?

expenses for employees in the same competitive market are allowed while the courts have not allowed general organizing expenses.[28] This also raises significant practical issues—especially whether calculating the amount of allowable expenses can be done at the national union level, or must be done separately for each local.[29]

Union and agency shop clauses are frequently used in conjunction with a dues checkoff provision in which employees can agree to have their union dues automatically deducted from their paychecks and deposited directly with the union. This provides the union with a predictable revenue stream and saves union leaders from having to spend valuable time and energy collecting dues from each individual worker—though this individual contact might develop stronger linkages between union leaders and rank and file workers and prevent the leadership from becoming detached from the membership.[30]

Unions typically try to negotiate union shop or agency shop clauses (in non—right-to-work states) to counter the free-rider problem of bargaining unit members benefiting from the union without paying for it. As will be discussed shortly, labor law requires that unions fulfill a duty of fair representation by representing *all* employees—members and nonmembers alike—so unions argue that it is unfair to allow free-riders to benefit from union representation without sharing the costs by paying dues. Majority rule is also a basic feature of democratic institutions, and any dues-paying requirements are subject to majority approval. On the other hand, right-to-work advocates label this "compulsory unionism" and

[28] *Food and Commercial Workers Locals 951, 1036, and 7 (Meijer, Inc.),* 329 NLRB No. 69 (1999). Christopher David Ruiz Cameron, "The Wages of Syntax: Why the Cost of Organizing a Union Firm's Non-Union Competition Should Be Charged to 'Financial Core' Employees," *Catholic University Law Review* 47 (Spring 1998), pp. 979–1003.

[29] Jeff Canfield, "What a Sham(e): The Broken *Beck* Rights System in the Real World Workplace," *Wayne Law Review* 47 (Fall 2001), pp. 1049–74.

[30] Rick Fantasia and Kim Voss, *Hard Work: Remaking the American Labor Movement* (Berkeley: University of California Press, 2004).

argue that it violates individual freedoms by depriving workers of their "right-to-work," that is, the right to freely choose whether or not to become a union member and pay union dues. In the public sector, there are more restrictions on union security clauses—in other words, there are more right-to-work laws for the public sector (including the federal sector) than the private sector.[31] On the other hand, a few states such as Minnesota and Hawaii mandate the agency shop. Agency shop payments in the public sector are frequently called fair share payments, and various states have legislated processes for determining their amount.[32]

In return for the various rights that a union might be granted by clauses in the union contract, it is obligated to live up to the terms of the complete contract. In particular, unions usually give up the right to strike over grievances and instead must pursue the orderly resolution of disputes over the application of the contract through the grievance procedure. This includes respecting the terms of any arbitration awards. Unions can be sued in court for violating a collective bargaining agreement.

Another union obligation, and a central issue in contract administration for labor unions, is the **duty of fair representation**.[33] Recall from Chapter 5 that under the NLRA a union that wins an NLRB election becomes the *exclusive* bargaining agent for that bargaining unit. Similar principles apply under the Railway Labor Act and in the public sector (in jurisdictions with bargaining laws). As early as 1944, the Supreme Court ruled that in return for this privilege of being the exclusive representative, unions have an obligation to fairly and without discrimination represent all of the bargaining unit employees.[34] This obligation applies to both contract negotiation and administration, though it is frequently discussed in terms of administration. In particular, a union "may not arbitrarily ignore a meritorious grievance or process it in a perfunctory fashion" in a discriminatory or bad faith manner.[35] As specific examples, unions cannot ignore the grievances of African-American workers because of racial discrimination or advocate less strenuously for nonmembers because they haven't joined the union or ignore the grievance of a member that is an outspoken political opponent of the union leadership. This does not mean that unions have to pursue every grievance all the way to arbitration, but it does mean that unions must have valid reasons for not pursuing a grievance (in particular, that the grievance truly lacks merit). Note carefully that since the duty of fair representation is rooted in Supreme Court applications of labor law, this obligation is universal and does not depend on the presence of specific clauses in a union contract.

MANAGEMENT RIGHTS AND OBLIGATIONS

As labor relations is frequently concerned with balancing competing interests of various stakeholders, it should be unsurprising that union contracts also provide rights to management—especially through conveniently named **management rights clauses.** Management rights

---

[31] B. V. H. Schneider, "Public-Sector Labor Legislation—An Evolutionary Analysis," in Benjamin Aaron, Joyce M. Najita, and James L. Stern (eds.), *Public-Sector Bargaining,* 2nd ed. (Washington, DC: Bureau of National Affairs, 1988), Chapter 6.

[32] John Lund and Cheryl L. Maranto, "Public Sector Labor Law: An Update," in Dale Belman, Morley Gunderson, and Douglas Hyatt (eds.), *Public Sector Employment in a Time of Transition* (Madison, WI: Industrial Relations Research Association, 1996), Chapter 1.

[33] Jean T. McKelvey (ed.), *The Changing Law of Fair Representation* (Ithaca, NY: ILR Press, 1985). Taylor and Witney, *Labor Relations Law.*

[34] *Steele v. Louisville and Nashville Railroad,* 323 U.S. 192 (1944). *Wallace Corporation v. NLRB,* 323 U.S. 248 (1944). *Ford Motor Co. v. Huffman,* 345 U.S. 330 (1953). Deborah C. Malamud, "The Story of *Steele v. Louisville and Nashville Railroad*: White Unions, Black Unions, and the Struggle for Racial Justice on the Rails," in Laura J. Cooper and Catherine L. Fisk (eds.), *Labor Law Stories* (New York: Foundation Press, 2005), pp. 55–105.

[35] *Vaca v. Sipes,* 386 U.S. 171, 191 (1967).

clauses embody management's longstanding insistence on maintaining sole authority over traditional management functions such as hiring, firing, assigning work, determining job content, and deciding what to produce and how and where to make it.[36] Such clauses are found in 80 percent of private sector contracts. In the public sector, management rights clauses are also frequently found in union contracts, and even specified by law in the federal sector by the Civil Service Reform Act and in the state and local sectors by some state bargaining laws.

Two examples are shown in Box 10.5—note the close similarities even though one covers unskilled workers in the private sector and the other covers skilled professional workers in the public sector. It is common to trace management rights clauses all the way back to the UAW's strike against General Motors in 1945–46. Even after 113 days of being struck, General Motors refused to relinquish its right to manage—in both the corporate boardroom and on the factory floor. This established the postwar pattern of union negotiations over wages, benefits, and work rules, but not managerial decisions. Management rights clauses are now deeply engrained in U.S. labor relations.[37] In fact, management rights clauses are even found in collective bargaining agreements in which the employer is a union and the workers are regular employees of that union (in such situations, the employees are represented by a different union, such as the Office and Professional Employees International Union).

Consider again the two management rights clauses in Box 10.5. In the hotel contract, "management shall have the right to direct the work force and to determine the policies and methods of operating its Hotel, *except as expressly limited by the specific provisions of this Agreement*" (emphasis added). In the community college contract, "Any term or condition of employment *not specifically established by this Contract* shall remain solely within the discretion of the Employer to modify, establish or eliminate" (emphasis added). These two provisions capture the **reserved rights** (or residual rights) **doctrine** of management rights—all management rights not explicitly limited, restricted, or modified by the union contract are reserved by management. Many arbitrators uphold the reserved rights doctrine even if this specific language is not in the contract.[38] The detailed work rules often found in traditional union contracts are a natural reaction by organized labor to this doctrine. If management retains authority over all issues that are not limited, restricted, or modified, then of course unions will seek to explicitly limit, restrict, and modify managerial authority where it serves workers' interests.

These limitations, restrictions, and modifications largely represent management's obligations under union contracts. Many of these have already been mentioned in the previous sections: disciplining and discharging workers only for just cause, using seniority as a factor in layoffs and promotions, assigning work to specific job classes, providing call-in pay, allowing shop stewards to investigate grievances, and the like. Union contracts also frequently specify safety standards that management must fulfill. And like both employees and unions, employers are obligated to resolve grievances peacefully through the grievance procedure and to abide by the terms specified not only by the contract, but also by arbitration awards.

There are thousands of union contracts in the U.S. private and public sectors and many elements of these contracts are similar. This is true across all four categories of contract clauses discussed so far: employee rights and obligations, job rights and obligations, union rights and obligations, and management rights and obligations. But these contracts are not

[36] Howell John Harris, *The Right to Manage: Industrial Relations Policies of American Business in the 1940s* (Madison: University of Wisconsin Press, 1982).
[37] Bluestone and Bluestone, *Negotiating the Future.*
[38] Ruben, *Elkouri and Elkouri.*

Private Sector Hotel Contract

"The Employer and the Union specifically agree that management shall have the right to direct the workforce and to determine the policies and methods of operating its Hotel, except as expressly limited by the specific provisions of this Agreement and longstanding custom and past practice. Such management rights and responsibilities shall include, but not be limited to, the following: the right to select the employees it will hire; the right to establish or revise work schedules; to determine the size and composition of its working force; to determine the number and type of equipment, material, products and supplies to be used or operated; to discipline or discharge employees for just cause; to maintain efficiency of employees; to determine assignments of work; to discontinue all or any part of its business operations; to expand, reduce, alter, combine or transfer, assign, or cease any job, department or operation for business purposes; to introduce new, different or improved methods and procedures in its operations; and to otherwise generally manage the Hotel, except as expressly restricted by the provisions of this Agreement."

Public Sector Community College Faculty Contract

"It is recognized that except as expressly stated herein the Employer shall retain whatever rights and authority are necessary for it to operate and direct the affairs of the colleges in all of their various aspects, including, but not limited to, the educational policies of the colleges; the right to select, direct, and assign faculty members; to schedule working hours; to determine whether goods or services should be made or purchased; to make and enforce reasonable rules and regulations affecting terms and conditions of employment that are uniformly applied and enforced in accordance with the provisions of the rules or regulations. Any term or condition of employment not specifically established by this Contract shall remain solely within the discretion of the Employer to modify, establish or eliminate."

entirely identical. There are frequently distinctive provisions specific to various bargaining units depending on its industry, occupation, location, history, and the like. Several examples of unique contract clauses are shown in Box 10.6.

GRIEVANCE PROCEDURES

The elements of union contracts discussed in the previous sections often contain ambiguities and are open to varying interpretations. Does maternity leave include adoption? Is swearing at a supervisor just cause for being fired? How is it determined if two individuals have equal ability when promoting someone? Do management's traditional powers allow it to create new job categories or does the inclusion of job classifications in the union contract make this is an issue to be negotiated? Conflicts over the interpretation, application, and enforcement of the contract inevitably occur and contract administration to settle these rights disputes—grievances—is a key topic in U.S. labor relations.

Consider the alternatives for settling grievances. In nonunion situations, employers are essentially free to resolve employee complaints in any way they see fit and issue unilateral decisions (as long as antidiscrimination and other laws are not violated). Employees who do not like their employer's decision are free to quit. Managerial control is therefore one option for settling grievances. This option might include labor's use of economic weapons to pressure employers—as occurs in interest disputes that involve strikes, slowdowns, and the like (Chapter 9). Another option for resolving rights disputes is union control through internal union mechanisms, including grievance procedures or review boards operated by local unions.[39] And yet another option is to litigate grievances in court by relying on judges to interpret and apply union contracts.

[39] Howard R. Stanger, "The Evolution of an Alternative Grievance Procedure: The Columbus Typographical Union No. 5, 1859–1959," in David Lewin and Bruce E. Kaufman (eds.), *Advances in Industrial and Labor Relations,* Volume 10 (Amsterdam: Elsevier Science, 2001), pp. 75–113.

1. "There will be no contact work (e.g., "live" blocking, tackling, pass rushing, bump-and-run) or use of pads (helmets permitted) at minicamps." [Professional football]

2. "The Local Safety and Health Committee shall promote the cause of safety and health by . . . 5. Reviewing local dog bite prevention efforts." [Post Office]

3. "In the exercise of academic freedom, the faculty member may, without limitation, discuss her/his own subject in the classroom, but s/he should not introduce into his/her teaching controversial matter which is not related to her/his subject. . . . There is an obligation to respect the dignity of others, to acknowledge their right to express differing opinions and to foster and defend intellectual honesty, freedom of inquiry, and instruction. A faculty member must follow course outlines as developed by and with her/his colleagues in the department(s)." [Community college]

4. "The loss of any employee's property resulting from a hold-up, robbery, accident, violence or riot, which occurs while the employee is on duty, shall be reimbursed by the Employer. Such reimbursement shall be paid upon submission of replacement receipt, or laundry or dry cleaning expense. Property shall mean: regulation watch (not to exceed $100 in value), prescription eyeglasses, regulation uniform at Employer cost; and any other equipment issued by the Employer in the performance of the employee's duties shall be replaced." [Bus company]

5. "Reporters may take pictures and photographers may write stories, but a reporter's competence shall in no instance be judged by his work with a camera and a photographer's work shall in no instance be judged by his work with a typewriter." [Newspaper]

6. "When a pilot is assigned by the Company to deadhead to a station for the purpose of being scheduled out of that station as a pilot, or from a station having flown into that station as a pilot, such deadhead time shall be credited for pay time and credit time purposes at the rate of full pay time and credit time for each hour of such deadhead time." [Commercial airline]

7. "Following a job-related exposure to blood or body fluids, the Hospital will provide, upon request of and without cost to the affected nurse, screening for AIDS. Such screening will be done by a reputable independent laboratory and confidential results will be provided to the nurse. Results shall not be a part of the nurse's personnel or employee health record." [Hospital]

8. "The Employer/Producer agrees to notify the Union if smoke, fog, and/or pyrotechnics are scheduled to be used. Such notification shall be given, in writing, as soon as the Employer/Producer makes the decision to use these materials. If the Union requests a meeting, it will be scheduled within a reasonable time and shall include representative(s) of the Union and the Employer/Producer at which meeting the parties will discuss any planned special effects such as smoke/fog and/or pyrotechnics and/or any other health and safety problem that either party feels might arise in the production." [Theatrical production association]

All three of these alternatives have largely been rejected in contemporary U.S. labor relations. Management is unwilling to concede control to unions, and vice versa. In fact, unilateral management control undermines the whole point of collective bargaining—without a balanced dispute resolution procedure for grievances, workers and workplace justice are at the mercy of employers and markets which is exactly the situation that the NLRA and public sector bargaining laws seek to improve upon. Resorting to economic weapons destroys the goal of industrial peace. In particular, the advantage to employers of signing union contracts is to achieve stability and predictability through employee and union adherence to negotiated rules. This advantage is lost if strikes frequently erupt over these rules. And relying on the courts also has significant drawbacks—it's costly, slow, largely beyond the parties' control, and generally lacks expertise in labor or business issues.

As a result, the near-universal method for resolving rights disputes—grievances—over the interpretation, application, and enforcement of union contracts in U.S. labor relations is through a **grievance procedure** that is negotiated into the contract. While grievance procedures could occasionally be found in the 1800s, the explosion in their adoption and usage came during World War II when the U.S. government leaned heavily on labor and management to resolve disputes through grievance procedures, not strikes, so as not to interrupt vital war production.[40] Today, nearly every union contract in the United States—in both the private and public sectors—contains a grievance procedure to resolve allegations by employees and/or the union that the employer has violated the contract.[41] Note that employees and unions react to managerial actions and raise complaints by filing grievances if they think a contractual violation has occurred—in other words, "management acts and the union grieves."

The grievance procedure provides a fair, orderly, and generally efficient method for resolving rights disputes and enforcing union contracts and is therefore relatively unique in U.S. labor relations to the extent that it receives broad approval from scholars, policymakers, and labor and management practitioners. Employers benefit from an institutionalized system of conflict resolution that avoids strikes and other disruptions. Both employers and unions benefit from continuity, consistency, and a prescribed channel of communication. And employees benefit from due process—the right to have a hearing, be assisted by an advocate if desired, and present evidence in one's defense. In other words, the unionized grievance procedure incorporates accepted standards of justice into the workplace. Nonunion grievance procedures—such as open door policies, peer review panels, or ombudspersons—typically lack due process protections.[42]

An example of a typical grievance procedure is shown in Box 10.7. This example has four steps. The first step involves discussions between the employee who has a grievance (the grievant) and his or her supervisor. If the grievant is not satisfied with the outcome of step one, the grievance can be appealed to step two at which time a union representative and a management official from the employee's department try to settle the dispute. The employee can further appeal the results of the second step to step 3 which is like step 2, but involves higher-level union and management officials. Lastly, the union can appeal the step 3 resolution to step 4—binding arbitration.

The number of steps varies across union contracts, but multistep procedures with between two and four steps are the norm. The example in Box 10.7 provides for a verbal grievance at first; other grievance procedures might require an initial written grievance. Most grievances are settled in the early steps.[43] Time limits for filing grievances and for appealing to the next step are also important components of unionized grievance procedures. Note that during the grievance process, unions have dual roles as both advocates and processors. As advocates, unions provide assistance and expertise to help grievants win their cases. As processors, unions determine how far to pursue grievances. In particular, unions (not grievants) decide whether or not to appeal grievances to arbitration, subject to their obligations to make these decisions fairly under the duty of fair representation.

The average grievance filing rate is perhaps 10–15 grievances per 100 employees per year, but there are huge variations in this rate across workplaces and industries—in other words, "formal grievance disputes may be inevitable in unionized workplaces, but the rate at which they emerge certainly is not."[44] Individual and organizational characteristics appear to partly determine whether grievances are initiated—for example, grievance filers are on

[40] Atleson, *Labor and the Wartime State.* Lichtenstein, *Labor's War at Home.*

[41] Bain, "Third Party Dispute Resolution—Rights Disputes." *Basic Patterns in Union Contracts.* Jill Kriesky, "Trends in Dispute Resolution in the Public Sector," in Adrienne E. Eaton and Jeffrey H. Keefe (eds.), *Employment Dispute Resolution and Worker Rights in the Changing Workplace* (Champaign, IL: Industrial Relations Research Association, 1999), Chapter 8.

[42] Alexander J. S. Colvin, "The Relationship Between Employment Arbitration and Workplace Dispute Resolution Procedures," *Ohio State Journal on Dispute Resolution* 16 (2001), pp. 643–68.

[43] David Lewin, "Theoretical and Empirical Research on the Grievance Procedure and Arbitration: A Critical Review," in Adrienne E. Eaton and Jeffrey H. Keefe (eds.), *Employment Dispute Resolution and Worker Rights in the Changing Workplace* (Champaign, IL: Industrial Relations Research Association, 1999), Chapter 5.

[44] Feuille, "Dispute Resolution Frontiers in the Unionized Workplace," p. 31.

A Police Contract's Grievance Procedure   Box 10.7

Purpose

A grievance is a good faith complaint of one or a group of employees, or a dispute between the City and the Police Officers Association involving the interpretation, application, or enforcement of the express terms of this Agreement. The purposes of this procedure are (a) to resolve grievances informally at the lowest possible level, and (b) to provide an orderly procedure for reviewing and resolving grievances promptly.

Step One

An employee who believes he/she has cause for grievance may contact his/her supervisor alone or with his/her union representative. If after discussions with the supervisor, the employee does not feel the grievance has been properly adjusted, the grievance shall be reduced to a written grievance statement that includes (a) the nature of the grievance, (b) the facts on which it is based, (c) the article(s) and section(s) of this Agreement allegedly violated, and (d) the remedy or correction requested of the City. The grieving employee's Deputy Chief shall assign the first level review to the employee's supervisor, and will give his/her answer to the grievance in writing within five (5) standard workdays from the time he/she receives the grievance in writing. Any grievance not appealed in writing to Step 2 within five (5) standard workdays shall be considered waived. No matter shall be considered as a grievance under this Article unless it is presented in writing within thirty (30) calendar days after occurrence of the events on which the grievance was based.

Step Two

An appeal to the second step shall be made within five (5) standard workdays. The hearing of the grievance will be held within five (5) standard workdays of the second step appeal. The Association representative and designated Department representative will meet in an effort to settle the matter. The City's answer will be made five (5) standard workdays after the hearing is held. The employee has five (5) standard workdays

to determine whether or not to appeal the grievance to the third step. Any grievance not appealed in writing to step 3 within five (5) standard workdays shall be considered waived.

Step Three

The Association's representative and the designated representative of the City will meet to hear grievance appealed to the third step. A grievance appealed to the third step of the grievance procedure shall be heard within ten (10) standard workdays after the appeal to the third step of the grievance procedure. A written answer will be made within ten (10) standard workdays after the hearing, stating the City's position.

Step Four: Arbitration

a. If the third step answer is not satisfactory to the employee, the Association may appeal the grievance to arbitration. The request for arbitration must be given in writing to the designated City representative by the Association within ten (10) standard workdays from the date of the third step answer. Any grievance not appealed in writing to Step 4 within ten (10) standard workdays shall be considered waived.

b. An arbitrator may be selected by mutual agreement between the Association's representative and the City's representative. Should the representatives fail to mutually agree on an arbitrator, they shall make a joint request to the State Mediation and Conciliation Service or the American Arbitration Association for a list of five (5) qualified arbitrators. The parties shall each strike two (2) names from the list and the remaining person shall be accepted as the arbitrator. The first party to strike will be determined by the flip of a coin.

c. It is understood that the arbitrator will only interpret this Agreement and will in no instance add to, delete from, or amend any part thereof. The arbitrator's decision shall be final and binding on the City, the Association, and employee.

d. All fees and expenses for the arbitrator will be borne equally by the Association and the City.

average younger than employees who do not file grievances, and grievances are more likely to be filed when employees interact with aggressive supervisors and union stewards and when employees perceive that their power is higher.[45] Grievances are also more likely just

[45] Brian Bemmels, "The Determinants of Grievance Initiation," *Industrial and Labor Relations Review* 47 (January 1994), pp. 285–301. Lewin, "Theoretical and Empirical Research on the Grievance Procedure and Arbitration." Samuel Bacharach and Peter Bamberger, "The Power of Labor to Grieve: The Impact of the Workplace, Labor Market, and Power-Dependence on Employee Grievance Filing," *Industrial and Labor Relations Review* 57 (July 2004), pp. 518–39.

before contract negotiations begin.[46] This result suggests that the grievance procedure provides not only employees with due process, but also unions with an avenue for pressuring management to further its bargaining goals. Lastly, the grievance procedure also appears to contain an element of organizational discipline and punishment. On average, grievance filers and their supervisors both experience lower performance ratings and promotion opportunities as well as increased job turnover relative to nonfilers and their supervisors after their grievances are settled.[47] Moreover, grievance activity can reflect management's monitoring of worker effort, and slight increases in grievance activity can be associated with increased productivity.[48]

GRIEVANCE ARBITRATION

The grievance procedure is intended to provide an orderly and fair dispute resolution method. But suppose management just ignores the union's arguments and evidence at each step of the procedure. What is there to ensure that the process is fair and respects workers' rights? The answer is **rights arbitration**—also called grievance arbitration. Like interest arbitration, rights arbitration involves a hearing before a third-party neutral (the arbitrator) who then issues a decision that is binding on the parties. Unlike interest arbitration, rights arbitration focuses on rights disputes—grievances. An interest arbitrator is a contract writer who establishes new terms and conditions of employment; a rights arbitrator is a contract reader who interprets the existing terms and conditions of employment.

Throughout the steps of the grievance procedure, the threat of a binding decision by a neutral third party provides labor and management with the incentive to try to settle grievances fairly and to respect due process. Nearly all contracts in both the private and public sectors include binding rights arbitration as the last step of the grievance procedure, and a few states even require it for public sector contracts. In return for management's acceptance of binding arbitration, most unions waive the right to strike during the life of the contract by agreeing to a no-strike clause.

Some very important Supreme Court rulings cemented the viability and importance of grievance arbitration in U.S. labor relations.[49] First, in 1957 the Court ruled that if a union contract contains binding arbitration as the final step of the grievance procedure, then the employer is legally bound to adhere to this agreement and submit unresolved grievances to binding arbitration.[50] Second, in 1960 the Court issued three decisions on the same day all involving the United Steelworkers of America—these decisions are collectively referred to as the ***Steelworkers Trilogy.*** The first two cases deal with employers who refuse to submit unresolved grievances to binding arbitration—even though it is in their union contracts—by claiming that either the grievance has no merit or that the subject of the

[46] James W. Kuhn, *Bargaining in Grievance Settlement: The Power of Industrial Work Groups* (New York: Columbia University Press, 1961). David Lewin and Richard B. Peterson, *The Modern Grievance Procedure in the United States* (New York: Quorum, 1988).

[47] Lewin and Peterson, *The Modern Grievance Procedure in the United States.* David Lewin and Richard B. Peterson, "Behavioral Outcomes of Grievance Activity," *Industrial Relations* 38 (October 1999), pp. 554–76.

[48] Morris M. Kleiner, Gerald Nickelsburg, and Adam Pilarski, "Monitoring, Grievances, and Plant Performance," *Industrial Relations* 34 (April 1995), pp. 169–89.

[49] Theodore J. St. Antoine, "The Law of Arbitration," in James L. Stern and Joyce M. Najita (eds.), *Labor Arbitration Under Fire* (Ithaca, NY: ILR Press, 1997), Chapter 1. Douglas E. Ray, Calvin William Sharpe, and Robert N. Strassfield, *Understanding Labor Law* (New York: Mathew Bender, 1999). Taylor and Witney, *Labor Relations Law.* Ruben, *Elkouri and Elkouri.*

[50] *Textile Workers Union of America v. Lincoln Mills,* 353 U.S. 448 (1957).

particular grievance is not covered by the arbitration provision. In the first, the Court ruled that in deciding whether a case is subject to arbitration, the courts should not look at the merits of the arbitration case—that is the role of the arbitrator.[51] In the second, the Court ruled that unless a subject is explicitly excluded from arbitration by the contract, it is subject to arbitration.[52] Both of these decisions support the importance of grievance arbitration by making it difficult for management to refuse to arbitrate a grievance when binding arbitration is specified in the union contract. The third case pertains to a different issue— can an arbitrator's decision be reviewed and overturned by the courts? The Supreme Court essentially ruled that the answer is no.[53] The courts cannot overrule an arbitrator's ruling as long as it "draws its essence from the collective bargaining contract"—it is not the role of the courts to second-guess arbitrators.

Taken together, the three decisions of the *Steelworkers Trilogy* provide very strong legal support for the grievance arbitration process and are frequently cited as directly responsible for the centrality of grievance arbitration in U.S. labor relations.[54] The standards established by the *Trilogy* cases have also been adopted in a number of states for public sector labor relations.[55] There are now roughly 10,000 arbitration awards issued each year.[56] Moreover, under the NLRB's *Collyer* doctrine, some grievances that allege a violation of the contract that can also be considered unfair labor practices will be deferred to arbitration under the grievance procedure rather than litigated by the NLRB.[57] But the supremacy of grievance arbitration is clouded when the grievance overlaps with employment laws and public policies. For example, the scope for reviewing an arbitration award is significantly greater if the grievance alleges racial discrimination that violates not only the union contract, but also the antidiscrimination provisions of the Civil Rights Act.[58] Somewhat in reverse, the use of arbitration is expanding into the nonunion sector where it is being used instead of the courts to resolve employment law claims, though this trend is quite controversial because of potential imbalances between employers and individual nonunion employees. Nonunion employment arbitration will be discussed later in this chapter.

In practical rather than legal terms, as grievance arbitration was developing in the 1950s, a major debate was whether arbitration should have a problem-solving or judicial character— this debate is often referred to as the Taylor-Braden debate because of the leading proponents of each perspective.[59] If grievance arbitration is an exercise in problem solving, then the arbitrator can be creative in methods (such as using mediation tactics) and solutions (such as adapting the union contract to fit current problems). If grievance arbitration is a judicial activity, then the arbitrator's sole job is to interpret—not adapt or modify—the contract just as a judge interprets the law. The latter won—there is no debate today that grievance arbitration is a formal, quasijudicial process. Note that in the sample grievance

---

[51] *United Steelworkers of America v. American Manufacturing Co.,* 363 U.S. 564 (1960).

[52] *United Steelworkers of America v. Warrior and Gulf Navigation Co.,* 363 U.S. 574 (1960).

[53] *United Steelworkers of America v. Enterprise Wheel and Car Corp.,* 363 U.S. 593 (1960).

[54] Feuille, "Dispute Resolution Frontiers in the Unionized Workplace." Katherine V. W. Stone, "The *Steelworkers' Trilogy*: The Evolution of Labor Arbitration," in Laura J. Cooper and Catherine L. Fisk (eds.), *Labor Law Stories* (New York: Foundation Press, 2005), pp. 149–89.

[55] Harry Graham, "Grievance Arbitration in State and Local Government in the 1990s and Beyond," in James L. Stern and Joyce M. Najita (eds.), *Labor Arbitration Under Fire* (Ithaca, NY: ILR Press, 1997), Chapter 3.

[56] Dennis R. Nolan and Roger I. Abrams, "Trends in Private Sector Grievance Arbitration," in James L. Stern and Joyce M. Najita (eds.), *Labor Arbitration Under Fire* (Ithaca, NY: ILR Press, 1997), Chapter 2.

[57] *Collyer Insulated Wire,* 192 NLRB 837 (1971). Taylor and Witney, *Labor Relations Law.*

[58] *Alexander v. Gardner-Denver,* 415 U.S. 36 (1974).

[59] Nolan and Abrams, "Trends in Private Sector Grievance Arbitration."

procedure in Box 10.7, the second-to-last provision explicitly states that "It is understood that the arbitrator will only interpret this Agreement and will in no instance add to, delete from, or amend any part thereof." Such contract language is very common in the private and public sectors, and in the public sector is occasionally even specified by law.

An arbitration hearing is therefore like a courtroom hearing, and extensive preparation by both labor and management advocates is important (see Box 10.8).[60] The union and the employer each make an opening statement, the moving party (typically employers in discipline and discharge cases since they have the burden of proving just cause, and unions in other cases since they have the burden of proving that the contract was violated) presents witnesses and evidence, these witnesses are cross-examined, the other party presents witnesses and evidence, these witnesses are cross-examined, and each side presents a closing statement. The traditional legal rules of evidence are not strictly applied—for example, circumstantial evidence might be allowed—but arbitrators nevertheless need to determine the credibility and persuasiveness of the evidence presented. Two to three months after the hearing, the arbitrator issues a written decision upholding or denying the grievance in whole or in part. If the grievance is upheld, a remedy is also awarded. The arbitrator's decision is binding on all of the parties.

In making a decision, the arbitrator's task is to interpret the contract and apply it to the situation at hand. Disputes for which the contract is crystal clear are likely to be settled early in the grievance procedure, so arbitrators are frequently confronted with difficult and ambiguous matters of interpretation. Suppose a contract reads "Employees who are unable to work because of being on jury duty will be reimbursed the difference between jury duty pay and their regular earnings."[61] An employee who works the day shift is obviously "unable to work because of being on jury duty" but what about an employee that works a night shift? A night-shift employee might claim that s/he is "unable to work" because of physical and mental exhaustion that would result from having eight hours of jury duty and then eight hours of work in the same day. The employer might argue that "unable to work" applies strictly to direct scheduling conflicts and therefore does not apply to night-shift employees. The arbitrator's task is to interpret "unable to work" and apply it to this particular situation.

To interpret the contract, arbitrators use three elements: contractual language, intent, and past practices.[62] In looking at the contractual language, arbitrators try to use the ordinary and popular meaning of words and place more weight on specific clauses than on general ones. If this fails to resolve the ambiguity of the language, arbitrators look to intent —what meaning did the parties intend when they negotiated the clause? For example, suppose the jury duty clause used to read "unable to report to work" and it was changed in the last negotiation to read "unable to work." This might indicate an intent to broaden the jury duty clause and therefore apply it to night-shift employees. Sometimes notes from previous negotiating sessions might be used to determine intent. Lastly, past practice is also important in determining how to interpret contract clauses. For the jury duty dispute, how have other night-shift employees been treated in the past? Have employees worked a double shift in the past (indicating that employees are able to work after eight hours of jury duty)? In

[60] Charles S. Loughran, *How to Prepare and Present a Labor Arbitration Case: Strategy and Tactics for Advocates* (Washington, DC: Bureau of National Affairs, 1996). Nolan and Abrams, "Trends in Private Sector Grievance Arbitration." Ruben, *Elkouri and Elkouri.*

[61] Arnold M. Zack, *Grievance Arbitration: Issues on the Merits in Discipline, Discharge, and Contract Interpretation* (Lexington, MA: Lexington Books, 1989), p. 154.

[62] Carlton J. Snow, "Contract Interpretation," in Theodore J. St. Antoine (ed.), *The Common Law of the Workplace: The View of Arbitrators*, 2nd ed. (Washington, DC: Bureau of National Affairs, 2005), Chapter 2. Ruben, *Elkouri and Elkouri.*

Handling grievances and preparing for arbitration hearings involve largely the same tasks for both labor and management officials:

- *Gathering evidence.* This might include interviewing potential witnesses, collecting information from personnel files, and reviewing past practices, previous grievances, other arbitration awards that might serve as precedents, the contract, and the bargaining history of any relevant clauses.

- *Collecting facts.* This includes evaluating the reliability, credibility, and consistency of the evidence to determine the facts that come from the evidence.

- *Constructing arguments from the facts.* Rarely do "the facts speak for themselves." Rather, they need to be carefully assembled and sequenced into a logical argument as to how the contract was violated or not.

- *Preparing questions for witnesses.* This includes determining the best way to present your case and also for cross-examining the other side's witnesses.

- *Anticipating evidentiary issues.* Will the other side challenge the credibility or admissibility of your evidence? Is the other side's evidence credible and reliable? If not, how can you demonstrate this?

Questions

1. Which of these tasks are applicable to all grievances and which are specific to arbitration hearings?

2. How can successful completion of these tasks help prevent grievances from getting to arbitration?

3. Are these tasks backward or forward looking? In other words, do they support the use of the grievance procedure and arbitration for problem solving or for litigating contractual disputes?

Sources: Charles S. Loughran, *How to Prepare and Present a Labor Arbitration Case: Strategy and Tactics for Advocates* (Washington, DC: Bureau of National Affairs, 1996). Mark I. Lurie, "The Eight Essential Steps in Grievance Processing," *Dispute Resolution Journal* 54 (November 1999), pp. 61–65.

sum, arbitrators' decisions are based on the **common law of the workplace**—the written rules and unwritten customs developed in each workplace by the union contract, intent of the negotiators, and past practices.[63]

While grievance arbitration can incorporate accepted standards of justice into workplace dispute resolution, it has also been criticized along several dimensions. As noted in the introduction to this chapter, the bureaucratic nature of traditional grievance procedures and the importance of stewards, union officials, and attorneys rather than individual workers is attacked by labor activists for stifling rank and file involvement in their unions.[64] Some unions are trying to create an organizing rather than servicing model of unionism by involving workers more in their own grievance resolution (see Chapter 14). A second criticism of grievance arbitration that comes from all parties is that it can be lengthy (perhaps a year from grievance filing to arbitrator decision) and costly.[65] The costs of an arbitrator are split equally between the union and the employer and might amount to $1,600 each, assuming an average arbitrator rate of $800 per day for four days. Attorney's fees are frequently more than this, so a typical arbitration hearing might cost a total of $10,000 or more. In response, some bargaining pairs have experimented with using grievance mediation, typically as a step in the grievance procedure

[63] Theodore J. St. Antoine (ed.), *The Common Law of the Workplace: The View of Arbitrators*, 2nd ed. (Washington, DC: Bureau of National Affairs, 2005).

[64] Klare, "Workplace Democracy and Market Reconstruction." Moody, *An Injury to All*. Stone, "The Post-War Paradigm in American Labor Law." Fantasia and Voss, *Hard Work*.

[65] Peter Feuille, "Grievance Mediation," in Adrienne E. Eaton and Jeffrey H. Keefe (eds.), *Employment Dispute Resolution and Worker Rights in the Changing Workplace* (Champaign, IL: Industrial Relations Research Association, 1999), Chapter 6. Nolan and Abrams, "Trends in Private Sector Grievance Arbitration."

just before arbitration. This process appears quite successful, and it remains a puzzle why more parties do not adopt this method.[66]

Lastly, grievance procedures in general, and arbitration in particular, are also criticized as excessively legal, formal, and reactive. By reactive, it is meant that the grievance procedure looks backward at what happened to determine if the contract was violated or not.[67] Grievance arbitration is a quasijudicial process focused on determining the "guilt" or "innocence" of managerial actions that have already occurred. The process is not a forward-looking, problem-solving venue. As such, traditional grievance procedures are potentially inconsistent with recent efforts to involve workers in workplace decision making through high performance work practices such as teams or quality circles. Reactive grievance processing needs to be complemented with proactive problem solving.[68]

EMPLOYEE DISCIPLINE

One of the most important areas of contract administration is employee discipline and discharge. Employers particularly want to be able to discipline and terminate employees who are substandard performers and employees don't want to lose their jobs, especially unfairly. In fact, more grievance arbitration hearings pertain to discipline and discharge than any other topic by a wide margin in both the private and public sectors.[69] Under the employment-at-will doctrine that governs the U.S. employment relationship in the absence of specific statutory restrictions (such as antidiscrimination statutes), employees can be discharged at any time for any reason: "for good cause, for no cause or even for cause morally wrong" (Chapter 1).[70] In a sharp departure from the employment-at-will doctrine, however, over 90 percent of private sector union contracts, and many public sector ones as well, specify that employees can only be disciplined and discharged for "cause" or "just cause."

Just cause is therefore an important concept in labor relations. In short, the requirement that employees be disciplined or discharged only when there is just cause means that there must be valid, job-related reasons for being disciplined or fired. Because the quasijudicial nature of grievance arbitration includes published arbitration decisions and the use of previous decisions as precedents (just as published court decisions often serve as precedents in other court cases), an extensive system of precedents has developed which can guide labor and management thinking about just cause (and numerous other issues).[71] In other words, we should ask what do arbitrators use to decide whether the standards of just cause have been fulfilled?

One common method is to apply the seven tests that Arbitrator Carroll Daugherty set forth in a frequently cited 1966 arbitration decision (see Box 10.9).[72] First, did the disciplined or discharged worker receive advance notice or a warning of the consequences of certain conduct? Some forms of conduct are so obvious and severe that it is assumed that

[66] Feuille, "Grievance Mediation."

[67] Lewin, "Theoretical and Empirical Research on the Grievance Procedure and Arbitration."

[68] Michelle Kaminski, "New Forms of Organization and Their Impact on the Grievance Procedure," in Adrienne E. Eaton and Jeffrey H. Keefe (eds.), *Employment Dispute Resolution and Worker Rights in the Changing Workplace* (Champaign, IL: Industrial Relations Research Association, 1999), Chapter 7.

[69] Graham, "Grievance Arbitration in State and Local Government in the 1990s and Beyond." Nolan and Abrams, "Trends in Private Sector Grievance Arbitration."

[70] *Payne v. Western and Atlantic R.R. Co.,* 81 Tenn. 507, 519–20 (1884), *overruled on other grounds, Hutton v. Watters,* 179 S.W. 134, 138 (Tenn. 1915).

[71] Adolph Koven and Susan L. Smith, *Just Cause: The Seven Tests,* 2nd ed. (Washington, DC: Bureau of National Affairs, 1992). St. Antoine, *The Common Law of the Workplace.* Ruben, *Elkouri and Elkouri.*

[72] *Enterprise Wire Company,* 46 LA 359 (1966). Koven and Smith, *Just Cause.*

The Seven Tests of Just Cause

Box 10.9

1. Was the worker given advance warning of the consequences of his/her conduct?
2. Was the rule, order, or standard reasonably related to employee performance?
3. Was the alleged violation thoroughly investigated before discipline?
4. Was the investigation fair and objective?

5. Did the investigation reveal convincing proof of guilt?
6. Was the employer's discipline nondiscriminatory?
7. Was the discipline reasonably related to the worker's record and the severity of the conduct?

Source: Arbitrator Carroll Daugherty, *Enterprise Wire Company*, 46 LA 359 (1966).

---

workers will know the consequences—violence, theft, or vandalism, for example. But for many other actions, it does not seem fair to impose discipline for something that the employee does not know is against company policy—leaving work during a break, leaving a workstation without a supervisor's permission, posting something on a bulletin board, using a company phone to make a local personal call, to name just a few. Second, was the workplace rule, management order, or performance standard that the employee violated reasonably related to employee performance? In other words, just cause discipline requires job-related reasons.

The next three of the seven tests pertain to management's investigation surrounding the discipline or discharge of an employee. Was the alleged violation thoroughly investigated *before* the discipline was imposed? Was the investigation fair and objective? Did the investigation reveal convincing proof of guilt? Negative answers to any of these questions undermines due process and just cause. Investigating an employee after imposing discipline looks like an attempt to find evidence to support a predetermined desire to discipline the employee. Just cause, however, is rooted in explicit, job-performance behaviors that trigger discipline. Investigations that are not fair and that do not reveal proof of guilt also cannot be used to support just cause discipline and discharge because they also fail to demonstrate that a valid, job-performance issue caused the discipline. Rather, clear and convincing evidence that is objective and credible is needed.

The final two tests of the seven tests of just cause focus on whether the employer's disciplinary action was appropriate under the circumstances. Was the employer's discipline nondiscriminatory? Was the disciplinary action reasonably related to the worker's record and the severity of the conduct? The first of these two underscores the importance of past practice. If other employees have not been disciplined in the past for the same misconduct, how is it justified to discipline the current offender? Such discipline is discriminatory, not just. The second of these two emphasizes the importance of progressive or corrective discipline. Arbitrators do not look favorably upon punitive penalties that are intended to punish workers. Rather, progressive or corrective discipline provides the opportunity for employees to remedy their poor behavior by having penalties that increase as the misconduct is repeated or gets more severe. As such, issues such as absenteeism might start off with a warning. If the problem continues, a suspension should be given, and then if it still persists, discharge is appropriate. Severe issues like violence, theft, vandalism, and gross insubordination might warrant immediate discharge without the need for progressive or corrective discipline. When arbitrators decide discharge cases, one of three outcomes are typical: the discharge is upheld as being consistent with just cause, the employee is exonerated and reinstated with full backpay, or an intermediate option is awarded in which the employee is reinstated but without full backpay (in effect, reducing the discharge to an unpaid suspension).

These seven tests are not the only method for analyzing the components of just cause, but they reveal the major issues that should be considered—job performance, the nature of the investigation and evidence, and the appropriateness of the degree of discipline. With the proliferation of unjust dismissal lawsuits in the nonunion sector, these are important issues for managers and employees in nonunion as well as unionized situations. Additionally, along with the duty of fair representation, the seven tests can shed light on a popular criticism of unions—that they help undeserving workers keep their jobs. Because of the duty of fair representation, unions have an obligation to represent all workers fairly and thus unions are sometimes put in the awkward role of advocating on behalf of a poor performing worker—but this is their legal obligation. Moreover, based on the seven tests, if the union is able to help a poor performing worker keep his/her job, management must not be fulfilling the standards of just cause—perhaps the performance has not been documented adequately, or the appropriate corrective steps have not been taken.

A final important issue for the topic of employee discipline is an employee's right to representation. The Supreme Court has interpreted the right of employees to engage in concerted activity for mutual protection (as provided by section 7 of the NLRA) to mean that an employee who believes that discipline will result from a meeting with management can insist that a union representative be present.[73] This is called an employee's **Weingarten rights** after the name of the initial 1975 Supreme Court decision.[74] The union representative is entitled to assist the employee, but not obstruct reasonable questioning by the employer. An ongoing controversy is whether nonunion employees have a similar right to have a co-worker present when they expect discipline—after all, section 7 does not pertain solely to unionized situations. During the administration of President Clinton, the NLRB extended *Weingarten* rights to nonunion workers[75], but this extension was overturned by a more conservative Bush-era NLRB in 2004 (recall Box 5.23); it is again the case that only union workers are entitled to *Weingarten* rights.[76]

DO THESE CONTRACT CLAUSES MATTER?

An important question in labor relations that swirls around contract clauses and their administration is what effect they have on the employment relationship. As discussed in Chapter 2, research on the effects of unions generally estimates that wages of union-represented workers are approximately 15 percent higher than similar nonunion workers—this is the union wage premium.[77] Unions also frequently compress the wage structure within a workplace by narrowing the differentials between lower and higher paid workers.[78] Unionized workers are significantly

---

[73] Feldacker, *Labor Guide to Labor Law.*

[74] *NLRB v. J. Weingarten, Inc.,* 420 U.S. 251 (1975).

[75] *Epilepsy Foundation of Northeast Ohio,* 331 NLRB No. 92 (2000).

[76] *IBM Corp.,* 341 NLRB No. 148 (2004). Christine Neylon O'Brien, "The NLRB Waffling on *Weingarten* Rights," *Loyola University Chicago Law Journal* 37 (Fall 2005), pp. 111–46.

[77] Alison L. Booth, *The Economics of the Trade Union* (Cambridge: Cambridge University Press, 1995). H. Gregg Lewis, *Union Relative Wage Effects: A Survey* (Chicago: University of Chicago Press, 1986). Barry T. Hirsch, "Reconsidering Union Wage Effects: Surveying New Evidence on an Old Topic," *Journal of Labor Research* 25 (Spring 2004), pp. 233–66. David G. Blanchflower and Alex Bryson, "What Effect Do Unions Have on Wages Now and Would Freeman and Medoff Be Surprised?" *Journal of Labor Research* 25 (Summer 2004), pp. 383–414.

[78] Richard B. Freeman, "Union Wage Practices and Wage Dispersion Within Establishments." *Industrial and Labor Relations Review* 36 (October 1982), pp. 3–21. Freeman and Medoff, *What Do Unions Do?* David Card, Thomas Lemieux, and W. Craig Riddell, "Unions and Wage Inequality," *Journal of Labor Research* 25 (Fall 2004), pp. 519–62.

more likely than comparable nonunion workers to receive health insurance, pensions, and other employee benefits.[79] Unions are also estimated to increase the likelihood of seniority rights, grievance procedures, and just cause discipline and discharge provisions.[80]

Evaluating the importance of the grievance procedure specifically is more difficult. The basic operating statistics of unionized grievance procedures support the delivery of due process protections to employees: the grievance procedure is widely used both in terms of employees and issues, grievants are assisted by union officials, neutral arbitrators are used to resolve the most difficult conflicts, employees win a significant fraction of grievances, unfairly dismissed workers are reinstated, and all parties usually accept the results of the grievance procedure.[81] This evidence strongly suggests that grievance procedures do matter. On the other hand, analyses of what happens to individual grievants and their supervisors are less favorable. After grievances are resolved, grievance filers and their supervisors receive lower performance ratings and are more likely to quit (grievants) or be fired (their supervisors).[82] Unfortunately, research cannot identify what would have happened to these individuals if their issues had occurred under an alternative system (such as no grievance procedure in a nonunion situation), so we don't know whether a grievance procedure makes the best of a lousy situation, or makes a lousy situation even worse. Most believe the former, but the research just mentioned clouds the issue.

In any case, a major consequence of union representation and the traditional contract provisions is reduced job turnover. This likely stems from the value that workers place on higher wages, better benefits, and objective seniority rights as well as the ability to address problems through the grievance procedure. Nonunion workers who lack a grievance procedure have more limited options for addressing problems—namely, quitting.[83] In fact, unionized workers with stronger grievance procedures are less likely to quit than unionized workers with weaker grievance procedures.[84] Taking into account differences in working conditions and workplace climate between union and nonunion workplaces, there does not appear to be a significant union–nonunion difference in job satisfaction.[85]

---

[79] Thomas C. Buchmueller, John DiNardo, and Robert G. Valletta, "Union Effects on Health Insurance Provision and Coverage in the United States," *Industrial and Labor Relations Review* 55 (July 2002), pp. 610–27. Budd, "Non-Wage Forms of Compensation." Richard B. Freeman, "The Effect of Unionism on Fringe Benefits." *Industrial and Labor Relations Review* 34 (July 1981), pp. 489–509. Richard B. Freeman, "Unions, Pensions, and Union Pension Funds," in David A. Wise (ed.), *Pensions, Labor, and Individual Choice* (Chicago: University of Chicago Press, 1985), pp. 89–121. Freeman and Medoff, *What Do Unions Do?*

[80] Richard B. Freeman and Morris M. Kleiner, "The Impact of New Unionization on Wages and Working Conditions," *Journal of Labor Economics* 8 (January 1990), pp. S8–S25. Tom Juravich, Kate Bronfenbrenner, and Robert Hickey, "Significant Victories: An Analysis of Union First Contracts," in Richard N. Block et al. (eds.), *Justice on the Job: Perspectives on the Erosion of Collective Bargaining in the United States* (Kalamazoo, MI: Upjohn, 2006), pp. 87–114.

[81] Lewin, "Theoretical and Empirical Research on the Grievance Procedure and Arbitration."

[82] Lewin and Peterson, *The Modern Grievance Procedure in the United States.* Lewin and Peterson, "Behavioral Outcomes of Grievance Activity."

[83] Richard B. Freeman, "The Exit-Voice Tradeoff in the Labor Market: Unionism, Job Tenure, Quits, and Separations," *Quarterly Journal of Economics* 94 (June 1980), pp. 643–73. Tove Helland Hammer and Ariel Avgar, "The Impact of Unions on Job Satisfaction, Organizational Commitment, and Turnover," *Journal of Labor Research* 26 (Spring 2005), pp. 241–66.

[84] Daniel I. Rees, "Grievance Procedure Strength and Teacher Quits," *Industrial and Labor Relations Review* 45 (October 1991), pp. 31–43.

[85] Jeffrey Pfeffer and Alison Davis-Blake, "Unions and Job Satisfaction: An Alternative View," *Work and Occupations* 17 (August 1990), pp. 259–83. Michael E. Gordon and Angelo S. DeNisi, "A Re-Examination of the Relationship Between Union Membership and Job Satisfaction," *Industrial and Labor Relations Review* 48 (January 1995), pp. 226–36. Keith A. Bender and Peter J. Sloane, "Job Satisfaction, Trade Unions, and Exit-Voice Revisited," *Industrial and Labor Relations Review* 51 (January 1998), pp. 222–40. Alex Bryson, Lorenzo Cappellari, and Claudio Lucifora, "Does Union Membership Really Reduce Job Satisfaction?" *British Journal of Industrial Relations* 42 (September 2004), pp. 439–59.

Another important aspect of the effects of unions and union contracts is organizational performance. Many aspects of union contracts are predicted to reduce productivity—seniority rights can reduce the employer's ability to allocate jobs on the basis of merit, requirements that certain tasks be assigned to skilled workers and other restrictive work rules can reduce flexibility, time spent resolving grievances is time away from production, and the like. On the other hand, grievance procedures, seniority provisions, just cause discipline requirements, and other provisions which promote fair treatment, increase morale, and reduce turnover, can also improve productivity.[86] So what happens in practice? The evidence is mixed. Some studies find that unions increase productivity, others find the opposite.[87] The effect of unionism on productivity appears to be determined by the specifics of each situation rather than the nature of U.S. unionism and contract clauses in general. But as many elements of union contracts increase labor costs—especially higher wages and more generous benefits—even when productivity increases, the increase is not sufficient to offset the increased labor costs; in other words, unions reduce profits.[88]

NONUNION WORKPLACE DISPUTE RESOLUTION

A critical difference between union and nonunion U.S. workplaces is the nature of dispute resolution. Unionized grievance procedures that embrace union representation and assistance for grievants as well as final hearings (if needed) before neutral arbitrators create systems of workplace justice that provide due process to individual employees. Such systems can also benefit employers by avoiding strikes and excessive employee turnover and by providing a channel of communication between employees and employers. Contrast this with nonunion workplaces. First, note carefully that conflicts in *all* workplaces are inevitable—employees might feel unfairly treated, harassed, cheated out of vacation days, overlooked for promotions, or deserving of a raise in any workplace, union or nonunion. Thus, methods of conflict resolution are needed in both union and nonunion workplaces.

Nonunion workplaces have traditionally lacked formal dispute resolution systems, and therefore by default have relied heavily on managerial control. Employees discuss their concerns and complaints with their managers. Employees that are dissatisfied by the managers' responses (or lack thereof) are free to quit. This type of dispute resolution system is often labeled an open door policy because the manager's door is open for employees who want to discuss their concerns. But the other open door should not be overlooked: the exit door for those who are dissatisfied. Many nonunion workplaces still rely on open door policies to resolve workplace disputes, but there has also been significant growth in formal policies, and by some estimates, perhaps as many as half of nonunion companies have a formal workplace dispute resolution procedure.[89]

[86] Freeman and Medoff, *What Do Unions Do?*

[87] Barry T. Hirsch, "What Do Unions Do for Economic Performance?" *Journal of Labor Research* 25 (Summer 2004), pp. 415–55. Christos Doucouliagos and Patrice LaRoche, "What Do Unions Do to Productivity? A Meta-Analysis," *Industrial Relations* 42 (October 2003), pp. 650–91.

[88] Brian E. Becker and Craig A. Olson, "Labor Relations and Firm Performance," in Morris M. Kleiner et al. (eds.), *Human Resources and the Performance of the Firm* (Madison, WI: Industrial Relations Research Association, 1987), Chapter 2. Hirsch, "What Do Unions Do for Economic Performance?" Richard S. Ruback and Martin B. Zimmerman, "Unionization and Profitability: Evidence from the Capital Market," *Journal of Political Economy* 92 (December 1984), pp. 1134–57.

[89] Colvin, "The Relationship Between Employment Arbitration and Workplace Dispute Resolution Procedures." David Lewin, "Workplace Dispute Resolution," in David Lewin, Daniel J. B. Mitchell, and Mahmood A. Zaidi (eds.), *The Human Resource Management Handbook Part II* (Greenwich, CT: JAI Press, 1997), pp. 197–218.

The basic element of formal nonunion dispute resolution procedures is an open door policy that is formalized by specifying a process for appealing the decision of the worker's immediate manager. This appeal process typically consists of appealing the grievance to higher levels of management with the final decision being issued by senior management, such as the vice president for human resources, or by an appeal board of managers. This type of grievance procedure lacks many elements of due process.[90] In particular, employees generally lack representation or assistance in presenting their grievances and the decision makers are all members of management. One or more elements are sometimes added to this basic nonunion grievance procedure: ombudspersons, peer review panels, and arbitration.

An ombudsperson is a neutral facilitator between employees and managers who assists them in resolving workplace disputes. An ombudsperson might investigate disputes, but almost always on an informal basis and with the goal of helping employees resolve their complaints. In other words, the ombudsperson is much more of a mediator than arbitrator or fact finder.[91] Note carefully, however, that the ombudsperson is an employee of the company and therefore this type of nonunion dispute resolution procedure runs the risk of favoring the company's interests over neutrality, confidentiality, and due process. Ombudspersons might also assist grievants in preparing their cases, but since they are paid by the company, this advocacy role is limited. As such, while there is somewhat greater neutrality than in stand-alone open door policies, employee representation in processing grievances is limited in ombudsperson systems.[92]

Some nonunion procedures add a peer review panel to the appeal process. In this system, grievances can be appealed to a review panel in which employees (not managers) comprise the majority of the panel members—hence the name *peer* review panel. Peer review panels are established to counter perceptions that dispute resolutions systems, in which managers make the final decisions, are unfair.[93] In fact, nonunion systems that include a nonmanagerial decision maker have higher grievance filing rates than nonunion systems in which decisions are made by managers, which suggests that employees are more accepting of nonunion grievance procedures in which managers do not make the final decision.[94] In some instances, arbitration is the final step of a nonunion workplace dispute resolution system, but this is the exception, not the norm.[95] Moreover, nonunion arbitration of grievances might still provide less due process to employees than unionized grievance arbitration if there are limitations on discovery (how much information the grievant can collect from the company), if the use of outside advocates such as attorneys is restricted, if employees cannot afford several thousand dollars of arbitration expenses, and if arbitrators favor management to increase their chances of getting selected for future cases (since individual employees are less likely than companies to know an arbitrator's reputation).[96]

[90] Colvin, "The Relationship Between Employment Arbitration and Workplace Dispute Resolution Procedures."

[91] Mary Rowe, "Dispute Resolution in the Non-union Environment: An Evolution Toward Integrated Systems for Conflict Management" in Sandra E. Gleason (ed.), *Workplace Dispute Resolution: Directions for the Twenty-First Century* (East Lansing: Michigan State University Press, 1997), Chapter 4.

[92] Lewin, "Workplace Dispute Resolution."

[93] Colvin, "The Relationship Between Employment Arbitration and Workplace Dispute Resolution Procedures."

[94] Alexander J. S. Colvin, "The Dual Transformation of Workplace Dispute Resolution," *Industrial Relations* 42 (October 2003), pp. 712–35.

[95] Joseph F. Gentile, "The Structure and Workings of Employer-Promulgated Grievance Procedures and Arbitration Agreements," in James L. Stern and Joyce M. Najita (eds.), *Labor Arbitration Under Fire* (Ithaca, NY: ILR Press, 1997), Chapter 6.

[96] John L. Zalusky, "A Union View of Nonrepresented Employees' Grievance Systems," in James L. Stern and Joyce M. Najita (eds.), *Labor Arbitration Under Fire* (Ithaca, NY: ILR Press, 1997), Chapter 8.

Another use of nonunion arbitration is increasing and is also controversial—the use of mandatory arbitration instead of the courts to resolve employment law claims.[97] In order to avoid costly court cases over alleged discrimination, harassment, or other employment law violations, some employers are requiring employees to agree in advance to waive their rights to court action and to instead arbitrate these claims. These agreements have been upheld by the Supreme Court, but the use of compulsory arbitration agreements is very controversial because of potential imbalances between employers and individual nonunion employees that undermine the fairness of employment arbitration in nonunion situations (see Box 10.10).[98] Quality standards for nonunion employment arbitration have therefore been proposed that include making arbitration agreements voluntary once a claim arises (rather than mandatory in advance of any disputes), ensuring employee access to relevant information, sharing expenses in a fair and affordable way, preserving a full range of remedies such as punitive damage awards, and allowing for judicial review of arbitrators' decisions.[99]

There are three possible explanations for the increased adoption of nonunion workplace dispute resolution systems in recent years.[100] First, formal dispute resolution procedures can be part of a human resource management strategy to increase organizational commitment and performance by treating employees fairly and by identifying problem areas. Second, these procedures might be implemented to try to avoid costly lawsuits. Third, since grievance procedures are a major feature of unionized workplaces, the implementation of a grievance procedure in a nonunion workplace might be part of a union substitution strategy (Chapter 6) to prevent unionization. Research supports all three explanations with peer review systems being linked with human resources and union substitution strategies and with employment arbitration being linked with a desire to avoid costly lawsuits. As such, formal dispute resolution systems in nonunion workplaces are not always implemented to enhance employee due process: "the impetus for the adoption of these procedures is the protection of the firm against institutional pressures from outside the organization. Like walls around a citadel, these procedures help prevent intrusion by outside actors—notably, in this case, unions and the courts."[101]

A DIFFERENT APPROACH TO CONTRACT ADMINISTRATION

This chapter describes the major elements of traditional union contracts in U.S. labor relations, including the grievance procedure that is used to administer contracts by enforcing and resolving disputes over clauses in the rest of the contract. By increasing compensation and benefits, using seniority as at least one factor in many personnel decisions, limiting employee discipline

[97] Richard A. Bales, *Compulsory Arbitration: The Grand Experiment in Employment* (Ithaca, NY: ILR Press, 1997). Michael H. Leroy and Peter Feuille, "Judicial Enforcement of Predispute Arbitration Agreements: Back to the Future," *Ohio State Journal on Dispute Resolution* 18 (2003), pp. 249–341. Katherine V. W. Stone, "Mandatory Arbitration of Individual Employment Rights: The Yellow Dog Contract of the 1990s," *Denver University Law Review* 73 (1996), pp. 1017–50.

[98] *Gilmer v. Interstate/Johnson Lane Corp.*, 500 U.S. 20 (1991). *Circuit City Stores, Inc. v. Adams,* 532 U.S. 105 (2001).

[99] Commission on the Future of Worker–Management Relations, *Report and Recommendations* (Washington, DC: U.S. Departments of Labor and Commerce, 1994). Richard A. Bales, "The Laissez-Faire Arbitration Market and the Need for a Uniform Federal Standard Governing Employment and Consumer Arbitration," *Kansas Law Review* 52 (2004), pp. 583–603.

[100] Alexander J. S. Colvin, "Institutional Pressures, Human Resource Strategies, and the Rise of Nonunion Dispute Resolution Procedures," *Industrial and Labor Relations Review* 56 (April 2003), pp. 375–92.

[101] Colvin, "Institutional Pressures, Human Resource Strategies, and the Rise of Nonunion Dispute Resolution Procedures," p. 377.

Nonunion Arbitration of Employment Law Claims

Box 10.10

No company wants to be sued for discrimination, harassment, or other violations of employment law. Legal fees, negative publicity, and the potential for huge monetary damages awarded by unpredictable juries can all harm a company's reputation and economic performance. An employee who seeks redress in the court system faces lengthy delays and significant lawyer's fees. In an attempt to reduce these delays and expenses in all kinds of court cases (not just employment law), since the 1970s the legal system has been promoting ADR—alternative dispute resolution. ADR includes mediation, arbitration, and other methods for avoiding court trials. As part of this movement, Congress amended the Civil Rights Act in 1991 to encourage the use of arbitration to resolve discrimination lawsuits (though not necessarily the form of compulsory arbitration described next).

Some employers reacted to these developments by requiring their employees to sign agreements to arbitrate rather than litigate (that is, not sue in court) any alleged violations of employment law. Such agreements have generally been enforced by the courts, including by the Supreme Court in *Gilmer v. Interstate/Johnson Lane Corp.* (1991) and *Circuit City Stores, Inc. v. Adams* (2001). Note carefully that these are compulsory agreements to arbitrate future disputes—these are not situations where an employer and employee who have an existing dispute voluntarily agree that they would both prefer to use arbitration rather than a lengthy, costly jury trial. As such, compulsory arbitration agreements are the subject of intense debate.

Because these compulsory arbitration agreements are required as a condition of employment, some fear that the employer can abuse its power and force an unfair rather than fair arbitration procedure on the employees. There are examples of one-sided arbitration agreements in which employees are required to waive their rights to discovery (which is essential to gather evidence) and to some remedies (such as reinstatement). Other one-sided examples include agreements in which employers unilaterally select the arbitrator and which impose significant expenses (such as arbitration fees) on low-paid workers. The courts have refused to enforce some of the most blatantly unfair arbitration procedures, but if the courts need to review significant numbers of cases, then the goal of resolving disputes out of court will be undone.

Arbitration of employment law disputes can offer significant benefits with respect to speed, cost, and the specialized expertise of arbitrators, but finding the appropriate policy requires finding a balance between these benefits and the potential destruction of employees' rights if the compulsory arbitration process unfairly favors employers.

Sources: Richard A. Bales, *Compulsory Arbitration: The Grand Experiment in Employment* (Ithaca, NY: ILR Press, 1997). Michael H. Leroy and Peter Feuille, "Judicial Enforcement of Predispute Arbitration Agreements: Back to the Future," *Ohio State Journal on Dispute Resolution* 18 (2003), pp. 249–341. Katherine V. W. Stone, "Mandatory Arbitration of Individual Employment Rights: The Yellow Dog Contract of the 1990s," *Denver University Law Review* 73 (1996), pp. 1017–50. John L. Zalusky, "A Union View of Nonrepresented Employees' Grievance Systems," in James L. Stern and Joyce M. Najita (eds.), *Labor Arbitration Under Fire* (Ithaca, NY: ILR Press, 1997), Chapter 8.

and discharge to situations of just cause, placing restrictions on work assignments, and providing for the orderly and fair resolution of disputes, union contracts clearly have important effects on employees, organizational performance, and the employment relationship. Whether one evaluates these effects more positively or negatively depends to a large degree on the intellectual framework used to analyze the employment relationship—neoclassical economics, human resource management, critical industrial relations, or pluralist industrial relations (Chapter 2).

Moreover, the traditional emphasis of U.S. labor relations on detailed, legally enforceable contracts can be criticized as ill-suited for the employment relationship of the 21st century—especially because of a lack of worker involvement and organizational flexibility. Therefore, even though union grievance procedures promote workplace justice through due process protections, new forms of contract administration might be necessary in the future if the nature of union contracts change. More flexible contracts likely require more flexible methods of administration. To stimulate thinking in this direction, this chapter closes with an alternative example which involves a different type of union contract and contract administration process: a chemical plant in Sarnia, Ontario, owned partly by Shell Canada, in which the workers are represented by the Communications, Energy, and Paperworkers Union of Canada.[102]

Rather than using traditional job classifications and a strict supervisory hierarchy, the chemical plant is operated by six self-directed work teams that are empowered to make the necessary operating decisions, including assignment of work, on a day-to-day basis. Instead of a single, traditional union contract, there are three agreements negotiated between the company and union: a philosophy statement, a collective bargaining agreement, and a Good Works Practices Handbook. The philosophy statement defines the basic principles of the plant such as extensive communication, commitment, employee discretion, and collaborative problem solving. The collective bargaining agreement, which is less than 20 pages long, outlines the existence of basic issues such as shift premiums and the number of vacation days. Administration of these items, however, is not pursued through the contract —as is typical with traditional union contracts. Rather, a separate Good Works Practices Handbook is used to administer the contract and provides general guidelines for the teams to follow when implementing the contractual provisions.

Note carefully the significant impact of this distinction between the contract and the Good Works Practices Handbook. The contract specifies the fundamental rights of each party which are often stable and involve conflicts of interest (distributive conflicts)—such as the number of vacation days. Implementation of these rights is typically a more flexible process and involves potential for mutual gain (integrative conflicts)—such as scheduling vacation. As such, separating the contract and the Handbook can facilitate joint problem solving in the administration phase without the necessity of interpreting the contract in a quasijudicial, formal fashion. In fact, the Handbook is continually modified to suit the needs of labor and management —this is only possible by separating administration of rights from the collective bargaining agreement. This continuous updating does not threaten the union's gains in compensation, benefits, and fundamental rights because the contract is a separate document.

In sum, a traditional union contract is the typical outcome of the New Deal industrial relations system. The major processes of this system which are the focus of Part II of this book—organizing, bargaining, and contract administration—all lead to the implementation of such contracts, and in this way, strive for a balance between efficiency, equity, and voice. But as discussed next in Part III, this system and these processes are under severe pressures in the global economic environment of the 21st century. These pressures for flexible and empowered workplaces, however, do not alter the fundamental objective of the labor relation system: striking a balance. An understanding of the existing labor relations processes and traditional union contracts is important not only for knowing how the current system works, but also for providing the foundation for thinking about how to strike a new balance in the global economic environment of the 21st century.

Key Terms

contract administration, *342*	duty of fair representation, *351*	rights arbitration, *357*
rights disputes, *342*	management rights clause, *351*	*Steelworkers Trilogy, 357*
seniority, *344*	reserved rights doctrine, *352*	common law of the workplace, *360*
union security clauses, *349*	grievance procedure, *354*	just cause, *361*
Beck rights, *349*		*Weingarten* rights, *363*

[102] Tom Rankin, *New Forms of Work Organization: The Challenge for North American Unions* (Toronto: University of Toronto Press, 1990).

Reflection Questions

1. Seniority is central in many private and public sector union contracts in the United States. What are the advantages to both employers and employees of using seniority to allocate employment opportunities? What are the disadvantages? How can a balance be struck between the interests of employers and employees?

2. What are the advantages and disadvantages of having the workplace governed by a legally enforceable contract supported by rights arbitration? Is this a good model for the workplace of the 21st century?

3. There is significantly more research on grievance initiation (for example, trying to identify under what circumstances grievances are filed) than on the effectiveness of unionized grievance procedures. What are some different ways of defining the effectiveness of a grievance procedure? How would you research these issues? Is grievance procedure effectiveness an issue for policymakers or is it strictly a private affair between employees, their unions, and their employers?

4. For each of the grievance discussion cases (Boxes 10.11–10.20), develop supporting arguments for the grievant and the employer. As an arbitrator, how would you rule? Why?

Internet Exploration

1. Various unions have contracts online and there are also databases of contracts (such as *socrates.berkeley.edu/~iir/library/contracts/index.html* and *www.opm.gov/cplmr/lairs .html-ssi*). Explore some of these contracts. Can you find the prominent clauses discussed in this chapter (such as a recognition clause, just cause discharge, seniority rights, union bulletin boards and access to the workplace, and management rights)? How similar are these clauses across different contracts? Try to also find unique clauses in some contracts—how do these relate to a specific occupation, industry, or location? How do various clauses serve efficiency, equity, and/or voice?

2. Browse through some arbitration decisions at *www.lawmemo.com/arb/award/all.htm*. What types of issues are being arbitrated? What pieces of evidence appear to have persuaded the arbitrator to rule the way s/he did? Did the arbitrator rely on any precedents (previous arbitration awards)?

3. Find rules and codes of conducts for arbitrators on the site of the American Arbitration Association (*www.adr.org*) and National Academy of Arbitrators (*www.naarb.org*). What things are emphasized? Why? Is there anything missing?

Additional Reading

Gleason, Sandra E. (ed.), *Workplace Dispute Resolution: Directions for the Twenty-First Century* (East Lansing: Michigan State University Press, 1997).

Grievance Guide, 11th ed. (Washington, DC: Bureau of National Affairs, 2003).

Koven, Adolph, and Susan L. Smith, *Just Cause: The Seven Tests,* 2nd ed. (Washington, DC: Bureau of National Affairs, 1992).

Lewin, David, "Theoretical and Empirical Research on the Grievance Procedure and Arbitration: A Critical Review," in Adrienne E. Eaton and Jeffrey H. Keefe (eds.), *Employment Dispute Resolution and Worker Rights in the Changing Workplace* (Champaign, IL: Industrial Relations Research Association, 1999), Chapter 5.

Prosten, David, *The Union Steward's Complete Guide* (Annapolis, MD: Union Communication Services, 1997).

Ruben, Alan Miles (ed.), *Elkouri and Elkouri: How Arbitration Works*, 6th ed. (Washington, DC: Bureau of National Affairs, 2003).

Stern, James L., and Joyce M. Najita (eds.), *Labor Arbitration Under Fire* (Ithaca, NY: ILR Press, 1997).

Grievance Discussion Case 1:
Is an Adoptive Mother Entitled to Maternity Leave?

Box 10.11

Background

Carol Fern has been employed by Bainbridge Borough for 18 years as a tax clerk. The tax clerk position in Bainbridge Borough is part of the bargaining unit represented by Local 10 of the American Federation of State, County and Municipal Employees (AFSCME).

When Carol and her husband found out that she was unable to conceive, they decided to adopt a child. The Ferns were notified on April 22 that a three-month-old baby girl was available and they could adopt her in three days. However, Carol told the adoption agency that she thought it was unfair to leave Bainbridge Borough on such short notice because April is a busy tax month. Adoption was therefore delayed until May 2.

On April 27, Carol requested two weeks of paid vacation for the period May 2 to May 17. This request was granted. The day before she was to return from her paid vacation, Carol asked for six months of unpaid maternity leave. This request had to be approved by the Bainbridge Borough Council which rejected the request by a 4–3 vote. However, the Council did offer Carol two successive 90-day Reasonable Purpose Leaves (amounting to six months of leave). On June 1, the following grievance was filed:

> According to Article X, Section 4.A—Unpaid Leaves 5. Maternity on page 13 of the final Agreement between Bainbridge Borough and Local Union 10—Maternity Leaves not to exceed six months shall be granted at the request of an employee. Maternity leaves shall, upon the request of the employee, be extended or renewed

for a period not to exceed six months. Relief or Remedy Sought: Granting of the just and deserved leave requested.

Potentially Relevant Contract Provisions

ARTICLE X. LEAVES OF ABSENCE
Section 4.A: Unpaid Leaves
1. *Reasonable Purpose*
   a. Leaves of absence for a limited period without pay—not to exceed ninety days—shall be granted for any reasonable purpose. Extension to be granted with approval of Borough Council.
   b. Reasonable purpose in each case shall be agreed upon by the Union and the Borough.
   . . .
5. *Maternity*
   a. Maternity Leaves—not to exceed six months—shall be granted at the request of the employee. Maternity leaves shall, upon the request of the employee, be extended or renewed for a period not to exceed six months.

Questions

1. As an attorney for Bainbridge Borough, develop a case to support the Council's rejection of Carol Fern's unpaid maternity leave request.

2. As an attorney for AFSCME Local 10, develop an argument to support your client's contention that the Council's rejection of Carol Fern's unpaid maternity leave request violates the collective bargaining agreement.

3. As an arbitrator, how would you rule? Why?

Background

The Picasso Company's paint gun factory includes three shifts of machinists who are represented by Lodge 821 of the International Association of Machinists and Aerospace Workers (IAM). Historically, the day shift did not have a Leader position unlike the second and third shifts. However, a group of first shift (day) employees presented management with a petition calling for a first shift Leader. The employees also developed a list of qualifications for the job. After some investigation, the factory manager, Sharon Murphy, decided that this was a good idea and began the process of selecting an employee for first shift Leader.

Murphy first developed her own list of qualifications for the position which turned out to be quite similar to the employees' list. In particular, it was felt that the position required "a knowledgeable employee to whom others could turn for help and who would troubleshoot and offer suggestions, or do whatever else was necessary to make the operation run more smoothly and efficiently." Moreover, Murphy thought the position needed "a self-starter who did not need to be told what to do."

When the position was posted, there were two applicants: Machinist First Class Robert Elder (seniority date March 10, 1987) and Machinist Second Class Mary Younger (seniority date July 6, 1991). Younger is rated as qualified for Machinist First Class, but has not received a promotion because of a lack of vacancies. Elder was a second and third shift Leader for five years until he voluntarily resigned as Leader to bump into a day shift position so that he could spend more time with his family. There is a $0.93 per hour pay differential between Machinist First Class and Second Class. Leaders receive $0.43 per hour above the Machinist First Class rate. In the past, the second and third shift Leader position was awarded to the senior applicant the majority of the time. No grievances were ever filed when the less senior person was selected. There is no record of a Second Class Machinist ever being promoted to Leader.

Murphy interviewed both individuals and also discussed the candidates with a supervisor, Rick Hatch. In the interviews, Murphy asked questions regarding initiative, communication skills, decision-making abilities, and scheduling flexibility. Supervisor Hatch evaluated Younger higher than Elder: he felt Younger had better interpersonal skills and greater initiative (Younger would take it upon herself to act whereas Elder would wait to be asked).

Hatch also indicated some flexibility and communication concerns stemming from when Elder had been third shift Leader. In particular, Hatch wanted Elder to arrive early enough to discuss instructions and problems with the second shift Leader, but Elder rarely was able to because he was in a carpool. Elder never arrived late. In fact, Elder has never been disciplined and has achieved near-perfect attendance. Hatch also communicated to Murphy that he encouraged Elder to operate a machine with a longer cycle time (in fact, the same machine Younger uses) when he was third shift Leader so that he could spend more time with other employees. Elder, however, felt it would be unfair to the other employees if he didn't rotate machines like everyone else. As the third shift Leader, Elder was in possession of the building keys and alarm codes after the Supervisor clocked out each night.

After her interviews with Elder and Younger and her conversations with Hatch, Murphy selected Younger for the first shift Leader position. Her decision was based on "her assessment of Younger as having the edge in interpersonal skills, communication skills, initiative, and attitude in that Younger seemed to enjoy doing the kinds of things that would be required of a Leader." She also felt "employees would be more comfortable going to Younger with their questions" and stated that "she considered seniority in making the decision."

Subsequently, Elder filed a grievance claiming the company has violated the collective bargaining agreement by failing to give full consideration to Elder's seniority and qualifications and by promoting the more junior employee.

Potentially Relevant Contract Provisions

SECTION 20.1. Awarding a Job Bid. When job openings occur or there are vacancies in classifications covered by this Agreement, excluding Leader classifications, the Corporation shall post on its bulletin boards a notice of such opening or vacancy, indicating the rate of pay for a period of three (3) days, in order to afford employees an opportunity to qualify for such opening or vacancy on the basis of seniority and ability to perform the available work. The Corporation shall not be required to consider the bid of a probationary employee. At the end of the third (3rd) day, the job opening or vacancy shall be filled by the employee who qualifies as soon as possible, but not to exceed ten (10) working days.

Continued

. . .

SECTION 20.4. The provisions of this Section, however, shall not be construed to prevent the Corporation from immediately filling vacancies in order to maintain scheduled production requirements, subject to the posting provisions of this Section. In filling vacancies in Leader positions covered by this Agreement, the Corporation agrees to give full consideration to seniority and the qualifications of employees in filling such vacancies.

Questions

1. As the president of IAM Lodge 821, how would you try to convince an arbitrator that the selection of Mary Younger violates the collective bargaining agreement?

2. As the human resources manager, develop a case for your contention that the selection of Mary Younger does not violate the contract.

3. As an arbitrator, how would you rule? Why?

Grievance Discussion Case 3: Safety Gloves Discharge, With Just Cause? Box 10.13

BARRERA RECYCLING COMPANY
LOS ANGELES RECLAMATION

REGLAS DE SEGURIDAD

11. Zapatos de seguridad y lentes deben ser usados todo el tiempo. Otras de seguridad deben ser usadas si lo indica el supervisor.

Background

This notice is posted on the lunch room bulletin board of the Los Angeles Reclamation facility of the Barrera Recycling Company. Rafael Gomez is the general manager of this facility and Erin McNamara is an employee with approximately 20 years of seniority and is represented by Local 37 of the United Paperworkers International Union.

McNamara's usual task was handling bundles of newsprint which were bound with plastic straps. McNamara cut the plastic straps and placed the newsprint into a baling machine. The plastic straps, however, were tight so it was difficult to slide a hand under the strap to lift the bundle and cut the strap. Consequently, McNamara and other employees would not wear the company's bulky safety gloves when lifting the bundles and cutting the straps. Occasionally, and not on a fixed schedule, McNamara would be required to sort loose paper, tin cans, and bottles which arrived in 30-gallon plastic bags. Many of the bottles arrived broken and the tin cans contained sharp edges so it was very important to wear safety gloves. McNamara eats her lunch in her pickup truck and has never been to the lunch room. She does not speak or read Spanish.

McNamara was transferred to this facility from a Long Beach facility in January and in October was imposed with a disciplinary three-day suspension by Gomez. Prior to this suspension, Gomez had six or seven conversations, which he considered verbal reprimands, with McNamara over work performance and safety issues. One (according to McNamara) or two (according to Gomez) of these conversations dealt with McNamara sleeping through safety meetings. Two others pertained to McNamara's failure to wear safety gloves, another the failure to wear a hard hat (McNamara had accidentally left it in her truck), and still another the failure to wear appropriate safety glasses. McNamara had been issued safety glasses without side panels at the Long Beach facility but Gomez insisted on glasses with side panels. The company, however, pays for one set of eyeglasses per year and upon being informed of this benefit, McNamara obtained the appropriate eyewear. The seventh and final conversation

Continued

Continued

before the suspension occurred on October 26 when Gomez noticed McNamara reading *Sports Illustrated* during working hours. On October 28, McNamara was suspended for three days and her disciplinary notice contained the following warning:

> Should you violate any Barrera rules or regulations during the next 12 months, you will be immediately discharged from Barrera employment.

No grievance was filed protesting this suspension.

December 9 began like nearly every day for McNamara: lifting the bundles of newsprint, cutting the plastic straps, and putting the paper into the baler—not wearing safety gloves since it was more efficient. However, a little while later an unexpected delivery of 30-gallon plastic bags arrived and McNamara and several other employees had to sort the paper, tin cans, and bottles. The other employees donned their safety gloves for this task, but McNamara had left hers in her pickup truck since the delivery was not expected. Thirty minutes later Gomez wandered by and observed McNamara sorting the materials without safety gloves. After explaining that they were in her pickup truck, she was ordered to go get them. Three minutes later she returned with the gloves and continued sorting—this time with the safety gloves.

Gomez, however, felt that discipline was appropriate and fired her. Consequently, Local 37 filed a grievance protesting the discharge on the grounds that the company did not have just cause.

Potentially Relevant Contract Provisions
Article I—General Purpose of Agreement
The general purpose of this Agreement is, in the mutual interest of the Plants and the employees, to provide for the operation of the Plants hereinafter mentioned under methods which shall further to the fullest extent possible, the safety of the employees, economy of operations, cleanliness of Plants, and protection of property. It is recognized by this Agreement to be the duty of the Plants and the employees to cooperate fully, individually, and collectively for the advancement of said conditions.
Article XIX—Non-Discrimination
Neither the Company nor the Union shall discriminate against any employee because of race, color, religion, sex, age, handicap or national origin. The parties further agree that they shall not discriminate against qualified handicapped individuals, qualified disabled veterans or qualified veterans of the Vietnam Era.
Article XX—Causes for Immediate Discharge
Section 1. Causes for immediate discharge are as follows:

1. Bringing intoxicants into or consuming intoxicants in the Plants or on Plant premises;
2. Reporting for duty under the influence of liquor;
3. Disobedience;
4. Smoking in prohibited areas;
5. Deliberate destruction or removal of Plant or another person's property;
6. Neglect of duty;
7. Refusal to comply with Plant rules, provided that such rules shall be posted in each department where they may be read by all employees and further, that no changes in present rules or no additional rules shall be made that are inconsistent with this Agreement, and further provided that any existing or new rules or changes in rules may be the subject of discussion between the Standing Committee and the Local Plant Manager and in case of disagreement, the procedure for other grievances shall apply;
8. Disorderly conduct;
9. Dishonesty;
10. Sleeping on duty;
11. Giving or taking a bribe of any nature as an inducement to obtaining work or retaining a position;
12. Reading books, magazines or newspapers while on duty, except where required in line of duty;
13. Failure to report for duty without bona fide reasons;
14. Reporting to work under the influence of any drug, marijuana, alcoholic beverage or any other mind altering substances; or the possession or use, thereof during work, on work premises or in Plantowned/leased vehicles.

Section 2. Discharge or suspension of an employee (not including a temporary layoff) shall be based on just and sufficient cause with a full explanation given to the employee.
Article XXI—Adjustment of Complaints
Section 5.
a. It is recognized and understood that management's right to discipline shall include the right to reprimand or warn an employee. The receipt of a written reprimand or warning shall be subject to the grievance procedure as set forth herein.
b. Provided further, all written reprimands of which a record is kept will be stricken from the Plant's files and the employee's work record after a period of one (1) year in which the employee received no reprimands.

Questions
1. As the person responsible for labor relations at Barrera Recycling Company, articulate a case to support your contention that there was just cause for the discharge of Erin McNamara.
2. As the Chief Steward for Local 37, how would you substantiate your allegation that the dismissal violates the collective bargaining agreement?
3. As an arbitrator, how would you rule? Why?

Grievance Discussion Case 4: Concealment of Education on a Job Application

Background

Jim Norbuck was born in rural central Pennsylvania and graduated from high school in the same town. He subsequently attended Bucknell University for two years and then transferred to the University of Illinois. He graduated from Illinois with a B.A. degree with an English major and a Philosophy minor. Jim then attended the University of Wisconsin where he received a Master of Arts degree. Jim started working on a Ph.D., but then decided that he was tired of school and wanted to work. Consequently, he moved back to Pennsylvania where he was a substitute high school teacher and taught as an instructor at a local college. Much to his dismay, the pay was quite poor and he needed a higher paying job.

On August 7, Jim Norbuck applied for a job at the nearby Leech Industries plant. From some friends, Jim had learned that Leech Industries' policy was not to hire people with a college education for blue collar jobs (because management firmly believed that college-educated individuals become bored faster in blue collar jobs which increases the cost of production). As part of the job application process Jim filled out a written job application form. In the education section, Jim circled the number "12" next to the heading "Highest Grade Completed" and left the block pertaining to college blank. In the experience section of the application, Jim did not mention any of his prior teaching experience. The company did not verify any of the answers provided by Mr. Norbuck. On October 22, Jim was hired by Leech Industries and commenced work as a Utility Person in the Tube Plating Department working the third shift from 11:00 P.M. to 7:00 A.M. After 30 days, his wage was increased because he had successfully completed the probationary period for new employees.

The steel industry experienced a business slowdown, however, and Jim was laid off in December. On January 3, he was recalled to work as a Labor Pool Person in the Foundry Department. On January 9, he was recalled to his original position as a third shift Utility Person in the Plating Department. All of the positions are part of a bargaining unit represented by the United Steelworkers.

Meanwhile, the collective bargaining agreement between the United Steelworkers of America Local 55 and Leech Industries expired on January 18. The negotiators were unable to reach an agreement and the union went out on strike. During the strike, Jim was actively involved in supporting the union and wrote several pamphlets. These pamphlets were distributed to striking workers and urged them to maintain solidarity so that the union would be successful in winning new contract gains for the bargaining unit.

Susan Napoli, Assistant Director of Human Resources at the plant, noticed these pamphlets and heard rumors that Jim Norbuck was college educated. Thus, Ms. Napoli initiated an investigation into Jim's background—both his previous employment and his education. Jim was the only employee for whom Ms. Napoli conducted such an investigation.

The strike ended at the end of February and Jim was recalled back to work on March 8 as a Labor Pool Person in the Foundry Department (business was slow so there were no openings in the Plating Department). On April 17, Ms. Napoli, Local 55's Grievance Committee Chairperson, and Jim discussed Ms. Napoli's investigation and her findings about his previous education and work experience. Jim was subsequently terminated for falsifying his employment application. After two additional meetings failed to resolve the dispute, the union filed the following grievance:

> Grievance No. 35. The aggrieved charges the company with discharging him on April 17 without just cause. The union is hereby requesting the company to reinstate Mr. Jim Norbuck with full seniority, and all lost wages and other benefits spelled out in the Agreement.

Potentially Relevant Contract Provisions

Article VIII. Suspension and Discharge.

Section 1. Procedure. Suspensions, discharges, and disciplinary actions shall be first discussed with the Shop Steward and/or Grievance Committee before being put into effect. Failure to discuss will result in rescinding any action taken.

Section 2. Differences. Any difference of opinion between the parties as to the facts and/or judgment shall result in a formal meeting between the parties and if not resolved to the satisfaction of both parties, it shall be referred to an impartial arbitrator for a final and binding decision. . . .

Article XI. Seniority.

Section 1. Basis of Seniority. (a) Plant seniority is defined as the length of continuous service with the Company and shall continue until terminated for reasons set forth under paragraph (b) of this Section. . . .

(b) Plant seniority shall be terminated for the following reasons:

Continued
375

Continued

1. Dismissal for cause . . .

(d) New employees shall be required to serve a probationary period of thirty (30) calendar days. Such probationary period may be extended by mutual agreement between the parties for a period not to exceed fifteen (15) calendar days. During this time the Company shall judge the fitness of such employees and will be free to discharge or lay-off such employees without regard to seniority. After completion of their probationary period the employee's plant seniority shall start from the first day worked. . . .

Article XII.

Section 1. Management Rights. (a) The right to hire and maintain order and efficiency is the sole responsibility of the Management.

(b) The right to promote, and the right to discipline and discharge for just cause, are likewise the sole responsibility of the Management.

Potentially Relevant Pennsylvania Legal Definition

Under Pennsylvania Law, deceit is interpreted to consist of a fraudulent misrepresentation of material facts in a business transaction which is calculated to induce reliance, and which actually causes reasonable and justifiable reliance to the detriment of the reliant. Note: the arbitrator's authority is derived from the collective bargaining agreement and his/her job is to interpret the agreement. The arbitrator's job is not to enforce legal statutes, but often an arbitrator looks to statutes, and their interpretation, to aid in the interpretation of the collective bargaining agreement.

Questions

1. Assume the role of Ms. Napoli. How would you try to convince an arbitrator that the dismissal is legitimate?

2. Assume the role of Local 55's Grievance Committee Chairperson. How would you try to convince an arbitrator that the dismissal violates the collective bargaining agreement?

3. As an arbitrator, how would you rule? Why?

Background

Lisa Vincent has been employed as a Police Officer by the Town of Stevenson for four years. The police officers at the Stevenson Police Department are represented by the American Federation of State, County and Municipal Employees (AFSCME) Local 7.

Article 3 of the collective bargaining agreement specifies that there shall be eight police cars on each shift. If, for whatever reason, there are not enough officers to staff a certain shift, officers are called on a voluntary basis. This is called a "callback." If the callback method fails to obtain sufficient personnel for the shift in question, police officers are ordered back to work—this is called an "orderback." In orderback situations, the Department is first required to order officers scheduled to work the next shift in early.

On May 29, the Police Department was understaffed for the second shift. The voluntary callback procedure did not yield sufficient personnel so the Department started an orderback. Officer Vincent was scheduled to work the third shift at 3:00 P.M. However, under the orderback Officer Vincent was ordered to report to work at 11:00 A.M. instead of 3:00 P.M. Officer Vincent had previously arranged for a babysitter to care for her three children during her regularly scheduled shift beginning at 3:00 P.M., but was unable to find anyone on such short notice to care for them between 11:00 A.M. and 3:00 P.M. She was thus unable to report for the orderback, but instead reported to work for her scheduled shift at 3:00 P.M.

Since Officer Vincent did not report when ordered in, the Town suspended her without pay for five days. The Union subsequently filed a grievance stating that Officer Vincent's failure to report for the orderback was not insubordination, but rather is analogous to the situation in which an officer is unable to report due to sickness.

Potentially Relevant Contract Provisions

ARTICLE 3: HOURS OF WORK

Section 2. The Shift hours of the PATROL DIVISION, DISPATCHERS AND CORPORALS shall be as follows, except in a justifiable emergency:

Shift #1.	11:00 P.M. to 7:00 A.M.
Shift #2.	7:00 A.M. to 3:00 P.M.
Shift #3.	3:00 P.M. to 11:00 P.M.

On Shift #1, there shall be eight (8) cars; on Shift #2, there shall be eight (8) cars; and on Shift #3, there shall be eight (8) cars. The number of cars assigned to each sub-shift, shall be determined by the Chief.

ARTICLE 8: SICK LEAVE AND HOSPITALIZATION BENEFIT
Section A. SICK LEAVE POLICY AND PROCEDURES

1. Sick leave shall be provided for Police Officers, as insurance against loss of income when a Police Officer is unable to perform assigned duties because of illness or injury.

2. Police Officers shall be entitled to 96 hours of sick leave each calendar year.

3. Police Officers absent from work on account of illness or injury shall report intended absence to their Division head or supervisor as soon as practical, but no later than fifteen (15) minutes after commencement of the Police Officer's duty shift unless justified by emergency circumstances.

4. Sick leave in excess of 16 hours for any one illness shall be documented by a written certification from a licensed practicing and attending physician, that during the period of leave, the Police Officer was prevented by illness from discharging the duties required by his or her office or position of employment. Such certification shall also be required of any Police Officer claiming sick leave benefits for an absence not reported in compliance with subsection (3) hereof or at such other times at which verification is requested by a supervisor or department head.

Questions

1. As an attorney for the Town of Stevenson, develop a case to support the Department's just cause in suspending Officer Vincent.
2. As an attorney for AFSCME Local 7, develop an argument to support your client's contention that just cause does not exist for suspending Lisa Vincent.
3. As an arbitrator, how would you rule? Why?

Background

John Arnett is a truck driver for Saga Food Services. He is part of a bargaining unit represented by Teamsters Local 444. John's normal workweek consists of four 10-hour workdays, Tuesday through Friday. The Labor Day holiday falls on a Monday and as is past practice, those employees who are normally not scheduled to work Monday observe the holiday on Tuesday.

Thus, John's Labor Day holiday was actually scheduled for Tuesday. At 11:00 P.M. on Tuesday night, John called the company via telephone and informed the clerk on duty that he was not coming to work on the following day because he was taking a personal leave day. John did not receive permission from his shift manager or any supervisor to take Wednesday as a personal leave day. However, as established by past practice, the Company cannot and does not (and did not in this case) refuse a personal leave day if the leave is requested an hour and a half or more before a worker's schedule shift starting time.

In sum, Labor Day is on a Monday, but John is not scheduled to work Mondays so his Labor Day holiday is on Tuesday. John then took a personal leave day on Wednesday. The Company subsequently refused to pay John for his holiday (Tuesday) claiming that he did not fulfill the requirements of the collective bargaining agreement.

The Union filed a grievance requesting that John Arnett be paid his holiday pay because he fulfilled the requirement for holiday pay computation set forth in the collective bargaining agreement.

Potentially Relevant Contract Provisions

ARTICLE 7: HOLIDAYS

Section 7.03. Holiday pay allowances will be given subject to the following terms and conditions:

. . .

(B) The employee shall have worked his full scheduled work day immediately before and immediately after the holiday except for proven sickness or injury. The shift manager may offer to waive this rule in advance of the holiday and acceptance thereof by an employee or employees shall be on a seniority basis.

Article 23: Leaves of Absence

Section 23.06. Each present employee will be entitled to four (4) days of personal leave per contract year. Said personal leave will be non-cumulative and said personal days will be paid if not used.

Questions

1. Assume the role of Director of Human Resources for Saga Food Services. How would you present your case that John Arnett is not entitled to his holiday pay for Labor Day?

2. As a business agent for Local 444, how would you argue that John Arnett is due his holiday pay?

3. As an arbitrator, how would you rule? Why?

Background

Local 4417 is the authorized bargaining agent for all employees, except clerical, supervisory and security employees, at the Tiger Oil Mill in Mississippi. On January 5, an electric motor broke causing the mill to shut down. Shortly thereafter, the Mill Superintendent Frank Tempest assigned Bob White and Michael Johnson to clean the mill's cyclone. This assignment required the two employees to go up on the mill roof 50 feet above the ground, hold onto the cyclone with one hand and clean the cyclone with the other hand. There is no railing or catwalk surrounding the cyclone. The temperature was 24°F and there were strong winds.

Bob and Mike worked on cleaning the cyclone for approximately 20 minutes, but then returned to the mill. The Superintendent asked if the cyclone had been cleaned and, upon finding out that it had not been, asked for an explanation. The employees responded that the severe cold combined with slippery conditions made the job unsafe. Frank ordered the two employees to go back on the roof to clean the cyclone.

Consequently, Bob and Mike returned to the cyclone, but found that they could not clean the cyclone due to the hazardous conditions. Upon returning to the mill the second time, the employees were again confronted by the Superintendent. Frank ordered them to "clean the damn cyclone."

What happened next is unclear (even after testimony). A "cursing tirade" between Frank and Bob ensued, but it is not clear who initiated it. The course of this conversation is disputed: Frank claims that Bob voluntarily quit by saying he was going home instead of going up on the roof in that weather. Bob claims that Frank ordered him off company premises because of his refusal to obey a clear directive: clean the cyclone. Bob further claims that he asked for another job assignment. There is no doubt that Bob used profanity towards his supervisor.

The end result was that Bob left work and his employment at the Tiger Oil Mill ceased (but it is unclear whether he quit or was discharged—even after testimony and cross-examination). Subsequently, the Union filed a grievance on behalf of Bob White claiming the Company violated the collective bargaining agreement by discharging Bob White without just cause.

Potentially Relevant Contract Provisions

Article XI—Miscellaneous

(A) The Company will only discipline and discharge employees for just cause.

. . .

(J) In addition to the grounds for temporary suspension or permanent discharge hereinbefore in this section enumerated, employees guilty of the following activities shall be the subject of permanent dismissal or other disciplinary action at the discretion of the Employer; (1) insubordination, (2) using materials or machinery contrary to instructions, (3) inefficiency, spoilage or negligent waste of materials, (4) throwing materials about the plant or out of windows, (5) boisterous talk, profanity or horseplay, (6) gambling on employer's premises, (7) theft of employer's or private property, (8) smoking anywhere inside the plant fence or in any of the employer's departments, (9) drunkenness, obscenity or immorality, (10) bringing intoxicating liquors on employer's property, (11) interference with production by slowdown or sit-down, (12) violations of plant or department rules or regulations, or (13) padding pay reports, or any other form of dishonesty.

Potentially Relevant Arbitration Precedent

Standard arbitrator practice is that safety and health reasons are potentially valid reasons for not carrying out a work assignment. The following portion of an arbitration award sums up the accepted standard:

> An employee may refuse to carry out a particular work assignment if, at the time he is given the work assignment, he reasonably believes that by carrying out such work assignment he will endanger his safety or health. In such an instance the employee has the duty, not only of stating that he believes there is a risk to his safety or health, and has the reason for believing so, but he also has the burden, if called upon, of showing by appropriate evidence that he had a reasonable basis for his belief. In the case of dispute, . . . the question to be decided is not whether he actually would have suffered injury but whether he had a reasonable basis for believing so. [*Laclead Gas Co.*, 39 LA 833 (1962)]

Questions

1. As the labor relations rep for the Tiger Oil Mill, develop a case for your contention that the discharge of Bob White was proper.

2. As the Chief Steward for Local 4417, how would you try to convince an arbitrator that the dismissal violates the collective bargaining agreement?

3. As an arbitrator, how would you rule? Why?

(*Hint:* pay careful attention to issues of burden of proof.)

Grievance Discussion Case 8:
Is Purchasing Parts
from a Catalog Subcontracting?

Box 10.18

Background

The Bangs Manufacturing Company makes heavy equipment used primarily for rock crushing and asphalt paving. Although this business is very seasonal and cyclical, the company normally employs approximately 850 production and maintenance employees (on two shifts) at its production facility. These production and maintenance employees are represented by the International Association of Machinists and Aerospace Workers Lodge 138. Due to the cyclical and seasonal nature of the industry and the fear of job loss, the union fought hard to win contract provisions pertaining to subcontracting.

All of the heavy equipment which the company manufactures use belt conveyors which are supported by a wide variety of wing pulleys. The company has made these pulleys themselves for many years. In fact, making and painting these pulleys was the primary job of several employees. The pulleys were traditionally painted orange.

During the fall, a salesman from The Pulley Place made an unsolicited visit to the company's Director of Procurement Harold Hill. The Pulley Place makes nothing but pulleys. The salesman showed Mr. Hill a variety of pulleys in The Pulley Place catalog that could be used directly on the machinery made by the Bangs Manufacturing Company without any necessary alterations.

Intrigued by the idea, Mr. Hill had some others in the company verify that the pulleys in The Pulley Place catalog could be used in the manufacturing process without any alterations or modifications. While the pulleys were a slightly different size, the results showed that the pulleys could be used "as is" and at an estimated savings of 30–60 percent. Thus, the company subsequently ordered pulleys directly from The Pulley Place catalog. No specifications were given to The Pulley Place and the pulleys were ordered by a catalog number. To help avoid confusion, the traditional (Bangs Manufacturing Company) part numbers were affixed to the pulleys by The Pulley Place. The pulleys were gray.

Earlier in the year, 295 bargaining-unit employees were laid off due to economic conditions. Several months later, a substantial number had been recalled, but there were still many employees on layoff. At this time, the workers started noticing that the pulleys they were using to assemble the heavy equipment were gray, not orange. Upon further investigation, the union discovered that the pulleys were being shipped in from outside. The union subsequently filed the following grievance:

> By utilizing pulleys made elsewhere, the Company is in violation of the collective bargaining agreement because work customarily performed by bargaining-unit employees is being performed by outside sources while bargaining-unit employees are laid off. Further, the work is to be returned to the bargaining-unit employees and all affected employees are to be fully reimbursed for lost rewards stemming from this violation.

Potentially Relevant Contract Provisions

ARTICLE XVII. GRIEVANCE PROCEDURE.

Step 6. . . . The arbitrator shall conduct a hearing on the grievance within a reasonable time and shall be empowered to rule on all disputes concerning the effect, interpretation and application of this Agreement. However, he shall have no power to add to, subtract from, or modify any of the terms of this Agreement or any other Agreement made supplementary hereto.

Article XXVII. SUB-CONTRACT.

During the periods of layoff the Company will not have any work that is normally done by Bangs Manufacturing performed by any outside source, either in or outside the plant except:

1. There is no machine or plant capacity at Bangs Manufacturing.

2. Where we do have machine or plant capacity and the provisions of the Contract have been followed and additional employees are needed, the Company will ask the laid-off employees seniority-wise if they would return to work on said jobs which would be voluntary. If they accepted, the regular provision of the Contract would apply. This would apply only when sub-contracting is involved.

3. No employees are laid off from development involved.

4. Any work farmed out will be returned to the Company within 48 hours from date layoff notice goes out, except paragraph 5 below.

5. The following items are made at Bangs Steel and Iron Works at any time—truck frames, elevating wheels, bins, columns, hoppers, feed chutes, drier drums, bolsters, lifting flights, dust collectors, elevator housings, cyclones, smoke boxes, exhaust washers, feeder frames.

Continued

Continued

Potentially Relevant United States Legal Definition
"A contract for the sale of articles then existing, or such as the seller in the ordinary course of his business manufactures or procures for the general market, whether on hand at the time or not, is a contract for the sale of goods to which the statute applies; but if the goods are to be manufactured for the buyer on his special order, and not for the general market, it is not a contract of sale" [but rather a contract for work, labor and materials] (*American Jurisprudence*, section 250). Note: the arbitrator's authority is derived from the collective bargaining agreement and his/her job is to interpret the agreement. The arbitrator's job is not to enforce legal statutes, but often an arbitrator looks to statutes, and their interpretation, to aid in the interpretation of the collective bargaining agreement.

Questions
1. Develop an argument supporting the Company's right to use pulleys from The Pulley Place.
2. Assume the role of Lodge 138's Grievance Committee Chairperson. How would you try to convince an arbitrator that the company's action violates the collective bargaining agreement?
3. As an arbitrator, how would you rule? Why?

Grievance Discussion Case 9: Is Upward Bumping an Unauthorized Promotion?   Box 10.19

Background
A plant manufactures approximately 1,200 different aluminum shapes. About 450 of the shapes are anodized by attaching the aluminum shapes to a rack and then dipping the rack into an anodizing tank. Anodizing is done by sets of teams of two Rackers each. Each Racker must do a careful job of securing the aluminum to the rack. Aluminum pieces that are not racked properly can be ruined which causes significant financial loss to the Company.

Local 491 of the International Chemical Workers Union is the authorized bargaining agent for the production workers of this plant. Christine Hinds was hired by the Company on September 15, 1990, and at the time of the grievance, was working as an Anodyne Racker. Ray Davies was hired on July 30, 1990, and is the grievant.

While employed by the Company, Davies has been classified as a Packer Helper, Saw Helper, Head Sawer (which is the same job grade as Racker), Fork Truck Operator, and Die Cleanup, but never as a Racker. On December 3, Tom was laid off by the Company due to economic reasons. Thus, he filed a grievance claiming that the Company violated the collective bargaining agreement by retaining a worker with less seniority (namely, Christine Hinds who was a Racker). At the time of the grievance filing, Ray was employed as a Saw Helper which is two job grades below Racker.

Testimony at the Arbitration Hearing
At the grievance hearing, Ray testified that while he never was actually classified as a Racker, he learned racking while working as a second shift Fork Lift Operator. He stated that he learned how to be a Racker by filling in for 15 or 20 minutes at a time and also by observing Rackers at other times. He further testified that he has become a "Jack-of-all-Trades" and could have satisfactorily performed the duties of a Racker if paired with an experienced Racker.

At the grievance hearing, the Plant Manager also testified regarding several points. First, had Ray been retained as a Racker, he would have been paired teamed with a regular Racker. Second, Ray is a willing and cooperative worker and would be able to do any job after training. Third, in the Plant Manager's estimation, Ray would probably have required 30 days training to become as efficient as a normal Racker. Fourth, four men bumped into being Rackers during the layoffs—one of them was a Rack Maker who had acquired some experience being a Racker by filling in during lunch breaks.

Continued

Continued

Potentially Relevant Contract Provisions

ARTICLE IX.

Section 1: Seniority shall be on a plantwide basis.

Section 2: In all matters of promotion, demotion, transfer, job training, shift preference, layoff, and recall, the following will be the determining factors:

a. seniority.

b. ability to do the work required.

Questions

1. As the labor relations manager for the company, how would you argue a case supporting your client's actions?

2. Assume the role of Local 491 Chief Steward. How would you support your contention that the Company has violated the collective bargaining agreement?

3. As an arbitrator, how would you rule? Why?

Grievance Discussion Case 10: Are Special Skills the Same as Merit?

Box 10.20

Background

The City of Ditchburn is located in south Florida. Nearly 90 percent of Ditchburn residents are Hispanic. Additionally, many residents only speak Spanish. Many of the city's civil service jobs, including the Fire Dispatcher, comprise the bargaining unit represented by the American Federation of State, County and Municipal Employees (AFSCME) Local 3.

Jose Obradors was a Fire Dispatcher for the City of Ditchburn on the 7:00 A.M. to 3:00 P.M. shift. A regular dispatcher on the 11:00 P.M. to 7:00 A.M. shift started maternity leave on November 23 which caused a temporary (six month) vacancy on this shift. To temporarily fill this vacancy until a six-month replacement could be found, Fire Chief Dave Franz transferred Jose to the 11:00 P.M. to 7:00 A.M. shift because Jose is bilingual.

The Chief then posted a vacancy notice for a temporary dispatcher for the 11:00 P.M. to 7:00 A.M. shift and stated that the dispatcher must be bilingual. However, no one volunteered so the Chief transferred Jose to fill the position until the prior dispatcher returned from maternity leave six months later. While Jose was the most junior bilingual dispatcher, he was not the most junior dispatcher. In fact, Jose had enough seniority to work a shift other than 11:00 P.M. to 7:00 A.M. and the transfer was made in spite of his objection. The City freely admits that Jose was transferred because of his ability to speak Spanish.

Jose, however, did not want to work the 11:00 P.M. to 7:00 A.M. shift and thus filed a grievance requesting to be transferred back to his day shift immediately because the City violated the collective bargaining agreement.

Testimony at the Arbitration Hearing

At the grievance hearing, the City's Personnel Director testified that the City has considered language ability as a factor in establishing schedules for the last 10 years, especially for the Fire Dispatcher and Police Complaint Officer positions. In fact, the City's schedules specify the number of bilingual persons required per shift. Consequently, shift assignments have not been based solely on seniority, but also on language ability. Examples could be cited of junior employees who were promoted instead of more senior employees because of language ability. Finally, the City's recently enacted hiring policy requires all new Fire Dispatchers to be bilingual.

Both parties agreed that Jose Obradors' transfer was based on his language ability and that he had the seniority to work a different shift.

Potentially Relevant Contract Provisions

ARTICLE 6: MANAGEMENT RIGHTS

Section 1. The Union agrees that the City has and will continue to retain, whether exercised or not, the right to operate and manage its affairs in all respects; that the powers or authority which the City has not officially abridged, deleted, or modified by

Continued

the express provisions of this Agreement are retained by the City. The rights of the City, through its management officials, shall include, but shall not be limited to: the right to determine the organization of City Government; to determine the purpose of each of its constituent departments; to exercise control and discretion over the organization and efficiency of operations of the City; to set standards for service to be offered to the public; to direct the employees of the City, including the right to assign work and overtime, to hire, examine, classify, promote, train, transfer, assign, and schedule employees in positions with the City; to suspend, demote, discharge, or take other disciplinary action against employees for proper cause; to increase, reduce, change, modify or alter the composition and size of the work force, including the right to relieve employees from duties because of lack of work or funds; to determine the location, methods, means, and personnel by which operations are to be conducted, including the right to determine whether goods or services are to be made or purchased; to establish, modify, combine or abolish job pay positions; to change or eliminate existing methods of operations, equipment or facilities; to determine the methods, means and number of personnel needed or desirable for carrying out the City's mission and to direct the work force.

. . .

Section 5. Delivery of municipal services in the most efficient, effective and courteous manner is of paramount importance to the City of Ditchburn. Such achievement is recognized to be a mutual obligation of both parties in their respective roles and responsibilities.

ARTICLE 10: NO DISCRIMINATION

Section 1. The City and the Union agree that the provisions of the Agreement shall be applied equally to all employees in the Bargaining Unit without discrimination as to age, sex, marital status, race, color, creed, national origin or political affiliation.

ARTICLE 30: LAYOFF AND RECALL

Section 2. Recall

A. Employees shall be called back from layoff according to the same criteria for layoff (i.e. the most senior person will be recalled) unless in the City's judgment special skills are required.

ARTICLE 31: SENIORITY

Section 1. All provisions within this Article shall constitute the basis for establishing a uniform procedure of seniority for vacations, shift transfers and days off preference, and overtime.

. . .

Section 4. It is recognized that the principle of merit must be given consideration in any "efficiency conscious" organization; therefore, the Department/Division Heads reserve the right to final determination in regards to employee transfer, shift assignment, days off and vacation time.

Questions

1. As the City of Ditchburn Personnel Director, how would you present your case that the transfer of Jose Obradors did not violate the Agreement?
2. As a local union official, how would you argue that the City's action regarding Jose Obradors' transfer violated the contract?
3. As an arbitrator, how would you rule? Why?

Part **Three**

Issues for the 21st Century

Part II has examined contemporary U.S. labor relations with an emphasis on the development and operation of the New Deal industrial relations system. In this system, labor relations emphasizes four processes—organizing, bargaining, dispute resolution, and contract administration. But with changes in the external economic and business environment, U.S. labor relations in the 21st century is under great pressure. The next two chapters explore the central components of this pressure: the drive for increased workplace flexibility and employee involvement combined with intense globalization.

Chapter Eleven

Flexibility and Employee Involvement

Advance Organizer

When successful, the processes described in the previous chapters result in a union contract. Typically, these contracts are detailed and reinforce bureaucratic forms of work organization. Contrast that with what you've probably heard about today's workplace and the calls for flexibility, empowerment, and cost competitiveness. This chapter discusses how these pressures conflict with traditional U.S. labor relations practices and the controversies that result.

Learning Objectives

By the end of the chapter, you should be able to:

1. **Identify** the importance of the structure of work for labor relations.
2. **Explain** the pressures for increased workplace flexibility and employee involvement in the contemporary employment relationship, and strategies for implementation.
3. **Compare** the conflicts between workplace flexibility and employee involvement on the one

hand, and the traditional U.S. model of job control unionism on the other.

4. **Understand** the debates over new forms of work structures—methods for empowering workers and enhancing competitiveness, or for making employees work harder for less?
5. **Understand** the debates over nonunion employee representation—vehicles of legitimate employee voice, or for preventing unionism?

Contents

Many of the central policies and practices of contemporary U.S. labor relations date back to earlier eras. The major provisions of labor law were enacted in 1935 and 1947. A pragmatic business unionism focus on improving wages and working conditions has been emphasized by U.S. unions since the early days of the American Federation of Labor in the late 1800s. Managerial insistence on retaining their right to manage by maintaining unchallenged authority to make business decisions was formalized in the 1940s. Multiyear contracts that are renegotiated with great formality only upon expiration began in the 1950s, and the importance of grievance arbitration to settle disputes during the life of the contract was cemented during World War II in the early 1940s.

But consider the changes in the global economic system, business practices, labor force education levels, and technology that have occurred since these earlier eras. From the end of World War II up to the oil crisis in 1974, U.S. manufacturers dominated both the U.S. and world economies.[1] Monopoly profits were often captured by a handful of large firms in each industry. After the oil crisis, increased domestic and international competition ended this dominance and put downward pressure on profits, employment, and wages. The strong U.S. economic growth between the 1940s and 1970s was based on a stable system of mass manufacturing with narrowly defined, routine jobs in which economies of scale created falling labor costs and increases in productivity.[2] But in the 21st century, routine jobs can be shifted to low-cost countries. U.S. companies can no longer be competitive in the global marketplace using traditional mass manufacturing methods.

Rather, for U.S. companies to create a competitive advantage, they must now produce high-quality goods and services that respond to quickly changing consumer tastes.[3] At a minimum, this requires replacing the traditional and bureaucratic mass manufacturing methods with more flexible employment systems. Moreover, because the U.S. workforce is more highly educated than in previous generations and because technology is more sophisticated, many advocate not only for increased flexibility, but also for greater levels of employee involvement in workplace decision making.[4] Compared to hierarchical work systems, participatory systems are believed to better harness the skills of employees, create loyal and motivated employees, and produce higher quality products. Lastly, competitive pressures are undermining traditional patterns of employment stability and job security and are instead creating short-term, market-driven employment relationships.[5] Putting all of these trends together, the mass manufacturing system with stable employment is nearly dead—management's 21st-century workplace goals increasingly focus on greater employee involvement and especially on increased flexibility. The push for flexibility and employee involvement is present in both nonunion and union workplaces, and contains far-reaching implications not only for U.S. labor relations, but also for human resource management.

THE CHANGING STRUCTURE OF WORK

Box 11.1 summarizes the development of the major trends in how to organize work—from early craft-based production systems, to mass manufacturing systems based on a specialized division of labor, to flexible and participatory workplaces that require teamwork and employee involvement. The dominant paradigm for how to structure work in much of the 20th century was **scientific management.** Expanding on the logic of the famous economist Adam Smith who praised the efficiency benefits of using 18 distinct steps to make a single pin in 1776, Frederick Winslow Taylor and others developed scientific management in the early 20th century to maximize efficiency through carefully studying work tasks and

[1] Barry Bluestone and Irving Bluestone, *Negotiating the Future: A Labor Perspective on American Business* (New York: Basic Books, 1992). Edward E. Potter and Judith A. Youngman, *Keeping America Competitive: Employment Policy for the Twenty-First Century* (Lakewood, CO: Glenbridge Publishing, 1995).

[2] Eileen Appelbaum and Rosemary Batt, *The New American Workplace: Transforming Work Systems in the United States* (Ithaca, NY: ILR Press, 1994).

[3] Michael J. Piore and Charles F. Sabel, *The Second Industrial Divide: Possibilities for Prosperity* (New York: Basic Books, 1984).

[4] Appelbaum and Batt, *The New American Workplace.* Bluestone and Bluestone, *Negotiating the Future.* David I. Levine, *Reinventing the Workplace: How Business and Employees Can Both Win* (Washington, DC: Brookings, 1995).

[5] Peter Cappelli, *The New Deal at Work: Managing the Market-Driven Workforce* (Boston: Harvard Business School Press, 1999).

18th century Industrial Revolution—the rise of factories, mills, and mines

19th century Dominance of skilled crafts in production

1911 Frederick Winslow Taylor publishes *The Principles of Scientific Management*—scientific management (or Taylorism) comes to dominate 20th century thinking

1913 Henry Ford starts producing cars on an assembly line (Taylorism + assembly line = Fordism)—skilled crafts are replaced by unskilled mass production workers

1920s The rise of welfare capitalism, including employee representation plans (company unions)

1935 Section 8(a)(2) of the National Labor Relations Act (NLRA) bans company-dominated employee representation plans

1946 UAW strike at General Motors fails to win employee input into managerial decisions; management's right to manage is cemented

1950s Institutionalization of job control unionism—emphasis on stability, predictability, and seniority

Two Americans, W. Edwards Deming and Joseph Juran, launch the quality movement in Japan

1972 General Motors Lordstown strike reflects the blue collar blues and worker alienation—first generation quality of working life (QWL) programs start to spread

1980s Total quality management (TQM) returns to the United States with increased efforts at using quality circles and other initiatives

Japanese auto manufacturers open U.S. plants using lean production techniques

1981 Desktop computing era begins with the launch of the IBM Personal Computer

1990 Production starts at Saturn based on extensive employee involvement in production and business decisions—highlights a new model of high performance work systems

1992 The *Electromation* ruling finds some forms of labor–management committees to be illegally dominated employee representation plans under section 8(a)(2) of the NLRA

1993 The first hypertext browser is released paving the way for the World Wide Web and the Internet age

Reengineering the Corporation: A Manifesto for Business Revolution advocates an end to Taylorism

1996 The TEAM Act to amend section 8(a)(2) is vetoed by President Bill Clinton

21st century Emphasis on flexibility, pay-for-performance, employee involvement, and continuous change

scientifically determining the one best way of completing a task.[6] For example, in the 1890s Taylor spent four months timing and measuring the amount of different types of coal a worker could shovel using different shovel sizes to determine that the optimal shovel size is 21 pounds.[7] More generally, time and motion studies were used to reduce jobs into their most basic components, stopwatches were used to calculate the optimal time required for each task, and instruction cards listed each specific operation—sometimes to the fraction of a second. Taylor assumed that workers were motivated by pay and once the time standards were established, differential piece-work wage rates—perhaps to three decimal places—could be used to encourage high production. Taylor saw this as a "win-win" situation: productivity and profits would increase, employees would earn more, and labor unrest would disappear. On the other hand, critics saw scientific management as degrading work through extreme specialization of jobs, competition between workers, the speedingup of the work

[6] Robert Kanigel, *The One Best Way: Frederick Winslow Taylor and the Enigma of Efficiency* (New York, Penguin, 1997). Frederick Winslow Taylor, *The Principles of Scientific Management* (New York: Harper and Brothers, 1911).

[7] Kanigel, *The One Best Way,* p. 334.

pace, and hostility towards labor unions.[8] To the craft unions of the AFL, the time-study man with the stopwatch was seen as an affront to the judgment, freedom, and dignity of skilled craft workers, and strikes against time studies and incentive pay plans resulted.[9]

The intense specialization of work and division of labor became known as Taylorism. This specialization of work serves efficiency by allowing workers to become proficient through repetition; standardization promotes efficiency through the use of carefully determined processes and the ease of training unskilled workers in rote tasks. Note carefully that as scientifically trained managers determine each job's one best way, Taylorism creates a divide between management and labor: management determines job content, optimal job processes, and does the planning; labor provides the muscle to implement management's directions. Workers are a cog in a standardized machine. Box 11.2 vividly illustrates the emphasis on creating detailed specifications for narrowly defined, standardized jobs with little opportunities for employee discretion—the left-hand column on Box 11.2 specifies that the worker's left hand should spend one second getting a U bolt, 1.20 seconds putting this bolt in place, and 11 seconds holding it in place while the right-hand column provides similarly narrow directions for the workers' right hand.

In 1913 Henry Ford also broke jobs down into their basic components while adding another innovation—assembly line production. This method of mass manufacturing using very narrowly defined jobs combined with assembly lines became known as Fordism. But Taylorism is not limited to manufacturing or assembly lines—banks, credit card processing centers, and other service-oriented workplaces were traditionally organized on the basis of repetitive, specialized tasks. In fact, clerical office tasks were restructured using scientific management methods between 1900 and 1930, a development that coincided with the feminization of clerical jobs.[10] Time and motion studies can be applied to making beds in a hotel, and McDonald's hamburgers are a classic example of a standardized product.[11] Designing a camera using separate camera body designers, shutter designers, film advance mechanism designers, and the like is a scientific management approach to product design.[12] The cartoon from the time of Frederick Winslow Taylor and Henry Ford shown in Box 11.3 portrays the ideal early 20th-century army recruit—all muscle and no brains. Because of the dominance of Taylorism and Fordism for much of the 20th century, this is arguably also the ideal worker.

The bureaucratic control of scientific management is well-suited to the mass production of standardized goods and services in a stable economy. Unstable economic markets in the 1970s, however, challenged the dominance of mass manufacturing methods because companies could no longer sell massive quantities of identical products and could not react quickly to changing consumer demands.[13] Moreover, simple, repetitive job tasks can cause boredom, alienation, and mental and physical fatigue. A focus on monetary motivation ignores

---

[8] Kanigel, *The One Best Way*. Daniel Nelson, "Scientific Management in Retrospect," in Daniel Nelson (ed.), *A Mental Revolution: Scientific Management Since Taylor* (Columbus: Ohio State University Press, 1992), Chapter 1.

[9] David Montgomery, *Workers' Control in America: Studies in the History of Work, Technology, and Labor Struggles* (Cambridge: Cambridge University Press, 1979). Clayton Sinyai, *Schools of Democracy: A Political History of the American Labor Movement* (Ithaca, NY: Cornell University Press, 2006).

[10] Lisa M. Fine, *The Souls of the Skyscraper: Female Clerical Workers in Chicago, 1870–1930* (Philadelphia: Temple University Press, 1990). Sharon Hartman Strom, *Beyond the Typewriter: Gender, Class, and the Origins of Modern American Office Work, 1900–1930* (Urbana: University of Illinois Press, 1992). Simon Head, *The New Ruthless Economy: Work and Power in the Digital Age* (New York: Oxford University Press, 2003).

[11] Kanigel, *The One Best Way*.

[12] Michael Hammer and James Champy, *Reengineering the Corporation: A Manifesto for Business Revolution* (New York: HarperBusiness, 1993).

[13] Piore and Sabel, *The Second Industrial Divide*.

BOX 11.2
Standardizing the Assembly of Cable Clamps

Source: Benjamin W. Niebel, *Motion and Time Study,* 7th ed. (Homewood, IL: Irwin, 1982), p. 160. The McGraw-Hill Companies.

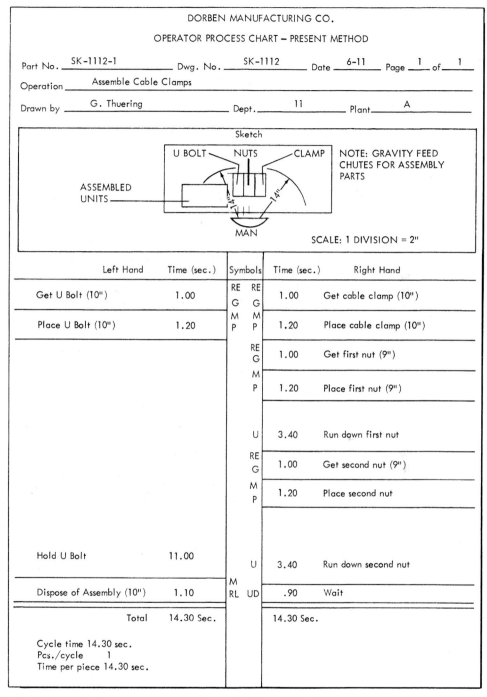

DORBEN MANUFACTURING CO.

OPERATOR PROCESS CHART – PRESENT METHOD

Part No. SK-1112-1   Dwg. No. SK-1112   Date 6-11   Page 1 of 1

Operation   Assemble Cable Clamps

Drawn by   G. Thuering   Dept.   11   Plant   A

Sketch

U BOLT   NUTS   CLAMP

ASSEMBLED UNITS

MAN

NOTE: GRAVITY FEED CHUTES FOR ASSEMBLY PARTS

SCALE: 1 DIVISION = 2"

Left Hand	Time (sec.)	Symbols	Time (sec.)	Right Hand
Get U Bolt (10")	1.00	RE RE G G	1.00	Get cable clamp (10")
Place U Bolt (10")	1.20	M M P P	1.20	Place cable clamp (10")
		RE G	1.00	Get first nut (9")
		M P	1.20	Place first nut (9")
		U	3.40	Run down first nut
		RE G	1.00	Get second nut (9")
		M P	1.20	Place second nut
Hold U Bolt	11.00	U	3.40	Run down second nut
Dispose of Assembly (10")	1.10	M RL UD	.90	Wait
Total	14.30 Sec.		14.30 Sec.	

Cycle time 14.30 sec.
Pcs./cycle 1
Time per piece 14.30 sec.

Note: Specific left-hand and right-hand operations are specified to the tenth of a second.

intrinsic motivators such as satisfaction from achievement, interest in a task, and responsibility. These factors can cause absenteeism, turnover, shirking, and low-quality output. All of these issues—both the macrolevel economic shocks and the microlevel issues with employee satisfaction—caused a competitive crisis in U.S. business in the 1970s and launched efforts at changing forms of work organization, human resources practices, and more generally, business strategies.

BOX 11.3

"At last, a perfect soldier." And under scientific management for much of the 20th century, a perfect worker

Source: *The Masses* (July 1916).

Since the 1970s, these efforts have intensified, not lessened. In fact, globalization and technology have resulted in what some have labeled market chaos and hypercompetition:

> Since any element in a company's value chain can be produced by an independent external party specializing in that activity, companies no longer compete just with other companies in their "industries." They must compete laterally with the best-in-world producer of that activity, wherever that producer may be. Everyone is competing with everyone else. . . . To deal with this, wholly new strategies—focusing on core competencies, strategic outsourcing, alliances, and highly disaggregated organizations—now link enterprises and nations in new ways. All center on developing, managing, and leveraging intellectual capabilities much more effectively.[14]

Strategies for corporate reform have therefore included continuous improvement and reengineering. Continuous process improvement is often associated with a Japanese management style (*kaizen*) and focuses on creating a corporate culture of constant change and small improvements. Total quality management (TQM) is an example of a continuous process improvement strategy in which statistical methods to measure defects are used to guide efforts at constantly improving the quality of manufactured products and customer service.[15]

While continuous process improvement emphasizes gradual change, reengineering targets large, one-time improvements in business processes:

> To reinvent their companies, American managers must throw out their old notions about how businesses should be organized and run. They must abandon the organizational and operational principles and procedures they are now using and create entirely new ones. . . . For two hundred years people have founded and built companies around Adam Smith's brilliant discovery that industrial work should be broken down into its simplest and most basic *tasks*. In the postindustrial business age we are now entering, corporations will be founded and built around the idea of reunifying those tasks into coherent business *processes*.[16]

---

[14] James Brian Quinn, Jordan J. Baruch, and Karen Anne Zein, *Innovation Explosion: Using Intellect and Software to Revolutionize Growth Strategies* (New York: Free Press, 1997), pp. 32–33. Richard A. D'Aveni, *Hypercompetitive Rivalries: Competing in Highly Dynamic Environments* (New York: Free Press, 1994).

[15] John S. Oakland, *Total Quality Management: The Route to Improving Performance,* 2nd ed. (East Brunswick, NJ: Nichols Publishing, 1993).

[16] Hammer and Champy, *Reengineering the Corporation,* pp. 1–2 (emphasis in original).

Replacing narrowly focused order fulfillment, engineering, or compensation specialists with generalist customer service, product design, or human resources teams are examples of reunifying tasks into processes that contain value for the organization.

These strategies for reforming corporate structures, processes, and strategies have tremendous implications for human resources practices and the organization of work. New business models consistently emphasize the replacement of traditional, bureaucratic human resources practices and scientific management systems of work with dynamic, team-oriented, flexible practices and systems that reward and empower employees. Continuous process improvement programs often include quality circles or other forms of teamwork in which all levels of employees can openly share ideas. Reengineering emphasizes multidimensional rather than narrowly specialized jobs combined with empowered rather than tightly controlled employees (see Box 11.4). It is also common for business strategists to encourage companies to focus on their core competencies—"a bundle of skills and technologies that enables a company to provide a particular benefit to customers."[17] This, too, requires empowered employees.

Scientific management forms of work organization are being replaced with flatter, team-oriented work structures that serve flexible specialization and employee involvement rather than mass manufacturing. Narrowly defined jobs are being replaced by job rotation, cross-training, and job enrichment. Wage rates are becoming less tied to job classifications and more tied to individual and organizational performance. Intrinsic as well as extrinsic motivators are recognized as important determinants of employee behavior and performance. While once looked at as simply muscle, workers are now asked to provide input into process improvements, and perhaps granted authority to make decisions such as in self-directed work teams. Many of these changes can be summarized as a managerial drive for flexibility. Some organizations pursue flexibility in a piecemeal fashion, often emphasizing reduced labor costs. More ambitiously, other organizations strive to implement high performance work systems—coherent systems of mutually supporting human resources practices that combine flexibility with employee involvement in decision making. Both strategies—flexibility alone or with employee involvement—place very significant pressures on established labor relations practices. The never-ending push for flexibility can also greatly strain individuals—as workers, and as people.[18]

FLEXIBILITY

The overall business goal of flexibility is underscored by the calls for creating the nimble organization and the boundaryless organization.[19] In the context of human resources, there are four types of flexibility: employment flexibility, wage flexibility, functional flexibility, and procedural flexibility (see Box 11.5).[20] Flexible employment, or a typical employment, includes part-time employment and temporary or contract work and other methods for

[17] Gary Hamel and C. K. Prahalad, *Competing for the Future* (Boston: Harvard Business School Press, 1994), p. 199. Gary Hamel, *Leading the Revolution* (Boston: Harvard Business School Press, 2000).

[18] Mike Parker and Jane Slaughter, *Choosing Sides: Unions and the Team Concept* (Boston: South End Press, 1988). Richard Sennett, *The Corrosion of Character: The Personal Consequences of Work in the New Capitalism* (New York: Norton, 1998).

[19] Daryl R. Conner, *Leading at the Edge of Chaos: How to Create the Nimble Organization* (New York: John Wiley and Sons, 1998). Ron Ashkenas, Dave Ulrich, Todd Jick, and Steve Kerr, *The Boundaryless Organization: Breaking the Chains of Organizational Structure* (San Francisco: Jossey-Bass, 1995).

[20] Muneto Ozaki (ed.), *Negotiating Flexibility: The Role of the Social Partners and the State* (Geneva: International Labour Office, 1999). Nick Wailes and Russell D. Lansbury, "Collective Bargaining and Flexibility: Australia," LEG/REL Working Paper (Geneva: International Labour Office, 1999).

Workplace Changes Resulting from Reengineering

Box 11.4

Work Units *Change*	. . .	*From* Functional Departments *to* Process Teams
Jobs *Change*	. . .	*From* Simple Tasks *to* Multidimensional Work
People's Roles *Change*	. . .	*From* Controlled *to* Empowered
Job Preparation *Changes*	. . .	*From* Training *to* Education
Performance Measures *Change*	. . .	*From* Activity *to* Results
Compensation *Changes*	. . .	*From* Activity *to* Results
Advancement Criteria *Change*	. . .	*From* Performance *to* Ability
Values *Change*	. . .	*From* Protective *to* Productive
Managers *Change*	. . .	*From* Supervisors *to* Coaches
Organizational Structures *Change*	. . .	*From* Hierarchical *to* Flat
Executives *Change*	. . .	*From* Scorekeepers *to* Leaders

Source: Michael Hammer and James Champy, *Reengineering the Corporation: A Manifesto for Business Revolution* (New York: HarperBusiness, 1993), Chapter 4.

BOX 11.5 Employment Relationship Flexibility

Goals	Examples	Employee Concerns
Employment Flexibility Change labor utilization through varying work hours or number of employees.	Part-time employment Temporary employment Seasonal employment Outsourcing	Lack of sufficient hours to earn enough income to take care of basic needs and raise a family. Uncertainty. Periods of unemployment. Stress.
Pay Flexibility Make compensation responsive to changes in competitive pressures and organizational performance.	Pay-for-performance Profit sharing Ending wage indexation	Risky. Compensation is uncertain and may decrease. Potential for managerial abuse. Organizational performance beyond individual or work group control. Stress.
Functional Flexibility Easily shift workers into different jobs in response to changing customer demands and production needs.	Job enrichment Work teams Cross-training	Potential for replacing high-wage, skilled employees with low-wage, unskilled employees. Disguised old-fashioned work speed-up? Stress.
Procedural Flexibility Change production methods, technology, and work organization.	Unilateral management authority to restructure the workplace	Lack of a voice in the absence of unions or works councils. Stress.

Source: Muneto Ozaki (ed.), *Negotiating Flexibility: The Role of the Social Partners and the State* (Geneva: International Labour Office, 1999). Nick Wailes and Russell D. Lansbury, "Collective Bargaining and Flexibility: Australia," LEG/REL Working Paper (Geneva: International Labour Office, 1999).

varying the number of employees and hours worked. Employment flexibility is a significant management concern because it allows businesses to adjust to changing levels of customer demand. Overtime provisions can restrain working-time flexibility while union-negotiated no-layoff provisions or public policies that require generous severance pay packages for discharged workers can restrict employment-level flexibility. European examples of the latter are often blamed for persistently high unemployment rates whereas the employment-at-will doctrine in the United States is applauded for allowing employers to freely adjust their employment levels as needed.[21] Farming out production to other companies through subcontracting and outsourcing—or privatization in the public sector—are additional strategies for attaining employment flexibility.

Pay flexibility seeks to make employee compensation more responsive to individual or group performance, organizational profitability or ability-to-pay, and competitive pressures. Examples of pay flexibility therefore include pay-for-performance and other incentive plans as well as profit-sharing and gainsharing plans.[22] Pay flexibility also includes the ability to reduce wage rates in response to competitive pressures. Efforts to facilitate downward wage flexibility include the weakening or abolishment of minimum wage requirements and the ending of wage indexation—that is, the explicit linking of wage increases to inflation.[23] Collective bargaining in many countries is becoming more decentralized so that pay rates can better reflect company specific-profitability (see Chapter 13).

Functional flexibility is the ability to easily shift workers to different tasks and functions in response to changing customer demands, market opportunities, and production needs. Functional flexibility is also consistent with continuous improvement efforts such as total quality management. Attempts to increase functional flexibility often explicitly attack the specialized division of labor created by scientific management systems of work organization. A worker trained narrowly in a limited set of tasks cannot be easily deployed to another role when demand shifts. As such, numerous, narrow job classifications are being replaced by a handful of broad jobs, and workers are being cross-trained in multiple skills. Work teams in which several workers are jointly responsible for completing a number of tasks can also promote functional flexibility.[24] Alternative work systems for achieving functional flexibility are discussed later in this chapter.

Procedural flexibility is the ability to introduce changes, such as new technology and forms of work organization. This flexibility is needed to respond to changing market opportunities and to embrace emerging forms of technology and work organization in a world of flexible specialization.[25] Procedural flexibility also underlies strategies to reengineer corporations and focus on core competencies.[26] The most unrestrained source of procedural flexibility is unilateral management action. Limitations on procedural flexibility—to

[21] Francine D. Blau and Lawrence M. Kahn, *At Home and Abroad: U.S. Labor-Market Performance in International Perspective* (New York: Russell Sage Foundation, 2002).

[22] John A. Fossum and Brian P. McCall, "Pay and Reward for Performance," in David Lewin, Daniel J. B. Mitchell, and Mahmood Zaidi (eds.), *The Human Resource Management Handbook Part 3* (Greenwich, CT: JAI Press, 1997), pp. 111–43.

[23] Ozaki, *Negotiating Flexibility.*

[24] Richard S. Wellins, William C. Byham, and Jeanne M. Wilson, *Empowered Teams: Creating Self-Directed Work Groups That Improve Quality, Productivity, and Participation* (San Francisco: Jossey-Bass, 1991). Ronald E. Purser and Steven Cabana, *The Self-Managing Organization: How Leading Companies Are Transforming the Work of Teams for Real Impact* (New York: Free Press, 1998).

[25] Piore and Sabel, *The Second Industrial Divide.*

[26] Hammer and Champy, *Reengineering the Corporation.* Hamel and Prahalad, *Competing for the Future.* Hamel, *Leading the Revolution.*

varying degrees—include collective bargaining agreements, legal requirements to consult with works councils (see Chapter 13), explicit employment contracts, and laws.[27]

While business continually extols the virtues of flexibility, it's equally important to appreciate the potential dark sides of flexibility. The last column of Box 11.5 describes some prominent employee concerns with various forms of flexibility. Weakening union-won protections such as seniority rights have the potential to increase opportunities for managerial abuse. Impatient U.S. financial markets force companies into operating for the short-term and the resulting push for flexibility—including downsizing, restructuring, asset sales, and the use of contingent employees—increases economic and social inequality.[28] Moreover, while a psychological contract between an employer and employee does not legally restrict the employer, there may be negative consequences of reduced job satisfaction and performance if procedural flexibility breaks this psychological contract (see Box 11.6).[29] Beyond the implications for job satisfaction and performance, others question the broader psychological and social effects of a hyperflexible culture:

> 'Who needs me?' is a question which suffers a radical challenge in modern capitalism. The system radiates indifference. It does so in terms of the outcomes of human striving, as in winner-take-all markets, where there is little connection between risk and reward. It radiates indifference in the organization of absence of trust, where there is no reason to be needed. And it does so through reengineering of institutions in which people are treated as disposable. Such practices obviously and brutally diminish the sense of mattering as a person, of being necessary to others.[30]

JOB CONTROL UNIONISM

As emphasized in Part II of this book, the dominant philosophy of U.S. unions is business unionism with a pragmatic, workplace focus. Before the competitive crisis that began in the 1970s, two widespread managerial practices were job standardization (as in scientific management) and the insistence on maintaining sole authority over traditional management functions such as hiring, firing, assigning work, determining job content, and deciding what to produce and how and where to make it—in other words, management rights.[31] In the New Deal industrial relations system, therefore, union pursuit of equity and voice for workers was largely limited to wages, benefits, and fair employment policies—not employee involvement in managerial decision making—that built upon the Taylorist systems of work with narrow job classifications. The resulting pattern of traditional unionized practices and policies in the postwar period is called **job control unionism**.[32] In short, job control unionism seeks to protect workers against managerial abuse by controlling the rewards and allocation of jobs. Job control unionism replaces managerial subjectivity and favoritism with the objective measure of seniority as the primary method for determining layoffs, promotions, and transfers. Similarly, subjectivity is removed from wage outcomes by closely linking wage rates to job classifications, not individuals.

---

[27] Ozaki, *Negotiating Flexibility.*

[28] Bennett Harrison, *Lean and Mean: The Changing Landscape of Corporate Power in the Age of Flexibility* (New York: Basic Books, 1994).

[29] Cappelli, *The New Deal at Work.*

[30] Sennett, *The Corrosion of Character,* p. 146.

[31] Howell John Harris, *The Right to Manage: Industrial Relations Policies of American Business in the 1940s* (Madison: University of Wisconsin Press, 1982).

[32] Harry C. Katz, *Shifting Gears: Changing Labor Relations in the U.S. Automobile Industry* (Cambridge: MIT Press, 1985). Thomas A. Kochan, Harry C. Katz, and Robert B. McKersie, *The Transformation of American Industrial Relations* (New York: Basic Books, 1986).

Box 11.6

Ethics in Action: Breaking the Psychological Contract

Many, if not all, of the portions of the contract or bond between employer and employee are unwritten, and many are probably never even explicitly discussed. Rather, employees work hard for an employer because they *perceive* that they will be rewarded. This is a psychological contract. These perceptions are shaped through personal experience and longstanding past practices. In the postwar period, the dominant psychological contract in the U.S. employment relationship has consisted of employees' expectations that their hard work, loyalty, and investments in firm-specific skills will be rewarded with increased compensation, promotions, and job stability.

By many accounts, this psychological contract has now been unilaterally broken by employers in pursuit of flexibility. Employers no longer expect that they will provide stable, near-lifetime employment security to loyal workers. Compensation, promotions, and job security are now a function of short-term market pressures, not longer-term psychological commitments. Individual employees, not companies, are responsible for career management and skill acquisition.

Question

Is this breaking of the psychological contract ethically acceptable? *Hint:* use the ethical analysis template from Chapter 3.

Sources: Peter Cappelli, *The New Deal at Work: Managing the Market-Driven Workforce* (Boston: Harvard Business School Press, 1999). Denise M. Rousseau, *Psychological Contracts in Organizations: Understanding Written and Unwritten Agreements* (Thousand Oaks, CA: Sage, 1995).

Detailed work rules further control how work is performed and allocated. These work rules are essentially the union response to the reserved rights (or residual rights) doctrine of management rights. Recall from Chapter 10 that the reserved rights doctrine means that all management rights not explicitly limited, restricted, or modified by the union contract are reserved by management—management therefore has sole authority over all of the unmodified managerial issues.[33] As a result, unions have sought to explicitly limit, restrict, and modify managerial authority where this is perceived to serve the workers' interests. Examples include requirements that discipline and discharge only be done if there is just cause, restrictions on subcontracting work, limitations on work speed, and specifications of the job duties that must be done by union-represented workers. Detailed rules also specify how seniority systems operate—some auto industry contracts contain 50 pages or more of such rules. Sometimes-complex flow charts further delineate seniority ladders that employees can climb up and down through promotions or layoffs (see Box 11.7).

The traditional U.S. union contract within job control unionism is a lengthy, detailed, legalistic document. Disputes over the contract's provisions are resolved through a formal grievance procedure (see Chapter 10). Over time, arbitration awards and past practices establish precedents and create a common law of the workplace which further reinforces the legalistic nature of job control unionism. This system of job control unionism was widespread in the postwar U.S. industrial relations system because it served both management and union needs. It supported the mass-manufacturing requirements for stable and predictable production while also fulfilling union leaders' needs for countering managerial authority without having to resort to wildcat strikes that could undermine their own leadership

---

[33] Alan Miles Ruben (ed.), *Elkouri and Elkouri: How Arbitration Works, 6th ed.* (Washington, DC: Bureau of National Affairs, 2003).

BOX 11.7
Auto Plant Seniority Ladder—Final Truck Assembly (circa 1988)

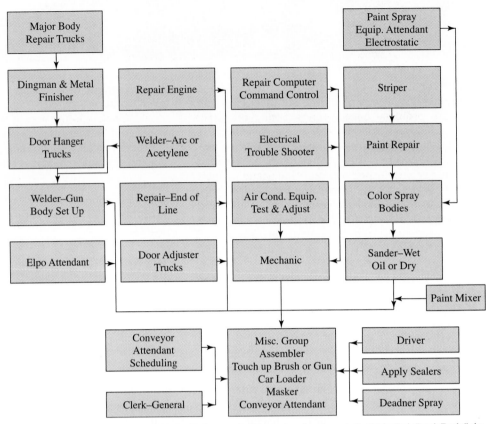

Note: Arrows denote bumping sequence during layoffs. For example, if the number of employees in the "Major Body Repair Trucks" classification is reduced, those with the least seniority move down to the "Dingman and Metal Finisher" classification, and so forth. The miscellaneous group including Assemblers is at the bottom of the seniority ladder.

positions.[34] Efficiency and equity were served through the peaceful, quasilegal application of workplace rules and contracts that fulfilled industrial justice; voice was provided through collective bargaining.[35] It's important to emphasize that job control unionism was more than just convenient—it embodied a very strong sense of industrial justice: justice through wages that were based on jobs rather than unfair manipulation of piece rates, justice through promotions and layoffs based on seniority rather than managerial favoritism, justice through quasilegal interpretation of contractual rules rather than by arbitrary decisions.[36] Justice was bureaucratic, however, and worker influence over day-to-day work issues was not part of the bargain.[37]

Currently, however, job control unionism is under fire (see Box 11.8). In fact, job control unionism is antithetical to all of the elements of flexibility that are so strongly emphasized

[34] Charles C. Heckscher, *The New Unionism: Employee Involvement in the Changing Corporation* (New York: Basic Books, 1988). Nelson Lichtenstein, "Great Expectations: The Promise of Industrial Jurisprudence and its Demise, 1930–1960," in Nelson Lichtenstein and Howell John Harris (eds.), *Industrial Democracy in America: The Ambiguous Promise* (Washington, DC: Woodrow Wilson Center Press, 1993), Chapter 6.

[35] John W. Budd, *Employment with a Human Face: Balancing Efficiency, Equity, and Voice* (Ithaca, NY: Cornell University Press, 2004).

[36] David Brody, "Workplace Contractualism in Comparative Perspective," in Nelson Lichtenstein and Howell John Harris (eds.), *Industrial Democracy in America: The Ambiguous Promise* (Washington, DC: Woodrow Wilson Center Press, 1993), Chapter 8.

[37] David Fairris, *Shopfloor Matters: Labor–Management Relations in Twentieth-Century American Manufacturing* (London: Routledge, 1997).

BOX 11.8   Job Control Unionism under Fire

Job Control Unionism	Today's Business Concerns
Wages are tied to jobs, not individuals.	Runs counter to paying for performance—cannot reward individual merit, productivity, skills, or organizational performance.
Jobs are very narrowly defined.	Difficult to deploy workers to different tasks. Problems with employee boredom and alienation. Workers are not responsible for monitoring their own quality. Teamwork is absent.
Seniority is a major determinant of promotions, layoffs, and transfers through seniority ladders.	Hard to promote the best performers or lay off the worst performers. Extensive bumping results in disruptive adjustment to changes in labor demand.
Extensive work rules.	Flexibility to move workers around, change job definitions, and adjust production methods is restricted. Layoffs and/or subcontracting might also be restricted.
Union contracts are very detailed and legalistic. Grievance procedures provide a quasilegal forum for resolving disputes.	Difficult to break with past practices. Change is slow. Innovation is stifled.
No employee involvement in business and production decision making; these are *management* rights.	Opportunities for harnessing workers' ideas for productivity improvements are limited. Innovation is stifled.
Employee voice is limited to the grievance procedure and periodic collective bargaining.	Change is slow. Issues are only solved through formalized procedures. Problems accumulate until the next round of bargaining.

by business in the 21st century. Standardized wages tied to jobs that are independent of both individual merit and company ability-to-pay prevent wage flexibility and pay-for-performance. Detailed systems of narrow job classifications are a barrier to functional flexibility—it is difficult to shift workers to different tasks in response to changes in market demands. Narrowly defined jobs also prevent teamwork and may lead to worker alienation. Restrictive work rules similarly limit functional flexibility and may also restrict employment flexibility through limitations on the use of part-time or temporary workers, subcontracting, or layoffs. Seniority-based procedures make it difficult to transfer and promote workers on the basis of skills and merit. Extensive bumping rights make frequent changes in deploying labor very cumbersome. This longstanding focus on seniority rather than skills also hampers training and other developmental opportunities. Detailed, lengthy, and legalistic union contracts that are only renegotiated every few years inhibit procedural flexibility and stifle innovation. The system of grievance arbitration and its continued reliance on past precedents similarly makes change and innovation difficult. The sharp divisions between labor that provides the brawn and management that provides the brains limit the benefits that business can reap from listening to its employees' ideas for process improvement. And job control unionism's limitation of employee voice to the bargaining table similarly deprives both companies and workers of the benefits of increased employee involvement in workplace decision making.

Consequently, one of the most important conflicts in U.S. labor relations in the 21st century is the clash between the bureaucratic model of job control unionism and the desire for flexibility. This is not to say that unions are opposed to moving away from job control unionism; but unions clearly have reservations about giving away their hard-won gains on terms that are deemed too unfavorable to the workers. The greatest resistance is probably in

Public Sector Labor Relations:Privatization   Box 11.9

Under pressure to deliver services at less cost, public sector governments and agencies sometimes opt to privatize some operations. Privatization transfers responsibility for delivering a service to a private sector company. Examples of privatizations in the United States include contracting out municipal water, sewer, and sanitation services, the provision of training and welfare payments, and prisons. What can public sector employees and unions do to combat public sector privatization (and similarly, private sector outsourcing)? Consider the following strategies inspired by the plays of William Shakespeare:

- Sly: I'll not budge an inch (*The Taming of the Shrew*)

This strategy is resistance to all attempts at privatization. This can be a short-sighted strategy, especially if pursued without financial analyses that reveal the true state of the problems and allow the employees to develop serious alternatives.

- Doctor: Therein the patient
      Must minister to himself (*Macbeth*)

This alternative is internal restructuring. If a union can help restructure work such that savings are achieved without privatization, then privatization can be prevented. This strategy may include developing a bid submitted by the public sector union to compete with bids submitted by private sector organizations.

- Edmund: Thou hast spoken right, 'tis true
      The wheel is come full circle; I am here
      (*King Lear*)

Similar to the previous strategy, employees can try to form their own business (such as through an employee stock ownership plan) to compete with other private sector organizations in submitting a bid for the privatized work.

- Hamlet: For 'tis the sport to have the engineer
      Hoist with his own petard (*Hamlet*)

In this strategy, the employees agree that the management function of some service be contracted out, but that the private sector organization that assumes this management function retains the original employees.

- Miranda: O brave new world (*The Tempest*)

Another alternative is for unions to negotiate clauses (such as a successorship clause) in their collective bargaining agreements that require the employers to only privatize operations to third parties that agree to recognize the union.

Source: Michael Glanzer, "Union Strategies in Privatizations: Shakespeare-Inspired Alternatives," *Albany Law Review* 64 (2000), pp. 437–500.

---

the area of employment flexibility. The Teamsters strike at UPS in 1997 graphically highlighted union opposition to undue corporate reliance on part-time work—with a significant degree of public sympathy for this aspect of the strike. Shifting production to other companies through subcontracting and outsourcing—and in the public sector, privatization—are additional methods for attaining employment flexibility. A number of union strategies are possible for trying to counter these efforts (see Box 11.9).

For the other dimensions of flexibility, there are a greater number of examples where labor and management have experimented with moving beyond traditional job control unionism. The UAW contracts with Ford, General Motors, and DaimlerChrysler now include a profit-sharing plan in which hourly workers receive an annual profit-sharing bonus based on overall company profitability (in some years this bonus is not paid because a company fails to meet the specified profit target).[38] Skill-based pay has been successfully introduced in a variety of unionized settings.[39] There are significant examples of quality circles, self-managed work teams, labor representatives on corporate boards of directors,

[38] Harry C. Katz, John Paul MacDuffie, and Frits K. Pil, "Autos: Continuity and Change in Collective Bargaining," in Paul F. Clark, John T. Delaney, and Ann C. Frost (eds.), *Collective Bargaining in the Private Sector* (Champaign, IL: Industrial Relations Research Association, 2002), Chapter 2. Harry C. Katz and Noah M. Meltz, "Profit Sharing and Auto Workers' Earnings: The United States vs. Canada," *Relations Industrielles* 46 (Summer 1991), pp. 515–29.

[39] Kenneth Mericle and Dong-One Kim, "From Job-Based Pay to Skill-Based Pay in Unionized Establishments: A Three-Plant Comparative Analysis," *Relations Industrielles* 54 (Summer 1999), pp. 549–78.

and other initiatives to involve workers in business decision making in unionized establishments.[40] In fact, the AFL–CIO endorses a new model of work organization that includes pay flexibility, functional flexibility, and procedural flexibility—when labor is treated as an equal partner to management (see Box 11.10). This model of work organization moves beyond a simple focus on flexibility and requires employee involvement in decision making. As described in the next section, these changes are not without their detractors.

EMPLOYEE INVOLVEMENT

In the 1940s, two staff members of the United Steelworkers union, Clinton Golden and Harold Ruttenberg, developed principles for getting employees more involved in their work.[41] The basic idea is simple: workers perform their job tasks over and over and therefore often have good ideas for improving productivity, increasing quality, and lowering costs. Moreover, they argued that employee discretion in their work will increase job satisfaction and create better employees. Golden also predicted—accurately and coming from a union leader, ironically—that management's insistence on retaining the right to manage and the accompanying scientific-management distinction between management's thinking and labor's action "might well restrict the flexibility so necessary to efficient operation."[42] While other countries such as Germany and Japan have longer traditions of involving employees in decision making (see Chapter 13), U.S. management categorically rejected this thinking for much of the 20th century. The competitive crisis in the 1970s, however, challenged this wisdom of treating workers as unthinking cogs in a machine.

In 1972, workers at the General Motors plant in Lordstown, Ohio, went on strike over the exhausting pace of work, confrontational methods of discipline, harassment, and a backlog of over 10,000 grievances.[43] This strike became symbolic of the blue-collar blues—worker alienation resulting from repetitive and exceptionally narrow (in other words, boring) jobs that leads to absenteeism, poor quality, and even sabotage. Concern with this growing issue of worker alienation led to experimentation with **quality of working life (QWL) programs** in the 1970s. These programs focused on improving the work environment—such as through improved ventilation—and the nature of employee—supervisor relations. While there was some experimentation with team-based production, most QWL programs were "off-line" programs that were simply added on top of the existing structure of scientific management and job control unionism.[44] The underlying principle was that if working conditions were made more humane, then job satisfaction and product quality would increase; alienation, absenteeism, and grievances—the blue-collar blues—would decrease.[45] In the 21st century, similar ideas are embodied in the use of employee assistance programs and family-friendly benefits.

As these first-generation QWL programs did not change the underlying structure of work organization, success was limited. Intensified competitive pressures in the 1980s, however, redoubled corporate efforts at restructuring the workplace for a competitive edge. Since that time,

---

[40] Appelbaum and Batt, *The New American Workplace.* Bluestone and Bluestone, *Negotiating the Future.* Heckscher, *The New Unionism.*

[41] Clinton S. Golden and Harold J. Ruttenberg, *The Dynamics of Industrial Democracy* (New York: Harper and Brothers, 1942). John P. Hoerr, *And the Wolf Finally Came: The Decline of the American Steel Industry* (Pittsburgh: University of Pittsburgh, 1988).

[42] Hoerr, *And the Wolf Finally Came,* p. 280.

[43] John Russo, "Lordstown, Ohio, Strike of 1972," in Ronald L. Filippelli (ed.), *Labor Conflict in the United States: An Encyclopedia* (New York: Garland Publishing, 1990), pp. 283–86.

[44] Katz, *Shifting Gears.*

[45] Bruce Nissen, "Unions and Workplace Reorganization," in Bruce Nissen (ed.), *Unions and Workplace Reorganization* (Detroit: Wayne State University Press, 1997), Chapter 1.

The AFL–CIO's Perspective on the New American Workplace

Box 11.10

"It is possible to discern five principles which together define a model for a new system of work organization.

- **First, the model begins by rejecting the traditional dichotomy between thinking and doing, conception and execution.** Workers—the individuals who actually do what it is the organization is doing—are in the best position to decide how their work can most efficiently and effectively be accomplished. Such decisions are never final but should be constantly revisited through an ongoing process in which change is the only constant. This process requires a fundamental redistribution for decision-making authority from management to teams of workers. These workers must not only be given such decision-making authority but also must be afforded the opportunity to develop and refine analytic and problem-solving skills so that they will be able to make the best possible work decisions.

- **Second, in the new model, jobs are redesigned to include a greater variety of skills and tasks and, more importantly, greater responsibility for the ultimate output of the organization.** Workers are organized into work groups (or teams); the workers learn not merely a particular task but an understanding of the overall process of producing a good or service and often they are trained to perform the various functions required for that process. Moreover, workers are given the authority, and the training, to exercise discretion, judgment, and creativity on the job. Workers' ingenuity is viewed as a key to success; workers are free to do the right thing, rather than being compelled to do the prescribed thing.

- **Third, this new model of work organization substitutes for the traditional, multi-layered hierarchy a flatter management structure.** At the same time, the role of the manager is transformed since the aim of the system is no longer to assure that workers do prescribed tasks, in prescribed manners, for prescribed intervals. In this less authoritarian work culture, the aim is to enable workers to be self-managers who are responsible for their own performance, and the work teams are often self-managed with responsibility for scheduling work, ordering materials, hiring workers, and the like. The foreman is replaced by a team leader; the role is to lead rather than mandate.

- **Fourth, the new model goes beyond the workplace level to insist that workers, through their unions, are entitled to a decision-making role at all levels of the enterprise.** Just as workers understand best how the work should be organized, workers—through their representatives—have expertise to contribute to strategic decision as well including, for example, about what new technologies should be acquired or about what changes to make in products or services. Moreover, as stakeholders in the enterprise, workers have a vital interest in the strategic decisions which ultimately determine how much work will be done, where, and by whom. Because workers have long-term ties to their jobs, they bring a long-term perspective and can be counted on to promote policies designed to insure that businesses have long-term futures and can provide long-term employment at decent wages. Thus, in this new model such strategic decisions are to be jointly made by workers—acting through their unions—and the other stakeholders.

- **Fifth and finally, the new model of work organization calls for the rewards realized from transforming the work organization to be distributed on equitable terms agreed upon through negotiations between labor and management.** This means, in the first instance, a negotiated agreement to protect income and employment security to the maximum extent possible. Of equal importance, it means a negotiated agreement to compensate workers fairly for their enhanced contribution to the success of the organization. This may be achieved through increases in base wages or, in other cases, through agreements providing for some form of supplementary contingent compensation (such as gain sharing, profit sharing, stock ownership, or the like). What is most important is that the worker's share is not set as an act of grace by managers and owners but is the product of a negotiated agreement between the employer and the union representing the workers.

These five principles form an integrated whole—a vision of a new system of work organization. They combine *individual participation* through restructured work processes and redesigned jobs, with *collective representation,* through restructured decision-making processes from the shop floor to corporate headquarters. The aim of this approach is to achieve work organizations which at one and the same are more productive *and* more democratic. Therein lies the source of its legitimacy and its power. . . ."

Source: AFL–CIO Committee on the Evolution of Work, *The New American Workplace: A Labor Perspective* (Washington, DC: American Federation of Labor–Congress of Industrial Organizations, 1994), pp. 8–9 (emphases in original). This document is also available in Bruce Nissen (ed.), *Unions and Workplace Reorganization* (Detroit: Wayne State University Press, 1997).

Union Representation on Corporate Boards of Directors

Box 11.11

A corporation's decisions regarding investment, mergers and acquisitions, product lines, and other strategic issues are ultimately controlled by the corporation's board of directors. The emphasis on the shareholder model of corporate governance in the United States means that these corporate directors primarily act in the interests of the shareholders (owners) of the company. But many strategic decisions made by boards of directors have significant effects on employees as well as shareholders—closing a plant is just one obvious example. In some cases, unions have therefore sought representation on corporate boards of directors, such as by having the union president be a director or by having a union-nominated director (who might be a retired union leader, college professor, or other interested individual).

Union representation on corporate boards of directors have typically occurred in two situations. One, unions have received board seats when employees become owners of significant amounts of stock. This has occurred through employee stock ownership plans in the steel industry as the workers have purchased struggling steel companies and in the airline industry when stock has been granted in return for significant wage and benefit concessions. In these situations, board seats are viewed as a way to protect the workers' investments in the company. The other scenario in which unions have obtained board representation is when a union and company negotiate a strategic partnership arrangement and create high performance work systems. In this scenario, board representation extends workplace-level employee involvement into the corporate boardroom. Rather than being viewed as a protection of the employees' investment, board representation in these situations is viewed as facilitating employee input into strategic decision making.

In either case, union representatives on corporate boards of directors face significant challenges, especially the legal and normative emphasis on directors as the champion of shareholders' interests. Union representatives are also frequently significantly outnumbered by the other directors. Many experiments with board representation seem to die out as unions pursue other bargaining priorities such as when the UAW essentially gave up its seat on Chrysler's board in 1991. Nevertheless, union representation on corporate boards of directors can provide employees with information and can potentially influence strategic corporate decision making. In fact, some European countries mandate that representatives of employees and other stakeholders be included on corporate boards of directors (Chapter 13). As such, U.S. experiments with board representation are likely to continue.

Source: Eileen Appelbaum and Larry W. Hunter, "Union Participation in Strategic Decisions of Corporations," in Richard B. Freeman, Joni Hersch, and Lawrence Mishel (eds.), *Emerging Labor Market Institutions for the Twenty-First Century* (Chicago: University of Chicago Press, 2005), pp. 265–91. Larry W. Hunter, "Can Strategic Participation Be Institutionalized? Union Representation on American Corporate Boards," *Industrial and Labor Relations Review* 51 (July 1998), pp. 557–78.

---

unions and companies have experimented with various forms of employee involvement. The extent to which employees are actively involved in decision making varies widely. In gainsharing programs such as a Scanlon Plan or a Rucker plan, workers make suggestions for process improvement, and a portion of the gains (reduced labor and nonlabor costs) are shared with the workers through an explicit formula. **Quality circles** provide a forum for workers to make suggestions about how to improve productivity and quality through regular group meetings with supervisors. Quality circles are a frequent component of continuous improvement programs such as total quality management. Other types of joint labor–management committees might be formed to address ad hoc issues, or to address establishment-wide issues such as increasing trust between labor and management. Employee involvement in strategic decision making can come through a labor representative on a corporation's board of directors (see Box 11.11).[46] As

[46] Larry W. Hunter, "Can Strategic Participation Be Institutionalized? Union Representation on American Corporate Boards," *Industrial and Labor Relations Review* 51 (July 1998), pp. 557–78. Robert B. McKersie, "Union-Nominated Directors: A New Voice in Corporate Governance," in Thomas A. Kochan and David B. Lipsky (eds.), *Negotiations and Change: From the Workplace to Society* (Ithaca, NY: ILR Press, 2003), Chapter 12.

an example from the public sector, in 1993 then-President Clinton mandated labor–management partnerships for agencies of the federal government. These partnerships ultimately covered more than 800,000 workers and though President Clinton's order was repealed by President Bush in 2001, research on these partnerships indicates that they were successful in creating a better labor–management climate, reducing disputes, and improving targeted performance outcomes such as customer service.[47]

All of these initiatives, however, do not necessarily change the underlying scientific management system of work organization. The most extensive efforts to restructure the workplace involve not only increasing employee involvement in decision making, but also changing how work is organized. In other words, these efforts try to create **high-performance work systems**—systems of mutually supporting human resources practices that combine flexibility with employee involvement in decision making. Four major categories of team-oriented, high-performance work systems that support flexible specialization and employee involvement rather than mass manufacturing are summarized in Box 11.12.[48] The first two have received the greatest attention in U.S. labor relations. **Lean production** is generally regarded as the Japanese approach to mass manufacturing—and as the traditional U.S. assembly line system is referred to as "Fordism," lean production is sometimes referred to as "Toyotism" or the "Toyota production system." Lean production emphasizes just-in-time inventories, the smooth flow of materials, teamwork, and off-line quality circles to deliver continuous process improvement. The sociotechnical systems approach is structured around **self-directed work teams**—autonomous groups of employees that are responsible for a set of job tasks as well as routine maintenance tasks. In lean production, work teams have little authority and are managed by a supervisor; self-directed work teams in a sociotechnical system are empowered to manage their internal affairs without a supervisor and the teams can make their own decisions regarding job pacing, task assignment, and quality control.

The effects of high-performance work systems are the focus of many academic debates. Surveys reveal that various elements of high-performance work systems—quality circles, job rotation, teams, total quality management, and the like—are becoming more prevalent.[49] But are they good for firms? Or for workers? Systems or bundles of human resources practices (but perhaps not individual practices) have been found to reduce employee turnover and increase productivity.[50] But such findings are not universal and also do not necessarily translate into improved corporate profitability.[51] The adoption of high performance work practices also does not necessarily yield higher wages or reduced

[47] Marick F. Masters, Robert R. Albright, and David Eplion, "What Did Partnerships Do? Evidence from the Federal Sector," *Industrial and Labor Relations Review* 59 (April 2006), pp. 367–85.

[48] Appelbaum and Batt, *The New American Workplace.*

[49] Casey Ichniowski and Kathryn Shaw, "Beyond Incentive Pay: Insiders' Estimates of the Value of Complementary Human Resource Management Practices," *Journal of Economic Perspectives* 17 (Winter 2003), pp. 155–80. Paul Osterman, "Work Reorganization in an Era of Restructuring: Trends in Diffusion and Effects on Employee Welfare," *Industrial and Labor Relations Review* 53 (January 2000), pp. 179–96.

[50] Rosemary Batt, "Work Organization, Technology, and Performance in Customer Service and Sales," *Industrial and Labor Relations Review* 52 (July 1999), pp. 539–64. Mark A. Huselid, "The Impact of Human Resource Management Practices on Turnover, Productivity, and Corporate Financial Performance," *Academy of Management Journal* 38 (June 1995), pp. 635–72. Ichniowski and Shaw, "Beyond Incentive Pay." Casey Ichniowski, Kathryn Shaw, and Giovanna Prennushi, "The Effects of Human Resources Management Practices on Productivity: A Study of Steel Finishing Lines," *American Economic Review* 87 (June 1997), pp. 291–313.

[51] Peter Cappelli and David Neumark, "Do 'High-Performance' Work Practices Improve Establishment-Level Outcomes?" *Industrial and Labor Relations Review* 54 (July 2001), pp. 737–75. John Godard, "A Critical Assessment of the High-Performance Paradigm," *British Journal of Industrial Relations* 42 (June 2004), pp. 349–78.

Lean Production

Production by work teams, but supervisors make decisions, not team members. Emphasis on quality through off-line quality circles rather than online worker decision making. Production is "lean" because of just-in-time inventories and a focus on the smooth flow of materials. Competitive advantage: price and mass scale quality Example: high-quality, high-volume automobiles such as Toyota (Japan)

Sociotechnical Systems

Formal, autonomous work teams have responsibilities for functional as well as routine maintenance tasks. Teams control their own internal affairs (such as pacing, task assignment, quality control) and also pursue problem solving and continuous improvement. Competitive advantage: quality and customization Example: high-quality, low-volume niche automobiles such as Volvo and Saab (Sweden)

Flexible Specialization

Small-scale production of diverse items using flexible networks of employers. Production often through small work groups with some level of autonomy. Competitive advantage: innovation Example: apparel (Italy)

Diversified Quality Production

Quality through broadly skilled, highly trained crafts workers.

Competitive advantage: quality and customization Example: high-quality, high-performance automobiles such as BMW and Mercedes Benz (Germany)

Source: Eileen Appelbaum and Rosemary Batt, *The New American Workplace: Transforming Work Systems in the United States* (Ithaca, NY: ILR Press, 1994).

---

layoffs.[52] Moderate adoption of such practices appear to increase employee satisfaction, esteem, and commitment, but extensive adoption can reduce employee well-being because of higher levels of stress.[53] Research has also linked the use of quality circles, work teams, and job rotation to higher levels of cumulative trauma disorders such as carpal tunnel injuries.[54] As such, some research supports the great promise of high-performance work systems, but other research reveals some possible pitfalls and therefore questions whether these promises are overstated.[55] These debates provide the backdrop for a more detailed consideration of the labor relations issues stemming from lean production and self-directed work teams.

Lean production has been popularized in the United States through the spread of total quality management (TQM) and the opening of Japanese auto plants in the United States—Honda in Ohio, Nissan in Tennessee, Subaru in Indiana, Toyota in Kentucky, and a joint General Motors–Toyota venture in California (NUMMI)—in the 1980s. Lean production is associated with TQM because workers participate in quality circles to make suggestions for continuous improvement (*kaizen*). The American version of lean production, however, is often quite centralized with management still tightly in control of decision

---

[52] Osterman, "Work Reorganization in an Era of Restructuring." Sandra E. Black, Lisa M. Lynch, and Anya Krivelyova, "How Workers Fare When Employers Innovate," *Industrial Relations* 43 (January 2004), pp. 44–66. Michael J. Handel and Maury Gittleman, "Is There a Wage Payoff to Innovative Work Practices?" *Industrial Relations* 43 (January 2004), pp. 67–97.

[53] John Godard, "High Performance *and* the Transformation of Work? The Implications of Alternative Work Practices for the Experiences and Outcomes of Work," *Industrial and Labor Relations Review* 54 (July 2001), pp. 776–805.

[54] Mark D. Brenner, David Fairris, and John Ruser, " 'Flexible' Work Practices and Occupational Safety and Health: Exploring the Relationship between Cumulative Trauma Disorders and Workplace Transformation," *Industrial Relations* 43 (January 2004), pp. 242–66.

[55] Godard, "A Critical Assessment of the High-Performance Paradigm."

making.[56] As such, this model is often not very well-received by the U.S. labor movement that questions the extent to which workers are involved or empowered in lean production systems. In fact, critics have labeled lean production as "management by stress."[57] This label comes from lean production's constant pressure to reduce inefficiencies such as idle time and from the peer pressure created by teams that must cover for absent workers:

> Work standards are constantly *kaizened* upward so that team members work fifty-seven out of sixty seconds; buffers are eliminated so that workers cannot pace themselves and create a break; relief personnel are reduced or eliminated and absent workers are not replaced; responsibility for handling these disruptions is forced downward; the supervisor is therefore pressured to fill out more papers and take on more tasks; he protects himself by holding out the team leader for production breakdowns, which means team members cannot get bathroom relief when they need it. The result that management desires is for workers to pressure each other to reduce absenteeism and bathroom breaks.[58]

This view clashes sharply with supporters of lean production that see team members as empowered to make decisions over their work and that highlight the quality and productivity advantages—especially the quality and labor hour differences between the U.S. and Japanese auto manufacturers.[59] There is no easy way to resolve these conflicting perspectives, but they continue to reflect a very important debate within U.S. labor relations.

These conflicting perspectives further underscore an important use of language that students of labor relations should be aware of. In discussing workplace restructuring, it is common for management to use the phrase "labor-management cooperation" whereas unions are more likely to talk about "involvement" or "participation." To labor, this is more than semantics. When managers emphasize cooperation, unions often interpret this as a push for unions and workers to quietly go along with management-driven initiatives. In effect, "cooperation" is seen as a way to weaken unions as the representative of the workers. As such, to the extent that it requires abandoning its advocacy role, unions are opposed to cooperation. Rather, unions want substantive changes in work organization and decision-making authority. Instead of cooperation, labor is looking for worker empowerment through "involvement" and "participation" (recall Box 11.10).

Turning to the sociotechnical systems approach, the most widely discussed U.S. example of the extensive use of self-directed work teams is the Spring Hill, Tennessee, plant of the Saturn subsidiary of General Motors.[60] Saturn developed in the mid-1980s out of a joint labor–management study of worldwide auto manufacturing practices that resulted in a new partnership embracing team-based production and co-managed decision making by the Saturn and the union (the UAW) (see Box 11.13). A series of formal joint labor–management committees, called Decision Rings, are empowered with decision-making authority over extensive issues. The UAW is further recognized as a legitimate stakeholder and therefore participates in business decisions over technology, supplier selection, pricing,

---

[56] Appelbaum and Batt, *The New American Workplace.* Steve Babson (ed.), *Lean Work: Empowerment and Exploitation in the Global Auto Industry* (Detroit: Wayne State University Press, 1995). Fairris, *Shopfloor Matters.*

[57] Parker and Slaughter, *Choosing Sides.* Mike Parker and Jane Slaughter, "Unions and Management by Stress," in Steve Babson (ed.), *Lean Work: Empowerment and Exploitation in the Global Auto Industry* (Detroit: Wayne State University Press, 1995), Chapter 2.

[58] Parker and Slaughter, "Unions and Management by Stress," pp. 45–46.

[59] James Womack, Daniel Jones, and Daniel Roos, *The Machine That Changed the World* (New York: Rawson Associates, 1990).

[60] Bluestone and Bluestone, *Negotiating the Future.* Heckscher, *The New Unionism.* Saul A. Rubinstein and Thomas A. Kochan, *Learning from Saturn: Possibilities for Corporate Governance and Employee Relations* (Ithaca, NY: ILR Press, 2001).

WORK UNIT MEMBER: An individual Saturn employee.

WORK UNIT: An integrated team of 6–15 Work Unit members. The Work Unit is self-directed with the authority to, *inter alia,* assign jobs, approve vacations, undertake scrap control and supply acquisition, keep records, handle absenteeism, select new members, and elect its own leader. There are approximately 600 teams at Saturn.

WORK UNIT MODULE: A grouping of Work Units that are interrelated by geography, product, process, or technology that has two (jointly selected) advisors (one from the represented [i.e., union] workforce, one not). Each Work Unit Module has a weekly Decision Ring consisting of the Work Unit Module advisors and Work Unit leaders.

BUSINESS UNIT: An integration of Work Unit Modules according to the business area (Body Systems, Powertrain, or Vehicle Systems) with various common advisors. Each Business Unit has a weekly Decision Ring consisting of the Work Unit Module advisors and representatives of Saturn and the union.

MANUFACTURING ACTION COUNCIL (MAC): A weekly Decision Ring of Business Unit advisors and representatives of Saturn and the union. This council focuses primarily on internal (to the plant) issues and decisions (e.g., broad manufacturing problems).

STRATEGIC ACTION COUNCIL (SAC): A weekly Decision Ring of representatives of Saturn and the union. This is the top executive management of Saturn that is responsible for long-range objectives and planning and focuses primarily on external issues (e.g., pricing, advertising, dealers).

Sources: Saul Rubinstein, Michael Bennett, and Thomas Kochan, "The Saturn Partnership: Co-Management and the Reinvention of the Local Union," in Bruce E. Kaufman and Morris M. Kleiner (eds.), *Employee Representation: Alternatives and Future Directions* (Madison, WI: Industrial Relations Research Association, 1993), Chapter 10. Barry Bluestone and Irving Bluestone, *Negotiating the Future: A Labor Perspective on American Business* (New York: Basic Books, 1992).

business planning, training, business systems development, budgeting, quality systems, productivity improvement, job design, new product development, recruitment and hiring, maintenance, and engineering. In terms of production, roughly 700 self-directed work teams of 6–15 employees each are responsible for their part of the production process. These teams are further empowered to make decisions regarding work pace, planning and scheduling, vacation approvals, and training and are responsible for safety and health, inventory, quality and scrap control, repair, maintenance, and other issues.

As the structure of work at Saturn is very different from the traditional scientific-management workplace, so too is the nature of labor relations at Saturn very different from the traditional model of job control unionism. Most visibly, the union contract at Saturn has considerably fewer pages than usual union contracts in the United States (recall Box 1.10). Teams and decision rings are empowered to make numerous decisions so detailed work rules and a management rights clause are not necessary. But because the decision-making processes were negotiated between the UAW and Saturn, protections are built into the structure and the union can ensure that employees receive support and due process. In particular, formal grievances are allowed and during contract renegotiations, the union can strike. In fact, Saturn employees authorized a strike in 1998 during contract negotiations over decision-making issues and production and quality bonuses.

Extensive levels of employee empowerment as well as union co-management of business operations further present numerous challenges for the operation of the local union.[61] To match the participatory nature of employee involvement in workplace decision making, the local union created participatory structures to promote employee involvement in union decision making. These structures include town hall meetings, rap sessions, and a twice-a-month congress meeting involving 450 union leaders, and are supplemented by an extensive

[61] Saul A. Rubinstein, "A Different Kind of Union: Balancing Co-Management and Representation," *Industrial Relations* 40 (April 2001), pp. 163–203. Rubinstein and Kochan, *Learning from Saturn.*

annual membership survey. Nevertheless, conflicts persist between the union's dual functions of co-management and representation, that is, between being a strategic business partner and an advocate for the workers. First, note that "while union leaders need to add value to the firm through their roles in the governance or management process, if this is all they do, they are undifferentiated from other competent managers."[62] Second, union leaders must be careful that their efforts at adding value do not come at the expense of representing individual employees.[63]

To put it more bluntly, there are some in the labor movement who see this form of strategic business partnership as selling out. In this view, when unions are concerned with business decisions, they are no longer fully looking out for employee interests to the fullest extent possible: "at Saturn, the union has made meeting the needs of the business *its* business. This means that there are two parties looking after management's interests (or one and a half), and only half a party looking after the [union] members' interests."[64] Moreover, it is argued that this form of unionism fails to develop a power base independent of the company and is therefore too weak to challenge management on a sustained basis.[65] What one sees as a slimmer union contract that promotes flexibility and increased employee discretion, another sees as a lack of well-defined standards that can be exploited by managers. As with the debates over lean production, there are no easy answers to questions over whether the system of union representation at Saturn represents an advance or retreat from the traditional system of job control unionism, but these are critical questions for U.S. labor relations in the 21st century.

While Saturn is a particularly extensive example of employee empowerment, other examples can be found in many industries and locations. A municipality in Washington reorganized its maintenance department into four self-directed work teams that are complemented by a joint labor–management group for problem solving.[66] Xerox completely re-designed its manufacturing methods in the 1980s around autonomous work teams and business area work groups that incorporated both employee and union involvement in decision making.[67] During contract negotiations for 9,000 nurses represented by the Minnesota Nurses Association at 13 hospitals in the Minneapolis–St. Paul metropolitan area in 2001, one of the critical issues was staffing shortages. Six of the hospitals, three of them after a 23-day strike, agreed to a contractual provision that allowed nurses to temporarily close units to new patient admissions if they are understaffed and can't handle any additional patients. Within a framework negotiated through collective bargaining—that therefore provides nurses with certain rights and protections—individual employees are empowered with the discretion to make business decisions. This is a limited example of employee empowerment because it is confined to a single issue, but illustrates the possibilities of moving away from a narrow model of job control unionism. These examples further reinforce the need for unions to continue challenging the parts of systems of work organization that workers view as exploitative while strengthening the aspects that are empowering.[68]

[62] Rubinstein, "A Different Kind of Union," p. 195.

[63] Rubinstein, "A Different Kind of Union."

[64] Mike Parker and Jane Slaughter, "Advancing Unionism on the New Terrain," in Bruce Nissen (ed.), *Unions and Workplace Reorganization* (Detroit: Wayne State University Press, 1997), Chapter 11 at p. 218.

[65] Parker and Slaughter, "Advancing Unionism on the New Terrain."

[66] U.S. Department of Labor, *Working Together for Public Service* (Washington, DC: Government Printing Office, 1996).

[67] Joel Cutcher-Gershenfeld, "The Impact on Economic Performance of a Transformation in Workplace Relations," *Industrial and Labor Relations Review* 44 (January 1991), pp. 241–60.

[68] Adrienne Eaton, "The Role of the Union and Employee Involvement in Lean Production," in Steve Babson (ed.), *Lean Work: Empowerment and Exploitation in the Global Auto Industry* (Detroit: Wayne State University Press, 1995), Chapter 4.

EMPLOYEE REPRESENTATION: ARE UNIONS REQUIRED?

Many of the corporate strategies to improve competitiveness and quality explicitly include some form of employee voice. For example, the rationale for quality circles and joint labor–management committees is providing an explicit way for workers and managers to discuss workplace issues. Employees can share their ideas for improving productivity, enhancing quality, and resolving specific problems. The impetus for self-directed work teams takes this premise one step further by allowing teams to make some decisions on their own without managerial approval. Beyond the benefits to the corporation that result from hearing the ideas of workers, employees may also be more loyal and committed to the organization if they feel that they have input into workplace decision making.[69] As such, it is expected that absenteeism and turnover will decline and individual productivity will increase. Moreover, by listening to employee concerns, managers can better tailor human resources policies and practices to the preferences of the employees which is also expected to reduce absenteeism and turnover while improving individual productivity. This might also partly be an attempt to prevent workers from forming a union.

In terms of competitiveness or efficiency, an ongoing debate is whether the presence of an independent labor union increases the effectiveness of these voice mechanisms. Some research suggests workers will more freely participate in these initiatives when a union is present to provide protections such as job security or just cause discipline and discharge provisions, and thus, employee involvement efforts are more successful when a union is present.[70] This is an interesting and important question, but there is no well-accepted consensus on the extent to which unions increase the effectiveness of high-performance work practices. And this question is often overshadowed by the larger question of whether nonunion voice mechanisms legitimately benefit workers or are instead management tools for suppressing unionization and true employee voice.

As discussed in Chapter 4, around the time of World War I, some U.S. companies created nonunion **employee representation plans** in which a group of employees would meet with managers to discuss employment conditions.[71] For example, one popular plan included equal numbers of managers and workers; the managers were appointed by senior executives and the worker members were elected by the employees. A significant number of these nonunion employee representation plans were part of a larger welfare capitalism package of human resources practices to create a motivated, loyal, and efficient workforce. By definition, these *representation* plans focused on collective voice; they were not mechanisms of individual voice or empowerment. These plans were also always nonunion: employee representation plans were

[69] Tove Helland Hammer, "Nonunion Representational Forms: An Organizational Behavior Perspective," in Bruce E. Kaufman and Daphne Gottlieb Taras (eds.), *Nonunion Employee Representation: History, Contemporary Practice, and Policy* (Armonk, NY: M. E. Sharpe, 2000), Chapter 8.

[70] Adrienne E. Eaton and Paula B. Voos, "Productivity-Enhancing Innovations in Work Organization, Compensation, and Employee Participation in the Union versus the Nonunion Sectors," in David Lewin and Donna Sockell (eds.), *Advances in Industrial and Labor Relations, Volume 6* (Greenwich, CT: JAI Press, 1994), pp. 63–109. Saul R. Rubinstein "The Impact of Co-Management on Quality Performance: The Case of the Saturn Corporation," *Industrial and Labor Relations Review* 53 (January 2000), pp. 197–218. Sandra E. Black and Lisa M. Lynch, "How to Compete: The Impact of Workplace Practices and Information Technology on Productivity," *Review of Economics and Statistics* 83 (August 2001), pp. 434–45.

[71] Bruce E. Kaufman, "Accomplishments and Shortcomings of Nonunion Employee Representation in the Pre-Wagner Act Years: A Reassessment," in Bruce E. Kaufman and Daphne Gottlieb Taras (eds.), *Nonunion Employee Representation: History, Contemporary Practice, and Policy* (Armonk, NY: M. E. Sharpe, 2000), Chapter 2. Daniel Nelson, "The AFL and the Challenge of Company Unionism, 1915–1937," in Bruce E. Kaufman and Daphne Gottlieb Taras (eds.), *Nonunion Employee Representation: History, Contemporary Practice, and Policy,* Chapter 3.

established unilaterally by management—management determined the structure, the issues covered, the extent of the plan's authority, and its continued existence (or not). While rarely having the power of an independent labor union—and while interactions between the employee and company representatives would not be characterized as collective bargaining as we now conceive of it—some employee representation plans were able to influence management decision making and the employees' terms and conditions of employment. But there were also notable examples, especially in the early 1930s, of management manipulation of employee representation plans with the primary purpose of preventing employees from forming an independent labor union.[72] Because Senator Wagner and others viewed nonunion employee representation plans as sham company unions, section 8(a)(2) of the National Labor Relations Act (NLRA) therefore prohibits employer domination of labor organizations (see Chapter 5).

The 1930s debate over employee representation plans as legitimate (albeit limited) vehicles of employee voice or as company-dominated tools for preventing unionization returned to labor relations with full force in the 1990s and continues as an important issue of contention in the 21st century. To set the stage for this debate, first note that neither the Railway Labor Act nor Canadian labor law restrict nonunion employee representation to the same extent as the NLRA—in spite of their very strong similarities with the overall NLRA framework.[73] As will be discussed in Chapter 13, a number of European countries even go one step farther and *mandate* employee representation plans—usually called works councils—for both efficiency and voice reasons.

Under the Railway Labor Act in the United States, Delta Airlines, for example, has a nonunion employee representation plan for its flight attendants.[74] This plan, the Flight Attendant Forum, consists of one elected representative for every 100 flight attendants that meet quarterly at local flight attendant bases to discuss employee issues. A subset of these representatives also meet on a national basis with Delta's senior management. Delta also created the Delta Personnel Board in 1996 consisting of one employee representative from seven major employee groups to be a major communication path between employees and the board of directors. This personnel board tries to make sure that employee concerns are known when the board of directors makes decisions. Neither of these plans involve formal bargaining, but both have addressed issues pertaining to benefit levels as well as work rules and other policies.

In Canada, nonunion employee representation is not widespread, but there are notable examples.[75] At Imperial Oil—Canada's premier oil and gas company that is owned by ExxonMobil—a system of joint industrial councils have been in operation since 1919.[76] The joint industrial councils have equal numbers of management and employee representatives. The employee representatives are elected every two years. Local councils meet monthly to discuss local workplace issues; local councils also send delegates to a district-level joint industrial council that discusses issues that affect multiple work sites. One district council's mission statement reads:

[72] Kaufman, "Accomplishments and Shortcomings of Nonunion Employee Representation in the Pre-Wagner Act Years." Nelson, "The AFL and the Challenge of Company Unionism, 1915–1937."

[73] Samuel Estreicher, "Nonunion Employee Representation: A Legal/Policy Perspective," in Kaufman and Taras (eds.), *Nonunion Employee Representation: History, Contemporary Practice, and Policy*, Chapter 9. Daphne Gottlieb Taras, "Portrait of Nonunion Employee Representation in Canada: History, Law, and Contemporary Plans," in Kaufman and Taras (eds.), *Nonunion Employee Representation: History, Contemporary Practice, and Policy*, Chapter 6.

[74] Cathy Cone, "Delta Personnel Board Council," in Kaufman and Taras (eds.), *Nonunion Employee Representation: History, Contemporary Practice, and Policy*, Chapter 23.

[75] Taras, "Portrait of Nonunion Employee Representation in Canada."

[76] Daphne Gottlieb Taras, "Contemporary Experience with the Rockefeller Plan: Imperial Oil's Joint Industrial Council," in Kaufman and Taras (eds.), *Nonunion Employee Representation: History, Contemporary Practice, and Policy*, Chapter 11.

Our Joint Industrial Council is committed to working together in an open and honest dialogue on any subject of importance to the Employees and the Company. Through trust and cooperation we can all achieve excellence.[77]

An extensive case study of these joint industrial councils found that they are neither manipulative management schemes to prevent unionization nor perfect participatory vehicles to create labor–management harmony.[78] The councils are clearly weaker than unions—management ensures that each item is treated individually and evaluated against the company's business needs, some employees fear reprisal for speaking out, and the higher-level corporate office ultimately makes important decisions unilaterally. Moreover, the councils have helped management prevent unionization by providing information about employee dissatisfaction and by socializing workers to focus their voice into the councils rather than a union. At the same time, employees are able to have a voice in decision making that is not completely powerless. The joint industrial councils receive more information than many unions, the district councils provide the means for workers from multiple work sites to share information and work together, and the threat of unionization provides an incentive for management to ensure that the workers see tangible gains from the councils. Interestingly, in some respects the workers have a greater voice than if they were unionized because of the broad issues that are tackled by the joint industrial councils—issues that are typically considered management rights and therefore not relinquished in collective bargaining.

THE *ELECTROMATION* CONTROVERSY

The employee representation plans at Delta Airlines and Imperial Oil would violate the NLRA's section 8(a)(2) ban on company-dominated labor organizations. As U.S. companies have sought to create quality circles and other mechanisms for discussing workplace issues, this ban has become sharply debated. In essence, U.S. business argues that section 8(a)(2) prevents legitimate efforts to increase competitiveness and quality through employee involvement.[79] As an example, review the labor law discussion case in Box 11.14 before reading further. The ruling that has received the greatest attention is the National Labor Relations Board (NLRB)'s 1992 *Electromation* decision.[80] Electromation, a small manufacturing company, established several committees with a handful of employees and two managers to discuss working conditions and policies. These committees were formed to better understand the employees' concerns and to improve the company's policies when feasible—there is no evidence that these committees were established because of a union organizing drive. The NLRB ruled that these committees were labor organizations under the NLRA because they dealt with management—there was some type of bilateral exchange between workers and managers regarding wages, hours, or other terms and conditions of employment. Moreover, the NLRB ruled that these committees were dominated labor organizations—and thus in violation of section 8(a)(2)—because management controlled their structure (such as how many employees would serve and how they would be selected), the issues, and their continued existence. In other words, "when the impetus behind the formation of an organization of employees emanates from an employer and the organization

---

[77] Taras, "Contemporary Experience with the Rockefeller Plan," p. 240.

[78] Taras, "Contemporary Experience with the Rockefeller Plan."

[79] Potter and Youngman, *Keeping America Competitive.*

[80] *Electromation, Inc. and International Brotherhood of Teamsters, Local Union No. 1049, AFL–CIO,* 309 NLRB 990 (1992), enforced 35 F.3d 1148 (7th Cir. 1994). Robert S. Moberly, "The Story of *Electromation*: Are Employee Participation Programs a Competitive Necessity or a Wolf in Sheep's Clothing?" in Laura J. Cooper and Catherine L. Fisk (eds.), *Labor Law Stories* (New York: Foundation Press, 2005), pp. 315–51.

Background

Tratelemonioc is a manufacturer of electrical components located in Elkhart, Indiana, and employs approximately 200 employees. None of the employees are represented by a union. The company was experiencing severe financial losses and decided that changes were needed to keep the company viable. To reduce costs, the company decided not to give a wage increase for the year, but instead paid employees a lump-sum bonus which depended on length of service. Additionally, the existing employee attendance bonus policy was dropped. In early January, 68 employees signed a petition expressing dissatisfaction with the new attendance policy. In response, the company decided to meet directly with the employees.

On January 11, the company met with a group of eight randomly chosen employees and discussed a wide range of issues, including wages, bonuses, incentive pay, attendance programs, and the leave policy. After this meeting, the company president concluded

> it was very unlikely that further unilateral management action to resolve the problems was going to come anywhere near making everybody happy . . . and we thought the best course of action would be to involve the employees in coming up with solutions to these issues.

The company decided that the employees' concerns could be divided into five categories (absenteeism/infractions, no smoking policy, communications, pay progression for premium positions, attendance bonus program). Thus, the company's management decided to form five "Issues Committees" to involve the employees in trying to resolve these problems.

A week later, the eight employees were informed of the proposal to create five Issues Committees of six employees and two managers each. The employees were told by the company president that the committees would meet to try to find solutions to problems and that if the company believed the solutions "were within budget concerns and they generally felt would be acceptable to the employees, that we would implement these suggestions or proposals." It was agreed that the Issues Committee employees would not be chosen at random. After the meeting, management drafted the goals and responsibilities of the committees.

On January 19, Tratelemonioc sent a memo to each employee announcing the formation of five Issues Committees. Also, sign-up sheets were posted for each committee. The sign-up sheets contained the goals and responsibilities of each committee. The company determined the number of employees who were allowed to sign up for the committees and restricted several employees to only serve on one committee. From the sign up sheets management was to select the members of the committee, although this proved to be unnecessary.

Tratelemonioc's Employee Benefits Manager, Elaine Nixon, served as coordinator of the committees, was the discussion facilitator in the committee meetings, and was "in charge of the Issues Committee program." The Issues Committees began weekly meetings in late January in a company conference room with the employees being paid for their time and with supplies being provided by the company. The employees were informed that they were expected to "kind of talk back and forth" with the other employees in the plant to get their ideas.

On February 13, International Brotherhood of Teamsters, Chauffeurs, Warehousemen and Helpers of America Local 1049 requested that Tratelemonioc recognize them as the authorized bargaining agent of the employees. There is no evidence that the company was aware of the Teamsters organizing drive. Subsequently, Nixon informed each Issues Committee that management could no longer participate, but that the employees could keep meeting if they wanted. Three committees decided to keep meeting on company premises and on company time. The Attendance Bonus Committee devised a proposed solution which was rejected by the company's controller because it was too expensive. Subsequently, the employees met again and drafted a second proposal. The company controller accepted this proposal, but it was never presented to the company president because of the union organizing drive.

On March 15, the company president informed employees that because of the Teamsters organizing drive, the company "would be unable to participate in the committee meetings and could not continue to work with the committees until after the election." A representation election was scheduled for March 31.

Questions

1. Do the Issues Committees constitute a labor organization?
2. Assuming that the Issues Committees are a labor organization, do they violate the NLRA?
3. If Tratelemonioc violated the NLRA, what is the appropriate remedy?
4. If Tratelemonioc violated the NLRA, does this ruling mean that labor law needs to be reformed to allow for employee participation plans?

has no effective existence independent of the employer's active involvement, a finding of domination is appropriate."[81]

Because of the apparent innocent or legitimate motivation of the company—to improve employee relations and competitiveness, not bust a union—the *Electromation* ruling created a large uproar among business. Consider another scenario:

> An employer wants to try to accommodate working parents by allowing more flexible scheduling. However, the employer does not know which employees want a more flexible schedule or how to make a series of flexible schedules fit the organization's daily work requirements. A committee of employees and managers is formed and charged to discuss the matter with coworkers and develop a new scheduling plan. The committee eventually produces a plan that the employer considers and implements with some modifications.[82]

This committee would likely be illegal because of the company union ban of the NLRA. However, survey evidence indicates that employees want a voice in the workplace.[83] Thus, the Teamwork for Employees and Managers (TEAM) Act was introduced in Congress in 1995 to modify section 8(a)(2) to explicitly exclude labor–management committees that do not seek to negotiate collective bargaining agreements (see Box 11.15). The **TEAM Act** was passed by Congress, but vetoed by President Clinton in 1996.

Opposition to the TEAM Act—and by extension, support for the strong 8(a)(2) ban on even loosely defined company unions—emphasizes the ability to manipulate nonunion employee representation plans.[84] In contrast to the view that some voice is better than none, labor advocates argue that only freely selected and independent employee representatives—that is, labor unions—have the power and legitimacy to make collective voice meaningful.[85] As noted in *Electromation,* one important danger is that a representation plan looks like a bilateral mechanism to the employees—they perceive a legitimate back-and-forth exchange between labor and management—and thus the employees feel there is no need for a union. But a finding of a company-dominated labor organization implies that there is not a truly bilateral mechanism—the formation, structure, nature, and continued existence of the plan is controlled unilaterally by management. Managers can mollify the workers by occasionally giving the representation plan a "victory" without truly granting the employees any power. In other words, labor law can be viewed as a truth-in-advertising requirement that seeks to prevent employee representation plans that look like unions, but really are quite different. A closely related concern is the potential for management to convey subtle and not-so-subtle antiunion messages in quality circles and other representation plans.[86]

NLRB rulings in other 8(a)(2) cases illustrate these concerns. In *du Pont* (1993), the NLRB ruled that the employer illegally established and dominated some labor–management committees covering workers that were already represented by a union.[87] In one instance,

---

[81] *Electromation,* p. 996.

[82] Michael H. LeRoy, "Employee Participation in the New Millennium: Redefining a Labor Organization Under Section 8(a)(2) of the NLRA," *Southern California Law Review* 72 (September 1999), pp. 1651–723 at 1657.

[83] Richard B. Freeman and Joel Rogers, *What Workers Want* (Ithaca, NY: ILR Press, 1999).

[84] Jonathan P. Hiatt and Laurence E. Gold, "Employer–Employee Committees: A Union Perspective," in Bruce E. Kaufman and Daphne Gottlieb Taras (eds.), *Nonunion Employee Representation: History, Contemporary Practice, and Policy,* Chapter 28.

[85] Patricia A. Greenfield and Robert J. Pleasure, "Representatives of Their Own Choosing: Finding Workers' Voice in the Legitimacy and Power of Their Unions," in Bruce E. Kaufman and Morris M. Kleiner (eds.), *Employee Representation: Alternatives and Future Directions* (Madison, WI: Industrial Relations Research Association, 1993), Chapter 5.

[86] Guillermo J. Grenier, *Inhuman Relations: Quality Circles and Anti-Unionism in American Industry* (Philadelphia: Temple University Press, 1988).

[87] *E.I. du Pont and Co.,* 311 NLRB 893 (1993).

An ACT

To amend the National Labor Relations Act to allow labor management cooperative efforts that improve economic competitiveness in the United States to continue to thrive, and for other purposes.

Section 1. Short Title

This Act may be cited as the "Teamwork for Employees and Managers Act of 1995."

Section 2. Findings and Purposes
a. FINDINGS—Congress finds that—

1. the escalating demands of global competition have compelled an increasing number of employers in the United States to make dramatic changes in workplace and employer–employee relationships;

2. such changes involve an enhanced role for the employee in workplace decisionmaking, often referred to as 'Employee Involvement,' which has taken many forms, including self-managed work teams, quality-of-worklife, quality circles, and joint labor–management committees;

3. Employee Involvement programs, which operate successfully in both unionized and nonunionized settings, have been established by over 80 percent of the largest employers in the United States and exist in an estimated 30,000 workplaces;

4. in addition to enhancing the productivity and competitiveness of businesses in the United States, Employee Involvement programs have had a positive impact on the lives of such employees, better enabling them to reach their potential in the workforce;

5. recognizing that foreign competitors have successfully utilized Employee Involvement techniques, the Congress has consistently joined business, labor and academic leaders in encouraging and recognizing successful Employee Involvement programs in the workplace through such incentives as the Malcolm Baldrige National Quality Award;

6. employers who have instituted legitimate Employee Involvement programs have not done so to interfere with the collective bargaining rights guaranteed by the labor laws, as was the case in the 1930's when employers established deceptive sham 'company unions' to avoid unionization; and

7. Employee Involvement is currently threatened by legal interpretations of the prohibition against employer-dominated "company unions."

b. PURPOSES—The purpose of this Act is—

1. to protect legitimate Employee Involvement programs against governmental interference;

2. to preserve existing protections against deceptive, coercive employer practices; and

3. to allow legitimate Employee Involvement programs, in which workers may discuss issues involving terms and conditions of employment, to continue to evolve and proliferate.

Section 3. Employer Exception

Section 8(a)(2) of the National Labor Relations Act is amended by striking the semicolon and inserting the following: "Provided further, That it shall not constitute or be evidence of an unfair labor practice under this paragraph for an employer to establish, assist, maintain, or participate in any organization or entity of any kind, in which employees who participate to at least the same extent practicable as representatives of management participate, to address matters of mutual interest, including, but not limited to, issues of quality, productivity, efficiency, and safety and health, and which does not have, claim, or seek authority to be the exclusive bargaining representative of the employees or to negotiate or enter into collective bargaining agreements with the employer or to amend existing collective bargaining agreements between the employer and any labor organization, except that in a case in which a labor organization is the representative of such employees as provided in section 9(a), this proviso shall not apply;"

Section 4. Limitation on Effect of Act

Nothing in this Act shall affect employee rights and responsibilities contained in provisions other than section 8(a)(2) of the National Labor Relations Act, as amended.

Notes: The TEAM Act (as H.R. 743) was passed by the House of Representatives on September 27, 1995 (221–202). On July 10, 1996, the Senate passed this bill (as S. 295) 53–46. On July 30, 1996, President Clinton vetoed the TEAM Act saying "this legislation, rather than promoting genuine teamwork, would undermine the system of collective bargaining that has served this country so well for many decades" and "rather than encouraging true workplace cooperation, this bill would abolish protections that ensure independent and democratic representation in the workplace." Nancy Kassebaum (R–Kan.), who sponsored S. 295, charged President Clinton with "buckling to pressure from the AFL–CIO during an election year."

a welder complained of poor ventilation. The union was unable to win improvements, so the welder took his complaint to the labor–management committee which was able to obtain a new welding shop. In another instance, the union unsuccessfully tried to obtain recreational facilities through bargaining, but then the labor–management committee was able to create such facilities. Occurrences such as these can be used to manipulate employee loyalty and undermine the legitimacy of the union. Box 11.16 presents another NLRB decision that is revealing. Read the first part of the case in Box 11.16. The plant council at Webcor seems like a legitimate employer initiative to enhance employee input and participation in a nonunion setting. But now look at the second part of the case—during the subsequent union organizing drive, the company explicitly put forward the plant council as an equivalent alternative to unionization. But the plant council has no independent authority. The danger of this situation is that employees choose the plant council and then once the union threat is removed, the plant council is weakened, or entirely disbanded—remember, management ultimately has complete control over the plant council.

At the same time, other NLRB rulings further reveal some of the distinctions between legal and illegal employee involvement and representation plans. First, remember that one concern of labor law is the illusion of a true bilateral, give-and-take relationship between labor and management. Thus, plans which are obviously one way are legal. Brainstorming sessions in which employees provide ideas to management or information-sharing sessions in which employers share information with employees are legal.[88] In these situations, there is no give and take; or, in the legal language of section 2(5), there is no "dealing with" in these situations. At the other end of the spectrum, plans in which employees have final decision-making authority also do not "deal with" management. Self-directed work teams are legal because workers have legitimate decision-making authority.[89] Similarly, committees that can issue final rulings on grievances are also legal.[90]

Second, recall that the NLRA focuses on concerted—that is, group—activity. Employee involvement plans in which employees speak for themselves as individuals, not as representatives of their co-workers, do not violate U.S. labor law.[91] Third, the NLRA also focuses on wages, hours, and terms and conditions of employment. Nonunion plans that are primarily concerned with business issues such as quality and productivity are therefore outside of the domain of the NLRA and are legal.[92] The Employee Involvement Steering Committee in Box 11.16 was found to be legal on this basis. Lastly, section 8(a)(2) bans management domination, not involvement. Plans in which the employees have some control over structure and function are acceptable.[93] In other words, labor law allows employee involvement and representation over wages and working conditions when employees have sufficient power. But the NLRA seeks to prevent false empowerment (see Box 11.17).

In trying to prevent this false empowerment, there are many who argue that the NLRA is too restrictive.[94] In this view, there are legitimate initiatives that serve both employee and employer interests that are unnecessarily restricted. The TEAM Act described above is the most concrete example of a reform proposal in this vein. However, it's important to remember that the main concern of the NLRA in terms of section 8(a)(2) is the potential for management to prevent unionization. Therefore, many commentators favor a broader set of reforms that include both a weakening of section 8(a)(2)—as in the TEAM Act—and

[88] *Sears, Roebuck and Co.,* 274 NLRB 230 (1985). *du Pont.*

[89] *Crown Cork and Seal,* 334 NLRB No. 92 (2001). *General Foods,* 231 NLRB 1232 (1977).

[90] *John Ascuaga's Nugget,* 210 NLRB 275 (1977). *Mercy Memorial Hospital,* 231 NLRB 1108 (1977).

[91] *du Pont.*

[92] *Webcor Packaging Inc. and Local 332, International Brotherhood of Teamsters, AFL and Local 332, International Brotherhood of Teamsters, AFL–CIO,* 319 NLRB No. 142 (1995).

[93] *Chicago Rawhide Mfg. Co. v. NLRB,* 221 F.2d 165 (7th Cir. 1955).

[94] LeRoy, "Employee Participation in the New Millennium."

Background

On February 13 employees at Webcor Packaging's corrugated box plant in Burton, Michigan, received a memo from the plant superintendent establishing the Webcor Plant Council. As outlined in this memo, the Plant Council "will consist of five hourly employees who will be elected by the hourly work force" and three management employees and "will function as a policy development body . . . involved with the development of plant policies, the employee handbooks, the creation of a grievance procedure that will involve council member representation, and with the process of hourly compensation and benefits." The memo further stated that "all matters of plant policy, procedure, and compensation will be jointly reviewed prior to implementation by the Plant Council and management." The hourly employees were notified that an election would be held in a week and each employee was to vote for five of the hourly employees who would serve on the council for a year (unless promoted to management).

When the election was held on February 22, 18 of the 28 ballots were blank and 4 of the 5 people with the most votes refused to serve. Robert Sikorsky, vice president for operations and an owner of Webcor, then ordered that the Plant Council process be suspended. In early May a second vote was held. This time employees were asked to volunteer and employees voted for five of the volunteers. This election was successful in choosing five hourly employees for the Plant Council.

Sikorsky is a self-described employee involvement apostle. Before arriving at Webcor the previous year, Sikorsky had been a manager at a different box plant where he was convinced that employee involvement generated quality levels higher than at Webcor. He believes that "quality and low cost [can be achieved] by involving all the people in our operation . . . not checking their brains at the door, but thinking about and participating in how we are going to get better at what we do." Consequently, upon arrival at Webcor Sikorsky established an Employee Involvement Steering Committee composed of three hourly employees (chosen randomly from volunteers) and two managers. This committee was to focus on quality, waste reduction, housekeeping, and productivity.

The Employee Involvement Steering Committee began weekly meetings in January and employees submitted items for discussion. For example, overtime issues, being paid for lunch breaks, vacation pay, and reimbursement for safety shoes were brought up for discussion. Since these issues were not directly concerned

with quality or productivity, Sikorsky decided to create the Plant Council to handle policy issues.

After the successful Plant Council election in May, it began holding regular meetings. Webcor provided necessary supplies and paid members for their time. A different member of the council chaired each meeting and decisions were typically made by consensus. A suggestion box was created and placed in the plant for workers who were not on the council to submit concerns. After reaching agreement, policies of a "substantive nature" would be taken "very seriously" by management and approved or rejected. Policies dealing with "lesser issues" were implemented by the council.

Since its inception, the Plant Council has drafted policies regarding company purchase of employee tools and overtime equalization. In the latter case, the policy developed by the Plant Council specified that overtime would be allocated by first offering overtime hours to the employee in the relevant job category with the lowest amount of overtime, then offering the extra hours to the employee with the second lowest amount, etc., irrespective of seniority. Additionally, the council has reviewed parts of Webcor's attendance policy and proposed increasing the safety shoe reimbursement from one pair per year to two. In reviewing the attendance policy, the council circulated a proposed revision to all employees and asked them to respond with comments. The council also discussed whether employees should be granted paid bereavement leave after a grandparent's death. The tools, overtime equalization, and safety shoes policies were approved by management and implemented.

None of the employees at Webcor are represented by a union.

Questions

1. Does the Employee Involvement Steering Committee violate the NLRA? *Hint:* remember to consider both section 2(5) and section 8(a)(2).
2. Does the Plant Council violate the NLRA? *Hint:* remember to consider both section 2(5) and section 8(a)(2).

After Considering These Questions, Read On:

In late-January, some Webcor employees approached Local 332 of the International Brotherhood of Teamsters, Chauffeurs, Warehousemen, and Helpers of America about organizing the Webcor plant. A petition for a certification election was filed with the National Labor Relations Board (NLRB) on February 19 and an election was scheduled for April 18.

Continued

Continued

During March, Webcor management distributed the following campaign literature to the hourly employees (note: these exhibits contain actual statements, but are not exact replicas):

IF THE UNION WINS THE ELECTION

- All wages are subject to change.

- All benefits are subject to change.

- Policies, rules, etc. are subject to change.

There is NO guarantee that those items will be as good as they are now.

IF THE UNION LOSES THE ELECTION:

As we stated prior to this organizing drive, We, the owners of Webcor:
GUARANTEE:

- The Employee handbook will not be changed unless it is changed through the Employee Involvement/Plant Council Process.

Dear Valued Employee:

An NLRB election will be held on April 18 to determine whether you will be unionized by the Teamsters. You are a valuable employee and it is unnecessary to let a third party disrupt our relationship. There are many reasons why you should vote against the Teamsters. Reason No. 1 is our commitment to Employee Involvement. Reason No. 2 is the implementation of the Plant Council.

The choice you will make on election day is a simple one. Either you will choose to hire Teamsters #332 as the sole and exclusive agent. Or you will choose to continue a relationship with Webcor based on Employee Involvement.

Bob

The results of the April 18 NLRB election were:

Teamsters Local 332   14
No Union   21

Question

3. Do the organizing drive events change your answers to the previous questions?

---

changes that strengthen the ability of workers to organize a union—such as increased union access to employees, quicker representation elections, and steeper penalties for companies that illegally discharge union supporters.[95] Similarly, section 2(5) could be revised to more narrowly define "labor organization" as an independent worker group that seeks collective bargaining rights—again, paired with reforms to the certification procedures in the NLRA.[96] In this way it is felt that perhaps the best of both worlds can be achieved: nonunion employee representation can be used when it's what the employees truly desire, but cannot be used to undermine their efforts to form an independent labor union when that is what they prefer.

[95] Samuel Estreicher, "Labor Law Reform in a World of Competitive Product Markets," *Chicago-Kent Law Review* 69 (1993), pp. 3–46. Samuel Estreicher, "Employee Involvement and the 'Company Union' Prohibition: The Case for Partial Repeal of Section 8(a)(2) of the NLRA," *New York University Law Review* 69 (April 1994), pp. 125–61.

[96] Bruce E. Kaufman and Daphne Gottlieb Taras, "Nonunion Employee Representation: Findings and Conclusions," in Bruce E. Kaufman and Daphne Gottlieb Taras (eds.), *Nonunion Employee Representation: History, Contemporary Practice, and Policy* (Armonk, NY: M. E. Sharpe, 2000), Chapter 31.

BOX 11.17 **False Employee Empowerment as Illustrated by Dilbert**

DILBERT: © Scott Adams/Dist. by United Feature Syndicate, Inc.

There are therefore three major views of nonunion employee representation—good, bad, and better than nothing. Disputes over these views split the field of human resources and industrial relations in the 1930s and are again dividing the field in the 21st century.[97] As such, there are no easy answers. But returning to the framework presented in Part I of this book, the avenue to understanding these debates is twofold: (1) recognizing the divisions as competing visions for the delivery of efficiency, equity, and voice, and (2) recognizing that the roots of these competing visions lie in different beliefs over the nature of the employment relationship as captured by the human resource management and pluralist industrial relations schools of thought.

STRATEGIC IMPLEMENTATION

An organization that wants to increase its flexibility and its level of employee involvement faces the tough task of implementing and executing a new workplace strategy. This task is challenging in any organization and many of the issues are similar in both unionized and nonunion situations—communicating change, building competencies, establishing supportive policies and cultures, and providing incentives and leadership (see Box 11.18).[98] But at the same time, there are particular aspects of unionized employment relationships that make change efforts different—not *always* better or worse, easier or more difficult, but definitely different—when the employees are represented by a union. In particular, as emphasized in Part II, when employees are represented by a certified union, management has an obligation to bargain over wages, hours, and terms and conditions of employment. Recall further that effects bargaining requires companies to negotiate the effects of many managerial actions even if the actions themselves are business rather than employment issues that do not require bargaining. An organization therefore cannot unilaterally impose whatever changes it wants in a unionized setting—this is a critical difference with nonunion situations.[99] Additionally,

---

[97] Bruce E. Kaufman, "John R. Commons and the Wisconsin School on Industrial Relations Strategy and Policy," *Industrial and Labor Relations Review* 57 (October 2003), pp. 3–30.

[98] Jay A. Conger, Gretchen M. Spreitzer, and Edward E. Lawler III (eds.), *The Leader's Change Handbook: An Essential Guide to Setting Direction and Taking Action* (San Francisco: Jossey-Bass, 1999). John P. Kotter, *Leading Change* (Boston: Harvard Business School Press, 1996). Arthur A. Thompson and A. J. Strickland, *Strategic Management: Concepts and Cases,* 12th ed. (Boston: McGraw-Hill/Irwin, 2001).

[99] Kirk Blackard, *Managing Change in a Unionized Workplace: Countervailing Collaboration* (Westport, CT: Quorum Books, 2000).

1. Building an organization with the competencies, capabilities, and resource strengths to carry out strategy successfully.

2. Developing budgets to steer ample resources into those value chain activities critical to strategic success.

3. Establishing strategy-supportive policies and procedures.

4. Instituting best practices and pushing for continuous improvement in how value chain activities are performed.

5. Installing information, communication, e-commerce, and operating systems that enable company personnel to carry out their strategic roles successfully day in and day out.

6. Tying rewards and incentives to the achievement of performance objectives and good strategy execution.

7. Creating a strategy-supportive work environment and corporate culture.

8. Exerting the internal leadership needed to drive implementation forward and keep improving on how the strategy is being executed.

Questions

1. How do these tasks apply to the specific context of moving from a traditional scientific management work organization system to a flexible, team-based production system with high degrees of employee empowerment?

2. In a unionized environment, should these tasks be pursued by management alone or jointly with the union? What is the role of the collective bargaining process?

Source: Arthur A. Thompson and A. J. Strickland, *Strategic Management: Concepts and Cases,* 12th ed. (Boston: Mc-Graw-Hill/Irwin, 2001), p. 347.

the presence of a union introduces another institution into the change process. Relative to a nonunion setting, the presence of a union can either add another layer of resistance to change or provide opportunities for improving the quality of change.[100]

There are therefore three change strategies for managers in unionized situations: escape, force, or foster.[101] Escape means escaping from the company's bargaining obligation by relocating operations to a nonunion site—perhaps in another country—or by subcontracting work or by decertifying the union. Engaging in surface bargaining to prompt a strike, using permanent strike replacements to replace the striking union members, and winning a decertification election is an escape strategy—albeit one that violates U.S. labor law and that might be risky and costly for other reasons.[102] In a unionized situation, forcing change means to pressure the union and employees to accept changes—often wage and work rule concessions—through hard bargaining. This strategy might require taking a strike to convince the employees to accept concessions, but this is not a strike to break a union as in the escape strategy. Concession bargaining that was widespread in the 1980s and which has returned most visibly in the airline industry since September 11, 2001, is an example of a forcing change strategy.

Lastly, the fostering change strategy focuses on developing a new labor–management partnership based on a recognition of both labor and management goals and the opportunities

---

[100] Blackard, *Managing Change in a Unionized Workplace.*

[101] Richard E. Walton, Joel E. Cutcher-Gershenfeld, and Robert B. McKersie, *Strategic Negotiations: A Theory of Change in Labor–Management Relations* (Boston: Harvard Business School Press, 1994).

[102] Jonathan D. Rosenblum, *Copper Crucible: How the Arizona Miners Strike of 1983 Recast Labor–Management Relations in America,* 2nd ed. (Ithaca, NY: ILR Press, 1998). Rick Fantasia and Kim Voss, *Hard Work: Remaking the American Labor Movement* (Berkeley: University of California Press, 2004).

for mutual gain. The Saturn example discussed earlier in this chapter is an advanced and extensive example of a fostering strategy. A fostering change strategy involves the bargaining process, and often results in a set of trade-offs in which wage and work rule concessions are granted in return for gains for workers.[103] For example, job security provisions such as no layoff guarantees have been won by unions in return for agreeing to wage restraint (or cuts), reductions in job classifications, or significant weakening of existing work rules in many industries. But a successful fostering change strategy typically involves much more than negotiating changes at the bargaining table, and more than creating quality circles or self-directed work teams. In the terminology of the bargaining subprocesses from Chapter 8, a fostering change strategy requires not only distributive and integrative bargaining to change the specific terms and conditions of employment, but also attitudinal structuring to shape the climate of the labor–management relationship. In fact, an examination of labor relations in the airline industry indicates that to improve organizational performance, improving the quality of labor–management relationships is more important than changing structural factors such as reducing wages or adding labor representatives to a company's board of directors.[104]

A successful fostering change strategy requires that management takes the necessary steps to ensure that the union is a positive force rather than an additional source of resistance. A very significant labor union fear of efforts to increase flexibility and employee involvement is co-optation—that these changes will intentionally or unintentionally reduce the union to an irrelevant and powerless outsider.[105] The initial union reaction to proposed changes is therefore likely to be resistance. How can managers overcome this resistance to foster change? Common strategies for overcoming resistance to change are listed in Box 11.19.

Fostering change uses a combination of the first three strategies in Box 11.19. To be successful, unions should be provided with full information, be involved in training, and participate in designing and implementing changes. In other words, unions should be recognized as legitimate full partners by being fully incorporated into the decision-making process, and not relegated to junior partners by marginalizing their participation and influence—"if the union is a junior partner, it will generally become a high-profile partner in blame and silent partner in success."[106] Unions should be allowed to participate in the evaluation of ongoing efforts. In this way, unions will feel that by being involved in workplace change, "they are an extension of union advocacy, not sellouts."[107] Fulfilling these requirements often rests on a multipronged strategy that involves training, communication, formal and informal participation structures, interest-based bargaining, joint monitoring arrangements, pay-for-performance or other incentive programs, extensive information sharing, and ethical leadership by both corporate and union leaders.[108] These are significantly different behaviors than those that dominated the traditional New Deal industrial relations system, and reflect the pressures for flexibility and employee involvement in a global economy.

---

[103] Ozaki, *Negotiating Flexibility.*

[104] Jody Hoffer Gittell, Andrew von Nordenflycht, and Thomas A. Kochan, "Mutual Gains or Zero Sum? Labor Relations and Firm Performance in the Airline Industry," *Industrial and Labor Relations Review* 57 (January 2004), pp. 163–80.

[105] Edward Cohen-Rosenthal and Cynthia E. Burton, *Mutual Gains: A Guide to Union–Management Cooperation,* 2nd ed. (Ithaca, NY: ILR Press, 1993).

[106] Cohen-Rosenthal and Burton, *Mutual Gains,* p. 30.

[107] Cohen-Rosenthal and Burton, *Mutual Gains,* p. 30.

[108] Blackard, *Managing Change in a Unionized Workplace.* Cohen-Rosenthal and Burton, *Mutual Gains.* U.S. Department of Labor, *Working Together for Public Service.* Walton, Cutcher-Gershenfeld, and McKersie, *Strategic Negotiations.*

BOX 11.19   Dealing with Resistance to Change

Strategy	Used When Resistance Stems from . . .	Example	Advantages	Disadvantages
Education and Communication	. . . inaccurate or incomplete information about the change.	Make presentations about the proposed change.	People will be more cooperative after being persuaded.	Can be slow and cumbersome.
Participation and Involvement	. . . power to resist (such as those resisting having needed information or skills for the change to be effective).	Create a team to design and implement the change.	People will be more committed and can share their knowledge and skills.	Can be slow and cumbersome. Loss of control.
Facilitation and Support	. . . difficulties of adjusting to the change.	Provide training or counseling.	Effective for addressing adjustment problems.	Time-consuming and potentially expensive and ineffective.
Negotiation and Agreement	. . . being made worse off by the change.	Increase wages in return for implementing a change.	Can buy out resistance; also see education and participation.	Potentially expensive, especially if it sets a precedent.
Manipulation and Co-optation	. . . any source (but be careful!).	Superficially involve a popular leader in the change.	Quick and inexpensive.	Loss of cooperation if people feel manipulated.
Explicit and Implicit Coercion	. . . any source, and if the initiators have power (but be careful!).	Threaten with job loss or demotion.	Quick and effective (in the short run).	Sharpened resistance if people feel threatened and/or get angry.

Source: Adapted from John P. Kotter and Leonard A. Schlesinger, "Choosing Strategies for Change," *Harvard Business Review* 57 (March–April 1979), p. 106–14.

Key Terms

scientific management, *388*
job control unionism, *396*
quality of working life program, *401*
quality circle, *403*

high-performance work system, *404*
lean production, *404*
self-directed work team, *404*

employee representation plan, *409*
Electromation, 411
TEAM Act, *413*

Reflection Questions

1. Consider the four types of flexibility summarized in Box. 11.5. How do increases in each of these forms of flexibility promote or impair efficiency? equity? voice? Should these forms of flexibility be tempered to strike a balance between efficiency, equity, and voice? If so, how?

2. What are the major strengths of job control unionism? The major weaknesses? Has job control unionism outlived its usefulness?

3. Recall the pluralist industrial relations and unitarist human resource management schools of thought from Chapter 2. Assume that labor leaders adhere to the pluralist industrial relations school of thought and that management adheres to the human resource management school of thought. How does the contrast between these two schools help increase the understanding of management's emphasis on "cooperation" versus labor's

emphasis on "participation"? How do the two schools help increase the understanding of different perspectives on nonunion representation and the TEAM Act?

4. While not sharing its concern for psychological motivators and rewards, Frederick Winslow Taylor's views demonstrate the human resource management school's perspectives on employment relationship conflict and labor unions. Explain.

5. Is the TEAM Act a beneficial reform to U.S. labor law? Are there forms of nonunion employee representation that are good for employees? Bad for employees? How can the law distinguish between the two?

Internet Exploration

1. Explore the Kaiser Permanente labor–management partnership Web site at *http://www.lmpartnership.org*. How do the contracts differ from traditional union contracts? What other supports (skills, practices, training, and the like) are used to support this partnership arrangement?

2. President Clinton's Executive Order 12871 (October 1, 1993) required U.S. federal agencies to create labor–management partnerships and partnership councils. President Bush revoked this requirement in Executive Order 13203 (February 17, 2001), so federal agencies are allowed to create labor–management partnerships, but partnerships are not required. Search the Internet for materials on federal-sector labor–management partnerships. Putting aside political sympathies for either President Clinton or President Bush, is it better for these labor–management partnerships to be mandated or voluntary?

3. Find Web sites for area- or industry-focused labor–management councils (search for "labor–management councils"). What types of activities do these councils do? How do these activities support changing labor–management relationships for the 21st century?

Additional Reading

Bluestone, Barry, and Irving Bluestone, *Negotiating the Future: A Labor Perspective on American Business* (New York: Basic Books, 1992).

Head, Simon, *The New Ruthless Economy: Work and Power in the Digital Age* (New York: Oxford University Press, 2003).

Heckscher, Charles C., *The New Unionism: Employee Involvement in the Changing Corporation* (New York: Basic Books, 1988).

Kaufman, Bruce E., and Daphne Gottlieb Taras (eds.), *Nonunion Employee Representation: History, Contemporary Practice, and Policy* (Armonk, NY: M. E. Sharpe, 2000).

Levine, David I., *Reinventing the Workplace: How Business and Employees Can Both Win* (Washington, DC: Brookings, 1995).

Nissen, Bruce (ed.), *Unions and Workplace Reorganization* (Detroit: Wayne State University Press, 1997).

Ozaki, Muneto (ed.), *Negotiating Flexibility: The Role of the Social Partners and the State* (Geneva: International Labour Office, 1999).

U.S. Department of Labor, *Working Together for Public Service* (Washington, DC: Government Printing Office, 1996).

Chapter **Twelve**

Globalization

Advance Organizer

The New Deal industrial relations system developed when U.S. corporations dominated world markets and did not face significant international competition. But as trade barriers fall and capital mobility increases, the global economy becomes more integrated. Globalization therefore yields competitive pressures that are putting great strain on the New Deal industrial relations system and that raise questions about how to govern the global workplace.

Learning Objectives

By the end of the chapter, you should be able to:

1. **Discuss** the key elements of globalization and how they affect the employment relationship and labor relations.
2. **Outline** alternative arrangements for governing the global workplace and the implications of each for labor relations.

3. **Explain** various strategies for representing workers in a global economy.
4. **Understand** the labor relations challenges for managers in multinational companies.

Contents

Globalization. The term is frequently used—often negatively—but what does it mean? And what does it have to do with labor relations? In short, **globalization** is increased economic integration among countries, and it is one of the most important pressures on labor relations—and employment more generally—in the United States and around the world in the 21st century. Increasing foreign trade puts competitive pressures on, and opens up new opportunities for, companies and workers. Expanding multinational corporations undermine nationally focused labor unions and government regulations while also demanding new skills and knowledge for managers. Increasing capital mobility makes it easier to move jobs around the globe. In terms of the labor relations environment, increased globalization both decreases the demand for unskilled labor in the United States and makes labor easier to replace.[1] In other words, and in more technical terms, globalization makes labor

---

[1] Dani Rodrik, *Has Globalization Gone Too Far?* (Washington, DC: Institute for International Economics, 1997).

demand more elastic which, as was described in Chapters 3 and 8, reduces labor's bargaining power. U.S. unions are therefore struggling to preserve the legitimacy of collective bargaining in the face of the pressures of globalization. This has been a painful process in industries such as steel and textiles that have collapsed and reduced manufacturing communities in the Northeast and Midwest United States to a rustbelt.

Globalization also raises broader issues. Deepening economic integration brings increased social and political integration that threaten local cultures, standards, and ways of life. Options for foreign subsidiaries, outsourcing, joint ventures, and the like bring both opportunities and challenges for managers and labor leaders. These options are shaped by various international institutional arrangements such as the World Trade Organization (WTO), European Union, or the North American Free Trade Agreement (NAFTA)—and by the responses of organized labor and other groups that push for enforceable international labor standards, antisweatshop codes of conduct for corporations, and transnational collective bargaining. As each of these subjects are presented in more detail in this chapter, note how the institutional arrangements enhance or undermine the viability of traditional collective bargaining. Moreover, as a group these institutional arrangements also represent the range of alternatives for governing the global workplace to strike a balance between efficiency, equity, and voice. Understanding globalization—its components, debates, and institutions—is therefore important not only for labor relations, but also for broader employment, business, and social issues.

THE DEBATE OVER GLOBALIZATION

Globalization has four major dimensions: international trade, foreign direct investment, international investment portfolios, and immigration (see Box 12.1).[2] To varying degrees, all four dimensions have been linked in theory to employment opportunities, working conditions, living standards, income inequality, consumer choices, prices, life expectancy, child mortality, educational attainment, cultural diversity, endangered species and biodiversity, deforestation, pollution, crime, democracy, peace, and human rights.[3] In fact, increased globalization has been accused of both improving *and* worsening all of these critical elements of human life. Moreover, with the collapse of state-socialism and communism in the former Soviet Union and Eastern Europe by the early 1990s and with China trying to increase foreign investment and trade, it is important to note that capitalism, international investment, and multinational corporations have penetrated virtually every corner of the globe. In fact, the world can now be characterized as flat—because of information technology, "it is now possible for more people than ever to collaborate and compete in real time with more other people on more different kinds of work from more different corners of the planet and on a more equal footing than at any previous time in the history of the world"; as "the global competitive playing field [is] being leveled . . . the world [is] being flattened."[4] Globalization is therefore the subject of intense debates (see Box 12.2).

[2] Kenneth F. Scheve and Matthew J. Slaughter, *Globalization and the Perception of American Workers* (Washington, DC: Institute for International Economics, 2001).
[3] United Nations Development Programme, *Human Development Report 1999* (New York: Oxford University Press, 1999).
[4] Thomas L. Friedman, *The World Is Flat: A Brief History of the Twenty-first Century* (New York: Farrar, Straus, and Giroux, 2006), p. 8.

BOX 12.1
**The Dimensions
of Globalization**

Source: Kenneth F. Scheve,
and Matthew J. Slaughter,
*Globalization and the Percep-
tion of American Workers*
(Washington, DC: Institute for
International Economics, 2001).

International Trade	Cross-border flow of goods and services. Exports and imports.
Foreign Direct Investment (FDI)	Cross-border flow of multinational corporation investment. Purchasing or establishing foreign subsidiaries and joint ventures.
International Investment Portfolios	Cross-border flow of investment securities. Investing in foreign stocks and bonds (but no control over the foreign enterprise in contrast to FDI).
Immigration	Cross-border flow of people. Migrating from one country to another.

International Trade

The first dimension of globalization is international trade—the cross-border flow of goods and services: in other words, imports and exports. The value of world merchandise trade in 2004 was $8.9 trillion for goods and $2.1 trillion for services and is growing steadily.[5] In the United States, increased international trade is reflected in the fact that in 1960 slightly more than 10 percent of merchandise production was exported, but the fraction has now jumped to 40 percent. Moreover, U.S. imports amount to more than 12 percent of gross domestic product (GDP).[6]

The benefits of international trade are clearly revealed in textbook economic models as well as in Adam Smith's 1776 classic *The Wealth of Nations*.[7] In short, free trade across countries allows consumers and producers to benefit from specialization. If one country has a comparative advantage in producing one product, such as computer software because of an educated population, and another has a comparative advantage in something else, such as clothing, then both countries are better off by specializing in what they are best at and trading for the other goods. Scarce resources are used more efficiently, productivity is higher, and greater income is produced. Additional benefits from free trade arise from increasing the size of markets (so that companies can take advantage of increased economies of scale) and by reducing the monopoly power of domestic companies (so that domestic companies become more efficient). Countries benefit from increased growth and income while consumers enjoy lower prices and greater choices. Increased wealth can also be used to conserve the environment, promote public health, and improve education.

Detractors criticize the textbook economics model of free trade in at least four ways. One, there are winners and losers as an economy adjusts to increased free trade. Removing trade barriers that were protecting an inefficient industry will likely cause job losses in that industry. Increased trade also makes it easier for companies to effectively shift some of their production elsewhere by outsourcing—purchasing components from low-cost foreign suppliers rather than producing them in-house.[8] In the textbook model, these job losses are more than offset by increases in other sectors that benefit from trade, but in the real world, how are the losers compensated by the winners?[9] Two, there are also short-run

[5] World Trade Organization, *International Trade Statistics 2005* (Geneva, 2005).
[6] Douglas A. Irwin, *Free Trade Under Fire* (Princeton, NJ: Princeton University Press, 2002), pp. 5 and 8.
[7] Irwin, *Free Trade Under Fire*. Scott C. Bradford, Paul L. E. Grieco, and Gary Clyde Hufbauer, "The Payoff to America from Global Integration," in C. Fred Bergsten (ed.), *The United States and the World Economy: Foreign Economic Policy in the Next Decade* (Washington, DC: Institute for International Economics, 2005), pp. 65–109.
[8] Rodrik, *Has Globalization Gone Too Far?*
[9] Lori G. Kletzer and Howard Rosen, "Easing the Adjustment Burden on US Workers," in C. Fred Bergsten (ed.), *The United States and the World Economy: Foreign Economic Policy in the Next Decade* (Washington, DC: Institute for International Economics, 2005), pp. 313–41.

Globalization: The Good, the Bad, and the Unequal

Box 12.2

THE GOOD

Trade promotes increased economic growth and income through the more efficient use of scarce resources and opportunities for increasing returns to scale. Trade also lowers prices and increases choices through competition.

Foreign direct investment boosts technology, infrastructure, and productivity.

Foreign portfolio investment provides capital for entrepreneurs and financing for government debt.

Improving property rights, reducing subsidies, and increasing wealth can lead to practices that conserve the environment.

THE BAD

Low-cost competition from countries that violate labor rights causes domestic job losses and erosion of income and working conditions.

Foreign multinational companies exploit workers and the environment in poor countries that are desperate for any investment and income. Low income countries and families cannot afford to protect the environment.

Volatile flows of foreign portfolio investment destabilize fragile, developing country banking systems and economies.

Economic integration with concentrated economic power undermines democracy, national sovereignty, and indigenous cultures.

THE UNEQUAL

The richest 20 percent of the world's population enjoy 75 percent of the world's income; the poorest 20 percent, enjoy less than 2 percent. The income of the wealthiest 500 individuals exceeds the income of more than 400 million people. More than a billion people have to live on less than $1 a day. Roughly 40 percent of the world's population has to live on less than $2 a day.

The world's largest corporations are bigger than the economies of many countries. Corporations in developed countries receive 95 percent of the world's patent royalties.

Developed countries have policies to attract skilled immigrants while limiting unskilled immigrants. More than 115 million primary school-age children do not attend school, mostly in Africa and South Asia.

Child mortality rates in Sub-Saharan Africa are 29 times higher than in high-income developed countries; moreover, this gap has doubled since 1980.

Sources: Douglas A. Irwin, *Free Trade Under Fire* (Princeton, NJ: Princeton University Press, 2002). United Nations Development Programme, *Human Development Report 2005* (New York, 2005).

versus long-run concerns. For example, increased growth may increase pollution and environmental degradation in the short-run, but then improve these issues in the long-run as income increases further.[10] A similar pattern may be true for income inequality and working conditions.[11]

For both of these criticisms, it is important not to gloss over the human and social costs of job loss. With the decline of the U.S. steel industry, for example, single cities saw the

[10] Gene M. Grossman and Alan B. Krueger, "Economic Growth and the Environment," *Quarterly Journal of Economics* 110 (May 1995), pp. 353–77. Daniel C. Esty, "Bridging the Trade-Environment Divide," *Journal of Economic Perspectives* 15 (Summer 2001), pp. 113–30.

[11] Simon Kuznets, "Economic Growth and Income Inequality," *American Economic Review* 45 (March 1955), pp. 1–28.

disappearance of thousands of good-paying jobs and the resulting sharp increase in unemployment, small business failures, and crime. The loss of 40,000 manufacturing jobs in the Youngstown, Ohio, area triggered the closing of 400 local businesses, the loss of $414 million in personal income, and significant reductions in tax revenues for public schools (as much as 75 percent in some cases).[12] In terms of the personal costs, consider the recollection of one ex-steelworker in Homestead, Pennsylvania:

> When [the steel mill] shut down, and when guys did lose their jobs—people with fifteen, twenty, thirty years on the job—the psychological and social damage was a hundred times more than the economic. . . . Within four years of the place shutting down, I had eighty-one guys that I knew of personally—not just knew of, but knew personally—who died of strokes, cancer, heart attacks—including seven suicides—within a period of three-and-a-half years after the mill shut down. All under the age of sixty.[13]

Similar stories are repeated in other communities with the decline of autos, textiles, and other industries. Images of the decline of Flint, Michigan, in particular are starkly captured by the film *Roger and Me*.

The third criticism of the textbook model of free trade is that the emphasis on comparative advantage and factors of production overlooks the importance of corporate strategies, product quality and differentiation, industry structure, national culture, and other factors.[14] In other words, the usual focus on *comparative* advantage should instead be on *competitive* advantage. In this thinking, there can be a positive role of government policy beyond simply reducing trade barriers. Government policies can establish product standards, stimulate demand for early or sophisticated products, encourage the expansion of clusters such as Silicon Valley, foster new business formation, and establish national goals.[15]

Four, market imperfections can cause the benefits of international trade to be distributed unevenly. Recall the fundamental industrial relations assumption of unequal bargaining power between corporations and individual employees (especially those lacking savings, education, and a social safety net). Just as the United States struggled with the labor problem of worker exploitation in the early 20th century, developing countries are now struggling with similar labor problems in the early 21st century. With unequal bargaining power, the benefits of trade flow disproportionately towards shareholders while some employees are left with low wages, long hours, and dangerous working conditions.

This situation raises concerns with **social dumping.** In international trade, dumping is when a foreign competitor is able to unfairly sell at a lower price than domestic producers, where *unfairly* means because of a subsidy, not because of greater efficiencies. Social dumping occurs when a foreign competitor is able to unfairly sell at a lower price because of lower labor or environmental standards—for example, no minimum wage floors, lack of safety regulations, or absence of pollution standards. Note that in the *maquiladora* region along Mexico's border with the United States, the average wage in Mexico is $3.52 per hour; and that's high for low-wage countries—garment workers in the Dominican Republic

[12] Robert Bruno, *Steelworker Alley: How Class Works in Youngstown* (Ithaca, NY: Cornell University Press, 1999), p. 149.

[13] Steve Mellon, *After the Smoke Clears: Struggling to Get By in Rustbelt America* (Pittsburgh: University of Pittsburgh Press, 2002), pp. 14–15.

[14] Robert Gilpin, *The Challenge of Global Capitalism: The World Economy in the 21st Century* (Princeton, NJ: Princeton University Press, 2000). Michael E. Porter, *The Competitive Advantage of Nations* (New York: Free Press, 1990).

[15] Porter, *The Competitive Advantage of Nations*.

earn an average of 57¢ an hour.[16] Social dumping can be a problem if it undermines the tighter labor and environmental standards of the domestic country by making it difficult for companies to remain competitive while respecting these standards. As discussed below, labor and environmental groups in the United States and Europe therefore continue to push for fair trade rather than free trade, that is, the addition of labor and environmental standards for international trade.

Foreign Direct Investment

A second component of globalization is foreign direct investment (FDI) which consists of cross-border flows of investment by multinational corporations to establish partial or full ownership in foreign businesses. A multinational corporation's purchase of a foreign operation or opening of a factory in another country are examples of FDI. In 2004, global FDI exceeded $600 billion; 26 percent of this total was invested in China.[17] FDI can benefit countries by bringing jobs and new technology and therefore providing the base for economic development and growth. Foreign subsidiaries of multinational companies pay higher wages than local domestic companies and share in the profits of the multinational parent.[18] FDI has been instrumental in some developing country success stories such as Singapore and Malaysia.[19]

At the same time, FDI can be used to exploit workers with no alternatives, degrade the environment in the absence of protections or incentives, and threaten domestic workers with plant closings unless concessions are made. These problems are thought to be especially acute in export processing zones.[20] Export processing zones are special areas of developing countries dedicated to attracting and supporting multinational investment and production. Developing countries hope these zones create employment, bring in foreign exchange, and stimulate economic development. Export processing zones typically include explicit incentives such as duty-free importing and exporting, reduced taxes, and publicly provided infrastructure. Critics also believe that some areas include under-the-table inducements like lax enforcement of labor laws and government assistance in keeping out independent unions. An important example of an export processing zone is the *maquiladora* sector in Mexico along the U.S. border (see Box 12.3).

The experience of RCA television assembly production from the 1930s to the present illustrates organized labor's fears with export processing zones in particular, and FDI more generally. But this example also reinforces the fact that managerial strategies to find low-cost production strategies are not limited to the global context.[21] After a sometimes violent conflict, RCA workers successfully unionized their New Jersey radio set assembly plant in 1936. As a result, management decided to move the plant elsewhere, and in the 1940s much of the radio production was shifted to nonunion locations in Indiana with significantly

---

[16] Geri Smith, "The Decline of the *Maquiladora*," (*BusinessWeek,* April 29, 2002), p. 59. David Jessup and Michael E. Gordon, "Organizing in Export Processing Zones: The Bibong Experience in the Dominican Republic," in Michael E. Gordon and Lowell Turner (eds.), *Transnational Cooperation Among Labor Unions* (Ithaca, NY: ILR Press, 2000), Chapter 9.

[17] The World Bank, *World Development Indicators 2006* (Washington, DC, 2006).

[18] Brian Aitken, Ann Harrison, and Robert E. Lipsey "Wages and Foreign Ownership: A Comparative Study of Mexico, Venezuela, and the United States," *Journal of International Economics* 40 (May 1996), pp. 345–71. John W. Budd, Jozef Konings, and Matthew J. Slaughter, "International Rent Sharing in Multinational Firms," *Review of Economics and Statistics* 87 (February 2005), pp. 73–84.

[19] Joseph E. Stiglitz, *Globalization and Its Discontents* (New York: W. W. Norton, 2002).

[20] Michael E. Gordon, "Export Processing Zones," in Michael E. Gordon and Lowell Turner (eds.), *Transnational Cooperation Among Labor Unions* (Ithaca, NY: ILR Press, 2000), Chapter 4.

[21] Jefferson Cowie, *Capital Moves: RCA's Seventy-Year Quest for Cheap Labor* (Ithaca, NY: Cornell University Press, 1999).

The *maquiladora* program was started in 1965 as the Border Industrialization Program under which U.S. parts assembled in the northern part of Mexico along the border with the United States shipped back into the United States would be nearly duty or tariff-free. Mexican factories that assemble U.S. components for export to the United States are called *maquiladoras.* The program is no longer limited to the border region, but the term *maquiladoras* is popularly associated with factories close to the border in Tijuana, Nogales, Ciudad Juárez, Matamoros, and other cities.

With an explicit emphasis on assembly of premade parts, the early *maquilodora* workforce was largely young, single women doing simple assembly tasks and largely managed by American managers and engineers. A typical early example is apparel. However, assembly methods have now become more complex, the workforce is less dominated by women, and the managerial staffs include many more Mexican managers and engineers. Typical recent examples are now autos and electronics. Some *maquiladora* plants now use flexible, team-based production methods and some include sophisticated technology. Employee turnover is high and bonus systems are used to reduce absenteeism.

The *maquiladora* program started as a way to provide jobs to Mexican workers who were no longer allowed to work in the U.S. agricultural industry—and as a way for U.S. companies to take advantage of low labor costs—but has since been expanded into a major economic development strategy for Mexico. Because of the pressures to attract foreign investment for economic development, *maquiladoran* labor relations is controversial. In particular, critics assert that government control and suppression of unions is used to keep labor costs low at the expense of workers and their families. Unions appear to be weaker or more tightly controlled in the western areas than in the eastern ones. In the eastern area (bordering Texas), there is a stronger tradition of strong unions in the petroleum industry and unions in *maquiladoras* appear stronger. In this region, pay has been higher and workweeks shorter. In the western region, there is interunion conflict in Tijuana which undermines union power and yellow unionism (government-controlled unions) is frequent in Nogales. A yellow union might accept conditions lower than the minimums specified by law, and its presence can be used to keep out more aggressive unions.

As *maquilidoras* compete with U.S. factories and increasingly with Mexican factories as well, government control of wages and benefits affects workers throughout the United States and Mexico. But the *maquiladora* sector is also struggling with the pressures of globalization. The North American Free Trade Agreement (NAFTA) phased out the *maquiladoras'* duty-free status, wages have been rising, and corporate tax subsidies have been reduced. Consequently, production has been shifting out of Mexico to lower-cost countries. Since 2001, Sanyo moved some TV production to China and Indonesia, Canon moved ink-jet printer production to Vietnam, and others have moved to Guatemala.

Sources: Altha J. Cravey, *Women and Work in Mexico's Maquiladoras* (Lanham, MD: Rowman and Littlefield, 1998). Alfredo Hualde, "Industrial Relations in the Maquiladora Industry: Management's Search for Participation and Quality," in Maria Lorena Cook and Harry C. Katz (eds.), *Regional Integration and Industrial Relations in North America* (Ithaca, NY: Institute of Collective Bargaining, Cornell University, 1994), pp. 207–17. Kathryn Kopinak, *Desert Capitalism: Maquiladoras in North America's Western Industrial Corridor* (Tucson: University of Arizona Press, 1996). Geri Smith, "The Decline of the *Maquiladora*," (*BusinessWeek*, April 29, 2002), p. 59.

lower wages. The Indiana workers later unionized and production switched to televisions. After three strikes in the mid-1960s, management started shifting work first to Tennessee and then, after more labor conflict, to a *maquiladora* plant in Mexico.

After a decade of concessions, Indiana RCA workers rejected a 20 percent wage cut in 1998 and their plant closed. In all, 10,000 jobs eventually transferred to Mexico where wages in Mexico were perhaps 1/10th the level in the United States. This is U.S. labor's fear of FDI: loss of jobs and downward pressure on the remaining jobs. Economists argue that free trade creates better jobs to make up for these lost jobs.[22] But more Americans than not believe that globalization destroys jobs and lowers wages.[23] Moreover, the textbook

[22] Irwin, *Free Trade Under Fire.*
[23] Scheve and Slaughter, *Globalization and the Perception of American Workers.*

Boeing works with over 15,000 suppliers in more than 80 countries, such as . . .	
Tail Sections and Miscellaneous Components	China
Aircraft Doors	France
Cabin Lighting	Germany
Landing Gear	Japan
Wing Tips	Korea
Engineering	Russia, Spain

Source: *www.boeing.com.*

story is that unskilled jobs will move to low-wage countries while skilled jobs are retained in the United States. But one business research company predicts that 3.3 million U.S. white-collar jobs will be lost to low wage countries by 2015.[24] Rather than rehiring skilled engineers and technicians from their post-September 11, 2001 layoffs, Boeing shifted some of these skilled jobs to Russia where engineers earn 1/7th the salary of U.S. engineers (see Box 12.4). Many technical jobs are being moved to India—including software programmers, computer engineers, and financial analysts. As further question marks about where the cycle ends, Mexico and India are no longer among the lowest-wage countries: production has been shifting out of Mexico to China, Vietnam, and other areas while China is increasingly bidding away customer service jobs from India.[25] The jobs that can now be done by anyone from anywhere in the world are seemingly limitless.[26] Even the saying of special intentions (requests by individuals for a priest to pray for a family member or friend) has been outsourced by the Catholic Church to India. Labor cost savings are undoubtedly an important consideration in the cycle of outsourcing and FDI, but it's also important not to oversimplify the complexities of globalization. Beyond the labor cost savings, companies invest in other countries for many reasons.[27] Investing in Chinese factories, for example, builds a positive corporate image in China and helps win contracts to sell products to Chinese businesses and the government.

International Investment Portfolios

International investment portfolios—cross-border flows of investment securities like stocks and bonds—are a third dimension of globalization. The magnitude of this activity is captured by the fact that foreign exchange markets handle $1.5 trillion of transactions *each day*, up from $10–20 billion in the 1970s.[28] International investment can be beneficial—it provides working capital for local companies and financing for foreign government operations. It allows improved risk-sharing across borders and allows investments to find their most productive uses.[29] But with an exceptionally short-term focus, international financial

[24] Pete Engardio et al., "Is Your Job Next?" *BusinessWeek* (February 3, 2003), pp. 50–60.
[25] Bruce Einhorn, "Move Over, India," *BusinessWeek* (August 11, 2003), pp. 42–43. Geri Smith, "Is the Magic Starting to Fade for Manufacturing in Mexico?" *BusinessWeek* (August 6, 2001). Pete Engardio, "The Future of Outsourcing," *BusinessWeek*, (January 30, 2006).
[26] Friedman, *The World Is Flat*.
[27] Mario F. Bognanno, Michael P. Keane, and Donghoon Yang, "The Influence of Wages and Industrial Relations Environments on the Production Location Decisions of U.S. Multinational Corporations," *Industrial and Labor Relations Review* 58 (January 2005), pp. 171–200.
[28] United Nations Development Programme, *Human Development Report 1999*, p. 25.
[29] Maurice Obstfeld, "The Global Capital Market: Benefactor or Menace?," *Journal of Economic Perspectives* 12 (Fall 1998), pp. 9–30.

transactions can be extremely volatile. During the East Asia crisis in 1997, international financial flows for Thailand went from inflows equal to 15 percent of its GDP to outflows equal to 20 percent in just one year.[30] This volatility greatly destabilizes fragile developing-country economies. In fact, real manufacturing wages during the growth period of the early 1990s in Indonesia, Korea, and Mexico grew between 5.6 and 7.6 percent per year; during the economic downturn that followed in the mid-1990s, real wages declined by between 5 and 25 percent per year.[31] In Turkey, the swing was from a real wage growth rate of 16 percent to a real wage decline of 25 percent annually. It's easy to imagine what this volatility does to employment, and to living standards. While financial capital is important in the global economy, institutional controls to provide stability, especially for developing countries with fragile banking systems, might be needed.[32]

Immigration

The fourth and final dimension of globalization is immigration, the cross-border flow of people. Upwards of 150 million people live outside of their country of birth.[33] Like the other dimensions of globalization, immigration can be beneficial. As FDI and international portfolio flows provide the opportunity for capital to seek its highest rate of return, immigration provides labor with the same opportunity. In other words, immigration provides an avenue for people to find a better life and escape persecution in a new country. By taking jobs that no one else wants or that no one else is qualified for, both unskilled and skilled immigrants can also benefit the destination country if labor demand exceeds supply. Immigrants can also bring new cultures, foods, and ideas.

But like the other dimensions of globalization, immigration is controversial because it also has disadvantages and can create winners and losers. In particular, most immigrants to the United States are low-skilled. This does not negatively affect most workers, but it does appear to provide additional competition for low-skilled workers, especially high school dropouts.[34] These workers therefore suffer from lower wages while their employers and consumers benefit from lower labor costs and prices. Because of language barriers, fears of reprisals, cultural differences, and other factors, immigrant workforces also bring challenges and opportunities for union organizing (recall Box 7.15).[35] A majority of Americans acknowledge the benefits that immigrants bring yet are in favor of restricting immigration because of fears—rightly or wrongly—of increased unemployment and lower wages.[36]

U.S. TRADE POLICY

Free trade has not always been the goal of U.S. economic policy, but debates over tariffs—taxes on imported goods—extend back to the American Revolution. Historically, tariffs were a critical source of government revenue. Before the federal income tax was created in

---

[30] United Nations Development Programme, *Human Development Report 1999,* p. 41.
[31] United Nations, *Trade and Development Report 2000* (New York, 2000), p. 64.
[32] Stiglitz, *Globalization and Its Discontents.*
[33] United Nations Development Programme, *Human Development Report,* p. 32.
[34] George J. Borjas, *Heaven's Door: Immigration Policy and the American Economy* (Princeton, NJ: Princeton University Press, 1999). Gordon H. Hanson, "Challenges for US Immigration Policy," in C. Fred Bergsten (ed.), *The United States and the World Economy: Foreign Economic Policy in the Next Decade* (Washington, DC: Institute for International Economics, 2005), pp. 343–72.
[35] Ruth Milkman (ed.), *Organizing Immigrants: The Challenge for Unions in Contemporary California* (Ithaca, NY: ILR Press, 2000). Immanuel Ness, *Immigrants, Unions, and the New U.S. Labor Market* (Philadelphia: Temple University Press, 2005).
[36] Scheve and Slaughter, *Globalization and the Perception of American Workers.*

BOX 12.5   Economic Integration Arrangements

	Reciprocal Trade Liberalization	Free Trade Within Area	Common External Tariffs	Free Capital and Labor Mobility Within Area	Common Monetary and Fiscal Policy	Examples
International Trading System	√					World Trade Organization
Free Trade Area	√	√				NAFTA
Customs Union	√	√	√			
Common Market	√	√	√	√		European Union
Economic Union	√	√	√	√	√	↓

Source: Adapted from Ali M. El-Agraa, *Economic Integration Worldwide* (New York: St. Martin's Press, 1997).

1913, the U.S. government received nearly half of its income from tariffs.[37] Tariffs were also used extensively to protect and promote the development of specific industries deemed important for economic development or the public interest. Tariffs are often ad valorem tariffs which means that the tariff rate is expressed as a percentage of the value of the imported item (similar to sales tax). With the passage of the Smoot-Hawley Tariff Act on the eve of the Great Depression in 1930, average U.S. tariff rates exceeded 50 percent.[38] During the Depression, the Wagner Act was intended to boost workers' purchasing power in the domestic arena (Chapter 5). At the same time, the Reciprocal Trade Agreements Act of 1934 sought to open up foreign markets to U.S. companies to further stimulate economic prosperity.[39]

The Reciprocal Trade Agreements Act authorized the President of the United States to negotiate tariff reductions with other countries on a product-by-product basis. The principle of reciprocity is essential: under this Act, U.S. trade policy was based on negotiating equal tariff reductions with other countries.[40] Around this time, the concept of most-favored nation status was also developed. Most-favored nation trade agreements are nondiscriminatory—a country agrees to extend the same tariff terms to all of its most-favored nation trading partners. The twin principles of reciprocity and most-favored nation provide the foundation for today's multilateral global trading system under the World Trade Organization (WTO). In other words, the WTO provides the framework for over 140 countries, including the United States, to negotiate reciprocal, nondiscriminatory trade agreements that reduce tariffs and other barriers to trade. This is a primary component of U.S. trade policy. The United States has also pursued more extensive arrangements with specific countries, most notably the North American Free Trade Agreement (NAFTA) with Canada and Mexico. Free trade agreements seek to remove all tariffs and trade barriers among the participating countries. Going even farther, the European Union is a free trade area that also includes free capital and labor mobility as well as common monetary and fiscal policies (see Box 12.5).

[37] Dana Frank, *Buy American: The Untold Story of Economic Nationalism* (Boston: Beacon Press, 1999), p. 16.
[38] Irwin, *Free Trade Under Fire.* John M. Rothgeb, *U.S. Trade Policy: Balancing Economic Dreams and Political Realities* (Washington, DC: CQ Press, 2001).
[39] Frank, *Buy American.*
[40] Rothgeb, *U.S. Trade Policy.*

THE WORLD TRADE ORGANIZATION

The dominant institution for reducing trade barriers and pursuing free trade on a global scale is the **World Trade Organization (WTO).** The WTO is an international organization of over 140 member countries that provides the forum for negotiating and enforcing global trade agreements. At the end of World War II, the philosophy of the U.S. Reciprocal Trade Agreements Act was expanded to a number of countries that agreed to the General Agreement on Tariffs and Trade (GATT). The GATT was an international agreement among signatory countries to reduce tariffs on specific products and was negotiated in several major rounds beginning with 23 countries in 1947 and ending with 109 countries in 1994.[41] The last agreement, the Uruguay round agreement, was so complex—it contained 22,000 pages and weighed 385 pounds—that a permanent organization was created to administer the GATT provisions and to handle future trade negotiations.[42] This organization is the WTO which came into existence on January 1, 1995, and is headquartered in Geneva, Switzerland.

The WTO promotes free trade through the reduction of trade barriers. The most obvious trade barrier is a tariff, but there are numerous others. Nontariff trade barriers include quotas (numerical restrictions on imported units), domestic subsidies (which make it more difficult for foreign firms to compete with a subsidized domestic firm), discriminatory government procurement policies (which also favor domestic producers), and regulations such as import licensing and product standards which can be manipulated to favor domestic companies. The WTO seeks to reduce all of these trade barriers. Additional factors that affect international trade, such as transportation costs, language barriers, and exchange rate risk, are beyond the scope of the WTO.

Recall that in 1930, average U.S. tariff rates exceeded 50 percent. Because of the GATT and now the WTO, average tariff levels on manufactured goods have fallen to less than 4 percent.[43] Moreover, quotas are illegal except in limited circumstances and regulations in the form of product standards must be supported by scientific evidence. Equal market access must be provided to all member countries (the most-favored nation principle), and domestic and foreign products must be treated equally (the national treatment principle).[44] Nevertheless, relative to pure free trade, the WTO system is incomplete. Some manufactured goods, such as textiles and clothing, continue to have quotas or high tariff levels. Outside of manufacturing, many trade barriers remain in agriculture and services. Outstanding issues persist with respect to the lack of uniformity of intellectual property rights and antitrust policies across countries. As a consequence, WTO members now negotiate continuously rather than during formal rounds as was the case under GATT.

One of the key ongoing controversies is the debate between free trade and fair trade. Free trade is the removal of all trade barriers. **Fair trade** is the incorporation of labor, environmental, pubic health, and other standards into trade agreements and the ability to impose trade sanctions on countries that violate these standards. This is labeled fair trade because it is believed that the addition of these social clauses to trade agreements can prevent social dumping and avoid a race to the bottom in terms of wages and working conditions.

---

[41] Irwin, *Free Trade Under Fire.*

[42] Gilpin, *The Challenge of Global Capitalism,* p. 101.

[43] Irwin, *Free Trade Under Fire.* Roger B. Porter, "Efficiency, Equity, and Legitimacy: The Global Trading System in the Twenty-First Century," in Roger B. Porter, Pierre Sauvé, Arvind Subramanian, and Americo Beviglia Zampetti (eds.), *Efficiency, Equity, and Legitimacy: The Multilateral Trading System at the Millennium* (Washington, DC: Brookings Institution Press, 2001), Chapter 1.

[44] Irwin, *Free Trade Under Fire.* Jeffrey J. Schott (ed.), *The WTO After Seattle* (Washington, DC: Institute for International Economics, 2000).

In other words, promoters of fair trade distinguish between legitimate and illegitimate (socially unacceptable) sources of comparative or competitive advantage.[45] An abundance of natural resources or differences in worker productivity are legitimate, but what about slavery? Should a country be able to enjoy a comparative advantage because it uses slaves? If not, this means an acceptance of the principle of fair trade. The debate then becomes what other practices are illegitimate: Child labor? Racial discrimination? Suppression of unions? Abuse of the environment? To date, most countries have opposed the inclusion of such standards in the WTO's free trade system and this heated issue boiled over in the form of the "Battle in Seattle" protests against the WTO during its third ministerial conference in 1999 (see Box 12.6).

Note, however, that the WTO system allows countries to establish standards that are "necessary to protect human, animal or plant life or health" or conserve "exhaustible natural resources" as long as such standards are not trade barriers. As an example, the United States established the requirement that all tuna be caught with nets that are safe for dolphins. Labor activists would like to see the United States and other countries refuse to import goods from a country that violates basic labor standards as well as environmental standards. Other countries, however, claim that such requirements are disguised trade barriers. The WTO has the authority to resolve trade disputes over these issues and a country found in violation must change its trade policy or pay damages. Refusal to do so can result in trade sanctions.

Those that emphasize the efficiency gains of free markets (recall the neoclassical economics school from Chapter 2), see free trade as optimal and therefore think national standards like dolphin-safe nets should be invalidated by the WTO as illegal as trade barriers.[46] For those that question the fairness of free markets (recall the industrial relations school from Chapter 2), fair trade with a set of basic standards for labor and the environment is desired. This can be achieved through a broader interpretation of the WTO allowance of standards that are "necessary to protect human, animal or plant life or health" but this has not yet happened on a widespread basis; rather, WTO rulings in trade disputes generally support free trade and the removal of national standards.[47] This is very important for labor relations because it means that the labor movement and other supporters of workers' rights have been unable to attach labor standards to trade on a global basis.

Alternatively then, labor standards can be pursued through the creation and enforcement of explicit international labor standards, increased enforcement of national laws, transnational employee representation or unionism, or voluntary corporate codes of conduct. These alternatives parallel the alternatives for governing the workplace discussed in Chapter 2. The current WTO structure is a free market mechanism for global workplace governance. Enforceable labor standards are analogous to using government regulation to govern the global workplace. Two options are discussed below: worldwide standards through the International Labor Organization (ILO) and increased compliance of existing national laws through the NAFTA side agreements. Using corporate codes of conduct to establish labor standards in the global arena is similar to relying on human resources policies to establish standards in the domestic

[45] Rodrik, *Has Globalization Gone Too Far?* Clyde W. Summers, "The Battle in Seattle: Free Trade, Labor Rights, and Societal Values," *University of Pennsylvania Journal of International Economic Law* 22 (Spring 2001), pp. 61–90.
[46] Irwin, *Free Trade Under Fire.* Drusilla K. Brown, "Labor Standards: Where Do They Belong on the International Trade Agenda?" *Journal of Economic Perspectives* 15 (Summer 2001), pp. 89–112.
[47] Salman Bal, "International Free Trade Agreements and Human Rights: Reinterpreting Article XX of the GATT," *Minnesota Journal of Global Trade* 10 (Winter 2001), pp. 62–108. Michael J. Trebilcock and Robert Howse, "Trade Policy and Labor Standards," *Minnesota Journal of Global Trade* 14 (Summer 2005), pp. 261–300. Lori Wallach and Michelle Sforza, *The WTO: Five Years of Reasons to Resist Corporate Globalization* (New York: Seven Stories Press, 2000).

As part of the World Trade Organization (WTO) framework, the trade ministers of each member country meet every two years. The third ministerial conference took place in 1999 in Seattle, Washington, and was accompanied by intense protests and demonstrations that received worldwide publicity. The biggest demonstrations occurred on the scheduled opening day of the ministerial meetings—November 30, 1999. An estimated 30,000 students, environmentalists, labor unionists, farmers, feminists, and other human rights activists marched in downtown Seattle and succeeded in delaying the start of the WTO meeting. Among the most memorable were 200 activists in turtle costumes symbolizing the endangered sea turtles that were the subject of an adverse WTO ruling that detractors see as promoting free trade at the expense of the environment.

While nearly all of the protesters were peaceful and nonviolent, trouble was caused by a few anarchists who broke some windows. Around the globe, television newscasts repeatedly broadcast a broken Starbucks window and a dumpster fire. Perhaps fearing the worst, police used tear gas, pepper spray, and rubber bullets to break up the protests, and numerous people were arrested. In contrast to standard media reports, many protesters prevented looting and the police often initiated aggressive tactics. The fire department was ordered to spray fire hoses on the crowds and refused. Over the next several days, the demonstrations gained momentum as many protested perceived civil rights violations by the police. A narrow media focus on limited violence and a small minority of aggressive protesters overshadowed the message of the peaceful protesters.

At the core of the protests was frustration with what protesters felt was the WTO's promotion of free trade without any consideration for the environment, labor rights, and human rights. A perceived lack of democracy and voice—for example, with many WTO decisions made behind closed doors by ministers focused solely on economic concerns—was also significant. Some wanted to stop trade while many others pushed for fair trade—trade with environmental, labor, and human rights standards and protections. The U.S. labor movement was very active in the protests, especially the International Longshore and Warehouse Workers (ILWU) and the United Steelworkers. At one rally, the ILWU president summed up many protesters' views:

And let us be clear. Let's not allow the free traders to paint us as isolationist anti-traders. We are for trade . . . When we say we demand fair trade policies, we mean we demand a world in which trade brings dignity and fair treatment to all workers, with its benefits shared fairly and equally, a world in which the interconnectedness of trade promotes peace and encourages healthy, environmentally sound, and sustainable development, a world that promotes economic justice, social justice, and environmental sanity. The free traders promote economic injustice, social injustice, and environmental insanity.

In contrast, inside the WTO meeting the goal of the WTO ministers was to start another round of global trade negotiations to further remove trade barriers, refine the WTO's dispute resolution system, and address other issues. After a couple of days, the WTO meeting collapsed in failure. While the protests disrupted the WTO meetings, and added to the tension, the collapse can ultimately be traced to disagreements among the WTO countries. Most visible are the divides between developed and developing countries. Reflecting the protests in the streets, the United States was pushing for greater incorporation of labor and environmental standards. Developing countries, however, view these initiatives as disguised protectionist trade barriers. Moreover, many countries—developed or developing—emphasize reducing trade barriers in sectors that they have an advantage. The United States wants to reduce barriers in financial services and agriculture but not textiles, European countries want to protect agriculture, and developing countries want to reduce trade barriers in textiles. As such, the Battle in Seattle occurred both on the streets and in the meeting halls. These battles reflect fundamental issues in a global economy, and disagreements are likely to continue to be sharp—between developing and developed countries, between individual countries, and between promoters of free trade and fair trade.

Sources: Jeffrey J. Schott (ed.), *The WTO After Seattle* (Washington, DC: Institute for International Economics, 2000). Clyde W. Summers, "The Battle in Seattle: Free Trade, Labor Rights, and Societal Values," *University of Pennsylvania Journal of International Economic Law* 22 (Spring 2001), pp. 61–90. Janet Thomas, *The Battle in Seattle: The Story Behind and Beyond the WTO Demonstrations* (Golden, CO: Fulcrum Publishing, 2000). The quote is from p. 142.

arena—in both cases, compliance is voluntary and relies on education and self-interest. Transnational employee representation is analogous to unionization and other forms of employee representation in the domestic context. Two alternatives are presented below: European Works Councils in the European Union and various attempts at transnational collective bargaining and labor solidarity. Because of the importance of globalization—for labor relations and business—each of these subjects are important in their own right. But the WTO, ILO core labor standards, NAFTA and its side agreement, the European Union and its European Works Councils, examples of transnational collective bargaining, and corporate codes of conduct should also be considered as a group as the alternatives for governing the global workplace.

THE INTERNATIONAL LABOR ORGANIZATION

The **International Labor Organization (ILO)** is a specialized agency of the United Nations focused on the promotion of social justice and internationally recognized human and labor rights. The ILO was created in 1919 as part of the peace settlement that ended World War I, and became the United Nations' first specialized agency at the end of World War II. With over 170 member countries, most countries now belong to the ILO. The ILO has a unique tripartite structure in that each country sends two government representatives plus a worker representative and an employer representative. The ILO is the undisputed chief international authority on labor standards, and its primary activity is adopting and then promoting conventions which specify minimum labor standards on particular issues. Nearly 200 conventions have been adopted to date. Technical assistance to help implement these standards is also provided.[48]

Against the backdrop of growing concern with labor issues and globalization, the ILO adopted the Declaration on Fundamental Principles and Rights at Work in 1998. This declaration establishes a set of **core labor standards:** freedom of association and collective bargaining, the abolition of forced labor, no discrimination in employment and pay, and the elimination of child labor which are all declared to be "fundamental to the rights of human beings at work" (recall Box 6.13). Proposals to add a social clause for labor issues to the WTO system of global trade are frequently based on this set of core labor standards.[49] Some would also add a living wage requirement, but the common definition of core labor standards does not include a wage standard.[50] Labor standards—core or otherwise—are not legally enforceable at this time, however. The ILO relies on publicity, diplomacy, and technical assistance, not legal or economic punishment, to encourage compliance with its labor standards.[51]

The WTO has the authority to issue rulings and trade sanctions while the ILO has expertise in establishing labor standards. Consequently, one way to establish enforceable global standards for labor issues is to marry the expertise of the ILO with the power of the

[48] Arturo Bronstein, "The Role of the International Labour Office in the Framing of National Labor Law," *Comparative Labor Law and Policy Journal* 26 (Spring 2005), pp. 339–69.

[49] Kimberly A. Elliott, "Getting Beyond No . . . ! Promoting Worker Rights and Trade," in Jeffrey J. Schott (ed.), *The WTO After Seattle* (Washington, DC: Institute for International Economics, 2000), Chapter 12. Robert Howse, "The World Trade Organization and the Protection of Workers' Rights," *Journal of Small and Emerging Business Law* 3 (Summer 1999), pp. 131–72. Summers, "The Battle in Seattle."

[50] Elissa Alben, "GATT and the Fair Wage: A Historical Perspective on the Labor–Trade Link," *Columbia Law Review* 101 (October 2001), pp. 1410–47. J. M. Spectar, "Pay Me Fairly, Kathie Lee! The WTO, the Right to a Living Wage, and a Proposed Protocol," *New York Law Journal of International and Comparative Law* 20 (2000), pp. 61–92.

[51] Daniel S. Ehrenberg, "From Intention to Action: An ILO–GATT/WTO Enforcement Regime for International Labor Rights," in Lance A. Compa and Stephen F. Diamond (eds.), *Human Rights, Labor Rights, and International Trade* (Philadelphia: University of Pennsylvania Press, 1996), Chapter 8.

WTO.[52] The addition of a social clause to global trade agreements mandating that countries adhere to the ILO's core labor standards would allow the WTO to impose trade sanctions on countries that violate these standards (as is currently the case for countries that establish illegal trade barriers such as tariffs). This type of trade–labor rights linkage, however, is very controversial.

In fact, demands for enforceable labor (and environmental) standards were at the root of the sometimes violent protests in the "Battle of Seattle" that accompanied the WTO meeting in 1999. At the same time, there was a (nonviolent) battle within the WTO meeting over a U.S. proposal to create a working group to study the issue of core labor standards. Developing countries (and free trade economists) see labor standards as protectionist trade measures (to protect U.S. jobs) in disguise. To promote their low-cost exports, developing countries strongly object to such standards. To promote efficiency, free trade economists similarly object to linking labor and environmental standards with trade. This is not a new debate, and will likely continue.[53]

With that said, some steps in the direction of creating enforceable labor standards have occurred. In 2006, the World Bank announced that companies that borrow money from its International Finance Corporation must agree to follow the ILO's core labor standards. But while enforceable labor standards are a possibility, they are not yet a reality on a comprehensive basis. Lastly, note that enforceable global labor standards–for example, proposals for WTO enforcement of ILO–established core labor standards—are essentially a government regulation model of governing the workplace (recall Chapter 2) on a global scale. A uniform set of rules and standards are established and violations can be punished. The debates over enforceable labor standards therefore parallel debates over the wisdom of government regulation, especially the difficulty of establishing laws that are universally applicable and the negative efficiency consequences of interfering in free markets.

NAFTA

With or without free trade agreements, the proximity of the United States, Canada, and Mexico has facilitated substantial trade between the countries, and Canada continues to be the largest trading partner of the United States. In the 1980s and before, the majority of exports from Canada and Mexico went to the United States.[54] To maintain access to the U.S. market and to attract foreign investment, Canada negotiated a free trade agreement with the United States in 1988 and Mexico initiated negotiations in 1990. The U.S. agreed to Mexico's initiative as a way to increase investment and sales opportunities for U.S. companies and to stem the tide of illegal immigrants and drugs from Mexico. Agreement by all three countries on the North American Free Trade Agreement (NAFTA) was reached in 1992. NAFTA eliminates tariff and nontariff trade barriers over a 10–15-year period, allows companies of any of the three countries to invest, sell services, and bid on government contracts in all three countries, and protects intellectual property rights. Also important are

[52] Ehrenberg, "From Intention to Action." Elliott, "Getting Beyond No . . . !" Howse, "The World Trade Organization and the Protection of Workers' Rights." Virginia A. Leary, "Workers' Rights and International Trade: The Social Clause (GATT, ILO, NAFTA, U.S. Laws)," in Jagdish Bhagwati and Robert E. Hudec (eds.), *Fair Trade and Harmonization: Prerequisites for Free Trade*? Volume 2: *Legal Analysis* (Cambridge: MIT Press, 1996), Chapter 4.
[53] Ehrenberg, "From Intention to Action." Elliott, "Getting Beyond No . . . !" Leary, "Workers' Rights and International Trade." Summers, "The Battle in Seattle." Andrew T. Guzman, "Global Governance and the WTO," *Harvard International Law Journal* 45 (Summer 2004), pp. 303–51.
[54] Rothgeb, *U.S. Trade Policy.* Sidney Weintraub, "The North American Free Trade Agreement," in Ali M. El-Agraa (ed.), *Economic Integration Worldwide* (New York: St. Martin's Press, 1997), Chapter 8.

detailed rules of origin which specify that products must contain a minimum amount of North American content—for example, 62.5 percent for automobiles—in order to be part of the North American free trade zone. Note, however, that there is an important asymmetry in NAFTA that is also common in other free trade arrangements (except the EU): companies are free to invest in all three NAFTA countries, but individuals are not free to work outside their home country. In other words, NAFTA provides for capital mobility but not labor mobility.

Before being ratified, NAFTA was a major issue during the 1992 U.S. presidential election campaign, and prior to the election Bill Clinton expressed support for NAFTA on the condition that labor and environmental safeguards be added to the agreement. This was meant to address labor's fears that low Mexican wages would undercut U.S. competitiveness, put downward pressure on U.S. wages and working conditions, and cause widespread plant closings—independent presidential candidate Ross Perot's "giant sucking sound" of jobs moving to Mexico. In other words, U.S. and Canadian labor unions were afraid of social dumping from Mexico. After winning the presidential election, the Clinton administration negotiated the NAFTA side agreements, the **North American Agreement on Labor Cooperation** (NAALC) and an environmental pact, to pursue labor and environmental issues.

The NAALC provides 11 guiding principles that the three countries commit to promote—including union activity, nondiscrimination, equal pay, minimum wages, and workplace safety—but these are not uniform standards and they are not enforced through trade sanctions (see Box 12.7). Rather, the explicit emphasis in the NAALC is on cooperation to promote compliance with existing domestic laws. No new laws are required nor are there restrictions on future laws. Article 2, for example, explicitly recognizes "the right of each [country] to establish its own domestic labor standards" (see Box 12.7); the NAALC's intent is to ensure that those domestic labor standards—whatever they may be—are enforced. Each country must establish a National Administrative Office (NAO) to collect information. If someone feels that a domestic labor law is not being enforced, they can file a complaint with that country's NAO. If the NAO feels a labor law violation has occurred, it can recommend that the relevant Secretaries of Labor consult with one another. There are also complex provisions for additional hearings and even arbitration with penalties if consultation fails to resolve certain complaints, but these provisions are full of limitations, restrictions, and provisos.[55] As such, the NAALC dispute resolutions procedures are best thought of as public consultation without significant enforcement powers.[56] Compliance is dependent on the "sunshine factor"—adverse publicity that stems from the public nature of the NAALC proceedings—or in other words, the "naming and shaming" of violators.[57]

Between 1994 and 2005, thirty-four submissions were filed with an NAO alleging a violation of domestic labor law.[58] Most complaints named multinational companies as the violators, but some alleged violations by one of the three governments as a public sector

---

[55] Roy J. Adams and Parbudyal Singh, "Early Experience with NAFTA's Labour Side Accord," *Comparative Labor Law Journal* 18 (Winter 1997), pp. 161–81. Mario F. Bognanno and Jiangfeng Lu, "NAFTA's Labor Side Agreement: Withering as an Effective Labor Law Enforcement and MNC Compliance Strategy?" in William N. Cooke (ed.), *Multinational Companies and Global Human Resource Strategies* (Westport, CT: Quorum Books, 2003), Chapter 18.

[56] Edward Mazey, "Grieving Through the NAALC and the Social Charter: A Comparative Analysis of Their Procedural Effectiveness," *Journal of International Law* 10 (Summer 2001), pp. 239–79.

[57] Bognanno and Lu, "NAFTA's Labor Side Agreement." George Tsogas, *Labor Regulation in a Global Economy* (Armonk, NY: M. E. Sharpe, 2001), p. 164.

[58] Bureau of International Labor Affairs, *Status of Submissions under the North American Agreement on Labor Cooperation* (Washington, DC: U.S. Department of Labor, 2006), available at *http://www.dol.gov/ ILAB/programs/nao/status.htm* [accessed July 12, 2006].

Excerpts from the North American Agreement on Labor Cooperation (1993):

Article 1: Objectives

The objectives of this Agreement are to:

1. improve working conditions and living standards in each Party's territory;

2. promote, to the maximum extent possible, the labor principles set out in Annex 1;

3. encourage cooperation to promote innovation and rising levels of productivity and quality;

4. encourage publication and exchange of information, data development and coordination, and joint studies to enhance mutually beneficial understanding of the laws and institutions governing labor in each Party's territory;

5. pursue cooperative labor-related activities on the basis of mutual benefit;

6. promote compliance with, and effective enforcement by each Party of, its labor law; and

7. foster transparency in the administration of labor law.

Article 2: Levels of Protection

Affirming full respect for each Party's constitution, and recognizing the right of each Party to establish its own domestic labor standards, and to adopt or modify accordingly its labor laws and regulations, each Party shall ensure that its labor laws and regulations provide for high labor standards, consistent with high quality and productivity workplaces, and shall continue to strive to improve those standards in that light.

Article 3: Government Enforcement Action

1. Each Party shall promote compliance with and effectively enforce its labor law through appropriate government action . . .

    . . .

Annex 1: Labor Principles

The following are guiding principles that the Parties are committed to promote, subject to each Party's domestic law, but do not establish common minimum standards for their domestic law. They indicate broad areas of concern where the Parties have developed, each in its own way, laws, regulations, procedures and practices that protect the rights and interests of their respective workforces.

1. **Freedom of association and protection of the right to organize**
The right of workers exercised freely and without impediment to establish and join organizations of their own choosing to further and defend their interests.

2. **The right to bargain collectively**
The protection of the right of organized workers to freely engage in collective bargaining on matters concerning the terms and conditions of employment.

3. **The right to strike**
The protection of the right of workers to strike in order to defend their collective interests.

4. **Prohibition of forced labor**
The prohibition and suppression of all forms of forced or compulsory labor, except for types of compulsory work generally considered acceptable by the Parties, such as compulsory military service, certain civic obligations, prison labor not for private purposes and work exacted in cases of emergency.

5. **Labor protections for children and young persons**
The establishment of restrictions on the employment of children and young persons that may vary taking into consideration relevant factors likely to jeopardize the full physical, mental and moral development of young persons, including schooling and safety requirements.

6. **Minimum employment standards**
The establishment of minimum employment standards, such as minimum wages and overtime pay, for wage earners, including those not covered by collective agreements.

7. **Elimination of employment discrimination**
Elimination of employment discrimination on such grounds as race, religion, age, sex or other grounds, subject to certain reasonable exceptions, such as, where applicable, *bona fide* occupational requirements or qualifications and established practices or rules governing retirement ages, and special measures of protection or assistance for particular groups designed to take into account the effects of discrimination.

8. **Equal pay for women and men**
Equal wages for women and men by applying the principle of equal pay for equal work in the same establishment.

Continued

9. **Prevention of occupational injuries and illnesses**
Prescribing and implementing standards to minimize the causes of occupational injuries and illnesses.

10. **Compensation in cases of occupational injuries and illnesses**
The establishment of a system providing benefits and compensation to workers or their dependents in cases of occupational injuries, accidents or

fatalities arising out of, linked with or occurring in the course of employment.

11. **Protection of migrant workers**
Providing migrant workers in a Party's territory with the same legal protection as the Party's nationals in respect of working conditions.

. . .

Note: The full text is available at *www.naalc.org*.

employer. The U.S. NAO received the most complaints (21), followed by Mexico (6), and Canada (5). Less than half reached the ministerial consultation stage and no submissions have advanced past this consultation stage. Evaluation of the NAALC cases fails to reveal a strong pattern of victories for organized labor and workers' rights advocates.[59] One success story appears to be a complaint about pre- and postemployment discrimination against pregnant women in Mexico's *maquiladora* sector (U.S. NAO case 9701). While preemployment discrimination against women is legal in Mexico, postemployment discrimination is not and as a result of the publicity generated by this NAALC case, the Mexican government has increased inspections and education on this issue. On the other hand, in cases involving freedom of association and collective bargaining, violations do not appear to have been remedied. Workers fired for union activity, for example, are not reinstated and independent unions in Mexico that challenge state- or company-dominated unions have yet to gain recognition. Instead, workshops and academic studies have been the frequent product of ministerial consultations (see Box 12.8). The number of complaints filed also appears to have declined, which suggests that labor unions and workers' rights organization do not feel that the process is effective.[60]

In spite of this poor track record, some remain optimistic that the NAALC can promote the 11 principles outlined in Box 12.7.[61] This optimism stems from at least three factors. One, the NAALC partners have been successful in educational activities and in increasing cross-border understanding. Perhaps this provides a foundation for greater protection of rights in the future. Two, the sunshine aspect of the NAALC procedures provides the opportunity to generate public concern with trade and labor issues. While the existing process does not work perfectly, it might be a starting point for building stronger public forums to examine trade–labor linkages. Three, the submission process also provides the opportunity for greater cross-border cooperation among unions. Perhaps more aggressive coordinated action can increase the effectiveness of the NAALC procedures. In any case, with both its pitfalls and potentials, the NAALC framework illustrates another alternative for trying to balance efficiency, equity, and voice in the global workplace. In fact, the United States has extended this NAALC model to bilateral and regional trade agreements negotiated after NAFTA, such as those with Jordan (2000), Chile (2003), Central America (2004), and

[59] Bognanno and Lu, "NAFTA's Labor Side Agreement." Clyde Summers, "NAFTA's Labor Side Agreement and International Labor Standards," *Journal of Small and Emerging Business Law* 3 (Summer 1999), pp. 173–87.
[60] Bognanno and Lu, "NAFTA's Labor Side Agreement."
[61] Adams and Singh, "Early Experience with NAFTA's Labour Side Accord." Tsogas, *Labor Regulation in a Global Economy*.

A Sony subsidiary in Mexico's *maquiladora* sector was the subject of an early case under the North American Agreement on Labor Cooperation (NAALC) which was added to NAFTA to facilitate enforcement of existing domestic labor laws. On paper, Mexican labor law is quite favorable to workers—much more favorable than U.S. labor law—but in reality, unions are frequently weak, state-controlled extensions of the government's economic development strategy. Such unions are often affiliated with the *Confederación de Trabajadores México* (CTM, Confederation of Mexican Workers) and are used to prevent the formation of more aggressive, independent unions.

At Sony, workers were frustrated with the CTM-affiliated union's acquiescence to management demands and they therefore tried to form their own independent union. The CTM union held a fraudulent election to prevent dissidents from winning any leadership positions and police broke up a resulting peaceful protest. The Mexican Conciliation and Arbitration Board (CAB) rejected a petition for a decertification election on a technicality. Dissident workers who were involved in the organizing drive were threatened and fired. By many accounts, Sony, the government-controlled CTM union, and the government's CAB conspired to prevent the formation of an independent union.

Within the NAALC procedures, two human rights organizations from Mexico and two from the United States filed a complaint with the U.S. National Administrative Office (NAO) alleging that these actions violated existing Mexican labor law (NAO Submission No. 940003, 1994). After a hearing, the NAO report found sufficient questions about the enforcement of Mexican law with respect to unjust dismissals and the union registration process in this case that it recommended ministerial consultations.

Subsequently, the U.S. Secretary of Labor and the Mexican Secretary of Labour consulted with each other and agreed to a program of workshops, seminars, and studies to improve understanding of the union registration procedures. Mexican government officials also agreed to meet with employees, Sony management, and local CAB officials to discuss the case. A follow-up report by the NAO six months later found that the discharged workers had not been reinstated and no election for the independent union had been held.

Sources: Clyde Summers, "NAFTA's Labor Side Agreement and International Labor Standards," *Journal of Small and Emerging Business Law* 3 (Summer 1999), pp. 173–87. George Tsogas, *Labor Regulation in a Global Economy* (Armonk, NY: M. E. Sharpe, 2001).

Australia (2005). In each of these, the signatory countries pledge to respect the core ILO labor standards through enforcement of their respective domestic labor laws; no changes to the existing labor laws are required, even if they appear inadequate.[62]

THE EUROPEAN UNION

Part of the rationale for creating a North American free trade zone through NAFTA was to counter the expanding European Union (EU).[63] The EU is an integrated community of 25 European nations that are progressing towards a true economic union. As such, the EU is more integrated than a simple free trade area like the one created by NAFTA (see Box 12.5). In fact, the EU includes common external tariffs, extensive capital mobility across the member countries, elements of common monetary and fiscal policies such as a common currency (the euro), and even attempts to coordinate foreign policies. Unlike free trade arrangements under the WTO and NAFTA, residents of the EU are allowed to freely work in any EU country. An additional five countries have applied for membership and the EU is working towards allowing them to join over the next 10 years (see Box 12.9).

[62] Stacie E. Martin, "Labor Obligations in the U.S.-Chile Free Trade Agreement," *Comparative Labor Law and Policy Journal* 25 (Winter 2004), pp. 201–26. Marisa Pagnattaro, "Leveling the Playing Field: Labor Provisions in CAFTA," *Fordham International Law Journal* 29 (January 2006), pp. 386–431.
[63] Weintraub, "The North American Free Trade Agreement."

BOX 12.9
The European Union

<u>1957</u>	<u>1981</u>	<u>2004</u>
Belgium	Greece	Cyprus
Germany		Czech Republic
France	<u>1986</u>	Estonia
Italy	Portugal	Hungary
Luxembourg	Spain	Latvia
The Netherlands		Lithuania
	<u>1995</u>	Malta
<u>1973</u>	Austria	Poland
Denmark	Finland	The Slovak Republic
Ireland	Sweden	Slovenia
United Kingdom		

Candidate Countries: Bulgaria, Croatia, Macedonia, Romania, Turkey

The primary objectives of European unification have been more political than economic in nature. In particular, the main driving force has been peace—World War II is only the most recent in a long series of destructive European wars and the goal of European integration is to prevent further wars.[64] As such, the foundations of the EU date back to the conclusion of World War II. The primary methods to achieve integration, however, have been economic in nature. One forerunner of today's EU is the European Coal and Steel Community that was created in 1951 by France, Germany, and four neighboring countries. By creating a common market for the coal, steel, and iron industries, no one country could gain an advantage in the production of war materials. From this beginning, economic integration has expanded to include all industries in a true single market that includes cross-border mobility of labor as well as capital, coordinated monetary policy, a common currency, and the addition of more countries.

Politically, the member countries have delegated authority to central EU-level institutions for handling issues of common interest.[65] The European Commission consists of representatives from the member countries and acts as an executive body and drafts legislation. The most powerful decision-making authority is the Council of the European Union, which includes each country's minister for the issue under discussion—for example, the Minister of Labor when considering employment issues or the Minster of Finance when considering monetary issues. Depending on the topic, the council consults or co-decides with the European Parliament that contains representatives elected directly by the citizens of the countries. These bodies can issue regulations (which are binding on member states), directives (which are binding, but each country can decide how to pursue the required results), recommendations (which are not binding, but national-level courts should use them for guidance), and opinions (which are also not binding). A Court of Justice fulfills the judicial functions for EU-level matters.

Noninflationary economic growth, not labor and social standards, is the explicit priority of the EU so economic concerns prevail over labor and social concerns in the EU (and also in the WTO and NAFTA). In other words, the EU has long embraced the "reasoning that the social caboose would be pulled by the economic locomotive."[66] Nevertheless, there has been concern with labor standards because of respect for basic human dignity and fears of

---

[64] Desmond Dinan, *Ever Closer Union: An Introduction to European Integration,* 2nd ed. (Boulder, CO: Lynne Rienner, 1999). Ali M. El-Agraa, *Economic Integration Worldwide* (New York: St. Martin's Press, 1997).

[65] Dinan, *Ever Closer Union.* El-Agraa, *Economic Integration Worldwide.*

[66] Roger Blanpain, *European Labour Law,* 6th ed. (The Hague: Kluwer, 1999), p. 91.

social dumping from member countries with lower standards and labor costs—such as Portugal—to countries with more generous standards and higher labor costs—such as Germany.[67] As a result, the Community Charter of Fundamental Social Rights of Workers (or "Social Charter") was adopted by the Council of the European Union in 1989.[68] This is a declaration of workers' rights that outlines desired standards pertaining to freedom of movement, fair remuneration, equal treatment for men and women, health and safety protections, working conditions, vocational training, freedom of association and collective bargaining (including the right to strike), and information, consultation and participation rights for workers. The Social Charter is in the process of being replaced by the Charter of Fundamental Rights which combines the workers' rights from the Social Charter with other civil, political, and economic rights. This is unlikely to result in substantive changes in the implementation of EU labor standards, but it will likely raise public awareness of these rights.

By itself the Social Charter is more of a moral or political document outlining aspirations than a legal document granting enforceable rights. But because the EU is more than simply a free trade zone, the EU-level political institutions can issue follow-up laws that enact specific sections of the Social Charter. A number of binding directives have been passed by the European Council of Ministers that obligate the EU member countries to achieve specific results.[69] For example, to implement the Social Charter's section on improving working conditions, a 1993 directive mandates a 48-hour maximum workweek. Regarding equal treatment of men and women, a 1992 directive specifies that pregnant women should receive at least 14 weeks leave that is paid equal to sick leave pay. Of particular interest to the subject of labor relations and employee representation is the 1994 directive "on the establishment of a European Works Council or a procedure in Community-scale undertakings and Community-scale groups of undertakings for the purposes of informing and consulting employees" (generally referred to as the "European Works Council directive").[70]

As discussed in the next chapter, a works council is a workplace-level committee of employees elected to represent all of the workers (except senior executives)—skilled and unskilled, blue and white collar, union members and nonmembers—in dealings with management. Works councils are legally distinct from unions and generally have three types of rights: (1) codetermination rights (that is, joint decision making with management) over some issues such as work rules or safety issues, (2) consultation rights over operational changes, and (3) rights to information about the company. While in practice union members are likely to be active in the works councils and unions help provide training and expertise, a works council's existence is mandated by law and does not depend on a local union presence. In various forms, works councils are found in many continental European countries.[71]

For companies with significant operations in at least two EU countries, a **European Works Council** is a transnational, company-level committee of employees from these different operations that has consultation and information rights, but not codetermination

[67] Christopher L. Erickson and Sarosh Kuruvilla, "Labor Costs and the Social Dumping Debate in the New European Union," *Industrial and Labor Relations Review* 48 (October 1994), pp. 27–47.

[68] John T. Addison and W. Stanley Siebert, "The Social Charter of the European Community: Evolution and Controversies," *Industrial and Labor Relations Review* 44 (July 1991), pp. 597–625. John T. Addison and W. Stanley Siebert, "Recent Developments in Social Policy in the New European Union," *Industrial and Labor Relations Review* 48 (October 1994), pp. 5–27. Mazey, "Grieving Through the NAALC and the Social Charter."

[69] Addison and Siebert, "Recent Developments in Social Policy in the New European Union."

[70] Janice R. Bellace, "The European Works Council Directive: Transnational Information and Consultation in the European Union," *Comparative Labor Law Journal* 18 (Spring 1997), pp. 325–61.

[71] Joel Rogers and Wolfgang Streeck (eds.), *Works Councils: Consultation, Representation, and Cooperation in Industrial Relations* (Chicago: University of Chicago Press, 1995).

rights, on issues that affect workers in more than one country. Because EU directives allow individual countries to determine implementation details, the European Works Council directive specifies minimum standards: councils must meet with management at least once a year, must be informed and consulted regarding the "progress of the business," and that

> The meeting shall relate in particular to the structure, economic and financial situation, the probable development of the business and of production and sales, the situation and probable trend of employment, investments, and substantial changes concerning organization, introduction of new working methods or production processes, transfers of production, mergers, cut-backs or closures of undertakings, establishments or important parts thereof, and collective redundancies (Annex 2).

A company's European Works Council can also request a meeting with management when there are exceptional circumstances, such as a plant closing. Expenses are paid by the company. Additional details such as the council's size, allocation of members, location and duration of meetings, and procedure for consultation are left up to individual companies and their employees. The requirements for what information must be provided and whether employee representatives are elected by the employees or appointed by elected union officials are determined by the national law of the country in which the company is headquartered.

The rationale for this directive is to enhance employees' rights to consultation and information as it pertains to their company and employment situation. Note carefully that this does not grant workers the right to bargain: specific terms and conditions of employment such as wages are not being negotiated by European Works Councils (though within each country, some workers might be represented in collective bargaining by national unions). Rather, a European Works Council provides employees with the opportunity to learn about their company's financial health and future plans (the information aspect) and to have a voice in providing feedback and ideas about these plans (the consultation aspect). These are viewed as important workers' rights, but the EU directive also states the belief that "harmonious" development of economic activities will be aided by informing and consulting with employees. Rather than creating a bargaining relationship, the European Works Council directive is intended to create a cooperative dialogue between labor and management.

In practice, European Works Councils can be divided into four categories: symbolic, service, project-oriented, and participative.[72] Symbolic European Works Councils are passive and fulfill the minimum requirements of the directive by a single annual meeting in which management provides limited information and the representatives do not make an effort to engage in a dialogue. A service European Works Council has a more active information flow but primarily services national unions by passing along the information received by the council. Activities are confined to information. Project-oriented European Works Councils build their own internal capabilities and pursue projects—such as a comparison of employment conditions across plants in the company—beyond the scope of the required meetings with management. A participative European Works Council is the most advanced form and includes active consultation and perhaps joint projects with management.

While symbolic European Works Councils contribute little towards employee representation, the other forms have greater potential. At BMW, the activities of the European Works Council have been modest, but they provided a mechanism for British and German union leaders to develop communication and trust which then was important when the British union leaders were engaged in traditional negotiations with BMW management.[73]

[72] Wolfgang Lecher, Hans-Wolfgang Platzer, Stefan Rüb, and Klaus-Peter Weiner, *European Works Councils: Developments, Types, and Networking* (Aldershot, Hampshire: Gower, 2001).
[73] Michael Whittall, "The BMW European Works Council: A Cause for European Industrial Relations Optimism?" *European Journal of Industrial Relations* 6 (March 2000), pp. 61–83.

The European Works Council at Nestlé is an example of a participative council. The works council and management established a consultation procedure for discussing plant closures and for implementing equal opportunity policies.[74] At Unilever, the European Works Council has actively pursued activities outside of the annual meeting with management. The top two officials meet monthly and this European Works Council has developed an information system to integrate information received by the European-level council and the workplace-level works councils in each country. A handbook of guidelines for corporate restructuring has also been developed and the European Works Council has been actively involved with management in implementing Unilever's restructuring initiatives.

A common thread with many success stories, however, is the presence of strong national unions. The BMW, Nestlé, and Unilever examples all include union leaders as council members. The General Motors European Works Council similarly has strong union participation and linkages (see Box 12.10). In contrast, McDonald's has been successful in marginalizing a union presence in its European Works Council, and in fact, a majority of the council members are salaried managers even though 90 percent of McDonald's employees are hourly workers, and the council is therefore merely symbolic.[75] With a lack of strong codetermination rights (in contrast with the traditional works councils discussed in the next chapter) and absence of union strength and expertise, management can keep European Works Councils symbolic.[76] European Works Councils are an intriguing option for representing employee interests in a global economy, but the exact route to make them effective remains an open question.

TRANSNATIONAL COLLECTIVE BARGAINING

With increased globalization and increased multinational corporate activity, labor unions are under pressure to collaborate across international borders.[77] This transnational collaboration ranges from simple messages of solidarity to sympathy strikes, from sharing of information to conducting coordinated lobbying or public pressure campaigns, from helping establish unions in developing countries to coordinated collective bargaining. The global initiatives of corporations are facilitated by free trade arrangements such as the WTO and NAFTA, but—with the limited exception of the European Works Council directive—international activities by labor unions are not. In fact, laws restricting sympathy strikes, secondary boycotts, and affiliations of labor unions with international federations all hamper transnational collaboration.[78] The one exception is European Works Councils which unions can use to develop networks and alliances with other unions (see Box 12.10).[79] Otherwise, unions cannot rely on international treaties or public policies to facilitate transnational collaboration, and the labor movement has instead created its own institutions for international solidarity.

[74] Lecher, Platzer, Rüb, and Weiner, *European Works Councils.*

[75] Tony Royle, "Where's the Beef? McDonald's and Its European Works Council," *European Journal of Industrial Relations* 5 (November 1999), pp. 327–47.

[76] Wolfgang Streeck, "Neither European nor Works Councils: A Reply to Paul Knutsen," *Economic and Industrial Democracy* 18 (May 1997), pp. 325–37. Jane Wills, "Great Expectations: Three Years in the Life of a European Works Council," *European Journal of Industrial Relations* 6 (March 2000), pp. 85–107.

[77] Michael E. Gordon and Lowell Turner, "Going Global," in Michael E. Gordon and Lowell Turner (eds.), *Transnational Cooperation Among Labor Unions* (Ithaca, NY: ILR Press, 2000), Chapter 1.

[78] Jean-Michel Servais, "Labor Law and Cross-Border Cooperation Among Unions," in Michael E. Gordon and Lowell Turner (eds.), *Transnational Cooperation Among Labor Unions* (Ithaca, NY: ILR Press, 2000), Chapter 3.

[79] Bob Hancké, "European Works Councils and Industrial Restructuring in the European Motor Industry," *European Journal of Industrial Relations* 6 (March 2000), pp. 39–59.

The European Works Council and Union Solidarity at General Motors Europe   Box 12.10

In December 2000, General Motors (GM) Europe told its European Works Council that it planned to cut 6,000 jobs in Europe over the next two years. Hardest hit was to be a Vauxhall plant outside of London. This announcement was controversial for a couple of reasons. First, GM's commitment to consult with its European Works Council was questioned because these cuts were announced to the works council and the media simultaneously. In fact, because Britain was just beginning to adhere to European Union labor directives such as the European Works Council directive, Vauxhall workers were not included in the GM European Works Council and learned of the job cuts through the media. Second, the Vauxhall cuts seemed to violate an earlier job security agreement that included loans from the British government.

The European Works Council therefore initiated a European Action Day to protest GM's actions. This day of protest occurred on January 25, 2001 with more than 40,000 workers participating, including

7,000 in Belgium, 16,000 in Germany, 11,000 in Great Britain, 1,000 in Portugal, and 5,000 in Spain. While the national and local unions were instrumental in leading these demonstrations, the GM European Works Council organized the action because the council includes representatives from all of the countries (except Britain).

As a result, GM agreed to negotiate a framework agreement with the European Works Council. This framework agreement specified important principles to guide GM's restructuring. National unions were involved in administering this agreement in each country and in making sure the principles were followed. The European Works Council was not able to stop GM's restructuring and the job cuts, but it was able to make sure that employee voices were heard during the implementation of the restructuring plan.

Source: *www.igmetall.de/nachrichten/betriebe/general_motors/ablauf_engl.html* (accessed July 30, 2002).

The apex of international labor organizations is the **International Trade Union Confederation** (ITUC).[80] The ITUC is a worldwide federation of national union federations. National union federations such as the AFL–CIO (U.S.), Trades Union Congress (Great Britain), *Deutscher Gewerkschaftsbund* (DGB, German Federation of Trade Unions), and over 300 others from more than 150 countries representing 166 million union members from around the world are members of the ITUC. The ITUC resulted from the 2006 merger of two longstanding federations, the western-oriented International Confederation of Free Trade Unions and the leftist World Federation of Trade Unions, to try to strengthen international union solidarity and have more influence in the global socio-political-economic system.

The ITUC's main objectives are to facilitate consultation, communication, and cooperation among unions. To pursue these objectives, the ITUC collects and publishes information and research to keep unions abreast of developments in other countries. The ITUC also provides education and training to union leaders, and financial assistance for emerging labor movements. In the international arena, the ITUC is an important advocate for organized labor, especially when lobbying transnational organizations such as the World Trade Organization. The ITUC is also pushing for multinational corporations to adopt codes of conduct that respect basic workers' rights (discussed in the next section).

---

[80] Michael E. Gordon, "The International Confederation of Free Trade Unions: Bread, Freedom, and Peace," in Michael E. Gordon and Lowell Turner (eds.), *Transnational Cooperation Among Labor Unions* (Ithaca, NY: ILR Press, 2000), Chapter 5.

The ITUC cooperates closely with 10 global union federations (formerly known somewhat confusingly as "international trade secretariats"). Global union federations are "international associations of national trade unions representing workers in specific industries, industry groups, occupations, professions, or other sectors of employment such as the public services."[81] For example, the International Metalworkers' Federation (IMF) is an umbrella organization for over 200 unions, with nearly 25 million members, from various metalworking industries (such as iron and steel, automobiles, and electrical products) in over 100 countries. The International Transport Workers' Federation (ITF) is comprised of unions from over 140 countries that represent workers in various transportation industries such as railroads, trucking, airlines, shipping, and longshoring. While these are international federations like the ITUC, the global union federations are composed of national unions, not national union federations (see Box 12.11). The global union federations promote transnational collaboration through information exchange, publicity, education, and various

BOX 12.11
The Structure of the International Labor Movement

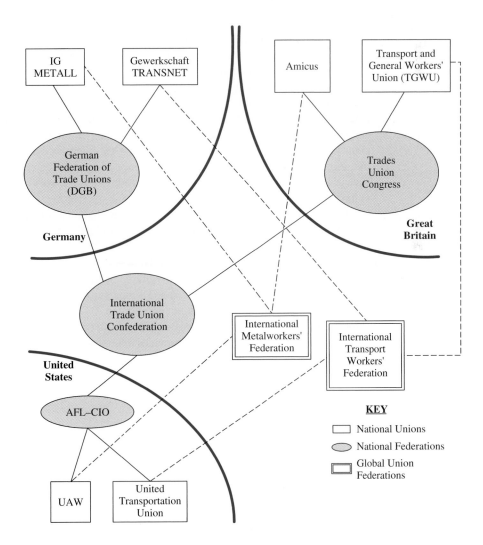

[81] John P. Windmuller, "The International Trade Secretariats," in Michael E. Gordon and Lowell Turner (eds.), *Transnational Cooperation Among Labor Unions* (Ithaca, NY: ILR Press, 2000), Chapter 6 at p. 102.

solidarity actions. The IMF, for example, has established a number of company councils that bring together union leaders from the operations of one company such as General Motors or General Electric from around the world. While these company councils have not directly engaged in collective bargaining, they can be important sources of information and support.

There are significant barriers to transnational labor collaboration—language barriers, cultural, religious, and ideological differences, fears of losing domestic autonomy, legal constraints, differences in union structures and goals, and employer resistance.[82] Moreover, true transnational collective bargaining—in which unions in more than one country negotiate jointly with the same company—is exceptionally rare.[83] U.S. and Canadian Chrysler workers were covered by a single UAW contract in the 1970s, but the U.S. and Canadian situations were very similar, so one can question whether this is truly international. Some transnational collective bargaining occurs in flag-of-convenience shipping—shipping companies who are granted flags from developing countries for a small fee. Without a real attachment to these countries, these companies are effectively unregulated by national laws. The ITF has negotiated roughly 150 contracts with shipping companies that have been able to dodge national unions. These agreements, however, must be enforced by national unions at their local ports—for example, by refusing to unload a ship if it does not demonstrate compliance with the negotiated standards for wages and hours.[84] While not true transnational collective bargaining, global union federations are being increasingly successful in getting multinational corporations to agree to sign international framework agreements in which the corporations pledge to respect workers' rights such as the right to organize labor unions and to safe workplaces. Some of the agreements go further—for example, the food industry global union federation negotiated framework agreements with the French food company Danone and banana giant Chiquita that specify standards pertaining to union access to corporate information, training, and other items. The implementation of framework agreements is left to unions in each country.[85] But if unions have little leverage, these framework agreements are reduced to voluntary corporate codes of conduct (discussed in the next section).

Unions are also increasingly trying to pursue international solidarity in support of bargaining disputes in one country. The ITF was actively involved in supporting an acrimonious dockworkers strike in Australia in 1998 (see Box 12.12). The ITF World Council of UPS Unions was also active in promoting international labor solidarity during the U.S. UPS strike in 1997 (see Box 12.13). During a United Mine Workers of America coal strike, unions in Australia, Colombia, and South Africa conducted 24-hour sympathy strikes at mines and factories owned by the same multinational parent corporation.[86] The United Electrical, Radio, and Machine Workers of America has a strategic alliance with the Mexican union *Frente Autentico del Trabajo* (Authentic Labor Front) that provides mutual support, especially in trying to organize

[82] Gordon and Turner, "Going Global."

[83] Burton Bendiner, *International Labour Affairs: The World Trade Unions and the Multinational Companies* (Oxford: Clarendon Press, 1987).

[84] Clifford B. Donn and G. Phelan, "Australian Maritime Unions and Flag of Convenience Vessels," *Journal of Industrial Relations* 33 (September 1991), pp. 329–39. Sigrid Koch-Baumgarten, "Trade Union Regime Formation Under the Conditions of Globalization in the Transport Sector: Attempts at Transnational Trade Union Regulation of Flag-of-Convenience Shipping," *International Review of Social History* 43 (December 1998), pp. 369–402. Nathan Lillie, "Global Collective Bargaining on Flag of Convenience Shipping," *British Journal of Industrial Relations* 42 (March 2004), pp. 47–67.

[85] International Confederation of Free Trade Unions, *A Trade Union Guide to Globalization* (Brussels, 2001). Lone Riisgaard, "International Framework Agreements: A New Model for Securing Workers Rights?" *Industrial Relations* 44 (October 2005), pp. 707–37.

[86] Kenneth S. Zinn, "Solidarity Across Borders: The UMWA's Corporate Campaign Against Peabody and Hanson PLC," in Michael E. Gordon and Lowell Turner (eds.), *Transnational Cooperation Among Labor Unions* (Ithaca, NY: ILR Press, 2000), Chapter 11.

Unionized dockworkers in Australia are represented by the Maritime Union of Australia (MUA), which is affiliated at the national level with the Australian Council of Trade Unions and at the international level with the International Transport Workers' Federation (ITF). In a surprise move in April 1998, one of the two dominant companies, Patrick Stevedores, fired all 1,400 of its MUA–represented dockworkers and brought in nonunion dockworkers in an outsourcing scheme to rid itself of the MUA. It is clear that the Australian government was complicit in this scheme and it quickly loaned the company $250 million to cover the required severance payments. The government had also been involved in an earlier attempt to train soldiers as dockworkers to be used as replacements.

The ITF announced that workers worldwide would refuse to unload ships that originated from the docks where the MUA was locked out. Unionized longshoring workers in the United States, Japan, and elsewhere demonstrated in support of the Australian unions and pledged to support the ITF's statement by refusing to unload disputed ships. Demonstrations were held outside Australian embassies in Japan, Korea, India, the Philippines, and Russia. The ITF was even sued (unsuccessfully) by Patrick Stevedores in English court (the ITF is headquartered in London) to try to prevent it from coordinating international solidarity in support of the MUA workers.

In May, the *Columbus Canada* arrived in Los Angeles from the disputed docks in Australia. The unionized U.S. dockworkers refused to unload the cargo, and after two weeks, the ship returned to Australia with its cargo. Ships were also reportedly turned away in India and Japan. After adverse legal rulings, and likely because of these displays of ITF–led international solidarity, Patrick Stevedores settled with the MUA in September 1998. The MUA agreed to concessions and workforce reductions (with severance packages) but was not broken by Patrick Stevedores (and the Australian government).

Source: International Confederation of Free Trade Unions, *A Trade Union Guide to Globalization* (Brussels, 2001).

unions in companies that operate in both countries.[87] The extent to which such efforts either develop into true transnational bargaining or suffice by themselves to provide domestic unions with sufficient leverage to confront the pressures of globalization remains to be seen.

CORPORATE CODES OF CONDUCT

A **corporate code of conduct** is a written statement of standards that a company voluntarily pledges to follow in its business activities. The codes can be created by transnational governmental organizations (such as the ILO) or by national and local governments, but are more frequently established by labor unions and other allied organizations or by individual corporations on their own. There is broad diversity in the content of different codes, but often they specify fair business practices, labor standards, environmental concerns, corporate citizenship and ethics, and respect for relevant laws.[88] In terms of labor practices, the common concerns are child labor, discrimination, and health and safety.[89] Freedom of association (to form unions) and collective bargaining are included less frequently. Since these codes are always voluntary, compliance cannot be legally enforced.

[87] Robin Alexander and Peter Gilmore, "A Strategic Organizing Alliance Across Borders," in Ray M. Tillman and Michael S. Cummings (eds.), *The Transformation of U.S. Unions: Voices, Visions, and Strategies from the Grassroots.* (Boulder, CO: Lynne Rienner Publishers, 1999), Chapter 14.

[88] Bob Hepple, "A Race to the Top? International Investment Guidelines and Corporate Codes of Conduct," *Comparative Labor Law and Policy Journal* 20 (Spring 1999), pp. 347–63.

[89] Tsogas, *Labor Regulation in a Global Economy.*

The Teamsters strike against UPS in 1997 has been widely cited as an example of how organized labor can be successful by mobilizing greater rank and file participation and by emphasizing issues that resonate with the public—in this case, the plight of part-time workers. However, the UPS strike also involved significant actions of international labor solidarity by UPS unions in other countries. Before the strike, the International Transport Workers' Federation (ITF) created the ITF World Council of UPS Unions which included representatives from the United States, Belgium, Brazil, Canada, France, Germany, Ireland, Italy, the Netherlands, Spain, and the United Kingdom. This council provided a forum for members to share information about UPS business strategies as well as working conditions, including common concerns with part-time workers and lifting injuries.

The council subsequently led a UPS World Action Day in May 1997 that included actions at 150 locations around the world. Most actions were demonstrations or information distribution efforts, but half-day strikes occurred in Spain and Italy. In August, 185,000 U.S. UPS workers went on strike for 15 days. During the strike, British workers engaged in a sick-out (a "brown flu" because of the color of their uniforms), workers in Belgium struck to resolve outstanding health and safety issues, and demonstrations in Spain and the Philippines temporarily disrupted package deliveries. Workers in France, Germany, and the Netherlands voted to authorize sympathy strikes, but the U.S. strike ended before the sympathy strikes occurred. These actions also raised the public profile of issues pertaining to safety and part-time workers in many countries that furthered empowered workers in those countries to address those issues.

Source: Andrew Banks and John Russo, "The Development of International Campaign-Based Network Structures: A Case Study of the IBT and ITF World Council of UPS Unions," *Comparative Labor Law and Policy Journal* 20 (Summer 1999), pp. 543–68.

In 1977, the ILO issued a model corporate code of conduct, the ILO Tripartite Declaration of Principles Concerning Multinational Enterprises and Social Policy, which includes all of the ILO's core labor standards—freedom of association and collective bargaining, the abolition of forced labor, the elimination of child labor, and equal opportunity and pay—as well as providing information to employee representatives, refraining from threats to move production to prevent union organizing or influence collective bargaining, providing advance notice of layoffs, avoiding arbitrary dismissal policies, promoting job stability and income protection, and in developing countries, paying a living wage. Compliance is voluntary. In 2003, the United Nations Sub-Commission on the Promotion and Protection of Human Rights issued a set of corporate norms, rooted in human rights instruments, that declares that companies have an obligation to respect human rights, including providing a safe workplace, a living wage, and freedom of association to form unions and engage in collective bargaining.[90]

Private sector initiatives can be traced back to the antiapartheid Sullivan Principles in the 1970s and 1980s.[91] U.S. multinationals were pressured to follow these principles

[90] David Weissbrodt and Muria Kruger, "Norms on the Responsibilities of Transnational Corporations and Other Business Enterprises with Regard to Human Rights," *American Journal of International Law* 97 (October 2003), pp. 901–22.

[91] Mark B. Baker, "Tightening the Toothless Vise: Codes of Conduct and the American Multinational Enterprise," *Wisconsin International Law Journal* 20 (Winter 2001), pp. 89–142. Lance A. Compa and Tashia Hinchliffe Darricarrére, "Private Labor Rights Enforcement Through Corporate Codes of Conduct," in Lance A. Compa and Stephen F. Diamond (eds.), *Human Rights, Labor Rights, and International Trade* (Philadelphia: University of Pennsylvania Press, 1996), Chapter 9. Robert J. Liubicic, "Corporate Codes of Conduct and Product Labeling Schemes: The Limits and Possibilities of Promoting International Labor Rights Through Private Initiatives," *Law and Policy in International Business* 30 (Fall 1998), pp. 111–58.

by desegregating their South African workplaces and promoting advancement opportunities for black South Africans. Another effort in 1984 took the same approach to fighting discrimination against the Catholic minority in Northern Ireland, and more recent efforts have targeted Mexico's *maquiladora* sector and its substandard working, living, and environmental conditions.[92] In a joint development effort that included businesses, human rights groups, and, at least initially, organized labor, 12 apparel and footwear companies agreed to abide by a Workplace Code of Conduct for their overseas factories and contractors.[93] This code of conduct forbids forced labor, child labor, harassment or abuse, discrimination, dangerous working conditions, and excessive daily and weekly working hours. The code of conduct also states that the companies will respect rights of freedom of association and collective bargaining and will pay at least the legal minimum wage or prevailing wage. The code is monitored by the Fair Labor Association that includes the participating companies and various human rights groups. The monitoring system requires that employees be informed of the standards and provided with opportunities to report noncompliance. Accredited external monitors also conduct inspections. Companies that are in compliance can use a product label demonstrating their compliance. Spurred by an outpouring of student activism in the form of an antisweatshop movement by college students, over 190 colleges and universities require the producers of their licensed apparel to adhere to the Fair Labor Association standards.

Many individual companies have also established their own codes of conduct.[94] Reebok's code is one of the most extensive (see Box 12.14). Standards address nondiscrimination, working hours/overtime (including a 60-hour, six-day maximum workweek), no forced or child labor, fair wages and benefits (at least a legal minimum or prevailing wage), freedom of association and the right to bargain collectively, no harassment, and workplace safety and health. Reebok's corporate code of conduct also includes a nonretaliation policy that states "Factories must publicize and enforce a nonretaliation policy that permits factory workers to express their concerns about workplace conditions without fear of retribution or losing their jobs. Workers should be able to speak without fear directly to factory management or Reebok representatives." Reebok's code of conduct applies not only to its own operations, but also to contractors, subcontractors, suppliers, and other business partners. Reebok's code of conduct, however, should not be taken as representative of other companies' codes. Reebok has been involved in numerous human rights promotions, including sponsorship of a rock band tour promoting human rights and support for Amnesty International, and its code is more extensive than most—and many companies don't have a code at all.[95]

Corporate codes of conduct are therefore another strategy for addressing labor issues in a global economy. This strategy has been particularly prominent in the apparel and footwear industries in which brand-conscious retailers such as Reebok, Nike, Levi Strauss, Liz Claiborne, and Polo Ralph Lauren utilize extensive contractors, subcontractors, and suppliers in Indonesia, Thailand, China, Mexico, and other low-wage developing countries. With sufficient public and consumer pressure, these codes can address some of the worst abuses. Publicity may also foster increased government enforcement of existing

---

[92] Compa and Darricarrère, "Private Labor Rights Enforcement Through Corporate Codes of Conduct."

[93] Liubicic, "Corporate Codes of Conduct and Product Labeling Schemes." Tsogas, *Labor Regulation in a Global Economy.*

[94] Compa and Darricarrère, "Private Labor Rights Enforcement Through Corporate Codes of Conduct." Liubicic, "Corporate Codes of Conduct and Product Labeling Schemes." Tsogas, *Labor Regulation in a Global Economy.*

[95] Compa and Darricarrère, "Private Labor Rights Enforcement Through Corporate Codes of Conduct."

Human Rights for Reebok's Production Workers

Box 12.14

The following notice is translated into nearly 30 languages and posted in the factories that produce Reebok's products "Reebok International Ltd. has made a commitment to ensuring decent conditions for workers at factories that make our products by obligating factory management to respect the following standards:

I. Non-discrimination

Reebok will seek business partners who do not discriminate in hiring and employment practices, and who make decisions about hiring, salary, benefits, training opportunities, work assignments, advancement, discipline and termination solely on the basis of a person's ability to do the job.

II. Working Hours/Overtime

Workers shall not be required to work more than 60 hours per week, including overtime, except in extraordinary circumstances. In countries where the maximum workweek is less, that standard shall apply. Workers shall be entitled to at least one day off in every seven-day period.

III. No Forced or Compulsory Labor

No factory making Reebok products shall use forced or other compulsory labor, including labor that is required as a means of political coercion or as punishment for holding or expressing political views.

IV. Fair Wages

Reebok will seek business partners committed to the betterment of wage and benefit levels to the extent appropriate in light of national practices and conditions. Reebok will not select business partners who pay less than the minimum wage required by applicable law or who pay less than the prevailing local industry wage.

V. No Child Labor

Reebok will not work with business partners that use child labor. The term "child" refers to a person who is younger than 15, or younger than the age for completing compulsory education in the country of manufacture, whichever is higher.

VI. Freedom of Association

Reebok will seek business partners that share its commitment to the right of employees to establish and join legal organizations of their own choosing. Reebok recognizes and respects the right of all employees to organize and bargain collectively.

VII. Non-harassment

Reebok will seek business partners that treat their employees with respect and dignity. No worker will be subject to any physical, sexual, psychological, or verbal harassment or abuse.

VIII. Safe and Healthy Work Environment

Reebok will seek business partners that assure employees a safe and healthy workplace that does not expose workers to hazardous conditions.

All factories accepting Reebok International Ltd. orders agree:

- to apply Reebok's Human Rights Production Standards;
- to implement a grievance system and address complaints by workers; and
- to permit workers to freely assist in Reebok's process for assessing workplace conditions.

Source: Reprinted with the permission of Reebok International Ltd.

laws, and when the codes of conduct protect freedom of association, they can also spur unionization (see Box 12.15).[96]

At the same time, because these codes are voluntary and rely on publicity rather than legal power, the most important problems with corporate codes of conduct are content and enforcement.[97] When companies create their own codes, they can define or exclude standards to serve their self-interest with greater attention on public relations than working

[96] Liubicic, "Corporate Codes of Conduct and Product Labeling Schemes."
[97] Baker, "Tightening the Toothless Vise." Compa and Darricarrère, "Private Labor Rights Enforcement Through Corporate Codes of Conduct." Hepple, "A Race to the Top?" Liubicic, "Corporate Codes of Conduct and Product Labeling Schemes." Tsogas, *Labor Regulation in a Global Economy.*

The Mexmode *maquiladora* factory in Atlixco, Mexico, is owned by the South Korean-based Kukdong International and makes licensed college apparel for Nike, including sweatshirts for the Universities of Arizona, California–Berkeley, Connecticut, Illinois, Michigan, North Carolina, and Oregon as well as Boston College, Georgetown, and Purdue. Mexmode had signed a collective bargaining agreement with the Revolutionary Confederation of Workers and Peasants union (ironically abbreviated "CROC") that did not contain any wage or benefit provisions above the legal minimums. In 2001, the 800 Mexmode workers—many of them young, single mothers—tried to form an independent union to fight sexual harassment, long hours, unhealthy plant cafeteria food, and low wages (less than $40 per week). The workers first boycotted the cafeteria and then went on strike when the boycott leaders were fired. Mexican police broke up the strike.

Nike's code of conduct, however, pledges to respect workers' rights to freedom of association and collective bargaining. Moreover, Nike is a member of the Fair Labor Association and its Workplace Code of Conduct also recognizes the right to collective bargaining. Consequently, the antisweatshop group the Workers Rights Consortium, several U.S. labor unions, and other organizations launched an investigation and a global solidarity campaign that resulted in 6,000 letters of protest to Nike urging the company to follow its own corporate code of conduct. Nike relented and pressured Mexmode to recognize a new independent union. In September, the fired workers were reinstated and the new union was recognized. In April 2002, wages and benefits were improved and an attendance program with significant bonuses was introduced.

Sources: *AFL–CIO News* (Washington, DC: AFL–CIO, 2001) available at *www.aflcio.org/news/2001/1130_workers.htm* (accessed July 24, 2002). *www.workersrights.org/Report_Kukdong_2.pdf* (accessed July 25, 2002). *www.cleanclothes.org/appeals_archive.htm* (accessed July 25, 2002).

conditions. Such codes frequently omit any reference to freedom of association or collective bargaining.[98] The Union of Needletrades, Industrial, and Textile Employees (UNITE) refused to agree to the apparel industry Workplace Code of Conduct because the code contains weak language on minimum or prevailing wages rather than stronger language on a living wage. With respect to monitoring and enforcement, corporate codes of conduct that rely on self-monitoring can be manipulated by controlling publicly released information. Some codes are monitored by human rights groups or other outsiders, including professional social auditors, but even this is controversial.[99] For example, UNITE also objected to the apparel industry monitoring system because factories for inspection were not selected at random and the inspections were not a surprise because the companies scheduled them (these provisions were later changed).

Lastly, a visible legal battle involving Nike raises the issue of whether companies can be sued for false claims about fulfilling their codes of conduct. In 1998, Nike was sued for false advertising by an activist who alleged that Nike's statements that its sneakers were not produced under sweatshop conditions were untrue. Nike argued that these claims are "political speech" dealing with social issues protected by the Constitution's guarantee of free speech. In contrast, the suit argued that statements about working conditions are "commercial speech" about the product itself and therefore must be truthful—otherwise, the company is guilty of false advertising. The California Supreme Court came down on the side of commercial speech and ruled that Nike could be held liable for its statements if they were false. To avoid further litigation, Nike settled the case by paying $1.5 million to the Fair Labor Association in 2003. This perhaps opens a small window for activists to use the legal

[98] Hepple, "A Race to the Top?"
[99] Tsogas, *Labor Regulation in a Global Economy.*

system to enforce corporate codes of conduct, but it remains to be seen whether this strategy can be effective.[100]

In the global arena, the use of corporate codes of conduct to address labor issues is analogous to the use of human resource management to govern the workplace (recall Chapter 2). Like human resource management, the use of corporate codes of conduct admits that working conditions are not entirely dictated by market forces—rather, companies have choices and establishing conditions more favorable to workers than the market minimums can be mutually beneficial for both the company and workers. As stated in Reebok's code, "We believe that the incorporation of internationally recognized human rights standards into our business practice improves worker morale and results in a higher quality working environment and higher quality products." This is similar to the human resource management philosophy that treating workers with respect increases morale and effectiveness. In other words, the use of corporate codes of conduct rejects the market-oriented conception of labor as a commodity and also the assumption of perfect competition that protects employees from abuse, but is based on the unitarist belief of shared interests between labor and management—just like the philosophy of human resource management (again, recall Chapter 2). But as is also true in human resource management, corporate codes of conduct are ultimately a unilateral mechanism for establishing employment conditions that lacks a rigorous set of minimum standards and an external enforcement mechanism. Many companies might be entrusted to this voluntary mechanism, but with the potential for abuse, it is reasonable to question whether the global workplace should rely entirely on corporate codes of conduct to balance efficiency, equity, and voice.

INTERNATIONAL MANAGEMENT

The intensified competition resulting from globalization is widely associated with pressures to restrain wage and benefit costs and to increase employment flexibility (recall Chapter 11). But globalization also adds significant complexities to the practice of management in multinational corporations. A multinational corporation's global strategy has two central dimensions: configuration and coordination.[101] Configuration involves the location of various activities such as whether production is concentrated in one country and exported to other markets or production is globalized into various countries through foreign direct investment. The location of suppliers and subcontractors is another element of configuration. Note that configuration decisions are not limited to production but also include research and product development, marketing, and other functions. The coordination dimension consists of the degree to which activities in different countries are harmonized or autonomous. The extent to which human resource management strategies and production techniques are required to follow one consistent model throughout the local operations of a multinational corporation is a key element of this coordination dimension.

The configuration dimension affects labor relations through its effects on relative bargaining power between corporations and employees. The threat of moving production to a lower wage country lowers labor's bargaining power.[102] Multiple production locations make it more difficult for a strike to place significant financial pressure on a company. Transfer pricing—the terms at which goods and services are exchanged within a company—can be

[100] Julia Fisher, "Free Speech to Have Sweatshops? How *Kasky v. Nike* Might Provide a Useful Tool to Improve Sweatshop Conditions," *Boston College Third World Law Journal* 26 (Spring 2006), pp. 267–310.
[101] Porter, *The Competitive Advantage of Nations.*
[102] Cowie, *Capital Moves.* Gordon and Turner, "Going Global."

used to hide the true profitability of specific operations from labor unions.[103] Complex international joint ventures or subcontracting arrangements can also make it more difficult for unions to discern the true state of a company's operations and financial situation.

The coordination dimension of global strategy and international management represents a central conflict in multinational corporations between centralization—global integration and efficiency—and decentralization—national and local responsiveness and autonomy. A critical task of international managers is balancing this tension—it is not a case of choosing one or the other, but rather of finding the appropriate mix of both sides of this centralization–decentralization or global integration–local responsiveness duality.[104] An organization in which all units are fully autonomous lacks a source of global competitive advantage such as standardized products, economies of scale, or organizational learning. In other words, where is the global synergy if all units act independently? On the other hand, a multinational corporation in which all decisions are centralized and all practices follow global uniform policies lacks the ability to capitalize on local differences and opportunities. In other words, there is little respect for diversity and a lessened sense of accountability, participation, and entrepreneurial activity. The task of international management is to find the appropriate balance between integration and autonomy. The difficulty in seeking this balance, however, is magnified by the complexity of communication within multinational corporations.[105] Communication gaps can result not only from distance—which is at least partially alleviated by advances in information technology such as e-mail—but also from differences in language and culture.

For labor relations, the tension between integration and autonomy manifests itself in the extent to which local labor relations practices and strategies are shaped by local managers and environmental conditions versus determined by corporate-wide policies and strategies. The general international management prescription of "organize one way, manage the other way" is equally valid for labor relations in multinational corporations.[106] If formal labor relations processes and structures are centralized, then local managers should strive for ways to incorporate local responsiveness and problem solving. If labor relations processes are decentralized, then local managers should build networks across the organization to facilitate coordination and learning.

Some amount of national responsiveness is required by international differences in relevant laws. For example, the U.S. Family and Medical Leave Act requires companies to provide 12 weeks of unpaid leave to care for newborn children and for other family and medical purposes. In the European Union, however, parental leave laws typically require 14 to 16 weeks of leave and some laws also require at least partial compensation. Ensuring compliance with these different national standards is an important challenge of multinational corporations.[107] The legal and institutional differences

[103] Harvie Ramsay and Nigel Haworth, "Managing the Multinationals: The Emerging Theory of the Multinational Enterprise and its Implications for Labour Resistance," in Stewart R. Clegg (ed.), *Organization Theory and Class Analysis: New Approaches and New Issues* (Berlin: Walter de Gruyter, 1990), pp. 275–97.

[104] Paul Evans, Vladimir Pucik, and Jean-Louis Barsoux, *The Global Challenge: Frameworks for International Human Resource Management* (Boston: McGraw-Hill/Irwin, 2002).

[105] Harvie Ramsay, "Know Thy Enemy: Understanding Multinational Corporations as a Requirement for Strategic International Laborism," in Michael E. Gordon and Lowell Turner (eds.), *Transnational Cooperation Among Labor Unions* (Ithaca, NY: ILR Press, 2000), Chapter 2.

[106] Evans, Pucik, and Barsoux, *The Global Challenge*, p. 83.

[107] Kathryn L. Morris, "A Matter of Compliance: How Do U.S. Multinational Corporations Deal with the Discrepancies in the Family and Medical Leave Act of 1993 and the European Union Directive on Parental Leave; Is an International Standard Practical or Appropriate in This Area of Law?," *The Georgia Journal of International and Comparative Law* 30 (Spring 2002), pp. 543–68.

in labor relations across different countries—such as the British system of voluntary recognition of unions and labor contracts or the tightly specified German system that provides specific codetermination rights to employees—are presented in the next chapter. These differences must be appreciated by successful international managers and union leaders.

GLOBALIZATION: ECONOMICS AND ETHICS

It is easy to reduce globalization to a purely economic phenomenon dominated by discussions of trade statistics, trade barriers, and foreign direct investment. In the textbook economics model, increased economic integration, free trade, and international capital mobility improve aggregate welfare in the long run, and short-run issues are dismissed as "adjustment costs." The economics of globalization are certainly important and should not be overlooked, but it is also critical to not overlook the broader effects of globalization on individuals, unions, communities, cultures, the environment, and nations. Globalization has brought many benefits to people around the world but has also closed U.S. factories, hollowed out entire communities, brought sweatshops to other countries, and placed great strains on the environment. Globalization therefore raises very important ethical issues (see Box 12.16).[108] It can further be argued that everyone—including corporations and consumers—has a moral obligation to do their fair share in addressing these ethical challenges and in improving human rights around the world.[109]

With respect to labor relations, private sector unions are struggling to maintain the viability of collective bargaining in the face of the pressures of globalization. The threat of moving production to low-wage countries has labor on the defensive and undermines labor standards. Traditional industrial unions like the United Steelworkers and United Auto Workers have lost thousands of members in their core industries and are now general unions with very diverse memberships. With the New Deal industrial relations system under fire from globalization, it is important to consider alternative institutional mechanisms for governing the global workplace. Some of these arrangements, especially enforceable international labor standards and transnational collective bargaining, have the potential to support domestic-level collective bargaining, while a continued emphasis on free trade rather than fair trade is likely to keep labor on the defensive in many countries. Sharp disagreements persist as to which institutional arrangements will best provide efficiency, equity, and voice in the 21st century. The key to understanding these disagreements lies in appreciating the different models of the employment relationship—neoclassical economics, human resource management, pluralist industrial relations, and critical industrial relations.

[108] Hoyt N. Wheeler, "Globalization and Business Ethics in Employment Relations," in John W. Budd and James G. Scoville (eds.), *The Ethics of Human Resources and Industrial Relations* (Champaign, IL: Labor and Employment Relations Association, 2005), pp. 115–40.

[109] Michael A. Santoro, *Profits and Principles: Global Capitalism and Human Rights in China* (Ithaca, NY: Cornell University Press, 2000).

Jack Welch, the legendary ex-CEO of General Electric (GE), was interviewed by business journalist Lou Dobbs on CNN's *Moneyline* on December 8, 1998:

Dobbs: . . . Jack, no one, very few people, I should say, have as certainly widespread diverse set of businesses and assets as does GE, as do you. Give us your sense about the economy in the year going forward, where you'd expect to see pressures as your outlook.

Welch: Well, it's clear that the deflationary pressures continue, whether it's copper hitting new lows, oil hitting new lows. Almost every key raw material hitting new lows. There's clearly a mood of deflation in the air. That's sets capacity in all global markets. Price compression in financial services offering margin squeezes, so there is real competitive pressure. And yet, there are enormous opportunities at the same time. Japan is opening up its financial markets. We've made a number of moves, have a number more on the drawing board. We've never had better opportunities to sources in joint ventures around the globe, to be more competitive.

Ideally, you'd have every plant you own on a barge, to move with currencies and changes in the economy. You can't do that. But the job of a company has to be agile, and to capitalize on these things. But it's a tough economy. It's a very tough economy, whether you're in financial services, where there is excess capacity, or whether you're in a manufacturing sector.

* * *

General Electric has been an unabashed champion of globalization: "Globalization is not only striving to grow revenues by selling goods and services in global markets. It also means globalizing every activity of the company, including the sourcing of raw materials, components, and products. Globalization especially means finding and attracting the unlimited pool of intellectual capital—the very best people—from all around the globe." GE has also been very successful financially. Its operating margin is close to 20 percent and its operating profit is around $15 billion annually. Its stock price consistently outperforms the broader market.

According to *BusinessWeek,* "GE's U.S. workforce has been shrinking for more than a decade as Welch has cut costs by shifting production and investment to lower-wage countries." In recent years, non–U.S. employment nearly doubled while U.S. employment fell by almost 50 percent. Moreover, U.S. unionized employment at GE is only one third of its early 1980s level while GE has expanded in Mexico, India, and other low-wage countries. There is also evidence that GE has pressured its suppliers to relocate to Mexico and other areas. All of the GE gas ranges and most of the electric stoves and side-by-side refrigerators sold in the United States are now produced in Mexico. However, production of mini-bar refrigerators was moved from Mexico to China in search of lower labor costs.

Reflection Questions

1. Use the Ethical Analysis Template from Chapter 3 to analyze the ethical content of putting factories on a barge to find the best labor costs deal around the world.

2. What is the role of ethics for managers in the global economy? for union leaders?

Sources: Cable News Network Financial, *Moneyline* (December 8, 1998, Transcript #98120800FN-L10). *www.ge. com/en/company/companyinfo* (accessed July 12, 2006). Aaron Bernstein, "Welch's March to the South," *BusinessWeek* (December 6, 1999). Geri Smith, "Is the Magic Starting to Fade for Manufacturing in Mexico?," *BusinessWeek* (August 6, 2001).

Key Terms

globalization, *423*
social dumping, *427*
World Trade
Organization, *433*
fair trade, *433*
International Labor

Organization, *436*
core labor
standards, *436*
North American
Agreement on Labor
Cooperation, *438*

European Works
Council, *443*
International Trade Union
Confederation, *446*
corporate code of
conduct, *449*

Reflection Questions

1. In a concise paragraph, paraphrase what you have learned about globalization to explain to a policymaker why globalization has profound implications for domestic employment issues. Based on these implications, should enforceable labor standards (a social clause) be added to free trade agreements? If so, what should the standards be and how should they be enforced?

2. Free trade agreements commonly include enforceable intellectual property rights but not labor standards. Is it consistent to have enforceable property rights but not labor standards?

3. Is coordinated, transnational collective bargaining a good idea for unions and workers? If so, how should it be promoted?

4. How does increased globalization affect U.S. managers, labor leaders, and workers in a unionized workplace? Does labor law need to be reformed because of these effects? If so, how?

5. Globalization represents a major change in the labor relations environment, but ethics should not be overlooked. For many, the push for free trade and increased economic integration is based on the belief that "the social caboose [is] pulled by the economic locomotive."[110] Which ethical frameworks in Chapter 3 are consistent with this belief? How would the remaining ethical frameworks challenge this belief?

Internet Exploration

1. Explore the Web sites of the International Trade Union Confederation (*www.ituc-csi.org*) or of a global union federation such as Education International (*www.ei-ie.org*) or the International Transport Workers' Federation (*www.itfglobal.org*). What are some of the current campaigns? What campaigns can you find that pertain to collective bargaining? Is there a transnational aspect to this collective bargaining situation?

2. Explore the Web sites for the Fair Labor Association (*www.fairlabor.org*) and the Workers Rights Consortium (*www.workersrights.org*). Is this an effective method for combating sweatshops in developing countries? Or is it a public relations scheme? Find the lists of participating colleges and universities. Does your school participate in either of these anti-sweatshop organizations? Should it?

3. Compare the Web pages of the World Trade Organization (*www.wto.org*) and other organizations that advocate free trade with the Web pages of the Trade Observatory (*www.tradeobservatory.org*), the Public Citizen's Global Trade Watch (*www.citizen.org/trade/*), or other organizations that are more critical of free trade. Why are there such differences between the two groups?

Additional Reading

Elliott, Kimberly Ann, and Richard B. Freeman, *Can Labor Standards Improve under Globalization?* (Washington, DC: Institute for International Economics, 2003).

Evans, Paul, Vladimir Pucik, and Jean-Louis Barsoux, *The Global Challenge: Frameworks for International Human Resource Management* (Boston: McGraw-Hill/Irwin, 2002).

Friedman, Thomas L., *The World Is Flat: A Brief History of the Twenty-first Century* (New York: Farrar, Straus, and Giroux, 2006).

Gordon, Michael E., and Lowell Turner (eds.), *Transnational Cooperation Among Labor Unions* (Ithaca, NY: ILR Press, 2000).

Irwin, Douglas A., *Free Trade under Fire* (Princeton, NJ: Princeton University Press, 2002).

Mellon, Steve, *After the Smoke Clears*: *Struggling to Get By in Rustbelt America* (Pittsburgh: University of Pittsburgh Press, 2002).

Scheve, Kenneth F., and Matthew J. Slaughter, *Globalization and the Perception of American Workers* (Washington, DC: Institute for International Economics, 2001).

Tsogas, George, *Labor Regulation in a Global Economy* (Armonk, NY: M. E. Sharpe, 2001).

[110] Blanpain, European Labour Law p. 91

Part **Four**

Reflection

The previous parts provide an intellectual framework for studying labor relations, a description of how the New Deal industrial relations system works, and an overview of the intense contemporary pressures on this system. The final two chapters explore labor relations systems in other countries and possibilities for the future of the U.S. labor relations system. This provides the opportunity to reflect upon where the U.S. labor relations system has been, and where it should go in the future.

Chapter Thirteen

Comparative Labor Relations

Advance Organizer

The previous chapters present the U.S. labor relations system in detail, but labor relations in other countries can be very different. The scope of bargaining, the extent of legal protection, and the nature of labor unions vary from country to country. Studying labor relations in other countries provides a richer understanding of the subject, can present ideas for reforming the U.S. system, and is also important for working professionals in a global economy.

Learning Objectives

By the end of the chapter, you should be able to:

1. **Compare** the basic features of labor relations systems in the major industrialized, democratic countries around the world.
2. **Identify** the basic features of labor relations systems in the transition and less developed economies of eastern Europe and Asia.
3. **Understand** various options in labor relations systems for reacting to the pressures of globalization, decentralization, and flexibility while trying to balance efficiency, equity, and voice.
4. **Analyze** the extent to which the labor relations experiences of other countries can provide ideas and lessons for reforming the U.S. labor relations system.

Contents

Comparative labor relations is the study of labor relations systems in different countries, and the goal of this chapter is *comparing* the U.S. labor relations system to other systems. A comparative perspective on labor relations is important for three reasons. The intellectual reason is that consideration of labor relations in multiple countries provides a rich way for thinking broadly about the underlying problem of balancing efficiency, equity, and voice and for obtaining a stronger understanding of the primary issues in labor relations. The public policy reason is that comparative analyses of labor relations can provide ideas for reforming the U.S. system. Aspects of labor relations in Canada, Germany, and Japan have all been championed as proposals for reforming U.S. labor relations. The practical reason is that if you work for an organization that does business in another country or for a labor

BOX 13.1   Common Dimensions of Industrialized Labor Relations Systems Around the Globe

	Dimension	Features	Examples
centralized	Social Partnership	Peak-level labor, business, and government agreements on broad economic and social issues	Austria, Finland, Ireland, Sweden
	Sector Bargaining	Collective bargaining with employers' associations to produce industrywide contracts	France, Germany, Sweden
	Centralized Awards	Occupational arbitration awards	Australia (pre-1997), New Zealand (pre-1991)
decentralized	Enterprise Unionism	Unions limited to one company	Japan
	Exclusive Representation/ Majority Rule*	Representation and bargaining only if a union represents a majority of the employees	Canada, United States
	Codetermination	Workplace-level shared decision making including works councils and board-level representation	France, Germany, Sweden
	Voluntarism*	Representation and bargaining based on economic power, not legal backing	Great Britain, Ireland, New Zealand (1991–2000)

*Bargaining in a system of exclusive representation or voluntarism can be centralized or decentralized depending on the parties, but it is commonly decentralized.

union that has strategic alliances with labor unions in another country, it is important to understand that country's labor relations framework. This chapter, therefore, outlines the major features of labor relations in Canada, Great Britain, Ireland, France, Germany, Sweden, Australia, and Japan (see Box 13.1). These countries are representative of the types of labor relations systems found in industrialized, democratic countries. Labor relations in Mexico, eastern Europe, and selected less developed Asian countries is also discussed.

A traditional claim is that U.S. labor relations is exceptional: low levels of support for unionization, lack of a socialist movement, legal protection of individuals rather than unions, and intense employer resistance to unions are all claimed to be relatively unique to the United States among industrialized, democratic countries—in other words, support for unionization, a socialist movement, legal rights for unions, and low employer resistance to unions are widely present in industrialized, democratic countries *except* the United States.[1] In this vein, when considering the labor relations systems of other countries, note the sometimes great differences with the U.S. system—exclusive representation is not always present, contracts are not always legally enforceable, and business unionism isn't always the dominant philosophy. Moreover, not only are unions often organized differently, but so too are employers. In many countries outside of North America, employers' associations rather than individual companies dominate collective bargaining. Box 13.2 also shows that in many other countries, union membership is not as closely associated with being covered by a union contract as it is in the United States. In Spain, France, and Austria, over 80 percent of employees are covered by a collective bargaining agreement, yet union density is less than 50 percent—and is only 10 percent in France.

At the same time, labor relations around the globe is similar in other respects. The contemporary pressures on labor, management, and government are universal—globalization,

[1] Larry G. Gerber, "Shifting Perspectives on American Exceptionalism: Recent Literature on American Labor Relations and Labor Politics," *Journal of American Studies* 31 (August 1997), pp. 253–74. Sanford M. Jacoby, "American Exceptionalism Revisited: The Importance of Management," in Sanford M. Jacoby (ed.), *Masters to Managers: Historical and Comparative Perspectives on American Employers* (New York: Columbia University Press, 1991), Chapter 8. Kim Voss, *The Making of American Exceptionalism: The Knights of Labor and Class Formation in the Nineteenth Century* (Ithaca: Cornell University Press, 1993).

BOX 13.2
Labor Relations around the Globe: Union Membership ≠ Contract Coverage

	Bargaining Coverage	Union Density
United States	14%	13%
Japan	15+	22
New Zealand	25+	23
United Kingdom	30+	31
Canada	32	28
Germany	68	25
Norway	70+	54
Spain	80+	15
Portugal	80+	24
Australia	80+	25
Italy	80+	35
France	90+	10
Belgium	90+	56
Finland	90+	76
Sweden	90+	79
Austria	95+	37

Notes: Figures are for 2000. + indicates a lower-bound estimate.
Source: OECD, *Employment Outlook* (Paris: Organization for Economic Cooperation and Development, 2004), p. 145.

decentralization, and flexibility. Moreover, the fundamental issues of labor relations are constant across all countries. The objectives of the employment relationship are efficiency, equity, and voice, there is a need to balance labor rights and property rights, and labor relations outcomes are determined by the environment and individual decision making. As such, the U.S. New Deal labor relations system is one possible method of pursuing these objectives, but the comparative study of labor relations in other countries reveals that there are many alternative possibilities as well. Therefore, this chapter outlines the labor relations systems of a number of representative countries. There are innumerable ways to order these countries, so as to avoid confusion the tour here proceeds geographically from North America to Europe to Asia. The chapter concludes by revisiting the question of globalization— in an integrated world economy, is it possible to have unique national labor relations systems, or does integration force convergence of national institutions?

CANADA

In broad terms, Canada and the United States have similar economic, institutional, and legal features, comparable demographic, occupational, and industrial structures, interdependent product markets, and many of the same corporations. With respect to labor relations specifically, labor unions in the two countries have similar structures, many Canadian workers are represented by U.S. unions, and Canadian labor law is patterned after the U.S. Wagner Act (but not the Taft-Hartley Act).[2] Exclusive representation, bargaining structures

[2] Daphne Gottlieb Taras, "Collective Bargaining Regulation in Canada and the United States: Divergent Cultures, Divergent Outcomes," in Bruce E. Kaufman (ed.), *Government Regulation of the Employment Relationship* (Madison, WI: Industrial Relations Research Association, 1997), Chapter 8.

and strategies, and the resulting union contracts are therefore similar.[3] However, there are some cultural and small yet important legal differences that have caused outcomes to diverge from those in the United States.

With respect to labor law, first note that Canadian labor law is not centralized as it is in the United States. Rather, each province has its own similar yet unique law that governs labor relations in that province. While largely modeled after the National Labor Relations Act (NLRA), there are some important differences between the provincial laws and the NLRA (see Box 13.3).[4] First, Canadian labor law makes it easier to establish and maintain

BOX 13.3

U.S. and Canadian Labor Law: Small Differences That Matter?

Topic	United States	Canada
Legal Jurisdiction	Centralized: private sector governed by federal law.	Decentralized: governed by provincial laws.
Union Certification	National Labor Relations Board election procedure. Employers can campaign and use delay tactics.	Some provinces allow card-check certification or instant elections.
First Contract Arbitration	No.	Provided in some provinces.
Decertification Elections	Strike replacements can vote and permanently replaced strikers can only vote for 12 months.	Some provinces exclude replacement workers from voting or prohibit decertification petitions during a strike.
Nonunion Representation	Illegal.	Company-domination and interference with organizing are illegal, otherwise legal.
Union Security	Right-to-work laws in 22 states forbid union and agency shops.	No right-to-work laws. Unions are guaranteed at least an agency shop in many provinces.
Technological Change	Not a mandatory bargaining item.	Equivalent of a mandatory bargaining item in some provinces.
Strike Replacements	Except in unfair labor practice strikes, permanent and temporary replacements are allowed.	Most provinces ban the use of permanent replacements. Two provinces ban all replacements.

Sources: Steven E. Abraham, "The Relevance of Canadian Labour Law to US Firms Operating in Canada," *International Journal of Manpower* 18 (October 1997), pp. 662–74. John W. Budd, "Canadian Strike Replacement Legislation and Collective Bargaining: Lessons for the United States," *Industrial Relations* 35 (April 1996), pp. 245–60. Daphne Gottlieb Taras, "Collective Bargaining Regulation in Canada and the United States: Divergent Cultures, Divergent Outcomes," in Bruce E. Kaufman (ed.), *Government Regulation of the Employment Relationship* (Madison, WI: Industrial Relations Research Association, 1997), Chapter 8. Daphne Gottlieb Taras and Allen Ponak, "Mandatory Agency Shop Laws as an Explanation of Canada–U.S. Union Density Divergence," *Journal of Labor Research* 22 (Summer 2001), pp. 541–68.

[3] John Godard, *Industrial Relations, the Economy, and Society,* 3rd ed. (Concord: Ontario: Captus Press, 2005). Mark Thompson and Daphne G. Taras, "Employment Relations in Canada," in Greg J. Bamber, Russell D. Lansbury, and Nick Wailes (eds.), *International and Comparative Employment Relations: Globalisation and the Developed Market Economies* (London: Sage, 2004), pp. 91–118.

[4] Steven E. Abraham, "The Relevance of Canadian Labour Law to US Firms Operating in Canada," *International Journal of Manpower* 18 (October 1997), pp. 662–74.

a union. In contrast to the sometimes lengthy National Labor Relations Board certification election procedure in the United States, some Canadian provinces provide for card-check recognition (certification based on authorization cards without a secret-ballot election) and instant elections that occur within a couple of days of filing the election petition. These quick processes reduce the scope for contentious campaigning and antiunion managerial tactics.[5] When newly organized unions fail to reach a first contract, some Canadian provinces provide for arbitration to establish a contract. Canadian labor relations also lacks right-to-work laws banning union security agreements, and, in fact, the larger provinces require at least an agency shop which strengthens the financial base of Canadian unions.[6] Second, Canadian labor law also makes it more difficult for employers to break an existing union. Some provinces do not allow decertification elections during a strike, and where they are allowed, strike replacements are often not considered part of the bargaining unit and therefore not allowed to vote. Moreover, most of the provinces ban permanent strike replacements or provide striking workers with immediate reinstatement rights; in Quebec and British Columbia, even temporary replacements are prohibited.[7]

Relative to the processes in the rest of the world, Canadian labor relations processes are very similar to those in the United States, but subtle legal differences and some cultural factors appear to support a more stable labor relations system in Canada.[8] Union density has remained more stable, though Canada also has a larger public sector that accounts for at least some of this difference with the United States. During the concession bargaining period of the 1980s, Canadian unions fared better in wage bargaining than their U.S. counterparts.[9] In contrast to the U.S. business unionism philosophy, Canadian unions are moving towards a social unionism philosophy in which labor has more of a militant, social activist role. For advocates of a stronger labor movement and greater employee representation in the workplace, the small legal differences pertaining to union organizing and strike replacements form the basis for proposals to reform U.S. labor law.

MEXICO

The increased economic integration of the United States, Canada, and Mexico via the North American Free Trade Agreement (NAFTA) has focused increased attention on the labor relations system of Mexico. The Mexican system is therefore important in its own right, but it is also presented here as broadly representative of labor relations in developing countries. In essence, the primary theme is appearance versus reality—on paper, Mexican law provides very strong protections for workers and unions, but the extent of enforcement

---

[5] Paul Weiler, "Promises to Keep: Securing Workers' Rights to Self-Organization Under the NLRA," *Harvard Law Review* 96 (June 1983), pp. 1769–827. Chris Riddell, "Union Certification Success under Voting versus Card-Check Procedures: Evidence from British Columbia, 1978–1998," *Industrial and Labor Relations Review* 57 (July 2004), pp. 493–517.

[6] Daphne Gottlieb Taras and Allen Ponak, "Mandatory Agency Shop Laws as an Explanation of Canada–U.S. Union Density Divergence," *Journal of Labor Research* 22 (Summer 2001), pp. 541–68.

[7] John W. Budd, "Canadian Strike Replacement Legislation and Collective Bargaining: Lessons for the United States," *Industrial Relations* 35 (April 1996), pp. 245–60.

[8] Taras, "Collective Bargaining Regulation in Canada and the United States." Thompson and Taras, "Employment Relations in Canada." Seymour Martin Lipset and Noah M. Meltz, with Rafael Gomez and Ivan Katchanovski, *The Paradox of American Unionism: Why Americans Like Unions More Than Canadians Do but Join Much Less* (Ithaca, NY: Cornell University Press, 2004).

[9] John W. Budd, "Union Wage Determination in Canadian and U.S. Manufacturing, 1964–1990: A Comparative Analysis," *Industrial and Labor Relations Review* 49 (July 1996), pp. 673–89.

is questionable.[10] Moreover, labor negotiations and unions have traditionally been controlled by the government as part of a larger economic development strategy. As in many other developing countries, this results in sharp clashes between the government and independent labor unions because of the government's focus on competitiveness and foreign investment at the expense of democracy and working conditions.

Quite strikingly, social and economic rights for workers are written directly into Mexico's constitution of 1917. In fact, this was the first constitution or basic national charter worldwide to explicitly include workers' rights.[11] Article 123 guarantees the right to organize unions, bargain collectively, and strike, provides protections against unjust dismissal and dangerous working conditions, and mandates minimum wages, overtime pay, profit sharing, an eight-hour day, a six-day workweek, and pregnancy and childbirth leave. Under Mexican labor law, a union must have at least 20 employees and can be an industrial union, craft union, or enterprise union (representing workers only at one company). In rural areas where there is difficulty meeting the 20-worker minimum, general unions are also allowed. To have legal rights, unions must register with the government as one of these types. A union does not need to represent a majority of employees to engage in collective bargaining, but it does to legally strike. All contracts automatically include the minimum provisions mandated by the constitution. Once approved by the government, contracts are legally enforceable.

There is no explicit obligation for management to bargain; rather, this is enforced through the strike-related aspects of labor law. Once the legal standards for a strike are fulfilled and mediation fails, a strike can occur. Red and black flags are flown at the entrances to the workplace and all employees must stop working except those necessary to protect raw materials and equipment.[12] Interestingly, it is the union that is legally responsible for protecting the company's materials and equipment. The employer must cease operations and permanent strike replacements are prohibited. As such, the legal protections for workers and unions are much greater in Mexico than in the United States—at least on paper.[13]

In practice, there are questions about the effectiveness of these protections. For 50 years, the most influential union federation was the *Confederación de Trabajadores México* (CTM, Confederation of Mexican Workers). The CTM was very closely connected to the longtime ruling party—the *Partido Revolucionario Institucional* (PRI, Institutional Revolutionary Party)—and was therefore frequently criticized as making the labor movement subservient to the government.[14] CTM-affiliated union leaders are portrayed if not as puppets of the government, then as more loyal to the PRI than to their unions. Similarly, collective bargaining agreements are alleged to be more of a function of the government's overall economic development strategy than the product of independent collective bargaining. To wit, as the government privatized industries and embraced free trade, union density fell from 30 percent to 20 percent from 1984 to 2000.[15]

---

[10] Stephen F. Befort and Virginia E. Cornett, "Beyond the Rhetoric of the NAFTA Treaty Debate: A Comparative Analysis of Labor and Employment Law in Mexico and the United States," *Comparative Labor Law Journal* 17 (Winter 1996), pp. 269–313.

[11] Commission for Labor Cooperation, *Labor Relations Law in North America* (Washington, DC, 2000).

[12] Commission for Labor Cooperation, *Labor Relations Law in North America.*

[13] Befort and Cornett, "Beyond the Rhetoric of the NAFTA Treaty Debate."

[14] Altha J. Cravey, *Women and Work in Mexico's Maquiladoras* (Lanham, MD: Rowman and Littlefield, 1998). Richard A. Morales, "Mexico," in Miriam Rothman, Dennis R. Briscoe, and Raoul C. D. Nacamulli (eds.), *Industrial Relations Around the World: Labor Relations for Multinational Companies* (Berlin: Walter de Gruyter, 1992), pp. 285–95. Alberto Aziz Nassif, "The Mexican Dual Transition: State, Unionism, and the Political System," in Maria Lorena Cook and Harry C. Katz (eds.), *Regional Integration and Industrial Relations in North America* (Ithaca, NY: Institute of Collective Bargaining, Cornell University, 1994), pp. 132–41.

[15] David Fairris and Edward Levine, "Declining Union Density in Mexico, 1984–2000" *Monthly Labor Review* 127 (September 2004), pp. 10–17.

Government control of labor unions is facilitated by Mexican labor law. To have legal rights, unions must register with the government. This is supposed to be purely an administrative requirement, but there is scope for favoritism and control. Government-controlled unions are referred to as "yellow unions" or "ghost unions" and by some estimates, such sham unions are widespread.[16] Government agencies also play significant roles in determining the legality of strikes and in approving contracts. The extent to which labor law and unions are manipulated and controlled by the government is probably overstated by critics, but nevertheless is at least partially true.[17] The independence, and therefore legitimacy, of the Mexican labor movement has been a concern nationwide. Such concerns are particularly acute in the *maquiladora* industry because of the need to attract foreign investment (recall Box 12.3). At the same time, the rank and file are not universally passive and struggles for democratic unions and free collective bargaining occur within and outside the official (government-approved) labor movement (see Box 13.4).[18]

Such struggles have sharpened in the first decade of the 21st century. After seven decades in power, the PRI was ousted by the conservative *Partido Acción Nacional* (PAN, National Action Party) with the election of Vincente Fox to Mexico's presidency in 2000. Fox was elected on a platform of government reform and transparency, and was supported by independent unions who saw these reforms as ending the government's control of the labor movement. But after taking office, Fox pushed a pro-business agenda of privatization, budget cuts, and labor law reform.[19] Moreover, independent unions see the Fox administration as continuing the legacy of government control over the labor movement, such as when Napoleón Gómez Urrutia was removed as president of the Mine Workers union in 2006. New federations of independent unions such as the National Union of Workers have sprung up and massive protests against the Fox administration have occurred. The contested presidential election of July 2006 further added to the turmoil in the intersection between labor and politics in Mexico. As such, Mexico continues to be broadly representative of labor relations in developing countries: strong labor rights on paper, but in reality, a high degree of state control (although not as repressive as in some regimes) which creates conflicts with independent labor movements.

GREAT BRITAIN

The labor relations system in Great Britain illustrates the very important concept of **voluntarism.** Unlike U.S. and Canadian labor relations in which the law requires unions and companies to negotiate if the union represents a majority of the workers, in Great Britain collective bargaining traditionally only occurred if the parties "voluntarily" agreed. "Voluntary" refers to the absence of legal force—labor and management use their economic power, not legal rights, to get the other side to do something, especially to bargain or abide by a contract. When management "voluntarily" agrees to bargain, for example, it is because the economic costs of refusing to bargain, such as strikes or poor morale, are greater than the costs of bargaining. Representation questions have traditionally been settled through economic force, not elections as in the U.S. system. Management will recognize a union when the union is powerful enough to make it costly for the firm to refuse.

[16] Dan La Botz, "Mexico's Labor Movement in Transition," *Monthly Review* 57 (June 2005), pp. 62–72.

[17] Befort and Cornett, "Beyond the Rhetoric of the NAFTA Treaty Debate."

[18] Maria Lorena Cook, *Organizing Dissent: Unions, the State, and the Democratic Teachers' Movement in Mexico* (University Park: The Pennsylvania State University Press, 1996). La Botz, "Mexico's Labor Movement in Transition."

[19] La Botz, "Mexico's Labor Movement in Transition."

The teachers' union in Mexico illustrates the tension between rank and file union members, union leaders, and the government in Mexico—and other countries in which the government tries to control the labor movement. The *Sindicato Nacional de Trabajadores de la Educación* (SNTE, National Union of Education Workers) was formed in 1943 and is now the largest union in Mexico with more than one million members. Similar to the private sector unions affiliated with the *Confederación de Trabajadores México* (CTM, Confederation of Mexican Workers), the SNTE has traditionally been a typical "official" union—a centralized structure with leaders who are very closely connected to the government and the ruling party, especially the *Partido Revolucionario Institucional* (PRI, Institutional Revolutionary Party) before 2000.

SNTE leaders generally were more interested in pleasing the PRI than the union's members—if they could keep the rank and file teachers tranquil, they would be rewarded by the PRI, and movement into government positions was common. But it is important not to oversimplify the tension—over time, relations between union leaders and the government shifted, alliances changed, and priorities varied such that new accommodations and compromises were often being pursued. Moreover, the rank and file teachers were not always passive, and at various times, their discontent pressured the SNTE leadership and the government.

In the late 1950s, a dissident movement among teachers grew out of frustration with declining real wages and the SNTE's undemocratic practices. In Mexico City, a member of the dissident group won a local election, but the national leadership refused to recognize the results of the election and this refusal was ultimately supported by the Federal Conciliation and Arbitration Board. A strike a few years later, which is illegal in the public sector, was repressed and the dissident movement broken—for the time being.

In 1972, the head of the SNTE was ousted—physically—in a coup by members of another faction. This move, too, was sanctioned by the Federal Conciliation and Arbitration Board. In effect, the labor boss loyal to the previous President of Mexico was replaced by a new labor boss loyal to the new President. While the coup was undertaken allegedly in defense of union democracy, the new leadership further centralized the union and repressed dissent. The links between PRI and the SNTE also strengthened.

The early 1980s witnessed the return of important dissident movements among teachers. This again reflected grassroots frustration with both economic and antidemocratic issues. A 29-day strike in the southern state of Chiapas in September 1979—essentially against both the government and the national SNTE—for increased cost-of-living supplements led to the founding of the *Coordinadora Nacional de Trabajadores de la Educación* (CNTE, National Coordinating Committee of Education Workers). The CNTE's major objective was to work within the structure of the SNTE to instill greater democracy. In the early 1980s, local branches of the CNTE were active in several states in leading strikes and other forms of protest against the government's working conditions and the SNTE's unresponsiveness or repression. Marches to state and federal government offices were common, and sometimes accompanied by a takeover of the office or violence against the marchers. CNTE groups were successfully elected to leadership positions in Chiapas and Oaxaca, but the SNTE effectively repressed the dissident movement elsewhere. Moreover, in the mid 1980s, the national SNTE frustrated the Chiapas and Oaxaca locals through delays in authorizing local elections to renew the authority of the CNTE-supported leaders.

A renewed national struggle for democracy within the SNTE followed the controversial election of Salinas to the presidency of Mexico in 1988. Led by the CNTE and fueled again by frustration with declining real wages and with the lack of democracy in the SNTE, numerous strikes, marches, and hunger strikes erupted in 1989 and the government ousted the head of the SNTE. Under the new leadership, reforms were enacted that included secret ballot elections and official disaffiliation with the PRI. The PRI was replaced in 2000 by the conservative *Partido Acción Nacional* (PAN, National Action Party) when Vicente Fox was elected President of Mexico. Nevertheless, dissidents continue to push for democratic reforms and the SNTE continues to be embroiled in national and regional politics. After a key SNTE leader was pushed out of the PRI in 2004, the union launched a New Alliance Party which ran a candidate in the controversial 2006 Mexican presidential elections. A strike by teachers in Oaxaca in 2006 for higher pay turned violent when police tried to clear the strikers from town plazas; subsequently, huge

Continued

Continued

demonstrations of more than 100,000 protesters called for the resignation of the provincial governor. As such, the tenuous relationship between unions and the government in Mexican labor relations is exemplified by the teachers' union, as are the recurring struggles not only between the union and the government, but also between the rank and file and their leaders.

Source: Maria Lorena Cook, *Organizing Dissent: Unions, the State, and the Democratic Teachers' Movement in Mexico* (University Park: The Pennsylvania State University Press, 1996).

More recently, the Employment Relations Act (1999) provides for statutory recognition of a union under specified majority demonstration provisions, but still encourages voluntary recognition.[20] Another major component of British voluntarism is that contracts are not legally enforceable. Labor and management "voluntarily" agree to abide by the contract—as long as the costs of following the contract are smaller than the costs of breaking it. Contracts are thus enforced by economic force, not the legal system.

British voluntarism can be traced back to the late 19th century. At that time, production was largely craft-based and skilled workers were able to shape workplace practices through formal and informal negotiations in individual workplaces using the scarcity of their skills as bargaining leverage.[21] Based on this tradition of unregulated bargaining, both labor and management feared unfavorable, restrictive government involvement—unions did not want restrictions on strikes and boycotts while management did not want restrictions on their freedom to manage. Thus, a voluntarism system emerged and has essentially been maintained. This does not mean that British labor relations is not regulated. The Trades Disputes Act facilitates voluntarism by making labor unions immune from being sued for breach of contract and for striking. Moreover, various pieces of legislation passed by the Conservative government of Margaret Thatcher in the 1980s restrict labor's ability to conduct secondary boycotts, outlaw the closed shop, and require unions to follow certain democratic procedures for electing officers and determining membership support for a strike.[22] Voluntarism in labor relations is therefore a relative term, not an absolute one—British labor relations is voluntaristic relative to labor relations in many other countries that have more extensive legal regulation of labor relations, but it is not absolutely free of all regulation.

As a result of its craft origins, the British labor movement historically consisted of numerous occupationally focused unions. Recent mergers have resulted in more general unions. Relative to the United States, there are still a large number of unions and the largest are UNISON (representing public sector workers), the Transport and General Workers' Union, the General, Municipal, and Boilermakers' Union, and the Amalgamated Engineering and Electrical Union.[23] Many unionized workplaces have multiple unions. There is one union federation, the Trades Union Congress (TUC), and its role in British labor relations is similar to the AFL–CIO's role in the United States—political lobbying, education, and

[20] Gregor Gall (ed.), *Union Organizing: Campaigning for Trade Union Recognition* (London: Routledge, 2003). Nancy Peters, "The United Kingdom Recalibrates the U.S. National Labor Relations Act: Possible Lessons for the United States," *Comparative Labor Law and Policy Journal* 25 (Winter 2004), pp. 227–56.

[21] Paul Edwards et al., "Great Britain: From Partial Collectivism to Neo-Liberalism to Where?," in Anthony Ferner and Richard Hyman (eds.), *Changing Industrial Relations in Europe* (Oxford: Blackwell Publishers, 1998), Chapter 1.

[22] Edwards et al., "Great Britain." Mick Marchington, John Goodman, and John Berridge, "Employment Relations in Britain," in Greg J. Bamber, Russell D. Lansbury, and Nick Wailes (eds.), *International and Comparative Employment Relations: Globalisation and the Developed Market Economies* (London: Sage, 2004), pp. 36–66.

[23] Marchington et al., "Employment Relations in Britain."

union coordination, but not collective bargaining. Another notable feature of the British labor movement is its close association with the Labour Party—one of Great Britain's major political parties—which in fact was founded in 1900 by British unions and the TUC in order to increase labor's legislative representation in the House of Commons.[24] While the Labour Party has tried to distance itself from the unions recently, before the 1980s there were periods in which Labour governments worked closely with the labor movement, for example, in linking wage restraint to industrial relations reform.[25]

The current issues facing British unions are very similar to those in the United States. The number one issue is probably the decline in union density. While the British decline began much later (1979) than in the United States (mid-1950s), since 1979 British union membership has fallen by more than 5 million members and the fraction covered by collective bargaining agreements has plummeted from 70 percent to 36 percent.[26] This decline appears to stem from structural changes in the economy, labor market weakness, and the previously mentioned Conservative government legal changes enacted in the 1980s.[27] A second major issue for unions in Great Britain is the challenge of employer demands for flexibility and "cooperation." As in the United States, changes in workplace practices are diverse and widespread and this presents a great challenge for unions.[28] A third issue is the future course of public policy. As their power has waned with the legal reforms of the Conservative government, British labor is starting to look more toward the European Union (EU) as a method for leveraging labor standards and public policy in favor of workers and their representatives.[29] For example, the European Works Council directive discussed in the previous chapter was enacted by the British government in 1999 and the EU's Information and Consultation Directive in 2004. Under the latter, an employer must consult with employees on business changes that might affect employment if 10 percent of the employees request consultation. Movement toward a European type of representation, however, entails significant change from the voluntaristic and adversarial traditions of British labor.

The balance between efficiency, equity, and voice in a voluntaristic system to a large extent depends on markets and the economic leverage of the two parties. In the early 1960s, low unemployment gave workplace shop stewards significant leverage and many strikes were called to win grievances and other gains—recall that the contract is enforced by economic force, not legal procedures.[30] As a result, British labor relations developed a reputation of being adversarial and turbulent and therefore harmful to efficiency and competitiveness (see Box 13.5). In the 1980s and 1990s when unemployment was higher, management had the upper hand and efficiency-enhancing policies dominated equity and voice concerns.

[24] Robert Taylor, "Out of the Bowels of the Movement: The Trade Unions and the Origins of the Labour Party 1900–18," in Brian Brivati and Richard Heffernan (eds.), *The Labour Party: A Centenary History* (London: Macmillan Press, 2000), pp. 8–49.

[25] Brian Brivati and Richard Heffernan (eds.), *The Labour Party: A Centenary History* (London: Macmillan Press, 2000).

[26] Harry C. Katz and Owen Darbishire, *Converging Divergences: Worldwide Changes in Employment Systems* (Ithaca, NY: ILR Press, 2000).

[27] Brian Towers, *The Representation Gap: Change and Reform in the British and American Workplace* (Oxford: Oxford University Press, 1997).

[28] Katz and Darbishire, *Converging Divergences*. Towers, *The Representation Gap*. John Kelly, "Social Partnership Agreements in Britain: Labor Cooperation and Compliance," *Industrial Relations* 43 (January 2004), pp. 267–92.

[29] Edwards et al., "Great Britain." Marchington et al., "Employment Relations in Britain."

[30] Towers, *The Representation Gap*.

The singular watershed event in U.S. labor relations in the last 50 years is arguably the illegal Professional Air Traffic Controllers Organization (PATCO) strike in 1981 (recall Box 4.23). President Ronald Reagan's firing of the 11,000 striking air traffic controllers is often cited as the event that made it acceptable for private sector companies to aggressively fight unions in organizing drives, at the bargaining table, and by using replacement workers for strikers. In Great Britain, the analogous watershed event is the National Union of Mineworkers (NUM) 12-month strike against the government-run National Coal Board (NCB) in 1984–85, often now referred to simply as the Great Strike.

By many accounts, the roots of the 1984–85 NUM strike go back to large coal strikes in 1972 and 1974 which were at least partly responsible for the downfall of the Conservative government of Edward Heath. When Conservative leader Margaret Thatcher was elected in 1979, she was determined to not let this happen again, and perhaps also to extract some revenge. An equally aggressive personality with polar opposite political views became leader of the NUM in 1981: the militant socialist Arthur Scargill. Adding to the mix of strong personalities was Thatcher's 1983 appointment to head the NCB: Ian MacGregor, who had already shed thousands of jobs at the nationalized (and unprofitable) British Steel. For NUM, this was a sign that Thatcher wanted a confrontation.

The strike was triggered by the NCB's March 1984 announcement that it was closing a mining pit in Yorkshire and by its *unilateral* insistence that a total of 20 pits be closed—in violation of earlier promises and agreements. While the coal board claimed that most of the 20,000 lost jobs would come through attrition, NUM was prepared to fight unilateral pit closures to protect their jobs and their communities, and went on strike without a strike vote. At the height of the strike, 150,000 miners were on strike, but 25,000 miners in Nottinghamshire refused to strike until a strike vote was taken. Their later strike vote rejected striking. With this large division within its own ranks, NUM garnered little support from the rest of the British labor movement. The lack of an initial strike vote also came back to haunt NUM as the strike was declared illegal because NUM's constitution required a strike vote, and its funds were sequestered.

The primary issue of the strike was pit closings—the government's right to unilaterally close mining pits versus the destruction of jobs and rural mining communities. With such a difficult issue dividing them, both NUM and the NCB took a hard line in negotiations. Depending on which side is to be believed, these hard line bargaining stances were backed up by violent miners on the picket lines or by overly aggressive police supported by complicit judges. There were numerous violent clashes between miners and police and it is estimated that 1,700 injuries and a couple of deaths resulted. Nearly 10,000 striking miners were arrested. A warm winter, some domestic mining, and increased imports of coal and oil generally offset the loss of coal production due to the strike. With no end in sight and more miners returning to work, the miners voted to end the strike without a collective bargaining agreement after 51 weeks.

Politically, the strike was extremely divisive. It highlighted north (poor) versus south (rich) divisions within Britain, created fissures within the labor movement and the Labour party, and questioned the fabric of British society. Thatcher's opposition was so intense that she labeled the miners "the enemy within." It was later revealed that MI5, Britain's domestic CIA, led a widespread surveillance effort that included infiltration of NUM, bugging restaurants frequented by NUM leaders, and tapping the phone of every NUM branch. At the end of the strike, Thatcher remained concerned about future strikes, and in 1990, NUM leader Scargill was accused in the media of using donations from Libya and the Soviet Union for his personal gain rather than helping striking miners. The accusations proved to be false and evidence points towards an MI5 conspiracy to plant these false accusations in the media.

As in the PATCO strike in the United States, the NUM strike of 1984–85 arguably established a climate in Britain of aggressive antiunionism. British union density has continued to decline and the Labour party continues to distance itself from the labor movement that founded it. And nearly all of the pit mines have been closed.

Ironically, however, for many miners' wives and other women the strike was a very empowering event. In stories that parallel the Women's Emergency Brigade in the General Motors sit-down strike in 1936–37 or the women's auxiliary in the Phelps Dodge strike in 1983 in the United States, women became actively involved in the NUM strike in running soup kitchens, speaking to groups around Great Britain to develop support for the strike, and picketing. The following two quotes from participants in the strike are revealing:

Continued

"The NUM, as far as I can see, put all its eggs in the picketing basket, as they traditionally have, and made no particular provision for dealing with destitution amongst the families. So the women began to see that as well as campaigning there was a need to support the families. That meant going far beyond the traditional housewife role of the mining women. There has been large-scale catering, feeding five and six hundred people in a day; having to raise the money for that, learning to argue for it, to earn it in all sorts of ways, by speaking at meetings and rallies, by collecting on the streets. What they did was to set up an alternative welfare system, and an effective one at that. And these women who had never done anything outside the home before, learning to speak on public platforms to enormous audiences. The change in those women is tremendous." (A daughter, mother, and ex-wife of miners in South Yorkshire)

"The strike has brought me out of my shell. I am not a quiet person, but I am not particularly outgoing. Now, if I thought something was wrong, or if someone needed my support, I would do it. I'm glad it happened, because we got up and shook ourselves." (A self-described "little simple housewife" (before the strike, and miner's wife in southeastern Wales)

Sources and additional reading: Teresa Ghilarducci, "When Management Strikes: PATCO and the British Miners," *Industrial Relations Journal* 17 (Summer 1986), pp. 115–28. Ian MacGregor, *The Enemies Within: The Story of the Miners' Strike, 1984–5* (London: Collins, 1986). Seamas Milne, *The Enemy Within: MI5, Maxwell, and the Scargill Affair* (London: Verso, 1994). Vicky Seddon (ed.), *The Cutting Edge: Women and the Pit Strike* (London: Lawrence and Wishart, 1986). The two quotes are from Seddon, *The Cutting Edge*, pp. 29 and 229.

Additional viewing: The entertaining movie *Billy Elliot* is set against the backdrop of the 1984–85 strike.

Because a voluntaristic system lacks legal standards for representation and bargaining, strong employer leverage can result in representation mechanisms that are illegal elsewhere. As a graphic example, consider Nissan and Toyota's recognition of the Amalgamated Engineering and Electrical Union at their British plants. Because of their economic leverage, the companies were able to insist that broad managerial prerogatives remain the sole function of management. In addition to production methods and standards, these prerogatives include core labor issues such as employee communications, transfers, and promotions. Moreover, wages and terms and conditions of employment are established not through bargaining, but through a joint employee–management company council in which the union has no formal role, strikes are not allowed, and the company retains final decision-making authority.[31] This essentially nonunion form of employee representation is illegal in the United States both because of mandatory bargaining items and restrictions on company-dominated unions, but voluntarism allows the agreement of any arrangement that is mutually acceptable, where "acceptable" is determined by bargaining power.

IRELAND

Labor relations in Ireland is an interesting contrast with the British system. At its core, Irish labor relations is very similar to British labor relations. When Ireland gained independence from Great Britain in 1922, the existing British laws for labor relations continued under the new Irish government. Consequently, the British system of voluntarism and labor union immunity from common law liabilities underlies Irish as well as British labor relations.[32] Collective bargaining was therefore also traditionally adversarial and produced restrictive work rules, and until 1980, Ireland was perceived as one of the most strike-prone countries in Europe.[33] The

[31] Katz and Darbishire, *Converging Divergences.*

[32] Patrick Gunnigle, Gerard McMahon, and Gerard Fitzgerald, *Industrial Relations in Ireland: Theory and Practice,* 2nd ed. (Dublin: Gill and Macmillan, 1999).

[33] Ferdinand von Prondzynski, "Ireland: Corporatism Revived," in Anthony Ferner and Richard Hyman (eds.), *Changing Industrial Relations in Europe* (Oxford: Blackwell Publishers, 1998), Chapter 2.

Industrial Relations Act of 1990 implemented reforms similar to the British changes in labor law in the 1980s initiated by the Thatcher government—restrictions on secondary activity and picketing plus requirements for secret ballot strike votes—but the basic labor relations framework remains voluntarism. Union density declined after 1980 from 55 percent to about 45 percent in the late 1990s which, compared to the British and U.S. experience, is a mild decline.[34]

The striking contrast with British labor relations is the Irish inclusion of **social partnership** on top of its voluntaristic labor relations system. Social partnership can mean various things, but here social partnership is used in a corporatist sense: a social partnership of labor, business, and the government which results in a series of peak-level agreements on social and economic issues.[35] Peak-level organizations are the highest national groups representing the public, employees, and employers. For the public, this is the government, for labor it is the major labor union federation, and for employers it is the major employers' association. In a corporatist political system, these key peak-level organizations are integrated into the political decision-making process (as will be described next). This stands in contrast to a pluralist political system (as in the United States) in which interest groups such as the labor movement and employers' associations compete for influence by pressuring and lobbying lawmakers, but are not formally incorporated into the decision-making process.

The peak-level organizations in the Irish case include the major union federation—the Irish Congress of Trade Unions (ICTU)—and the Irish Business and Employers' Confederation (IBEC) representing employers. Prompted by a growing economic crisis in the 1980s—including stagnant personal income and sharply increasing unemployment and government debt—the government, the ICTU, and the IBEC negotiated a social partnership agreement called the Programme for National Recovery (PNR) in 1987. The goal of the PNR was to create a fiscal and monetary climate that was conducive to economic growth and a reduction in government debt. This included changes in the tax system, increased employment opportunities, and private sector pay guidelines (a 6-month pay freeze followed by 2.5 percent annual increases). This three-year social partnership agreement has been followed by six additional agreements (see Box 13.6). In a break from the earlier agreements, the seventh partnership agreement "Towards 2016" negotiated in 2006 lasts for 10 years (except the wage agreement which covers the first 27 months).

On one level, these social partnership agreements reflect a system of centralized bargaining. Each of the agreements established pay guidelines for the Irish economy, and while some local bargaining occurred, collective bargaining for wages was essentially done by the one major union federation and employers' association on an economy-wide basis. But this is more than just centralized collective bargaining. In addition to labor and management, the government participates as a third pillar, and in the 1990s a fourth pillar of community groups was added to the partnership process.[36] Recent social partnership talks have therefore included representatives from organizations such as the Irish Farmers Association, the Irish National Organization of the Unemployed, and the Conference of Religious of Ireland; the resulting agreements reflect a *social* partnership much broader than a limited economic or workplace agreement. Far-ranging economic and social issues are tackled in these agreements: government spending and taxation, unemployment, housing, access to health care,

---

[34] Gunnigle, McMahon, and Fitzgerald, *Industrial Relations in Ireland.*

[35] Hans Slomp, *Between Bargaining and Politics: An Introduction to European Labor Relations* (Westport, CT: Praeger, 1996).

[36] Paul Teague and James Donaghey, "The Irish Experiment in Social Partnership," in Harry C. Katz, Wonduck Lee, and Joohee Lee (eds.), *The New Structure of Labor Relations: Tripartism and Decentralization* (Ithaca, NY: Cornell University Press, 2004), pp. 10–36.

The Programme for National Recovery (PNR), 1987–1990

Objectives: Creation of a fiscal and monetary climate that is conducive to economic growth and a reduction in government debt.

Provisions: Changes in the tax system, increased employment opportunities, and private sector pay guidelines (a 6-month pay freeze followed by 2.5 percent annual increases).

The Programme for Economic and Social Progress (PESP), 1990–1994

Objectives: Sustained economic growth, increased employment, development of greater social rights (education, health, and housing), worker participation, women's rights, and consumer rights.

Provisions: Pay guidelines and a pledge by labor and management to maintain industrial harmony and to resolve bargaining differences through formal dispute resolution machinery (such as the Labour Court).

The Programme for Competitiveness and Work (PCW), 1994–1997

Objectives: Pay stability and creation of climate for growth (similar to the PNR).

Provisions: Primarily pay guidelines, but also employment and training programs, and tax reform.

Partnership 2000 for Inclusion, Employment and Competitiveness, 1997–2000

Objectives: Continued development of an efficient, internationally competitive economy, employment growth, and social inclusion.

Provisions: Tax relief, government debt reduction targets, creation of a national framework for creating labor–management partnerships at the enterprise level, attempts at tackling "social exclusion," a framework for resolving union recognition questions, and pay guidelines.*

The Programme for Prosperity and Fairness, 2001–2003

Objectives: Promote competitiveness, further economic prosperity, improvements in the quality of life and living standards for all, and a fairer and more inclusive Ireland.

Operational Frameworks: Living Standards and Workplace Environment (including pay standards, workplace partnerships, and flexibility), Prosperity and Economic Inclusion, Social Inclusion and Equality, Successful Adaptation to Continuing Change, and Renewing Partnership.

Sustaining Progress, 2003–2005

Objectives: To continue progress toward economic inclusion (based on full employment, consistent economic development that is socially and environmentally sustainable, social inclusion and a commitment to social justice, and continuing adaptation to change) by sustaining economic growth and high levels of employment while strengthening the economy's competitiveness.

Provisions: Pay guidelines with strengthened enforcement mechanisms, a commitment to seek specific labor law reforms, enhanced severance pay, and affordable housing targets.

Towards 2016, 2006–2015

Objectives: Fulfill a longer-term vision for Ireland that links social policy and economic prosperity, develops a vibrant knowledge-based economy, increases the integration of the island of Ireland, and successfully handles diversity.

Provisions: Pay guidelines, increased penalties for employment law violators, social welfare payments linked to average wage level, increased provision of affordable housing, child care and health care, infrastructure spending targets, greater investments in education.

*Social exclusion captures the idea that those often in poverty are often excluded not only from jobs, but also from political rights, health care, and education. This might stem from racism, religious discrimination, lack of education, being an immigrant, or other reasons.

poverty and social exclusion, and education and lifelong learning. Moreover, while the agreements are not legally binding contracts, they do provide a very public framework that the parties generally try to adhere to. The resulting stability and predictability—for the aggregate economy as well as workplace labor relations—are widely credited with laying the foundation for

Ireland's exceptional economic performance during the 1990s.[37] The extent to which a climate of partnership has extended to the workplace, however, can be questioned.[38]

Various forms of social partnerships or corporatism have been prevalent, albeit not continuously, in the smaller European countries such as Austria, Belgium, Denmark, the Netherlands, Norway, and Switzerland.[39] The benefits of the participation of labor, business, government, and other groups in the development of a national plan for both economic and social development are inclusion, stability, predictability, and a climate of consensus rather than conflict. Government policy can also be depoliticized in that labor and business are also involved in establishing economic and social policy.[40] For unions, a social partnership arrangement provides greater social relevance as the voice for all workers, and perhaps consumers and taxpayers as well. This voice is on a national level, however, not in the workplace, and unions need to be careful not to lose their workplace voice. Echoing the workplace-level debates over unions and high performance work systems (Chapter 11), there can also be a fine line for unions in a social partnership arrangement between collaboration and "selling out."[41] Lastly, while social partnerships can promote stability and consensus, the centralized nature of this form of labor relations is under pressure at the workplace level as management seeks greater flexibility, increased pay-for-performance, and other decentralized, efficiency-enhancing human resource management innovations.

FRANCE

Labor relations in France consists of an interesting mixture of militant, often politically oriented unions but weak collective bargaining, very low union density but very high coverage by industry-level agreements, and several mechanisms for workplace-level representation.[42] As shown in Box 13.7, there are seven major union federations; recall that the United States until 2005, Britain, and Ireland each had or have one. Unlike the U.S. emphasis on business unionism, the French union federations often have distinct political or ideological perspectives. The CGT has traditionally been communist and therefore acted as Lenin's transmission belt for conveying Communist Party priorities to the working class, though it is moving away from this platform. While also becoming more pragmatic in recent years, the FO and CFDT have traditionally been associated with socialist ideals of worker control while the CFTC has a Christian orientation. The CFTC supports collective bargaining, but note that in very general terms, communist and socialist unions have not

---

[37] Gunnigle, McMahon, and Fitzgerald, *Industrial Relations in Ireland*. Séamus Ó'Móráin, "The European Employment Strategy—A Consideration of Social Partnership and Related Matters in the Irish Context," *International Journal of Comparative Labour Law and Industrial Relations* 16 (Spring 2000), pp. 85–101.

[38] Patrick Gunnigle, "More Rhetoric than Reality: Enterprise Level Industrial Relations Partnerships in Ireland," *The Economic and Social Review* 28 (October 1997), pp. 179–200. Teague and Donaghey, "The Irish Experiment in Social Partnership."

[39] Anthony Ferner and Richard Hyman (eds.), *Changing Industrial Relations in Europe* (Oxford: Blackwell Publishers, 1998).

[40] Slomp, *Between Bargaining and Politics.*

[41] Richard Hyman, *Understanding European Trade Unionism: Between Market, Class and Society* (London: Sage, 2001).

[42] Unless otherwise noted, this section draws heavily on these two sources: Anthony Daley, "The Hollowing Out of French Unions: Politics and Industrial Relations After 1981," in Andrew Martin and George Ross (eds.), *The Brave New World of European Labor: European Trade Unions at the Millennium* (New York: Berghahn Books, 1999), Chapter 5. Janine Goetschy, "France: The Limits of Reform," in Anthony Ferner and Richard Hyman (eds.), *Changing Industrial Relations in Europe* (Oxford: Blackwell Publishers, 1998), Chapter 13.

BOX 13.7
French Union
Confederations

	Membership	Works Committees Elections
Industrial Unions		
Confédération générale du travail (CGT)—General Confederation of Labor *Traditionally Communist though moving away from Marxist orthodoxy.*	800,000	22.1%
Confédération français democratique du travail (CFDT)—French Democratic Confederation of Labor *Radical support of worker control in 1960s, but recently a more moderate focus on union adaptation to economic change.*	850,000	22.6
Force ouvriére (FO)—Workers' Strength *Anti-Communist and militant.*	270,000	12.7
Confédération français des travailleurs chrétiens (CFTC)—French Confederation of Christian Workers *Christian orientation, anticlass struggle, pro-collective bargaining.*	100,000	6.7
Occupational Unions		
Union nationale des syndicats autonomes (USNA)—National Federation of Independent Unions *Mostly public sector workers, especially teachers.*	350,000	Only has sectoral-level representative status
Confédération française de l'encadrement-Confédération générale des cadres (CFE-CGC)—French Confederation of Professional and Managerial Staff–General Confederation of Managerial Staffs *Focus on economic issues for engineers, technicians, supervisors, sales representatives and others.*	80,000	6.6
Fédération syndicale unitaire (FSU)—Unitary Union Federation *Primarily teachers with more of a left-wing orientation than those affiliated with the USNA.*	150,000	Only has sectoral-level representative status
	Others:	6.1
	Nonunion:	23.2

Sources: Janine Goetschy and Annette Jobert, "Employment Relations in France," in Greg J. Bamber, Russell D. Lansbury, and Nick Wailes (eds.), *International and Comparative Employment Relations: Globalisation and the Developed Market Economies* (London: Sage, 2004), pp. 176–210. "2003 Works Council Election Results and New Worker Representation Rules for SMEs," *EIRO On-line* (Dublin: European Foundation for the Improvement of Living and Working Conditions, 2005), available at *http://www.eiro.eurofound.eu.int/2005/10/feature/fr0510103f.html* [accessed July 15, 2006]. Membership and election statistics are circa 2002–03.

always supported collective bargaining because signing a contract limits worker freedom and legitimizes capitalism.[43] With such sharp ideological differences between unions, and between labor and employers, a stable social partnership arrangement is nearly impossible to achieve. Rather, political mobilization and political strikes motivated by each union's ideological focus have been as important, if not more important, than collective bargaining in French labor relations. For example, brief national strikes and massive protests by workers and students—sometimes involving more than a million protesters—in 2006 caused the French government to withdraw a legislative proposal that would make it easier for companies to dismiss younger workers. As such, France is an example of political or **ideological unionism.** Other southern European countries such as Italy and Spain are broadly similar in this regard. Moreover, this is a pluralist model of political unionism rather than a corporatist model—unlike in the Irish social partnerships, the French unions (as "outsiders") pressure the government to enact policies favorable to the unions' agendas rather than participating directly in policymaking (as "insiders").

Continuing competitive and economic problems led to government initiatives to regularize French labor relations, and since the 1980s, collective bargaining and workplace representation have increased in importance. Bargaining takes place on three levels: multi-industry, industry, and company. The multi-industry and industry agreements provide the broad parameters and minimum standards for individual companies to follow regarding flexibility and working time (multi-industry) and pay (industry). Company-level agreements implement specific pay and working conditions provisions. Note carefully that there is no feature of exclusive representation—French law essentially mandates company-level bargaining irrespective of whether a majority of employees authorize a single union as their representative. Thus, an employer may negotiate with a committee comprised of individuals from varying unions. Moreover, as is true in a number of other European countries, French law provides for the extension of industry agreements to all companies within the same industry—irrespective of the number of union members (if any) at a specific company. Thus, while union density is very low, the fraction of workers covered by collective bargaining agreements is very high (recall Box 13.2). On the other hand, collective bargaining agreements in France are weak by U.S. standards—though this is perhaps offset by national legislation that often favors workers, such as a 35-hour work week.

Lastly, French law provides for several forms of workplace-level employee representation separate from labor unions. Employee delegates are required to handle grievances and to monitor the enforcement of both labor laws and collective bargaining agreements. Works committees are entitled to information and to consultation on workplace and companywide decisions (see the discussion of German codetermination in the next section). Employee delegates and works committee representatives are elected via secret ballot by all workers. The union confederations listed in Box 13.7 (excepting the USNA and FSU) are entitled to provide the first slate of candidates, but as shown in Box 13.7, nearly one-quarter of works committee representatives are not members of a union. A single works committee likely has members of different unions. French labor law also guarantees workers a right of expression, so workers are entitled to voice their opinions regarding the nature of their work. That French law struggles with trying to balance efficiency, equity, and voice is captured by this description of reforms in the early 1980s: "The Auroux laws were intended to foster a mutual learning process within the enterprise, with employers becoming more aware of their social employment responsibilities and unions more attentive to the firm's economic constraints."[44]

---

[43] Hyman, *Understanding European Trade Unionism.*

[44] Goetschy, "France," p. 379.

GERMANY

The labor relations system of Germany (formerly, West Germany) is best known for its system of codetermination, but this important feature must be understood in conjunction with a second major feature, sector bargaining. In contrast to France, there is one dominant union federation, *Deutscher Gewerkschaftsbund* (DGB, German Trade Union Confederation), that accounts for over 80 percent of German union membership and has eight affiliated unions each of which represents a specific industry.[45] Employer federations are also organized by industry. As such, each major industry or sector has a dominant union and employer association and these two bodies engage in **sector bargaining**—industry-wide bargaining that produces a contract for the entire sector.

Sector bargaining often takes place at a regional level, but it is tightly coordinated by the national organizations and the first regional agreement sets a strong pattern for the other regions. For example, a regional branch of *Gesamtmetall,* the metal and electrical industry employers' association, and the regional branch of *IG Metall,* the metal and electrical industry union, will negotiate basic agreements on wages, pay structures, working time, and working conditions under the direction of their parent organizations. These agreements establish minimum labor standards that apply to *all* members of the employers' association—the number of union members at each company is unimportant. Moreover, the agreements can be extended to other companies by the government. As such, the contract coverage rate is very high (see Box 13.2). Strikes are illegal during the life of an agreement. A company cannot invalidate the contract by leaving the employers' association, so it is difficult to become nonunion in Germany.[46] As in many other countries, competitive forces are pressuring the German collective bargaining system to become more decentralized. As a result, local exceptions to the industry standards are increasing and some companies have negotiated independently rather than through their employers' association—Volkswagen is the prominent example—but because of strong traditions and institutions, these deviations are still the exception rather than the norm.[47]

Collective bargaining in Germany, therefore, largely occurs at a centralized industry (sector) level. This is complemented in the workplace by **codetermination**—an institutionalized system of employee voice in which employees are entitled to participate in workplace decision making. German codetermination has two components: works councils and employee-representation on corporate supervisory boards. A **works council** is a workplace-level committee of employees elected to represent all of the workers (except senior executives)—skilled and unskilled, blue and white collar, union members and nonmembers—in dealings with management. Works councils in various forms are also found in France, Spain, the Netherlands, Austria, Italy, and Belgium, but the German example is perhaps the most well-known.[48]

---

[45] Berndt K. Keller, "Employment Relations in Germany," in Greg J. Bamber, Russell D. Lansbury, and Nick Wailes (eds.), *International and Comparative Employment Relations: Globalisation and the Developed Market Economies* (London: Sage, 2004), pp. 211–53.

[46] Katz and Darbishire, *Converging Divergences.* Gerhard Bosch, "The Changing Nature of Collective Bargaining in Germany: Coordinated Decentralization," in Harry C. Katz, Wonduck Lee, and Joohee Lee (eds.), *The New Structure of Labor Relations: Tripartism and Decentralization* (Ithaca, NY: Cornell University Press, 2004), pp. 84–118.

[47] Bosch, "The Changing Nature of Collective Bargaining in Germany."

[48] Ferner and Hyman, *Changing Industrial Relations in Europe.* Joel Rogers and Wolfgang Streeck (eds.), *Works Councils: Consultation, Representation, and Cooperation in Industrial Relations* (Chicago: University of Chicago Press, 1995). Mark Carley, Annalisa Baradel, and Christian Welz, "Works Councils: Workplace Representation and Participation Structures," *EIRO Thematic Features* (Dublin: European Foundation for the Improvement of Living and Working Conditions, 2005), available at *http://www.eiro.eurofound. eu.int/other_reports/works%20councils_final.pdf* [accessed July 16, 2006].

German law entitles all workers in companies with at least five employees to form a works council if some employees wish—generally only 5 percent of the employees need to sign a list of candidates to trigger an election of employee representatives to a works council (or a minimum of two employees in very small establishments and a maximum of 50 in large workplaces). Do not confuse this with a drawn-out and sharply contested NLRB representation election as in the United States (Chapter 7)—"once the procedure is initiated by employees, the election of a works council is to all intents and purposes automatic."[49] More than 90 percent of establishments with at least 500 employees have a works council, but less than 10 percent of small establishments do; changes to the German Works Constitution Act in 2001 therefore further simplified the election process in small establishments.[50]

German works councils have codetermination, consultation, and information rights regarding various workplace issues and are legally distinct from unions—their existence does not depend on a local union presence. Nevertheless, in practice union members are likely to be active in the works councils, and unions help provide training and expertise.[51] The size of works councils vary with the size of the workforce: a 500-person establishment has an 11-member works council (including one full-time member) while a 5,000-person establishment has a 29-person works council (including seven full-time members). The works council must meet with an employer at least once a month and the company pays for a works council's expenses. Companies with multiple establishments must also establish company-wide works councils. The law mandates that "the employer and the works councils shall work together in a spirit of mutual trust . . . for the good of the employees and of the establishment." A works council cannot strike, but it can sue if an employer does not fulfill its legal obligations of codetermination, consultation, and information provision.

Granting codetermination rights to works councils means that a company must jointly determine with the works council issues pertaining to work rules and discipline, daily working hours, leave schedules, performance-based pay and bonuses, overtime, safety and health, training, and personnel selection methods (see Box 13.8). In other words, on these matters the employer cannot take action without the agreement of the works council. Negotiated agreements on codetermined issues are incorporated into works agreements. The second set of rights granted to works councils are consultation rights—the works council must be consulted before an employer changes the nature of work. Thirdly, a firm's works council must be given financial information regarding the firm's balance sheet, investment and marketing plans, and other corporate intentions (see Box 13.8).

Remember that industry-wide collective bargaining agreements specify minimum standards and other broad parameters for the workplace. As such, works councils are left to work out specific details, especially pertaining to implementation issues, for each workplace.[52] Moreover, when the labor market is strong, some works councils are able to negotiate extra wage increases, and conversely, when a firm's financial health is weak, some works councils agree to concessions below the collective bargaining agreement's standards ("wildcat cooperation").[53] Works councils are also viewed as generally supportive of workplace

[49] John T. Addison et al., "The Reform of the German Works Constitution Act: A Critical Assessment," *Industrial Relations* 43 (April 2004), pp. 392–420 at 398.

[50] Addison et al., "The Reform of the German Works Constitution Act."

[51] Walther Müller-Jentsch, "Germany: From Collective Voice to Co-Management," in Joel Rogers and Wolfgang Streeck (eds.), *Works Councils: Consultation, Representation, and Cooperation in Industrial Relations* (Chicago: University of Chicago Press, 1995), Chapter 3.

[52] Müller-Jentsch, "Germany."

[53] Otto Jacobi, Berndt Keller, and Walther Müller-Jentsch, "Germany: Facing New Challenges," in Anthony Ferner and Richard Hyman (eds.), *Changing Industrial Relations in Europe* (Oxford: Blackwell Publishers, 1998), pp. 190–238.

74. Principles of collaboration

(1) The employer and the works council shall meet together at least once a month for joint conferences. They shall discuss the matters at issue with an earnest desire to reach agreement and make suggestions for settling their differences.

(2) Industrial action between the employer and the works council shall be unlawful; the foregoing shall not apply to industrial action between collective bargaining parties. The employer and the works council shall refrain from activities that interfere with operations or imperil the peace in the establishment.

85. Works council's role in dealing with grievances

(1) The works council shall hear employees' grievances and, if they appear justified, induce the employer to remedy them.

Social Matters

87. Right of co-determination

(1) The works council shall have a right of codetermination in the following matters in so far as they are not prescribed by legislation or collective agreement:

1. matters relating to the order by operation of the establishment and the conduct of employees in the establishment;

2. the commencement and termination of the daily working hours including breaks and the distribution of working hours among the days of the week;

3. any temporary reduction or extension of the hours normally worked in the establishment;

4. the time and place for and the form of payment of remuneration;

5. the establishment of general principles for leave arrangements and the preparation of the leave schedule as well as fixing the time at which the leave is to be taken by individual employees, if no agreement is reached between the employer and the employees concerned;

6. the introduction and use of technical devices designed to monitor the behavior or performance of the employees;

7. arrangements for the prevention of employment accidents and occupational diseases and for the protection of health on the basis of legislation or safety regulations;

8. the form, structuring and administration of social services whose scope is limited to the establishment, company or combine;

9. the assignment of and notice to vacate accommodation that is rented to employees in view of their employment relationship as well as the general fixing of the conditions for the use of such accommodation;

10. questions related to remuneration arrangements in the establishment, including in particular the establishment of principles of remuneration and the introduction and application of new remuneration methods or modification of existing methods;

11. the fixing of job and bonus rates and comparable performance-related remuneration including cash coefficients;

12. principles for suggestion schemes in the establishment.

13. principles governing the performance of group work; group work within the meaning of this provision is defined as a group of employees performing a complex task within the establishment's workflows, which has been assigned to it and is executed in a largely autonomous way.

Structuring, Organization and Design of Jobs, Operations and the Working Environment

90. Information and consultation rights

(1) The employer shall inform the works council in due time of any plans concerning

1. the construction, alteration or extension of works, offices and other premises belonging to the establishment;

2. technical plants;

3. working procedures and operations or

4. jobs

and submit the necessary documents.

(2) The employer shall consult the works council in good time on the action envisaged and its effects on the employees, taking particular account of its impact on the nature of their work and the resultant demands on the employees so that suggestions and objections on the part of the works council can be taken into account in the plans.

91. Right of co-determination

Where a special burden is imposed on the employees as a result of changes in jobs, operations or the working environment that are in obvious contradiction to the established findings of ergonomics relating to the tailoring of jobs to meet human requirements, the works council

Continued

may request appropriate action to obviate, relieve or compensate for the additional stress thus imposed.

92. Manpower planning

(1) The employer shall inform the works council in full and in good time of matters relating to manpower planning including in particular present and future manpower needs and the resulting staff movements and vocational training measures and supply the relevant documentation. He shall consult the works council on the nature and extent of the action required and means of avoiding hardship.

95. Guidelines for selection

(1) Guidelines for the selection of employees for recruitment, transfer, regrading and dismissal shall require the approval of the works council.

98. Implementation of vocational training in the establishment

(1) The works council shall participate in the decisions relating to the implementation of vocational training programs in the establishment.

102. Co-determination in the case of dismissal

(1) The works council shall be consulted before every dismissal. The employer shall indicate to the works council the reasons for dismissal. Any notice of dismissal that is given without consulting the works council shall be null and void.

Financial Matters

106. Finance committee

(1) A finance committee shall be established in all companies that normally have more than 100 permanent employees. It shall be the duty of the finance committee to consult with the employer on financial matters and report to the works council.

(2) The employer shall inform the finance committee in full and in good time of the financial affairs of the company and supply the relevant documentation in so far as there is no risk of disclosing the trade or business secrets of the company and demonstrate the implications for manpower planning.

111. Alterations

In establishments that normally have more than twenty employees with voting rights the employer shall inform the works council in full and in good time of any proposed alterations which may entail substantial prejudice to the staff or a large sector thereof and consult the works council on the proposed alterations.

---

changes and the implementation of new processes and technologies if the company and its workforce will be strengthened, and management can utilize works councils to help implement such changes.[54] German companies are introducing the same types of flexible work systems as in other countries, but the legal rights of works councils—which again are independent of union membership—give them the power to ensure that employee interests are represented when these changes are implemented.[55] Research on works councils fails to uncover significant effects on economic efficiency; in other words, it is difficult to conclude that works councils either improve or harm productivity, employee turnover, and the like.[56] Supporters of works councils, however, see them as mechanisms for providing equity and especially voice, not efficiency.

Complementing works councils is the other major component of German codetermination: employee representation on corporate supervisory boards. German corporations have two boards for managing the company—a management board controls the day-to-day management of the firm and reports to the higher-level supervisory board that sets strategic policies and appoints upper-level managers. The supervisory board generally meets four times per year. Employees are entitled to minority representation (1/3 of representatives) on the supervisory board of companies with more than 500 employees and to nominally equal parity in companies with more than 2,000 employees. For these firms, employees

---

[54] Müller-Jentsch, "Germany."

[55] Katz and Darbishire, *Converging Divergences.* Lowell Turner, *Democracy at Work: Changing World Markets and the Future of Labor Unions* (Ithaca, NY: Cornell University Press, 1991).

[56] Addison et al., "The Reform of the German Works Constitution Act." John T. Addison, Claus Schnabel, and Joachim Wagner, "The Course of Research into the Economic Consequences of German Works Councils," *British Journal of Industrial Relations* 42 (June 2004), pp. 255–81.

are entitled to half of the supervisory board members, though this is not true parity because shareholders elect the chairperson who has the power to decide dead-locked issues. In the coal and steel industry, employees have true parity on the supervisory board and can also appoint a labor director to the management board. German supervisory boards are less powerful than U.S. boards of directors, but employee representation nevertheless provides workers with a voice when strategic decisions are being considered.[57] In the United States, unions occasionally obtain a single board seat, often as part of a significant package of employee wage and work rule concessions, but significant board-level representation is mandated by law in Germany.

Lastly, note that since union membership is not linked to industry-level collective agreements, workplace-level works council representation, or supervisory board representation, the decision to join a union is very different than in the United States. In Europe "joining a trade union is as much an act of political commitment as it is a step to support collective bargaining. It is more an act of solidarity than simply a means to secure personal gains."[58] Similarly, European unions traditionally have not focused solely on winning economic improvements for their members. Rather, advocacy of broad working class interests—either within capitalism or in opposition to it—and integration of workers into broader political movements have been as important, and frequently more important, than collective bargaining.[59]

SWEDEN

The major dimensions of labor relations in Sweden and the other Nordic countries appear broadly similar to those in Germany: a very high contract coverage rate and a dual representation structure with centralized, industry-wide collective bargaining and strong workplace representation.[60] An important difference, however, is that while workplace representation in Germany is institutionalized by law in the form of works councils that are technically independent of labor unions, until recently workplace representation in Sweden has been institutionalized by culture and tradition in the form of strong workplace-level unions. Like the United States, workplace representation in Sweden relies on unions; unlike the United States, union density in Sweden is very high (see Box 13.2) so workplace representation is widespread. As in other countries around the world, economic pressures are causing greater decentralization in bargaining: peak-level negotiations have been sporadic since 1980, industry-wide agreements have become less detailed, and local agreements have become both more important and more diverse.[61] The traditional goal of the Swedish labor movement was a "solidaristic wage policy" which consisted of equal pay for equal work across companies (so that company ability to pay is unimportant) and a compression of wage outcomes within an establishment. New forms of work organization, however, have reoriented this objective more towards a "solidaristic work policy" in which unions are involved

---

[57] Kirsten S. Wever, *Negotiating Competitiveness: Employment Relations and Organizational Innovation in Germany and the United States* (Boston: Harvard Business School Press, 1995). Felix FitzRoy and Kornelius Kraft, "Co-determination, Efficiency and Productivity," *British Journal of Industrial Relations* 43 (June 2005), pp. 233–47.

[58] Slomp, *Between Bargaining and Politics,* pp. 21–22.

[59] Hyman, *Understanding European Trade Unionism.* Slomp, *Between Bargaining and Politics.*

[60] Anders Kjellberg, "Sweden: Restoring the Model?" in Anthony Ferner and Richard Hyman (eds.), *Changing Industrial Relations in Europe* (Oxford: Blackwell Publishers, 1998), Chapter 3.

[61] Katz and Darbishire, *Converging Divergences.* Kjellberg, "Sweden." Olle Hammarström, Tony Huzzard, and Tommy Nilsson, "Employment Relations in Sweden," in Greg J. Bamber, Russell D. Lansbury, and Nick Wailes (eds.), *International and Comparative Employment Relations: Globalisation and the Developed Market Economies* (London: Sage, 2004), pp. 254–76.

in the transformation of work to ensure that workers as well as companies benefit from these changes.[62] In particular, the solidaristic work policy advocates self-directed work teams, training, job and skill development, and compensation for skills and responsibilities. The extent to which U.S. unions might also be less resistant to workplace change if they had the institutional and cultural security of Swedish unions is a thought-provoking question.

EASTERN EUROPE

After World War II, labor relations in the Soviet Union and the communist countries of eastern Europe was characterized by **Stalinist unionism,** after the Soviet dictator Joseph Stalin.[63] In centrally planned Stalinist economies, managers of state-owned enterprises and unions were both controlled by the government (the Communist Party). Unions were a critical part of this economic and political system, primarily as a transmission belt for delivering the Communist Party's agenda to the working class (*not* as a transmission belt in the reverse direction: conveying the concerns of the working class to the ruling party)—Stalin's predecessor, Vladimir Ilyich Lenin, developed the concept of the transmission belt and this political role of unions can be described as Leninist. In the workplace, unions in a Stalinist system had dual roles: to facilitate the state's production goals (such as through maintaining discipline) and to protect individual workers from abusive managers (such as by refusing to approve employee dismissals).[64] As transmission belts of the Communist Party, the first role was much more important than the second. Unions also administered the government's various social benefits such as housing and recreational programs and therefore membership rates were very high (approaching 100 percent). There was no collective bargaining because wages and other items were determined by central planners—"the official trade unions in the Soviet Union were never designed to represent workers' interests, since official ideology held that there could be no conflict of interests between the working class and its vanguard that ran the economy, the Communist Party."[65] As such, strikes and independent unions were illegal. Unions were tightly controlled by the Communist Party, typically structured along industry lines, and, following the model of the Communist Party, very centralized.

There were some deviations from this strict model during the Cold War, for example in Hungary and most visibly in Poland. Led by electrician Lech Walesa, 17,000 workers conducted a sit-down strike at the Lenin Shipyards in Gdansk, Poland, in 1980.[66] The most important demand of the strikers was the right to form free labor unions independent of the

[62] Rianne Mahon, "'Yesterday's Modern Times Are No Longer Modern:' Swedish Unions Confront the Double Shift," in Andrew Martin and George Ross (eds.), *The Brave New World of European Labor: European Trade Unions at the Millennium* (New York: Berghahn Books, 1999), Chapter 4. Åke Sandberg, "Justice at Work: Solidaristic Work Policy as a Renewal of the Swedish Labor Market Model?" *Social Justice* 21 (Winter 1994), pp. 102–14.

[63] Simon Clarke and Peter Fairbrother, "Post-Communism and the Emergence of Industrial Relations in the Workplace," in Richard Hyman and Anthony Ferner (eds.), *New Frontiers in European Industrial Relations* (Oxford: Blackwell Publishers, 1994), Chapter 14. Derek C. Jones, "The Transformation of Labor Unions in Eastern Europe: The Case of Bulgaria," *Industrial and Labor Relations Review* 45 (April 1992), pp. 452–70. Hans Slomp, Jacques van Hoof, and Hans Moerel, "The Transformation of Industrial Relations in Some Central and Eastern European Countries," in Joris Van Ruysseveldt and Jelle Visser (eds.), *Industrial Relations in Europe: Traditions and Transitions* (London: Sage, 1996), Chapter 9.

[64] Robert J. Flanagan, " Institutional Reformation in Eastern Europe," *Industrial Relations* 37 (July 1998), pp. 337–57.

[65] Sarah Ashwin, "Social Partnership or a 'Complete Sellout'? Russian Trade Unions' Responses to Conflict," *British Journal of Industrial Relations* 42 (March 2004), pp. 23–46 at 24.

[66] Lawrence Goodwyn, *Breaking the Barrier: The Rise of Solidarity in Poland) (New York: Oxford University Press, 1991).*

Communist Party and the Solidarity union (*Solidarność*) was born. The strike was a major victory and Solidarity's membership jumped to 10 million workers. In 1981 additional strikes were used to pressure the Polish government for free elections. However, under pressure from the Soviet Union, the Polish government imposed martial law in December 1981, outlawed Solidarity, and jailed its leaders. Strikes in 1988 again pressured the government to legalize Solidarity and it was allowed to participate in free elections in 1989. Solidarity was very successful in these elections and was able to form a coalition government. Walesa won the Nobel Peace Prize in 1983 and in 1990 he became Poland's first popularly elected president.

In addition to the Solidarity movement in Poland, the fall of the Berlin Wall in 1989 marked the end of communist East Germany and by the end of that year, communism was collapsing throughout eastern Europe. In 1991 the Soviet Union dissolved into Russia and a number of independent states. These events were triggered by the Solidarity movement, which underscores the power of collective action and the need for independent labor movements in society. All of these countries, however, have been struggling with the transition to capitalist, free market economies, and democratic, pluralistic political systems since that time. Stable systems of labor relations have yet to emerge and unions have struggled to find their most effective roles in the new transition economies.[67] Are they workplace advocates, or independent political representatives of the working class in a pluralist political system, or part of governing coalitions responsible for shaping new economic and political institutions?

Collective bargaining, economic strikes, and independent labor unions have been legalized in eastern Europe. The emergence of independent unions has resulted in significant interunion competition, though in many of the countries the largest unions continue to be reformed versions of the preexisting communist unions.[68] Because of the traditional importance of the government in economic affairs in these countries before the collapse of communism, the governments of many of the post-communist countries remain actively involved in economic activities generally, and in labor relations specifically. Tripartite bodies involving unions, employers associations (albeit nominally because private ownership is still emerging), and the government have therefore been used in Bulgaria, Hungary, and elsewhere.[69] As in other social partnerships (recall the discussion of Ireland above), such arrangements have dealt with establishing wage guidelines, reforming labor law, and dispute resolution. These accomplishments might be more symbolic than real, however, and political and economic instability, interunion competition, and a legacy of dependence on management and the state undermine the prospects for successful social partnerships in the years to come.[70]

The Stalinist model left behind a legacy of weak unions at the enterprise and workplace levels with no experience in collective bargaining and with little rank and file involvement. Enterprise-level collective bargaining is now emerging, but remains in its infancy because

[67] Heribert Kohl and Hans-Wolfgang Platzer, *Industrial Relations in Central and Eastern Europe: Transformation and Integration—A Comparison of the Eight New EU Member States* (Pete Burgess, transl.) (Brussels: European Trade Union Institute, 2004).

[68] Flanagan, "Institutional Reformation in Eastern Europe." Slomp, van Hoof, and Moerel, "The Transformation of Industrial Relations in Some Central and Eastern European Countries."

[69] Lajos Héthy, "Tripartism in Eastern Europe," in Richard Hyman and Anthony Ferner (eds.), *New Frontiers in European Industrial Relations* (Oxford: Blackwell Publishers, 1994), Chapter 12.

[70] Paul Thompson and Franz Traxler, "The Transformation of Industrial Relations in Postsocialist Economies," in Gerd Schienstock, Paul Thompson, and Franz Traxler (eds.), *Industrial Relations Between Command and Market: A Comparative Analysis of Eastern Europe and China* (New York: Nova Science Publishers, 1997), pp. 291–314. Ashwin, "Social Partnership or a 'Complete Sellout'?"

of this weak history and because many enterprises are still state-owned.[71] As such, "bargaining" is still often conducted with the government, so wage settlements reflect political power and maneuverings rather than economic conditions and bargaining tactics. Works councils have been implemented in Hungary, but were either not legislated or were enacted and then repealed elsewhere, and unions are struggling to develop influence in the workplace. Unions have frequently been marginalized in industries that have been privatized and turned over to private ownership. It will be interesting to watch what types of employment systems emerge when the eastern European economies develop greater economic and political stability—will existing Western systems be adopted or will new methods for balancing efficiency, equity, and voice be created—and to see whether unions have a significant role to play.

AUSTRALIA AND NEW ZEALAND

While unions in Germany and Sweden are examples of unions organized primarily along industry lines, unions in Australia were traditionally organized mostly on a craft or occupational basis. Unions typically had members in more than one industry and managers often had to deal with multiple unions—in the 1980s, the average number of unions per Australian firm was 12.[72] Union density, however, has declined sharply since the mid-1970s from above 50 percent to around 25 percent.[73] Consequently, since the late 1980s the Australian labor movement has actively pursued union mergers and amalgamations to transform a relatively large number of small unions into a smaller number of industry-based or general unions. By 1995, nearly all union members belonged to one of 20 unions.[74] This strategy attempts to counter the decline in union density by increasing the number of services that larger, industry-focused unions can provide to potential members.[75] Such merger activity, however, raises the same issue that faces the U.S. labor movement: how to balance union strength with responsiveness to the needs of individual workers and workplaces (see Box 13.9).

The drive to increase the power of Australian unions through rationalization along industry lines also stems from the trend towards decentralization of Australian labor relations. The central feature of labor relations in Australia has traditionally been a centralized system of arbitration awards. In this **awards system,** a federal or state arbitration commission (or tribunal) issues an award that specifies the minimum standards for pay and working conditions, often for an occupation. This arbitration system dates back to the early 1900s and was devised to prevent strikes. For a number of years, the basic federal award established a minimum wage for unskilled workers to fulfill "the normal needs of an average employee, regarded as a human being living in a civilized community" based on a family

[71] Denis MacShane, "The Changing Contours of Trade Unionism in Eastern Europe and the CIS," in Richard Hyman and Anthony Ferner (eds.), *New Frontiers in European Industrial Relations* (Oxford: Blackwell Publishers, 1994), Chapter 13. Gerd Schienstock, Paul Thompson, and Franz Traxler (eds.), *Industrial Relations Between Command and Market: A Comparative Analysis of Eastern Europe and China* (New York: Nova Science Publishers, 1997).

[72] John Niland and Dennis Turner, *Control, Consensus, or Chaos? Managers and Industrial Relations Reform* (Sydney: Allen and Unwin, 1985).

[73] Russell D. Lansbury and Nick Wailes, "Employment Relations in Australia," in Greg J. Bamber, Russell D. Lansbury, and Nick Wailes (eds.), *International and Comparative Employment Relations: Globalisation and the Developed Market Economies* (London: Sage, 2004), pp. 119–45.

[74] Lansbury and Wailes, "Employment Relations in Australia."

[75] Braham Dabscheck, *The Struggle for Australian Industrial Relations* (Melbourne: Oxford University Press, 1995).

In response to a decline in union density and an increased decentralization in labor relations, Australian unions have aggressively merged and amalgamated since the late 1980s. The goal of these mergers is to produce larger unions with greater resources that are therefore more powerful and better able to provide services to members. However, there is a trade-off between power and centralization on the one hand, and grassroots participation and responsiveness to local needs on the other. The experience of the Musicians' Union of Australia (MUA) highlights these conflicts.

The MUA represents approximately 5,000 musicians, vocalists, musical producers, and others in the music business and includes members in symphony orchestras, jazz ensembles, and rock bands. The union has a decentralized structure with nine branches that largely control their own activities and finances. This structure parallels the nature of its members' employment: most are employed together in small groups at clubs, hotels, and other venues on a local basis.

As part of the Australian union merger mania of the 1990s, the MUA contemplated merging with two other groups. The MUA considered merging with the Federated Miscellaneous Workers Union—itself a recent amalgamation of the Liquor Trades Union and a union of miscellaneous workers. Because of the large number of MUA members who work in clubs and hotels, there are some shared interests with the liquor trades, but orchestra members of MUA were not in favor of aligning with this group. The MUA's decentralized structure also conflicted with the centralized structure of the Federated Miscellaneous Workers Union.

The other merger considered by the MUA was with the Media, Entertainment and Arts Alliance (MEAA)—also a recent amalgamation, in this case between the Actors Equity of Australia, a theatrical employees union, and a union of journalists. The MUA membership ultimately rejected affiliating with the MEAA for several reasons. Like the Federated Miscellaneous Workers Union (and many others), the MEAA has a centralized structure and MUA members did not want to lose the autonomy of their local branches. Compounding this fear was the fact that the MEAA was having financial trouble, so MUA members feared that the MEAA was interested in the MUA for its assets. MUA members were also concerned about a loss of influence within a larger union. In particular, MEAA voting rules give more votes to members who have higher income and dues payments. As such, full-time journalists have more votes than part-time club musicians. Lastly, some bad feelings continued over from an earlier dispute in which the actors union failed to support the MUA's fight against allowing dancers represented by the actors union to dance to taped music, a trend that threatened employment opportunities for MUA–represented musicians. All of these issues illustrate the conflicts in labor unions around the globe between power through centralization and local responsiveness through decentralization.

Source: Grant Michelson, "Out of Tune? Union Amalgamations and the Musicians Union of Australia," *Journal of Industrial Relations* 39 (September 1997), pp. 303–31.

of five. A series of wage differentials for skilled occupations were established relative to this basic wage award. The federal awards established the pattern for state and industry-level awards. In periods of labor market tightness, unions were successful in using collective bargaining with individual employers to negotiate "over-award" pay more generous than the arbitration awards. Working conditions were established separately from the arbitration awards through workplace-level bargaining, often informally and with high levels of wildcat strikes. But because of the importance of the national and regional awards, overall this was a very centralized system of labor relations in which arbitration, not collective bargaining, was the centerpiece.

Since 1987 Australian labor relations has pushed away from centralized awards towards greater decentralization and enterprise-level bargaining. This effort is the product of both the government (due to macroeconomic problems such as an exchange rate crisis) and employers (to improve labor–management cooperation, flexibility, and responsiveness to firm-specific conditions). In other words, Australia is also struggling with globalization, decentralization, and flexibility. In the 1990s, the role of the federal arbitration commission shifted away from issuing awards (except for a national minimum wage) to approving enterprise-level agreements negotiated through collective bargaining and finally to only ensuring that enterprise-level agreements meet a small number of minimum standards. Moreover, Australian workplace agreements—nonunion agreements negotiated by employers directly with employees—are now allowed. The Work Choices Act in 2005 replaced the federal arbitration commission with an Australian Fair Pay Commission and furthered the earlier trends toward greater use of workplace agreements with fewer binding standards. The centralized awards system has decreased in importance and enterprise agreements between employers and unions have increased; the impact of Australian workplace agreements remains to be seen.[76]

Labor relations in New Zealand exhibits a similar trend, albeit with even more radical reforms. New Zealand's arbitration system, in fact, dated back to 1894 and therefore predated Australia's, and operated in a similar fashion. A federal arbitration commission issued awards for minimum conditions while collective bargaining, often on a multiemployer basis, established above-award terms. Moreover, an employer could unilaterally establish terms and conditions of employment as long as they exceeded the minimum provisions established by the relevant arbitration award. Unlike the Australian initiative to decentralize labor relations by weakening the arbitration awards system, New Zealand has pursued decentralization by abolishing its award system. The 1991 Employment Contracts Act replaced the awards system with voluntarism (recall Great Britain's system described earlier in this chapter). The Employment Contracts Act created a voluntaristic system so it did not require bargaining of any type—unions could negotiate collective contracts, but only if they had explicit authorization from each worker and if the employer wanted to bargain; otherwise, individual nonunion contracts are used.[77] The Employment Relations Act 2000 moves New Zealand industrial relations away from a pure voluntarism system. Individual employment contracts are still allowed, but unlike under the 1991 Employment Contracts Act, employers have an obligation to bargain in good faith with a union if a set of employees request it. It is also illegal for employers to pressure or discriminate against employees in order to encourage or discourage union membership.

JAPAN

The primary institutional feature of Japanese labor relations is enterprise unionism. An **enterprise union,** such as the Hitachi Workers' Union, only represents workers in a single company (enterprise). The dominant type of enterprise union in Japan represents *all* regular (not temporary or part-time) employees in a single company, including white collar workers except higher level managers. At some companies, however, several enterprise unions coexist and compete, but note that even in these cases, each union only represents workers within the one enterprise.[78] As such, while union density is approximately 22 percent, there are nearly 70,000 labor unions.[79] In addition to a close alignment between enterprises and unions, there are also close ties between management and the union leadership. Supervisors are generally part of the enterprise union and union leaders are

---

[76] Katz and Darbishire, *Converging Divergences*. Marian Baird and Russell D. Lansbury, "The Changing Structure of Collective Bargaining in Australia," in Harry C. Katz, Wonduck Lee, and Joohee Lee (eds.), *The New Structure of Labor Relations: Tripartism and Decentralization* (Ithaca, NY: Cornell University Press, 2004), pp. 166–91.

[77] Ellen J. Dannin, *Working Free: The Origins and Impact of New Zealand's Employment Contracts Act* (Auckland: Auckland University Press, 1997).

[78] Hirosuke Kawanishi, *Enterprise Unionism in Japan* (London: Keegan Paul International, 1992).

[79] Yasuo Kuwahara, "Employment Relations in Japan," in Greg J. Bamber, Russell D. Lansbury, and Nick Wailes (eds.), *International and Comparative Employment Relations: Globalisation and the Developed Market Economies* (London: Sage, 2004), pp. 277–305.

often career-type employees who continue their promotions within the enterprise up through the management ranks after being a union leader.

This system of enterprise unionism is embedded in a broader system of human resource management structured around lifetime employment, seniority and firm-based wages, and broad job classifications. These features are not universal, but they have traditionally been central for core employees in large firms. Lifetime employment is an arrangement in which employees normally are never laid off and stay with a single firm until retirement. Cyclical and seasonal burdens are shifted to temporary workers who are not covered by this implicit—not contractual—lifetime employment tradition (and are usually not covered by the union either). Wages for regular employees are generally based on seniority plus a large annual bonus which partly reflects firm or industry profitability.[80] Japanese firms also often use broad job classifications, and workers are rotated across jobs to increase their skills. All of these features mean that employees identify with an enterprise—its internal labor market and financial performance—not a specific job.

Enterprise unionism fits well with this strong enterprise identification among employees and Japanese labor relations is often characterized as cooperative or consensual.[81] Enterprise unions are very concerned with the company's performance and tailor demands and agreements accordingly. A number of companies also have joint labor–management consultation bodies in which information about the firm is shared with employees, and employees are consulted about personnel matters and working conditions. Although enterprise unions are entitled to bargain over wages and working conditions, some argue that a more cooperative and less adversarial relationship can develop if these issues are settled through a consensual approach in a joint consultation committee. By some accounts, joint consultation is therefore more important than collective bargaining in Japanese labor relations.[82] Enterprise-level consultation and bargaining are complemented by an annual wage negotiation process called Shunto (see Box 13.10).

The Japanese system is a very important contrast for U.S. labor relations. The two countries share a broadly similar labor law framework. In fact, Japanese labor law was established by the U.S. occupation authorities at the end of World War II and based on the U.S. model of using unfair labor practices to support employee rights to organize and bargain collectively. There is limited use of exclusive representation and majority rule, however.[83] Also, enterprise unions are not mandated by law—there are isolated examples of industrial and other forms of unions in Japan—and have essentially developed within a Wagner Act framework. Because of the economic success of Japan in recent decades—witness the sharp increase in the popularity of Japanese cars in the United States—the cooperative model of Japanese labor relations, with high levels of employee participation and union concern for firm profitability, is often advocated as a model for U.S. labor relations to emulate. As discussed in Chapter 11, it is often argued that U.S. unions should be more cooperative and do more to enhance productivity and quality. These arguments are frequently rooted in an idealized view of a cooperative and productive Japanese labor relations system of enterprise unionism. On the other hand, what some view as cooperative enterprise unions, others see as management-dominated sham unions. This is a major debate in both countries. For example, the prevalence of enterprise unions in Japan is characterized by some as stemming from worker concern for an efficient enterprise and by others as resulting from management suppression of industrial unions in the 1950s.[84]

---

[80] Katz and Darbishire, *Converging Divergences.*

[81] Takashi Araki, "The Japanese Model of Employee Representational Participation," *Comparative Labor Law Journal* 15 (Winter 1994), pp. 143–54. Kuwahara, "Employment Relations in Japan."

[82] Araki, "The Japanese Model of Employee Representational Participation."

[83] William B. Gould, *Japan's Reshaping of American Labor Law* (Cambridge: The MIT Press, 1984).

[84] Araki, "The Japanese Model of Employee Representational Participation." Kawanishi, *Enterprise Unionism in Japan.* Turner, *Democracy at Work.*

In Japan, labor–management agreements on issues except pay are reached through joint labor–management committees or through collective bargaining with enterprise unions. Pay bargaining, however, occurs each April and May in an annual spring offensive called Shunto. Dating back to the 1950s, Shunto has traditionally been a very important feature of Japanese labor relations in which unions coordinate bargaining across enterprises to win greater wage gains. But in 2002, influential companies in the automotive, electrical machinery, shipbuilding, and steel industries did not offer any across-the-board pay increases. This was especially striking at the very profitable Toyota. Moreover, Toyota's union subsequently declined to demand a wage increase in the next three Shunto rounds. In a move thought to signal a shift toward greater linkages between pay and company performance, Toyota did agree to its union's demands for bonuses. It was not until 2006 that Toyota workers again won a wage increase. The labor movement in the 2006 Shunto round also tried to return to the earlier practice of coordinated, uniform wage demands. But business prefers to have wages depend on business conditions at individual firms and based on the experiences of the past several years, the labor movement is unlikely to consistently obtain uniform wage increases. So while it appears that Shunto will survive, the changes occurring in this annual spring offensive reflect the difficulties of centralized negotiations in a competitive global environment in which management emphasizes decentralization and flexibility.

Source: "Japan Labor Flash" (Tokyo: The Japan Institute for Labour Policy and Training, various issues), available at *http://www.jil.go.jp/emm/whatjlf.htm.*

Lastly, note that in a system of enterprise unionism, existing unions have little incentive to organize new unions at other establishments and overall labor movement solidarity is low.

ASIAN DEVELOPING COUNTRIES

The history of labor relations in the developing countries of Asia parallels the major concerns in other countries. As emphasized in Parts II and III of this book, the U.S. labor relations system has evolved from a mid-20th-century emphasis on economic growth through industrial peace to a 21st-century struggle with competitiveness through flexibility. Asian industrial relations is undergoing this same evolution—earlier policies emphasized industrial peace to promote industrial development while contemporary policies focus on achieving global competitiveness through flexibility.[85] As with developed countries, the developing countries of Asia have taken different approaches in designing specific labor systems to promote similar objectives. In fact, by this point in the chapter the types of systems found in Asia should be familiar: a high-level tripartite or corporatist model (Singapore—recall Ireland), a pluralist model with varying combinations of political representation and collective bargaining (the Philippines and India—recall Germany, France, Canada, and the United States), and a government-control model (Malaysia and Indonesia—recall Mexico) as well as systems that are in flux (China and South Korea—recall eastern Europe).[86]

Within these developing countries, however, the government frequently exercises tighter control over unions and labor relations than in developed countries. In Singapore's tripartite system, unions participate with the government and employers at high levels to craft wage guidelines and various social policies, but control over workplace-level labor relations is exercised through restrictions on bargaining items, limitations on strikes, and government approval

[85] Sarosh Kuruvilla and Christopher L. Erickson, "Change and Transformation in Asian Industrial Relations," *Industrial Relations* 41 (April 2002), pp. 171–227.

[86] Sarosh Kuruvilla and C. S. Venkataratnam, "Economic Development and Industrial Relations: The Case of South and Southeast Asia," *Industrial Relations Journal* 27 (March 1996), pp. 9–23.

of collective bargaining agreements (agreements not deemed consistent with Singapore's economic development interests can be rejected).[87] Moreover, the labor movement is closely intertwined with the ruling political party and in the early 1980s, the government (not the unions) restructured the labor movement by forming Japanese-style enterprise unions. Similarly, the early postwar labor relations system in the Philippines was inherited from its colonial ruler—the United States—but evolved into a system with greater government control.[88] Changes in the 1970s restricted strikes, allowed permanent strike replacements, and required unions to belong to a single government-controlled federation. Government control over labor relations is more explicit in Malaysia and Indonesia. In Malaysia, for example, the government controls the structure and size of unions by selectively approving or rejecting the required union registration applications and has used this administrative power to force Japanese-style enterprise unions rather than industrial unions.[89] In the export-focused electronics industry in particular, the government has used the registration requirements to keep unions weak.[90]

An important underlying thread in all of these developing country models of labor relations is the subservience of labor relations to the country's industrial development strategy.[91] When the Philippines was pursuing an import substitution strategy in which domestic industries were protected from foreign competition, a pluralist labor relations model was allowed because international cost competitiveness was not critical. But when the industrial development strategy switched to an emphasis on exports, the government stepped in to exercise greater control over labor relations to keep costs low and attract foreign investment. The supremacy of industrial development strategies underlies another theme in developing country labor relations: appearance versus reality. Malaysian law, for example, might appear to allow collective bargaining, but the reality of the situation is that government control of union registration can be manipulated to keep unions weak, as was also discussed for Mexico earlier in this chapter.

Lastly, several of the Asian developing countries are experiencing significant economic or political transitions similar to the situation in eastern Europe. Perhaps most notably, the Republic of Korea (South Korea) became a democracy in 1987 and China's economic system has been moving from state-socialism to a mixed economy with important elements of private ownership and competition. In Korea, political democratization loosened the government's grip on labor relations—unions were given greater freedoms to strike and collective bargaining became more important.[92] Note, however, that a second labor federation

---

[87] Sarosh Kuruvilla, "Linkages Between Industrialization Strategies and Industrial Relations/Human Resource Policies: Singapore, Malaysia, the Philippines, and India," *Industrial and Labor Relations Review* 49 (July 1996), pp. 635–57.

[88] Kuruvilla, "Linkages Between Industrialization Strategies and Industrial Relations/Human Resource Policies."

[89] Stephen J. Frenkel and David Peetz, "Globalization and Industrial Relations in East Asia: A Three-Country Comparison," *Industrial Relations* 37 (July 1998), pp. 282–310. Wesley J. Hiers and Ponniah Arudsothy, "From Ostensible Voluntarism to Interventionism in Malaysian Industrial Relations: The Colonial Experience as an Important Variable," in Sarosh Kuruvilla and Bryan Mundell (eds.), *Colonialism, Nationalism, and the Institutionalization of Industrial Relations in the Third World* (Stamford, CT: JAI Press, 1999), pp. 103–54.

[90] Kuruvilla, "Linkages Between Industrialization Strategies and Industrial Relations/Human Resource Policies."

[91] Sarosh Kuruvilla, "Economic Development Strategies, Industrial Relations Policies and Workplace IR/HR Practices in Southeast Asia," in Kirsten S. Wever and Lowell Turner (eds.), *The Comparative Political Economy of Industrial Relations* (Madison, WI: Industrial Relations Research Association, 1995), Chapter 4. Kuruvilla, "Linkages Between Industrialization Strategies and Industrial Relations/Human Resource Policies."

[92] Kuruvilla and Erickson, "Change and Transformation in Asian Industrial Relations." Wonduck Lee and Joohee Lee, "Will the Model of Uncoordinated Decentralization Persist? Changes in Korean Industrial Relations after the Financial Crisis," in Harry C. Katz, Wonduck Lee, and Joohee Lee (eds.), *The New Structure of Labor Relations: Tripartism and Decentralization* (Ithaca, NY: Cornell University Press, 2004), pp. 143–65. Young-bum Park and Chris Leggett, "Employment Relations in the Republic of Korea," in Greg J. Bamber, Russell D. Lansbury, and Nick Wailes (eds.), *International and Comparative Employment Relations: Globalisation and the Developed Market Economies* (London: Sage, 2004), pp. 306–28.

that challenged the longtime government-recognized federation was not legalized until 1999. Korean labor relations is therefore still in a period of transition—a period made more difficult by the Asian financial crisis of the late 1990s and the resulting job losses.

In China, change has been driven by economic rather than political change. While the economic system is moving from socialism to a mixed economy (sometimes called market socialism) as in eastern Europe, there is little loosening of the Communist Party's control over the political system.[93] Prior to the start of this economic transition in the 1980s, labor relations was similar to the eastern European Stalinist model and unions served as transmission belts for the Communist Party. The weakening of the party's control over economic activities and the growth of private ownership and market mechanisms mean that an explicit transmission belt probably no longer exists, but organized labor is not yet completely free and, as in many other countries, economic development trumps labor rights. New labor laws in 1994 ostensibly promote collective bargaining, but close interrelationships between union leaders and the Communist Party remain, there is only one legal union federation (the All-China Federation of Trade Unions, ACFTU), and strikes are still restricted.[94] Independent union representation is also undermined by the emphasis in Chinese labor law on regulating outcomes rather than promoting processes, such as collective bargaining, that require the Communist Party to give up some control.[95] On paper, unions are mandatory in foreign-owned businesses, but this is not universally enforced by local authorities fearful of losing foreign investment.[96] Moreover, in workplaces where unions are present, they are generally dependent on and integrated with management. It's important to remember that Communism and socialism were seen as solving capitalism's deep-seated conflict between capital and labor; in other words, the official ideology of Communist and socialist states insists that Communism and socialism achieve a unitarist employment relationship (recall Chapter 2) where the interests of workers, managers, and the state are all aligned. So unions in China have no experience with, or even conception of, representing workers' interests in opposition to employers' interests as in a pluralist employment relationship.[97] In fact, while the ACFTU is probably the world's largest labor movement with perhaps 100 million members, it might also be the world's largest "paper tiger" because the ACFTU is more of a "quasi-government organ" than a labor union.[98]

BARGAINING OR LEGISLATING LABOR STANDARDS?

From these descriptions of labor relations systems in different countries, it is apparent that there are numerous possibilities for structuring labor relations (recall Box 13.1). The U.S. emphasis on exclusive representation and majority support is often absent outside of North America. Consultation between labor and management through peak-level organizations at a national level and through works councils at a workplace level occurs throughout Europe. Some countries have centralized industry-wide bargaining arrangements while others

[93] Trini Wing-Yue Leung, "Trade Unions and Labor Relations Under Market Socialism in China," in Gerd Schienstock, Paul Thompson, and Franz Traxler (eds.), *Industrial Relations Between Command and Market: A Comparative Analysis of Eastern Europe and China* (New York: Nova Science Publishers, 1997), pp. 239–89. Bill Taylor, Chang Kai, and Li Qi, *Industrial Relations in China* (Cheltenham: Edward Elgar, 2003).

[94] Frenkel and Peetz, "Globalization and Industrial Relations in East Asia."

[95] Taylor et al., *Industrial Relations in China.*

[96] Kuruvilla and Erickson, "Change and Transformation in Asian Industrial Relations."

[97] Simon Clarke, Chang-Hee Lee, and Qi Li, "Collective Consultation and Industrial Relations in China," *British Journal of Industrial Relations* 42 (June 2004), pp. 235–54.

[98] Leung, "Trade Unions and Labor Relations Under Market Socialism in China," p. 264. Taylor et al., *Industrial Relations in China*, p. 207.

focus on enterprise-level unions. Moreover, while U.S. union contracts are highly complex, legally enforceable documents that specify a wide range of employment terms, in many other countries union agreements provide more of a skeletal specification of minimum terms. In some countries, contracts are not legally enforceable.

The political activities of the labor movement in many countries outside of the United States are also at least as important as their workplace activities, if not more so. Rather than the U.S. labor movement's philosophy of business unionism, European labor movements often embrace social movement unionism. Gains for workers are won through social and political activism as well as through bargaining with employers, and unions are often closely aligned with left-wing political parties.[99] In Great Britain, the Trades Union Congress founded the Labour party. One of the major parties that sometimes rules Australia is the Australian Labor party. In Sweden and Germany, the labor movement is closely aligned with social democratic parties. French and Italian unions are closely connected with communist and socialist political parties, and political strikes to win gains for workers are common. Advocates of a stronger U.S. labor movement see this type of political and social activism as the avenue to more power.[100] Such activism can bolster the labor movement's voice in the political arena, and can result in laws supporting union activities.

Political strength can also result in labor standards that are legislated for all workers rather than confined to workers covered by collective bargaining. Outside of the United States, many employment conditions, especially pertaining to employee benefits, are established by government regulations. For example, while the United States does not mandate any vacation days, workers in Sweden are entitled to 32, in Spain to 30, and in Germany to 18.[101] The importance of legislated rather than negotiated labor standards is further demonstrated by job security protections. U.S. workers are subject to the employment-at-will doctrine and can therefore be laid off or fired at any time. In addition to legislative restrictions against discriminatory discharge, the major exception to this doctrine is a just cause provision in a union contract. Thus, only the 15 percent of U.S. workers covered by union contracts are protected against dismissals except for valid reasons related to job performance or economic conditions. This is in stark contrast to the widespread unjust dismissal protections in much of the rest of the industrialized, democratic world granted by national legislation. Legislation in many countries also places limits on employers' abilities to lay off workers.

In Germany, for example, after a six-month probationary period, only "socially justified" employee discharges are legal. In other words, employees can only be dismissed with just cause due to poor performance or economic necessity: discharge must be justified by "the conduct of the employee or by pressing reasons connected with the enterprise." Note carefully that in contrast to the United States, this protection is provided by law and is not dependent on union representation. Disputes are resolved by a federal labor court and coverage is nearly universal. Belgium, France, Great Britain (except for part-time or temporary workers), Italy, and Spain all have similar legislative protections to those found in Germany.[102] In Mexico, after a 30-day probationary period, employees may be laid off for

[99] Hyman, *Understanding European Trade Unionism*.

[100] Gregory Mantsios (ed.), *A New Labor Movement for the New Century* (New York: Garland, 1998). Kim Moody, *An Injury to All: The Decline of American Unionism* (London: Verso, 1988). Ray M. Tillman and Michael S. Cummings (eds.), *The Transformation of U.S. Unions: Voices, Visions, and Strategies from the Grassroots* (Boulder, CO: Lynne Rienner Publishers, 1999). Rick Fantasia and Kim Voss, *Hard Work: Remaking the American Labor Movement* (Berkeley: University of California Press, 2004).

[101] Lawrence Mishel, Jared Bernstein, and John Schmitt, *The State of Working America, 2000–2001* (Ithaca, NY: ILR Press, 2001).

[102] Hoyt N. Wheeler and Jacques Rojot (eds.), *Workplace Justice: Employment Obligations in International Perspective* (Columbia: University of South Carolina Press, 1992).

BOX 13.11
Employees Covered by Unjust Dismissal Protections.

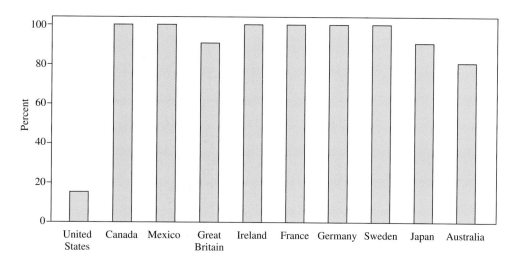

Source: See text.

economic reasons or dismissed only for just cause—and these protections are written into Mexico's constitution.[103] In Japan, the doctrine of abusive dismissal protects workers against unjust dismissal. This doctrine has been extended to all employees with the exception of short-term, contract employees who have yet to have their initial contract renewed.[104] Even in Canada, employees must either be dismissed for just cause or provided with several weeks of advance notice.[105] In contrast, workers in the United States are dependent on union representation for protections against unjust dismissal, and only 15 percent of the workforce is covered by collective bargaining agreements. As such, the United States stands alone with such a low level of coverage for protections against unjust dismissal (see Box 13.11). But in many countries, such protections were obtained through the legislative rather than the bargaining process. This political aspect of comparative labor relations should not be overlooked, and an important question for the future is whether labor standards should be negotiated or legislated (or neither).

GLOBALIZATION RECONSIDERED

Analyzing national labor relations systems from around the world is important. A comparative approach provides rich material for thinking broadly about the underlying labor relations problem of balancing efficiency, equity, and voice. Examining the pros and cons of other countries' policies and practices can aid efforts to reform law and practice in the United States to better strike this balance. And understanding how labor relations works in other countries is critical for managers and union leaders who have professional activities involving other countries. Describing the broad outlines of the traditional workings of

[103] Befort and Cornett, "Beyond the Rhetoric of the NAFTA Treaty Debate."

[104] Vai Io Lo, "Atypical Employment: A Comparison of Japan and the United States," *Comparative Labor Law Journal* 17 (Spring 1996), pp. 492–525. Kazuo Sugeno, *Japanese Employment and Labor Law*, Leo Kantowitz (trans.) (Durham: Carolina Academic Press, 2002).

[105] James C. Oakley, "Employee Duty of Loyalty—A Canadian Perspective," *Comparative Labor Law Journal* 20 (Winter 1999), pp. 185–203. Alexander J. S. Colvin, "Flexibility and Fairness in Liberal Market Economies: The Comparative Impact of the Legal Environment and High-Performance Work Systems," *British Journal of Industrial Relations* 26 (March 2006), pp. 73–97.

labor relations systems of a number of representative developed and developing countries is therefore the primary objective of this chapter.

But recall from the previous chapter that a major feature of the labor relations environment in nearly every country is globalization. Globalization raises a key question for comparative labor relations in the 21st century: in an integrated world economy, is it possible to have unique national labor relations systems, or does integration force convergence of national institutions? In a competitive world, free trade should harmonize labor standards if countries with higher standards have higher labor costs and are unable to compete with lower-cost countries. If certain labor relations practices are more productive than others, then competitive pressures are expected to cause others to adopt those practices—such as U.S. attempts to emulate the more cooperative style of Japanese labor relations. More ambitious efforts at political and legal as well as economic integration, such as in the European Union, should further weaken national differences as common standards and policies are enacted. The **convergence thesis** therefore predicts that labor relations practices and policies across countries will converge to a common set of practices and policies, and national differences will disappear.

The evidence, however, does not support this convergence thesis.[106] In particular, arguably the most important effects of globalization on labor relations across many countries are declining union strength and intense corporate pressures for increased workplace flexibility (Chapter 11). These two factors have caused increased decentralization of labor relations activities in many countries.[107] Even though collective bargaining in Germany, for example, has traditionally been much more centralized than in the United States, the bargaining structure in both countries has become more decentralized than in earlier years. This decentralization is key: increasing decentralization causes local-level labor relations practices to *diverge* as companies and local workplaces experiment and try to tailor employment practices to the specific needs and constraints of individual workplaces. Uniform convergence, therefore, is not occurring. However, there appear to be several standard models that are followed across workplaces such as an antiunion, low-wage approach, a traditional human resource management approach, and a high-performance work systems approach. As such, labor relations practices within countries are becoming more diverse, but are simultaneously embracing several common patterns. In other words, rather than a strict convergence, there appears to be "converging divergences."[108]

Increased divergence on a local level as well as convergence can undermine the importance of national-level labor relations systems.[109] So in the face of globalization and decentralization, does it continue to make sense to discuss *national* labor relations systems? In a word, yes. The laws and institutions that characterize the labor relations systems of different countries—whether it be exclusive representation with majority support in the United States, voluntarism in Great Britain, codetermination in Germany, enterprise unionism in Japan, government control in Malaysia, and so forth—shape the choices faced by companies

---

[106] Stephen Frenkel and Sarosh Kuruvilla, "Logics of Action, Globalization, and Changing Employment Relations in China, India, Malaysia, and the Philippines," *Industrial and Labor Relations Review* 55 (July 2002), pp. 387–412. Katz and Darbishire, *Converging Divergences.* Richard M. Locke, "The Demise of the National Union in Italy: Lessons for Comparative Industrial Relations Theory," *Industrial and Labor Relations Review* 45 (January 1992), pp. 229–49.

[107] Harry C. Katz, "The Decentralization of Collective Bargaining: A Literature Review and Comparative Analysis," *Industrial and Labor Relations Review* 47 (October 1993), pp. 3–22. Harry C. Katz, Wonduck Lee, and Joohee Lee (eds.), *The New Structure of Labor Relations: Tripartism and Decentralization* (Ithaca, NY: Cornell University Press, 2004).

[108] Katz and Darbishire, *Converging Divergences.* Paul Marginson and Keith Sisson, *European Integration and Industrial Relations: Multi-Level Governance in the Making* (London: Palgrave/Macmillan, 2004).

[109] Locke, "The Demise of the National Union in Italy."

and unions when confronted with competitive pressures (Chapter 3). National-level institutions are therefore still important determinants of labor relations practices and employment outcomes.[110] Even in the European Union (EU), the greatest convergence towards uniformity has been in minimum standards through European-wide directives for health and safety requirements, gender equity, and other labor standards.[111] With the limited exception of the European Works Councils mandate (Chapter 12), EU policies have not erased national differences in the labor relations processes in individual countries; rather the employment relationship in Europe and elsewhere is increasingly characterized by a multilevel system of governance with important institutions and outcomes embedded in the workplace, company, sector, national, *and* supra-national levels.[112]

In sum, globalization is causing converging divergences of labor relations practices across countries through pressures for decentralization and flexibility. National-level institutions nevertheless remain important for shaping the responses of companies and unions to these pressures. Studying how labor relations works in different countries is therefore still an important component of understanding labor relations. Moreover, these local practices and national institutions can both be evaluated against the objectives of efficiency, equity, and voice.[113] Comparative labor relations therefore reveals numerous labor relations possibilities for tackling the challenges of the 21st-century employment relationship and striking an effective balance between the objectives of employers and workers.

Key Terms

voluntarism, *467*

social partnership, *473*

ideological unionism, *477*

sector bargaining, *478*

codetermination, *478*

works council, *478*

Stalinist

unionism, *483*

awards system, *485*

enterprise union, *487*

convergence thesis, *494*

Reflection Questions

1. In moments of frustration, some U.S. labor leaders have claimed that U.S. unions would be better off with a deregulation of labor law and a return to the "law of the jungle." How would a return to voluntarism affect U.S. unions? workers? employers?

2. What are the pros and cons of adopting the German system of mandatory works councils in the United States?

3. Are Japanese-style enterprise unions effective vehicles of voice that align worker interests with firm interests, or are they weak, company-dominated, sham unions?

4. Labor unions can be important players in three different political systems: pluralism, corporatism, and Leninism. Give examples of each and describe the key roles of unions. What are the pros and cons of pluralism and corporatism for both organized labor and employers? Should U.S. unions play a stronger role in U.S. politics?

[110] Frenkel and Peetz, "Globalization and Industrial Relations in East Asia." Katz and Darbishire, *Converging Divergences.* Colvin, "Flexibility and Fairness in Liberal Market Economies." John Godard, "Institutional Environments, Employer Practices, and States in Liberal Market Economies," *Industrial Relations* 41 (April 2002), pp. 249–86.

[111] Slomp, *Between Bargaining and Politics.*

[112] Marginson and Sisson, *European Integration and Industrial Relations.*

[113] John W. Budd, *Employment with a Human Face: Balancing Efficiency, Equity, and Voice* (Ithaca, NY: Cornell University Press, 2004).

496 Part Four   *Reflection*

Internet Exploration

1. Search for union Web sites in other countries. How are they different and/or similar to union Web sites in the United States?

2. Explore the Web sites of employers' associations that engage in collective bargaining (for example, Gesamtmetall at *www.gesamtmetall.de/Gesamtmetall/MEOnline.nsf/id/ HomepageEN* or the Korean Employers Federation at *eng.kef.or.kr*). What themes are emphasized by these associations? Why are employers' associations less likely to be important actors in U.S. collective bargaining relative to some other countries? What are some advantages to greater participation in collective bargaining by employers' associations?

3. Browse the recent national reports or other articles at the European Industrial Relations Observatory online (*www.eiro.eurofound.eu.int/annualreports.html*). Are there commonalities in current labor relations developments across different countries?

Additional Reading

Bamber, Greg J., Russell D. Lansbury, and Nick Wailes (eds.), *International and Comparative Employment Relations: Globalisation and the Developed Market Economies* (London: Sage, 2004).

Ferner, Anthony, and Richard Hyman (eds.), *Changing Industrial Relations in Europe* (Oxford: Blackwell Publishers, 1998).

Katz, Harry C., and Owen Darbishire, *Converging Divergences: Worldwide Changes in Employment Systems* (Ithaca, NY: ILR Press, 2000).

Kuruvilla, Sarosh, and Bryan Mundell (eds.), *Colonialism, Nationalism, and the Institutionalization of Industrial Relations in the Third World* (Stamford, CT: JAI Press, 1999).

Schienstock, Gerd, Paul Thompson, and Franz Traxler (eds.), *Industrial Relations Between Command and Market: A Comparative Analysis of Eastern Europe and China* (New York: Nova Science Publishers, 1997).

Turner, Lowell, *Democracy at Work: Changing World Markets and the Future of Labor Unions* (Ithaca, NY: Cornell University Press, 1991).

Wever, Kirsten S., and Lowell Turner (eds.), *The Comparative Political Economy of Industrial Relations* (Madison, WI: Industrial Relations Research Association, 1995).

Chapter **Fourteen**

What Should Labor Relations Do?

Advance Organizer

The goal of a labor relations system is to balance efficiency, equity, and voice. The previous chapters analyze the development and operation of the U.S. labor relations system, the major pressures on this system, and varied international examples. This chapter looks to the future by exploring alternatives for unions, employers, and labor policy for balancing efficiency, equity, and voice in the 21st century.

Learning Objectives

By the end of the chapter, you should be able to:

1. **Outline** alternative directions for union strategies in the 21st century.

2. **Describe** alternative directions for corporate behaviors in the 21st century.

3. **Identify** alternative directions for labor relations public policies in the 21st century.

4. **Understand** strategic management and leadership issues pertaining to labor relations for managers and union leaders in the 21st century.

Contents

At the start of the 21st century, the U.S. labor relations system is under fire from many angles and perspectives. Proponents of free markets and human resource management see unions as negatively interfering with markets and managers. Advocates of employment relationship flexibility criticize union policies as restrictive barriers to competitiveness. Proponents of greater labor–management cooperation and employee involvement attack U.S. labor law as adversarial and overly restrictive, especially with respect to the National Labor Relations Act's (NLRA) section 8(a)(2) limitations on nonunion employee representation plans. Globalization and the need to create high performance workplaces are therefore placing great strains on the U.S. labor relations system (Chapters 11 and 12). The current state of U.S. labor relations is also sharply criticized by proponents of labor unions and workers' rights. The seemingly unrelenting management drives for flexibility and team-based work systems are attacked as old-fashioned speed-ups—workers are forced to work harder for lower pay and less security. Organized labor believes that U.S. labor law is exceptionally weak and fails to prevent antiunion employer actions like firing union supporters or replacing striking workers. Labor activists further criticize the traditional business unionism approach of U.S. unions for failing to develop a vibrant labor movement based on grassroots participation. To varying degrees, all of these criticisms reflect frustration with the current state of efficiency, equity, and voice in the U.S. employment relationship.

Comparative examples from other countries indicate that there are many institutional arrangements and behaviors for seeking the common underlying goal of balancing efficiency, equity, and voice (Chapter 13). In other words, if the U.S. system no longer effectively serves its purposes, there are plenty of alternative options. This chapter therefore builds on all of the earlier chapters to look towards the future. What should unions do in the 21st century? Labor unions have a variety of options such as becoming more militant or cooperative, and for changing their structures and strategies. What should companies do? Companies, too, have a variety of options ranging from a continued short-term focus on shareholder returns to broader visions of the importance of embracing stakeholders and corporate responsibility. What should labor policy do? Labor law can be deregulated, strengthened, loosened, or rewritten from a clean slate to reflect a new environment and set of priorities. Putting all of these questions together yields the concluding subject for this book's investigation of labor relations—what should labor relations do?

WHAT SHOULD UNIONS DO?

Labor unions are the representatives of workers. As such, unions champion the interests and aspirations of workers, not vice versa. Unions do not determine these aspirations, but rather must shape their strategies and structures to respond to them—the early AFL craft unions, the CIO industrial unions in the 1930s, and the public sector unions in the 1960s created strategies and structures to fit with the blossoming needs of skilled craftsmen, mass manufacturing workers, and government employees, respectively.[1] As the employment relationship changes in response to the pressures of globalization, flexibility, and decentralization, as the nature of work changes in response to changing workforce demographics (including ethnicity, gender, and education) and increased employee involvement, and as the U.S. economy experiences shifts in industries and occupations, workers in the 21st century will likely create a unique sense of workplace justice different from the earlier eras. Unions will have to adapt to these changes.

As the world and work are changing in diverse ways, there are numerous alternative directions for U.S. unions. U.S. unions can try: to become more powerful, or more cooperative; to emphasize greater social activism, or greater individual empowerment; to network like a professional association, or buy firms and become owners (see Box 14.1). As such, there are various proposals for reforming union strategies and structures. The most important possibilities are summarized in Box 14.2. Before considering these options in more detail, a number of cautionary notes are important. One, the categories are presented here as intentionally broad to stimulate wide-ranging reflection and debate. Two, not all of the categories are necessarily mutually exclusive—some can be complementary. In fact, it is common to argue that reviving U.S. labor unions requires discarding the servicing model by actively engaging individual workers.[2] Most of the options presented here share this theme, albeit in different ways. Moreover, some proposals for a new unionism are drawn on several of the categories outlined here.[3] Three, even with the broad categories presented in Box 14.2, it's not obvious that there should be one best model of unionism. In other words,

[1] David Brody, "Labor's Crisis in Historical Perspective," in George Strauss, Daniel G. Gallagher, and Jack Fiorito (eds.), *The State of the Unions* (Madison, WI: Industrial Relations Research Association, 1991), Chapter 8. Richard W. Hurd and John Bunge, "Unionization of Professional and Technical Workers: The Labor Market and Institutional Transformation," unpublished paper (Cornell University, 2002).

[2] Samuel Bacharach, Peter Bamberger, and William Sonnenstuhl, *Mutual Aid and Union Renewal: Cycles of Logics of Action* (Ithaca, NY: Cornell University Press, 2001).

[3] Thomas A. Kochan, *Restoring the American Dream: A Working Families' Agenda for America* (Cambridge, MA: MIT Press, 2005).

BOX 14.1
Directions for U.S. Labor Unionism

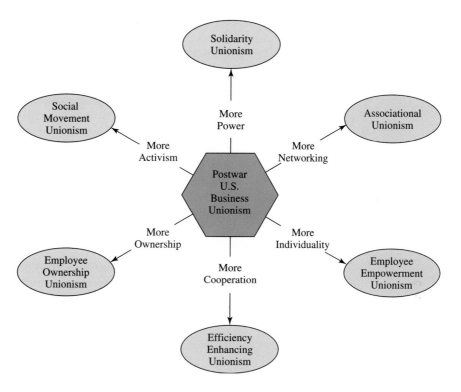

BOX 14.2   Possibilities for 21st-Century Labor Unions

Possibilities	Unions As . . .	Emphases	Concerns
Solidarity Unionism	Powerful Solidarity Alliances	Strong worker advocacy in the workplace through bargaining backed up by strikes and solidarity across workplaces.	More adversarial than cooperative. More rules-based than flexible. How to achieve competitiveness and quality?
Social Movement Unionism	Community and Political Activists	Social and political militancy and activism. Alliances with community groups.	What about workers' workplace concerns?
Efficiency Enhancing Unionism	Productivity and Cooperation Enhancers	Concern with establishing participatory structures to serve competitiveness and quality. Rewards based on performance. Training initiatives.	What is the source of employee power? Is there solidarity across workplaces? Who's looking out for employee interests?
Employee Ownership Unionism	Employee Owners	Control over employment conditions through employee ownership of companies.	Is employee ownership efficient? How are business decisions made? Is it too risky for employees when their savings are invested in their company?
Employee Empowerment Unionism	Individual Empowerment Supporters	Bargaining for procedures that empower individual decision making. Inclusion of procedural safeguards and minimum standards.	What is the source of employee power? Is there solidarity across workplaces?
Associational Unionism	Loose Networks of Professional Associations	Flexible, multiple forms of representation and networks based on multiple concerns. More than just bargaining. No exclusive representation.	What is the source of employee power?

you should question whether one-size-fits-all, or whether diverse workers, companies, industries, and occupations are best suited to diverse forms of unionism. And four, some proposals are consistent with existing U.S. labor law, others require legal changes.

Solidarity Unionism

Proposals that focus on increasing the traditional bargaining power of U.S. unions can be grouped together in a category of **solidarity unionism**—so-called because they generally rely on increasing labor power through enhanced solidarity within and across workplaces. Of the options listed in Box 14.2, solidarity unionism is the closest to the existing model of business unionism—as illustrated by solidarity unionism's focus on strengthening collective bargaining. Relative to some proposals that emphasize greater responsiveness to business concerns, proponents of solidarity unionism make no apologies for championing a strong labor movement as the protector of worker interests in opposition to management. Unions are seen as a needed force of worker power and protection; the problem with the current weakness of unions

> is not that most American workers have no representative to develop and to express their views on the business strategies and tactics, or the personnel policies and benefits, chosen by their employers. The problem is that American workers have lost power—power to extract a larger share of the returns of American enterprise and power to protect individual employees from arbitrary, unjust, or discriminatory treatment by their managers.[4]

The solution, then, is to mobilize workers. For example, immigrant workers who are segregated into ethnic enclaves in American workplaces and communities develop strong collective bonds through their shared struggles and are ripe for unionization efforts that build upon this solidarity.[5]

Part of the strategy to regain labor power involves using more aggressive organizing and bargaining tactics.[6] Graduate teaching assistants at Yale University refused to hand in grades (a grade strike) and also later conducted a conventional strike to try to pressure the university to recognize their union. Other unions are also increasingly trying to organize outside of the National Labor Relations Board (NLRB) election process (Chapter 7). Corporate campaigns—that is, social and financial pressure on companies through adverse publicity—involve another set of nontraditional tactics that labor can use to increase its power (Chapter 9). During a strike against the Ravenswood Aluminum Company in the early 1990s, the United Steelworkers pressured beverage companies to stop buying Ravenswood's aluminum for cans, filed charges of safety violations with the Occupational Safety and Health Administration (OSHA), and publicized the shady deal-making practices of its secretive owner throughout Europe (who had fled a U.S. indictment for mail fraud and tax evasion) (recall Box 9.12).[7]

Many of these tactics include developing greater solidarity linkages with other workers. The Yale graduate assistants struck at the same time as clerical and food service workers; the Ravenswood campaign included developing alliances with allied European unions.

[4] Michael C. Harper, "A Framework for the Rejuvenation of the American Labor Movement," *Indiana Law Journal* 76 (Winter 2001), pp. 103–33 at 104.

[5] Immanuel Ness, *Immigrants, Unions, and the New U.S. Labor Market* (Philadelphia: Temple University Press, 2005).

[6] Kate Bronfenbrenner et al. (eds.), *Organizing to Win: New Research on Union Strategies* (Ithaca, NY: ILR Press, 1998). Mike Parker and Jane Slaughter, *Choosing Sides: Unions and the Team Concept* (Boston: South End Press, 1988). Ray M. Tillman and Michael S. Cummings (eds.), *The Transformation of U.S. Unions: Voices, Visions, and Strategies from the Grassroots* (Boulder, CO: Lynne Rienner Publishers, 1999).

[7] Tom Juravich and Kate Bronfenbrenner, *Ravenswood: The Steelworkers' Victory and the Revival of American Labor* (Ithaca, NY: Cornell University Press, 1999).

Within a union, increased solidarity among the rank and file members is also emphasized. The development of this solidarity often focuses on harnessing an organizing model of representation.[8] Recall from Chapter 6 that in contrast to the servicing model, an organizing model seeks to create widespread rank and file participation in the life of the union. These efforts are closely related to efforts to increase internal union democracy thereby creating a vibrant and powerful labor movement through rank and file involvement.[9] Unions are also being encouraged to negotiate members-only agreements by bargaining on behalf of their supporters in workplaces in which majority support has not yet been achieved.[10] Such unions would be **nonmajority unions**—that is, unions that have the support of a minority rather than a majority of employees in a workplace. Nonmajority unions can gain a foothold in new workplaces and demonstrate to reluctant workers the firsthand benefits of unionism, and ultimately achieve majority support—as often was the case in the 1930s.

Some proposals for increasing labor's power involve going beyond new strategies to also change the structure of unions. Unions need to reduce their bureaucracy and avoid traditional jurisdictional conflicts as outsourcing and other labor market changes make work more fluid and drive some work into the informal sectors of the economy. Moreover, unions need to be willing to lend financial and institutional support to diverse grassroots organizations while also promoting their autonomy.[11] Another proposed change in union structure is the call for moving beyond industrial unionism to occupational unionism.[12] Occupational unionism represents a partial return to earlier forms of craft unionism in that occupational unionism emphasizes a worker's identity with his/her occupation rather than his/her specific employer. It moves beyond craft unionism, however, in not being limited to skilled crafts. Waitresses, flight attendants, and janitors, for example, can have strong occupational interests that are tied more closely to those same occupations at other companies than to other workers at their same company (see Box 14.3). These occupational interests are the basis for solidarity across employers. This model might be well-suited to the 21st century if the trends toward increased use of contingent workers and increased job switching (rather than stable, lifetime employment) continue.

Social Movement Unionism

Social movement unionism rejects the narrow business unionism focus on workplace-based collective bargaining and instead sees labor unions as the representatives of the entire working class and as part of a broader social movement of community, social, and political activist groups.[13] Conceptually, social movement unionism largely wins gains for workers through social and political channels rather than only through narrow workplace bargaining, and is frequently associated with social democratic labor movements in Europe.[14] In practical

---

[8] Andy Banks and Jack Metzgar, "Participating in Management: Union Organizing on a New Terrain," *Labor Research Review* 14 (Fall 1989), pp. 1–55. Bill Fletcher, Jr. and Richard W. Hurd, "Beyond the Organizing Model: The Transformation Process in Local Unions," in Kate Bronfenbrenner et al. (eds.), *Organizing to Win: New Research on Union Strategies* (Ithaca, NY: ILR Press, 1998), pp. 37–53.

[9] Tillman and Cummings, *The Transformation of U.S. Unions.*

[10] Charles J. Morris, *The Blue Eagle at Work: Reclaiming Democratic Rights in the American Workplace* (Ithaca, NY: Cornell University Press, 2005).

[11] Ness, *Immigrants, Unions, and the New U.S. Labor Market.*

[12] Dorothy Sue Cobble, *Dishing It Out: Waitresses and Their Unions in the Twentieth Century* (Urbana: University of Illinois Press, 1991). Dorothy Sue Cobble, "Lost Ways of Unionism: Historical Perspectives on Reinventing the Labor Movement," in Lowell Turner, Harry C. Katz, and Richard W. Hurd (eds.), *Rekindling the Movement: Labor's Quest for Relevance in the Twenty-First Century* (Ithaca, NY: ILR Press, 2001), Chapter 4.

[13] Tillman and Cummings, *The Transformation of U.S. Unions.*

[14] Richard Hyman, *Understanding European Trade Unionism: Between Market, Class and Society* (London: Sage, 2001).

Occupational Unionism Among Waitresses   Box 14.3

Between the 1900s and 1960s, significant numbers of waitresses were represented by the Hotel Employees and Restaurant Employees International Union (HERE). In fact, in the 1940s a majority of waitresses were unionized in New York, Detroit, and San Francisco. Interestingly, the local waitress unions emphasized occupational rather than employer-specific standards. They developed standards for good waitressing and established work boundaries (such as excluding menial clean-up duties). Employment security in the local industry, not at a specific restaurant, was emphasized. Restaurant managers retained broad rights to discharge waitresses except in retaliation for union activity; discharged waitresses would simply return to the local hiring hall to await an opening at another restaurant. And the union would discipline workers for poor performance to maintain the standards of the union and the craft. Benefits were provided through union welfare funds, not by specific employers. Some union contracts only specified minimum wage rates and individual waitresses were free to earn more.

Later restrictions on closed shops in U.S. labor law, however, removed the waitress unions' ability to control their occupation, and with the passage of the Civil Rights Act in 1964, the all-female waitress unions were merged into other hospitality unions and took on a more traditional industrial union flavor. But this model of occupational rather than job-specific unionism—including the provision of training, job opportunities, and occupational standards—might have appeal for today's professional service sector workers.

Sources: Dorothy Sue Cobble, *Dishing It Out: Waitresses and Their Unions in the Twentieth Century* (Urbana: University of Illinois Press, 1991). Dorothy Sue Cobble, "Organizing the Postindustrial Workforce: Lessons from the History of Waitress Unionism," *Industrial and Labor Relations Review* 44 (April 1991), pp. 419–36.

---

terms, social movement unionism is often a key element of efforts to create forms of solidarity unionism in the United States, and therefore strengthen union bargaining power. In other words, advocates of a stronger U.S. labor movement see greater social activism as one route to more power in society and at the bargaining table.[15] Efforts to increase grassroots participation and mobilization can serve both social movement unionism and solidarity unionism.

A popular example of using community activism and union alliances with social, religious, and political groups to increase labor's effectiveness is the Justice for Janitors campaigns.[16] These campaigns expand the drive to organize janitors in major cities such as Los Angeles or Washington, D.C., from a workplace issue to a community issue. Public demonstrations, strong ties with immigrants rights and religious groups, and active participation by janitors—not just union leaders—give these campaigns social vibrancy, and have been successful in winning bargaining rights and contracts (see Box 14.4). Cesar Chavez and the United Farm Workers in the 1960s famously created a social movement ("La Causa") by tightly linking organizing of California field workers with religious groups and community activists through nationwide grape and lettuce boycotts.[17] Labor-religious alliances between

---

[15] Gregory Mantsios (ed.), *A New Labor Movement for the New Century* (New York: Garland, 1998). Kim Moody, *An Injury to All: The Decline of American Unionism* (London: Verso, 1988). Peter Rachleff, *Hard-Pressed in the Heartland: The Hormel Strike and the Future of the Labor Movement* (Boston: South End Press, 1993). Tillman and Cummings, *The Transformation of U.S. Unions.* Dan Clawson, *The Next Upsurge: Labor and the New Social Movements* (Ithaca, NY: Cornell University Press, 2003). Rick Fantasia and Kim Voss, *Hard Work: Remaking the American Labor Movement* (Berkeley: University of California Press, 2004).

[16] Roger Waldinger et al., "Helots No More: A Case Study of the Justice for Janitors Campaign in Los Angeles," in Kate Bronfenbrenner et al. (eds.), *Organizing to Win: New Research on Union Strategies* (Ithaca, NY: ILR Press, 1998), Chapter 6. Jane Williams, "Restructuring Labor's Identity: The Justice for Janitors Campaign in Washington, D.C.," in Ray M. Tillman and Michael S. Cummings (eds.), *The Transformation of U.S. Unions: Voices, Visions, and Strategies from the Grassroots* (Boulder, CO: Lynne Rienner Publishers, 1999), Chapter 11.

[17] Susan Ferriss and Ricardo Sandoval, *The Fight in the Fields: Cesar Chavez and the Farmworkers Movement* (New York: Harcourt Brace, 1997).

Justice for Janitors as Social Movement Unionism

Box 14.4

One of the most prominent examples of social movement unionism in the United States is the Justice for Janitors campaigns created by the Service Employees International Union (SEIU) in the 1980s to organize janitors at large commercial properties in major cities (recall Box 7.15). Janitors in many major cities include large numbers of immigrant workers; the work is low-paid and isolating. In response, the Justice for Janitors campaigns have relied on creating solidarity and power through social demonstrations and alliances with community groups. During a campaign in Washington, D.C., in 1995, the SEIU led multiple mass demonstrations. These demonstrations blocked traffic, marched through city streets, and picketed various locations. But they did not simply demand better wages—the campaign highlighted the social issues revealed by the janitors' conditions. The low pay and sexual harassment of janitors was contrasted with the massive tax breaks granted to the property owners and the resulting decline in school funding and other city services. In the words of one SEIU official:

> Civil disobedience by a cross-section of supporters, including religious and other community leaders, helps

draw attention to the janitors' plight. The themes of the campaign play a role here: "Justice" as opposed to "wage" slogans help broaden the appeal of the workers' struggle. The problems of the working poor, mistreatment of minority groups, sexual harassment, and lack of health insurance are issues that will attract a diverse constituency. [The] Justice for Janitors picket line gives sympathizers a vehicle for expressing their diverse concerns.

The Justice for Janitors campaigns clearly reject a narrow business unionism approach and try instead to create a broad-based social movement in which organized labor champions workers' issues in their social context beyond the confines of individual workplaces.

Source: Jane Williams, "Restructuring Labor's Identity: The Justice for Janitors Campaign in Washington, D.C.," in Ray M. Tillman and Michael S. Cummings (eds.), *The Transformation of U.S. Unions: Voices, Visions, and Strategies from the Grassroots* (Boulder, CO: Lynne Rienner Publishers, 1999), Chapter 11. The quote is from p. 212.

---

unions and the Chicago Catholic archdiocese and an interdenominational committee helped organize O'Hare airport concession workers.[18] These types of initiatives underscore an important aspect of creating a vibrant, socially focused labor movement: unions explicitly embracing diversity by reaching out to workers not traditionally included in the labor movement, especially in leadership positions—women, minorities, and immigrant workers.[19]

The emphasis on community is echoed in calls for citizen unionism.[20] Instead of the occupational focus of craft unions or the industry focus of industrial unions, a citizen union has a geographical focus and seeks to organize all employees in a specific geographical area. Bargaining, public pressure such as negative publicity and boycotts, and political power are used to make sure that all companies in a local area are good employers and social

---

[18] Ronald Peters and Theresa Merrill, "Clergy and Religious Persons' Roles in Organizing at O'Hare Airport and St. Joseph Medical Center," in Kate Bronfenbrenner et al. (eds.), *Organizing to Win: New Research on Union Strategies* (Ithaca, NY: ILR Press, 1998), Chapter 10.

[19] Sharon Kurtz, *Workplace Justice: Organizing Multi-Identity Movements* (Minneapolis: University of Minnesota Press, 2002). José La Luz and Paula Finn, "Getting Serious About Inclusion: A Comprehensive Approach," in Gregory Mantsios (ed.), *A New Labor Movement for the New Century* (New York: Garland, 1998), pp. 197–211. Ruth Milkman (ed.), *Organizing Immigrants: The Challenge for Unions in Contemporary California* (Ithaca, NY: ILR Press, 2000). Ruth Needleman, "Women Workers: Strategies for Inclusion and Rebuilding Unionism," in Gregory Mantsios (ed.), *A New Labor Movement for the New Century* (New York: Garland, 1998), pp. 175–96. Ness, *Immigrants, Unions, and the New U.S. Labor Market*.

[20] Katherine V. W. Stone, *From Widgets to Digits: Employment Regulation for the Changing Workplace* (Cambridge: Cambridge University Press, 2004).

citizens. With a geographical focus, citizen unions can also provide portable benefits and other services such as training, child care, and legal assistance that help contingent workers and other frequent job changers. A union that includes all employees in a locality regardless of occupation or industry could also be a strong advocate for community issues: "by reconceptualizing workers as citizens who collectively have an interest in the health, education, well-being, and employability of the entire population," labor issues become issues of general, community-wide concern.[21]

On a national scale, another significant aspect of increased labor activism is reasserting influence in national U.S. politics. Labor's influence with the Democratic party fell to an all-time low in the 1970s and since that time the AFL–CIO and individual unions have devoted renewed attention to political activities.[22] Since John Sweeney became president of the AFL–CIO in 1995, organized labor has created a vibrant grassroots effort that involves many rank and file workers in campaigning for pro-labor political candidates and in get-out-the-vote efforts. Nevertheless, organized labor continues to face a hostile political environment. This is most evident under the Republican administrations of Ronald Reagan, George Bush, and George W. Bush, but even during the Democratic administration of Bill Clinton, efforts to reform health insurance and labor law failed. Some labor supporters have therefore called for the creation of an independent labor party as an additional component of a social movement unionism strategy.[23]

Efficiency Enhancing Unionism

Solidarity unionism and social movement unionism include diverse initiatives or proposals that can generally be thought of as militant or activist and that embody a strong need to represent workers' interest *in opposition to* employers' interests. The remaining alternatives in Boxes 14.1 and 14.2 seek to create new forms of unionism that are not as adversarial or oppositional. As such, some see these alternatives as more productive, others see them as weak. The most extreme case of the nonoppositional—that is, cooperative—approach can be labeled **efficiency enhancing unionism.** Efficiency enhancing unionism sees labor unions as strategic business partners that can help advance productivity, quality, and competitiveness.

One proposal for this type of unionism argues for replacing the typical, detailed union contract with an enterprise compact.[24] Note the cooperative philosophy:

> A *contract* is essentially adversarial in nature, representing a compromise between the separate interests of each party to the agreement. In contrast, a *compact* is fundamentally a cooperative document, providing for a mutual vision and a joint system for achieving common goals that foster the general well-being of all stakeholders in a given endeavor.[25]

An enterprise compact therefore specifies the principles of a labor–management relationship based on union and employee involvement in business decision making in return for greater union commitment to competitiveness, and increased sharing by employees in both the risks and rewards of the company (see Box 14.5). A leading example of this approach

---

[21] Stone, *From Widgets to Digits*, p. 228.

[22] Taylor E. Dark, *The Unions and the Democrats: An Enduring Alliance* (Ithaca, NY: ILR Press, 2001). Nelson Lichtenstein, *State of the Union: A Century of American Labor* (Princeton, NJ: Princeton University Press, 2002). Robert H. Zieger and Gilbert J. Gall, *American Workers, American Unions: The Twentieth Century,* 3rd ed. (Baltimore: Johns Hopkins Press, 2002).

[23] Tony Mazzocchi, "Building a Party of Our Own," in Gregory Mantsios (ed.), *A New Labor Movement for the New Century* (New York: Garland, 1998), pp. 281–93.

[24] Barry Bluestone and Irving Bluestone, *Negotiating the Future: A Labor Perspective on American Business* (New York: Basic Books, 1992).

[25] Bluestone and Bluestone, *Negotiating the Future,* pp. 24–25 (emphases in original).

"What we advocate is not an expansion of traditional trade-union structures or an atavistic return to the good old days of hardheaded adversarial collective bargaining. Instead, given the nature of the contemporary world economy, we believe it is necessary to build a new union movement based on the principle of a shared set of labor and management rights and responsibilities. . . . The technical details of the Enterprise Compact must be negotiated between labor and management in much the same way that collective bargaining has been used to nail down the traditional Workplace Contract. But at the core of the Enterprise Compact, as we envision it, are seven major provisions:

1. The union and management agree to pursue mutually established productivity growth targets.

2. Wage and compensation goals are set consistent with productivity growth in order to maintain global competitiveness.

3. Price setting in the company is subject to joint action by union and management.

4. Quality is a 'strikable' issue, to assure that products and services meet or exceed international standards.

5. Employment security is guaranteed for the company's work force.

6. Extra financial rewards are provided through profit and gain sharing throughout the enterprise.

7. The union and management agree to joint decision making throughout the firm, including labor representation on the company's Board of Directors. With this, the last remnants of the traditional Workplace Contract's 'management's rights' clause are abolished."

Source: Barry Bluestone and Irving Bluestone, *Negotiating the Future: A Labor Perspective on American Business* (New York: Basic Books, 1992), pp. 25–26.

is the automaker Saturn. Recall from Chapter 11 that the union and managers at Saturn jointly make strategic business decisions and that teams of workers are empowered to make production and work decisions. Recall further that supporters of this form of unionism view this as a way to serve the company's interests of competitiveness and quality while providing a richer, positive work environment for individual employees; critics see it as selling out and leaving workers without strong protections against management.[26]

Another approach to efficiency enhancing unionism is through active union involvement in providing training. For example, the Wisconsin State AFL–CIO has been instrumental in establishing and running the Wisconsin Regional Training Partnership (WRTP).[27] In cooperation with both private sector companies and public sector agencies and technical colleges, the WRTP provides training across the broad spectrum of workforce needs—from basic job and language skills up to advanced technical skills. Elsewhere across the country, unions have been involved in providing training for hotel, hospital, and child care workers, to name just a few. This cooperative approach has the potential to increase workers' incomes while providing a more skilled—and therefore more efficient and competitive—workforce to employers.

Employee Ownership Unionism

Another approach to incorporating workers' interests more squarely into the business aspects of employers is through employee ownership.[28] If employees own stock in a company, they may work harder to promote the profitability of their company. More importantly, if

[26] Peter Lazes and Jane Savage, "New Unionism and the Workplace of the Future," in Bruce Nissen (ed.), *Unions and Workplace Reorganization* (Detroit: Wayne State University Press, 1997), Chapter 10. Mike Parker and Jane Slaughter, "Advancing Unionism on the New Terrain," in Nissen (ed.), *Unions and Workplace Reorganization,* Chapter 11.

[27] Eric Parker and Joel Rogers, "Building the High Road in Metro Areas: Sectoral Training and Employment Projects," in Lowell Turner, Harry C. Katz, and Richard W. Hurd (eds.), *Rekindling the Movement: Labor's Quest for Relevance in the Twenty-First Century* (Ithaca, NY: ILR Press, 2001), Chapter 11.

[28] Hoyt N. Wheeler, *The Future of the American Labor Movement* (Cambridge: Cambridge University Press, 2002).

ownership comes with voting rights in corporate governance and/or direct representation on a corporation's board of directors, then employees can participate in business decision making at the highest levels of the corporation (recall Box 11.11). Through these channels of influence, companies might weigh employees' interests (such as job security) more heavily when making strategic decisions. **Employee ownership unionism,** therefore, seeks to represent workers by facilitating employee ownership of companies.

Some examples of union involvement in employee ownership efforts include employee stock ownership plans (ESOPs) in the steel, trucking, and airline industries. These ESOPs usually occurred when the companies were struggling and involved employees trading wage and benefit concessions for stock ownership. To date, organized labor has therefore entered into ESOPs as a defensive rather than as a proactive representation strategy. Moreover, the difficulty of using employee ownership to advocate for employee interests is underscored by the fact that only a tiny minority of ESOPs include employee representatives on corporations' boards of directors.[29]

Another potential direction of employee ownership unionism focuses on the investment policies of pension funds. Employee pension funds have a total worldwide value of $13 trillion (an amount equal to almost half of the world's gross national product) and U.S. pension funds have over $7 trillion in assets invested in stocks, bonds, and other instruments—this is labor's capital.[30] Various efforts are underway to try to use the power of these assets to promote workers' interests by creating "worker–owner" investment objectives that pursue a broader larger social agenda than simply short-term financial returns. Union pension funds are leading a movement of shareholder activism in which workers use their rights as shareholders to submit shareholder proposals and resolutions to limit executive compensation, ensure the independence of outside board members, and bring about other changes in corporate strategies and governance.[31] These proposals and resolutions are voted on by shareholders and even if they do not pass, the publicity can cause companies to make changes. One potential for employee ownership unionism is expanding shareholder resolutions to encompass employment practices as well as corporate governance issues. A second method is using union pension funds to directly make worker-friendly investments, such as in unionized construction projects.[32] The use of labor's capital to promote efficiency, equity, and voice is an important labor relations development to watch in the 21st century.

Employee Empowerment Unionism

A frequent concern with the traditional, postwar model of U.S. business unionism is its emphasis on uniformity and standardization through rules.[33] Not only does this job control unionism approach clash with managerial drives for flexibility (Chapter 11), but it is also reasonable to question whether this is what workers want. In **employee empowerment**

---

[29] Joseph R. Blasi and Douglas L. Kruse, *The New Owners: The Mass Emergence of Employee Ownership in Public Companies and What It Means to American Business* (New York: HarperBusiness, 1991), p. 245.

[30] Robin Blackburn, *Banking on Death or Investing in Life: The History and Future of Pensions* (London: Verso, 2002), p. 6. Archon Fung, Tessa Hebb, and Joel Rogers (eds.), *Working Capital: The Power of Labor's Pensions* (Ithaca, NY: Cornell University Press, 2001).

[31] Marleen O'Connor, "Labor's Role in the Shareholder Revolution," in Fung, Hebb, and Rogers (eds.), *Working Capital: The Power of Labor's Pensions* (Ithaca, NY: Cornell University Press, 2001), Chapter 4. Stewart J. Schwab and Randall S. Thomas, "Realigning Corporate Governance: Shareholder Activism by Labor Unions," *Michigan Law Review* 96 (February 1998), pp. 1018–90.

[32] Michael Calabrese, "Building on Success: Labor-Friendly Investment Vehicles and the Power of Private Equity," in Archon Fung, Tessa Hebb, and Joel Rogers (eds.), *Working Capital: The Power of Labor's Pensions* (Ithaca, NY: Cornell University Press, 2001), Chapter 5.

[33] Cobble, "Lost Ways of Unionism." Charles C. Heckscher, *The New Unionism: Employee Involvement in the Changing Corporation* (New York: Basic Books, 1988).

unionism, unions negotiate processes rather than outcomes and thus provide the framework for greater individual autonomy, discretion, and empowerment (Chapter 6).[34] Unlike systems installed unilaterally by employers, negotiated processes can include minimum standards and procedural safeguards (ultimately backed up by a strike threat). Unions can also provide expertise and support to individual employees as needed.

In professional sports and the entertainment industry, unions typically only negotiate minimum salaries. Within the processes negotiated by the unions, individual players or actors negotiate their own salaries (see Box 14.6). As an example among office workers, the clerical workers at Harvard University negotiated joint committees and problem-solving systems instead of rules and a traditional grievance procedure. In this way, individual employees are empowered to participate in their own determination of working conditions, within a union-negotiated framework and with the union's support (see Box 14.7).[35] Employee empowerment unionism can overlap with efficiency enhancing unionism in workplaces run by self-directed work teams. At Saturn, for example, teams of workers are empowered to make a range of decisions, but these decisions are made within a framework that was negotiated by the UAW and Saturn. As such, protections are built into the structure and the union can ensure that employees receive support and due process. Perhaps most graphically, employees can file grievances and the UAW can strike during contract negotiations.

Associational Unionism

Another possible direction for employee representation is called **associational unionism.**[36] This perspective is rooted in a contrast with the postwar model of industrial unionism and U.S. labor law. These postwar institutions are premised on a balance of power between (often large) unions and (often large) corporations. In a mass manufacturing economy, this balance was achieved through rules-based contracts; stability was achieved through uniformity of contracts across an industry. In other words, both union representation and production were very bureaucratic. Proponents of associational unionism argue that this bureaucratic balance of power no longer matches the need for nimble, flexible, and competitive organizations. Perhaps more importantly, the traditional sharp distinction between "labor" and "management" no longer matches large numbers of today's semiprofessional, professional, and knowledge workers. These workers have multiple interests—personal, occupational, industry-specific, and company-specific—and often look to professional associations to serve their interests in a flexible, positive, and nonadversarial way such as through training and the establishment of professional standards. But professional associations, such as the Society for Human Resource Management (SHRM), generally lack or even pursue power in the workplace.

Associational unionism attempts to blend the multiple-interest philosophy and services of professional associations with the power of unions to create a new organizational form that is more powerful than an association, but is more decentralized and flexible than a typical U.S. union.[37] Associational unions (if they existed) could strike, but like a professional association they could also use other tactics such as political pressure and publicity. Such unions could also negotiate contracts with employers, but because of the multiple interests

---

[34] John W. Budd, *Employment with a Human Face: Balancing Efficiency, Equity, and Voice* (Ithaca, NY: Cornell University Press, 2004).

[35] John Hoerr, *We Can't Eat Prestige: The Women Who Organized Harvard* (Philadelphia: Temple University Press, 1997).

[36] Heckscher, *The New Unionism.*

[37] Heckscher, *The New Unionism.*

In the entertainment industry, collective bargaining agreements for the Screen Actors Guild, the American Federation of Television and Radio Artists, the Writers Guild of America, and the Directors Guild of America contain a set of sometimes complicated minimum rates, the framework for individual negotiations, and industrywide standards on residual payments. Actors, writers, and directors are explicitly allowed to negotiate their own compensation above the negotiated minimums. Moreover, this model is not limited to superstars: the International Alliance of Theatrical and Stage Employees (IATSE) takes the same approach for below-the-line craft employees in the television and film industry who handle cameras, sound, lighting, and other production aspects.

Through typical collective bargaining, IATSE negotiates Basic Agreements with various associations of producers, such as the Alliance of Motion Picture Television Producers or the Association of Independent Commercial Producers, and with production companies, such as Walt Disney or Twentieth Century Fox. The Basic Agreements are similar to typical union contracts and include union recognition and security clauses, benefits, standards for rest and meal periods, overtime provisions, no strike clauses, and a grievance procedure. The critical differences between these Basic Agreements and a typical U.S. union contract, however, are that there are no just cause provisions and the wage rates are minimums. Individual IATSE members are explicitly allowed to negotiate higher rates—often referred to as "better conditions"—on their own. In other words, "IATSE's collective bargaining agreement is simply an umbrella that contains and defines the parameters of embedded individual bargains." This embedded bargaining fits well with IATSE's membership because of their episodic employment patterns. Specific jobs, such as making a commercial or a movie, only last a few days or months, so the self-representation aspect provides producers and employees the ability to tailor wages and hours for each project. At the same time, the umbrella collective bargaining agreement provides a set of minimum standards and also continuity of benefits.

Sources: Alan Paul and Archie Kleingartner, "The Transformation of Industrial Relations in the Motion Picture and Television Industries: Talent Sector," in Lois S. Gray and Ronald L. Seeber (eds.), *Under the Stars: Essays on Labor Relations in Arts and Entertainment* (Ithaca, NY: ILR Press, 1996), Chapter 5. Katherine V. W. Stone, "The New Psychological Contract: Implications of the Changing Workplace for Labor and Employment Law," *UCLA Law Review* 48 (February 2001), pp. 519–661. The quote is from p. 635.

that they represent, associational unions would also have to become skilled in multilateral negotiations, not just bilateral negotiations with a single employer. In fact, this proposed system is not based on exclusive representation; rather, workers can belong to various associations that reflect their interests and ideals. As a hypothetical example, an African-American human resource manager might look to a national professional association for the establishment of national standards for HR professionals while also belonging to a local group of minority business professionals for advocacy on diversity issues and also affiliating with other professionals within his or her company to lobby the company for better educational benefits. In other words, associational unions coordinate employee networking with others that share similar interests.

In sum, there are a number of possible directions for U.S. labor unions in the 21st century. As summarized in Box 14.2, there are pros and cons to all of these directions. These alternatives can also be analyzed against the critical dimensions of the employment relationship: efficiency, equity, and voice. Efficiency is emphasized most strongly by efficiency enhancing unionism, but employee ownership unionism can also promote efficiency if stock ownership motivates employees or if social investing produces stable companies with high-performance employment systems. Moreover, the flexibility and individual discretion aspects of employee empowerment unionism and associational unionism can also be consistent

Recall from Chapter 7 that the Harvard Union of Clerical and Technical Workers (HUCTW) successfully unionized clerical and technical workers at Harvard University in the 1980s by emphasizing nontraditional tactics. In particular, the HUCTW relied heavily on building one-to-one relationships with the workers and by trying to create the HUCTW as a vehicle for employee empowerment, not for institutional confrontation with Harvard (recall the slogan, "It's not anti-Harvard to be prounion."). This approach was based on trying to counter the paternalism of Harvard towards the predominantly female clerical workers.

But once the organizing drive was successful, what then? A standard union contract with narrow work rules and a quasilegal grievance procedure (in the tradition of the servicing model of representation) is inconsistent with the empowerment philosophy of the HUCTW (an organizing model of representation). In fact, this type of contract would simply replace the paternalism of Harvard with the paternalism of the union. Consequently, using an inclusive and participative bargaining structure, the HUCTW negotiated a nontraditional contract. Rather than restrictive work rules, the contract explicitly recognizes that "Each school and administrative unit of Harvard has a unique culture and therefore an employee participation program must be flexible to accommodate the needs of the school or administrative department and its staff."

To support employee participation and flexibility, a two-part system was established that consists of (1) joint committees to discuss and seek consensus on "workplace matters which have a significant impact on staff," and (2) problem-solving teams to resolve problems. The principles guiding these procedures include consensus building, open communication, and developing individual problem-solving skills. If an individual has a workplace problem (a "grievance" in traditional lingo), the first step is employee–supervisor discussions. Employees can rely on the HUCTW for support, but the explicit goal is for employees to resolve their own issues. If the problem is not resolved at this level, it can be referred to a joint problem-solving team, and ultimately to mediation. In cases of impasse, the mediator can issue a binding decision.

Clerical and technical workers have therefore created a system of self-representation at Harvard. Through joint councils and an individual problem resolution system, individual workers are empowered to participate in the determination of their conditions of employment, backed up by the expertise and negotiating power of their union.

Source: John P. Hoerr, *We Can't Eat Prestige: The Women Who Organized Harvard* (Philadelphia: Temple University Press, 1997).

with increased competitiveness. Equity is stressed most sharply in solidarity unionism and social movement unionism and is pursued through strong bargaining and social power. In contrast, employee empowerment unionism seeks equity through minimum standards and procedural safeguards. Social voice is an important feature of social movement unionism while workplace voice is delivered in alternative ways in some of the other models. Employee ownership unionism provides workplace voice through participation in corporate governance while employee empowerment and associational unionism emphasize a combination of individual and collective voice mechanisms.

Lastly, discussions of the future of unionism should not ignore the current weak state of the U.S. labor movement. In particular, can weak unions successfully pursue more cooperative strategies such as efficiency enhancing or employee empowerment unionism? Cooperative behavior from a position of weakness likely promotes efficiency, but is unlikely to revive the labor movement and to make positive contributions to equity and voice. Moreover, weak unions that feel that their very existence is threatened might turn to militant, adversarial strategies to increase their power. As such, the extent to which unions are institutionally secure in the economic, political, and social system of the 21st century can shape which direction U.S. unions move in Box 14.1. Whether unions are secure or threatened depends not only on choices that the labor movement must make, but also on corporate behavior and public policies.

WHAT SHOULD COMPANIES DO?

In looking towards the future of labor relations, it is equally important to consider possible directions for employers as well as for unions. While many might argue that there is less need to change existing labor relations strategies and structures on the corporate side than on the union side, there are nevertheless important alternatives to consider (see Box 14.8). In many ways, these alternatives boil down to the question of what is the social responsibility of corporations?

> The baseline answer to this important (and highly debated) question is to make a profit: Few trends could so thoroughly undermine the very foundations of our free society as the acceptance of corporate officials of a social responsibility other than making as much money for their stockholders as possible. . . . The view has been gaining widespread acceptance that corporate officials . . . have a "social responsibility" that goes beyond serving the interest of their stockholders. . . . This view shows a fundamental misconception of the character and nature of a free economy. In such an economy, there is one and only one social responsibility of business—to use its resources and engage in activities designed to increase profits so long as it stays within the rules of the game, which is to say, engages in open and free competition, without deception or fraud.[38]

This view embraces essentially utilitarian and libertarianism ethical views (see Chapter 3), but is also rooted in a distinct legal view of corporate governance. This U.S. view of corporate governance is the **shareholder model**.[39] Shareholders are viewed as the key group in the corporation because they invest their money and bear the risk of making a profit or loss. As such, for both economic and legal reasons, shareholders are recognized as the owners of the corporation. Managers have a primary legal obligation to act in the best interests of the shareholders.[40] Maximizing shareholder value has come to be the primary emphasis of U.S. corporations—and maximizing shareholder value is now equated with maximizing short-term stock prices.[41] This

BOX 14.8
Directions for Corporate Governance and Norms

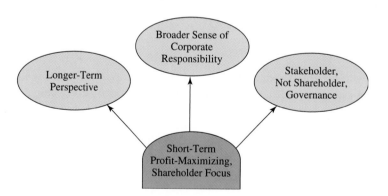

[38] Milton Friedman, *Capitalism and Freedom* (Chicago: University of Chicago Press, 1962), p. 133.

[39] Margaret M. Blair, *Ownership and Control: Rethinking Corporate Governance for the Twenty-First Century* (Washington, DC: Brookings, 1995). Mary O'Sullivan, *Contests for Corporate Control: Corporate Governance and Economic Performance in the United States and Germany* (Oxford: Oxford University Press, 2000). Sanford M. Jacoby, *The Embedded Corporation: Corporate Governance and Employment Relations in Japan and the United States* (Princeton, NJ: Princeton University Press, 2005).

[40] C. A. Harwell Wells, "The Cycles of Corporate Social Responsibility: An Historical Retrospective for the Twenty-first Century," *Kansas Law Review* 51 (November 2002), pp. 77–140.

[41] Marjorie Kelly, *The Divine Right of Capital: Dethroning the Corporate Aristocracy* (San Francisco: Berrett-Koehler, 2001). Allan A. Kennedy, *The End of Shareholder Value: Corporations at the Crossroads* (Cambridge, MA: Perseus, 2000).

strong shareholder value model of corporate governance therefore establishes a corporate pre-occupation with short-term financial results that treats employees as labor costs and also usually denies employees or unions meaningful participation in corporate governance and decisions over investments, mergers, and other major business activities.

While this short-term, financial focus can have benefits for short-term wealth maximization and efficiency, and has many supporters, it is not without critics. More specifically, critics argue that corporate social responsibility is broader than profit-maximization. In ethical terms, recall from Chapter 3 that the ethics of duty (in the tradition of Kant) and virtue (in the tradition of Aristotle) reject a sole focus on outcomes (such as profit-maximization) without regard for actions (such as how people are treated). The ethics of justice further gives weight to the fairness of economic outcomes. Thus, business is viewed as a human activity—seeking profits through efficiency and competitiveness is important but must be balanced with respect for the humanity of people and the corporation's role in society.[42] From a legal perspective, it is argued that stockholders have important rights but that corporations are legally sanctioned by governments and thus shareholder rights are not unlimited. In particular, because of a perceived public interest, the law grants shareholders limited liability (if you own stock in a bankrupt company, creditors cannot take your house); in return, corporations must serve the public interest. In other words, corporations are viewed as social rather than purely private institutions.[43]

As a result, an alternative to the shareholder model of corporate governance is the **stakeholder theory** of the corporation. Stakeholder theory asserts that *all* stakeholders—employees, customers, suppliers, local communities, and others in addition to shareholders or owners—are sufficiently affected by corporate actions to deserve the right to be considered in corporate decision making.[44] In other words, a corporation exists not just for the benefit of shareholders, and should be operated for the benefit of all those who have a stake in it. In fact, 32 states have adopted constituency statutes in which company directors are explicitly allowed to consider interests beyond those of the shareholders.[45] In its most extensive form, stakeholder theory advocates greater legal changes in corporate governance, especially mandated representatives of employees and other stakeholders on corporate boards of directors. This is the case in other countries such as Germany (Chapter 13).[46]

More commonly, supporters of a stakeholder approach in the United States advocate the need for changing corporate and societal norms, and stop short of calling for legal changes. At the workplace level, it is argued that employee dignity in daily work requires new norms for management behavior that respect workers' interests and rights.[47] In terms

[42] Norman E. Bowie, *Business Ethics: A Kantian Perspective* (Malden, MA: Blackwell, 1999). Kelly, *The Divine Right of Capital.* Robert C. Solomon, *Ethics and Excellence: Cooperation and Integrity in Business* (New York: Oxford University Press, 1992). Joel Bakan, *The Corporation: The Pathological Pursuit of Profit and Power* (New York: Free Press, 2004).

[43] E. Merrick Dodd, Jr., "For Whom Are Corporate Managers Trustees?" *Harvard Law Review* 45 (May 1932), pp. 1145–63.

[44] Blair, *Ownership and Control.* Thomas Donaldson and Lee E. Preston, "The Stakeholder Theory of the Corporation: Concepts, Evidence, and Implications," *Academy of Management Review* 20 (January 1995), pp. 65–91. R. Edward Freeman, *Strategic Management: A Stakeholder Approach* (Boston: Pitman, 1984).

[45] Edward S. Adams and John H. Matheson, "A Statutory Model for Corporate Constituency Concerns," *Emory Law Journal* 49 (Fall 2000), pp. 1085–135.

[46] Sanford M. Jacoby, "Employee Representation and Corporate Governance: A Missing Link," *University of Pennsylvania Journal of Labor and Employment Law* 3 (Spring 2001), pp. 449–89. Kelly, *The Divine Right of Capital.* O'Sullivan, *Contests for Corporate Control.*

[47] Randy Hodson, *Dignity at Work* (Cambridge: Cambridge University Press, 2001). Michael A. Santoro, *Profits and Principles: Global Capitalism and Human Rights in China* (Ithaca, NY: Cornell University Press, 2000).

of human resources and industrial relations strategies, for example, high-performance work practices in which employees have decision-making authority can be used instead of confrontational methods of supervision (Chapter 6); in union organizing drives, employers can choose a policy of neutrality instead of union suppression (Chapter 7).

Similar arguments about the need to respect workers' interests and rights are made for policies and institutions at a national level.[48] And changing corporate norms towards a stakeholder view has also become prominent in international discussions of employment issues. The United Nations is trying to establish a Global Compact with business in which corporations agree to voluntarily respect human labor and environmental concerns while the United Nations promotes trade and open markets.[49] The United Nations has also developed a model code of conduct for companies with respect to human rights based partly on the belief that corporate citizenship is good for business and partly on the foundation that "business enterprises have increased their power in the world . . . with power comes responsibility."[50] The International Labor Organization's campaign for "decent work" is based on similar principles.[51]

A stakeholder rather than shareholder approach to labor relations would represent a significant change from past U.S. experiences. High-performance work systems with extensive employee involvement would likely be more widespread (Chapter 11). Employers would probably maintain neutrality in union organizing drives (Chapter 7). Labor–management negotiations would likely have more of an integrative or win-win, problem-solving approach than a distributive and adversarial character (Chapter 8). Grievance resolution would probably be more flexible and informal (Chapter 10). Companies might be less likely to move production to different locations in response to union activity or modest labor cost differentials. Significantly greater amounts of information would probably be shared with employees and their representatives, and employees would have a voice in strategic decision making. And unions might adopt less militant strategies and structures (see above).

Is there any prospect for moving from a shareholder to a stakeholder model of corporate governance? The fallout from the corporate scandals at Enron, WorldCom, and elsewhere has raised the issue of corporate ethics and responsibility. Using pension fund assets to pursue shareholder activism and targeted investing as described in the employee ownership unionism section earlier in this chapter might provide additional pressure for change. In the meantime, the primacy of shareholders and the focus on short-term profitability are firmly entrenched. Nevertheless, discussions of the future of U.S. labor relations should not overlook questions of corporate governance, responsibility, and business norms.[52]

THE FUTURE OF U.S. LABOR RELATIONS POLICY

Any discussion of the future of U.S. labor relations is incomplete without considering alternative directions for U.S. public policies pertaining to labor relations—in other words, the question of labor law reform. This is a tremendously important issue and has ramifications that extend far beyond the small fraction of U.S. workplaces that are unionized. In particular, recall from Chapter 2 the question of workplace governance: Who gets to make the rules

[48] Budd, *Employment with a Human Face.*

[49] *http://www.unglobalcompact.org.*

[50] David Weissbrodt, "Principles Relating to the Human Rights Conduct of Companies," E/CN.4/Sub.2/2000/WG.2/WP.1 (New York: United Nations Commission on Human Rights, 2000), p. 4.

[51] International Labour Organization, *Decent Work* (Geneva, 1999).

[52] Budd, *Employment with a Human Face.* Jacoby, "Employee Representation and Corporate Governance." Jacoby, *The Embedded Corporation.*

of the workplace? The marketplace? Management? Government (through laws)? Workers? Or employers and employees (or their representatives) together? Whoever gets to make the rules gets to govern the workplace. U.S. labor law is a critical determinant of workplace governance—the absence of laws means that markets and managers govern the workplace; strong laws promoting a certain form of labor–management negotiations—whether traditional U.S. unions, works councils, associational unions, or other options—establish a joint mechanism for rule-making. The issue of whether U.S. labor law needs to be reformed is therefore, in broad terms, a question of how the workplace should be governed.

There is perhaps widespread agreement that U.S. labor law needs to be reformed—across the entire spectrum of beliefs on labor unions or employee representation, supportive and not. U.S. labor law dates back to the 1930s and 1940s. Think of the drastic changes in technology, demographics, industries and occupations, globalization, and other areas of economic and social life that have occurred since that time. There is certainly good reason to question whether U.S. labor law—and by extension, the current system of workplace governance—still makes sense more than a half century later. Many argue that in one way or another, the system indeed no longer makes sense—but for very different reasons—and thus, that U.S. labor law needs to be reformed—but in very different ways. It is instructive to consider four major directions for the future of U.S. labor policy: strengthening, loosening, deregulating, and transforming the National Labor Relations Act (NLRA) system (see Box 14.9).

Strengthening the NLRA

Union membership as a fraction of the U.S. workforce—that is, union density—has been declining in the U.S. private sector since the 1950s (Chapter 1). One explanation for this decline is that weaknesses in the law allow employers to suppress unionization efforts. Direct evidence on this contention is difficult to obtain, but proponents of this view cite the existence

BOX 14.9
Directions for U.S. Labor Law

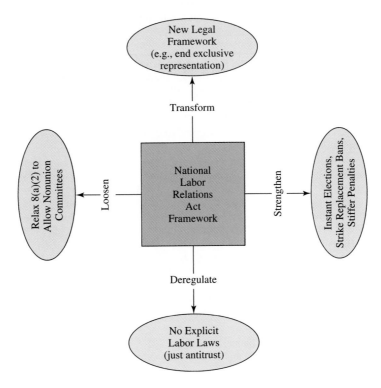

of a representation gap: significant numbers of employees say that they want more representation in the workplace than they have.[53] Moreover, the union density rate is much higher in the public sector than in the private sector and it is commonly believed that public sector employers have fewer opportunities to fight unionization than private sector employers—the local board of education cannot threaten to shut down a school and move it to China in response to a union organizing drive. Consequently, organized labor and workers' rights supporters believe that weaknesses in the NLRA are an important cause of the frail health of today's unions. When combined with a pluralist industrial relations view that sees unions as needed counterweights to corporate power, the logical consequence of this thinking is to advocate for strengthening the NLRA. From one perspective, the NLRA's weaknesses are the result of decades of unfavorable court decisions that have effectively rewritten the law.[54] In this vein, the route to strengthening the NLRA is to educate judges about labor issues and reverse these legal decisions to restore the original intent of the law. More common, however, is the belief that the NLRA's weaknesses stem from management exploitation of the NLRA.[55] In this vein, congressional rather than judicial action to revise and amend the NLRA is seen as an urgent necessity. Such calls for strengthening the NLRA are increasingly rooted in the argument that the current NLRA framework fails to fulfill international human rights standards pertaining to freedom of association and collective bargaining (recall Chapter 6).[56]

Box 14.10 lists the major options for strengthening the NLRA. It is useful to consider two categories: remedial and substantive changes.[57] Remedial changes include increasing the penalties for violating the NLRA—including both monetary penalties and stronger remedial directives such as bargaining orders—and reducing delays in the organizing process that stem from legal challenges. Substantive changes include expanding the coverage of the NLRA to include low-level supervisors, removing restrictions on secondary boycotts, and widening the scope of bargaining items. The two substantive issues that receive the most attention, however, are representation elections and strike replacements.

Criticisms of the election process include problems with delay and the asymmetries between managers and union organizers, especially with respect to access to employees.[58] Recall from Chapter 7 that employers can force employees to listen to their views in captive audience

---

[53] Richard B. Freeman and Joel Rogers, *What Workers Want* (Ithaca, NY: ILR Press, 1999). Richard B. Freeman and Joel Rogers, "Who Speaks for Us? Employee Representation in a Nonunion Labor Market," in Bruce E. Kaufman and Morris M. Kleiner (eds.), *Employee Representation: Alternatives and Future Directions* (Madison, WI: Industrial Relations Research Association, 1993), Chapter 1. Brian Towers, *The Representation Gap: Change and Reform in the British and American Workplace* (Oxford: Oxford University Press, 1997).

[54] Ellen Dannin, *Taking Back the Workers' Law: How to Fight the Assault on Labor Rights* (Ithaca, NY: Cornell University Press, 2006).

[55] Stephen F. Befort, "Labor and Employment Law at the Millennium: A Historical Review and Critical Assessment." *Boston College Law Review* 43 (March 2002), pp. 351–460. Charles B. Craver, *Can Unions Survive? The Rejuvenation of the American Labor Movement* (New York: New York University Press, 1993). Sheldon Friedman, Richard W. Hurd, Rudolph A. Oswald, and Ronald L. Seeber (eds.), *Restoring the Promise of American Labor Law* (Ithaca, NY: ILR Press, 1994). William B. Gould, *Agenda for Reform: The Future of Employment Relationships and the Law* (Cambridge: MIT Press, 1993).

[56] Human Rights Watch, *Unfair Advantage: Workers' Freedom of Association in the United States under International Human Rights Standards* (Washington, DC, 2000). Roy J. Adams, "Choice or Voice? Rethinking American Labor Policy in Light of the International Human Rights Consensus," *Employee Rights and Employment Policy Journal* 5 (2001), pp. 521–48. James A. Gross (ed.), *Workers' Rights as Human Rights* (Ithaca, NY: Cornell University Press, 2003).

[57] Craver, *Can Unions Survive?*

[58] Craver, *Can Unions Survive?* Cynthia L. Estlund, "Labor, Property, and Sovereignty After *Lechmere*," *Stanford Law Review* 46 (January 1994), pp. 305–59. Gould, *Agenda for Reform.* Paul Weiler, "Promises to Keep: Securing Workers' Rights to Self-Organization Under the NLRA," *Harvard Law Review* 96 (June 1983), pp. 1769–827.

Strengthening the NLRA: Common Reform Proposals

Box 14.10

Remedial Reforms

- **Create Strict Timetables for Unfair Labor Practice Processing** to prevent "justice delayed is justice denied."

- **Penalize Violators with Fines,** such as triple backpay for illegal firings.

- **Provide Immediate Reinstatement** of illegally fired workers.

- **Allow Bargaining Orders** when an employer's illegal actions prevent a union from obtaining majority support.

Substantive Reforms

- **Expand Coverage** to include independent contractors and supervisors.

- **Provide Equal Access** to employees by unions and managers during organizing drives. Union organizers should be able to give a captive audience speech if management does.

- **Limit Management and Union Campaigning** to prohibit lies and to restrict statements that imply negative consequences will result from supporting a union (such as a plant closure).

- **Require Instant Elections** so that elections occur soon after a petition is filed to remove opportunities for negative campaigning and selective discharges. Card-check elections is another similar reform.

- **Require Arbitration of First Contracts** if bargaining fails to produce a contract for a newly organized unit.

- **Broaden the Scope of Mandatory Bargaining Items** to include plant closures, subcontracting, introduction of new technology, and other issues that directly affect working conditions and job security.

- **Ban Permanent Strike Replacements** so that companies can use temporary workers during a strike, but strikers will not lose their jobs. Temporary replacements could also be prohibited from participating in decertification elections.

- **Relax the Secondary Activity Ban** so that unions could pursue secondary boycotts during a strike.

Sources: Charles B. Craver, *Can Unions Survive? The Rejuvenation of the American Labor Movement* (New York: New York University Press, 1993). William B. Gould, *Agenda for Reform: The Future of Employment Relationships and the Law* (Cambridge: MIT Press, 1993).

---

speeches while using private property rights to bar union organizers from the workplace. Union organizers are instead relegated to trying to contact employees in their homes. Commonly proposed reforms, therefore, include instant or card-check elections which avoid a long and contentious campaigning period, restrictions on management campaigning and/or equal access to union organizers, punitive damages and immediate reinstatement for illegally discharged union supporters, and first contract arbitration. Many of these reforms are included in the Employee Free Choice Act which was introduced in Congress in 2003 and 2005, but as of mid-2006, had not been debated or voted on.

For workers who are already unionized, the biggest perceived weakness in U.S. labor law is the ability of companies to hire permanent replacement workers during a strike. Recall from Chapter 9 that if replacement workers are designated as permanent, then striking workers are not entitled to immediate reinstatement to their jobs at the conclusion of a strike. Because a strike is by far a union's most powerful weapon, critics see the use of permanent replacements as fundamentally stripping the union of its power, and therefore of reducing collective bargaining to collective begging.[59] The obvious reform proposal from this

[59] Craver, *Can Unions Survive*? Samuel Estreicher, "Collective Bargaining Or 'Collective Begging'?: Reflections On Antistrikebreaker Legislation," *Michigan Law Review* 93 (December 1994), pp. 577–608. Gould, *Agenda for Reform*. Paul Weiler, "Striking a New Balance: Freedom of Contract and the Prospects for Union Representation," *Harvard Law Review* 98 (December 1984), pp. 351–420.

point of view is to ban the use of permanent strike replacements, though specific proposals vary on whether this ban should be indefinite or for a specific time period (such as the first six months of a strike). Note in conclusion that labor law debates over union access and the use of strike replacements involve an important theme in this book: how to balance property rights versus labor rights, and by extension how to balance efficiency, equity, and voice.

Deregulating the NLRA

Directly opposed to the viewpoint that the NLRA should be strengthened is the belief that U.S. labor law should be deregulated—that is, completely repealed or discarded (Box 14.9). This view is strongly rooted in mainstream, neoclassical economics thinking and the closely related philosophy of libertarianism (described in Chapter 3). Recall from Chapter 2 that neoclassical economics emphasizes free-market transactions because of the belief that perfect competition maximizes efficiency and aggregate welfare. Monopolies, laws, and other barriers to competition are bad. From this perspective, unions are labor market monopolies.[60] They cause harmful economic effects by using strikes to raise wages higher than the competitive market rate. As such, the NLRA is complicit in reducing aggregate welfare by protecting monopoly unions, forcing unwilling employers to bargain with them, and in some situations, making unwilling employees pay union dues.

Rather than strengthening the NLRA, therefore, others advocate for its repeal (see Box 14.11).[61] Consistent with mainstream economic thought, unions should not be protected by any special legislation. Rather, they should be subject to the same antitrust (antimonopoly) regulations that limit other business organizations from engaging in anticompetitive practices. At the same time, consistent with the libertarian emphasis on individual freedom and liberty, advocates of deregulation generally do not push for legal restrictions on unions beyond antitrust regulations. Rather, as long as individuals and unions abide by the common law principles that outlaw fraud, violence, and threats, then individuals should be free to *voluntarily* form unions—but not with explicit legal protections. If an employer feels that bargaining with a union is in its best interests, then the employer should be free to *voluntarily* bargain. But the law should not compel action because this interferes with free markets and encroaches on individual freedoms. Thus, in this viewpoint, the NLRA should be deregulated.

It's important to note that advocates of deregulating labor law have a very different interpretation of the longstanding decline in U.S. union density than those that support strengthening the NLRA. Whereas the latter group believes that managerial exploitation of weaknesses in the NLRA is responsible for this decline, deregulation proponents feel that this decline stems from a reduced need and desire for unions among workers. In other words, there has been a decline in the demand for unions.[62] In this view, competitive labor markets force employers to be responsive to employee needs and to treat them well through human resource management policies. As such, workers are seen as preferring a system of

---

[60] Milton Friedman and Rose Friedman, *Free to Choose: A Personal Statement* (New York: Harcourt Brace Jovanovich, 1980). Dan C. Heldman, James T. Bennett, and Manuel H. Johnson, *Deregulating Labor Relations* (Dallas: Fisher Institute, 1981). Morgan O. Reynolds, *Power and Privilege: Labor Unions in America* (New York: Universe Books, 1984).

[61] Richard A. Epstein, "A Common Law for Labor Relations: A Critique of the New Deal Labor Legislation," *Yale Law Journal* 92 (July 1983), pp. 1357–408. Heldman, Bennett, and Johnson, *Deregulating Labor Relations*. Reynolds, *Power and Privilege*. Morgan O. Reynolds, *Making America Poorer: The Cost of Labor Law* (Washington, DC: Cato Institute, 1987). Morgan Reynolds, "A New Paradigm: Deregulating Labor Relations," *Journal of Labor Research* 17 (Winter 1996), pp. 121–28.

[62] Henry S. Farber and Alan B. Krueger, "Union Membership in the United States: The Decline Continues," in Bruce E. Kaufman and Morris M. Kleiner (eds.), *Employee Representation: Alternatives and Future Directions* (Madison, WI: Industrial Relations Research Association, 1993), Chapter 3.

Deregulating Labor Law

Box 14.11

"If deregulation in product markets can foster price competition and increase productivity, jobs, and the array of new products and services, why not in [labor] markets too? There are no real intellectual obstacles. It's mostly a matter of superstitions that free labor markets are "different" and exploitative, combined with the familiar tyranny of an entrenched status quo. . . . Whether judged by the criteria of justice, liberty, equality of income, social conflict, or general productivity, the special-interest legislation supporting adversarial unions and compelling employers to deal with them and forcing unwilling workers to be represented by them should be repealed. . . . To be clear, government should not intervene to help nor hinder unions, but simply stick to its fundamental duty, that is, enforce ordinary property, contract, tort, and criminal law in an impartial manner. Only in this way can the framework of peaceful social cooperation assure a maximum rate of progress."

Source: Morgan Reynolds, "A New Paradigm: Deregulating Labor Relations," *Journal of Labor Research* 17 (Winter 1996), pp. 121–28 at 123.

individual rather than collective representation.[63] And thus, if the decline in union density is voluntary (rather than forced by management suppression), then there is no need to strengthen the NLRA. In fact, if unions are only monopolies that interfere with competitive markets, then labor law should be deregulated by repealing the NLRA.

Loosening the NLRA

Between the two arguments for strengthening and deregulating the NLRA is somewhat of a middle compromise position—loosening the NLRA. This view primarily focuses on the NLRA's section 8(a)(2) restriction on company-dominated labor organizations. Recall from Chapter 11 that the NLRA defines labor organizations quite broadly and can include labor–management committees as well as formal unions. In some instances, therefore, workplace committees have been ruled to be illegal—most notably in the *Electromation* case. To some, these rulings demonstrate that the NLRA needs to be loosened to allow for legitimate employee participation mechanisms that give workers a voice and that promote cooperation and competitiveness.[64] In other words, labor law is viewed as partially obsolete and no longer in tune with the realities of global competition and flexibility.

The most concrete example of a proposal to loosen the NLRA is the TEAM Act which sought to modify section 8(a)(2) to allow for labor–management committees that do not seek to negotiate collective bargaining agreements (Chapter 11). The TEAM Act, however, was vetoed by President Clinton in 1996, so it did not become law. Critics of a TEAM Act-type loosening of section 8(a)(2) emphasize the ability of employers to manipulate nonunion employee representation plans to prevent the formation of independent unions and therefore would label the TEAM Act a "weakening" rather than a "loosening" of labor law.[65] Advocates of reform do not view this as a weakening because of the belief that the NLRA's company union ban unnecessarily restricts some legitimate initiatives that serve both employee and employer interests.[66]

[63] Leo Troy, *Beyond Unions and Collective Bargaining* (Armonk, NY: M. E. Sharpe, 1999).

[64] Edward E. Potter and Judith A. Youngman, *Keeping America Competitive: Employment Policy for the Twenty-First Century* (Lakewood, CO: Glenbridge Publishing, 1995).

[65] Jonathan P. Hiatt and Laurence E. Gold, "Employer–Employee Committees: A Union Perspective," in Bruce E. Kaufman and Daphne Gottlieb Taras (eds.), *Nonunion Employee Representation: History, Contemporary Practice, and Policy* (Armonk, NY: M. E. Sharpe, 2000), Chapter 28.

[66] Michael H. LeRoy, "Employee Participation in the New Millennium: Redefining a Labor Organization Under Section 8(a)(2) of the NLRA," *Southern California Law Review* 72 (September 1999), pp. 1651–723.

With that said, many academic commentators do not want a TEAM Act-type change to undermine workers' abilities to form an independent union when they prefer this over a nonunion representation plan. It is therefore common for reform proposals to loosen the NLRA to include both narrowing the scope of section 8(a)(2) and strengthening the ability of workers to organize a union—such as increased union access to employees, quicker representation elections, and steeper penalties for companies that illegally discharge union supporters.[67] In fact, this was the recommendation of the last blue-ribbon panel investigation of U.S. labor relations—the Commission on the Future of Worker–Management Relations created by President Clinton in 1993 (popularly known as the Dunlop Commission).[68] The common theme of these various proposals for loosening the NLRA are based on the view that labor law needs to be reformed—not deregulated—to promote greater cooperation and competitiveness to benefit both employees and employers.

Transforming the NLRA

The fourth possible direction for U.S. labor law is to transform the NLRA into something brand new for the 21st century by completely rewriting labor law. Proponents of this view believe that the New Deal industrial relations system performed admirably in the stable, mass manufacturing era immediately following World War II, but that this framework no longer matches the global, competitive environment of the 21st century. Compared to strengthening or loosening the NLRA, the arguments for transforming the NLRA are based in the belief that the basic NLRA framework is obsolete—a complete overhaul is therefore necessary; modifications will not suffice. Put differently, transformation proponents believe that there is a mismatch between the assumptions of the New Deal industrial relations system and the world of work in the 21st century. This perspective shares the deregulation camp's desire to repeal the NLRA, but because of their pluralist industrial relations foundation, supporters of a transformation believe that new institutions should be created to place checks and balances on free markets. In fact, the strengthening, loosening, and transforming platforms are all rooted in the industrial relations school of thought, but they differ in their beliefs about the form of employee representation that will best provide equity and voice in the environment of the 21st century—traditional unions, a combination of unions and nonunion representation plans, or new forms of unionism, respectively.

Perhaps the primary basis cited for needing to transform the NLRA system into something completely different is **adversarialism**. Adversarialism is a culture of conflict.[69] In U.S. labor relations, adversarialism is typically equated to traditional, distributive negotiations that revolve around a power struggle—every labor–management interaction is a contest of strength and each side assumes the other is always trying to gain the upper hand. *If* adversarialism is harmful for both employees and employers in a global economy, and *if* this culture of conflict is embedded in the provisions of the NLRA, then the NLRA should be

---

[67] Samuel Estreicher, "Labor Law Reform in a World of Competitive Product Markets," *Chicago-Kent Law Review* 69 (1993), pp. 3–46. Samuel Estreicher, "Employee Involvement and the 'Company Union' Prohibition: The Case for Partial Repeal of Section 8(a)(2) of the NLRA," *New York University Law Review* 69 (April 1994), pp. 125–61. Bruce E. Kaufman and Daphne Gottlieb Taras, "Nonunion Employee Representation: Findings and Conclusions," in Bruce E. Kaufman and Daphne Gottlieb Taras (eds.), *Nonunion Employee Representation: History, Contemporary Practice, and Policy* (Armonk, NY: M. E. Sharpe, 2000), Chapter 31. LeRoy, "Employee Participation in the New Millennium." Paul C. Weiler, "A Principled Reshaping of Labor Law for the Twenty-First Century," *University of Pennsylvania Journal of Labor and Employment Law* 3 (Winter 2001), pp. 177–206.

[68] Commission on the Future of Worker–Management Relations, *Report and Recommendations* (Washington, DC: U.S. Departments of Labor and Commerce, 1994).

[69] Roy J. Adams, *Industrial Relations Under Liberal Democracy: North America in Comparative Perspective* (Columbia: University of South Carolina Press, 1995).

discarded and replaced with a completely transformed system. Proponents of transforming labor law believe that adversarialism is bad for unions and employees because it makes effective representation more difficult in today's environment; business attacks adversarialism as inimical to developing the level of cooperation needed in a competitive environment.[70]

And transformation proponents further believe that adversarialism is caused by specific features of U.S. labor law. This belief is not universally accepted—adversarial U.S. labor relations might stem from inherent conflicts of interest in the employment relationship between labor and management rather than from any specific provisions of the NLRA—but how might the NLRA create a culture of conflict? The primary culprit is the centrality of exclusive representation and majority support in U.S. labor law. Because a union must garner the support of a majority of workers to have any workplace rights, the representation process becomes a battle for support between labor and management. To create support for a union, management is attacked as abusive, and an us-versus-them adversarial culture is established. Moreover, this culture of conflict is perpetuated because existing unions must continue to maintain majority support or be decertified. It is also argued that the NLRA's sharp distinctions between labor and management reinforce an us-versus-them mentality.

As a result, many proposals to transform U.S. labor law would replace or supplement exclusive representation and majority support with alternative arrangements. One option is to explicitly provide legal support for nonmajority unions—as noted earlier, these are unions that have the support of a minority rather than a majority of employees in a workplace. This legal support might include full collective bargaining rights for members-only bargaining in which contracts would apply only to members, not the entire bargaining unit. Technically, the NLRA might not even need to be reformed because refusing to bargain with a nonmajority union might already be a section 8(a)(1) unfair labor practice (recall Box 5.11).[71] But explicit legal reform to endorse nonmajority unions is probably necessary to make them a reality. Alternatively, a nonmajority union might be limited to consultation rights—in fact, this arrangement is already in use by U.S. federal government employees (see Box 14.12).

A second option is to replace the certification process with mandated works councils—as widely found in Europe.[72] The trigger to create a works council is typically significantly less than majority support, and might be quite low—perhaps just a handful of employees wanting a works council would suffice. Employees would then elect their works councils' representatives from among existing employees. A works council is typically entitled to jointly determine certain issues and to have information and consultation rights with respect to other issues. In most proposals, U.S. works councils would lack the right to strike. The emphasis on joint determination and consultation, rather than bargaining and strikes, underscores the cooperative rather than adversarial aspect of works councils. And giving workers more influence over their work might increase their sense of legitimacy and justice, thereby increasing cooperation and productivity.[73] Before anyone rejects these proposals too quickly, note that some states already require joint labor–management safety and health committees.

Lastly, in support of nonmajority unions, works councils, and other forms of employee voice, other elements of a transformation of U.S. labor law might include additional

[70] Adams, *Industrial Relations Under Liberal Democracy.* Heckscher, *The New Unionism.* Potter and Youngman, *Keeping America Competitive.*

[71] Morris, *The Blue Eagle at Work.*

[72] Adams, *Industrial Relations Under Liberal Democracy.* Befort, "Labor and Employment Law at the Millennium." Freeman and Rogers, "Who Speaks for Us?" Paul C. Weiler, *Governing the Workplace: The Future of Labor and Employment Law* (Cambridge: Harvard University Press, 1990).

[73] David Fairris, *Shopfloor Matters: Labor–Management Relations in Twentieth-Century American Manufacturing* (London: Routledge, 1997).

Union representation in the U.S. private sector is an all or nothing affair—with majority support, a union is the exclusive representative of all employees and is entitled to bargain over wages, hours, and terms and conditions of employment. But without majority support, unions have few rights. This stands in sharp contrast to European labor relations in which works councils have codetermination, consultation, and information rights even if only a few workers desire such representation. But for employees of the U.S. federal government, it is possible for a union that represents less than a majority of employees to have consultation rights.

More specifically, the Civil Service Reform Act includes the following:

Sec. 7113. National consultation rights

(a) If, in connection with any agency, no labor organization has been accorded exclusive recognition on an agency basis, a labor organization which is the exclusive representative of a substantial number of the employees of the agency, as determined in accordance with criteria prescribed by the Authority, shall be granted national consultation rights by the agency. . . .

(b)1. Any labor organization having national consultation rights in connection with any agency under subsection (a) of this section shall—

(A) be informed of any substantive change in conditions of employment proposed by the agency, and

(B) be permitted reasonable time to present its views and recommendations regarding the changes.

(2) If any views or recommendations are presented under paragraph (1) of this subsection to an agency by any labor organization—

(A) the agency shall consider the views or recommendations before taking final action on any matter with respect to which the views or recommendations are presented; and

(B) the agency shall provide the labor organization a written statement of the reasons for taking the final action.

(C) Nothing in this section shall be construed to limit the right of any agency or exclusive representative to engage in collective bargaining.

The Federal Labor Relations Authority (FLRA) specifies that "substantial number of employees" means at least 3,500 or 10 percent of the civilian employees of a specific government agency (whichever is smaller). Unlike in the U.S. private sector, federal government employees can be represented by a union through consultation if the union only represents 10 percent of the employees.

The U.S. Department of Agriculture (USDA) has consulted with the American Federation of Government Employees (AFGE) and the National Federation of Federal Employees (NFEE) over issues pertaining to equal employment opportunity procedures, reasonable accommodation procedures, telecommuting, mentoring, childcare, and tuition subsidies. Other examples of consultation pertain to changing the Veterans Administration's policy of providing nurses with annual wage comparability increases to match the local labor market and a National Guard Bureau's policy change allowing national guard personnel to fill positions previously filled by civilian technicians represented by the National Association of Government Employees (NAGE).

Consultation is not the same as bargaining because management only needs to consider the union's views; it does not have to try to reach agreement before acting. Nevertheless, consultation has the potential to provide employee voice when a union does not represent a majority of the employees (as in the U.S. federal sector) or over a broader range of issues than just working conditions (as in Europe).

employee rights such as employee free speech, unjust dismissal protections, and the right to workplace information.[74] Transforming U.S. labor law might also involve encouraging employee ownership and representation on corporate board of directors, for example,

---

[74] Heckscher, *The New Unionism.*

through legal changes or tax subsidies.[75] Or it might change the legal conception of bargaining units and items to allow workers from multiple employers in a community to negotiate local standards for wages, portable benefits, and training programs.[76] And the most effective transformation will be one that integrates labor relations reform into the broader context of the changing employment relationship—such as the importance of information technologies, flexibility, diversity, work-family conflicts, and the growth of contingent employees—and that overhauls both employment and labor law.[77]

STRATEGIC LABOR RELATIONS AND LEADERSHIP

The previous three sections have an institutional focus—in what direction should labor unions, corporate behavior, and labor law move in the future? But questions of future directions for U.S. labor relations also involve individual-level issues for managers and union leaders. Insights from strategic management have been applied to human resource management, and they can be equally useful for labor relations—for both management and labor practitioners. Human resource managers have three roles: a builder, a change partner, and a navigator.[78] The builder assembles the basic building blocks of an organization's human resource management function in a coherent way—staffing, compensation, and the like. The change partner reshapes the human resources functions in response to changes in the external environment, often in partnership with others in the organization. Changing forms of pay and work organization in response to the need for greater flexibility is a common example. Note that the builder is focused internally on making sure the pieces of the puzzle fit together while the change partner is focused externally on fitting organizational practices with the outside environment. In the third role, the navigator must continuously develop organizational competencies and performance by balancing these internal and external pressures. An effective organization has both flexibility and control, change and stability, and responsiveness to the demands of markets and the needs of employees. Each of these pairs of contrasts constitutes a **duality**—a tension that is best managed through balancing rather than choosing one option over the other (as might be the case if either internal or external fit is the sole focus).[79]

This three-part framework is insightful for thinking about the roles of labor relations managers and union leaders (see Box 14.13). On the corporate side, managers must build labor relations functions that have high internal fit. Long-term contracts, formalized grievance-handling, and adversarial negotiations served mass manufacturing modes of production in which stability and labor costs were important concerns. But as the environment has changed, labor relations managers as change agents must restructure the labor relations function to fit with an external environment that demands flexibility and quality. This is a major challenge of contemporary managers. But the third role is the

[75] Jacoby, "Employee Representation and Corporate Governance." David I. Levine, *Reinventing the Workplace: How Business and Employees Can Both Win* (Washington, DC: Brookings, 1995).

[76] Stone, *From Widgets to Digits.*

[77] Befort, "Labor and Employment Law at the Millennium." Paul Osterman, Thomas Kochan, Richard Locke, and Michael J. Piore, *Working in America: A Blueprint for the New Labor Market* (Cambridge: MIT Press, 2001). Kochan, *Restoring the American Dream.* Cynthia Estlund, *Working Together: How Workplace Bonds Strengthen a Diverse Democracy* (Oxford: Oxford University Press, 2003). Stone, *From Widgets to Digits.*

[78] Paul Evans, Vladimir Pucik, and Jean-Louis Barsoux, *The Global Challenge: Frameworks for International Human Resource Management* (Boston: McGraw-Hill/Irwin, 2002).

[79] Evans, Pucik, and Barsoux, *The Global Challenge.*

BOX 14.13   *HR Strategy*: **The Strategic Roles of Managers and Union Leaders**

Role	Major Focus	Labor Relations Managerial Issues	Union Leader Issues
Builder	Internal Fit/ Coherence	Creating processes for negotiating and administering contracts that fit with other organizational needs.	Building internal competencies like leadership and strategic planning skills to support organizing, bargaining, and other core activities; creating democratic structures.
Change Partner	External Fit/ Responsiveness	Shaping contracts and labor–management partnerships that promote competitiveness in a global economy.	Creating strategies for representing workers that fit changing demographics, globalization, and other external trends.
Navigator	Balancing Competing Internal and External Pressures (Dualities)	Respecting union and employee needs while promoting competitiveness; creating flexibility from union and employee security.	Balancing centralized power with decentralized responsiveness to local needs, control with discretion, solidarity with individuality.

Source: Columns 1 and 2 are adapted from Paul Evans, Vladimir Pucik, and Jean-Louis Barsoux, *The Global Challenge: Frameworks for International Human Resource Management* (Boston: McGraw-Hill/Irwin, 2002).

most challenging: managers must also navigate (or steer) the labor relations function so as to balance the competing internal and external concerns (dualities). It is often difficult to force flexibility onto unionized employees; rather, navigating means negotiating change and creating flexible systems that are also responsive to employee needs. This might require managing the paradox of making unions and employees feel more secure so that they will be more flexible.

While often overlooked, union leaders face these same tasks in managing their own organizations.[80] On an internal level, union leaders must build union structures to fulfill the labor movement's basic functions, such as organizing, bargaining, contract administration, and political lobbying. These structures must be internally consistent—as an example, the Justice for Janitors campaigns have emphasized organizing through intense rank and file activism, but after successfully winning bargaining rights, contract negotiations and administration have reverted to traditional methods without significant rank and file involvement, to the frustration of the workers.[81] These structures must also be consistent with the fact that unions are democratic organizations. At the same time, that unions are democratic is not an excuse for not building core management skills relating to budgeting, strategic planning, and benchmarking.[82]

Union leaders must also be change partners—they must partner with rank and file employees to construct new forms of representation that fit with changes in the external environment, including greater workforce diversity, greater educational levels, and increased competitive pressures on their employers. The six alternative directions for unions discussed earlier in this chapter are responses to the external environment.

---

[80] John T. Dunlop, *The Management of Labor Unions: Decision Making with Historical Constraints* (Lexington, MA: Lexington Books, 1990).

[81] La Luz and Finn, "Getting Serious About Inclusion." Williams, "Restructuring Labor's Identity."

[82] Thomas A. Hannigan, *Managing Tomorrow's High-Performance Unions* (Westport, CT: Quorum Books, 1998). David Weil, *Turning the Tide: Strategic Planning for Labor Unions* (Lexington, MA: Lexington Books, 1994).

Effective leadership is the result of a number of factors—such as vision, personality traits, specific behaviors, skills, courage, and power. Focusing on this last factor, leadership power can be categorized into five sources:

- Legitimate Power: the authority or right to order someone to do something (followers comply because they have to)
- Reward Power: influence that comes from the ability to hand out rewards (followers comply to obtain rewards)
- Coercive Power: influence that comes from the ability to hand out punishments (followers comply to avoid punishments)
- Referent Power: influence that derives from appealing personal characteristics (followers comply because of admiration or emulation)
- Expert Power: influence that stems from knowledge and expertise (followers comply because they believe the action is wise)

Labor relations constrains some of these sources of power. Labor law denies managers and union leaders the legitimate power to order individuals to support or not support a labor union and similarly bans the use of reward and coercive power to influence support for a union. Union contracts also often specify limitations on management's legitimate, reward, and coercive power—discipline and discharge must be with just cause and rewards are often seniority-based.

But these are turbulent times for labor relations. The institutions of labor relations—both labor law and unions—are widely regarded as weak. As such, in many cases these restrictions on a manager's power are more theoretical than real. At the same time, managers are under great pressure in a hypercompetitive global economy.

Questions

1. Provide labor relations examples of a manager's use of these five types of power that would support good leadership. Provide labor relations examples in which uses of these five types of power undermine good leadership.
2. It's often argued that integrity is a key component of good leadership and that leaders should adhere to high ethical standards. Why?
3. With weak labor laws and labor unions, is it more or less important that leaders have high ethical standards?

Source: Thomas S. Bateman and Scott A. Snell, *Management: Competing in the New Era,* 5th ed. (Boston: McGraw-Hill/Irwin, 2002).

Finally, union leaders must also be navigators that balance the dualities created by internal and external pressures. Important dualities in labor unions include the tension between organizing new members and servicing existing members, between centralized power and decentralized responsiveness to local conditions, between centralized control and democratic participation, and between solidarity across workplaces and concern for individual needs.

This book can help make you a more effective management or union leader by understanding the dualities that need to be navigated. By studying labor relations in a framework that recognizes multiple perspectives or schools of thought on the employment relationship, you can better understand others that you may have to interact with in the workplace—be it a manager, a union leader, an employee, or a government official. Without needing to agree with all alternative viewpoints, this understanding will make you a better leader. Leadership issues were also discussed in Chapters 8 and 11 in the context of resistance to change and strategies for change in moving to integrative bargaining and to a more flexible work system. Lastly, the ethical framework presented in this book has important ramifications for effective leadership (see Box 14.14).

STRIKING A BALANCE

One of the major goals of this book is to present an intellectual framework for understanding labor relations that provides an effective foundation for not only understanding the development and operation of the New Deal industrial relations system and how the current U.S. labor relations processes work, but also for critically evaluating this system, these processes, and the need for reform. To do this, we need to go beyond an examination of how the processes work (though this is important) and ask what the processes are trying to accomplish. Studying any aspect of the employment relationship, in fact, should be rooted in the objectives of the employment relationship: efficiency, equity, and voice. Efficiency is the effective use of labor to promote competitiveness and economic prosperity, equity encompasses fair labor standards in terms of both material outcomes and personal treatment, and voice is the ability to have meaningful input into decisions.

The framework for studying labor relations used in this book is therefore how employee representation—typically through independent labor unions—contributes towards the achievement of efficiency, equity, and voice. The goal of the U.S. labor relations system is to balance efficiency, equity, and voice through balancing property rights and labor rights (Part I). Laws, processes, and behaviors should seek to handle employment relationship conflict and power imbalances between employees and employers in ways that promote effective organizations, a healthy economy, equitable outcomes, respect for human dignity, and fulfillment of the principles of democracy. In the language of the previous section, labor relations and labor law must navigate a number of critical dualities: tensions between property rights and labor rights, between work rules and flexibility, between bilateral negotiation and unilateral control, and between efficiency, equity, and voice.

Different schools of thought on the nature of the employment relationship have varying beliefs on the best way to fulfill these goals.[83] Conventional economic thought emphasizes providing the greatest good for the greatest number through free market exchange. The foundation of this thinking is perfect competition. The human resource management school focuses on management-led policies and practices that can simultaneously benefit both employers and employees. This perspective is rooted in unitarist employment relationship conflict. Critical, or Marxist, industrial relations emphasizes radically changing capitalist institutions to give workers more control in the workplace and throughout society. The basis for this school of thought is conflict between labor and capital that is pervasive throughout society—not narrow economic conflict limited to the employment relationship. Mainstream U.S. industrial relations focuses on adding institutional checks and balances to the employment relationship. This perspective is rooted in pluralist employment relationship conflict—conflict that includes some win-win opportunities for mutual gain and some win-lose, zero-sum clashes of interests.

The New Deal industrial relations system is a critical centerpiece of the pluralist industrial relations system of employment relationship checks and balances. U.S. labor law explicitly protects workers' rights to form unions and collectively bargain because it is believed that these protections balance efficiency, equity, and voice. Efficiency is served through industrial peace and increased consumer purchasing power through increased labor bargaining power. Efficiency is also promoted through the relatively limited incursions of labor law—employee rights are confined to wages and working conditions, not business decision making, and rather than a government bureaucracy imposing specific outcomes, the parties fashion their own agreements to shape their particular circumstances (the principle of subsidiarity). Equity is fulfilled through collective rather than individual

---

[83] Budd, *Employment with a Human Face.*

labor power to better equalize corporate bargaining power. This collective power can prevent exploitation (recall the labor problem of the early 20th century from Chapter 2) and promote a more equitable distribution of economic rewards. Voice is achieved through replacing unilateral managerial authority with the requirement that employee issues must be negotiated with employee representatives. As such, workers have input into decisions that affect them. Understanding the major processes of the U.S. labor relations system—union organizing, bargaining contracts, resolving conflicts, and administering grievances—is therefore the major goal of Part II of this book.

But as discussed in Part III, the traditional operation of the processes such as adversarial negotiations and the typical postwar outcomes such as detailed contracts are under heavy pressure to change because of global competition and the need for workplace flexibility and employee involvement. At this juncture it is critical to remember that the New Deal industrial relations system's processes and work rules are not important in their own right—the processes and work rules are only important to the extent that they promote efficiency, equity, and voice. Labor relations processes are means to greater ends, not ends in themselves and are therefore not untouchable. As such, Part IV—the previous chapter on comparative labor relations and this chapter on alternative directions—reveals that there are various alternatives to the traditional New Deal system for promoting efficiency, equity, and voice. Understanding the current system, the role of labor unions, and future systems of employee representation all require the appreciation of the same fundamental principle: striking a balance.

The major concluding question of this book is therefore what type of system for governing the workplace—and in particular, what form(s) of employee representation—will best achieve the goals of the employment relationship in the economic, social, technological, and global environment of the 21st century? Creating the ideal system likely requires changing union and corporate strategies, social norms, and public policies—which are ultimately rooted in the choices that all of us make as workers, managers, consumers, investors, and citizens. With respect to policy, there are four major possible directions for U.S. labor law in the 21st century—the NLRA can be strengthened, deregulated, loosened, or transformed. Note how these different directions imply different systems of workplace governance—a continued reliance on traditional labor unions, a renewed emphasis on free markets, greater forms of nonunion employee representation, or some new model of representation, respectively. As such, labor law reform cannot and should not be separated from the larger question of how the employment relationship of the future will be structured.

Furthermore, as described in Chapter 12, international debates over free trade and fair trade and other issues in the global economy are closely related to the issue of governing the global workplace and the viability of domestic unions. And there are also various options for changing corporate governance structures. All of these governance issues are closely interrelated, and the direction of reforms for all three should be mutually supporting rather than addressed in isolation from each other. Put differently, a free trade model of global governance and the continued primacy of the shareholder in corporate governance can potentially undermine systems of workplace governance that seek a balance between employers and employees. These inter-linkages should not be overlooked—workplace practices, national labor laws, corporate governance norms, and international treaties must all work together to strike a balance.

Lastly, in considering the various aspects of what labor relations should do in the future and the various perspectives on the need to potentially reform labor unions, corporate behavior, and labor law, there is the difficult question of law versus behavior. If U.S. labor law is a major determinant of outcomes, then the law likely needs to be changed. But if the law provides only the broad skeleton of the system and various outcomes are possible, then perhaps it is behavior—not the law—that needs reforming. To wit, if the union density decline stems from weaknesses in the NLRA, then many argue the law needs changing. But if the union density decline reflects a lack of worker demand for unionization, then what probably needs reforming is union behavior rather than the law. As a second example, does the NLRA force labor and management into an adversarial relationship with little employee involvement and flexibility? Perhaps. But there are notable examples under the NLRA of very productive labor–management partnerships. As such, is it the law or behavior—of both labor and management—that needs reforming? Like many other things in labor relations, the truth likely lies in the middle, and thus, a careful examination of multiple perspectives is required.

Key Terms

solidarity unionism, *500*
nonmajority union, *501*
social movement
unionism, *501*
efficiency enhancing

unionism, *504*
employee ownership
unionism, *506*
employee empowerment
unionism, *506*

associational unionism, *507*
shareholder model, *510*
stakeholder theory, *511*
adversarialism, *518*
duality, *521*

Reflection Questions

1. Employers commonly try to portray unions in a negative light by characterizing them as outside, third-party organizations. Is this accurate if unions are comprised of employees? Describe how the pluralist industrial relations school of thought sees value in having a union as both an outsider and an insider. In what direction(s) should U.S. labor unions go to serve these roles in the 21st century?

2. What is a corporation's social responsibility? Are there corporate labor relations practices that should be unacceptable? If so, how should these standards be enforced?

3. Many argue that U.S. labor relations is broadly characterized by adversarialism. In what ways is adversarialism the result of U.S. labor law? In what ways is adversarialism caused by the behavior of companies and unions rather than by the legal system?

4. Is it still necessary for laws to promote and protect some form of unionism? If so, outline the needed reforms to U.S. labor law.

Internet Exploration

1. Find the Report of the Dunlop Commission (the Commission on the Future of Worker–Management Relations) online. Are efficiency, equity, and voice well-served by this report? Outline an argument that the report does not go far enough to promote employee rights. Outline an argument that the report does not go far enough to promote competitiveness in the 21st century environment.

2. Browse some union-related Web sites at random (*http://www.webring.org/cgi-bin/ webring?ring=unionring&id=_&random*). Can you find examples of the different forms of unionism described in Box 14.2?

3. The United States has the world's freest labor market (*Forbes*, January 30, 2003). Explore the AFL–CIO's Job Tracker database (*www.workingamerica.org/jobtracker/*) to see some of the negative aspects of loosely regulated markets in your community. In contrast, what are the benefits of free labor markets? Is there a need for government regulation?

Additional Reading

Budd, John W., *Employment with a Human Face: Balancing Efficiency, Equity, and Voice* (Ithaca, NY: Cornell University Press, 2004).

Craver, Charles B., *Can Unions Survive? The Rejuvenation of the American Labor Movement* (New York: New York University Press, 1993).

Dannin, Ellen, *Taking Back the Workers' Law: How to Fight the Assault on Labor Rights* (Ithaca, NY: Cornell University Press, 2006).

Fung, Archon, Tessa Hebb, and Joel Rogers (eds.), *Working Capital: The Power of Labor's Pensions* (Ithaca, NY: Cornell University Press, 2001).

Kochan, Thomas A., *Restoring the American Dream: A Working Families' Agenda for America* (Cambridge, MA: MIT Press, 2005).

Lichtenstein, Nelson, *State of the Union: A Century of American Labor* (Princeton, NJ: Princeton University Press, 2002).

Tillman, Ray M., and Michael S. Cummings (eds.), *The Transformation of U.S. Unions: Voices, Visions, and Strategies from the Grassroots* (Boulder, CO: Lynne Rienner Publishers, 1999).

Troy, Leo, *Beyond Unions and Collective Bargaining* (Armonk, NY: M. E. Sharpe, 1999).

Turner, Lowell, Harry C. Katz, and Richard W. Hurd (eds.), *Rekindling the Movement: Labor's Quest for Relevance in the Twenty-First Century* (Ithaca, NY: ILR Press, 2001).

Wheeler, Hoyt N., *The Future of the American Labor Movement* (Cambridge: Cambridge University Press, 2002).

Appendix **A**

Selected Laws and Declarations

Contents

U.S. CONSTITUTION (1789)

We the people of the United States, in order to form a more perfect union, establish justice, insure domestic tranquility, provide for the common defense, promote the general welfare, and secure the blessings of liberty to ourselves and our posterity, do ordain and establish this Constitution for the United States of America.

Article I

. . .

Section 8. The Congress shall have power to lay and collect taxes, duties, imposts and excises, to pay the debts and provide for the common defense and general welfare of the United States; but all duties, imposts and excises shall be uniform throughout the United States;

To borrow money on the credit of the United States;

To regulate commerce with foreign nations, and among the several states, and with the Indian tribes;

To establish a uniform rule of naturalization, and uniform laws on the subject of bankruptcies throughout the United States;

To coin money, regulate the value thereof, and of foreign coin, and fix the standard of weights and measures;

To provide for the punishment of counterfeiting the securities and current coin of the United States;

To establish post offices and post roads;

To promote the progress of science and useful arts, by securing for limited times to authors and inventors the exclusive right to their respective writings and discoveries;

To constitute tribunals inferior to the Supreme Court;

To define and punish piracies and felonies committed on the high seas, and offenses against the law of nations;

To declare war, grant letters of marque and reprisal, and make rules concerning captures on land and water;

To raise and support armies, but no appropriation of money to that use shall be for a longer term than two years;

To provide and maintain a navy;

To make rules for the government and regulation of the land and naval forces;

To provide for calling forth the militia to execute the laws of the union, suppress insurrections and repel invasions;

To provide for organizing, arming, and disciplining, the militia, and for governing such part of them as may be employed in the service of the United States, reserving to the states respectively, the appointment of the officers, and the authority of training the militia according to the discipline prescribed by Congress;

To exercise exclusive legislation in all cases whatsoever, over such District (not exceeding ten miles square) as may, by cession of particular states, and the acceptance of Congress, become the seat of the government of the United States, and to exercise like authority over all places purchased by the consent of the legislature of the state in which the same shall be, for the erection of forts, magazines, arsenals, dockyards, and other needful buildings;—And

To make all laws which shall be necessary and proper for carrying into execution the foregoing powers, and all other powers vested by this Constitution in the government of the United States, or in any department or officer thereof.

Bill of Rights (first 10 amendments, adopted 1791)

Amendment I

Congress shall make no law respecting an establishment of religion, or prohibiting the free exercise thereof; or abridging the freedom of speech, or of the press; or the right of the people peaceably to assemble, and to petition the government for a redress of grievances.

Amendment II

A well regulated militia, being necessary to the security of a free state, the right of the people to keep and bear arms, shall not be infringed.

Amendment III

No soldier shall, in time of peace be quartered in any house, without the consent of the owner, nor in time of war, but in a manner to be prescribed by law.

Amendment IV

The right of the people to be secure in their persons, houses, papers, and effects, against unreasonable searches and seizures, shall not be violated, and no warrants shall issue, but upon probable cause, supported by oath or affirmation, and particularly describing the place to be searched, and the persons or things to be seized.

Amendment V

No person shall be held to answer for a capital, or otherwise infamous crime, unless on a presentment or indictment of a grand jury, except in cases arising in the land or naval forces, or in the militia, when in actual service in time of war or public danger; nor shall any person be subject for the same offense to be twice put in jeopardy of life or limb; nor shall be compelled in any criminal case to be a witness against himself, nor be deprived of life, liberty, or property, without due process of law; nor shall private property be taken for public use, without just compensation.

Amendment VI

In all criminal prosecutions, the accused shall enjoy the right to a speedy and public trial, by an impartial jury of the state and district wherein the crime shall have been committed, which district shall have been previously ascertained by law, and to be informed of the nature and cause of the accusation; to be confronted with the witnesses against him; to have compulsory process for obtaining witnesses in his favor, and to have the assistance of counsel for his defense.

Amendment VII

In suits at common law, where the value in controversy shall exceed twenty dollars, the right of trial by jury shall be preserved, and no fact tried by a jury, shall be otherwise reexamined in any court of the United States, than according to the rules of the common law.

Amendment VIII

Excessive bail shall not be required, nor excessive fines imposed, nor cruel and unusual punishments inflicted.

Amendment IX

The enumeration in the Constitution, of certain rights, shall not be construed to deny or disparage others retained by the people.

Amendment X

The powers not delegated to the United States by the Constitution, nor prohibited by it to the states, are reserved to the states respectively, or to the people.

Other Selected Amendments

Amendment XIII (1865)

Section 1. Neither slavery nor involuntary servitude, except as a punishment for crime whereof the party shall have been duly convicted, shall exist within the United States, or any place subject to their jurisdiction.

Section 2. Congress shall have power to enforce this article by appropriate legislation.

Amendment XIV (1868)

Section 1. All persons born or naturalized in the United States, and subject to the jurisdiction thereof, are citizens of the United States and of the state wherein they reside. No state shall make or enforce any law which shall abridge the privileges or immunities of citizens of the United States; nor shall any state deprive any person of life, liberty, or property, without due process of law; nor deny to any person within its jurisdiction the equal protection of the laws.

Amendment XV (1870)

Section 1. The right of citizens of the United States to vote shall not be denied or abridged by the United States or by any state on account of race, color, or previous condition of servitude.

Section 2. The Congress shall have power to enforce this article by appropriate legislation.

Amendment XIX (1920)

The right of citizens of the United States to vote shall not be denied or abridged by the United States or by any state on account of sex.

Congress shall have power to enforce this article by appropriate legislation.

THE NATIONAL LABOR RELATIONS ACT (U.S. CONGRESS, 1935, AS AMENDED 1947 AND LATER)

Author's note: The most up-to-date version of the National Labor Relations Act (NLRA) can be found in the United States Code at Title 29, Chapter 7. The NLRA was first enacted by the Wagner Act on July 5, 1935. It was significantly amended on June 23, 1947 by the Taft-Hartley Act (the Labor–Management Relations Act). Some further changes were implemented by the Landrum-Griffin Act on September 14, 1959, and other pieces of legislation in various years.

What follows are the separate introductions to the Wagner Act and the Taft-Hartley Act followed by the current NLRA. The portions of the NLRA that appeared in the Wagner Act are in italics; the Taft-Hartley Act additions are in roman type; post–1947 additions are underlined. Repealed text is not shown.

The Wagner Act: Findings and Policies

Sec. 1. *The denial by employers of the right of employees to organize and the refusal by employers to accept the procedure of collective bargaining lead to strikes and other forms of industrial strife or unrest, which have the intent or the necessary effect of burdening or obstructing commerce by (a) impairing the efficiency, safety, or operation of the instrumentalities of commerce; (b) occurring in the current of commerce; (c) materially affecting, restraining, or controlling the flow of raw materials or manufactured or processed goods from or into the channels of commerce, or the prices of such materials or goods in commerce; or (d) causing diminution of employment and wages in such volume as substantially to impair or disrupt the market for goods flowing from or into the channels of commerce.*[1]

The inequality of bargaining power between employees who do not possess full freedom of association or actual liberty of contract and employers who are organized in the corporate or other forms of ownership association substantially burdens and affects the flow of commerce, and tends to aggravate recurrent business depressions, by depressing wage rates and the purchasing power of wage earners in industry and by preventing the stabilization of competitive wage rates and working conditions within and between industries.

Experience has proved that protection by law of the right of employees to organize and bargain collectively safeguards commerce from injury, impairment, or interruption, and promotes the flow of commerce by removing certain recognized sources of industrial strife and unrest, by encouraging practices fundamental to the friendly adjustment of industrial disputes arising out of differences as to wages, hours, or other working conditions, and by restoring equality of bargaining power between employers and employees.

It is hereby declared to be the policy of the United States to eliminate the causes of certain substantial obstructions to the free flow of commerce and to mitigate and eliminate these obstructions when they have occurred by encouraging the practice and procedure of

---

[1] Author's note: The Taft-Hartley Act qualified this statement to find that "some employers" (rather than "employers") deny the rights of employees to organize and accept the procedure of collective bargaining, and also added a fourth paragraph:

Experience has further demonstrated that certain practices by some labor organizations, their officers, and members have the intent or the necessary effect of burdening or obstructing commerce by preventing the free flow of goods in such commerce through strikes and other forms of industrial unrest or through concerted activities which impair the interest of the public in the free flow of such commerce. The elimination of such practices is a necessary condition to the assurance of the rights herein guaranteed.

collective bargaining and by protecting the exercise by workers of full freedom of associa-
tion, self-organization, and designation of representatives of their own choosing, for the
purpose of negotiating the terms and conditions of their employment or other mutual aid
or protection.

The Taft-Hartley Act: Short Title and Declaration of Policy

Sec. 1. (a) This Act may be cited as the "Labor Management Relations Act, 1947."

(b) Industrial strife which interferes with the normal flow of commerce and with the full production of articles and commodities for commerce, can be avoided or substantially minimized if employers, employees, and labor organizations each recognize under law one another's legitimate rights in their relations with each other, and above all recognize under law that neither party has any right in its relations with any other to engage in acts or practices which jeopardize the public health, safety, or interest.

It is the purpose and policy of this Act in order to promote the full flow of commerce, to prescribe the legitimate rights of both employees and employers in their relations affecting commerce, to provide orderly and peaceful procedures for preventing the interference by either with the legitimate rights of the other, to protect the rights of individual employees in their relations with labor organizations whose activities affect commerce, to define and proscribe practices on the part of labor and management which affect commerce and are inimical to the general welfare, and to protect the rights of the public in connection with labor disputes affecting commerce.

The National Labor Relations Act (as amended)

Definitions

Sec. 2. *When used in this Act—*

(1) *The term "person" includes one or more individuals, labor organizations, partnerships, associations, corporations, legal representatives, trustees, trustees in bankruptcy, or receivers.*

(2) *The term "employer" includes any person acting as an agent of an employer, directly or indirectly, but shall not include the United States or any wholly owned Government corporation, or any Federal Reserve Bank, or any State or political subdivision thereof, or any person subject to the Railway Labor Act as amended from time to time, or any labor organization (other than when acting as an employer), or anyone acting in the capacity of officer or agent of such labor organization.*

(3) *The term "employee" shall include any employee, and shall not be limited to the employees of a particular employer, unless the Act explicitly states otherwise, and shall include any individual whose work has ceased as a consequence of, or in connection with, any current labor dispute or because of any unfair labor practice, and who has not obtained any other regular and substantially equivalent employment, but shall not include any individual employed as an agricultural laborer, or in the domestic service of any family or person at his home, or any individual employed by his parent or spouse,* or any individual having the status of an independent contractor, or any individual employed as a supervisor, or any individual employed by an employer subject to the Railway Labor Act, as amended from time to time, or by any other person who is not an employer as herein defined.

(4) *The term "representatives" includes any individual or labor organization.*

(5) *The term "labor organization" means any organization of any kind, or any agency or employee representation committee or plan, in which employees participate and which exists for the purpose, in whole or in part, of dealing with employers concerning grievances, labor disputes, wages, rates of pay, hours of employment, or conditions of work.*

(6) *The term "commerce" means trade, traffic, commerce, transportation, or communication among the several States, or between the District of Columbia or any Territory of the United States and any State or other Territory, or between any foreign country and any State, Territory, or the District of Columbia, or within the District of Columbia or any Territory, or between points in the same State but through any other State or any Territory or the District of Columbia or any foreign country.*

(7) *The term "affecting commerce" means in commerce, or burdening or obstructing commerce or the free flow of commerce, or having led or tending to lead to a labor dispute burdening or obstructing commerce or the free flow of commerce.*

(8) *The term "unfair labor practice" means any unfair labor practice listed in section 8.*

(9) *The term "labor dispute" includes any controversy concerning terms, tenure or conditions of employment, or concerning the association or representation of persons in negotiating, fixing, maintaining, changing, or seeking to arrange terms or conditions of employment, regardless of whether the disputants stand in the proximate relation of employer and employee.*

(10) *The term "National Labor Relations Board" means the National Labor Relations Board provided for in section 3 of this Act.*

(11) The term "supervisor" means any individual having authority, in the interest of the employer, to hire, transfer, suspend, lay off, recall, promote, discharge, assign, reward, or discipline other employees, or responsibly to direct them, or to adjust their grievances, or effectively to recommend such action, if in connection with the foregoing the exercise of such authority is not of a merely routine or clerical nature, but requires the use of independent judgment.

(12) The term "professional employee" means—

(a) any employee engaged in work (i) predominantly intellectual and varied in character as opposed to routine mental, manual, mechanical, or physical work; (ii) involving the consistent exercise of discretion and judgment in its performance; (iii) of such a character that the output produced or the result accomplished cannot be standardized in relation to a given period of time; (iv) requiring knowledge of an advanced type in a field of science or learning customarily acquired by a prolonged course of specialized intellectual instruction and study in an institution of higher learning or a hospital, as distinguished from a general academic education or from an apprenticeship or from training in the performance of routine mental, manual, or physical processes; or

(b) any employee, who (i) has completed the courses of specialized intellectual instruction and study described in clause (iv) of paragraph (a), and (ii) is performing related work under the supervision of a professional person to qualify himself to become a professional employee as defined in paragraph (a).

(13) In determining whether any person is acting as an "agent" of another person so as to make such other person responsible for his acts, the question of whether the specific acts performed were actually authorized or subsequently ratified shall not be controlling.

(14) <u>The term "health care institution" shall include any hospital, convalescent hospital, health maintenance organization, health clinic, nursing home, extended care facility, or other institution devoted to the care of sick, infirm, or aged person.</u>

National Labor Relations Board

Sec. 3. (a) The National Labor Relations Board (hereinafter called the "Board") created by this Act prior to its amendment by the Labor Management Relations Act, 1947, is continued as an agency of the United States, except that the Board shall consist of five instead of three members, appointed by the President by and with the advice and consent of the Senate. Of the two additional members so provided for, one shall be appointed for a term of five years and the other for a term of two years. Their successors, and the successors of the other members, shall be appointed for terms of five years each, excepting that any individual chosen to fill a vacancy shall be appointed only for the unexpired term of the member whom he shall succeed. The President shall designate one member to serve as Chairman of the Board. Any member of the Board may be removed by the President, upon notice and hearing, for neglect of duty or malfeasance in office, but for no other cause.

(b) Board is authorized to delegate to any group of three or more members any or all of the powers, which it may itself exercise. The Board is also authorized to delegate to its regional directors its powers under section 9 to determine the unit appropriate for the purpose of collective bargaining, to investigate and provide for hearings, and determine whether a question of representation exists, and to direct an election or take a secret ballot under subsection (c) or (e) of section 9 and certify the results thereof, except that upon the filing of a request therefore with the Board by any interested person, the Board may review any action of a regional director delegated to him under this paragraph, but such a review shall not, unless specifically ordered by the Board, operate as a stay of any action taken by the regional director. *A vacancy in the Board shall not impair the right of the remaining members to exercise all of the powers of the Board,* and three members of the Board shall, at all times, constitute a quorum of the Board, except that two members shall constitute a quorum of any group designated pursuant to the first sentence hereof. *The Board shall have an official seal, which shall be judicially noticed.*

(c) *The Board shall at the close of each fiscal year make a report in writing to Congress and to the President summarizing significant case activities and operations for that fiscal year.*

(d) There shall be a General Counsel of the Board who shall be appointed by the President, by and with the advice and consent of the Senate, for a term of four years. The General Counsel of the Board shall exercise general supervision over all attorneys employed by the Board (other than administrative law judges and legal assistants to Board members) and over the officers and employees in the regional offices. He shall have final authority, on behalf of the Board, in respect of the investigation of charges and issuance of complaints under section 10, and in respect of the prosecution of such complaints before the Board, and shall have such other duties as the Board may prescribe or as may be provided by law. In case of vacancy in the office of the General Counsel the President is authorized to designate the officer or employee who shall act as General Counsel during such vacancy, but no person or persons so designated shall so act (1) for more than forty days when the Congress is in session unless a nomination to fill such vacancy shall have been submitted to the Senate, or (2) after the adjournment sine die of the session of the Senate in which such nomination was submitted.

Sec. 4. (a) *Each member of the Board and the General Counsel of the Board shall be eligible for reappointment, and shall not engage in any other business, vocation, or employment. The Board shall appoint an executive secretary, and such attorneys, examiners, and regional directors, and such other employees as it may from time to time find necessary for the proper performance of its duties.* The Board may not employ any attorneys for the purpose of reviewing transcripts of hearings or preparing drafts of opinions except that any attorney employed for assignment as a legal assistant to any Board member may for such Board member review such transcripts and prepare such drafts. No administrative law judge's report shall be reviewed, either before or after its publication, by any person other than a member of the Board or his legal assistant, and no administrative law judge shall advise or consult with the Board with respect to exceptions taken to his findings, rulings, or recommendations. *The Board may establish or utilize such regional, local, or other agencies, and utilize such voluntary and uncompensated services, as may from time to time be needed. Attorneys appointed under this section may, at the direction of the Board, appear for and represent the Board in any case in court. Nothing in this Act shall be construed to authorize the Board to appoint individuals for the purpose of conciliation or mediation, or for economic analysis.*

(b) *All of the expenses of the Board, including all necessary traveling and subsistence expenses outside the District of Columbia incurred by the members or employees of the Board under its orders shall be allowed and paid on the presentation of itemized vouchers therefore approved by the Board or by any individual it designates for that purpose.*

Sec. 5. *The principal office of the Board shall be in the District of Columbia, but it may meet and exercise any or all of its powers at any other place. The Board may, by one or more of its members or by such agents or agencies as it may designate, prosecute any inquiry necessary to its functions in any part of the United States. A member who participates in such an inquiry shall not be disqualified from subsequently participating in a decision of the Board in the same case.*

Sec. 6. *The Board shall have authority from time to time to make, amend, and rescind,* in the manner prescribed by the Administrative Procedure Act, *such rules and regulations as may be necessary to carry out the provisions of this Act.*

Rights of Employees

Sec. 7. *Employees shall have the right to self-organization, to form, join, or assist labor organizations, to bargain collectively through representatives of their own choosing, and to engage in other concerted activities for the purpose of collective bargaining or other mutual aid or protection,* and shall also have the right to refrain from any or all such activities except to the extent that such right may be affected by an agreement requiring membership in a labor organization as a condition of employment as authorized in section 8(a)(3).

Unfair Labor Practices

Sec. 8. (a) *It shall be an unfair labor practice for an employer—*

(1) *to interfere with, restrain, or coerce employees in the exercise of the rights guaranteed in section 7;*

(2) *to dominate or interfere with the formation or administration of any labor organization or contribute financial or other support to it: Provided, That subject to rules and regulations made and published by the Board pursuant to section 6, an employer shall not be prohibited from permitting employees to confer with him during working hours without loss of time or pay;*

(3) *by discrimination in regard to hire or tenure of employment or any term or condition of employment to encourage or discourage membership in any labor organization: Provided, That nothing in this Act, or in any other statute of the United States, shall preclude an employer from making an agreement with a labor organization (not established, maintained, or assisted by any action defined in section 8(a) of this Act as an unfair labor practice) to require as a condition of employment membership therein* on or after the thirtieth day following the beginning of such employment or the effective date of such agreement, whichever is the later, (i) if such labor organization is the representative of the employees as provided in section 9(a), in the appropriate collective-bargaining unit covered by such agreement when made, and (ii) unless following an election held as provided in section 9(e) within one year preceding the effective date of such agreement, the Board shall have certified that at least a majority of the employees eligible to vote in such election have voted to rescind the authority of such labor organization to make such an agreement: Provided further, That no employer shall justify any discrimination against an employee for non-membership in a labor organization (A) if he has reasonable grounds for believing that such membership was not available to the employee on the same terms and conditions generally applicable to other members, or (B) if he has reasonable grounds for believing that membership was denied or terminated for reasons other than the failure of the employee to

tender the periodic dues and the initiation fees uniformly required as a condition of acquiring or retaining membership;

(4) *To discharge or otherwise discriminate against an employee because he has filed charges or given testimony under this Act;*

(5) *To refuse to bargain collectively with the representatives of his employees, subject to the provisions of section 9(a).*

(b) It shall be an unfair labor practice for a labor organization or its agents—

(1) To restrain or coerce (A) employees in the exercise of the rights guaranteed in section 7: Provided, That this paragraph shall not impair the right of a labor organization to prescribe its own rules with respect to the acquisition or retention of membership therein; or (B) an employer in the selection of his representatives for the purposes of collective bargaining or the adjustment of grievances;

(2) To cause or attempt to cause an employer to discriminate against an employee in violation of subsection (a) (3) or to discriminate against an employee with respect to whom membership in such organization has been denied or terminated on some ground other than his failure to tender the periodic dues and the initiation fees uniformly required as a condition of acquiring or retaining membership;

(3) To refuse to bargain collectively with an employer, provided it is the representative of his employees subject to the provisions of section 9(a);

(4)(i) To engage in, or to induce or encourage <u>any individual employed by any person engaged in commerce or in an industry affecting commerce</u> to engage in, a strike or a refusal in the course of his employment to use, manufacture, process, transport, or otherwise handle or work on any goods, articles, materials, or commodities or to perform any services; <u>or (ii) to threaten, coerce, or restrain any person engaged in commerce or in an industry affecting commerce,</u> where in <u>either case</u> an object thereof is—

(A) forcing or requiring any employer or self-employed person to join any labor or employer organization <u>or to enter into any agreement which is prohibited by section 8(e)</u> subsection (e) of this section;

(B) <u>forcing or requiring any person to cease using, selling, handling, transporting, or otherwise dealing in the products of any other producer, processor, or manufacturer, or to cease doing business with any other person, or</u> forcing or requiring any other employer to recognize or bargain with a labor organization as the representative of his employees unless such labor organization has been certified as the representative of such employees under the provisions of section 9: <u>Provided, That nothing contained in this clause (B) shall be construed to make unlawful, where not otherwise unlawful, any primary strike or primary picketing;</u>

(C) forcing or requiring any employer to recognize or bargain with a particular labor organization as the representative of his employees if another labor organization has been certified as the representative of such employees under the provisions of section 9;

(D) forcing or requiring any employer to assign particular work to employees in a particular labor organization or in a particular trade, craft, or class rather than to employees in another labor organization or in another trade, craft, or class, unless such employer is failing to conform to an order or certification of the Board determining the bargaining representative for employees performing such work:

Provided, that nothing contained in this subsection shall be construed to make unlawful a refusal by any person to enter upon the premises of any employer (other than his own employer), if the employees of such employer are engaged in a strike ratified or approved by a representative of such employees whom such employer is required to recognize under this Act: <u>Provided further, That for the purposes of this paragraph (4) only, nothing contained in such paragraph shall be construed to prohibit publicity, other than picketing, for the purpose of truthfully advising the public, including consumers and members of a labor</u>

organization, that a product or products are produced by an employer with whom the labor organization has a primary dispute and are distributed by another employer, as long as such publicity does not have an effect of inducing any individual employed by any person other than the primary employer in the course of his employment to refuse to pick up, deliver, or transport any goods, or not to perform any services, at the establishment of the employer engaged in such distribution;

(5) To require of employees covered by an agreement authorized under subsection (a)(3) the payment, as a condition precedent to becoming a member of such organization, of a fee in an amount which the Board finds excessive or discriminatory under all the circumstances. In making such a finding, the Board shall consider, among other relevant factors, the practices and customs of labor organizations in the particular industry, and the wages currently paid to the employees affected;

(6) To cause or attempt to cause an employer to pay or deliver or agree to pay or deliver any money or other thing of value, in the nature of an exaction, for services which are not performed or not to be performed; and

(7) To picket or cause to be picketed, or threaten to picket or cause to be picketed, any employer where an object thereof is forcing or requiring an employer to recognize or bargain with a labor organization as the representative of his employees, or forcing or requiring the employees of an employer to accept or select such labor organization as their collective-bargaining representative, unless such labor organization is currently certified as the representative of such employees:

(A) Where the employer has lawfully recognized in accordance with this Act any other labor organization and a question concerning representation may not appropriately be raised under section 9(c) of this Act,

(B) Where within the preceding twelve months a valid election under section 9(c) of this Act has been conducted, or

(C) Where such picketing has been conducted without a petition under section 9(c) being filed within a reasonable period of time not to exceed thirty days from the commencement of such picketing: Provided, That when such a petition has been filed the Board shall forthwith, without regard to the provisions of section 9(c)(1) or the absence of a showing of a substantial interest on the part of the labor organization, direct an election in such unit as the Board finds to be appropriate and shall certify the results thereof: Provided further, That nothing in this subparagraph (C) shall be construed to prohibit any picketing or other publicity for the purpose of truthfully advising the public (including consumers) that an employer does not employ members of, or have a contract with, a labor organization, unless an effect of such picketing is to induce any individual employed by any other person in the course of his employment, not to pick up, deliver or transport any goods or not to perform any services.

Nothing in this paragraph (7) shall be construed to permit any act, which would otherwise be an unfair labor practice under this section 8(b).

(c) The expressing of any views, argument, or opinion, or the dissemination thereof, whether in written, printed, graphic, or visual form, shall not constitute or be evidence of an unfair labor practice under any of the provisions of this Act, if such expression contains no threat of reprisal or force or promise of benefit.

(d) For the purposes of this section, to bargain collectively is the performance of the mutual obligation of the employer and the representative of the employees to meet at reasonable times and confer in good faith with respect to wages, hours, and other terms and conditions of employment, or the negotiation of an agreement or any question arising there under, and the execution of a written contract incorporating any agreement reached if requested by either party, but such obligation does not compel either party to agree to a proposal or require the making of a concession: Provided, That where there is in effect a collective-bargaining contract covering employees in an industry affecting commerce, the duty to bargain collectively shall also mean that no party to such contract shall terminate or modify such contract, unless the party desiring such termination or modification—

1. serves a written notice upon the other party to the contract of the proposed termination or modification sixty days prior to the expiration date thereof, or in the event such contract contains no expiration date, sixty days prior to the time it is proposed to make such termination or modification;
2. to meet and confer with the other party for the purpose of negotiating a new contract or a contract containing the proposed modifications;
3. the Federal Mediation and Conciliation Service within thirty days after such notice of the existence of a dispute, and simultaneously therewith notifies any State or Territorial agency established to mediate and conciliate disputes within the State or Territory where the dispute occurred, provided no agreement has been reached by that time; and
4. continues in full force and effect, without resorting to strike or lockout, all the terms and conditions of the existing contract for a period of sixty days after such notice is given or until the expiration date of such contract, whichever occurs later.

Whenever the collective bargaining involves employees of a health care institution, the provisions of this section 8(d) shall be modified as follows:

(A) The notice of section 8(d)(1) shall be ninety days; the notice of section 8(d)(3) shall be sixty days; and the contract period of section 8(d)(4) shall be ninety days.

(B) Where the bargaining is for an initial agreement following certification or recognition, at least thirty days' notice of the existence of a dispute shall be given by the labor organization to the agencies set forth in section 8(d)(3).

(C) After notice is given to the Federal Mediation and Conciliation Service under either clause (A) or (B) of this sentence, the Service shall promptly communicate with the parties and use its best efforts, by mediation and conciliation, to bring them to agreement. The parties shall participate fully and promptly in such meetings as may be undertaken by the Service for the purpose of aiding in a settlement of the dispute.

The duties imposed upon employers, employees, and labor organizations by paragraphs (2), (3), and (4) shall become inapplicable upon an intervening certification of the Board, under which the labor organization or individual, which is a party to the contract, has been superseded as or ceased to be the representative of the employees subject to the provisions of section 9(a), and the duties so imposed shall not be construed as requiring either party to discuss or agree to any modification of the terms and conditions contained in a contract for a fixed period, if such modification is to become effective before such terms and conditions can be reopened under the provisions of the contract. Any employee who engages in a strike within any notice period specified in this subsection, or who engages in any strike within the appropriate period specified in subsection (g) of this section, shall lose his status as an employee of the employer engaged in the particular labor dispute, for the purposes of sections 8, 9, and 10 of this Act, but such loss of status for such employee shall terminate if and when he is reemployed by such employer.

(e) It shall be an unfair labor practice for any labor organization and any employer to enter into any contract or agreement, express or implied, whereby such employer ceases or refrains or agrees to cease or refrain from handling, using, selling, transporting or otherwise dealing in any of the products of any other employer, or cease doing business with any other person, and any contract or agreement entered into heretofore or hereafter containing such an agreement shall be to such extent unenforceable and void: Provided, That nothing in this subsection (e) shall apply to an agreement between a labor organization and an employer in the construction industry relating to the contracting or subcontracting of work to be done at the site of the construction, alteration, painting, or repair of a building, structure, or other work: Provided further, That for the purposes of this subsection (e) and section 8(b)(4)(B) the terms "any employer," "any person engaged in commerce or an industry affecting commerce," and "any person" when used in relation to the terms "any other producer, processor, or manufacturer," "any other employer," or "any other person" shall not include persons in the relation of a jobber, manufacturer, contractor, or subcontractor working on the goods or premises of the jobber or manufacturer or performing parts of an integrated process of production in the apparel and clothing industry: Provided further, That nothing in this Act shall prohibit the enforcement of any agreement which is within the foregoing exception.

(f) It shall not be an unfair labor practice under subsections (a) and (b) of this section for an employer engaged primarily in the building and construction industry to make an agreement covering employees engaged (or who, upon their employment, will be engaged) in the building and construction industry with a labor organization of which building and construction employees are members (not established, maintained, or assisted by any action defined in section 8(a) of this Act as an unfair labor practice) because (1) the majority status of such labor organization has not been established under the provisions of section 9 of this Act prior to the making of such agreement, or (2) such agreement requires as a condition of employment, membership in such labor organization after the seventh day following the beginning of such employment or the effective date of the agreement, whichever is later, or (3) such agreement requires the employer to notify such labor organization of opportunities for employment with such employer, or gives such labor organization an opportunity to refer qualified applicants for such employment, or (4) such agreement specifies minimum training or experience qualifications for employment or provides for priority in opportunities for employment based upon length of service with such employer, in the industry or in the particular geographical area: Provided, That nothing in this subsection shall set aside the final proviso to section 8(a)(3) of this Act: Provided further, That any agreement which would be invalid, but for clause (1) of this subsection, shall not be a bar to a petition filed pursuant to section 9(c) or 9(e).

(g) A labor organization before engaging in any strike, picketing, or other concerted refusal to work at any health care institution shall, not less than ten days prior to such action, notify the institution in writing and the Federal Mediation and Conciliation Service of that intention, except that in the case of bargaining for an initial agreement following certification or recognition the notice required by this subsection shall not be given until the expiration of the period specified in clause (B) of the last sentence of section 8(d) of this Act. The notice shall state the date and time that such action will commence. The notice, once given, may be extended by the written agreement of both parties.

Representatives and Elections

Sec. 9 (a) *Representatives designated or selected for the purposes of collective bargaining by the majority of the employees in a unit appropriate for such purposes, shall be the exclusive representatives of all the employees in such unit for the purposes of collective bargaining in respect to rates of pay, wages, hours of employment, or other conditions of employment: Provided, That any individual employee or a group of employees shall have the right at any time to present grievances to their employer* and to have such grievances adjusted, without the intervention of the bargaining representative, as long as the adjustment is not inconsistent with the terms of a collective-bargaining contract or agreement then in effect: Provided further, That the bargaining representative has been given opportunity to be present at such adjustment.

(b) *The Board shall decide in each case whether, in order* to assure to employees the fullest freedom in exercising the rights guaranteed by this Act, the unit appropriate for the purposes of collective bargaining shall be the employer unit, craft unit, plant unit, or subdivision thereof: Provided, That the Board shall not (1) decide that any unit is appropriate for such purposes if such unit includes both professional employees and employees who are not professional employees unless a majority of such professional employees vote for inclusion in such unit; or (2) decide that any craft unit is inappropriate for such purposes on the ground that a different unit has been established by a prior Board determination, unless a majority of the employees in the proposed craft unit votes against separate representation or (3) decide that any unit is appropriate for such purposes if it includes, together with other employees, any individual employed as a guard to enforce against employees and other persons rules to protect property of the employer or to protect the safety of persons on the employer's premises; but no labor organization shall be certified as the representative of employees in a bargaining unit of guards if such organization admits to membership, or is affiliated directly or indirectly with an organization which admits to membership, employees other than guards.

(c)(1) Whenever a petition shall have been filed, in accordance with such regulations as may be prescribed by the Board—

(A) by an employee or group of employees or any individual or labor organization acting in their behalf alleging that a substantial number of employees (i) wish to be represented for collective bargaining and that their employer declines to recognize their representative as the representative defined in section 9(a), or (ii) assert that the individual or labor organization, which has been certified or is being currently recognized by their employer as the bargaining representative, is no longer a representative as defined in section 9(a); or

(B) by an employer, alleging that one or more individuals or labor organizations have presented to him a claim to be recognized as the representative defined in section 9(a); the Board shall investigate such petition and if it has reasonable cause to believe that a question of representation affecting commerce exists shall provide for an appropriate hearing upon due notice. Such hearing may be conducted by an officer or employee of the regional office, who shall not make any recommendations with respect thereto. If the Board finds upon the record of such hearing that such a question of representation exists, it shall direct an election by secret ballot and shall certify the results thereof.

(2) In determining whether or not a question of representation affecting commerce exists, the same regulations and rules of decision shall apply irrespective of the identity of the persons filing the petition or the kind of relief sought and in no case shall the Board deny a labor organization a place on the ballot by reason of an order with respect to such labor organization or its predecessor not issued in conformity with section 10(c).

(3) No election shall be directed in any bargaining unit or any subdivision within which, in the preceding twelve-month period, a valid election shall have been held. Employees <u>engaged in an economic</u> strike who are not entitled to reinstatement shall be eligible to vote <u>under such regulations as the Board shall find are consistent with the purposes and provisions of this Act in any election conducted within twelve months after the commencement of the strike</u>. In any election where none of the choices on the ballot receives a majority, a run-off shall be conducted, the ballot providing for a selection between the two choices receiving the largest and second largest number of valid votes cast in the election.

(4) Nothing in this section shall be construed to prohibit the waiving of hearings by stipulation for the purpose of a consent election in conformity with regulations and rules of decision of the Board.

(5) In determining whether a unit is appropriate for the purposes specified in subsection (b) the extent to which the employees have organized shall not be controlling.

(d) *Whenever an order of the Board made pursuant to section 10(c) is based in whole or in part upon facts certified following an investigation pursuant to subsection (c) of this section and there is a petition for the enforcement or review of such order, such certification and the record of such investigation shall be included in the transcript of the entire record required to be filed under section 10(e) or 10(f), and thereupon the decree of the court enforcing, modifying, or setting aside in whole or in part the order of the Board shall be made and entered upon the pleadings, testimony, and proceedings set forth in such transcript.*

(e)(1) Upon the filing with the Board, by 30 per centum or more of the employees in a bargaining unit covered by an agreement between their employer and labor organization made pursuant to section 8(a)(3), of a petition alleging they desire that such authorization be rescinded, the Board shall take a secret ballot of the employees in such unit and certify the results thereof to such labor organization and to the employer.

(2) No election shall be conducted pursuant to this subsection in any bargaining unit or any subdivision within which, in the preceding twelve-month period, a valid election shall have been held.

Prevention of Unfair Labor Practices

Sec. 10. (a) *The Board is empowered, as hereinafter provided, to prevent any person from engaging in any unfair labor practice (listed in section 8) affecting commerce. This power shall not be affected by any other means of adjustment or prevention that has been or may be established by agreement, law, or otherwise:* Provided, That the Board is empowered by agreement with any agency of any State or Territory to cede to such agency jurisdiction over any cases in any industry (other than mining, manufacturing, communications, and transportation except where predominately local in character) even though such cases may involve labor disputes affecting commerce, unless the provision of the State or Territorial statute applicable to the determination of such cases by such agency is inconsistent with the corresponding provision of this Act or has received a construction inconsistent therewith.

(b) *Whenever it is charged that any person has engaged in or is engaging in any such unfair labor practice, the Board, or any agent or agency designated by the Board for such purposes, shall have power to issue and cause to be served upon such person a complaint stating the charges in that respect, and containing a notice of hearing before the Board or a member thereof, or before a designated agent or agency, at a place therein fixed, not less than five days after the serving of said complaint:* Provided, That no complaint shall issue based upon any unfair labor practice occurring more than six months prior to the filing of the charge with the Board and the service of a copy thereof upon the person against whom such charge is made, unless the person aggrieved thereby was prevented from filing such charge by reason of service in the armed forces, in which event the six-month period shall be computed from the day of his discharge. *Any such complaint may be amended by the member, agent, or agency conducting the hearing or the Board in its discretion at any time prior to the issuance of an order based thereon. The person so complained of shall have the right to file an answer to the original or amended complaint and to appear in person or otherwise and give testimony at the place and time fixed in the complaint. In the discretion of the member, agent, or agency conducting the hearing or the Board, any other person may be allowed to intervene in the said proceeding and to present testimony.* Any such proceeding shall, so far as practicable, be conducted in accordance with the rules of evidence applicable in the district courts of the United States under the rules of civil procedure for the district courts of the United States, adopted by the Supreme Court of the United States pursuant to section 2072 of title 28, United States Code.

(c) *The testimony taken by such member, agent, or agency, or the Board shall be reduced to writing and filed with the Board. Thereafter, in its discretion, the Board upon notice may take further testimony or hear argument. If upon the preponderance of the testimony taken the Board shall be of the opinion that any person named in the complaint has engaged in or is engaging in any such unfair labor practice, then the Board shall state its findings of fact and shall issue and cause to be served on such person an order requiring such person to cease and desist from such unfair labor practice, and to take such affirmative action including reinstatement of employees with or without backpay, as will effectuate the policies of this Act:* Provided, That where an order directs reinstatement of an employee, back-pay may be required of the employer or labor organization, as the case may be, responsible for the discrimination suffered by him: And provided further, That in determining whether a complaint shall issue alleging a violation of section 8(a)(1) or section 8(a)(2), and in deciding such cases, the same regulations and rules of decision shall apply irrespective of whether or not the labor organization affected is affiliated with a labor organization national or international in scope. *Such order may further require such person to make reports from time to time showing the extent to which it has complied with the order. If upon the preponderance of the testimony taken the Board shall not be of the opinion that the person named in the complaint has engaged in or is engaging in any such unfair labor practice, then the Board shall state its findings of fact and shall issue an order dismissing the said complaint.* No order of the Board shall require the reinstatement of any individual as an employee who has been suspended or discharged, or the payment to him of any back-pay, if such individual was suspended or discharged for cause. In case the evidence is presented before a member of the Board, or before an administrative law judge or judges thereof, such member, or such judge or judges, as the case may be, shall issue and cause to be served on the parties to the proceeding a proposed report, together with a recommended order, which shall be filed with the Board, and if no exceptions are filed within twenty days after service thereof upon such parties, or within such further period as the Board may authorize, such recommended order shall become the order of the Board and become affective as therein prescribed.

(d) Until the record in a case shall have been filed in a court, *as hereinafter provided, the Board may at any time, upon reasonable notice and in such manner as it shall deem proper, modify or set aside, in whole or in part, any finding or order made or issued by it.*

(e) *The Board shall have power to petition any court of appeals of the United States, or if all the courts of appeals to which application may be made are in vacation, any district court of the United States, within any circuit or district, respectively, wherein the unfair labor practice in question occurred or wherein such person resides or transacts business, for the enforcement of such order and for appropriate temporary relief or restraining order, and shall file in the court* the record in the proceeding, as provided in section 2112 of title 28, United States Code. *Upon the filing of such petition, the court shall cause notice thereof to be served upon such person, and thereupon shall have jurisdiction of the proceeding and of the question determined therein, and shall have power to grant such temporary relief or restraining order as it deems just and proper, and to make and enter a decree enforcing, modifying and enforcing as so modified, or setting aside in whole or in part the order of the Board. No objection that has not been urged before the Board, its member, agent, or agency, shall be considered by the court, unless the failure or neglect to urge such objection shall be excused because of extraordinary circumstances. The findings of the*

Board with respect to questions of fact if supported by substantial evidence on the record considered as a whole shall be conclusive. *If either party shall apply to the court for leave to adduce additional evidence and shall show to the satisfaction of the court that such additional evidence is material and that there were reasonable grounds for the failure to adduce such evidence in the hearing before the Board, its member, agent, or agency, the court may order such additional evidence to be taken before the Board, its member, agent, or agency, and to be made a part of the* record. *The Board may modify its findings as to the facts, or make new findings, by reason of additional evidence so taken and filed, and it shall file such modified or new findings, which findings with respect to question of fact if supported by substantial evidence on the record considered as a whole shall be conclusive, and shall file its recommendations, if any, for the modification or setting aside of its original order.* Upon the filing of the record with it *the jurisdiction of the court shall be exclusive and its judgment and decree shall be final, except that the same shall be subject to review by the appropriate United States court of appeals if application was made to the district court as hereinabove provided, and by the Supreme Court of the United States upon writ of certiorari or certification as provided in section 1254 of title 28.*

(f) *Any person aggrieved by a final order of the Board granting or denying in whole or in part the relief sought may obtain a review of such order in any United States court of appeals in the circuit wherein the unfair labor practice in question was alleged to have been engaged in or wherein such person resides or transacts business, or in the United States Court of Appeals for the District of Columbia, by filing in such court a written petition praying that the order of the Board be modified or set aside. A copy of such petition shall be forthwith* transmitted by the clerk of the court to the Board, *and thereupon the aggrieved party shall file in the court the record in the proceeding, certified by the Board, as provided in section 2112 of title 28, United States Code. Upon the filing of such petition, the court shall proceed in the same manner as in the case of an application by the Board under subsection (e) of this section, and shall have the same jurisdiction to grant to the Board such temporary relief or restraining order as it deems just and proper, and in like manner to make and enter a decree enforcing, modifying and enforcing as so modified, or setting aside in whole or in part the order of the Board;* the findings of the Board with respect to questions of fact if supported by substantial evidence on the record considered as a whole shall in like manner be conclusive.

(g) *The commencement of proceedings under subsection (e) or (f) of this section shall not, unless specifically ordered by the court, operate as a stay of the Board's order.*

(h) *When granting appropriate temporary relief or a restraining order, or making and entering a decree enforcing, modifying and enforcing as so modified, or setting aside in whole or in part an order of the Board, as provided in this section, the jurisdiction of courts sitting in equity shall not be limited by the Norris-LaGuardia Act."*

(i) [Repealed, 1984].

(j) The Board shall have power, upon issuance of a complaint as provided in subsection (b) charging that any person has engaged in or is engaging in an unfair labor practice, to petition any United States district court, within any district wherein the unfair labor practice in question is alleged to have occurred or wherein such person resides or transacts business, for appropriate temporary relief or restraining order. Upon the filing of any such petition the court shall cause notice thereof to be served upon such person, and thereupon shall have jurisdiction to grant to the Board such temporary relief or restraining order as it deems just and proper.

(k) Whenever it is charged that any person has engaged in an unfair labor practice within the meaning of paragraph (4)(D) of section 8(b), the Board is empowered and directed to hear and determine the dispute out of which such unfair labor practice shall have arisen, unless, within ten days after notice that such charge has been filed, the parties to such dispute submit to the Board satisfactory evidence that they have adjusted, or agreed upon methods for the voluntary adjustment of, the dispute. Upon compliance by the parties to the dispute with the decision of the Board or upon such voluntary adjustment of the dispute, such charge shall be dismissed.

(l) Whenever it is charged that any person has engaged in an unfair labor practice within the meaning of paragraph (4)(A), (B), or (C) of section 8(b), or section 8(e) or section 8(b)(7), the preliminary investigation of such charge shall be made forthwith and given priority over all other cases except cases of like character in the office where it is filed or to which it is referred. If, after such investigation, the officer or regional attorney to whom the matter may be referred has reasonable cause to believe such charge is true and that a complaint should issue, he shall, on behalf of the Board, petition any United States district court within any district where the unfair labor practice in question has occurred, is alleged to have occurred, or wherein such person resides or transacts business, for appropriate injunctive relief pending the final adjudication of the Board with respect to such matter. Upon the filing of any such petition the district court shall have jurisdiction to grant such injunctive relief or temporary restraining order as it deems just and proper, notwithstanding any other provision of law: Provided further, That no temporary restraining order shall be issued without notice unless a petition alleges that substantial and irreparable injury to the charging party will be unavoidable and such temporary restraining order shall be effective for no longer than five days and will become void at the expiration of such period: Provided further, That such officer or regional attorney shall not apply for any restraining order under section 8(b)(7) if a charge against the employer under section 8(a)(2) has been filed and after the preliminary investigation, he has reasonable cause to believe that such charge is true and that a complaint should issue. Upon filing of any such petition the courts shall cause notice thereof to be served upon any person involved in the charge and such person, including the charging party, shall be given an opportunity to appear by counsel and present any relevant testimony: Provided further, That for the purposes of this subsection district courts shall be deemed to have jurisdiction of a labor organization (1) in the district in which such organization maintains its principal office, or (2) in any district in which its duly authorized officers or agents are engaged in promoting or protecting the interests of employee members. The service of legal process upon such officer or agent shall constitute service upon the labor organization and make such organization a party to the suit. In situations where such relief is appropriate the procedure specified herein shall apply to charges with respect to section 8(b)(4)(D).

(m) Whenever it is charged that any person has engaged in an unfair labor practice within the meaning of subsection (a)(3) or (b)(2) of section 8, such charge shall be given priority over all other cases except cases of like character in the office where it is filed or to which it is referred and cases given priority under subsection (1).

Investigatory Powers

Sec. 11. *For the purpose of all hearings and investigations, which, in the opinion of the Board, are necessary and proper for the exercise of the powers vested in it by section 9 and section 10—*

(1) The Board, or its duly authorized agents or agencies, shall at all reasonable times have access to, for the purpose of examination, and the right to copy any evidence of any person being investigated or proceeded against that relates to any matter under investigation or in question. The Board or any member thereof, shall upon application of any party to such proceedings, forthwith issue to such party subpoenas requiring the attendance and testimony of witnesses or the production of any evidence in such proceeding or investigation requested in such application. Within five days after the service of a subpoena on any person requiring the production of any evidence in his possession or under his control,

such person may petition the Board to revoke, and the Board shall revoke, such subpoena if in its opinion the evidence whose production is required does not relate to any matter under investigation, or any matter in question in such proceedings, or if in its opinion such subpoena does not describe with sufficient particularity the evidence whose production is required. *Any member of the Board, or any agent or agency designated by the Board for such purposes, may administer oaths and affirmations, examine witnesses, and receive evidence. Such attendance of witnesses and the production of such evidence may be required from any place in the United States or any Territory or possession thereof, at any designated place of hearing.*

(2) *In case on contumacy or refusal to obey a subpoena issued to any person, any United States district court or the United States courts of any Territory or possession, within the jurisdiction of which the inquiry is carried on or within the jurisdiction of which said person guilty of contumacy or refusal to obey is found or resides or transacts business, upon application by the Board shall have jurisdiction to issue to such person an order requiring such person to appear before the Board, its member, agent, or agency, there to produce evidence if so ordered, or there to give testimony touching the matter under investigation or in question; and any failure to obey such order of the court may be punished by said court as a contempt thereof.*

(3) [Repealed, 1970].

(4) *Complaints, orders and other process and papers of the Board, its member, agent, or agency, may be served either personally or by registered or certified mail or by telegraph or by leaving a copy thereof at the principal office or place of business of the person required to be served. The verified return by the individual so serving the same setting forth the manner of such service shall be proof of the same, and the return post office receipt or telegraph receipt therefore when registered or certified and mailed or when telegraphed as aforesaid shall be proof of service of the same. Witnesses summoned before the Board, its member, agent, or agency, shall be paid the same fees and mileage that are paid witnesses in the courts of the United States, and witnesses whose depositions are taken and the persons taking the same shall severally be entitled to the same fees as are paid for like services in the courts of the United States.*

(5) *All process of any court to which application may be made under this Act may be served in the judicial district wherein the defendant or other person required to be served resides or may be found.*

(6) *The several departments and agencies of the Government, when directed by the President, shall furnish the Board, upon its request, all records, papers, and information in their possession relating to any matter before the Board.*

Sec. 12. *Any person who shall willfully resist, prevent, impede, or interfere with any member of the Board or any of its agents or agencies in the performance of duties pursuant to this Act shall be punished by a fine of not more than $5,000 or by imprisonment for not more than one year, or both.*

Limitations

Sec. 13. *Nothing in this Act,* except as specifically provided for herein, *shall be construed so as either to interfere with or impede or diminish in any way the right to strike* or to affect the limitations or qualifications on that right.

Sec. 14. Nothing herein shall prohibit any individual employed as a supervisor from becoming or remaining a member of a labor organization, but no employer subject to this Act shall be compelled to deem individuals defined herein as supervisors as employees for the purpose of any law, either national or local, relating to collective bargaining.

(b) Nothing in this Act shall be construed as authorizing the execution or application of agreements requiring membership in a labor organization as a condition of employment in any State or Territory in which such execution or application is prohibited by State or Territorial law.

(c)(1) The Board, in its discretion, may, by rule of decision or by published rules adopted pursuant to the Administrative Procedure Act, decline to assert jurisdiction over any labor dispute involving any class or category of employers, where, in the opinion of the Board, the effect of such labor dispute on commerce is not sufficiently substantial to warrant the exercise of its jurisdiction: Provided, That the Board shall not decline to assert jurisdiction over any labor dispute over which it would assert jurisdiction under the standards prevailing upon August 1, 1959.

(2) Nothing in this Act shall be deemed to prevent or bar any agency or the courts of any State or Territory (including the Commonwealth of Puerto Rico, Guam, and the Virgin Islands), from assuming and asserting jurisdiction over labor disputes over which the Board declines, pursuant to paragraph (1) of this subsection, to assert jurisdiction.

Sec. 15. [Obsolete]

Sec. 16. If any provision of this Act, or the application of such provision to any person or circumstances, shall be held invalid, the remainder of this Act, or the application of such provision to persons or circumstances other than those as to which it is held invalid, shall not be affected thereby.

Sec. 17. This Act may be cited as the "National Labor Relations Act."

Sec. 18. [Obsolete]

Individuals With Religious Convictions

Sec. 19. Any employee who is a member of and adheres to established and traditional tenets or teachings of a bona fide religion, body, or sect which has historically held conscientious objections to joining or financially supporting labor organizations shall not be required to join or financially support any labor organization as a condition of employment; except that such employee may be required in a contract between such employee's employer and a labor organization in lieu of periodic dues and initiation fees, to pay sums equal to such dues and initiation fees to a nonreligious, non-labor organization charitable fund exempt from taxation under section 501(c)(3) of title 26 of the Internal Revenue Code, chosen by such employee from a list of at least three such funds, designated in such contract or if the contract fails to designate such funds, then to any such fund chosen by the employee. If such employee who holds conscientious objections pursuant to this section requests the labor organization to use the grievance-arbitration procedure on the employee's behalf, the labor organization is authorized to charge the employee for the reasonable cost of using such procedure.

Title II

Conciliation of Labor Disputes in Industries Affecting Commerce: National Emergencies

Sec. 201. It is the policy of the United States that—

(a) sound and stable industrial peace and the advancement of the general welfare, health, and safety of the Nation and of the best interest of employers and employees can most satisfactorily be secured by the settlement of issues between employers and employees through the processes of conference and collective bargaining between employers and the representatives of their employees;

(b) the settlement of issues between employers and employees through collective bargaining may be advanced by making available full and adequate governmental facilities for conciliation, mediation, and voluntary arbitration to aid and encourage employers and the representatives of their employees to reach and maintain agreements concerning rates of pay, hours, and working conditions, and to make all reasonable efforts to settle their differences by mutual agreement reached through conferences and collective bargaining or by such methods as may be provided for in any applicable agreement for the settlement of disputes; and

(c) certain controversies which arise between parties to collective bargaining agreements may be avoided or minimized by making available full and adequate governmental facilities for furnishing assistance to employers and the representatives of their employees in formulating for inclusion within such agreements provision for adequate notice of any proposed changes in the terms of such agreements, for the final adjustment of grievances or questions regarding the application or interpretation of such agreements, and other provisions designed to prevent the subsequent arising of such controversies.

Sec. 202. (a) There is created an independent agency to be known as the Federal Mediation and Conciliation Service (herein referred to as the "Service," except that for sixty days after June 23, 1947, such term shall refer to the Conciliation Service of the Department of Labor). The Service shall be under the direction of a Federal Mediation and Conciliation Director (hereinafter referred to as the "Director"), who shall be appointed by the President by and with the advice and consent of the Senate. The Director shall not engage in any other business, vocation, or employment.

(b) The Director is authorized, subject to the civil service laws, to appoint such clerical and other personnel as may be necessary for the execution of the functions of the Service, and shall fix their compensation in accordance with sections 5101 to 5115 and sections 5331 to 5338 of title 5, United States Code, and may, without regard to the provisions of the civil service laws, appoint such conciliators and mediators as may be necessary to carry out the functions of the Service. The Director is authorized to make such expenditures for supplies, facilities, and services as he deems necessary. Such expenditures shall be allowed and paid upon presentation of itemized vouchers therefore approved by the Director or by any employee designated by him for that purpose.

(c) The principal office of the Service shall be in the District of Columbia, but the Director may establish regional offices convenient to localities in which labor controversies are likely to arise. The Director may by order, subject to revocation at any time, delegate any authority and discretion conferred upon him by this Act to any regional director, or other officer or employee of the Service. The Director may establish suitable procedures for cooperation with State and local mediation agencies. The Director shall make an annual report in writing to Congress at the end of the fiscal year.

(d) All mediation and conciliation functions of the Secretary of Labor or the United States Conciliation Service under section 51 [repealed] of title 29, United States Code, and all functions of the United States Conciliation Service under any other law are transferred to the Federal Mediation and Conciliation Service, together with the personnel and records of the United States Conciliation Service. Such transfer shall take effect upon the sixtieth day after June 23, 1947. Such transfer shall not affect any proceedings pending before the United States Conciliation Service or any certification, order, rule, or regulation theretofore made by it or by the Secretary of Labor. The Director and the Service shall not be subject in any way to the jurisdiction or authority of the Secretary of Labor or any official or division of the Department of Labor.

Functions of the Service

Sec. 203. (a) It shall be the duty of the Service, in order to prevent or minimize interruptions of the free flow of commerce growing out of labor disputes, to assist parties to labor disputes in industries affecting commerce to settle such disputes through conciliation and mediation.

(b) The Service may proffer its services in any labor dispute in any industry affecting commerce, either upon its own motion or upon the request of one or more of the parties to the dispute, whenever in its judgment such dispute threatens to cause a substantial interruption of commerce. The Director and the Service are directed to avoid attempting to mediate disputes which would have only a minor effect on interstate commerce if State or other conciliation services are available to the parties. Whenever the Service does proffer its services in any dispute, it shall be the duty of the Service promptly to put itself in communication with the parties and to use its best efforts, by mediation and conciliation, to bring them to agreement.

(c) If the Director is not able to bring the parties to agreement by conciliation within a reasonable time, he shall seek to induce the parties voluntarily to seek other means of settling the dispute without resort to strike, lockout, or other coercion, including submission to the employees in the bargaining unit of the employer's last offer of settlement for approval or rejection in a secret ballot. The failure or refusal of either party to agree to any procedure suggested by the Director shall not be deemed a violation of any duty or obligation imposed by this Act.

(d) Final adjustment by a method agreed upon by the parties is declared to be the desirable method for settlement of grievance disputes arising over the application or interpretation of an existing collective-bargaining agreement. The Service is directed to make its conciliation and mediation services available in the settlement of such grievance disputes only as a last resort and in exceptional cases.

(e) The Service is authorized and directed to encourage and support the establishment and operation of joint labor management activities conducted by plant, area, and industry wide committees designed to improve labor management relationships, job security and organizational effectiveness, in accordance with the provisions of section 205A.

(f) The Service may make its services available to Federal agencies to aid in the resolution of disputes under the provisions of subchapter IV of chapter 5 of title 5, United States Code. Functions performed by the Service may include assisting parties to disputes related to administrative programs, training persons in skills and procedures employed in alternative means of dispute resolution, and furnishing officers and employees of the Service to act as neutrals. Only officers and employees who are qualified in accordance with section 573 of title 5 may be assigned to act as neutrals. The Service shall consult with the agency designated by, or the interagency committee designated or established by, the President under section 573 of title 5 in maintaining rosters of neutrals and arbitrators, and to adopt such procedures and rules as are necessary to carry out the services authorized in this subsection.

Sec. 204. (a) In order to prevent or minimize interruptions of the free flow of commerce growing out of labor disputes, employers and employees and their representatives, in any industry affecting commerce, shall—

1. exert every reasonable effort to make and maintain agreements concerning rates of pay, hours, and working conditions, including provision for adequate notice of any proposed change in the terms of such agreements;
2. whenever a dispute arises over the terms or application of a collective-bargaining agreement and a conference is requested by a party or prospective party thereto, arrange promptly for such a conference to be held and endeavor in such conference to settle such dispute expeditiously; and
3. In case such dispute is not settled by conference, participate fully and promptly in such meetings as may be undertaken by the Service under this Act for the purpose of aiding in a settlement of the dispute.

Sec. 205. (a) There is created a National Labor–Management Panel which shall be composed of twelve members appointed by the President, six of whom shall be elected from among persons outstanding in the field of management and six of whom shall be selected from among persons outstanding in the field of labor. Each member shall hold office for a term of three years, except that any member appointed to fill a vacancy occurring prior to the expiration of the term for which his predecessor was appointed shall be appointed for the remainder of such term, and the terms of office of the members first taking office shall expire, as designated by the President at the time of appointment, four at the end of the first year, four at the end of the second year, and four at the end of the third year after the date of appointment. Members of the panel, when serving on business of the panel, shall be paid compensation at the rate of $25 per day, and shall also be entitled to receive an allowance for actual and necessary travel and subsistence expenses while so serving away from their places of residence.

(b) It shall be the duty of the panel, at the request of the Director, to advise in the avoidance of industrial controversies and the manner in which mediation and voluntary adjustment shall be administered, particularly with reference to controversies affecting the general welfare of the country.

Sec. 205A. (a)(1) The Service is authorized and directed to provide assistance in the establishment and operation of plant, area and industry wide labor management committees which—

A. have been organized jointly by employers and labor organizations representing employees in that plant, area, or industry; and

B. are established for the purpose of improving labor management relationships, job security, organizational effectiveness, enhancing economic development or involving workers in decisions affecting their jobs including improving communication with respect to subjects of mutual interest and concern.

(2) The Service is authorized and directed to enter into contracts and to make grants, where necessary or appropriate, to fulfill its responsibilities under this section.

(b)(1) No grant may be made, no contract may be entered into and no other assistance may be provided under the provisions of this section to a plant labor management committee unless the employees in that plant are represented by a labor organization and there is in effect at that plant a collective bargaining agreement.

(2) No grant may be made, no contract may be entered into and no other assistance may be provided under the provisions of this section to an area or industry wide labor management committee unless its participants include any labor organizations certified or recognized as the representative of the employees of an employer participating in such committee. Nothing in this clause shall prohibit participation in an area or industry wide committee by an employer whose employees are not represented by a labor organization.

(3) No grant may be made under the provisions of this section to any labor management committee which the Service finds to have as one of its purposes the discouragement of the exercise of rights contained in section 7 of the National Labor Relations Act, or the interference with collective bargaining in any plant, or industry.

(c) The Service shall carry out the provisions of this section through an office established for that purpose.

(d) There are authorized to be appropriated to carry out the provisions of this section $10,000,000 for the fiscal year 1979, and such sums as may be necessary thereafter.

National Emergencies

Sec. 206. Whenever in the opinion of the President of the United States, a threatened or actual strike or lockout affecting an entire industry or a substantial part thereof engaged in trade, commerce, transportation, transmission, or communication among the several States or with foreign nations, or engaged in the production of goods for commerce, will, if permitted to occur or to continue, imperil the national health or safety, he may appoint a board of inquiry to inquire into the issues involved in the dispute and to make a written report to him within such time as he shall prescribe. Such report shall include a statement of the facts with respect to the dispute, including each party's statement of its position but shall not contain any recommendations. The President shall file a copy of such report with the Service and shall make its contents available to the public.

Sec. 207. (a) A board of inquiry shall be composed of a chairman and such other members as the President shall determine, and shall have power to sit and act in any place within the United States and to conduct such hearings either in public or in private, as it may deem necessary or proper, to ascertain the facts with respect to the causes and circumstances of the dispute.

(b) Members of a board of inquiry shall receive compensation at the rate of $50 for each day actually spent by them in the work of the board, together with necessary travel and subsistence expenses.

(c) For the purpose of any hearing or inquiry conducted by any board appointed under this title, the provisions of sections 49 and 50 of title 15, United States Code (relating to the attendance of witnesses and the production of books, papers, and documents) are made applicable to the powers and duties of such board.

Sec. 208. (a) Upon receiving a report from a board of inquiry the President may direct the Attorney General to petition any district court of the United States having jurisdiction of the parties to enjoin such strike or lockout or the continuing thereof, and if the court finds that such threatened or actual strike or lockout—

(i) affects an entire industry or a substantial part thereof engaged in trade, commerce, transportation, transmission, or communication among the several States or with foreign nations, or engaged in the production of goods for commerce; and

(ii) if permitted to occur or to continue, will imperil the national health or safety, it shall have jurisdiction to enjoin any such strike or lockout, or the continuing thereof, and to make such other orders as may be appropriate.

(b) In any case, the provisions of the Norris-LaGuardia Act shall not be applicable.

(c) The order or orders of the court shall be subject to review by the appropriate United States court of appeals and by the Supreme Court upon writ of certiorari or certification as provided in section 1254 of title 28, United States Code.

Sec. 209. (a) Whenever a district court has issued an order under section 208 enjoining acts or practices which imperil or threaten to imperil the national health or safety, it shall be the duty of the parties to the labor dispute giving rise to such order to make every effort to adjust and settle their differences, with the assistance of the Service created by this Act. Neither party shall be under any duty to accept, in whole or in part, any proposal of settlement made by the Service.

(b) Upon the issuance of such order, the President shall reconvene the board of inquiry which has previously reported with respect to the dispute. At the end of a sixty-day period (unless the dispute has been settled by that time), the board of inquiry shall report to the President the current position of the parties and the efforts which have been made for settlement, and shall include a statement by each party of its position and a statement of the employer's last offer of settlement. The President shall make such report available to the public. The National Labor Relations Board, within the succeeding fifteen days, shall take a secret ballot of the employees of each employer involved in the dispute on the question of whether they wish to accept the final offer of settlement made by their employer, as stated by him and shall certify the results thereof to the Attorney General within five days thereafter.

Sec. 210. Upon the certification of the results of such ballot or upon a settlement being reached, whichever happens sooner, the Attorney General shall move the court to discharge the injunction, which motion shall then be granted and the injunction discharged. When such motion is granted, the President shall submit to the Congress a full and comprehensive report of the proceedings, including the findings of the board of inquiry and the ballot taken by the National Labor Relations Board, together with such recommendations as he may see fit to make for consideration and appropriate action.

Compilation of Collective-Bargaining Agreements, etc.

Sec. 211. (a) For the guidance and information of interested representatives of employers, employees, and the general public, the Bureau of Labor Statistics of the Department of Labor shall maintain a file of copies of all available collective bargaining agreements and other available agreements and actions there under settling or adjusting labor disputes. Such file shall be open to inspection under appropriate conditions prescribed by the Secretary of Labor, except that no specific information submitted in confidence shall be disclosed.

(b) The Bureau of Labor Statistics in the Department of Labor is authorized to furnish upon request of the Service, or employers, employees, or their representatives, all available data and factual information which may aid in the settlement of any labor dispute, except that no specific information submitted in confidence shall be disclosed.

Exemption of Railway Labor Act

Sec. 212. The provisions of this title shall not be applicable with respect to any matter which is subject to the provisions of the Railway Labor Act, as amended from time to time.

Conciliation of Labor Disputes in the Health Care Industry

Sec. 213. (a) If, in the opinion of the Director of the Federal Mediation and Conciliation Service, a threatened or actual strike or lockout affecting a health care institution will, if permitted to occur or to continue, substantially interrupt the delivery of health care in the locality concerned, the Director may further assist in the resolution of the impasse by establishing within 30 days after the notice to the Federal Mediation and Conciliation Service under clause (A) of the last sentence of section 8(d) (which is required by clause (3) of such section 8(d)), or within 10 days after the notice under clause (B), an impartial Board of Inquiry to investigate the issues involved in the dispute and to make a written report thereon to the parties within fifteen (15) days after the establishment of such a Board. The written report shall contain the findings of fact together with the Board's recommendations for settling the dispute, with the objective of achieving a prompt, peaceful and just settlement of the dispute. Each such Board shall be composed of such number of individuals as the Director may deem desirable. No member appointed under this section shall have any interest or involvement in the health care institutions or the employee organizations involved in the dispute.

(b)(1) Members of any board established under this section who are otherwise employed by the Federal Government shall serve without compensation but shall be reimbursed for travel, subsistence, and other necessary expenses incurred by them in carrying out its duties under this section.

(2) Members of any board established under this section who are not subject to paragraph (1) shall receive compensation at a rate prescribed by the Director but not to exceed the daily rate prescribed for GS–18 of the General Schedule under section 5332 of title 5, United States Code, including travel for each day they are engaged in the performance of their duties under this section and shall be entitled to reimbursement for travel, subsistence, and other necessary expenses incurred by them in carrying out their duties under this section.

(c) After the establishment of a board under subsection (a) of this section and for 15 days after any such board has issued its report, no change in the status quo in effect prior to the expiration of the contract in the case of negotiations for a contract renewal, or in effect prior to the time of the impasse in the case of an initial bargaining negotiation, except by agreement, shall be made by the parties to the controversy.

(d) There are authorized to be appropriated such sums as may be necessary to carry out the provisions of this section.

Title III

Suits by and Against Labor Organizations

Sec. 301. (a) Suits for violation of contracts between an employer and a labor organization representing employees in an industry affecting commerce as defined in this Act or between any such labor organization, may be brought in any district court of the United States having jurisdiction of the parties, without respect to the amount in controversy or without regard to the citizenship of the parties.

(b) Any labor organization which represents employees in an industry affecting commerce as defined in this Act and any employer whose activities affect commerce as defined in this Act shall be bound by the acts of its agents. Any such labor organization may sue or be sued as an entity and in behalf of the employees whom it represents in the courts of the United States. Any money judgment against a labor organization in a district court of the United States shall be enforceable only against the organization as an entity and against its assets, and shall not be enforceable against any individual member or his assets.

(c) For the purposes of actions and proceedings by or against labor organizations in the district courts of the United States, district courts shall be deemed to have jurisdiction of a labor organization (1) in the district in which such organization maintains its principal offices, or (2) in any district in which its duly authorized officers or agents are engaged in representing or acting for employee members.

(d) The service of summons, subpoena, or other legal process of any court of the United States upon an officer or agent of a labor organization, in his capacity as such, shall constitute service upon the labor organization.

(e) For the purposes of this section, in determining whether any person is acting as an "agent" of another person so as to make such other person responsible for his acts, the question of whether the specific acts performed were actually authorized or subsequently ratified shall not be controlling.

Restrictions on Payments to Employee Representatives

Sec. 302. (a) It shall be unlawful for any employer or association of employers or any person who acts as a labor relations expert, adviser, or consultant to an employer or who acts in the interest of an employer to pay, lend, or deliver, or agree to pay, lend, or deliver, any money or other thing of value—

1. to any representative of any of his employees who are employed in an industry affecting commerce; or
2. to any labor organization, or any officer or employee thereof, which represents, seeks to represent, or would admit to membership, any of the employees of such employer who are employed in an industry affecting commerce;
3. to any employee or group or committee of employees of such employer employed in an industry affecting commerce in excess of their normal compensation for the purpose of causing such employee or group or committee directly or indirectly to influence any other employees in the exercise of the right to organize and bargain collectively through representatives of their own choosing; or
4. to any officer or employee of a labor organization engaged in an industry affecting commerce with intent to influence him in respect to any of his actions, decisions, or duties as a representative of employees or as such officer or employee of such labor organization.

(b)(1) It shall be unlawful for any <u>person</u> to request, <u>demand, receive,</u> or accept, or agree to receive or accept, <u>any payment, loan, or delivery</u> of any money or other thing of value <u>prohibited by subsection (a).</u>

(2) <u>It shall be unlawful for any labor organization, or for any person acting as an officer, agent, representative, or employee of such labor organization, to demand or accept from the operator of any motor vehicle (as defined in part II of the Interstate Commerce Act) employed in the transportation of property in commerce, or the employer of any such operator, any money or other thing of value payable to such organization or to an officer, agent, representative or employee thereof as a fee or charge for the unloading, or in connection with the unloading, of the cargo of such vehicle: Provided, That nothing in this paragraph shall be construed to make unlawful any payment by an employer to any of his employees as compensation for their services as employees.</u>

(c) The provisions of this section shall not be applicable (1) in respect to any money or other thing of value payable by an employer <u>to any of his employees whose established duties include acting openly for such employer in matters of labor relations or personnel administration or</u> to any representative <u>of his employees, or to any officer or employee of a labor organization</u> who is <u>also</u> an employee or former employee of such employer, as compensation for, or by reason of, his service as an employee of such employer; (2) with respect to the payment or delivery of any money or other thing of value in satisfaction of a judgment of any court or a decision or award of an arbitrator or impartial chairman or in compromise, adjustment, settlement, or release of any claim, complaint, grievance, or dispute in the absence of fraud or duress; (3) with respect to the sale or purchase of an article or commodity at the prevailing market price in the regular course of business; (4) with respect to money deducted from the wages of employees in payment of membership dues in a labor organization: Provided, That the employer has received from each employee, on whose account such deductions are made, a written assignment which shall not be irrevocable for a period of more than one year, or beyond the termination date of the applicable collective agreement, whichever occurs sooner; (5) with respect to money or other thing of value paid to a trust fund established by such representative, for the sole and exclusive benefit of the employees of such employer, and their families and dependents (or of such employees, families, and dependents jointly with the employees of other employers making similar payments, and their families and dependents): Provided, That (A) such payments are held in trust for the purpose of paying, either from principal or income or both, for the benefit of employees, their families and dependents, for medical or hospital care, pensions on retirement or death of employees, compensation for injuries or illness resulting from occupational activity or insurance to provide any of the foregoing, or unemployment benefits or life insurance, disability and sickness insurance, or accident insurance; (B) the detailed basis on which such payments are to be made is specified in a written agreement with the employer, and employees and employers are equally represented in the administration of such fund, together with such neutral persons as the representatives of the employers and the representatives of employees may agree upon and in the event the employer and employee groups deadlock on the administration of such fund and there are no neutral persons empowered to break such deadlock, such agreement provides that the two groups shall agree on an impartial umpire to decide such dispute, or in event of their failure to agree within a reasonable length of time, an impartial umpire to decide such dispute shall, on petition of either group, be appointed by the district court of the United States for the district where the trust fund has its principal office, and shall also contain provisions for an annual audit of the trust fund, a statement of the results of which shall be available for inspection by interested persons at the principal office of the trust fund and at such other places as may be designated in such written agreement; and (C) such payments as are intended to be used for the purpose of providing pensions or annuities for employees are made to a separate trust which provides that the funds held therein cannot be used for any purpose other than paying such pensions or annuities; (6) with respect to money or other thing of value paid by any employer to a trust fund established by such representative for the purpose of pooled vacation, holiday, severance or similar benefits, or defraying costs of apprenticeship or other training programs: Provided, That the requirements of clause (B) of the proviso to clause (5) of this subsection shall apply to such trust funds; (7) with respect to money or other thing of value paid by any employer to a pooled or individual trust fund established by such representative for the purpose of (A) scholarships for the benefit of employees, their families, and dependents for study at educational institutions, (B) child care centers for preschool and school age dependents of employees, or (C) financial assistance for employee housing; Provided, That no labor organization or employer shall be required to bargain on the establishment of any such trust fund, and refusal to do so shall not constitute an unfair labor practice: Provided further, That the requirements of clause (B) of the proviso to clause (5) of this subsection shall apply to such trust funds; (8) with respect to money or any other thing of value paid by any employer to a trust fund established by such representative for the purpose of defraying the costs of legal services for employees, their families, and dependents for counsel or plan of their choice: Provided, That the requirements of clause (B) of the proviso to clause (5) of this subsection shall apply to such trust funds: Provided further, That no such legal services shall be furnished: (A) to initiate any proceeding directed (i) against any such employer or its officers or agents except in workman's compensation cases, or (ii) against such labor organization, or its parent or subordinate bodies, or their officers or agents, or (iii) against any other employer or labor organization, or their officers or agents, in any matter arising under the National Labor Relations Act, or this Act; and (B) in any proceeding where a labor organization would be prohibited from defraying the costs of legal services by the provisions of the Labor-Management Reporting and Disclosure Act of 1959; or (9) with respect to money or other things of value paid by an employer to a plant, area or industry wide labor management committee established for one or more of the purposes set forth in section 5(b) of the Labor Management Cooperation Act of 1978.

(d) Any person who willfully violates any of the provisions of this section shall, upon conviction thereof, be guilty of a misdemeanor and be subject to a fine of not more than $10,000 or to imprisonment for not more than one year, or both.

(e) The district courts of the United States and the United States courts of the Territories and possessions shall have jurisdiction, for cause shown, and subject to the provisions of rule 65 of the Federal Rules of Civil Procedure (relating to notice to opposite party) to restrain violations of this section, without regard to the provisions of the Clayton Act, and the Norris-LaGuardia Act.

(f) This section shall not apply to any contract in force on June 23, 1947, until the expiration of such contract, or until July 1, 1948, whichever first occurs.

(g) Compliance with the restrictions contained in subsection (c)(5)(B) upon contributions to trust funds, otherwise lawful, shall not be applicable to contributions to such trust funds established by collective agreement prior to January 1, 1946, nor shall subsection (c)(5)(A) be construed as prohibiting contributions to such trust funds if prior to January 1, 1947, such funds contained provisions for pooled vacation benefits.

Boycotts and Other Unlawful Combinations

Sec. 303. (a) It shall be unlawful, for the purpose of this section only, in an industry or activity affecting commerce, for any labor organization to engage in any activity or conduct defined as an unfair labor practice in section 8(b)(4) of the National Labor Relations Act.

(b) Whoever shall be injured in his business or property by reason of any violation of subsection (a) may sue therefore in any district court of the United States subject to the limitation and provisions of section 301 hereof without respect to the amount in controversy, or in any other court having jurisdiction of the parties, and shall recover the damages by him sustained and the cost of the suit.

Title IV
Creation of Joint Committee to Study and Report on Basic Problems Affecting Friendly Labor Relations and Productivity
Secs. 401–407. Omitted.

Title V
Definitions
Sec. 501. When used in this Act—

(1) The term "industry affecting commerce" means any industry or activity in commerce or in which a labor dispute would burden or obstruct commerce or tend to burden or obstruct commerce or the free flow of commerce.

(2) The term "strike" includes any strike or other concerted stoppage of work by employees (including a stoppage by reason of the expiration of a collective-bargaining agreement) and any concerted slowdown or other concerted interruption of operations by employees.

(3) The terms "commerce," "labor disputes," "employer," "employee," "labor organization," "representative," "person," and "supervisor" shall have the same meaning as when used in the National Labor Relations Act as amended by this Act.

Saving Provision
Sec. 502. Nothing in this Act shall be construed to require an individual employee to render labor or service without his consent, nor shall anything in this Act be construed to make the quitting of his labor by an individual employee an illegal act; nor shall any court issue any process to compel the performance by an individual employee of such labor or service, without his consent; nor shall the quitting of labor by an employee or employees in good faith because of abnormally dangerous conditions for work at the place of employment of such employee or employees be deemed a strike under this Act.

Separability
Sec. 503. If any provision of this Act or the application of such provision to any person or circumstance, shall be held invalid, the remainder of this Act or the application of such provision to persons or circumstances other than those as to which it is held invalid, shall not be affected thereby.

DECLARATION OF PHILADELPHIA (INTERNATIONAL LABOR ORGANIZATION, 1944)

Declaration concerning the aims and purposes of the International Labor Organization
The General Conference of the International Labor Organization meeting in its Twenty-sixth Session in Philadelphia, hereby adopts this tenth day of May in the year nineteen hundred and forty-four the present Declaration of the aims and purposes of the International Labor Organization and of the principles which should inspire the policy of its Members.

I. The Conference reaffirms the fundamental principles on which the Organization is based and, in particular, that—

(a) labor is not a commodity;

(b) freedom of expression and of association are essential to sustained progress;

(c) poverty anywhere constitutes a danger to prosperity everywhere;

(d) the war against want requires to be carried on with unrelenting vigor within each nation, and by continuous and concerted international effort in which the representatives of workers and employers, enjoying equal status with those of governments, join with them in free discussion and democratic decision with a view to the promotion of the common welfare.

II. Believing that experience has fully demonstrated the truth of the statement in the Constitution of the International Labor Organization that lasting peace can be established only if it is based on social justice, the Conference affirms that—

(a) all human beings, irrespective of race, creed or sex, have the right to pursue both their material well-being and their spiritual development in conditions of freedom and dignity, of economic security and equal opportunity;

(b) the attainment of the conditions in which this shall be possible must constitute the central aim of national and international policy;

(c) all national and international policies and measures, in particular those of an economic and financial character, should be judged in this light and accepted only in so far as they may be held to promote and not to hinder the achievement of this fundamental objective;

(d) it is a responsibility of the International Labor Organization to examine and consider all international economic and financial policies and measures in the light of this fundamental objective;

(e) in discharging the tasks entrusted to it the International Labor Organization, having considered all relevant economic and financial factors, may include in its decisions and recommendations any provisions which it considers appropriate.

III. The Conference recognizes the solemn obligation of the International Labor Organization to further among the nations of the world programs which will achieve:

(a) full employment and the raising of standards of living;

(b) the employment of workers in the occupations in which they can have the satisfaction of giving the fullest measure of their skill and attainments and make their greatest contribution to the common well-being;

(c) the provision, as a means to the attainment of this end and under adequate guarantees for all concerned, of facilities for training and the transfer of labor, including migration for employment and settlement;

(d) policies in regard to wages and earnings, hours and other conditions of work calculated to ensure a just share of the fruits of progress to all, and a minimum living wage to all employed and in need of such protection;

(e) the effective recognition of the right of collective bargaining, the cooperation of management and labor in the continuous improvement of productive efficiency, and the collaboration of workers and employers in the preparation and application of social and economic measures;

(f) the extension of social security measures to provide a basic income to all in need of such protection and comprehensive medical care;

(g) adequate protection for the life and health of workers in all occupations;

(h) provision for child welfare and maternity protection;

(i) the provision of adequate nutrition, housing and facilities for recreation and culture;

(j) the assurance of equality of educational and vocational opportunity.

IV. Confident that the fuller and broader utilization of the world's productive resources necessary for the achievement of the objectives set forth in this Declaration can be secured by effective international and national action, including measures to expand production and consumption, to avoid severe economic fluctuations to promote the economic and social advancement of the less developed regions of the world, to assure greater stability in world prices of primary products, and to promote a high and steady volume of international trade, the Conference pledges the full cooperation of the International Labor Organization with such international bodies as may be entrusted with a share of the responsibility for this great task and for the promotion of the health, education and well-being of all peoples.

V. The Conference affirms that the principles set forth in this Declaration are fully applicable to all peoples everywhere and that, while the manner of their application must be determined with due regard to the stage of social and economic development reached by each people, their progressive application to peoples who are still dependent, as well as to those who have already achieved self-government, is a matter of concern to the whole civilized world.

UNIVERSAL DECLARATION OF HUMAN RIGHTS (UNITED NATIONS, 1948)[2]

Preamble

Whereas recognition of the inherent dignity and of the equal and inalienable rights of all members of the human family is the foundation of freedom, justice and peace in the world,

Whereas disregard and contempt for human rights have resulted in barbarous acts which have outraged the conscience of mankind, and the advent of a world in which human beings shall enjoy freedom of speech and belief and freedom from fear and want has been proclaimed as the highest aspiration of the common people,

Whereas it is essential, if man is not to be compelled to have recourse, as a last resort, to rebellion against tyranny and oppression, that human rights should be protected by the rule of law,

Whereas it is essential to promote the development of friendly relations between nations,

Whereas the peoples of the United Nations have in the Charter reaffirmed their faith in fundamental human rights, in the dignity and worth of the human person and in the equal rights of men and women and have determined to promote social progress and better standards of life in larger freedom,

Whereas Member States have pledged themselves to achieve, in co-operation with the United Nations, the promotion of universal respect for and observance of human rights and fundamental freedoms,

Whereas a common understanding of these rights and freedoms is of the greatest importance for the full realization of this pledge,

Now, therefore, The General Assembly,

[2] Adopted and proclaimed by the General Assembly of the United Nations on December 10, 1948.

Proclaims this Universal Declaration Of Human Rights as a common standard of achievement for all peoples and all nations, to the end that every individual and every organ of society, keeping this Declaration constantly in mind, shall strive by teaching and education to promote respect for these rights and freedoms and by progressive measures, national and international, to secure their universal and effective recognition and observance, both among the peoples of Member States themselves and among the peoples of territories under their jurisdiction.

Article 1

All human beings are born free and equal in dignity and rights. They are endowed with reason and conscience and should act towards one another in a spirit of brotherhood.

Article 2

Everyone is entitled to all the rights and freedoms set forth in this Declaration, without distinction of any kind, such as race, color, sex, language, religion, political or other opinion, national or social origin, property, birth or other status. Furthermore, no distinction shall be made on the basis of the political, jurisdictional or international status of the country or territory to which a person belongs, whether it be independent, trust, non-self-governing or under any other limitation of sovereignty.

Article 3

Everyone has the right to life, liberty and security of person.

Article 4

No one shall be held in slavery or servitude; slavery and the slave trade shall be prohibited in all their forms.

Article 5

No one shall be subjected to torture or to cruel, inhuman or degrading treatment or punishment.

Article 6

Everyone has the right to recognition everywhere as a person before the law.

Article 7

All are equal before the law and are entitled without any discrimination to equal protection of the law. All are entitled to equal protection against any discrimination in violation of this Declaration and against any incitement to such discrimination.

Article 8

Everyone has the right to an effective remedy by the competent national tribunals for acts violating the fundamental rights granted him by the constitution or by law.

Article 9

No one shall be subjected to arbitrary arrest, detention or exile.

Article 10

Everyone is entitled in full equality to a fair and public hearing by an independent and impartial tribunal, in the determination of his rights and obligations and of any criminal charge against him.

Article 11

1. Everyone charged with a penal offence has the right to be presumed innocent until proved guilty according to law in a public trial at which he has had all the guarantees necessary for his defense.
2. No one shall be held guilty of any penal offence on account of any act or omission which did not constitute a penal offence, under national or international law, at the time when it was committed. Nor shall a heavier penalty be imposed than the one that was applicable at the time the penal offence was committed.

Article 12

No one shall be subjected to arbitrary interference with his privacy, family, home or correspondence, nor to attacks upon his honor and reputation. Everyone has the right to the protection of the law against such interference or attacks.

Article 13

1. Everyone has the right to freedom of movement and residence within the borders of each state.
2. Everyone has the right to leave any country, including his own, and to return to his country.

Article 14

1. Everyone has the right to seek and to enjoy in other countries asylum from persecution.
2. This right may not be invoked in the case of prosecutions genuinely arising from nonpolitical crimes or from acts contrary to the purposes and principles of the United Nations.

Article 15

1. Everyone has the right to a nationality.
2. No one shall be arbitrarily deprived of his nationality nor denied the right to change his nationality.

Article 16

1. Men and women of full age, without any limitation due to race, nationality or religion, have the right to marry and to found a family. They are entitled to equal rights as to marriage, during marriage and at its dissolution.
2. Marriage shall be entered into only with the free and full consent of the intending spouses.
3. The family is the natural and fundamental group unit of society and is entitled to protection by society and the State.

Article 17

1. Everyone has the right to own property alone as well as in association with others.
2. No one shall be arbitrarily deprived of his property.

Article 18

Everyone has the right to freedom of thought, conscience and religion; this right includes freedom to change his religion or belief, and freedom, either alone or in community with others and in public or private, to manifest his religion or belief in teaching, practice, worship and observance.

Article 19

Everyone has the right to freedom of opinion and expression; this right includes freedom to hold opinions without interference and to seek, receive and impart information and ideas through any media and regardless of frontiers.

Article 20

1. Everyone has the right to freedom of peaceful assembly and association.
2. No one may be compelled to belong to an association.

Article 21

1. Everyone has the right to take part in the government of his country, directly or through freely chosen representatives.
2. Everyone has the right of equal access to public service in his country.
3. The will of the people shall be the basis of the authority of government; this will shall be expressed in periodic and genuine elections which shall be by universal and equal suffrage and shall be held by secret vote or by equivalent free voting procedures.

Article 22

Everyone, as a member of society, has the right to social security and is entitled to realization, through national effort and international co-operation and in accordance with the organization and resources of each State, of the economic, social and cultural rights indispensable for his dignity and the free development of his personality.

Article 23

1. Everyone has the right to work, to free choice of employment, to just and favorable conditions of work and to protection against unemployment.
2. Everyone, without any discrimination, has the right to equal pay for equal work.
3. Everyone who works has the right to just and favorable remuneration ensuring for himself and his family an existence worthy of human dignity, and supplemented, if necessary, by other means of social protection.
4. Everyone has the right to form and to join trade unions for the protection of his interests.

Article 24

Everyone has the right to rest and leisure, including reasonable limitation of working hours and periodic holidays with pay.

Article 25

1. Everyone has the right to a standard of living adequate for the health and well-being of himself and of his family, including food, clothing, housing and medical care and necessary social services, and the right to security in the event of unemployment, sickness,

disability, widowhood, old age or other lack of livelihood in circumstances beyond his control.

2. Motherhood and childhood are entitled to special care and assistance. All children, whether born in or out of wedlock, shall enjoy the same social protection.

Article 26

1. Everyone has the right to education. Education shall be free, at least in the elementary and fundamental stages. Elementary education shall be compulsory. Technical and professional education shall be made generally available and higher education shall be equally accessible to all on the basis of merit.

2. Education shall be directed to the full development of the human personality and to the strengthening of respect for human rights and fundamental freedoms. It shall promote understanding, tolerance and friendship among all nations, racial or religious groups, and shall further the activities of the United Nations for the maintenance of peace.

3. Parents have a prior right to choose the kind of education that shall be given to their children.

Article 27

1. Everyone has the right freely to participate in the cultural life of the community, to enjoy the arts and to share in scientific advancement and its benefits.

2. Everyone has the right to the protection of the moral and material interests resulting from any scientific, literary or artistic production of which he is the author.

Article 28

Everyone is entitled to a social and international order in which the rights and freedoms set forth in this Declaration can be fully realized.

Article 29

1. Everyone has duties to the community in which alone the free and full development of his personality is possible.

2. In the exercise of his rights and freedoms, everyone shall be subject only to such limitations as are determined by law solely for the purpose of securing due recognition and respect for the rights and freedoms of others and of meeting the just requirements of morality, public order and the general welfare in a democratic society.

3. These rights and freedoms may in no case be exercised contrary to the purposes and principles of the United Nations.

Article 30

Nothing in this Declaration may be interpreted as implying for any State, group or person any right to engage in any activity or to perform any act aimed at the destruction of any of the rights and freedoms set forth herein.

Appendix **B**

Collective Bargaining Simulation: The Zinnia and Service Workers Local H-56

Collective bargaining simulations in which student teams representing management and a union negotiate a union contract are a common and important component of many labor relations courses. Unlike other texts, however, the simulation that accompanies *Labor Relations: Striking a Balance* is online. The simulation is titled "The Zinnia and Service Workers Local H-56" and involves a fictitious 300-room hotel in Minneapolis (The Zinnia) and a fictitious local union, Local H-56 of the International Union of Service Workers and Allied Employees. Rather than reading a textbook narrative, students explore the Web sites of The Zinnia and Local H-56 to learn about the expiring contract, the environment, their priorities, and their constraints. This use of technology and the need for Web exploration make for a very engaging exercise. As with other simulations, bargaining can take place in person, or if the instructor arranges, via e-mail, chat, or instant messaging. All of the needed materials are on the Web site at *www.thezinnia.com*, including an Excel spreadsheet for contract costing and Word documents for creating bargaining goals. Additional instructions for instructors can be found in the instructor's manual.

www.thezinnia.com

Name Index

Note: page numbers followed by *n* indicate material in footnotes.

Subject Index

Note: page numbers followed by *n* indicate material in footnotes; persons listed in this index are discussed as subjects in text; full listings for all names are found in Name Index.